SPORTS LAW
Third Edition

Cavendish
Publishing
Limited

This book is supported by a Companion Website, created to keep *Sports Law* up to date and to provide enhanced resources for both students and lecturers.

Key features include:

- termly updates
- links to useful websites
- 'ask the author' – your questions answered

www.cavendishpublishing.com/sportslaw

SPORTS LAW
Third Edition

Simon Gardiner, BA (Hons), MA
and
Mark James, LLB (Hons), PhD
John O'Leary, LLB (Hons), M Phil
Roger Welch, LLB (Hons), M Phil
with
Ian Blackshaw, LLM
Simon Boyes, LLB (Hons), LLM
Andrew Caiger, LLB (Hons), LLM

Cavendish
Publishing
Limited

Third edition First Published in Great Britain 2006 by
Cavendish Publishing Ltd

This edition reprinted 2006
by Routledge-Cavendish
2 Park Square, Milton Park, Abingdon, Oxon, OX14 4RN

Simultaneously published in the USA and Canada
by Routledge-Cavendish
270 Madison Avenue, New York, NY 10016

Reprinted 2007

Routledge-Cavendish is an imprint of the Taylor & Francis Group

© Gardiner, Simon; James, Mark; O'Leary,
John; Welch, Roger; Blackshaw, Ian; Boyes,
Simon; Caiger, Andrew   2006
First edition   1998
Second edition   2001

British Library Cataloguing in Publication Data
Gardiner, Simon
Sports law – 3rd edn
1 Sports – Law and legislation – Great Britain
I Title
344.4'1099

Library of Congress Cataloging in Publication Data
Data available

ISBN 10: 1-85941-894-5
ISBN 13: 978-1-859-41894-9

Printed and bound in Great Britain by Antony Rowe Ltd, Chippenham, Wiltshire

FOREWORD

I am honoured and delighted to write this Foreword to the third edition of *Sports Law*.

During the time that I have been Director of Legal Affairs at the International Olympic Committee, beginning in 1985, sport has continued to grow as a global phenomenon, and the impact of the law on sport and sports events has increased significantly. It is fair to say that a discreet body of what one may now call 'sports law' has developed – and is continuing to do so – in many parts of the world.

Sports law has also spawned a new generation of lawyers specialising in this particular field. This book will provide them with very useful material and analysis of the many complex legal issues confronting sport today. A review of the Table of Contents will illustrate how much and in what ways the law now impacts on the area of sport. The book also provides essential information for persons involved in the administration and regulation of sport and sporting events, including the promotion, marketing and broadcasting thereof.

Simon Gardiner and his team of sports law experts and practitioners are to be warmly thanked and congratulated for producing this comprehensive and comparative survey.

This is a book which I can sincerely recommend; it is one that persons involved in the practice of sport would benefit from reading and referring to in the course of their work of promoting and upholding the Olympic ideals and values inherent in sport in which the 'Rule of Law' also plays a significant role.

Howard M Stupp
Director of Legal Affairs
The International Olympic Committee
Chateau de Vidy, Lausanne
Switzerland
August 2005

PREFACE

The third edition of *Sports Law* reflects the reality of the growth of the subject of sports law in Britain as an important area of academic inquiry. This growth over the seven years since the first edition was published corresponds to the growth in legal practice of sports law – significant numbers of lawyers spend a considerable amount of their professional time on sports related legal issues, with some firms having dedicated sports law practices. During the 1990s the subject has grown in stature. The creation of the British Association for Sport and the Law in 1992 was an important development. There are now a significant number of undergraduate modules in sports law on UK law degrees and it has become an important part of the curriculum in the plethora of sports studies courses that have developed in Britain in recent years. A number of postgraduate courses have also developed in UK Universities.

In addition, the sports law literature has expanded considerably. Books such as Craig Moore's *Sports Law Litigation*, David Griffith-Jones' *The Law and Business of Sport*, Richard Verow *et al*'s *Sport, Business and the Law*, Michael Beloff *et al*'s *Sports Law* and Adam Lewis and Jonathan Taylor's *Sport: Law and Practice* are focused primarily at practitioners; Steve Greenfield and Guy Osborne's edited collection, *Law and Sport in Contemporary Society* and William Stewart's edited collection, *Sports Law: The Scots Perspective* are focused primarily on a wider academic examination; and of course Edward Grayson's *Sport and the Law*, now in its fourth edition, provides his uniquely detailed and dense account of the development of sports law.

Specialisms have also developed: David McArdle's *From Bootman to Bosman: Football, Society and Law*, John O'Leary's edited collection, *Drugs and Doping in Sport: Socio-Legal Perspectives* and Hazel Hartley's *Exploring Sport and Leisure Disasters: A Socio-legal Perspective* are examples. European sports policy and regulation has been a specific focus with Andrew Caiger and Simon Gardiner's edited collection, *Professional Sport in the European Union: Regulation and Re-regulation* and Richard Parrish's *Sports Law and Policy in the European Union*. A number of UK-based sports law journals provide updated information and commentary: *World Sports Law Report*, *Sport and the Law Journal*, *Sports Law Administration and Practice* and the *International Sports Law Journal*. No doubt new publications will be added to this list in the years ahead. Sports law is now a mature academic discipline. It has intellectual rigour and there are intellectually challenging issues with which to engage.

In the preface to the first edition in 1998 it was stated: 'there is clearly a growing interest in the academic study of the legal regulation of sport and now is the time to produce a book that attempts to not only provide an exposition of the growing sports law jurisprudence, but provide a full analysis and critical evaluation of its operation, reflecting the growing maturity of this legal subject.' The first edition provided the first rigorous academic analysis of the role that law has in sport in Britain. This third edition continues this mission.

The approach has been to develop a text and materials book with extensive extracts from primary and secondary sources. We provide detailed analysis of this material and the major issues in sports law. This analysis will be of value to sports lawyers, sports administrators and students at sub-degree, undergraduate and postgraduate level; studying sports law, or sports studies.

This third edition of *Sports Law* updates the issues covered in the second edition. To fully understand the issues and complexities of sports law, it is vital that a thorough theoretical examination informs practice and vice versa. The two approaches are intertwined, but it is vital that a rigorous theoretical underpinning of sports law practice is made explicit. Sport has immense cultural significance. Its future regulation is increasingly subject to external legal norms. If lawyers are to play an increasingly influential role as the custodians of sport, they need to take on this responsibility in an informed and dependable way.

For sport, as for society in general, legal regulation and litigation are a reality of modern life. The law has expertise and values that can contribute to the running and organisation of modern sport. However, there is still debate over the legitimacy and extent to which the law should be involved with sport. What role should the law have in the 'regulatory space' surrounding sport? The recent debate concerning the future development and application of European Union policy to sport is an example of where the intervention of the law is contested: should sport have a special exemption or should it be subject to the general regulation of European law?

In the preface to the first edition of this book, it was stated that a major issue was whether this subject of legal inquiry should be labelled 'sports law' or merely 'sport and the law'. This debate may still linger in some individuals' eyes that see the area as merely the application of traditional legal principles to the sports industry. To others it may be seen as essentially an abstract esoteric argument. However, in Britain the speedy emergence of a recognisable and distinct set of principles and doctrine concerning the legal regulation of the sports world that can be designated as a distinct legal area can be discerned. As with other legal disciplines, for example, information technology law and entertainment law, the same argument applies. It was no accident that this book is entitled *Sports Law*. The publication of subsequent texts entitled similarly may not only reflect the notion that 'imitation is truly the sincerest form of flattery'. Sports law has now arrived as a legitimate legal subject. As a generic term, more publications will appear in the area of sports law. Law has a crucial role to play in contemporary sport and the growing body of statutory and case law specific to sport is a testimony to this fact. Similar to the growth of a *lex mercatoria* in the Middle Ages, a *lex sportiva* is fast developing.

This book provides an analysis of the legal regulation of sport clearly within the socio-cultural and political context of contemporary sport. The focus is, inevitably, on elite professional sport, although it should not be forgotten that the vast majority of participation in sport is on an amateur and recreational level. Football also tends to dominate the analysis of legal issues. It is, of course, Britain's primary national sport, but every attempt has been made to cover as wide a range of sports as possible. The term 'sports athlete' is used extensively throughout the book to denote an individual who participates in both team and individual sports.

A primary focus has been to highlight the contingencies as to how certain areas of law are developing in sport. The areas of uncertainty have been highlighted in the hope that this will lead to further research and inquiry in these areas. Sports law is an area where different types of legal research methodology, ranging from traditional library based methods to socio-legal empirical approaches, are possible. The book attempts to explain quite technical and formal bodies of law and also to put the development of sports law into a socio-economic context, in order to help understand the reasons for the increasing role of the law in regulating sport.

This book has been a co-operative effort with a number of contributors. The same team of myself, Mark James, John O'Leary, Roger Welch with Ian Blackshaw, Simon Boyes and Andrew Caiger bring their own particular areas of expertise to this third edition. All have been involved in the growth of the academic study of sports law in Britain. A major strength of the book is that it represents the work of a research-active group who have applied their individual interests and areas of expertise to respective areas of sports law.

As with the second edition, this third edition has been divided into five sections, each of which is sub-divided into chapters, which has the aim of providing a coherent and unfolding account of the dominant issues in sports law. Due to the differing nature of the subjects involved, each chapter differs in the amount of case law and statutory law discussed and the use of extracts of primary and secondary sources.

Section 1: Sport, Law and Society

This section provides a context within which sports law is located. It is vital to have a full understanding of the cultural and historical significance of sport, in attempting to understand the contemporary role that law has in regulating sport. Regulation is a key word. As with other 'social fields', how best to regulate is a complex question.

Simon Gardiner writes Chapter 1 entitled 'Historical and Cultural Perspectives on Sport Regulation'. It provides an introduction to the historical and socio-cultural role that law has had in regulating sport. Some foundational material attempts to explain how sport is defined, particularly necessary in the context of arguments supporting the need for a legal definition of sport. The history of the law's greater involvement in sport regulation is explored.

Simon Gardiner also writes Chapter 2 entitled 'Theoretical Models of the Regulation of Sport'. It considers the reasons why law is increasingly used as a primary form of regulating sport. The relationship between law and the other normative rules, primarily the internal rules of the sport itself, are explored. Basic models of regulation are examined. An attempt is made to provide a theoretical framework for understanding the role of law in modern sport, premised largely, but not exclusively, on the reality of the commercialised nature of much of contemporary professional sport.

Chapter 3 by Simon Gardiner is entitled 'Sport and the Role of the State in Britain'. Various institutional bodies are examined in terms of their role in terms of promoting sport as a form of social policy. Four examples of the intervention of the law in sport are analysed: whether boxing should be banned; the role of animals in sport, with a focus on fox hunting; the regulation of spectator racism; and the protection of child athletes from forms of abuse. The policy arguments for legal intervention and other non-legal initiatives are evaluated.

Section 2: The Governance of Sport

This section provides a number of national, European and international perspectives on the role that the law has in supporting and, in some ways, enforcing effective governance in sport and the resolution of sporting disputes. The control of doping in sport is a major issue of governance.

Simon Gardiner and Simon Boyes write Chapter 4 entitled 'Governance of Sport: National, European and International Perspectives'. The characteristics of good governance are considered. What lessons can be learned from corporate governance? The increasing role that the European Commission has as a form of 'supervised autonomy' to sport and the development of a recognisable European Union sports policy is discussed. The wider globalisation of sport and the development of an international sports law are also examined.

Simon Boyes writes Chapter 5 entitled 'The Legal Regulation of Sports Governing Bodies'. On a UK national basis, the role that the courts have in reviewing the operation and decisions of sports governing bodies is critically evaluated. Grounds for such examination, such as restraint of trade and natural justice, are considered. The impact of the European Union and specifically the European Court of Justice and the relevant jurisprudence on sport is also evaluated.

Ian Blackshaw writes Chapter 6 entitled 'Alternative Dispute Mechanisms in Sport'. The primary ADR mechanism in sport is the Court of Arbitration in Sport. Its function and operation, together with its role in formulating an international sports law, is explored. Other forms of arbitration and mediation are considered, including the relatively new UK Sports Dispute Resolution Panel. The effectiveness of ADR in sport, particularly mediation, is evaluated.

John O'Leary writes Chapter 7 entitled 'The Legal Regulation of Doping'. The focus is the major issue of how national and international sports governing bodies should regulate doping in sport. The regulation of drugs in sport is highly contentious, as it is generally in society. An evaluation is made of the impact of the World Anti-Doping Agency and the effectiveness of internal sport anti-doping procedures and the role of the law in re-enforcing and challenging these procedures.

Section 3: The Commercial Regulation of Sport

Sport at the professional and elite level is clearly big business. The sports industry accounts for over 3% of world trade. The role of the law in sport can be premised on the argument that, as law regulates business, it therefore must regulate sport in a similar way. However, it is clear sport is not like any other business – it has a number of very specific characteristics.

Simon Gardiner writes Chapter 8 entitled 'Sport and Money: Accountability and Regulation'. The regulation of financial dealings in sport is examined. There is a clash between the values associated with financial probity generally found in business and the idiosyncratic way that financial dealings and transactions have traditionally been carried out in sport. The recent corruption scandals in sport generally, and particularly football, cricket and the International Olympic Committee are examined. The move to professionalisation in a greater number of sports and in expanding parts of the world is also discussed.

Andrew Caiger writes Chapter 9 entitled 'Sport and Competition Policy'. The purpose of competition law is analysed and the impact of the new UK Competition Act and the European provisions applicable to the sports world are considered. The question posed is whether sport is a case for special treatment. A comparative examination is taken of the ways in which sport can be regulated through competition law provisions. There is a particular focus on the issues surrounding the sale of broadcasting rights and the monopoly position that many sports governing bodies hold.

Ian Blackshaw writes Chapter 10 entitled 'Intellectual Property Rights and Sport'. The protection that individual sports athletes have for the intellectual property rights they have in their own person are examined. An examination is carried out of the various forms of IP rights, including trade marks and copyright, and how these can protect the sports athlete, event organisers and sports governing bodies. There is a particular focus on how these rights can be protected with the advent of new technologies such as the Internet.

Ian Blackshaw also writes Chapter 11 entitled 'Sports Marketing, Sponsorship and Ambush Marketing', which has become an enormous industry with sponsorship and advertising deals bringing vast amounts of money into sport. The chapter provides a practical insight into the legal regulation and practice surrounding 'brand protection' and 'ambush marketing'. Again, there are many issues concerning the protection of sponsorship and other sports related commercial rights linked to new technologies whose commercial exploitation transcends national boundaries.

Section 4: Regulation of the Sports Workplace

The dynamics of the employment of sports athletes is complex. Not only is their working life usually quite short, their contractual position is often unclear – are they an employee or independent contractor? The power relations between sports governing bodies and sports athletes have often led to highly inequitable situations. The impact of *Bosman* on team sports has challenged many of the restraints that have been found within the sporting world. A number of discriminatory practices have also begun to be challenged.

Roger Welch writes Chapter 12 entitled 'Sport and Contracts of Employment'. The role that employment law has in sport and on the formation of sporting employment contracts and the rights that sports athletes enjoy is the focus. The contractual terms of sports athletes have in the past reflected the unequal position they have with club owners and sports promoters. This relationship has been subject to increased legal challenge under concepts such as restraint of trade. The 1995 decision of the European Court of Justice in *Bosman* is analysed at length.

Roger Welch also writes Chapter 13 entitled 'Termination of Contracts of Employment in Sport'. The focus is on the termination of employment in sport. Participation in sport at elite levels is always precarious in the context of the never-ending spectre of career breaking or ending injuries. Loss of form is always around the corner too. Sports athletes are also subject to rigorous and specific internal sporting rules as far as conduct and discipline are concerned. Disciplinary rules in a number of sports are evaluated and the dynamics of how contracts come to an end are discussed.

Chapter 14 by Roger Welch is entitled 'Sports Participants and the Law of Discrimination'. The primary issues discussed are discrimination in terms of sex, race and disability. A major social aim of sport during the recent past has been the promotion of equal opportunities for participation in sport: 'sport for all' policies. However, much of the structural discrimination found generally in the work place is found in sport and the effectiveness of the legal remedies that exist are analysed. Additionally, the sport specific programmes to counter discrimination are evaluated.

Section 5: Safety in Sport: Legal Issues

In the early 1990s, this was a primary focus of sports law in the UK, particularly in the aftermath of the Hillsborough Disaster in 1989. A specific regulatory approach to ensuring safety in sports stadiums has developed with an emphasis on risk assessment and management. In addition, the law has intervened increasingly in terms of potential liability between participants in sporting activities.

Mark James writes Chapter 15 entitled 'The Criminal Law and Participator Violence'. The focus is on the relationship between the criminal law and the internal rules within sport regulating physical force and interaction between sports athletes that is an essential part of much sport. Excessive force can often be characterised as 'sports violence' and has been constructed as one of the major problems in contemporary sport. How should criminal law liability be constructed in such circumstances?

Mark James also writes Chapter 16 entitled 'Tort, Compensation and Alternative Dispute Resolution for Participator Violence'. The civil law application to sports injuries and the case law that has developed in this area of liability is evaluated. The distinction between legitimate and illegitimate, legal and illegal play within sport is a vital issue in terms of how liability is determined for participants, coaches and officials. This is an area where there is a continuing tension concerning the competing claims of sports bodies through internal mechanisms and developing ADR procedures on the one hand, and the courts and lawyers on the other, in providing the most effective remedies. For example, the development and dissemination of risk management programmes in sport is examined.

John O'Leary writes Chapter 17 entitled 'Spectators, Participants and Stadiums'. The focus is on the legal regulation of sports stadiums and spectating. Sporting events attract large numbers of people and, as with any congregation of people, their regulation and control needs to be carefully managed. One of the major events in recent sporting history in Britain was the Hillsborough tragedy, which led to the Taylor Report. The subsequent regulatory framework for safety is analysed in depth. The role of the civil and criminal law is evaluated in how it directs relationships between sports spectators, participants, the police and sports organisers.

The Authors

All the seven co-authors are keen sports fans and all try to continue to compete on a recreational level in a number of sports. Fandom is, of course, an important part of participation within the sports world. Those of you who know us will be well aware of our sporting allegiances: football dominates but since the last edition, the fortunes of our respective teams (very sadly on my part) have fluctuated. Premier League rivalry continues between John, 'a true blue' Chelsea supporter, red-scouser Mark and his beloved Liverpool, and Roger with his devotion of his adored Pompey. Having 'lived the dream', and then the nightmare, I look forward to better times with the finest United in England – Leeds of course! The other Simon provides foundational and inspirational support for us all – dreaming about the future glories of Scarborough FC.

During the summer what is there to do – no football! Cricket provides a welcome juxtaposition. While we all enjoy the improving performance of the England team and the winning of 'the Ashes', a healthy form of north – south rivalry exists between the two Simons and their allegiance for the mighty White Rose of Yorkshire and the softy southerners Roger and John who follow Essex and Middlesex respectively. Andrew and Ian enjoy more leisurely pursuits. Ian is a keen swimmer and enjoys walking in the French and Swiss Alps and also admits to following Real Madrid. Andrew is an aficionado of the Wimbledon fortnight and now is able to watch the exploits of Ajax Cape Town.

We hope the foci of our sporting devotion are not too obvious in our respective commentaries. Enjoy.

Simon Gardiner
Bishop's Stortford
October 2005

INTRODUCTION

Sports law roughly divides into the money matters and the misconduct matters, although the two get mixed up when the sin is greed and corruption. Some issues relate to the organisation of competitions, property rights, and the participation and payment of the players. Other issues belong to the 'ethical crisis' as sport exacts a toll of injuries[1] and sees endless examples of men behaving badly. The two categories are both true to the transport element in the word 'sport': the money matters deal with carrying away the cash, while the misconduct matters deal with carrying on, getting carried away and carrying things too far. These mixed problems of money, morality and masculinity are certainly not new in sports law. The 1890s began with the Master of the Rolls horrified to learn that football teams played to win and that they paid salaries to professionals.[2] At the end of the decade, a court had to rule on the legal consequences of women cyclists wearing 'rational' bloomers in a hotel.[3]

In the five years since the publication of the second edition of Simon Gardiner's *Sports Law*, sport has been squarely on the ethical backfoot as headlines have focused on issues of safety and misconduct both on and off the field.[4] Athletes continue to be implicated in a variety of sexual and non-sexual crimes, including a current example of a hockey player charged with conspiring to murder his agent.[5] There are further cases of abuse and sexual harassment involving coaches and other supervisors. The sidelines witness ugly behaviour by fanatical parents, and 'rink rage' has even extended to beating a coach to death.[6] The field of play offers no refuge since there are further instances of player violence in the course of games.[7] The paradox in all of this is that most of this conduct is not particularly deviant as it is firmly rooted in the values and structures of contemporary sport. The fault is in our stars, but is also in our games. The alleged and actual sexual assaults spring from the culture that tolerates the booze-driven wildness of aggressive, well-paid 'lads'.[8] Abusive coaches are able to exploit their physical opportunities and positions of power in activities that celebrate the eroticism of the body beautiful.[9] The violent spectator takes the tribalism and loyalty of fandom a bit too far, and the thuggish player is simply showing his competitive commitment, hardness and will to beat down the opposition. Further examples relate to discrimination and doping. An endeavour that emphasises the physical performance of young males is structured to exclude women, older persons and the disabled. Doping, meanwhile, is merely an extension of the performance-enhancing technologies developed by sports scientists. Doping control's appeal to 'fun' and 'the spirit of sport'[10] is strangely nostalgic and ignores the reality that medals are now won in the training lab.[11]

---

1 The annual cost of sports injuries in Australia is estimated at A$1.6 billion: 'The walking wounded of the fitness fad' *Sydney Morning Herald*, 19 December 2003.

2 *Radford v Campbell* (1890) 6 TLR 488 (CA). See further, Introduction to the second edition (2001).

3 *R v Sprague* (1899) 63 JP 233.

4 Ethical issues in sport are discussed at www.ethicalsport.ca.

5 Mike Danton of the St Louis Blues was arrested in April 2004 in an alleged murder-for-hire scheme.

6 In January 2002, Thomas Junta was convicted of involuntary homicide after he fought with another hockey father in Reading, Mass. The deceased had been serving as supervising coach at a game for 10-year-olds.

7 In March 2004, the NHL saw its latest major incident when Todd Bertuzzi of the Vancouver Canucks struck Steve Moore of Colorado and caused a neck fracture.

8 Germaine Greer has commented that professional footballers are denied adult status: 'They are "lads" or "boys" to be bought and sold, transferred or dropped or left on the bench; as they are denied autonomy, we can't be surprised if they lack responsibility': 'Nothing new about ugly sex' *The Guardian*, 16 December 2003.

9 Scanlon, TF, *Eros & Greek Athletics* (New York: Oxford University Press, 2002).

10 'Introduction' to the *World Anti-Doping Code* (2003), 'Fundamental rationale'.

11 Cf. 'In the case of sport we have an activity nominally known as play but raised to such a pitch of technical organization and scientific thoroughness that the real play-spirit is threatened with extinction': J Huizinga, *Homo Ludens: A Study of the Play-Element in Culture* (Boston: Beacon Press, 1938, 1955), p 199.

Although sport is morally frayed in its basic fabric and actual practice, this has not diminished the Victorian[12] faith that it is good for health and character development. Sport is even promoted as the cure for the 'obesity crisis', despite the discouraging model of sport-obsessed America and the close associations with beer and pies, chocolate sponsorships and the couch in front of the television.[13] We are all encouraged to go out and be active, although this is sometimes contradicted by tort reforms that tell us, 'don't expect to be able to sue'.[14] In Canada, there have been significant initiatives to renew sports policy and achieve the objective of a healthy and accessible sports system. The preamble to the new *Physical Activity and Sport Act*[15] recognises that, 'physical activity and sport are integral parts of Canadian culture and society and produce benefits in terms of health, social cohesion, linguistic duality, economic activity, cultural diversity and quality of life'. Section 4 incorporates the following 'sport policy principles':

> The Government of Canada's policy regarding sport is founded on the highest ethical standards and values, including doping-free sport, the treatment of all persons with fairness and respect, the full and fair participation of all persons in sport and the fair, equitable, transparent and timely resolution of disputes in sport.

This legislation is particularly 'fair' to sports lawyers since the vast majority of the provisions deal with the establishment of the Sport Dispute Resolution Centre of Canada.[16] The federal Act is accompanied by two national policy documents[17] endorsed by all government jurisdictions. *The Canadian Sport Policy* (2002) and the *Canadian Strategy for Ethical Conduct in Sport* (2002) incorporate a vision for the desired state of sport by 2012. This vision includes the respectful treatment of all parties and the achievement of the goals of enhancing participation, excellence, capacity and interaction. The shared policies and strategies are certainly to be welcomed, but the goal of achieving practical change in values and structures is indeed ambitious.

Ultimately, the misconduct matters may be dictated by money matters. Violence and scandal can be good for the sports business since there is nothing worse than being ignored by the media. On this basis, we can expect more of the same, and sports lawyers can look forward to more cases as sport becomes increasingly troubled and regulated. There is, however, the Victorian tradition that makes an explicit correlation between good sport and sound morals, and this approach may be the new marketing tool:

> This tradition is still encouraged for the purposes of making money. If you have perceived moral value – they call it being a role model – then you make more money in endorsements.[18]

If athletes and leagues determine that there is cash in ethics, then we may see signs of progress.

I am pleased to introduce the third edition of *Sports Law* and congratulate the team on once again getting the result. Simon Gardiner and his colleagues effectively survey the wide range of issues and

---

12 There has been a useful recent reminder to beware of Victorian values: 'This was a ruthless, grabbing, competitive, male-dominated society, stamping on its victims and discarding its weaker members with all the devastating relentlessness of mutant species in Darwin's vision of Nature itself': Wilson, AN, *The Victorians* (London: Hutchinson, 2002), p 120.

13 The 'obesity crisis' succeeds the 'thinness and anorexia crisis' in women's sports.

14 Australia has responded to the 'compensation culture' and the 'liability and insurance crisis'. Australian jurisdictions have implemented tort reforms that provide protection to defendants and emphasise participants' personal responsibility for 'obvious risks'. See, for example, *Civil Liability Act*, 2002 (NSW).

15 SC 2003, c 2. The Act repeals the *Fitness and Amateur Sport Act* of 1961.

16 See further, www.adrsportred.ca.

17 The Policies are available through Sport Canada at www.pch.gc.ca.

18 Simon Barnes, 'Why we are indebted to Johnson' *The Times*, 24 July 2001.

continue the valuable approach that combines practical legal information with analysis of the social and political context of sport. The book shows that United and Wanderers may have their ups and downs, but sport and sports law will always fascinate.

John Barnes

Research Centre for Sport in Canadian Society, University of Ottawa

Author of *Sports and the Law in Canada* (3rd edn, 1996)

June 2005

AUTHOR BIOGRAPHIES

Ian Blackshaw is an International Sports Lawyer and is Visiting Professor at the FIFA International Centre for Sports Studies at Neuchatel University, Switzerland, where he lectures on intellectual property, licensing and merchandising and EU competition and sport. He writes regularly on topical sports legal issues for several journals, including *The International Sports Law Journal*, of which he is Contributing Editor, and also for *The Times*. He is a regular contributor to BBC Sports programmes. He is also a member of the Court of Arbitration for Sport in Lausanne, Switzerland, and the UK Sports Dispute Arbitration and Mediation Panels. He is the author of *Mediating Sports Disputes* (2002) and Editor of *Sports Image Rights Europe* (2004) and *The Court of Arbitration for Sport: The First Twenty Years* (2004), all published by the TMC Asser Press in The Hague.

Simon Boyes is a legal academic at Nottingham Law School, Nottingham Trent University. He teaches on Nottingham Law School's LLM Sports Law, as well as a Sports Law module on the undergraduate law programme. His primary research interests are in the self-regulatory aspects of sport and their relationship with the law, and his published work is primarily in this area including 'The Regulation of Sport and the Impact of the Human Rights Act 1998' [2000] 6 *European Public Law* 517. He also has an interest in the impact of European Union Law on sport. Recent publications include 'In the Shadow of *Bosman*: The Regulatory Penumbra of Sport in the EU' [2003] 12 *Nottingham Law Journal* 72 and 'Protecting Sporting Events for Free-to-Air Broadcast' [2001] 10 *Nottingham Law Journal* 41.

Andrew Caiger is a member of the Cape Town Bar in South Africa. He returned to South Africa after an academic career in the UK of over fifteen years. His current research interests include contract and competition law as it relates to sport. He has read conference papers worldwide including in the UK, USA and South Africa. He teaches a sports law class at the University of South Africa and is a member of the South African Sports Law association. Recent publications include co-editor of *Professional Sport in the European Union: Regulation and Re-regulation* (2000, Asser) (with Simon Gardiner) and 'Shift in the power of English professional football' (2000) *New Zealand Journal of Industrial Relations* (with John O'Leary). He is on the Editorial Board of the *International Sports Law Journal*.

Simon Gardiner is a legal academic at Middlesex University. He is also Senior Research Fellow at the Asser International Sports Law Center, TMC Asser Institute at The Hague. He has been involved in consultancy for a range of sports bodies and has worked with the European Union in terms of anti-doping provisions and the regulation of football hooliganism and the Council of Europe in the area of Conflict Dispute in Sport. He has been an active researcher in the area for over ten years and has an international reputation. His particular research interests include sports governance and the regulation of sports related corruption, racism in sport and the construction of national identity and athlete mobility in sport. He has published widely in sports law, including being co-editor of *Professional Sport in the European Union: Regulation and Re-regulation* (Asser Press, 2000) (with Andrew Caiger) and author of 'UK Sports Law', in Hendrickx, F & Blanpain, R (eds), *International Encyclopaedia of Sports Law* (2006, Kluwer). He is editor of the *Sport and the Law Journal* and co-editor of the *International Sports Law Journal*. He writes a monthly column for *Sport Business International*. He is a member of the Board of Directors of the International Association of Sports Law.

Mark James is a legal academic at the Manchester Metropolitan University's School of Law. His main research interests cover issues of criminal and tortious responsibility for player violence (the subject matter of his PhD) and government regulation of sports fans, on which he has read conference papers in the UK, Europe, the USA and Australia. His recent publications include 'The Trouble with Roy Keane' (2002) 1(3) *Entertainment Law* 72 and 'Virtually Foul or Virtually Fair', in Greenfield, S and Osborn, G, *Readings in Law and Popular Culture*, (2004, Routledge). He is currently working on a series of articles examining the liability of governing bodies for injuries that occur in their sports. He has also had a number of shorter articles published in the *New Law Journal*, *International Sports Law Journal* and the *Sports Law Bulletin*. He is the Assistant Editor of the *Sport and the Law Journal* and the Reviews Editor of *Entertainment Law* and currently supervises a number of LLM and PhDs on a wide range of topics in the fields of sports law and law/popular culture.

John O'Leary is a legal academic at Anglia Polytechnic University. He is also head of the University's Sports Law Unit and Course Leader for the LLM International Sports Law. He has published widely in the areas of doping, stadium safety and sports contracts. He acts as a consultant to sports governing bodies and was co-author of a report on doping for the European Commission. His recent publications include editor of *Drugs and Doping in Sport: Socio-Legal Perspectives* (2000, Cavendish Publishing) and co-author of 'The re-regulation of football and its impact on employment contracts', in Collins, H (ed), *The Legal Regulation of the Employment Relation* (2000, Kluwer) (with Andrew Caiger).

Roger Welch is a legal academic at the University of Portsmouth. His teaching and research interests are primarily in the area of employment law. He has published widely in the area of sports law including 'Sport, Racism and the Limits of Colour Blind Law', in Carrington and McDonald (eds), *Race, Sport and British Society* (2001, Routledge) (with Simon Gardiner); Show Me the Money: Regulation of the Migration of Professional Sportsmen in Post-*Bosman* Europe, in Caiger and Gardiner (eds), *Professional sport in the EU: Regulation and Re-regulation* (2000, The Hague) (with Simon Gardiner); 'A Snort and a Puff: Recreational Drugs and Discipline in Professional Sport', in O' Leary (ed), *Drugs and Doping in Sport*, (2001, Cavendish). He has been a regular contributor to *Sports Law Bulletin*. He has also written extensively on trade union rights. This work includes: *Trade Union Rights in South Africa: The Labour Relations Act 1995* (2000, Institute of Employment Rights); and 'Into the twenty-first Century – The Continuing Indispensability of Collective Bargaining as a Regulator of the Employment Relation', in Collins, Davies and Rideout (eds), *The Legal Regulation of the Employment Relation* (2000, Kluwer).

ACKNOWLEDGMENTS

Grateful acknowledgment is made for the following:

Bale, J, *Landscapes of Modern Sport* (1994), Leicester: Leicester UP

Barnes, J, *Sports and the Law in Canada* (1996), Toronto: Butterworths

Birley, D, *Sport and the Making of Britain* (1993), Manchester: Manchester UP

Bitel, N, 'Ambush marketing' (1997) 5(1) Sport and the Law Journal

Blake, A, *The Body Language: The Meaning of Modern Sport* (1996), London: Lawrence and Wishart

Boyes, S, 'The regulation of sport and the impact of the Human Rights Act 1998' [2000] 6(4) EPL 517

Brackenridge, C, *Spoilsports: Understanding and Preventing Sexual Exploitation in Sport* (2001), London: Routledge

Brearly, M, 'Cricket: Atherton Affair: the dirt that is in all our pockets', *The Observer*, 31 July 1994

Brown, WM, 'Paternalism, drugs and the nature of sport' (1994) XI Journal of the Philosophy of Sport

Cagier, A and Gardiner, S, *Professional Sport in the EU: Regulation and Re-regulation* (2000), The Hague: Asser

Cashmore, E, *Making Sense of Sports* (1996), London: Routledge

Chaudhary, V, 'Asians can play football, too' *The Guardian*, 17 August 1994

Couchman, N, 'IP rights in website content' (2000) 7 Sports and Character Licensing

De Knop, P, 'Globalization, Americanization and localization in sport' (2000) 2 International Sports Law Journal 20

Deloitte & Touche, *Annual Review of Football Finances*, August 2000

Downes, S and Mackay, D, *Running Scared: How Athletics lost its Innocence* (1996), Edinburgh: Mainstream

Dyer, G, 'In the noble art, even failure contains greatness' *The Guardian*, 27 February 1995

Fitzsimons, P, *The Rugby War* (1996), Sydney: HarperSports

Foster, K, 'Developments in sporting law', in Allison, L (ed), *The Changing Politics of Sport* (1993), Manchester: Manchester UP

Foster, K, 'How sport can be regulated', in Greenfield, S and Osborn, G (eds), *Law and Sport in Contemporary Society* (2000), London: Frank Cass

Fraser, D, *Cricket and the Law: The Man in White is Always Right* (1993), Sydney: Institute of Criminology

Gardiner, S, 'The law and hate speech: "Ooh aah Cantona" and the demonstration of "the other" ', in Brown, A (ed), *Fanatics! Power, Identity and Fandom in Football* (1998), London: Routledge

Goldman, B and Klatz, R, *Death in the Locker Room 2* (1992), Chicago: Elite Sports Medicine Publications

Grayson, E, *Sport and the Law* (1994), 2nd edn, London: Butterworths

Haigh, G, *Cricket War: The Inside Story of Packer's World Series Cricket* (1993), Melbourne: Text Publishing Company

Hargreaves, J, *Sport, Power and Culture: A Social and Historical Analysis of Popular Sports in Britain* (1986), Cambridge: Polity

Holt, R, *Sport and the British: A Modern History* (1989), Oxford: Clarendon

Lazic, V, 'Conference on ADR in sports disputes' (2001) 5/6 International Sports Law Journal 35

Leaman, O, 'Cheating and fair play in sport', in Morgan, W (ed), *Sport and the Humanities: A Collection of Original Essays* (1981), Educational Research and Service, University of Tennessee

Long, J, Tongue, N, Spacklen, K and Carrington, B, *What's the Difference? A Study of the Nature and Extent of Racism in Rugby League* (1995), School of Leisure and Sports Studies, Leeds Metropolitan University

Longmore, A, 'Absurd cup rule obscures football's final goal' *The Times*, 1 February 1994

Mason, T, *Sport in Britain* (1988), London: Faber & Faber

McVicar, J, 'Violence in Britain: the sporting life of crime' *The Guardian*, 19 September 1995

Monnington, T, 'Politicians and sport: uses and abuses', in Allison, L (ed), *The Changing Politics of Sport* (1992), Manchester: Manchester UP

Morris, P and Little, G, 'Challenging sports bodies' determinations' (1998) 17 Civil Justice Quarterly

Nelson, G, *Left Foot Forward* (1995), London: Headline

Redhead, S, *Unpopular Culture: The Birth of Law and Popular Culture* (1995), Manchester: Manchester UP

Regan, T, 'Why hunting and trappings are wrong', in William, J and Meier, K (eds), *Philosophical Inquiry in Sport* (1995), Champaign: Human Kinetics

Reid, R, 'Report of the FA Premier League Seminar', 8 January 1996, British Association for Sport and Law

Ryan, J, *Little Girls in Pretty Boxes* (1995), New York: Warner

Sheard, K, 'Aspects of boxing in the Western civilising process' (1997) 32(1) International Review for the Sociology of Sport

Sutcliffe, P, 'The noble art?', *Total Sport*, February 1996

Verow, R, Lawrence, C and McCormick, P, *Sport, Business and the Law* (1999), Bristol: Jordan

Whannel, G, *Fields in Vision: Television, Sport and Cultural Transformation* (1992), London: Routledge

Williams, J, 'Support for all?', *121 When Saturday Comes*, March 1997

HarperCollins Australia for permission to reproduce extracts from Brasch, R, *How Did Sports Begin?* (1986)

The Institute for the Study and Treatment of Delinquency, King's College London, Strand, London, WC2R 2LS; email: istd.enq@kcl.ac.uk; website: www.kcl.ac.uk/orgs/istd for permission to reproduce extracts from Robins, D, 'Sport and crime prevention: the evidence of research' (1996) 23 Criminal Justice Matters

SDRP for Rules for Arbitration (issued on 13 October 1999)

British Medical Association for *The Boxing Debate* (1993)

IAAF for IAAF Procedural Guidelines for Doping Control 1996

Virgin Publishing Ltd for permission for the extract taken from *Football Babylon*® Russ Williams (1996)

'Anzla News Ltd's Super League Appeal Success', Anzla Newsletter Update, January 1997

We would like to thank the Court of Arbitration for Sport, the Council of Europe, the European Commission, the English Football Association, the International Cricket Council, the International Olympic Committee, the Organisers of 'The Rules of the Game' – Europe's first conference on the Governance of Sport (www.governance-in-sport.com) and the UK Sports Dispute Resolution Panel for reproduction of materials.

There are many people to thank who have provided formal and informal comments on ideas and issues that have become part of this book. We are particularly grateful to John Barnes, Michael Beloff QC, Adam Brown, Brian Doyle, Jonathan Fitchen, Ken Foster, Andy Gibson, James Gray, Barrie Houlihan, Vicki Latta, Dave McArdle, Paul McCutcheon, Phillip Morris, Steve Morrow, Urvasi Naidoo, Michael Nash, Richard Parrish, Nades Raja, Fraser Reid, Robert Siekmann, Janwillem Soek, Sue Taylor, Michelle Verroken, Emile Vrijman, Stephen Weatherill, John Wolohan, for the support they have provided. A number of materials have been included from these writers, especially from contributions to *Sports Law Bulletin*. We would like to thank colleagues at Cavendish Publishing for their patience and continued support.

We would also like to thank all the undergraduate and postgraduate students who we have taught over the last few years who have always been prepared to enter a dialogue and have provided many useful insights to the whole range of sports law issues.

We thank those who have allowed the inclusion of their work. Every effort has been made to trace all the copyright holders but if any have been inadvertently overlooked the publishers will be pleased to make the necessary arrangement at the first opportunity.

CONTENTS

SECTION 1: SPORT, LAW AND SOCIETY

SECTION 2: THE GOVERNANCE OF SPORT

SECTION 4: REGULATION OF THE SPORTS WORKPLACE

To all our families. Thank you for all your support, and in particular for Alexander, Maighraed, Niamh and Orfhlaith – the sports lawyers of tomorrow.

TABLE OF CASES

TABLE OF STATUTES

TABLE OF STATUTORY INSTRUMENTS

TABLE OF EU SECONDARY LEGISLATION

SPORT, LAW AND SOCIETY

CHAPTER 1

HISTORICAL AND CULTURAL PERSPECTIVES ON SPORT REGULATION

The rule of law in sport is as essential for civilisation as the rule of law in society generally. Without it generally anarchy reigns. Without it in sport, chaos exists.[1]

THE CONTEMPORARY SIGNIFICANCE OF SPORT

Sport is a truly global phenomenon. As a social activity, whether it is in terms of participation as a recreational pastime, competitive playing at amateur levels, the elite and mainly professional level or in terms of spectating, sport assumes immense cultural significance.[2]

Sport is going through significant changes: the context within which law has assumed an increasingly important role in regulating sport will be analysed during this chapter. The chapter is divided into three sections. First, the cultural and political significance of sport will be evaluated together with a discussion of various sociological theories that have developed to explain the role that sport plays. Second, a question will be posed, namely 'what is sport?' This will be answered by both looking at various social definitions of sport and the historical origins of its development and identification. Third, the historical regulatory environment of sport in Britain will be examined and a link made with contemporary areas of sporting activity subject to legal regulation.

Sport is very much a part of popular culture and our consumption of it is increasingly mediated through television, radio, newspapers and a myriad of 'new technologies'. In Britain, more sport is shown on television than ever before. Satellite television, in the guise of Rupert Murdoch's BSkyB with numerous dedicated sports channels and, to a lesser extent, the other terrestrial and cable channels, has had an immense impact upon the financial contours of contemporary elite sport. Sport is a major element on both national and local radio. Sport has also become a major part of the circulation battle between national newspapers, and the number of lavish magazines on sport and recreation have multiplied. Sport books are often in the best sellers list and a number have clear literary merit.[3] The academic study of sport has mushroomed in the last 30 years with many university centres focusing on the scientific, philosophical, sociological, historical and legal study of sport; and there is a huge associated volume of work.

Blake, A, *The Body Language: The Meaning of Modern Sport*

... sport is very much part of popular culture. Many people participate in it, either as amateurs or professionals and many people observe it as spectators inside stadia or by listening to the radio or

---

1   Grayson, E, former President of the British Association for Sport and Law, in his inaugural presidential address (1993) 1(1) Sport and the Law Journal.

2   For an examination of many of the cultural issues concerning sport see Tomlinson, A (ed), *The Sports Studies Reader: Sport, Culture and Society* (2001), London: Routledge; Cashmore, E (ed), *Sports Culture: An A–Z Guide* (2000), London: Routledge; and *Making Sense of Sport* (2000), 3rd edn, London: Routledge.

3   Football books include Hopcraft, A, *The Football Man: People and Passions in Football* (1968), London: Penguin; Davies, H, *The Glory Years*; Davies, P, *All Played Out – The Full Story of Italia '90* (1990), London: Mandarin; Hornby, N, *Fever Pitch* (1992), London: Indigo; Hamilton, I, *Gazza Agonistes* (1993), London: Granta; Winner, D, *Brilliant Orange: The Neurotic Genius of Dutch Football* (2000), London: Bloomsbury. A cricket masterpiece is James, C, *Beyond a Boundary* (1996), London: Serpent's Tail. On boxing see Remnick, D, *The King of the World* (2000), London: Picador; Michell, K, *War Baby* (2001), London: Random House.

watching television. At any rate, sport is continuously visible elsewhere in the world. Indeed, as this book will argue, sport is a crucial component of contemporary society, one very important way through which many of us understand our bodies, our minds and the rest of the world. This is true not only because of mass participation and observation: sport saturates the language that surrounds us. Sporting activity is reported in every newspaper; it forms an important part of the wider literary culture of magazines and books. Take the annual American journal of record, the *Britannica Yearbook for 1994*. In the section devoted to reviewing the previous year's events, Sports and Games form by far the longest entry. Forty pages are devoted to reports of events from the world of sport and a further 28 pages give 'the sporting record' of performance statistics (winners, newly broken records, times and distances); both national and global events are covered, from archery through gymnastics and rodeo to wrestling. By contrast, there are only 20 pages on economic affairs and coverage of the arts is far thinner, with only four pages each on dance, music (covering both classical and popular) and publishing.

Sport is also perpetually audible and visible through the electronic media. Television and radio devote a great deal of time to sport. There are whole departments of most networks devoted to sport as current affairs, providing everything from the brief reporting of results on news programmes to the saturation coverage of events like the Olympics, World Cups and national championships in team sports on both mainstream and dedicated programmes and channels. Sport is arguably one of the most powerful presences within broadcasting. Both on television and radio, the principle of live coverage is often taken to mean that sporting events have priority over others. As well as driving other programming from the screen at certain times of the year, sport can instantly reshape television in a way which can only be matched by political crises or disasters involving loss of life. Unexpectedly rearranged fixtures or more routinely, late finishing matches, disrupt published broadcast schedules, to the distress of people who do not wish to stay up late or people who have programmed their video recorders to record scheduled programmes. This prioritised saturation coverage means that even those uninterested in sport or hostile to it, cannot escape its nagging presence, as an ongoing part of the 'background noise' of contemporary culture.[4]

Another perspective on the cultural significance of sport presents a theory of the relationship between sport and culture in the context of power relations:

Hargreaves, J, *Sport, Power and Culture*

When we refer to culture in the substantive sense, then, we mean first those activities, institutions and processes that are more implicated in the systematic production and reproduction of systems of meaning and/or those not concerned mainly or immediately with economic or political processes but which instead encompass other kinds of vital activities. We are referring here to major institutions, such as religion, education, science, the arts, the media of communication, the family, leisure and recreation, as well as sports – and, in fact, to much of the routine practice of everyday life. Secondly we find it useful to employ the ethnographer's substantive sense of culture as a 'whole way of life' of a particular group of people. Culture here refers to the way different threads of similarly placed individuals' lives – work, leisure, family, religion, community, etc are woven into a fabric or tradition, consisting of customs, ways of seeing, beliefs, attitudes, values, standards, styles, ritual practices, etc giving them a definite character and identity. It is thus we speak here of working-class culture, men's and women's culture, black culture, bourgeois culture and youth culture. Cultures in this sense are profound sources of power, reproducing social divisions here, challenging and rebelling against them there, while in many ways accommodating subordinate groups to the social order. We will be at pains to develop the theme throughout this study that the function and significance of sports varies with the type of culture in question and even does so within cultures. We will be arguing that it is precisely because sport plays different roles in relation to different cultures that it is able to reproduce power relations.

---

4   Blake, A, *The Body Language: The Meaning of Modern Sport* (1996), London: Lawrence & Wishart, pp 11–12.

We contend that, in addition, the linkages between sport and power cannot be elucidated without reference to two other forms of culture – popular culture and consumer culture. As the term implies, popular culture engages 'the people' and although, therefore, it is not the product or possession of any one specific group, popular culture does overlap to a perplexing degree with working-class culture and the culture of subordinate groups as a whole. While expressing in its content and idiom the experience of those whom it engages, like its political counterpart 'populism', it does so ambivalently, facing simultaneously in a radical and in a conservative direction – for popular culture as we know expresses a certain critical penetration of the power structure, while also manifesting a complicity in it. The long historical association between sports and popular culture, culminating in sport becoming a major component of the national popular culture is, we argue, highly significant for the character of sport. Accordingly, one of our major themes will be the ambivalent relation between sport and power, exemplified best perhaps, in that mixture of respectable family entertainment, violence, rebellion and chauvinism that characterises modern day professional football.

Consumer culture, by which we mean the way of life associated with and reproduced through the operations of consumer capitalism, clearly in many ways also overlaps with working-class and popular culture, to the extent that many aspects of the latter, notably sports, seem to have been in effect appropriated by consumer culture. We will be exploring the significance of the increasing tendency of sport to become one more commodity and attempting to specify the extent to which sporting activity, as an aspect of working-class and of popular culture, remains autonomous. In particular we are rather sceptical of the notion that sport has been absorbed into a manipulated form of culture supposedly exercising a uniformly conservative influence over 'the masses'; and we will be attempting to pinpoint ways in which, as far as commodified sport is concerned, it also exhibits an ambivalent tendency to, on the one hand, accommodate subordinate groups and on the other hand, to stimulate resistance and rebellion in certain ways.[5]

SPORT AND POLITICS

Sport tells us much about the dynamics of social change in society. It represents a powerful political force: organisations such as the Fédération Internationale de Football Associations (FIFA)[6] and the International Olympic Committee (IOC)[7] are more influential than many countries:

Yallop, D, *How They Stole the Game*

He [Dr Joao Havelange] saw himself as the most powerful man in the world. He was in charge of the world's greatest religion and the coming summer's ceremonies would be watched on television by a cumulative audience of forty billion people. More than six times the population of the world. An aide hurried forward and muttered in the ear of His Majesty. The aide had to reach on tiptoe to reach the royal ear. In his eighty-second year, the Sun King still stood six feet tall. The athletic muscle tone of his youth had softened slightly but though his weight was now some ten kilos more than in his prime, he remained

---

5   Hargreaves, J, *Sport, Power and Culture: A Social and Historical Analysis of Popular Sports in Britain* (1986), Cambridge: Polity, pp 9–10.

6   For a discussion of the role of FIFA, see Yallop, D, *How They Stole the Game* (1999), London: Poetic Products; Duke, V, and Crolley, L, *Football Nationality and the State* (1996), Harlow: Longman; Sugden, J and Tomlinson, A, *FIFA and the Contest for World Football* (1998), London: Polity; and 'Who rules the people's game? FIFA versus UEFA in the struggle for control of world football', in Brown, A (ed), *Fanatics! Power, Identity and Fandom in Football* (1998), London: Routledge.

7   For a discussion of the role of IOC, see Jennings, A, *The New Lords of the Rings* (1996), London: Pocket Books; *The Great Olympic Swindle: When the World Wanted Its Games Back* (2000), London: Simon & Schuster; Tomlinson, A; Whannel, G (eds), *Five Ring Circus – Money, Power and Politics at the Olympic Games* (1984), London: Pluto; and Hill, C, *Olympic Politics* (1992), Manchester: Manchester UP.

an imposing figure. His face, which usually resembled a well-kept grave, hovered on a smile, then reverted to a baleful stare, but it was still obvious that he was savouring the moment. 'Do excuse me, ladies and gentlemen. I have to take a phone call from President Chirac.' Presidents. Kings and Queens. Heads of State. Prime Ministers. He has met every world leader. His Holiness the Pope has been granted a number of audiences. The Sun King has a very clear view of his place in the world order. 'Do you consider yourself the most powerful man in the world?' Most men asked such a question would demur. Would dismiss it with a laugh. Dr Joao Havelange, President of Federation Internationale de Football Association – FIFA – did not demur and he certainly did not laugh. 'I've been to Russia twice, invited by President Yeltsin. I've been to Poland with their President. In the 1990 World Cup in Italy I saw Pope John Paul II three times. When I go to Saudi Arabia, King Fahd welcomes me in splendid fashion. In Belgium I had a one and a half hour meeting with King Albert. Do you think a Head of State will spare that much time to just anyone? That's respect. That's the strength of FIFA. I can talk to any President, but they'll be talking to a President too on an equal basis. They've got their power, and I've got mine: the power of football, which is the greatest power there is. That's the Havelenge version of "yes" '.8

The selection process of host cities for the summer and winter Olympics has created some disquiet for many years. However, it was not until 1998 that the full situation was exposed. Andrew Jennings comments:

Jennings, A, *The Great Olympic Swindle: When the World Wanted Its Games Back*

There was no problem until people outside the Olympic family found out, and that wrecked Christmas 1998, the world's press united in disgust at the notion that bribery should taint the near sacred Olympics, and the family set about defending what credibility it had left ... he [President Samaranch] personally selected five trusty IOC members to investigate their peers ... there was bad behaviour, they said, and the hosts were the culprits. Those people were so insistent, and persistent, and well, so darned friendly down in Utah that some vulnerable members thought that those lovely gifts were about personal friendship, nothing to do with the business of getting the games. A few Olympic heads rolled.9

Not only has the selection procedure been exposed as corrupt,10 it represents the interstices of complex political interests of the bidders, the IOC and other nation states. The choice for the host city for the 2008 summer Olympics is a good example. Beijing, after narrowly losing out in the past, developed another bid and was successful. The human rights record in China came under the spotlight, and the 'practicalities' of deciding how relevant an issue this should be in the IOC's determination was vigorously contested.

Chaudhary, V, 'This decision will allow a police state to bask in reflected glory'

The decision to award Beijing the 2008 Olympic Games was greeted with concern and criticism from around the world, particularly over how China might exploit the games to cover up its poor human rights record and maintain a totalitarian regime. The American Government, which has tense relations with China, said its athletes would compete in Beijing and that the decision about where the games take place was up to the International Olympic Committee.

Condoleezza Rice, George Bush's national security adviser, said: 'We understand that this was a decision for the IOC to take. What we do know is that American athletes are going to go there, and they're going to compete and hopefully bring home lots of gold medals.' President Bush was said to be neutral on the issue. Ms Rice said the US remained concerned about the state of human rights in China. She said: 'The President has made very clear that human rights will be on the agenda. We have a human rights agenda with China, I think the Chinese expect it and we'll continue to pursue that in our bilateral relationship.'

---

8   *Op cit*, fn 6, Yallop (1999), pp 11–12.
9   *Op cit*, fn 7, Jennings (2002), p 2.
10   See pp 314–318 on the investigation of IOC corruption.

A spokesman for the British Government said: 'We very much hope that the Olympics will play a positive role in China.'

The island state of Taiwan, which is not officially recognised by China, said it hoped that the decision to award Beijing the games would decrease tension in the region. The Tibetan Government in exile, which is based in India, criticised the IOC for awarding the games to Beijing. China has been accused of carrying out widespread human rights abuses in Tibet after invading the region in 1950.

Kalon TC Tethong, spokesman for the exiled Tibetan Government, said the Olympic Games would mean more repression, referring to 'the suffering that will be unleashed on ordinary people by a totalitarian one-party state which will assume that it has received international permission for its horrendous repression'.

While officially western governments remained tight-lipped, individual politicians said the IOC was wrong to choose Beijing. In Washington, Tom Lantos, the house international relations committee's leading Democrat, said: 'It truly boggles the mind. This decision will allow the Chinese police state to bask in the reflected glory of the Olympic Games despite having one of the most abominable human rights records in the world.'

In Europe, the French were most critical of China's human rights record and the IOC's decision. François Loncle, the head of parliament's foreign affairs committee, said: 'Following the example of Nazi Germany in 1936 and the Soviet Union in 1980, communist China will use the games as a powerful propaganda instrument destined to consolidate its hold on power.'[11]

Although the focus of this book is on the regulation of British sport, it has already been stated that this cannot be understood purely in national terms. The wider supra-national and international regulatory environment needs to be considered and as will be considered later, the process of globalisation as it applies to sport is a crucial factor. Football is probably the one true global sport:[12]

Gardiner, S and Felix, A, 'Juridification of the football field: strategies for giving law the elbow'

The cultural significance of football is enormous. Its ubiquity as the world's premier sport provides it with a unique position. Kitchen has called football the only 'global idiom' apart from science. It is truly a global sport with the majority of the world's nations members of the Federation Internationale de Football Associations (FIFA). The influence of FIFA should not be understated. From its Geneva headquarters it has direct contacts with many heads of State. It has in the past applied for observer status at the United Nations. The President, Joao Havelange, has largely been responsible for elevating the influence of FIFA and accommodating external pressures such as television. He was nominated for the Nobel Peace Prize in 1988. Bill Shankly's often quoted belief that football is not just a matter of life or death – it is more important – may seem an exaggeration of reality but for many its influence is as profound as any fundamentalist religion. For example in 1964, during a match between Peru and Argentina in Lima, it was estimated that 318 people died in rioting that was initiated largely due to the result. The murder of the Colombian player, Andres Escobar, after his own-goal in the 1994 World Cup, displays the extreme response that can be engendered by failure.

What cannot be refuted however is the growth of football as the global game and essentially in most countries as an important element of working-class culture. As with other mass participation and spectator sports, football is highly significant in popular discourse. Both in national and international contexts, football personifies the sectarianism of class, regional and national rivalry. The mass media play a crucial role in its representation magnifying the significance of these competitive elements. Football has undergone

---

11   Chaudhary, V, 'This decision will allow a police state to bask in reflected glory' *The Guardian*, 14 July 2001.

12   Over two billion people were estimated to have watched the 1994 World Cup final between Brazil and Italy (*The Times*, 18 July 1994), with a cumulative audience of 31 billion people – more than five times the population of earth.

many changes. Commercialisation has brought incremental change. Today it is increasingly commodified and developing as an integral part of the leisure industry ... In England the emergence of the Premier league or 'Premiership' as 'whole new ball game', reflects the view of football's potential as a big money maker. Players have also been the winners with incomes changing the financial contours of the game.[13]

Within both the national and the international community, the relationship between sport and formal politics is complex.[14] The argument that sport is apolitical in the sense of being neutral and value-free in terms of cultural values is often promulgated. Is sport really separate from formal politics? There are many examples where sport has become a part of the political arena and has been 'used' for political ends. Sporting boycotts have been used many times in recent history – it is a question of conjecture how effective they have been:

Monnington, T, 'Politicians and sport: uses and abuses'

The characteristic forceful intervention of Mrs Thatcher in policy implementation, which was much in evidence during the passage of the Football Spectators Bill, had been similarly apparent earlier in her administration in 1980, again in the sports arena. The major debate in international politics in 1980 was the Soviet Union's actions in Afghanistan. It was not only the intervention of that country in the domestic affairs of another sovereign State, but also the reported atrocities perpetrated there that aroused international concern. Direct action was impossible by either the British or American Governments. In an endeavour to cause as much embarrassment to the Soviet Government as possible the Carter administration in the USA implemented a boycott of the forthcoming Olympic Games in Moscow that summer. Mrs Thatcher intervened personally in support of the American Games boycott and called on British athletes and the British Olympic Association to boycott the Games also.

The very limited success of this British boycott is again well-documented history, but its significance less so. The real diplomatic value of the American boycott in influencing the government of the USSR, according to a study by J H Frey, was minimal. He revealed that analysis of top-level contacts between the USA and USSR Governments around the time of the Moscow Games made no reference to the boycott. The use of sport in this context was more for media and public consumption.

The consequence for the British political scene was not only an early indication of Thatcher's tendency to become involved directly in a wide range of policy matters, but also her willingness to ride roughshod over the heads of her ministers. The then Minister for Sport, Hector Munroe, was not even called to speak in the House of Commons debate on the Moscow Olympics, held in March 1980.

For Mrs Thatcher her intervention into the sporting arena proved to be a political disaster. Although she was not prepared to go as far as Jimmy Carter in withdrawing the British competitors from the Games, she did consider seizing the passports of British competitors until advised as to the likely illegality of such an action. Attempts to persuade the British Olympic Association to refuse to send a team met with a frosty response.

Threats of dismissal were even made to members of the British team who were public employees if they chose to take their holidays at a time that would allow them to travel to Moscow for the Games. Several of the athletes faced with this threat resigned from their jobs rather than acquiesce to this overt pressure. In the end, with only a limited number of enforced absences, a British team attended the Games, competing under the Olympic flag. For the British Government and Mrs Thatcher in particular the entire incident was an embarrassment, an example of political naivety and a failed attempt to bring British sport into the Cold War political arena.

---

13   Gardiner, S and Felix, A, 'Juridification of the football field: strategies for giving law the elbow' (1995) 5(2) Marquette Sports Law Journal 189, p 191.

14   See Arnaud, P and Riordan, J, *Sport and International Politics: Impact of Fascism and Communism on Sport* (1998), London: Routledge.

Five years later, when the Heysel Stadium incident was debated in Cabinet, it was Mrs Thatcher and her senior ministers who were involved, not Colin Moynihan. Moynihan had, as Macfarlane suggested, 'become a member of the smallest and most unimportant trade union in the House, the Trade Union of Ministers with special responsibility for Sport'.

The forceful diplomatic stand that Mrs Thatcher took with respect to the Soviet intervention into Afghanistan and her support for the American boycott of the Moscow Olympics contrasts with her position on South Africa. She maintained the support of the British Government for the Gleneagles Agreement signed by Callaghan in 1977, which discouraged sporting links with South Africa. But she has often been criticised as selective in her isolation policy with respect to that country by maintaining diplomatic and trade links. Sport was apparently an easy public policy weapon, without any real diplomatic or political recoil, to express the British Government's opposition to another country's conduct in its domestic affairs.

Mrs Thatcher's reluctance to take such a firm stand over sporting contacts with South Africa as she had with respect to the USSR in 1980, along with her obvious eagerness to avoid bringing South Africa to its knees through the imposition of economic sanctions, alienated many of the member nations of the British Commonwealth. The policy consequence for many of these nations was the boycott of the 1986 Commonwealth Games in Edinburgh. Mrs Thatcher was held to be personally responsible for their absence from the Games.

There are several other areas where sport has experienced the consequences of 'Thatcherism'. These have occurred when reforms such as compulsory competitive tendering, local management of schools, the 'opting-out' of schools from local authority control and actual local authority restructuring have been implemented. In addition, the current debate over the national curriculum in physical education bears the imprint of Thatcherism. But it is important to appreciate a subtle, yet important, difference here. Sport is affected in these instances as a consequence of policy, rather than being used as an instrument of policy implementation.

A final consideration must be the relationship of Mrs Thatcher to the Sports Council. She came to power with a 'New Right' ideological belief that government 'quangos' (quasi-autonomous non-governmental organisations) should be curtailed in power and number. The reality was that after 11 years in office the importance of such bodies was not significantly reduced. In particular, the Sports Council remained in existence, with an enhanced role and a much increased grant from government. However, it too did not remain isolated from the tentacles of Thatcherism. Increasingly, the Council was subjected to 'clientism' as successive Ministers for Sport, closely directed by Mrs Thatcher, more rigidly interpreted the Council's Royal Charter and regarded the body as an 'executive arm of government'. In particular the Council increasingly mirrored the government's stance on the role of sport in the maintenance of public order. A coincidental policy match or an example of the guiding hand of government? Have the most appropriate policy initiatives for sport that the Sports Council should have been pursuing, been compromised or stifled as a result of government interference?

The hand of Thatcher with respect to sport, despite her apparent indifference to the activity itself, was clearly evident during her Premiership. Sport was used and perhaps abused in a very distinctive manner. The jury remains out, however, still considering its verdict on the consequences of her policies for sport.

Thus two highly visible politicians, Margaret Thatcher and Ronald Reagan have in their own particular manner utilised sport as a valuable medium to further their own political objectives. They both left office when their finest hours were perhaps already behind them. But they have left a political legacy that is both significant in terms of policy successes as well as failures, and also in terms of style. The 'Gipper' and the 'Iron lady' have assured themselves a place in the annals of both political, as well as sporting, history.[15]

---

15 Monnington, T, 'Politicians and sport: uses and abuses', in Allison, L (ed), *The Changing Politics of Sport* (1992), Manchester: Manchester UP, p 128.

Gardiner, S and Felix, A, 'Juridification of the football field: strategies for giving law the elbow'

The relationship between sport and formal politics is however conversely best categorised as one that 'lacks invisibility'. Although sport in general, and football in particular, have been projected as autonomous from political values, they have been used both in terms of liberation and the soliciting of legitimacy. The role of sport in the war against apartheid in South Africa cannot be overstated. Conversely there are a number of examples of the role sport has played in deception and distortion of political reality. The Brazilian national football team has been used to symbolise harmony and well-being in general life. The 'beautiful game' can be easily used to promote the beautiful life. In 1970 the winning of the World Cup was used to distract concern away from the injustices of military rule. Today similarly the exploits of Romario, Babeto et al and the winning of another World Cup (in 1994) have been used to attempt to deflect national and international concern away from the infanticide being practised by the 'Justiceros' vigilante squads. Ironically, one sure way for street kids to escape the likelihood of an early death is to excel at football.[16]

Largely due to sport's immense cultural importance, politicians are prone to see sport as a powerful political tool. Of course this does not always have negative connotations. Sport can be used to support very positive values of community and co-operation. It can also powerfully show disapproval. Many influential commentators have argued that the sports boycott of South Africa during the apartheid era played an important role within the general political and economic boycott.[17] The Gleneagles Agreement adopted by the Commonwealth heads of government was intended:

> ... [To urge member governments] to combat the evil of apartheid by withholding any form of support for, and by taking every practical step to discourage contact or competition by their nationals with sporting organizations, teams or sportsmen from South Africa.[18]

Sport has also increasingly been seen as an area of human activity with which the European Union should be involved; mainly because of its commercial structure, but also because of its cultural significance and ability to transcend national barriers.

SOCIOLOGY OF SPORT

The role of sport in society needs explanation: traditional sociological theories develop competing perspectives:[19]

Coakley, J, *Sport in Society: Issues and Controversies*

Sociology provides a number of theoretical frameworks that can be used to understand the relationship between sport and society and each takes us in a different direction ... we focused on four of those frameworks: functionalism, conflict theory, critical theory and symbolic interactionism. The purpose of this chapter was to show that each framework has something to offer, helping us understand sport as a social phenomena. For example functionalist theory offers an explanation for positive consequences associated with sport involvement in the lives of both athletes and spectators. Conflict theory identifies serious problems in sports and offers explanations of how and why players and spectators are oppressed and exploited for economic purposes. Critical theory suggests that sports are connected with social

---

16 *Op cit*, fn 13, Gardiner and Felix (1995), pp 194–95.

17 See Osborne, P, *Basil D'Oliveira: Cricket and Controversy* (2004), Little Brown: London.

18 *The Gleneagles Agreement on Sporting Contacts with South Africa* (1981), London. See Nafziger, J, *International Sports Law* (1988), New York: Transnational; Booth, D, *The Race Game: Sport and Politics in South Africa* (1998), London: Frank Cass, for a discussion on the effects of the agreement and other moves by the United Nations.

19 For both general reading and explanation of both general and specific theories see Coakley, J, *Sport in Society: Issues and Controversies* (1994), St Louis: Mosbey; op cit, fn 5, Hargreaves (1986); Jarvie, G and Maguire, J, *Sport and Leisure in Social Thought* (1994), London: Routledge, p 179; *op cit*, fn 2, Cashmore (2000).

relations in complex and diverse ways and that sports change as power and resources shift and as there are changes in social, political and economic relations in society. Social interactionism suggests that an understanding of sport requires an understanding of the meanings, identities and interaction associated with sport involvement.

It is also useful to realise that each theoretical perspective has its own weaknesses. Functionalist theory leads to exaggerated accounts of the positive consequences of sports and sport participation; it mistakenly assumes that there are no conflicts of interests between groups within society; and it ignores powerful historical and economic factors that have influenced social events and social relationships. Conflict theory is deterministic, it overemphasises the importance of economic factors in society and it focuses most of its attention on top-level spectator sports, which make up only a part of sport in any society. Critical theory provides no explicit guidelines for determining when sports are sources of opposition to the interests of powerful groups within society and it is only beginning to generate research on the everyday experiences of people involved in struggles to define and organise sport in particular ways. Symbolic interactionism does a poor job relating what goes on in sports with general patterns of social inequality in society as a whole and it generally ignores the body and physical experiences when it considers the self and issues of identity ... Which theory or theoretical framework will lead us to the truth about sports?[20]

Coakley's account of the main theoretical perspectives identifies functionalism,[21] conflict theory,[22] critical theory[23] and symbolic interactionism.[24] There is not enough space to discuss any of these in detail. They all have some validity in understanding sport as a social phenomenon, and particular theoretical perspectives are used as the basis of research methodology for individual researchers' own projects within this discipline.

The descriptions of the various areas of sports law in this book have not adopted a theoretical approach, although there is a dominant ideology in Western jurisprudence of legal positivism, in seeing law as autonomous and separate from political values. These alternative sociological theoretical perspectives listed above are applied to the study of the sociology of law as they are to the sociology of sport. This book explicitly assumes a view of the law as a political instrument. Law is not value free; it is not democratic in terms of its construction. Law reflects the dynamic of power relations in society and changes as social, political and economic relations shift. Law is not a neutral mechanism, separate from societal values.

The use of law in regulating sport needs therefore to be understood in the context and recognition of it being used in a contingent and ideological way. Critical theory in sports sociology is probably the theoretical perspective, which is the most plausible in the subsequent theoretical explanation of law's intervention in sport. The concept of 'hegemony', largely introduced by the Italian Marxist, Antonio Gramsci,[25] and developed in the sport context by John Hargreaves, is central to this theoretical view.[26] What it characterises 'is the achievement of consent or agreement' to dominant ideologies in

---

20 *Ibid*, Coakley (1994), pp 49–50.

21 See Uschen, G, 'The interdependence of sport and culture', in Loy, J *et al* (eds), *Sport, Culture and Society* (1981), Philadelphia: Lea and Febiger; Wohl, A, 'Sport and social development' (1979) 14(3) International Review of Sport Sociology 5–18.

22 See Hammond, D, *Foul Play: A Class Analysis of Sport* (1993), London: Ubique.

23 See *op cit*, fn 5, Hargreaves (1986); Messner, M, *Power at Play: Sports and the Problem of Masculinity* (1992), Boston: Beacon; Donnelly, P (ed), 'British cultural studies and sport' (1992) 9(2) Special Issue of Sociology of Sport Journal.

24 Coakley, J and White, A, 'Making decisions: gender and sport participation amongst British adolescents' (1992) 9(1) Sociology of Sport Journal 20.

25 Gramsci, A, *The Prison Notebooks* (1971), London: Lawrence & Wishart.

26 See earlier, pp 11–12.

society, those determined by the groups who hold social, economic and political power and promoted as being in the interests of the whole of society. Sport, as an immensely powerful cultural institution, is seen as helping to carry out this process.

Feminist Theories of Sport

Men have historically monopolised sports participation in all capacities. In recent years, however, the involvement of women has increased despite many forms of resistance. Coakley recognises feminist theories as a form of critical theory which are becoming more important in the study of sport:

Coakley, J, *Sport in Society: Issues and Controversies*

Feminists describe sports as 'gendered' activities. The fact that organised sports were developed to emphasise competition, efficiency and performance ranking systems and to devalue supportiveness and caring contributions to the 'gendered' character. To say that sports are 'engendered' activities and to say that sports organisations are 'gendered' structures means that they have been socially constructed out of the values and experiences of men.[27]

Jarvie, G and Maguire, J, *Sport and Leisure in Social Thought*

It might be suggested that some or all of the following concerns have been central to many feminist accounts of sport and leisure: (a) to consider the structures which have historically exploited, devalued and often oppressed women; (b) to consider various strategies which are committed to changing the condition of women; (c) to adopt a critical perspective towards intellectual traditions and methods which have ignored or justified women's oppression; (d) to explain women's involvement in and alienation from different sport and leisure contexts and practices; and (e) to highlight the engendered nature of sport and leisure organisation, bureaucracies and hierarchies.[28]

Although there are many varieties of feminist methodology–liberal, radical, black and post-modern–the focus has been on why women are devalued in sport.[29] Areas of inquiry include levels of participation in sport; legitimate use of the female body; barriers to participation and consumption; and biological myths surrounding performance.[30] The law has provided some provision for challenging sex discrimination in sport and this will be considered in Chapter 14.

Figurational Theory

One applied theoretical position that has been massively influential on the British sociology of sport movement is that of 'Figuration' as espoused by Norbert Elias and developed by Eric Dunning.[31] Elias argues that British society since the late Middle Ages has become increasingly codified with rules and norms gradually being introduced to govern human activity.

---

27 *Op cit*, fn 19, Coakley (1994), p 38.
28 *Op cit*, fn 19, Jarvie and Maguire (1994), p 179.
29 See a good discussion in Scraton, S and Flintoff, A, *Gender and Sport Reader* (2001), London: Routledge.
30 See Tomlinson, A (ed), *Gender, Sport and Leisure* (1995), Brighton: University of Brighton; Hargreaves, J, *Sporting Females: Critical Issues in the History and Sociology of Women's Sport* (1994), London: Routledge; Humberstone, B (ed), *Researching Women and Sport* (1997), London: Macmillan.
31 See Elias, N, *The Civilising Process* (1939), Oxford: Blackwell; and Dunning, E, *Sport Matters: Sociological Studies of Sport, Violence and Civilisation* (1999), London: Routledge.

Blake, A, *The Body Language: The Meaning of Modern Sport*

Since the 1950s the so-called 'figurative sociology', the work of Norbert Elias and his followers, has become influential. Elias has always been interested in sports and his theories have always been applied to sports as much as to other aspects of society. The argument involves a particular interpretation of history. Here is the outline of the argument. Elias and friends argue that since the Middle Ages, western society has become more 'civilised', by which they mean better behaved, more temperate and less violent. Medieval sport was a violent part of a violent society: aristocratic tournaments, wild boar hunting and quarterstaff fighting could all involve the serious injury, even death, of the participants. They claim that new forms of public discipline, which were first practised at medieval courts spread down the social scale. First the ruling elite became less military and more political and learned. In Britain, castles were gradually replaced by magnificent but indefensible, country houses, as the ruling classes gave up the civil wars and rebellions which had been routine in high politics before their apex, the 17th century civil war. After this point, disagreements amongst gentlemen increasingly tended to take the form of parliamentary debate. At the same time, the gentlemanly elite began to set up the first nationally organised sports, cricket and horse racing. Then the middle classes sought to emulate the aristocracy and gentry, by gaining a classical education; sure enough the school system expanded massively during the 19th century and sure enough the universities set up the next wave of nationally organised sports, the newly rationalised games such as soccer and rugby. The values expressed in the ways that these games were taught and played – values such as public restraint and fair play within the rules – then spread to those who took up the team sports with such enthusiasm, the skilled working class ... Sport is an example of the 'civilising process' in two ways. As well as providing a very necessary public arena for the display of public emotions, it displays or demonstrates, the containing and disciplining of public violence. However violent they appear, Elias and followers argue, the new team sports show how high the threshold of public toleration of resistance has risen since the time of the Roman gladiatorial arena or the medieval tournament, in which people quite routinely killed others in front of cheering crowds.[32]

Elias presents a historical view of sport having increasingly become codified, regulated and a part of civil society. This presents a very specific view of history and one that can be contended. As Blake argues:

Elias and company offer a vision of 'progress' that is deeply Euro centric, elitist (claiming that change spreads from the top of the social scale downwards) and masculinised. Many people would argue that the replacement of public confrontation and uprising by parliamentary discourse has merely disempowered people. In other words, by following rules, which conveniently protected the lives and property of an elite, we have gravely damaged the potential for radical social change.[33]

Elias uses the term 'sportisation' to refer to a process in the course of which the framework of rules applying to sport becomes stricter, including those rules attempting to provide for fairness and equal chances to win for all. The rules become more precise and explicitly differentiated, and the supervision of rule-observance becomes more efficient. In the course of the same process, self-control and self-discipline reach a new level, while in the games contests themselves a balance is established between the possibility of attaining a high level of 'combat-tension' and reasonable protection against injury. Rules are therefore a development to attain competition – seen, of course, as an integral part of sport.

Figurational theory is therefore useful to apply to the contemporary regulation of sport. The increasing presence of 'regulatory law' could be argued as being a continuation of the codifying and 'civilising process'.[34] Sport has clearly become more rule-bound and is now augmented (and indeed

---

32 *Op cit*, fn 4, Blake (1996), pp 48–49.

33 *Ibid*, pp 49–50.

34 See Agozino, B, 'Football and the civilizing process: penal discourse and the ethic of collective responsibility in sports law' (1996) 24 International Journal of the Sociology of Law 163–88.

challenged) by the rules of law. Conversely, can the law's involvement oppose the claim of increased civilisation of sport as supported by figurational theory, especially in areas such as sports violence and drug abuse, which can in fact be best explained by conflict or critical theories supporting law being used as a mechanism of control? These competing theoretical models will help underpin a theoretical model of sports law developed in Chapter 2.

WHAT IS A SPORT?

This is a fundamental question that needs to be posed to help demarcate the disciplinary area of sports law. A good starting point is to see sport as a human activity that exists somewhere along the continuum from work to play. There is a need to demarcate sport from recreational activities in general and games and play specifically. But an attempt at a definition reveals the dynamic and changing nature of sport. In modern elite sport, professionalisation has led to an increasing transformation of sport into a type of work with the world of 'amateur play' seemingly contracting quickly.[35] There are also a number of anomalies in the way participation in sport is described. Some sports such as football, rugby and golf are seen as being 'played', and the participants are 'players'. These are the sports most akin to work. There are other sports where it is uncommon to talk of those involved as being players; with fishing, archery and hunting the sport is not 'played' but, in contrast to the former group, it is closer to play and leisure than work.

There are positive reasons for needing to provide definitional clarity. An activity defined as a sport has a number of financial and legal advantages. Where are the lines going to be drawn between sport, games, recreation, leisure, work and play?

Social Definition

A historical examination of the development and meaning of sport provides a powerful view of what we mean by sport and its social import. This will be addressed shortly. However, the historical perspective also needs a clear social context. The use of the term sport in its expansive meaning is one that is a product of modernity. The definitional problems are alluded to by Slusher when he analogises between sport and religion:

> Basically sport, like religion defies definition. In a manner it goes beyond definitive terminology. Neither has substance which can be identified. In a sense both sport and religion are beyond essence.[36]

There is a considerable body of sociological and cultural literature concerning the definition of sport.[37] It is important to have clear definitions of the concepts that are being studied. In the sociology of sport a good working definition helps an understanding of the role that sport has as a part of social life. Similarly, the study of sport and the law needs the same definitional clarity.

---

35 This can be illustrated by the move away from the distinction between amateurs and gentlemen in cricket shortly after the Second World War and the recent professionalisation of rugby union during the 1990s.

36 Slusher, H, *Men, Sport and Existence: A Critical Analysis* (1967), Philadelphia: Lea and Febiger.

37 See Loy, J, 'The nature of sport: a definitional effort', in Loy, J and Kenyon, G (eds), *Sport, Culture and Society: A Reader on the Sociology of Sport* (1969), New York: Macmillan; Coakley, J, *Sport in Society: Issues and Controversies* (1994), 5th edn, St Louis: Mosbey; Sprietzer, E, *Social Aspects of Sport* (1967), Englewood Cliffs, New Jersey: Prentice Hall; Mandel, R, *Sport: A Cultural History* (1981), Oxford: Clarendon; and Dunning, E (ed), *The Sociology of Sport: A Selection of Readings* (1971), Oxford: Blackwell.

One approach to a clear definition of sport is to look at the level of the sporting activity. Are games or individual pursuits at elite level more likely to be termed sport than kids playing on a patch of wasteland? Do we want to develop a definition of sport that differentiates it from mere physical recreation, aesthetic and conditioning activities and informal games?

There are considerable problems in attempting to provide answers. For example, what of activities such as mountain climbing, which have been developed as an indoor competitive 'sport' of wall climbing, and mountain biking, an activity that takes place within a continuum from the use of bikes being purely about mobility, through their use for recreational leisure, to involvement in highly competitive national and international competitions such as the Tour de France. It may also be important to consider the subjective intention and motivation of the participant; this may distinguish between involvement in sport rather than mere play or entertainment.

Using the above guidelines, can we define activities such as jogging as a sport? What about synchronised swimming, darts, fox hunting, skin diving, chess? What about hybrid sports[38] and those that are more likely to be viewed as forms of recreation and entertainment?[39] One common claim is that sport needs some notion of being a physical activity, in that there is 'the use of physical skill, physical prowess or physical exertion'.[40] Chess and other board games clearly need a minimal amount of physical effort either in terms of complex physical skills or vigorous exertion; the skills required are essentially cognitive.[41]

Such a definitional approach emphasising physical effort could potentially include all physical activities, including sex, as a sport! In *R v Brown*,[42] a case involving the legality of consensual sadomasochistic homosexual activity, an argument was expressed that the participants might have gained protection and exemption from criminal liability under the law of assault if they could be seen as being involved 'in the course of properly conducted games or sports'.[43] The application of 'rules of play', which evidence showed often existed in sadomasochistic sex, and the policing by an official were suggested as characteristics of a would-be sport!

To distinguish sport from recreational activity, it is necessary to consider the context or conditions of the physical activity and to determine whether it needs to take place in some institutionalised situation. This can help distinguish between formally organised competitive activities compared with those carried out in an ad hoc unstructured form; for example, the distinction between a Premier League football match and a number of children kicking a football in a park. Elements that characterise the former are perhaps standardised rules, official regulatory agencies, importance of organisational and technical aspects and the learning of strategies, skills and tactics by participants.

This process can be applied to the codification of the two branches of football, rugby and association, in the late 19th century. It can also be illustrated with the emergence and institutionalisation of body-building, which has developed from an activity based on aesthetics and health objectives to one open to competitions and being considered a sport. Such an approach produces an essentially objective understanding of a sport. Meier argues that subjective perceptions

---

38 For example, bicycle polo, octopush, a form of underwater hockey, and horseball, and an amalgam of rugby, basketball and horse riding. See 'Horsing around with a ball' *The Times*, 21 April 1997.

39 Note also World Wrestling Entertainment (WWE, formerly the WWF) professional wrestling, ballroom dancing and dragon boat racing.

40 *Op cit*, fn 19, Coakley (1994), p 13.

41 See 'Chess – a sport or just a game' (1999) 2(2) Sports Law Bulletin 16.

42 [1993] 2 All ER 75.

43 This exemption from liability short of grievous bodily harm (serious injury) that was consented to factually during a sporting activity was laid down in *Attorney General's Reference (No 6 of 1980)* [1981] 2 All ER 1057.

of participants are irrelevant in determining the nature of sport.[44] Some writers, however, have considered that the motivations of the participants in the sport help determine its meaning. Coakley claims that a 'play spirit' based on the internal motivations of the participant is an important element in determining whether the activity in question can be termed as a sport.[45] Huizinga describes play as:

> ... a free activity standing quite consciously outside 'ordinary' life as being 'not serious' but at the same time absorbing the player intensely and utterly ... it proceeds within its own proper boundaries of time and space according to fixed rules and in an orderly manner.[46]

Stone argues that sports are composed of two types of behaviour which he characterises as 'play' and 'dis-play'.[47] Play is where the participant's motivations are concerned with that individual's relationship with the activity. Dis-play, on the other hand, is participation being essentially concerned with spectators to the activity – the notion of a spectacle becomes more important than the sport. External motivations such as money and fame, especially if they replace the internal motivations for participating in the activity, lead to this danger. The dangers of increased commercialisation and commodification of sport together with the spectacularisation of contemporary sport are clear. Two sports where such dangers arise are boxing and wrestling:

Michener, J, *Sports in America*

In 1946, boxing and wrestling and roller derbies were taken seriously but when they began to grab the nearest dollar, the quickest laugh, the most grotesque parody of violence, their credibility was destroyed. When enough people begin laughing at the exaggerations of any sport, it is doomed.[48]

Stone, G, 'American sports: play and dis-play'

Play and dis-play are precariously balanced in sport and, once that balance is upset, the whole character of sport in society may be affected. Furthermore, the spectacular element of sport may, as in the case of American professional wrestling, destroy the game. The rules cease to apply and the 'cheat' and the 'spoilsport' replace the players. Yet even here counter forces are set in motion. If we may discontinuously resume our analysis of wrestling, we would note that there is always the 'hero' who attempts to defeat the 'villain' within the moral framework of the rules of the game. It is a case of law versus outlaw, cops and robbers, the 'good guys' versus the 'bad guys'. Symbolically the destruction of the game by the spectacle has called into existence forces of revival that seek to re-establish the rules, but these forces are precisely symbolic – representative. They are seldom able to destroy the spectacular components of the display. They are part of the spectacle itself.

The point may be made in another way. The spectacle is predictable and certain; the game, unpredictable and uncertain. Thus spectacular display may be reckoned from the outset of the performance. It is announced by the appearance of the performers – their physiques, costumes and gestures. On the other hand, the spectacular play is solely a function of the uncertainty of the game. The spectacular player makes the 'impossible catch' – 'outdoes himself'. He is out of character. The 'villains' and 'heroes' of the wrestling stage are in character. They are the *dramatis personae* of a pageant – an expressive drama. Consequently their roles have been predetermined. The denouement of the contest has been decided at its inception and the hero is unlikely to affect the course of events.[49]

---

44 Meier, K, 'On the inadequacies of sociological definitions of sport' (1981) 16(2) International Review of Sports Sociology 79.

45 *Op cit*, fn 19, Coakley (1994), p 16.

46 Huizinga, J, *Homo Ludens – A Study of the Play-Element in Culture* (1955), Boston: Beacon.

47 Stone, G, 'American sports: play and dis-play' (1965) 9 Chicago Review 83; and see also Dunning, E (ed), *The Sociology of Sport: A Selection of Readings* (1971), London: Frank Cass, p 47.

48 Michener, J, *Sports in America* (1976), New York: Fawcett, p 540.

49 *Op cit*, fn 47, Stone (1965), p 59.

This can be illustrated by the disintegration of the professional boxing regulatory organisations and the emergence of a plethora of world governing bodies offering their own world titles.[50] In professional wrestling, the emergence of World Wrestling Entertainment (WWE), formerly the World Wrestling Federation (WWF),[51] has clearly demarcated itself from amateur wrestling still mainly played for Stone's internal reasons. WWE has become purely a spectacle where characters such as 'The Undertaker' and 'The Rock' present a slick entertainment televised throughout the world in artificially created championships, 'The Royal Rumble', 'The King of the Ring' and 'Wrestle Mania', a paradigm example of the spectacularisation of sport – content has been sacrificed for image.[52]

Hargreaves, J, *Sport, Power and Culture*

The extent to which a given cultural formation is enabled to feed the power network also depends crucially, on its own particular character, that is on those autonomous features which distinguish it from others as a specific type of cultural formation. The realm of sport encompasses a bewildering diversity of radically different kinds of activity, which defies a watertight definition – from the local hunt and pub darts match, village cricket, inter-collegiate rowing and little league football, to professionalised mass entertainment like the Football League, the Wimbledon Tennis Championships, heavyweight boxing and horse racing. Some of this activity plainly has little, if any, connection with power. Despite the complexity, in our view sufficient distinguishing characteristics can be identified, which enable us to analyse how, in specific conditions, the sport-power relation may be constituted. First, sports to one or other degree embody an irreducible element of play. Play is a type of activity having no extrinsic purpose or end and as such it is a form of activity which enjoys a universal appeal. Sports play is not always unalloyed by other motives or considerations – financial gain, prestige, etc – and in specific instances (politicised and professional sport for example) play may be by no means the most important element. But the ludic impulse is, nevertheless, always present to some degree at least, existing in tension with disciplined organised aspects of sporting activity.

Secondly sports play tends to be highly formalised: in many cases it is governed by very elaborate codes or statutes. Sports play in this sense is far from being spontaneous: it is by convention rule orientated and to have no rules would be a contradiction in terms. Whether the rules are, in fact, being followed, is therefore an ever present issue in the conduct of sports and in this sense we could say that not only are sports rule orientated – they can be rule-obsessed. Rule-structured play, like play in general, 'suspends reality' but in this case through the acceptance of formal codes ordering the use of space, time and general behaviour. In choosing to structure their activity thus, both participants and onlookers are indulging in a form of 'play acting'and in this respect the activity can be said to be 'unserious' or set aside from normal life. Play acting is also involved in sporting activity when 'display' before an audience is one of the objectives. In addition, many sports were associated historically with the great festivals and to varying extents are still conducted in a spirit of festivity, a spirit which, by 'turning the world upside down', suspends while simultaneously challenging reality.

Thirdly, sports involve some element of contest between participants. The rules which structure sporting contests, however, unlike those that structure competition and conflict in the real world, deliberately set out to equalise conditions of participation, that is, they are intended to be neutral, so that no one party to the contest has an advantage over the other(s). Since a contest within neutral rules makes the outcome inherently uncertain and in principle unpredictable, the very point of the activity is negated when either the rules are biased in favour of one or other party or when the contestants are matched unevenly, for then the outcome does indeed become predictable. The uncertainty of the contest's outcome and the

---

50 For example, see the World Boxing Association (WBA), the World Boxing Council (WBC), the World Boxing Organisation (WBO) and the International Boxing Federation (IBF).

51 See litigation that led to name change- *(1) WWF – World Wide Fund For Nature (Formerly World Wildlife Fund) (2) World Wildlife Fund Inc v World Wrestling Federation Entertainment Inc.* (2002) IPD 25023.

52 See cultural resistance to the sometime gratuitous violence 'Singapore Broadcasting Authority blasts WWF', 17 May 2001, www.sportbusiness.com.

attendant tension it creates lends a unique excitement to sports, compared with other activities involving play and it is probably one of the main reasons why sports become so often the subject of intense interest and emotion. Paradoxically, the deep commitment which sports often arouse also makes them deadly serious affairs as well as unserious ones.

Three other attributes of sporting activity which have received much less attention are crucial in any consideration of the sport–power relation. The play acting, contest and uncertainty elements ensure that sports are an intrinsically dramatic means of expression and an audience in addition transforms them into a form of theatre. We argue that sports fall within the province of 'the popular' and in so far as they take on the attribute of a dramatic performance they can be said to constitute a form of popular theatre, arguably the most popular contemporary form of theatre.[53]

Competition is a fundamental prerequisite for sport. Some of the contemporary issues around the regulation of sporting competition will be examined later in this book, whether it be anti-doping measures or the need to have some measure of equal distribution and ability of talent between teams within the same professional league.

SPORT: A NEED FOR A LEGAL DEFINITION

There is no precise legal definition of sport in English law.[54] Nevertheless, it has been necessary in cases to provide a view of whether a sporting activity is taking place. In *R v Oxfordshire County Council and Others ex p Sunningwell Parish Council*,[55] there was an appeal by the local parish council from the decision of the Court of Appeal refusing leave to apply for judicial review against the decision of the respondent council not to register the glebe (village green) in their village as common land, under s 13(b) of the Commons Registration Act 1965. Section 22(1) of the Act contains a three-part definition of a town or village green:

> . . . [a] land which has been allotted by or under any Act for the exercise or recreation of the inhabitants of any locality or [b] on which the inhabitants of any locality have a customary right to indulge in lawful sports and pastimes or [c] on which the inhabitants of any locality have indulged in such sports and pastimes as of right for not less than 20 years.

The issue was whether under s 22(1)(c) of the Act, the phrase 'as of right' was to be construed as meaning that the right to indulge in sports and pastimes on the green must be exercised in the belief that it was a right enjoyed by the inhabitants of the village to the exclusion of all other people. The respondent argued *inter alia* that the nature of the activities on the glebe did not include anything, which could properly be called a 'sport' as required by the definition in the 1965 Act.

R v Oxfordshire County Council and Others ex p Sunningwell Parish Council [1999] 3 WLR 160

Lord Hoffmann: The first point concerned the nature of the activities on the glebe. They showed that it had been used for solitary or family pastimes (walking, tobogganing, family games) but not for anything which could properly be called a sport. Miss Cameron said that this was insufficient for two reasons. First, because the definition spoke of 'sports and pastimes' and therefore, as a matter of language, pastimes were not enough. There had to be at least one sport. Secondly, because the 'sports and pastimes' in class c had to be

---

53   *Op cit*, fn 5, Hargreaves (1986), pp 10–11.
54   See Gardiner, S, 'Sport: a need for A legal definition?' (1996) 4(2) Sport and the Law Journal 31, for a fuller discussion. There is no definition in the Act of a lawful sport in the Commons Registration Act 1965, which provides registration for land which can be used by local inhabitants to indulge in 'lawful sports and pastimes' see Samuels, A, 'Getting greens registered' (1995) Solicitors Journal 948.
55   (1999) 3 WLR 160.

the same sports and pastimes as those in respect of which there could have been customary rights under class b and this meant that there had to be some communal element about them, such as playing cricket, shooting at butts or dancing round the maypole. I do not accept either of these arguments. As a matter of language, I think that 'sports and pastimes' is not two classes of activities but a single composite class which uses two words in order to avoid arguments over whether an activity is a sport or a pastime. The law constantly uses pairs of words in this way. As long as the activity can properly be called a sport or a pastime, it falls within the composite class. As for the historical argument, I think that one must distinguish between the concept of a sport or pastime and the particular kind of sports or pastimes which people have played or enjoyed at different times in history. Thus in *Fitch v Rawling* (1795) 2 H Bl 393, Buller J recognised a custom to play cricket on a village green as having existed since the time of Richard I, although the game itself was unknown at the time and would have been unlawful for some centuries thereafter: see *Mercer v Denne* [1904] 2 Ch 538–39, 553. In *Abercromby v Town Commissioners of Fermoy* [1900] 1 I R 302 the Irish Court of Appeal upheld a custom for the inhabitants of Fermoy to use a strip of land along the river for their evening passeggiata. Holmes LJ said, at p 314 that popular amusement took many shapes: 'legal principle does not require that rights of this nature should be limited to certain ancient pastimes'. In any case, he said, the Irish had too much of a sense of humour to dance around a maypole. Class c is concerned with the creation of town and village greens after 1965 and in my opinion sports and pastimes includes those activities which would be so regarded in our own day. I agree with Carnwath J in *R v Suffolk County Council ex p Steed* (1995) 70 P & CR 487, 503, when he said that dog walking and playing with children were, in modern life, the kind of informal recreation which may be the main function of a village green. It may be, of course, that the user is so trivial and sporadic as not to carry the outward appearance of user as of right. In the present case, however, Mr Chapman found 'abundant evidence of use of the glebe for informal recreation' which he held to be a pastime for the purposes of the Act.[56]

The appeal was allowed and Oxfordshire County Council directed to register the glebe as a village green.[57]

Sports Violence

Another area where discussion has taken place concerning the legal definition of sport concerns sports participant violence. The Law Commission Consultation Paper[58] concerning the issue of criminal liability for injury caused by participation in 'a recognised sport' suggests that the most important defining criteria are those concerning safety and risk of injury.[59] The existence of rules that deal with these issues within a sport and the absence of wider political, ethical or moral reasons why the sport should not exist may provide us with some vague definition but one that is imprecise. This may well make it difficult to define developing activities as sports in the future. The Law Commission proposes that criminal liability for sporting injuries should be so constructed that:

> . . . a person should not be guilty of an offence of causing injury if he or she caused the relevant injury in the course of playing or practising a **recognised** sport in accordance with its rules (emphasis added).[60]

Liability is therefore only possible outside the rules of a particular sport. The Law Commission identified the need to produce a corresponding definition of what is a 'lawful sport'[61] so that the internal rules or regulations of such a sport can be verified or recognised. This they see as particularly

---

56 *Ibid, per* Lord Hoffmann, pp 171–72.
57 Also see *R (on the application of Pamela Beresford) v Sunderland City Council* [2004] 1 All ER 160.
58 Law Commission Consultation Paper No 139, *Criminal Law: Consent in the Criminal Law* (1995), London: HMSO.
59 *Ibid*, para 13.11.
60 *Ibid*, para 12.68.
61 *Ibid*, para 13.1.

important in the context of what they called 'martial arts activities', a number of which have failed to be recognised as sports.

The national Sports Councils (for example, Sports England, Sports Scotland etc) believe that a lawful sporting activity is one:

> ... with a reasonably responsible attitude to minimising risks of harm ... unless Parliament takes the view that it is so dangerous that it should be outlawed.[62]

The Sports Councils, however, already have a set of recognition criteria for sports. They have a number of statutory duties that require them to identify sports: deciding those sports that should be associated with and developed; to advise local authorities and other bodies on those activities they should promote; advise on safety in sport; to evaluate competence of organising and supervising sporting bodies; and evaluate the financial support to be given to a sport by the Council. The process of recognition is two-fold. The sporting activity is first recognised and then the sports organisational structure needs to be recognised in terms of competency to administer any government funds it may receive. The sports governing body 'must maintain and demonstrate an agreed level of management and financial accountability'. The Sports Councils use the following criteria:

Sport England – 'Recognition of activities and governing bodies'

The sports councils, including Sport England, currently recognise 112 activities. From time to time we are asked to consider the recognition of new activities, but this does not mean that we decide what is or is not a sport. Rather, we operate a recognition procedure – agreed jointly with the other four sports councils – for identifying those activities with which we should be associated and which we want to see develop.

Recognition criteria

New activities

The principal criteria against which the councils assess new activities are that the activity must involve: physical skills, physical effort, and physical challenge

Other criteria include whether the activity:

- Is unique
- Is accessible
- Has established rules and organised competition
- Includes strategy and tactics as elements for success
- Has a minimum of 5000 regular participants in the UK

Governing bodies

The recognition of an activity does not automatically lead to the recognition of a governing body for that activity. Applicant bodies are assessed against a number of criteria. These include the requirement for applicant bodies to:

- Be responsible for a recognised activity that does not already have a recognised governing body
- Have as members a reasonable proportion of the total number of participants in the activity
- Be democratic, with an appropriate written constitution and committee structure

---

62   *Ibid*, para 13.6.

- Have an appropriate level of management and financial accountability
- Be able to support financially their core administrative responsibilities
- Make their services and membership available to all
- Have been in operation for at least three years[63]

These criteria can be divided into two basic groups, those that are to demarcate a physical sport from a recreation, hobby or pastime and those that are based on safety and ethical considerations together with the legitimate structure of the sports organisation. In terms of sports being given recognition for protection from the involvement of the criminal law, the second grouping of criteria would seem to be the most important. In the context of potential liability for participant assaults, the Law Commission suggests that the Sports Councils[64] would be the obvious choice as the appropriate recognition body for determining a 'legal sport' in consultation with other sporting bodies including existing sports governing bodies, local authorities and the Central Council of Physical Recreation.

In the context of eligibility for National Lottery funding, the Sports Councils have been looking at the definition and recognition of sports. It has ruled that camping and caravanning are no longer sports but model aircraft flying, folk dancing, skipping, rambling, caving and lifesaving are sports. Some controversy was caused when darts was derecognised and effectively deselected as a sport.[65] Recognition also has other financial implications including exemption from VAT. In the past, the Sports Council considered that darts involved insufficient physical activity by the participants. The British Darts Organisation believed they had been singled out due to snobbery:

> They wrote to us and said that they do not simply decide what is and is not a sport but 'identify sports and governing bodies with which they want to be associated'. They are really saying that they do not want to be associated with fat blokes with fags in their mouth but that is such an outdated image of the sport.[66]

In 2005, however, Sport England has reselected darts under the auspices of the BDA as a sport.[67] So can we conclude on a working definition of sport that can be used in terms of legal proceedings? The European Sports Charter provides this definition:

> 'Sport' means all forms of physical activity which through casual or organised participation aimed at expressing and improving physical fitness and mental well-being, forming social relationships or obtaining results in competition levels.[68]

Coakley believes:

> Sports are institutionalised competitive activities that involve vigorous physical exertion or the use of relatively complex physical skills by individuals whose participation is motivated by a combination of intrinsic and extrinsic factors.[69]

---

63   See www.sportengland.org/recognition_of_activities.htm, which includes a full list of recognised activities.
64   See later, pp 97–98 for more details of these bodies.
65   See 'When octopussy comes to shove h'appeny, it isn't "croquet" ' *The Observer*, 18 February 1996; 'When is a sport not a sport?' *The Daily Telegraph*, 27 February 1996.
66   'Darts swept from the board' *The Guardian*, 14 February 1996.
67   'Bull's-eye! Darts achieves sporting recognition', *The Guardian*, 25 March 2005.
68   The Council of Europe, *The European Sports Charter*.
69   *Op cit*, fn 19, Coakley (1994), p 21.

Singer similarly sees sport as:

> ... a human activity that involves specific administrative organisations and historical background of rules which define the objective and limit the pattern of human behaviour; it involves competition and/or challenge and a definite outcome primarily determined by physical skill.[70]

An exact definition of sport seems to be impossible, but some common elements of the existence of a recognisable organisational structure, rules, physical exertion and competition need to be present.

HISTORY OF SPORT

The term 'sport' derives from the French determined Middle English verb *sporten*, to divert[71] and also the Latin term *desporto*, literally 'to carry away'. The emphasis is therefore on it being a distraction, something that gives pleasure. Throughout the Middle Ages sport in England meant mainly hunting of a variety of animals. Archery, bowls and horse racing can be seen as early sports dating from the 16th century.[72] One of our main cultural and historical identifications with sport is with the original Greek Olympics held in 686 BC.[73] Going further back in time, the earliest evidence of boxing's existence is recorded in Ethiopian hieroglyphics around 4000 BC. The world's oldest ball game is thought to have been played as early as 1400 BC in Mexico.[74]

Hunting can be seen as the precursor of much of modern sport. The fact that forms of hunting still persist today indicates its longevity. It is likely that as a sport it originally grew out of a form of play that early man took part in, especially in childhood, as a training for the reality of life: that being a 'hunter gatherer' included the killing of animals to survive:

Brasch, R, *How Did Sports Begin?*

In the beginning, sport was a religious cult and a preparation for life. Its roots were in man's desire to gain victory over foes seen and unseen, to influence the forces of nature and to promote fertility among his crops and cattle. Sport, as a word, is an abbreviation: the shortened form of disport, a diversion and an amusement. Rooted in Latin, it literally means 'carry away' (from *desporto*). In our time millions of people, whether spectators or participants, amateurs or professionals, are carried away by the sport they love from the cares of their daily toil, their anxieties and frustrations, to a world of relaxation and emulation, excitement and thrill. However going back to the very beginning of sport as such, we find that far from being restricted, it started as part of man's history and is bound up closely with his very being. Sport was not merely a diversion or pastime but an essential feature of man's existence. An inborn impulse and a basic need caused primitive man to play games, even though it might be only hitting a stone with a branch. It eased his tension, helped him to get aggressiveness out of his system and, altogether, served as an innocuous outlet for otherwise harmful urges. After all, to hit an object was so much better than to hit a friend. Thus sport fulfilled a primary want of man and, spontaneously taken up, games catered to it, giving satisfaction and a sense of achievement and overcoming.

Sport was a natural result of a universal love of play and man's innate desire to compete with and to excel, if not dominate, others. Another mainspring of sport was man's need effectively to defend himself, his tribe and later on, his country. In panic and fear when escaping from danger, he learned to run, jump and swim. To avoid defeat or to subdue opponents, he invented archery, judo and karate. And in order to

---

70 Singer, R, *Physical Education: Foundations* (1976), New York: Holt, Rinehart and Winston.
71 *Webster's New Collegiate Dictionary* (1995), New York: Websters.
72 *Op cit*, fn 1, Grayson (1993), p 36.
73 See Toohey, K and Veal, A, *The Olympic Games: A Social Science Perspective* (2000), New York: Cabi.
74 'When did sport begin?' (1998) 1(3) Sports Law Bulletin 12.

be ready for combat, at all times he practised them and new sports evolved out of his martial training. Even football and baseball carry vestiges of battles between tribes. Muscular strength and alertness served well in the repulse or conquest of foes. Sports taught man endurance and courage, essential qualities in a fighter and man was a fighter from the very beginning. However in some parts of the world where the severity of the elements and a low protein diet endangered his life, man's healthy instinct led him to create sports for yet another reason. In cold climates, games provided vital exercise, making the blood course through the veins and keeping man warm and resistant to the hazards of nature and the harshness of the weather. Man's wish to survive, in this world and the next, explains the origin of a majority of sports. They were not deliberately invented but arose, almost inevitably, out of man's quest to exist and to overcome the countless enemies that threatened him: natural and supernatural, man and beast. He had to ward them off everywhere. Most of all, sports began as fertility magic, to ensure birth, growth and the return of spring. Therefore sport to begin with was mainly a magical rite. It tried to attain human survival by supernatural means. Numerous examples of this are at hand in ancient records and the practices of primitive races. For instance, for the Zunis, a Mexican tribe that lived in arid zones, rain was the prime necessity for life. Droughts were frequent and it was because of them that the Zunis first played games. They were convinced that these would magically bring rain for the crops.

Other primitive tribes established a fraternity of rain-making priests. The sole task of this first team of professional players was to join in games of chance, which, they believed, would force nature to precipitate rain. With the approach of the whaling season, Mach Indians played a primitive type of hockey, using whalebone for ball and bat, the latter symbolising the war god's club. A hill tribe in Assam, India, arranged a regular tug of war to expel demons. The ceremony – it was not then a sport – took place at a fixed time each year. Two bands of men (the original teams) stood on opposite banks of a river, each tugging at the end of a rope stretched across the water. One team represented the forces of evil, the other those of increase in nature. On the result of the struggle depended whether trouble would haunt the tribe or the sun would shine, literally. Wrestling bouts were practised in southern Nigeria. They took the form also of a religious act to strengthen the growth of the crop by sympathetic magic. In suspense, huge crowds watched the contestants. They were not reluctant to interfere should either of the fighters show weakness, anger or fatigue, lest these deficiencies cause any ill-effect on the reproductive forces of nature. Games were highly important in winter and at the coming of spring. They were considered essential to hasten the return of the sun and ensure a fruitful season. Some of the games took place between groups of single men and women, representing the unprolific and married people, symbolising fecundity. The Wichita tribe, on the Red River of Oklahoma, conducted a sporting event very similar to modern field hockey. This, too, enacted symbolically a contest between winter and spring, to assist in the renewal of life and the conquest of the evil forces of winter. For a similar reason, some Eskimos had seasonal games. In spring, the players used a kind of cup and ball – to catch the sun. In the autumn, when the sun was going south, a sort of cat's cradle of seal gut was used to enmesh the sun and delay its departure.

Sport thus assumed even cosmic significance. Definite rules in primitive ball games were religiously observed to direct the winds, the bringers of life. The two teams represented earth and sky and as no one would dare to cheat the gods, an umpire was unnecessary. No wonder that primitive man believed that sport if not divine itself, was a gift of the gods. He was firmly convinced that 'to play the game' meant to accelerate the revival of nature and the victory of vegetation. The association of games with religious worship continued from prehistoric times well into the classical period. The Olympic Games were centred on the magnificent temple of Zeus at Olympia and were played in his honour. The Python Games were closely linked with the oracle of Apollo and his shrine at Delphi. It was from those magical roots of primitive faith that our sports mainly grew. With the passing of time and frequent repetition of games, their original purpose was forgotten and people enjoyed the contests for their own sake, discovering in them a source of excitement, amusement and strength. All these pursuits can be called 'natural' sports, as they 'naturally' evolved from early rites, training for warfare and defence against threats of nature, whether of the animate or inanimate kind. Equally prominent in this class are sports now taken up for mere pleasure, which developed out of man's search for sustenance: hunting for food, catching fish, rowing and sailing across rivers and the sea. In the practice of these skills, he acquired as well a liking for them, independent of their primary aim and pursued them even after their original purpose no longer applied. A means to an end here became an end in itself. And that is how hunting, angling, yachting and shooting became sports. There is no doubt that the present day probing of outer space sooner or later will create a modern 20th (or 21st) century sport, perhaps called cosmonauts. Finally, of course, there are those sports which do not constitute relics of man's previous preoccupation with his fate or which are not the by-products of vital tasks. They were artificially created and from the very beginning designed as sports and nothing else. New technological advance may account for the origin of such sports as car racing and flying. Mostly, the motive was to present a new type of exercise, demanding different skills and a novel kind of recreation when older games could not be played or, for one reason or another, had lost their appeal. In one case, however, ten pin bowling, a new sport was devised simply as a legal subterfuge. And yet, unconsciously, even the latest of sports continues to answer some of the identical needs that had urged our ancestors in the dim past to play games.

Some of the earliest statutes emphasised the power and agility of man. Sporting pictures adorned the walls of Egyptian temples. The Pharaohs and their nobles enjoyed sport, not merely as spectators but as participants. A hieroglyphic inscription lauds Pharaoh Amenophis II as a perfect athlete – 'strong of arm', 'long of stride', 'a skilled charioteer', an efficient oarsman and a powerful archer. Gradually, sport soon became part and parcel of man's social life. Even the Bible, though interested mainly in the spiritual aspect of existence, could not ignore sporting activities altogether. Hebrew Scripture mentions the use of the sling and the bow. Some authorities have even suggested that it contains certain allusions to weightlifting, either as a test of strength or a means to toughen one's muscles (Zechariah XII: 3). Contests and tournaments were known and with them, the selection of champions. The New Testament abounds in references to games and St Paul, especially, aware of how much they belonged to everyday life, makes frequent metaphorical use of them. In the Epistle to the Corinthians, for instance, he recalls the spirit of contest to illustrate the strenuous and glorious issue of the Christian fight. Foot races, boxing and wrestling alike supplied him with memorable phrases to express essential lessons. Paul thus speaks of man's wrestling against the powers of darkness, his fighting the good fight and finishing the race. Describing his mission and the task of the faithful Christian, he could say: 'I do not run aimlessly, I do not box as one beating the air but I pommel my body to subdue it.' A notable passage in the Epistle to the Hebrews compares the vast multitude of men and women who have borne testimony to their faith in God, to the enormous crowd of spectators at a foot race in which the contestant discards all unnecessary encumbrance. He needs patience to go forward perseveringly and to gain the prize conferred by the umpire, who judges all. The terminology of sports has its own story. The word 'game' recalls an Old English and Teutonic term that referred to 'participation' and a 'gathering' for fun. The scoring of points is linked with primitive methods of counting and recording. 'Score' is derived from an Old Norse word for 'notch'. Notches made on a stick served to register the correct number of hits, wins or killings. Score also came to indicate units of 20. In earliest days, dents were cut into pieces of wood to mark every 20, possibly, first of all, when sheep were being counted. Originally, 'umpire' – from the Latin *non par* – described an 'odd' man who was called upon to settle differences. Amateurs (from the Latin *amare*, 'to love') played for the love of the game. Civilisation has been defined as what man does with his leisure time. Its wise use for the practice of sports has had its beneficial effect not only on his physical health and the promotion of numerous skills but on his moral character. All sports, irrespective of their origin, developed in man faculties that have enriched his life manifold. They trained him in endurance, hard work and vigorous self control, gave him stamina and the will to do his best, no matter what. Some of the greatest lessons of life have come out of the world of sport. They have taught man to be undaunted by any challenge. Athletics, from the Greek, embodies the 'prize' (athlon) awarded to the winning contestant. Yet, failing to gain it, the true sportsman also knows how to take defeat. He will always be ready to try again and strive to attain what has never before been achieved. Sports, not least, have had their impact on the social ethics of man. Not accidentally do we speak of 'playing the game', it 'not being cricket', to 'abide by the rules of the game' or 'hitting below the belt' and being a 'spoilsport'.[75]

---

75 Brasch, R, *How Did Sports Begin?* (1986), Sydney: Angus and Robinson, pp 1–5.

HISTORICAL PERSPECTIVES ON SPORTS REGULATION

David Birley in his two volumes on the history of British sport, *Sport and the Making of Britain*[76] and *Land of Sport and Glory – Sport and British Society 1887–1910*,[77] believes that the Celts that came to Britain around 1000 BC developed boar hunting as a form of military sport. This could be seen as the birth of hunting as a recognisable sport. Birley also speculates that the Romans brought with them ball games and chariot racing. During the Dark Ages until the Norman Conquest, he provides some scant evidence of other developing sports: swimming, running, archery and horse racing. He also chronicles early prohibition of sport: hunting was limited to the ruling classes and certain areas of land; the Church tried to control the misuse of holy days; for example, in 747 AD the Council of Clofeshoh in the North of England forbade sports and horse racing on Rogation Days (the three preceding days before Ascension Day, itself 40 days after Easter, which should be set aside for prayer).

Below are a number of extracts from *Sport and the Making of Britain*, which chart both the origins and development of recognisable sports and their control and prohibition by the State. Greater State control appeared with the coming of the Normans:

> In Normandy bloodthirsty fights between barons and knights had long been a menace that defied control ... But the melees and skirmishes that were rife on the continent were held in check by the force of William and his judicious distribution of largesse (clemency).[78]

Restrictions on hunting that had been in force before the Norman Conquest continued, especially amongst the 'lower orders', with only rabbit and the wolf open to 'hunting for all'. The law has consistently controlled hunting rights on private land to the modern age. Formal jousting, however, became a common event. Sport became not only exclusive to rural life and, with the first meaningful urbanisation towards the end of the 12th century, new sporting forms developed:

> Shrove Tuesday, the great carnival before Lent, was a special day for schoolboys. In the morning, on receipt of his cock-penny, the master would cancel lessons so that his pupils could match the fighting cocks they had trained for the occasion. This educational custom survived for many years and its passing was bemoaned by traditionalists. Cock fighting itself remained a fashionable and popular diversion, declining in reputation as the squeamish middle classes grew in influence but still an attraction to the raffish, rich and poor alike, in the 19th century.

> For the medieval students of London and their counterparts in industry the holiday was not over. After lunch they went to play 'the famous game of Ball' (*ad ludum Pilae celebrem*) on a level ground near the city (probably Smithfield). Scholars from every place of learning and workers in the various occupations of the town played their own games of Ball, whilst older men, fathers and rich men from the city on horseback, watched the young men's contests, being young along with them in their own way, showing a natural excitement at so much action and sharing in the uninhibited pleasures of youth.

> We are told no more about these games but they may have included football, which was so prominent in the later history of Shrove Tuesday sport. Annual tussles, village against village with the ball being captured and carried home in triumph or married versus single, with the ball provided by newly weds, were part of ancient manorial custom. They were tolerated and even encouraged by parish clergy, some of whom provided the ball, as part of the pre-Lenten carnival, a good way of letting off steam. Lords of the manor were often hosts at the celebrations, and later, in more urban communities, Shrove Tuesday football matches were sponsored by the various craft gilds with special reference to the initiation of apprentices.[79]

---

76   Birley, D, *Sport and the Making of Britain* (1993), Manchester: Manchester UP.
77   Birley, D, *Land of Sport and Glory – Sport and British Society 1887–1910* (1995), Manchester: Manchester UP.
78   *Ibid*, p 16.
79   *Ibid*, pp 20–21.

Control of urban sporting activity began in the 13th century:

London needed special attention. In 1285 after years of political dissidence, corruption and violent crime Edward I manoeuvred the civic authorities into a situation where he could impose direct rule on the city. He immediately banned tournaments and swordplay. The statute, referring to 'fools who delight in their folly', prohibited the teaching of swordsmanship in the city on pain of 40 days' imprisonment. It did not close the fashionable fencing schools but it drove them underground, confirming their reputation as hotbeds of drinking, gambling and brawling. Nothing of course could prevent sword fights when it was the right and duty of every freeman to bear arms. Military swords were too cumbersome for pedestrian use and the classes obliged to go on foot carried staves for protection and support, especially in the country or on journeys. Daggers, of varying length, were widely used, either openly or concealed. In a ball game, probably football, at Ukham, Northumberland on Trinity Sunday 1280, Henry de Ellington was accidentally killed when, jostling for the ball, he impaled himself on another player's knife. But ball games could be dangerous even without knives. Three years earlier a 10 year old boy killed a 12 year old companion by hitting him on the ear after a clash of sticks in a hockey game (*ad pilam ludendo altercantes*). And there was growing fear of public nuisance especially in towns. In 1303 an Oxford student from Salisbury was killed – allegedly by Irish fellow students – whilst playing football in the High. By 1314, calling for restraint during Edward II's forthcoming absence in the resumed wars with the Scots, the Lord Mayor of London issued a proclamation on the King's behalf forbidding rumpuses with large footballs (*rageries de grosses pelotes de pee* in Norman French) in the public fields.[80]

The curb on civilian sports continued. In 1369 the King sent his sheriffs throughout England a list of the games they were to ban. As well as cock fighting these included *jactus lapidem, lignum et ferrum*, throwing stone, wood and iron. Casting the stone we have already encountered in Fitzstephen's account of London amenities. Such tests of strength were amongst the earliest and most basic of sports: reputedly early Irish and Scottish chieftains would keep a rock or two by their doors for the purpose. Throwing a lump of iron (called a diskos) was one of the events in Patroclus's funeral games in The *Iliad* when iron working was part of the new technology and *jactus ferrum* no doubt included contests with shot, discus or quoits.

Similarly, throwing wood could include tossing the caber (Celtic for beam) or the more domesticated (English) axletree. The chances are, however, that the terms also embraced bowling and skittles and such variants as *loggats, kayles* and *doish*, prohibited by name in later statutes. Bowls itself was traced back to the 13th century by Joseph Strutt, who illustrates three types: players trying to hit each other's bowl, bowling at small cones and bowling to a jack in the modern manner.

The other main category of prohibitions was that of games *ad pilam manualem, pedalem et baculoream, et cambucam*: handball, football, dub ball and cam buck. This last, also called cammock, may have been, as a contemporary commentator believed, a game in which a small wooden ball was propelled forward with a curved stick or mallet (and thus an ancestor of golf, pall mall and croquet), or, equally likely, an early form of hockey, also known as bandy, shinty, hurling and camogie, games that were played with the bent or knobbed stick from which cammock got its name. From the law enforcement point of view, of course, it did not matter if the categories were overlapping: overlap was better than under lap. Thus *pila baculorea*, club ball or stickball, could also refer to the hockey group of games. Club ball, however, was the term later used to denote the rounders-type game illustrated in early manuscripts and believed by Strutt (but not his later editors) to be the source of cricket.

The two remaining games in the prohibition were to cause the authorities great concern over the years. Football, *pila pedalis*, was banned, as Strutt put it 'not, perhaps from any particular objection to the sport in itself but because it cooperated, with other favourite amusements, to impede the progress of archery'. Handball, *pilamanualis*, no doubt took many forms about which the same could be said. The kind that

---

80   *Ibid*, p 32.

caused most trouble later, however, was the French game *jeu de paume*, later known as tennis, played in an open quadrangular space, making use of surrounding roofs buttresses and grilles.[81]

In the late 14th century, hunting restrictions increased:

Parliament had been given a fright and clamped down even harder on the peasants. In 1388 hunting laws were introduced which applied not just in the royal forest but throughout the land. Noting that 'artificers and labourers and servants and grooms' were in the habit of keeping 'greyhounds and other dogs' and that 'on holy days, when good Christian people be at Church' they went hunting 'in parks, warrens and coneyries of lords and others, to the very great destruction of the same', the new law forbade, on pain of a year's imprisonment, laymen with holdings worth less than forty shillings and clerics with benefices less than ten pounds a year to keep greyhounds or other hunting dogs or to use 'ferrets, hayes, rees, hare pipes, cords and other engines to take or destroy the deer, hares or coneys'. The legislation also renewed the ban on 'importune games' with particular reference to the servant and labourer class, forbidding all ball games whether handball or football, together with quoits, dice and casting the stone.[82]

. . .

Henry IV and V regularly renewed Edward III's ban on popular sports, with new Acts in 1401, 1409, 1410 and 1414 and they tried to apply the same disciplinary standards to the upper classes of society as to the lower orders.[83]

During the reign of Henry VIII, with the war against France continuing, prohibitions against sport were made in 1526 in order to boost the war effort:

Two years later with peace restored Wolsey introduced a revised measure which whilst equally draconian was more socially selective. It gave the county commissioners appointed under his 1526 legislation power to enter private houses in search of illicit crossbows and handguns and to enter hostelries, inns and alehouses to 'take and burn' tables, dice, cards, bowls, cloches, tennis balls and other instruments of the devil. Tennis was forbidden only if courts were not properly conducted: similarly bowls was condemned 'because the alleys are in operation in conjunction with saloons or dissolute places' which denied it the status of a true sport.[84]

Animal sports continued to be popular:

The death of Henry VIII left a power vacuum. Then the pendulum swung between the extreme Protestantism of the boy Edward VI (1547–53), who completed his father's asset stripping of the Roman church by dissolving the chantries and the avenging Catholicism of his equally pious half sister Mary who burnt at the stake some 300 enemies of the faith. There was no apparent conflict between religious belief and personal cruelty.

At Christmas 1550 the saintly Edward had publicly rebuked Mary for popish practices like 'conjured bread and water': then after dinner on the feast of the Epiphany he watched a bear baiting with the 17 year old Princess Elizabeth. When, as Queen, Mary was persuaded by her devious Philip of Spain to visit Elizabeth at her country house at Hatfield she was treated to a bear baiting, with which 'their highnesses were right well content'. And when Elizabeth herself became Queen in 1558 it was natural entertainment she offered to foreign ambassadors would include bear baiting.

The royal family had its own private bear gardens but there were public bear gardens in London of which the most famous was behind the Globe Theatre, Bankside. Because of their cost bears were usually kept alive (it was the dogs that died) but as they grew battle-scarred they could expect no mercy; as

---

81   *Ibid*, pp 35–37.
82   *Ibid*, p 38.
83   *Ibid*, p 41.
84   *Ibid*, pp 56–57.

a German visitor pointed out: 'to this entertainment there often follows that of whipping a blind bear, which is performed by five or six men, standing in a circle with whips, which they exercise upon him without any mercy'.

Bulls were more readily available and expendable, though if they fought well they too might be retained for further service. They could do a lot of damage with their fearsome horns and the trick was for the bulldog to get in underneath and grab the muzzle, the dewlap or 'the pendant glands'. If it got a hold it clung on and either tore the flesh away and fell or had to be pulled off, with the aid of flour blown up the nostrils to make it let go. This tenacity so inspired the populace that the bulldog became an emblem of the British character. There was a convenient superstition that bulls needed to be baited to improve the taste of beef and in some parts of the country bylaws required this to be done.[85]

The masses were excluded from gentleman's sports:

Tudor licensing laws were much concerned with keeping out 'men of base condition' from fashionable games like tennis and bowls. In 1592 Thomas Bedingfield, seeking permission to keep houses in London and Westminster for dice, cards, tables, bowls and tennis, proposed exemplary rules: no play before noon on weekdays or during hours of religious service on Sundays, no swearing or blaspheming and 'none but noblemen, gentlemen and merchants or such as shall be entered in the Book of Subsidies at £10 in land or goods'.[86]

In the late 16th century, common concerns on how the working masses spent their leisure time became prominent:

Yet it was old religious allegiances that brought sport to the centre of the political stage requiring the intervention of the King himself. There was a new twist to the old concern about the way the lower orders spent their leisure time. Now that archery practice had ceased to be thought desirable they were supposed to spend it reading the Bible or thinking improving thoughts. Catholic magistrates generally allowed games-playing after divine service but this was thought outrageous and provocative in Puritan circles, which were widening all the time. In Edinburgh games 'sic as gof' had been banned all day on the Sabbath since 1592. On a tombstone at Llanfair Church, South Wales, appeared the warning:

Who ever hear on Sunday

will practis playing at Ball

It may be before Monday

The Devil will Have you all.

In 1607 young men of Aberdeen were arraigned for profaning the Sabbath by 'drinking, playing football, dancing and roving from parish to parish'. At Guisborough, Yorkshire, in 1616 a man was charged with 'making a banquet for football players' on a Sunday.

The question for Puritans, as expressed by Stubbes, was whether 'the playing at foot ball, reding of mery bookes and such like delectations' profaned the Sabbath day. They had only one answer. But Puritanism was essentially a middle class movement. A day of quiet contemplation each week was all very well for those who had leisure on weekdays for more exciting activities but a bit hard on the average man in the fields. Matters came to a head in Lancashire, a county of extremes. Many of the aristocracy and their rustic followers clung obstinately to the old faith but Puritanism was also strong. Sunday sport was an inevitable source of conflict. In 1616 the Manchester justices banned 'piping, dancing, bowling, bear and bull baiting' or any other 'profanation' at any time on the Sabbath and similar restrictions were imposed in surrounding districts.

---

85 *Ibid*, pp 62–64.
86 *Ibid*, p 68.

The following year as James was returning from Scotland a party of Lancashire villagers met him at Myerscough with a petition complaining about the attempt to ban their customary amusements. The King made an impromptu speech promising them protection. They took him at his word and the following Sunday there were complaints from churchgoers in the vicinity that their worship had been disturbed by music, piping, dancing, shouting and laughter outside. The outcome was a declaration drawn up on the King's instructions by the local bishop to be read from pulpits throughout Lancashire. It was a rambling document but it answered the purpose, which was compromise. The King rebuked certain 'Puritans and precise people' for interfering with the people's 'lawful recreations' and ordained that after divine service on Sundays and other holy days piping, dancing, archery, 'leaping and vaulting and other harmless recreations were to be allowed'. Yet he maintained existing legislation which forbade bear and bull baiting and interludes on Sundays and bowling 'for the meaner sort of people' at all times.

James was so impressed by the success of his Solomon-like judgment in Lancashire that in 1618 he ordered an expanded version to be read in every pulpit in England and Scotland, adding approval of May games, Whitsun ales, Morris dances and the like 'in due and convenient time' to his bounty. James's Book of Sports, as it came to be known, was a setback for extreme Puritanism. Its arguments, taken at face value, were hard to counter – the people would turn from the church if it allowed them no amusement; they would be 'less able for war'; if denied sport they would spend more time in the alehouse. Most telling of all when would 'the common people have leave to exercise if not upon Sundays and holy days, seeing they must apply their labour and win their living in all working days?'[87]

In the 17th century, a more moderate approach to team sports and games seemed to be supported:

It was 1667 before new laws 'for the better observation of the Lord's Day' were enacted and they were not specifically directed at sport ... Indeed when in 1664 a law was passed against 'deceitful, disorderly and excessive gaming' the preamble declared that, properly used, games were innocent and moderate recreations: it was when they were misused that they promoted idleness and dissolute living and circumventing, deceiving, cozening and debauchery of many of the younger set.[88]

Violence against animals continued to be sport:

Bears, which had higher social status and did not toss dogs about, were in shorter supply. Bulls were therefore the standard fare, not only for baits but for rustic variants such as the traditional bull running at Stamford and the bizarre goings on at Tutford. The lowest level of baiting was of badgers all that could be afforded in some country districts. The connoisseur's sport was cock fighting. Charles Cotton grew lyrical:

Cocking is a great sport or pastime so full of delight and pleasure that I know not any game ... to be preferred before it and since the Fighting Cock hath gained so great an estimation among the gentry in respect of this noble recreation I shall here propose it before all the other games of which I have afore succinctly dismissed.

Fighting cocks had metal spurs tied to their heels, often of silver, fashioned by expert craftsmen, proud to engrave their name on each pair. Cockspur Street in London took its name from this sophisticated craft. Huge sums were wagered on choice birds by the highest in the land.[89]

Public demonstrations of violence against the criminal classes were very violent and very visible and this was reflected in continued enjoyment of blood sports during the early 18th century:

Hanging and whipping were greatly enjoyed as public spectacles and what the literary set saw as cruelty in sport enthusiasts saw as a desirable emblem of virility. Thus cock fighting was proclaimed a valuable way of diverting the English gentry from effeminate dancing, whoring and drinking 'which are three evils grown almost epidemical' and a more manly occupation than 'to run whooting after a

---

87   *Ibid*, pp 79–80.
88   *Ibid*, p 91.
89   *Ibid*, p 94.

poor, timorous hare'. Its ancient lineage was generally cited in its favour and at least one writer, a Scottish fencing master, cited Aristotle, with salacious intent.[90]

The distinction between the way football and cricket were viewed by the State was clear:

> ... opposition to football grew, not only for its lack of decorum but for fear of what it bred, idleness and what it could conceal, subversives. In England, football was sometimes a symbol of resistance to authority or to change ... In East Anglia, which had its own popular variant, campball, it frequently marked objections to Fenland drainage schemes or enclosures ... Amidst this turmoil cricket was better suited both to gambling and to the preservation of the social order.[91]

Field sports were going through a period of transition in the mid 18th century, with shooting becoming more popular. Grouse, pheasants and the like began to be protected:

> The notion of game as property fitted well into the modern scheme of things. Thirty two game laws were enacted in George III's reign and gamekeepers proliferated. Despite this – or perhaps because of it – poaching was rife. When the law made it illegal to buy and sell game both poachers and gamekeepers found it profitable to sell a few brace on the side. Animal predators, as ever, were a serious problem. Farmers' enemies, especially if they were edible like hares and rabbits, were more likely to be snared than shot but for bigger nuisances, like the fox, either shooting or stopping up their earths and digging them out was common.[92]

The preceding extracts show that the State has been involved in regulating sport for centuries.[93] Historically this has revolved around a number of issues. The control of land and the rights to hunting has been a perennial issue dividing clearly on class grounds between the aristocracy, landowners and the masses. The needs of war dictated the legitimacy of many sporting activities until the late Middle Ages. The maintenance of order has been a major concern, both in nationalistic terms with alarm of foreign influence being attained by certain sports, and in the disorder implicit in many team sports. The spectre of the mob, the uncontrollable rabble, was a constant fear. The dysfunctional effects of gambling on sport have also clearly been an increasing concern.

It is certainly possible to speculate which of the above continue to be current concerns: the debate about fox hunting and the use of land;[94] the influx of 'foreign players' in a number of sports continues;[95] the regulation of sports crowds especially in the context of football hooliganism; restriction on sports gambling; to name just a few.

---

90 *Ibid*, p 106.

91 *Ibid*, p 115.

92 *Ibid*, p 131.

93 For other historical perspectives on sport, particularly of the 19th and 20th century see Holt, R, *Sport and the British: A Modern History* (1989), Oxford: Clarendon; Mangan, J, *Athleticism in the Victorian and Edwardian Public School* (1981), Cambridge: CUP; Mason, T, *Sport in Britain* (1988), London: Faber & Faber; Mason, T (ed), *Sport in Britain: A Social History* (1989), Cambridge: CUP; and Vamplew, W, *Pay up and Play the Game* (1989), Cambridge: CUP. On specific sports, see Vamplew, W, *The Turf: A Social and Economic History of Horse Racing* (1976), London: Frank Cass; Walvin, J, *The People's Game: A Social History of British Football* (1975), London: Allen Lane; Murray, B, *Football: A History of the World Game* (1994), London: Scholar; Taylor, R and Ward, A, *Kicking and Screaming: An Oral History of Football in England* (1995), London: Robson and the BBC television series of same name (1995); Brookes, C, *English Cricket: The Game and Its Players Through the Ages* (1978), London: Frank Cass; *The People's Century: Sporting Fever*, BBC Television (1996); Birley, D, *A Social History of English Cricket* (2000), London: Aurum; and Smith, S, *The Union Game: A Rugby History* (1999), London: BBC Books.

94 See Chapter 3, pp 122–28.

95 A debate raged in the 1970s and 1980s concerning the large number of 'foreign players' in English cricket and the adverse impact that it was having on the performance of the English Test team led to current regulations that limit this to one per team. Similarly in recent years this has happened in football and the impact post-*Bosman* of foreign players in both the Premier League and the Football League.

THE VICTORIAN AGE: ORIGINS OF MODERN SPORT

The early years of Queen Victoria's reign began a period of the modernising of sport in a number of ways, including the regulation of blood sports:

Birley, D, *Sport and the Making of Britain*

Cock fighting became illegal in 1849 but it continued nevertheless, especially outside the range of the metropolitan police. In the capital there were two compensatory vogues in the sporting inns. One was ratting. Perhaps the most famous rat pit was that of Jeremy Shaw, an expugilist, where the turnover was between 300 and 700 rats a week, and where handling rats dead and alive was a mark of virility. The dogs pitted against them were often little bigger than the rats: Henry Mayhew, the journalist, described the two lb wonder, Tiny, who wore a lady's bracelet as a collar and had killed 200 rats. Another London attraction was dog fighting; in some hostelries there were contests every night and for some it was the sole topic of conversation. George Borrow recalled the scorn of a dog fancier when the topic of religion came up: 'Religion, indeed! If it were not for the rascally law my pit would fill better on Sundays than any other time. Who would go to church when they could come to my pit? Religion! Why the parsons themselves come to my pit'.[96]

During the Victorian era sport became increasingly codified and the formal rules of the major British sports were initiated. National governing bodies that exist today in their original or modified form were originated.[97] Team sports became an important part of social life, both in terms of playing and spectating. The first concerns about spectator hooliganism, particularly in football, were raised. Concern also continued about the propensity of gambling and betting on sport.

Barnes, J, *Sports and the Law in Canada*

In the late 18th century, Britain began to change into the urban industrial society that would eventually produce modern-organised sport. Before this time, sport bore the badges of 'Merrie Englande': landed society had its field sports, horse racing and cricket; the common people had rural folk games; and both classes patronised prize fights for their attractive combination of gore and gambling. The initial phase of the industrial revolution was then accompanied by a campaign against the lower class traditions as Puritanism affected the urban middle class. From the 1780s to the 1840s, State intervention in popular play was usually 'penal and restrictive'. The traditional folk sports were associated with taverns and with seasonal fairs and holidays; typical events included local versions of riotous football, smock races, greasy poles, pugilism and animal baiting. These customary festivities had pagan roots and brought associated problems of disorder, gambling and intemperance but they enjoyed the patronage of rural squires. Their slow decline occurred as public land was lost to enclosure and as authorities responded to the demands of evangelicals and industrial employers. The new morality called for personal salvation, seriousness, domesticity and a disciplined workforce. Such recreation as respectable reformers allowed had to be self-improving and 'rational'. Local magistrates and national legislators moved to ban fairs, street football and lower class cruel sports and sought to promote Sunday observance; employers meanwhile cut the number of holidays. Many traditional forms of play nevertheless survived and popular interest remained to be recaptured by the controlled and standardised sports of a later generation.

By the 1850s, the stage was set for the Victorian reconstruction of sport. A positive games ethic first developed in the elite public schools, which had recently undergone moral renewal through the

---

96   *Op cit*, fn 76, Birley (1993), p 208.
97   These include the Amateur Boxing Association in 1880, the Amateur Athletics Association in 1880, the Football Association in 1863, the Rugby Football Union in 1871, the Amateur Swimming Association in 1886, the English Football League in 1888, the Scottish Football League in 1891 and the Rugby League in 1894.

supposed influence of Thomas Arnold of Rugby. The reformed schools catered to the new upper middle class by assimilating their sons into the gentlemanly traditions of the aristocracy. Arnold's successors first promoted organised games to discipline boys' spare time and instill the manly virtues of courage, fair play and character but games soon became an end in themselves. The athletic culture then spread because it appealed to those shades of dominant Victorian opinion that saw sports as an effective means of preparing leaders. Educators and 'Sparto-Christians' found a favourable link with the ancient Greeks. Traditionalists and the Tory establishment saw sports as patriotic activities imbued with heroism and chivalry and serving as a training ground for military service and empire building. Social Darwinians and the commercial middle-class appreciated the notional 'equality' of sports, where success goes to the healthy, industrious competitor who struggles for the survival of the fittest. The Victorians found the ultimate attraction in sport's capacity to distinguish the social classes and separate the sexes. Sport was useful in class conciliation but aristocratic patronage and the new code of amateurism ensured exclusivity. Medical myths, aesthetics and decency limited womens' exercises to appropriate feminine pursuits. In codifying games, the society pursued goals that were also central to the movement to restructure criminal law: the new sports and the new criminal law both sought to instill character and responsibility and looked to maintain disciplinary controls based on age, class and sex.

Conditions were now right for the growth of approved sports. Legitimate physical recreation emerged as cities provided parks and facilities and as 'muscular Christians', driven by an ideal of public service, began to incorporate lower class participation. These social missionaries had their greatest conversion when working men adopted the newly codified version of football (soccer). Rule structures and elite governing bodies began to emerge in the 1860s and 1870s: the Football Association in 1863, the Amateur Athletic Club in 1865, boxing's Queensbury Rules in 1867, the Rugby Union in 1871 and the Wimbledon Lawn Tennis Tournament in 1877. Cricket was revitalised as a spectacle during the 1870s by the county championship and the exploits of WG Grace. The new games were suited to urban constraints of time and space and were seen as useful remedies for the problems of 'health, morality and discipline that affected city life'. They also conformed to the Victorian tendency to measure, regulate, structure and improve. Playing and watching were made possible by advances in transportation and by the more regular pattern of work and leisure time in industrial society. General interest in standardised sports was spread through the new system of public education and through communications technology and the popular press. By the 1880s, sports became important forms of mass entertainment. Soccer, in particular, emerged as a commercial spectacle played by professionals and offering a regular schedule of games through the Football League.

British traditions of class, religion and commerce thus found a way to tame and approve popular sports. The final vision of terraces packed with spectators was not exactly what the early reformers had had in mind but sports were now at least incorporated into the moral order: they had shifted from being the crimes of the idle to become well-drilled, respectable recreation that safely preserved class distinctions. The rationalised sports were capable of worldwide diffusion, so that they came to transcend all cultures. The British duly spread their games and in the 1890s an Anglophile French aristocrat revived the Olympics. North America in the 19th century offered especially strong possibilities: with their serious, clean, profitable Protestantism, sports seemed American to the core.[98]

The importance of sport in society grew considerably during this period. The concept of 'muscular Christianity' became a powerful cipher of the time: sport could be used as a means of purifying the body by participation in rational recreation. This form of Christian socialism and social engineering was used as a mechanism of social control. Hand in hand with the codification of sport, attempts were made to increasingly codify and control society.

---

98 Barnes, J, *Sports and the Law in Canada* (1996), Toronto: Butterworths, pp 4–7.

In Chapter 3, the contemporary role of the State in British sport will be examined and further parallels with the past drawn.

THE CONTEMPORARY REGULATION OF SPORT

The 20th century saw significant developments in its form and regulation. This change has arguably accelerated in recent years. Edward Grayson, acknowledged as the 'founding father' of British sports law, has strongly supported the involvement of law in the operation of sport over this period. His early writings culminating in the book *Sport and the Law*, the first edition of which was published in 1988,[99] have been crucial in identifying and recognising this area of law. He argues:

> ... the law can and should come to the help of sport; and indeed, how sport with its high profile and image can come to the help of the law. For sport without rules and their control creates chaos. Society without laws and their enforcement means anarchy.[100]

Supporting Corinthian values, Grayson argues that:

> ... if sport and its rulers cannot or will not try to preserve that Corinthian tradition, which the citations throughout ... and the inspiration for this book demonstrate is an ideal realistically and recognised and capable of attainment to aim for, if not always achieved, then the courts can and will do it for them, through the law of the land at both criminal and civil levels and certainly if adequate compensation is required.[101]

Grayson sees that the essential amateur Corinthian values are the epitome of sportsmanship and are an increasingly dissipating ethos in modern sport. The view that these were in fact the dominant values in sporting history has already been questioned. Much of sport in the past has been violent, secular, partisan and competitive. Sportsmanship is clearly a positive virtue as far as participation in sport is concerned. Players of the post-war era such as footballers Bobby Charlton and Gary Lineker and cricketers Dennis Compton[102] and David Gower embody that ethos.[103] Grayson uses cricketers such as GO Smith and CB Fry and the Corinthian cricket and football teams to support the view that sport was played with absolute adherence to the letter and spirit of the rules.[104] The one fact that these sportsmen and teams shared in the early 1900s was their upper-class background of public school education and privilege. Grayson believes it was their background and professional lives as 'doctors, lawyers (sic) and schoolmasters' that provide them with this outlook on sport. He presents a view of the past where sport was purely played for the love of participation.

Gamesmanship and 'shamateurism' in sports history have existed for many years and will be discussed later in the context of examples of 'cheating' in cricket. For example, the 'amateur' cricketer, WG Grace, earned £8,835 in 1895 and an estimated £120,000 during his lifetime, equivalent today to

---

99 Grayson, E, *Sport and the Law* (1988), London: Butterworths; also see *Police Review*, 19 November 1969; 'On the field of play' [1971] NLJ 413; 'The day sport died' [1988] NLJ 9; 'Keeping sport alive' [1990] NLJ 12.

100 Grayson, E, *Sport and the Law*, 2nd edn (1994), London: Butterworths, p vii.

101 Ibid, p xxxvi.

102 On Compton's death in 1997, see 'Cricketing cavalier who dazzled a nation' *The Daily Telegraph*, 24 April 1997.

103 Also see 'Professional touch from the last Corinthian' *The Daily Telegraph*, 26 April 1997 on the rugby player, Lawrence Dallaglio.

104 See Grayson, E, *Corinthian and Cricketers – And Towards a New Sporting Era* (1996), Harefield: Yore. Also see Grayson, E, 'Sports and the law: a return to Corinthian values?', Inaugural professorial lecture, Lord's Cricket Ground, 15 January 1998, and 'Casuals stroll on defiantly' *The Observer*, 19 January 1997.

many hundreds of thousands of pounds.[105] Corinthian values such as fair play and the joy of participation still are powerful values in contemporary sport – but limited largely to recreational and amateur levels. The commercial reality of contemporary sport is that participation has other motivations and, especially at the elite level, the nature of sport is much more complex. Grayson clearly supports the argument that modern sporting bodies cannot be trusted to uphold these Corinthian values (or perhaps better stated as being the custodians of ethical positions) and that the rule(s) of law is needed. Commenting on the reasons for writing *Sport and the Law*, he once again stresses that dispute resolution should not be left to sports administrators:

Grayson, E, *Sport and the Law*

Many within both sport and the law could not see any need for bringing the law into sport believing, with the author, that it ought always to be enjoyed for fun and, at times, as a spectators' entertainment. Indeed they were generally hostile to such a position. For whatever the true meaning and the position of sport in society may be, if ever all of its elements can be defined, too many thought that sport was cocooned in a world of its own, sealed off from reality and the rule of law. The vagaries and limitations upon human conduct and contact however, preclude such idealism in an ever-growing intensively competitive and commercially orientated sporting climate. Thus the creation of a book which explored that theme required justification, notwithstanding the existence for over a century of intervention by the courts and of Parliament, in relation to specific sporting issues. I was placed in a defensive position six years ago in 1988 in order to justify the subject of sport and the law. That defence was against a combination of abuse, ignorance, ridicule and hostility linked to the arrogance of feudalism based on an absence of awareness of the past which has permeated so much of sporting administration and still lingers again. The intervening six years, however, have changed all that. Indeed, anyone who seeks to challenge the need for law to partner sport for the benefit of each discipline in 1994 should examine his or her conscience ... today no one can argue that the subject of sport and law does not exist.[106]

Wither sport and the law: what direction should sport take today? Whatever route is taken, the rule of law, on and off the field, alone can and must guide it within a rapidly revolving social setting whose pace can hardly match the kaleidoscopic changes daily imposed upon the public mind and eye.[107]

Whether it is a loss of the Corinthian values in sport or not, in many people's eyes there is a dissatisfaction with what sport has become in the modern world. Some detect a loss of innocence, a fading away of the essential spirit and values of sport that has been replaced by cynicism, gamesmanship, and commercial excess.[108] It may well be, however, that past generations have had this same view of the deterioration of what they understand as sport and nostalgia for a lost notion of true sport and sportsmanship. This is not just a British phenomenon. For example, in the United States a number of disputes, notably the baseball strike that wiped out the second half of the 1994 season and the World Series, led to widespread spectator disillusionment.[109]

---

105 Not only was he paid very well for his services, he was infamous for his tactics of gamesmanship; see Midwinter, E, *WG Grace: His Life and Times* (1981), London: Frank Cass; Holt, R, *Sport and the British: A Modern History* (1989), Oxford: Clarendon; and Sandiford, K, *Cricket and the Victorians* (1994), London: Frank Cass.

106 *Op cit*, fn 100, Grayson (1994), pp xxxi–xxxii.

107 *Ibid*, p 418.

108 See 'The corruption of our sporting life' *The Sunday Times*, 18 December 1994, pp 2–20; 'Hijacking of our dreams' *The Observer*, 9 April 1995; 'Every little breeze seems to whisper new sleaze' *The Observer*, 19 March 1995.

109 For details, see 'America's field of bad dreams' *The Times*, 12 March 1995; 'Baseball strikes in the field of nightmares' *The Independent on Sunday*, 26 March 1995; 'Why sports don't matter anymore' *The New York Times Magazine*, 2 April 1995, p 50; Cosell, H, *What's Wrong with Sports* (1991), New York: Pocket Books; Weiller, P, *Levelling the Playing Field* (2000), Cambridge, Mass: Harvard UP.

In Britain, sport has been subject to numerous sporting scandals during the 1990s and into the new millennium: drug use, cheating, corruption and others. The national game, football, seems to have been the most scandal bound.[110] This can be combined with a lack of success of British sports teams and individual athletes on the world stage, perhaps crystallised with the small number of medals won at the Atlanta Olympic games in 1996.[111] In comparison, the relative success at the Sydney Olympics in 2000 boosted the 'feel good factor' that sport has the power to create.[112]

Any cursory review of the daily newspapers reveals an increasing propensity of the law to be involved in the regulation of sport. This is not an absolutely new phenomenon: as we have seen, the State has been involved in regulating sporting activity for centuries, largely on grounds of policy-driven aims of prohibition. But today the law is intervening in sport in increasingly diverse ways and into all the interstices of the sporting world.[113] Of course the general law that regulates social activities and relations in all areas of social life is involved in sport, in spheres such as the regulating of contracts of employment and services, revenue law taxing sport as a business and personal injuries law. But not only has there been the emergence of sports-specific legislation;[114] sports law related litigation is widespread. This may of course reflect a more litigious society generally,[115] but over the last few years a number of lawyers have begun to spend a considerable amount of their professional time on sports related legal issues and a small number of firms have sizeable sports law workloads.[116] A process that will be identified and discussed in the next chapter is the increased juridification of sport; that is, that sporting relations and disputes are increasingly primarily being understood in legal terms.

This leads to the question: does the law have a legitimate role to play in sport? This is a contentious issue. Clearly there are areas of sport where the law needs to intervene in terms of facilitating commercial dealings and supporting sports athletes' rights – here its role is uncontroversial. However, there are areas where this intervention is contested. At various points in the book, this issue will be highlighted. It needs to be remembered that in opposition to the by-line to this chapter,[117] the law may not always be the saviour of sport and the most effective form of regulation.

The causes of this greater role of the law will be evaluated. In Chapters 2 and 8 and at other points in the book, the increasingly commercialised nature of sport, particularly at the elite level, will be

---

110 See 'How soccer sold its soul' *The Observer*, 3 December 1995; 'Football's drug crisis' *The Guardian*, 17 June 2001; 'Men behaving badly in version of the Mad Hatter's tea party' *Daily Telegraph*, 21 September 1996.

111 See 'Our athletes under cloud at Olympics' *The Sunday Times*, 4 August 1996; 'Troubled legacy of blighted games' *The Observer*, 4 August 1996.

112 See 'Success at Sydney' *The Times*, 30 September 2000.

113 See Grayson, E, *Sport and the Law* (2000), 3rd edn, London: Butterworths; Moore, C, *Sports Law Litigation* (1997), Birmingham: CLT; Griffith-Jones, D, *The Law and Business of Sport* (1997) London: Butterworths; Verow, R, Lawrence, C and McCormick, P, *Sport, Business and the Law* (1999), London: Jordan: Beloff, M, Kerr, T and Demetriou, M, *Sports Law* (1999), Oxford: Hart; and Stewart, WJ (ed), *Sport and the Law: The Scots Perspective* (2000), Edinburgh: Butterworths, focused primarily at practitioners. Greenfield, S and Osborn, G (eds), *Law and Sport in Contemporary Society* (2000), London: Frank Cass; Caiger, A and Gardiner, S (eds), *Professional Sport in the European Union: Regulation and Re-regulation* (2000), The Hague: Asser, are focused primarily on a wider academic examination. More focused books have appeared too – McArdle, D, *From Bootman to Bosman: Football, Society and Law* (2000), London: Cavendish Publishing; O'Leary, J (ed), *Drugs and Doping in Sport: Socio-Legal Perspectives* (2000), London: Cavendish Publishing. A number of UK-based sports law journals provide updated information and commentary: *Sports Law Bulletin* (www.sportslawbulletin.com), *Sport and the Law Journal*, *Sports Law and Administration* and the *International Sports Law Review*.

114 Most notably in football, ie Football Spectators Act 1989, Football (Offences) Act 1991, Football (Offences and Disorder) Act 1998 Football Disorder Act 2000.

115 But see Armstrong, N, 'The litigation myth' (1997) 147 NLJ 1058.

116 See 'Legal eagles have landed' *The Observer*, 25 September 1995.

117 *Op cit*, fn 1, Grayson (1993).

examined. Legal issues concerning sport are, however, not solely concerned with commercial law – a wide variety of sports law issues have become a part of the general discourse of sport.

It can also be argued that much sport has been commercialised and professionalised for many years. Professional football clubs have been run, sometimes badly, as commercial entities since the late 1880s. Nonetheless, large areas of sport have been essentially amateur or have masqueraded under this guise in terms of 'shamateurism'; athletics and rugby are two such sports. However, commercialisation around sport in recent years, for example with the vast increases in sponsorship, marketing and merchandising operations, has led to modern sport being a huge business.[118] The mediation of large amounts of elite sport, primarily by television but increasingly by other technologies, has helped change its financial contours.[119] The significant and relevant case law concerning sport in the UK will be examined in the following chapters together with an explanation and evaluation of the issues around this intervention. As stated earlier, it is of course very difficult to restrict our understanding of sports law to national boundaries and the developments within the European Union concerning the regulation of sport and more widely on an international stage are vital to consider. Not only is this the reality of the regulation of elite professional sport; it provides comparative models as to 'best practice'. The next chapter will attempt to put this expansion of sports law within a theoretical context of why it is happening and how best we can understand it, and will consider whether there is an area of 'sporting autonomy' into which outside regulation and the law should not intrude.

KEY SOURCES

Birley, D, *Sport and the Making of Britain* (1993), Manchester: Manchester UP.

Cashmore, E, *Making Sense of Sport* (2000), 3rd edn, London: Routledge.

Gardiner, S, 'Sport: a need for a legal definition?' (1996) 4(2) Sport and the Law Journal 31.

Grayson, E, *Sport and the Law* (2000), 3rd edn, London: Butterworths.

McArdle, D, *From Boot Money to Bosman: Football, Society and Law* (2000), London: Cavendish Publishing.

---

118 See, for example, 'United put finishing touches to £300 m kit deal', *The Guardian*, 4 November, 2000 – a 13 year deal concerning the playing kit has been agreed between Manchester United and Nike worth £302.9 m – the most lucrative tie-up in sporting history.

119 The Premier League TV rights deal for the three seasons from 2001–04 is worth £1.3 billion; see Spink, P and Morris, P, 'The TV rights in professional football', in Caiger, A and Gardiner, S (eds), *Professional Sport in the European Union: Regulation and Re-regulation* (2000), The Hague: Asser.

CHAPTER 2

THEORETICAL MODELS OF THE REGULATION
OF SPORT

INTRODUCTION

Sport is now big business. It has developed into a global industry and represents more than 3% of world trade.[1] And it is worth more than 1% of the gross national product (GNP) of the European Union (EU).[2] In the EU alone, two million new jobs have been created directly or indirectly by the sports industry.[3] In the UK, sport provides employment for some 420,000 people, and is worth £12 billion a year in consumer spending.[4]

This phenomenal growth in the value of the sports industry is largely due to the increase in the broadcast coverage of sports events and the concomitant rise in the fees paid by broadcasters for the corresponding rights. An audience of 3.9 billion individuals watched Olympic broadcasts at least once during the Athens Olympics in summer 2004.[5] The final of the 2002 FIFA World Cup between Brazil and Germany in Yokohama attracted in excess of 1.1 billion – the largest TV audience in footballing history. The Korea/Japan based tournament recorded total viewing figures in excess of 28.8 billion. Television and other media rights have soared in value. Increased television coverage has also led to a spectacular rise in the value of sports sponsorship, by national and multinational companies wishing to associate themselves and their products and services with major national and international sports events, such as the Olympic Games. It has been estimated that the value of global sponsorship reached an all time high of US$26.2 billion in 2003 – up 7.4% from $24.4 billion in 2002.[6]

The increase in leisure time in the developed world has also played a significant part in the meteoric rise of the sports industry with more people participating in and watching sport than ever before. This, in turn, has seen the rise of sports men and women as sports personalities with salaries, especially footballers – the age of £100,000 per week footballers – sponsorship and endorsement deals akin to the fabulous incomes of Hollywood 'stars'.[7] In fact, sport is now very much a part of the world-wide entertainment industry.[8]

All of this, combined with the development of the internet and other new forms of new media, including mobile phones, to deliver sports programming, content and information (for example the latest cricket score), the value of the sports industry is set to grow even further in the future – new media companies have used sport as very much the driving force in advertising new technologies.

With all this money and wealth 'sloshing' around in sport, winning is now everything – the privilege and satisfaction alone of taking part is passé. And, with the increasing use of performance

---

1   European Commission, *The European Model of Sport* (1999).
2   *Ibid.*
3   Monti, M, excerpts of a speech given at a Commission-organised conference on sports, Brussels, 17 April 2000; see http://europa.eu.int.
4   Department of Culture, Media and Sport figures – see www.culture.gov.uk.
5   'IOC reports record global TV audience for Athens Games', www.woodtv.com/Global/story.asp?S=2420459.
6   Ardi Khola Maximising The Value Of Sponsorship, Sport Business International @ London (2003).
7   *Annual Report on Football Finance 2000*, Deloitte & Touche, August 2000; see www.footballfinance.co.uk/publications.
8   See, for example, the sponsorship of the new Union of European Basketball League, the SuproLeague, formed in July 2000 and sponsored by the Spanish telecommunications giant, Telephonica; see *Soccer Investor Weekly*, 19 September 2000.

enhancing drugs by sports persons, it seems to be a case of winning at all costs. For top sports persons, winning means money and riches. So, in line with the old adage, where there is money to be fought over there are likely to be disputes, it is not surprising that sports litigation is also on the increase.

This chapter will provide a theoretical basis for the law's intervention and regulation of sport within this context of greater commercialisation. This will be carried out in three connected ways:

Regulatory Regimes

First, alternative regulatory regimes concerning sport will be examined. British sporting organisations are of course varied in size and form. They range from the small sports club, invariably one that is in the eyes of the law, an 'unincorporated association', its members contractually bound together towards compliance with the rules of the association. There are tens of thousands of them around the country. Governing bodies in sport are likely to be 'incorporated' as limited liability companies. These sporting organisations have traditionally been seen as autonomous and private 'self-regulating' bodies. The question that is increasingly asked is, within this overtly commercialised sporting world, can these bodies be trusted to continue to be the 'custodians' of their sport and essentially be self-policing? Periodic financial scandals and allegations of corruption have made this question more immediate.[9] Within the overtly commercialised world of elite professional sport, there is the danger that sport's requirement of uncertainty as to result and a degree of equality between clubs and individual athletes to be able to participate in 'real competition' – the essence of sport – is increasingly compromised. Essentially the argument can be summarised in the form that if law is the regular form of regulation for market relations and if sport is now essentially commercialised, it needs to be subject to similar regulation.

The two opposing models that will be considered are on the one hand, the continuation of self-regulation or on the other, external regulation of some sort. This latter model can clearly be of a variable degree. The debate concerning the ability of the law to intervene into these 'private' and 'autonomous bodies' to challenge decisions and procedures through judicial review will be examined later in the next section – 'The Governance of Sport'. A simple distinction can be made between sports regulation and governance. Although intertwined, regulation concerns outside supervision of some type, while governance concerns the procedures and issues of power within the organisation or body itself.

To illustrate the issue of sports regulation, it is football that will primarily be examined. Calls for external regulation have been partly premised on the observation that effective governance of football by the authorities has failed. Not only is football culturally the primary British national sport; it has been impacted upon by the changes in the surrounding commercial dynamics more than any other sport. On a general level the sports industry has distinct and unusual commercial characteristics that need to be carefully understood in terms of regulation. The 1999 report, *Commercial Issues*, produced by the Football Task Force, will be used to illustrate alternative regulatory regimes as they might apply to football.

The Rules of Sport

The second concern of the chapter will be to examine the normative rule structure concerning sport. Sport as a social practice is highly rule-bound. Individual sports are regulated by their own

---

9   See Chapter 8 for a further examination of these issues.

constitutional rule book and adjudication machinery. The volume of rules varies between different sports. Some are particularly multifarious. Rules in sport exist for both its organisation and playing. Explicit codes of ethics are also relatively new developments as largely informal but written normative statements. Sport is also surrounded by strategies and practices that are not explicitly stated and recorded but partly amount to the working or 'playing culture' of particular sports. The interaction of sports' internal rules and the influence of the law are also important; the internal rules of sport need to be examined before the role of the law in sport can be fully evaluated.

Both of these approaches concern the essential issue: to what extent should the internal rules and norms be superceded by external legal norms. Put more bluntly, to what extent do sports bodies need to comply with the law? The courts, particularly the European Court of Justice, have made careful distinctions between internal rules of sport that can be considered 'sporting rules' and those that are open to external legal examination and compliance with legal provisions – invariably those that have an economic impact.[10] As has been stated earlier, sports law decreasingly can be understood merely in national (UK) terms – European and international regulation is increasingly pervasive.[11]

A short history of the development of the internal sporting rules will be examined to better understand the dynamics and structure of these rules. The process and motivations for rule changes will be considered, as will the dynamics surrounding infringement and 'bending of the rules' – when does this amount to 'cheating'?

Competing perspectives on the reason for the contemporary involvement of law in sport beyond the obvious commercial reasons for law's greater presence, which have already been briefly noted. It may be too simplistic to see law's intervention as being purely due to increasing commercialisation; doing so may hide some of the other causal reasons for the greater role of the law in sport. The relationship between greater legal regulation and the commercialisation of sport will be dealt with at length in Section Three – 'The Commercial Regulation of Sport'.

The process of juridification will be analysed and presented as a potential danger for sport – that is, that sporting relations are increasingly viewed as essentially legally constructed. The law therefore becomes the primary remedy that will be sought, and the discourse of the law becomes the language employed. This has arguably happened with doping in sport – no longer have disputes surrounding drug use essentially been constructed as sporting ones around concepts such as fair play. These disputes have gone through a process over the years of being professionalised – initially becoming a medical issue with drug testing procedures becoming endemic, they are now fundamentally legal disputes to be resolved in relevant tribunals and courts. This may be good news for lawyers, but a vital question is whether it is in the long term interests of sport. There are many ethical issues to be determined in sport, and the law has a role to play in helping provide solutions.

Is There a Sports Law?

The final section will evaluate what some may think is an abstract and esoteric argument. Is the concern in this legal discipline one that is best termed 'Sports Law' or 'Sport and the Law'? The

---

10 Notably Cases C-51/96 and C-191/97 *Deliège v Liège Ligue Francophone de Judo,* judgment of 11 April 2000 and Case C-176/96 *Lehtonen & Castors Canada Dry Namur-Braine v FRBSB (Belgian Basketball Federation),* judgment of 13 April 2000.

11 See Caiger, A and Gardiner, S (eds), *Professional Sport in the European Union: Regulation and Re-Regulation* (2000), The Hague: Asser.

Preface to this book has clearly indicated what the authors' position is on this issue. The resolution of this debate is important within the recognition of Sports Law as an intellectually rigorous and increasingly mature legal discipline. If the many problematic issues that currently face sport are to be effectively challenged and the law is to have a well reasoned and appropriate role within the general regulatory framework, sports lawyers and administrators need to have a sound theoretical understanding of the backgrounds, reasons and implications of law's involvement. The chapter will conclude by arguing that a sports law or *lex sportiva* is fast developing – indeed, a legal discipline that can be seen as analogous to a *lex mercatoria* – that needs to be understood both in national legal terms but, perhaps more importantly when it comes to the regulation of sport, in supra-national (European) and international terms.

COMMERCIALISATION OF SPORT

The argument has already been made that the commercial orientation of contemporary sport is not a new phenomenon. However, the vast amounts of money currently found in sport make it one of the most commercially powerful forms of business. The extract below shows that players and athletes have become members of the super-rich. This is primarily due to their earning power as vehicles for advertising, not the salaries from actual performing.

'Forbes Celebrity 100 – 2004'

Tiger Woods is the world's highest-paid athlete, earning $80.3 million in the last year, according to Forbes magazine's 'Celebrity 100' issue. Formula One driver Michael Schumacher of Germany was second on the list with $80 million in earnings. The rest of the top 10 are: Indianapolis Colts quarterback Peyton Manning ($42 million); the retired Michael Jordan ($35 million); Los Angeles Lakers center Shaquille O'Neal ($31.9 million); Minnesota Timberwolves forward Kevin Garnett ($29.7 million); tennis star Andre Agassi ($28.2 million); soccer icon David Beckham ($28 million); New York Yankees third baseman Alex Rodriguez ($26.2 million); and Lakers guard Kobe Bryant ($26.1 million). No female athletes made the list of the top 50.[12]

It may have been generally accepted in the past that although sport was a form of business, sporting success should traditionally outweigh financial profit as the primary aim. However, the pursuit of money has increasingly come to represent the aim of sport. Massive amounts of income have been generated from the selling of television rights. The broadcast rights to the Sydney 2000 Games were sold for a record US$1.3 billion – five times more than those for the 1984 Los Angeles Games. In the summer of 2003, the TV rights to The Premier League in England for the next three seasons were sold for over £1 billion.[13] Sport is clearly 'big business'. Britain is catching up with the United States in this regard where this has been the reality for many years.

Hofmann, D and Greenberg, MJ, *Sport$biz*

Sports has become a modern merchandising monster. And it eats money. Incredible amounts of money. Mind-boggling mounds of money. *Sports Inc* magazine conducted a study in 1987 to try to find out just how much money, and the results were right out of a Pentagon budget session. The magazine pegged the gross national sports product at $50.2 billion.

---

12   See www.forbes.com.

13   For further information see Spink, P and Morris, P, 'The battle for TV rights in professional football', in Caiger, A and Gardiner, S (eds), *Professional Sport in the European Union: Regulation and Re-regulation* (2000), The Hague: Asser.

That is more than we spend in this country on oil and coal and even automobiles. It is about 1% of the gross national product. In other words, for every hundred dollars that changes hands in the United States, a buck finds its way to one kind of game or another.

Not only that, but the creature gets bigger every year. Most of us play or watch something. If we do not, we buy products or services from companies with big investments in athletes or athletics. Even little old ladies in tennis shoes get the shoes with Boris Becker's autograph on them.[14]

Sport has become an ideal medium for sponsorship and advertising, mainly due to the vast exposure on television. This has led to a debate concerning the extent to which sport is in control of sponsors and television companies. Ethical issues have been raised concerning particular types of advertising; for example, whether there should be prohibitions on alcohol and tobacco advertising.[15] It is interesting to see how some sports in Britain became commercialised in the early years of being in an organised form, and others did not. Wray Vamplew notes how at the end of the 19th century, some sports such as football became fully commercialised and others, such as cricket, decided not to go down that path; and indeed he shows how the cricket establishment positively resisted commercial opportunities.[16] Although football has been run as a business since the birth of the professional game, it has rarely been seen as a serious way to make money. The investors have often been local business people uninterested in a return on their money.

The Business of Football

However, for the most successful football clubs today, a return on investment is considered vital.[17] During the 1990s, multimillionaire benefactors such as Jack Warner at Blackburn Rovers and Jack Hayward at Wolverhampton Wanderers emerged, individuals portrayed as indulging their philanthropy in childhood allegiances. Although having no traditional allegiance with Chelsea, Roman Abramovich can be seen in the same mould. Britain has also seen the rise of entrepreneurs such as Sir John Hall at Newcastle and Milan Mandaric at Portsmouth, who sees a football club as he would any other business: they provide an opportunity to make money and must be run as such. Since the early 1990s, there has been a trickle of clubs including Manchester United and Tottenham Hotspur that have become Public Limited Companies listed on the Stock Exchange. In recent years this development has increased.[18] Setting aside BSkyB's abortive takeover of Manchester United,[19]

---

14   Hofmann, D and Greenberg, MJ, *Sport$biz* (1989), Champaign, Illinois: Leisure Press, p xi.

15   In the US, for example, these types of sport related advertising are heavily regulated. See Pearl, I, 'Kicking the habit: the battle to rid sport of tobacco' (2001) 4(1) Sports Law Bulletin 15.

16   Vamplew, W, *Pay up and Play the Game* (1989), Cambridge: CUP.

17   For books on football business see Corry, D, Williamson, P and Moore, S, *A Game Without Vision: The Crisis in English Football* (1993), London: Institute for Public Policy Research; Boon, G, 'Is football a going concern' (1994) 3(3) Sport and the Law Journal 24; Fynn, A and Guest, L, *Out of Time* (1994), London: Pocket Books; and Boon, G and Thorpe, D, 'Going concern considerations in relation to football clubs' (1995) 3 Sport and the Law Journal 44, for an analysis of the financial state of football; Morrow, S, The People's Game?: Football, Finance and Society (2003), London: Palgrave Macmillan; Banks, S Going Down: Football in Crisis (2002), Edinburgh: Mainstream; Hamil, S (ed), *The Changing Face of the Football Business* (2000), London: Frank Cass; Szymanski, S and Kuypers, T, *Winners and Losers: The Business Strategy of Football* (1999), London: Viking; Conn, D, *The Football Business* (1997), Edinburgh: Mainstream; Hamil, S, Michie, J and Oughton, C (eds), *The Business of Football: A Game of Two Halves* (1999), Edinburgh: Mainstream; Hamil, S, Michie, J, Oughton, C and Warby, S (eds), *Football in the Digital Age: Whose Game is it Anyway?* (2000), Edinburgh: Mainstream.

18   See Watford's listing on the Alternative Investment Market (AIM), the junior stock market for small and growing companies; http://news.bbc.co.uk/hi/english/business/newsid_1411000/1411472.stm.

19   See later, p 313 for more.

media companies including BSkyB, NTL, Granada and Carlton have purchased significant shares in a number of the top clubs.[20] However, the financial picture for the vast majority of the 92 professional football clubs in England is not very rosy.[21] The decision by the European Court of Justice (ECJ) in *Bosman*[22] has had a seismic impact on not only on the dynamics of UK and European professional football, but also on the global game. Indeed its impact continues to be felt, for example with the changes to the transfer system in football. A detailed analysis of *Bosman* is found later in this book.[23] The importance of *Bosman* has principally been its questioning of the legality of the transfer system. The *Bosman* decision ruled on Art 39 of the Treaty of Rome and freedom of movement provisions. The likelihood of a successful challenge under European law was one that had been noted for quite a period of time – it was perhaps only a question of when someone would bring a discrimination case to court.[24] Contrary to the arguments raised by the Opinion of Advocate-General Lenz,[25] the ECJ largely ignored the position as far as Arts 81–82 concerning controls on anti-competitive practices. The impact that the competition rules have had on sport has occurred in other fora.[26]

A major issue in British Football is that the gap between the rich elite clubs and the smallest clubs in the lower professional leagues has widened. *Bosman* has contributed to the increasing of this division. There could well be a terminal threat to the lower division professional or semi-professional clubs. The accountants Deloitte have provided an annual review of English football finances since 1993 and for the Premier League since 1998. They provide a yearly 'snap-shot' of the changing financial contours of the game – particularly illuminating due to the dramatic changes over the last decade.[27]

An ongoing debate has focused the impact that the transfer system has had on the movement of money between the clubs in the different leagues. It is argued that the transfer system has acted in the past as 'a powerful mechanism for redistributing wealth'.[28] This redistributive effect of the transfer system is, however, one that has been contested. What is clear is that new money, vast amounts of it, has entered English professional football in recent years from the sale of TV and other media rights and the expansion in sponsorship and marketing opportunities. However, it seems that the top clubs, in particular Manchester United and the top players, have been the main beneficiaries. With clubs there are clearly the 'haves' and the 'have-nots'. As far as players, there are the super-rich, the merely comfortable and an increasingly growing number who, although reasonably paid, face greater uncertainty when it comes to contract renewal as clubs cut the size of playing squads.

Boon, G, '1996 football survey'

The financing of clubs in the lower divisions is clearly a cause for concern. With escalating wage bills and less money filtering down from the top clubs, some difficult decisions will have to be taken if

---

20 See 'Football club dealings' (1999) 2(6) Sports Law Bulletin 6.

21 See recent financial crises for Leeds United, Bradford City and Leicester City amongst others.

22 Case C-415/93 *Union Royale Belge des Sociéitiés de Football ASBL v Bosman* [1995] ECR I-4921; [1996] 1 CMLR 645, para 237.

23 See pp 500–19.

24 See the arguments pre-*Bosman* in Weatherill, S, 'Discrimination on grounds of nationality in sport', in *Yearbook of European Law 1989* (1990), Oxford: Clarendon, p 55 and Miller, F and Redhead, S, 'Do markets make footballers free?', in Bale, J and Maguire, J (eds), *The Global Sports Arena: Athletic Talent Migration in an Interdependent World* (1994), London: Frank Cass.

25 See pp 501–07.

26 See later, Chapter 9.

27 Copies can be obtained at www.footballfinance.co.uk.

28 Lee, M, 'A game of two halves: putting the boot in' (1995) New Statesman and Society 27.

professional football in England is to remain in its present form. The transfer market has historically been the saviour of many clubs, not only the smaller ones, and if this source of funding diminishes then an alternative mechanism of distributing monies to the lower divisions' clubs, perhaps through a re-distribution of TV income, will have to be found to save clubs from either going part-time or out of business completely.[29]

The latest Deloitte *Annual Review of Football Finance* confirms some of the trends identified over the last few years. The following are some of the highlights of the Report.

Highlights of the Deloitte *Annual Review of Football 2004*

Europe's premier leagues

The European football market (leagues, clubs and Federations covered by UEFA's 52 members) was worth £7.2 billion in 2002/03.

- Total income generated by the top divisions of the 'Big Five' leagues was £3.9 billion in 2002/03. This was a 7% increase on the previous season and a near tripling of income since 1995/96.

- Each of the 'Big Five' top divisions experienced revenue growth in 2002/03, with the English Premiership enjoying the largest growth, therefore widening the gap between it, the highest revenue generator at £1.2 billion, and the Italian Serie A, the second highest earner at £0.8 billion. France's Ligue 1 generated the lowest revenue of the five top divisions with £0.5 billion.

- Broadcast income remained the most important revenue source for all 'Big Five' leagues in 2002/03 with Serie A the most reliant, where the revenue stream contributed 55% of total income. The German Bundesliga was the least reliant on broadcast income at 33%, having dropped from 40% in 2001/02 due to the collapse of the league's broadcasting deal.

- Total wages and salary costs for the 'Big Five' top divisions stabilised at £2.5 billion in 2002/03, approximately equal to the previous year's total.

- Two leagues, Serie A and the Bundesliga, achieved a decrease in wages and salary costs compared to the previous year, the first time during the period analysed that any league has exhibited a year on year decrease. As a consequence Italy's wages to turnover ratio has dropped from 90% to 76%, whilst Germany had the lowest ratio at 45%.

- The variation in operating profit performance between the four leagues analysed is vast. The English Premier League has recorded cumulative operating profits of over £600 m since 1995/96 – the most of any league; Serie A has recorded combined losses of £0.8 billion over the same period. Encouragingly, whilst England and Germany showed increased profits in 2002/03, Serie A and the French Ligue 1 also halted a worrying increase in the scale of losses over the previous two years.

- The estimated broadcast income from 'Big Five' league domestic live and highlights deals in 2002/03 was £1.3 billion although the changing broadcast landscape in several countries has affected rights values. There is a disparity in the capacity to earn broadcast income between clubs within the same league, which is exacerbated in those leagues where clubs sell rights individually.

- Each of the 'Big Five' leagues has experienced the regulator's influence on their media rights selling strategies in recent seasons. The industry should be wary of assuming any particular judgment or ruling from another league or 'market' will apply universally as each situation is unique. Whilst recognising the regulator's well meaning intentions, football must continue to 'sell its case' regarding the specific benefits its arrangements bring – in solidarity between clubs and a coherent product for fans, to name but two.

---

29 Boon, G, '1996 Football survey' (1996) 4(2) Sport and the Law Journal 46.

- The Bundesliga's average attendance was 35,048 in 2003/04, the highest amongst the 'Big Five' leagues, and the first time since 1998/99 that the English Premiership hasn't been the highest. Despite this, the Premiership's average stadium utilisation was 95% compared to the Bundesliga's 78%.

Profitability of English clubs

- In 2002/03 the 92 top professional clubs generated total revenue of £1,658 m – up 4% from 2001/02.

- The total revenue of Premiership clubs was £1,246 m, up 10% on 2001/02 (£1,132 m) maintaining the League's position as the 'European and world champions' in terms of revenue generation.

- The loss of ITV Digital monies resulted in total Football League clubs' revenue falling by 12% to £412 m – the majority of the drop occurring in Division One (down 14% to £255 m).

- Manchester United headed the Premiership 'revenue league table' at £175 m, followed by Liverpool and Arsenal (both at £104 m). At the other end of the table was West Bromwich Albion (£28 m). In 2002/03, the average Premiership club generated revenue of £62.3 m.

- Premiership clubs' matchday income increased to £363 m – driven by a 3% increase in Premiership attendances, more European matches and increased ticket yield.

- Commercial revenue was almost unchanged, at £340 m in total, in part reflecting the tough market for sponsorship and advertising.

- The Premiership clubs' largest source of revenue came from broadcasting – 44% of the total at £543 m. Looking back a few years, broadcasting was the smallest revenue source. In 1996/97, broadcasting monies were less than £100 m, representing just 21% of Premiership clubs' total revenue and, in 1991/92, were less than 10% of revenues at a mere £15 m.

- In the 2003/04 season just ended Premiership clubs are estimated to have generated turnover of £1.33 billion, which we forecast will increase further to £1.36 billion by 2004/05.

- Premiership clubs reported overall operating profits of £124 m – a record high since the formation of the Premier League and a healthy 10% margin – with 16 of the clubs making operating profits. By contrast, pre-tax losses rose to £153 m and only five of the clubs made a pre-tax profit.

- The apparent paradox – of a record level of Premiership clubs' operating profits and pre-tax losses in the same year – is largely the product of high player amortisation costs (a legacy of high transfer spending in the past) and much reduced profits on player disposals (as transfer spending was much reduced in 2002/03).

- Contrary to the speculation from some commentators that media values might collapse, the deals announced so far by the Premier League, and press comment about other deals yet to be announced, indicate that monies to Premiership clubs for the next period should be in line with the previous broadcast deals.

- The four English clubs competing in the Champions' League in 2002/03 – Manchester United (to Quarter Final), Arsenal (2nd round group stage), Newcastle United (2nd round group stage) and Liverpool (1st round group stage) – received approximately £49 m from UEFA between them.

- The gap between the Premiership and Division One grew again in 2002/03, with the average Premiership club having revenue almost six times greater than its Division One counterpart.

- The 2004 prize for Crystal Palace winning promotion to the Premiership (even if the club 'yo-yo's' straight back down) was around £35 m – making the Division One Play-Off Final the 'richest game on earth'.

- Manchester United were again top in terms of operating profit. Their profit of £47.8 m increased their Premiership record (previously £34.5 m in 2001/02). Furthermore, their cumulative 5 year operating profits of £174 m were well over three times those of their nearest rival – Newcastle United at £52 m.

Player costs – wages and transfers

- In the 2002/03 season, Premiership clubs' total wages and salaries (ie not just players' wages) grew by 8% to £761 m, the lowest rate of increase since the formation of the Premier League, and well below the average annual increase of c25% over the previous ten years.

- The 15 clubs for whom we have accounts and who were in Division One in both 2002/03 and in 2001/02 saw total wages and salaries drop by 2%. For the division as a whole however, the wage bill grew slightly to £228 m (a 6% increase). Lower down the pyramid, total wages and salaries amongst clubs in Divisions Two and Three declined in absolute terms.

- With some notable exceptions, it appears that clubs have also been relatively restrained, in terms of wage increases, in the 2003/04 season.

- The ratio of total wages to turnover – a key financial performance indicator in football – for the average Premiership club fell to 61% in 2002/03 (2001/02: 62%). West Bromwich Albion, Manchester United and Newcastle United all had ratios below 50%. The equivalent ratio for Sunderland, Fulham and Leeds United was over 80% in each case.

- The surplus of Premiership clubs' turnover over total wages was at a record high of £485 m (2001/02: £426 m).

- The average total wages and salaries cost for a Premiership club in 2002/03 was £38 m (2001/02: £35 m). Manchester United had the highest total wages costs (as was the case in 2001/02) of £79.5 m and the lowest was West Bromwich Albion (£11.5 m).

- As in the previous season, in 2002/03 there were five Premiership clubs with a total wages cost (not just players) over £50 m – Manchester United (£79.5 m), Arsenal (£60.6 m), Leeds United (£56.6 m), Chelsea (£54.4 m) and Liverpool (£54.4 m).

- Unfortunately, the reduction in turnover – which was somewhat outside their control – for clubs in Divisions One and Two was greater than the amount by which clubs managed to reduce their wages and salaries costs. Hence, the overall wages to turnover ratio in each of those divisions increased in 2002/03 to 89% and 85% respectively.

- The average wages to turnover ratio for clubs in Division Three – the least affected by ITV Digital's demise – reduced to a more sustainable level of 68%. This improvement appears to have been further reinforced in 2003/04, the first season of implementation of the 'salary cost management protocol', that is to be extended to Division Two clubs from 2004/05.

- Total payments in respect of players (wages plus transfers) have fallen by 5% to £852 m. This is a monumental change – the first recorded year on year decrease in player spending since we started producing the Annual Review 12 years ago.

- The total of transfer fees committed by English clubs in 2002/03 (of £203 m) was down 50% on the total in the previous season (2001/02: £407 m).

- The total of transfer fees committed by Premiership clubs in 2002/03 (of £187 m) was down 42% on the total in the previous season (2001/02: £323 m) and transfer spending by Football League clubs fell dramatically from £84 m in 2001/02 to only £16 m in 2002/03, a decrease of 81%.

- The most significant change in 2002/03 was the reduction in the amount of money spent by Premiership clubs on buying players from non-English clubs. In 2002/03 transfer spending by Premiership clubs with non-English clubs was down 48% to £101 m (2001/02: £195 m), thereby keeping more money within the English game.

- Of the £187 m committed by Premiership clubs, a net £32 m was re-distributed to Football League clubs – this is almost double the £18 m re-distributed in 2001/02.

- Significant transfer spending by Chelsea over the past year – reportedly over £120 m (aggregate of summer 2003 and January 2004 windows) – means we expect that total transfer spending by Premiership clubs in 2003/04 will have risen again, to around £260 m. However, this is still well below the peak of £364 m in 2000/01, which is unlikely to be exceeded again.

- Over the 12 year life of the Premier League, Premiership clubs have provided a total of around £600 m in transfer fees to Football League clubs.

- Since the end of the 2002/03 season, transfer spending by Football League clubs has continued to be minimal. Clubs are no longer prepared to, nor need they, spend significant sums on acquiring player registrations. As we predicted, the 2001/02 season was a watershed and the subsequent financial results demonstrate that the market has changed.

- The January 2004 transfer window spending by Premiership clubs was estimated by Deloitte at under £50 m, and non-English clubs barely spent at all (less than £10 m across Italy, Spain, Germany and France).

- The summer 2004 transfer market has continued the trend from the January 2004 transfer window, with transfer activity remaining relatively muted even after Euro 2004.

Stadium development

- Total spending by English clubs on stadia and facilities in 2002/03 was £176 m, taking the total investment in the post-Taylor era to over £1.6 billion.

- Spending by Premiership clubs on stadia and facilities was £133 m in 2002/03. This was the sixth successive year when facilities investment by Premiership clubs exceeded £100 m and brings spending, since 'Taylor', to almost £1.2 billion.

- Arsenal was, by far, the club who invested most in facilities in 2002/03, comprising £80 m of the £176 m total. Arsenal is expected to stay at the head of the investment list until completion of Ashburton Grove – which is planned in time for the 2006/07 season.

- In 2002/03, average attendances at Premiership matches topped the 35,000 mark – the largest top division average since the 1950/51 season, and a 3% increase on the previous season. Overall capacity utilisation rose to 93.8%.

- Largely due to a change in the 'mix' of clubs, the average Premiership attendance in the 2003/04 season just ended fell back a shade to 35,008, although capacity utilisation improved further to 94.7%.

- The total capacity of Premiership stadia in 2003/04 (of 739,000) is 89,000 (14%) greater than six years ago (1997/98: 650,000).

- Whilst capacity utilisation now stands at 94%+, Deloitte estimate that there was still around £19 m worth of empty seats at Premiership matches in 2002/03 and around £16 m in 2003/04 – a further opportunity – along with more sophisticated pricing of existing sales – for the application of yield management techniques to maximise revenues.

- Football League attendances totalled 15.9 m in 2003/04, a 7% increase on the previous season. Aggregate attendances for the three divisions below the top flight are now at their highest level since 1963/64 and more than double the aggregate crowds for these games in the mid 1980s. The average Division One attendance in 2003/04 was 15,890, a healthy 45% of the size of the average attendance at a Premiership game.

Financing the clubs

- There was £1.05 billion of total 'Capital Employed' amongst Premiership clubs in summer 2003. Only 18% was from bank borrowings – bank loans and overdrafts, net of cash at bank, was £187 m. Total borrowings were £704 m, such that the overall gearing ratio (of debt to shareholders' funds) was 204% (2002: 137%).

- Over recent years, several Premiership clubs have used alternative financing mechanisms – in particular, securitisation of ticket receipts and specialised player financing methods – to supplement traditional finance sources. Generally, these monies are included in other loans, which stood at £505 m for Premiership clubs at summer 2003. The flow of such deals appears to have 'dried up' in 2003.

- Net Interest charges from finance providers increased to £44 m (2001/02: £30 m), but interest cover remained in excess of 21/2 times.

- Dividend payments to shareholders were a modest £14 m (2001/02: £11 m).

- At summer 2003, Fulham (£133 m) topped the table for net debt, albeit £91 m of the balance was 'soft' loans. The next two clubs in the table of net debt were Leeds United (£78 m) and Chelsea (£75 m). In both cases, albeit in rather different circumstances, there has been a restructuring of each club's finances since their last annual financial statements.

- At summer 2003, Manchester United (£157 m) topped the table for net assets, more than double their nearest rival (Arsenal – £76 m). Overall net assets for Premiership clubs were £345 m.

- Amongst Division One clubs, bank borrowings (£115 m; 57% of capital employed) are a relatively more important source of financing than for Premiership clubs (£186 m; 18% of capital employed).

- A record number of clubs entered insolvency proceedings during 2002 and 2003 (seventeen Football League clubs in total). As we predicted, the Football League has come through a particularly challenging couple of years with a full complement of clubs intact (just!).

- Division One clubs had a deficit in shareholders' funds of £78 m at summer 2003, compared to a surplus of £37 m the previous year – a 'swing' of £115 m. This is largely due to the change in mix of clubs between seasons and losses in the 2002/03 season.

- There is an increased air of financial realism at Football League clubs. Better financial management is being further encouraged and supported by structural changes such as sporting sanctions for insolvency, limits on wage spending, parachute payments between the divisions of the Football League and division dependent pay levels for players.

- There is an increasing amount of supporter involvement in the ownership and operation of clubs, particularly below the Premiership. Primarily this has been driven by the supporters' trust movement that has contributed over £2 m of fundraising to clubs in 2002/03. While this amount itself is relatively small, in the overall context; the principle, and achievements, of supporters trust involvement has had a big impact. A strong relationship between club and community is also good for business.

Football and tax

- The football industry continues to generate substantial tax receipts for Government. Clubs in the top four divisions of English football paid around £550 m of tax to Government in 2002/03.

- The estimated annual tax take of around £550 m is almost four times greater than in 1995/96 (£149 m). And, the tax burden is increasing – the rate of compound annual growth in the tax take (21%) exceeds the rate of growth in football's income (18%) over that period.

- The Premiership clubs are estimated to have paid around £394 m in tax (PAYE/income tax; National Insurance; VAT and corporation tax) in 2002/03.

- During the 12 year life of the Premier League, Premiership clubs have provided a total of around £2.5 billion of tax receipts for Government. The total contribution by clubs in the top four divisions, over that same period, is over £3 billion.

- The substantial tax contribution, together with the investments by clubs into grassroots and social initiatives, mean that the clubs are a significant contributor of funds for the wider public benefit, estimated to be over £600 m for 2002/03.[30]

The relationship between the powerful top clubs and the lower divisions is changing. A growing development is the lower division clubs acting as training and farming clubs for the elite. Such a

---

30 www.deloitte.com

system exists in professional sports in the United States such as baseball and in football in countries such as Spain. The elite clubs own the 'farm club' or 'nursery club' and the promising player learns his trade playing at the lower level and then hopefully will progress. In English football, such relationships cannot operate due to prohibitions on multiple ownership. However, informal relationships can develop such as the one that has existed between Liverpool and Crewe Alexandra.[31]

One of the problems with a formal structure is that this hierarchical relationship also breaks the normal dynamics of relegation and promotion. Farm teams cannot compete with their parent and could not be promoted to a higher league if the parent is there already. In all the four major US team sports, there is no promotion to or relegation from the top league. The farm team will always be the poor relation and the inability of these smaller clubs to break through into the big time increases the centralisation and oligopoly of a small number of elite clubs. Even without the development of such a formal system, it is thought by many that the emergence and rise of clubs such as Watford, Wigan and Wimbledon will no longer be possible in the post-*Bosman* era. Connected with this argument is the view that the elite clubs need to invest more money in finding and nurturing home grown talent. However, there is evidence that this can lead to very sharp practices by clubs desperate to sign promising youngsters with many questionable inducements. The FA has investigated clubs such as Manchester United and Arsenal.[32]

It is clear that the early corporatism of professional clubs in England, in the sense of each club being mutually reliant on each other, is a thing of the past. There may be alliances between groups of clubs but these are shifting ones and tend to be around particular single issues. But as generally with sport, and unlike most other businesses, football clubs have a mutual interest in each other's business health. Each club plays each other. In team sport the product to be marketed is the game itself. Therefore no single team can sell the product itself. A team needs to play another in a league or cup. There is a need for competition and although this may be keen on the field, the clubs are dependent on each other to a much greater extent than in other businesses.

THE ECONOMICS OF SPORT

A major issue is how sports are to be structured and financed in the professional world of team sports. There are various economic models that can be applied to the structure of sport. One useful model distinguishes between 'win maximisation' where the main goal is sporting success with profits being reasonably unimportant, and 'profit maximisation' where generating of profits is the main aim. The former model reflects the traditional view of team sports in Europe where even in football most professional clubs make a loss in the long run. The latter model characterises American team sport.[33]

---

31 'Small clubs have to accept hand that feeds them' *The Times*, 3 March 1997, p 37; also note international links that have developed, eg Arsenal and Saint Etienne, Coventry and Juventus and Ajax and Ajax Cape Town; see Gardiner, S and Welch, R, '"Show me the money": regulation of the migration of professional sportsmen in post-*Bosman* Europe', in Caiger, A and Gardiner, S (eds), *Professional Sport in the European Union: Regulation and Re-regulation* (2000), The Hague: Asser, pp 114–16.

32 See 'Coaching and poaching', *Fair Game*, Channel 4, 3 June 1996.

33 See Gratton, C and Taylor, P, *Economics of Sport and Recreation* (2001), London: Spon; Sandy, R, Sloane, P and Rosentraub, M, *The Economics of Sport: An International Perspective* (2004), London: Palgrave.

In American sport, a number of systems work to provide a financial structure particularly in terms of regulation of the labour market.[34] In the early days of all the main American sports, a player reservation system of 'reserve clauses' gave clubs exclusive rights over the services of each player registered to them. The player was only free if the rights were traded to another club. This process was similar to the transfer system in a number of European sports. As a mechanism for even distribution of player talent between teams, it seems that the reserve clause or transfer system is not very effective.[35] In terms of wealth distribution, the transfer system has worked to some degree and in England has facilitated the perpetuation of 92 professional football clubs.

Some professional team sports in the United States, such as Gridiron football and baseball, have accepted a system of revenue sharing between clubs in order to help guarantee a reasonable degree of competition and uncertainty of outcome. In American football, the gate receipts are split 60/40 between home and away team and broadcasting rights are almost equally divided.

Another attempt to improve the competitive balance in US sports leagues is the salary cap. This is a league-wide maximum on team payrolls, but not on individual salaries. It has been suggested that a salary cap is the most effective way to bring about competitive balance in a league.[36] With the same overall money spent by each team on their players, all teams have roughly the same strength. Enforcement problems exist, though: the large teams have to stay below the cap, the small teams have a problem affording it and may need subsidising. The National Basketball Association (NBA) has perhaps been the most successful professional league and has seen enormous growth over the last 10 years. The salary cap that has operated reflects the growth in the revenue capacity of the NBA: it was set at $3.6 million in the 1984–85 season, rose to $23 million in the 1995–96 season and is at $43.84 million for the 2003–04 season – the highest in NBA history. It can decrease though: for the 2002–03 season, the figure dropped from $42.5 million to $40.27 million – the first drop since the salary cap system was adopted for the 1984–85 season. Built upon stars such as 'Magic' Johnson and Michael Jordan, the NBA has been a great business success.[37]

Within European sport there is a search for appropriate regulatory mechanisms that provide this 'competitive balance', without necessarily adopting American-designed approaches.[38] There is a strong case for the development of hybrid mechanisms – for example, greater revenue sharing which has happened in an ad hoc basis in the past in English football – that acknowledge the deep-rooted traditions and characteristics of European sport.[39]

Késenne, S, 'Player market regulation and competitive balance in a win maximizing scenario'

If European sports clubs are indeed non-profit organisations as distinct from the American clubs, the results of economic research show that there is a case for some regulation of the sector by the league authorities in order to guarantee a more balanced competition. However the transfer system turns out to be totally ineffective in that respect. If the salary cap seems to be effective in the profit maximising US

---

34   For further information, see Gray, J, 'Regulation of sports leagues, teams, athletes and agents in the United States', in *op cit*, fn 31, Caiger and Gardiner (2000).

35   See Cooke, A, *The Economics of Leisure and Sport* (1994), London: Routledge; El-Hodri, M and Quirck, J, 'An economic model of a professional sport league' (1971) Journal of Political Economy; Cairns, J, Njennet, S and Sloane, P, 'The economics of professional team sports: a survey of theory and evidence' (1986) 8(2) Journal of Economic Studies.

36   Quirk, J and Fort, RD, *Pay Dirt: The Business of Professional Team Sports* (1992), Ewing, New Jersey: Princeton UP. Also see Farrell, R, 'Salary caps and restraint of trade' (1997) 5(1) Sport and the Law Journal 53.

37   See Greenberg, MJ, 'The NBA – a model for success' (1995) 3 Sport and the Law Journal 9; 'The NBA needs to do some Globetrotting' *Business Week*, 19 July 1999.

38   On the use of salary caps in UK Sport, see Bitel, N, 'Salary Caps: Lawful, Workable and Imminent' (2004) 12(1) Sport and the Law Journal 132.

39   See later, pp 179–81, concerning this debate.

world of professional sports, it raises some doubts in the non-profit European sports sector. If one conclusion from our research can be drawn for European professional team sports, this conclusion will be that revenue sharing between teams in a league is the best way to guarantee a more balanced competition without running into the ethical and legal problems of the transfer market.[40]

CHARACTERISTICS OF SPORT BUSINESS

There are important distinctive and unusual characteristics of the sports industry. They are illustrated below by examples from professional football:

- **Cut-throat competition is limited** – sporting clubs are mutually dependent on each other's well-being. Although cartels operate in many industries (and are often regulated through the law) and there may be some notion of mutual interest in each other's business strength, sporting entities are actually economically dependent. In sport there is a critical need for sporting competition and 'uncertainty of outcome'. Each team needs another team or opponent to play, and there is a need for some sort of level playing field as without it, sport loses its unpredictability and dies. Dominance by one team or a small number of teams in a league can adversely affect the whole 'product'. In the English Premier League, a number of leagues 'within a league' have been identified, with Manchester United almost in a league of its own. The traditional 'corporatism' in professional football, evidenced by the sharing of gate receipts and television rights deals, has increasingly dissipated over the last 20 or so years. Clubs often see their 'individual interests' as paramount over the other clubs in a league.

- **The search for talent** – sports businesses are able to subsidise a number of losses in their quest for the periodic 'big hit'. As with the wider entertainment industry, the Hollywood film companies are a good example; a number of losses can be sustained by the periodic big hit and accompanying financial reward. In club football, the ultimate prize is qualification for the European Champions League: the aim of the vast majority of Premier League clubs – for the others it is simply to avoid relegation. This dynamic of the sports business world leads to business practices that would be seen as irrational in regular industries.

- **The aim of winning** – traditionally European clubs have primarily aimed to win competitions and not make money – this move from a primarily 'win-maximisation' model to a 'profit-maximisation' model has been noted above. The increasing tendency for football clubs to seek plc status has created tensions that control decision making in clubs, for example, on the purchases of new players and the move to improve stadiums. Who is the main constituency to be consulted – the shareholders or the fans?

- **Who is the sports consumer?** – there is confusion as to who are the ultimate consumers: paying spectators or TV viewers. The demands of TV, 'he who controls the purse strings, calls the tune', have lead to concerns over ownership of the game. The voice of the fan and the notion of 'fan equity' – the social and cultural rights football fans have in the game – have increasingly been marginalised and ignored.[41]

---

40 Késenne, S, 'Player market regulation and competitive balance in a win maximizing scenario', in Jeanrenaud, C and Késenne, S (eds), *Competition Policy in Professional Sports: Europe after the Bosman Case* (1999), Antwerp: Standard Editions, p 121.

41 A good example of 'fan equity' and the power relations between clubs and supporters is the fight that some Newcastle United season ticket holders had when their seats were moved due to ground improvements; see *Duffy and Others v Newcastle United Football Club, The Times*, 7 July 2000; (2000) 3(5) Sports Law Bulletin 6.

- **National element to sport** – team games have historically been primarily limited to competition within national boundaries. However, with the developments of 'Europeanisation' on the one hand, the emergence of European Leagues[42] and European teams[43] – and 'globalisation' on the other, with wider international competition of club teams[44] – this parochialism has been challenged. Within Europe there are also the proposed development of regional competitions; for example, the so-called Atlantic League.[45] International competition between national teams has, of course, a long history. Some of the greatest rivalries include football between England and Scotland, and the 'fight' for 'The Ashes' between England and Australia in cricket. However, there are increasing tensions becoming visible; for example, the 'country versus club battle' in football for the services of a player, and the introduction of 'central contracts' paid by the national association in addition to the club contract. A connected debate has surrounded the justification for quotas that restrict the number of 'foreign' players who can play for clubs in domestic leagues, due to the adverse effect that the lack of opportunities for indigenous players might have on the quality and performance of the national team.[46]

- **Idiosyncratic labour market** – the working life of most professional athletes is reasonably limited. As already stated, there is a continual search for talent – specific rules of supply and demand apply. This results in managers and coaches in football and other sports such as ice hockey looking widely for potential players. This has lead to complex patterns of player migration.[47] The use of fixed term contracts is normal and in football, the search for contract stability within the post-*Bosman* years has lead to distinct contractual dynamics.

Ken Foster, who has written extensively on the legal regulation of sport, presents alternative models of the Sports Market to assist in determining appropriate regulatory regimes.

Foster, K, 'How can sport be regulated?'

Models of Sports Market

1 The Pure Market Model

This model treats sport purely as a business. Money comes before sporting success and unregulated economic competition occurs. The prevailing ideology is 'competition is the best regulator'. Governing bodies of sport have broad functions but mainly provide a loose regulatory framework in which profit maximisation occurs. The public interest is ignored and fans have limited power to resist their exploitation. There is a network of contracts between economic units with an individualistic ideology. The normal form of regulation is through the market and the predominant legal instrument is the contract.

2 The Defective Market Model

The limitations of the pure market model are manifest. The major one is that free markets tend to eliminate the weakest economic units. Sport cannot tolerate this market logic for too long for good sporting competitions need near equal teams or players. Monopoly of success is bad for sport;

---

42   eg the FIBA *SuproLeague* in basketball, which started in 2000.
43   eg the European Ryder Cup team in golf.
44   In rugby league, annual games are played between English and Australian clubs.
45   See *op cit*, fn 31, Caiger and Gardiner (2000), p 7 for a discussion on the proposed league of leading clubs from small national football markets, such as Scottish clubs Glasgow Rangers and Celtic, Dutch clubs Ajax PSV and Portuguese clubs, Sporting Lisbon and Porto.
46   See later, pp 576–88.
47   Lanfranchi, P and Taylor, M, *Moving with the Ball: The Migration of Professional Footballers* (2001), Oxford: Berg.

unpredictable outcomes are a key value. Governing bodies of sport, and the competitions they licence, are often monopoly controllers of sport. They can use this power to restore the sporting balance by reallocating resources. The main legal method of regulation in a defective market is competition policy. If the market fails, competition law can be used to counter balance the tendency to monopoly, or to correct an abuse of a dominant position.

3 The Consumer Welfare Model

This model addresses the other main limitation of the pure market model. Different interests may be linked through contracts but there can be very unequal economic power and bargaining power between contracting parties. The fan has weak market power against the football club. Players historically had limited economic power against their clubs. Players and clubs may need protecting against sporting federations who can take decisions over them with major economic consequences. The legal form of regulation is protective legislation to protect the weaker party, or to allow a greater protection of the wider public interest.

4 The Natural Monopoly Model

One of the arguments to support statutorily backed regulation is that the regulated industry is a natural monopoly and therefore market competition is absent. A natural monopoly is said to be characterized by a single seller, a unique product and barriers to easy entry to the market. Sport, it is claimed, has these characteristics. It therefore needs a regulatory structure that assumes it is a private monopoly that is likely to ignore the public interest. Competition law is an inappropriate mechanism of regulation because the market cannot be freed if there is a natural monopoly. An alternative regulatory strategy is needed.

5 The Socio-Cultural Model

This model argues that sporting values are dominant and that profit is ancillary. It also stresses the social and cultural significance of sport. It rejects all the assumptions behind the free market model. The importance of autonomy for sport is emphasized. The form of governance has historically been the private club, for example the Jockey Club. Clubs are ideally not-for-profit organisations with limited scope for maximising profits. Fans are seen as stakeholders in 'their' clubs. The difficult question to answer is what form of regulation best suits this model. The private club, with amateur voluntary administrators, has been one solution with consensus regulation in the 'best interests of the sport'. But commercialism can and has undermined this voluntarism and autonomy. Nevertheless, the sporting judgment of governing bodies needs to be protected from commercial interests to preserve the best features of this model. The preferred regulatory strategy may be 'supervised self-government'. This allows governing bodies to be autonomous and to regulate the sport without external interference in sporting matters. But this sporting autonomy must be matched by an internal constitutionalism, due process and good governance. This has links with the concept of 'enforced' or 'mandated' self-regulation. It shares with the pure market model a preference for 'non-intervention' but for diametrically opposed reasons. The pure market model argues for *laissez-faire* minimum interference to protect commercial interests. The socio-cultural model argues for autonomous self-government with 'constitutional' safeguards to protect sporting values.[48]

---

48 Foster, K, 'How can sport be regulated?', in Greenfield, S and Osborn, G (eds), *Law and Sport in Contemporary Society* (2000) London: Frank Cass, pp 268–270.

These models can be represented in a table:

Model	Values	Form of regulation	Governing bodies
Pure Market	profit/private interest (shareholders)	contract/intellectual property	maximise commercial opportunities
Defective Market	equal sporting competition (teams and players)	competition law	reallocate
Consumer Welfare	fans and viewers	protective legislation	widen democracy and accountability
Natural Monopoly	public interest	independent regulator	overcome rival organisations
Socio-cultural (traditional)	private club	immunity/ voluntarism	preserve sporting values
Socio-cultural (modern)	fairness, internal constitutionism and rule of law	supervised self government	preserve sporting values with due process

This typology of the sports market suggests that the development of effective regulatory is problematic – the sports industry or market is a complex one with availability of alternative regulatory regimes. Foster indicates that there are many interests to balance and potential ways to attempt to achieve this. In English football there are many tensions concerning power: between the football authorities, potential external regulators, shareholders of clubs, the increasingly powerful top players and, importantly, the fans.

COMMODIFICATION

This creeping commercialisation that has been outlined in football is mirrored in other sports to varying degrees and has brought incremental changes to sport. The financial base of sport has become increasingly dependent on sponsorship and marketing activities. Sports clubs have become a brand image and have a corporate identity as distinctive as Disney or McDonalds. In world sport, none is more powerful than Manchester United.[49] Built on a combination of tragedy and glory, the United plc has seen staggering growth in the 1990s. In 1996 it was valued at £429.85 million; in 1998, it was valued at £623 million by BSkyB in their aborted take-over;[50] in March 2000 it reached a value in excess of £1.02 billion.[51] In 2004, profits were down to £27.9 million in the year to July 31. This includes revenue of over £60 million on merchandising such as the sales of replica shirts. However,

---

49 They have been top of the 2001 Deloitte/*Four Four Two* Twenty Richest Clubs in the World list from 1997–2004. In 2004 they generated income of over €250 million – see www.footballfinance.co.uk .

50 See p 313 for more.

51 'Man Utd pass a billion', http://bbc.co.uk/news, 8 March 2000.

this unprecedented sporting business success over the last decade may be heading for an uncertain future, especially in the context of spiralling player salary costs:

> With more sponsorship and television money flooding in this year and next, the immediate future looks bright enough. But businesses which can't control their costs are inherently fragile. And football may still be more of a religion than a business.[52]

Sport is developing as an integral part of the leisure industry as a 'brand' and 'product' that can be consumed in recognisable and discrete entities. As such it is increasingly indistinguishable from other sectors of the entertainment business.

The process of the commodification of sport as an extension of the process of commercialisation is important to explain. The theory has developed within the discipline of cultural studies and can be seen originating in the work of the Italian political writer, Antonio Gramsci.[53] He developed the concept of hegemony, that is, the achievement of consent or agreement to dominant ideology (values and ideas) in society. Those groups who have most social, economic and political power in any particular society create these ideas. The argument is that the masses largely agree to and accept these ideas and values even though they are not in their best interests, because they are transmitted and reinforced by the many different institutions in society, such as education and the media.

This process of hegemony has been identified with the commodification of culture, commodity fetishism and the creation of 'false needs'. Writers such as Marcuse,[54] Horkheimer and Adorno,[55] aligned with the Frankfurt School of Political Thought, indicate how individuals are seduced into compliance in capitalist society by the attraction of superficial commodities, especially entertainment. Sport falls neatly into this theoretical analysis. Modern sport is used to make money through attracting spectators, selling satellite subscriptions and increasingly by selling sports merchandise. We as sports fans seem happy to accept it.

Through this process of commodification of increasing areas of social life such as sport, the argument is that the masses increasingly become compliant and in agreement with capitalism. However, it has been acknowledged that an absolute notion of hegemony is never attained, with cultural resistance or counter-hegemonic strategies coming from sub-cultures expressing antipathy towards these dominant views. Perhaps some of the football fans' pressure groups and activities such as fanzines are good examples of this:

Strinati, D, *An Introduction to Theories of Popular Culture*

> The cultivation of false needs is bound up with the role of the culture industry. The Frankfurt School sees the culture industry ensuring the creation and satisfaction of false needs, and the suppression of true needs. It is so effective in doing this that the working class is no longer likely to pose a threat to the stability and continuity of capitalism.[56]

The Frankfurt School has developed a neo-Marxist analysis seeing culture and in this context, sport, promoted as a 'product'; to be consumed to help pacify the populous and achieve consent to the existing social order. This of course is in opposition to theoretical perspectives that see sport as a natural human activity. It is clearly true that the modern form of elite sport is increasingly mediated and packaged. This has led to complaints that the nature of modern sport has changed for the worse.

---

52 'It's a funny old game' *The Economist*, 10 February 2001.
53 See Gramsci, A, *The Prison Notebooks* (1971), London: Lawrence & Wishart.
54 Marcuse, H, *One-Dimensional Man* (1968), London: Abacus.
55 Horkheimer, M and Adorno, T, *The Dialectic of Enlightenment* (1973), London: Allen Lane.
56 Strinati, D, *An Introduction to Theories of Popular Culture* (1993), London: Routledge, p 63.

Certainly TV companies have had enormous impact upon how and when particular sports are played.[57] The argument is that no longer is sport something to admire in terms of its virtue; sport is sullied by commercial priorities, gamesmanship and a 'winner takes all' mentality. There may be some revisionism in terms of the way that sport in the past is viewed, a false nostalgia of a perfect past where 'playing the game' was the sole aim. In fact, the historical evidence suggests that sport has been subject to these unsportsmanlike characteristics throughout its history.[58]

MODELS OF REGULATION

The alternative forms of regulation that might be applied to sport have been presented earlier. There is a 'turf war' in terms of the right to govern: international and national governing bodies and sports administrators or the government through agencies, lawyers and the courts. In Britain there has been increasing concern about the ineffectiveness of sports administrators in the modern commercialised world of sport. Conversely there has been a view from sports administrators that, as Foster states, 'legal intervention disrupts the good administration of sport'.[59]

In Britain, football has seen the strongest calls for external regulation.

FOOTBALL TASK FORCE

In July 1997, soon after coming into power, the Labour Government appointed a Task Force comprising different interest groups in football. In 1996, whilst in opposition, the Labour Party had produced a *Charter for Football*. Therein a Football Task Force was promised that would *inter alia* consider the restructuring of the Football Association, investigate links between football and television, consider the treatment of fans and the financing of football and look at the future development of the game. The subsequent remit of the Task Force changed somewhat and was divided into seven areas of work, including issues of racism and participation by ethnic minorities,[60] improving access to disabled spectators[61] and the responsibility that players have as role models in the community.[62] The other areas had a financial context:

- encourage greater supporter involvement in the running of clubs;
- encourage ticketing and pricing policies that are geared up to reflect the needs of all on an equitable basis, including, for cup and international matches;
- encourage merchandising policies that reflect the needs of supporters as well as commercial considerations;
- reconcile the potential conflict between the legitimate needs of shareholders, players and supporters where clubs are floated on the Stock Exchange.[63]

---

57 Premier League football matches are played on Sundays and Mondays together with the traditional Saturday afternoon. The US network NBC, who paid over £1,000 million for the TV rights to the Sydney 2000 and Salt Lake 2001, time-delayed all the coverage from Sydney 2000; see Moss, T, 'OK, the cameras are ready, start the race' *The Guardian*, 11 September 2000.
58 See Gardiner, S and Felix, A 'Juridification of the football field: Strategies for giving law the elbow' (1995) 5(2) Marquette Sports Law Journal 189.
59 *Op cit*, fn 48, Foster (2000).
60 Football Task Force, *Eliminating Racism* (1998), London.
61 Football Task Force, *Improving Disabled Access* (1998), London.
62 Football Task Force, *Investing in the Community* (1999), London.
63 Football Task Force, *Commercial Issues* (1999), London, p 1, para 1.3.

The consideration of these issues lead to the fourth and main report entitled *Commercial Issues* – how football should best be governed in the future and how the interests of the governing bodies, clubs and supporters reconciled. In fact there were two conflicting reports: one representing the perceptions of football fan groups sitting on the Task Force – 'the Majority Report'; the other from the football establishment, the FA and the Premier and Football Leagues sitting on the Task Force – 'the Minority Report'.

Football has of course been the focus of government regulation in recent years, where football's ability to self-regulate the game has been adjudged to have failed. The Hillsborough Disaster in 1989 led to the Taylor Report[64] in 1990 and the subsequent legislative framework concerning safety at football matches and football hooliganism. The perception that football needed to be regulated as a business was, however, a new development:

Summary of Main Proposals in Commercial Issues Report (1999)

Report One – The Majority Report: The Fans' View

Summary of Recommendations:

Regulation

A Football Audit Commission

The Task Force proposes that a Football Audit Commission be established, properly resourced, as a permanent standing body with terms of reference to include the following:

- the FAC will seek to achieve a greater accountability of clubs to a range of stakeholders, including supporters and shareholders;

- ensure the implementation of Task Force recommendations;

- specify objectives and reporting requirements on football clubs and authorities to cover financial management, involvement of supporters, development of new models of ownership, redistribution of income within the game, management of partnerships and resources, customer satisfaction and impact on society;

- set performance targets and monitor compliance;

- deal with non-compliance through sanctions if necessary;

- the FAC should be composed of members from a range of backgrounds appointed by the Secretary of State, under Nolan rules, and chosen for their expertise, experience, appropriate skills and commitment to and interest in football;

- the FAC will, where necessary, oversee the appointment of auditors for all football clubs and require them to publish a range of performance indicators relating to the social and economic impact of football clubs, customer satisfaction, and relationships with supporters and other stakeholders;

- the FAC will use this information to produce an annual report on commercial issues, highlighting areas where targets are not being met, and describing compliance with the Code of Practice;

A Football 'Ombudsfan':

- the Task Force recommends the establishment of an 'Ombudsfan' who investigates individual complaints and reports to the FAC;

---

64 Taylor LJ, *The Hillsborough Stadium Disaster: Final Report* (1990), London: HMSO, see Chapter 17 for a further discussion.

- he/she would be appointed by the FAC in consultation with the Minister, football authorities and fans' groups;

- the Ombudsfan would have powers to requisition evidence and call on the FAC to impose sanctions/solutions;

- this person would be a credible independent individual;

- the Ombudsfan will operate within clear terms of reference and guidelines and have the power to fine clubs in clear cases of maladministration.

Financial Compliance Unit:

- the Football Task Force supports the FA's proposals to establish a financial compliance unit;

- to introduce a 'fit and proper persons' requirement for persons wishing to own a substantial number of shares in a football club;

- the Task Force would expect the compliance unit to review club business plans on an annual basis;

- this Unit would also be subject to review by the FAC.

Code of Practice:

- a prerequisite of more effective regulation of football is the development of a coherent, constitutionally entrenched and detailed Code of Practice for the game, on and off the field;

- this code should be drawn up by the FAC in consultation with the governing bodies, clubs and supporters;

- the Code of Practice will set out minimum standards to be met by their clubs in their treatment of supporter-customers and all clubs should be expected to reach them;

- the FAC's Code of Practice should take as its starting point all of the appropriate recommendations contained in the four reports of the Task Force;

- the FAC will keep this code under review and in consultation with the game will develop new rules to reflect changing circumstances.

Ticketing Policies

The Football Audit Commission should:

- receive reports from all clubs annually on how they have widened access to fans who would otherwise have been excluded;

- encourage and ensure compliance on best practice amongst clubs on issues of ticketing policy, aiming to encourage accessibility to all supporters;

- review regularly all matters relating to the treatment of away fans.

All clubs should:

- stretch the range of prices offered, so that fans paying the highest prices are effectively cross subsidising those who pay new, lower prices;

- for the lower priced tickets, increase prices annually by no more than the rate of inflation in the Retail Price Index;

- reduce prices for restricted view seats and those at the very front or to the sides of major goal end areas;

- offer better access for fans who have difficulty paying current prices by being more flexible and imaginative in the marketing of less popular matches;

- extend concessionary tickets to embrace a wider section of the population particularly those who have felt excluded from football;

- under-16s and those in full-time education should be offered half-price tickets for all competitive matches covering at least 10 per cent of ground capacity (both home and away);

- offer payment for season ticket by instalment, over the six months from June to December. Clubs should not charge interest that is higher than base rate;

- limit the number of season tickets they sell in order to encourage home support from those who cannot afford to buy a season ticket;

- increase the proportion of tickets available for away fans wherever possible;

- at the beginning of each season be required to provide the FAC with details of their pricing policies. At the end of the season each should also report on how they have offered better access to fans who might otherwise have been excluded from matches because of price.

Clubs should not:

- charge away fans higher prices than home fans for the same facilities;

- restrict ticket sales to club members;

- offer tickets for away matches, including for European competition, on condition that supporters have to purchase travel from the club.

Merchandising

All football clubs and the FA so far as these measures are relevant to the sale of England kits, should:

- ensure that each strip has a minimum life-span of two full seasons;

- consult supporters on the design of new kits and take care to ensure it is in keeping with club traditions;

- carry a 'sell-by' date in the collar of the shirt indicating when the shirt will be replaced;

- adhere to the assurances given to the Director General of Fair Trading on retail price maintenance;

- the FAC should work with all clubs to encourage best practice on merchandising issues.

Supporter Involvement in the Running of Clubs

The FAC should promote best practice amongst clubs in consulting and working with supporters' groups.

- Supporters' associations should be encouraged as far as possible to be represented at national level with a single voice.

All clubs should:

- establish democratic forums through which all fans can be involved in decision-making;

- recognise and encourage as a collective body supporter trusts and supporter shareholder associations; this could involve promoting a representative from a trust, group or shareholders' association on to the board in a director or observer capacity;

- as far as practical provide appropriate financial and administrative support to the supporter bodies and the proper functioning of their elected representatives' duties;

- consult supporters on major decisions being taken by the club, such as ground relocation, stock market flotation, major sale of shares or changes in pricing policy;

- provide an opportunity, at least once a year, for a supporters' representative to discuss their concerns at boardroom level;
- where no other mechanism for supporter liaison exists, work with a supporter liaison committee.

The football authorities should:

- continue to provide a forum for regular consultation with supporters' representatives on the major issues facing the game;
- provide sufficient funding for the proper running and effective functioning of a national supporter representative body.

Reconciling Conflict in Football Club plcs

- Where a club is intending to float on the Stock Exchange or other public market in shares, or sell a majority of its shares, or perform any act substantially affecting its constitution or its football stadium, it must satisfy the FAC that it is intending to do so in the best long term interests of the club and all sections of its supporters and of the game of football itself.
- A minimum of twenty five per cent of shares in any club intending to take up a public listing must be offered to season ticket holders, subject to Stock Market rulings.
- All floated clubs and all clubs with more than 5000 season ticket holders should produce a public statement of intent and should organise twice-yearly meetings at which matters of club policy and structure can be debated.
- The club shall where possible consult supporters about all aspects of flotation.

The Government should:

- ensure that all clubs should be subject to the Department for Trade and Industry's referral criteria for take-overs;
- encourage communities, through local councils, to take an equity stake in their club.

The FAC should:

- ensure that all floated clubs adhere to football's new Code of Practice;
- investigate means of encouraging democratic supporter representation at floated clubs through the collectivisation of supporters' shareholdings; this should include advising supporter-shareholders, including current shareholders, how to hold their shares in a collective or mutual trust form;
- hold a legal charge over the ground of every club so that they cannot be sold without the consent of the FAC;
- in consultation with club-companies and supporters, develop detailed rules designed to reconcile the potential conflict between the needs of shareholders and supporters. These rules, to govern member club companies, including floated companies, would be designed to preserve the long term interests and survival of the companies as football clubs, working to the broad principle of balancing commercial requirements with responsibilities to promoting the aims of football and the Football Association.

Report Two – The Minority Report: The Football Authorities

The Football Association, the FA Premier League and the Football League have completed their own report after considering the majority report. Their recommendations can certainly be characterised as very much less radical and essentially about keeping the status quo. Their shared view is that football needs to be understood as a leading international industry with significant revenue and cost demands, a sporting business in a modern leisure market. The report focuses on a number of issues:

Ticketing:

- whilst supporting the promotion of good practice concerning ticket pricing and distribution, there is an acceptance that each club is an individual business and should be able to make its own 'sensible and balanced decisions on the right ticket policy';
- the report emphasises the role of concessionary tickets and the need to 'stretch' the range of ticket prices. The main emphasis is on the availability and distribution of tickets rather restrictions on pricing.

Merchandising:

- the report notes that purchase of a range of products is not an essential part of watching football and they dismiss calls for 'sell-by-dates' on replica kits;
- they do however acknowledge that all clubs 'should have a published, well-communicated kit cycle policy' particularly on any proposed changes.

Clubs and their supporters:

- clubs should consult their fans as stakeholders on a regular basis, through forums, questionnaires and focus groups and through the publication of current policy on major issues in an easily digested format;
- clubs should take steps wherever possible to promote supporter and community liaison. To that end each club should be encouraged to produce a customer charter that would cover the following: what can the customer reasonably expect from the club; how will this service be delivered; how can a customer feed back to the club; and what recourse do they have.

Financial compliance:

- although it is stressed that the financial affairs of each club remains with that club, the FA proposes to create a financial compliance team that would review annual returns from clubs and monitor financial health, help clubs to set up their own business processes.

Regulation:

- the football authorities note that in their view 'English football is not an under-governed sport';
- they state that there are an interlocking set of rules, regulations and codes of conduct which across the three bodies have recently been subject to amongst other things, modernisation, consistency, improved independent scrutiny and promoted best practice;
- the football authorities state that they 'do not believe that the overall well-being of the game will be helped by new layers of regulation or bureaucracy';
- the view is that especially in the global market that many football clubs exist, the creation of an additional set of rules is not appropriate;
- however the football authorities acknowledge they need to 'actively demonstrate their commitment to the good governance of the game'. They see improved self-regulation and more obvious public accountability as necessary aims;
- this aim they see as being achieved by the creation of an Independent Scrutiny Panel. Carrying out a function not dissimilar to the British Standards Institution, it would not sit permanently but carry out work from time to time and produce an audit report every two years. It would provide an independent assessment of the quality of regulation, best practice and governance, evaluation of compliance and non-compliance and recommendations for improving performance.[65]

---

65 'Football Task Force: commercial issues' (2000) 3(1) Sports Law Bulletin 1.

The Majority Report that represented the fan groups' perspective supported a radical interventionist approach with support for the creation of a permanent standing body, the Football Audit Commission (FAC), and the establishment of a new consumers' voice for football, the *Ombudsfan*. Supporters' groups would have formal involvement in the FAC. In addition, where a club intended to float on the Stock Exchange, the long term interests of the club ought to be considered.

The Minority Report from the football authorities', perspective was significantly more conservative. It argued that increased regulation was not needed for what is 'not an under-governed sport'. They recommended the emphasis should be on self-regulation, but found merit in supporting an advisory body, the Independent Scrutiny Panel (ISP), to provide assessment of the quality of regulation, best practice and governance found within individual clubs. This body would merely provide advice and no powers to intervene.

Adam Brown was a member of the Task Force and was a co-author of the Majority Report.

Brown, A, 'In my opinion: the Football Task Force final report'

The Government's Football Task Force concluded its business in December with a split Final Report on commercial issues. Having published three unanimous reports on racism, disabled access and football in the community, it was the controversial areas of regulation, ticket policies, supporter representation, merchandising and 'floated' clubs which were always going to test the body most.

This is not to say that the project has been a failure: far from it. The Task Force represents the biggest consultation exercise with English football ever undertaken – we saw 73 fans groups and 30 clubs amongst others as well as commissioning key research. The Task Force has also seen, for the first time, all elements of the game sitting around the same table. The Government is already committed to alter laws on racist chanting; to improve disabled facilities; and to create a dedicated unit to help fans form shareholding trusts (instrumental in the salvation of a number of clubs in the lower leagues). The Premier League have also promised to reinvest 5% of its TV revenue from the next television deal, reportedly worth some £1 billion, in the grass roots.

However, the Final Report now presents a dilemma for the Government's Sports Minister, Kate Hoey. The minority report, representing the football establishment, advocates an Independent Scrutiny Panel for football, of 3–5 people sitting for just four weeks a year to assess the performance of the FA, as well as a token Code of Conduct. The majority report, representing fans organisations and independent members have called for a much more thorough Football Audit Commission, and a series of robust recommendations on the key areas tickets, representation and commercial activities.

I have supported the latter because it promises that the performance of football authorities and clubs will be thoroughly examined by an independent body which will also include a fans' champion in the form of a football 'Ombudsfan' to investigate individual complaints. We have recommended that firm measures are needed to ensure that the top level of football does not price supporters out of attending and to make sure fans' interests are represented at all levels. Whilst some recommendations are shared by both sides – such as the need for clubs to 'stretch' prices, lowering the 'bottom end', some changes to merchandising policies and for some independent regulation – there is a gulf between the perceptions of the game. One sees it as a business which should be able to operate virtually unfettered; the other recognises football's importance in local communities and the lifeblood of the game that is the loyalty of ordinary supporters.

For 'our side', which includes the Chair and Vice Chair, the football establishment were simply not able to move far enough to satisfy both what we and the thousands of fans who made testimony to us wanted to see: namely, effective independent auditing of football's relationship to its community, protection for its customers and measures to try and balance some of the inequities in modern football. A limit on price increases, meaningful representation of fans at club and national level and checks on the effects of clubs floating, as well as calls for better redistribution of wealth in football to the lower leagues, were all key planks of our report. These went too far for the football establishment and top clubs and the Government, who established the Task Force to get a better deal for fans, must now choose.

11 full members of the Task Force (out of 17), including Chair, Vice Chair, all fans groups and all independent members, together with Pamela Taylor (of Water UK) from the Working Group, have written to Kate Hoey asking her to meet us and them to implement the majority report. This is backed by unanimous support from the the All Party Football Group of MPs, and an Early Day Motion to which nearly 100 MPs have put their names. However, word is that Number 10 is reluctant to pick a fight with the football authorities and public pressure needs to be maximised in the coming weeks, with a fans' lobby of Parliament due on March 2nd. Watch this space.[66]

The two Reports, although sharing some areas of commonality, seem far apart particularly on the issues of governance and accountability. The highly interventionist FAC favoured by the Majority Report is a very different form of regulation from that of the ISP, favoured by the Minority Report. The FAC would essentially see the existence of two bodies overseeing English football: the FA controlling the playing side of the game, including supervising rule changes and enforcing disciplinary matters, and the FAC controlling financial and commercial issues concerning the individual professional clubs.

The ISP was supported in the Minority Report with the view that:

... in our view English football is not an under-governed sport[67] ... English football does not need an additional set of imposed rules which prohibit and restrict the ability of clubs to make their own footballing and commercial decisions, particularly given the globalisation of the market place within which they are operating.[68]

The Independent Football Commission

In October 2000, plans were announced for the creation of an Independent Football Commission – a regulatory body very much in the form of the ISP supported by the Minority Report. The football authorities seemed to have heavily influenced the development of what will be an essentially 'soft-touch' independent monitoring body. As Brown comments:

Brown, A, 'The Football Task Force and regulation'

The division of the Task Force was also one of philosophical disagreement about what football is and should be – a business first or foremost, or a sport with too much cultural and social importance for it to be left to market forces. Given other developments, such as the increasing influence of media corporations in the ownership and future directions of the game, the decision of the government on which report to support is even more crucial.[69]

The IFC came into being in March 2002.

Independent Football Commission, 'Terms of Reference'

1. To review and report on the promotion by the FA, The F A Premier League and The Football League ('the governing bodies') of best practice in commercial and financial matters within professional football, particularly with regard to customer service. In particular to review and report on:
   - the establishment of a code of best practice, customer charters and customer relations units by each of the governing bodies, and by individual clubs.

---

66 Brown, A, 'In my opinion: the Football Task Force final report' (2000) 3(1) Sports Law Bulletin 2.
67 'Football's response to the Football Task Force', Football Task Force, *Commercial Issues* (1999), London, para 125.
68 *Ibid*, para 128.
69 Brown, A, 'The Football Task Force and regulation', in Greenfield, S and Osborn, G (eds), *Law and Sport in Contemporary Society* (2000), London: Frank Cass, pp 268–70.

- the governing bodies' establishment of a complaints resolution hierarchy based on the Code of Best Practice, with the Independent Football Commission as the final step in that hierarchy: and
- the establishment of a Financial Advisory Unit by the Football Association which will review and monitor aspects of clubs' financial performances and promote best practice

The IFC is to have particular regard to:-

- Ticket prices
- Accessibility to matches
- Merchandise; and
- Supporter and other stakeholder involvement.

2. To review the rules and regulations of the governing bodies relating to financial and business matters within their competitions, and the Code of Best Practice, and to recommend changes where appropriate.

3. To review and report on the adoption and/or promotion (as appropriate) by the governing bodies of the customer service related in the recommendation in the Football Task Force Reports 1–3.

4. To publish their findings by way of an annual public report.

The IFC was met with a largely cynical view as to its likely effectiveness.[70] A major perceived problem is that it is fully funded by the football authorities and therefore open to charges that it is not truly independent. It has produced two Annual Reports focusing on such issues as the financial crisis at club level and governance in the game and racism. The IFC has indicated that as a body it is pretty impotent in its ability to engage with the pressing financial and socio-cultural problems in English football.[71] The vast majority of professional clubs are in a parlous financial state. The collapse of ITV Digital in 2002 has severely damaged the financial dynamics in the Football League clubs.[72] The FA continues to be seen as one of the worst examples of sports governance.[73] The conduct of professional players, a significant number highly paid, continues to be under scrutiny.[74] The arguments for effective external regulation are strong.

In May 2004, the IFC published a 'Report on Self Regulation', a document partly reviewing its role and partly suggesting proposals on alternative structures that could be employed beyond its initial two-year terms of reference. These alternatives are:

- discontinue the IFC;
- do nothing;
- extend the IFC terms of reference and increase its funding;
- a radically revised role and structure for the IOC;

---

70 'The IFC's flawed potential', 13 March 2002, www.news.bbc.co.uk; Chaudhary, V, 'Soccer watchdog "has no bite"' *The Guardian*, 14 March 2002.

71 Bower, B, *Broken Dreams: Vanity, Greed and the Souring of British Football* (2003), London: Simon & Schuster.

72 'ITV Digital: Where did it all go wrong?' 30 April 2002, www.bbc.co.uk/news; also see information on the failed attempt by the Football League to seek dmagse against Carlton and Granada TV: 'League loses football cash battle', 1 August, 2002, www.bbc.co.uk/news; see *Carlton Communications Plc (2) Granada Media Plc v Football League* (2002) EWHC 1650 (Comm), LTL 1/8/2002 (unreported elsewhere).

73 'Minister wants FA to face review', 24 October 2004, www.bbc.co.uk/news.

74 On the criminal trial of Leeds United players Lee Bowyer and Jonathan Woodgate for assault, see Redhead, S, Leeds United on Trial (2002) 1(3) Entertainment Law 98–106.

- immediate revolution; or
- statutory regulation.

The IFC believes that it has 'lack of power, inadequate resources, restrictive terms of reference and limited access to information'. In evaluating the options presented, the first five options will perpetuate self-regulation; options 2–5 will continue to see the IFC having a role; option 6 would lead to direct government intervention through legal provisions and an end to self-regulation. Option 4 is the one favoured by the IFC. The IFC believes that keeping the status quo is not a realistic option. The FA is a particular target whose dual role of a regulatory function of the English game and a representative function within the international game is seen as problematic. The IFC sees the FA as not being wholly independent, with many inadequacies including tensions around the national team and club interests, the handling of commercial interests, lack of accountability and a lack of codes of practice.

In addition, a Parliamentary Report in February 2004 from the All Party Football Group has also proposed that the powers of the IFC are increased. The Report also focuses on reforms in the context of the financial realities of English football. Some selected recommendations are:

All Party Football Group, *Inquiry into Football and its Finances*

- Premier League to double to 10% the broadcasting revenue it re-distributes to the rest of football
- More re-distribution of TV rights money within the Premier League
- Detailed research into the financial impact of the transfer window
- Consultation between football authorities and all clubs on the re-introduction of gate-sharing
- Strong support for severe points deduction for clubs going into administration
- Wage-capping to be considered by Premier League if experiment in Football League/Conference proves successful
- Immediate introduction of the `Fit & Proper Person' test for club directors
- Supporters' views represented at board level and FA to be more representative of modern Britain
- All professional clubs to have budgets approved two seasons in advance
- Introduction of an agents' levy to be re-distributed to grass-roots game
- Future Premier League contracts to include limited number of games to be broadcast by free-to-air channels
- Decisive England qualifying matches to become Listed Events
- The norm for a majority of a club's home league fixtures to kick off at 3pm on a Saturday.[75]

As the IFC argues, English football must demonstrate more clearly that it has the ability and will to regulate itself, and that it must be prepared to shoulder the responsibilities that go with self-regulation. The IFC have put the ball in the court of the football authorities to see if they are prepared to cede more power to a body such as the IFC so as to have more of a risk than essentially just passive scrutiny. The response is awaited.

---

75 See www.allpartyfootballgroup.org.uk/inquiry.htm.

THE NORMATIVE RULE STRUCTURE OF SPORT

As indicated earlier, sport as an area of social life is extremely 'rule-bound'. An examination of the rule structure is required. There is clearly a structure or hierarchy of such rules. The term 'normative' indicates that they are designed to be prescriptive and are concerned with 'ought (not) may (not) or can (not), in relation to behaviour'.[76] Both sport's informal and formal rules are subject to frequent change which creates a dynamic relationship with new tactics being developed by sports coaches and participants.[77] This is the context within which the rules of law operate. The consequential tripartite amalgam of normative rules – sport rules, sport's working culture, and the law – leads to many issues of demarcation.

History of Rules of Sport

Rules are needed for specific sports to be played. The historical development of the 'codification' of sport and the creation of formal rule structures has been outlined above. They can generally be divided into those having the goal of ensuring safety and those regulating the dynamics of play.

In boxing, the rules developed to codify prize fighting in the 18th century were motivated by safety:

> That a square of a Yard be chalked in the middle of the Stage; and on every fresh set-to after a fall or being parted from the rails, each Second is to bring his Man to the side of the square and place him opposite to the other and till they are fairly set-to at the Lines, it shall not be lawful for one to strike at the other.[78]

These are the first crude rules set down in print to govern boxing that were written by Jack Broughton in 1743, two years after he had killed George Stevenson in a prize-ring in Tottenham Court Road. They are couched in language that reflects the peculiarly muscular decency of the times. These rules were further codified in 1867 under the auspices of the Marquis of Queensbery. As noted earlier, the late 1800s saw the formal codification of many sports.

The combinations of safety rules and the rules determining the mechanics of play can be termed as any particular sport's 'constitutive rules':

Simon, R, *Fair Play: Sports, Values and Society*

> If players were unaware of such rules or made no attempt to follow them they logically could not be playing basketball (although minimal modifications might be acceptable in informal play or other special contexts). Constitutive rules should be distinguished sharply from rules of strategy such as 'dribble only if there is no faster way of advancing the ball up the court'. Rules of strategy are general suggestions as to how to play the game well; constitutive rules determine what counts as a permissible move within the game itself.[79]

---

76 Twining, W and Miers, D, *How to do Things With Rules* (1999), 4th edn, London: Butterworths, p 123. This is a good starting point in terms of examining the rule as the basic 'working tool' of the law.

77 See 'Do not change the balls or tinker with the rules please' *The Times*, 6 July 1994.

78 'Sportsview: why they can't close school of hard knocks' *The Observer*, 29 October 1995, p 10.

79 Simon, R, *Fair Play: Sports, Values and Society* (1991), Boulder: Westview, pp 14–15.

Playing Culture

Rules of strategy are therefore separate from the constitutive rules of the game or sport. They may be formally written in coaching manuals, etc or they may be informal rules. In addition, conventions and customs also have a powerful normative impact on play in a number of sports. These are informal and rarely defined except in very wide terms.[80] In fact there are numerous informal and unwritten rules in sports that guide athletes in how they play the game. For example, in rugby, there is a convention to tackle an opponent 'hard and low' early in a game to achieve a consequential advantage. It also includes 'psyching out' an opponent. As David Fraser says of 'sledging' (the practice of talking to or at a batsman in derogatory terms in cricket), 'while it is almost certainly illegal, sledging is a current and "accepted" ethical practice in some cricket circles'.[81] There is a view that there is more intimidation between opposing players in international cricket than ever before.[82] These actions can be defined as the working or 'playing culture' of sport.

These playing cultures develop to gain an advantage within the formal rule structure. This behaviour challenges the formal playing rules and the adjudication of the referee or umpire in that it may be illegal. Indeed, certain practices that are contrary to the playing rules may be followed so frequently that it becomes 'customary' to break the law of the game. On a wider philosophical level, probably the most powerful value within liberal democracies and legal liberalism is the 'rule of law'. The duty to follow the law and not break it is seen as fundamental. On the contrary, however, theories of civil disobedience provide support for breaking the law in circumstances of injustice and in fact in certain circumstances, a 'moral duty' to so act.[83] Similarly in sport, violating the rules may be the right thing to do. Ice hockey can be used as an example:

Fraser, D, *Cricket and the Law: The Man in White is Always Right*

There are some sport sociologists who argue that no violation of the rules should be encouraged or permitted, just as there are jurists who argue that there is neither a right nor a duty to engage in acts of civil disobedience. An example of such formalism can be found in the recent soccer World Cup, for example, where FIFA instructed referees to issue a red card (expel) to any player committing a 'professional foul'.

On the other hand, our experience of sport indicates that rule-violating behaviour like the 'professional foul' is directly and intentionally integrated into the existential norms of participants and others who interpret the particular sport/text. Studies of ice hockey violence in Canada, for example, demonstrate that while fist-fights are illegal, they are accepted by all participants as an important and integral part of the game. Indeed, to refuse to fight, ie, to refuse to break the rules, will lead to ostracism and shaming by peer and other reference groups (eg parents).

Moreover, as other studies show, some rule-violating behaviour may be functional as a deterrent to other more serious rule-breaking. Again, the example of ice hockey violence indicates that there is a clear distinction between legitimate (although illegal) fighting (fist-fights) and illegitimate (and still illegal) violence (using the stick as a weapon). Not only is a player who uses his stick as a weapon ostracised and stigmatised as a 'cheap shot artist', but using a stick can cause serious, career-ending injury. Participants in the sport, and spectators and fans, see fist-fighting as legitimate not only because it functions to physically intimidate opponents (a skill or attribute which is honoured and legitimated when it occurs

---

80 See later, pp 606–12.
81 Fraser, D, *Cricket and the Law: The Man in White is Always Right* (1993), Sydney: Institute of Criminology, p 185.
82 See 'Lord's cracks down on appeals' *The Guardian*, 22 November 2000, and 'Cork's dumb insolence proves costly' *The Guardian*, 8 June 2001.
83 See Waldron, J, *The Law* (1990), London: Routledge.

within the rules), thereby making it easier to win in a 'collision' sport, but it is also legitimate because it prevents the occurrence of more violent and dangerous instances of illegality by providing a relatively harmless outlet for aggression. Just as in the world of criminal law and criminological theory, in sport not all illegal acts can be simply lumped into a single category. More specificity and detail are required than simply and simplistically labelling an act 'illegal', if we are truly to understand the act and its place in a complex whole.[84]

This relationship between the formal rules and informal 'playing or working culture' of the sport can help determine when the law intervenes:

Gardiner, S, 'The law and the sports field'

The reality is that in contact sports there is a continued risk of injury. The rules of sport are designed to avoid serious injury. They are a crucial guide in determining criminal liability. In the absence of proof of intent or recklessness to injure, participants who cause injury within the reasonable application of the rules of the sport can rely on the victim's consent to potential harm. An injury caused due to an illegal tackle that amounts to a foul within the rules of the sport is also likely to be seen as consensual. It may be contrary to the rules of the game but may well be inside the 'code of conduct' or 'working culture' of the sport. Consent is not limited solely by the formal rules in contact sports.[85]

The informality of the playing culture of sport can be exploited illegitimately, especially perhaps in the context of the winner-takes-all mentality of modern sport. The spectre of cheating is raised.[86] But playing cultures are pervasive in all sports.

Supplementing the Rules – Codes of Ethics

Increasingly in sport, codes or charters of ethical behaviour and fair play have been developed, stressing the need to play fairly.[87] The focus on ethics in sport has grown in recent years, largely due to the wide range of ethical dilemmas faced in sport including the use of violence; drug abuse; and exploitation of young athletes. These codes target not only sports participants but also administrators, coaches, spectators, etc. In terms of sports participants, though, they encourage ethical behaviour within the general context of the sport being played. It provides a balance to the legitimacy of participation beyond the exact application of the rules but within the playing culture. Two examples can be provided by way of illustration:

Council of Europe, *Code of Sports Ethics: Fair Play – The Winning Way*
(Qui joue loyalement est toujours gagnant)

Aims

The basic principle of the Code of Sports Ethics is that ethical considerations leading to fair play are integral, and not optional elements, of all sports activity, sports policy and management, and apply to all levels of ability and commitment, including recreational as well as competitive sport.

---

84 *Op cit*, fn 81, Fraser (1993), p 28. On ice hockey and the culture of physical force, see Whitson, D and Gruneau, R, *Hockey Nights in Canada* (1993), Toronto: Garamond.

85 Gardiner, S, 'The law and the sports field' [1994] Crim LR 514. This will be looked at further concerning liability for participant violence; see Chapter 15.

86 See later, p 74, for some examples.

87 See Parry, S and McNamee, M, *Ethics and Sport* (1998), London: Routledge; Malloy, D, Ross, S and Zakus, D, *Sports Ethics: concepts and Cases in Sport and Recreation* (2003) 2nd edn, Toronto: Thompson Education; and for some additional resources, the Canadian Centre for Ethics in Sport at www.cces.ca.

The Code provides a sound ethical framework to combat the pressures in modern day society which appear to be undermining the traditional foundations of sport – foundations built on fair play and sportsmanship, and on the voluntary movement.

The primary concern and focus is Fair Play for children and young people, in the recognition that children and young people of today are the adult participants and sporting stars of tomorrow. The Code is also aimed at the institutions and adults who have a direct or indirect influence on young people's involvement and participation in sport.

The Code embraces the concepts of the right of children and young people to participate and enjoy their involvement in sport, and the responsibilities of the institutions and adults to promote fair play and to ensure that these rights are respected.

Defining Fair Play

Fair play is defined as much more than playing with the rules. It incorporates the concepts of friendship, respect for others and always playing within the right spirit. Fair play is defined as a way of thinking, not just a way of behaving. It incorporates issues concerned with the elimination of cheating, gamesmanship, doping, violence (both physical and verbal), thwe sexual harassment and abuse of children, young people and women, exploitation, unequal opportunities, excessive commercialisation and corruption.

Fair play is a positive concept. Sport is a social and cultural activity which, practised fairly, enriches society and the friendship between nations. Sport is also recognised as an individual activity which, played fairly, offers the opportunity for self-knowledge, self-expression and fulfilment; personal achievement, skill acquisition and demonstration of ability; social interaction, enjoyment, good health and well-being. Sport promotes involvement and responsiblity in society with its wide range of clubs and leaders working voluntarily. In addition, responsible involvement in some activities can help to promote sensitivity to the environment.

Responsibility for Fair Play

Involvement and participation in sport among children and young people takes place within a wider social environment. The potential benefits to society and to the individual from sport will only be maximised where fair play is moved from the peripheral position it currently occupies to centre stage. Fair play must be given the highest priority by all those who, directly or indirectly, influence and promote sporting experiences for children and young people. These include:

– Governments: at all levels, and including agencies working with Government. Those involved in formal education have a particular responsibility.

– Sports and Sports-Related Organisations including Sports Federations and Governing Bodies; Physical Education Associations, Coaching Agencies and Institutes, Medical and Pharmacological Professions and the Media. The commercial sector, including sports goods manufacturers and retailers and marketing agencies, also has a responsibility to contribute to the promotion of fair play.

– Individuals including Parents, Teachers, Coaches, Referees, Officials, Sports Leaders, Administrators, Journalists, Doctors and Pharmacists; and those role models who have achieved levels of sporting excellence and fame; those who work on a voluntary or on a professional basis. Individuals may also have responsibilities in their capacity as spectators.

Each of these institutions and individuals has a responsibility and a role to play. This Code of Sports Ethics is addressed to them. It will only be effective if all involved in sport are prepared to take on the responsibility identified in the Code.

Governments

Governments have the following responsibilities:

– To encourage the adoption of high ethical standards in all aspects of society within which sport operates.

- To stimulate and support those organisations and individuals who have demonstrated sound ethical principles in their work with sport.

- To encourage the education profession to include the promotion of sport and fair play as a central part of the physical education curriculum.

- To support initiatives aimed at promoting fair play in sport, particularly amongst the young, and encouraging institutions to place fair play as a central priority in their work.

- To encourage research both nationally and internationally which improves our understanding of the complex issues surrounding young people's involvement in sport and which identifies the extent of poor behaviour and the opportunities for promoting fair play.

Sports and Sports-Related Organisations

Sports and sports related organisations have the following responsibilities:

In setting a proper context for Fair Play

- To publish clear guidelines on what is considered to be ethical or unethical behaviour and ensure that, at all levels of participation and involvement, consistent and appropriate incentives and/or sanctions are applied.

- To ensure that all decisions are made in accordance with a Code of Ethics for their sport which reflects the European code.

- To raise the awareness of fair play within their sphere of influence through the use of campaigns, awards, educational material and training opportunities. They must also monitor and evaluate the impact of such initiatives.

- To establish systems which reward fair play and personal levels of achievement in addition to competitive success.

- To provide help and support to the media to promote good behaviour.

When working with Young People,

- To ensure that the structure of competition acknowledges the special requirements of the young and growing child and provides the opportunity for graded levels of involvement from the recreational to the highly competitive.

- To support the modification of rules to meet the special needs of the very young and immature, and put the emphasis on fair play rather than competitive success.

- To ensure that safeguards are in place within the context of an overall framework of support and protection for children, young people and women, both to protect the above groups fropm sexual harassment and abuse and to prevent the exploitation of children, particularly those who demonstrate precocious ability.

- To ensure that all those within or associated with the organisation who have a responsibility for children and young people are qualified at an appropriate level to manage, train, educate and coach them, and in particular that they understand the biological and psychological changes associated with children maturation.

Individuals

Individuals have the following responsibilities:

Personal Behaviour

- To behave in a way which sets a good example and presents a positive role model for children and young people; not in any way to reward, to demonstrate personally, nor to condone in others unfair play and to take appropriate sanctions against poor behaviour.

– To ensure that their own level of training and qualification is appropriate to the needs of the child as they move through different stages of sporting commitment.

When working with Young People,

– To put as a first priority the health, safety and welfare of the child or young athlete and ensure that such considerations come before vicarious achievement, or the reputation of the school or club or coach or parent.

– To provide a sporting experience for children that encourages a life long commitment to health related physical activity.

– To avoid treating children as simply small adults but be aware of the physical and psychological changes that occur during maturation and how these affect sporting performance.

– To avoid placing expectations on a child unrelated to his or her capacity to meet them.

– To put the enjoyment of the participant as a priority and never place undue pressure which impinges on the rights of the child to choose to participate.

– To take equal interest in the less talented as in the talented and emphasise and reward personal levels of achievement and skill acquisition in addition to more overt competitive success.

– To encourage young children to devise their own games with their own rules, to take on the roles of coach, official and referee in addition to participant; to devise their own incentives and sanctions for fair or unfair play; and to take personal responsibility for their actions.

– To provide the child and young person and child's family with as much information as possible to ensure awareness of the potential risks and attractions of reaching levels of high performance.

Summary

Fair play is an essential and central part of successful promotion, development and involvement in sport. Through fair play, the individual, the sports organisations and society as a whole all win. We all have a responsibility to promote 'fair play – the winning way'.[88]

A second example comes from the world of surfing:

British Surfing Association, *Code of Conduct for Surfers*

- All surfers must be able to swim at least 50 metres in open water.

- Ensure that you are covered by Public Liability Insurance for surfing.

- Keep your surfing equipment in good condition.

- Always wear a surf leash to prevent you from losing your surfboard (or body board). For you your board is a safety device, for others it may be a lethal weapon.

- Have consideration for other water users including anglers.

- Never surf alone or immediately after eating a meal.

- Never mix surfing with alcohol or drugs.

- Always wear a wetsuit when surfing in Britain.

- If you are new to the sport never hire a surfboard without first having a surfing lesson (given by a qualified instructor).

- Be considerate of other beach users especially when carrying your board to and from the water.

---

88   Council of Europe, *Code of Sports Ethics: Fair Play – The Winning Way* (adopted by the Committee of Ministers on 24 September 1992). Also see Council of Europe, *Fair Play – The Winning Way Code of Sports Ethics* (1996), Sports Council leaflet.

- When possible use a lifeguard patrolled beach. Obey the lifeguard's instructions and be prepared to assist them if required.

- Where possible surf in a recognised surfing area (eg in between the black and white checked flags).

- When paddling out avoid surfers who are riding waves.

- When taking a wave see that you are clear of other surfers. Remember, if someone else is already riding the wave you must not take off.

- Be environmentally friendly. Always leave the beach and other areas as you would wish to find them.[89]

The Council of Europe's 'Fair Play Charter' is essentially an attempt to provide an ethical context for the enjoyment and pursuit of sport. It supports the cultural importance of sport, but acknowledges the pressures that are the reality of contemporary sport, can undermine notions of fair play and sportsmanship. The surfing code is more specifically about risk management – engaging with what is inherently a dangerous sport.[90] The emergence of more 'extreme sports' makes the development of these types of codes increasingly important.

The Increasing Conformity of Playing Rules

So the formal rules of sport (of the variety that have been discussed) have developed very much as a product of modernity. As John Bale argues, they have produced an increasingly uniform activity:

Bale, J, *Landscapes of Modern Sport*

It is a plausible claim that 'the first laws ever to be voluntarily embraced by men *(sic)* from a variety of cultures and backgrounds are the laws of sports' and these laws are crucial to the contents of this book. Without laws which were accepted over large areas, inter-regional competition was difficult if not impossible and the laws of sports were drawn up to make competition between geographically dispersed teams more meaningful. To enforce these laws, national (or in large countries, regional) bureaucracies (ie sports associations) were set up. In western nations the cumulative frequency curves for the growth of such associations display a pattern of initially slow but subsequently rapid (late 19th century) growth, characteristic of many cultural innovations.

As sports diffused internationally the formation of national governing bodies was followed by similar global organisations but western sports did not simply take root in virgin soil; they were often firmly implanted – sometimes ruthlessly by imperialists, while in other cases indigenous elites sought to imitate their masters in order to gain social acceptance. Such sports colonisation was at the expense of indigenous movement cultures and as cultural imperialism swept the globe, sports played their part in westernising the landscapes of the colonies – tennis courts and golf courses, race tracks and football pitches becoming permanent features of the cultural environment while evidence of indigenous games often became relict features of the landscape. The laws drawn up by the sports bureaucracies almost always included the spatial parameters within which the sporting action was to take place. It is this explicitly spatial character of the globally applied rules of sport which has such an important impact on the sports environment since it facilitates global 'body trading', permitting people from different cultures to make sense of the sports landscape by encouraging 'sameness' wherever it might be in the world. Although the 'globalisation' of culture is not the same as its 'homogenisation', the globally enforced rules

---

89   British Surfing Association, *Code of Conduct for Surfers*. For more information contact BSA, Champions Yard, Penzance, Cornwall TR18 2SS.

90   For more on safety and regulation of surfing, see Fitzgerald, B and Clarke, G (eds), 'Law Culture and Knowledge of Surfing' (2002) 6 Southern Cross University Law Review (www.scu.edu.au/schools/lawj/law_review/law_of_surf_number2.pdf).

of sport encourage sameness, homogenisation and placelessness to an extent not so commonly found in such global common denominators as tourism, leisure or work. Even if one was to accept the rather unconventional view that modern sport is essentially the same as its antecedents in that each are 'the ritual sacrifice of physical energy', the modernity of sport (in the sense that word is used in this book) is demonstrated by its standardised spatial and environmental forms. Today, a squash court or a running track is essentially the same whether it is in London or in Lagos. Sports, therefore, are versions of what Appadurai calls 'technoscapes', each having roots in a number of multinational organisations (sports' governing bodies) which, with the help of modern technology insist on certain standardised landscapes within which sport is allowed to take place.[91]

Bale shows how sport has become more uniform wherever it is played through the development of rules as far as play and the increasingly standardised spatial dimensions of play; for example, football pitches need to be within certain size limits, international boxing rings need to meet a number of criteria on surface and size and environmental factors such as wind velocity need to be inside certain parameters for the validity of international records in athletics. He also shows how certain sports facilities are increasingly regulating environmental factors; the Sky Dome in Toronto with its retractable roof, for example. He uses the terms 'placelessness' to describe this process of increasing standardisation of the places that sport is played. As he says:

> The modern sports landscape can be described as tending towards placelessness in its geographical sense of places looking and feeling alike with 'dictated and standardized values'.[92]

Interestingly, this is one of the complaints concerning the introduction of all-seater football stadia since the Taylor Report after the Hillsborough disaster – grounds have become too soulless without recognisable ends and lacking the atmosphere of old. There have been recent calls for a return of a limited amount of standing 'terracing' areas at Premier League grounds.[93] In his geographical examination of sport, Bale highlights the greater than ever importance of the rule framework of sport.

RULE CHANGES

Another issue is to what extent and frequency the rules of games should be modified. One argument is that changes are merely tinkering and are often carried out with the aim of short term expediency. This is often to placate external pressures such as sponsors and television, for example, the introduction of the back-pass rule in football to speed the game up; or to curb the excellence of particular participants, for example, the changes in the rules of Formula One motor racing largely to curb the past dominance of the Williams team;[94] and similarly the constant changes in cricket to the short pitch delivery rules have been carried out to control fast bowlers, particularly the dominance of the West Indian bowlers during the 1980s and 1990s.[95]

The opposing argument is that rule changes are needed to secure the integrity of modern support in the context of the commodification and globalisation of sport. New variants of a traditional sport

---

91 Bale, J, *Landscapes of Modern Sport* (1994), Leicester: Leicester UP.

92 *Ibid*, pp 94–95.

93 'Football split over terrace return', www.bbc.co.uk/sport, 22 December 2000.

94 'Do not change the balls or tinker with the rules please' *The Times*, 6 July 1994, p 42; 'Law-makers struggle to keep pace with the law-breakers' *The Guardian*, 16 September 1994; 'Scots urge IB to speed up game' *The Guardian*, 4 October 1994; 'The dangers of playing for time-out' *The Independent on Sunday*, 9 April 1995; 'FIFA to hit taller keepers by moving the goalpost' *The Guardian*, 3 January 1996.

95 'Bouncer law is changed' *The Guardian*, 7 July 1994.

are periodically introduced, such as one-day cricket in 1963 and 20 : 20 cricket in 2003. Coaches and players are under increasing pressure to succeed and therefore exploit the limitations of existing rules. Rule changes are then required to try to re-establish the vitality and balance in a particular sport. New skills and strategies then develop to confront the new rules. This allows the sport to be dynamic and reflects the character of rules as being both certain and being pliant.

Rules certainly do have an elasticity and, together with the players' 'playing culture', are only part of the regulation of the sport. Without this acknowledgment and the ability to modify rules, sport are subject to predictability and ossification. But in most sports, rule changes have significantly accelerated in the last 30 years. Increasing external pressures may well be the cause. Too many changes can be counterproductive and damage the balance of particular sports. Some sports such as American Gridiron have numerous and complex rules. Others such as football have a simplicity that is derived from a small number of rules. Coherent rule changes are made for these reasons: to promote safety, assist the fluidity of the game and to allow the skilful to shine. Some are not fundamental changes in the rules, but different interpretations of existing ones. There is, however, a danger that rule changes in sport are developing an increasingly sanitised game for mass global consumption.

There is a complex interaction between the playing rules and the officials that enforce them. At particular points in time, governing bodies instruct referees or umpires to enforce the rules more or less strictly.[96] This can lead to disquiet from players and more or less formal infringements and fouls during the game.[97] The statistics may indicate a fall or increase in foul play but it is unlikely to be primarily about changes in the style of play, becoming more violent, for example. It is much more about officials' attitudes towards actual and potential perpetrators during the game.[98]

Increasingly, the human vulnerability of officials is being questioned. A number of sports are using various forms of technology to aid officials in coming to decisions. In sports such as horse racing and athletics, cameras have been used for many years. In tennis, line decisions are determined electronically. The use of video cameras as an aid to the officials on the field of play or as a guide to 'third umpire' as the final arbiter have been used in sports such as cricket and rugby league in Britain for some years. There are interesting issues concerning whether this undermines the officials' authority, and makes a game too clinical, or whether human error needs to be minimised as much as possible when a wrong decision may have an enormous financial cost.[99] Where does justice lie in terms of adjudicating sporting performance? It reflects the debate concerning judging within the law – whether disputes should be treated consistently with the minimum of discretion, the notion of formal justice or formalism (prioritising the unquestioned application of law), or whether the individual issues of the case should be considered specifically, the notion of substantive justice.

Some rule creations and changes, as with the law itself, can also be clearly dysfunctional and sometimes utterly bizarre:

Longmore, A, 'Absurd cup rule obscures football's final goal'

The law, they say, is an ass and more of an ass in sport than most walks of life but not even the bigwigs at the Football Association could have concocted a rule so daft that both sides ended a competitive cup

---

96 'UEFA orders referees to stay tough' *The Guardian*, 11 June 1996, p 22.

97 'Referees must go with the flow' *The Observer*, 18 September 1994, p 6.

98 *Op cit*, fn 81, Fraser (1993), makes some interesting comparisons between umpires (officials) and judges; see Chapter 6, 'The man in white is always right: umpires, judges and the rule of law'. The comparison between styles of umpiring, being interventionist or not, frequently (using discretion) reflect the theorising of the jurist, Karl Llewellyn, concerning his formal and grand style of judging; see Twining, W, *Karl Llewellyn and the Realist Movement* (1973), London: Weidenfeld & Nicolson.

99 See Gardiner, S, 'The third eye: video adjudication in sport' (1999) 7(1) Sport and the Law Journal 20.

match attacking their own goals, the farcical situation that occurred at the end of a recent match between Barbados and Grenada in the final group match of the Shell Caribbean Cup.

Needing to beat Grenada by two clear goals to qualify for the finals in Trinidad and Tobago, Barbados had established a 2–0 lead midway through the second half and were seemingly well in control of the game. However an own goal by a Bajan defender made the score 2–1 and brought a new ruling into play, which led to farce. Under the new rule, devised by the competition committee to ensure a result, a match decided by sudden death in extra time was deemed to be the equivalent of a 2–0 victory. With three minutes remaining, the score still 2–1 and Grenada about to qualify for the finals in April, Barbados realised that their only chance lay in taking the match to sudden death. They stopped attacking their opponents' goal and turned on their own. In the 87th minute, two Barbadian defenders, Sealy and Stoute, exchanged passes before Sealy hammered the ball past his own goalkeeper for the equaliser.

The Grenada players, momentarily stunned by the goal, realised too late what was happening and immediately started to attack their own goal as well to stop sudden death. Sealy, though, had anticipated the response and stood beside the Grenada goalkeeper as the Bajans defended their opponents' goal. Grenada were unable to score at either end, the match ended 2–2 after 90 minutes and, after four minutes of extra time, Thorne scored the winner for Barbados amid scenes of celebration and laughter in the National Stadium in Bridgetown.

James Clarkson, the Grenadian coach, provided an unusual variation on the disappointed manager's speech: 'I feel cheated,' he said. 'The person who came up with these rules must be a candidate for the madhouse. The game should never be played with so many players on the field confused. Our players did not even know which direction to attack. Our goal or their goal. I have never seen this happen before. In football, you are supposed to score against the opponents to win, not for them', he added. Nobody should tell the organising committee of the World Cup. They might get ideas.[100]

CHALLENGING THE RULES: CHEATING AND SPORTSMANSHIP

Is the above example and the actions of the Barbadian team an example of cheating? The issue of cheating and its regulation in perhaps the two main sporting contexts of violence and drugs will be discussed later in the book. Codes of ethics are able to challenge the playing culture, which in elite professional sport has invariably developed to circumvent the rules of play to the advantage of the athlete. Two examples can illustrate this position.

It's Just Not Cricket

In a one-day cricket international between the West Indies and Australia in Bridgetown, Barbados in April 1999, crowd disturbances included bottles thrown from the stand, causing the match to be stopped. The disturbances were initiated when West Indies opener and local hero Sherwin Campbell was given run-out, after colliding with bowler Brendon Julian as the West Indies chased Australia's 252 9. Julian appeared to body-check non-striker Campbell as he went for a quick single and, with the batsman left lying on the floor complaining, Michael Bevan completed the run-out.

Australian captain Steve Waugh led his players from the field and attempts were made to restore calm. After a long delay while the outfield was cleared of broken glass, match referee Ramon Subba Row decided, at the suggestion of the Australians, that the game could continue as long as Campbell

---

100 Longmore, A, 'Absurd cup rule obscures football's final goal' *The Times*, 1 February 1994, p 44.

was reinstated. Under a revised total it was declared that West Indies needed 58 runs to win from 11 overs.

Subba Row said: '... the Australians have very graciously said they would like Campbell to be brought back to continue his innings. We feel it was six of one and half a dozen of the other.' News of Campbell's reinstatement was greeted with cheers from fans in the Kensington stand where the trouble broke out.

Discretion was clearly used in a tense situation in deciding to reinstate Campbell and continue the game. The cricketing rules are silent about how the umpires should react when there is bodily contact between a fielder and an opposing batsman, although s 7 of Law 42 states that 'it shall be considered unfair if any fieldsman wilfully obstructs a batsman in running'. The umpire in such a situation should call a dead ball. The video replay of the incident indicated that this was no accident but an intentional body-check. The West Indies went on to win the match.

A similar event testing the match official's discretion occurred in the fifth round FA Cup-tie between Arsenal and Sheffield United in the 1999–2000 season. A Sheffield United player kicked the ball out of play so that an injured team mate could receive medical attention. As the ball was thrown back to a Sheffield player, an Arsenal player chased on to it and crossed the ball for a goal. At the time the game was a draw – this goal put Arsenal into the lead. The referee did not disallow the goal. There is a convention in football that when a player is injured the ball is kicked out of play so that the game can be stopped and the player can receive medical help. From the throw-in, the ball is then returned to the opposing team who were previously in possession. This is constructed as 'good sportsmanship'.

Arsenal subsequently won the match but the Arsenal manager, Arsene Wenger, offered to replay the match. He stated: 'It was the only answer to a difficult situation.' The English FA supported the move. FIFA, perhaps correctly, stalled on giving their full blessing to the rematch; a meeting of its International Board, football's law makers, highlighted that although the ball was not given back, a rule was not broken, merely a convention, and replaying a game in such circumstances created a problematic precedent.[101]

In both these incidents, if discretion had not been exercised the aggrieved party may well have attempted to seek a legal remedy. They highlight the gaps within the playing rules; just as with law, there will always be *casus omissus* – gaps in the rules of the sport. A response by the cricket law makers to the type of incident between the West Indies and Australia has been to introduce a ruling concerning the 'Spirit of Cricket'.

The Laws of Cricket, 2000 Code – 'The Preamble, the Spirit of Cricket'

Cricket is a game that owes much of its unique appeal to the fact that it should be played not only within its Laws but also within the Spirit of the Game. Any action which is seen to abuse this spirit causes injury to the game itself. The major responsibility for ensuring the spirit of fair play rests with the captains.

1 There are two Laws which place the responsibility for the team's conduct firmly on the captain.

Responsibility of captains

The captains are responsible at all times for ensuring that play is conducted within the Spirit of the Game as well as within the Laws.

Player's conduct

In the event of a player failing to comply with instructions by an umpire, or criticising by word or action the decisions of an umpire, or showing dissent, or generally behaving in a manner which might

---

101 For more on this incident, see Demetriou, G, 'In the spirit of football?' (1999) 2(3) Sports Law Bulletin 2.

bring the game into disrepute, the umpire concerned shall in the first place report the matter to the other umpire and to the player's captain, and instruct the latter to take action.

2 Fair and unfair play

According to the Laws the umpires are the sole judges of fair and unfair play.

The umpires may intervene at any time and it is the responsibility of the captain to take action where required.

3 The umpires are authorised to intervene in cases of:

- Time wasting
- Damaging the pitch
- Dangerous or unfair bowling
- Tampering with the ball
- Any other action that they consider to be unfair

4 The Spirit of the Game involves RESPECT for:

- Your opponents
- Your own captain and team
- The role of the umpires
- The game's traditional values

5 It is against the Spirit of the Game:

- To dispute an umpire's decision by word, action or gesture
- To direct abusive language towards an opponent or umpire
- To indulge in cheating or any sharp practice, for instance:

  (a) to appeal knowing that the batsman is not out

  (b) to advance towards an umpire in an aggressive manner when appealing

  (c) to seek to distract an opponent either verbally or by harassment with persistent clapping or unnecessary noise under the guise of enthusiasm and motivation of one's own side

6 Violence

There is no place for any act of violence on the field of play.

7 Players

Captains and umpires together set the tone for the conduct of a cricket match. Every player is expected to make an important contribution to this.

The players, umpires and scorers in a game of cricket may be of either gender and the Laws apply equally to both. The use, throughout the text, of pronouns indicating the male gender is purely for brevity. Except where specifically stated otherwise, every provision of the Laws is to be read as applying to women and girls equally as to men and boys.[102] This provision gives more formal discretion to the umpires to respond to incidents such as that above, together with the captains. This provision however has been used very sparingly up to July 2001.[103]

---

[102] The Laws of Cricket, 2000 Code – 'The Preamble, the Spirit of Cricket', MCC, www.ecb.co.uk.

[103] See 'Jacobs banned for three games' *The Guardian*, 6 July 2001. West Indian wicket keeper Ridley Jacobs was found to have transgressed the spirit of the game by indulging in 'cheating or any sharp practice' when he stumped Virender Shewag without the ball in his gloves in a one-day international against India. Also see 'Speed urges better behaviour', www.bbc.uk.co/sport, 18 July 2001, and demands from ICC Chief Executive, Malcolm Speed, for better compliance with rules by players.

What is Cheating?

But what do we mean by 'cheating'? It is invariably seen as actions that are contrary to the rules of the sport; but can it be reconciled with the working culture of the sport; when does the law have a role to play in regulating it? Leaman has attempted to define cheating:

Leaman, O, 'Cheating and fair play in sport'

It is not as easy as it might initially be thought to define cheating in sport and it is just as difficult to specify precisely what is wrong morally with such behaviour and why fair play should be prized. In this article I intend to try to throw some light on the notions of both cheating and fair play and to suggest that stronger arguments than those so far produced in the literature are required to condemn the former and approve the latter.

Let us try to deal first with the definitional problem of what sorts of behaviour constitute cheating and come to the ethical issue later. Gunther Luschen boldly starts his essay on cheating in sport with this definition:

> Cheating in sport is the act through which the manifestly or latently agreed upon conditions for winning such a contest are changed in favour of one side. As a result, the principle of equality of chance beyond differences of skill and strategy is violated.

A problem with this definition is that it omits any consideration of intention. After all, if a player unwittingly breaks the rules and thereby gains an unfair advantage he will not necessarily have cheated. For example, if a boxer has a forbidden substance applied to bodily damage without his knowledge, then he has not cheated even though the rules have been broken to his advantage. Were he to be penalised or disqualified, it would not be because of his cheating but due to the rules having been broken by those who attend to him in the intervals.

A superior account of cheating is then provided by Peter McIntosh, who claims that:

> Cheating ... need be no more than breaking the rules with the intention of not being found out ... Cheating, however, implies an intention to beat the system even although the penalty, if the offender is found out, may still be acceptable.

But McIntosh next claims that:

> This definition, however, is too simple. It is not always the written or even the unwritten rule that is broken; tacit assumptions which one contestant knows that the other contestant acts upon may be rejected in order to gain an advantage. A more satisfactory definition is that of Luschen.

McIntosh's adaptation of Luschen's account makes possible the useful distinction between intending to deceive, which he calls cheating and breaking the rules without having that intention. He concludes that 'Cheating is an offence against the principles of justice as well as against a particular rule or norm of behaviour'.

If people undertake to play a game, then they may be taken to have understood and agreed to the rules of the game and the principle upon which any fair victory in the game must rest ... Yet what are 'the rules of the game' to which players supposedly commit themselves when they enter a game? If we look at the ways in which some sports are played it becomes evident that the rules of the game involve following the formal rules in so far as it is to the advantage of one's own side and breaking them when that is perceived, perhaps wrongly, to be to the side's advantage, where the possibility of suffering a penalty is taken into account. The existence of an authority in games enshrines cheating in the structure of the game; the authority is there to ensure that cheating does not interfere with the principle of fairness in a game. He is there to regulate cheating so that it does not benefit one side more than the other except where one side is more skilful at cheating than the other and to see that the amount of cheating which takes place is not so great as to change the general form of a particular game. That is, the formal rules of the game must in general be adhered to by all players since otherwise in a clear non-moral sense the game is not being played. But if we are profitably to discuss the notion of the rules of the game and of cheating and fair play, we must address ourselves to the ways in which players and spectators perceive those rules rather than to an abstract idea of the rules themselves. The next step is to determine what notion of fair play is applicable within the context of the ways in which players actually participate in sporting activities. An injection of realism into philosophical discussions of cheating and fair play in sport is long overdue.[104]

Cheating is therefore a complex philosophical phenomenon.[105] Three examples from the cricket world will be used to illustrate this concept.

1. Bodyline

Holt, R, *Sport and the British: A Modern History*

All this brings us to 1932 and the 'bodyline' tour. The bones of the business can be set out quite simply. After being soundly beaten by Australia in England in 1930 mainly as a result of the remarkable batting of Bradman, whose 334 at Headingley broke the existing Test record, England had to find a way to contain the 'Don' and win back the Ashes. The England captain, Douglas Jardine, for all his Oxford amateurism, was a grim competitor. Like some of his Australian critics, he did not believe simply in 'playing the game for its own sake' and being a 'good loser'. Jardine had only one advantage in comparison to Bradman's Australia. He had a formidable pace attack at his disposal in the form of Larwood, Voce, Bowes and Allen. To be able to draw upon four fast bowlers was extremely rare in the days when spin was still regarded as essential for a balanced side. The fact that Harold Larwood was possibly the fastest bowler of all time gave Jardine a potentially strong hand to play. It was the way he played that hand which caused the trouble.

Bradman had proved a magnificent player of spin bowling. If he had any weakness at all it was perhaps a tendency to play too much off the back foot and to hook the high fast ball on the line of the body. Whether the 'bodyline' assault was coldly premeditated by Jardine or it was Larwood himself who hit upon it while bowling to a momentarily nervous Bradman during the 1930 series may never be fully resolved. What is more important is that both captain and bowler were determined to use intimidatory bowling to unsettle Bradman. Larwood always claimed it was a fair tactic but it was precisely the legitimacy of playing this way which was at the heart of the controversy. Though he was slightly built, mentally Larwood was a tough professional, an ex-miner, who believed the batsmen who got the glory had to be able to take punishment and show courage when it was needed. Jardine also felt intimidatory bowling was legitimate. He set a leg-side field and waited for a simple catch as the batsman tried to protect himself from a sharply bouncing ball aimed at the upper body and an unprotected head. In brief, the tactic seemed to work. Bradman's test average slumped from over a hundred to a mere 50 – still well ahead of the rest – but England regained the Ashes.

The real trouble came in the third Test at Adelaide when the Australian captain was felled by a short pitched but straight ball from Larwood. What really incensed the crowd was Jardine's switch to a full leg-field immediately after the accident. Later the Australian wicket keeper Oldfield was struck on the head, again from a straight delivery from Larwood and the crowd roared angry abuse at the England team. Jardine, who was believed to loathe Australians and to enjoy baiting them by his supercilious attitude, silk

---

104 Leaman, O, 'Cheating and fair play in sport', in Morgan, W (ed), *Sport and the Humanities: A Collection of Original Essays* (1981), Educational Research and Service, University of Tennessee, pp 25–30.

105 See Luschen, G, 'Cheating in sport', in Landers, D (ed), *Social Problems in Athletics* (1977), Urbana: University of Illinois; Intosh, P, *Fair Play: Ethics in Sport and Education* (1994), London: Heinemann; Meier, W and K (eds), 'Part IV – fair play, sportsmanship and cheating', in *Philosophical Inquiry in Sport* (1995), 2nd edn, Champaign: Human Kenetics; Simon, R, *Fair Play: Sports Values and Society* (1991), Boulder: Westview.

handkerchief and Harlequin cap, was the main target. When drinks were brought out, a voice from the crowd was heard to shout, 'Don't give him a drink, let the bastard die of thirst'. Jardine had been barracked in the earlier 1928–29 tour of Australia and was said to have deeply resented it. He had even requested that spectators be forbidden to attend net sessions. At the end of the day's play the England manager, 'Plum' Warner, who had been born in Australia and captained several successful pre-war tours, went to enquire about the injuries after the game and received what has since become the best known rebuke in the history of the game: 'Of two teams out there,' said Woodfull, 'one is playing cricket, the other is making no effort to play cricket'. There are several versions of the precise form of words he used but the message was unmistakable and Warner left deeply hurt. Privately he urged Jardine to desist from the tactic but without success. 'Not cricket?' roared the Australian popular press and matters became much worse when the Australian Cricket Board surprisingly made public a telegram they sent to the MCC which read 'Bodyline bowling has assumed such proportions to menace the best interests of the game ... in our opinion it is unsportsmanlike'. To have been a fly on the wall of the Long Room at Lord's when this arrived would have been a rare treat. The MCC have diplomatically 'lost' the records of their discussions but their icy reply insisting the 'unsportsmanlike' be withdrawn and offering to cancel the tour is well known. By implication the Australian cricketing authorities and public were questioning the good faith of the British in the common morality that bound them together ... the MCC could not contemplate the public humiliation of accepting that their side was 'not playing the game'. So the MCC had to stick by its man for the duration of the series and the Australians withdrew the word 'unsportsmanlike'. But in the time honoured traditions of the British establishment Jardine was quietly ditched despite his success and Larwood was never selected for England again. At this time in the 1930s this style of bowling was labelled as cheating. It would be interesting to see whether it would be viewed in the same way in modern cricket.[106]

2. Ball Tampering I: Dirt in the Pocket

The second example comes from a Test match against South Africa in 1994, when the England cricket captain, Mike Atherton, was fined £1,000 by the Test and County Cricket Board (forerunner of the England and Wales Cricket Board), after he admitted not telling the whole truth over 'all tampering' allegations. Atherton was seen on television putting his hands in his pockets and apparently rubbing something on the ball. Atherton said that he had dirt in his pockets, which he was using to dry his fingers on a clammy day. There is nothing wrong with this – but it would be illegal to use it on the ball contrary to the Laws of Cricket and Law 42(5):

Law 42 Unfair Play

(5) Any member of the fielding side may polish the ball provided that such polishing wastes no time and that no artificial substance is used. No one shall rub the ball on the ground or use any artificial substance or take any action to alter the condition of the ball. In the event of a contravention of this Law, the Umpires, after consultation, shall change the ball for one of similar condition to that in use prior to the contravention. This Law does not prevent a member of the fielding side from drying a wet ball or removing mud from the ball.[107]

On the face of it the act was the time-honoured behaviour of a man doing something illegal to make the ball swing. However, Atherton, when challenged by the match referee Peter Burge to explain his actions, said he was drying his hands in his pockets and did not mention the dirt in there. With

---

106 Holt, R, *Sport and the British: A Modern History* (1989), Oxford: Clarendon, p 233, by permission of OUP. See Le Quesne, L, *The Bodyline Controversy* (1983), London: Macmillan; and Fraser, D, *The Man in White is Always Right: Cricket and the Law* (1993), London: Blackwell, for further discussion of the bodyline strategy.

107 The Laws of Cricket, 1980 Code, MCC.

reference to the rule, a number of questions were left unanswered. Did Atherton rub dirt on the ball? What is an artificial substance? This raised interesting issues of interpretation:

Fraser, D, 'Balls, bribes and bails: the jurisprudence of Salim Malik'

The case of Michael Atherton with its legal, interpretative difficulties may well be more accurately classified as a case of 'perjury' or perversion of the course of justice' rather than as a case of 'ball tampering'. Nonetheless it remains true that it originally started off as what appeared to be a clear-cut case of 'ball tampering' and remains classified as such by many observers of the game. Whatever jurisprudential taxonomy one decides to apply in this case, however, it is clear that it was treated by all concerned, almost from the outset, as something different from a 'Pakistani ball tampering case'. It serves as a classic example of the way in which the apparently neutral discourses and practices surrounding the legal and ethical issues in question actually serve to establish a dual system of legal rules and ultimately of 'justice'. This epistemological and juridical duality is confirmed by recent events.[108]

Fraser goes on to recount how Atherton's misdemeanours were largely forgotten when he batted for almost 15 hours to save the Test against South Africa at Johannesburg in the return series in 1995. 'Atherton was treated as a hero of the great colonial struggles of yore.'[109]

Brearley, M, 'Cricket: Atherton affair: the dirt that is in all our pockets'

'Unfamiliar action', as the Test and County Cricket Board statement put it, it certainly was. I had never heard of a cricketer pocketing dirt to dry his hands. What is less clear is whether, in the same statement's second quaint phrase, 'there was nothing untoward', this strange little incident contains, concealed in pockets about its person, several dubious psychological substances. The poets were right to see 'a World in a Grain of Sand' and 'fear in a handful of dust'! These issues touch us all. Are we not all inclined, to some degree, to be both over-suspicious and naive; to be self-righteous and to turn a blind eye? Do we not all have deep-seated responses to the possible downfall of the Great and the Good, ranging from horror to salacious triumph? This pocketful of dirt – does it epitomise the dirt we all carry, usually hidden, however white our gear?

In a society where cricket is supposedly synonymous with fair play, is the burden of expectation on England's captain too great? What, too, is the role of the cricket Establishment? Have they done all they could to be seen to be both fair and stringent? Do we have one standard for our own and another for others? (And this can work both ways: we can condemn our own man, like Caesar's wife, simply for being suspected – which in a world of lascivious suspiciousness may be simply unjust – or we may refuse to believe that one of us is dishonest while assuming dishonesty in, say, a Pakistani bowler.) And what, exactly, was Michael Atherton up to? If dishonest, he seemed so unconcerned; if honest, so disinclined to come clean.

First, the evidence; and then, as the Michelin guides have it, a little history. I start with the sequences shown on television news on Monday. To my eyes, Atherton looks like a man taking a little pinch of snuff from his pocket; instead of sniffing it, he appears to drop it on the ball. The stuff looks like fine, grey dust. He then polishes the ball and hands it to the bowler, Gough, who takes it with finger and thumb, presumably touching only the seam, gingerly, as if the rest of the ball were made of china. When questioned about what had happened, Atherton at first failed to mention the dirt in his pocket. Later he said that he had used it to dry his hands but that he didn't apply it to the ball. The umpires stated that the condition of the ball had not been altered. Later, Illingworth fined him £1,000 for doing whatever he was doing with the ball and £1,000 for not coming clean about the dirt with the match referee. I gather that Atherton had picked up the dust from the footholes not long before.

---

108 Fraser, D, 'Balls, bribes and bails: the jurisprudence of Salim Malik' (1995), Law and Popular Culture Research Group working papers, Manchester Metropolitan University, p 12.
109 *Ibid*, Fraser (1995), p 12.

Now for the history. In England the traditional way of interfering with the ball has been to raise its seam with the nail. This practice is not, I think, endemic but it is certainly not rare. Seam picking goes on because English pitches often permit movement and the slightly raised seam makes such movement slightly more likely. Most professionals would tend to shrug their shoulders at a minor degree of seam raising. They would also be angered by the few who have gone further and more substantially and systematically altered the seam. From time to time umpires are instructed to check the condition of the ball frequently. Such spot checks eradicate the habit for the time being. Overseas the ball moves off the seam less and the likelier form of minor cheating has been to put skin cream or lip salve on the ball and thereby heighten the polish. This helps orthodox swing, that is, swing where the bowler delivers the ball with its shiny half on the side from which the ball is to swing; this shinier side meets less resistance and travels faster through the air. Sweat, a natural substance, is permitted for this purpose.

More recently, in Pakistan, where the ball tends to get roughened by the bare ground quicker than elsewhere, a new technique – reverse swing – has been developed. Apparently the essential requirement for this is an oldish ball whose non-shiny side is kept dry; hence the need for dry hands. For some reason reverse swing usually means in-swing. In Gough, England now have a bowler capable of doing this. Reverse swing can transform the game, since, as the innings goes on, it can make batting suddenly much harder rather than, as one would usually expect, easier. It also means that there is less need for spin bowlers, who usually do most of their work with the old ball. I first encountered this sharp, old ball in-swing batting against Sarfraz Nawaz in Karachi in 1972 but had no idea how he did it. Keeping the rough side dry is not the only aid to reverse swing. Bowlers have been accused of lifting the quarter-seam and scuffing and gouging the rough side. This, if practised, is ball tampering writ large. But I find it hard to understand why regular spot checks don't rule out such practices.

If I am right, that Atherton put a pinch of dust on the ball, then it is not true that he was using it only to dry his hands. (And wouldn't he need to dry both hands, not only his right hand? Why not two pockets of dirt?) However, the umpires say the ball's condition was not altered and I see no reason to doubt this. The fine dust was probably used only to dry sweat from the ball. Moreover, the law does not say that no substances may be applied to the ball, only artificial ones. Presumably the intention was to rule out all substances except sweat; but dust, though perhaps artificial in contrast to sweat, is not artificial in contrast to sun cream. Nowadays, the ball may not be rubbed in the dirt but the laws don't explicitly rule out dirt being rubbed in the ball. (As far as gravediggers are concerned, the man going to the water is a different matter from the water coming to the man: *Hamlet* Act V Scene 1.)[110]

This particular Cricket Law in the new 2000 Code has been expanded considerably to attempt to address this perceived problem. As with the law generally, are more sporting rules necessarily going to be 'good laws' and provide better regulation? They often create very specific problems of interpretation.

The Laws of Cricket, 2000 Code – Law 42, Fair and Unfair Play

3   The match ball – changing its condition

    (a)   Any fielder may

        (i)   polish the ball provided that no artificial substance is used and that such polishing wastes no time;

        (ii)   remove mud from the ball under the supervision of the umpire;

        (iii)   dry a wet ball on a towel.

    (b)   It is unfair for anyone to rub the ball on the ground for any reason, interfere with any of the seams or the surface of the ball, use any implement, or take any other action whatsoever which is likely to alter the condition of the ball, except as permitted in (a) above.

---

110 Brearley, M, 'Cricket: Atherton affair: the dirt that is in all our pockets' *The Observer*, 31 July 1994, p 10; also see 'Cheating art that's not just cricket' *The Observer*, 31 July 1994.

    (c)   The umpires shall make frequent and irregular inspections of the ball.

    (d)   In the event of any fielder changing the condition of the ball unfairly, as set out in (b) above, the umpires after consultation shall

         (i)   change the ball forthwith. It shall be for the umpires to decide on the replacement ball, which shall, in their opinion, have had wear comparable with that which the previous ball had received immediately prior to the contravention;

        (ii)   inform the batsmen that the ball has been changed;

      (iii)   award 5 penalty runs to the batting side. See 17 below;

      (iv)   inform the captain of the fielding side that the reason for the action was the unfair interference with the ball;

       (v)   inform the captain of the batting side as soon as practicable of what has occurred;

      (vi)   report the occurrence as soon as possible to the Executive of the fielding side and any Governing Body responsible for the match, who shall take such action as is considered appropriate against the captain and team concerned.

    (e)   If there is any further instance of unfairly changing the condition of the ball in that innings, the umpires after consultation shall

         (i)   repeat the procedure in (d)(i), (ii) and (iii) above;

        (ii)   inform the captain of the fielding side of the reason for the action taken and direct him to take off forthwith the bowler who delivered the immediately preceding ball. The bowler thus taken off shall not be allowed to bowl again in that innings;

      (iii)   inform the captain of the batting side as soon as practicable of what has occurred;

      (iv)   report this further occurrence as soon as possible to the Executive of the fielding side and any Governing Body responsible for the match, who shall take such action as is considered appropriate against the captain and team concerned.[111]

3. Ball Tampering II: In the High Court

The legitimacy of ball tampering has become an ongoing debate within the cricket world.[112] The third and last example, the libel action by ex-English test cricketers Ian Botham and Allan Lamb, against the accusations of the ex-Pakistani test cricketer Imran Khan, had a complex underlying narrative concerning cheating. The dispute which resulted in the costly High Court action can be traced back to the summer of 1992, when the Pakistan cricket team arrived in England with allegations of cheating being made against them. The 1992 series, which Pakistan won 2–1, was described in court as savage and ugly, with accusations of cheating being made by the tabloid press against Pakistan's two fast bowlers, Wasim Akram and Waqar Younis. There were headlines like 'Paki cheats' and claims that the two Pakistan bowlers, had regularly been tampering with the ball, by either picking the seam or scratching it on one side, to make it swing more than it should. Some even suggested that this contributed to their World Cup win against England months earlier.

    The controversy resurfaced in 1994 when Imran admitted in a biography that he had scratched a ball with a bottle top while playing for Sussex in a county match. Imran claimed in court that he was merely trying to highlight the unacceptable face of ball tampering which he claimed had gone on in English cricket for years. Picking the seam with your fingers or applying a bit of grease to one side of the ball was 'tacitly accepted' but using outside agents like bottle tops was overstepping the limit. 'That is what I would call cheating,' Imran confessed while giving evidence during the trial.

---

111 The Laws of Cricket, 2000 Code – Law 42, Fair and Unfair Play – see www.ecb.co.uk.

112 Khan, I, 'ICC need to come to grips with laws' *The Daily Telegraph*, 24 January 1996.

Lamb and Botham responded swiftly to the Imran biography. In May 1994, Lamb contributed an article to *The Sun* newspaper in which Imran was accused of cheating and teaching Younis and Akram how to tamper with the ball. This was followed by an article in *The Daily Mirror* in which Botham called for a full investigation into Imran's ball tampering and demanded his resignation from the International Cricket Conference. Less than a week later, Imran, who by now had retired from Test Cricket and was concentrating on building a cancer hospital in his native Lahore, responded by giving an interview to *The Sun*. Under the headline 'World's greatest bowlers have all doctored the ball', he once again claimed that ball tampering was an accepted part of English cricket.

With England–Pakistan cricket relations at an all-time low, matters deteriorated when extracts from an interview given by Imran to *India Today* magazine appeared in the British press. He was quoted as calling Botham and Lamb racists, claiming that their approach to the whole issue of ball tampering was 'irrational' because they were 'lower-class and uneducated'. It was this interview that led Botham and Lamb to bring their libel action against Imran while Botham alone was suing him for *The Sun* article, claiming that Imran had called him a cheat. At the trial a material issue discussed at some length concerned technical details of what happens to a cricket ball when it is scratched, has its seam picked or lip salve is applied. The issue of what constitutes cheating in cricket became crucial and the darker side of cricket was publicly exposed, with successive players, including England captain Mike Atherton and ex-test cricketer and television commentator Geoffrey Boycott, admitting that ball tampering was part and parcel of the game. At the end of the day it was a tussle between three cricket giants with egos to match who refused to back down once heated words were exchanged over what is cheating in their sport.

This was the second time Lamb had been in a libel action. He was fined £5,000 by the Test and County Cricket Board after accusing Pakistani bowlers of ball tampering in 1992. The following year he was sued for libel by former Northamptonshire and Pakistani paceman Sarfraz Nawaz. The case was settled out of court but effectively ended his England career after 79 Tests, three as captain.[113]

Evaluating Cheating

In which of these situations can cheating be identified? Are the actions cheating when institutionalised over a period into the working culture of the particular sport?[114] Are the intentions of the perpetrator a salient issue – cheating only occurs with a clear cognition on the part of the athlete?[115] Do these examples illustrate the inadequacies of the internal rules of sport and maybe the need for the law to intervene, or do they in fact identify the flexibility of rules and the real problems of precise interpretation? This would seem to present a good example of 'rule scepticism', identified with the jurisprudential movement, the American Realists, most prominent in the first half of this century, with its emphasis on the inherent problem of reducing law into a precise form of a set of rules. The American Realists promoted rule scepticism concerning the possibility of making exact interpretations of legal or non-legal rules. The Atherton example is a good illustration of this problem. This scepticism may well provide caution to the view that the law can provide exact solutions to the problems of sport.

---

113 See 'Judge raises finger to expansive Boycott' *The Guardian*, 27 July 1996, p 3 and 'Botham libel case: an exercise in futility' *The Guardian*, 1 August 1996, p 9. For other sporting libel cases see *Tolley v Fry* [1931] AC 333 (HL) and *Williams v Reason* [1988] 1 WLR 96 (CA) (both concerning allegations of shamateurism).

114 See 'Par for the Courts' *The Guardian*, 28 April 1994 concerning cheating in golf and Greenberg, M and Gray, J, 'The legal aspects of the Tonya Harding figure skating eligibility controversy' (1994) 2(2) Sport and the Law Journal 16.

115 Note the debate surrounding the concept of 'strict liability' in anti-doping controls; see later, Chapter 5.

The paradigm example of the construction of cheating in sport today is doping. The discussion on this will be expanded later.[116] The use of new technology in terms of equipment and increasing sports science expertise that is pushing the boundaries of the physiological capabilities of the human body is relevant. The spectre of genetic engineering with manipulation of the 'human geno' – the creation of the super athlete – will present immense ethical dilemmas in the sports world in the coming years.[117] Legal intervention can attempt to at least protect the rights and interests of athletes, when the sporting rules fail. As Beloff *et al* claim:

> ... more lawyers in sport does not necessarily mean more justice in sport, but it may do, and it should do. The growth of legalism in sport is borne of a desire for higher standards of justice.[118]

The Normative Rule Milieu

What has been identified is that sport is internally governed and subject to a complex interaction of normative rules: playing and administrative rules; unwritten conventions and values that have developed informally; sports' complex playing cultures that develop to gain advantage and circumvent the formal rules (that may or not be constructed as cheating); and the engagement of codes of ethics to challenge perceived deficiencies in the behaviour regulated by this normative structure.[119] Lastly, the dynamics of internal policing of and adjudication over sports' internal regulatory structure are inconsistent. If this internal regulation of sport is ineffective, does the law of the land have a role to play? How does it fit into this already crowded normative rule structure? An attempt will be made to provide an answer in the following section.

JURIDIFICATION OF SPORT: THE ROLE OF LAW

A major danger attending the intervention of law into new 'sporting arenas' is juridification: here what were intrinsically social relationships between humans within a 'social field' become imbued with legal values and are understood as constituting legal relationships – thus social norms become legal norms.[120] If a dispute then befalls the parties, a legal remedy is seen as the primary remedy. This invariably changes the nature and perception of the dispute and the relational connection between the parties.

Foster, K, 'Developments in sporting law'

> Juridification ... at a simple level, it merely reproduces the traditional idea of private and public realms, with private areas increasingly being subject to public or judicial control, a move from voluntarism to legalism. But it offers also a more complex version which stresses the interaction as legal norms are used to reorder the power relations within the social arena.[121]

---

116 *Ibid*.

117 See Miah, A, 'The engineered athlete: human rights in the genetic revolution' (2000) 3(3) Culture, Sport and Society; Miah, A, *Genetically Modified Athletes: Biomedical Ethics, Gene Doping and Sport* (2004), London: Routledge.

118 Beloff, M, Kerr, T and Demetriou, M, *Sports Law* (1999), Oxford: Hart, p 6.

119 It may be that the influence of ethics increasingly means that the informal playing culture is an amalgam of (il)legitimate strategy and codes of ethics.

120 See Bourdieu, P, 'The force of law: towards a sociology of the juridical field' (1987) 38 Hastings Law Review 814.

121 Foster, K, 'Developments in Sporting Law', in Allison, L (ed.), *The Changing Politics of Sport* (1993), Manchester: MUP, p 108.

Sport is not alone as being a social field that has increasingly become legally regulated. The 'private area' of the family, for example, has increasingly become regulated by the law; examples include the development of remedies for domestic violence, particularly against women; the recognition of child abuse as a real social problem; and the initiation of the Child Support Agency to bring to account errant fathers. There may be criticism of how the law actually works in these and connected areas, but few would argue that the family should not be subject to this 'public' legal regulation. That law should never be involved in regulating sport is clearly absurd. The question is when and to what extent it should be involved.

An important part of this process is the ability of lawyers to develop new areas of work. The involvement of lawyers in sport can be compared with their involvement in other environments where their participation is contested. As Bankowski and Mungham argue, concerning tribunals of both a legal and a wider quasi-legal nature:

> The creation and maintenance of legal problems by lawyers follows a ... pattern ... when 'proper' becomes synonymous with 'legal' and 'paid' then there is created a pressure to abandon extra-legal means of dispute settlement in favour of legal ones.[122]

Similarly, Flood and Caiger in their examination of lawyers' rivalry with non-lawyers to control arbitration mechanisms in the construction industry argue:

> Lawyers are in a strong position to effect colonisation because of their power over the discourse of legalism. They have the power of appropriation.[123]

The danger is that the law too easily becomes the primary regulatory mechanism to be used to provide remedies. However, it is increasingly argued, particularly by Alan Hunt, that law is best understood in contemporary society, not in the classic formulation of English jurisprudence as a collection or model of rules but as a form of 'governance' or regulation. He stresses that this occurs not only through law but other quasi-legal and non-legal mechanisms:

Hunt, A, 'Law as a constitutive mode of regulation'

> The model of law as regulation can be seen as a shift towards public law that focuses on the varied means whereby extensive fields of social life are made subject to regulatory intervention ... we should recognise the diversity of legal phenomena and avoid falling into the presumption of a unitary entity 'the law' ... on the one hand law exists as an increasingly detailed and particularistic regulation of ever more specific situations and relations in which any boundary between law and non-law is difficult if not impossible to identify. On the other hand this important recognition of the diversification and pluralisation of law and regulation should not lead us to forget about the role that law plays as the medium of an ever-expanding State.[124]

This view fits in with the interaction of law with the internal sporting rules. The reluctance of the courts until quite recently to judicially review sporting bodies' internal rule-based decisions perhaps indicates the contrary view that sports should govern themselves and are separate from the law of the land. Law's increased intervention in sport in recent years provides the mix of legal and quasi-legal regulation.

---

122 Bankowski, Z and Mungham, G, *Images of Law* (1976), London: Routledge, p 62.

123 Flood, J and Caiger, A, 'Lawyers and arbitration: the juridification of construction disputes' (1993) 56(3) MLR 412.

124 Hunt, A, 'Law as a constitutive mode of regulation', in *Explorations in Law and Society: Towards a Constitutive Theory of Law* (1993), London: Routledge, p 307.

Hunt uses the work of the French philosopher Michel Foucault as the basis of his study of the sociology of governance.[125] He sees Foucault's contention that though law was important in the pre-modern world as a form of control, in modern society (from the end of the 18th century) law has largely given way to 'governance' and 'policing', a more complex multidimensional form of regulation. One of Foucault's most persistent influences on political philosophy is his ideas on discipline and surveillance, in that increasingly the State uses bodies of knowledge to intervene as a form of power. As Hunt says:

> ... the picture that he is taken to have painted is of ever extending and ever more intrusive mechanisms of power that insert themselves into every nook and cranny of social and personal life.[126]

One aim of this for Foucault is the stated aim for increasing 'normalisation' and the search for new sites of disciplinary intervention. Can sport be seen as one of these sites needing regulation? Of course, some of the sociological perspectives discussed earlier see sport itself as a form of social control. In a wider context, Steve Redhead sees the law's intervention in popular culture generally (sport being a significant part of this culture) as closely associated with the regulation of social activities that are considered to be morally reprehensible, a threat to social order.[127] The earlier historical extracts showed how this has occurred particularly concerning team sports, especially those seen as the wrong type, notably football and the control of the crowd. Redhead sees the regulation of football as a clear example.[128] The work of Geoffrey Pearson is pertinent with his focus on the State's control of football and surrounding culture by its construction as something that was a threat and should be feared, what Pearson calls 'respectable fears'.[129] This construction of social problems has also been termed 'moral panics'.[130] Although football has persistently been subject to such condemnation, Redhead sees that much of popular culture has been censured since the end of the last century:

Redhead, S, *Unpopular Culture: The Birth of Law and Popular Culture*

The whole field of 'law and popular culture' (or law and 'play' to coin another phrase) is of increasing scholarly interest in the field of legal, social and cultural studies, not least in the massive body of regulatory instruments (court cases and statutes, local authority bylaws) now in place which require interpretation and application. In Britain, for instance, such laws seem to be literally everywhere. For example, consider the following Bills: the Entertainment (Increased Penalties) Act 1990 (dubbed the 'Bright' Bill or 'Acid House' Bill in the press) and its attack on the organisation of what have been called pay parties or legal or illegal 'raves'; the Football Spectators Act 1989 and its abortive compulsory identity card scheme to combat soccer hooliganism with its introduction of new measures to stop soccer fans travelling abroad and ban convicted offenders attending designated matches; the Football (Offences) Act 1991 with its attempt to outlaw racist abuse, pitch invasions and other 'hooligan' activity at domestic soccer matches; the strengthening of licensing laws to close down certain clubs through the Licensing Act 1988; the calls for changes in the environmental and other laws to curb the noise of all night dance parties and the nuisance of the 1990s folk devils such as 'New Age travellers' and 'ravers' in various parts of town and countryside ... the moral panics about ecstasy (MDMA), LSD, cannabis and other 'recreational' (as defined by users) drug taking amongst large swathes of late 20th century global youth.

---

125 Foucault, M, *Discipline and Punish: The Birth of the Prison* (1977), London: Penguin.

126 *Op cit*, fn 124, Hunt (1993), p 288.

127 Also see Stanley, C, *Urban Excess and the Law: Capital Culture and Desire* (1996), London: Cavendish Publishing.

128 Also see the calls to have legislative intervention to regulate crowds at cricket matches in (2001) 4(4) Sports Law Bulletin 3.

129 See Pearson, G, *Hooligan: A History of Respectable Fears* (1983), London: Macmillan.

130 See Cohen, S, *Folk Devils and Moral Panics: The Creation of Mod Rockers* (1972), London: MacGibbon & Kee, for an explanation and analysis of moral panics.

These regulatory regimes all exhibit familiar features of the relationship between law, market and the State in the 1990s and illustrate contemporary attempts to regulate, discipline and police popular culture in the late 20th century which apply generally to many countries outside the national boundaries from where specific examples are drawn. Indeed such boundaries are part of the problem, as technologies and other changes make control on such border/lines almost impossible. But these aspects of legal discourse are for some commentators plainly what might be termed more or less 'repressive' in that they are seen to be part of a larger network of what many theorists persist, even in the 1990s, in calling 'social control' through criminal justice and penal systems which have in the past been theorised as part of the 'law and order control culture'. In the cruder, over-simplified versions of this conception, the State, through law, is seen as capable only of acting negatively – or repressively – against a group, class individual. Power is conceived in much of this mode of theorising as a thing, an instrument, which is wielded by one group, class or individual against another ... such theorisation of legal discourse and agency is often unsatisfactory – though Foucauldian alternative theorisations of the productivity of power can be equally problematic – especially when it is focusing on new instances of folk devils, moral panics or law and order campaigns.[131]

Moral panics can therefore be seen as having justified some legal intervention in sport. Their creation in popular culture and sport are produced by a complex amalgam of social pressures, the media having a central role in their amplification. Recent social examples are the allegations of satanic abuse, dangerous dogs, and the perceived widespread problem of road rage. Redhead presents a number that have justified State intervention in regulating popular culture. In sport, football has been the most prone to this effect and this will be discussed at some length in Chapter 3.[132] The consequence is 'panic law' that is invariably ineffective and feckless. It fits in with the wider regulatory view of law colonising new social fields and expanding its sphere of influence.

There is a wider jurisprudential debate concerning the role of law within this complex regulatory milieu. There are those that see 'autonomous law' increasingly replaced by a bureaucratic regulation;[133] there are those that see a positive development in this diversification of legal regulation.[134] What can be seen, however, is that the boundaries between formal law and other normative rules are increasingly blurred.

This development reflects the jurisprudential theory of 'legal pluralism', associated with the work of writers such as Boaventura de Sousa Santos:

> The legal regulation of social relations is not the exclusive attribute of any [one] form of normative order, it is rather the end result of a combination of the different forms of law and the modes of production thereof.[135]

---

131 Redhead, S, *Unpopular Culture: The Birth of Law and Popular Culture* (1995), Manchester: Manchester UP, pp 7–8.

132 See Greenfield, S and Osborn, G, 'Criminalising football supporters: ticket touts and the Criminal Justice and Public Order Act 1994' (1995) 3(3) Sport and the Law Journal 36; Greenfield, S and Osborn, G, 'After the Act: the (Re)construction and regulation of football fandom' (1996) 1(1) Journal of Civil Liberties 7; Greenfield, S and Osborn, G, 'When the whites go marching in? Racism and resistance in English football' (1996) 6(2) Marquette Sports Law Journal 315; Gardiner, S, 'The law and hate speech: "Ooh aah Cantona" and the demonstration of "the other" ', in Brown, A (ed), *Fanatics! Power, Identity and Fandom in Football* (1998), London: Routledge.

133 See Hayek, F, *Law, Legislation and Liberty* (1973–79), three volumes, London: Routledge; Posner, R, 'The decline of an autonomous discipline' (1987) 100 Harvard Law Review 761.

134 See Luhmann, N, *A Sociological Theory of Law* (1985), London: Routledge; Teubner, G (ed), *Dilemmas of Law in the Welfare State* (1986), New York: Walter de Gruyter.

135 Santos, B, 'On modes of production of law and social power'(1985) 13 International Journal of the Sociology of Law 299, 307; also see Teubner, G, Legal Pluralism in the World Society in Teubner, G, (ed), *Global Law Without a State* (1997), Andover: Dartmouth.

A problem with legal pluralism is that it fails to provide a convincing account of law in a general sense, that is, the argument that State law is in competition with other forms of legal order. State law may not have a monopoly but it is evidently a dominant force. It is, however, in specific contexts or social fields such as sport where legal pluralism seems credible and illuminating in terms of that areas regulation. The work of Stewart Macaulay on the non-contractual and therefore non-legal forms of business relations is an example of such a 'specific context'.[136] On sport, Macaulay has said:

> There is an official law, but there are complimentary, overlapping, and conflicting private legal systems as well ... spectator sports offer versions of law that differ from that found in law schools. They also offer alternative resources from which people fashion their own understandings of what is necessary, acceptable and just.[137]

There is a complex interaction between the rules of sport and the rules of law that are increasingly intervening within a complex regulatory framework of various types of rules and quasi-law. Legal pluralism provides use with a theoretical context to make sense of this complex setting. It also provides us with a principle with which to challenge the too pervasive interventionist role of the law in sport and the importance of other non-legal forms of regulation.

VIVA SPORTS LAW – SPORT AND THE LAW *RIP*

In the context of the increasing body of law that has been specifically developed for sport generally and sports such as football in particular, the penultimate section in this chapter will consider whether there is any such identified legal subject known as 'sports law' or whether it is more accurate to talk of merely a relationship of 'sport and the law'. The view of two practitioners first:

Grayson, E, *Sport and the Law*

No subject exists which jurisprudentially can be called sports law. As a soundbite headline, shorthand description, it has no juridical foundation; for common law and equity creates no concept of law exclusively relating to sport. Each area of law applicable to sport does not differ from how it is found in any other social or jurisprudential category ... When sport hits the legal and political buffers, conventional and ordinary principles affecting the nature of the appropriate sporting issue concerned including parliamentary legislation are triggered into action.[138]

Woodhouse, C, 'The lawyer in sport: some reflections'

I have often said there is no such thing as sports law. Instead it is the application to sport situations of disciplines such as contract law, administrative law (disciplinary procedures), competition law, intellectual property law, defamation and employment law ... I hope the next generation of sports lawyers will enjoy it as much as I have over the past 25 years. But do remember there is no such thing as sports law.[139]

---

136 Macaulay, S, 'Non-contractual relations in business: a preliminary study' (1963) 28 American Sociological Review 55.
137 Macaulay, S, 'Images of law in everyday life: the lessons of school, entertainment, and spectator sports' (1987) 21 Law and Society Review 185.
138 Grayson, F, *Sport and the Law* (1999), London: Butterworths, p xxxvii.
139 Woodhouse, C, 'The lawyer in sport: some reflections' (1996) 4(3) Sport and the Law Journal 14.

Legal academics not surprisingly have a wider and more reasoned analysis:

Barnes, J, *Sports and the Law in Canada*

Sports law deals with State interests and the resolution of conflicts according to general legal norms. Sports maintain internal rules and structures to regulate play and organise competition. In sports law, the wider legal system impinges on this traditionally private sphere and subjects the politics of the sports game to the politics of the law game. The result is a double drama as the deep human concern for play combines with the concern for social justice. Sports law addresses basic ethical issues of freedom, fairness, equality, safety and economic security. The subject matter of sports law includes State control and subsidy of sport, rights of access, disciplinary powers and procedures, commercial and property rights, employment relations and compensation for injuries. Sports law is grounded in the material dimensions of sport and includes a study of the life and times of its heroic practitioners.

State interest in sport and recreation has a long history and there are early Canadian instances of civil litigation and prosecutions for violent play but the flowering of sports law dates from the 1970s when a 'daily barrage of socio-legal crises' began to fill newspaper sports pages. Law, politics and finance have since become prominent features of sports culture and various factors explain this trend: sports now offer lucrative commercial rewards so that participants look to protect their economic interests through legal and industrial relations processes; governments have addressed social problems in sport and have been involved in sports administration; and sports have been affected by emancipation movements seeking wider recognition of legal and constitutional rights. Sports management has always relied on legal power to control the enterprise and retain the prime slice of the pie. Conflict has grown as the underpaid, the injured and the excluded have acquired remedies and gained the organisational strength necessary to further claims. The legal profession has been happy to appropriate this conflict.

The most familiar court battles occurred in the North American professional sports leagues. Some disputes involved the community interests affected by the establishment or relocation of team franchises but most cases dealt with the rights and freedoms of players. Litigation in the United States has partly emancipated professional athletes from restraints that limit them in selling their services to the highest bidder. The formation of rival leagues first offered alternative markets and anti-trust actions and collective bargaining then brought further mobility and prosperity. These developments inevitably affected Canadian members of American based leagues and the new freedoms served as models for Canadian athletes. Litigation has not, however, been limited to the major leagues. Sports organisations at all levels in Canada have been forced to respond to members who are more willing to seek judicial remedies and question restrictive regulations and disciplinary powers.

After a quarter century of intense conflict, litigation fatigue may now have set in and there is some yearning to revert to a lost 'pre-legal' ideal. The dissatisfaction with sports law reveals itself in public impatience over labour disputes and the lofty levels of professional salaries but a more concrete threat comes from the excesses of the war on drugs. Some feel that general legal principles should not intrude unduly into the sports world and that athletes' rights can only go so far.[140]

Opie, H, 'Sports associations and their legal environment'

'Sports law' is one of those fields of law which is applied law as opposed to pure or theoretical law. Rather than being a discipline with a common legal theme such as criminal law, equity or contract law, sports law is concerned with how law in general interacts with the activity known as sport. Hence, the label applied is law. Yet there is an increasing body of law which is specific to sport. This produces debate among scholars over whether one should use the term sports law, which indicates a legal discipline in its own right or 'sport and law' which reflects the multifarious and applied nature of the field. No doubt the

---

140 Barnes, J, *Sports and the Law in Canada* (1996), Toronto: Butterworths, pp 2–3.

general public would regard this as one of those sterile debates which are so attractive to inhabitants of ivory towers – if the public bothered to think about it!

Sport and the law is not the only field of law to be debated in this way. As new fields of law emerge it is almost customary for them to undergo this debate until they have been around long enough to establish themselves. This leads to an important observation: namely systematic attention to sport and law is a relatively new phenomenon in Australia. It is certainly something which has occurred only during the last 15 years. It is rare to find any seminar papers or learned articles on the topic prior to that period. Those which existed were regarded or presented almost as curiosities at their time of publication. There seems to have always been court cases concerning sport but these were isolated and are insignificant compared with the variety and volume of court proceedings that are to be observed today. A contributing factor to this prior inactivity is that in some fields of law the courts pursued a policy of non-intervention by holding that sport disputes were private matters which did not raise justiciable issues. Any informed observer will realise that the position is vastly different today. What has produced this change?[141]

These four accounts present alternative views on this issue: sport and the law or sports law? Grayson believes there is no such identifiable area of sports law. Woodhouse agrees. It is particularly depressing that this view still permeates the practice of law and sport. It is symptomatic of a narrow outlook and the fact that there has been little meaningful dialogue between practitioners and academics in Britain thus far. The wider picture of the significant changes taken place in the regulation of sport is seldom understood.

Although they come from arguably more advanced jurisdictions in terms of sports law, Canada and Australia respectively, Barnes suggests that the proliferation of sports legislation, litigation and arbitral decisions has led to some 'special doctrine' and Opie believes that it is possible to see a recognisable sports law, an 'applied' area of law. He notes the debate concerning whether an 'identifiable legal subject' exists has occurred in other developing and burgeoning areas.

It is, however, pleasing to see that there are more progressive practitioner observers who have acknowledged the importance of recognition of sports law. Michael Beloff and his co-authors consider that:

Beloff, M, Kerr, T and Demetriou, M, *Sports Law*

... the law is now beginning to treat sporting activity, sporting bodies and the resolution of disputes in sport, differently from other activities or bodies. Discrete doctrines are gradually taking shape in the sporting field ... English courts are beginning to treat decisions of sporting bodies as subject to particular principles.[142]

Similarly, Adam Lewis and Jonathan Taylor contend that although their book seeks not to address this distinction as it 'is an issue of academic rather than practical interest', they do:

Lewis, A and Taylor, J, *Sport: Law and Practice*

... share the belief of many writers in the field that in at least some areas, for example where international institutions such as the Court of Arbitration for Sport review the decisions of sports governing bodies, a separate and distinct body of law inspired general principles of law common to all states is in the process of development. Equally the extent of the adaptation by the English courts of existing principles of challenge to address the particular circumstances of sports governing bodies' decisions is well on the way to construction of model of review of such decisions analogous to the public law model, where previously there was much greater uncertainty.[143]

141 Opie, H, 'Sports associations and their legal environment', in McGregor-Lowndes, M, Fletcher, K and Sievers, S (eds), *Legal Issues for Non-Profit Associations* (1996), Sydney: LBC, pp 74–94.

142 *Op cit*, fn 118, Beloff, Kerr and Demetriou (1999), p 3.

143 Lewis, A and Taylor, J (eds) *Sport: Law and Practice* (2003) London: Butterworths.

The Emergence of Legal Disciplines

The development of this subject area of law's involvement in sport is part of a process that has happened to all legal areas in the past. Labour or employment law is a subject area that has only achieved relatively recent recognition. It has its origins in contract law in the employment context but no one would doubt that with the plethora of legislation during the post-war era regulating the workplace, it has become a subject area in its own right. Passing through various incarnations such as industrial law, it is now a mature legal subject.

The process by which legal areas are identified, constituted and named is a complex one and often to some extent arbitrary. There is no official recognition procedure. It is a process of legal practitioners and academics recognising the growing application of law to a new area of social life. Computer law is a good example to analogise with sports law. It is a relatively new legal subject, where specific laws dealing with this new technology are recent developments. In Britain two pieces of legislation, The Data Protection Act 1998 concerning access to information on computers and the Computer Misuse Act 1990 concerning criminalisation of unauthorised access to computer systems, have developed due to the inadequacies of the existing law to effectively regulate. As far as unauthorised access to computers or hacking, as it is commonly known, unsuccessful attempts had been made to apply the law of criminal damage to penalise such activities. The need for new legislation was overwhelmingly supported.

A significant body of computer law has developed. It falls into the 'applied law' classification that Opie describes. The development of legal areas which involves essentially the application of pure legal areas in the context of a human activity, in this case sport, moves from a loose association such as sport and the law to a more recognisable body of law such as sports law. It is true to say that it is largely an amalgam of interrelated legal disciplines involving such areas as contract, taxation, employment, competition and criminal law but dedicated legislation and case law have developed specific sports law related doctrines and principles and will continue increasingly to do so. As an area of academic study and extensive practitioner involvement, the time is right to accept that a new legal area has been born and is thriving in the 'bloom of its youth' – *Viva* sports law.

CONCLUSION: THE EMERGENCE OF A *LEX SPORTIVA*

To conclude, this chapter has shown that in Britain and elsewhere, there are a number of reasons for law's intervention in sport. The commercialisation of sport presents a palpable need for legal regulation. Many 'problems' in sport such as drug use and violence are presented as 'moral panics' in need of legal regulation. Two theoretical models of law's intervention have been developed in this and the previous chapter. They may not necessarily be oppositional and can be potentially complementary.

The first model is that the law's involvement is an extension along the road of the civilising process in sport in addition to the internal constitutive sports rules. The law is providing a functional role in the context of the modern commercial complexity of sport. This fits in with a figurational perspective on sport and society.

The second model is the law as a form of regulatory power, a form of control. Intervention is often legitimised in the context of the creation of moral panics.

Which is the most persuasive? The legal regulation of sport reflects the general increase of regulation of new social contexts or fields. In the regulation of sport there is evidence of pluralism with the interaction between different levels of normative rules. Sports law is an area on the periphery of the legal domain and as such, the law's role in regulating sport is open to continual analysis, debate and evaluation. The debate concerning the appropriate regulatory model for English professional football that has been examined is a good illustration.

Lawyers have seen sport as a social field ripe for colonisation and exploitation: the phenomenon of the greater activity of lawyers in sport is one that can fit into both models. A cynical view is that lawyers will always follow where there is work and where money can be made.

As stated already, sports law cannot be understood even primarily in purely national terms and this regulatory debate needs to be located within a European and indeed wider international context. Professional sport needs to be increasingly understood internationally with the substantial power that international sports federations have in determining how sports are organised and played.[144] In addition, it is a specific commodity that has developed complex and symbiotic relationships within the global media complex and sports marketing industry. This has been examined on a UK level with football. On the wider European regulatory level, this changing nature of sport has led to a number of governance issues. The regulatory aspects affecting sport are multidimensional and require a variety of responses.

Up until now sport and sports associations have enjoyed a measure of autonomy in rule making and enforcing. In short, sport has enjoyed 'relative autonomy'. A regulatory approach to this relative autonomy can be discerned in Europe:

Caiger, A and Gardiner, S (eds), *Professional Sport in the European Union: Regulation and Re-regulation*

This relative autonomy in sport is perhaps most closely mirrored by the *Lex Mercatoria*. The application of the *Lex Mercatoria* to the area of sport must be selective. There are two discernible approaches that may indicate a starting point for the re-regulation of professional sport in the EU:

'The "autonomist" approach conceives of an anational, autonomous, self-generating system of laws articulated by the international commercial community to regulate its activities. Its practices, usages and customs, supplemented by the general principles of law recognised by commercial nations form a – not yet fully developed – normative order that exists independent of any national system of law. On the other hand the "positivist" position views the *Lex Mercatoria* as having transnational origins, but only by virtue of states giving effect to conventions and uniform laws by ratification into municipal codes, and by trade usages that are articulated by international agencies.' (Wiener, J, *Globalization and the Harmonization of Law* (1999), London: Pinter, p 161.)

This formulation explains much of what is now occurring in sports governance. When sports rules and governance are challenged – whether from a competition point of view or from a mobility point of view – the national court, or the Commission or ECJ is asked to recognise or validate the sports usage as represented in the rules of a particular sporting association. These institutions and courts must decide to what extent they are prepared to recognise these rules, customs and usages. This in fact is what has happened with every legal challenge thus far. This interaction between the sports world and the normative order is helping to build, redefine and establish a distinct *Lex Sportiva*. For the purposes of this analogy it is not essential to decide which of the two approaches may be the most appropriate.

This analogy with the *Lex Mercatoria* allows sports law to develop distinctiveness and an incremental formation. It encourages sports organisations to reconsider their own rules and mode of governance in the light of the dominant legal norms. This process of acculturation allows and promotes a convergence between the *Lex Sportiva* and the dominant legal norms.[145]

---

144 Chapter 4 develops this debate in terms of whether there is an 'International Sports Law'; see pp 173–77.
145 Caiger, A and Gardiner, S (eds), *Professional Sport in the European Union: Regulation and Re-regulation* (2000), The Hague: Asser.

The analogy between *lex mercatoria* and a *lex sportiva* or sports law is germane: both respect a degree of autonomy, both acknowledge cultural specificities, both are part of a pluralistic and complex normative rule structure, and both acknowledge the need for international emphasis in terms of legal regulation. *Lex mercatoria,* or the Law Merchant, was the legal doctrine developed in the Middle Ages by special local courts in Britain and elsewhere.[146] These merchant courts had judges and jury who were merchants themselves and would apply the *lex mercatoria* as opposed to local law. An analogy can be made with the Court of Arbitration for Sport and the view that it is developing a specific doctrine of international sports law.

Sealey, L and Hooley, RJA, *Commercial Law: Text, Cases and Materials*

The *lex mercatoria* was an international law of commerce. It was based on the general customs and practices of merchants which were common throughout Europe and was applied almost uniformly by the merchant courts in different countries ... [it] derived its authority from the voluntary acceptance by the merchants whose conduct it sought to regulate ... it was flexible enough to adapt to new mercantile practices ... it was speedily administered by merchant courts which shunned legal technicalities and often decided cases *ex aequo yet bono* (in equity and good conscience).[147]

The relative autonomy of sport needs to be preserved – it is that special[148] – and what is needed is sensitivity to the particular specificity and needs of sport (and of distinct sports). A casuistic approach, allowing solutions to be found to solve particular problems that arise – what could be termed a *'horses for courses'* approach – is appropriate to recognise both the cultural significance of sport and the distinctions found between different sports. The law in terms of regulation together with other normative regulatory mechanisms has a role to supervise this relative autonomy – or to put it another way, that it has a role in guaranteeing 'supervised autonomy' for the good of sport.[149]

KEY SOURCES

Caiger, A and Gardiner, S (eds), *Professional Sport in the European Union: Regulation and Re-regulation* (2000), The Hague: Asser.

Foster, K, 'How can sport be regulated', in Greenfield, S and Osborn, G (eds), *Law and Sport in Contemporary Society* (2000), London: Frank Cass, pp 268–70.

Football Task Force, *Commercial Issues* (1999), London.

Fraser, D, *Cricket and the Law: The Man in White is Always Right* (2003), London: Frank Cass.

Weiller, P, *Levelling the Playing Field: How Can the Law Make Sport Better for Fans* (2000), Cambridge, Mass: Harvard UP.

---

146 The Laws of Oléron, an island of the French Atlantic coast, were of the highest persuasive authority, see Goode, R, *Commercial Law* (1995), London: Penguin, p 3.

147 Sealey, L and Hooley, RJA, *Commercial Law: Text, Cases and Materials* (1999), London: Butterworths.

148 Kerr, T, 'Is sport special?' (2001) 9(1) Sport and the Law Journal 78.

149 Term used by Ken Foster; see Foster, K, 'Can sport be regulated by Europe? An analysis of alternative models', in *op cit*, fn 145, Caiger and Gardiner (2000).

CHAPTER 3

SPORT AND THE ROLE OF THE STATE IN BRITAIN

INTRODUCTION

Compared with most other European countries, the British State's formal involvement in sport has been fairly minimal. Sports bodies are treated as autonomous independent bodies and self-regulation has been the tradition. Even when promoting and effectively 'managing' sport, the State has played a passive role. Within Europe a distinction can be made between northern countries, which share this approach, and southern 'Mediterranean' countries, where there is a tradition of specific regulation.[1] As outlined in Chapter 1, there has been a long history of legal prohibition of certain types of sport in Britain. However, it is also true to say that in recent years in Britain, there has been a steady move to greater regulatory involvement.[2]

Obvious examples of direct State (albeit delayed) intervention in British sport were made in response to a number of stadium disasters (almost all concerning football) that occurred during the last 50 years. There were official reports after the 1946 disaster at Bolton (33 deaths), the 1972 disaster at Ibrox in Glasgow (66 deaths), the Bradford fire in 1985 (55 deaths), and most notably the 1989 Taylor Report on the Hillsborough disaster where 96 died. It was not until this last report that the British Government positively acted to legislate for sports stadium safety.[3]

The lack of recent success in Britain's national sporting teams and the sporadic accomplishment of its individual sportsmen and women has intensified the debate concerning the effective role that the State can play in sport. Increasing pressure has been brought to bear upon the State to provide greater financial and material assistance to British sport through national lottery funding, for example.

This chapter will initially consider the framework through which the State may intervene in British sport. Such intervention can be through various methods including financial support and the promotion of sport as an activity that has health and social benefits. The use of sport as a form of social policy to fight crime and social exclusion will also be considered, and the role of bodies such as the Sports Councils will be briefly discussed.

Five different sports related issues will be considered, each allowing the debate concerning the role of State intervention via social policy and legal method to be evaluated. The historic prohibition of certain sports on policy grounds, that is, boxing and fox hunting, will be considered. There are periodic calls for boxing to be banned. Hunting foxes with hounds has been subject to attempts to pass legislation to restrict its operation. Sport is a social area that is subject to general societal problems that are subject to legal regulation. In Britain, football has been the sport most subject to the gaze of sport largely due to the problem of football hooliganism. In the context of the issue of racism, the sports world can be seen as a microcosm of society. How effective are anti-racist measures in sport? Finally the focus will be on child protection in sport that, as in society in general, has become recognised as a 'real' problem in Britain since the mid-1980s. Sport, which involves participation by many children, has grappled with the existence of potential abuse and a responsibility to protect child athletes.

---

1   See Council of Europe, *Study of National Sports Legislation in Europe* (1999); see details of a number of European countries including Michel, A, 'Sports policy in France', in Chalip, L, Johnson, A and Stachura, L (eds), *National Sports Policies: An International Handbook* (1996), Westport, CT: Greenwood.
2   See Lewis, A and Taylor, J (eds), *Sport: Law and Practice* (2003), London: Butterworths, pp 1–44.
3   See Chapter 17 for a fuller discussion.

FRAMEWORK OF SPORT IN BRITAIN

Until the Second World War, other than Acts of prohibition of some sporting activity, there was virtually no direct State involvement in the framework and organisation of sport. All that existed were a number of private federations for particular sports, tracing their origins from the end of the 19th century. These organisations were, on the whole, controlled by establishment figures with close connections to the politically powerful. One significant development was the creation of what is now the Central Council of Physical Recreation (CCPR) in 1935: this was initiated as a non-governmental voluntary organisation, an 'umbrella body' of sporting organisations funded from private sources.

In 1957 the CCPR appointed a committee to report on 'the future of sporting administration in promoting the general welfare of the community'. The subsequent Wolfenden Report in 1960 concluded with 57 paragraphs of recommendations. It indirectly led to other key developments in the State intervention of sport: the appointment of a Minister of Sport in 1962 and the birth of the Sports Council in 1966.

Today the CCPR and the Sports Councils are the two main organisations enforcing sports policy in Britain.[4] There are a number of other bodies that are worthy of mention. A British Sports Forum has been in existence since the early 1990s. There are organisations such as Sports Coach UK (formerly the National Coaching Foundation), which provides educational and advisory services for coaches in all sports. In addition to the many sports organisations under the umbrella of the CCPR, there is the British Olympic Association, founded in 1905, which is the National Olympic Committee for Britain.

The Central Council of Physical Recreation

The CCPR, as the representative body of many British sports governing bodies, identifies its modern role as being:

(1) the umbrella organisation for the National Governing and Representative Bodies of sport and recreation in the UK;

(2) speaks and acts to promote, protect and develop the interests of sport and physical recreation at all levels;

(3) at the forefront of sports politics, providing support and services to those who participate in and administer sport and recreation;

(4) completely independent of any form of government control;

(5) having no responsibility for allocating funds;

(6) strictly non-party and will support or oppose proposed measures only on the basis of their perceived value to sport and recreation.

CCPR – *How We Work*

- As the voice of British sport and recreation, all of CCPR's work is aimed at promoting and protecting the interests of sport and recreation and to supporting the organisations involved in their provision and administration

---

4   See Hargreaves, J, *Sport, Power and Culture* (1986), London: Polity, for an analysis of the operation of these bodies and State intervention in general.

- We provide a central focus for all the national bodies and authorities who administer and run sport and recreation

- We are an effective lobbying organisation, representing the view of our members to all authorities whose decisions impact sport and recreation

- We offer opinions and advice to policy making organisations whose decisions impact sport and recreation

- We provide a collective platform developing policies which benefit sport and recreation

- We provide members with advice and information on issues relating to the running of their sport and their 'business'

- We ensure that members are kept informed of changes in Government policy and UK and EU law[5]

The Sports Councils

The concept of the 'Sports Council' has gone through a number of changes since its inception in 1966. In contrast to the CCPR, they are publicly funded official advisory bodies to the government. In 1972, the structure was modified by the creation of the Great Britain Sports Council and three additional Councils for the other parts of the United Kingdom (Scotland, Wales and Northern Ireland) with extended powers. At the end of 1996, The Great Britain Sports Council was divided into the UK Sports Council (now 'UK Sport') and the English Sports Council (now 'Sport England'), with the three other home country Sports Councils continuing unchanged (Sports Council of Northern Ireland, Sports Council of Wales, Sports Scotland). They are all national, non-departmental public bodies (sometimes known as quangos), which receive funding from, and are accountable to, the Department of Culture, Media and Sport. There is a Secretary of State for this Department and a Parliamentary Under-Secretary of State, known as the Minister for Sport. The House of Commons scrutinises the work of the United Kingdom Sports Council and the English Sports Council via the relevant Select Committee and Public Accounts Committee.

The UK Sports Council

The UK Sports Council has a small staff and acts as a co-ordinating body for the four home country Sports Councils (England, Northern Ireland, Scotland and Wales).[6] It deals with areas of common interest at UK level. These include:

UK Sport – *About UK Sport*

Established by Royal Charter in 1996, UK Sport works in partnership with the Home Countries and other agencies to drive the development of a world-class high-performance system in the UK. This will result in more winning athletes and greater world-class success. UK Sport is responsible for managing and distributing public investment (£29 million annually) and is a statutory distributor of funds raised by the National Lottery (9.2% of sport allocation). UK Sport is in a unique position to enhance and add value to the work of our partners through delivering on our primary and supporting goals:

Primary goal: World Class Performance- Building on the world-class athlete support established over the last four years, it is critical that we now focus on creating a system that continues to deliver world class success.

---

5   See www.ccpr.org.uk
6   See its guide, *Sport and Legislation in the UK* (1996), 2nd edn, London: UK Sports Council.

Supporting goal: Worldwide Impact- The 2012 Olympic bid places UK Sport's international work in the spotlight.

Supporting goal: World Class Standards- UK Sport will promote the highest standards of sporting conduct and explore its wider social applications. We will continue to lead a world-class anti-doping programme for the UK and be responsible for improving the education and promotion of ethically fair and drug-free sport. The critically important modernisation of National Governing Bodies (NGBs) will be integrated into mainstream funding programmes.[7]

Sport England

As with the other Sports Councils from the home countries, in recent years the emphasis has increasingly been on the grass roots development of sport.

The Sport England Mission

Our vision

Making England an active and successful sporting nation.

Our mission

Working with others to create opportunities to get involved in sport, to stay in sport and to excel and succeed in sport at every level.

Our role

1. To be the strategic lead for sport in England.
2. To make focused investments through partners.
3. To provide advice, support and knowledge to partners and customers.
4. To influence the decision-makers and public opinion on sport.

Our business objectives

1. Start – increase participation in sport in order to improve the health of the nation, with a focus on priority groups.
2. Stay – retain people in sport and active recreation through an effective network of clubs, sports facilities, coaches, volunteers and competitive opportunities.
3. Succeed – achieve sporting success at every level.
4. Internal efficiency – ensure that we operate and allocate our resources with maximum effectiveness.[8]

The work of Sport England includes the promotion of women in sport, sport for people with disabilities and sustainable sport in the countryside. UK Sport is now the main focus for elite sport and the promotion of excellence. Since the mid-1990s, there has been a shift towards promoting excellence in sport with the government indicating a more pro-active role in sport.[9]

---

7 See www.uksport.gov.uk.
8 See www.sportengland.org.
9 See the latest policy position in *A Sporting Future for All* (2001), London: HMSO; Sporting Britain (2004) DCMS, www.culture.gov.uk.

SPORT AND SOCIAL POLICY

Sport and Social Inclusion

The Labour Government came into power in 1997 with a declared policy aim to encourage the involvement of those individuals whose participation in mainstream society had been restricted. Such groups included women, the elderly, those from lower socio-economic categories such as the long term unemployed and those from certain ethnic minorities. A Social Exclusion Unit located at the Cabinet Office was created. Sport has been identified as a social activity that can be used to help fight social exclusion.[10] Claims have been made that sport can help 'to tackle the issues around social exclusion and cut crime, improve health, education and employment prospects in deprived communities through teamwork, discipline, responsibility and creative expression'.[11]

Many initiatives are taking place. The increasing social policy claims made for sport are reflected in the rhetoric of the European Commission:

European Commission, *The Development and Prospects for Community Action in the Field of Sport*

Sport is unique in that it performs five functions:

(1) An education function: active participation in sport is an excellent way of ensuring balanced personal development for all age groups;

(2) A public health function: physical activity offers an opportunity to improve people's health; it is an effective means of combating certain illnesses such as heart disease and cancer and help to maintain good health and quality of life among the elderly;

(3) A social function: sport is a suitable tool for promoting a more inclusive society and for combating intolerance, racism, violence, alcohol and drug abuse; sport can also assist in the integration of people excluded from the labour market;

(4) A cultural function: sport gives people an additional opportunity to put down roots, to get to know an area better, to integrate better and to protect the environment to a greater degree;

(5) A recreational function: sporting activity is an important leisure occupation and provides personal and collective entertainment.

Employed in the correct way, sport is therefore a particularly effective weapon in the fight against intolerance, racism, violence, alcohol and narcotics abuse. It is therefore particularly affected by the development of voluntary work as an expression of social solidarity.[12]

Claims have been made for sport as an effective tool for fighting crime and juvenile delinquency. This is, however, a contested issue: some argue that sport can positively influence and decrease anti-social acts; others argue that sports' impact upon social behaviour is far more limited.

McVicar, J, 'Violence in Britain: this sporting life of crime'

Despite this upsurge of concern about violence in sport, playing these games continues to be seen as character building; an assumption reinforced by John Major's recent governmental commitment to promoting excellence in sport. Doubtless he wants to incorporate it in his English vision of village greens and early morning mists. Yet one of the most glaring links between sport and violence is the way so

---

10 See Collins, M, *Sport and Social Exclusion* (2001), London: Routledge.

11 European Sports Council, *A Sporting Future for All*, p 46.

12 European Commission, *The Development and Prospects for Community Action in the Field of Sport* (1998).

many in organised crime began as useful sportsmen and continue to show an avid interest in sport throughout their criminal career.

This connection receives scant attention from social scientists, lawyers, sports administrators or government officials; yet go into any prison gymnasium and who is in the thick of the action? Not rapists – except Mike Tyson – but robbers, gangsters and others who figure in the criminal pecking order. Similar observations can be made at any big fight or in the stands at Highbury where north London's leading criminal family and their favoured hit man can be seen cheering on Arsenal. I was reminded of all this by two recent books by our great men of crime. In *Memoirs of a Life of Crime*, Mad Frankie Fraser talks about his lifelong obsession with boxing and football (he played park football into his 50s). Now in his mid 70s, Frank is a regular at Highbury and is ringside at all the big fights. And this love and involvement in sport is virtually the norm among heavy-duty professional criminals. Take the latest piece of – forgive me for mentioning the name – Kray memorabilia, *The Krays' Lieutenant* by Albert Donaghue. In this, one of the twins' old henchmen talks about Ronnie and Reggie being like 'two hunting dogs' as they sniffed out victims for their brainless mayhem; but their taste and capacity for violence had been honed during their long careers as amateur and professional boxers.

Obviously, an apprenticeship in sport is neither sufficient nor necessary for graduating into organised crime. But, given other factors, a solid grounding in sport can and often does make crime an attractive proposition. What factors? Well, first, this relationship applies almost solely to males: organised crime, like physical sport, is virtually a male preserve. Secondly sport and crime tend to coalesce only at the bottom of society. Sportsmen from higher up the social scale often develop for example, through playing rugby – a hyper-masculine identity but other circumstantial factors, such as family background, education and their social networks, militate against this being conducive to a life of crime. Finally, the sporting apprenticeship should not be too successful, as that is likely to catapult the athlete into a sporting career, diverting him from the temptations of crime. If Ronnie and Reggie Kray had been champion boxers, they would almost certainly not have become murderers, nor, as a consequence, spent most of their lives in prison.

What is it about physical sports, though, that helps equip the young plebeian male for a life of crime? What qualities does it impart that make him better at crime and more likely to choose it as a career? (Incidentally, career criminals are nothing to do with the stage army of petty criminals who clog the courts and overcrowd the prisons. These inadequates invariably have disturbed upbringings that render them incapable of playing anything organised or disciplined; they are neither good at sport or crime.) Contact sports, which are premised on mock war or combat, are not solely about orchestrating warrior virtues but the latter are clearly by-products of boxing, rugby, football and so on. Even if some don't teach a youngster how to look after himself, they all increase his strength and speed, his physical prowess. Males from the lowest level of society, though, find such qualities far more useful than their more socially privileged peers because violence, and its threat, figures far more in the regulation of their social life than it does on other social levels. Violent skills, even familiarity with violence, fitness, strength and so on, are also functional in the commission of crime. They confer, as it were, occupational advantages on the career criminal. Moreover, a capacity or potential for violence is also important in regulating relationships between criminals. Career criminals are enmeshed in a network of criminal relationships, the integrity of which rests upon their nature and content being hidden from the police. Thus all enduring criminal groups develop a prohibition against cooperating with law enforcement officials and others, such as journalists, who would be likely to pass on information to the police. This is the cornerstone of the criminal way of life.[13]

Robins, D, 'Sport and crime prevention: the evidence of research'

The idea that engaging in sports and outdoor activities has a morally redemptive quality was very popular with Victorian social reformers. Bold claims are sometimes made today. But how effective are sports and outdoor pursuits in crime prevention?

---

13   McVicar, J, 'Violence in Britain: this sporting life of crime' *The Guardian*, 19 September 1995, p 6.

Mistaken assumptions

The assumption that participation in sport, or the provision of sports facilities affects levels of delinquency, is made in the absence of any supporting evidence. Coalter (1987), in his review of the literature on the subject commissioned by the Scottish Sports Council felt 'unable to conclude a correlation between high level of sports participation/low level of delinquency holds good in the UK'. Mason and Wilson alluded to the myriad of variables that have to be taken into account before the relation between sport and delinquency can be ascertained. My own (1990) study concluded that there is no sound theoretical basis for the use of sport and outdoor adventure activities to combat or prevent juvenile crime.

The view that participation in sport has little effect is shared by many of those who work professionally with offenders. Many are deeply sceptical of sport as prevention. But the power of the sports lobby is strong. Not for the first time, the findings of the researchers and the experiences of the practitioners are at odds with the decisions of the policy makers.

Sport as prevention

The use of sports, games and rigorous PE sessions are just as much the core feature of today's young offender institutions as they were of the borstals. The use of outdoor adventure in treatment programmes for youth at risk is also commonplace. Considerable amounts of public funds and private charitable donations are deployed in this direction. When asked to propose solutions for young offenders who for the most part are destined to spend their lives trying to survive in the jungles of the cities, politicians of all political persuasions will evoke windswept rock faces and speak of Challenges Overcome and Lessons Learnt. Even Britain's leading expert on young offenders, Professor David Farrington of Cambridge University, has invoked the supporting, and discredited, safety valve theory expounded by the Victorians by suggesting that 'if offending is linked to boredom, excitement seeking and impulsiveness then it might be reduced by some kinds of community or recreational programmes that provide socially approved opportunities for excitement and risk-taking'. For your average tearaway a socially approved 'buzz' is a contradiction in terms. This sort of thinking also implies that the best way to handle hyped up, manic and self-destructive kids, is to give them more and better opportunities to 'act out'.

The belief in 'sport as prevention' also occurs in community development capital programmes aimed at improving sport and recreational facilities in deprived areas. This approach aims to reduce delinquency rates by encouraging a positive use of leisure time. There is of course nothing objectionable about greater investment in sport and recreational provision in these areas. But it cannot be stressed enough that there is no evidence of concomitant reductions in juvenile crime following such developments. On the contrary, gleaming sports centres have become the foci for young people's negative projections and the targets for violent attacks.

Failed dreams

In October 1990 the French high rise suburb of Vaulx en Velins was engulfed in a week of bloody clashes between police and local youths, during which new community facilities were set on fire and destroyed. Immediately before the disturbances a brand new sports centre, including a gymnasium and a swimming pool, had been opened in a euphoric mood of self-congratulation. A climbing wall inaugurated a few days earlier had been seen as the culmination of a successful programme based on the idea of providing constructive sports pursuits for people with time on their hands. At the height of the disturbances, several hundred riot police had to be deployed to protect the sports centre.

Some new treatment programmes attempt to blend the joys of sport and outdoor adventure with group confrontation therapy techniques. Sending 'bad boys' up mountains to find themselves, confronting childhood trauma with more trauma in group therapy: these are the alternatives to the customary verbal beating by the magistrate followed by the custodial sentence. I have found that advocates of such programmes are often propelled by a sort of aggressive optimism which acts as a defence against the hopelessness felt when confronting the destructive nihilism of criminalised youth. (Of course this is preferable to the attitude adopted by the present Home Secretary, Mr Michael Howard. He appears to be driven purely by a need to punish children.)

Policy makers and criminal justice professionals need to be reminded of the essential futility of sports and outdoor pursuits, the fact that they make no direct contribution to the wealth of the community, or to a fairer society. At the risk of sounding old fashioned, to privilege such programmes is to denigrate more cerebral activities. Intellectual qualities – a sceptical, questioning attitude towards authority and convention, broadening horizons, acquiring a more educated view of society – are not required. The old socialist belief in the educational, and intellectual, advance of working-class youth has been abandoned.

There is no evidence that participation in physical endeavour based programmes, whether punitive or 'liberal', prevents criminality. But another incontrovertible fact is that sports and games are massively popular. A staggering three million people play football on a regular basis. Every youth worker and prison officer knows that football is a priceless lowest common denominator of activity designed to hold the attention of young men who are otherwise uncooperative, and who have successfully resisted the lessons of the classroom. The sad consequence of the failure to find real educational solutions for young offenders is that the purely instrumental aspects of sport become the main rationale for provision.[14]

The view that sport can be the magical cure for juvenile crime is naive. Participation in sporting endeavour can of course be a positive channelling of energies and can help teach positive life values; however, it is unlikely to have a significant impact upon the underlying social reasons for criminality. The causes of crime are highly complex and contested. Sport has a role to play in helping fight crime, but one must be realistic about its limitations.

SPORT AND PUBLIC POLICY

Contemporary State Regulation in Sport

The major role of the State in sport continues to lie in the regulating and prohibiting of sporting activities. This role is not straightforward: to regulate or not to regulate, to prohibit or not to prohibit? These are complex issues that are not easily reconciled. The legitimacy of the State protecting individuals from certain activities can be explained as 'paternalism' where essentially the State acts as a parent, guiding behaviour. This has its origins in the ideas of the philosopher, John Stuart Mill,[15] who thought that human activities could be justifiably regulated or prohibited when they cause 'harm' to others or to oneself.[16]

The counter-view is the belief that the State is too interventionist in people's lives: the nanny State. This view develops a libertarian approach that essentially argues people should be able to do as they wish; in this case, in the sporting context. The restrictions on the ownership of handguns in the

---

14 Robins, D, 'Sport and crime prevention: the evidence of research' (1996) 23 Criminal Justice Matters 26. Also see Coalter, F, *Sport and Delinquency* (1987), unpublished; Mason, G and Wilson, P, *Sport Recreation and Juvenile Crime* (1988), Canberra: Australian Institute of Criminology; Robins, D, *Sport as Prevention* (1990), Oxford: Centre for Criminal Research; Farrington, D, Implications of criminal career research for the prevention of offending' (1990) 13 Journal of Adolescence 93; Jones, V, 'Football and crime prevention' and Dulop, D, 'Can sport reduce crime amongst young people?' both (1996) 23 Criminal Justice Matters 24; Nichols, G and Crow, I, 'Measuring the impact of crime reduction interventions involving sports activities for young people' (2004) 43(3) Howard Journal of Criminal Justice, 267–283.

15 Mill, JS, *On Liberty* (1962), Everyman Edition, London: Fontana.

16 The work of Mill will be discussed at greater length in the context of how combat sport should be regulated or prohibited; see later, p 620.

wake of the 1996 Dunblane tragedy provide a good example.[17] This reform had wide public support, but those who took part in the sport of shooting vociferously decried it as an 'overreaction' and a denial of their rights.

The State's policy driven involvement in sport will be examined in the following five ways:

(1) the regulation of football hooliganism;

(2) safety concerns in boxing;

(3) arguments for/against the banning of fox hunting;

(4) engaging with racism in sport;

(5) protection of child athletes from abuse.

These areas are a disparate collection of areas of controversy and 'perceived problems' which exist in contemporary sport. In all these areas of sporting activity, the role of the law will be considered. It is vital to bear in mind the discussion in Chapters 1 and 2 concerning the role of the law in regulating areas of social life. The law increasingly operates together with other normative rules such as the existing internal rules: that is, sporting rules and codes of practice. The major area of contention is whether law can offer an effective mode of regulation. Law can produce positive results, but it is not always the best way of providing solutions to perceived problems, and has to be understood as part of a wider regulatory framework.

FOOTBALL HOOLIGANISM

Elsewhere in this book, there are extensive materials on the regulation of sports stadia and in particular football grounds and employment issues concerning those involved in hooligan activity.[18] This section provides some of the historical and policy background to the current legal regulation of football hooliganism.[19] As discussed in Chapter 1, folk games akin to modern football have been played for many centuries. Often in terms of the participants, they were highly physical and bloody. But there are few indications that there was physical disorder in the 'crowds' that watched up until the period when the game became codified during the second half of the nineteenth century. The historical and sociological aetiology of what we contemporarily understand as football hooliganism is uncertain.

Football hooliganism has often been termed the 'English disease', one which is often portrayed as a modern phenomenon which developed in the 1970s. In reality it is likely that crowds within the era of organized football from the end of the nineteenth century have always been the locus for disorder. It has been suggested that over 4000 incidents of what one might term 'football hooliganism' (rather than just individual fights) occurred in the 20 years before the First World War.[20] This has not only been limited to English football.[21] In 1909, goalposts were torn down and over 100 people were

---

17 See the Firearms (Amendment) Act 1997.
18 See Chapters 13 and 17.
19 For excellent accounts of the these issues, see McArdle, D, *From Boot Money to Bosman: Football, Society and the Law* (2000), London: Cavendish Publishing and Greenfield, S and Osborn, G, *Regulating Football: Commodification, Consumption and the Law* (2001), London: Pluto Press.
20 Dunning, E, Murphy, P, Willaims, J and Maguire, J, 'Football Hooliganism in Britain Before the First World War' (1984) 19 International Review of the Sociology of Sport 215.
21 *Op cit*, fn 19, McArdle (2000), p 64.

injured in a pitched battle between fans and police after the Scottish Cup Final in Glasgow. Similarly, Kuper provides many examples of crowd disorder at professional games in both the Netherlands and Germany during the Second World War.[22] Further afield many examples of hooligan activity can be found historically in a number of South American countries.[23] Although only subject to specific State scrutiny in the UK over the last 30 years or so, it has existed as a social phenomenon for much longer. The modern era of football hooliganism is often viewed as starting in 1961, where a major riot occurred after an equalising goal during a Sunderland versus Tottenham game in 1961. 'That the hooligans were seen on television, *The Guardian* later said, provided . . . encouragement to others.'[24]

There is an extensive body of sociological literature concerning the study of football hooliganism.[25] Marxist analysis competes with functionalist analysis in attempting to explain its existence. The work of Norbert Elias and his figurational analysis informed some of the early academic research, much of it carried out at Leicester University. Subsequently a good deal of research has come from wider perspectives including anthropological studies based on participant observation.[26] Popular culture has also provided many accounts, often from the professional 'reformed' hooligan.[27] But why football hooliganism exists as a social phenomenon remains contested.

Not only has hooliganism been recognized as a national 'problem' within the English game; fans travelling to see the England side have been involved in numerous incidents. Complex issues of nationalism and national identity are being played out in football fandom, of course within the more general contemporary political and social momentum towards a more formalised integrationist Europe and additionally the continuing decline of the British Empire.

Legal Responses

What is contested and unclear as far as football hooliganism is concerned, is what social policy and legal responses should be made on both a national and European level. In England, significant amounts of legislation have been enacted, often in response to particular incidents that have led to significant media coverage. Two such incidents in 1985 televised matches at the grounds of Chelsea FC and Luton Town are of import. Both games involved spectators gaining access to the playing area and mass fights ensuing between opposing groups.[28] Also in that year, a government inquiry leading to the Popplewell Report took place after the fire at the Bradford City ground, which led to the death

---

22 Kuper, S, *Ajax, the Dutch, the War: Football in Europe During the Second World War* (2003), London: Orion.

23 Archetti, EP, 'Death and violence in Argentinean football', in Giulianotti, R, Bonney R, and Hepworth, M, *Football, Violence and Social Identity* (1994), London: Routledge.

24 See useful materials on football hooliganism at www.sirc.org.

25 See for example Armstrong, G and Harris, R, 'Football Hooligans: Theory and Evidence' (1991) 39(3) Sociological Review 427; Williams, J, Dunning, E and Murphy, P, *Hooligans Abroad: The Behaviour of English fans at Continental Matches* (1989), 2nd edn, London: Routledge; Dunning, E, Murphy, P and Waddington, I, 'Anthropological versus sociological approaches to the study of soccer hooliganism: some critical notes' (1991) 39(3) Sociological Review 459; Taylor, I, 'On the sports violence question: soccer hooliganism revisited', in Hargreaves, J (ed), *Sport, Culture and Ideology* (1981), London: Routledge; Marsh, P, Rosser, E and Harre, R, *The Rules of Disorder* (1978), London: Routledge; and Hobbs, D and Robins, D, 'The boy done good: football violence, changes and continuities' (1991) 39(3) Sociological Review 551.

26 For example, see Armstrong, G, *Football Hooligans: Knowing the Score* (1998), London: Berg.

27 See Buford, B, *Amongst The Thugs* (1993), New York: Vintage; Brimson, D, *Capital Punishment: London's Violent Football Following* (1997), London: Headline; Brimson, D, *The Crew* (2000), London: Headline.

28 Until the 1990s and the creation of all-seater stadia in the higher professional leagues, the most ardent younger fans often stood on a terrace behind one goal and the away supporters behind the other goal. The aim of invading the pitch and 'taking an end' was prized.

of 54 people. The recommendations were also based on an analysis of the tragedy at the Hazel Stadium in Brussels at the UEFA Cup Final. This tragedy led to a number of recommendations concerning safety on the one hand and the consideration of a membership scheme for all football spectators on the other. Although enabling legislation was introduced in the form of the Football Spectators Act 1989, a compulsory membership scheme was never introduced.

The other pivotal event of course was the death of 95 Liverpool fans at the FA Cup semi-final in 1989 at the Hillsborough Stadium in Sheffield. Although it is now recognised that this was caused primarily by safety defects and failures of policing, it was initially portrayed as being the latest manifestation of hooligan activity. The subsequent government inquiry produced the Taylor Report.[29] Again similar to the earlier Popplewell Report, recommendations were divided into ones concerning safety at stadiums, most notably the introduction of all-seater stadia at the top professional clubs and further specific football-related legislative provisions that led to the amending of the Football Spectators Act 1989, then passing through Parliament, and the enacting of the Football (Offences) Act 1991, which criminalized entry on to the playing area, throwing missiles and racist chanting. Significant amounts of legislation have been passed without any real analysis of the causes of football hooliganism.

Greenfield, S and Osborn, G, *Regulating Football: Commodification, Consumption and the Law*

Two distinct strands to the issue can be detected during the conservative administrations that enacted the legislation from 1985 to 1994. First it was seen as football's problem, as something to be controlled by the sport's governing bodies. Second, if it couldn't be dealt with in this manner it would be treated as a public-order problem and subject to firm policing. There was no attempt to understand and, more important, why, outbreaks of hooliganism occurred; the symptoms would merely be tackled in an authoritarian manner.[30]

As discussed earlier, such measures can be seen as 'panic law'.[31] The subsequent Football (Offences and Disorder) Act 1999 and Football Disorder Act 2000 have amended and strengthened many of the provisions in the earlier 1989 and 1991 Acts.[32] In addition, the normal Public Order Act offences apply together with sports specific alcohol legislation introduced in the 1980s.[33] Adding to this the measures introduced by the Criminal Justice and Public Order Act 1994,[34] which criminalized the practice of ticket touting, what is now in place is an extensive legislative framework. Many people see the current legislative framework in the UK as having 'criminalized' the ordinary football fan.[35]

The location of hooliganism has shifted over a period of time. Whereas it 'traditionally' took place in or near to stadiums, it has relocated away from the highly regulated environment of modern football grounds to other points where rival supporters can meet. Football stadia portray a powerful cultural identity.

McArdle, D, *From Boot Money to Bosman: Football, Society and the Law*

Many of the most illuminating recent discussions of hooliganism have been predicated upon John Bale's exploration of the significance of space as a social and cultural construct. For Bale, space provides an

---

29 *The Hillsborough Stadium Disaster (Final Report)*, ('Taylor' Report) CM 962 (1990) – see later, Chapter 17.
30 *Op cit*, fn 19, Greenfield and Osborn (2001), p 6.
31 See earlier, Chapter 2 p 87.
32 See later discussion, Chapter 17, p 690.
33 See later discussion, Chapter 17, p 692.
34 See later discussion, Chapter 17, pp 693–94 and *R (on the application of Brown) v Inner London Crown Court* (2003) concerning provision of banning order on conviction for ticket touting, LTL 15/12/2003 (unreported elsewhere).
35 For a review of the legislative framework, see Home Office Guidance on Football-Related Legislation, HC 34/2000.

outlet for the personal and collective expression of social agency, and for the imposition and exercise of power. For a football club's supporters, the football ground is the space that provides this outlet, and this is the case for the most sedate supporters as much as it is for those with a propensity for hooligan activity.[36]

For the real football hooligans, the spatial significance of the ground has been transformed by segregation. Prior to the erection of the fences, the ground had been the only forum in which rivalries were played out. In the years after segregation, hooligan confrontations increasingly occurred in train stations and to a lesser extent, in pubs and towns, city centres and the streets surrounding them.[37]

The policing of matches by the police and club stewards, together with the widespread use of CCTV,[38] would suggest that the various legal prohibitions concerning football fandom would be rigorously enforced. So what are the rates of arrest and prosecution under these various offences? Although there is national co-ordination in the 'fight' against football hooliganism with the National Criminal Intelligence Service taking a leading role,[39] it might be suspected that the local policy and actual practice of policing these offences will be an important factor in determining these rates. Each year the Home Office produces an analysis of the past football season's figures:

Football Offences Season 2003–2004 – Statistical Highlights

- Arrests for football related offences down by 10%, to 3,982 from 4,413

- Level of arrests reflects the lingering domestic football disorder problems

- Substantial increase in the number of football banning orders, up to 2,596 on 18 October 2004, from 1,794 on 14 August 2003

- Targeted police operations resulted in hundreds of high quality football banning orders. 1,263 new bans were made between 15 August 2003 and 18 October 2004

- Arrest levels remain low – the highest league attendances for 34 years, 29,197,510 produced 3,010 arrests – an arrest rate of 0.01%

- Vast majority of matches remain trouble-free – 50% of Premiership, 72% of 1st Division, 82% of 2nd Division and 89% of 3rd Division matches had one arrest or less. Overall, during the 2003–2004 season there was an average of 1.62 arrests per game

- 69% increase in the number of arrests for domestic breach of football banning order (from 37 to 63) reflecting an increased crackdown on individuals acting in breach of the terms of their order. No arrests, or evidence of anyone subject to a banning order attempting to travel overseas

- 57% of the total arrests were made outside of grounds, 85% of arrests for violent disorder outside of grounds

- 25% of matches completely police free

- Arrests of England fans decreased from 261 to 70 reflecting a highly successful Euro 2004 tournament

36 *Op cit*, fn 19, McArdle (2000), p 62; see also Bale, J, 'Playing at Home', in Williams, J and Wagg, S (eds), *British Football and Social Change* (1994), Leicester: Leicester University Press.

37 *Ibid*, p 69.

38 See Taylor, N, 'Closed Circuit Television: The British Experience' (1999) Stanford Technology Law Review 11.

39 See www.ncis.gov.uk.

- Statistics for football-related arrests tell only part of the story and need to be placed in context. Some incidents, especially public disorder outside of grounds, may result in few arrests whereas, in other cases, a large number of arrests may be indicative of preventative police action.[40]

The figures suggest that out of around 36 million attendances at professional games in England and Wales during the 2003–04 season, the amount of arrests per fan and per game are low.

Banning Orders

The figures also show the increased use of domestic and international banning orders, which can be seen as having increasingly successfully limited the movement of and excluded (from stadiums and surrounding areas) potential offenders. The 1999 and 2000 Acts have strengthened the ability for the courts to make both domestic and international banning orders when individuals are convicted of 'football-related' criminal offences. This extends to, for example, police officers refusing an individual fan the ability to travel abroad where the officer has 'reasonable suspicion' that the individual may be involved in hooligan activity.

Gough v Chief Constable of Derbyshire [2002] 2 All ER 985

Appeal by Gough and Smith ('the appellants') from a decision of the Divisional Court dismissing their appeals by way of case stated against banning orders for two years made against them under s 14B Football Spectators Act 1989 as amended by the Football Disorder Act 2000. The appellants had been convicted of violent offences in 1998 and 1990 respectively. In addition, each was the subject of a 'profile' prepared by the police that indicated repeated involvement in or near incidents of violence at or around football matches. By this appeal the appellants contended that: (i) the banning orders derogated from the positive rights on freedom of movement and freedom to leave their home country conferred on them by Art 1 and Art 2 Council Directive 73/148/EEC because it was not permissible to justify a banning order on public grounds, alternatively that no such grounds were made out on the evidence; (ii) the 2000 Act was contrary to Community law and therefore inapplicable insofar as it imposed mandatory restrictions on free movement within the Community on criteria that were not provided for or permitted by Community legislation; and (iii) it was contrary to the Community law principle of proportionality to ban an individual from travelling anywhere within the Community even if the relevant match or tournament was not taking place within the Community. The appellants further contended that the procedures for the imposition of banning orders infringed Art 6 and/or Art 8 European Convention on Human Rights because: (a) only the civil standard of proof was required to be satisfied; (b) there were insufficient procedural safeguards appropriate to the 'criminal charge' that a notice of application for a banning order constituted; and (c) the geographical scope of the orders was unacceptably broad.

HELD: (1) The court was satisfied that there was a public policy exception to Art 2 of the Directive. There was no absolute right to leave one's country. (2) Although it might initially appear disproportionate to ban all foreign travel, the court was satisfied that such a reaction was unsound. Banning orders were only to be imposed where there were strong grounds for concluding that the individual had a propensity for taking part in football hooliganism. It was proportionate that those who had shown such a propensity should be subject to a scheme that restricted their ability to indulge in it. (3) Although the civil standard of proof applied, that standard was flexible and had to reflect the consequences that would follow if the case for a banning order were made out. This should lead magistrates to apply an exacting standard of proof which, in practice, would be hard to distinguish from the criminal one (see *B v Chief Constable of Avon and Somerset Constabulary* [2001] 1 WLR 340 and *R v Manchester Crown Court, ex parte McCann* [2001] 1 WLR 1084). (4) Banning orders were not 'criminal charges', yet the standard of proof to be applied was akin to the

---

40 See the Home Office website for more statistical information on these figures – www.homeoffice.gov.uk.

criminal standard. In such circumstances, the Art 6 challenge failed. (5) If a banning order were properly made, any interference with an individual's Art 8 rights would be justified under Art 8(2) because it was necessary for the prevention of disorder. (6) On the facts, and even though the correct standard of proof had not been applied, the case for a banning order on each of the appellants was amply made out.

Appeals dismissed.[41]

Gough held that international banning orders under the Football Spectators Act 1989 as amended by the Football Disorder Act 2000 contravened neither European law on free movement of persons nor the European Convention on Human Rights. However, the feeling still continues that the civil liberties of football supporters that may have some football-related conviction are being restricted.[42]

BOXING: THE NOBLE ART?

Boxing occupies a curious position in English law. This will be discussed in detail later, but legal authority suggests that only sparring (practising) between boxers is lawful; actual boxing has no specific legal precedent and seems to be treated as an anomaly.[43] What is clear is that its legality and legitimacy has been debated over the last few years in the wake of deaths and critical injuries to a number of boxers in professional bouts. A number of Private Members' Bills have been initiated in Parliament to attempt to ban boxing.[44] There have also been numerous internal changes within boxing to promote safety. In amateur boxing, head guards have been worn for a number of years.[45] In 1982 the number of rounds in professional fights was reduced from 15 to 12 by the world's two main boxing authorities. This followed the death of the South Korean lightweight Duk Koo Kim after he was knocked out in the 14th round of a fight against the American Ray Mancini. In Britain, the deaths of Steve Watts, Bradley Stone[46] and James Murray[47] and the serious brain-damage of Michael Watson,[48] Gerald McClellan[49] and Paul Ingle[50] amongst others have led to the polarised opinions about whether boxing can be justified within contemporary society.

Boxing as a sport has not only been criticised in terms of safety issues; cynicism towards its commercialisation, spectacularisation and exploitation has grown. Mike Tyson is perhaps the epitome of such cynicism. Tyson's biting off the top of his opponent's ear in the course of his fight with

---

41 *Gough v Chief Constable of Derbyshire* [2002] 2 All ER 985 CA (Civ Div). Also see *R v Winkler* [2004] EWCA Crim 1590; (2004) 168 JPN 720 (CA (Crim Div)).

42 Beckham, G, 'The Price Of Passion: The Banishment Of English Hooligans From Football Matches In Violation Of Fundamental Freedoms' (2001) 25 Hastings International and Comparative Law Review 41; Pearson,G, 'Legitimate Targets? The Civil Liberties of Football Fans' (1999) 4(1) Journal of Civil Liberties 37. For a review of regulatory frameworks for football hooliganism in other European countries, see Siekmann, R, Gardiner, S, Soek, J, Offers, M and Mojet, H, *Football Hooliganism with an EU Dimension: Towards an International Legal Framework*, Agis Programme 2003, Project Jai/203/Agis/138, October 2004, TMC Asser Instituut, The Hague, The Netherlands.

43 For a detailed discussion see Gunn, M and Omerod, D, 'The legality of boxing' (1995) 15(2) Legal Studies 192; Pannick, D (QC), 'What's so special about boxing?' *The Times*, 14 March 1995; Brayne, H, Sargeant, L and Brayne, C, 'Could boxing be banned: a legal and epidemiological perspective' (1998) BMJ 1813; also see later, p 621.

44 See Parpworth, N, 'Parliament and the boxing Bill' (1996) 4(1) Sport and the Law Journal 24.

45 For their role in another sport, see Lennon, J, 'Head protectors in Gaelic games' (2000) 3(5) Sports Law Bulletin 12.

46 See 'Boxer's life in danger after bout' *The Guardian*, 28 April 1994.

47 'Your son is brain dead, surgeon tells boxer's parents' *The Observer*, 15 October 1995, p 3.

48 See 'Boxing: board bows before surgeon's advice' *The Guardian*, 17 October 1991, p 20.

49 Near-tragedy brings fresh calls for ban on boxing' *The Guardian*, 27 February 1995, p 3.

50 'Health Minister rejects calls to ban boxing' *The Guardian*, 18 December 2000, p 3.

Evander Holyfield in 1997, led to the revocation of his licence and a $3 million fine.[51] The two fighters had, however, shared nearly £40 million. Tyson's tirade after his win against Lou Savarese in Scotland led to another fine.[52] On this occasion there was already considerable controversy on whether he should have been allowed into Britain due to his previous conviction for rape.[53] The plethora of world boxing championships is also a symptomatic; the WBO (World Boxing Organisation), WBC (World Boxing Council), WBA (World Boxing Association) and IBF (International Boxing Federation) all compete to be seen as the leading world body in what is a highly fragmented regulatory framework.[54]

Should Boxing be Banned?

For supporters of boxing, the sport is about bravery and determination in the face of extreme physical danger. Boxing is seen as 'the noble art', the epitome of man's instinct to fight, a fine way of teaching self-discipline.[55] The history of sport discussed in Chapter 1 indicates that boxing can be seen as a continuum of the need for man to be able to fight to survive.

Opponents say that a civilised society should not tolerate organised brutality, however brave and heroic it might appear.[56] Professional boxing, in contrast to the highly regulated amateur game, is banned in Sweden, Norway and Iceland.[57] Such boxing is seen as far too violent and barbaric.[58] Boxing, compared with other sports, is distinguished by a clear goal of the infliction of physical injury upon the opponent:

R v Brown [1994] 1 AC 212

Lord Mustill: for money, not recreation or personal improvement, each boxer tries to hurt the opponent more than he is hurt himself, and aims to end the contest prematurely by inflicting a brain injury serious enough to make the opponent unconscious, or temporarily by impairing his central nervous system through a blow to the midriff, or cutting his skin to a degree which would ordinarily be well within the scope of s 20 (Offences Against the Persons Act 1861). The boxers display skill, strength and courage, but nobody pretends that they do good to themselves or others. The onlookers derive entertainment, but none of the physical and moral benefits, which have been seen as the fruits of engagement in many sports.[59]

Increasingly there is a middle ground of opinion that has started to question the legitimacy of boxing as currently organised. Greater safety and regulation are seen as a necessary development by almost

---

51 'Tyson faces fight for future after ear biting' *The Daily Telegraph*, 30 June 1997.

52 Arguments were raised at his disciplinary hearing that the fine breached the Human Rights Act 1998; see pp 235–41 for more information on the impact of the Act.

53 A judicial review of the Home Secretary's decision failed; see *Rape Crisis Centre v Sandly Brindley* (2001) LT 389; see also Naidoo, U, 'Return of the rapist' (2000) 97 Law Soc Gazette 14; Naidoo, U, 'Tyson rules' (2000) 3(3) Sports Law Bulletin 7; 'Update: Tyson' (2000) 3(4) Sports Law Bulletin 7.

54 See Mitchell, K, 'The King and I' *Observer Sports Monthly*, July 2000, p 44.

55 For a wide examination of boxing, see Sugden, J, *Boxing and Society: An International Analysis* (1996), Manchester: Manchester UP.

56 'Boxing – ban it?' *Panorama*, BBC Television, 25 October 1995 and 'Boxing on the ropes', www.bbc.co.uk/news, 18 December 2000.

57 Note also call for ban in Australia, see 'Another boxing ban call', www.bbc.co.uk/sport, 28 April 2001.

58 Though note the problem of defining violence and sports violence, see Gardiner, S, 'Tackling from behind: interventions on the playing field', in Greenfield, S and Osborn, G (eds), *Law and Sport in Contemporary Society* (2000), London: Frank Cass, pp 91–115.

59 *R v Brown* [1994] 1 AC 212, p 265.

everyone, especially in the professional game. The following extracts will assist the evaluation competing perspectives on the legitimacy of boxing:

Sutcliffe, S, 'The Noble Art?'

James Murray's death last year polarised opinion about the future of boxing. A disciplined forum for innate aggression or unreformable barbarism inviting brain damage and worse?

Dr Helen Grant is one of a handful of specialists who have looked inside the skull of a dead boxer. An expert on diseases of the nervous system, in 1986 she examined Steve Watt, who collapsed and went into a coma after being stopped in the 10th round of a Southern area title fight. 'He died, as Bradley Stone did last year, and Michael Watson and Gerald McClellan nearly died, of an acute bleed from a severed vein which led to rapid accumulation of blood squashing the brain stem down against the base of the skull. Although he was treated in hospital for a couple of days, it was clear that he had been brain dead in the ambulance.'

But the fatal injury was not all Grant saw when she examined Watt's brain. 'There were about 20 lesions in his brain from that fight and hundreds of scars from old lesions. Each one was about the size of a cherry. Such lesions heal after about six weeks. But the scars represent lost brain cells. In addition, the septum dividing the two ventricles (main cavities) was torn away; that was also old damage. Steve Watt was 29. He had been boxing for 10 years, I think. In my opinion, he was on the slippery slope to punch-drunk syndrome. The only logical place to hold a boxing match is in the operating theatre of a neurosurgical hospital,' she concludes. 'But major traumas are not the main point. It is the long-term diminution of the man's ability that is awful. If you take part in boxing for long, a great deal of your grey matter bites the dust, that is what it amounts to. I say that with every respect for boxers. I think they are the bravest people in the world.'

In 1982, prompted by concern over the hazards of *dementia pugilistica* and recurring ring fatalities, the British Medical Association (BMA), representing 80% of doctors, called for the abolition of boxing, professional and amateur. Their argument was that any punch to the head causes the soft tissue of the brain to 'swirl' in what by some evolutionary aberration is the skull's 'inhospitable environment' of internal bumps and ragged edges: damage is therefore inevitable and cumulative even where not traumatic. Ever since, the BMA has been an energetic and persuasively credible focus for the campaign against the sport in the UK. So began the latest phase of the boxing debate, a sporadic war of words in which a new volley is fired after every tragedy – most recently when James Murray died on 17 October last year. But the entrenched battle lines never move. They cannot. As presented, it is a for or against issue. To box or not to box.

Both combatants summon up science to state their case. The BMA is keen on the Haslar report which 'finds evidence of brain impairment among amateur boxers in the armed forces'. Boxing counters with the Butler report which found 'no evidence of cumulative effect'. Then both sides will quote the John Hopkins University Stewart Study of 'central nervous system function in US amateur boxers', the biggest research project ever undertaken on the sport. It notes an association between a large number of bouts and diminished performance in selected cognitive domains', as the BMA points out. Yet it also says that 'none of the changes we have observed to date, however, are clinically significant' – delighting the International Amateur Boxing Association so much that they published the whole report in a booklet of encouraging medical evidence 'to offensively counteract the permanent and unfounded attacks on Olympic style boxing'.

To the layman watching this ultimately pathetic ping-pong of tentative conclusions and prudent reservations, it soon becomes plain that the scientific jury is still out. Then a further cogent thought occurs: while both sides are keen to establish a hard-fact justification for their enthusiasms, that is not the heart of the debate at all. Nobody significant on the pro-boxing side denies the risk of brain damage. They would dispute only matters of quantity and degree. What really counts for both sides is their own gut feelings about common sense, decency and civilised behaviour.

BMA spokeswoman Dr Fleur Fisher insists that the anti-boxing campaign is scientific, not moral or emotional, yet she moves on to say 'it is difficult for doctors to see trauma inflicted on that most exquisite computer, the brain, and not take action. It would be unethical for us not to speak up. It is bizarre that it is utterly ungentlemanly to hit a man in the balls and OK to hit him in the brain. I see Nigel Benn fighting, psyched up, I think "Ooh" (cry of pain and frustration), you recognise the bravery, the determination but, in that McClellan fight, you see his head bouncing around, you are in agony watching it, thinking what the cost could be. After the Murray tragedy I watched the boxing world go through mourning in a state of denial, still trying to say it's a wonderful sport'.

Nicky Piper, chair of the Professional Boxers Association (PBA), the fighters' trade union, does say 'it is a wonderful sport. It is the oldest of all sports. It is man's instinct to want to fight and it is far better done in a civilised form with rules and controls. It comes down to knowing the risks, freedom of choice, making your own decision'. 'Boxing really does teach discipline,' adds Dr Adrian Whiteson, chief medical officer of the British Boxing Board of Control and chair of the World Boxing Council's medical commission. 'Diet, not smoking, very little drink, certainly no drugs, getting up early in the morning to do your roadwork, training, sparring. To do all this properly adds up to being true to yourself. Then it gives people from underprivileged areas – I know it sounds trite – a chance to better themselves.'

That is a traditional line Fisher particularly detests: 'What a terrible slur on our society if boxing was the only way that the enormous force of character in a young man like James Murray could have shone through.' Thus the spirit and substance of the stand-off between the BMA and the boxing world. It is impossible to say whether the feud has stimulated or set back progress to reduce the level of risk to boxers. Perhaps its value has been as a sort of moral background music accompanying more practical developments. But despite Fisher's assertion that 'the issue has moved' and that boxing is 'just unacceptable to society' in the aftermath of Murray's death, it is interesting to note that none of the three main political parties currently supports abolition.

For anyone who seriously cares about boxers, the realities of the sport's future are surely all about improving safety. The measures recommended by the medical panel convened by the Board after Bradley Stone's death in April 1994, will obviously help, despite the remaining grey areas which worry Nicky Piper and the PBA – for instance, qualified anaesthetists not compulsory at ringside – because they are not necessarily the best people for a war situation', says Whiteson and electrolyte drinks between rounds still banned in face of the venerable addiction to plain water.

Probably the most important rule change arose from a relatively recent realisation that pre-fight dehydration to make the weight could have deadly effects because, as well as weakening the body, it actually shrinks and therefore 'loosens' the brain. Conversely, rehydrating rapidly by slinging down three or four pints of water in half an hour can cause cerebral swelling. Basically, a dehydrated fighter is a disaster waiting to happen. In response, weigh-ins have been brought forward to at least 24 hours in advance of the fight. That has been followed up by introducing a sequence of weight checks through the fortnight ahead of major championships. If a boxer is outside carefully calculated parameters at any stage the bout will be cancelled or postponed. Enforced conscientiously, this could all but guarantee that boxers operate in their natural divisions.

Some of the best ideas are still being worked on. St John's Ambulance are devising a boxing-specific first-aid course, which will then be compulsory for all trainers. A government department is researching the possibility of reducing the impact of punches by altering glove materials and design. The World Boxing Council will probably back a British inspired study of psychometric testing – which hopefully would reveal mental malfunction even earlier than a scan would visually reveal an abnormality.

However Piper is very pleased that the Board is now championing annual and post-stoppage MRI (Magnetic Resonance Imaging) scans, replacing the cruder CT. MRI shows 'the architecture of the brain'. While the BMA stresses that it can only pick up damage already done – 'When the boxer is already doomed' by Dr Grant's reckoning – Whiteson says that it will enable the Board to withdraw boxers' licences at the first sign of anything amiss. His guiding principle, after all, is damage limitation because damage elimination is impossible without closing the sport down.

All the same, Whiteson has a militant warning for Piper about the coming of MRI scans and then psychometric testing: 'When we tell a boxer he has to stop, he must accept it and the PBA have to agree with us too, no going to law to get his licence back.' 'It is not a simple situation for us,' says Piper, diplomatically. 'I think if a test shows a problem we would invariably recommend the boxer to accept the Board's decision. But we are here to represent our members and we would have to take each case individually.' Whiteson won't wear any such ambivalence. 'You cannot ride two horses on this one,' he says, then raises the stakes a little further. 'Anyway when these test results start to come in the PBA may get the biggest shock of their lives. Who knows? Some of the biggest names may find they're not boxing any more.' It is a hint of the future that might give even the BMA their first and last laugh out of boxing. *Reductio ad absurdum pugilisticum*: the Board's safety measures could become so exacting that they have to refuse all professional boxers a licence, thereby delivering the quietus to a sport which, in truth, the abolitionists have barely laid a glove on.

If British boxing is to survive through the 21st century, it will have to bind itself together better than ever and, paradoxically, the sport's foot soldiers – the boxers – are going to have to lead the way. In one important detail government help is needed. For the 'official' sport to prosper, professional and amateur, and secure the safety standards developed at such cost, unlicensed boxing with its unsupervised and dangerous conditions must be made illegal.[60]

Boxing can be subject to Elias's 'civilising process' as discussed in Chapter 1. Perhaps the increased safety provisions in recent years are an extension of a continuing regulatory approach to boxing that has been going on since the mid-19th century when prize fighting (pugilism), where the winner took all, was a popular 'sport'. The facets of such a regulatory approach are outlined below:

Sheard, K, 'Aspects of boxing in the western "civilising process" '

There is little doubt that the pugilists of the 18th and 19th centuries would have difficulty recognising the boxing of today as being the same activity as the prize-fighting of their own time. In the intervening period the rules governing the sport have become increasingly complex, the bureaucratic organisations controlling it have become more powerful, and the law of the land has become more intrusive, more protective, than ever before. The violence of boxing has been controlled and contained. Prize-fighting, like fox hunting, can be said to have gone through a 'sportisation' process as it metamorphosed into boxing.

Using the framework developed by Dunning ... the modern sport of boxing can be said to have become more 'civilised' by a number of interrelated processes which include the following:

(1) Boxing in the early period of its development – ie from approximately the mid-17th to the early decades of the 19th century – was by present standards an extremely violent, brutal and bloody activity. However this aspect of the sport has since become increasingly regulated by a complex set of formal written rules. These rules not only define and control the sorts of violence which are permitted, but also outlaw violence in certain forms. The type of violent blow permitted and the areas of the body allowed to be attacked have been carefully delineated. Thus in the early stages of the sport's development it was possible to use a variety of what we would now call 'wrestling' holds to subdue an opponent. For example, the 'cross-buttock' throw, in which the opponent could be thrown over one's hip to the ground, was allowed. This could then be followed by a leap upon the fallen adversary, smashing one's knees into his exposed ribcage. Eyes could be gouged, hair pulled, and the testicles attacked. The natures of the punch, and the shape of the fist, have also been more carefully defined. The 'target' must be hit with the knuckle part of the hand. Hitting with an open glove – 'slapping' – is not allowed, possibly because it once permitted one's opponent to be injured by the lacing of the glove. 'Straight finger' blows to the eyes are also banned.

---

60   Sutcliffe, P, 'The Noble Art?' *Total Sport*, February 1996, pp 92–94.

(2) The rules also allow for penalties to be imposed upon boxers who infringe these rules. For example, points may be lost by boxers who hit 'below the belt', use the head illegally, or who receive constant warnings for holding and hitting. As early as 1838, under the London Prize Ring Rules, if a fighter went down deliberately without being hit or thrown – thus allowing him to rest for a while or corruptly 'throw' the fight – he could be disqualified and thus prevented from gaining any pecuniary or other advantage from the ploy. Under modern conditions champions who refuse to defend their titles within a specified time period, or who turn up to defend their titles overweight, may have the titles taken from them.

(3) Weight divisions have been introduced in an attempt to equalise conditions for all boxers. In the early days of the prize-ring, there were no weight divisions and men fought each other irrespective of poundage. It was not until the 1880s, after the widespread adoption of the Queensberry Rules of 1865, that a real effort was made to standardise weight divisions both in Britain and the United States. This innovation, of course, allowed boxing skill to have a greater impact upon the outcome of a contest than extra poundage or extra reach.

(4) Boxing has also been civilised by having restrictions placed upon the length of contests and the length of 'rounds'. These restrictions differ according to the experience of the boxers and the nature of the contest, for example whether or not a fight is for a title or whether it is an amateur or a professional fight. Most professional championship contests in Britain now follow the lead given by the European Boxing Union and are fought over 12 rounds. In America until relatively recently the stipulated 'distance' was 15 rounds. And before this – in both the US and Britain – the usual distance was twenty rounds of three minutes each. By contrast, prior to the 1860s, a round ended with a fall, and fights would be fought to a finish or until one of the fighters could not continue for any reason. In Britain, the largest number of rounds to be fought under this system was the 276 fought between Jack Jones and Patsy Tunney, in Cheshire in 1825.

(5) Physical protection has been introduced to protect boxers from the permitted and accidental violence they can inflict upon each other. For example, padded gloves, gum shields, head guards and groin protectors have all been introduced over the years. Gloves are claimed to have been first introduced in 1747, by Jack Broughton, an ex-prize-fighter, early 'entrepreneur' and boxing tutor, and supposed originator of the first code of written rules governing the 'sport' of boxing.[61]

The British Medical Association has been a particularly vociferous campaigner for the abolition of boxing. Their arguments are primarily on medical grounds, not only as far as the risk of traumatic tragedy is concerned, but also in terms of the cumulative damage that almost inevitably occurs during a prolonged boxing career:

BMA – 'Second report of the BMA Board of Science Working Party on Boxing'

The BMA's first working party report on boxing (1984) concluded that damage occurred to the brain and eye in both amateur and professional boxing and the BMA first called for a ban on boxing in 1987. Although there has been sustained opposition to a total ban (the British Boxing Board of Control and others described the report as relying too heavily on studies of boxing in other countries), there was also support from many quarters and widespread debate of the subject in the profession, in sporting circles, in the media and in parliament. The BMA has taken part in such discussions at all levels. The continued deaths and serious injuries to boxers have been widely reported and these, too, have provoked widespread debate about the dangers of boxing.

In 1992, following a review of the evidence on boxing published since 1984, the BMA stated that '. . . . this meeting calls for a total ban on amateur and professional boxing in the UK' and that '. . . as the next stage of our campaign against boxing we should seek a ban on children below the age of consent from boxing.'

---

61 Sheard, K, 'Aspects of boxing in the western "civilising process" ' (1997) 32(1) International Review for the Sociology of Sport 35, p 36.

The BMA's second report The Boxing Debate found no evidence to suggest that boxing was any safer in 1998 than it was when the BMA began its campaign. Pro-boxing arguments point out the fact that other sports result in injury, but the major concern over boxing is the brain damage sustained cumulatively rather than in any one recorded instance. Many people think that boxing could be made safer – by the use of head guards or shorter rounds, for example. Evidence suggests that these changes have minimal effect and in some cases might even have the reverse effect. Even the existence of medical specialists at the ring-side would not protect boxers suffering acute haematomas, for example. Boxing does not provide a unique opportunity for working class boys to 'better' themselves, which is a popular, if patronising, argument. However, the BMA believes that the Government should give more consideration to the provision of leisure facilities for the young, particularly in inner cities.

The BMA will continue to campaign for a total ban on boxing, while concentrating on areas such as boxing among children and the armed forces and doctors' involvement in the sport.

Injuries sustained during boxing

Brain: Whereas much of the rest of a boxer's body is protected by bone, fat, skin and well developed muscle, the brain is encased only by the skin-covered skull and attached to its interior by fine filaments of blood vessels and nerves. (One of the most useful models to describe the structure is that of a jelly suspended in a box by threads on all sides.) When a boxer sustains a direct blow to the head – which has been likened to the effect of being hit by a 12 lb padded, wooden mallet travelling at 20 mph – the head rotates sharply and then returns to its normal position at a much slower speed. In addition, the different densities of the different parts of the brain also move at different rates and the overall result is to create a 'swirling' effect inside the brain. Resulting damage: surface damage from brain hitting against inner surface of skull; tears to nerve networks; tension between brain tissue and blood vessels may cause lesions and bleeding; pressure waves created causing differences in blood pressure to various parts of the brain; (rarely) large intracerebral clots (Michael Watson).

Effect on boxer; grogginess, weakness, paralysis, weakening of limbs, inability to focus, possible loss of consciousness, ie the 'knock-out'. Long-term effects are cumulative and may not show immediately after a match. Most signs of damage are more likely to appear towards the end of a boxer's career or even after retirement. Stretched fibres may recover after many weeks but cut nerve fibres do not repair. Ex-boxers are less able to sustain natural ageing of brain or diseases of brain and may be more likely to suffer diseases such as Alzheimer's and Parkinsonism. Boxers' brains are smaller, surface grey matter is thinner, fluid-containing ventricles enlarged because of the decrease in white matter.

Injury to eye: Eye protected by very hard bone on a many sides but very vulnerable to direct hits from below. Damage may result from direct contact or from shock waves set up in fluid contents. Depending on force of blow damage may result in injury to retina (possible detachment – eg Frank Bruno), retinal haemorrhage, choroidal ruptures, etc.

Methods of detecting neurological injury

Computed Tomography (CT) and Magnetic Resonance Imaging (MRI) indicate structural changes to brain but don't show up deficiencies in brain function. This requires techniques such as electroencephalography (EEG), neuropsychometric testing and clinical neurological examination.

Professional boxers: studies confirm findings of 1984 report – professional boxers suffer from cumulative effect of damage to the brain, often resulting in 'punch drunk' syndrome. This damage may not show up until after the boxer has retired. The BBBC criticised the 1984 report for using studies which related to non-UK boxers and to boxers fighting before the introduction of strict controls. This report uses evidence collected since the introduction of these controls and using neuropathology studies derived almost exclusively from UK material.

Amateur boxers: evidence is far less clear cut – a number of studies found no evidence of cumulative brain damage. The sample populations were relatively tiny and most authors felt that it would be difficult to extrapolate their findings with any degree of certainty. Also, rules and regulations of boxing and medical controls differed widely from country to country, so very hard to make comparisons.

The BMA has been calling for more studies of boxers to be undertaken over long periods of time. In addition it suggests that the BBBC and the Amateur Boxing Association (AMA) are in a unique position to assist in recording injuries to both brain and eye.[62]

The danger that banning boxing will drive it underground is also a fear that is often raised: the spectre of an increase in prize fighting could be the consequence.[63] However, unlicensed boxing or prize fighting still occurs.[64] In addition, there is also a hybrid of unregulated boxing and martial arts, 'Extreme Fighting', that first emerged in a number of US States, and has been commercially promoted in the UK. It is a form of fighting where two bare-knuckled combatants are pitted against each other in a ring until only one is left standing. There are no rounds, no time-outs and no holds barred – just a lot of punching, kicking, choking, nose pinching, ear yanking and groin kneeing. Only eye gouging and biting are forbidden.[65]

Sheard, K, 'Aspects of boxing in the western "civilising process" '

Donnelly's belief that, if banned, boxing as we now know it would be driven underground is valid. Indeed, such a ban would probably have all sorts of unintended and unanticipated consequences. Boxers fighting under such circumstances might be at greater risk than they are at present. Donnelly's claim that 'the sport may, under present social conditions, be defensible' might also be concurred with. However it is doubtful whether the 'dominant class' or 'culture' is deterred from legislative action by a fear that death or serious injury might befall a few working-class young men. The debate, as Donnelly implicitly recognises, is primarily about the morality of boxing and the 'bad example' which it sets, and not the pain and suffering it causes. If boxing were to be made illegal and pushed behind the scenes as prize-fighting was in the nineteenth century – and even if it continued to exist in a subterranean way – this would indeed be a reflection of greater 'civilisation' as the term is used here.[66]

The fight between Nigel Benn and Gerald McClellan in 1995, that left McClellan with severe brain damage, was universally seen as a brutal fight where the protagonists went to the absolute brink. As is common, the bout was built up as a grudge fight.[67] This fight and others have crystallised the debate about the continued legitimacy of boxing in the context of an activity between two humans that has an essential natural link to our drive to survive.

Dyer, G, 'In the noble art, even failure contains greatness'

A couple of years ago, discussing boxing with an acquaintance, I was taking my usual line that boxing was an art form and so forth. If you ever see people fighting in the street it is ugly, hideous. In the ring, however, with the complex of rules governing what can and cannot be done, what begins in ugliness can become magnificent. Ban boxing and you ban the possibility of there being events like the

---

62 Report from 2001 – see www.bma.org.uk; also see BMA, *The Boxing Debate* (1993) London: BMA. Also see Constantoyannis and Partheni, Fatal Head Injury from Boxing: a Case Report from Greece, (2004) 38, British Journal of Sports Med 78–79.

63 See Parpworth, N, 'Boxing and prize fighting: the indistinguishable distinguished?' (1994) 2(1) Sport and the Law Journal 5; Jones, R, 'Deviant sports career: towards a sociology of unlicensed boxing' (1997) 21(1) Journal of Sport and Social Issues 37–52; *op cit*, fn 61, Sheard (1997); 'Raw scrap from boxing's underbelly' *The Guardian*, 23 May 1997, p 6; 'How bare-knuckled savagery became a noble art' *The Times*, 30 June 1997.

64 Darling, A, 'You cannot beat a good right hander' *Total Sport*, August 1997.

65 Mitchell, K, 'Mortal combat' *Observer Sport Monthly*, April 2001; Hall, S, 'Opposition grows to new sport of total fighting' *The Guardian*, 28 February 2000.

66 *Op cit*, fn 61, Sheard (1997), p 54. Also see Donnelly, P, 'On boxing: notes on the past, present and future of a sport in transition' (1989) 7(4) Current Psychology: Research and Reviews 331.

67 'Hype that stirs bad blood' *The Independent on Sunday*, 5 March 1995.

Leonard–Hagler or Ali–Foreman fights. The history of the century would be impoverished without them. 'But what you want to see,' interrupted my acquaintance, 'is two blokes beating the shit out of each other'. There is no refuting this claim. Since then, although I have continued to follow boxing, I accept that everything else one might say about the sport is predicated on this brutal truth. By these terms Saturday's encounter between Nigel Benn and Gerald McClellan was pretty much the ideal fight: two blokes smashing the shit out of each other.

My acquaintance, I should add, was speaking not as a critic of boxing but as a fan. Boxers do not fight for their fans. They do it for themselves. Nor, despite what Chris Eubank is always saying, do they box just for the money, any more than Martin Amis wrote his new novel for the money. Marvin Hagler said that if, when he died, his head was opened up all you would find would be a boxing glove because that is all there was in his life: boxing. Boxers box to prove something, to make their mark on the world, to become themselves. The price is often high but, as Robert Redford's film Quiz Show demonstrates, people will ruin themselves for more paltry things than a world boxing title. Besides, all sorts of activities take our lives away. A lifetime of factory work almost killed my father. First it wore him down and then, when he was exhausted, it came close to killing him. Ban factories and then ban boxing. As for the arts, music, painting and writing, they devour people. Greatness rarely comes cheap. Failure costs even more. Jazz begins with Buddy Bolden who, as Jelly Roll Morton said, 'went crazy because he really blew his brains out through the trumpet' . . .

As with Bolden so with boxers: they remind us how far most of us fall short of living our lives to the full. Anyone with any desire to live would gladly have traded places with McClellan, knowing what might happen. Benn was nervous, frightened before the fight. To stand any chance of beating McClellan he had to overcome not simply his opponent but himself. This ex-squaddie thereby achieved what for Nietzsche was the highest possible affirmation: to go to meet what was simultaneously your greatest desire and your greatest fear. McClellan used up his life in 30 minutes on Saturday, bringing to bear every fibre of his being, everything he had been born with, everything he had learned. In sport we often talk of athletes finding a second wind. Even those of us who have played only amateur sports have found this second wind. For boxers, though, as the trainer tells the battered protagonist of Tom Jones's The Pugilist at Rest, 'there is a third wind. It is between here and death'. Ali found it in his fight with Foreman; Eubank found it in his second fight with Watson (like most fighters he will never dare to look for it again). Benn and McClellan both found it on Saturday. For 10 rounds McClellan wrung out of his destiny every last drop that it could concede. Wrung it dry. Even in his failure there was greatness. The rest of us languish, content to let destiny pass us by, to happen to other people. Now McClellan is on a life-support machine. For most of us life is little more than a life-support machine.

Boxing is terrible, tragic. It is awful. That is why it exerts such power over us. The job of our lives, perhaps of evolution itself, is to become gentler, more pacific. But the raw materials we are dealing with have scarcely changed in thousands of years. As a species human beings have hardly changed physically since antiquity. When we watch boxers we feel exactly the same awe, horror and respect expressed by Plutarch in a passage from his Life of Theseus: 'At that time there were men who, for deftness of hands, speed of legs and strength of muscles, transcended normal human nature and were tireless. They never used their physical capacities to do good or to help others, but revelled in their own brutal arrogance and enjoyed exploiting their strength to commit savage, ferocious deeds, conquering, ill-treating, and murdering whosoever fell into their hands.'43

Safety in Other Sports

The debates concerning the legitimacy of boxing will no doubt continue, especially in the aftermath of periodic tragedies in the ring. Will there be a tragedy too far some time in the future? Now women

---

68   Dyer, G, 'In the noble art, even failure contains greatness' The Guardian, 27 February 1995, p 18.

are able to apply for licences and box, would the death or serious injury of a female boxer lead to a ban?[69] A paternalistic approach based on the protection of fighters is often advanced. Although it is argued that the incidents of catastrophic and traumatic injuries such as blood clots are less common and medical treatment has meant that the consequences are less severe, there is growing evidence of the cumulative nature of repetitive injuries to the head that can lead to degenerative brain conditions and possibly Parkinson's Disease.[70] Medical assistance ring-side and improved medical techniques have assisted in dealing with traumatic injuries, but the litigation that has arisen from the Michael Watson tragedy against the British Boxing Board of Control has put the responsibility on governing bodies to provide the most up to date medical support. In terms of risk management, this has sent a clear warning to governing bodies in other sports.[71]

'Safety measures in boxing'

In 2001, the BBBC introduced new safety measures:

For championship fights:
(1) Initial and secondary weight checks
For boxers:

(2) Training diaries
(3) Random weight checks
(4) Late arrival for official weigh-in will constitute a breach of the regulations
(5) Compulsory courses for trainers and seconds with particular respect to weight reduction, diet and nutrition
(6) The investigation of an amendment to permit the taking of isotonic drinks between rounds to combat dehydration[72]

There are some involved in boxing who argue that when compared with sports such as mountaineering and rock-climbing, the risks of boxing are minimal.[73] Boxing can usefully be compared with the equestrian sport of Three Day Eventing, another sport that has suffered a number of fatalities to riders (in addition to their horses) in recent years.

Latta, V, 'Report on the Eventing International Safety Committee Recommendations'

Following five fatalities in eventing in as many months in Britain last year (in the first half of 2000, there were a further five deaths – one in each of Britain, Switzerland and the USA, and two in Australia), the International Safety Committee was formed jointly by the *Fédération Equestre Internationale* (FEI) and the British Horse Trials Association (BHTA), the body responsible for administration of eventing in Britain. Its task was to review the findings from the fatalities, consider any areas of commonality and put forward recommendations to the FEI (as the world governing body) for making the sport safer. Although

---

69 Felix, A, 'The "Fleetwood Assassin" strikes a blow for female boxing' (1998) 1(3) Sports Law Bulletin 1.
70 Claims have been made that Muhammad Ali's illness is linked to punishing fights he was involved in towards the end of his career. In Britain, there have been attempts to prove links between heading footballs, especially in the 1950s and 1960s when old style leather balls were used that would soak up water and become extremely heavy, and medical conditions such as pre-senile dementia. If such a link can be proven, an individual could be eligible for Industrial Disability Benefit; see 'Industrial disability (Billy McPhail)' (1998) 1(4) and (1999) 2(3) Sports Law Bulletin 3 and 'Heading the ball killed striker' *The Guardian*, 12 November 2002, where South Staffordshire coroner Andrew Haigh recorded a verdict of 'death by industrial disease' on the former West Bromwich Albion striker.
71 For a further analysis of this case see later, p 650.
72 See 'Safety measures in boxing' (2001) 4(2) Sports Law Bulletin 7.
73 Statistics discussed in a Parliamentary debate on a Private Members' Bill in 1991, stated that between 1969 and 1980 in Britain, compared with two deaths in professional boxing, there were 93 in mountaineering and rock climbing, *Hansard*, 4 December 1991, col 293.

a large number of events come under national, rather than international control, the Committee expressed the hope that national federations adopt the recommendations as 'a positive step in the development of the sport'. The establishment by the FEI of a system for overall monitoring was considered necessary and could be established under the rules of membership.

The main objective of the Committee was to try and minimise the risk of horses falling and thereby to reduce the chances of riders being seriously injured. The majority of fatalities have been as a result of horses falling on the riders, some fatalities however have occurred as a result of horses crushing the riders against an obstacle. One of the recommendations was that a statistical database be established and maintained by the FEI for collation of information about accidents and to monitor safety provisions. In this way earlier recognition of common features in accidents could be detected. Mandatory rider passports were suggested. This would include details of three day event results (qualifying events for progression through the international levels), medical information regarding falls and any disciplinary measures. Such a system would alert organisers and officials to riders who had been recently injured, those disciplined for actions likely to give rise to problems and it would enable qualifications to be verified.

The Committee considered courses to have become too technical and the suggestion was for a limitation on the 'intensity of effort'. The recommendation was made to reduce the distance of the roads and tracks phase and add another compulsory break at three day events, also to reduce speeds where conditions warrant and at one day events. These proposals are designed to ensure horses are fresher for the cross-country phase thus reducing the likelihood of falls from tiredness. While falls can result with tired horses, they can result where horses are too fresh – particularly as they are generally ridden faster!

Fence construction was noted as important in helping minimise the risk of horses falling. While there has been discussion regarding 'deformable' fences, it was considered much more research is needed before such fences are introduced. This would include studies on their impact on the rules. Olympic and World Champion Blyth Tait broke his leg last year in a fall where his horse crushed him against a fence. Had the rail collapsed with the impact, Blyth believes his horse would have fallen on him.

Looking at the recommendations, many are sensible suggestions for constant monitoring and keeping abreast of changes in the sport and to ensure the sport is kept as safe as possible. It has to be remembered though that riding half a ton of animal with a mind of its own, involves risk. When you introduce undulating terrain, speed and obstacles into the equation, the risks increase ... Increased effort has been put into making courses safer and more inviting since the three horse fatalities at Badminton in 1992. Maybe those changes have resulted in a reduced consciousness of the risks. What has to be kept in mind is that a healthy respect for the fences is necessary to keep riders alert to the risks involved.

Different combinations of factors have been involved in each of the recent deaths in England. There is no common denominator of fence type, level of competition, conditions, and speed or experience of either horse or rider. In each case mistakes have been made by either horse or rider or in the communication between the two. Such incidents always bring greater awareness of the risks, particularly when involving someone you know. Unfortunately the nature of the sport makes those risks unavoidable.

In the final analysis, it is a risk sport. While all parties must work towards ensuring the sport is as safe as possible, riders must take ultimate responsibility for their actions. Changes will from time to time be necessary but hopefully they will not alter the character of the sport completely.[74]

There have been no concerted calls for the banning of Three-day Eventing. A risk management approach has been adopted to attempt to minimise the risk and learn more about the causes.[75] The

---

74 Latta, V, 'Report on the Eventing International Safety Committee Recommendations' (2000) 3(4) Sports Law Bulletin 4.
75 See later, pp 725–31 on discussion of risk management; also see Singer, E, Saxby, F and French, N, A Retrospective Case Control Study of Horse Falls in the Sport of Horse Trials and Three Day Eventing (2003) 35(2) *Equine Veterinary Journal* 139–145.

number of fatalities has dropped.[76] There is now a plethora of adventure and 'extreme' sports with continued inherent risks.[77] However, the distinguishing feature of boxing is its 'intentional' infliction of injury and a belief by some that it is increasingly anachronistic.

SPORT AND ANIMALS

As was discussed in Chapter 1, animals have been involved with human sport from the earliest times. The more barbaric forms of animal sport, involving fighting often to the death, are for the main part unlawful in modern Britain. The modern involvement of animals in sporting activities can clearly be labelled sport albeit a specific sub-division: they share the characteristics of sport that have been identified earlier. The recent attempts in Britain to prohibit fox hunting with hounds will be a focus of this section. The use of animals in sporting activities is varied. Animal sports can be divided into three categories:

Sporting Synergy of Humans and Animals

The first category is sports in which humans use animals in the pursuit of athletic excellence. These are mainly horse related sports; horse racing, show jumping, and polo. The so called 'sport of kings', horse racing, has a long history and remains immensely popular. Indeed, there is a substantial body of law surrounding the equine industry with issues such as riding accidents litigation, disciplinary issues concerning jockeys in horse racing and those concerned with protecting the pedigree of horses.

The Prohibition of Fighting Animals

The second category is sports where the animal is pitted against another animal either in competition of athletic prowess, for example, greyhound racing and pigeon racing, or fighting involving combat often to the death, for example, dog, quail and cock fighting.

The history of governmental regulation of animal fighting has already been chronicled.[78] Regulation clearly continues: prosecutions for cock fighting and dog fighting are not uncommon. The legal banning of these activities has often been based on their barbarity. Is this prohibition an example of Elias' 'civilising process' or rather moralistic government control?

Cashmore, E, *Making Sense of Sports*

Hugh Cunningham, in his *Leisure in the Industrial Revolution*, relates a Sunday morning meeting in London in 1816 at which several hundred people were assembled in a field adjoining a churchyard. In the field, 'they fight dogs, hunt ducks, gamble, enter into subscriptions to fee drovers for a bullock'. The Rector of the nearby church observed: 'I have seen them drive the animal through the most populous parts of the parish, force sticks pointed with iron, up the body, put peas into the ears, and infuriate the beast.'

---

76 But note 'Silent tribute for UK rider', www.bbc.co/sport, 5 September 2004.

77 See Gardiner *et al, Sports Law* (1998), 1st edn, London: Cavendish Publishing, pp 131–35, and the regulation of certain types of adventure holidays by the Activity Centres (Young Person's Safety) Act 1995, as a response to the Lyme bay canoe tragedy. Also see Grant, D, 'Is the activity tourism industry paying enough for safety?' (1999) 2(1) Sports Law Bulletin 11.

78 See earlier, Chapter 1.

Although condemned systematically from the eighteenth century, blood sports persist to this day, most famously in the Spanish bull rings and in the streets of Pamplona. England's bull ring in Birmingham reminds us that such events were not always confined to Spain; bull running ceased in England in 1825, a year after the founding of the Royal Society for the Prevention of Cruelty to Animals (RSPCA). The same organisation brought pressure against cock fighting, which was banned in 1835, only to go 'underground' as an illicit, predominantly working-class pursuit.

The decline of cock fighting, bull baiting and the like coincided with cultural changes that brought with them a range of alternative leisure pursuits. The whole spectrum of changes were part of what some writers have called the civilising process ... But, before we are tempted into assuming that barbaric tastes and activities have completely disappeared, we should stay mindful of Holt's caution: 'The tendency by members of all social classes to maltreat animals for excitement or gain is by no means dead even today.' Dog fighting in particular persists in the West to this day and dogs are bred for the specific purpose of fighting. In the early 1990s, amid a panic over the number of ferocious breeds proliferating, Britain banned the import of American pit bulls (such animals are required to be registered in Britain under the Dangerous Dogs Act 1991; there are about 5,000 unregistered pit bulls trained for fighting rather than as pets).[79]

Parker, C and Thorley, J, *Fair Game*

Cock fighting, like the baiting of dogs and badgers, is an illegal and secretive practice which legislation has failed to eliminate. It has an ancient history, probably originating in Greece about 500 BC. In Britain, it was the sport of all classes and its general acceptance made it difficult to ban. Edward III prohibited it as early as 1365, as did subsequently Henry VIII, Elizabeth I and Cromwell, but all with little success.

In England and Wales, a further attempt to stop cock fighting was made in the Cruelty to Animals Act 1835, which was followed with tougher penalties in 1849. However the sport continued quite openly throughout the country, most fights being too well-organised for the police and RSPCA to obtain evidence to sustain a conviction.

As late as 1930, a cock pit where the Chief Constable and magistrates were spectators was guarded by local police. Today, cock fighting does not have such powerful defenders, but the clandestine nature of the sport makes it difficult to enforce the law against it.[80]

Prosecutions for illegal cock fighting continue to be brought periodically:

Bowcott, O, '17 held in raid on cock fight by police and RSPCA'

RSPCA inspectors and police using a surveillance helicopter arrested 17 people yesterday when they raided a cock fight on a travellers' site in southeast London. Among those detained was a boy aged eight. Seven dead birds and several cock fighting spurs were seized from a shed on land between an industrial estate and the Thames marshes at Erith. The coordinated operation follows one last month when six people were arrested in a shed on allotments in Kelloe, Co Durham, and 14 dead cockerels, spurs, a weighing machine, a board listing birds' names and betting odds were found. The gathering was described as a well-organised event with seating around a fighting ring. The RSPCA yesterday condemned cock fighting as a barbaric blood sport. It had been outlawed since 1849, but still attracts a regular following.[81]

---

79 Cashmore, E, *Making Sense of Sports* (2000), 3rd edn, London: Routledge, p 70.
80 Parker, C and Thorley, J, *Fair Game* (1994), London: Pelham, p 271.
81 Bowcott, O, '17 held in raid on cock fight by police and RSPCA' *The Guardian*, 10 April 1995, p 2. For continued activity abroad, see 'Deadly game for the birds of play', *The Guardian*, 20 December 1996, p 6; also see 'Cockfighting' (2001) 4(4) Sports Law Bulletin 4 and 'Ten guilty of cock-fight charges', 12 April 2005, www.bbc.co.uk/news.

Legal Regulation of Blood Sports

The third category includes sports where the animal becomes pitted against human in test of athletic excellence by use of a gun, other instrument or animal agency. These can be termed 'blood sports'. Examples include angling, one of the most popular sports in Britain with a myriad of regulatory legislation,[82] hunting, and although not carried out in Britain, bull fighting.

It is this point that philosophical arguments may raise: can blood sports be morally justified? Hunting includes not only fox hunting, but connected activities such as deer, stag and mink hunting, and also hare coursing. These are all lawful within the qualifications of legal safeguards.

The historical regulation of blood sports was discussed in Chapter 1. They can be divided into three types: baiting including bear, bull and badger baiting; fighting including with dogs and cocks; and hunting, including birds and foxes. Fox hunting is now unlawful, and the debate about its legitamacy will be evaluated shortly, but first a short summary of the legal position of hunting sports is provided.

Activity	Lawful	Legal Prohibition or Qualification
Deer hunting	Yes	*Deer Act 1991*
Hare coursing	Yes	*Hares Act 1848; Protection of Animals Act 1911*
Mink hunting	Yes	*Protection of Animals Act 1911*
Bird shooting	Yes	*Wildlife and Countryside Act 1981; Games Act 1831 and Games Act 1971*
Cock fighting	No	*Cock fighting Act 1952; Protection of Animals Act 1911*
Dog fighting	No	*Protection of Animals Act 1911; Protection of Animals (Amendment) Act 1911*
Badger baiting	No	*Protection of Badgers Act 1992*
Angling	Yes	*Salmon and Freshwater Fisheries Act 1975; Control of Pollution (Angler's Lead Weight) Regulations 1986*
Fox hunting	No	*Protection of Animals Act 1911*

This table summarises the main statutory regulation of blood sports in Britain. Those activities that are lawful are lawful in a qualified sense: they are typically subject to temporal and species based restrictions. There are also various general Acts; for example, the Protection of Animals Act 1911 prohibits cruelty to domestic or captive animals; the Wildlife and Countryside Act 1981 protects birds such as the golden eagle and animals such as the otter. Additionally, there exists a large body of law concerning poaching and land used for blood sports.

The regulatory framework has been developed often in a piecemeal and arbitrary way. Extensive campaigning has often been needed to improve legal prohibition and protection of the hunted animals. A good deal of the legislation has been initiated in the form of Private Members' Bills. One

---

82   See Gregory, M, *Angling and the Law* (1992), London: Charles Knight. There have been calls for similar prohibitions on angling as with fox hunting, eg 'Moves are launched to untangle legal lines' *The Times*, 10 July 1997, p 45, concerning a new regulatory framework for angling, but the Labour Government since 1997 has argued that fishing is not cruel and not in need of additional controls.

activity that has been controlled by a series of legislative controls is badger baiting. First controlled in 1835 at the same time as prohibition of baiting of other captive animals such as bears and bulls, badger baiting nevertheless continued. Subsequently Parliament enacted the Badgers Act 1973 which made it a criminal offence for a person to 'wilfully kill, injure or take, or attempt to kill, injure or take, any badger'. Due to pressure from fox hunters, the legislation contained an exemption allowing landowners and their agents to persecute badgers living on their land. The subsequent Wildlife and Countryside Act 1981 strengthened the law to make it an offence to be in possession of a badger or part of one; however, the growing trend of attacking badger setts with dogs was not specifically prohibited, although the Wildlife and Countryside (Amendment) Act 1985 placed the burden of proof upon the accused. Two Private Members' Bills attempted to improve the regulatory framework. The first failed[83] but the second became the Badger Bill 1991[84] and subsequently the Protection of Badgers Act 1992. It is now an offence to interfere with a badger sett without a government licence.

Fox Hunting

The legitimacy and legality of fox hunting has continually been questioned in recent years. The whole issue of fox hunting is one that is highly charged. The debate has two well-organised protagonists: the League Against Cruel Sport[85] and the Countryside Alliance, an umbrella coalition formed in 1995 to campaign against any prohibition on hunting and the general way of life in the country.[86] Underlying the debate are complex questions of morality and the rights of animals. The controversy surrounding fox hunting persists. Many issues have surrounded the use of land for hunting, first the rights of those participating in the hunt and second, the rights of protesters.[87]

Although many blood sports including animals have been severely regulated or banned, the lawfulness of fox hunting until recently indicates the deep-seated role the activity has played in British Society. Fox hunting's longevity needs to be explained:

Cashmore, E, *Making Sense of Sports*

Blood sports in general, and fox hunting in particular, are seen as having central importance by Norbert Elias and his collaborator Eric Dunning. The 'civilising' of society demanded greater personal self-control and a stricter constraint on violence, but the process of hunting or just observing allowed 'all the pleasures and the excitement of the chase, as it were, mimetically in the form of wild play' (1986). While the passion and exhilaration associated with hunting would be aroused, the actual risks would be absent in the imagined version (except for the animals, of course) and the effects of watching would be, according to Elias and Dunning, 'liberating, cathartic'. The comments could be applied without alteration to all of the activities considered so far. They are products of a human imagination ingenious enough to create artificial situations that human evolution has rendered irrelevant. But, once created, they have seemed to exert a control and power of their own, eliciting in both participants and audience a pleasurable excitement that encapsulates the thrill or 'rush' of a hunt, yet carries none of the attendant risks.[88]

---

83   Badger Sett Protection Bill 1989, introduced by Tony Banks MP.

84   Introduced by Roy Hughes MP.

85   See www.league.uk.com and *Wildlife Protection: The Case for the Abolition of Hunting and Snaring* (1992), London: League Against Cruel Sports.

86   See www.countryside-alliance.org.

87   They are regulated by the Criminal Justice and Public Order Act 1994, which criminalised the normally civil law wrong of trespass with hunt saboteurs seen to be the major target; see Bailey, S, Harris, D and Jones, B, *Civil Liberties: Cases and Materials* (1995), 4th edn, London: Butterworths; *The Unacceptable Face of Protest* (1993), London: British Field Sports Society.

88   *Op cit*, fn 79, Cashmore (2000), pp 66–67.

Fox hunting is Elias's favourite example. Once synonymous with the word 'sport', fox hunting is now an anachronism and pressure against it would have no doubt prompted its demise were it not a pursuit practiced exclusively by England's landowning elite. Developing in the late 18th century, this peculiarly English sport was quite unlike the simpler, less regulated, and more spontaneous forms of hunting of other countries and earlier ages where people were the main hunters and foxes were one amongst many prey (boar, red deer, and wolves being others). Fox hunting (itself an example of a figuration) was bound by a strict code of etiquette and idiosyncratic rules, such as that which forbade killing other animals during the hunt. Hounds were trained to follow only the fox's scent, and only they could kill, while humans watched.

The fox itself had little utility apart from its pelt; its meat was not considered edible (not by its pursuers, anyway) and, while it was considered a pest, the fields and forests were full of others which threatened farmers' livestock and crops. The chances of anyone getting hurt in the hunt were minimised, but each course in the wall of security presented a problem of how to retain the immediacy and physical risk that were so important in early times. Elias believes that the elaboration of the rules of hunting were solutions. The rules served to postpone the outcome, or finale of the hunt and so artificially prolong the process of hunting. 'The excitement of the hunt itself had increasingly become the main source of enjoyment for the human participants.' What had once been foreplay to the act of killing became the main pleasure. So the fox hunt was a virtual 'pure type' of autotelic hunt: the thrill for participants came in the pace and exhilaration of the chasing and the pleasure of watching violence done without actually doing the killing.

But the influence of the civilising spurt is apparent in the restraint imposed and exercised by the participants. The overall trend was to make violence more repugnant to people, which effectively encouraged them to control or restrain themselves. Elias stresses that this should be seen not as a repression but as a product of greater sensitivity. The fox hunters did not secretly feel an urge to kill with their own hands; they genuinely found such an act disagreeable, but could still find pleasure in viewing it from their horses – what Elias calls 'killing by proxy'.

Despite all attempts to abolish them, hunts persist to this day, probably guided by appetites similar to those whetted by the sight of humans being masticated by sharks. Hundreds of millions of *Jaws* fans can attest to the enjoyable tension provided by the latter, albeit through the medium of film. While Elias does not cover the modern hunts, we should add that their longevity reveals something contradictory about the civilising trend and the impulse to condone or even promote wanton cruelty. To ensure a long and satisfying chase, and to be certain that foxes are found in the open, 'earth stoppers' are employed to close up earths (fox holes) and badger sets in which foxes may take refuge. Many hunts maintain earths to ensure a sufficient supply of foxes through the season (foxes used to be imported from the continent). The hunt does not start until after 11 am to allow the fox time to digest its food and ensure that it is capable of a long run. During the course of a hunt, a fox may run to ground and will either survive or be dug out by the pursuant dogs, a virtual baiting from which even the dogs emerge with damage. New hounds are prepared by killing cubs before the new season, a practice observed and presumably enjoyed by members of the hunt and their guests.

In Elias's theory, fox hunting was a solution to the problems created by the accelerating trend toward civilisation and the internal controls on violence it implied. The closing up of areas of excitement, which in former ages had been sources of pleasurable gratification (as well as immense suffering), set humans on a search for substitute activities and one which did not carry the risks, dangers, or outright disorder that society as a whole would find unacceptable what Elias, in the title of one of his books, calls the Quest for Excitement. The English form of fox hunting was only one example of a possible solution, but Elias feels it is an 'empirical model', containing all the original distinguishing characteristics of modern sport. Other forms of sport, such as boxing, soccer, cricket, and rugby showed how the problem was solved without the use and abuse of animals.[89]

---

89 *Ibid*, pp 81–83.

The argument in favour of fox hunting tends to focus on the practical need to control the fox because of it being a great pest to the farmer. Philosophically hunters focus on fox hunting as a part of the natural order:

Ortega, Y and Gasset, J, 'The ethics of hunting'

Every authentic refinement must leave intact the authenticity of the hunt, its essential structure, which is a matter of a confrontation between two unequal species. The real care that man must exercise is not in pretending to make the beast equal to him, because that is a stupid utopia, a beatific farce, but rather in avoiding more and more the excess of his superiority. Hunting is the free play of an inferior species in the face of a superior species. That is where one must make some refinement. Man must give the animal a 'handicap', in order to place him as close as possible to his own level, without pretending an illusory equivalence, which, even if it were possible, would annihilate ipso facto the very reality of the hunt. Strictly speaking, the essence of sportive hunting is not raising the animal to the level of man, but something much more spiritual than that: a conscious and almost religious humbling of man, which limits his superiority and lowers him toward the animal.

I have said 'religious' and the word does not seem excessive to me. As I have already pointed out, a fascinating mystery of nature is manifested in the universal fact of hunting: the inexorable hierarchy among living beings. Every animal is in a relationship of superiority or inferiority with regard to every other. Strict equality is exceedingly improbable and anomalous. Life is a terrible conflict, a grandiose and atrocious confluence. Hunting submerges man deliberately in that formidable mystery and therefore contains something of religious rite and emotion in which homage is paid to what is divine, transcendent, in the laws of nature.[90]

Arguments against fox hunting focus both on the falsity of the view that foxes are a major problem in the country and that hunting is the best way to counter it. They also focus on the 'rights' of animals not to be hunted:

Regan, T, 'Why hunting and trappings are wrong'

Since animals can pose innocent threats and because we are sometimes justified in overriding their rights when they do, one cannot assume that all hunting or trapping must be wrong. If rabid foxes have bitten some children and are known to be in the neighbouring woods, and if the circumstances of their lives assure future attacks if nothing is done, then the rights view sanctions nullifying the threat posed by these animals. When we turn from cases where we protect ourselves against the innocent threats wild animals pose, to the activities of hunting and trapping, whether for commercial profit or 'sport', the rights view takes a dim view indeed. Standard justifications of the 'sport' of hunting – that those who engage in it get exercise, take pleasure in communion with nature, enjoy the camaraderie of their friends, or take satisfaction in a shot well aimed – are lame, given the rights view. All these pleasures are obtainable by engaging in activities that do not result in killing any animal (walking through the woods with friends and a camera substitutes nicely) and the aggregate of the pleasures hunters derive from hunting could only override the rights of these animals if we viewed them as mere receptacles, which, on the rights view, they are not.

The appeal to tradition – an appeal one finds, for example, in support of fox hunting in Great Britain – has no more force in the case of hunting than it does in the case of any other customary abuse of animals – or humans. All that appeals to tradition signal in this case, and all they signify in related contexts, is that it is traditional to view animals as mere receptacles or as renewable resources. These appeals to tradition, in other words, are themselves symptomatic of an impoverished view of the value animals have in their own right and thus can play no legitimate role in defending a practice that harms

---

90 Ortega, J and Gasset, Y, 'The ethics of hunting', in Morgan, W and Meier, K, *Philosophic Inquiry in Sport* (1995), 2nd edn, Champaign, Illinois: Human Kenetics.

them. Such appeals are as deficient in Great Britain, when made in behalf of the 'sport' of fox hunting, as they are when made in Japan or Russia in defence of commercial whaling, or in Canada in defence of the annual slaughter of seals. To allow these practices to continue, if certain quotas are not exceeded, is wrong, given the rights view, for reasons that will become clearer as we proceed ...

The rights view categorically condemns sport hunting and trapping. Though those who participate in it need not be cruel or evil people, what they do is wrong. And what they do is wrong because they are parties to a practice that treats animals as if they were a naturally recurring renewable resource, the value of which is to be measured by, and managed by reference to, human recreational, gustatory aesthetic, social and other interests.[91]

The Burns Report

The Labour Party came into power in 1997, promising a free vote on fox hunting. In June 1997, a Private Members' Bill had its first hearing, but was considered to have little hope of successfully progressing without some compromise on its total ban.[92] Campaigners on both sides of the argument were vociferous in stating their cases. The Burns Inquiry was convened to prepare a report on:

(1) the practical aspects of different types of hunting with dogs and its impact on the rural economy, agriculture and pest control, the social and cultural life of the countryside, the management and conservation of wildlife, and animal welfare in particular areas of England and Wales;

(2) the consequences for these issues of any ban on hunting with dogs; and

(3) how any ban might be implemented.[93]

One of the issues raised was whether a total ban would be illegal under the Human Rights Act 1998.

> **Burns Report,** *Report of the Committee of Inquiry into Hunting with Dogs in England and Wales*
>
> Compatibility with the European Convention on Human Rights (ECHR)
>
> **10.5** A fundamental argument put to us by the Countryside Alliance was that a ban on hunting would be incompatible with the ECHR. This matter was considered at some length in the papers prepared by the Countryside Alliance and Deadline 2000 and was also discussed fully at the seminar itself. The papers helpfully included Opinions by distinguished Counsel on both sides. Counsel's Opinion, relied on by Deadline 2000 specifically addressed a draft Bill which had been prepared, whilst Counsel for the Countryside Alliance had considered the matter in principle.
>
> **10.6** Counsel for the Countryside Alliance (Edward Fitzgerald QC) concluded that, in his opinion, there was 'a serious argument that the proposed ban on hunting with dogs will violate [both] Article 1 of Protocol I and Article 8'. Counsel for IFAW (David Pannick QC, Richard Drabble QC and Rabinder Singh), relied on by Deadline 2000, concluded that, in their opinion, 'a ban on hunting wild mammals with dogs would be compatible with the Convention'.
>
> **10.7** The Convention rights will become part of national law from 2 October 2000, when the key provisions of the Human Rights Act 1998 come into force. Under the Act the higher courts will be able to make a declaration of incompatibility with the Convention in relation to an Act passed by Parliament.

---

91 Regan, T, 'Why hunting and trappings are wrong', in William, J and Meier, K (eds), *Philosophical Inquiry in Sport* (1995), 2nd edn, Champaign, Illinois: Human Kinetics, p 46; see also Brooman, S and Legge, D, *Law Relating To Animals* (1997), London: Cavendish Publishing, for full discussion on arguments for and against fox hunting and also generally on issues concerning animals and sport.

92 'Foxhunters scent victory as ban recedes' *The Independent*, 30 July 1997, p 1.

93 Burns Report, *Report of the Committee of Inquiry into Hunting with Dogs in England and Wales* (2000); see www.huntinginquiry.gov.uk.

10.8 It was clear to the Committee from the submissions and Opinions on both sides that the main argument centred on two Articles in the Convention: Article 8, which deals with respect for private life, and Article 1 of Protocol I, which deals with the right to peaceful enjoyment of property. (Although there has also been some discussion in this context of Articles 5 (right to liberty and security), 6 (right to a fair trial), 11 (freedom of assembly and association) and 14 (prohibition of discrimination), it does not appear that a strong case could be mounted for arguing that a Bill to ban hunting would infringe any of these articles.)

Article 8

10.9 Article 8 provides as follows:

1 Everyone has the right to respect for his private and family life, his home and correspondence.

2 There shall be no interference by a public authority with the exercise of this right except such as is in accordance with the law and is necessary in a democratic society in the interests of national security, public safety or the economic well-being of the country, for the prevention of disorder or crime, for the protection of health or morals, or for the protection of the rights and freedoms of others.

10.10 There are two main issues: whether hunting with dogs can be regarded as coming within the concept of 'private life' and, if it does, whether interference is justified on the grounds set out in Article 8 (2). On the first issue, both sides agree that 'private life' may encompass certain aspects of social interaction with others. But they disagree on whether a ban on hunting with dogs would constitute an interference with this right. The Countryside Alliance contend that it is an activity which is strongly identified with the ethos of a local community. They also point out that it takes place, at least in part, on private land. Deadline 2000, on the other hand, argue that the nature of the activity, even when it takes place on private land, is essentially public in character. The Fitzgerald Opinion concluded that a ban would 'probably constitute an interference with Article 8 rights', albeit not 'one of the more intimate or core aspects of private life'. The Pannick Opinion concluded that 'we do not consider that hunting with dogs falls within the concept of private life at all'.

10.11 If it were the case that private life is interfered with, the issue of a legitimate objective (ie the protection of morals) seemed to the Committee to be crucial. That question seemed to the Committee to turn on two key factors: first, whether hunting with dogs is viewed as inherently or necessarily causing unnecessary suffering; second, whether, if it was so seen by members of the public or Parliament, this could constitute sufficient 'moral' grounds in the absence of objective, scientific evidence.

10.12 Both sides agree that, if Article 8 (1) is engaged, the key tests are whether the interference has a legitimate basis (ie whether interference is necessary 'for the protection of morals'), whether there is 'a pressing social need' for the interference and whether it is proportionate. In reaching a judgment on the former, the European Court of Human Rights would allow a State a 'wide margin of appreciation' – on the basis that States are better able to judge what is appropriate in their particular circumstances. Similarly, the domestic court would be likely, we understand, to afford Parliament 'a discretionary area of judgment'. The Countryside Alliance argue, however, that it would not be sufficient simply to assert that hunting with dogs is immoral: there would need to be objective evidence that hunting involves unnecessary suffering, including by reference to that involved in other methods. They also point out that this argument is particularly relevant to the draft Bill prepared by Deadline 2000 since the latter would penalise hunting *per se*, without any need to prove unnecessary suffering. Deadline 2000, on the other hand, argue that the test would be met in the light of the fact that Parliament would have decided on a free vote, after an inquiry and much public debate, that hunting is morally wrong and cruel. The question of a permissible approach to 'moral' grounds was also addressed in supplementary representations: a closing submission by the Countryside Alliance and a further opinion for IFAW, relied on by Deadline 2000.[543]

10.13 The Countryside Alliance also argue that a ban would fail the 'proportionality' test. This is in the light of what they regard as the lack of firm scientific evidence in respect of unnecessary suffering and the impact that a ban would have on rural communities and people's lives and livelihoods. Deadline 2000 argue, on the other hand, that their draft Bill meets the test since it does only what is necessary to achieve its purpose – to ban hunting with dogs – and because it contains suitable exceptions and limitations.

Article 1 of Protocol I

10.14 Article 1 of Protocol I provides as follows:

'Every natural or legal person is entitled to the peaceful enjoyment of his possessions. No-one shall be deprived of his possessions except in the public interest and subject to the conditions provided for by law and by the general principles of international law.

The preceding provisions shall not, however, in any way impair the right of a state to enforce such laws as it deems necessary to control the use of property in accordance with the general interest or to secure the payment of taxes or other contributions or penalties.'

10.15 Both sides agree that Article 1 of Protocol I is engaged, in the sense that a ban on hunting, though it would not actually deprive someone of the use of land or the animals involved, would constitute a control on their use (according to Deadline 2000) or an interference with the substance of ownership (according to the Countryside Alliance). The issue then turns on whether this is justified in accordance with 'the general interest' and whether a fair balance is struck between the general public interest and the interference with the fundamental rights of individuals.

10.16 Both sides also agree that the 'general interest' test is interpreted by the European Court with considerable latitude to national authorities. The approach to which we were referred is to ask whether Parliament's judgment as to what was in the public interest is 'manifestly without reasonable foundation'. The Countryside Alliance, however, question whether this 'general interest' test is satisfactorily met. They also argue that, even if the court held that it was met, there is a strong likelihood that a balance would require economic compensation for owners of packs and for landowners. Deadline 2000, on the other hand, argue that the Bill meets the 'general interest' test since it is concerned with the protection of morals and the prevention of cruelty and that it is proportionate to these aims. They also take the view that any losses to landowners would be speculative – other activities such as shooting and humane trapping would be unaffected – and that, in any event, no form of compensation scheme would be required.

Conclusions

10.17 Legislation to ban hunting might be open to challenge under Article 1 Protocol I (property rights) and, possibly, Article 8 (respect for private life) of the European Convention on Human Rights. We are not qualified to express an opinion on whether any challenge along these lines would succeed. Key questions would be whether the undoubted interference with property, and possibly with private life, was justified under Convention principles, bearing in mind the nature of the interference and the latitude enjoyed by the national authorities. An important consideration would be whether legislators could point to unnecessary suffering or some other reference point beyond mere disapproval, to reflect the general interest (or, to the extent necessary, the protection of morals and pressing social need). A relevant issue would be the form of the Bill: one which required proof of unnecessary suffering, or some similar test, would be less open to argument than one which banned hunting *per se*.[94]

Article 1 might be the most likely challenge to a total ban on hunting with dogs. The provision would allow a landowner to claim 'every natural or legal person is entitled to the peaceful enjoyment of his possessions'. As indicated in the Report, the principle of proportionality is crucial. This general principle of the ECHR has been expressed as the 'fair balance' test, which is 'struck between the demands of the general interest of the community and the requirements of the protection of the individual's fundamental rights'.[95] If the interference with the property (not being able to use it for hunting) is disproportionate to the aim being pursued (the ban), there may well be a violation of

---

94   *Ibid*, paras 10.5–10.17.
95   See *Sporrong and Lonnroth v Sweden* (1982) 5 EHRR 35, para 69; for more on impact of the Human Rights Act 1998 on sport, see pp 217–22.

Art 1. In balancing these claims, a crucial question is the morality of hunting and whether the hunted animal does in fact suffer unnecessarily. This argument relates to a fundamental issue concerning whether landowners (or more widely property owners) can resist the State's right to criminalise activities that may impact upon the property owners' rights to enjoy use over that property.[96]

Conclusion

In November 2000, a Bill was introduced concerning hunting with dogs but ran out of parliamentary time due to the June 2001 General Election. In 2004, another vote on a reintroduced bill took place:

Hunting Bill 2004

1 Hunting wild mammals with dogs

A person commits an offence if he hunts a wild mammal with a dog, unless his hunting is exempt.

2 Exempt Hunting

(1) Hunting is exempt if it is within a class specified in Schedule 1.

(2) The Secretary of State may by order amend Schedule 1 so as to vary a class of exempt hunting.

3 Hunting: assistance

(1) A person commits an offence if he knowingly permits land which belongs to him to be entered or used in the course of the commission of an offence under section 1.

(2) A person commits an offence if he knowingly permits a dog which belongs to him to be used in the course of the commission of an offence under section 1.

The Bill was supported by 339 to 155 votes and although there was considerable resistance in the House of Lords, the Government applied the Parliamentary Act 1949 to force through the legislation without the agreement of the House of Lords. The Hunting Act 2004 came into force on 18 February 2005.[97] Legal challenges have been made questioning the legality of the Act on grounds that the Government should not have been able to impose the Parliamentary Act.[98]

RACISM IN SPORT

Racism in sport as with racism generally in society is an endemic problem in Britain.[99] Institutionalised racism has been accepted to exist in many areas of society.[100] The focus of this section

---

96 For further discussion, see Rook, D, 'A ban on hunting with dogs' [2001] NLJ 373. She believes in fact that a claim under Art 1 of the ECHR would fail in these circumstances as 'the legislation (a total ban) pursues a legitimate aim and is proportionate to the attainment of that aim'; also 'Fox hunt ban "breaches human rights law" ' *The Guardian*, 25 November 2003.

97 See 'Hunt ban to be policed "as usual" ', www.bbc.co.uk/news, 24 February 2005.

98 *R (on the application of Jackson) v Attorney-General* [2005] EWCA Civ 126 (2005) *The Times*, 17 February 2005.

99 For a number of perspectives on this issue, see McDonald, I and Carrington, B (eds), *'Race', Sport and British Society* (2001), London: Routledge including Gardiner, S and Welch, R, 'Sport, racism and the limits of "colour blind" law', pp 133–151.

100 See MacPherson, W (Sir), *The Stephen Lawrence Inquiry: Report on the Inquiry by Sir William Macpherson of Cluny*, Cm 4262 (1999), London: HMSO. The report followed the public inquiry into the killing of Stephen Lawrence in South London in 1994. The report considered that institutionalised racism is 'not solely through the deliberate actions of a small number of bigoted individuals, but through a more systematic tendency that could unconsciously influence police performance generally' (para 6.5). Also see 'Amnesty attacks racism in criminal justice system' *The Guardian*, 25 July 2001.

will be on the regulation of spectator racism against those participating in sport, although there are other types of racism or racist issues found in sport. Growing concern has been voiced about the low levels of representation of sports administrators or coaches from ethnic minority backgrounds, especially from ex-sports men and women. Another is that sporting excellence by black athletes, that is, those from an Afro-Caribbean background, has become itself a racist issue; many racist myths and scientific half-truths have been spun to provide psychological, physiological and genetical explanations between blacks and whites.[101] A third issue is the way that it seems Afro-Caribbean school children are channelled into sport due to lack of available alternative opportunities. This is often in deference to perceived stereotypes that blackness is synonymous with physical prowess but intellectual backwardness. This section will provide a background and link to discussion on racism in sport in the context of employment[102] and the regulation of sports stadiums.

Sport and race have a complex and self-perpetuating symbiotic role in constructing social understanding of racial difference.[103] Sport is a useful measure of how far we have come and how far there is to go in terms of race relations and racial integration. In the USA, things have come a long way since Jackie Robinson's breaking of the 'colour bar' in professional baseball in the late 1940s, when he played for the Brooklyn Dodgers. Although in many sports such as professional basketball and notably the National Basketball League, the representation of African Americans is very high, in others such as professional golf it is very low. However, in the higher echelons of professional sport in positions such as team managers, whites 'rule' supreme.[104] In the UK, similarly, few ethnic minority ex-players have been able to progress into coaching and management positions and change seems to be painfully slow.[105]

Greater participation of athletes from ethnic minority backgrounds in British sport is often used to illustrate the belief in greater tolerance in contemporary society to racial difference. Some sports such as athletics seem to have been at the cutting edge of equal opportunities. However, in an array of other sports, for example, swimming, snooker, golf and horse racing, there is virtually no representation from ethnic minority groups. Britain clearly has ethnic minority stars: Kelly Holmes, Amir Khan and Rio Ferdinand. In recent years two who reached the top of their respective sports were Linford Christie and Frank Bruno. They provide an interesting contrast. Bruno is probably the most loved black athlete of the last decade, an 'honorary white'. His 'blackness' has never been very visible, due to his own lack of racial self-promotion and the conflation of blackness and boxing. In contrast, Christie, who is arguably the greatest British sportsman of the 1990s, has never had his achievements appropriately acknowledged. He has never hidden his colour; some see him as 'an opinionated, arrogant, fast black man focused on winning'. As Hill argues:

> Unlike the loveable loser Bruno, Christie does not play up to a recognisable British character role ... he is deemed at least in part an outsider in his own land.[106]

---

101 The recent assertion by Dr Roger Bannister that black athletes have better developed tendons due to climatical factors illustrates the vicissitudes of explaining racial differences; see *The Times*, 23 November 1995. Also see the debate in the United Hoberman, J, *Darwin's Athletes: How Sport Has Damaged Black America and Preserved the Myth of Race* (1997), New York: Mariner; Entine, J, *Taboo: Why Black Athletes Dominate Sports and Why We're Afraid to Ask* (2000) Public Affairs: New York.

102 See Chapter 14.

103 See Cashmore, E, *Black Sportsmen* (1982), London: Routledge, and Jarvie, G (ed), *Sport, Racism and Ethnicity* (1991), London: Falmers.

104 See Shropshire, K, *In Black and White: Race and Sports in America* (1996), New York: New York UP.

105 'Racism bars way to top jobs in football' *The Guardian*, 19 February 1996; 'Football is "too white" off pitch', www.bbc.co.uk/news, 11 October 2004; also see Commission for Racial Equality Report – Welch, M, Spracklen, K and Pilcher, A, *Racial Equality in Football*, CRE Survey Findings No 2004/1.1.

106 'Unlevel fields' *The Guardian (Section 2)*, 21 March 1995, p 2.

Racism in social life can be brutally visible both in terms of physical attacks and a clear denial of the fundamental freedoms accepted in contemporary liberal society. However, it also exists in the hidden interstices of society. Verbal racism is more insidious, but as all ethnic minority sportsmen will know in Britain, it is only too real. Racism has been a part of sport as long as sport has been played. The aetiology of spectator racism in sport is as complex as it is of racism generally in society:

Hammond, D, *Foul Play: A Class Analysis of Sport*

The success of blacks in professional sports such as soccer has not, of course, eradicated racism either from the changing room or the terracing, but it has clearly made a difference. It is very difficult for racists to continually abuse blacks while supporting a team that is peppered with blacks, especially if the team is successful and the black players can be seen to be an integral part of that success.

Perhaps this effect should not be over estimated though. Terrace language still refers to 'our niggers' as opposed to 'theirs', and equally disturbing when a team reverts to an all white line-up the abuse heaped on blacks playing for the opposing team increases. Blacks are undoubtedly still racially abused albeit on a smaller scale, and they have still yet to make the breakthrough into senior positions on the coaching staff and that management jobs are not available to blacks after their playing days are over must be a consideration before they take up serious sport in the first place. The effect of ignoring other opportunities to take up a sport that will eventually leave one uneducated and unemployed can be catastrophic.[107]

Racism in sport becomes more apparent at times of lack of success in sporting terms. The controversy within cricket in 1995 as far as the doubted 'application' of Asian or black players to the cause of the English team is a contemporary example. Perhaps it is not surprising that at times of national decline in sports such as cricket, the focus of blame falls on those who are different. The causality of racism is complex, as are the solutions. If we accept that racism in sport is a reflection of general societal-wide racism, as Bowling says:

The historical records show that violent racism waxes and wanes with social, economic and political forces . . . we must hope . . . no one becomes complacent during those periods when the extent and ferocity of violent racism wanes.[108]

A major issue is what role the law has in addressing racism in sport and what extra-legal policies should be developed.

Racism in Football

English football has become, in terms of ethnicity, cosmopolitan. Over the last three decades, the participation of players of Afro-Caribbean descent has dramatically increased. Many of these players have been second or third generation children of immigrants from the Caribbean who came to Britain in the 1950s and 1960s. Today, in English professional football, players of Afro-Caribbean descent are over-represented in relation to the general population. However, representation by players from other ethnic minorities, for example, those of Asian descent, is significantly lower than in the general population.[109] Black players have had to fight to achieve prominence despite the dominant values within football culture. The stereotyped but long held wisdom that 'coloured players', as they were

---

107 Hammond, D, *Foul Play: A Class Analysis of Sport* (1993), London: Ubique, p 52.

108 Bowling, B, *Violent Racism* (1998), Oxford: OUP, p 317.

109 There are virtually no Asian professional footballers. See 'Asians can't play barrier' *The Guardian*, 10 February 1996 and 'Ooh, aah . . . Jaginder' *The Independent Magazine*, 17 August 1996.

called for many years, did not have suitable temperament, 'lacked heart' and 'would not be able to stand the cold' is still present in modified forms.[110]

As with the causes of football hooliganism generally, the causes of spectator racism are complex.[111] The *Bosman* decision has been a cause of this increasing cosmopolitanism with the signing of more foreign players. English football has always had players from the other home countries of the United Kingdom. It was not until the emergence of black players, during the 1960s, that the first manifestation of any real identifiable spectator reaction became evident. Some of these early players seem to have been grudgingly tolerated.[112] Perhaps it was not until the late 1970s, when the number of Afro-Caribbean players began to increase significantly, that they became 'visible' and began to represent a perceived threat. Sections of spectators, at some clubs more than others, began to react actively, through stereotyping racial comments and abuse, monkey chants, and the throwing of bananas on to the ground.[113] It has been termed 'the English Disease', although it clearly is a worldwide phenomenon.[114]

L'Affaire Cantona

There is evidence that the racial nature of football hooliganism has increasingly become politicised and co-ordinated throughout Europe.[115] Legal and non-legal initiatives have had some positive impact upon manifestations of spectator racism within football.[116] 'L'Affaire Cantona' in 1995 can be used to speculate that racial abuse and indifference has spread beyond the black/white demarcation that has been constructed over the last 30 years. As the four professional divisions become increasingly diverse in terms of ethnic origins and nationality, especially within the ambiguity and instability of the New Europe, the fear of difference may escalate.

Gardiner, S, 'The law and hate speech: "Ooh aah Cantona" and the demonisation of "the Other" '

The Cantona incident in south London in early 1995 needs careful explanation. He was sent off after kicking out at a Crystal Palace player. He was walking along the touch-line towards the exit to the dressing rooms when Matthew Simmons, a Crystal Palace supporter, ran down to the front of the crowd

---

110 See later, p 609.

111 See Greenfield, S and Osborn, G, 'When the whites come marching in' (1996) 6(2) Marquette Sports Law Journal 315; Fleming, S and Tomlinson, A, 'Football, racism and xenophobia in England (I) Europe and the Old England'; Garland, J and Rowe, M, 'Football, racism and xenophobia in England (II) challenging racism and xenophobia', in Merkel, U and Tokarski, W (eds), *Racism and Xenophobia in European Football Sports, Leisure and Physical Education Trends and Developments* (1996), Aachen: Meyer and Meyer Verlag, Vol 3; and Back, L et al, *Changing Face of Football: Racism, Identity and Multiculture in the English Game* (2001) London: Berg Publishers.

112 It is interesting to compare Albert Johanneson, a South African, who played for Leeds United from 1960–70 and Clyde Best, a Bermudian, who played for West Ham from 1967–77. Johanneson's career petered out and, suffering from chronic alcoholism, he died in late 1995 in poverty in Yorkshire. In comparison, Best returned to the Caribbean at the end of his career and is a successful business man.

113 Note the belated acknowledgment on the FA's part of its past inaction on responding effectively to this matter; see 'FA issues public apology for decades of racism' *The Guardian*, 4 July 2001.

114 There have been a number of racist incidents in Italian football in 1999–2000 and 2000–01 seasons; see Colantuoni, L, 'Italian update 2000' (2000) 3(4) Sports Law Bulletin 14; also see the FIFA anti-racism campaign launched in July 2001, www.fifa.com.

115 The crowd disorder, which caused the abandoning of the international game between the Republic of Ireland and England in Dublin in early 1995, was seen as involving organised hooligan groups such as 'Combat 18'. See 'Troublemakers caught police on the hop' *The Guardian*, 16 February 1995.

116 It is important not to see this as a problem only limited to football. A report compiled for The Rugby League Association showed levels of racial abuse by spectators. See below, p 136.

and 'verbally and digitally' abused Cantona ('Cantona hits fan, faces lengthy ban', The *Guardian*, 26 January 1995). He was reported as saying the immortal words: 'Fucking, cheating French cunt. Fuck off back to France, you mother fucker'. Cantona reacted by leaping over the advertising hoardings with a two-footed kick against Simmons' chest. He struck him a number of times before the two were parted by police, stewards and team officials.

Simmons' version of the outburst was rather different. He told the police after the event that he actually had walked eleven rows down to the front because he wanted to go to the toilet and said: 'Off! Off! Off! Go on, Cantona, have an early shower.' In court he said: 'The crowd was very noisy, everyone was cheering and shouting, everyone was pleased that he [Cantona] had been sent off, me included. Like any normal fan, I joined in with this and was just shouting 'Off, off, off' and pointing towards the dressing rooms' ('It was business as normal', says Cantona case accused', *The Guardian*, 1 May 1996).

Cantona was charged with common assault and pleaded guilty at his trial. He was initially given a two-week prison sentence by magistrates, justified at the time largely because 'he is a high profile public figure looked up to by many young people' *(The Guardian*, 24 March 1995). This was commuted to 120 hours community service teaching school children football skills, and he was also banned from playing for eight months by the English Football Association. Cantona's own obscure observation concerning the immense public interest in his case was: 'When seagulls follow a trawler, it is because they think sardines will be thrown into the sea' (Ridley 1995: 42).

As Redhead observes, the incident was 'caught clearly on camera and has been repeatedly shown via the international airwaves almost as many times as the Zapruder film of the JFK assassination in Dallas'. He compares it with the way that an incident involving Paul Ince was dealt with by the football authorities, one that was not clearly mediated by the TV cameras. Ince was charged with assaulting another Crystal Palace supporter, Dennis Warren, shortly after the Cantona incident. He was not given any ban before his trial and was acquitted on the charge of assault. Warren had four previous convictions for football violence and drunkenness, belonged to a right-wing fascist group and had been banned from acting as a manager in 1993 by Surrey Football Association for shouting instructions to his players to, 'get the nigger', on the opposing team. The power of the video image and its ability to reify events and actions is well illustrated by the distinctions in the respective censuring of Cantona and Ince.

Simmons, over a year after the incident, was convicted of threatening behaviour ('Cantona tormentor jailed for court kick', *The Guardian*, 3 May 1996). At his trial he did however turn the tables on Cantona, although not targeting him as the victim: he launched his own drop-kick attack on the prosecuting lawyer, seconds after hearing he had been found guilty of provoking the Manchester United star. He threw himself at Jeffrey McCann, grabbing him around the neck, trying to haul him over a table and appearing to kick him in the chest. McCann had asked magistrates to bar Simmons from all football grounds. Six police officers rushed in to restrain Simmons, who then rushed at the press box shouting: 'I am innocent. I swear on the Bible. You press, you are scum.' Simmons was fined £500 for threatening behaviour, banned from all professional football grounds for 12 months, and sentenced to seven days in prison for contempt of court. During his trial there had been unsubstantiated claims that Simmons was linked with right-wing fascist groups.[117]

Individualising Racist Chanting

This incident highlighted the issue of control of racist 'hate speech'. Is legislation the best answer to the xenophobia of the likes of Simmons? He was convicted under public order offences for racial hatred. He could not be charged under s 3 of the Football (Offences) Act 1991 for indecent and racist

---

117 Gardiner, S, 'The law and hate speech: "Ooh aah Cantona" and the demonisation of "the other" ', in Brown, A (ed), *Fanatics! Power, Identity and Fandom in Football* (1998), London: Routledge. Also see 'The Kick that Stunned Football' *The Observer Sport Monthly*, 24 November, 2004.

chanting because he fell outside the scope of this legislation due to his actions being solitary. At that time liability only occurred when in a designated football match, 'words or sounds are chanted in concert with one or more others which are threatening, abusive or threatening to a person by reason of his colour, race, nationality or ethnic or national origins'.

The Act has been the second dedicated piece of legislation for the regulation of football stadiums. The first Act was the Football Spectators Act 1989, which like the 1991 Act had its origins in the recommendations of the Taylor Report based on the Hillsborough disaster. The Taylor Report considered that the provisions of the Public Order Act 1986 concerning 'threatening, abusive or insulting words or behaviour' did not adequately cover indecent or racist chanting. This was due to the need to have a clearly identifiable victim to establish liability, in that either another person believed 'unlawful violence will be used against him or another',[118] or the chanting was 'within the hearing or sight of a person likely to be caused harassment, alarm or distress'.[119] Under the 1991 Act, no recognisable individual is needed, although the racial abuse will generally be directed at a particular player.

The Simmons/Cantona incident highlighted the limitation of the 1991 Act to chanting in concert with one or more others.[120] During the parliamentary progress of the legislation it was argued that to criminalise a single racist or indecent remark would have created 'too low' a threshold. After the Cantona incident, there were calls for the legislation to be extended to include individual acts.

In 1995, the Labour Party proposed that the offence should be individualised.[121] The Football Task Force interim report, *Eliminating Racism from Football*,[122] as one of its key recommendations asked the Government to 'amend the Football (Offences) Act 1991 as a matter of urgency to make it an offence for individuals to use racist comments inside football grounds'.

Football Task Force, *Eliminating Racism from Football*

5(a) 14 The introduction of the Football Offences Act may have contributed to this culture change by giving spectators more confidence to challenge unacceptable behaviour. Yet, this success should not obscure the fact that the Act is no longer fulfilling the purpose for which it was introduced. Rather, it should strengthen our resolve to amend it as it suggests that good legislation can be an effective deterrent against unacceptable behaviour.

5(a) 15 Kick It Out argues that the phrasing of the Act has 'significantly reduced the chances of the police mounting arrests that can be successfully prosecuted'. Home Office figures show that only 10 arrests were made during the last football season under this section of the Act.[123]

In 1998, the Home Office produced a *Review of Football-Related Legislation*.[124] Amongst a number of recommendations, it was suggested again that the offence should be able to be committed by a lone individual. Around this time there was some conjecture over whether spectator racism was increasing

---

118 Public Order Act 1986, s 4, 'Fear or Provocation of Violence'.

119 *Ibid*, s 5, 'Harassment, Alarm or Distress'. An additional offence has recently been created with s 4A of the Public Order Act 1986, 'Intentional Harassment, Alarm or Distress', as substituted by s 154 of the Criminal Justice and Public Order Act 1994, again needing an identifiable victim.

120 See 'It takes two to chant, court decides' *The Times*, 23 January 1993 and Pendry, T, *A Law with a Flaw, Kick It Again: Uniting Football Against Racism* (1995), London: Commission for Racial Equality.

121 *A New Framework for Football: Labour's Charter for Football* (1995), London: Labour Party.

122 Football Task Force, *Eliminating Racism from Football* (1998), London.

123 *Ibid*, para 5.

124 *Review of Football-Related Legislation* (1998), London: Home Office – Operational Policing Policy Unit. Copy can be found at www.football-research.org; see Gardiner, S, 'New powers to fight football hooliganism' (1998) 1(6) Sports Law Bulletin 1.

or decreasing. From the commencement of the Act in the early 1990s until early 1998, there were only about 180 convictions. In the season 1998–99 there were 33 convictions.[125] Section 3 of the 1991 Act has been little used, suggesting that it has been used primarily symbolically as an official indication that 'something was being done'. As Chambliss and Seidmann argue, the way to identify legal symbolism is to measure the levels of enforcement.[126] If they are low, symbolism is likely. One of the major problems is the issue of policing even though closed circuit television cameras are used to aid identification of perpetrators during matches.

The dominant discourse within the Football Association has been that the problem is decreasing, if not completely eradicated. There is, however, strong evidence that incidents of racist activity are still perpetuated by individuals and small groups that operate 'in complex and often contradictory ways ... racist abuse in grounds occurs in an intermittent fashion'.[127] The location and form, the expression of racism has changed – it is, however, unclear whether the extent of the problem has altered significantly. Caution is vital in alluding to the reduction of the problem.[128]

The offence was individualised with s 9 of the Football (Offences and Disorder) Act 1999. The effect of the amendment is that an individual who engages in such chanting on his own can commit the offence.[129] It seems however that the offence still must amount to 'chanting' albeit by an individual. A single abusive shout will not suffice.[130] A major question is whether or not the individualising of the offence would arguably be even harder to enforce, with police and ground stewards finding it difficult to identify the cries of a lone racist. As Parpworth argues:

> There is a certain futility in creating statutory offences, which are effectively moribund due to difficulties associated with detection.[131]

The future policing of this provision and the number of consequential convictions will be interesting to monitor. One case has given guidance on an unfortunately not uncommon chant in games between certain clubs. In *DPP v Stoke on Trent Magistrates' Court*[132] the court acquitted the defendant Ratcliffe, who admitted taking part together with a number of other Port Vale supporters in the chant 'You're just a town full of Pakis', directed at Oldham supporters, in a match between the two clubs. He was tried and acquitted on a submission at the end of the prosecution case that the words used were not of a racialist nature. The district judge's reasons included that the phrase had been 'mere doggerel' and amounted to no more than aimlessly stating that 'our town is better than your town'. On a prosecution appeal by way of case stated against an acquittal, the appeal was allowed and the case remitted to the District Judge with a direction that he should on the evidence convict Ratcliffe of the offence.

DPP v Stoke On Trent Magistrates' Court [2004] 1 Cr App R 4

The words "of a racialist nature" meant, as provided by section 3(2)(b), that the chant consisted of, or included, matter that was threatening, abusive or insulting to a person, by reason of his colour, race,

---

125 In season 2002–03 there were 78 arrests; in season 2003–04 there were 63 arrests.

126 Chambliss, W and Seidmann, R, *Law, Order and Power* (1982), 2nd edn, New York: John Wiley.

127 Back, L, Crabbe, T and Solomos, J, 'Racism in football: patterns of continuity and change', in *op cit*, fn 117, Brown (1998).

128 See Garland, J and Rowe, M, 'Policing racism at football matches: an assessment of recent developments in police strategies' (1999) 27(3) International Journal of the Sociology of Law 251.

129 Gardiner, S, 'The continuing regulation of football supporters: the Football (Offences and Disorder) Act 1999' (1999) 2(4) Sports Law Bulletin 1.

130 See Greenfield, S and Osborn, G, 'The Football (Offences and Disorder) Act 1999: amending s 3 of the Football (Offences) Act 1991' (2000) 5(1) Journal of Civil Liberties 55.

131 Parpworth, N, 'Football and racism: a legislative solution' (1993) Solicitors Journal, 15 October.

132 *DPP v Stoke On Trent Magistrates' Court* [2004] 1 Cr App R 4; also see (2003) 6(5) Sports Law Bulletin.

nationality or ethnic or national origins. It was immaterial whether persons of the racial group referred to in the alleged offending words were present so as to hear them or, if so present, were offended or affected in any way by them. (2) The word "Paki" was in most contexts racially offensive. It went beyond a convenient and/or affectionate abbreviation of a description of a nationality such as "Aussie" or "Brit". The use of the word had to be looked at in its context on a case by case basis. (3) On the facts found by the District Judge there was no doubt that R and his fellow Port Vale supporters were using the word as part of their chant in a racially derogatory or insulting sense. R's admitted behaviour fell squarely within the definition of racialist chanting in the Act.

The debate about the extension and individualising of racist hate speech on the football field reflects the argument for the existence of legislation that provides a discrete offence for racial attacks.[133]

The Crime and Disorder Act 1998, s 28

Assaults can be dealt with in a more serious form if they are seen as being 'racially aggravated'. This occurs if:

a) either at the time of committing the offence, or immediately before or after doing so, the offender demonstrates towards the victim of the offence hostility based on the victim's membership (or presumed membership) of a racial group; or

b) the offence is motivated (wholly or partly) by hostility towards members of a racial group based on their membership of that group.

As with the increasing criminalisation of spectator racism, there is a counter view that a major problem with the creation of a 'racially aggravated' offence of assault is the lack of implementation of existing provisions by the police and other enforcement agencies, suggesting a failure in practice of these agencies to take racial violence and abuse seriously:

Francis, P, 'Race attacks: do we need new legislation?'

What the evidence does highlight is the overall paucity of political discussion on tackling racial attacks and the absence of any realistic assessment of existing legal and extra-legal provision ... further legislation will suffer the same problem existing legislation has encountered, and may not even provide symbolic importance. Rather what is needed is a genuine commitment from government and existing agencies to an imaginative use of existing powers, coupled with the continuing development, monitoring and evaluation of extra-legal provision.[134]

Gardiner, S, 'Ooh aah Cantona: racism as hate speech'

The process of criminalisation of problems such as racist hate speech can often be used to deflect political responsibility for them, as failures of social policy. It is convenient if such incidents can be seen as a criminal issue based on individual responsibility and wickedness. Legislation has a role to play, but it should not be at the expense of other non-legal social practices.[135]

Non-legal Approaches to Regulating Sports-Related Racism

There is a strong argument that the use of legislation can be seen as diverting attention and resources from educational and social policy initiatives, which might more successfully eliminate the causes of the problem. Football stadiums have become one of the most overtly regulated public spaces. There is an increasing danger that this regulatory approach to social problems by the use of the law will create

---

133 See Brennan, F, 'Racially motivated crime: the response of the Criminal Justice System' [1999] Crim LR *Op cit*, fn 108, Bowling (1998).

134 Francis, P, 'Race attacks: do we need new legislation?' (1994) 16 Criminal Justice Matters 10.

135 Gardiner, S, 'Ooh aah Cantona: racism as hate speech' (1996) 23 Criminal Justice Matters 23.

increasingly anodyne environments where freedom of expression and movement is overtly suppressed through the law. Law is often made too hastily to deal with what is seen as a pressing problem. Panic law is invariably bad law. The alternative approach is the use of campaigns such as that conceived in 1993, when the Professional Footballers' Association and the Commission for Racial Equality (CRE) launched the 'Let's Kick Racism out of Football' Campaign.[136] The campaign has been periodically re-launched. In addition, many clubs have developed their own policies against racism with the 'football in the community' programme. Anti-racist fanzines have also developed as an informal method of campaigning.

The main objective of the 'Let's Kick Racism Out of Football' Campaign was to 'encourage all those associated with the game of football to improve standards of behaviour, especially with reference to racial abuse, harassment, and the discrimination in and around grounds and to make grounds safe for spectators, and to motivate public opinion generally against all forms of racism associated with the game and other spheres of life'. In 1997, the campaign changed its name to 'Kick it Out' and became independent of the CRE. The campaign's priorities are:

'Kick it Out' Campaign

Professional football

Working with the professional game by offering advice and guidance on all aspects of race equality within professional football.

Young people

Using the appeal of the game to address young people within schools, colleges and youth organisations, by the development of resources and delivery.

Amateur football

Working at grassroots and amateur levels to tackle racial abuse and harassment from parks football.

Asians in football

Helping to raise the issue of the exclusion of south Asians as players from the game.

Black communities

Capacity building local ethnic minority communities to engage with professional clubs and the structures of the game.

European football

Developing partnerships to raise the debate and tackle racism in European football.[137]

Rugby League

The issue of racism has also been highlighted in other sports, including rugby league:

Long, J, Tongue, N, Spracklen, K and Carrington, B, *What's the Difference?*
A Study of the Nature and Extent of Racism in Rugby League

Having accepted the challenge of trying to cast light on the nature and extent of racism in rugby league, we recognised that we were not going to get the answer but would unearth different shades of meaning.

---

136 See Greenfield, S and Osborn, G, 'When the whites come marching in?' (1996) 6(2) Marquette Sports Law Journal 330–31 for further details.

137 For further information see www.kickitout.org; also see Football Against Racism in Europe (FARE) – www.farenet.org.

These we have tried to present here to represent the range of views expressed during the course of the research. At the same time we have tried to respect the confidences shared with us. We are most grateful to those who took part in the various surveys, ensuring through their cooperativeness high levels of response, which lend credibility to the findings. The rugby league fans in particular were very tolerant of those crazy researchers. This, we believe, represents their desire to be involved in everything associated with the game, a commitment that can be used to good effect by the RFL and the individual clubs.

Discussing racism in the sport you love (which was how most of our respondents regarded rugby league) is uncomfortable, because for most of us it is one of those things that is 'not nice' and we would prefer it if it were not really there. That meant we felt we had to be especially careful with the questions we asked and the way they were presented in the surveys.

We cannot speculate on the views of those who did not respond, but the following quotes represent two of the most commonly held positions:

- I feel we could be highlighting a problem, which by and large does not exist. Our supporters are not moronic flag-waving National Front supporters (Club Official 102).
- We need to stop racism before it spreads. It is there in the game and there is no point hiding it (Club Official 89).

Our research suggests that the first of these views is probably the more frequently held, and there is a third set of people who flatly deny that there is any racism in rugby league. However while our research confirmed that racism in professional rugby league is not on a par with what has been evidenced in professional soccer, there is a small but significant problem. Our evidence also suggests that although the intensity may vary, racism is evident throughout the game and should not be dismissed as simply being the preserve of a minority of rogue clubs. People on the inside refer to rugby league as the greatest game, which has been taken as the name of one of the fanzines. This kind of pride is obviously one of the game's great strengths, but can also encourage complacency, making it difficult to alert people to significant issues. It is important that people should be honest enough to recognise problems and seek to address them appropriately. It should be possible to appeal to the pride that fans have in the game to enlist their support in ridding the game of racism and setting an example for other sports to follow.

Among the supporters almost half had heard chanting against black players. While 87% feel that it is not acceptable for players to be abused because of the colour of their skin, that still leaves 13%; while 90% disagreed that black players are lazy, that still leaves 10%. There is still a message to be conveyed that while an individual player who happens to be black may be lazy (or have any number of other attributes, including positive ones), it is not because they are black that they are lazy.

Fewer club officials reported hearing chanting against black players, but a third were aware of it even at their own club and over half had witnessed racist behaviour at other clubs. Almost all clubs were named or included within a more general category so would be ill-advised to consider racism as just somebody else's problem. Many of the club officials (especially the chairmen) had stereotypical views of the attributes of ethnic minority players, most commonly relating to the athletic prowess of Afro-Caribbean players. Black players experiencing racism are rather ambivalent about that kind of stereotyping because some of it appears favourable to them. Other aspects about suitability only for certain positions may be very limiting.

Players were more aware of racism within the game than the coaches and other club officials. All the players interviewed acknowledged that there is racist chanting from the stands and terraces. They know that it is a small number but identified a significant problem. The players were also aware that racial abuse was not just confined to the stands and terraces. All the black players and some of the white players talked about the racial abuse they were aware of on the pitch. While this was considered to be a 'winding-up' tactic, the players felt there was no justification for it. Not surprisingly, players were reluctant to point the finger at their own team, but some of the dressing room jokes were not felt to be funny. Some coaches were also identified as adopting racist stereotypes.

It is important for it to be recognised that abuse because of the colour of a player's skin is racist and not just one of those things that can be laughed off. Clubs can and should do something. On balance the feeling of club officials was that the anti-chanting campaigns had had a beneficial effect, and the supporters also thought they had been a good idea. However, beyond that, club officials identified very little that had been done to date to counter racism and promote the game within ethnic minority communities. There have been some notable exceptions like the Keighley Classroom and the Batley free ticket scheme. But Asian and black people are still extremely rare among rugby league crowds. The players in particular saw the need for development initiatives to make sure that as many as possible be introduced to a great game and that talent be encouraged.

The black players we interviewed felt that when they encountered racism they just had to get on with the game, but did not see why they should have to accept it. Whether or not racist abuse was directed at them personally, they as black players were affected by it. There was also a feeling that many had been deterred along the way, deciding that if that was what the game was going to be about there were better directions they could go in. Of course, there are many reasons why people stop playing, but any sport should be concerned about an avoidable loss of talent. Moreover, experiencing racism like this may affect the form of black players, so it is in the interest of coaches and team mates to try to counter anything that has a detrimental effect on their players.

Not surprisingly, when confronted with racist chanting the majority of supporters ignored it. In the pressures of the crowd it is not easy for the individual to know what to do. Part of the 'Let's Kick Racism Out of Football' campaign was to suggest to fans what they could do if they came across racist behaviour in football.

While beginning to question that it is, people do still want to see rugby league as a family sport and an environment in which racism is evident is not conducive to that image. If racism were to spread it could hit clubs in their pockets through lower attendances.

For the white players it was clear that rugby league is indeed very much a family game. Their families and network of family friends and social contacts had been instrumental in introducing them to rugby league clubs. Lacking that kind of introduction, Asian and black players had had to find other routes into the game. To avoid missing out on talent in the various ethnic minority communities, rugby league needs to offer the kind of support that few youngsters will get from their networks of family and friends.

We have tried not to create a scare about 'a cancer sweeping through the game'. We are persuaded that such a conclusion would be unwarranted. However we also believe it would be wrong for those in rugby league to shirk their responsibility and hide behind the protestations that there is no issue to address. Although racism is a problem in society at large, that is no reason for inaction within the game, which should instead acknowledge its social responsibility. There is an opportunity for rugby league to take an initiative for the good of the game and the communities that support it.[138]

The report was a significant reason for the CRE in 1996 to launch an anti-racism campaign in rugby league.[139]

---

[138] See Long, J, Tongue, N, Spracklen, K and Carrington, B, *What's the Difference? A Study of the Nature and Extent of Racism in Rugby League* (1995), School of Leisure and Sports Studies, Leeds Metropolitan University, pp 43–45.

[139] Also note similar scheme in cricket, 'Clean Bowl Racism'; McDonald, I, 'Why we must hit racism for six', in *Hit Racism for Six: Race and Cricket in England Today* (1995), London: Roehampton Institute; McDonald, I and Sharda, U, *Anyone for Cricket?* (1999), London: Centre for New Ethnicities Research, UEL; Gardiner *et al*, *Sports Law*, 2nd edn (2001), London: Cavendish Publishing, pp 150–154; Williams, J, *Cricket and Race* (2001), London: Berg.

CRE, 'A 13-point action plan for rugby league clubs to tackle racism'

Professional clubs undertake to observe the following articles in the fight to keep racism out of rugby league:

1 Clubs will formulate a statement to be published in each and every match programme and displayed on permanent notice boards around their grounds, to the effect that they will not tolerate racism of any kind and will take action against spectators who engage in racist chanting or abuse or intimidation.

2 Clubs will undertake to prevent spectators who indulge in racist chanting or abuse or offensive behaviour from attending matches at their grounds.

3 Clubs will make public address announcements during matches to condemn any racist chanting which arises, and to warn that swift and comprehensive action will be taken against offenders.

4 Clubs will engage season ticket holders in a contract, which forbids them from taking part in racist chanting or abuse or any other offensive behaviour.

5 Clubs will ensure that there is no sale or distribution of racist literature in or around their grounds on match days.

6 Clubs will insist upon a code of conduct for players and officials, which prohibits them from making racially abusive remarks against fellow players officials and supporters at any time.

7 Clubs will maintain communications with other clubs and with Rugby Football League headquarters, through a nominated club officer, to facilitate the efforts to keep racism out of the game.

8 Clubs will maintain a strategy for dealing with racist chanting and abuse and offensive behaviour, and will ensure that all active stewards and, where necessary the police, are aware of their responsibilities and courses of action in this regard.

9 Clubs will ensure that all parts of their grounds are entirely free of racist graffiti.

10 Clubs will adopt an equal opportunities policy in the areas of employment and service provision.

11 Clubs will undertake to cooperate to the best of their endeavours with such other groups and agencies as seek to promote awareness of race issues and to combat racism in all levels of society.

12 Clubs will ensure that their development strategies as carried out by their nominated Academy/Youth Development manager are positively weighted to encourage the paling of rugby league, particularly at junior levels, among such ethnic minority communities as are included within their catchment areas.

13 Clubs will ensure that all youth, community and general development programmes conducted in accordance with the Rugby Football League's 'Framing the Future' policy document reflect the needs for such ethnic minority communities as are included within their catchment areas.[140]

In 2000, a racial discrimination case by Paul Sterling against Leeds 'Rhinos' Rugby League Club may be some way to measure the effectiveness of this code.[141] Sterling was 36 years old and towards the end of his career. In early 2000, the team's coach decided that he had six players to choose two from for the wing position where Sterling played and that the applicant was sixth in order of preference and he would not be picked that season. On 5 May 2000, the applicant with support from

---

140 For further details see www.cre.gov.uk.
141 Case 1802453/00, *Sterling v Leeds Rugby League Club and Others* (2000) (ET); see (2000) 4(2) Sports Law Bulletin 3.

the CRE presented an originating application to claim that the decision had been made on racial grounds. The tribunal found that there was evidence of discrimination and that it was proper to draw an inference that the principal reason for the decision not to allow the applicant the chance to compete for a place in the fist team was the applicant's racial origin.

The tribunal noted that the team coach had indicated that Afro-Caribbean players were not as well suited to playing rugby league in Australia. He had replied to questioning by the tribunal when he stated that 'those boys' play basketball and other sports. This remark had rung alarm bells in the mind of each member of the tribunal. This case illustrates that although racism in rugby league both in terms of spectator actions and within employment practices has been recognised – for example, Leeds Rhinos had a plan called 'Tackle it' against racism and the Club had an equal opportunities clause implied into employment contracts – there are still identifiable problems.

CHILD PROTECTION: SPORTS COACHES AND CHILD ATHLETES

The issue of the treatment of children in sport mirrors increasing awareness of the rights of children generally in society.[142] Although the focus is on participation in sport, there is evidence of considerable exploitation of children within the wider sports industry.[143] Sport provides many positive opportunities for young people to participate individually or more commonly in groups. This is generally at a recreational 'play' level; however, increasingly young people are taking part in highly competitive and sometimes elite level sport. The image of parents shouting at their children and haranguing the officials has become not uncommon in school and Sunday morning football: even at this level winning is all.[144] In sports such as tennis, swimming and gymnastics the age of participants at elite level has become ever younger.

Awareness of the existence and extent of sexual and physical abuse of children has appeared fairly recently in sport as it has generally in society.[145] The need to provide more effective protection of exploitation of children in sport has grown in recent years.[146] This exploitation ranges from clear acts of sexual and physical abuse at one extreme to oppressive encouragement at the other. Clear acts of abuse are almost inevitably going to be contrary to the criminal law. Oppressive encouragement is much more problematic to regulate. However, detection of all forms of exploitation in sport is difficult.

The main area of concern has been with the relationship between coaches and child athletes. In Britain over the last few years, there have been a number of criminal trials of sports coaches. The most notable has been the conviction of the swimming coach Paul Hickson who was the British team coach at the 1988 Olympics in Seoul. He was sentenced for 17 years after he was found guilty of two rapes, 11 indecent assaults and two other serious sexual offences. He was cleared of two other indecent

---

142 See the Children Act 1989.

143 *A Sporting Chance* (1997), Christian Aid, p 217, concerning exploitation of children in India, some, as young as 10, stitching footballs for about 10 pence a ball. Pieri, M, 'Labour standards in the manufacture of sporting goods: a tarnished trophy?' (1999) 2(2) Sports Law Bulletin 10; see Christian Aid Report at www.oneworld.org/christian_aid.

144 See 'Soccer brawl father is told to pay £750' *The Daily Telegraph*, 15 February 1997.

145 See *Report of the Inquiry into Child Abuse in Cleveland 1987*, Cm 412 (1988), London: HMSO.

146 Research from Huddersfield University suggests that 52% of children know their abuser through community based organisations such as swimming clubs; see 'Child abuse in sport' (2001) 4(2) Sports Law Bulletin 7.

assaults. Hickson had denied all charges, saying he was the victim of teenage girls' fantasies. One of his victims, who was 13 when he first molested her, was reported as saying 'he was evil, a monster':

> The woman, an undergraduate, was angry that the Amateur Swimming Association seems to have failed to investigate complaints by three senior swimmers in 1986 about Hickson's behaviour towards women. The Association said yesterday that there had been no allegations of criminality, but it would re-examine the way it protects athletes. The woman said: 'Investigations should have been made because some people were aware that something was not quite right'. The woman cannot bring herself to utter the name of Hickson, who fondled her and forced her to perform oral sex. 'I was so young', she said, 'and I just felt that what he was doing was something I had to endure, something that was necessary. I trusted in everything that he told me'.[147]

The case of Hickson came to light almost accidentally when an off-duty policeman at a party overheard some teenage girls recounting allegations against Hickson. He had been reprimanded in 1987 by his employer, the University of Wales at Swansea, for telling a woman to strip for a 'naked fitness' test, and then undressing himself. He subsequently moved to the public school, Millfield, as swimming coach.

One real problem is that often allegations are viewed with disbelief from those associated with the individuals in question. Victims often believe that they are the only ones involved and only find out later that other fellow athletes were subject to similar treatment. The sports coach–child athlete relationship is one where the coach has immense power and influence over the child and it is difficult for the child to raise the alarm. Celia Brackenridge has produced a significant body of work concerning the causes of abuse in sport, particularly against women, and she shows how abusive coaches take care and time to 'groom' their athletes so that they will submit to their advances.[148] Child sport, as with other activities involving working with children, attracts those with a propensity to paedophilia. What has arisen is a rightful awareness of the reality of this problem, but also confusion and uncertainty: issues such as how to deal with false allegations, as with the suicide of Cliff Temple, the athletics correspondent of *The Sunday Times* after false allegations of sexual harassment,[149] and the problem of how to develop good practice for sports coaches when working with child athletes so that both parties are not inhibited from working effectively together. Hickson's case has subsequently led to many more prosecutions and heightened awareness.[150] There continues to be a clash of cultures that construct particular incidents in different ways. The then Chelsea FC coach Graham Rix's consensual underage sex with a 15 year old girl is an example.[151] Should Rix and Hickson's acts be similarly defined? What is clear is that more effective mechanisms need to be put in place in sport to protect children from exploitation and abuse.

---

147 'Olympic coach jailed for rapes' *The Times*, 28 September 1995, p 1. See also 'Swimmer blew whistle on Hickson nine years ago' *The Times*, 28 September 1995, p 5; 'The great betrayal' *The Sunday Times*, 1 October 1995, p 14.

148 See Brackenridge, C, 'He owned me basically . . . : women's experience of sexual abuse in sport' (1997) 32(2) International Review for the Sociology of Sport; 'Sexual harassment and sexual abuse in sport', in Clarke, G and Humberstone, B (eds), *Researching Women and Sport* (1997), London: Macmillan; 'In my opinion' (1999) 2(2) Sports Law Bulletin 2; *Spoilsports: Understanding and Preventing Sexual Exploitation in Sport* (2001), London: Routledge.

149 See Downes, S and Mackay, D, *Running Scared* (1996), Edinburgh: Mainstream.

150 See cases of Cecil Mallon, a gym coach jailed for indecent assault; and David Low, an athletics coach given 18 months' probation for sending obscene questionnaires to young girls. Also see TV programmes, 'Bad sports', *On the Line*, BBC2 Television, 26 January 1994 (on sexual misconduct in US sport); *On the Line*, BBC2 Television, 25 August 1993 (on sexual harassment and sexual abuse in UK sport); and *Diverse Reports*, Channel 4 Television, 23 January 1997 (on sexual abuse in English football).

151 'Chelsea to stand by jailed Rix' *The Guardian*, 27 March 1999.

Defining Abuse

Clear proven allegations of sexual and physical abuse can be subject to the general criminal and civil law. What is more problematic is how oppression, short of abuse of child athletes, should be defined and regulated.[152] Of course, as has already been noted, brutality is sanctioned in sports, whose 19th century origins lie in:

> ... militarism and muscular Christianity, the Chariots Of Fire ethos: a Bible under one arm and a ball under the other ... Sport promotes and protects bad behaviour, because it is not politically responsible. The coaches' word is law, they dominate players' every waking moment – it is not about empowerment or democracy. It is like a cult.[153]

A number of graphic accounts have been made of the treatment of children, to which girls especially are subject. In gymnastics, there has been growing concern of the pressures on girls to conform to a certain body size and weight seen as most likely to lead to success. There is evidence that puberty is artificially delayed and its effects minimised.[154]

Joan Ryan's *Little Girls in Pretty Boxes* provides a moving account of elite female gymnasts and ice skaters who, every four years, captivate millions by the seemingly effortless skill and grace at the Olympic Games. However, she provides a very different image of the frail, tiny figures performing feats of co-ordination and power and exposes the suffering and sacrifice they have endured, and the hundreds who didn't make it, broken in their early teens by the demands of their sport. Unerringly, Ryan, one of America's leading sports journalists, presents a catalogue of what she describes as 'legal, even celebrated child abuse', in which girls starve themselves (her research shows that 60% of college gymnasts in the US suffer from eating disorders), risk osteoporosis, curvature of the spine, and untold psychological damage, at the behest of brutal, self-promoting coaches, and parents driven by misguided sentiment. As far as coaches' impropriety, Ryan focuses on the Romanian Bela Karolyi who spotted Nadia Comaneci as a six year old and groomed her to Olympic stardom. His coaching approach:

Ryan, J, *Little Girls in Pretty Boxes*

> ... was based on militaristic control. His gymnasts lived in dormitories at the gym in Romania, trained seven to eight hours a day, fit in a few hours of school and ate only what the Karolyi fed them. There was no talk or fooling around inside the gym. The only proper response to Karolyi's instructions was a nod. He trained them like boxers, like little men, introducing rigorous conditioning and strengthening exercises to their workouts, transforming their bodies into muscled machinery. Karolyi insisted on small young girls for his team, not only for their pliability and resilience but for the little doll look he believed enchanted the spectators and swayed the judges.[155]

After his defection to the United States, Ryan produces evidence of continued physical and emotional exploitation by Karolyi:

> He rushed the gymnasts back in the gym sooner than doctors recommended, rationalising that the doctors were simply concerned with (legal) liability ... Kristie Phillips, for instance, trained for three years with a fractured wrist because Karolyi did not feel it was serious enough to warrant full rest.

---

152 See Nelson, M, *The Stronger Women Get, the More Men Love Football: Sexism and the Culture of Sport* (1996), New York: The Women's Press.

153 Brackenridge, C, quoted in Campbell, B, 'Why the coast is clear' *The Guardian*, 7 November 1996, p 4.

154 See 'Hungry For Success', *Fair Game*, Channel 4, 10 June 1996.

155 Ryan, J, *Little Girls in Pretty Boxes* (1995), New York: Warner, pp 198–99.

Nearly ten years later the wrist barely bends ... Similarly before the 1991 World Championships a Karolyi doctor diagnosed Kim Zmeskal's wrist injury pain as a sprain, leading Karolyi to suggest on national television that the injury was more in Zmeskal's head than in her wrist. It turned out that Zmeskal's problem was a fracture of the distal radius, or growth plate – a common injury amongst elite gymnast but one with which Karolyi's doctor was apparently unfamiliar.[156]

Injuries had no place in Karolyi's carefully designed formula for producing a star every four years. He built his program around the girl with the most talent. 'Your top athlete is a very strange creature', Karolyi explains. 'Of course, I never studied psychology, but through these years these little guys have taught me. We paid our dues on our mistakes, praising our little guys and cheering and clapping and showing our enthusiasm and baying them. And those are the ones who turn around and show disappreciation, ignorance and even arrogance. They take advantage of your sincere urge to show your appreciation. Give them everything in the world and ensure you're getting a big, big, big, big slap. She is the first to turn her back.'

So Karolyi constructed a training environment that kept his star athlete questioning her worth. In selecting five other gymnasts to train with her, he carefully chose each to play a specific role. Perhaps the most tortuous position was that of the secondary star: like the understudy in a play, the girl was just talented enough to present a threat to the star's status. Nadia had Teodora Ungureaunu, Dianne Durham had Mary Lou Retton, Kristie Phillips had Phoebe Mills, and Kim Zmeskal had Betty Okino. The four remaining gymnasts were the 'crowd', as Karolyi called them, chosen as much for their personality traits as their talents. One girl from the 'crowd' was always chosen as his pet. She might be the least talented, but she possessed the qualities he wanted to reinforce in his star: hard work, discipline and stoicism. Karolyi would praise her lavishly and hold her up as an example, angering the more talented gymnasts who resented his favouritism. Anger, Karolyi knew, was a powerful motivator.[157]

Development of an Effective Child Protection Policy

In the United States, many strategies to expose and eradicate exploitation of child athletes have been developed including criminal and civil law remedies, organisation awareness and pro-active development of plans, specific codes of conduct, screening potential coaches etc.[158] In Britain the issue of developing greater awareness and recognition of child abuse and promotion of good practices for working with children has also become a priority. In response to the Hickson case, the Amateur Swimming Association has been at the forefront of confronting child abuse in sport.

Gray, A, 'Swimming and child protection: the story so far'

Ensuring the safety of young persons to enjoy sport must surely be the highest priority of any sports governing body. The sport of swimming has over the last eighteen months been endeavouring to understand the problems of child abuse in all its various forms and to implement strategies to deal with the problems. It must be appreciated that child abuse is a problem in our society and sport is not immune. Recent highly publicised cases involving 'caring' services have illustrated that there exist many opportunities within society for those who would prey on our young children to gain the necessary intimate access to children. Amateur sport inevitably relies upon the efforts of thousands of volunteers who give so much in support of the development of children in sport. Herein lies the opportunity for that small minority of people who would harm our children to gain the necessary opportunities to abuse these children.

---

156 *Ibid*, p 209.

157 *Ibid*, p 211.

158 Fried, GB, 'Unsportsmanlike contact: strategies for reducing sexual assaults in youth sports' (1996) 6(3) Journal of Legal Aspects of Sport 155.

The starting point for the sport of swimming was the trial of Paul Hickson, Olympic Swimming Coach.

Convicted September 1995 on two counts of rape and eleven indecent assaults.

Sentenced to seventeen years' imprisonment.

This happened in the first few months of David Sparkes' period of office as Chief Executive of the Amateur Swimming Association.

Whilst the sport had been considering child protection issues prior to the Hickson trial what the case brought clearly into focus was the following:

Recognition of the fact that the sport of swimming was a sport of some 300,000 members of whom approximately 90% were under 16 years of age.

The sport's governing body needed to act swiftly and decisively to restore the confidence of the membership, its parents and the public at large.

To deal with these various problems of child abuse there was the need for the Association to develop short and medium term strategies.

Steps Which Were Taken by the Sport in the Light of Hickson

1 The sport entered into a wide consultation process including the Home Office, Sports Council and other agencies with expertise in the area of child protection.

As a result of this process there were produced clear procedures for recognising and acting upon suspicions of child abuse.

It is considered that there are two problem areas, which are not entirely distinct:

Physical and sexual abuse of children.

Emotional abuse (eg threatening and taunting of children) which may manifest itself in teaching and coaching and which are clearly unacceptable practices.

The Association sought to produce guidelines which were embodies in the publication 'Child Protection Procedures in Swimming'. The principles enshrined in the procedures are:

The child's welfare is paramount.

All children whatever their age, culture, disability, gender, language, racial origin, religious belief and/or sexual identity have the right to protection from abuse.

All suspicions and allegations of abuse will be taken seriously; and responded to swiftly and appropriately.

The procedures offer guidance in the recognition of child abuse and how to respond if abuse is suspected or alleged.

The NSPCC in particular provided great assistance to the Association in the formulation of this document, which was published in June 1996 and circulated to all affiliated clubs and organisations. It was recognised that clear and concise procedures for dealing with child abuse cases were necessary due to the perception that clubs had a tendency to react in panic to allegations eg ignoring the problem hoping it would go away/suspending the children.

The Guidelines also recognise and establish procedures for dealing with complaints of 'poor practice' in coaching or teaching.

2 Emergency powers were given to the Chief Executive by the sports governing body, the ASA Committee, to allow:

Temporary suspension of suspected child abusers who were the subject of a police investigation.

The withdrawal of teaching and coaching certificates of convicted offenders – thereby effectively excluding them from the sport.

The above represents the 'rapid response' phase of the Association's developing child protection procedures.

But ASA knew that it needed to do more to follow through this process.

The Medium Term

1 The Association set about establishing a child protection database upon which would be included details of all individuals with access to young swimmers.

It was considered a necessary starting point to find out who is involved in our sport at this level. A standard form questionnaire was produced which asked questions of previous criminal records and whether the individual was known to Social Services.

It also sought consent of the individual for the undertaking of police checks anticipating the amendments now contained in the Police Act.

Whilst in some quarters initially there were reservations with regard to the efficacy of a self-certification process the message from the experts was that paedophiles do not like lists and monitoring and their natural response to such vigilance and scrutiny will be to move on.

2 Working in conjunction with bodies representing teachers and coaches the Association produced a Code of Ethics (unacceptable coaching practices).

The purpose of the Code was principally to endeavour to instil good coaching practice amongst coaches/teachers by highlighting the unacceptable practices. Many of the practices may fall within the definition of emotional abuse as explained in the Child Protection Procedures.

However, it was considered of vital importance that coaches/teachers would 'buy into' this new development and accordingly there was wide consultation with bodies representing the interests of coaches and teachers.

3 To reinforce the Code from an educational perspective. It has been included as a syllabus item on all higher level teaching and coaching certificates.

4 The Association has substantially reviewed its domestic disciplinary Tribunals with effect from 1 April 1997 in the following respects:

Chairmen of Tribunals now have greater flexibility in the procedures they adopt for particular Tribunals to allow informal mediation in particular cases and for a Tribunal hearing to be held in a manner sensitive to cater for the needs of young children witnesses.
Chairmen may co-opt onto Tribunal panels specialists with expertise in the area of child protection (eg senior police officers in child protection units and employees of other agencies).

As with many sports the Association has detailed disciplinary rules with procedures for persons within the jurisdiction of the sport to be subject to disrepute charges in the event that, for instance, they bring the sport into disrepute. It has to be recognised that not all allegations of child abuse will result in a police charge and conviction but whether or not the police proceed (and they may not due to evidential or other difficulties) there is still the possibility of the child's family wishing to take action under the laws of the sport. Indeed due to the difficulties that may prevent a criminal prosecution proceeding it still may be appropriate for action to be taken within the sport – the Chief Executive is charged with the responsibility of considering the bringing of proceedings for alleged breaches of the Code of Ethics.

5 Having established clear procedures there is a need to ensure that there has been a general raising of awareness and acceptance on the ground. For that reason working very closely with the NSPCC the Association produced a series of road shows which very much presented the procedures to the clubs at a local level through a series of seminars and question and answer sessions.

The purpose of this was to:

Explain the procedures and their practical effect.

Identify persons within clubs at a local level who have the necessary skills to offer guidance and advice.

To ascertain further training needs, particularly of these individuals.

6 The Association has been in contact with Mr Tony Butler the Chief Constable of Gloucestershire and a leading representative of the ACPO (Association of Chief Police Officers) Child Protection Group.

Mr Butler has agreed to circulate the Guidelines produced to the 43 individual police forces. The purpose of this is to raise awareness of the steps that the sport of swimming is trying to make and at the same time we are looking for feedback on our procedures in order to see if there are ways in which things can be done better.

Recent Initiatives

1 We have established a standing Child Protection Working Group to monitor the practical operation of our procedures and to formulate and develop new strategies. The group includes representatives from all ASA affiliated district associations and the NSPCC.

We have established a 'hot line' known as Swimline (telephone number 0808 100 4001) manned by members of the Working group who are skilled counsellors and who will provide telephone assistance in the following areas:

To children and parents of children who have suffered child abuse (the intention is to complement Child line and other agencies by giving sport specific advice eg advice in relation to coaching practices and where this strays into the area of emotional abuse).

To coaches and teachers (individuals who are concerned as to how they should be acting).

Anyone telephoning Swimline has the option of being automatically transferred to the NSPCC Childline for emergency assistance.

Conclusion: Longer Term Strategies

1 The response of participants in the sport generally to the significant developments, which have taken place over the last three years, has been overwhelmingly supportive.

2 The Association believes that the amendments to legislation contained in the Police Act with regard to criminal record checks together with the proposed new ban on convicted offenders working with children are very positive moves which will help sport in its efforts to combat this problem of child abuse.

As is stated in the Foreword to our Procedures document undoubtedly some individuals will actively seek employment or voluntary work with children in order to abuse their position. Any steps that make this attempt more difficult have the support of the ASA. Our paramount aim is the welfare of our younger members.

3 But there is a need for coordination strategies within sport (indeed society) as a whole. One fear of the Association is that it will be successful but only at the expense of driving paedophiles from the sport of swimming into other sports which have similar disciplines or to which there is similar methodology in coaching and teaching.

4 To avoid this scenario that ASA believes that a coordinated approach is needed across all sports and that this should be regarded as a priority issue by the Home Office, CCPR, UK and Home Countries Sports Councils. However, recognising that there will necessarily need to be further consideration of the funding ramifications of this as an interim measure there needs to be greater information sharing between governing bodies which in turn depends upon their taking appropriate steps to ensure that they have in place the necessary Data Protection Act licenses to enable them to be free to disseminate information to other governing bodies regarding suspected offenders. The Association has in place

a licence enabling it to accept as a 'source' and to make 'disclosures' to other sporting bodies having as one of their areas of concern the protection of the welfare of young children in their sport.

The Association is always willing to sit down with other sporting bodies to share experiences in this area.[159]

Conclusion

Other sports have been praised for developing coherent child protection policies. Bodies such as the Child Protection in Sport Unit (partly run by the National Society for the Prevention of Cruelty to Children – NSPCC) and the Sports Coach UK (formerly the National Coaching Foundation) have produced considerable literature on this area.[160]

Brackenridge, C, *Spoilsports: Understanding and Preventing Sexual Exploitation in Sport*

Codes of Practice constitute an important part of an overall policy infrastructure that can guarantee safe and enjoyable sporting experiences. They set out expectations and help to delimit the boundaries between ethical and unethical practices ... However, they are also limited in that they provide only one view of ethical practice – a contractual one – that might militate against the notion of individual virtue and responsibility in sport ... a code of practice should be seen as only *one*, limited step towards the prevention or eradication of sexual exploitation ... sports managers therefore need to acknowledge the limitations of codes, without a comprehensive implementation strategy, they are often meaningless in practice.[161]

More effective vetting and screening of applicants to coaching positions needs to be implemented. The Criminal Records Bureau is available to be used by sports organisations both for employees and volunteers.[162] However, it is estimated that only a smell percentage of those with a propensity to abuse children have a criminal record. Brackenridge believes that:

What is certain is that the clamour for some form of official checking will continue in voluntary sport because of the widespread, mistaken belief that criminal checks will somehow, in themselves, purify sport of the dangers of sexual exploitation.[163]

Perhaps a register of convicted paedophiles who have, or attempt to get involved in sport needs to be initiated, similar to the Sex Offenders Register?[164]

There clearly is a problem of balance here. Young athletes need support and encouragement in their endeavours. In sport, all the emotions from elation to despair can be experienced. Coaches need to be able to show encouragement sometimes in a physical way, a hug of joy or a shoulder to cry on. In some sports, for example, gymnastics, physical contact is needed between coach and child to assist in certain techniques.

Oppressive encouragement and abuse in all its forms needs to be exposed and effectively eradicated. What is of importance is that a safe working environment for child athletes needs to be

---

159 Gray, A, 'Swimming and child protection: the story so far' (1999) 2(2) Sports Law Bulletin 8. See Myers, J and Barrett, B, 'In at the Deep End' (2002) NSPCC.

160 See www.thecpsu.org.uk and http://sportengland.org.

161 *Op cit*, fn 148, Brackenridge (2001), p 189.

162 Williams, Y, 'Child protection in sport' (2000) 8(1) Sport and the Law Journal 8; Williams, Y, Government sponsored Professional Sports Coaches and the Need for Protection (2003) 2(1) Entertainment Law 55.

163 *Op cit*, fn 148, Brackenridge (2001), p 189.

164 See the general provisions for regulation of convicted paedophiles in the Sex Offenders Act 1997.

guaranteed. The law has a role to play, perhaps, but this will need to be alongside other regulatory mechanisms such as codes of ethical practice. All parties need to be better informed of the distinction between acceptable and unacceptable behaviour.

CONCLUSION

These five examples of sporting areas, where either the law has a regulatory role or there are strong calls for its intervention, all illustrate the complex policy issues that exist. They all also demonstrate that law is only a part of a wider regulatory framework. The interaction between law and the other regulatory rules and policies is essential to understand as part of this wide and complex regulatory milieu.

KEY SOURCES

BMA, *The Boxing Debate* (1993), London: British Medical Association.

Brackenridge, C, *Spoilsports: Understanding and Preventing Sexual Exploitation in Sport* (2001), London: Routledge.

Burns Report, *The Report of the Committee of Inquiry into Hunting with Dogs in England and Wales* (2000); see www.huntinginquiry.gov.uk.

Collins, M, *Sport and Social Exclusion* (2001), London: Routledge.

Gardiner, S and Welch, R, 'Sport, racism and the limits of "colour blind" law', in McDonald, I and Carrington, B (eds), *'Race', Sport and British Society* (2001), London: Routledge.

THE GOVERNANCE OF SPORT

CHAPTER 4

GOVERNANCE OF SPORT: NATIONAL, EUROPEAN AND INTERNATIONAL PERSPECTIVES

INTRODUCTION

This chapter will focus on issues that have already been alluded to in Section One. First there will be a discussion of the issues concerning sports governance – that is, the internal running of a sport from the national governing body (NGB) through regional and county bodies to the individual sports club. This creates a pyramid structure with the NGB at the apex. Above this structure are of course European and international sports federations. In the recent past there has been an increasing belief that the sports governance in the UK has been sub-standard. The qualities of effective corporate governance, comparable to that needed in NGBs and international sports federations (ISF) will be considered.

Second, the need to understand the regulation and governance of UK as a part of the development of a European sports policy will be examined. The reality of sports as being big business and this recognition by the European Commission (EU) has led to an increasingly interventionist approach. This has happened primarily through the four Fundamental Freedoms and competition law provisions.[1] The development of a distinct EU sports policy will be charted. An analysis will be made of 'The European Model of Sport' that reflects the traditions and regulatory structures found within Europe. An alternative model is 'The American Model of Sport'. There is evidence that the structure of European sport is becoming increasingly 'Americanised' and this evidence will be evaluated.

Third, the developing international sports law framework will be examined; the reality that much of elite professional sport is internationalised and regulated by powerful ISFs. The regulatory framework that tries to ensure effective and fair governance within the organisations is crucial. The growing influence of bodies such as the Court of Arbitration for Sport is significant. This all needs to be understood within the process of globalisation. Sport is a paradigm example of this phenomenon. Sport, however, is paradoxical – it fits into notions of globalisation particularly with its symbiotic relationship with the global media complex, yet retains very powerful notions of specificity and localism.

GOVERNANCE

The move to professionalisation in Rugby Union during the mid-1990s was accompanied by Will Carling's description of the English Rugby Union Committee as '57 old farts running Rugby Union'.[2] The English Football Association has also been seen as out of touch with the realities of modern sport. There have been concerns voiced about the unwieldy nature of the FA's general committee.

In athletics similar disharmony has reigned:

Downes, S and Mackay, D, *Running Scared: How Athletics Lost Its Innocence*

Until 1990, British athletics was organised by 16 different governing bodies in a confusing miasma of administration, full of duplication, as well as conflicting and contradicting interests. The AAA (Amateur

---

1   The impact of EU and national competition law is discussed in Chapter 9.
2   'Amateur status "not accurate" ' *The Guardian*, 17 March 1995, p 21 and 'Commentary: time to tackle the thorny question of "shamateurs" ' *The Guardian*, 17 March 1995, p 24.

Athletics Association), the oldest athletics body in the world, which still governed the affairs of men's athletics in clubs throughout England, was the richest and most powerful and was not alone in its reluctance to cede its independence and authority to a new group. But after 30 years of debate, wrangling, consultation reports and more discussion, the sport finally, if somewhat reluctantly, came together under the umbrella of a single federation, the BAF (British Athletics Federation), in 1991.[3]

BAF went into administration largely due to the action by Diane Modahl.[4] It has been resurrected as UK Athletics. Often disputes within the administrative structure of sports have been disputes between competing governing bodies or internal power struggles or between governing bodies and players' associations as to the right to administer. There has been an awareness of a need to improve the standards of organisational governance and also a need for the operation of NGBs to comply with the external norms dictated by the law.

The traditional ethos of sports administrators has been built on a base of amateurism and voluntary contributions, with individuals rising through the ranks of the particular sport, driven primarily by their love of the sport. In recent years this has started to be replaced by individuals brought in from outside the sport with particular professional skills. The organisation of English cricket has gone through changes, with the Test and County Cricket Board becoming the English and Welsh Cricket Board in 1997. Major criticisms have been voiced over the years as to the lack of vision for the future of the game. The appointment of Lord MacLaurin, ex-chairman of the Tesco supermarket chain, was designed to inject new ideas and a more rational plan for the future of cricket. The Chief Executive of the FA from 1999 until 2002 was Adam Crozier, whose background was in advertising.

There has been support for the involvement of more lawyers in top positions in NGBs. What do lawyers have to offer to improve sports administration? In the United States, lawyers have been actively involved in running and regulating sport for some time.[5] The big four professional team sports in the USA, American football, basketball, baseball and ice hockey, all have lawyers as commissioners or presidents of their respective national associations.[6] There is big money to be earned: David Stern, the Commissioner of the National Basketball Association is extremely well remunerated.[7]

Lawyers clearly have qualities to offer: rational thinking, objectivity, foresight and development of preventive methods.[8] British sport may be learning from the United States. A number of sports administrators have a legal background, an acknowledgment that legal expertise has a role to play in sports administration.[9] The appointment of a lawyer to be Chief Executive of the English Premier League was, however, not a great success. Peter Leaver QC saw his contract terminated in 1999.[10]

---

3   Downes, S and Mackay, D, *Running Scared: How Athletics Lost Its Innocence* (1996), London: Mainstream, pp 29–30.

4   See later, p 203.

5   Judge Landis was commissioner of baseball from 1920–44; Clarence Cambell, a lawyer, was the National Hockey League President from 1946–77. See Kaplan, J, 'The most fun they've ever had: lawyers in the world of pro sports' (1992) 78 American Bar Association Journal 56; and Shulruff, L, 'The football lawyers' (1985) 71 American Bar Association Journal 45.

6   See 'Student note' (1990) 67 Denver University Law Review 110.

7   He is reported to earn over US$70 million per year; www.askmen.com/.

8   Common qualities discussed by lawyers generally and recounted in a series of interviews with leading sports lawyers in Britain in 1994 by the author. Generally, on lawyers', qualities and values see Cotterrell, R, *The Sociology of Law: An Introduction* (2003), 3rd edn, London: Butterworths.

9   See 'Why every FC will soon need its own QC' *The Guardian*, 1 March 1997, p 20.

10   See 'TV advisors get big pay-out' (2000) 3(2) Sports Law Bulletin 7.

Characteristics of Sports Governance

What has been increasingly apparent is that there has been a need to develop more effective mechanisms of governance within sports NGBs. This is partly due to the need to achieve compliance to the external legal norms, that is, to operate within the law. It is also about balancing all the interests that were discussed in Chapter 2.[11]

So what are the qualities of effective sports governance? Sport has looked to the world of corporate governance for guidance. In 1992, the *Cadbury Report* was published providing the values and standards required of corporate behaviour.[12] A Code of Best Practice was directed at the Boards of Directors of all listed companies in the UK:

Cadbury Report, 'Code principles'

3.2 The principles on which the Code is based are those of openness, integrity and accountability. They go together. Openness on the part of companies, within the limits set by their competitive position, is the basis for the confidence which needs to exist between business and all those who have a stake in its success. An open approach to the disclosure of information contributes to the efficient working of the market economy, prompts boards to take effective action and allows shareholders and others to scrutinise companies more thoroughly.

3.3 Integrity means both straightforward dealing and completeness. What is required of financial reporting is that it should be honest and that it should present a balanced picture of the state of the company's affairs. The integrity of reports depends on the integrity of those who prepare and present them.

Boards of directors are accountable to their shareholders and both have to play their part in making that accountability effective. Boards of directors need to do so through the quality of the information which they provide to shareholders, and shareholders through their willingness to exercise their responsibilities as owners.

The arguments for adhering to the Code are twofold. First, a clear understanding of responsibilities and an open approach to the way in which they have been discharged will assist boards of directors in framing and winning support for their strategies. It will also assist the efficient operation of capital markets and increase confidence in boards, auditors and financial reporting and hence the general level of confidence in business.[13]

These values of openness, integrity and accountability are the only relevant values of effective governance? Are they as appropriate to sports governing bodies as to general business? Perhaps it is not an exhaustive list.[14] Other terms can be substituted for these listed – values such as transparency are closely linked to openness. Transparency is partly about openness, but also allows outsiders to see, for example in sport, how disciplinary procedures operate and how decisions are made. It is also about the need for effective communication of key information in a form and way that is meaningful to target audiences. Can greater democracy be added? With companies, this is constructed in terms of the rights of the shareholders vis à vis the directors of a company. Some sporting bodies and clubs may have shareholders, but it is more accurate to talk of 'stakeholders' in sport including owners,

---

11 See p 53 – 'In English football there are many tensions concerning power, between the football authorities, potential external regulators, shareholders of clubs and the increasingly powerful top players and the fans.'

12 *Report of the Committee on the Financial Aspects of Corporate Governance* (1999), London: Gee.

13 *Ibid*, paras 3.2–3.5.

14 Note that there have been many more reports on corporate governance since the Cadbury Report, e.g. OECD – Principles of good practice (2004), see Birkbeck College's Football Governance Research Centre web site for copies of other Reports- www.football-research.org/library.htm.

administrators, fans, media and commercial interests. What say should these constituent groups have in the future direction of a sports body?

The value of compliance with external legal norms of sport could be added. With the tradition of self-regulation permeating sport, this is something that sport has had difficulty in engaging with. Lastly, the requirement that organizations should act with a 'social responsibility' has developed in recent years and this increasingly should apply also to sporting bodies.[15]

These values and goals are commendable, but an issue is always how are they 'policed' and how compliance is to be guaranteed. In addition, how should these values be applied to the sports world – how different are specific sporting to general organizations?

WHAT IS EFFECTIVE SPORTS GOVERNANCE?

In recent years sport governance has fallen into disrepute primarily because of the involvement of sports federations not only in the rules of the game but also in wide ranging commercial activities. Because of the monopolistic position of virtually all sports federations, this distinction which appeared so clear in the past when governing sport for the 'good of the game' has become blurred by commercial activities.

There have been increasing demands that sports NGBs are more responsive and democratic, together with other sports organisations lower in the pyramid structure. This will be examined later in the context of football. In Europe, the increasing pressure from the European Commission for NBGs and ISFs to comply with EU law and notably the competition law regime, together with the scandals that have enveloped the IOC, have put the spotlight on sports governance. DG IV (competency for competition issues) of the EU Commission and the European Court of Justice have on several occasions drawn attention to this dichotomy (rules for the governance of the game on the one hand and rules that have a commercial impact on the other).[16] Most recently this has occurred in the *Deliège*[17] and *Lehtonen*[18] cases. The European Competition authorities have on several occasions indicated that where the rules of sports federations have an economic or commercial dimension, they will attract the attention of European law; particularly the four basic freedoms, namely free movement of persons, of services, of goods and of the rights of establishment, as well as the competition rules pertaining to cartels and abuse of dominant positions. The majority of sport federations find themselves in a monopolistic position by virtue of the way in which their sport is organised. It is in this context that in March 2001, the First European Conference on the Governance of Sport was held.[19]

---

15 See (2003) 6(3) Sports Law Bulletin, 2 – this will include environmental concerns.

16 The Court of Arbitration for Sport has shown a distinction between issues involving technical decisions, standards or rules that essentially concern rules of the game are beyond arbitral ior judicials scrutiny and should not be reviewed, e.g. *M. v Assoc. Internationale de Boxe Amateur (AIBA)*, CAS Ad Hoc Div. (O.G. Atlanta 1996) reported in Reeb, M, *Digest of Awards of CAS Awards 1986–1998*, (1999), Berne: Staempfli, where case was made to review a referee's decision when Boxer M was disqualified for landing a below-the-belt punch on his opponent.

17 Cases C-51/96 and C-191/97 *Deliège v Liège Ligue Francophone de Judo*, judgment of 11 April 2000.

18 Case C-176/96 *Lehtonen & Castors Canada Dry Namur-Braine v FRBSB* (Belgian Basketball Federation), judgment of 13 April 2000.

19 *The Rules of the Game* – Europe's first conference on the Governance of Sport, see papers at www.governance-in-sport.com. The Conference was jointly organised by the FIA, the European Olympic Committee and lawyers, Herbert Smith. For more information, see Caiger, A and Gardiner, S, 'The rules of the game: Europe's first conference on the governance of sport' (2001) 4(2) Sports Law Bulletin 1, and *SportBusiness*, April 2001, p 26.

The intention of the conference was to encourage a debate as to how it may be possible to separate out the rules of the game of a non-economic nature from those that have an economic dimension. This dichotomy is clearly more important in the large federations than in the case of small ones where economic activity is insignificant and would probably fall within the *de minimus* rules of European law and be ignored.

An important example of the problems of dichotomy can be illustrated by the recent negotiations between the *Fédération Internationale de L'Automobile* (FIA) and DG IV. There have been many years of tension between the Competition Commission and Formula I racing; of particular concern has been the close relationship between the FIA and Formula One Administration, the company that markets the rights to Formula One racing. In June 1999, the EU Commission made formal objections to this relationship. The agreement announced in January 2001 lays down that the FIA will concentrate on managing the rules of the governance of the FIA whilst licensing their commercial rights for one hundred years to Bernie Ecclestone's 'F1 Races'.

Commission ended its monitoring of FIA/Formula One compliance with 2001 settlement.

The Commission is satisfied that the conflict of interests identified in the FIA regulations and the restrictions that had been put on circuit owners, F1 teams and TV broadcasters have been ended. This assessment comes after a period of monitoring compliance of the settlement reached in October 2001 with international motor racing body FIA and the Formula One companies. FIA's role is now limited to that of a sports regulator. Circuit owners can, if they wish, organise rival championships and car manufacturers will in the future be able to participate in races other than those organised by the Formula One company. Television contracts have also been significantly shortened, which allows broadcasters to bid for coverage of this popular sport at regular intervals.[20]

The 'corporate experience' provides valuable lessons for the development of higher and more consistent standards of governance in sport. The key governance principles developed for companies are also highly relevant to sports and sports' governing bodies. Two extracts from the papers given at the conference are particularly useful:

Gaved, M, 'Corporate governance today and its relevance to sport'

2 Differences between sports and companies

However, when reviewing the development of improved standards of governance in corporations, it is also important to recognise that there are a number of fundamental differences between sports organisations and companies. In general, these differences should make it easier to develop a general governance framework for sports and codes for individual sports. The three most important differences are:

(1) Members of sports organisations do not 'own' their sports in the way that shareholders own companies. Shares can be purchased and sold but membership of sports organizations generally cannot. The ownership of shares and companies is essentially a legal construct, whilst most sports organisations are associations of people with a common interest in:

    a the broad development and funding of their sports

    b training and participation;

    c competitions and events; and

    d the setting and application of rules. Shareholders and companies have interests in common but these are seldom as broad in their scope.

---

20   IP/03/1491, 31 October 2003 – see http://europa.eu.int/comm/sport.

(2) Members of sports organisations are also real people who typically belong to only one organisation. In contrast, most shares are owned by competing financial institutions who normally own shares in many – or sometimes hundreds – of companies. Historically, this diversification has made it difficult for shareholders to coordinate their common interests. The creation of common and widely supported codes of governance has made it considerably easier.

(3) Boards and shareholders are strongly focused on the commercial activities and performance of companies. Where companies have activities which are not aligned to the interests of shareholders, governance processes may have an important role to play. Whilst many sports now have a commercial element – and in some cases this has grown dramatically over the last few years – in Europe commercial activities are not sports' fundamental reason for existing.[21]

Rogge, J, 'Governance in sport: a challenge for the future'

As demonstrated earlier, governments or public authorities are linking the recognition of the role of sports governing bodies to the way they operate. The issue of governance and the *contend* sports bodies are ready to give to it are essential for the future relations between sports, its stakeholders and public authorities.

Governance is about clarification between the 'rules of the games' and the economic and commercial dimension related to the management of a sport. Because sports is based on ethics and fair competition, the governance of sport should fulfil the highest standards in terms of transparency, democracy and accountability.[22]

How best can bodies such as the EU Commission ensure sports governing bodies (NGBs and ISF) take seriously the need to seek greater compliance with external legal norms? Is it always possible to distinguish between sporting rules concerning governance of the game and those concerning the commercial dynamics of sport?

EUROPEAN SPORTS POLICY

There are two main European institutions of increasing influence upon sport. The European Commission is the most important such institution but the separate body, the Council of Europe also has a role.

The Council of Europe

The Council of Europe is an intergovernmental European cultural institution which comprises the majority of European countries. Set up in 1948 to support the concept of European unity in the aftermath of the Second World War, it is situated in Strasbourg and shares a site with the European Parliament of the European Union when in session. The Council of Europe is best known for its Human Rights Convention. It also does useful work in a number of areas such as the environment, education and local government. The Council of Europe has a directorate with sole responsibility for sport. Through this directorate, the European Ministers responsible for sport meet every three years to draw up guidelines for the Council of Europe's sports policy and to discuss problems arising in

---

21 Gaved, M, 'Corporate governance today and its relevance to sport', *The Rules of the Game* – Europe's first conference on the Governance of Sport; see papers at www.governance-in-sport.com.

22 Rogge, J, 'Governance in sport: a challenge for the future', *The Rules of the Game* – Europe's first conference on the Governance of Sport; see papers at www.governance-in-sport.com.

international sport. If so required, they may also hold informal meetings of European Ministers within the three year cycle.

The Steering Committee for the Development of Sport consists of national governmental and non-governmental officials and prepares and implements the ministers' decisions. It decides the annual work programme and organises seminars and workshops on sports related issues. It meets annually in February/March.

Council of Europe, 'Promoting tolerant, fair and democratic sport open to everybody'

The Council of Europe is active on two fronts to maintain the integrity and the virtues of sport, the first of which was emphasised at the second summit:

- promoting sport for all as a means of improving the quality of life, facilitating social integration and contributing to social cohesion, particularly among young people;

- fostering tolerance through sport and defending sport against the serious threats currently facing it.

- The Council of Europe is involved in these specific fields because it regards sport as important for the example it sets, for the part it plays in society and for the contribution it makes to the health of the population.[23]

There are a number of programmes:

- Democracy through and in sport, social integration and personal development: since 1992, the work of the Committee for the Development of Sport (CDDS) has been guided by the European Sports Charter (an update of the 1975 Charter).

- Personal well-being: the CDDS has initiated various activities to promote healthy lifestyles and participation in sport.

- EUROFIT: personal fitness tests covering flexibility, speed, endurance and strength was devised for children of school age and is used in many European schools.

- Doping: the Anti-Doping Convention (1989).[24]

- Soccer: the European Convention on Spectator Violence and Misbehaviour at Sports Events and in Particular at Football Matches (1985).[25]

- Sport and the environment: work on sustainable development and sport has resulted in a code being adopted at the 9th Ministerial Conference, which calls on all sectors of the sports world to take measures to establish a harmonious relationship between sport and the environment.

- Sport, tolerance and fair play: in May 1996 the CDDS, together with the Dutch authorities, held a highly successful Round Table on sport, tolerance and fair play. The aim is to encourage fair play in sport and to spearhead programmes to teach and encourage tolerance in sport.

- The Clearing House: a European documentation centre for sport (SIONET).

- Guidance on sports legislation.[26]

- Youth and Sport.[27]

---

23 Find more information at www.coe.int and *The Council of Europe's Work on Sport 1967–91* (1992) Council of Europe, Vol I and *The Council of Europe's Work on Sport 1967–91* (1992), Council of Europe, Vol II; Walker, G, 'Conventions of the Council of Europe on sport', in *Congress Internacional Del Dret Il'Esport Proceedings*, March 1992, Barcelona.

24 Find Convention at http://culture.coe.fr/sp/splist.html.

25 *Ibid.*

26 *Study of National Sports Legislation in Europe* (1999), Council of Europe.

27 Further information on youth activities of the Council of Europe can be found on their website at www.coe.fr/youth.

As indicated, two full Conventions, the Convention on Anti-Doping and the Convention on Spectator Violence at Sports Events, have been drawn up.

European Commission of the European Union

Over the last 10 years or so, there has been some debate concerning whether the European Commission should be actively involved in the regulation of sport. Most people would argue that sport is different from other areas of economic activity such as the Common Agricultural Policy. The European Commission have, however, noticed that sport is 'big business', and claim that the general provisions of the Treaty of Rome should apply to sport, that is, the four freedoms underpinning the single market – free movement of individuals, goods, capital and services.

In a paper in 1992 entitled, 'The European Community and sport',[28] the European Commission defined its overall approach to relations with the world of sport. For sports federations, this paper provided the first reference framework defining the scope of Community action. It marked the starting point for a constructive dialogue, to acknowledge the specificity of sport and its special characteristics.

The creation of the single market in 1992 has had serious consequences for European sport. It has helped facilitate sport becoming an identifiable industry; many aspects of sporting activities are now covered by Community law and are subject to the legal and institutional imperatives of the Community. A number of rulings by the European Court of Justice have spelled out the relationship between sport and the Community. The first was laid down in *Walrave and Koch v Union Cycliste Internationale*,[29] which ruled that sport, at the professional, but not amateur level, falls within the Treaty of Rome:

Case 36/74 *Walrave and Koch v Union Cycliste Internationale*

Having regard to the objectives of the Community, the practice of sport is subject to Community Law only as far as it constitutes an economic activity within the meaning of Article 2 of the Treaty.

This has clearly been reinforced by the *Bosman* case.[30] The European Commission has set up a specialised unit to serve as a focal point for Community action located within the Directorate General X.

The European Union has recognised two main things concerning sport over the last few years. First the huge financial reality of sport as a big business.[31] Sport can no longer be protected and excluded from the application of the Treaty provisions of the Union. It is clear that sports administrators, organisers and athletes should be subject to, and able to avail themselves of European law.

Second, the political value of sport is being identified. The role that sport has in promoting social solidarity has been actively supported as part of a clear socio-cultural policy. In addition, sport is seen as being able to achieve integration within the 'New Europe' in a way that other institutions cannot.

---

28 'The European Community and sport' (1992) Commission of the European Communities 2/1992.

29 Case C-36/74 [1974] ECR 1405; [1975] 1 CMLR 320. However, Case C-13/76 *Dona v Mantero* [1976] 2 CMLR 578; [1976] ECR 1333 was more cautious in the application of the Treaty of Rome, ruling that it was not applicable to national sporting associations.

30 Case C-415/93 *Union Royale Belge des Societes de Football Association ASBL v Jean-Marc Bosman*, 15 December 1995.

31 See the study by Coopers and Lybrand for DG X, *The Impact of European Union Activities on Sport* (1995), European Commission.

The European Commission in the surrounding issues of the *Bosman* case suggested that the development of a European football team might be a long term goal. At a time of political pressure from some Member States for greater unification, sport may be seen as one of the neutral mechanisms to market the European dream. Although not initiated by the European Commission, and predating it by many years, we have already been integrated in golfing terms: the dramatic victory of the European team over the USA in the Ryder Cup in 2002 and the more leisurely triumph in 2004 have been followed by millions. As rare events of a 'supra-national' team being widely supported, it helped reinforce the notion of being European.

The extent to which there is a general transference of being European into the general consciousness and popular culture is another question. The Europeanisation of our sporting teams and the nationality of players in national leagues seems likely to increase. These seem to be the very conditions in sport under which the spectre of extreme nationalism is raised. Sport can be a unifying factor, but it clearly is also an arena where 'difference' in numerous ways, importantly in terms of nationality, is highly visible.

The Development of a European Sports Policy

The development of any discernible policy in the European Union (EU) in any area is long and complex, given the range of general EU activity that impacts upon the operation of sport in Europe. This has been particularly true of the absence of a specific legal status for sport in the Treaties. As such, sport has been prone to fall victim to the unintended consequences of activity elsewhere in the EU. Nevertheless, a degree of order can be placed on the development of a 'sports policy' in the EU over the last 10 years. The following analysis identifies three phases in this development.

Parrish, R, 'The path to a "sports policy" in the European Union'

Phase One

The first phase of EU involvement in sport pre-dates the Single European Market (SEM) programme. A tenuous link between sport and the EU emerged post 1957 as the objectives of the Treaty of Rome became increasingly applied to the world of sport despite sport being granted no legal status in the Treaty.

Early European Court of Justice (ECJ) rulings established principles based on these objectives. In *Walrave and Koch v AUCI* (1974), the Court held that the practice of sport is subject to Community law only in so far as it constitutes an economic activity. In *Donà v Mantero* (1976) the Court held that discriminatory nationality rules in sport were incompatible with European Community (EC) law unless such rules were applied to matters of purely sporting interest such as national teams and not to those of economic interest.

The response of the other European institutions was patchy. The European Commission began negotiations with UEFA in 1978 over the use of quota systems limiting the number of foreign players being used by an employer and the use of a transfer fee system for players at the end of their contracts. The European Parliament responded with a number of reports in the early to mid 1980s covering such issues as sport and the Community and vandalism and violence in sport. The European Council's first direct response came in the form of the 1984 European Council when the integrationist qualities of sport were first recognised. Furthermore, in 1985 the Milan Summit adopted the Adonnino report including reference to sport and a people's Europe. In the meantime, the Council of Ministers continued to pass legislation not specifically directed at sport but increasingly being applied to it.

Phase Two

The second phase of EU involvement in sport was greatly influenced by the accelerated regulatory ethos of the SEM project. Today 18 out of 23 Directorate Generals (DGs) in the European Commission have some impact, direct or indirect on the operation of sport in Europe. The expanded range of EU policy competence fostered by the SEM programme has further sucked sport into the operation of the Single Market. Such expansion has meant that EU involvement in sport now includes areas such as free movement of persons, goods and services, health and safety, competition policy, animals in sport, environmental policy, taxation, economic and monetary union, funding for sport and people with disabilities. In only the last two areas of involvement can EU action be said to be specifically targeted at sport, yet a *de facto* 'sports policy' is emerging.

During this second phase, the most stark recognition of sports link to the Single Market came in 1995 with the *Bosman* ruling. In this case the Court held that transfer rules and UEFA nationality clauses were incompatible with Article 48 of the Treaty dealing with free movement of persons. The subsequent impact of the ruling has been profound.

The intergovernmental conference (IGC), launched in March 1996 provided an opportunity for the EU to clarify its relationship with the world of sport. The task of framing a new treaty led to intense lobbying for sport to be included by way of a protective article. The European Olympic Committees (EOCs) and the European Non Governmental Sports Organisations (ENGSO) hoped to minimise the effects of 'insensitive' EU legislation by pressing for the insertion of such an article that would ensure sporting interests be taken into account in the framing of new EU legislation. The results fell short of expectations.

Phase Three

The third phase started with the conclusion of the IGC process and the signing of the Treaty of Amsterdam. After concern raised by the European Commission regarding the prospect of Treaty exemptions stemming from the inclusion of a legally binding article for sport, a compromise was reached by the generally ambivalent Member States. The Heads of Government and State attached a non binding declaration to the Treaty which read . . .

> The conference emphasises the social significance of sport, in particular its role in forging identity and bringing people together. The conference therefore calls on the bodies of the European Union to listen to sports associations when important questions affecting sport are at issue. In this connection, special consideration should be given to the particular characteristics of amateur sport.

The declaration represented a belated acknowledgement by the Member States that the activities of the EU were having a profound impact on sport in Europe even though sport was not the intended target of legislation. A degree of uncertainty must characterise this third phase as the impact of the declaration remains unclear. Should this 'soft law' approach harden into a legally binding article, then phase four will have begun.[32]

THE EUROPEAN MODEL OF SPORT

The European Commission published two important documents in 1998. The first was a Commission working paper published by DG X entitled, *The Development and Prospects for Community Action in the Field of Sport*.[33] The paper identified sport as performing an educational, public health, social, cultural and recreational function. Sport is the key vehicle through which policy objectives in these fields could be pursued. It recognised that sport plays a significant economic role in Europe, and the Commission as guardian of the Treaties had a responsibility to ensure the even implementation of Community law.

---

32 Parrish, R, 'The path to a "sports policy" in the European Union' (1998) 2(1) Sports Law Bulletin 10.

33 Commission of the European Communities, *The Development and Prospects for Community Action in the Field of Sport* (1998), DG X, Brussels, found at http://europa.eu.int/comm/sport/index.html.

The paper advocated a dual approach to sport: on the one hand the integration of sport into different Community policies whilst on the other ensuring the implementation of Community law.

The second document was a consultation document entitled, *The European Model of Sport*.[34] This document attempted to identify the characteristics of European sport. Three main issues were identified: the structure of European sport, for example, the organisation, features and current changes and problems; sport and television focusing primarily on broadcasting rights; and lastly, the relationship between sport and society (in particular the role of sport in promoting social inclusion).

What are these specific characteristics of European sport? What particular problems does European sport face? The document acknowledged that the *Bosman* case had had huge financial repercussions for sport in Europe. It also indicated that revenues from sports events depend on the attractiveness of a sport for the general public, but foresaw problems, in that not every sport is as suited to television as football. There is a risk that only the commercially attractive sports will survive and other smaller sports will become endangered. The income received from the sale of broadcasting rights is transforming the sports world, widening the gulf between amateur and professional and between the top and bottom of sport in Europe.

The Commission of the European Communities, *The European Model of Sport: Consultation Document*

The characteristics of sport (uncertainty of results, equality of competitors) recognised by Advocate-General Lenz in the *Bosman* case make the sport market different from any other commercial market. The Advocate-General suggested that there should be a distribution of income in order to maintain a competitive balance. It is necessary to examine if and how sports income needs to be distributed among the clubs and associations. This can have consequences for the financing of sport in Europe.[35]

The document focuses on the structure of the 'European Model of Sport'. It was careful to note that from the end of the Second World War until the mid-1980s two different models of sport existed in Europe, namely the East and the West European model. The East was more or less ideologically oriented; sport was a part of propaganda. In western countries European sport developed a mixed model, in which actions performed by governmental and non-governmental organisations existed side by side. There was also the recognition that sport has grown in parallel with television, basically in an environment of exclusively public television.

The role of government in sport may be distinguished between different countries. Western European sport is thus the result of private and public activity. In the northern countries, the State does not regulate, whereas in the southern countries, the State plays a significant regulatory role in sport.[36]

The commercial reality of sport and the need for regulation is therefore clearly acknowledged, but as Richard Parrish argues:

Parrish, R, 'Reconciling conflicting approaches to sport in the European Union'

EU sports 'policy' is equally being shaped by a deep commitment to socio-political integration. This commitment has manifested itself in a desire to harness the socio-cultural and integrationist qualities of sport for political purposes. These include the use of sport to promote European solidarity and identity,

---

34 Commission of the European Communities, *The European Model of Sport: Consultation Document* (1998), DG X, Brussels, found at http://europa.eu.int/comm/sport/index.html.

35 *Ibid*, para 3.4.

36 See details of a number of European countries in Chalip, L, Johnson, A and Stachura, L (eds), *National Sports Policies: An International Handbook* (1996), Westport, CT: Greenwood.

the use of sport as a tool of urban and regional regeneration and the use of sport as a tool to combat social exclusion. This approach to sport is however incompatible with the economic and essentially regulatory approach being pursued elsewhere in the EU. As such a body of opinion has emerged in the EU seeking a more broad-based approach to sport that balances regulation with the promotion and protection of the socio-cultural dimension of sport.[37]

The Amsterdam Declaration in 1998 stated explicitly that sport has a role in forging identity and bringing people together. Sport represents and strengthens national or regional identity by giving people a sense of belonging to a group. It unites players and spectators, giving the latter the possibility of identifying with their nation. Sport contributes to social stability and is an emblem for culture and identity. Although sport in Europe has been confronted with globalisation, it often has a very obvious national and even regional specificity. The commitment to national identity or even regional identity is, therefore, one of the features of sport in Europe. This aim of social solidarity has been a continuing and important theme.

The documents reinforce the importance of Europe as a focus for world sport.

Commission of the European Communities, *The European Model of Sport: Consultation Document*

Traditionally the Member States of the European Union have hosted a significantly large percentage of world sports events: for example, 54% of Summer Olympics between 1896–1996 and 50% of football World Cups between 1930 and 1998. This remarkable concentration of world sport events within the EU has been partly a result of history. Europe saw the start of the industrial revolution. The ensuing development towards economic and social progress enhanced the development of sport in Europe. Traditionally sport has its origins on the European continent; the Olympic movement, for example, came about as the result of a European initiative. Moreover, most of the important international sport organisations are based in Europe. Europe can therefore be considered the powerhouse of world sport. The latest developments are evidence that sport in Europe is very dynamic.[38]

Characteristics of European Sport

Two key characteristics are:

Pyramidic Structure: the clubs form the base of the pyramid. Regional federations form the next level; the clubs are usually members of these organisations. National federations, one for each discipline, represent the next level. Usually all the regional federations are members of the respective national federation. The apex of the pyramid is formed by the European Federation, which are organised along the same lines as the national federations. The pyramid structure implies interdependence between the levels, not only on the organisational side but also on the competitive side, because competitions are organised on all levels. This can be compared very specifically with the horizontal structure of North American sport, where there is little connection between the professional leagues and the lower echelons of any particular sport.

Promotion and Relegation: this system of promotion and relegation is one of the key features of the European model of sport. In comparison, in the US has developed the model of closed championships/ leagues and multiple sport federations. The same teams, once in this championship, keep on playing in this league. It has to be recognised that however in Europe, there is a new tendency to try and

37 Parrish, R, 'Reconciling conflicting approaches to sport in the European Union', in Caiger, A and Gardiner, S (eds), *Professional Sport in the EU: Regulation and Re-regulation* (2000), The Hague: Asser.
38 *Op cit*, fn 34, Commission of the European Communities (1998), para 1.3.

combine both systems. UEFA (Union of European Football Associations) has suggested clubs could qualify for European competition not only by a system of promotion and relegation, but also by fulfilling economic and technical criteria. In addition to the proposal for a breakaway and 'closed League' outside UEFA, a 'European Super League' has been mooted for a number of years.[39] Within this league it would be very likely that there would be no system of promotion and relegation. It is a new form of competition, which has no link with the existing pyramidal structure. Although there have been changes to UEFA's distribution of Champions League revenues, it may well be that the top clubs continue to be interested in a Super League, with more monies directed to the participants rather than to the administrators of the competition.[40]

Is European Sport being 'Americanised'?

Can these changes be seen as an example of an *Americanisation* of the regulatory and economic framework of European sport?[41] If things develop as in the United States, where the system of closed competitions has existed for many years, the top clubs could increase their profits enormously. The new approach will see the big teams playing each other regularly, something the US has known for a long time with its major sports. UEFA has been forced to react by proposing a new initiative that seeks to combine the traditional system of promotion and relegation and the closed championship system. What UEFA is offering clubs is a bigger share of the revenues generated by the sale of broadcasting rights.

As mentioned in Chapter 2, in the context of professional team sports in the USA, there is a general assumption that clubs are 'profit-maximisers'. In comparison, the main underlying economic model of European professional sport can be characterised as 'win-maximisation'. The ongoing demise of the transfer system has led to a search for a new mechanism for financial distribution: there is a search for new economic models. Salary caps and revenue sharing are two such possibilities. An example of the latter was established by UEFA as a solidarity system in order to distribute Champions League TV revenues. According to UEFA this system serves to maintain a competitive and financial balance among the clubs and to promote football in general. It is hard to please everyone all the time. The large football clubs accuse UEFA of not being transparent in financing and distribution. The smaller clubs complain that more money should go to the lower levels of the pyramid.

There is a need therefore, to understand these American-determined mechanisms thoroughly. Their importance is developing – but what is vital is that Europe develops appropriate hybrid mechanisms to recognise the specific traditions and forms of European sport and also perhaps the deeply embedded nature and quality of sport itself. As Stephen Weatherill comments, 'it is emphatically *not* the case that European sport is being propelled down the American Road by the law of the Community'.[42]

What is needed is to carefully resist the 'McDonaldisation' of sport regulation[43] (or perhaps reflecting the impact upon sport of the global media complex, it could more appropriately be

---

39   'Super clubs face ban says Blatter' *The Guardian*, 26 September 1998.

40   See the views of G14, the representative group of top European clubs – www.g14.com.

41   See Hoehn, T and Szymanski, S, 'The Americanisation of European football' (1990) Economic Review 205.

42   Weatherill, S, 'The influence of "Americanization": the influence of European Community law on the "European sport model" ', in Greenfield, S and Osborn, G (eds), *Law and Sport in Contemporary Society* (2000), London: Frank Cass, pp 157–81.

43   See Ritzer, G, *The McDonaldization of Society* (1996), California: Fine Forge.

described as the 'Murdochisation' of sport). The regulatory framework must have supra-national (European) and national specificity and relevance. This model has been exported to almost all other continents and countries, with the exception of North America. Sport in Europe has a unique structure. For the future development of sport in Europe these special features should be taken into account.

The Road to Nice: Emergence of a Distinct EU Sports Policy

The findings of the consultation exercise initiated by the publication of 'The European Model of Sport' were discussed at the first EU conference on sport held in Olympia in 1999.[44] The conclusions of this conference led to *The Helsinki Report on Sport*.[45]

Parrish, R, 'The Helsinki Report on Sport: a partnership approach to sport'

Introduction

The existence of the Helsinki Report on Sport owes much to the increasing involvement of the European Union's member states in sporting matters. Following the 1995 Bosman ruling and the European Commission's execution of competition powers in relation to sport, calls intensified for sport to be granted 'special status' within the EU Treaty. In 1997, the member states, meeting at the Amsterdam Summit attached a non-legally binding declaration on sport to the treaty expressing the wish that the 'social significance' of sport be safeguarded. In 1998, as part of its response to the declaration, the Commission published two policy papers, 'The Development and Prospects for Community Action in the Field of Sport', followed shortly by 'The European Model of Sport'. The reports were used to prepare the first EU conference on sport, held in Greece in May 1999.

The conclusions of this exercise were used by the Commission to respond to the member states' request, made at the December 1998 Vienna European Council that the Commission should 'submit a report to the Helsinki European Council with a view to safeguarding current sports structures and maintaining the social function of sport within the Community framework'. Accordingly, in December 1999 the Commission submitted the Helsinki Report on Sport to the member states meeting in Finland. The bulk of the report is contained within three sections.

The development of sport in Europe risks weakening its educational and social function.

The report claims that the 'European approach' to sport has recently been affected by several important developments. These developments include the growth in the popularity of sport, the increasing internationalisation of sport and the unprecedented development of the economic dimension of sport. The advantages of these developments for the European economy are considerable. The number of jobs created directly or indirectly by the sports industry has risen by 60% in the past ten years to reach nearly 2 million. However, the above developments have also led to some 'tensions'. First, doping may be a bi-product of increased competition stemming from commercial developments. Second, commercialism may be squeezing traditional sporting principles out of sport. In particular, the social function of sport is being threatened. Third, commercial pressures may lead to the current single structure for sport being fragmented as some participants seek a more lucrative future in break-away leagues. This may jeopardise financial solidarity between professional and amateur sport. Finally, the above developments are putting an increasingly physical and mental strain on young sports people thus risking their subsequent switch to alternative employment.

The Community, its member states and the sporting movement need to reaffirm and strengthen the educational and social function of sport. In this connection the report makes two sets of recommendations.

---

44 Caiger, A, 'A report on the first European Union conference on sport' (1999) 2(3) and (4) Sports Law Bulletin 11.
45 Found at http://europa.eu.int/comm/sport/index.html.

First, in relation to enhancing the educational role of sport, the report suggests that Community educational and training programmes could focus on:

- improving the position of sport and physical education at school through Community programmes;
- promoting the subsequent switch to other employment and future integration onto the labour market of sportsmen and women;
- promoting convergence between the training systems for sports workers in each member state.

Second, concerning doping in sport, the report outlines the measures adopted by the Commission in relation to anti-doping policy. First, doping issues have been referred to the European Group on Ethics. Second, a world anti-doping agency (WADA) has been established following co-operation with the Olympic movement. Third, measures to improve legislative co-ordination with national anti-doping measures have been explored.

1 Clarifying the legal environment of sport

The third section of the report examines the thorny issue of the relationship between sport and EU law. The report examines how the commercialisation of the sports sector has contributed to an increase in the number of conflicts involving EU law. These conflicts have ranged from disputes concerning the sale of television rights to issues of club ownership and geographical location. Quoting the conclusions of the first EU Conference on Sport organised by the Commission held in Olympia in May 1999, the paper argues that 'sport must be able to assimilate the new commercial framework in which it must develop, without at the same time losing its identity and autonomy, which underpin the functions it performs in the social, cultural, health and educational areas'.

To enable the sports world to achieve this, the report identifies a need for a 'new approach' for dealing with sports related issues in the EU. As the report explains, 'this new approach involves preserving the traditional values of sport, while at the same time assimilating a changing economic and legal environment.' Action at three levels was recommended.

At Community level, central to this 'legal environment' is the application of EU competition law. In this connection, the report provides examples of:

- practices which do not come under the competition rules;
- practices that are, in principle, prohibited by the competition rules; and
- practices likely to be exempted from the competition rules.

At national level, the report proposes measures designed to protect the national single structure 'model' of sporting organisation. In particular, the report suggests that 'one way of safeguarding the national federal structures could be to provide for them to be recognised by law in each member state of the Union'.

Finally, at the level of sporting organisations, the report suggests that sporting federations should more clearly define their 'missions and statutes'. This recommendation clearly places the emphasis on the federations to define the particular characteristics of sport and the measures they themselves have taken to protect and nurture such characteristics. Where sporting operations have a commercial dimension, the report argues that such operations must be 'founded on the principles of transparency and balanced access to the market, effective and proven redistribution and clarification of contracts, while prominence is given to the specific nature of sport'. Furthermore, regulatory measures should be 'objectively justified, non-discriminatory, necessary and proportional'. If sporting rules conform to these 'tests', they should not conflict with treaty provisions.

Conclusion

At the heart of the Helsinki Report on Sport lies the concept of 'partnership', a concept widely employed by EU officials. In this context partnership means the knitting together the macro (EU institutions), meso (member states) and micro (sub-national groups and non state actors) levels of activity to ensure a more structured and co-ordinated approach to sport. Simultaneously of course, partnership also draws a wide range of actors into the regional integration process and serves to legitimise EU involvement in policy areas.

The report clearly links commercialisation with the 'juridification' of sport. As sporting operations practise increasingly on a commercial basis, so EU law seeps into the internal laws of sport. The clearest example of this, other than the infamous *Bosman* ruling is the application of EU competition law to the sports sector. The danger is that the 'special characteristics' of sport become squeezed between these commercial and legal developments. The paper makes clear that action at EU level alone will be insufficient to protect current structures and the social function of sport. Hence a 'partnership' approach is recommended.[46]

The conclusions of the meeting reflected a desire on the part of the Member States to see the EU adopt a more holistic approach to sport. This involves the EU promoting and safeguarding the socio-cultural dimension of sport in addition to recognising the economic dimension of sport. The Directors concluded:

... sport is an important resource that promotes people's well-being and health, the cultural dimension and social cohesion. Therefore, sport in its social significance should be seen as a broad-based sector.[47]

Discussions on the fight against doping in sport and the social dimension of sport were continued by the Portuguese Presidency in the first half of 2000. Following the Santa Maria da Feira European Council meeting, the Presidency Conclusions relating to sport read:

... the European Council requests the Commission and the Council to take account of the specific characteristics of sport in Europe and its social function in managing common policies.[48]

In December 2000, a European council summit was held at Nice, France.

European Commission, 'The Nice Declaration on Sport'

1 The European Council has noted the report on sport submitted to it by the European Commission in Helsinki in December 1999 with a view to safeguarding current sports structures and maintaining the social function of sport within the European Union. Sporting organisations and the Member States have a primary responsibility in the conduct of sporting affairs. Even though not having any direct powers in this area, the Community must, in its action under the various Treaty provisions, take account of the social, educational and cultural functions inherent in sport and making it special, in order that the code of ethics and the solidarity essential to the preservation of its social role may be respected and nurtured.

2 The European Council hopes in particular that the cohesion and ties of solidarity binding the practice of sports at every level, fair competition and both the moral and material interests and the physical integrity of those involved in the practice of sport, especially minors, may be preserved.

Amateur sport and sport for all

3 Sport is a human activity resting on fundamental social, educational and cultural values. It is a factor making for integration, involvement in social life, tolerance, acceptance of differences and playing by the rules.

4 Sporting activity should be accessible to every man and woman, with due regard for individual aspirations and abilities, throughout the whole gamut of organised or individual competitive or recreational sports.

---

46 Parrish, R, 'The Helsinki Report on Sport: a partnership approach to sport' (2000) 3(3) Sports Law Bulletin 16. The report can be found at http://europa.int/comm/sport.
47 Finnish Presidency Conclusions 18 and 20.
48 Portuguese Presidency Conclusions 19 and 20, June 2000.

5 For the physically or mentally disabled, the practice of physical and sporting activities provides a particularly favourable opening for the development of individual talent, rehabilitation, social integration and solidarity and, as such, should be encouraged. In this connection, the European Council welcomes the valuable and exemplary contribution made by the Paralympic Games in Sydney.

6 The Member States encourage voluntary services in sport, by means of measures providing appropriate protection for and acknowledging the economic and social role of volunteers, with the support, where necessary, of the Community in the framework of its powers in this area.

Role of sports federations

7 The European Council stresses its support for the independence of sports organisations and their right to organise themselves through appropriate associative structures. It recognises that, with due regard for national and Community legislation and on the basis of a democratic and transparent method of operation, it is the task of sporting organisations to organise and promote their particular sports, particularly as regards the specifically sporting rules applicable and the make-up of national teams, in the way which they think best reflects their objectives.

8 It notes that sports federations have a central role in ensuring the essential solidarity between the various levels of sporting practice, from recreational to top-level sport, which co-exist there; they provide the possibility of access to sports for the public at large, human and financial support for amateur sports, promotion of equal access to every level of sporting activity for men and women alike, youth training, health protection and measures to combat doping, acts of violence and racist or xenophobic occurrences.

9 These social functions entail special responsibilities for federations and provide the basis for the recognition of their competence in organising competitions.

10 While taking account of developments in the world of sport, federations must continue to be the key feature of a form of organisation providing a guarantee of sporting cohesion and participatory democracy.

Preservation of sports training policies

11 Training policies for young sportsmen and -women are the life blood of sport, national teams and top-level involvement in sport and must be encouraged. Sports federations, where appropriate in tandem with the public authorities, are justified in taking the action needed to preserve the training capacity of clubs affiliated to them and to ensure the quality of such training, with due regard for national and Community legislation and practices.

Protection of young sportsmen and -women

12 The European Council underlines the benefits of sport for young people and urges the need for special heed to be paid, in particular by sporting organisations, to the education and vocational training of top young sportsmen and -women, in order that their vocational integration is not jeopardised because of their sporting careers, to their psychological balance and family ties and to their health, in particular the prevention of doping. It appreciates the contribution of associations and organisations which minister to these requirements in their training work and thus make a valuable contribution socially.

13 The European Council expresses concern about commercial transactions targeting minors in sport, including those from third countries, inasmuch as they do not comply with existing labour legislation or endanger the health and welfare of young sportsmen and -women. It calls on sporting organisations and the Member States to investigate and monitor such practices and, where necessary, to consider appropriate measures.

Economic context of sport and solidarity

14 In the view of the European Council, single ownership or financial control of more than one sports club entering the same competition in the same sport may jeopardise fair competition. Where necessary, sports federations are encouraged to introduce arrangements for overseeing the management of clubs.

15 The sale of television broadcasting rights is one of the greatest sources of income today for certain sports. The European Council thinks that moves to encourage the mutualisation of part of the revenue from such sales, at the appropriate levels, are beneficial to the principle of solidarity between all levels and areas of sport.

Transfers

16 The European Council is keenly supportive of dialogue on the transfer system between the sports movement, in particular the football authorities, organisations representing professional sportsmen and - women, the Community and the Member States, with due regard for the specific requirements of sport, subject to compliance with Community law.

17 The Community institutions and the Member States are requested to continue examining their policies, in compliance with the Treaty and in accordance with their respective powers, in the light of these general principles.[49]

Parrish, R, 'The road to Nice'

The French Presidency in the second half of 2000 was dominated by three related developments. The first issue concerned the European Commission's objections to the international transfer system and the interest shown by the game's governing body at re-introducing nationality restrictions in European football. The nationality issue, despite being widely discussed throughout 2000, soon found itself playing second fiddle to the more immediate concern of the transfer dispute (see previous edition of the SLB). Nevertheless, FIFA and UEFA hoped that both issues could be addressed through the insertion of a protective protocol on sport in the Nice Treaty. A forum to discuss these issues was provided by the French Presidency and the Commission through the convening of the 9th European Sports Forum held in Lille on 26 and 27 October 2000.

The Lille Sports Forum was the second major development during the French Presidency. At this meeting, participants took the opportunity to stress the special characteristics of sport. In particular, they emphasised the social, health, cultural and integrationist qualities of sport and to this end welcomed efforts by the French Presidency to prepare a Declaration on sport to be discussed at the Nice European Council.

The third development, the negotiation of the Nice Treaty, gave the French Presidency the opportunity to present their sports related ideas to a wider forum whilst offering the European Council an opportunity to formally respond to the Helsinki Report on Sport. The protocol approach advocated by UEFA and FIFA was rejected by the member states in favour of a Declaration on sport presented as a Presidency Conclusion. The Declaration, reproduced in full below, is significant in that the member states have offered some guidance as to the immediate resolution of pending disputes (notably the transfer issue) whilst also laying down some signposts for the longer term future of EU involvement in sport.

The road to Nice began at Amsterdam and has been littered with 'soft' law measures designed to add clarity to the relationship between sport and the EU. The Nice Declaration, although legally even 'softer' than Amsterdam, is an important development in that it not only serves to guide the application of EU law to sport, but it also further 'hardens' sports policy in the EU. The scope and length of the Declaration clearly demonstrates that sport is now discussed at the highest political levels in the EU. Never before have the member states expended over 1000 words on sport. Furthermore, although not a legally binding measure, with such strong support from the member states to see EU involvement in sport respect the special characteristics of sport, it is inconceivable that those responsible for the application of EU law will ignore the Declaration.

---

49 'Declaration on the specific characteristics of sport and its social function in Europe', Presidency Conclusions, Nice European Council Meeting, 7–9 December 2000; found at http://europa.eu.int/comm/sport/index.html.

The immediate post-Nice future is therefore beginning to look clearer. Sport will not be granted a general exemption from EU law. However, neither will it simply be treated as any other commercial activity operating within the Single European Market. The Nice Declaration has acknowledged that sport may be 'special' and should be treated as such in the application of EU law (see point 1 of the Declaration). This is a crucial breakthrough for sport, but the word 'special' needs defining. Only sport itself can provide this definition and this gives sport an opportunity to state its case. In this connection, the Lille discussions on the 'Specific Nature of Sport' are an important contribution to this ongoing debate. In the future, the sports world must do two things. First, sporting organisations should clearly define their missions and statutes in order to identify those special characteristics of sport worthy of protection. They should also identify and review those measures they themselves have taken to protect and nurture such characteristics. Second, where sporting operations have a commercial dimension, sports rules must be *'founded on the principles of transparency and balanced access to the market, effective and proven redistribution and clarification of contracts, while prominence is given to the specific nature of sport'*. Furthermore, regulatory measures should be 'objectively justified, non-discriminatory, necessary and proportional' (the Helsinki Report on Sport, 1/12/99). If sporting rules conform to these 'tests', they should not conflict with Treaty provisions.

The Helsinki/Nice approach to sport in the EU offers sport an ideal opportunity to proactively shape the future of EU involvement in the sports world. History has however shown European sport to be a less than homogenous entity when faced with strategic political decisions. Having failed to even entertain the prospect of changing the international transfer system following the Commission's complaints, the football world is now divided on how to shut the stable door just as the horse looks like it might bolt. The less than common position adopted by FIFA, UEFA and FIFPRO over the transfer dispute should be a warning to sport that the Helsinki/Nice approach is an opportunity not to be missed.[50]

The Future for the EU Sports Policy

It seems as though there will continue to be a bifurcated approach to EU sports policy. It is highly unlikely that there will be a 'sporting exemption' from the provisions of EU law. There is recognition that although sport is an economic activity it is a 'special' case. Sport will, however, have to ensure that it complies with the provisions of EU law in areas such in competition law. The dialogue between the European Commission and the football federations concerning the changes to the transfer system is a good illustration of what seems to be a 'new realism'.[51]

In addition, the social-cultural dimension of sport is clearly recognised as being powerful and will continue to be actively promoted.[52] What has emerged in terms of an EU sports law is little 'hard law' that has legally binding force, but significant amounts of 'soft law', that is, 'rules of conduct which in principle have no legally binding force but which nevertheless may have a significant effect on policy and legal developments'.[53]

Parrish, R, *Sports Law and Policy in the European Union*

The use of soft law stems from the peculiarities of the EU's system of law and governance. The EU is obviously a multi-national organisation. The size, complexity and diversity of the EU results in

50 Parrish, R, 'The road to Nice' (2001) 4(2) Sports Law Bulletin 15.
51 See discussion in Chapter 9, pp 368–72.
52 Reading, V, *The European Community and Sport: From the Economic to the Social Dimension*, IXth Sports Forum of the Konrad Adenauer Foundation, Eichholz, 3 May 2001; found at http://europa.eu.int/comm/sport/index.html.
53 Parrish, R, *Sports Law and Policy in the European Union* (2003), Manchester: MUP, p 17. However, note continued periodic ECJ cases, eg Case C-438/00 *Deutscher Handballbund eV v Maros Kolpak* [2003] ECR I-4135.

protracted decision making at the best of times. In the absence of unanimity, member states often favour the use of soft law when they are unable to agree upon binding measures but nevertheless wish to place political pressure on the EU institutions for a change in policy direction. As such, sports law can be employed by the member states as an implied threat of taking further harder measures unless EU institutions change their approach. Soft law has therefore offered important guidance as to the interpretation and scope of the application of EU law. The Amsterdam Declaration is increasingly a frequently sourced reference in Commission competition law cases and ECJ cases. Politically, the commission must be sensitive not only to the interests of the member states, but also to the requirements of business operating in the Single Market. Soft law is therefore often used as the politically pragmatic option ... Soft law has therefore characterised much of the development of EU sports law. The lack of a formal Treaty base to take 'harder' measures in sport clearly also necessitates the use of soft law.[54]

Over many years the debate has rolled on whether or not to incorporate an article on sport into the Treaty. The Draft Treaty Establishing a Constitution for Europe has proposed a reference to sport in these terms:

Provisional Consolidated Version of the Draft Treaty Establishing a Constitution for Europe
Education, Youth, Sport and Vocational Training

1. The Union shall contribute to the promotion of European sporting issues, while taking account of its specific nature, its structures based on voluntary activity and its social and educational function of sport.

2. The Union action shall be aimed at:

  (g) developing the European dimension in sport, by promoting fairness in competitions and cooperation between bodies responsible for sport and by protecting the physical and moral integrity of sportsmen and sportswomen, especially young sportsmen and sportswomen.[55]

Creating a legal basis of this kind would enable the European Union to do more for sport, alongside the action taken by national bodies and sports associations. The role that the EU plays is to provide sports with a clear message that it is subject to what Foster terms 'supervised or limited autonomy', and to gain that autonomy it must be aware of a number of issues, including the rights of players, commitment to solidarity in sport and the interests of fans – the notion of 'fan equity'. As Foster states:

Foster, K, 'Can sport be regulated by Europe:? an analysis of alternative models'

Without these minimum conditions for limited autonomy, sports federations should expect further legal regulation to ensure that sport as a business is still run partly for the love of the game and not just for the love of money.[56]

Sports bodies need to comprehend that unless they comply with these values upheld in EU law and in effect exercise 'good governance' they will be subject to intervention. And this is a two-way street.

Parrish, R, *Sports Law and Policy in the European Union*

... sport should finally recognise that the EU is remarkably receptive to claims of special treatment. Working within the sports policy subsystem has allowed sports governing bodies to make these claims more coherently. It has also altered sport to what is and what is not possible ... [it] requires sport to abandon the rather feeble 'we know best' claim ... increasingly the ECJ and the Commission are

---

54 *Ibid*, 17.

55 Provisional Consolidated Version of the Draft Treaty Establishing a Constitutuion for Europe Part III, Chapter V, Section 4, CIG 86/04, 25 June 2004.

56 Foster, K, 'Can sport be regulated by Europe:? an analysis of alternative models', in *op cit*, fn 37, Caiger and Gardiner (2000).

emerging as a supranational sports regulator – not in the sense of establishing a legislative framework for sport but as a clearing-house for sports rules. Although the Helsinki Report's 'model of sport' cannot be imposed on sport, measures adopted by sport which undermine its principles are unlikely to be cleared by the EU. Although all parties reject the desirability of a supranational sports regulator, it is surely difficult to argue that current EU sports policy is not based on this reality.[57]

It is still very common to hear those involved in sports administration bemoan the intervention of the EU in sport and claim that it is detrimental. Regulation from the EU or elsewhere brings about change that challenges vested interests. But as elite sport is increasingly driven by money it does provide a counterbalance that reinforces the values and qualities that are inherent to sport.[58]

GLOBALISATION OF SPORTS LAW

The issues surrounding European Union regulation of sport also bring to bear the growing extent to which sport is regulated on a global level. Sports law issues are increasingly international in nature. There are a number of international sports bodies that have been noted: the *Fédération Internationale de Football Associations* (FIFA), the *International Olympic Committee* (IOC) and the *International Associations of Athletics Federations* (IAAF). Sports disputes often involve relationships between individual athletes and national and international bodies. Arbitration and mediation mechanisms, most notably the Court of Arbitration for Sport in Switzerland, are dedicated to resolving sports disputes, which often involve international issues. Issues of jurisdiction therefore become vital. The development of an 'international sports law' is becoming a practical necessity. As is highlighted in previous chapters, sport is a practice that has developed from being largely localised and uncodified in its earliest forms, to the current position where many sports have a universal code of laws and regulations and are regulated by organisations that purport to influence their sports wherever they might be played.

De Knop, P, 'Globalization, Americanization and localization in sport'

Introduction

Today's world is tomorrow's village. As a consequence of increased mobility, new communication technologies, exploding information networks, mass media and the all-embracing economy, we are now experiencing globalization in numerous areas. We are living in a world where national borders are becoming ever more porous and in which different globalization processes are occurring (Horseman and Marshall, 1996). Sport, too, is going through this globalization, which has great impact on the way it is managed.

Definitions

'Globalization can be defiled as the intensification of world-wide social relations which link distant localities in such a way that lot happenings are shaped by events occurring many miles away and vice versa. This is a dialectical process because such local happenings may move in an obverse direction from the very distanciated relations that shape them. Local transformation is as much a part of globalization as the lateral extension of social connections across time and space' (Giddens, 1990, p 64).

---

57 *Op cit*, fn 53, Parrish (2003), 219.
58 See earlier, Chapter 2, p 50. For a fuller analysis of the impact of the EU upon sport, see *op cit*, fn 37, Caiger and Gardiner (2000); fn 50, Parrish (2003); Weatherill, S, ' "Fair Play Please!": Recent Developments in the Application of EC Law to Sport' (2003) 40 CMLRev 51, 89; and Halgreen, L, *European Sports Law: A Comparative Analysis of the European and American Models of Sport* (2004), Copenhagen: Thomson.

Results – Globalization

That sport is going through a globalization process may be concluded from the facts enumerated hereunder.

1 A universalization of western sports, eastern combat sports, etc is taking place. Research in twenty different countries world-wide (De Knop *et al*, 1996) has found that there are hardly any major sport practised today which are exclusive to the youth of one (or only some) countries.

2 There is a marked presence of international 'sports heroes' such as Lewis, or Jordan, who are seen as universal role models. Some forms of sport contribute to globalization, not by contributing to the development of a metaculture, but rather through a fragmented and segmented culture, which regroups individuals independently from the national level. Such is the case, to a certain extent, for high-performance athletes whose identities are linked more to a network of training and competition than to any element of their national heritage, such as language or religion (Harvey and Houle, 1994).

3 (World) trade in sportswear and equipment is flourishing. Especially the large multinationals and sport brands such as Nike, Adidas and Reebok have stood to gain from the increased significance of sport. These three brands are undoubtedly the largest distributors of sportswear and sports shoes. It is striking, however, that the majority of people buying these brands never or hardly ever engage in sport of any kind. Sports goods have become world-wide fashion articles through world-wide promotional campaigns and sponsoring.

4 Due to ever increasing specialization, the manufacture of products has become fragmented. Reich (1991) provides an example of economic, technological, and industrial globalization anti interdependence in connection with sport: 'Precision hockey equipment is designed in Sweden, financed in Canada, and assembled in Cleveland and Denmark for distribution in North America and Europe, respectively, out of alloys whose molecular structure was researched and patented in Delaware and fabricated in Japan.' (p 112). The sports goods industry does not only aim at growing segments of a global market but also adopts global strategics of production, such as delocalization. A growing portion of the population in developing countries is engaged in the production of goods for the reproduction of the lifestyles of those living in developed countries.

5 The power of the international sports organizations (IOC, AGFI, FIFA, etc) has increased. This is illustrated by, for example, the fact that the IOC decides the allocation of the Games to the Olympic cities, but also the Olympic recognition of a sport and thereby, indirectly, its popularity. According to the Olympic Charter a sport must comply with the following criteria in order to be an Olympic sport: it must be widely practised by men in at least seventy-five countries and on tour continents and by women in at least forty countries and on three continents.

6 Public sports policy is discussed in a number of international structures, eg, in the Council of Europe.

7 International (European) legislation has come to play an important role in sports, sometimes with major consequences (eg, the *Bosman* case).

8 The Olympic Games, the Commonwealth Games, various world championships, and other uni- or multi-sports tournaments at a global level have gained in economic and political importance ...

Conclusion

To sum up, it may be concluded that there is clearly a globalizing trend in sport. At the same time we notice a growing apart, a polarization of, on the one hand, the ever more commercial top-class sports and, on the other, the revival of local recreational sports and local traditions. The revival of local popular sports, such as folk games or traditional games are examples of this.

So, globalization versus localization. This phenomenon was described by Featherstone (1990) as the 'paradox of culture', or, in other words, seemingly contradicting tendencies going hand in hand. Both globalization and localization are manifestations of an ever increasing differentiation in sport, which has great impact on the organization of sport.[59]

A paradox of sport can therefore be identified in terms of both its characteristics of 'globalisation' and 'localisation'.[60] However, it is clear that regional and international sports federations regulate by cutting across traditional boundaries. In effect it is often the case that these global regulators can override domestic sporting regulators, and even State authorities themselves, to effectively regulate activity within their 'jurisdiction'.

Nafziger, JAR, *International Sports Law*

Domestic law – local, state or federal – may ... be affected significantly by a variety of forces outside of the control of any of the local decision makers involved. Global forces may encourage new forms of economic and legal harmonisation across legal and economic systems.[61]

Indeed, the International Olympic Committee has been likened to a specialised body of the United Nations.[62] It appears that sport's regulations can tolerate a certain amount of latitude in terms of their interpretation and application, relative to the local cultural, economic, social and legal context of their conduct. This is characterised in the jargon of globalisation as 'resistance'. However, where that 'resistance' imposes a difference so great that the theoretical 'level playing field' becomes unworkable, two possible outcomes arise. In the first instance, where the resistant 'locale' is relatively weak, it appears that the global regulator will in effect be able to ignore that resistance, and the locale will either have to accept the imposition of the global standard or accept isolation from the world system. This, it appears, has often been the case as global sporting standards have been absorbed by domestic systems of law and regulation. However, globalisation is not just a homogenising process; it also works in other ways.

Ougaard, M, 'Approaching the global polity'

Much attention has been given to internationalisation's impact on domestic policy and institutions, but the discourses on 'two levelness' point to the reverse process: domestic forces and processes are increasingly penetrating international politics. A process of *mutual interpenetration* between the domestic and the international is underway. The dual nature of this phenomenon is important. If you focus solely on the first side, you get a picture of domestic forces being subjected to a powerful, actorless process of internationalisation. If you focus on the other side, an element of *empowerment* appears: individuals, political parties, interest groups, etc, can influence events in the outside world, including the politics of harmonisation.[63]

Thus, according to Ougaard, the second scenario is one where the local or regional resistance has sufficient sway to influence the operation of the global system as a whole. This second scenario can be seen very clearly in relation to the re-regulation of football's transfer system, highlighted above. Though the EU was concerned with – and indeed has jurisdiction limited to – activities taking place

---

59 De Knop, P, 'Globalization, Americanization and localization in sport' (2000) 2 International Sports Law Journal 20. Literature cited includes De Knop, P and Standeven, J, *Sport and Tourism: International Perspectives* (1999), Champaign, Illinois: Human Kenetics; Reich, Horseman and Marshall, in Donnelly, P, 'The local and the global; globalization in the sociology of sport' (1996) 11 Sociology of Sport Journal 239; Wagner, E, 'Sport in Asia and Africa: Americanisation or mundialization?' (1990) 7 Sociology of Sport Journal 399.

60 See Maguire, J, *Global Sport: Identities, Societies, Civilizations* (1999), Cambridge: Polity.

61 Nafziger, JAR, *International Sports Law* (1988), New York: Transnational, p 3.

62 Aman, A (Jr), 'Indiana journal of global legal studies: an introduction' (1993) 1(1) Indiana Journal of Global Legal Studies, available at www.law.indiana.edu/glsj/vol11/aman.html.

63 Ougaard, M, 'Approaching the global polity', Working Paper No 42/99, Centre for the Study of Globalisation and Regionalisation, p 14; emphasis in original. Available at www.csgr.org.

within EU Member States, the changes implemented in the transfer system are to be applied not only in respect of EU territories, but also across the footballing world.

The situation should not be seen as being a question of either the local or the global taking precedence. In truth, the issue is not quite so polarised; the shape of sporting regulation is the result of a complex web of values and incentives each pulling in different directions. The case of football's transfer system may, on the face of it, appear to be a clear victory for 'local' EU law over the autonomy of the global regulator FIFA. However, continuing suggestions that even the new transfer system may be contrary to EU law indicate that the new rules are in effect a compromise between the two, representing not so much a 'victory' for EU law over FIFA autonomy, but a shift in the power dynamic toward EU law.[64]

This issue has clear implications for accountability and legal regulation of sports governing bodies. If these global regulators are not subject to law as such, but can effectively 'bargain' with State actors to determine the scope of their powers, how are individuals to effectively secure their rights as against these bodies? One way is through the use of domestic law, though it is clear that domestic courts may not always be able, or in any case willing, to strictly impose domestic law on global actors. In relation to football, FIFA has given clear indications recently that it will not tolerate State interference with the operation of the game's regulation.[65] Though EU law has proven to be a potent weapon where economic rights require protection, it is only in exceptional cases that this has impacted upon the global system through the action of an individual.[66] The impact of globalising tendencies on the ability of individuals to seek redress is emphasised in the following extract:

Devetak, R and Higgot, R, *Justice Unbound? Globalisation, States and the Transformation of the Social Bond*

The language of globalisation ... has failed to recognise the manner in which the internationalisation of governance can also exacerbate the 'democratic deficit'. States are not only problem solvers, their policy élite are also strategic actors with interests of, and for, themselves. Collective action problem solving in international relations is couched in terms of effective governance. It is rarely posed as a question of responsible or accountable government, let alone justice.[67]

Increasing internationalisation, indeed 'globalisation', of sporting activity clearly raises concerns as to the accountability of the bodies that organise and regulate such activities. While many see this challenge as one to be addressed by domestic and transnational law,[68] others believe the solution to lie with a novel approach to the problem of globalisation:

Weatherill, S, 'After *Bosman*: tracking a sporting revolution'

Should the 'law' of international sporting bodies be treated as an autonomous system worthy of protection from disruption by state law or the law of transnational entities such as the EC? The intellectual case could be made that this is an internally coherent system, which responds to the special

---

64   For further discussion see Boyes, S, 'Globalisation, Europe and re-regulation of sport', in *op cit*, fn 37, Caiger and Gardiner (2000).

65   'FIFA asks Greek Government to refrain from interfering with football', FIFA media release, 20 March 2001; 'Guinea FA suspension maintained, national team excluded from 2002 FIFA World Cup', FIFA media release, 19 March 2001; 'FIFA suspends Football Association of Albania', FIFA media release, 27 November 1996: all available from www.fifa.com.

66   Note however, that EU is increasingly being put forward by athletes seeking redress in domestic courts. See, eg, *Edwards v BAF* [1997] EuLR 721 and *Wilander v Tobin* [1997] 2 Lloyd's Rep 293.

67   Devetak, R and Higgot, R, *Justice Unbound? Globalisation, States and the Transformation of the Social Bond*, Working Paper No 29/99, Centre for the Study of Globalisation and Regionalisation, p 10; available at www.csgr.org.

68   See below, Chapter 5.

interests of sport, and which should not be invaded by differently motivated, alien systems. To treat decisions of sporting associations as 'law' in their own right, rather than as private acts subordinate to 'real law', would argue for a differently conceived 'sports law' and would bring to mind questions surrounding choice of which legal order to apply in case of conflict.[69]

It has been suggested that such an approach might be furthered by the development of a World Sport Body, to oversee the regulation of sport at a global level.[70] While such an approach might be desirable, it appears that it is politically unlikely. However, this does support contentions that the manner in which sport is regulated needs to be conceived of in global terms, even if it is not organised in such a manner.

Global Sports Law or International Sports Law?

As the globalisation of sport has accelerated, the regulation of sport is increasingly in the hands of International Sports Federations. In turn the regulation of these ISFs and the domains that they in turn 'rule' has been variously described as both an international sports law and as a global sports law. Foster makes the distinction:

Foster, K, 'Is there a global sports law?'

International sports law can be applied by national courts. Global sports law by contrast implies a claim of immunity from national law. Some authors have used the concept '*lex sportiva*' in a superficial manner to describe what is happening with the globalisation of sports law. I argue that '*lex sportiva*' should be equated to 'global sports law'. To define it thus as 'global sports law' highlights that it is a cloak for continued self-regulation by international sports federations. It is a claim for non-intervention by both national legal systems and by international sports law. It thus opposes a rule of law in regulating international sport.[71]

Foster sees international sports law as universal principles of law that cannot be ignored by ISFs and they can and should be enforced by any available legal institution that has jurisdiction. This would include principles such as those of fair hearings and the doctrine of proportionality. James Nafziger is perhaps the leading authority on the international law aspects of sport.

Nafziger, J, *International Sports Law*

The term "international sports law" refers to a process that comprises a more or less distinctive body of rules, principles, institutions and procedures to govern important consequences of transnational sports activity. As a body of international law, it draws upon the general sources of law that are identified in the most widely accepted checklist, Article 38 of the Statutes of the International Court of Justice. The process of international sports law thus includes provisions of international agreements, international custom, as evidence of general principles accepted as law; general principles (including equity and general principles articulated in the resolutions of international organizations); and as subsidiary sources, judicial decisions (including those of both international and national tribunals) and scholarly writings.[72]

---

69 Weatherill, S, 'After *Bosman*: tracking a sporting revolution: the Bosman Lecture', May 2000, available at www.sportslaw.apu.ac.uk.

70 Blackshaw, I, 'Regulating sport globally: a challenge for the twenty-first century' [2000] NLJ 617.

71 Foster, K, 'Is there a global sports law?' (2003) 2(2) Entertainment Law.

72 Nafziger, J, *International Sports Law* (2004), Transnational: New York, 1; also see Nafziger, J, 'Globalizing sports law' (1999) 9(2) Marquette Sports Law Journal 225; see ICJ website for further details, www.icj-cij.org/ icjwww/icjhome.htm.

Global sports law as distinguished from international sports law is seen by Foster as:

Foster, K, 'Is there a global sports law?'

A transnational autonomous legal order created by the private global institutions that govern international sport. Its chief characteristics are first that it is a contractual order, with its binding force coming from agreements to submit to the authority and jurisdiction of international sporting federations and second that it is not governed by national legal systems.[73]

He goes on to claim that:

This clear distinction between international and global sports law shows that they are different concepts, which need careful analysis. To conflate the two concepts into a single concept, called *lex sportiva*, is misleading. In particular to describe what is happening with the globalisation of sports law as *lex sportiva* is to imply that international sporting federations are legally immune from regulation by national legal systems. This allows the private regimes of international sporting federations, such as the IOC or FIFA, to be legally unaccountable except by arbitration systems established and validated by those very same private regimes.[74]

This perceptive distinction has been one largely ignored by other writers in the area.[75] Indeed, the commentary at the end of Chapter 2 in this book provides support for an emerging *lex sportiva*.[76] Foster's understanding of 'global sports law' is understood as a guise or cloak for continued self-regulation by ISFs. Central to this is the role and prominence of the Court of Arbitration for Sport. It is this forum which is being claimed by some as the sources of these principles of a *lex sportiva*. The role of the CAS will be analysed later at length, and setting aside claims about its lack of independence and flawed procedural issues that question the 'objectivity' of its decision making, it may be inappropriate to talk about an emerging *lex sportiva* anyway. The term *lex specialis*, a less specific body of law, may be a more appropriate term at this stage in the development of international sports law. But even on this point, Nafziger strikes a note of caution:

The *lex sportive* is the product of only a few hundred arbitral decisions within a limited range of disputes over a historically short period of time. It is more of a *lex ferenda* than a mature *lex specialis*.[77]

CONCLUSION

This chapter has provided an examination of the appropriate qualities of sports governance. It has also charted the development of a European Union sports policy. It is clear that sports governing bodies need to comply with the external legal norms of the EU. It is also clear that sport needs to be

---

73 *Op cit*, fn 71, Foster (2003).

74 *Op cit*, fn 71, Foster (2003). Foster cites the distinction that Houlihan makes between 'internationalised sport', which 'like international law, is firmly based on nation states. Teams are defined by their country of origin. This sporting culture prefers national or regional competitions to global or Olympic games. Internationalised sport is often funded by state subsidy and has a national framework of regulation. 'Globalised sport' by contrast has nationally ambiguous or rootless teams, 'sport without a state', as in professional road cycling or Formula One motor racing where teams are named after corporate sponsors. Globalised sport has a uniform pattern of sport that diminishes national traditions and local diversity. Sports rely on commercial sponsorship rather than state funding; also see Houlihan, B, *Sport, Policy and Politics: A Comparative Analysis* (1997) London: Routledge.

75 For example, Beloff, M, *et al*, *Sports Law* (1999), Oxford: Hart; *op cit*, fn 37, Caiger and Gardiner (2000).

76 See Chapter 2, pp 91–92.

77 *Op cit*, fn 72, Nafziger (2004), p 49; *lex ferenda* can be seen as what the law ought to be in a particular area with norms in process of ripening into law.

aware of a developing set of international legal norms that are being applied to sport. The Court of Arbitration for Sport is an obvious source of these norms in some specific areas of sports law.[78] A study of any European national Sports Law system needs to be very firmly located in this European and international context.

KEY SOURCES

Caiger, A and Gardiner, S (eds), *Professional Sport in the EU: Regulation and Re-regulation* (2000), The Hague: Asser.

Weatherill, S, 'The influence of "Americanization": the influence of European Community law on the ' "European sport model" ', in Greenfield, S and Osborn, G (eds), *Law and Sport in Contemporary Society* (2000), London: Frank Cass, pp 157–81.

Europa Sports Site: http://europa.eu.int/comm/sport/index.html.

Parrish, R, *Sports Law and Policy in the European Union*, (2003), Manchester: MUP, p 17.

Nafziger, J, *International Sports Law* (2004), New York: Transnational.

---

78   See below, Chapter 6 on CAS and Chapter 7 on the role of CAS and anti-doping.

CHAPTER 5

THE LEGAL REGULATION OF SPORTS GOVERNING BODIES

INTRODUCTION

Bodies controlling sporting activity find themselves increasingly involved with the law.[1] Only rarely do sportspersons arrive at a disciplinary hearing without a team of lawyers at hand, ready to see that the governing body dispenses justice in the appropriate manner. Sports governing bodies are no strangers to the courts, as their determinations and their rules are subjected to scrutiny by the judiciary. Such scrutiny is clearly of some importance; these bodies are powerful regulators with the ability to ruin livelihoods and tarnish reputations. Diane Modahl's suspension for a failed dope test removed her trade and reputation at a stroke. The protracted litigation that followed illustrates the growing extent to which the courts are now being asked to intervene in the regulation of sport. It also emphasises the potential significance of such actions for both regulator and regulated. In Modahl's case her pursuit of the suit led to near financial ruin, while for the governing body – the British Athletics Federation (BAF) – it resulted in an administration and its replacement as the UK's governing athletics body. The consequent nervousness exhibited by governing bodies is exemplified by the caution displayed by the International Tennis Federation in a series of cases where the organization itself had supplied players with supplements which were suspected of causing positive drug tests in a number of players, most notably Greg Rusedski.[2]

Sports governing bodies are powerful organisations; they regulate particular niches of everyday life in much the same way as might be expected of the State. They lay down rules that affect not only the on-field activities of sportspersons, but also affect the commercial transactions which they may conduct, their employment relationships, personal conduct and drug use. Governing bodies engage in licensing, control safety standards and have significant powers to exclude individuals from their sport. One might wonder whether such activities would not ordinarily be carried out by organs closely related to the State – yet it must be remembered that, for the most part, sports governing bodies are private associations and not elements of the State. These private, self-regulating associations generally grew up during the late nineteenth century as sport developed out of disparate and localised games into the codified and uniform packages that exist today. While government may have been generally supportive of regulation of sports, because of the increased orderliness and control it brought to them, it took no significant part in the regulatory process. It seems sport was simply not important enough for the State to involve itself in. Should the question arise now it seems that the outcome could be quite different. Now government shows an increasing interest and involvement in sport, whether it be in controlling doping, lottery funding for sport, the development of national stadia, bidding for the right to host international events, availability of sport on television, the behaviour of spectators, the form of football's transfer system, or simply the price and availability of entry to sporting events.[3]

This is important because it highlights the immense significance of sport, both to its participants, at whatever level, and to society more generally. This raises questions as to the extent that sports

---

1   See generally, Hoult, P, 'The beautiful game' (2004) 101(12) LSG 26.
2   'Rusedski clears his name as tribunal attacks ATP actions' *The Independent*, 11 March 2004.
3   On interventionist and non-interventionist approaches see Lewis, A and Taylor J (eds), *Sport: Law and Practice* (2004), London: Butterworths, pp 5–7.

governing bodies are accountable for their actions, and the ability of individuals to obtain redress against them. The purpose of this chapter is to examine the accountability of these bodies through domestic and European courts. It also addresses broader questions as to the efficacy of the present situation and the pros and cons of the operation of sport on a self-regulatory basis.[4]

EVALUATING SELF-REGULATION

It has already been noted that self-regulatory bodies, such as those that govern sport, have the capacity to act governmentally while still possessing the institutional and legal structures and interests of private bodies. The general debate about self-regulation is helpful in understanding the legal approach to such bodies.

Self-regulation is perceived as having many benefits, most significantly that the costs of the regulation are largely 'internalised', thus reducing the burden on the public purse. Additionally, there are a number of perceived technical advantages in the utilisation of self-regulatory techniques in relation to expertise and efficiency. However, criticisms relating to the adoption of self-regulatory strategies focus upon the issues of mandate, accountability and procedural fairness.[5]

Expertise

Certain regulatory functions may require the exercise of expert judgment where a decision maker has to consider competing options or values and come to a balanced judgment on incomplete and shifting information. Then the regulator may claim legitimacy and support on the basis of expertise or specialist knowledge:[6]

Sinclair, D, 'Self-regulation versus command and control: beyond false dichotomies'

[E]ven with the best of intentions, regulators are often not in a strong position to determine the technical practicalities of regulating complex industrial processes. This is compounded in sectors where technology is rapidly changing, or with the advent of new, previously unregulated industrial activities, or with the discovery of previously unknown negative ... impacts ... It is in both government and industry's interests, therefore, for industry to constructively participate in the development of appropriate and effective regulatory strategies.[7]

Self-regulation usually has the ability to command higher levels of relevant expertise and technical knowledge than is possible with independent or State regulation. This knowledge includes that which the regulated parties will see as being a reasonable regulatory burden. The role of the sector in setting its own standards engenders a close sense of ownership meaning rules are more likely to be both acceptable and effective based on the expert knowledge of those actively involved in the area.[8] The potential for flexibility in a rapidly changing domain is enhanced. However, where matters of important policy are concerned, it may be that state organs will be less willing to cede regulatory

---

4   See generally, Weatherill, S, 'Do sporting associations make law or are they merely subject to it?' (1999) 13 Am Cur 24.

5   Baldwin, R and Cave, M, *Understanding Regulation: Theory, Strategy and Practice* (1999), Oxford: OUP, p 126.

6   *Ibid*, p 80.

7   Sinclair, D, 'Self-regulation versus command and control: beyond false dichotomies' (1997) Law and Policy 545–46.

8   Black, J, *Rules and Regulators* (1997) Oxford: Clarendon, pp 103, 219.

territory to private actors. Thus, in these specific areas regulatory arrangements might look different to those where mundane, narrow or technical matters are concerned and the state may be willing to bow to the greater expertise of those involved in the sphere of activity. Conceptions of high policy are thus extremely important in this regard: these rarely remain settled as political agendas shift and change. Notably, the entry of new actors, possibly inter- or supra-national bodies, can play a role in the compilation of political priorities.[9]

Efficiency

Self-regulators generally have easy access to those under control and experience low costs in acquiring the information necessary to formulate and set standards, with consequently low monitoring and enforcement costs.[10] They are able to adapt their regimes to changes in individual conditions in a flexible manner, because of the relative informality of their procedures.[11] As outlined above, conceptions of policy priorities may affect when high cost regulation will be considered acceptable.

Mandate

Because of their very nature, self-regulatory objectives can be drawn up by bodies with no or little democratic legitimacy. It is often hard to justify actions that affect parties outside of the association's membership structure – or to argue that the public interest is being served.[12] Indeed, it is difficult to justify the impact of self-regulation on the members of an association itself, where the decision making procedures of such an organisation are not founded upon internal democratic processes. It is often argued that self-regulatory bodies have a particularly poor record in protecting the public interest in the enforcement of standards.[13]

Accountability

Critics often perceive the existence of self-regulatory systems as being the manifestation of the capture of power by groups that are not accountable through 'normal' democratic demands.[14] Many democratic models make the assumption that legitimate authority to exercise 'public' power can only flow from a command of popular and legislative majorities.[15] On this basis, regulation should be subject to the scrutiny and effective control of the organs of the (democratic) State as a matter of necessity.

Regulation inevitably involves the exercise of 'public' power, yet it seems that this is not always subject to the scrutiny and control that is demanded by constitutionalists.[16] The key, where

---

9   Hancher, L and Moran, M, 'Organising regulatory space', in Baldwin, R, Scott, C and Hood, C (eds), *A Reader on Regulation* (1998), Oxford: OUP, p 162; Collins, H, *Regulating Contracts* (1999) Oxford: OUP, pp 63–64, 66.

10 Braithwaite, J, *Restorative Justice and Responsive Regulation* (2002) Oxford: OUP, p 247.

11 *Op cit*, fn 5, Baldwin and Cave (1999), p 127.

12 Ogus, A, 'Rethinking self-regulation' (1995) OJLS 97, p 99.

13 *Op cit*, fn 5, Baldwin and Cave (1999), p 129.

14 Graham, G, 'Self-regulation', in Richardson, G and Genn, H, *Administrative Law and Government Action: The Courts and Alternative Mechanisms of Review* (1994), Oxford: Clarendon, p 190.

15 *Op cit*, fn 9, Hancher and Moran (1998), p 150.

16 Black, J, 'Constitutionalising self regulation' (1996) 59 MLR 24.

self-regulating organisations are not underpinned by any legislative mandate, is the extent to which the courts can hold these associations to account, ensuring transparency and accountability. This is particularly so where bodies can often have an impact upon those outside of any legal relationship with the regulator. This would suggest that, in relation to sport at least, such self-regulatory bodies ought to be subject to scrutiny by the courts in order to meet the requirements of democratic legitimacy.

Procedural Fairness

Self-regulatory schemes tend to be prone to criticisms of unfairness in so far as non-members may be affected by regulatory decisions to which they have had poor or no proper access. Typically they will not have been involved in the negotiations that established the regulation in the first place. Courts may act so as to ameliorate this; however, they have generally proven to be reluctant to do so.[17] Nevertheless, there are areas which are traditionally self-regulatory that have become sufficiently important to warrant great concern over the extent to which their regulation is subject to scrutiny. These sectors of activity, of which sport should be considered a foremost example, have, in effect, changed their nature to the extent that their activities can now be regarded as truly 'public' in practice and thus of constitutional significance.[18]

THE DOMESTIC POSITION: JUDICIAL REVIEW

The traditional means by which public bodies are held to account through the courts is the claim for judicial review. The procedure operates in such a way that public bodies are required to exercise their powers in accordance with particular principles. Under this procedure the court does not hear an appeal against State measures or consider the merits of a decision; instead it undertakes a review of the legality of the decision making process. Where a decision has been made illegally it will not be allowed to stand. The court will not impose a decision of its own, but require the decision maker to repeat the process in a lawful fashion. The parameters of judicial review were set out by Lord Diplock:

Council of Civil Service Unions v Minister for Civil Service [1985] AC 375

To qualify as a subject for judicial review a decision must have consequences which affect some person (or body of persons) other than the decision maker, although it may affect him too. It must affect such other person either (a) by altering rights or obligation of that person which are enforceable by or against him in private law; or (b) by depriving him of some benefit or advantage which either (1) he had in the past been permitted by the decision maker to enjoy and which he can legitimately expect to be permitted to continue to do until there has been communicated to him some rational grounds for withdrawing it on which he has been given an opportunity to comment; or (2) he has received assurance from the decision maker will not be withdrawn without him giving him first an opportunity of advancing reasons for contending that they should not be withdrawn . . .

---

17 *Op cit*, fn 5, Baldwin and Cave (1999), p 132.

18 On regulation generally and for an assessment of different regulatory techniques see Better Regulation Task Force, *Imaginative Thinking for Better Regulation* (2003) available from www.brtf.gov.uk. See also Webb, K, 'Government, Private Regulation and the Role of the Market', Chapter 12 in MacNeil, M, Sargent, M and Swan P (eds), *Law, Regulation and Governance* (2002), Oxford: OUP.

For a decision to be susceptible to judicial review the decision maker must be empowered by public law (and not merely, as in arbitration, by agreement between the private parties) to make decisions that, if validly made, will lead to administrative action or abstention from action by an authority endowed by law with executive powers, which have one or other of the consequences mentioned in the preceding paragraph. The ultimate source of the decision making power is nearly always nowadays a statute or subordinate legislation made under the statute; but in the absence of any statute regulating the subject matter of the decision the source of the decision making power may still be common law itself, ie that part of the common law that is given by lawyers the label of 'the prerogative'. Where this is the source of the decision making power, the power is confined to executive officers of central as distinct from local government and in constitutional practice is generally exercised by those holding ministerial rank.[19]

The rules pertaining to judicial review were consolidated in a package of measures, Order 53 of the Rules of the Supreme Court, which was in turn endorsed by s 31 of the Supreme Court Act 1981. These measures had the effect of bundling together the 'prerogative writs' along with private law remedies so that they could be obtained by way of a unified process known as 'application for judicial review', now a 'claim for judicial review'. The reforms were instigated in order to streamline the public law process; however, new issues were also raised. The rules for the judicial review procedure are now contained within Part 54 of the Civil Procedure Rules.

The case of *O'Reilly v Mackman*[20] established the concept of procedural exclusivity – the restriction that application for relief by way of judicial review could only be allowed where a challenge was based solely on public law rights. In *O'Reilly* a group of prisoners sought declarations that a prison board of visitors' decision was *ultra vires*. Their application was struck out on the basis that they proceeded by way of a private law process when judicial review would have been available to them, thus subverting public law process. In *O'Reilly* the court was concerned to see that public bodies were able to carry out their functions efficiently and effectively.

O'Reilly v Mackman [1983] 2 AC 237

Now that ... all remedies for infringements of rights protected by public law can be obtained upon an application for judicial review, as can also rights under private law if such rights should be involved, it would in my view as a general rule be contrary to public policy, and as such an abuse of the process of the Court, to permit a person seeking to establish that a decision of a public authority infringed rights to which he was entitled to protection under public law to proceed by way of an ordinary action and by this means to evade the provisions of Order 53 for the protection of such authorities.[21]

A further important question raised by the 1977 reforms was whether the types of body subject to judicial review had been expanded. This was particularly pertinent in relation to sporting bodies, as they had traditionally been seen as excluded from the category of body subject to the prerogative writs.

Setting the Scene: *Law v National Greyhound Racing Club*

The issue was addressed soon afterwards in the seminal case of *Law v National Greyhound Racing Club Ltd*.[22] Law was a greyhound trainer, suspended after a dog in his charge was found to have been

---

19 *Council of Civil Service Unions v Minister for Civil Service* [1985] AC 375, pp 408–09.
20 [1983] 2 AC 237.
21 *O'Reilly v Mackman* [1983] 2 AC 237, p 285. Though cf *Clark v University of Lincolnshire & Humberside* [2000] 3 All ER 752.
22 [1983] 1 WLR 1302.

doped, contrary to the National Greyhound Racing Club (NGRC) rules. Law brought a private law action claiming a declaration that the NGRC had breached an implied contractual term that all actions taken to deprive him of his licence would be reasonable and fair and made on reasonable grounds, and that the decision was *ultra vires* and therefore void. The NGRC sought to strike out the motion, claiming that the action ought to have been brought by way of an application for judicial review as the claimant was alleging an abuse of power. Lawton LJ dismissed the suggestion that the power to suspend a licence had any public element, even though such a decision may affect the public.

Law v National Greyhound Racing Club Ltd [1983] 1 WLR 1302

In my judgment, such powers as the stewards had to suspend the claimant's licence were derived from a contract between him and the defendants. This was so for all who took part in greyhound racing in stadiums licensed by the defendants. A steward's inquiry under the defendants' Rules of Racing concerned only those who voluntarily submitted themselves to the stewards' jurisdiction. There was no public element in the jurisdiction itself. Its exercise, however, could have consequences from which the public benefited, as, for example, by the stamping out of malpractices, and from which individuals might have their rights restricted ... Consequences affecting the public generally can flow from the decisions of many domestic tribunals. In the past the courts have always refused to use the orders of certiorari to review the decisions of domestic tribunals.[23]

Lawton LJ also rejected any suggestion that the 1977 reforms had broadened the scope of the judicial review process:

The purpose of section 31 is to regulate procedure in relation to judicial reviews, not to extend the jurisdiction of the court ... It did not purport to enlarge the jurisdiction of the court so as to enable it to review the decisions of domestic tribunals.[24]

The finding of the Court of Appeal in Law has proved to be an important one. The contractual relationship between Law and the NGRC served to exclude the application for judicial review and emphasised that the scope of judicial review had not been extended to domestic tribunals (that is, those founded in contract, not on the basis of statute or the Royal prerogative) such as sports governing bodies.

Developing the Law: *Datafin*

The law in this regard developed through a number of decisions following the case of *R v City Panel on Take-overs and Mergers ex p Datafin*.[25] This case dealt with a challenge by Datafin, a company involved in a take-over bid, to a decision of the City Panel on Take-overs and Mergers. The Panel on Take-overs and Mergers (the Panel) is a self-regulating body that produced and manages the City Code on Take-overs and Mergers (the Code) governing the procedure to be followed in the take-over of listed public companies. The Panel has no direct statutory, prerogative or common law powers – no visible legal support – but is supported by a number of statutory provisions relating to the listing of companies on the Stock Exchange. Further, the Department of Trade and Industry has cited the

---

23 *Ibid*, p 1307.
24 *Ibid*, p 1308. In his judgment Fox LJ agreed with Lawton LJ's opinion that the authority of the stewards was derived wholly from contract and that the NGRC did not have rights or duties relating to members of the public as such: 'What the defendants do in relation to the control of greyhound racing may affect the public, or a section of it, but the defendants' powers in relation to the matters with which this case is concerned are contractual,' p 1309.
25 [1987] 1 All ER 564.

existence of the Code as a reason why there is little statutory intervention in the area of take-overs. Sir John Donaldson MR stated:

R v City Panel on Take-overs and Mergers ex p Datafin [1987] 1 All ER 564

As an act of government it was decided that, in relation to take-overs, there should be a central self-regulatory body which would be supported and sustained by a periphery of statutory powers and penalties wherever non statutory powers and penalties were insufficient or non-existent, or where EEC requirements called for statutory provisions. No one could have been in the least surprised if the panel had been instituted and operated under the direct authority of statute law, since it operates wholly in the public domain. Its jurisdiction extends throughout the United Kingdom.[26]

He went on to comment that the Panel was clearly performing an important public duty. Its decisions affected the rights of citizens, not all of whom had consented to being affected in this manner. The Panel's power was not only based upon moral persuasion and the assent of institutions and their members, but it was also provided with strength by the statutory powers exercised by the Department of Trade and Industry and the Bank of England. Donaldson MR continued:

I should be very disappointed if the courts could not recognise the realities of executive power and allowed their vision to be clouded by the subtlety and sometimes complexity of the way in which it can be exerted.[27]

Lloyd LJ endorsed and expanded upon this opinion, emphasising that the self-regulatory nature of the Panel did not make it any less appropriate for subjection to the scrutiny of judicial review.[28] He also commented that the source of the power was not the sole test in deciding upon a body's susceptibility to judicial review:

Of course the source of the power will often, perhaps usually, be decisive. If the source of the power is a statute, or subordinate legislation under a statute, then clearly the body in question will be subject to judicial review. If, at the other end of the scale, the source of power is contractual ... then clearly [this is] not subject to judicial review. But in between these extremes there is an area in which it is helpful to look not just at the source of the power but at the nature of the power. If the body in question is exercising public law functions, or if the exercise of its functions have public law consequences, then that may ... be sufficient to bring the body within the reach of judicial review ... [t]he essential distinction ... is between a domestic or private tribunal on the one hand and a body of persons who are under some public duty on the other.[29]

On its particular facts the application was rejected. However, the case is significant in that, despite not deriving its powers from statute or the exercise of the prerogative, the Panel was held to be a body susceptible to judicial review, because of its nature. This suggests three broad areas for consideration:

– whether a contractual relationship exists between the parties;

– whether the body challenged is one of a nature such that it is subject to judicial review; and

– whether the nature of the decision or act in question is of a nature that is affecting the public at large, which is susceptible to judicial review.[30]

26 Ibid, p 574.
27 Ibid, p 577.
28 Ibid, p 582.
29 Ibid. Nicholls LJ concurred.
30 R v Derbyshire County Council ex p Noble [1990] ICR 808.

Datafin appeared to signal a shift away from a strictly source-based test of amenability to judicial review towards a more general, functional test where the source of power was only one of a number of factors to be considered. *Datafin* resulted in questions being posed relating to the nature of bodies considered susceptible to judicial review, once again raising the possibility that sports governing bodies would be subject to the process. A number of the subsequent cases involved challenges to decisions of such bodies.

The Problem of Contract

In *R v Football Association of Wales ex p Flint Town United Football Club*[31] the appellant club was a member of the Football Association of Wales (FAW), playing in the Welsh Amateur League. The club sought to leave that league to join another one, administered by the English Football Association. According to the FAW's rules, by which the applicant was bound, the club required the consent of the FAW to play in a league administered by the English FA. The FAW refused permission and the applicant sought judicial review. In refusing the application at the leave stage,[32] the Divisional Court held that it was long established that certiorari (one of the prerogative writs available as a public law remedy) would not lie against private or domestic tribunals since their authority was derived solely from contract.[33] In *Flint Town* a contractual relationship existed between the parties; thus the court was bound by the decision in *Law*, and the remedy of certiorari could not lie against a domestic tribunal. *Datafin*, it appeared, had changed little where a contractual relationship existed between the parties.

In many cases sporting bodies possess a monopoly in their particular field. Those wishing to have significant involvement in association football or horse racing in England, for example, have little realistic choice but to submit themselves to the authority of the Football Association or the Jockey Club, respectively. It can be questioned, therefore, whether it is right to disqualify such a relationship from the courts' supervisory jurisdiction of judicial review on the basis that it is viewed as being 'contractual'. The rules making up the 'contract' are presented on a 'take it or leave it' or 'adhesionary' basis, with no opportunity for the negotiation of terms. Individuals have no choice but to accept the terms if they wish to be involved in the sport. Thus, to refuse to subject a body to judicial review on the basis that the relationship is based on consensual agreement is questionable. The adhesionary nature of the rules and regulations of sports governing bodies have, in fact, been recognised by the judiciary, albeit in the context of a private law action:

Enderby Town Football Club Ltd v The Football Association Ltd [1971] Ch 591

> The rules of a body like [the Football Association] are often said to be like a contract. So they are in legal theory. But it is a fiction – a fiction created by lawyers to give the courts jurisdiction ... Putting the fiction aside, the truth is that the rules are nothing more nor less than a legislative code – a set of regulations laid down by the governing body to be observed by all who are, or become, members of the association.[34]

The inherent risk in this approach is that those having a justifiable grievance may be denied redress. Further, the exercise of public power by those bodies that have clear links with the State is subjected

---

31 [1991] COD 44.
32 Before making a claim for judicial review an intending claimant must apply for leave to do so, stating the relief sought, the grounds upon which it is based, and provide an affidavit confirming the facts upon which the applicant is seeking to rely.
33 As established in *Law v National Greyhound Racing Club Ltd* [1983] 1 WLR 1302.
34 *Enderby Town FC Ltd v The Football Association Ltd* [1971] Ch 591, p 606, *per* Lord Denning MR.

to scrutiny not only through judicial review, but also through other means.[35] Decision makers more easily identified with the exercise of public power because of their proximity to government are more likely to be made accountable through the democratic process or through other more specific grievance redress mechanisms, such as Ombudsmen, which may be available to aggrieved individuals within the system of government. In contrast, sporting bodies which possess and utilise powers equivalent in effect to those exercised closer to government go relatively unscrutinised. Not only are they not accountable through the democratic process, but neither are there the internal governmental mechanisms by which they must justify their actions and decisions. This only serves to highlight the importance of judicial review of these bodies.

Applying *Datafin*: More Problems

Discrepancies in the application of the law post-*Datafin* are highlighted by the case of *R v Disciplinary Committee of the Jockey Club ex p Massingberd-Mundy*.[36] The applicant, Massingberd-Mundy, was a local steward appointed by the Jockey Club and was also on a list of stewards approved to act as chairman of stewards. He was chairman of stewards at a race meeting during which an incident took place that called for a stewards' inquiry. His conduct at that inquiry was criticised by the Jockey Club's Disciplinary Committee, which felt that he had taken too long to bring the inquiry to a conclusion. He was subsequently removed from the list of stewards approved to act as chairman. The applicant sought judicial review of the Jockey Club Disciplinary Committee's decision, by way of an order of certiorari.

The applicant argued that the decisions of bodies deriving their powers from statute or statutory instrument or from a Royal Charter are generally susceptible to judicial review. As the Jockey Club was reconstituted under a Royal Charter in 1970, the powers of the Jockey Club were now derived from its Charter, making it susceptible to judicial review. The applicant further suggested that the exercise of control over a large and important industry meant that the Disciplinary Committee of the Jockey Club was more than just a domestic tribunal. This 'special' position, it was argued, was underlined by the fact that the representatives of the horse racing industry on the Horse-Race Betting Levy Board were drawn exclusively from the Jockey Club.[37] The Jockey Club countered that it was a domestic body deriving its jurisdiction from contract and was not therefore susceptible to judicial review. Further, it argued, the fact of its incorporation by Royal Charter did not mean that its powers were derived from the prerogative any more than a public company's powers were derived from statute because of its incorporation under the Companies Act. Neill LJ decided that the Royal Charter was not the real source of the Club's power, it being more a sign of Royal 'approval', therefore it could not be properly regarded as deriving its power from prerogative.[38] This suggests a paradoxical approach has developed where the source of power question is determined. *Flint Town*, outlined above, was decided in the post-*Datafin* era. There the court did not attempt to look beyond the obvious, being satisfied to accept the superficial view of the FAW in terms of its source. However, in *Massingberd-Mundy* the court was quite prepared to discount the Charter status of the Jockey Club in determining its susceptibility to review. This suggests judicial reluctance to subject sport's governing bodies to judicial review rather than the development of any systematic approach to the basis of review in such cases.

---

35 Mullan, D, 'Administrative law at the margins', in Taggart, M (ed), *The Province of Administrative Law* (1997), Oxford: Hart, p 137; Alder, J, 'Obsolescence and renewal: judicial review in the private sector', in Leyland, P and Woods, T (eds), *Administrative Law Facing the Future; Old Constraints and New Horizons* (1997), London: Blackstone, p 165.
36 [1993] 2 All ER 207.
37 Betting, Gaming and Lotteries Act 1963, s 24.
38 *R v City Panel on Take-overs and Mergers ex p Datafin* [1987] 1 All ER 564, p 219.

Neill LJ did extend his examination to the nature of the powers exercised in making the decision, going on to state that the character of the Charter and of the powers conferred upon the Club strongly suggested that in some aspects of its work it operated in the public domain, and that its functions were at least in part public or quasi-public functions.[39] He continued:

R v Disciplinary Committee of the Jockey Club ex p Massingberd-Mundy [1993] 2 All ER 207

Accordingly, if the matter were free from authority, I might have been disposed to conclude that some decisions, at any rate, of the Jockey Club were capable of being reviewed by judicial review.[40]

Nevertheless, despite the introduction of a broader test in *Datafin*, the courts still have difficulty overcoming a tendency to base susceptibility to review on the basis of the body rather than the nature of the decision itself. Here the labelling of the Jockey Club as a 'domestic tribunal' meant the court felt unable to classify it as a body amenable to judicial review. Despite considering the nature of the decision, and accepting that certain decisions taken by the Jockey Club would be typically suitable for subjection to judicial review,[41] once again the nature of the body was decisive.

R v Jockey Club ex p RAM Racecourses Ltd[42] concerned a challenge to a Jockey Club decision not to allocate races to a new course following an internal report stating that 60 new fixtures ought to be allocated in 1990 and 1991 and that an unspecified number of fixtures ought to be made available to a new course. Copies of the report were distributed to existing racecourse owners and the Jockey Club announced that it would allocate an extra 30 fixtures in both 1990 and 1991. RAM Racecourses obtained a copy of the report, purchased a site and spent £100,000 on developing a new racecourse in anticipation of being allocated fifteen new fixtures in 1991. In June 1989 the applicant sent details of its development proposals to the Jockey Club, who replied stating that, notwithstanding the report, it had made no commitment as to the number of fixtures to be allocated to new racecourses. Shortly afterwards it was made clear by the Jockey Club that no fixtures would be allocated to the applicant's new racecourse in 1991 and that it would not indicate when such an allocation might be made. The applicant sought judicial review of the Jockey Club's decision, contending that the report had raised a legitimate expectation that the new racecourse would be granted a minimum of 15 fixtures for 1991.

On the substantive issue of whether the Jockey Club report had raised a legitimate expectation in the applicant that it would be awarded at least 15 fixtures in 1991, the applicant failed.[43] The judgment of Stuart-Smith LJ took a step back from the position in *Massingberd-Mundy*. He did not accept that the Jockey Club was affected by its Charter status:

R v Jockey Club ex p RAM Racecourses Ltd [1993] 2 All ER 225

[S]o far as its functions of issuing licences and controlling fixtures is concerned the Jockey Club is in no different a position from a practical point of view after the Charter than before.[44]

---

39 *Ibid.*

40 *Ibid.* Note Neill LJ felt bound by the decision in *Law v NGRC* [1983] 1 WLR 1302, in as much as it rejected the expansion of the application for judicial review to the actions of domestic tribunals.

41 On the facts it was held that no public right was infringed.

42 [1993] 2 All ER 225.

43 The Divisional Court held that there had been no clear and unambiguous representation in the report that a new racecourse would receive 15 fixtures as of right in 1991. The Jockey Club had not made any direct representation to the applicant as the report had not been made available to it, therefore it was not within the class of persons entitled to rely on the report. Nor was it reasonable for the applicant to rely upon any representation in the report without approaching the Jockey Club directly to check whether its assumption was correct.

44 *R v Jockey Club ex p RAM Racecourses Ltd* [1993] 2 All ER 225, p 243.

Stuart Smith LJ also affirmed the general principle that the majority of cases would be entirely domestic in character, being based upon a contractual relationship between the parties.[45] Simon Brown J gave the most expansive judgment to date, assuming a more pragmatic stance. The nature of the power being exercised by the Jockey Club in discharging its functions of regulating racecourses and allocating fixtures was noted as being strikingly akin to the exercise of a statutory licensing power. Similarly, there was no difficulty in regarding that particular function as one belonging to a public law body, giving rise to public law consequences.[46] Simon Brown J noted the close affinity with the type of decision making commonly accepted as reviewable by the courts and the inability to identify that particular exercise of power with that of an arbitrator or other domestic body, which would clearly be outside the court's supervisory jurisdiction.[47] In doing so Simon Brown J shifted towards the approach, outlined above, that the nature of the activity should be the focal point when deciding bodies' amenability to judicial review, not the label ascribed to the body carrying it out. Simon Brown J also disagreed with Stuart Smith LJ on the effect of the Jockey Club's Charter status. He accepted that it could not be a decisive consideration but stressed that it was not irrelevant when deciding upon the susceptibility of the Club to judicial review:

> It may indicate governmental (in the widest sense) recognition of the national importance of the Jockey Club's position, holding as it does monopolistic powers in this important field of public life.[48]

However, this approach still contrasts with the rigid approach taken where the basis of a body's powers are contractual. Simon Brown J failed to recognise the legislative nature of the rules of the Jockey Club in concluding that they made decisions which affected only those voluntarily and willingly subscribing to their rules and procedures, with an insufficient public interest to justify the application of judicial review. However, he did not see that as preventing the Club from being susceptible to review when operating in its occasional public law capacity, such as when exercising quasi-licensing powers.[49]

Developing the 'Governmentality' Test

The necessity for a body to be interwoven with, or underpinned by, government for it to be susceptible to judicial review was highlighted in *Datafin* and in *Massingberd-Mundy* and *RAM Racecourses*, where the Jockey Club's Royal Charter was argued to represent governmental support for its activities. This question was dealt with in greater detail in *R v Football Association Ltd ex p Football League* Ltd,[50] concerning an attempt by the Football League to prevent the Football Association (FA) forming the FA Premier League. The FA is the governing body of association football in England. Part of its role is to sanction various competitions; the most significant of which was, at the time, the Football League. In 1991 the FA chose to form and co-ordinate a Premier League, making alterations to their rules in order to facilitate this. The Football League brought an application for judicial review of the FA's decisions to set up the Premier League and to make the required amendments to its rules. The Football League provided three arguments for the FA's susceptibility to judicial review. First it had a monopoly control over association football. Secondly, its rules, despite being contractual in form, were in effect a legislative code for the game. Finally, the FA regulated an

---

45   *Ibid*, p 244.
46   *Ibid*, p 247.
47   *Ibid*.
48   *Ibid*.
49   *Ibid*.
50   [1993] 2 All ER 833.

important aspect of national life and, if it did not exist, the State would have to create a public body to perform its functions.

In the Divisional Court Rose J acknowledged the extension of the FA's powers beyond contract, suggesting this could characterise the FA as a body susceptible to judicial review, despite its private law constitution and accepting that its rules were effectively a legislative code.[51] Rose J went on to analyse the effect of the *Datafin* decision on the position of the FA, stating that prior to that case there was no argument for its susceptibility to judicial review. He accepted the effect of *Datafin* as extending the scope of judicial review to a non-statutory body not derived from the exercise of prerogative. He interpreted the *ratio* of the decision in *Datafin* such that a body may be susceptible to judicial review when regulating an important aspect of national life, with the support of the State, in that, but for its existence, the State would create a public body to perform its functions.[52] Rose J questioned the judgment of Simon Brown J in *R v Jockey Club ex p RAM Racecourses*, suggesting the decision in *Law* to be a better guide in relation to those bodies deriving power, *prima facie*, from contract and stated that the *Datafin* decision in no way altered the law in this area.[53] His conclusion was that the FA was not a body susceptible to judicial review, stating that it was:

R v Football Association Ltd ex p Football League [1993] 2 All ER 833

... a clear and inescapable conclusion ... that the FA is not a body susceptible to judicial review, either in general or, more particularly, at the instigation of the League, with whom it is contractually bound. Despite its virtually monopolistic powers and the importance of its decisions to many members of the public who are not contractually bound to it, it is, in my judgment, a domestic body whose powers arise from and duties exist in, private law only. I find no sign of underpinning directly or indirectly by any organ or agency of the state or any potential government interest, nor is there any evidence to suggest that if the FA did not exist that the state would intervene to create a body to perform its functions. On the contrary, the evidence of the commercial interest in the professional game is such as to suggest that if the FA did not exist that a far more likely intervener would be a television or similar company rooted in the entertainment business or a commercial company seeking advertising benefits such as presently provides sponsorship in one form or another.[54]

Again, the basis in private law is the prime consideration in deciding susceptibility to review, despite recognition of the potentially far-reaching and significant consequences of the FA's decisions. The key issues in this case are those of 'interweaving and underpinning', and 'substitution'. The question of 'substitution', that is to say whether government would step in to fill a body's functions if it did not exist, is a highly speculative inquiry, and particularly vague. In establishing this test the courts have failed to lay down any detailed criteria against which particular bodies can be tested. The test relies upon the notion that public power and government powers are analogous. As noted in the judgment of Simon Brown J in *RAM Racecourses*, this is not the case. Powers akin to those wielded by government are utilised outside of the governmental sphere. While it is true that the majority of the FA's powers will be entirely within the realms of private law, this is not a compelling argument for the total exclusion of judicial review. It might be argued that in applying this test the courts fail to recognise the reality of 'mixed' administration,[55] where a private body performing private law functions can also operate in a public law capacity. The question of substitution can also be criticised

51   *Ibid*, p 841.
52   *Ibid*, p 843.
53   *Ibid*, p 847.
54   *Ibid*, p 848.
55   Aronson, M, 'A public lawyer's response to privatisation and outsourcing', in Taggart, M (ed), *The Province of Administrative Law* (1997), Oxford: Hart, p 52.

as it is unlikely to be answered in the affirmative where government is in the process of actively downsizing,[56] delegating its functions and duties to the private sector. This may have the effect that private bodies, having powers analogous to those operated by sport's governing bodies but delegated directly from government, will be subjected to judicial review, whereas the bodies in the sporting sector will not. Despite the broad comparability in terms of the nature of power exercised, the same policy of decentralisation that would make the first body amenable to judicial review could prevent sporting bodies from becoming susceptible.

Similar arguments relate to the interweaving and underpinning test. There is little evidence of *visible* governmental support for sporting bodies in the way in which there was for the Panel in *Datafin*. Though the FA is not supported by a statutory framework, this does not necessarily indicate the absence of government support, in its narrow sense, for the activities of the FA. The reactive, rather than pro-active, nature of government may offer some clarification in this matter. Where a sport is generally seen as being well managed, there is unlikely to be any incentive for government to legislate for the sport's regulation.

The Court of Appeal Moves In: *Aga Khan*

Arguably the most important authority in this field is now *R v Jockey Club ex p Aga Khan*.[57] As an owner wishing to race horses in Great Britain, the Aga Khan was compelled to register with the Jockey Club, entering into a contractual agreement expressly submitting to the Rules of Racing and the Club's disciplinary powers. After winning a race, a horse owned by the Aga Khan was found to have a substance prohibited by the Rules of Racing in its urine. Following an inquiry by the disciplinary committee of the Jockey Club, the horse was disqualified and the trainer fined. It was not proved that the applicant or the trainer had caused or arranged for the doping of the horse, nor that its performance had been in any way affected. The Aga Khan claimed that the decision was damaging to his status as a religious leader and to his reputation as an owner and breeder of racehorses. He also contended that the value of the horse for breeding purposes had been significantly reduced and applied for judicial review of the disciplinary committee's decision to disqualify the horse. He contended that the Jockey Club, despite being a private club in form, was susceptible to judicial review. As the body that regulated horse racing in Great Britain the Jockey Club, in making decisions of this kind, was exercising a public function in the *de facto* control of a major national industry. Further, the Jockey Club's decisions represented the exercise of powers public in character.

The opinions of the Court of Appeal are worthy of careful attention in that they are often divergent. All three judges accepted the source of power was inconclusive, but not irrelevant, in determining justiciability, and that the nature of the power exercised was important.[58] Sir Thomas Bingham MR and Hoffmann LJ also recognised the position of the Jockey Club as having *de facto* control over an area of significant national activity.[59] Bingham MR stated that the powers exercised in this area were essentially of a public nature.[60] Hoffmann LJ disagreed, believing the power to be entirely private in its nature.[61]

---

56 *Op cit*, fn 36, Mullan (1997), p 153.
57 [1993] 1 WLR 909.
58 Sir Thomas Bingham MR, pp 915–16; Farquharson LJ, p 927; and Hoffmann LJ, p 931.
59 *R v Jockey Club ex p Aga Khan* [1993] 1 WLR 909, pp 916 and 932 respectively.
60 *Ibid*, p 916.
61 *Ibid*, pp 932–33.

In respect of the governmental nature of the body, Bingham MR accepted that if the body ceased to exist, the government would be required to fulfil its functions.[62] Farquharson LJ, however, stated:

R v Jockey Club ex p Aga Khan [1993] 1 WLR 909

I do not detect in the material available to us, any grounds for supposing that, if the Jockey Club were dissolved, any governmental body would assume control of racing.[63]

In addition to recognising the public nature of its powers, and that it could satisfy the substitution test, Bingham MR accepted that the Club exercised effective monopoly power over a significant national activity. However, he also accepted the contention of the Jockey Club that the Club's origin, history, constitution and membership did not reflect that of a public body.[64] Bingham MR did not just demand that the powers exercised be governmental in nature; he also required that they be interwoven into a system of governmental control of the sport. As with previous cases he was unable to identify such a relationship between the regulation of racing and government. The apparent effect of this was that the powers exercised by the Club were public, but not governmental. Thus the Club was not susceptible to judicial review.[65] Bingham MR's final comment was that the Jockey Club's power was based on consensual agreement. This was the case in spite of the effective monopoly of the Club and the recognition in previous judgments of the legislative nature of such 'agreements'.[66] The agreement established private law rights, which provided a basis for effective action in private law without need for resort to judicial review. Judicial review could not therefore be extended to encompass the Jockey Club.[67]

Evaluating the Case Law

The tests applied in discerning justiciability can themselves be criticised in that they do not deal with the reality of the power exercised, concentrating instead upon the body exercising it. However, not only have the tests themselves been shown to be potentially flawed, but the manner in which the courts have applied them can also be criticised. This raises the question as to whether the way in which these tests have been applied has been influenced by other considerations. In R v Football Association ex p Football League Rose J suggested that there was a giant conceptual step to be taken before sport's governing bodies could be considered as being susceptible to review:

R v Football Association ex p Football League [1993] 2 All ER 833

For my part, to apply to the governing body of football, on the basis that it is a public body, principles honed for the control of the abuse of power by government and its creatures, would involve what, in today's fashionable parlance would be called a quantum leap.[68]

---

62   *Ibid*, p 916.
63   *Ibid*, p 930.
64   *Ibid*.
65   *Ibid*.
66   *Russell v Duke of Norfolk* [1949] 1 All ER 109, pp 113–14, *per* Tucker J; *Enderby Town FC Ltd v The Football Association Ltd* [1971] Ch 591, p 606, *per* Denning LJ.
67   *R v Jockey Club ex p Aga Khan* [1993] 1 WLR 909, p 924. Farquharson LJ followed this final statement. He also recognised the absence of realistic choice in the Jockey Club's contractual relationship but denied that this in any way undermined the consensual nature of the agreement. His suggestion was that this was necessary for the control and integrity of the sport concerned.
68   *R v Football Association ex p Football League* [1993] 2 All ER 833.

Similarly in the *Aga Khan* case Hoffmann LJ commented:

R v Jockey Club ex p Aga Khan [1993] 1 WLR 909

Power can be private as well as public. Private power may affect the public interest and the livelihood of many individuals. This does not mean the rules of public law should be available in law for curbing the excesses of private power . . . I do not think that one should try to patch up the remedies available against domestic bodies by pretending that they are organs of government.[69]

In this respect, rather than arguing that sporting bodies do not fit a particular model or test, the underlying approach has been more straightforward. The judicial view is simply that judicial review is a mechanism for the control of the exercise of public power by government and that for all their legislative powers, governing bodies in sport are not part of this judicial view of government, and are therefore beyond the scope of judicial review. This is supported by the judgment of Sir John Donaldson MR in *Datafin* who referred to the control of *executive* rather than *public* power.[70] It is argued that the term *executive* used in relation to the nature of power, which will be subject to judicial review, implies a dual requirement that the power must be a *public* one exercised by *government*. If this two-fold test is accepted, then this would make it very difficult to argue the case for the susceptibility to judicial review of sport's governing bodies. Despite contending that it could be possible to view sporting bodies as being underpinned by or intertwined with government, it is not argued here that sporting bodies are *constituent parts* of government.

Whether or not this view is accepted, the case law in relation to the application for judicial review raises a number of important questions.[71] Is the judiciary predetermining the issue of susceptibility to review and then applying the law so as to meet the desired outcome? Have the courts simply decided that judicial review is a means of controlling power that is not only public, but also governmental in nature?

However, judicial review is only one part of a range of mechanisms for the control of the exercise of power, and the field of public law is not limited to judicial review: private law has absorbed principles from public law.[72] The question is whether the private law process can offer applicants sufficient protection in the light of the fact that judicial review is unavailable.

NATURAL JUSTICE

One way in which private law has adopted public law principles is in relation to the rules of natural justice. These rules make up part of one of the heads of judicial review, procedural impropriety, outlined by Lord Diplock in *CCSU v Minister for the Civil Service*.[73] However, as suggested, the rules

---

69   *R v Jockey Club ex p Aga Khan* [1993] 1 WLR 909, pp 932–33.

70   *R v Panel on Take-overs and Mergers ex p Datafin* [1987] 1 All ER 564, p 577.

71   For a critical view of the application of judicial review to sports governing bodies see: Pannick, D, 'Judicial review of sports bodies' (1997) 2(3) JR 150; Beloff, MJ and Kerr, T, 'Why *Aga Khan* was wrong' (1996) 1(1) JR 30. For a brief survey of the case law see Bond, C, 'Sporting bodies and judicial review' (1993) 1 SATLJ 7; and Belloff, M, Kerr, T, and Demetriou, M, *Sports Law* (1999) Oxford: Hart, pp 227–228. By contrast it has also been suggested that the distinction between public and private process has become irrelevant; see Lewis, A and Taylor J (eds), *Sport: Law and Practice* (2004), London: Butterworths, pp 123–127.

72   Taggart, M, 'The province of administrative law determined?', in Taggart, M (ed), *The Province of Administrative Law* (1997), Oxford: Hart, p 2.

73   [1985] AC 374.

are applied not only in the context of judicial review actions but also those founded in private law – including the private law relationships of sports governing bodies. There are two main rules of natural justice: the rule against bias (*nemo judex in sua causa*), and the right to a fair hearing (*audi alteram partem*). The initial development of the rules was in order to provide a minimum of protection for those appearing before bodies carrying out an adjudicative function. However, it was extended beyond this to take in bodies acting in an administrative capacity.[74] This position was not maintained during the first half of the 20th century; the rules were applied only in circumstances where a body was acting in a judicial rather than an executive or administrative capacity.[75] *Ridge v Baldwin*[76] signalled a change of approach; the circumstances in which the rules could be applied were redefined, with an emphasis upon the effect of a decision. An indication of this shift can be seen in the early case of *Russell v Duke of Norfolk*.[77] The case concerned the withdrawal by the Jockey Club of the claimant's licence to train racehorses and subsequent disqualification from having an involvement in racing in any capacity. The licence was withdrawn at an inquiry, held by the stewards of the Jockey Club and attended by Mr Russell, which arose after a horse trained by the claimant was found to have been doped, contrary to Jockey Club rules. The stewards of the Jockey Club acted under powers conferred upon them under the Club's rules, by which the claimant had agreed to be bound by making an application for a licence. The stewards intimated that the licence was withdrawn on the ground of misconduct, with the effect that he was effectively prevented from taking on any substantial role in the racing world. Because of the Jockey Club's practical monopoly over the holding of race meetings, this withdrawal effectively precluded the claimant from training racehorses.

Mr Russell brought an action arguing that he had been found guilty of misconduct and become a disqualified person without an inquiry being conducted in accordance with the demands of natural justice. At first instance the jury decided that the inquiry held by the stewards was fair.[78]

In the Court of Appeal Tucker LJ assumed the existence of a contract, providing the relationship between the claimant and the Jockey Club (that is, the Rules of Racing), though he doubted whether this was technically correct:

Russell v Duke of Norfolk [1949] 1 All ER 109

I have some doubt whether it is constituted a contract or whether it was not merely a licence issued on conditions binding both parties.[79]

The majority in the Court of Appeal chose to reject Mr Russell's claim on the basis that the contract did not require a hearing to take place at all, so to require any hearing to be in accordance with the rules of natural justice would be perverse. Denning LJ submitted an alternative view. He suggested that in a situation where the conditions of the licence gave the Jockey Club absolute discretion as to its withdrawal, it would be sufficient that the Club act honestly and in good faith in making such a decision. However, where the withdrawal of a licence was coupled with disqualification (from involvement in racing in any form) this was much more serious. It had the

---

74 eg, *Cooper v Wandsworth Board of Works* (1863) 14 CB NS 180. The rules were held to extend to administrative decisions affecting property rights.
75 *R v Electricity Commissioners* [1924] 1 KB 171.
76 [1964] AC 40.
77 [1949] 1 All ER 109.
78 [1948] 1 All ER 488.
79 *Ibid*, pp 113–14.

effect of taking away a person's livelihood:

> Common justice therefore requires that before any man be found guilty of an offence carrying such consequences, there should be an inquiry at which he has the opportunity of being heard ... It is very different from a mere dismissal of a servant or withdrawal of a licence, or even expulsion from a club.[80]

Denning LJ suggested such a disqualification could be contrary to public policy. He went on to note the position of the Jockey Club as having a 'monopoly in an important field of human activity. It has great powers and corresponding responsibilities'.[81] On the facts Denning LJ held that the hearing that had taken place was in conformity with the principles of natural justice. Thus the claimant's appeal was dismissed. The judgment of Denning LJ represents an indication of the way in which the case law concerning natural justice, both generally and with specific relation to sport's governing bodies, was to develop.

The fair hearing rule exists now such that courts and tribunals with similar functions as well as other bodies acting in a judicial capacity will be subject to the demands of the fair hearing rule. In exceptional circumstances the rule requiring a fair hearing will be applied solely upon the basis of the substantial effect of a decision upon an individual's rights. The rule can require a variety of things from decision makers, dependent upon the nature of the individual case. The rules may require prior notice of a decision, consultation and written representation, a duty to give adequate notice of a disciplinary charge, an oral hearing, the right to call and cross-examine witnesses, legal representation and a requirement to give reasons.[82]

The *audi alteram partem* rule has been invoked most readily where the loss of a person's livelihood or reputation has been at stake, highlighting that the application of the rules will be highly dependent upon the individual circumstances of each case. The extension of the rule following *Ridge v Baldwin* indicates an acknowldgment on behalf of the courts that it is not only statutory bodies that can affect rights and that statutory protection is not always sufficient: the approach favoured by Denning LJ in *Russell v Duke of Norfolk*. There it was recognised that the monopolistic nature of the Jockey Club combined with the significant effect that its decisions could have would be reason enough to subject it to the requirements of natural justice.

Natural Justice and Sporting Bodies

Lord Denning MR followed his judgment in *Russell* and demonstrated that the principles outlined in *Ridge v Baldwin* were applicable in relation to the actions of governing bodies of sport in *Enderby Town FC Ltd v The Football Association Ltd.*[83] The case concerned the ability of the FA to deny legal representation in the operation of its tribunals. The defendants, the FA, had control over association football, and the county associations affiliated to it. The claimants, Enderby Town, were fined and censured by their county association and made an appeal to the FA. They asserted the right to be represented by solicitor and counsel in their appeal hearing. The FA rejected this on the ground that their rule 38(b) excluded legal representation except where the chairman or secretary of the club being heard was a lawyer. The club sought an injunction restraining the FA from hearing the appeal without the club being legally represented. At first instance it was held that the provisions of the

---

80   *Ibid*, p 119.
81   *Ibid*.
82   See Lord Woolf, Jowell, J and Le Sueur, AP, *Principles of Judicial Review* (1999), London: Sweet & Maxwell, Chapter 8.
83   [1971] Ch 591.

contract entered into between Enderby Town and their county association should be observed. Lord Denning MR highlighted the invalidity of any attempt to 'oust the jurisdiction of the court, unreasonably shut out a man from his work or lay down procedure contrary to natural justice'.[84] However, the club's argument that legal representation was essential in their appeal to the FA, because of the difficulty of the points of law involved, was rejected by Lord Denning MR. The club, he decided, were perfectly entitled to bring an action for a declaration on those points before the court. This would allow legal representation. In any case, it would be preferable that such intricate points of law should be decided by the courts rather than by a body such as the FA.[85] Significantly, once again, this highlights the balance that has to be struck by the courts between the demands of justice and the requirement that a governing body be given sufficient latitude to carry out its tasks efficiently.

Enderby Town Football Club Ltd v The Football Association Ltd [1971] Ch 591

In many cases it may be a good thing for the proceedings of a domestic tribunal to be conducted informally without legal representation. Justice can often be done, in them, better by a good layman than by a bad lawyer ... But I must emphasise that the discretion must be properly exercised. The tribunal must not fetter its discretion by rigid bonds. A domestic tribunal is not at liberty to lay down an absolute rule.[86]

Lord Denning MR concluded that as long as a rule denying legal representation was merely directory and not imperative it would not be in breach of natural justice. He summarised:

The long and the short of it is that if the court sees that a domestic tribunal is proposing to proceed in a manner contrary to natural justice, it can intervene to stop it.[87]

This case serves to emphasise two key points. First, that the courts will use the combination of monopolistic control coupled with serious consequences for the individual to justify subjecting decisions to the demands of natural justice. However, secondly, there may be a tendency to avoid complicating sporting bodies' procedures too greatly.

The Limits of Natural Justice

Throughout the early case law the recurrent theme was one of generally expansive judgments, aimed at protecting individuals from the capricious and arbitrary exercise of monopoly powers. *McInnes v Onslow-Fane*[88] dealt with the question of the requirement for governing bodies to inform an applicant of the case against him and to provide that applicant with the opportunity of a hearing. The case represents a more conservative view of the courts' approach. In 1976 the claimant, McInnes, applied to the British Boxing Board of Control (BBBC) for a licence to permit him to act as a boxing manager, coupled with a request that he might be given an oral hearing and prior notice of anything that might prevent him from obtaining the licence. The board refused his application without acquiescing to his additional requests. McInnes had previously held licences to act as a promoter, a trainer and as a master of ceremonies; all of which were withdrawn in 1973. Between 1972 and 1975 McInnes had

---

84   *Ibid*, p 606.
85   *Ibid*, p 605.
86   *Ibid, per* Denning MR, p 605.
87   *Ibid*, p 606. Fenton, Atkinson and Cairns LJJ concurred with Lord Denning MR's judgment and the claimant's appeal was dismissed.
88   [1978] 1 WLR 1520.

made five applications for a manager's licence, all of which were refused. The claimant sought a declaration against the British Boxing Board of Control that it had acted in breach of natural justice and/or unfairly in refusing his application for a boxing manager's licence in that they failed to comply with his requests to be informed of the case against him, so as to allow him to reply prior to the consideration of his application, and that they failed to grant him an oral hearing. Additionally he sought a mandatory order that the BBBC should either grant him a manager's licence or, alternatively, that they inform him of the case against him and grant him an oral hearing.

Megarry VC questioned whether the situation was one in which the courts were entitled to intervene, emphasising the changes which had taken place in relation to the application of the rules of natural justice:

McInnes v Onslow-Fane [1978] 1 WLR 1520

The question is not one that is governed by statute or contract, with questions of their true construction or the implication of terms; for there is no statute, and there is no contract between the claimant and the board. Nevertheless, in recent years there has been a marked expansion of the ambit of the requirements of natural justice and fairness reaching beyond statute and contract.[89]

Megarry VC held that the courts could intervene in order to enforce the requirements of natural justice but questioned the requirements of natural justice in such circumstances. He distinguished between three types of situation: forfeiture cases, where a licence or membership is withdrawn; application cases, where an application for such a licence or membership is refused; and expectation cases, which are different from the application cases in that the applicant has some legitimate expectation from previous conduct that a licence will be granted.[90] The applicant had argued that the other licences that he had held entitled him to have a legitimate expectation that his application for a manager's licence would succeed. Megarry VC rejected this; the other licences were for different functions and thus there was no legitimate expectation that his application would succeed.[91]

Megarry VC also rejected the claimant's contention that the BBBC were under an obligation to provide reasons for their decision of an oral hearing. As the issue of a licence was not dependent upon particular criteria, the refusal did not place a slur upon the applicant's character. The judgment also highlighted the need for balance between protection of the individual and the needs of the particular sport as a whole to be taken into account by the regulator.[92] Megarry VC emphasised the need to keep procedures speedy and uncomplicated, with the result that they would be perfectly entitled to withhold reasons for any refusal of a licence.[93] The situation in this respect has been somewhat altered by later case law.[95] Megarry VC did, nonetheless, note that the Board was under a

---

89 *Ibid*, p 1528.

90 *Ibid*, p 1529.

91 *Ibid*, p 1531.

92 *Ibid*, p 1535.

93 *Ibid*, p 1536.

94 *R v Civil Service Appeal Board ex p Cunningham* [1991] 4 All ER 310 extended the position to one where a decision maker should give outline reasons for its decision where procedural fairness demands, in that reasons will aid the individual to ascertain whether the decision was lawful and thus help an individual in any potential litigation. In *R v Home Secretary ex p Doody* [1993] 1 WLR 154, it was judged that reasons could be required where a decision has severe consequences, though in *R v Higher Education Funding Council ex p Institute of Dental Surgery* [1994] 1 WLR 242, it was decided that where a body was making a decision on 'expert' or technical reasons which a court would not be competent to assess, then reasons would not be required. This appears to conform to the 'trust to my expertise' approach to self regulation. Though cf *R v University of Cambridge ex p Evans (No 1)* [1998] Ed CR 151; *R (a/o Asha Foundation) v Millennium Commission* [2003] EWCA Civ 88.

duty to reach an honest conclusion, without bias and not in pursuance of a capricious policy.[95] In dismissing the application Megarry VC commented:

> I think that the courts must be slow to allow any implied obligation to be fair to be used as a means of bringing before the courts for review honest decisions of bodies exercising jurisdiction over sporting and other activities, which those bodies are far better fitted to judge than the courts. This is so even where those bodies are concerned with the means of livelihood of those who take part in those activities. The concepts of natural justice and the duty to be fair must not be allowed to discredit themselves by making unreasonable requirements and imposing undue burdens. Bodies such as the board, which promote a public interest by seeking to maintain high standards in a field of activity, which might otherwise become degraded and corrupt, ought not to be hampered in their work without good cause.[96]

This approach manifested itself in the case of *Calvin v Carr*,[97] which involved a challenge to the decision of the Australian Jockey Club (AJC) to disqualify an owner of a horse. Here once again, the need to avoid over-juridification in the decision making processes of domestic bodies was highlighted:

Calvin v Carr [1980] AC 574

> It is undesirable in many cases of domestic disputes, particularly in which an inquiry and appeal process has been established, to introduce too great a measure of formal judicialisation. While flagrant cases of injustice, including corruption or bias, must always be firmly dealt with by the courts, the tendency in their Lordships' opinion in matters of domestic disputes should be to leave these to be settled by the agreed methods without requiring the formalities of judicial process to be introduced.[98]

The Rule Against Bias

Sports governing bodies are also required to act in accordance with the rule against bias. The rule requires an adjudicator to be free from any interest in a case. This can be financial, which automatically disqualifies the adjudicator,[99] or where there is the likelihood of the appearance of bias.[100]

Morris, P and Little, G, 'Challenging sports bodies' determinations'

> The rule is a distinct limb of natural justice and precludes a member of a disciplinary tribunal from sitting in any case where there is a reasonable likelihood or suspicion of bias; actual bias need not be established. In applying the rule stringently courts recognise its value as a tool in promoting confidence in the integrity of administrative justice. Factual circumstances in which the rule may be infringed are infinite, but there are particular instances of the rule in operation, which are particularly relevant to sports bodies' administrators when carrying out their role of designing and operating arrangements for the adjudication of disciplinary cases. First, the disciplinary code should make provision for the rigid demarcation of 'prosecutorial' and 'adjudicating' functions. Any intermingling of these functions such as 'the prosecutor' participating or appearing to participate in the adjudication is likely to infringe the rule unless the essential and historic function of a sports official dictates such participation, one example being horse racing stewards who have long performed an 'evidence gathering' function as well as sitting

---

95 *McInnes v Onslow-Fane* [1978] 1 WLR 1520, p 1533.

96 *Ibid*, p 1535.

97 [1980] AC 574.

98 *Ibid*, p 593. See also *Modahl v British Athletic Federation Ltd* [2002] 1 WLR 1192 *per* Latham LJ at para 67, Jonathan Parker LJ at para 87 and Mance LJ at para 116.

99 *Dimes v Grand Junction Canal Co* (1852) 3 HLC 759.

100 *R v Sussex Justices ex p McCarthy* [1924] 1 KB 256; *R v Gough* [1993] AC 646; *Locabail (UK) Ltd v Bayfield Properties* [2000] 1 All ER 65.

in an adjudicating capacity during a disciplinary inquiry (*Hall v New South Wales Trotting Club* (1977) 1 NSWLR 378, 397, *per* Moloney JA). Secondly, in general a sports body's disciplinary code should strive to ensure, in the case of appeals, that an individual who sits (or is entitled to sit) in at the initial hearing does not also participate as an adjudicator during the appeal (*Hannan v Bradford Corporation* [1970] 1 WLR 937). The rationale for this prohibition is clearly articulated by Lord Widgery CJ namely that 'when one is used to dealing with other people in a group or on a committee, there must be a built-in tendency to support the decision of that committee, even though one tries to fight against it' (at 946). Thirdly, it is perfectly proper for sports disciplinary tribunals to be composed exclusively or substantially of fellow sportsmen on the basis that the individual members of a profession or occupational group are ideally equipped to judge whether there has been a breach of the professional code of conduct and the gravity of it. This professional autonomy however is subject to the proviso that the architects of the disciplinary arrangements are 'careful in framing the constitution of the governing body, and of its disciplinary tribunal, to ensure that the task of presenting a complaint and the task of adjudicating upon it and, if it is proved, determining the appropriate sanction are in different hands' (*Re S, A Barrister* [1981] QB 670 at 683, *per* Vinelott J).

Perhaps the most pressing problem confronting sports' governing bodies in relation to the rule against bias is to resist the quite natural temptation to pack disciplinary tribunals with their own officials. Historically, governing bodies have succumbed to this temptation and the infamous *Don Revie* case (*The Times*, 14 December 1979) shows that it can contribute to a finding of bias by the courts.[101]

In *Revie* members of a Football Association disciplinary tribunal who had criticised Don Revie, the former England manager, before a hearing, were disqualified on the basis of a likelihood of bias. The tribunal's decision to impose a 10 year ban on Revie was subsequently revoked. In *Modahl* (discussed in greater detail below) the Court of Appeal adopted a similar line of reasoning to that in *Calvin v Carr* in determining that overall the athlete had a fair hearing.

The Modern Law: *Jones v WRFU*

A recent indicator of the way in which the law has developed in the area of natural justice more generally is the case of *Jones v Welsh Rugby Football Union*,[102] which involved a challenge to the disciplinary procedures operated by the Welsh Rugby Football Union (WRFU).

Mark Jones played for Ebbw Vale Rugby Football Club. He was sent off the field of play for fighting during the club's game against Swansea in November 1996. Jones appeared before the Disciplinary Committee of the WRFU in order to offer explanation and comment on the referee's report. He was denied legal representation, but due to a severe speech impediment, he was allowed to be represented by an official of the Ebbw Vale club. The club representative was a QC, but his function was to speak in place of Jones rather than to act as his advocate. Standard WRFU procedure was followed, the player's representative commented on the referee's report, and the referee commented and was questioned by the Disciplinary Committee. However, the Committee refused Jones' request that his representative be given permission to comment on the video of the incident, in order that it might be demonstrated that Jones was acting in self-defence. The Committee also refused to allow Jones' representative to cross-examine the referee. The Committee viewed the video of the incident in private, and again refused Jones or his representative the right to comment upon it. As a result of the hearing, the Disciplinary Committee decided that the referee had been correct in sending

---

101 Morris, P and Little, G, 'Challenging sports bodies' determinations' (1998) 17 Civ JQ 128, pp 139–40.

102 *The Times*, 6 March 1997, and *The Times*, 6 January 1998. See also Rose, N and Albertini, L, '*Jones v Welsh Rugby Union*: new law for the new era' (1997) 5(1) SATLJ 20.

Jones off and imposed a 30 day suspension upon him. The constitution of the WRFU granted power in relation to disciplinary matters to the Committee. These rules had the effect of conferring upon the Committee complete discretion in relation to the manner and form of its hearings.

Jones and his club, Ebbw Vale, proceeding by way of writ, sought a declaration that the decision to suspend was invalid, and an order obligating the WRFU to refrain from the imposition of the suspension until the completion of a new disciplinary process. Jones argued that any order should amend the disciplinary process in such a way as to allow him legal representation, to call and question witnesses, and to compel the Committee to examine or review evidence in his presence, giving him the right to make submissions pertaining to it.

Ebsworth J granted an interlocutory injunction preventing the imposition of a suspension prior to the final resolution of the issue.[103] In her judgment Ebsworth J agreed it was arguable that in refusing to vary its procedure, not on the basis of any rules but on the grounds of custom and practice, the Committee acted in a manner lacking in fairness. In this case Ebsworth J felt that it was arguable that the claimant had effectively been denied the right to defend himself properly.

Following the interlocutory decision of Ebsworth J, the WRFU was keen that the matter should be resolved as speedily as possible. In response to the judgment the WRFU implemented changes to its rules, granting a player or his representative the right to question the referee and to call and cross-examine witnesses. The amendments also required video evidence to be viewed in the presence of all the parties and provided that player's requests for legal representation should be treated on their merits, in conformity with the judgment of Lord Denning MR in *Enderby Town*.

The claimants then applied for an order restraining the WRFU from imposing any suspension related to the incident in the match against Swansea in November 1996 prior to the final resolution of the issue. Despite the argument of the WRFU that Ebsworth J's order was limited to the suspension imposed at the initial disciplinary hearing, Potts J granted the order requested by the claimants.[104]

The defendant appealed against both the decision of Ebsworth J and that of Potts J (heard in the Court of Appeal).[105] In his judgment Potter LJ recognised that the WRFU could well be successful in defending its actions if the case proceeded to trial. However, he refused its appeal against the decision of Ebsworth J on the basis that all that it was necessary for her to do when deciding upon the grant of an interlocutory injunction was to determine whether or not the claimants had an arguable case for relief. Potter LJ was willing to overturn the decision of Potts J, on the ground that in Potter LJ's view Ebsworth J's order related only to the first hearing: it was not apt to deal with any further hearing which could not be criticised on the ground of procedural unfairness.

Evaluating the Case Law

The case law relating to natural justice demonstrates a general acceptance on the part of the courts of the need to subject sport's governing bodies to scrutiny. The monopoly positions held by many of these bodies have been acknowledged as being reason enough to supervise their activities. The broad range of values deemed worthy of protection by the rules of natural justice have meant that an extensive array of situations have been deemed to fall for consideration by the courts.[106]

---

103 *The Times*, 6 March 1997.
104 (1997) unreported, 17 November.
105 *The Times*, 6 January 1998.
106 See also McCutcheon, JP, 'Sports discipline, natural justice and strict liability' (1999) 28(1) Anglo-Am LR 37.

However, though the courts have accepted the general susceptibility of the considerations of sport's governing bodies to the rules of natural justice, the application of those maxims has been less vigorous. There is concern that the courts should not inhibit the activities of such bodies to any great degree. Whilst it may be desirable that sporting bodies should be reasonably free to conduct their affairs as they wish, their monopoly position demands that they should be prevented from acting unfairly. It is clear that those who are subject to the disciplinary procedures of sporting bodies should be prevented from hiding behind deficiencies in such procedures in order to avoid censure. The courts have tended to err on the side of administrative efficiency rather than individual justice.

However, cases such as *Jones* do demonstrate that the rules of natural justice can be extremely useful in helping sporting bodies to avoid acting unfairly. The speedy and comprehensive amendment of the WRFU's rules in that case demonstrated a desire on the part of sporting bodies to avoid having their decisions challenged in the courts.[107]

The usefulness of the natural justice rules as a method by which to call sport's governing bodies to account is further limited. The rules are largely restricted to procedural elements of governing bodies' activities, and thus have a limited capacity to penetrate bodies' regulatory sphere. The character of the natural justice rules combined with the manner of their application has the effect that, despite the courts' general willingness to subject these bodies to scrutiny, the usefulness of the rules in calling sport's governing bodies to account is marginal.

THE CONTRACTUAL RELATIONSHIP

Throughout the judicial review case law, the importance of the 'contractual' relationships by which sport's governing bodies obtain their power is emphasised and cited as the primary ground upon which judicial review is withheld. Thus, the extent to which contract can be utilised in rendering bodies accountable is important. Bodies controlling sport take on the form of either incorporated or unincorporated associations.[108] In the case of unincorporated associations, each of the association's members enters into a contractual relationship – the rules of the club – with each of the other members, as such associations are not recognised as having legal personality. Where an association is incorporated by becoming a limited company (or by obtaining a Royal Charter), each of the members contracts with the company and is subjected to its rules. Such rules are usually to be found in the company's memorandum and articles of association, constituting the 'contract' by which members are bound.[109]

Perhaps in contrast to the position in relation to the application for judicial review, the courts have developed a zeal for examining the contractual relationships between governing bodies and those subjected to their rules. The question of excluding the courts' jurisdiction by contract has been considered in a number of cases. *Baker v Jones*[110] examined the capacity of the Central Council of the British Amateur Weightlifters' Association (BAWLA) to pay out of BAWLA funds the legal costs of its members who had been sued in relation to their activities on the council. BAWLA was an

---

107 Note: the amendments were made not in response to a final judgment that had condemned the relevant rules, but as a reaction to proceedings for an interlocutory injunction where it was considered only that it was *arguable* that the rules were unfair.

108 Beloff, MJ, 'Pitch, rink, pool . . . court? Judicial review in the sporting world' [1989] PL 96.

109 Kerr, T, 'Fortifying sport's governing bodies and clubs against legal challenge', paper presented at *Strategies for Sports: Developing Proactive Legal and Marketing Practices*, 4 December 1997, pp 2–3.

110 [1954] 2 All ER 553.

unincorporated body, which had its primary object set out in rule 2 of its constitution, 'to promote weightlifting as a sport and weight training as a means of physical improvement'. The power to govern BAWLA was granted to the Central Council[111] including the power to act as the sole interpreter of the rules of BAWLA, and to act in any matter not dealt with by the rules.[112] Rule 40 also purported to make decisions of the Central Council final. The claimant, Baker, was a member of BAWLA who objected to the legal costs, in respect of tort actions faced by members of the Central Council, being met from BAWLA funds. He sought a declaration, as against the officers of BAWLA and members of the Central Council, in that the payments made were unlawful, arguing that the rules did not give the Central Council the requisite authority. In response the defendants argued that the rules not only granted them such authority, but also meant the decision was final and impervious to challenge before the courts.

Lynskey J disagreed with the defendants' construction of the rules, stating that the rules constituted a contract and that public policy would prevent the ousting of the jurisdiction of the courts by such a contract. Thus the decision of the Council was open to scrutiny by the court.

On the facts in *Baker* Lynskey J accepted that there were no specific rules on the making of such payments and that the rules gave the Council power to decide matters not covered by the rules. However, he also stated that this broad power should be utilised with the primary objects of BAWLA in mind. The council would be unable to use BAWLA funds for purposes outside of the objects. The defendants argued those having their legal bills paid had been sued in their capacity as officers of BAWLA, Lynskey J was unable to construe the objects of the association, or a reasonably incidental purpose thereof, as extending to payment of the legal fees of its officers. The association was an unincorporated association with no legal personality and thus could not be liable for the tortious acts of its officers. Lynskey J ruled that there was no power under the rules for the council to authorise the payment of officer's legal fees and issued a declaration as requested by the claimant. This begins to suggest that there may be limits on sporting autonomy, in as much as they will be required to act in accordance with their own rules and regulations, and that the court will consider this in the light of the general aims and objectives of the body.

The extent of sports governing bodies' accountability on the basis of contract was demonstrated in *Davis v Carew-Pole*.[113] The claimant, Davis, was a stable keeper required to appear before the National Hunt Committee (NHC) to answer an allegation that he had trained a horse for a steeplechase contrary to the rules of the NHC, as he was unlicensed. Davis attended the NHC inquiry, at which two other allegations concerning his unlicensed training of horses were considered, without prior notice. At the inquiry Davis was declared to be a 'disqualified person' under the rules, thus depriving him of the ability to be involved in National Hunt racing at any level. Davis claimed a declaration that the decision of the NHC was *ultra vires* and void, and an injunction restraining the NHC from treating him as a disqualified person. Pilcher J set out his understanding of the situation, stating:

Davis v Carew-Pole [1956] 1 WLR 833

If the powers of the quasi-judicial body are set out in a code of rules to which the party aggrieved is in the circumstances subject, the quasi-judicial body is also bound by its own rules and can only mete out punishment in strict accordance with such rules.[114]

---

111 Rule 34.

112 Rule 40.

113 [1956] 1 WLR 833.

114 *Ibid*, pp 837–38. See also *Aberavon & Port Talbot RFC v WRU Ltd* [2003] EWCA Civ 584; *Towcester Racecourse Ltd v Racecourse Association* [2002] EWHC 2141; *Meggeson v Burns* [1972] 1 Lloyd's Rep 223. Though cf the judgment of Jonathan Parker LJ (dissenting) in *Modahl v British Athletic Federation Ltd* [2002] 1 WLR 1192 at paras 70–88.

On considering the facts and the rules of the NHC, Pilcher J held that they did not entitle the NHC to declare Davis a disqualified person. More importantly, he decided that there *was* a contractual relationship between Davis and the NHC, despite the fact that Davis was unlicensed by the committee. The contractual nexus, Pilcher J said, arose when the claimant submitted to the jurisdiction of the committee in attending the inquiry. On the basis of this generous interpretation of the contractual nexus Pilcher J ruled in favour of the claimant, issuing the declaration and injunction.

Questioning the Contractual Relationship: *Modahl v BAF*

The question of the existence or otherwise of a contract between governing bodies is not uncontroversial and was a key point in the litigation between Diane Modahl and the British Athletic Federation.[115] Modahl was suspended from participating in athletics events by the BAF when she was found to have committed a doping offence by a BAF disciplinary committee after being tested at an athletics meeting in Lisbon. Modahl appealed to an independent appeal tribunal, which lifted the ban after hearing new evidence that the samples on which the suspension was based could have affected the reliability of the test. Modahl brought an action for breach of contract, claiming damages for expenses and loss of income during the period of her suspension. This claim was on the basis that there had been a breach of an implied contractual term that the disciplinary committee would act fairly and without bias. At first instance it was held that there was no contract between the parties and that, in any case, the disciplinary committee had acted fairly and without bias. On appeal to the Court of Appeal there was extensive discussion of whether a contract existed between Modahl and the British Athletic Federation. The claimant put forward three arguments in favour of finding the existence of a contract. The first was based upon Modahl's membership of Sale Harriers Athletic Club. The Club's rules and regulations specifically required Modahl to adhere to the rules of the BAF. Secondly, Modahl argued that her participation in events overseas meant that she submitted to the jurisdiction of the BAF. Rule 6(4)(a) of the BAF required participants in overseas competition to obtain the organisation's permission to do so. It was argued that this submission to the rules of the IAAF gave the respondent a disciplinary function which could only be sensibly dealt with in the context of a contract. Thirdly, it was argued that Modahl's invocation of her right to appear before a disciplinary panel and the exercise of her right of appeal created a contractual relationship as in the case of *Davis v Carew-Pole*. In response the BAF argued that it was not possible to identify any intention to create legal relations, sufficient certainty as to the terms, or any consideration. On appeal the claim was dismissed, but there was disagreement amongst the Court of Appeal as to the existence or otherwise of a contractual relationship. Both Latham and Mance LJJ found that overall it was appropriate to find the existence of a contract, though arriving at this conclusion by different routes:

Modahl v British Athletics Federation (No 2) [2002] 1 WLR 1192

Per Latham LJ:

50 There is no doubt that over a period of many years the applicant accepted that if she entered meetings under the auspices of the respondent or of the IAAF, she would be subject to the relevant rules. Equally, it seems to me to be a proper inference that the respondent in its turn accepted the responsibility to administer those rules in relation to all subject to its jurisdiction who competed in those meetings. I see

---

115 *Modahl v British Athletic Federation (No 2)* [2002] 1 WLR 1192.

no difficulty, therefore, in identifying with certainty the basic obligations undertaken by both the athlete and the respondent. There is a benefit and a detriment to both. The benefit to the athlete is that he or she knows that every athlete competing will be subject to the same rules, and that to remain entitled to compete, both nationally and internationally, he or she must comply with those rules. The respondent accepted the burden of administering those rules, and the benefit of having recognised athletes compete both in national and international events . . . I therefore see no difficulty in determining the consideration which each provides . . . The basic structure for a contract is, in my view, readily identifiable.

51. The remaining question is whether or not the parties can have had an intention to create a legal relationship. This seems to me to be the difficult part of the problem. It could be said that in the context of a sport, that involves imposing an inappropriate legal structure on for what for many will be recreation. This could justify the conclusion that only in those cases in which an athlete is offered and accepts an express contractual obligation can it properly be said that there is a contract between him or her and a body such as the respondent. Further, an inevitable corollary of the existence of a contractual relationship is that both parties are bound by obligations, the breach of which are capable of giving rise to a claim for damages. It would follow that breaches by the athlete of his or her obligations would potentially give rise to a claim for damages on the part of a body such as the respondent. But that seems to me to beg, rather than answer, the problem. There are many contractual situations, the paradigm being employer and employee, where neither party may have applied their minds to or appreciated the consequence of the contractual obligations, namely that both parties are liable in damages for its breach, subject always to the proper construction of the relevant obligations under that contract.

52. In my judgment if a legally enforceable contract can be created, as seems to me is inevitable, where an athlete expressly agrees in an entry form to be bound by the relevant rules, I can see no escape from the conclusion that a contract can properly be implied when the circumstances make it clear that that is, in essence, what the athlete has promised. I consider for the reasons that I have already given, that the appellant, even on the facts that have been established in this case, undertook to be so bound, and the respondent in turn undertook the obligation to apply those rules. In my judgment, the contract extended in the present case to the meeting in Lisbon. Under the rules the appellant must have sought permission from the respondent to compete, and thereby accepted the offer to compete in the knowledge of the disciplinary consequences; and the respondent in giving permission obtained the benefit of her competing.

Per Mance LJ:

103. In the present case, although the language of the respondents' rules has the contractual aspects to which I have drawn attention, there is no conversation or document which can be identified as constituting an express agreement. Any contract must be implied from conduct, in the light of the rules. The rules, in my view, contain a framework of rights and duties of sufficient certainty to be given contractual effect, with regard to the athlete's entitlement and ability to compete. Consideration exists in the athlete's submission to the rules and to the respondents' jurisdiction, in the respondents' agreement to operate the rules and to permit the athlete to compete in accordance with them, and in both parties' agreement on the procedures for resolution of any disputes contained in the rules.

. . .

105. In my judgment, the necessary implication of the appellant's conduct in joining a club, in competing at national and international level on the basis stated in the rules and in submitting herself to both in and out of competition doping tests, is that she became party to a contract with the respondents subject to the relevant terms of the rules. I have already identified three respects in which the rules appear to point towards a contractual analysis. I find unpersuasive the submission that an athlete had no personal right to enforce the obligations and standards of behaviour imposed expressly or impliedly on the respondents under their rules. The submission that no-one can have intended this in a sporting context seems unrealistic in relation to the modern sporting scene, which, whatever the labels of amateurism, has aspects affecting substantially the career, livelihood and prosperity of participants.

However, Jonathan Parker LJ was not convinced that a contractual relationship existed between the parties:

72. In any event, I am not persuaded that there was any contract between Mrs Modahl and the BAF. There is no written or oral contract, but [Modahl's Counsel] Mr Julius puts forward three possible bases for implying a contract containing an obligation of fairness on the part of the BAF in relation to the disciplinary process . . . I will consider each of these suggested bases in turn.

The 'club basis'

. . .

74. I agree with the judge that on the material before the court the 'club basis' for implying a contract between Mrs Modahl and the BAF cannot succeed . . . [T]he form which Mrs Modahl signed when applying for membership of Sale Harriers in 1977 has not been produced, nor is there any secondary evidence as to its terms . . .

75. In my judgment, the requisite evidential foundation for the implication of a contract between Mrs Modahl and the BAF via her membership of Sale Harriers has simply not been laid.

The 'participation basis'

76. . . . In the instant case . . . the Lisbon event was an EAA event, in respect of which the responsibility for doping control lay with the Portuguese Athletic Federation. The BAF exercised no control over the Lisbon event. The involvement of the BAF in the Lisbon event derives solely from its obligation under the rules of the IAAF to carry into effect its disciplinary procedures . . . In the instant case . . . there is no evidence as to the terms of the form (if any) which Mrs Modahl signed when applying to enter the Lisbon event, or, for that matter, to whom any such form was addressed. On such facts as are known, it seems that the application might have been addressed to the IAAF, to the EAA, or to the Portuguese Athletic Federation . . .

77. Further, on the material available it seems to me unlikely, to put it no higher, that in applying to participate in the Lisbon event Mrs Modahl intended to create legal relations between herself and the BAF; still less that the BAF had such an intention. As already noted, the BAF was obliged under the IAAF rules to operate its disciplinary process in respect of Mrs Modahl. The inference which I would draw is that in so doing the BAF was doing no more, and was intending to do no more, than fulfil that obligation.

78. I accordingly conclude that Mrs Modahl does not succeed in implying a contract on the 'participation basis'.

The 'submission basis'

79. If there is a sound basis for implying a contract between Mrs Modahl and the BAF in relation to its disciplinary process then in my judgment this must be it. To my mind, however, the 'submission basis' gives rise to significant difficulties both as to intention to create legal relations and as to consideration.

80. As to intention to create legal relations, it seems to me that the natural inference is that in submitting herself to the BAF's disciplinary process Mrs Modahl's intention was merely to seek to defend herself against the finding of a positive drugs test and to avoid the imposition of a mandatory ban which would have had the practical effect of preventing her competing at national or international level for the period of the ban. As for the BAF, I have already stated my view that the natural inference is that its intention was merely to fulfil its obligation to the IAAF.

81. In my judgment, it is also material to bear in mind in this connection that the absence of a contract does not, on the authority of *Nagle v Feilden*, mean that Mrs Modahl is without a remedy should the sanction imposed as a result of the disciplinary process amount to an unreasonable restraint of trade. This is not, of course, a substitute for an action for damages for breach of contract, but it is a relevant feature of the context in which a contract is sought to be implied.

82. As to consideration, on the available evidential material I am unable to identify any benefit to the BAF capable of supporting the alleged contract, or for that matter any detriment to Mrs Modahl. As I see it, Mrs Modahl's interest in submitting to the BAF's disciplinary process was in maintaining her eligibility for national and international competition.

83. As Bingham LJ said in *Blackpool Aero Club v Blackpool BC* at 1202, 'contracts are not lightly to be implied'. In my judgment the fact that the factual context may be consistent with the parties having made a contract does not suffice for this purpose, nor (by the same token) does the fact that the parties would have acted no differently had a contract been concluded. To my mind, that is simply the starting-point for the inquiry whether a contract is to be implied. Something more is required. I am, however, unable to find anything more in the instant case.

The importance of establishing a contractual relationship between participants and governing bodies is clear. It has already been noted in this chapter that the claim for judicial review has been ruled out by the courts as a means of calling sports governing bodies to account. This has been done primarily on the basis that such relationships have their foundation in contract and thus are not strictly 'public law' affairs. The risk is that if no contractual relationship is deemed to exist, and the courts persist with the view that governing bodies are not subject to the claim for judicial review, there is the potential for a legal vacuum in which the individual may find themselves unable to effectively establish their rights and obligations in respect of governing bodies.[116]

Extending Justiciability

However, it appears to be generally accepted that the use of contract, by way of 'legal fiction' if not on a strict interpretation, is the most appropriate means by which to regulate sports governing bodies. The willingness to extend justiciability on this basis is emphasised by two further cases.

Nagle v Feilden[117] involved a female, Florence Nagle, who challenged the Jockey Club's consistent refusal to issue her with a licence to train racehorses on the sole basis of her gender. The claimant effectively trained racehorses; a licence to train was granted to her 'head lad' rather than her. Nagle brought an action claiming a declaration that the practice of the stewards in refusing a trainer's licence to any woman was void as against public policy and an injunction ordering the stewards to grant her a licence. At first instance and on appeal the claimant's case was struck out on the ground that, as there was no contractual relationship between the two parties, the application disclosed no cause of action.

In the Court of Appeal the claimant argued that the Jockey Club and their stewards operated a monopoly in the control of horse racing on the flat in Great Britain, and that as such they were under a duty to all those involved in the sport to exercise their control reasonably and lawfully, in accordance with the Rules of Racing, and not to exercise the discretion vested in them by those rules, capriciously. It was also maintained that the Jockey Club expressly and/or impliedly offered to prospective applicants that it would give consideration in accordance with the Rules of Racing to the bestowal of training licences. The claimant asserted that such an offer contained an implied term that when giving consideration to applications for training licences the stewards would act reasonably and would not exercise the discretion vested in them by the Rules of Racing with caprice. The systematic refusal of women applicants constituted a breach of the duty owed, as well as preventing females from earning a living in this area in restraint of trade and contrary to public policy.

---

116 On the indirect nature of contractual relationships between participants and governing bodies see Beloff, M, Kerr, T and Demetriou, M, *Sports Law* (1994) Oxford: Hart, pp 27–28.

117 [1966] 2 QB 633.

In the Court of Appeal Lord Denning MR decided that there was no contract between Nagle and the Jockey Club on the basis that the defendants had expressly declined to contract with the claimant.[118] However, Lord Denning MR was more receptive to the claimant's public policy argument, stressing the difference between the Jockey Club and social or other clubs. The Jockey Club was different as it was an operation administering a virtual monopoly in an important field of human activity and exercised significant power over individual livelihoods.[119] This had the effect that those wrongly rejected by the Jockey Club could have a remedy despite the absence of a contractual relationship.[120] Lord Denning felt that the right to work combined with capricious or arbitrary rejection constituted sufficient grounds for intervention by the courts, and thus that there was no need to imply a contract to give the claimant a cause of action:

Nagle v Feilden [1966] 2 QB 633

When an association, who have the governance of a trade, take it upon themselves to license persons to take part in it, then it is at least arguable that they are not at liberty to withdraw a man's licence – and thus put him out of business – without hearing him. Nor can they refuse a man a licence – and thus prevent him from carrying on his business – in their uncontrolled discretion.[121]

He then stated:

When authorities exercise a predominant power over the exercise of a trade or profession, the courts may have jurisdiction to see that this power is not abused ... If a practice in this respect is invalid as being contrary to public policy, there is ground for thinking that the court has jurisdiction to say so.[122]

An important point to stress in relation to this case is that no declaration was granted in favour of the claimant. The judgment in this case was that the claimant had an arguable case for claiming the relief sought on the ground that the practice of refusing a trainer's licence to a woman *could* be void as contrary to public policy, and thus the claimant's claim should not be struck out. The case may be analogous with the restraint of trade case law, discussed below; nevertheless, it is still useful in emphasising the extent to which the courts have gone in order to ensure accountability for governing bodies through the private law process.

There were a series of cases concerning the decision of the New Zealand Rugby Football Union (NZRFU) to send a touring team to the then apartheid state of South Africa, representing an extreme example of the broad manner in which the 'contracts' by which sports are regulated will be interpreted. In *Finnigan v NZRFU (No 1)*,[123] a number of local level players sought a declaration claiming that, in sending a team to South Africa, the NZRFU were in breach of their contractual obligation to 'promote, foster and develop New Zealand rugby', as stated in its rules and regulations. The applicants in the case were members of a rugby club, which was a member of a local union, which in turn was a member of the national union. In the High Court the NZRFU was successful in striking out the action, on the ground that the claimants lacked standing as not being members of the NZRFU. However, the result of the claimants' appeal to the New Zealand Court of Appeal was in stark contrast:

---

118 *Ibid*, p 643.

119 *Ibid*, p 644.

120 *Ibid*, p 646.

121 *Ibid*.

122 *Per* Lord Denning MR, p 647. Dankwerts LJ echoed the judgment of the Master of the Rolls by rejecting any contractual relationship but recognising the monopolistic nature of the Jockey Club's powers and the need to prevent those powers being exercised in a 'dictatorial' manner.

123 [1985] 2 NZLR 159.

Finnigan v NZRFU (No 1) [1985] 2 NZLR 159

Although not having contracts directly with the parent union, the claimants as local club members are linked to it by a chain of contracts . . . further the decision affects the New Zealand community as a whole, and so relations between the community and those specifically and legally associated with the sport . . . [and] may affect the international relations and standing of New Zealand.[124]

In allowing the appeal and according the claimants standing Cooke J commented:

While technically a private and voluntary sporting association, the NZRFU is, in relation to this decision, in a position of major national importance. Therefore we are not willing to apply to the question of standing the narrowest criteria that might apply, drawn from private law fields. In truth the case has some analogy with public law issues.[125]

The decision in this case, combined with that in *Nagle*, goes some way to allaying fears that a 'gap' may exist where a potential claimant could be denied redress through the courts by a combination of the rigid approach taken with regard to judicial review and a narrow construction of the nature of sports governing bodies in private law proceedings.

Clearly, these cases involved situations of unusually high public and political interest and could thus be regarded anomalous. However, the lengths to which the courts went to create a cause of action for the claimants in these cases, and the breadth of the duties which they imposed upon the governing bodies, give cause to suggest that the contractual approach to regulating the activities of sporting bodies should not be too readily criticised for being overly narrow.

However, there is case law that suggests that the contractual approach is not an adequate method by which to render sports governing bodies accountable. *Wayde v New South Wales Rugby League Ltd*,[126] an Australian case, demonstrated that the courts could also adopt a narrow approach. As in *Finnigan* the case involved a challenge to a governing body, claiming failure to serve the best interests of the game and its members. Article 76 of the New South Wales Rugby League articles of association empowered it to: 'conduct such competitions between teams representing all or any of the Clubs or Junior Leagues as the Board of Directors may, from time to time determine provided that the Board of Directors may at its discretion invite other clubs to participate in any competition pursuant to the provisions of this clause'.

Clause 3 of the memorandum of association provided the role of the Board of Directors as '(j) to determine which clubs shall be entitled to enter teams in the league and other competitions'. The contention of the claimant, Western Suburbs District RLFC (Wests), was that in reconstituting a league competition having the effect of excluding Wests, the NSWRL had failed in promoting the best interests of rugby league. The answer, from all five judges was clear and unambiguous:

Wayde v New South Wales Rugby League Ltd [1985] 59 ALJR 798

Given the special expertise and experience of the Board, the *bona fide* and proper exercise of the power in pursuit of the purpose for which it was conferred and the caution which the court must exercise . . . the appellants faced a difficult task in seeking to prove that the decisions in question were unfairly prejudicial to [the Club] and therefore not in the interests of the members as a whole.[127]

---

124 *Ibid* at p 179.
125 *Ibid*.
126 [1985] 59 ALJR 798.
127 *Per* Mason ACJ, Wilson, Deane and Danson JJ, p 801.

Brennan J went on to emphasise the specialist nature of such bodies:

> The directors had to make a difficult decision in which it was necessary to draw upon the skills, knowledge and understanding of experienced administrators of the game. There is nothing to suggest ... that reasonable directors with the special qualities possessed by specialist administrators would have decided that it was unfair to exercise their power as the League's directors did.[128]

This goes further towards emphasising the degree of regard and deference that the courts have demonstrated in regard of the specialist nature of the decisions made by governing bodies.

Evaluating the Case Law

In the contractual context, there can be demonstrated a general willingness on behalf of the courts to render sports governing bodies accountable. In *Enderby Town*, Lord Denning MR emphasised that such bodies would not be able to oust the jurisdiction of the courts through contract. Indeed, the courts have been willing to stretch the contractual nexus extensively in order to ensure accountability. Though the capacity to review bodies' activities has been fiercely protected, the courts have often been significantly less pro-active in utilising that competence. Though in *Wayde* there was no difficulty on the question of standing, a comparison with *Finnigan* and *Nagle* raises questions of inconsistency and certainty. Whereas in the former cases the courts were prepared to impose significant duties upon the NZRFU because of the magnitude of the decision it was taking, by contrast in *Wayde* the court refrained from questioning the decision taken by the NSWRL Board despite the serious consequences which would result to Wests. This perhaps suggests that the decisions in *Finnigan* and *Nagle* were somewhat anomalous and that courts will step in on this basis only where major public policy issues are at stake. In *Wayde*, and in common with the natural justice case law, the court preferred to rely on the specialist qualities of the board rather than examining the decision itself. This raises questions as to what extent should the specialist knowledge of bodies governing sport be acknowledged and at what point should courts feel competent to intervene in sports' self-regulatory processes. This relates closely to the general proposition, that when dealing with self-regulatory bodies the courts are likely to intervene only in matters of 'high policy', rather than in relation to more narrow, technical matters. The potentially devastating consequences of the decision in *Wayde* do raise considerable concerns that the threshold of intervention has been set particularly high. This is further emphasized by *Colgan v Kennel Club*[129] where Cooke J noted that the implied terms of the contract embodied by the rules were largely limited to requiring any disciplinary process to be conducted in accordance with the rules of natural justice.

Rendering sport's governing bodies accountable on a contractual basis raises further problems. It is clearly important that sporting bodies should not be able to operate in contravention of their own rules. However, testing the activities of governing bodies on this basis makes the basic assumption that the rules themselves are fair and reasonable. Even though the 'against the objects' approach, which has been adopted by the courts, mitigates this problem to a limited extent, the contractual approach achieves only partial penetration of the regulatory sphere thus leaving sport's governing bodies, on the whole, unaccountable. This problem is compounded by the fact that a claimant will rarely have a significant input on the form of the rules forming the 'contract'. This can have the effect that the rules can be changed in such a manner that once a sporting body has been successfully

---

128 *Ibid.*
129 Unreported, 26 October 2001, QBD. See generally Samuels, A, 'Some Problems for Domestic Tribunals' [2003] 8(1) JR 54.

challenged on the basis of its application of a particular rule, that rule can be altered unilaterally, so as to allow the challenged course of conduct to continue impervious to challenge.[130] The courts might be seen as treating the relationship between regulators and regulated as they might any 'ordinary' contractual relationship – with each party holding equal bargaining power. It is questionable whether this is the appropriate response when sports regulation has been acknowledged as both monopolistic and legislative in nature.

THE RESTRAINT OF TRADE DOCTRINE

This position is mitigated somewhat, when one considers the application of the restraint of trade doctrine which serves to outlaw agreements in which powerful bargaining positions are abused. The function of the restraint of trade doctrine is to render partially or wholly void contracts or agreements that are found to be unreasonably in restraint of trade. The doctrine in its current form evolved during the late 19th and early 20th century when the courts began to pursue a general policy of enforcing the right of every man to work and to offer his services without restriction. The doctrine can be expressed very simply: a contract[131] in unreasonable restraint of trade is void. A restraining contract will be deemed valid, if it satisfies the three elements outlined by Lord Macnaghten.

Nordenfelt v Maxim Nordenfelt Guns and Ammunition Co Ltd [1894] AC 535

The public have an interest in every person's carrying on his trade freely: so has the individual. All interference with individual liberty in action in trading, and all restraints in themselves, if there is nothing more, are contrary to public policy, and therefore void. That is the general rule. But there are exceptions; restraints of trade and interference with individual liberty of action may be justified by the special circumstances of a particular case. It is sufficient justification, and, indeed, it is the only justification, if the restriction is reasonable . . . reasonable that is, in the interests of the public, so framed and so guarded as to afford adequate protection to the party in whose favour it is imposed, while at the same time it is in no way injurious to the public.[132]

Thus in the absence of the following characteristics a restraining agreement will be considered in restraint of trade and be void:

- there must be an interest meriting protection;
- the restraint must be reasonable; and
- the restraint must not be contrary to the public interest.

The doctrine is based on the fluid concept of public policy in which it is important to emphasise the significant role of discretion. It is possible to highlight the general trends and development of the doctrine, but difficult to ascribe strict rules to it. Because of the doctrine's foundation on the general principles of public policy, cases characteristically involve the courts in performing a balancing act. In performing this function the courts seek to reconcile a competing range of subjective values.

---

130 Aronson, M, 'A public lawyer's responses to privatisation and outsourcing', in Taggart, M (ed), *The Province of Administrative Law* (1997), Oxford: Hart, p 47. Though it should be noted that these comments were made in relation to judicial review.

131 It should be noted that the restraint of trade doctrine is not strictly limited only to contractual situations, a matter considered in more detail below.

132 [1894] AC 535, p 565.

In the sporting context the doctrine has been primarily utilised in three areas: challenges to transfer systems; where a ban or suspension has been imposed; and where governing bodies purport to prevent a team or club from entering a competition.

Transfer Systems

Eastham v Newcastle United Football Club[133] first demonstrated the susceptibility of sports governing bodies to attack on the basis of restraint of trade. It concerned a challenge to the rules of the English FA and Football League relating to the system of 'retain and transfer', governing the movement of players between clubs.[134]

George Eastham, the claimant, was a professional footballer who had come to the end of a contract under which he played for Newcastle United. The combination of the rules of the FA and League had the effect that, even though his contract had ended, Newcastle could still retain him. Despite the absence of a contract between himself and Newcastle, the claimant was prevented from moving to another club without Newcastle's consent.

The claimant exhausted – unsuccessfully – all avenues of appeal open to him. Newcastle eventually capitulated to his demands for a transfer (to Arsenal) in an attempt to prevent proceedings from being brought. However, Eastham had spent three months out of professional football. He sought declarations against Newcastle United, the FA and the League that his agreement with the club, the rules of the FA and the regulations of the League relating to the 'retain and transfer' system were not binding upon him as being in unreasonable restraint of trade and in addition, or in the alternative, *ultra vires*.

Eastham argued that the retention system had the effect of impeding his ability to pursue further employment and make use of his abilities as a professional footballer after the termination of his contract.

In deciding that the retention system was in unreasonable restraint of trade, Wilberforce J demonstrated that the specialist abilities and knowledge of the governing body would not necessarily sway the courts:

Eastham v Newcastle United Football Club [1963] 1 Ch 413

The system is an employers' system, set up in an industry where the employers have succeeded in establishing a united monolithic front all over the world, and where it is clear that for the purpose of negotiation the employers are vastly more strongly organised than the employees. No doubt the employers all over the world consider the system a good system, but this does not prevent the court from considering whether it goes further than is reasonably necessary to protect their legitimate interests.[135]

On the question of *ultra vires* Wilberforce J decided that, although the rules formulating the retain and transfer system may not have been against the objects of the FA and League, 'it cannot be within the powers of associations such as these to commit their members to action which is against public policy'.[136] Thus the courts are able to examine the substance of a rule.,

The FA and the League argued that the claimant was a stranger to their rules, not being a member of either and that, even if the rules were in restraint of trade, this would merely make them

---

133 [1963] 1 Ch 413.

134 Edward Grayson highlights some earlier cases where the doctrine might have been invoked. See 'The Ralph Banks road to Bosman via Eastham, *Greig v Insole* and beyond' (1996) 4(1) Sport and the Law Journal 19.

135 *Eastham v Newcastle United Football Club* [1963] 1 Ch 413, p 438.

136 *Ibid*, p 440.

unenforceable, a stranger could not prevent the clubs continuing the practice on a voluntary basis. However, Wilberforce J disagreed:

> Is it open to an employee to bring an action for a declaration that the contract between the employers is in restraint of trade? To my mind it would seem unjust if this were not so. The employees are just as much affected and, indeed, aimed at by the employers' agreement as the employers themselves. Their liberty of action in seeking employment is threatened just as much as the liberty of the employers to give them employment, and their liberty to seek employment is considered by the law to be an important public interest.[137]

This contrasts with the law of judicial review, where the formalities of the relationship between the parties are highly significant. As has been noted in relation to private law challenges generally, there is a willingness to interpret the relationship broadly, to accept the reality of control by sporting bodies even though strictly there is no legal relationship.

Similarly in the case of *Pharmaceutical Society of Great Britain v Dickson*,[138] though not in a sporting context, even where a rule was not contained in a contract, in this case in a code, it could still be challenged on the basis of restraint of trade if, in effect, it was mandatory. This has been perceived as being particularly important,[139] implying that the doctrine could be applied to all restraints whatever their source. It also reinforces the suggestion that there may be non-proprietary interests that can be reasonably protected.[140]

Disciplinary Procedures

The application of restraint of trade law has not been limited to measures concerning player transfers. It has also been used to challenge the reasonableness of disciplinary measures.

Greig v Insole[141] involved a challenge to the rules of the International Cricket Council (ICC) and the Test and County Cricket Board (TCCB). The ICC controlled the playing of international matches and the TCCB administered and controlled the playing of first class cricket in the UK. In May 1977 World Series Cricket (WSC), a company managed by the Australian entrepreneur Kerry Packer, announced that it had secretly signed up 34 of the world's foremost cricketers to play in a series of 'test matches' in Australia. In July 1977 the ICC altered its rules so that players taking part or making themselves available to play in a match previously disapproved of by the ICC, after 1 October 1977, would be disqualified from taking part in test cricket without the express consent of the ICC. At the same time the ICC issued a resolution specifically disapproving of any match organised by WSC. The ICC also recommended that national governing bodies take similar action in respect of their domestic game. The TCCB then resolved to alter its rules so that any player who was subject to the test match ban would also be disqualified from taking part in first class cricket. Three cricketers, Tony Greig, Jon Snow and Mike Procter, all of whom had contracted with WSC to take part in the 'unofficial' tests,

---

137 *Ibid*, p 443.

138 [1970] AC 403 (HL).

139 Heydon, JD, *The Restraint of Trade Doctrine* (1971), London: Butterworths, p 74.

140 Koh, KL 'Professional ethics and restraint of trade' (1968) 31 MLR 70. For the application of *Eastham* see *Blackler v New Zealand Rugby Football League* [1968] NZLR 547; and *Buckley v Tutty* (1971) 125 CLR 353. For more general comment see Farrell, R, 'Transfer fees and restraint of trade' (1997) 5(1) Sport and Law Journal 54.

141 [1978] 1 WLR 302. Joined with *World Series Cricket v Insole*. World Series Cricket issued a writ seeking, in addition to the declaration of *ultra vires*, a declaration that the rules constituted an unlawful inducement to the cricketers to break their contracts.

issued a writ seeking against the TCCB and ICC, a declaration that the change of rules by the ICC and those proposed by the TCCB were *ultra vires* and in unlawful restraint of trade.

Slade J decided that both the ICC and TCCB had legitimate interests that they were entitled to protect. The ICC argued that it was acting reasonably in introducing rules that would effectively protect it from the competition provided by WSC. Test Match cricket provided a large proportion of the money through which the game at lower levels was financed. Thus, the ICC argued, it was acting reasonably in aiming to prevent players from taking part in a competition which could threaten the existence of Test Match cricket, and result in cricket suffering at all levels. Slade J did accept that WSC posed at least a short term threat, but that this was not particularly serious and indeed that the profile of cricket could be raised. However, the long term threat, Slade J decided, could be adequately met by the imposition of a *prospective* ban on players playing in unsanctioned games. Though such bans would not necessarily be valid, they could be more easily justified than the *retrospective* action taken. Though Slade J recognised that the imposition of a retrospective ban may have broader advantages, he regarded it as being both a serious and unjust step. It would be to deprive a professional cricketer of the opportunity to be employed in an important part of his professional field. The justifications proffered by the ICC for the suspension of the players from Test Match cricket were judged to be highly speculative and thus the ICC failed to justify its rule change. Thus the new rules of the ICC were held to be *ultra vires* and void as being in unreasonable restraint of trade.

The resolution of the TCCB to support the ICC bans at domestic level was regarded as being much more serious. Test cricket offered a limited opportunity to supplement a cricketer's income; first class cricket offered the only opportunity to earn a living by playing cricket. This was particularly relevant to players such as two of the claimants, Jon Snow and Mike Procter who, by reason of age and South African nationality respectively, were effectively out of contention for Test Match selection. Slade J also accepted that the length of their contracts with WSC combined with their ages would effectively mean that Snow and Procter would never play first class cricket again; a ban would be imposed. Again Slade J felt that the public interest demanded that top players such as the claimants should be allowed to play the first class game and that to remove them from it could prove injurious to the sport. The judge also considered that as WSC was more likely to be damaging to Australian domestic cricket and the TCCB was concerned almost exclusively with cricket in the UK, that the TCCB had less justification in supporting the suspensions than the ICC. Accordingly the TCCB was held to be acting *ultra vires* and in unreasonable restraint of trade.[142]

In *Gasser v Stinson*,[143] Sandra Gasser, a Swiss athlete given an automatic ban after having a prohibited substance found in her urine, challenged the rules of the International Amateur Athletic Federation (IAAF). Gasser had been found to have a prohibited substance in a urine sample taken after she had finished third in the 1987 World Athletic Championships women's 1,500 metres. Gasser claimed that the IAAF rules were in unreasonable restraint of trade. The rules of the IAAF did not permit Gasser to try to establish her innocence, even in mitigation. It was argued that this was unreasonable and unjustifiable on the basis that a finding of 'guilt' had the effect of imposing a mandatory suspensory penalty of fixed length. This had the effect that an athlete found 'guilty' under the rules of the IAAF and being suspended accordingly could in fact be 'morally innocent', where they had not intentionally or knowingly taken a prohibited drug. It was argued that to treat those who were 'morally innocent' in the same way as those who had knowingly cheated was unreasonable.

---

142 As regards WSC's case against the ICC and TCCB, Slade J agreed that there had been an unlawful inducement upon the players to break their contracts. See also *Hughes v Western Australian Cricket Association* [1986] 69 ALR 660.

143 (1988) unreported, 15 June (QBD).

The IAAF attempted to argue that Gasser's status as an amateur athlete precluded her from bringing such an action. Scott J held that because the rules of the IAAF allowed athletes to obtain an income through sponsorship, and that income was directly related to participation in events governed by the IAAF, a suspension from competition could be justifiably regarded as being a restraint of trade. Here, the court, while not severing the economic link, extended the doctrine to cover a larger group than might otherwise have access to the courts. Scott J agreed that the rules acted so as to restrain an athlete but also found them to be 'reasonable'. He accepted the argument put forward by the IAAF that the difficulty of proving 'moral innocence' would lead to an opening of the floodgates and that attempts to thwart drug taking would become futile. Thus the blanket application of penalties for doping offences could be justified by the importance of the need to eliminate drug taking in sports.[144] This demonstrates the likely limits of the doctrine as a tool for calling governing bodies to account. It also suggests that the courts still choose to give significant weight to the values applied by governing bodies, particularly in relation to a cause *célèbre* such as the 'war against doping in sport'. This is despite the fact that a restraint on these grounds may not always be objectively justifiable.[145]

This is apparent in *Wilander v Tobin*[146] where two tennis professionals, Matts Wilander and Karel Novacek, unsuccessfully challenged a similar rule of the International Tennis Federation (ITF). Lord Woolf MR, giving the leading judgment of the Court of Appeal, noted the limits of the restraint of trade doctrine:

Wilander v Tobin [1997] 2 Lloyd's Rep 293

The history of these proceedings discloses that the claimants have taken point after point with a view to defeating domestic disciplinary proceedings which in relation to sporting activities should be as uncomplicated as possible. While the courts must be vigilant to protect the genuine rights of sportsmen in the position of the claimants, they must be equally vigilant in preventing the courts' procedures being used unjustifiably to render perfectly sensible and fair procedures inoperable.[147]

Participation in Competition

The variety of situations in which the restraint of trade rules will be applied is demonstrated in two further cases that consider the restraint of trade rules as they apply to Club membership of leagues and associations. In the case of *Newport AFC Ltd v The Football Association of Wales*,[148] three Welsh football clubs, Newport, Caernarfon and Colwyn Bay, challenged a decision of the defendants, the Football Association of Wales (FAW), to pass a resolution preventing Welsh football clubs from playing in leagues making up part of the English pyramid system in order that a comparable Welsh competition could be established.[149] The three claimant clubs resigned their membership of the FAW

---

144 Note though that the IAAF has reduced the length of its mandatory suspension from four to two years, as a result of restraint of trade legislation in Germany, Russia and Spain. German athletes made successful applications for reinstatement after two years of the ban (*The Independent*, 1 July 1997). Also, in this particular instance a Swiss court refused to uphold the ban placed on Gasser by the national athletics body on the basis of her claim of 'moral innocence'.

145 See the chapter on the regulation of doping in this text.

146 *The Times*, 8 April 1996; [1997] 2 Lloyd's Rep 293. See also *Johnson v IAAF*, unreported, 25 July (Ontario Court (General Division)). Noted in Stoner, C, 'Recent developments in doping control' (1997) 4(7) Sports Law Administration and Practice 1.

147 [1997] 2 Lloyd's Rep 293, p 301. Millet and Potter LJJ concurred.

148 [1995] 2 All ER 87.

149 Resolution of the Football Association of Wales Ltd, 30 November 1991.

and joined the English Football Association to facilitate their continued participation in the English pyramid competition. This had potentially disastrous financial consequences for the claimant clubs and they sought an injunction against the FAW's decision to exclude them. The award, by Jacob J, of an interlocutory injunction, is further evidence of the courts' willingness to utilise the restraint of trade doctrine as a mechanism by which to scrutinise the substance of sports governing bodies' activities, rather than merely the procedural or contractual elements, as highlighted above.

The second case in this respect is *Stevenage Borough FC Ltd v The Football League Ltd*.[150] In May 1996 Stevenage Borough finished top of the GM Vauxhall Conference (GMVC) a position which in principle entitled them to take the place in the Football League of the team finishing bottom of Division Three, Torquay United. However, Football League rules stipulated that this promotion would be dependent upon the winner of the GMVC satisfying certain requirements relating to ground capacity and safety, by December of that winning season. Stevenage failed to meet the League's deadline but would have met the requirements in time for the beginning of the new season. On this basis the Football League refused Stevenage entry to the League.

Stevenage challenged the decision by the League to deny them promotion, on the grounds that the entry criteria were in unreasonable restraint of trade. They sought an injunction restraining the League from imposing the criteria for membership of the League so as to refuse entry to them.

In his judgment Carnwath J recognised that in normal circumstances the burden of demonstrating the reasonableness of the restraint would lie with the Football League, as it was the party seeking to impose it. Here, however, the restraint was a part of a regulatory system imposed by a body exercising control in the public interest, and therefore different considerations would arise. Carnwath J felt that the control exercised by the Football League could be attacked where it was 'arbitrary or capricious' or a 'pernicious monopoly'. In this case the Football League was operating in the public interest and so the onus was shifted upon the challenger to illustrate the unreasonableness of the rules.

Technically there was no legal relationship between the Football League and Stevenage when treated as strictly private bodies and therefore nothing unreasonable about the position adopted by the League. When viewed from this 'private aspect' Stevenage were nothing more than an applicant for entry to the League – a company owned by its member clubs each of whom were private trading organisations. From this point of view there was no need for the League to justify the restraint; it had no legal obligations binding upon it; neither were Stevenage prevented from conducting their business of playing football within the GMVC, or any other league willing to accept it as a member. However, Carnwath J felt this was too simplistic a view to take and that a broader approach was apt. When considered more generally, the Football League could be seen to be operating as a part of the complicated system of control operating for the organisation of professional football, in the interests of participants and the general public. The fact of the Football League's operation in the public interest was seen as a reasonable basis upon which to extend the ambit of the restraint of trade doctrine. Stevenage had objected to the entry requirements on the basis that they would have had to complete ground improvements long before it was clear whether or not they would win the GMVC and be eligible for promotion. Secondly, the League also imposed financial requirements upon entrance to Division 3, which were not demanded of existing member clubs. Carnwath J agreed that these requirements would be open to attack on the grounds of restraint of trade. However, he had reservations as to whether the criteria could be regarded as arbitrary or capricious. He also felt that

---

150 *The Times*, 1 August 1996.

there was an important question of discretion to be decided, considering the question of delay and prejudice to third parties. Stevenage had argued that it would be unfair to expect them to begin legal proceedings until they had satisfied the first criteria for promotion to the League by winning the GMVC. Carnwath J accepted this was reasonable as from Stevenage's point of view, but that did not take account of the need to be fair to all others that would be affected. Stevenage had the opportunity to challenge the criteria at the beginning of the season. Even though this involved an element of commercial risk, in that Stevenage might not benefit from success in litigation, this did not make it unreasonable to expect them to do so. That route would have allowed the rules to be tested before the December deadline with time for the making of alternative arrangements. Carnwath J also felt that Torquay United's position was of particular relevance; relegation to the GMVC would be very significant for them, and to leave them uncertain as to their future so close to the beginning of the new season was unfair.

However, the judge did feel that the Football League's rules did require reconsideration; failure to amend them would leave them open to challenge on restraint of trade grounds in the future. This highlights that even though an individual claimant may be unsuccessful in his action because of the overall situation, a judgment can still be effective in that rules are altered to be brought into line with the doctrine, as has now happened in this case. Carnwath J stated that the court would have jurisdiction in extreme cases to set aside rules such as these; however, the criteria had been accepted at the beginning of the season by Stevenage and all representative bodies including the GMVC of which Stevenage was a member. Stevenage's delay in bringing proceedings to challenge the rules of the Football League resulted in the court refusing to grant relief.

On appeal the Court of Appeal held that the issue of a declaration was a discretionary remedy, thus the judge's refusal to grant such, despite finding that the League's rules could be in unreasonable restraint of trade, was justifiable. Carnwath J was adjudged to have been correct to withhold a declaration on the basis of the overall justice of the situation.[151]

Evaluating the Case Law

The restraint of trade route has clearly been the most fruitful for those seeking to call sports governing bodies to account. Indeed, the doctrine has been applied more liberally in relation to sports governing bodies than has generally been the case. The doctrine itself is highly accessible; its invocation is not limited to those who are parties to the challenged agreement, and it can be utilised by a stranger to an agreement who is unreasonably restrained by its operation. The source of the restraint is not seen as being of particular significance; it is the effect that brings the doctrine into play. This has the result that the doctrine is not hindered by the procedural pitfalls found particularly in the context of judicial review. This is evident throughout the case law examined above.

The application of the doctrine has been pragmatic. In relation to sporting bodies the contractual and natural justice approaches have been found wanting. Though the concepts have recognised the relative position of those subject to governing bodies' rules, and used this as a justification for subjecting the bodies to scrutiny, this has largely failed to account for the imbalance between the parties. In contrast, restraint of trade law has demonstrated the capacity to reconcile these different positions. The doctrine is primarily concerned with the effect of the challenged provision upon the ability to trade and less preoccupied with the 'specialist' position of sporting decision makers. Sports governing bodies cannot hide behind their rules in order to avoid scrutiny. The very content of those

---

151 (1997) Admin LR 109. See also *Hearn v Rugby Football Union* (2003) *The Times*, September 15.

rules can be called into question and tested for reasonableness under the doctrine. This facilitates a more significant penetration of the regulatory sphere than previously encountered, though the operations of governing bodies are still protected where their aims and objects are legitimate and reasonable. It has been accepted that the doctrine will not extend to all decisions taken by governing bodies, only those that affect the ability of others to trade. This has been expanded somewhat by the decisions in *Newport* and more notably *Stevenage*, where it was the overall justice of the situation that was taken into account.

THE HUMAN RIGHTS ACT 1998

One approach to remedying this shortfall comes in the form of the Human Rights Act 1998. The effect of the Human Rights Act 1998 is to give further effect to the provisions of the European Convention on Human Rights (1950) in the UK.[152] This has been achieved primarily through the imposition of a new interpretative obligation upon domestic courts, with a responsibility to interpret legislation as far as possible as being in accordance with the Human Rights Act 1998.[153] In addition to this, courts and tribunals are required to take into account the jurisprudence of the Convention's Strasbourg institutions where relevant to proceedings before it.[154] The Act also compels public authorities to conduct themselves in a manner that is consistent with the principles set out in the Convention.[155] It seems possible that the Act will not only have an impact upon government in the narrowest sense, but also that it will impact upon the activities of self-regulating organisations such as those that govern sport.

Boyes, S, 'Regulating sport after the Human Rights Act 1998'

There appear to be two mechanisms by which the Convention rights incorporated by the Act are likely to impact upon the activities of sports governing bodies:

The first is what may be described as the 'horizontal effect' of the Act. The Act contains no explicit support for the extension of its provisions to the purely private relationships of private parties. However, whilst not creating a new and independent cause of action in these circumstances, it is possible that the provisions of the Act will exert an influence upon the courts as they interpret and develop pre-existing law ... [T]here does appear to be an argument that the Act will, even must, impact upon purely private relationships. Section 6(3)(a) of the Act defines those public bodies that are compelled by section 6(1) to act in accordance with the rights laid down as including a 'court or tribunal'. When considered in combination with section 2 of the Act, requiring the courts to take into account the case law of the Strasbourg institutions, it is well arguable that this may have an impact upon purely private relationships. However it is clear that the Act makes no provision for the creation of a new cause of action for potential litigants.

What is arguable is that where a cause of action already exists, the courts will necessarily be influenced in their decisions by the rights protected by the ECHR and expanded upon as case law has developed, on the basis of the obligations placed upon them as 'public authorities' under the Act. Thus where individuals are able to identify a cause of action against a sporting body they may well be able to argue that the Act should be taken into account where it is relevant to a case – in effect to 'attach' a Convention

---

152 The act incorporates Arts 2–12 of the convention itself as well as Arts 1–3 of the First Protocol and Arts 1–6 of the Sixth Protocol.

153 HRA 1998, s 3, with provision for a declaration of incompatibility where this is impossible (s 4).

154 HRA 1998, s 2.

155 *Ibid*, s 6.

right to a pre-existing cause of action. This might impact upon the manner in which the courts interpret the contractual relationship between athlete and governing body or the way in which they choose to apply the restraint of trade doctrine . . .

A more likely and immediate effect is likely to be felt as a result of the classification of sports governing bodies as 'quasi-public authorities'.

Section 6 of the Act provides for the enforcement of the Convention's fundamental rights against what are described as 'public authorities' . . . Section 6(3)(b) of the Act obliges 'any person certain of whose functions are functions of a public nature' – 'quasi-public authorities' – to meet the requirements of the Act. However, this requirement is limited *only* to the public acts of those persons and thus has no bearing upon their private activities, smartly avoiding the problem of the public–private divide so often encountered in the field of public law. . . . [T]he Act . . . requires the courts to consider the *nature* of the power employed in determining whether or not it will be subject to the requirements of the Act. Combined with section 7(1)(a) of the Act, permitting a victim of an act by a 'public authority' that infringes a protected Convention right to bring proceedings 'in the appropriate court or tribunal', this creates the possibility of the opening of a new avenue by which to challenge the activities of sports governing bodies. . . .

[O]f significance was the statement of the Home Secretary at the Committee stage of the Act's passage through Parliament, when he specifically drew attention to a sporting body as being of the type that he would expect to fall within the section 6(3)(b) 'quasi- public body' category:

> 'There will be occasions – it is the nature of British society – on which various institutions that are private in terms of their legal personality carry out public functions . . . I would suggest that it . . . includes the Jockey Club . . . The Jockey Club is a curious body: it is entirely private, but exercises public functions in some respects, and to those extents, but to no other, it would be regarded as falling within [this classification].'

> *(Hansard HC, 20 May 1998, col 1018.)*

This is likely to be of significance not only to the Jockey Club, but also to a range of other sports governing bodies. There is judicial support for Mr Straw's assertion that such bodies carry out public activities; this is particularly evident from the case law relating to the application for judicial review.[156]

The introduction of the Human Rights Act 1998 in the United Kingdom, it appears, has the potential to have an impact upon both the manner and substance of sporting regulation. As yet there is little sports specific case law related to the Act. However, it seems that the Act may impact in a growing number of areas. The following extract speculates as to the impact of particular provision of the European Convention on Human Rights on the regulation of sport.

Boyes, S, 'The regulation of sport and the impact of the Human Rights Act 1998'

Article 4: Freedom from Slavery, Servitude, and Forced or Compulsory Labour

Paragraph 1 of Article 4 deals with the prohibition of slavery and servitude, less relevant to the sporting world. However, more important is Paragraph 2 that prescribes that, 'no one shall be required to perform forced or compulsory labour'. . . .

It may seem unlikely that this would be applied in the context of sporting activity; however, there is an instance of a case being brought in respect of football's transfer system (Application 9322/81, *X v Netherlands* (1983) 32 DR 180). A Dutch player made a complaint under Article 4 after he had withdrawn

---

156 Boyes, S, 'Regulating sport after the Human Rights Act 1998' (2001) 151 NLJ 444–46.

from his contract with one club in order to join another. This transfer was prevented because of the prohibitive fee requested by the first club and the player was denied the opportunity to play for the second club because he was still registered as a player with the first. However, the European Commission on Human Rights dismissed the player's claim. This was done on the basis that the applicant freely entered into the contract with the first club, knowing that he would be affected in this way by the rules that governed the relationships between football clubs. The Commission decided that while this state of affairs might be inconvenient for those affected it was not considered 'oppressive' or an 'avoidable hardship'.

The Commission seems to have taken on board the idea that the player was not, in fact, being compelled to work for the first employer but merely being restrained from working for another. In fact it would seem that the player was not really complaining of being forced to work for the first club, but about his inability to work for an alternative employer in the same field. The approach taken by the Commission in this case seems to be in accordance with the more general one adopted under the ECHR; that where a profession has attached to it certain obligations it is implied that any person entering that profession accepts those obligations and thus there is no force or compulsion. This suggests the Commission has not recognised the reality of a professional footballer's situation. Being excluded from employment by all professional football clubs other than the one to which he is contracted will inevitably have the effect of compelling him to work for that club, or embark on an alternative career. It may be that this approach may be less relevant after the ruling of the European Court of Justice in *Bosman* (*Union Royale Belge des Sociétés de Football Association ASBL v Bosman* (C-415/93) [1996] 1 CMLR 603) . . . It seems that the requirements of freedom from forced and compulsory labour are unlikely to have a significant impact upon the club–player relationship, even after the introduction of the Human Rights Act. The relevant provisions of English law, most notably the restraint of trade doctrine, are significantly more facilitative of the right of the individual to pursue trade or employment than those under the Convention. However, Article 4 may still be of use as part of a package of measures used to challenge the system of registration and transfer as it stands in English football even after the *Bosman* ruling and the subsequent amendments to the transfer system.

Article 6: The Right to a Fair and Public Hearing

Article 6 of the ECHR is primarily concerned with the right to a fair hearing in respect of criminal charges. However, Article 6(1) also makes reference to the 'determination of civil rights or obligations'. The concept of 'a civil right or obligation' has been considered at length before both the European Court and Commission of Human Rights, which have developed a broad interpretation. Thus all that is required is a dispute relating to a right or obligation (Joined Applications 5145/71, 5246/71, 5333/72, 5586/72, 5587/72 and 5532/72, *Ringeisen v Austria* (1973) 43 CD 152) which must also be of a 'genuine and serious nature' (Applications 7151/75 and 7152/75, *Sporrong and Lönnroth v Sweden* (1982) 5 EHRR 35). Clearly this can be seen as including tribunals, which are used by sporting bodies in order to discipline those who take part in the activity, which they regulate. The right entitles the individual to a 'fair and public hearing within a reasonable time by an independent and impartial tribunal established by law'. To a large extent it is difficult to anticipate the extent to which this provision will have any impact upon the activities of tribunals established by sporting bodies. This is not because the provision itself is weak but, as noted above, English Courts have been keen to apply the rules of natural justice, which have developed in domestic law, against sports governing bodies. However, as noted above, the extent to which the rules are applied is often dependent upon the protection of an economic right. It is also significant that Article 6 of the Convention itself demands a lower standard in civil cases than in those pertaining to criminal matters.

Article 8: The Right to Respect for Privacy

The right to privacy has a potential impact in respect of the taking of urine and blood samples from participants in sport as a part of anti-doping policies pursued by governing bodies. There are a number of related cases that have been considered by the Commission of Human Rights in allied areas. In *X v the Netherlands* (1979) 16 DR 184, 189, the Commission decided that a blood sample, taken in connection with determining the amount of alcohol in the bloodstream for the purposes of road traffic legislation, would not contravene Article 8. The infringement upon the privacy of the individual was justified by the need to protect the rights of others. A blood sample taken for the purposes of a paternity test was justified on similar grounds (Application 8278/78, *X v Austria* (1980) 18 DR 155, 157). Whether the taking of samples for the purposes of a sport's dope-testing procedure would be justified on similar grounds remains questionable. It may be that this could be justified on the basis of the protection of health or morals as set out in Article 8(2). However, it must be noted that the Strasbourg institutions have been particularly keen to see that any infringement upon the rights protected meet the Convention requirement of being 'necessary in a democratic society', and that their interpretation of this principle has been particularly restrictive.

It is possible to draw some comparisons with the constitutional position of drug testing of athletes in the United States of America. The Fourth Amendment of the United States Constitution protects the right of the individual 'to be secure in their person . . . against unreasonable searches and seizures' and that this right shall not be violated without probable cause. Indeed the United States Supreme Court has held that the collection of urine for the purposes of drug testing necessarily involves a consideration of the Fourth Amendment right to privacy (*Skinner v Railway Labor Executions Ass'n* (1989) 109 SCt 1402). Breaches of the right to privacy must be justified by reference to the promotion of compelling government interests – similar to the 'pressing social need' test utilised in the context of the ECHR. In *O'Halloran v University of Washington* (1988) 679 F Supp 997, these compelling interests were accepted by the court to include: providing fair competition; protecting the health of athletes; and the deterrence of drug use. However, in a subsequent case it has been held that invasions of privacy are only justified on these grounds where there is 'reasonable suspicion' leading to the belief that banned substances have been used by a particular athlete and not by random subjection to drug testing (*Derdeyn v University of Colorado* (1991) Colorado Court of Appeals, Case No 89 CA 2044, Division 3). However, challenges on the basis of a breach of Fourth Amendment rights have generally fallen foul of the requirement that the infringement complained of be a state action (*Arlosoroff v NCAA* (1984) 746 F 2d 10109, 1021, *NCAA v Tarkanian* (1988) 109 SCt 1492. Though cf *Hennessey v NCAA* (1977) and *Parish v NCAA* (1975) where the court took the view that government would step in to organise intercollegiate athletics if the NCAA ceased to exist). If drug testing is considered a 'public function' for the purposes of the Human Rights Act, this public–private problem is unlikely to arise and sporting bodies will find their procedures subject to increased scrutiny, with the potential for there to be a reassessment of the conduct and rationale of drug testing procedures.

Article 10: Freedom of Expression

Freedom of expression is another right that has been fiercely protected under the auspices of the ECHR. It may also have a bearing in the sporting arena. It is suggested that the HRA may impact upon sports governing bodies' ability to discipline those subject to their jurisdiction for comments made that may 'bring the game into disrepute' ('FA gags may be ended by Human Rights Law' *The Times*, 31 October 1999). During the English football season it seems a weekly ritual to read of action taken against managers as a result of criticisms that they have made of a referee's performance. Questions have even been raised concerning the dismissal of the then England manager, Glenn Hoddle, as a result of his voicing of his religious convictions. ('On your head be it, my son' *The Times*, 9 February 1999). Of course any influence that the HRA will have will not completely disempower sports regulators. As with other freedoms encompassed within the ECHR, the right to freedom of expression has attached to it various responsibilities. Clearly Article 10 does not allow expression that might endanger public safety or prompt disorder, so sports regulators will still have the ability to discipline on this basis, particularly where the protection of officials is at issue (see for example Application 00025716/94, *Janowski v Poland*, judgment of July 8, 1999). ECHR case law pertaining to the regulation of professions does highlight that professional bodies should not utilise their powers in such a way as to disproportionately interfere with the ability of the individual to make beliefs known (*Ezelin v France* 14 EHRR 362, 26 April 1991, Series A, No 202).[157]

The discussion above is necessarily speculative. Even should the courts decide not to interpret the Act in the manner suggested, an action before the European Court of Human Rights would be likely to be successful. An aggrieved athlete could bring a case against the United Kingdom on the basis of a failure on the part of domestic law to adequately protect a particular Convention right.[158] It is notable that the Human Rights Act has not been utilised to any great degree in litigation pertaining to sports governing bodies as yet.[159] Nevertheless, it seems virtually certain that sports governing bodies will become susceptible to the new provisions as a result of their 'quasi'-public nature. Which activities of those bodies the courts will consider as being 'public acts' remains to be seen. However, without engaging the courts to any great extent the Human Rights Act appears to be having an impact upon the way in which sports governing bodies are carrying out their functions. The British Boxing Board of Control charged American boxer Mike Tyson after he continued to punch an opponent after a bout was stopped and subsequently aimed threatening and abusive language towards British heavyweight boxer, Lennox Lewis. The Board restrained themselves to a mere censure of Tyson for the second offence after his representative at the disciplinary hearing warned that an action under the Human Rights Act 1998 would be likely to be successful. Geoffrey Robinson QC suggested that to punish Tyson for his outburst would be in breach of Art 10 of the European Convention on Human Rights, protected by the Act.[160] The previously neglected interface between human rights law and the administration of sport has been subject to academic scrutiny in this regard. In particular the compatibility of drug testing procedures has come to be considered in more detail.[161] In other areas, most obviously in relation to the protection of private and family life under Article 8 of the ECHR, the courts have been relatively pro-active in evolving the law in the light of the introduction of the Human Rights Act 1998, though not as yet against sports governing bodies.[162] One leading instance of the application of the Act in relation to a sports governing body came in the case of *Jockey Club v Buffham*.[163] Here the High Court considered the obligation in s 12 of the Human Rights Act 1998 to take account of Article 10 of the ECHR (freedom of expression) when considering restricting freedom of the press. The case related to an attempt by the Jockey Club to restrain the BBC from broadcasting information by a former Director of Security for the Club, Roger Buffham. The information pertained to perceived problems with security in horse racing. The Jockey Club argued that Buffham was under a duty of confidence that also bound the BBC. In the event the court found that the public interest in important information coming to light outweighed the interest in upholding

---

157 Boyes, S, 'The regulation of sport and the impact of the Human Rights Act 1998' [2000] 6(4) EPL 517, pp 525–28. See also McArdle, D, 'Judicial Review, "Public Authorities" and Disciplinary Powers of Sporting Organisations' (1999) 30 Cambrian LR 31; Lewis, A and Taylor, J, (eds), *Sport: Law and Practice* (2004), London: Butterworths, pp 231–258.

158 See, eg, Application 7601/76, *Young and James v United Kingdom* (1977) 20 Yearbook 520; Application 7866/76, *Webster v united Kingdom* (1978) 12 D&R 168; and Application 4125/69, *X v Ireland* (1971) 14 Yearbook 198.

159 Though cf *Rubython v Federation Internationale De L'Automobile* (unreported, 6 March 2003, QBD) for a brief discussion of the classification of sports governing bodies as 'public authorities' for the purposes of the Human Rights Act 1998.

160 'Human Rights Act Saves Tyson', *The Guardian*, 23 August 2000.

161 See Rigozzi, A, Kaufmann-Kohler, G and Malinverni, G, 'Doping and fundamental rights of athletes: Comments in the Wake of the World Anti-Doping Code' [2003] 3 ISLR 39; Soek, J, 'The fundamental rights of athletes in doping trials' in O'Leary, J (ed), *Drugs and Doping in Sports: Socio-Legal Perspectives*, 2001, London: Cavendish, p 57; Donnellan, L, 'The Right to Privacy and Drug Testing: An Irish Perspective' (2002) 9(5) SLAP 11.

162 See generally, Phillipson, G, 'Transforming breach of confidence? Towards a common law right of privacy under the Human Rights Act' [2003] 66(5) MLR 726; *Campbell v MGN Ltd* [2004] 2 WLR 1232; *A v B* [2003] QB 195; *Theakston v MGN Ltd* [2002] EMLR 22; *Ashworth Hospital Authority v MGN Ltd* [2002] 1 WLR 2033; *Venables v News Group Newspapers Ltd* [2001] 2 WLR 1038.

163 [2003] QB 462.

confidentiality agreements. Though the Human Rights Act 1998 was not given as a primary reason for the outcome of the case, there is clear evidence of its influence in the balancing process.

The Act should be seen as contributing towards balance in the way that sports governing bodies are scrutinised under English law, and as a move towards subjecting their activities to greater public law scrutiny. Whilst domestic courts have been reasonably keen to prevent these bodies escaping scrutiny, this appears to have been done primarily with the intention of protecting economic rights. The introduction of the Human Rights Act 1998 offers a real possibility that parity between the protection of economic and fundamental rights may be achieved in the sporting field.

THE POSITION OF THE EUROPEAN UNION

Similar issues arise in the context of the application of European Union Law to sporting activity. Questions of whether or in fact how EU Law should deal with sporting issues have been met with a variety of responses over a period of years.[164] There is, as yet, no explicit Treaty basis for the Community to involve itself in sporting activity. However, the European Court of Justice's involvement in sport began with the case of *Walrave and Koch v Association Union Cycliste Internationale*,[165] relating to the ability of Dutch motorcycle pacemakers to pace nationals of other Member States during the World Cycling Championships. Walrave and Koch were prevented from doing so by the rules of the AUCI that required pacemakers to be of the same nationality as the team's cyclists. For the purposes of this chapter, the most interesting element of the case is the extent to which the ECJ saw sport as being an area in which it could intervene. The ECJ provided a clear view that sport is subject to Community law only in so far as it constitutes an economic activity within the meaning of Art 2 of the Treaty. Community law would not, for example, impact upon the composition of sports teams, especially national teams, where the composition of the team was of sporting rather than economic interest. Interestingly, the ECJ was keen to highlight that its jurisdiction would extend not only to the activities of state or public authorities, but would also include the activities of regulatory bodies encompassing particular spheres of economic activity, including those regulating sport. Indeed, the body seeking to regulate the sphere concerned need not even be based within the territory of a Member State of the EU; all that would be required was for the regulatory relationship to be entered into or take effect within the boundaries of the Community. These principles were reinforced by the ECJ in the case of *Donà v Montero*,[166] relating to the restriction on non-Italian nationals being employed as professional footballers in Italy; reasserting the economic nature of sporting activity as being the reason for ECJ intervention.

These early incursions into the regulation of sport can be perceived as being fairly minor; it was not until the decision in *Bosman*[167] that the potentially massive impact of EU law began to be recognised. The technical aspects of *Bosman* are dealt with at length elsewhere in this text. Here it suffices to say that the case dealt with the restrictions placed upon footballers at the end of their contracts. Richard Parrish highlights the issues raised by the case:

Parrish, R, 'Reconciling conflicting approaches to sport in the EU'

The European Commission's attitude towards discriminatory practices in sport in the aftermath of *Walrave* and *Donà* was somewhat contradictory. The Commission adopted a fairly consistent view that

---

164 See generally Bailey, D, 'The growing influence of European law and regulation on sport' (2003) 10(6) SLAP 4.
165 Case 36/74 [1974] ECR 1405.
166 Case 13/76 [1976] ECR 1333.
167 Case C-415/93 *Union Royale Belge de Societes de Football v Bosman* [1995] ECR I-4921.

discriminatory practices in sport should be abolished but took little action to ensure sports compliance with community law. Dialogue between the Commission and UEFA (European football's governing body) began in 1978 and culminated in the 1991 'gentleman's agreement' between the two parties. This agreement introduced the 1992 '3 + 2' rule permitting clubs to play three non-nationals in a team and two 'assimilated' players who had played in the country in question for five years without interruption including three years in junior teams. The Commission's position on sport was framed at a time when sport was barely practised as a significant economic activity. The rapid commercialisation of sport in the 1990s and the ruling in *Bosman* significantly altered the Commission's position.

Jean-Marc Bosman, a Belgian footballer, challenged UEFA's use of nationality restrictions and the international transfer system. Bosman's action was sparked by his inability to leave the Belgian first division football club SA Royal Club Liégois (RC Liége) following his rejection of a new (and diminished) contract offer. RC Liége was permitted to demand a transfer fee for Bosman and thus retain a financial interest in the player despite his contract having ended. In August 1990, Bosman began legal proceedings in the Belgian Courts in the hope of securing three main objectives. First Bosman wanted to gain compensation from his club and the Belgian football authority. Second he wanted the transfer rules amended which allowed a club to retain a financial interest in a player even after the expiry of a contract. Third, he wanted the case to be referred to the European Court of Justice for a preliminary ruling on the compatibility of international transfer rules and nationality restrictions in football with EU free movement and competition law. In June 1992 such a reference was made by the national court and although appealed, was confirmed by the Liége Court of Appeal in October 1993.

On 15 December 1995 the European Court of Justice delivered its ruling. The court answered the questions posed by the *Liége Cour d'Appel* by stating . . .

1. Article 48 of the EEC Treaty precludes the application of rules laid down by sporting associations, under which a professional footballer who is a national of one Members State may not, on the expiry of his contract with a club, be employed by a club of another Members State unless the latter club has paid the former club a transfer, training or development fee.

2. Article 48 of the EEC Treaty precludes the application of rules laid down by sporting associations under which, in matches in competitions which they organise, football clubs may field only a limited number of professional players who are nationals of other Member States.

The impact of the ruling has been profound. The significant effect has been felt by sports organisations. The internal organisation of professional football has been dramatically re-shaped. International and domestic transfer regimes have been dismantled and nationality restrictions relaxed in all games except in the composition of national teams. Furthermore, the ruling has confirmed sports linkage to the operation of the Single European Market whenever practised as an economic activity. Football is therefore not the only sport to be affected by the ruling. The second significant effect has been felt within the EU itself. In particular, the ruling sparked renewed regulatory interest in sport from elements within the European Commission. This interest served to galvanise support from within other elements of the EU who wanted sport to be afforded a higher level of protection from EU legislation. In particular, the socio-cultural coalition wanted the EU to give the socio-cultural and integrationist qualities of sport a higher priority.[168]

As Parrish highlights, it is not only the European Court of Justice that has been involved in EU regulation of sport; other institutions – most notably the European Commission – have taken a strong interest in the compatibility of sports rules and regulations with European Union Law. He also highlights the tensions that exist between the highly legalistic approach pursued by certain elements of

---

168 Parrish, R, 'Reconciling conflicting approaches to sport in the EU', in Caiger, A and Gardiner, S (eds), *Professional Sport in the EU: Regulation and Re-regulation* (2000), Hague: Asser, pp 28–29; Lewis, A and Taylor J, (eds), *Sport: Law and Practice* (2004), London: Butterworths, pp 431–439. NB Since the *Bosman* judgment the EC Treaty has been renumbered so that the provisions previously contained in Article 48 now fall within Article 39 of the EC.

the EU and those that would wish to adopt a more sympathetic approach to the question of the autonomy of sports governing bodies. This is perhaps reflected in two recent decisions of the European Court of Justice. In *Lehtonen*,[169] again a case taken on the basis of free movement rules, a Finnish basketball player sought to challenge transfer rules imposed by the Belgian Basketball Federation, which effectively prevented him from playing in particular games. Once again the ECJ was quick to rule out any argument based on the idea of any general organisational autonomy of sports associations. However, the court did accept that where there were good sporting reasons to justify some kind of economic restriction, these would not be considered to be illegal. This suggests that the court was taking into account similar considerations to those considered by the domestic courts – however, there appears to have been a much greater in-depth scrutiny of the rules than has taken place under English law, with a real need for governing bodies to identify and successfully argue 'sporting justifications' for restrictive rules. Similarly in the case of *Deliège*[170] – again brought on the basis of the free movement elements of the Treaty – the ECJ wrestled with the division between sporting and economic rules and regulations. Deliège was not selected for her national team in Judo, though she argued that her performance and ability made her suitable for selection. However, the ECJ was ready to concede that there would necessarily be restrictions on the numbers of participants in tournaments.

Cases C-51/96 and C191/97 *Deliège v Ligue Francophone de Judo et Disciplines Associées ASBL* [2000] ECR I-2549

67 It naturally falls to the bodies concerned, such as organisers of tournaments, sports federations or professional athletes' associations, to lay down appropriate rules and to make their selections in accordance with them.

69 [A] rule requiring professional or semi-professional athletes or persons aspiring to take part in a professional or semi-professional activity to have been authorised or selected by their federation in order to be able to participate in a high-level international sports competition, which does not involve international teams competing against each other, does not in itself, as long as it derives from a need inherent in the organisation of such a competition, constitute a restriction on the freedom to provide services prohibited by Article 59 of the Treaty.[171]

Interestingly, even though Deliège was essentially an amateur athlete the ECJ was still willing to consider the case, because Deliège obtained grants on the basis of results and this was also linked to sponsorship. Additionally, the ECJ saw that, while Deliège was not in receipt of direct economic benefits, the events in which she competed were commercial operations attracting sponsorship and broadcasting monies and that this too would allow the court to intervene in rules of the governing body.

In a similar fashion to the English Courts the ECJ has demonstrated some degree of restraint with regard to the activities of sporting bodies. It does appear, however, that it has delved much more deeply into the substance of sporting regulation and has refused to accept the arguments of 'organisational autonomy' and 'specialism' to the same degree as their English counterparts. This is of course an ongoing process, the application of EU law to sport is a relatively new phenomenon and the relationship naturally develops as the Union has itself evolved. Foster highlights the four stages of EU interest in sporting activity:

Foster, K, 'Can sport be regulated by Europe? An analysis of alternative models'

European regulation of sport has had four periods, each of which illustrates a different regulatory tactic. There was a long period of relative non-intervention that lasted until the judgment in *Bosman*. Early

---

169 Case C-176/96 *Jyri Lehtonen & Castors Canada Dry Namur-Braine v Fédération Royale Belge des Sociétés de Basketball ASBL*.
170 Cases C-51/96 and C-191/97 *Deliège v Ligue Francophone de Judo et Disciplines Associées ASBL* [2000] ECR I-2549.
171 [2000] ECR I-2549.

judicial decisions recognised that the Treaty of Rome governs sport in principle in so far as it involves economic activity. These decisions nevertheless suggested that amateur sport was not necessarily covered and that selection for national teams could be an exception to the Treaty, the Commission as a regulator intervened very little in sport. It limited itself to peripheral issues such as the sale of package tours linked to the purchase of tickets for the 1990 World Cup in Italy (Italia 90, OJ 1992 L326/31.) It had also begun to be interested in the sale of broadcasting rights by sporting bodies. There was some inter-governmental action in the Council of Europe on football hooligans and doping in sport. The Council adopted a European Sports Charter in 1992 but this contains only vague aspirations about co-operative measures. Overall the pattern was one of minimum regulation with little desire to intervene. A report in 1995 for the European Commission was a catalogue of piecemeal measures that hardly suggested widespread intervention in sport.

The *Bosman* decision marked the start of a second phase. The implications of the judgment for professional football were far-reaching. The legality of the transfer system was questioned. A labour market in which players out of contract could move without restriction was allowed, and the legality of transfer fees for players under contract questioned. *Bosman* also declared national quotas that limited the number of foreign players illegal. This made the preservation of local and national identity in sport more difficult. The principle of the single market that allowed no discrimination based on national origins overrode the sporting values of teams made up of mainly domestic players. The significant feature of *Bosman* was that it was a private right action brought by an individual player. By relying on Article 39 of the Treaty, *Bosman* was able to bypass the cosy regulatory regime that existed previously. The direct enforcement of the basic freedoms in the Treaty was a means of regulation that sidestepped the slow-moving Commission. They had been considering *Bosman*-type issues for many years and had only moved UEFA part of the way towards a free non-discriminatory labour market for footballers.

Bosman also highlighted the implications of competition law. Whilst not using Articles 81 and 82 of the Treaty as the basis of their decision, the European Court of Justice made it clear that when acting as a business, football was subject fully to competition law and policy. This began a third phase, that of Commission activity. It is much easier and cheaper to file a complaint with the Commission against sporting federations for acting in an anti-competitive manner than it is to bring a private right action. Suddenly the Commission became reactive as a flood of complaints reached it and proactive as they debated the automatic application of the competition rules to sport. To treat sport purely as a business implied that the ideology of the free market was the appropriate one for sport. The logic of a free and single market underpins Europe's competition policy. As Hoehn and Szymanski have argued, football does not have a single European market. It lacks a European league and is still segmented into national leagues. They propose that a 'transnational league' is the 'most plausible market solution'. But the question remains – can sport be regulated like any other business?

The Amsterdam Treaty of 1997 began a fourth period with a different strategy. The Treaty had a protocol emphasizing the social aspects of sport and its unique features. This was a political initiative with two aims. One was a warning shot across the bows of the Commission, encouraging it to develop policies that limited the automatic application of the competition rules to sport. The other purpose was to develop a separate policy strand of regulation that argued for sport's distinctive cultural and social importance. This purpose could be achieved by exempting sport from the Treaty entirely or by having a special competence for sport akin to the existing one for cultural affairs. The Helsinki Report on Sport in 1999 furthered this 'social role of sport' approach.[172]

Foster rightly highlights the Amsterdam Declaration on Sport as being an important shift in the EU's approach to the regulation of sport. The declaration is interesting as it represents a balance drawn by

---

172 Foster, K, 'Can sport be regulated by Europe? An analysis of alternative models', in *op cit*, Caiger and Gardiner (2000), pp 44–45

the Member States of the EU:

Amsterdam Declaration

The conference emphasises the social significance of sport, in particular its role in forging identity and bringing people together. The conference therefore calls on the bodies of the European Union to listen to sports associations when important questions affecting sports are at issue. In this connection, special consideration should be given to the particular characteristics of amateur sport.

While it is significant that the Member States may be seen as reigning in the Commission in its approach to the application of EU law to sports governing bodies, it must be equally significant that the Member States stopped short of legislating for a 'sporting exception' in order to make sport a special case. The message must be clear – EU law should be sympathetic to the particular needs of sport in its application; however, sport too must abide by the law as required. The overall impetus appears to be towards a position of co-operation, rather than the dogma that has so far characterised the approaches of both the Commission and the sporting federations with which it has dealt. This view is further supported by subsequent action in the field by the EU:

Weatherill, S, ' "Fair play please!": recent developments in the application of EC law to sport'

The refusal to exempt sport, but the temptation to garland it with laurel, also marks the negotiations at Nice. A Declaration on 'the specific characteristics of sport and its social function in Europe, of which account should be taken in implementing common policies' was annexed to the Conclusions of the Nice European Council held in December 2000. This concedes the absence of any direct Community powers in the area, but asserts the institutions of the Community must 'take account of the social, educational and cultural functions inherent in sport and making it special, in order that the code of ethics and the solidarity essential to the preservation of its social role may be respected and nurtured'.[173]

As suggested, it is not only discrimination provisions that touch upon the conduct of sporting activity – competition law too has had a significant impact. The application of competition law to sporting activity is dealt with in more detail elsewhere in the text. However, it is worthwhile highlighting the extent to which competition law has impacted on the governance of sporting activity. Indeed, arguments founded on competition law were put forward in *Bosman*, though the ECJ chose not to deal with them. The competition law of the EC, found in Arts 81 and 82 of the Treaty, has had as yet only a minor impact on the accountability of governing bodies. Both Clydebank (of the Scottish Football League) and Wimbledon (England) have considered moving their operations to Dublin and have met stubborn resistance from their respective regulators. Both might have considered asking the European Commission to consider this refusal in the light of competition laws. Perhaps the most striking instance of community action came with the Commission's attack on football's transfer fee, even after the *Bosman* imposed reforms. Initial reports suggested that transfer fees would be outlawed completely within the European Union. This would be the case even if the player were still under contract, where even post-*Bosman*, transfer fees are currently payable during the term of a player's contract.[174] The Commission after engaging with FIFA and UEFA in discussions found a compromise position, meaning that players will have the freedom to move whilst still under contract, dependent

---

173 Weatherill, S, ' "Fair play please!": recent developments in the application of EC law to sport' (2003) 40 CML Rev 51, 89.

174 FIFA, Regulations for the Status and Transfer of Players (2001) available at www.fifa.com/fifa/handbook/regulations/player_transfer/2003/Status_Transfer_EN.pdf; Transfer negotiations between European Commission and Football organisations finalised – agreement over principles reached, (5 March 2001), available at www.fifa.com/en/organisation/index/0,1521,22566,00.html?articleid = 22566.

upon their age and the length of the contract.[175] The ECJ has also broadened the impact of the application of free-movement provisions through its decision in *Kolpak* where it extended elements of the *Bosman* judgment to nationals of non-EU states having association agreements with the EU.[176]

EVALUATION

The Domestic Position

With the exception of judicial review, the English courts have demonstrated a general readiness to subject the activities of sports governing bodies to scrutiny at the behest of those subject to their rules.[177] However, this welcome general approach has been limited somewhat by a number of factors.

First, there has been a general unwillingness in the context of the contractual and natural justice cases to subject sports governing bodies to anything but the most limited scrutiny. Secondly, those approaches are somewhat limited in the influence they can have over the administration of sport, because of their very nature. Only in the restraint of trade approach has there been demonstrated a general willingness to subject sports governing bodies to the rules, a vigorous application of those rules, and that the approach is capable of having anything other than the most superficial effect on the bodies. It is only in the most extreme situations, involving serious public policy considerations, that the natural justice and contractual approaches have been shown to be similarly capable.

However, the restraint of trade doctrine is limited to those situations where the ability to trade freely is restricted and this will not extend to all situations. This has the effect that those adversely affected by the activities of a sports governing body will have to resort to the less useful mechanisms offered by natural justice and contract, if indeed they are applicable.

Judicial review might then be seen as a possible remedial tool in this respect. However, it is suggested that the courts have demonstrated a great deal of determination that they will not be moved from their present position in this respect. It may also be that the judicial review question is not just one that pertains to sports governing bodies and that litigants in such cases may well be the victims of a broader jurisdictional dispute.

In each of these instances there is a clear tension between the interventionist impulses of the courts in relation to matters concerning public policy and the desire to adopt a 'hands-off' approach where specialist, technical decisions arise. To date there appears to be broad satisfaction amongst the judiciary to reserve intervention for situations where major policy issues fall for consideration. This is particularly so where economic rights are at stake. Despite the extension of the economic relationship in *Gasser*, there appears to remain a key association between intervention and economic disadvantage. There appears to be little evidence, if any, of the courts stepping in to protect more

---

175 See generally Stewart, P and Gibson, D, 'The regulation of domestic soccer: Adapting to a new player regime' (2002) 9(4) SLAP 11.

176 Case C-438/00 *Deutscher Handballbund v Kolpak* [2003] ECR I-4135. See Boyes, S, 'In the Shadow of Bosman: The Regulatory Penumbra of Sport in the EU' [2003] 12(2) Nott LJ 72 and Van den Bogaert, S, 'And Another Upperecut from the European Court of Justice to Nationality Requirements in Sports Regulations' [2004] 29(2) EURLR 267.

177 For a comparative perspective see Beloff, MJ and Kerr, T, 'Judicial control of sporting bodies: the Commonwealth jurisprudence' (1995) 3(1) SATLJ 5; Stewart, WJ, 'Judicial control of sporting bodies: Scotland' (1993) 3(3) SATLJ 45; McCutcheon, JP, 'Judicial control of sporting bodies: recent Irish experiences' (1995) 3(2) SATLJ 20.

fundamental rights. Even in relation to the rules of natural justice, the requirements appear to be greater as the financial stakes grow. The question then is the extent to which the courts will protect more fundamental non-economic rights, as none of the above mechanisms seems to hold significant promise in this regard.

The EU Position

A comparison between the domestic and EU positions highlights a more interventionist approach to sporting regulation taken by European bodies, in particular the ECJ and the Commission, but also hints at some possible limitations. While the case law leading up to, and including, *Bosman* demonstrates a growing vigour in the application of EU law to sporting regulation, this may have reached its zenith. The collaborative and co-operative nature of the agreement between the football authorities and the Commission over transfer fees hints at a post-Amsterdam cooling of the Commission's zeal in its application of EU law. This tends to suggest that there is a certain degree of recognition by the Commission that sport ought to be allowed a degree of regulatory autonomy. In reaching a compromise position the Commission is clearly acknowledging football's position as being more than just a business and is demonstrating a degree of deference to the sporting autonomy of the governing bodies.

Nevertheless, the point is still proven that the EU has presented sporting authorities with significant difficulties and demanded major changes to the regulatory framework. FIFPro, the world footballers' union, still argue that the transfer system, even as amended, remains illegal under EU law. Any case brought before the ECJ in this regard will clearly represent a significant indicator of the extent to which EU law is likely to play a part in sporting regulation for the foreseeable future and thus determine the delicate balance between deference to sporting bodies and over regulation of their affairs.

KEY SOURCES

Black, J, 'Constitutionalising self regulation' (1996) 59 MLR 24.

Boyes, S, 'The regulation of sport and the impact of the Human Rights Act 1998' [2000] EPL 517.

Morris, P and Little, G, 'Challenging sports bodies' determinations' (1998) 17 CivJQ.

Parrish, R, *Sports Law and Policy in the European Union* (2003), Manchester: MUP.

Weatherill, S, 'Do sporting associations make law or are they merely subject to it?' (1999) 13 Am Cur 24.

CHAPTER 6

ALTERNATIVE DISPUTE MECHANISMS IN SPORT

INTRODUCTION

In this chapter, the possibilities of using, instead of the traditional forms of litigation and arbitration, alternative forms of dispute resolution (ADR), especially mediation, as a means of settling sports disputes will be examined. In view of the global nature of sport and sports disputes, a less insular and more comparative approach to this subject will be taken.[1]

But first, to put the subject into context and by way of background, there will be abrief consideration of the attitude of the courts generally to being involved in sports disputes.

The Courts and Sports Disputes

In England, there is a long tradition that the courts do not generally intervene in sports disputes. They tend to leave matters to be settled by the sports bodies themselves regarding them as being, as Vice Chancellor Megarry put it in the case of *McInnes v Onslow-Fane*: ' . . . far better fitted to judge than the courts.'[2] In similar vein, Lord Denning MR expressed the point in the following succinct and typical way in *Enderby Town Football Club Ltd v Football Association Ltd*: ' . . . justice can often be done in domestic tribunals better by a good layman than a bad lawyer.'[3] However, the courts will intervene when there has been a breach of the rules of natural justice (*Revie v Football Association*)[4] and also in cases of restraint of trade, where livelihoods are at stake (*Greig v Insole*).[5]

The position is the same in North America. In the United States, sports disputes are regarded as private matters. The attitude of the courts is well summarised by the Federal District Court in Oregon in the *Tonya Harding* case in 1994 as follows:

Harding v United States Figure Skating Association [1994] 851 F Supp 1476

> The courts should rightly hesitate before intervening in disciplinary hearings held by private associations . . . Intervention is appropriate only in the most extraordinary circumstances, where the association has clearly breached its own rules, that breach will imminently result in serious and irreparable harm to the plaintiff, and the plaintiff has exhausted all internal remedies. Even then, injunctive relief is limited to correcting the breach of the rules. The court should not intervene in the merits of the underlying dispute.[6]

US courts are willing to hear sports disputes only between sports bodies in accordance with federal law, and in breach of contract cases. In Canada, the position is well illustrated by the 1996 case of *McCaig v Canadian Yachting Association & Canadian Olympic Association*. There, the judge refused to

---

1   Nafziger, J, 'Globalizing sports law' (1999) 9(1) Marquette Sports Law Journal 225.
2   [1978] 1 WLR 1520, 1535.
3   [1971] 1 Ch 591, 605.
4   *The Times*, 19 December 1979.
5   [1978] 3 All ER 449.
6   (1994) 851 F Supp 1476.

order the Canadian Yachting Association to hold a second regatta to select the 'mistral class' sailing team to compete in the 1996 Olympics, remarking:

Case 90-01-96624 *McCaig v Canadian Yachting Association & Canadian Olympic Association* **(1996)**

> ... the bodies which heard the appeals were experienced and knowledgeable in the sport of sailing, and fully aware of the selection process. The appeals bodies determined that the selection criteria had been met ... [and] as persons knowledgeable in the sport ... I would be reluctant to substitute my opinion for those who know the sport and knew the nature of the problem (emphasis added).[7]

From this brief survey, it is clear that the courts do not object to sports disputes being resolved by ADR. Before ADR is examined in the sporting context, what is ADR and why has it become popular and grown in importance generally?

ADR: ITS BACKGROUND AND ADVANTAGES

ADR has been defined by the ADR Group, which is based in Bristol and claims to be the UK's first and largest private commercial dispute resolution service, as follows: 'Any process that leads to the resolution of a dispute through the agreement of the parties without the use of a judge or arbitrator.'[8] The ADR Group was established in 1989 by a group of lawyers, businessmen and professional mediators to provide a 'quick and inexpensive means of resolving disputes without the need to resort to the courts'.[9] It has affiliated offices in the USA, Canada and throughout the EU, and mediates in more than 12,000 cases annually, claiming a 94% settlement rate. The Group offers services in dispute prevention and management and training courses in negotiation and mediation.

The other body providing ADR services in the UK is the 'Centre for Effective Dispute Resolution' (CEDR), which is based in the City of London. CEDR was established one year after the ADR Group in 1990. CEDR also offers training programmes and its members include leading lawyers and law firms and many 'blue chip' companies. CEDR claims an 85% settlement rate.[10]

ADR has grown out of the need to provide parties to a dispute with an alternative to litigation as a means of settling their disputes. Over the years, litigation has come to be regarded, especially by businessmen, as an expensive, inflexible and dilatory method of dispute resolution. Arbitration, originally seen and embraced by the commercial community as a quicker and less expensive way of settling disputes, is also now regarded as suffering from similar defects.[11] The English courts have responded to these complaints by promoting attempts to settle cases in the early stages of the litigation process as part of the recent reforms of the Rules of Civil Procedure introduced on 26 April 1999 by Lord Woolf.[12]

> Gladiatorial-style litigation is losing its appeal. In its place, mediation – a conciliatory way to tackle disputes outside the courtroom – is finally taking off. These are the findings of a survey [by 'MORI'] into

---

7   Case 90-01-96624 (1996) (QB Winnipeg Centre).
8   See *Alternative Dispute Resolution: Explanatory Booklet* (2000), Bristol: ADR Group, www.adrgroup.co.uk.
9   *Ibid.*
10   For further information, see www.cedr.co.uk.
11   See Carroll, E and Mackie, K, *International Mediation – The Art of Business Diplomacy* (1999), London: Kluwer; Mackie, K Miles, D and Marsh, W. *Commercial Dispute Resolution – An ADR Practice Guide* (2002), 2nd edn, London: Butterworths; Dezaley, Y and Garth, B, *Dealing in Virtue: International Commercial Arbitration and the Construction of a New Legal Order* (1996), Chicago: University of Chicago Press.
12   Lord Woolf, *Access to Justice: Final Report* (1996), London: HMSO.

Lord Woolf's shake-up of civil justice. The message one year on is that the reforms have promoted a 'cultural shift' towards mediation.[13]

In fact, to encourage attempts at mediation, the courts may impose an adverse order for costs on a party refusing to mediate who is considered to have acted unreasonably. As the Lord Chancellor, Lord Irvine of Lairg, has remarked:

> There is no doubt that ADR can provide quicker, cheaper and more satisfactory outcomes than traditional litigation. I want to see ADR achieve its full potential.[14]

It is interesting to note, *en passant*, that, in the case of *Lennox Lewis v The World Boxing Council and Frank Bruno*,[15] the High Court ordered Lewis to try to settle the dispute with Bruno and the WBC over a fight with Mike Tyson, as required by the WBC Rules, by compulsory mediation, which the judge considered would be 'a perfectly proper independent process of mediation'. Like many other innovative business practices, ADR originated in the United States and has quickly spread around the world. For example, a number of US organisations, including one appropriately called 'JAMS', have been providing an ADR service to individuals and companies for more than 20 years, claiming a settlement rate of 90%. As CEDR puts it:

> All disputes, whether in difficult business negotiations or full-scale litigation, can become a drain on resources, sapping money, time and management focus, and destroying important commercial relationships.[16]

So, what are the advantages of ADR? ADR offers:

- **Speed** – ADR processes can be set up quickly and usually last only one or two days.

- **Cost Savings** – ADR costs a fraction of litigation.

- **Confidentiality** – ADR is confidential, thus avoiding any unwanted publicity.

- **Control and Flexibility** – Unlike a court hearing, the parties themselves remain in full control of the ADR process and any settlement agreed. If no settlement is reached, the parties retain their rights to sue. In other words, the ADR process is conducted on a 'without prejudice' basis.

- **Commercial Focus** – The parties' commercial and/or personal interests influence the outcome, thereby making more creative settlements possible.

- **Business relations** – ADR processes, being closer to business negotiations than adversarial courtroom procedures, can be better preserved or restored.

- **Independence** – Parties can benefit from rigorous and confidential analysis of their position by a genuinely independent mediator.

ADR can be used in conjunction with litigation and arbitration and in national and international disputes. It can also be used in almost any area of law or business. But, as the former Lord Chancellor, Lord Irvine of Lairg, has also pointed out: 'ADR is not a panacea, nor is it cost-free.'[17]

---

13 *The Times*, 4 April 2000.
14 CEDR Civil Justice Audit Conference, London, 7 April 2000.
15 (1995), unreported.
16 See www.cedr.co.uk.
17 Inaugural Lecture to the Faculty of Mediation and ADR, London, 27 January 1999; but note Nicholson, M, 'Does Speedy Disposal Mean Rough Justice?' (2003) 10 (2) Sports Law Administration and Practice, 12.

Forms of ADR

- **Conciliation** – The intervention of an independent third party in order to bring the disputing parties together to talk.

- **Mediation** – A voluntary private dispute resolution process in which a neutral person helps the parties to reach a negotiated settlement. The neutral third party would ordinarily play a more pro-active role than in conciliation. The mediator has no power to make any decision or award.

- **Med-Arb** – A combination of mediation to define the issues followed by arbitration to reach a settlement.

- **The Mini-Trial** – A voluntary non-binding procedure allowing both parties to present their case before senior executives from each party. They would normally do so in the presence of a neutral 'expert' who would assist the parties to settle and who may if necessary give a legal or technical view of the merits of the case or likely litigation outcome. This procedure has been described as being 'structured to reconvert a legal dispute back into a business dispute'. The neutral 'expert' could also be a mediator.

- **Neutral Evaluation** – The use of a neutral party to evaluate the facts and offer an opinion designed to help the parties reach a settlement.[18]

According to the ADR Group, CEDR, and other ADR service providers, the most popular form of ADR is mediation, with high success rates. Mediation is also taking off in the rest of Europe, which:

> ... is more receptive to mediation because on the whole the continent is less adversarial [with] fewer large law firms with strictly litigation departments [and] lawyers [who] do both corporate and litigation.[19]

COURT OF ARBITRATION FOR SPORT

Sports Disputes and the International Sports Federations

Dominating the international sports disputes resolution scene is the Court of Arbitration for Sport (CAS), based in Lausanne, Switzerland.[20] Almost all the International Sports Federations belonging to the Olympic Movement require sports disputes arising between themselves and the sportspersons, who come under their aegis, to be finally settled by the CAS. The IABA, the World Governing Body of Amateur Boxing, has its own Arbitral Tribunal and does not, therefore, refer its sports disputes to the CAS for settlement.

Other International Sports Federations, whose sports are not Olympic disciplines and do not, therefore, fall within the Olympic programme, such as the FIA, the world governing body of motor sports, also have their own dispute resolution bodies. For example, in 1993, a claim of bringing the sport of motor racing into disrepute was brought against Alain Prost, the Formula 1 driver, and the Williams Renault Team. The matter was satisfactorily resolved in a private proceeding, conducted by

---

18 *Op cit*, fn 8, ADR Group (2000).
19 *European Lawyer*, July 2000.
20 Also known as TAS (*Tribunal Arbitral du Sport*); see www.tas-cas.org

the FIA in a Paris Hotel, resulting in Prost escaping a possible ban from competing at the time in the rest of the Formula 1 Grand Prix series.[21]

In view of its importance, a detailed look at the organisation and operation of the CAS as a major international sports disputes resolution mechanism will be made. Some other sports dispute resolution bodies will also be mentioned.

What is the CAS?

The CAS is an arbitral tribunal created by the IOC in 1983.[22] It is based in Lausanne, Switzerland, and has two permanent outposts in Sydney, Australia, and New York, USA. During the Olympic Games, it operates an Ad Hoc Division (AHD) (see later). The CAS has a minimum of 150 arbitrators from 37 countries, who are specialists in arbitration and sports law. They are appointed by the International Council of Arbitration for Sport (ICAS) for four year renewable terms and must sign a 'letter of independence'. The CAS also has a permanent President, who is also President of ICAS. The CAS is dedicated to hearing and settling any disputes directly or indirectly relating to sport, including commercial issues; for example, a dispute over a sponsorship contract. Any natural person, for example an athlete, or legal person, for example an association or a company, may bring a case before the CAS. The parties must agree to do so in writing.

The CAS is a legal entity (a Foundation under Swiss law) administered and financed by ICAS. ICAS was established in November 1994 and is composed of 5 sportspersons; 5 independent persons, who are outside the Olympic Movement and sport generally; 5 persons from the IOC; 5 persons from the Association of Summer Olympics International Sports Federations (ASOIF) and the Association of Winter Olympics International Sports Federations (AIWF); and 5 persons from the Association of National Olympic Committees (ANOC). The members of ICAS are appointed for four year renewable terms. ICAS is also based in Lausanne, Switzerland.

The funding of CAS is shared between the constituents of ICAS as follows:

- 4/12 by the IOC;

- 3/12 by the ASOIF;

- 1/12 by the AIWF; and

- 4/12 by the ANOC.

---

21 Further information on governance issues in motor sports can be obtained from the FIA, Rue d'Arlon 50, B-1000 Brussels,

22 There is now an extensive body of literature on the CAS, including ADR; Gearhart, S, 'Sporting Arbitration and the International Olympic Committee Court of Arbitration ofSport' (1989) 6 Journal of International Arbitration 39; Ingelsey, R,'Court sponsored meditation: the case against mandatory participation' (1993) 56 MLR 441; Polvino, A, 'Arbitration as preventative medicine for Olympic ailments: the International Olympic Committee Court of Arbitration for Sport and the future of the settlement of international sporting disputes' (1994) 8 Emory International Law Review 347; Nafziger, J, 'International sports law as a process for resolving disputes' (1996) 45(130) ICLQ 143; Morris, P and Spink, P, 'Court of Arbitration for Sport', in Stewart, W, Sports Law: The Scots Perspective (2000), Edinburgh: T & T Clark, p 61.; McLaren, R, 'Sports Law Arbitration by CAS: Is it the same as International Arbitration?' (2001) Pepperdine Law Review; Nafziger, J, 'Dispute Resolution in the Arena of International Sports Competition' (2002) American Journal of Comparative Law Section II; and Naidoo, U and & Sarin, N, 'Dispute Resolution at Games Time' (2002) Fordham Intellectual Property, Media and Entertainment Law Journal.

The CAS also receives funding from UEFA and from some other international sports federations, such as the International Chess and Rowing Federations. In the ordinary procedure (see later), the parties pay the costs and fees of the arbitrators according to a fixed scale of charges, plus a share of the costs of the CAS. In the appeals procedure (see later), a court office fee of 500 Swiss francs only is payable. The budget of the CAS is currently 1.5 million Swiss francs.

At the time of writing, the CAS has dealt with more than 576 cases in its first 20 years of existence. Surprisingly, perhaps, there have been no cases from Africa or Asia so far, even though the CAS Panel of Arbitrators includes persons from both these regions.

How Does the CAS Function?

The CAS is governed by its own Statutes and Rules of Procedure – Statutes of the Bodies Working for the Settlement of Sports Related Disputes; Code of Sports Related Arbitration; and Mediation Rules.

On 3 December 2003, the ICAS amended the Code. The amendments respect the general structure of the previous Code and are aimed at codifying the regular practice of the CAS arbitrators and the CAS Secretariat. They also bring clarification to certain provisions, which caused interpretation problems. These amendments came into force on 1 January 2004. According to Arts S12, S20, R27 and R47 of the Code, the Appeals Arbitration Procedure is now open for the appeal against every decision rendered by a federation or club and no longer limited to disciplinary matters, especially doping cases. In addition, Art R57 of the Code empowers the CAS Panels not only to annul a certain decision, but also to replace a decision by a decision of the arbitrators, or to refer the case back to the issuing body. Finally, Art R58 of the Code authorises the Panel to apply the 'rules of law' it deems most appropriate for the case. Thus, the Panels may deviate from the law of the country in which the federation is domiciled and reach a decision on the basis of the laws of another country or other rules of law, such as general principles of law. Appellate jurisdiction in favour of CAS is also mandatory under Art 13 of the World Anti-Doping (WADA) Code. Art 13.2.3 of the WADA Code also allows appeals by certain sports governing bodies, such as international federations and WADA itself, even if they have not been a party to the proceedings. One further point of practice is as follows: in a new Memorandum issued to CAS members, para 3 introduces the following ethical rule: 'No CAS member may act concomitantly as a CAS arbitrator and as a counsel for a party in another procedure before the CAS.' This new directive is designed to further ensure the independence of CAS arbitrators and avoid any possible conflicts of interests.

Proceedings before the CAS are commenced by filing a written request for arbitration or a statement of appeal. The CAS has two divisions: the ordinary division and the appeals division. The former deals with commercial disputes. The latter reviews the facts and the law in relation to purely sporting matters, such as disciplinary cases, for example, doping and cruelty to horses, and constitutional/administrative matters, such as voting procedures of international sports federations.[23]

The CAS also issues so-called advisory opinions on matters, which are not the subject of an existing dispute or one that is likely to arise – for example, the interpretation of the rules of a federation.[24] There is a separate procedure – called 'the consultation procedure' – for issuing these

---

23 See Reeb, M, 'The Court of Arbitration for Sport' (2000) 3(4) Sports Law Bulletin 10.

24 See Advisory Opinion CAS 2000/C/267, *Australian Olympic Committee (AOC)*, 1 May 2000 rendered by RH McLaren (Canada) on the so-called 'Long John' swimsuits and their compliance with the FINA (International Amateur Swimming Federation) rules. For a critique of this Advisory Opinion, see Soek, J, 'You don't win

opinions, which are not legally binding.[25] The President of the CAS determines whether or not to admit the request for an opinion and, if so, what questions shall be put to the Panel, which shall consist of one or three CAS Arbitrators designated by him.[26]

Soek, J, 'You don't win silver – you miss gold'

The CAS Procedural Rules accord a prominent role to the President of the CAS in requests for advisory opinions. Not only does he decide whether the request will be dealt with and does he appoint – if he so decides – the arbitrators from the list to act on the panel, but he is moreover competent to rephrase the questions posed. His freedom to decide whether the panel shall consist of one or three arbitrators may have consequences for the outcome of the advisory opinion. His discretionary power to submit the questions asked to the panel in a different form than the one in which they were originally submitted might also bear a strong influence on the outcome of the advisory opinion. Even a change in the order of the questions asked might influence the outcome. . . . The requesting party cannot object to the changes the President makes to the questions; he can only ask the President to change the rephrasal [sic], but again, the decision lies with the President. In 'normal' arbitrations the President's powers are not nearly as extensive.[27]

In the so-called 'Long John' swimsuits Advisory Opinion, to which the above comments relate, FINA, the World Governing Body of Swimming, in authorising the use of the suits, was found by the sole CAS arbitrator to have acted within the terms of its authority. However, as Soek points out in the same article, the Opinion did not address the sporting question whether the use of the swimsuits by certain competitors could be considered to give them an unfair advantage over other competitors who did not wear them! However, in general, Advisory Opinions are useful in that they help to clarify the law and thus avoid full-blown litigation.

This was certainly true of the Advisory Opinion rendered by the author of this chapter on the question of whether the new scoring rules for badminton were legally introduced by the International Badminton Federation and also whether they discriminated unfairly between women and men players.[28] The Opinion found that they had not been lawfully authorised and that they could be held to be discriminatory on the particular facts of the case. The CAS also issues advisory opinions on matters that are not the subject of an existing dispute or one that is likely to arise – for example, the interpretation of the rules of a federation. There is a separate procedure for issuing these opinions, which are not legally binding.

Here are a couple of examples of the kinds of issues that have been the subject of deliberations by the CAS. Jessica Foschi complained to the CAS in 1996 about the actions of the International Amateur Swimming Federation (FINA). The question before the CAS was whether an international federation (the FINA) was competent to intervene in a doping case after a first sanction was imposed by a

---

silver – you miss the gold' (2000) 2 The International Sports Law Journal 15.; also quoted *in extenso* in Blackshaw, I, *Mediating Sports Disputes: National and International Perspectives* (2002), The Hague: The TMC Asser Press, pp 51–61.

25 See Arts R60, 61 & 62 of the CAS Code of Sports Related Arbitration, 3rd edn, January 2004.

26 Art R61, *ibid*.

27 (2000) 2 The International Sports Law Journal, 15.

28 See Advisory Opinion CAS 2003/C/445, *Canadian Olympic Committee*, 24 April 2003 rendered by IS Blackshaw (United Kingdom) on the legality of the new scoring rules introduced by the International Badminton Federation on 23 May 2002.

National Federation (USS), but reversed by a National Court. The CAS held that there was no violation of the principles of 'double jeopardy' for the following reasons:

Case TAS 96/156 *Ms Jessica K Foschi/USA v Federation Internationale de Natation Amateur (FINA)/CH*, 6 October 1997

> It is imperative that international sports federations be permitted to review the decisions of national sports federations in doping cases in order to prevent any bias of national federations spoiling fairness in international competition. If the international federations were not given this opportunity, there would be no safeguard against a national federation from 'overlooking' a (national) doping case in order to allow its athlete to compete in an international competition. The Panel does not therefore consider the fact that an international federation takes up a case of doping of its own accord to constitute, in principle, a breach of the principle forbidding double jeopardy. In each case, it will, however, depend upon the rules of the federation.[29]

Apart from the restrictions on ownership of Football Clubs in the UK, UEFA, the European governing body of football, recently introduced a rule that clubs with a common control may not play in the same UEFA Cup competition. Again, the rationale for this rule is sporting integrity – the interests of the game.

In 2000, this rule was challenged by AEK Athens and Slavia Prague Football Clubs, which are both controlled by the same UK Investment Company, English National Investment Company (ENIC), as being contrary to EU Competition Law. The case was actually brought before the Court of Arbitration for Sport (CAS) in Lausanne, Switzerland. In a 73 page Advisory Opinion, in which the EU competition law was reviewed, the CAS upheld the restriction as being pro-competitive.[30] The CAS argued that, within the relevant market for the ownership of interests in football clubs, reducing the number of owners of those clubs, by removing any specific restrictions on ownership, would lessen competition, from an economic and also a sporting point of view. Under the CAS Rules, Advisory Opinions are non-binding, but the ENIC case could be of *persuasive authority* in any similar case in the future.

The UEFA common ownership rule was subsequently investigated by the EU Commission as to whether or not it falls outside the EU Competition Rules as being an essential matter of sports governance. As part of this review, the Commission invited comments from third parties on whether the same sporting objective – namely, preserving the integrity of the European football competitions – could be achieved by less restrictive means (the 'proportionality' test). The Commission found that the UEFA rule was justified on sporting grounds and did not restrict fair competition in an economic sense; therefore it dismissed the complaint of ENIC.[31]

Ordinary Cases

In ordinary cases, generally there is a panel of three arbitrators – one appointed by each party from the CAS list and the third designated by the other two arbitrators. If the parties agree, or the CAS considers it appropriate, the dispute can be decided by a single arbitrator.[32] The arbitrators must be

---

29 Case TAS 96/156, 6 October 1997.
30 Case 98/200, 20 August 1999.
31 Case COMP/37 806: *ENIC/UEFA* 2002.
32 *Court of Arbitration for Sport – Guide to Arbitration, January 2000; Court of Arbitration for Sport – Code of Sports-Related Arbitration and Mediation Rules,* Janurary 2000.

independent: they must not have played any role in the case or have any connection with the parties. In ordinary cases, Swiss law is applied unless the parties agree on any other law.

The process normally takes between six and nine months from the filing of the request for arbitration to the rendering of the decision. It is, of course, quicker in those cases where only one arbitrator is appointed. Ordinary cases are by majority decision or, in the absence of a majority, by the President alone. Brief reasons must be given in the award.

Appeal Cases

In appeal cases, there is a panel of three arbitrators and the procedure is quicker, taking about four months from the filing of the statement of appeal to the rendering of the decision. The matter is decided according to the law chosen by the parties. In the absence of any such choice, the matter will be decided according to the law of the country in which the federation is domiciled. Again, the award is rendered by a majority decision, or, in the absence of a majority, by the President alone. Likewise, the award must give brief reasons.

General Procedure

Generally, a case proceeds as follows: after the filing of the request for arbitration or the statement of appeal, any additional statements are exchanged, following which the parties are summoned to an oral hearing at which evidence is taken and oral submissions are made. The parties can conduct their own cases, or be represented or assisted by another person of their choice, who may or may not be a lawyer. The proceedings before the CAS are conducted in English or French; another language may be used under certain conditions. By arrangement, it is possible for hearings to be conducted through conference telephone calls or video conferencing. It is also possible for the arbitrators to sit where the dispute arises – for example, in New Zealand in the case of a dispute between a New Zealand athlete and a New Zealand based Sports Federation. The parties may request interim and conservatory measures to be granted by the CAS, who may require security to be given.

Ordinary cases are confidential and, in principle, awards are not published. However, the parties may agree to waive their confidentiality. In appeal cases, there are no specific rules on confidentiality, but the arbitrators and the CAS staff are subject to a duty of confidentiality. Unless the parties agree otherwise, the award may be published by the CAS. The CAS issues binding arbitral awards, which, in principle, have the same legal status as enforceable judgments of the ordinary courts (see later).

Ad Hoc Division Cases

Special procedural rules apply for cases brought before the Ad Hoc Division (AHD) of the CAS. In 1996, for the first time, the CAS set up an AHD at the Olympic Games in Atlanta to deal with disputes arising in the course of the Games. In order to take part in the Games, all athletes were required to sign an entry form, which included an express and exclusive submission of all disputes to the CAS, including the following undertaking: 'I shall not constitute any claim, arbitration or litigation, or seek any other form of relief in any other court or tribunal.'

Under the special Rules for the AHD,[33] decisions were to be rendered within 24 hours of the request for arbitration being filed.[34] The AHD comprised a President, plus 6 or 12 arbitrators. The proceedings of the AHD were free of charge.[35] The AHD was not subject to any particular law, but was to 'rule on the dispute pursuant to the Olympic Charter, the applicable regulations, general principles of law and the rules of law, the application of which it deems appropriate'.[36] The AHD had power to grant a stay or give other appropriate preliminary relief,[37] and also full power to review the facts on which an application was based.[38] The parties may be assisted or represented by persons of their choice, including lawyers.[39]

Five cases were dealt with by the AHD at the Atlanta Games. They ranged from doping to eligibility to challenges against official sporting verdicts. According to Michael Beloff, QC, one of the members of the AHD in Atlanta:

> The Panel emphasised the general principles of fairness, ... and the importance of sufficiency of evidence ... They stressed the need to eliminate doping from sport ... to protect generally the referee's decision ... and to uphold the authority of duly constituted governing bodies ... [40]

The AHD operated in 1998 at the Winter Games in Nagano, again dealing with five cases. In the same year, the AHD was in session at the Commonwealth Games in Kuala Lumpur, where no cases were dealt with. In 2000, the AHD sat at the Euro 2000 Football Championships in Belgium and also at the Summer Olympics in Sydney.

The AHD is designed to deal with disputes arising in the course of the Games within 24 hours – or sooner if the competition schedule requires – and free of charge. The AHD first operated at the Atlanta Games in 1996, dealing with five cases. At the Nagano Games in 1998, it dealt with five cases, and at the Millennium Games in Sydney in 2000 – officially declared 'the best games ever' – its workload increased significantly to fifteen cases. It will also be in session in 2002 at the Winter Games in Salt Lake City, USA.

The CAS has published a digest of the cases handled by the AHD at the 2000 Sydney Summer Games. This provides not only interesting reading, but also useful reference material for students and practitioners of sports dispute resolution.[41] These cases covered a wide range of disputes and sports and were more complex than those handled at previous Games. Apart from the usual crop of doping cases, in which the CAS upheld the principle of strict liability, there were also novel cases, including athletes, who having changed their nationality, now wanted to compete in the Games for their new countries.

The cases of Angel Perez and Arturo Miranda, former Cubans, who wished to compete in the Games on behalf of the US and Canada respectively, not only involved questions of when a person legally acquires a new nationality, but also the impact of 'statelessness' under International Law, for the purposes of the eligibility provisions of the Olympic Charter.

---

33 Arbitration Rules for the Olympic Games of the XXVII Olympiad in Sydney, 29 November 1999.
34 *Ibid*, Art 18.
35 *Ibid*, Art 22.
36 *Ibid*, Art 17.
37 *Ibid*, Art 14.
38 *Ibid*, Art 16.
39 *Ibid*, Art 8.
40 'The Court of Arbitration for Sport at the Olympics' (1996) 4(2) Sport and the Law Journal 5.
41 Reeb, M (ed), *CAS Awards – Sydney 2000* (2000), ICAS: Lausanne. Copies obtainable from info@tas-cas.org.

The CAS also dealt with a variety of other cases, including the reliability of official timing equipment in rowing; the size of a sponsor's logo appearing on a rhythmic gymnast's clothing; and the disqualification of the winner of a 20 km race walk, for failing to keep at least one foot on the ground during the event. The CAS also upheld the decision of the IOC to strip the 16 year old Romanian Gymnast, Andrea Raducan, of her gold medal, because she had taken a flu remedy prescribed by her team doctor containing a banned substance, pseudoephedrine. The CAS said:

> The Panel is aware of the impact its decision will have on a fine, young, elite athlete … [but] in balancing the interests of Miss Raducan with the commitment of the Olympic Movement to drug-free sport, the Anti-Doping Code must be enforced without compromise.[42]

A harsh, but understandable decision of principle. But perhaps the most important legal principle to come out of the Sydney Olympics came not from the CAS, but from the Australian Courts. Before the Games, the CAS arbitrated in a selection dispute involving two Australian 'judokas'. The unsuccessful one, Angela Raguz, challenged the CAS award in the New South Wales Court of Appeal. The court held that the CAS agreement for arbitration form signed by the parties was not a 'domestic arbitration agreement' within the Commercial Arbitration Act 1984, but a foreign one, and so outside the jurisdiction of the Australian Courts. Although the physical place of arbitration was Sydney, Australia, the legal place of arbitration, as expressly stipulated in the agreement, was Lausanne, Switzerland – the 'seat' of the CAS. The CAS award could only, therefore, be challenged in a Swiss court under Swiss law – in limited circumstances (see later).

This decision – and the other rulings at the Sydney Games – contributed to the continuing development of the CAS as a global dispute resolution body serving the needs of an increasingly global sports community. They also lend credence to the claims of leading sports academics, such as James Nafziger, who are of the opinion that a discrete body of international sports law (if not a 'lex sportiva' then a 'lex specialis') is evolving and taking shape.[43]

The AHD was in session at the Salt Lake City Winter Olympics in 2002, and dealt with seven cases, including the usual crop of doping and eligibility cases. There was also a special AHD for the Manchester Commonwealth Games in the summer of the same year.[44] The AHD was in session at the Athens Summer Olympics of 2004 and dealt with nine cases, including eligibility, doping and judging appeals; and there was also a separate AHD to deal with any disputes arising during the Euro 2004 Football Championships in Portugal.

Lex Sportiva

During its 20 years of operation, the CAS has dealt with a substantial number of cases covering a wide range of sports related legal issues. Although CAS arbitrators are not generally obliged to follow earlier decisions or obey the sacred Common Law principle of 'stare decisis' (binding legal precedent),[45] in the interests of comity and legal certainty, they usually do so. As a result of this practice, a very useful body of sports law is steadily being built up.[46]

---

42   *Ibid*, para 1, p 122.
43   See *op cit*, fn 1, Nafziger (1999).
44   See Blackshaw, I, 'A sporting decision in just 24 hours' *The Times*, 23 July 2002.
45   See *UCI v J.* 7 NCB, CAS 97/176 Award of 28 August 1998, 14.
46   See further, Nafziger, J, 'Arbitration of Rights and Obligations in the International Sports Arena', (2001) 35(2) Valparaiso University Law Review 57; and Blackshaw, I, *Mediating Sports Disputes: National and International Perspectives* (2002), The Hague: TMC Asser Press.

The extent to which the CAS is contributing to a lex sportiva is a contested issue. Foster argues that the CAS as an institutional forum is not yet

> ... globally comprehensive ... [but] has improved by becoming more independent of the International Olympic Committee and thus satisfying Teubner's criterion of externalisation.[47]

The development by the CAS of a discreet body of sports law is a complex and continuing subject.

Nafziger, J, 'The Court of Arbitration for Sport: the emerging lex sportiva'

The CAS deserves acclaim for two decades of high quality, productive arbitration of sports-related disputes. Among its accomplishments is the gradual development of a new and useful jurisprudence derived from its awards. This lex sportiva, though still incipient, is emerging as a means of resolving and potentially helping avoid a broad range of sports-related disputes. Principles and rules derived from CAS awards are becoming more clear on such issues as the jurisdiction and review powers of the CAS; eligibility of athletes; and the scope of strict liability in doping cases. The conformity of these principles and rules with the process of international sports law underscores their legitimacy. A truly effective body of jurisprudence generated by CAS awards, however, will require more development before the emerging lex sportiva can become a truly effective regime of authority.[48]

Foster, K, 'Lex sportiva and lex judica: the Court of Arbitration for Sport's Jurisprudence'

The Court of Arbitration for Sport applies general legal principles to sport when it is dealing with good governance and procedural fairness; it sets minimum standards, if for no other reason than to forestall litigation before national courts. In this function, it is a form of alternative dispute resolution. But its distinct jurisprudence is its application of lex sportiva and lex ludica. The danger for the Court of Arbitration for Sport is that the use of 'lex sportiva' as a concept leads to the position that its principal function as a 'supreme court of world sport' excludes or modifies the other functions that it performs.

Arbitration systems ultimately get their legitimacy from the contractual agreement of the parties. When the issues before the Court of Arbitration for Sport are appeals against the exercise of disciplinary powers over athletes, who are forced to agree to its jurisdiction, then a contractual model is inoperative. Mandatory arbitration has many dangers. It can continue to act as the supreme court for the interpretation of lex sportiva. But its primary role must be to ensure individual justice and rights for athletes; this is what will reinforce its legitimacy and protect its own institutional autonomy and independence.[49]

One of the difficulties faced by CAS in developing a lex sportiva stems from the fact that, generally speaking, CAS proceedings and decisions are confidential to the parties – CAS, by its nature, is a private arbitral body. Art. R43 of the CAS Code of Sports-related Arbitration provides as follows:

> Proceedings under these Procedural Rules are confidential. The parties, the arbitrators and the CAS undertake not to disclose to any third party any facts or other information relating to the dispute or the proceedings.

However, the last sentence of the same article provides the following exceptions to this general rule of confidentiality: 'Awards shall not be made public unless the award itself so provides or all parties

---

47 Foster, K, (2003) 2 (2) 'Is there a Global Sports Law?' Entertainment and Sports Law Journal, 1. Teubner's criterion of externalisation applied to case is represented by an 'external arbitrator' who is able to make decisions amounting to 'official and organized' law.

48 Nafziger, J, 'The Court of Arbitration for Sport: the emerging lex sportiva' in Blackshaw, I, (ed), *The Court of Arbitration for Sport: The First Twenty Years* (2005), The Hague: TMC Asser Press.

49 Foster, K 'Lex sportiva and lex judica: the Court of Arbitration for Sport's Jurisprudence' in *op cit*, Blackshaw (2005).

agree.' In practice, however, more CAS Awards are being published,[50] especially on the CAS official website.[51] And, indeed, as the work of the CAS continues to expand and becomes more widely known and discussed, especially in press sports reports and articles, the need for such publicity also increases. In other words, a 'public interest' argument comes into play that needs to be satisfied.

One area of sports law in which the CAS is developing a particular body of jurisprudence is, sadly, in doping cases. The following extract[52] well illustrates the legal challenges and limitations facing CAS in developing a consistent approach to doping cases:

Oschutz, F, 'Doping cases before the CAS and the World Anti-Doping Code'

CAS – Awards Concerning Doping Cases

A. Basic Ideas

1. Parties' Interests in Doping Cases

CAS decisions in doping cases are held in a magnetic field between two poles: the protection of the rights of the athlete, who is accused of a doping offence, and the need for effective measures against doping in order to preserve the credibility of sport.

On the one hand, the CAS confirmed that every decision taken by a federation had to respect the principles of national and international law, and, in particular, the right to personality of the accused athlete and other human rights.[53] In the fight against doping, the CAS considers itself as an observer of that the law, the basic principle of innocence and the correct application of the rules of the federation.[54]

On the other hand, the CAS also emphasised the need for effective measures in the fight against doping. The arbitrators underlined that the high objectives and practical necessities of the fight against doping may justify the application of strict definitions and of rules without exemptions. For these reasons, (and until lately[55]) most of the panels were inclined to interpret the doping offence as a case of pure strict liability and were not convinced that this standard was unreasonable or contrary to natural justice, or that it constituted an unreasonable restraint of trade.[56]

2. Limitation to Interpretation

The CAS is not in a position to create its own material rules in the fight against doping. The CAS is a judicial authority, limited to the control of decisions, which are based on the rules of sports governing bodies. The CAS is bound to apply existing bodies of rules and the law to certain facts, cf Art R58 of the Code. In doing so, the arbitrators may interpret these rules according to certain standards, but they must refrain from rewriting them. Despite some general considerations in obiter dicta,[57] the panels have not – as yet – controlled the validity of the rules and regulations of the federations under the State law applicable to the case. The arbitrators only emphasised that the rules have to emanate from duly authorised bodies and need to be adopted in constitutionally proper ways.

---

50   The Secretary General of CAS, Matthieu Reeb has already published two Digests of a number of CAS cases covering the periods 1986–1998 and 1998–2000; other such Digests for subsequent years will also be published in due course.

51   See www.tas-cas.org.

52   Taken from *op cit*, fn 48, Blackshaw (2004).

53   IOC, CAS 86/02, Advisory opinion of 10 November 1986, CAS Compilation 1993, p 61.

54   *N v FEI*, CAS 91/56, Award of 13 August 1992, CAS Compilation 1993, p 19.

55   See now *A v FILA*, CAS 2001/A/317, Award of 9 July 2001, p 15; for case comment see Pfister, B, (2003) Sport Recht 16.

56   *USA Shooting & Q v UIT*, CAS 94/129, Award of 23 May 1995, CAS-Digest I, p 187, 194; *F v FINA*, CAS 96/156, Award of 6 October 1997, p 42.

57   See eg: *L v FINA* CAS 95/142, Award of 14 February 1996, CAS-Digest I, p 225, 238 and *USA Shooting & Q v UIT*, CAS 94/129, Award of 23 May 1995, CAS-Digest I, p 187, 194.

The CAS will annul a decision, which does not have a proper legal basis in the rules or regulations of the federation.[58] Only in one award, a CAS Panel was more relaxed. Although the disciplinary rules of the federation did not contain a doping offence, the Panel found it sufficient for a sanction that the introductory notes to the Medical Control Guide, which were prepared by the Chairman of the Medical board, mentioned that 'the presence of the drug in the urine constitutes an offence, irrespective of the route of administration.'[59] Bearing in mind the strict standards established in earlier cases, this decision was rather surprising. Fortunately, it has remained unique.

The Panels are not hesitant to criticise poor draftsmanship and the lack of clarity in the anti-doping rules.[60] Although the arbitrators are generally prepared to interpret the rules in a way that seeks to discern the intention of the rule maker, and not to frustrate it, they also held that rules might be interpreted contra stipulatorem if they are unclear. Athletes and officials should not be confronted with a thicket of mutually qualifying or even contradictory rules that can be understood only on the basis of the de facto practice over the course of many years by a small group of insiders. The test for anti-doping rules is whether an athlete, who has no legal education or experience, understands them clearly and unambiguously.

B. The Doping Offence

Since the CAS is limited to the interpretation of existing rules, the legal nature of a doping offence very much depends on the wording in the rules and regulations of the respective sports governing body. Since a harmonisation of anti-doping rules on the basis of the Olympic Movement Anti Doping Code could not be achieved, there is no general CAS definition of the doping offence. Notwithstanding, there have been clear trends towards a uniform interpretation of different doping regulations.

To put the result at the beginning, two concepts are rivalling. On the one hand, there are Panels, which have stressed that the nature of a doping offence is one of pure strict liability, that is, a liability without fault. Consequently, there is no need to address the issue of intent or negligence at any stage of the proceedings. If an athlete is found with a forbidden substance he has to be sanctioned for a doping offence – period. However, some Panels, which applied the rules of strict liability also felt the need to soften the harsh consequences of such a regime for athletes who committed the offence neither intentionally nor negligently. In the eyes of these arbitrators, the athletes should enjoy the right to escape liability by providing evidence that the violation of the anti-doping rule was committed without their fault. So, the intentional element – that does not exist in a strict liability offence – sneaked in by the back door. On the other hand, there are more and more awards in which the Panels applied a rebuttable presumption of guilt if an athlete is found with a forbidden substance in his body. This athlete may adduce evidence that he or she did neither act intentionally, nor negligently. Consequently, those Panels would not apply the concept of strict liability.[61] However, one may also perceive a certain degree of misunderstanding of those two different legal concepts in some CAS decisions.[62]

---

58 *M v FIC*, CAS 97/169, Court order of 15 May 1997, CAS-Digest I, p 539, 541; *R v IOC*, CAS OG 98/002, Award of 12 February 1998, CAS-Digest I, p 419; see also *H v FINA*, Award of 27 May 1999, CAS-Digest II, p 325, 326.

59 *NWBA v IPC*, Award of 5 March 1996, CAS-Digest I, p 173, 178.

60 See for example: *USA Shooting & Q v UIT*, CAS 94/129, Award of 23 May 1995, CAS-Digest I, p 187, 196; *AC v FINA*, CAS 96/149, Award of 13 March 1997, CAS-Digest I, p 251, 262; *F v FINA*, CAS 96/156, Award of 6 October 1997, p 52; *L v FILA*, CAS 2000/A/312; Award of 22 October 2001, p 11.

61 See for example: *W v FEI*, CAS 92/86, Award of 19 April 1993, CAS-Digest I, p 161, 163. A clarification of these concepts contains the award in *A v FILA*, CAS 2001/A/317, Award of 9 July 2001, p 15; see also *op cit*, fn 55, Pfister, (2003) 17; also see on developing jurisprudence of the CAS in doping cases, Soek, J, 'The Legal Nature of Doping Law' (2002) 2 The International Sports Law Journal 2.

62 Oschutz, F, 'Doping Cases before the CAS and the World Anti-Doping Code', (2001) (7) The International Sports Law Journal 22. Note more details of CAS doping cases in Fitchen, J, O'Leary, J, Gardiner, J and Gray, JT, 'Analysis of Doping Cases of The Court of Arbitration for Sport' (2001),a research project undertaken by European Commission for one-year drugs & public policy (in context of sport) research framework. Bid submitted by the TMC Asser Institute, The Hague, the Max Plank Institute, Munich & the University of Erlangen-Nurnberg, Germany; see www.sportslaw.nl for more information on this project.

Legal Status of CAS Awards

An arbitral award rendered by the CAS is final and binding on the parties from the time it is communicated to them. Like any other international arbitral award it can be enforced according to the usual rules of Private International Law and, in particular, in accordance with the provisions of the New York Convention on the Recognition and Enforcement of Foreign Arbitral Awards of 10 June 1958. Almost 100 countries have acceded to this Convention. The procedure for recognising and enforcing a foreign arbitral award under the New York Convention is laid down in Art IV. The status of the CAS is also recognised under the European Convention on the Recognition of the Legal Personality of International Non-Governmental Organisations.

If a party is dissatisfied with a CAS award, what legal action can be taken?

Challenges to CAS Awards

In Switzerland, it is possible to challenge a CAS Award before the Swiss Federal Tribunal in Lausanne under Swiss law, but in very limited circumstances:

Article 190(2) of the Swiss Federal Code on Private International Law of 18 December 1987

[The Award] can be attacked only:

a if a sole arbitrator was designated irregularly or the arbitral tribunal was constituted irregularly;

b if the arbitral tribunal erroneously held that it had or did not have jurisdiction;

c if the arbitral tribunal ruled on matters beyond the claims submitted to it or if it failed to rule on one of the claims;

d if the equality of the parties or their right to be heard in an adversarial proceeding was not respected;

e if the award is incompatible with Swiss public policy.

A CAS Award was challenged in February 1992 by a horse rider, Elmar Gundel. His horse had tested positive for a banned substance, as a result of which the horse and the rider had been banned from international competition by the International Equestrian Federation. So he appealed to the CAS, who upheld the ban, but reduced the period of suspension, and also fined the rider. The rider then appealed against the CAS ruling to the Swiss Federal Tribunal. His grounds for this appeal were that, as the CAS was funded by the IOC, it was not an independent tribunal.

On the 15 March 1993, the Swiss Federal Tribunal rendered its judgment in the case of *Elmar Gundel v FEI/CAS*.[63] The court held that the CAS is a real arbitral court, whose decisions properly constitute arbitral awards at the international level, and that the court is neutral and independent. Thus, the CAS, according to Swiss law, is an arbitral body that can render final and enforceable awards, which have the force of a judgment.

However, the Swiss Federal Tribunal noted, *en passant*, that, where the IOC is a party to a dispute before the CAS, the CAS is not an independent body. As a result of this case, the organisation of the CAS was changed with the establishment of the International Council for Arbitration in Sport (ICAS), which now administers and finances the CAS as described above. However, the CAS is still not entirely independent of the IOC, because of its substantial involvement in the ICAS, which, in turn,

---

63 [1949] All ER 109, 118.

appoints the 'judges' of the CAS, as well as the substantial funding of the CAS by the IOC and the Olympic Movement, ultimately controlled by the IOC.

> The independence of the CAS was legally challenged more recently before the Swiss Federal Tribunal by two Russian cross-country skiers, Larissa Lazutina and Olga Danilova, who were disqualified by the IOC for doping offences following the 2002 Salt Lake City Winter Olympics. The International Ski Federation (FIS) suspended both of them from competition for two years. After their appeal to the CAS to overturn the IOC and FIS rulings was turned down, they appealed against the CAS Awards to the Swiss Federal Tribunal claiming that the CAS was not an independent and impartial tribunal because of its association with the IOC. The Swiss Federal Appeal Tribunal rejected their appeal, holding that the CAS offered all the guarantees of independence and impartiality of a real tribunal and must be regarded as such, even where the IOC was a party to its proceedings.[64]

It is also possible to challenge a CAS Award before courts in other Countries. For example, in England, it is clear from the authorities that decisions rendered by private courts or bodies can be challenged if they act in an arbitrary and capricious way or disregard the rules of natural justice (see above). This will depend, however, on the circumstances of each case.

Russell v Duke of Norfolk [1949] All ER 109

> Tucker LJ: ... The requirements of natural justice must depend on the circumstances of the case, the nature of the inquiry, the rules under which the tribunal is acting, the subject matter that is being dealt with and so forth.[65]

However, in 1991, the Football League unsuccessfully challenged, in the High Court, the decision of the Football Association (FA) to establish and run the Premier League. In that case, the court held that the FA was 'not a body susceptible to judicial review'. The FA was a domestic body, whose powers derived from duties existing in private law only, despite the facts that the FA exercised almost monopolistic powers over the game of football and its decisions were important to many members of the public. The court held that it was not appropriate to apply to the FA, which was not a public body, principles intended to control abuses of power by government.

On the other hand, in cases involving restraint of trade, where the livelihood of an affected party is threatened, or other anti-competitive restrictions, the English courts can and do intervene. For example, in *Eastham v Newcastle FC*,[66] England's *Bosman* case, the court held that the combined effect of the rules of the FA on retention and transfer were an unreasonable restraint of trade. Likewise, in *Nagle v Feilden*,[67] the court intervened in relation to the refusal by the Jockey Club to grant a trainer's licence to a woman applicant purely on the grounds of gender, in order to protect her right to work.

It is also possible to challenge a CAS Award under Art 6 of the European Convention on Human Rights, which became part of the law in England and Wales on 2 October 2000 when the Human Rights Act of 1998 came into force. Article 6 requires that individuals receive a fair trial 'in the determination of [their] civil rights and obligations'. Likewise, a CAS Award, in so far as it is the result of an arbitration process based on a written arbitration agreement, can also be challenged under s 1 of

---

64 *Lazutina and Danilova v Court of Arbitration for Sport (CAS)* (2003) ATF Civ 27 May 2003. A further point on the question of the independence of the CAS from the IOC: it is interesting to note that the CAS headquarters moved in 2004 from its old building, owned by the IOC and adjacent to the IOC Museum, to entirely new independent and self-contained premises at the Chateau de Bethusy, Lausanne.

65 [1949] All ER 109, 118.

66 [1963] 3 All ER 139.

67 [1996] 2 QB 633.

the Arbitration Act of 1996. This provides that arbitration must be fair and conducted by an impartial tribunal, and also that the court will only intervene in certain defined circumstances. These circumstances include agreements to oust the jurisdiction of the courts, such agreements being void.[68]

THE UK SPORTS DISPUTE RESOLUTION PANEL

The SDRP is largely the 'brain child' of Charles Woodhouse, a former Legal Adviser to the Commonwealth Games Foundation. It was established on 1 January 2000 and is headquartered in London. It was set up to provide sports governing bodies, commercial organisations and individuals throughout the UK with 'a simple, independent and effective mechanism ... to resolve their differences fairly, speedily and cost effectively'.[69] It is modelled on the CAS. In addition to offering binding arbitration and providing non-binding advisory opinions, the SDRP also offers mediation. The mediation service has been set up with advice and assistance from CEDR and exhibits many of the features characteristic of the mediation process offered by CEDR, but adapted to a sporting context. The arbitration rules can be found on its website.[70] At the time of writing, the SDRP has completed four years of operations, and its Director, Jon Siddall, has issued the following upbeat report:

Siddall, J, 'The UK sports dispute resolution panel – four years on and aiming for gold'

As the world waits expectantly for the arrival of the teams in Athens for the Olympic and Paralympic Games after a four year cycle of intense and methodical preparation, it is perhaps timely to note the progress made by the Sports Dispute Resolution Panel ('SDRP') over the same period in providing a dedicated independent dispute resolution service to sport in the United Kingdom since it began its operations in early 2000. The swift and effective handling of selection and eligibility issues in the lead up to major games has been one notable feature of SDRP's work to date as it seeks to achieve its own gold standard.

Established by the key representative bodies of sport as a not for profit company limited by guarantee, and with support and increased funding from UK Sport, SDRP has worked independently on sport's behalf in providing a comprehensive range of dispute resolution (and prevention) services, designed to meet the needs of the sports market in the UK at all levels and in all forms of dispute resolution, including those of arbitration and mediation. The original organisations behind SDRP were the British Olympic Association; the BOA Athletes Commission (now superseded by the British Athletes Commission); the CCPR; the Institute of Professional Sport; the Institute of Sports Sponsorship; the Northern Ireland Sports Forum; the Scottish Sports Association; and the Welsh Sports Association. They remain fully supportive along with other key stakeholders.

SDRP is a forward-thinking initiative that, uniquely, has brought together all sides of sport in jointly tackling the major threat that disputes represent to sport, whether by acting as a drain on resources, tarnishing its image, straining the relationships that are key to its success, or simply detracting from the enjoyment that an involvement in sport offers to its participants. Growing commercialisation, the greater risk of legal challenge and litigation, and the need for sport to regulate itself in a modern and businesslike manner all combine to emphasise the merits of effective dispute resolution in sport, thus mirroring similar developments in ADR in other sectors.

---

68 *Baker v Jones* [1954] 2 All ER 553.
69 See SDRP Booklet, *Towards Successful Sports Dispute Resolution Planning and Practice*. Copies of all literature on the UK SDRP can be obtained from the Director, Jon Siddall,
70 www.sportsdisputes.co.uk.

The completion of SDRP's own first four year cycle provides a timely opportunity to reflect on the progress that SDRP has made towards delivering its mission of 'Just Sport' – just sport in the sense of creating a sporting environment that is free from the unwelcome and costly distraction of unresolved disputes and litigation, and just sport in the sense of achieving fairness in sport through the availability of an independent mechanism to resolve and prevent disputes.

SDRP recently achieved an important milestone when it handled its one hundredth referral. In addition, a similar number of enquiries have been received where SDRP's involvement, although not requiring a formal referral, has often assisted the process of resolving a dispute or identifying an appropriate mechanism to do so.

Referrals have come from some twenty-five sports to date, both professional and amateur, and from a number of sources, including governing bodies of sport, individual athletes, and those advising them. It has been an interesting feature that the disputes have covered a wide range of issues including discipline; selection; eligibility; doping; exclusion from membership; funding; contractual rights; commercial rights; employment; personal injury; discrimination and child welfare.

In delivering its service, SDRP has set itself the target operationally of being independent, expert, inclusive, flexible, comprehensive, speedy, robust and cost effective. The results to date reflect this and have enabled SDRP to achieve its initial key objective of gaining the trust and confidence of its service users. This is further reflected in the way in which sports organisations are now choosing to use SDRP. At the beginning, the vast majority of referrals – not surprisingly -arose on an individual case-by-case basis. However, the position is changing as more and more organisations make specific provision within their regulations and contracts to refer disputes (both commercial and non-commercial) to SDRP or alternatively to use SDRP to make independent appointments on their behalf.

This sits well with SDRP's intention both to complement existing governing body dispute resolution procedures and to provide an alternative dispute resolution mechanism, where appropriate, reflecting SDRP's overriding concern to provide a framework that is in the best interests of sport, rather than simply persuading sports organisations to refer all levels of disputes as a matter of course to SDRP. Ultimately, SDRP's work is concerned with promoting best practice in sports dispute resolution, as part of the broader modernisation agenda for sport.

SDRP's growing status is recognised by the arrangements that it now has with a number of sports governing bodies to provide agreed dispute resolution services to meet their specific needs. By way of illustration, SDRP has recently renewed its agreement with the English Football Association to appoint an independent chairman to all FA Appeal Boards and, from the 2004–2005 season, to appoint a second independent member from within the football community. Any appeal against the decision of the British Paralympic Association not to select individual athletes for the Athens Games will be considered by SDRP in much the same way that it dealt with eligibility issues for the Commonwealth Games Council for England in the run up to Manchester 2002. SDRP has similarly helped to resolve eligibility issues for the British Olympic Association, which also provides in its commercial contracts for arbitration and/or mediation through SDRP.

This growing level of partnership between SDRP (while retaining its complete independence) and the various stakeholders in sport is critical. In the key area of anti-doping, where the WADA Code is due for implementation during 2004, SDRP is working closely with UK Sport and other interested groups to develop an effective framework for dealing with doping cases in the UK, including the establishment of a national tribunal service. SDRP's central role is testament to its growing reputation.

In that context, a sample of some of the cases dealt with to date by the SDRP illustrates the considerable and diverse potential of the service offered:

- The parties had been in dispute for a period of nine months over an alleged infringement of intellectual property rights with no immediate prospect of a resolution, and with the major sports event at the centre of the dispute imminent. A framework was agreed and a specialist QC appointed as arbitrator. The dispute was then dealt with by written arbitration, thereby keeping costs to a minimum, and a decision issued within four weeks of initial referral.

- A dispute involving three complaints against a coach, his club, and the governing body regarding its handling of the matter complained of. The dispute had been running for almost 18 months with little sign of agreement even as to the process. The referral to SDRP gave the complainants the confidence to abandon their complaints in favour of an independent review by a leading QC into the governing body's handling of the matter. His subsequent report identified some 'best practice' lessons of general application to sport and led to a review of the governing body's dispute resolution procedures.

- A dispute between an athlete and their governing body over the contractual terms of an elite athlete funding agreement. After months of disagreement and ill feeling, the parties agreed to try and mediate their differences through SDRP with the assistance of the relevant sports councils. An acceptable arrangement was made and the athlete concerned was able to return to their sport, competing successfully at the highest level.

- A team appealed against the decision of the relevant league to exclude it from the division that it was due to play in. With the next season less than six weeks away, an arbitration was arranged within two weeks and a final outcome reached, thus enabling the fixture list to be confirmed.

- A dispute between a football manager and his club, following the termination of his contract, was successfully resolved through a one-day mediation.

- A club member was excluded from his club after raising a concern about the club with his governing body. A protracted dispute, which had taken up a considerable amount of time on the part of all the parties involved, was ultimately resolved through a half-day mediation.

Over the four-year period, SDRP has built up a considerable level of experience and expertise, due in great part to the continued support and involvement of the SDRP Panels of Arbitrators and Mediators. Much progress has already been made in recruiting leading experts in the arbitration and mediation fields, and SDRP is now able to call on the services of some 150 members of the Panel of Arbitrators and 50 members of the Panel of Mediators. There is an ongoing commitment to build on existing levels of expertise, so as to ensure that all areas of specialisation and experience are available throughout the UK. In developing the Panels, due emphasis will be given to the importance of mediation as an effective, but as yet not fully utilised, mechanism for resolving disputes in a sporting context.

As SDRP turns its attention to the next four years, there is good reason to be confident about the role that SDRP will play over this period in delivering a best practice and modernisation agenda within dispute resolution, thereby helping to reduce the impact and incidence of disputes. With the continued backing and support of sport, SDRP will be looking to consolidate the good progress that has been made in establishing a service that offers a truly independent, speedy and expert dispute resolution framework at an affordable cost.

In looking ahead, SDRP's work will be driven by some key guiding principles, which are designed to reflect sport's own requirements. Every organisation should aim to have fair, affordable, timely and effective dispute resolution, disciplinary and grievance procedures in place. Every individual and organisation in sport should have ready access to such procedures. Every dispute should be dealt with at a level and in a manner appropriate to the nature of the case and with a view to its early resolution, wherever possible without reference to the courts.

In the same way that the Court of Arbitration for Sport has really come into its own over the last ten years in providing a much-valued framework at the international level, the interests of sport in the UK will surely be met by the real emergence of SDRP as the UK-equivalent of CAS over the next few years. As this happens, it will form part of a developing trend, as a series of national dispute resolution bodies start to become established around the world. The priority that is given to SDRP's work in dispute resolution and planning, and the investment that is made in it, should result in a handsome return for sport as a whole.[71]

Advisory Opinions

As with CAS, the SDRP has the competence to provide an Advisory Opinion.

Sports Dispute Resolution Panel (SDRP) Rules for an Advisory Opinion

The following Rules (amended by the SDRP from time to time) shall govern the giving of an advisory opinion ('the Opinion') and the party or parties shall be taken to have agreed that the Opinion shall be given in accordance with these Rules.

1 The party or parties who wish to submit a request for an Opinion must sign an agreement with the SDRP in relation to costs before the SDRP will consider a request for an Opinion.

2 The request for an Opinion shall be in the SDRP's standard form and shall include:

   (a) the name of the party or parties requesting the Opinion;

   (b) copies of any documents which may be relevant to or have a bearing on the Opinion; and

   (c) a brief statement describing the nature and circumstances and background to the request and why it is requested.

3 The party or parties shall decide how many and which of the Arbitrators shall consider the request and give the Opinion and, if they fail to do so or in the absence of agreement, the Chairman of the SDRP shall so decide and shall notify the party or parties who made the request of his choice.

4 The Arbitrator(s) selected shall have absolute discretion to decide what documents and further information shall be supplied to the Arbitrator(s) and may consult with the party making the request or with any other party or relevant person or body before issuing an opinion.

5 Any costs relating to the Opinion as agreed with the SDRP, must be paid in full to the SDRP before the Opinion will be issued.

6 The Arbitrator(s) selected to give the Opinion shall have absolute discretion as to the form, length and content of the Opinion.

7 The Opinion shall not constitute a binding arbitral award.[72]

In practice, the possibility of being able to obtain a non-binding advisory opinion in a sports dispute is a very useful one for clarifying the legal issues. This can save time and money, as well as safeguarding relationships. But much will depend, in each case, on the standing of the 'Arbitrators' who render the opinion. The parties are free to select them from the Panel maintained by the SDRP.

---

71 Siddall, J, 'The UK sports dispute resolution panel – four years on and aiming for gold' (2004).
72 Sports Dispute Resolution Panel (SDRP) Rules for Arbitration (issued on 16 October 2002), pp 15–16.

MEDIATION AND SPORTS DISPUTES

Why Mediate?

Mediation enjoys the following main advantages:

- **Mediation is quick** – it can be arranged within days or weeks rather than months or years as in the case of litigation and can also be conducted in a very short time.

- **It is less expensive** – quick settlements save management time and legal costs.

- **It is confidential** – adverse publicity is avoided and unwanted parties, such as competitors or journalists, are not present.

- **It covers wider issues, interests and needs** – underlying issues and hidden agendas are exposed making creative solutions possible to satisfy the needs of all the parties.

- **It is informal** – a common sense and straightforward negotiation results.

- **It allows the parties to retain control** – the parties make the decisions rather than control being handed over to a judge or an arbitrator.

- **It is entirely 'without prejudice'** – the parties have nothing to lose, their rights are not affected by the mediation, thus litigation can be commenced or continued if the mediation fails to produce an agreed settlement.

Parsons, K, 'Hands across the table'

... mediation differs from other alternative dispute resolution methods, such as arbitration, because the outcome or solution is not imposed. It has to be concluded voluntarily by the parties on either side. The mediator facilitates by evaluating the dispute and proposing solutions, but does not make a judgment as happens in an arbitration or independent expert determination. This means the parties own the outcome, it is their problem but also their solution, therefore they are more likely to get an outcome that they can live with.[73]

And for all these reasons, mediation enjoys a high rate of success. The ADR Group claims a settlement rate of 94% of the mediation cases it handles, whilst CEDR claims a settlement rate of 85%.

So, what is mediation and how is it conducted?

The Idea of Mediation

Mediation is not a new thing. People have been mediating – that is, trying to reconcile differences between individuals and groups – for thousands of years. The Bible and other ancient texts are full of examples. However, in the last 20 years or so, mediation, as a method of settling commercial disputes, has grown in popularity in the business community and has taken on certain features and characteristics.[74]

---

73 Sam Passow, Head of Research at CEDR, quoted in Parsons, K, 'Hands across the table' *The European Lawyer*, July 2000.

74 For example, mediation in the shipping and insurance industries is frequently used and highly developed. It is also widely effective and successful.

Many learned books have been written and seminars given on the theory of mediation and the underlying principles of negotiation, as well as manuals published on its practical application to a range of disputes and issues. It is beyond the scope of this chapter to go into the theory of mediation and the part played by psychology, and its practical application in a dispute situation and context. Suffice to say that mediation, if not a science, is certainly an art, and there is need for mediators to be properly trained. Many professional training and accreditation courses are available, and many litigators have taken or are taking advantage of them. Mediation is growing as a new legal practice area to satisfy a developing need amongst an increasingly wide range of clients.

The Mediation Process

Mediation is a voluntary, non-binding, 'without prejudice' process that uses a neutral third party (mediator) to assist the parties in dispute to reach a mutually agreed settlement without having to resort to a court. It differs from litigation and arbitration in that a binding decision is not imposed on the parties by a judge or an arbitrator. The main advantage of the mediation process is to permit the parties to work out their own solution to their dispute with the assistance of the mediator.

Mediation is a natural extension of the most common method of resolving disputes, namely, negotiation. However, negotiations either break down or cannot be commenced for a variety of reasons. Mediation gives the parties in dispute the option to start or continue negotiations in a controlled setting. If the mediation is not successful, the parties are still free to go to court or arbitration, so nothing has been lost.

Common Concerns about Mediation

Many people regard agreeing to mediation as an admission of failure. This should not be the case. As previously mentioned, negotiations break down for various reasons, and so mediation gives the parties the chance of keeping the negotiations going. The negotiations have not concluded until mediation has been attempted. Putting the dispute in the hands of a mediator does not involve any loss of control by the parties. On the contrary, the control remains with the parties, as the mediator has no authority to render any decision or force any settlement. A settlement is only reached if and when the parties consider that the settlement proposed is fair and reasonable.

Mediation does not create extra work for the parties in dispute. In fact, in the long run, mediation saves time. The parties do have to invest some time and effort in the mediation, but most cases submitted to mediation settle, saving further time. Even in the minority of cases in which mediation does not lead to a settlement, the time spent on the mediation reduces the time needed for preparing for a trial. Neither does mediation create extra costs. Mediation reduces costs related to litigation through the early settlement of the dispute. It also, as already mentioned, reduces the trial preparation time required in those cases, which do not settle.

Many people shy away from mediation because they think that an opponent will use the mediation to gain more information about their case. In the mediation process, each party is completely in control of the information disclosed. If a party does not wish the other side to know something, they can keep it to themselves or disclose it to the mediator in confidence. However, if the information is something that might persuade the other party to accept a settlement, or is something they will find out about later on through discovery, there is little, in those particular circumstances, to be lost by disclosing that information.

The parties are entirely free to choose the mediator. In fact, they must agree on his or her appointment. Organisations, such as CEDR, that offer mediation services have a list of trained mediators with details of their qualifications and experience. Most mediations are quick, lasting a few hours or a few days, but the mediator will continue to work with the parties as long as they wish to continue with the mediation. It is often said that arbitration, rather than replacing litigation, tends to lead to litigation. On the other hand, mediation is not just an extra step in the dispute resolution process; it is usually the final step, as most cases settle.

As already mentioned, nothing is lost if the mediation is not successful. Because the mediation process is conducted on a 'without prejudice' basis, the parties are free to go to court or arbitration. It is as if the mediation did not take place. Nothing revealed in the mediation can be used by either party and neither can the mediator be required to give evidence on behalf of either party in any subsequent court or arbitration proceedings.

Applying Mediation to Sports Disputes

Perhaps the main advantage of using mediation to settle sports disputes is that the process preserves and even restores personal and business relationships.[75] It is well known that the sports world is a small one – everyone seems to know somebody – and relationships, and, indeed, reputations, are therefore more important and worth preserving. As Bernard Foucher, President of the French Board of Mediators, has put it: 'Mediation allows legal disputes to be resolved within the family of sport.'[76]

As the process is not adversarial, there is no winner and, therefore, no loser. Or, at the very most, the parties share the 'pain'. Mediation re-opens lines of communication, which have often broken down, requiring the parties to co-operate with one another in finding a solution to their problems. Mediation provides the opportunity for co-operative problem solving. Through careful probing by the mediator, the actual underlying reasons for the particular dispute can be identified and addressed. This goes a long way towards finding an appropriate solution to the parties' problems.

Dispute settlement through the courts or arbitration is backward looking, the decision or award being reached on the basis of past facts and historical background. Mediation, on the other hand, is forward looking, having regard to the future and future possibilities. Mediation is not seeking to apportion blame or fault, but to reach a solution. Mediation is more flexible than traditional forms of litigation and even arbitration, which has become rather technical and specialised. There are no set rules of procedure to get in the way. The approach is informal and flexible. Mediation is swift, and this is a particular advantage to sportspersons, who often have pressing event and other commitments and commercial deadlines.

This was one of the factors why a dispute in 1999 between Frank Warren, the well known boxing promoter, and Richie Woodhall, the former WBO super middleweight world champion, was successfully resolved by mediation. The case also illustrates other reasons for opting to settle disputes by mediation.[77]

---

75 See Blackshaw, I, 'Resolving sports disputes the modern way – by mediation' (2000) 18(1) Sport and the Law Journal; Blackshaw, I, 'Sporting settlements' (2001) 145(27) SJ; Newmark, C, 'Is mediation effective for resolving sports disputes?' (2000) 5/6 International Sports Law Journal 37; Slate, W, 'The Growth of Mediation and Mediation in Sports Disputes in the US' (2000) Paper presented at the CAS Symposium on Mediation, 4 November 2000.

76 Foucher, B, 'La Concilation Comme Mode de Reglement des Conflits Sportifs en Droit Français' (2000), Paper presented at the CAS Symposium on Mediation, Lausanne, 4 November 2000.

77 See CEDR Press Release, 21 July 1999.

The *Woodhall/Warren* Case

In April 1999, Richie Woodhall sought to terminate his management and promotion agreements with Frank Warren, claiming that Warren was in breach of them and also that the agreements were unenforceable. Woodhall refused to fight for Warren, and also started approaches to other boxing promoters. On the other hand, Warren refused to let Woodhall go, claiming that contracts were valid; that there was still some considerable time to run on them; and that he was not in breach of them. The parties were adamant in their respective positions.

Woodhall, therefore, started proceedings in the High Court in June 1999. He requested an early hearing of the case to enable him to fight the defence of his world title by September, as required by the rules of the World Boxing Organisation. As the agreements required that any disputes were to be referred to the British Boxing Board of Control, Warren, for his part, sought an order from the court to that effect.

This dispute had all the makings of a full-blown legal fight in the courts with lots of blood on the walls – and in the full glare of the media. As such, it would not only be time consuming and expensive to both parties, but also potentially damaging for their reputations. In addition, Woodhall was anxious to get back in the ring and, if he were to continue to be of any value to Warren, he needed to fight his mandatory defence to his world title within a short period of time. So, in all these circumstances, the question arose as to whether the court was the best forum in which to resolve this bitter dispute. It was decided to refer the dispute to mediation. And the court was prepared to adjourn the proceedings, for a short time, to enable the parties to see if they could settle their differences by this method. A hastily arranged mediation was set up and conducted by CEDR. Within 72 hours, the dispute was resolved, and Woodhall signed a new deal with Warren and continues to box for him.

As mediation is confidential, there is no official record or transcript of the process. It is not possible to have a 'blow by blow' account of what was said, the arguments adduced, why a settlement was reached and what were its terms. One thing can, however, be deduced from the known facts and circumstances of this dispute: there were sporting and commercial deadlines to concentrate the minds of the parties and act as a spur to reaching a compromise. There was also a pressing need for the parties not to 'wash their dirty linen in public'.

Other Sports Cases

For many years now, many labour disputes have been settled by mediation through private and official bodies, such as ACAS (Arbitration and Conciliation Advisory Service). With more and more sportspersons, especially footballers, being paid more and more for their services, more and more disputes are arising under their employment and service contracts. This is, therefore, a field in which many such disputes are capable of being successfully settled by mediation. This has certainly been the experience in the United States where labour disputes in the sporting context are quite commonplace.[78]

The Amateur Swimming Association (ASA) encourages 'informal mediation' in settling cases of alleged breaches of their Code of Ethics in 'suitable cases'. Also the ASA operates a 'Quick Justice'

---

78 For further information, see Weiller, P and Roberts, R, *Sports and the Law: Text, Cases, Problems* (1998), 2nd edn, St Paul, Minn: West.

system (a kind of mediation) for charges of 'brutality' in water polo. Cases must be brought within 30 days.[79]

A schedule of some other sports disputes recently mediated by CEDR, giving brief details of the nature of the dispute, the parties and the amounts involved, as well as the outcomes, follows:

- Frank Warren boxing contract (£300,000) – settled in 1 day.

- Fees over a golf club (£20,000) – settled in 1 day.

- Aircraft leasing within a parachute club (£340,000) – settled in 2 days.

- Contract over a rugby club and the Rugby Football League (£340,000) – settled in 1 day.

- Contract concerning yachting club (£1.5 m) – settled in 1 day.

- Defamation case between Premier football club and national broadsheet newspaper – settled in 1 day.

- Land dispute with Formula One company (£350,000) – settled in 1 day.

- Football club contract (£400,000) – settled in 1 day.

- Contract over a gliding club (£50,000) – settled in 1 day.

- Ground dispute between two rugby clubs (£500,000) – settled in 1 day.

- Shooting club and game (pheasant) supplier (£120,000) – settled in 1 day.[80]

Likewise, brief details of some sports disputes recently mediated by the ADR Group follow:

January 2000: a personal injury case involving a sportswoman injured in a track and field event (value about £150,000) was referred to mediation but did not proceed due to the parties settling after mediation was proposed. The other side was a Sports Council body. In my experience a small percentage of cases (5%) settle after the parties agree to mediate but before the edition take place – it appears that when parties begin to prepare for a mediation they get into 'settlement mode' and reach agreement without the mediator.

- January 2000: a personal injury action where a female spectator at a sports event sat on a fixed fold-down plastic chair which collapsed causing her severe back injury. The case was in excess of £200,000. It was mediated within three weeks of being referred to the ADR Group and was successfully settled. The other side was Trust responsible for the stadium.

- April 2000: the ADR Group was instructed to mediate in a case involving a disputed sporting goods and clothing sale and distribution agreement. The value was not that high (approx £80,000) but the parties wanted to mediate to try and preserve their existing business relationship. One party was the sports clothing manufacturer and the other was a high street sports retailer. Unfortunately the case did not settle on the day, although all parties felt the process had been tremendously useful in narrowing the issues in dispute. The case settled within a month of the mediation in bringing the parties closer together and enabled the settlement to be achieved after the mediation.

- All the above cases took place on a single day. The ADR Group try to arrange for all of the above mediations to take place on a single day, although we recognise that 'mega-mediations' may require more than a single day. In most of our cases mediation results in significant savings in legal costs.[81]

---

79   For further information, refer to ASA Legal Affairs Dept; see www.britishswimming.org.
80   CEDR report to author (2001).
81   CEDR Civil Justice Audit Conference (2001).

So, mediation was a great success in the *Woodhall/Warren* case and the majority of the other CEDR and ADR Group mediated sports disputes mentioned above. But, it must be said, mediation does have some limitations.

Mediation Limitations

Mediation, as a method of settling sports disputes (as opined by Lord Irvine), is not a panacea. Although it works in most cases, it does not work in all. Mediation is not suitable in those cases in which a legal precedent or an injunction is required – it is not, as previously noted, a legally based process. Neither is mediation appropriate where a sports body needs to make a public example of another party to the dispute in order to act as a deterrent to others. This point is illustrated by the banning by the FA of the Arsenal manager, Arsene Wenger, from the touchline for four weeks for 'threatening behaviour and physical intimidation' of an official.[82] He was also fined four weeks' wages amounting to £100,000. This sort of case raises a point of principle on which the FA is unlikely to compromise in a mediation, especially as the FA wishes to enforce its new hard-hitting disciplinary code of conduct designed to preserve the integrity of the game of football.

Being a voluntary and non-binding process until a settlement is agreed, written down and signed by the parties, mediation is not suitable either in those cases where the parties are not interested in trying to find a settlement by mediation or extra-judicial means. For example, the Rugby Football Union (RFU) is attempting to resolve a major dispute between the two top divisions in English rugby union involving 26 professional clubs and has suggested mediation. The chairman of the RFU considers that appointing an independent third party with specialist skills in resolving difficult disputes is the right way forward, whilst the head of English First Division Rugby is reported in 2000 as saying: 'It wouldn't make any difference if they brought the Queen in to arbitrate.'[83] The RFU may consider that mediation is a good idea, but if the teams in dispute do not, mediation will not work in such a case. Again, if the full glare of publicity is important, mediation is not the kind of dispute resolution method to adopt. It is an entirely confidential process.

Neither is mediation suitable for resolving doping and other disciplinary cases. Indeed, as has previously been noted, the mediation procedure of the CAS is expressly excluded for dealing with such cases (and this is also the considered opinion of David Richbell, Training Director of CEDR). Mediation may, however, be useful for dealing with the commercial fall out from such cases – for example, claims for financial compensation for losses suffered as a result of a wrongful 'conviction'.

The well known Dianne Modahl doping case would be a good example for mediation in relation to the financial claims and losses the athlete is currently seeking to recover, as a result of having been exonerated from taking a banned performance enhancing substance, from her world governing body, the International Amateur Athletic Federation, that wrongly imposed the suspension from competition in the first place. In deciding, however, whether mediation is suitable or not, it is often said by protagonists of mediation that the question to be asked is not 'is mediation appropriate?' but rather 'why is mediation not appropriate?' Each case has to be considered on its own merits.

Of the various forms of ADR available, it has already been noted above that mediation is proving to be a popular and effective means of settling disputes generally and is also gaining favour in the

---

82   *The Times*, 10 October 2000.
83   *The Guardian*, 20 October 2000.

sports arena. A number of sports bodies offer mediation, as an alternative to arbitration, as a means of settling sports disputes – or more correctly 'sports related' disputes.

The mediation competence of CAS will be examined together with the new UK Sports Dispute Resolution Panel (SDRP). As sport is now global in nature and disputes often transcend national boundaries and arise in various parts of the world, the mediation services offered by the Australian National Sports Disputes Centre, based in Sydney, and the conciliation procedure offered by a non-sports body, the International Chamber of Commerce, based in Paris, will also be examined.

CAS Mediation Process

The CAS is dedicated to hearing and settling any disputes directly or indirectly relating to sport, including commercial issues; for example, a dispute over a sponsorship contract. Any natural person, for example, an athlete, or legal person, for example, a sports association or a company, may bring a case before the CAS. The parties must agree to do so in writing. In May 1999, the CAS introduced a mediation service:

CAS Mediation Rules, Article 1, para 1

CAS Mediation is a non-binding and informal procedure, based on a mediation agreement in which each party undertakes to attempt in good faith to negotiate with the other party, and with the assistance of a CAS mediator, with a view to settling a sports-related dispute.[84]

The second paragraph of this article goes on to limit mediation to disputes under what is called the 'CAS ordinary procedure', and to exclude mediation in relation to any decision passed by a sports organisation and also disputes related to disciplinary matters and doping issues. The CAS ordinary procedure applies to cases brought in the CAS Ordinary Division, which is dedicated to resolving commercial disputes.

The CAS Mediation Rules ('the Rules') are as follows. A 'mediation agreement' is defined as one whereby the parties agree to submit existing or future sports related disputes to mediation, and further provides that it may take the form of a separate agreement or a mediation clause in a contract.[85] Such a clause may be along the lines, *mutatis mutandis*, of the following standard so-called 'comprehensive clause' of the ADR Group:

ADR Group, 'comprehensive clause'

In the event of any dispute arising between the parties in connection with this [agreement] [contract] the parties will in good faith seek to resolve that dispute through mediation under the auspices of the [ADR Group]. The mediator shall be agreed upon within [15] days of one party requesting mediation, failing which the mediator shall be appointed by the then President of The Law Society. Unless otherwise agreed the parties shall share equally the costs of the mediation. If the dispute is not resolved within [30] days, or one of the parties refuses to participate in mediation, the dispute shall be referred to [arbitration in accordance with the rules of the Chartered Institute of Arbitrators, whose rules are deemed to be incorporated by reference into this clause] or [litigation]. Nothing in this clause shall prevent either party seeking a preliminary injunction or other judicial relief at any time if in its judgement such action is necessary to prevent irreparable damage.[86]

---

84 CAS Mediation Rules (May 1999).

85 *Ibid*, Art 2.

86 The reference to the President of the Law Society may be considered to be vague and held to be invalid for uncertainty under English contract law, because there is more than one Law Society in the UK. To avoid this result, the correct reference should be to 'The Law Society of England and Wales'.

For agreements involving one or more non-UK parties, it is suggested that the London Court of International Arbitration be substituted for the Chartered Institute of Arbitrators as the arbitral body. Likewise, in relation to international mediations, the mediation clause should also include provisions on the language to be used in the mediation and who is responsible for providing necessary translations and who pays for them. Except where the parties agree otherwise, the version of the Rules in force at the time the written request for mediation is filed at the CAS shall apply.[87] Apparently, the parties may agree to apply other rules of procedure.[88]

The President of the CAS chooses the mediator from the list of CAS mediators, who, in turn, are chosen from the list of CAS arbitrators or from outside, where the parties themselves cannot agree on the mediator. The mediator appointed must be and remain independent of the parties.[89] The parties may be represented or assisted in their meetings with the mediator.[90] In line with the procedures of the CAS generally, the person representing the parties need not be a lawyer or legally qualified. The procedure to be followed in the mediation shall either be agreed by the parties themselves or determined by the mediator.[91] This is a slight deviation from the general principle, noted above, that the mediator is the one who controls the procedural aspects of the mediation.[92]

The mediation process is confidential and also lays down and spells out the 'without prejudice' principle on which the mediation shall be conducted.[93] There are provisions dealing with the questions of when and how the mediation may be terminated.[94] Any settlement of the mediation must be in writing and signed by the mediator and the parties.[95] There are provisions in the case of a failure to settle.[96]

Concerning the costs of the mediation,[97] in typical Swiss style, until the CAS fee is paid, the mediation proceedings cannot be started, and the CAS Court Office may require the parties to deposit an equal amount as an advance towards the mediation costs. The parties are required to pay their own mediation costs and share equally the other costs, which include the CAS fee, the mediator's fees, a contribution towards the costs of the CAS, and the fees of the witnesses, experts and interpreters. It may be mentioned here that the working languages of the CAS are French and English and, in the absence of agreement between the parties, the CAS shall select one of the two languages as the language of the proceedings. The parties can choose another language provided the court agrees, in which case the CAS may order the parties to pay all or part of the translation costs.[98]

Since its introduction on 18 May 1999, the CAS has only dealt with six mediations. Two of them related to administrative disputes involving International Sports Federations; the other four

---

87   *Op cit*, fn 84, CAS Mediation Rules (1999), Art 4.
88   *Ibid*, Art 3.
89   *Ibid*, Art 6.
90   *Ibid*, Art 7.
91   *Ibid*, Art 8.
92   *Ibid*, Art 9.
93   *Ibid*, Art 10.
94   Ibid, Art 11.
95   *Ibid*, Art 12.
96   *Ibid*, Art 13.
97   *Ibid*, Art 14.
98   CAS Procedural Rules, r 29.

concerned commercial disputes. On the whole, these CAS mediations led to settlements of the respective disputes.[99]

SDRP Mediation

The UK SDRP also offers a mediation service for the settlement of sports disputes.[100] Support has been given for the use of the SDRP in:

... resolving drugs cases through the new independent Sports Dispute Resolution Panel, and not through the disciplinary systems of individual sports' governing bodies.[101]

There are limits to mediation, however. Sports governing bodies jealously guard their rights and powers over disciplinary matters in their sports, and doping cases are not a suitable subject for mediation.[102]

The National Sports Dispute Centre

The National Sports Dispute Centre (NSDC), based in Sydney, Australia, was established in January 1996, to provide 'an inexpensive, fast and effective means of resolving sports disputes'.

NSDC Brochure

Sporting disputes have become an epidemic in Australia in the last five years. No longer are sports disputes settled by a friendly argument between mates over a beer. Sport is big business. Even amateur sports cannot escape the potential for a dispute. Faced with potential high costs, time delay and pressure associated with Court proceedings, sports organisations have been crying out for an alternative.[103]

It offers arbitration and mediation in 'sporting disputes', which it defines as 'including any dispute involving a person or organisation which has a connection with sport'.[104] It defines mediation as 'a process designed to assist parties resolve their dispute by agreement' and describes the mediator as 'an independent neutral third party who does not make a decision for the parties but facilitates honest and open discussions between them on all the matters raised'.[105]

The NSDC is an independent organisation jointly operated by the Australian Olympic Committee, the Australian Sports Commission, the Australian and New Zealand Sports Law Association and the Confederation of Australian Sport. It is managed by a Board comprising four experienced sports lawyers and administrators appointed by each of these four constituent bodies. Its mediation services are available to any individual, company or organisation whose activities are

---

99 For more details, see Blackshaw, I, 'The Court of Arbitration for Sport: An International Forum for Settling Disputes Effectively 'Within the Family of Sport' (2003) 2(2) *Entertainment Law*; also see Lazic, V, 'Conference on ADR in sports disputes' (2001) 5/6 International Sports Law Journal 35 for details of CAS held Symposium on 'ADR in Sports Disputes' at its headquarters in Lausanne on 3 and 4 November 2000.

100 Mediation rules can be found at www.sportsdisputes.co.uk.

101 Kate Hoey, the former UK Sports Minister, is quoted in Goodbody, J, 'Hoey aims to give Britain sporting chance' *The Times*, 12 July 2000, as saying that she favours using the SDRP for the settlement of all sports disputes, including doping cases.

102 See below, p 280.

103 Preamble to NSDC Brochure.

104 *Ibid*, para 2 of the NSDC Mediation Process.

105 *Ibid*, para 3.

sports related, including athletes, sports governing bodies, organising committees, sponsors and companies involved in sports broadcasting, print and electronic media.

Use of the services of the NSDC are purely voluntary: the NSDC can only act if the parties to a sports dispute agree, either at the time the dispute arises, or previously if agreed in the relevant rules or contract. So far, the NSDC has been requested to intervene in a wide range of sports cases, including the following:

- Disputes between athletes and sports bodies over such matters as selection, discrimination, restraint of trade;

- Disputes between athletes or event promoters or organisations and sponsors over money due or alleged failure to perform under sponsorship agreements;

- Disputes over television broadcast rights;

- Disputes between sports federations at different levels (eg between a state and a national organisation);

- Disputes between administrators and a sports organisation over employment issues;

- Disputes and appeals over penalties imposed by disciplinary tribunals including natural justice claims;

- Disputes between different sports over athletes involved in more than one sport over the use of venues;

- Damage claims by athletes for sports injuries.[106]

The NSDC has also been involved in the following matters:

- Nominating an independent person to oversee the review of a sports organisation's decision in relation to a coaching appointment;

- Convening a panel for conducting hearings for breaches of doping policies;

- Conducting tribunal hearings in relation to selection appeals;

- Appointing experts to sit on disciplinary tribunals;

- Providing referrals to qualified sports lawyers; and

- Assisting in mediation processes for sports bodies and athletes.[107]

And, according to Mark Fewel, mediation:

> ... is ideally suited to situations where disputes arise quickly, and need to be resolved quickly ... [and] ... [t]he business of sport certainly fits into this category.[108]

Doyle, B, 'Sports dispute resolution in Australia'

In 1992 the Australian and New Zealand Sports Law Association (ANZSLA) at its annual conference held a session specifically directed towards dispute resolution. At that time there were no facilities

---

106 *Ibid*, NSDC Brochure. Further information about the NSDC can be obtained from Tim Frampton, President of the Australia and New Zealand Sports Lawyers' Association, at the Law Firm of O'Donnell Frampton Salzano, Melbourne, Australia by email: tframpton@odonfs.com.au.

107 *Ibid*.

108 A member of the Board of the NSDC.

available in Australia that could effectively avoid the civil court system with all its disadvantages of expense, delay and the fracturing of sporting relationships.

The meeting urged the establishment of a registry of the Court of Arbitration for Sport to cover the Oceania region, and the Executor Director of the Confederation of Australian Sport (the umbrella organisation that lobbies on behalf of most Australian sports) called for the establishment of an independent disputes resolution service to be established for all sports when he said:

> The reality is that there are going to be severe disputes in sport which inevitably end up in the courts. Sport is emotional, it involves complicated commercial arrangements, it is often about personal and organisational power. It is multi-faceted and involves a veritable kaleidoscope of opinions – nearly all of them 'expert'. Ask an athlete, a coach, an administrator and a neutral observer about a sporting issue and receive four different perspectives.

Shortly after that conference ANZSLA prepared an issues paper on the role of alternative dispute resolution in sport, and that eventually led to the establishment of the ANZSLA Dispute Resolution Scheme which was launched at the Auckland annual conference in 1995.

The service had a number of arms:

- mediation
- arbitration
- providing assistance to sporting judiciaries/tribunals, and
- providing suitable people to carry out expert investigations.

The proposal for a separate mediation service was to overcome what we saw as a problem within the Court of Arbitration for Sport where the arbitrators were firstly to try to settle the dispute. Most people involved in mediation or arbitration accept that to try to settle a dispute, and in doing so hear the issues and the arguments, can cause a difficulty in then sitting as an arbitrator.

Perhaps the CAS arbitrators got over this by paying lip service to the requirement to mediate. There was an overwhelming response from qualified arbitrators and mediators with that special interest in sport that we required, and panels were formed throughout the States of Australia and in New Zealand. The value of having qualified people available to conduct independent inquiries was seen in the appointment of the then President of ANZSLA Hayden Opie to investigate problems within the gymnastics section of the Australian Institute of Sport. Allegations had been raised by (mostly) parents of some of the younger girls attending the Institute as to the conduct of some of the staff. Mr Opie conducted a long and very searching inquiry that required him to travel throughout Australia before presenting a very thorough report to the Australian Sports Commission.

The service suffered from lack of resources and funds but was nevertheless able to provide assistance to a number of sports in dispute.

In 1996 the establishment of an Oceania Registry of the Court of Arbitration for Sport in Sydney was announced. With the Olympic Games of 2000 being conducted in that city it was considered a priority to have a court up and running in the lead in to the Games.

At the same time the Australian Olympic Committee, the Confederation of Australian Sport, the Australian Sports Commission (ASC – the arm of the Federal Government that administers sport in Australia) and ANZSLA reached agreement on the establishment of a National Sports Dispute Centre Pty Limited (NSDC). Each of those organisations jointly owns an equal share in and operates the Centre, with a Director from each organisation and an appointed Registrar who is assisted in carrying out his duties by funding from the ASC.

The NSDC essentially took over the ANZSLA Dispute Resolution Service, and provides a:

- mediation,
- arbitration

- tribunal service.
- (and through its close association with ANZSLA) it can supply the names of qualified lawyers to people involved in the sports industry.

NSDC is a non-profit organisation, and its objective is to provide quick and inexpensive access to its services. There are no fees for general inquiries and the referral service, but parties using the mediation and arbitration service pay a fee, originally $100 and now $250 each. The costs of meeting rooms, mediator and arbitrators' fees are paid for by the parties.

The Centre provides:

- a quick decision
- an arbitrator (mediator) who is experienced in sports related disputes
- confidentiality
- a cost-effective system compared to court costs.

By way of example of its effectiveness during 1999 I was asked to assist in a dispute involving an Olympic sport – a minor sport in Australia. There had been allegations of sexual discrimination made against the national coach and when reported to the National Sports Disputes Centre on a Wednesday the Registrar was advised that the national team was due to depart for Europe on the following Monday. I was able to bring the witnesses together in Melbourne and travelled there (some 1,200 kilometres from my office) for interviews on the Friday, conducted a day long investigation and was able to speak with the President of the Sport on the Friday evening in Sydney and submit a written report to the Board of the sport by Saturday morning. The NSDC were able to satisfy their requirements of a relatively inexpensive inquiry, conducted promptly and with confidentiality.

Matters come to the Centre through provisions within constitutions and contracts that provide for disputes to be referred to the Centre or by agreement between the parties when the dispute arises. By way of example other disputes that have come before the NSDC include:

- nomination of independent persons to oversee the review of a sports organisation's decision on a coaching appointment
- convening of panels to conduct hearings for breaches of doping policies
- conducting tribunal hearings in respect of selection appeals.

The service currently suffers from a lack of publicity, however efforts are being made at the present time to remedy this by the distribution of brochures advertising the service through all sporting organisations. To some degree there may be competition between the service and CAS.

Currently within Australia there is a spate of selection disputes arising from the nomination of teams for the Olympic Games. The AOC has directed those disputes to CAS by requiring each of the Olympic sports to enter into contracts with their athletes to abide by a nomination criteria whereby their appeal rights are restricted to, initially an internal appeals tribunal within the sport, and thereafter to CAS. These appeals are to the exclusion of the ordinary courts of the land.

The value of the NSDC has been proved. Its future success will depend upon financing from the Australian Sports Commission, its ability to continue to publicise itself and the enthusiasm of the lawyers who sit as mediators, arbitrators or investigators.[109]

---

109 Doyle, B, 'Sports dispute resolution in Australia' (2000) 3(4) Sports Law Bulletin 13.

Conciliation by the International Chamber of Commerce (ICC)

As previously mentioned, sport is now a global business and, as such, many sports related disputes are international in nature and scope. For many years, international business disputes of various kinds have been successfully referred to arbitration by the ICC, based in Paris.[110]

Conciliation under such a prestigious, experienced, professional and independent body as the ICC – considered to be the world's leading business organisation – is another dispute resolution tool available to parties involved in all kinds of international commercial disputes, including sports related ones, which, in relation to the latter, it is suggested, may be overlooked at their peril. Furthermore, as doubts continue to be expressed about the independence of the CAS, despite the creation and interposition of the International Council of Arbitration for Sport, pursuant to the 'Paris Agreement' of 22 June 1994, this could be another reason for parties to international sports disputes opting for the conciliation services of a completely independent body such as the ICC.

EVALUATION OF SPORTS MEDIATION

Reasons for its Success

Although it has certain limitations, mediation is generally proving itself to be a modern effective alternative method of resolving disputes in general. As the *Woodhall/Warren* and other sports cases show (eg the dispute between Ellery Hanley, the rugby league coach, and his club's directors over some unflattering remarks he made publicly about them), mediation can be a most suitable way of settling sports disputes quickly, effectively and relatively cheaply.

The success of mediation in the *Woodhall/Warren* case is a clear sign that resort to the courts is no longer the only and perhaps not the best way of resolving disputes. And it also shows that opting for mediation should no longer be regarded as a sign of weakness on the part of any of the parties. As Frank Warren remarked: 'It was important to all concerned to have brought this matter to a speedy conclusion. We have shaken hands and look forward to resuming our successful partnership.'[111] For Richie Woodhall, speed was also 'of the essence': 'I am pleased this episode has now come to an end. I can tell my fans that I will be back in the ring within the next few weeks.'[112]

Mediation generally offers many advantages over traditional dispute resolution methods. In the sports field, in particular, the attraction of mediation has been well summarised by Frank Warren's Lawyer, Dominic Bray, in the following terms:

> Mediation can have real benefits, not only in terms of savings of management time and money, but also, and perhaps more significantly, in the preservation of ongoing relationships between the parties. These relationships are fundamental to any business, but particularly so in the sporting context.[113]

Not only must the case be suitable for mediation, but the success of the mediation will also, to a large extent, depend upon the qualities and skills of the mediator. On this point, Woodhall's lawyer,

---

110 ICC International Court of Arbitration – Rules of Arbitration and Conciliation, March 1999.
111 CEDR Press Release of 21 July 1999.
112 *Ibid.*
113 *Ibid.*

Richard Cramer, remarked: 'The mediator proved to be a very positive feature and focused the parties' minds on settlement.'[114]

He or she needs to have knowledge and understanding of sport as well as being a good mediator. As Robert Barker, a former Senior International In-house Counsel for The Coca-Cola Company, one of the world's major sponsors of major international sports events, including the Summer and Winter Olympic Games, has remarked in relation to the handling of sports disputes:

> If mediation . . . [is] required . . . traditional mediators . . . may not serve you well . . . [t]hey are not skilled in the industry of sports . . . sport is a unique industry . . . [and] . . . produces a product – a sporting event – that excites emotion in the industry's consumers. Emotion is a contributing factor to its uniqueness.[115]

In view of sport's uniqueness, he points out that, if, for instance, an intellectual property issue arises in connection with a sports dispute:

> . . . traditional mediators . . . are not skilled in the finer issues of intellectual property . . . [which] . . . is its own law merchant, and it probably does little good to have a [mediator] who will not recognise an IP right just because it might not be recognised at law . . . Like our judicial system today, traditional neutrals [ie mediators] tend to want to render equitable rulings, rather than enforcing the rights in a contract – particularly if those rights are hard fought and harsh . . . There is a need for a global solution to sport problems, not just solutions based on a case-by-case negotiation. If you are acting in a particular sector or sub-industry, encourage those in the industry to create a standard for mediation . . . Some sports lawyers are lucky enough today to be defining the rules for new leagues and sports for tomorrow. They should consider writing ADR into the governing documents of their leagues – and make it condition for all contracts with outsider parties.[116]

It is in the light of remarks such as these that suitably qualified mediators need to be chosen if the mediation is to be a successful one.

Mediation 'On Line'

With the rise and increasing use of the internet, it is not surprising that mediation 'on line', using video conferencing, is now being offered to parties in dispute. Where? In the US, of course. It will be interesting to see how this method of mediating develops. It would certainly seem to be attractive in international commercial disputes and, with access to the 'world wide web' becoming more widespread and the cost of going 'on line' becoming cheaper, it must save time and money, both of which are precious commodities as far as business people are concerned.[117]

Mediation by telephone is also now becoming popular and more use of this medium is being made. As mentioned above, the ADR Group offers a telephone mediation service. However, face to face discussions are, in the writer's view, more preferable as personal interaction and 'body language' are fundamental elements in the success of any mediation.[118]

---

114 *Ibid.*
115 *Resolving Sports Conflicts Centers on Rights' Analysis*, Center for Public Resources (CPR), New York, USA: info@cpradr.org.
116 *Ibid.*
117 For further information on the potential of 'On line dispute resolution' ('ODR' as it is known) for settling a range of commercial and other disputes, see Katsh, E and Rifkin, J, *Online Dispute Resolution: Resolving Conflicts in Cyberspace* (2001), London: Jossey-Bass.
118 Incidentally, it is not unknown for 'hearings' before the Court of Arbitration for Sport to be held by telephone – using conference calls and other 'hook-ups' – where the parties and their representatives (especially their lawyers) are spread across more than one continent or hemisphere.

Some International Experiences

In France, there is a special law of 13 July 1992 relating to the settlement of sports disputes by arbitration and mediation. This law has been strengthened by another law of 6 July 2000. Mediation is usually attempted in disputes between leading footballers (eg d'Anelka, Ginola and Vieira) and French and European football clubs, through the competent National Federations and/or FIFA, before invoking EU law.

In Germany, most of the national sports bodies, including the German Football Association, now include mediation in their statutes as a dispute resolution procedure, although, to date, mediation has been little used in sports cases.

Surprisingly, in the US – the home of ADR – mediation in sports disputes is also still, relatively speaking, virgin territory:

> ... mediation merits much greater attention than it has had as an alternative to both forms of adjudication – arbitration and litigation. In fact, of course, much informal mediation does go on, but is seldom reported.[119]

However, China, where a National Sports Policy is developing, is 'in the vanguard of the global trend' as far as the use of ADR, as a primary form of dispute resolution, is concerned.[120]

Internet Disputes and Mediation

The phenomenal rise in the popularity and use of the internet – not least in relation to sports content – has spawned its own peculiar kinds of disputes and produced a particular kind of mediation for settling them.[121]

For example, 'cybersquatting', which is abusive registration of 'domain names', is subject to a particular form of adjudication process under the auspices of the World Intellectual Property Organisation (WIPO), a specialised agency of the UN, headquartered in Geneva, Switzerland. Abusive registration of a domain name occurs where:

- a domain name complained of is identical or confusingly similar to a trade mark of another;
- is registered by a party who has no rights or legitimate interest in that domain name; and
- the domain name in question is registered and used in bad faith.

All three conditions must be satisfied for the complainant to succeed.

As to the bad faith requirement, the ICANN (Internet Corporation for Assigned Names and Numbers) Uniform Domain Name Dispute Resolution Policy provides examples of acts, which *prima facie* constitute evidence of bad faith. They are as follows:

- offering to sell the domain name to the trade mark owner or its competitor;
- an attempt to attract for financial gain internet users by creating confusion with the trade mark of another;

---

119 Author's conversation with James Nafziger
120 Nafziger, J and Li, W, 'China's sports law' (1999) AJCL.
121 See Blackshaw, I, 'Settling Sports Disputes in Cyberspace' (2004) 1, The International Sports Law Journal.

- registration of a domain name in order to prevent the trade mark owner from reflecting his trade mark in a corresponding domain name; and

- registration of the domain name in order to disrupt the business of the competitor.

Using the WIPO adjudication procedure, a number of sports disputes have been quickly and effectively settled – not surprisingly, over the internet itself!

For example, FIFA successfully challenged the use of its trade mark 'world cup' in 13 domain names by another party who had used some of the domain names in the address of his website, which not only related to the FIFA event, but also included copyrighted content from FIFA's official website.[122] In addition, the other party contacted FIFA with an offer to sell some of the domain names concerned prior to FIFA filing the complaint. WIPO found bad faith and ordered the other party to transfer those domain names to FIFA. However, in the same proceeding, WIPO refused to order the transfer of two competing domain names consisting of the letters 'wc', holding that these would not be unequivocally seen as an abbreviation of the name 'world cup' and were not sufficiently distinctive to constitute a trade mark. In line with this decision, WIPO disallowed a complaint made by a group of companies involved in the organisation of the Formula One Grand Prix Motor Racing Championship against the use of the domain name 'f1.com', on the grounds that 'F1' was its famous trade mark and an abbreviation of the mark 'Formula 1'. WIPO held that, because the trade mark 'F1' consists merely of a single letter and a numeral, it was not sufficiently distinctive. In order to claim a monopoly right over the use of the abbreviation 'F1', proof of considerable use of this mark would need to be adduced. Although the complainants were able to establish some reputation in this mark, they were not able to show that its use was so widespread as to be able to claim that any commercial use of it implied a connection with their activities.

On the other hand, a complaint by Jordan, owner of the Formula One motor racing team and proprietor of the registered trade mark 'JORDAN GRAND PRIX', as well as the domain name jordangp.com, against the use of the domain name jordanf1.com, was upheld by WIPO.[123] They considered that there was a real danger of confusion in this case, bearing in mind that the name Jordan is well known as being associated with Formula One and both the expressions 'Grand Prix', which forms part of its trade mark, and 'F1' will be associated with motor racing and therefore with Jordan. There was also other evidence of bad faith, including the fact that the other party had offered to sell the offending domain name to Jordan.

Complaints against other sporting domain names, uefachampionsleague.com and niketown.com, by UEFA and NIKE Inc respectively were also successfully and quickly resolved using the WIPO adjudication process.[124]

More recently, the WIPO domain names dispute resolution procedure was also successfully invoked in the 'f1.ferrari.com' case. A certain enterprising South Korean lady from Seoul, one Ms Lee Jo-Hee, had registered – but not used – the domain name 'f1.ferrari.com' with the domain registry 'eNom.' Ferrari were not best pleased with this unauthorised use of their famous name and trade mark in connection with their well-known Formula One sporting activities. So they complained on 5 November 2003 to WIPO. Ms Lee was given until 2 December 2003 to answer the complaint, but failed to do so. Within a week, a sole 'expert' adjudicator had been appointed to resolve the matter.

---

122 Case D2000–0034 *ISL Marketing AG and The Federation Internationale de Football Association v JY Chung*, 3 April 2000.

123 Case D2000–0233 *Jordan Grand Prix Ltd v Sweeney*, 11 May 2000.

124 Case D2000-0153 *Union des Associations Europeennes de Football v Alliance International Media*, 25 April 2000; Case D2000-0108 *NIKE Inc v Granger & Associates*, 2 May 2000.

On 18 December 2003, the expert found all the complaints of Ferrari proved and ordered the registry to transfer the domain name to them. In particular, the adjudicator considered that Ms Lee's use of such a well known trade mark as FERRARI – details of trade mark registrations held by them world wide running to some 103 pages, each page listing around 10 to 20 such registrations, had been submitted to him – without having any connection with the complainant was in itself evidence of 'opportunistic bad faith'. And there was further evidence of bad faith in that the telephone and fax numbers given by Ms Lee to the domain registry were false.

The Ferrari case is not only interesting for the speed in which it was dealt with – in just over a month – but also because, although there was no active use by the other party of the disputed domain name, the mere holding of it, although passive, was, in the view of the adjudicator, sufficient to constitute the legal requirement of 'bad faith'. He was following the test established in an earlier WIPO cybersquatting case, in which it was said that 'the relevant issue was not whether the other party was undertaking a positive action in bad faith in relation to the domain name, but instead whether, in all the circumstances of the case, it could be said that the other party was acting in bad faith.'[125]

However, as the above cases illustrate, all claims of 'cybersquatting' on the internet are decided on their own particular facts and merits, in line with the above bad faith criteria.

A SPORTS OMBUDSMAN?

Finally, for the sake of completeness, a word or two about a novel idea for settling sports disputes extra-judicially à la mediation: a Sports Ombudsman.

Morris, P, 'The role of the Ombudsman in sporting disputes: some personal thoughts'

The apparently relentless juridification of much professional sport both in the United Kingdom and abroad, which is an inevitable consequence of the massive commercial interests in the structures, processes and outcomes of modern sport, has prompted debate about the appropriate mechanisms for dispute resolution. The initial enthusiasm which accompanied increasing judicial intervention in sports administration has begun to wane, largely because of an increasing realisation that high profile, bitterly fought court battles between athletes and governing bodies do not necessarily serve the long term interests of sports governing bodies, athletes or indeed the sport itself. While academic and practising lawyers may view long running legal conflicts involving the likes of Jean-Marc Bosman, Butch Reynolds, Tonya Harding and Diane Modahl as providing fertile ground for research projects and fee income, these disputes leave significant problems in their wake.

While I can accept that some sporting disputes may make a significant and lasting contribution to the development of national and international sports law jurisprudence as well as leading to structural changes in a particular sport for the enduring benefit of athletes (*Bosman* is perhaps *the* outstanding example of this) I would, on an objective cost-benefit analysis, express serious concerns about the utility of court involvement in most sporting disputes. The costs, antagonism, bad publicity and (all too frequently) ineffectual remedies awarded all make a compelling case for confining court intervention to disputes raising novel or crucial issues of sporting or legal policy where a clear, binding precedent is of overriding importance. To argue in favour of a shift toward a greater measure of self-regulation is of course not new. What *is* now urgently needed though is a balanced assessment of the various modes

---

125 A full report on the Ferrrari case can be found at http://arbiter.wipo.int/domains/decisions/html/2003/d2003–0882.html.

of alternative dispute resolution potentially on offer, the interaction between them and whether it might be possible to design an integrated national and international sports dispute resolution structure.

Completion of this project requires sports lawyers to think seriously about the utility of the Ombudsman technique as a mechanism of redress. No longer confined to the province of government, Ombudsmen are now well entrenched both in the professions and in the financial services sector both in the United Kingdom and abroad. Indeed this year has witnessed the creation of a 'super' Financial Services Ombudsman scheme for the United Kingdom. The scheme is the largest Ombudsman institution in the world with 330 employees and an annual operating budget expected to exceed £20 million. In principle there is no reason why, albeit on a self-regulatory and much smaller basis, this model could not be replicated by major United Kingdom sports governing bodies. The obvious objection is that there is no room or need for the Ombudsman technique given the existence of distinct arbitration schemes operated by some governing bodies, the recent launch of the United Kingdom Sports Dispute Resolution Panel and, on the international plane, the increasingly important contribution of the Court of Arbitration for Sport.

Without wishing to understate the work of these bodies there are key advantages, I believe, offered by the Ombudsman model in the sporting context:

- An Ombudsman, unlike arbitration techniques, is not confined to strict legal standards but can draw upon his/her own subjective notions of fairness and good administration which together furnish athletes with enhanced protection.

- In performance of his/her adjudication and conciliation functions an Ombudsman does not characteristically focus on redress of individual grievance but may also use a complaint as a vehicle for improving administrative practices within the industry (the so-called 'quality control' dimension of an Ombudsman's work).

- Arbitration mechanisms continue to suffer from the lingering suspicion by athletes (even one as prestigious and well established as the Court of Arbitration for Sport) that they are not truly independent of governing bodies whereas Ombudsmen schemes can be designed, as the United Kingdom financial services industry experience shows, in such a way as to allay any such fears.

- Unlike arbitration, with its reliance on formal, court like hearings, Ombudsmen tend to prefer the use of inquisitorial, paper-based investigations which are user-friendly and more conducive to continuing harmonious relations between the athlete and the governing body.

- Where a dispute raises legal or policy issues more appropriately determined by a court it is possible, by use of a 'test cases' clause in the Ombudsman's terms of reference, to provide for the timely transfer of the dispute to a court provided the complainant consents and with the sports governing body meeting the erstwhile complainant's legal costs.

If one accepts the case for United Kingdom Sports Ombudsman the next issue is to delineate its main features. It could, I think, be created on a self-regulatory basis using the same 'blue print' as existing private sector schemes, that is to say membership of a private company, an independent Ombudsman Council to perform a 'buffer' function between the sponsoring governing bodies and the Ombudsman and a separate Board, composed of a majority of sports' governing bodies representatives, raising the finance for the scheme which would take the form of a fixed levy and a case fee for every formal complaint lodged with the Ombudsman.

Given the self-regulatory character of the scheme, achieving comprehensive membership by United Kingdom governing bodies would rest, ultimately, on persuading them of the benefits of membership in terms of cheapness, speed, informality and privacy compared with litigation and traditional arbitration. To avoid charges of ousting the athlete's 'constitutional' right of access to court for a determination as to his/her legal rights, use of the Ombudsman should be voluntary with a right to reject the Ombudsman's eventual recommendation and pursue the matter in court. I very much doubt whether many would opt to do so given that the Ombudsman unlike a court enjoys the capacity to transcend the parameters of legality by applying any relevant code of practice and his own subjective standards of fairness and good administrative practices.

Finally, if Ombudsman schemes along similar lines were established in other sporting nations an embryonic international extra-judicial dispute resolution structure could emerge by incorporating a final right of appeal for either party to the Court of Arbitration for Sport on the ground that the dispute involves important or novel issues of sports law or policy. The proliferation of national Sporting Ombudsmen and their integration with the Court in this manner could extend and strengthen its role as a pivotal institution in the development of a coherent and sophisticated corpus of sports law jurisprudence.[126]

Whilst recognising that the arbitration and mediation services offered by the SDRP and CAS may make a Sports Ombudsman redundant, Morris mentions a number of advantages that an Ombudsman could offer in the sporting context. An Ombudsman can draw on his/her own notions of fairness and good administration, thus enhancing the protection of athletes. An Ombudsman in performing his/her conciliation functions can not only provide redress, but also use a complaint for improving practices within the sports 'industry' (the so-called 'quality control' dimension). An Ombudsman acts totally independently of any sports bodies or interests.

The writer, having had a good and wide professional experience of the work of Ombudsmen in the Scandinavian countries in settling consumer disputes in relation to advertising and marketing complaints, considers that the idea of a Sports Ombudsman is worth pursuing. This is especially so if, as Morris also suggests, Ombudsman schemes are established in other sporting nations as part of what he calls 'an international extra-judicial resolution structure'.

Certainly, as sport has become transnational, there is a need for a coherent international sports disputes structure, which relies on effective alternative forms of dispute resolution whenever and wherever appropriate.

CONCLUSIONS ON ADR IN SPORTS DISPUTES

Alternative methods of dispute resolution are proving to have valuable advantages to offer to sport in appropriate cases, including speed, confidentiality and cheapness. Many sports bodies and other organisations have recognised this and are offering – and also promoting – arbitration, mediation and conciliation services at national and international levels.[127]

Much depends, as we have seen, on the personal skills and experience of the arbitrators and mediators, but success equally depends on the willingness of the parties to settle their disputes amicably and informally, wherever possible, and not regard this kind of approach as a sign of weakness.

As for mediation, one of its main advantages is that it is a 'without prejudice' process and so little, if anything, is lost if it fails. It is very much a case of 'nothing ventured nothing gained'. But mediation and other forms of ADR are not a universal solution for dispute settlement; in this way, it is very much a case of 'horses for courses'.

---

126 Morris, P, 'The role of the Ombudsman in sporting disputes: some personal thoughts' (2000) 3(4) Sports Law Bulletin 12.

127 At its extraordinary congress held in Buenos Aires on 5 July 2001, FIFA, the World Governing Body of Football, approved the creation of a new Independent Arbitration Tribunal for Football (to be known by its French acronym, CTAF) for the settlement of a wide range of disputes.

Neither is ADR cost-free. But savings in time are also saving in monetary terms. As an alternative to settling sports disputes by traditional means through the courts and by arbitration, alternative forms of dispute mechanisms have a great deal more to offer to all those involved in any way in the practice and promotion of sport, both nationally and internationally.

KEY SOURCES

Blackshaw, I, *Mediating Sports Disputes – National and International Perspectives* (2002), The Hague: TMC Asser Press.

Carroll, E and Mackie, K, *International Mediation – The Art of Business Diplomacy* (1999), London: Kluwer.

Mackie, K, *Commercial Dispute Resolution – An ADR Practice Guide* (2000), 2nd edn, London: Butterworths.

Nafziger, J, 'Globalizing sports law' (1999) 9 Marquette Sports Law Journal 225.

Reeb, M, 'The Role and Functions of the Court of Arbitration for Sport (CAS)' 2002 2 International Sports Law Journal 21.

CHAPTER 7

THE REGULATION OF DOPING IN SPORT

INTRODUCTION

There are few issues in sport more emotive than anti-doping. Athletes at the centre of doping controversies such as Ben Johnson and, more recently, Rio Ferdinand, Dwain Chambers and Greg Rusedski have received extensive media coverage. This is, in part, because drug taking is viewed by many as contrary to the very essence of sport. Top sporting performers are viewed as society's heroes and are often held out to our children as role models. Elite competitors' doping indiscretions, it is said, undermine not only their sport but also the very values on which our society is based.

The relationship between sportsmen and women and their governing bodies appears to be a contractual one, the terms of which include, *inter alia*, the doping regulations of that particular sport. Diane Modahl's action against the British Athletics Federation Ltd (BAF) was based on the breach of an implied contractual term that her hearing following a positive doping test would be fair and objective. The Court of Appeal discovered that Modahl, like all athletes, was affiliated to a club which, in turn, was affiliated to the BAF (who conducted the hearing), which was affiliated to the International Amateur Athletics Federation (IAAF) which drafted the rules of competition.

Modahl v British Athletics Federation Ltd 2001 WL 1135166

Lord Justice Latham: A court should not merely assume a contract to exist, but must consider all the surrounding circumstances to determine whether or not the contract can properly be implied. We are handicapped in the present case by a lack of basic factual material. Although the court has been provided with the rules of the IAAF and the respondent, the court has not seen any document setting out the constitution of either organisation, although we have been given a general description of both. We have not seen any documents which indicate whether or not any individual athlete on entering any relevant competition, signs any document by which he or she agrees to be bound by either set of rules; and in particular we have not been shown any documents in relation to the applicant's entry for the meeting at Lisbon. It may or may not be, therefore, that, contained in such documents was the sort of wording which enabled Lightman J to conclude that Mr Korda became contractually bound by the ITF Rules when entering the All England Lawn Tennis Championships. It is clear from documents that we have seen that the successor body to the respondent envisages that individual contracts may be entered into by athletes which could contain such express provisions. This suggests to me that there is nothing inherently improbable about the concept of a contractual obligation being entered into by an individual athlete which would create a contractual relationship between the athlete and the respondent. The question therefore is whether or not on the material which we do have, it is proper to infer such a contract.[1]

Latham LJ and Manse LJ agreed there was a contractual relationship. Jonathan Parker LJ disagreed. The view of Jonathan Parker LJ would have been supported fully by Lord Denning who, in cases such as *Nagle v Feilden*[2] and *Lee v The Showman's Guild of Great Britain*[3] expressed his concern that the identification of a contractual nexus in such situations was little more than a fiction. Lord Denning's proposal that, even without a contractual relationship an athlete could still achieve redress through

---

1   See earlier Chapter 5, pp 203–06 for extracts from case.
2   [1966] 2 QB 633.
3   [1952] 2 QB 329.

the courts by applying for a declaration or an injunction however, is of little use if the athlete's career has effectively been ended by the ban.

On an emotive level, doping 'cheats' often evoke far greater disdain and contempt than normally associated with the simple expedient of a breached contract. Not all breaches of this sports contract are considered to be 'cheating'. Most breaches such as the false start, the faulty baton change or the walker who runs are dealt with instantaneously by officials. The penalty imposed for such a breach may be the subject of a challenge by the competitor, but this is unusual. Generally there is no intention on the part of the competitor to breach rules of this nature. However, the reason for their exclusion is axiomatic – they flout the principle of fair competition. These banned activities, identified by the rules of the relevant sports governing body and, in most cases, imported into the contact between competitor and sports organisation are reinforced by a general consensus that the prohibited behaviour is undesirable.

Conversely, some activities that could carry the hallmark of cheating are deemed legitimate. One might, for example, argue that technological advantages such as high-tech bicycles, swimming and running suits and the sophisticated drinks of some marathon runners should constitute cheating because they establish an advantage that may be considered unfair. They are not, however, necessarily breaches of the contractual terms prescribed by the governing bodies.

The area where the outlawing of activities by the governing bodies of sport has become synonymous in the minds of the public with cheating is doping. Drug abuse or doping encompasses a wide range of behaviour. Doping consists not only of the taking of substances but also complex scientific processes, such as blood doping. Blood doping consists of taking blood from the athlete's body, re-oxygenating and then pumping it back into the athlete. Doping sanctions also extend to those who, for various reasons, do not comply with the testing regime (even though there is no evidence of doping), as Rio Ferdinand discovered to his cost. Sports regulators wage a continuing 'war' against the scientist and the doctor: each scientific development enabling the athlete to evade detection is countered by more complex testing procedures and rules.

Although doping in humans is used almost exclusively to enhance performance, the doping of racehorses, greyhounds and other animals is often a destructive technique aimed at adversely affecting performance. This chapter concentrates on the doping of humans but most of the issues raised are equally applicable to the doping of animals.

ANTI-DOPING INSTITUTIONS

The International Olympic Committee (IOC), is at the apex of world sports organisations and 'fights' a 'war' against dopers. The unyielding position, and rhetoric, adopted by the IOC and the governing bodies is based on the premise that doping is wrong. In 1999 the IOC restated its stance in a press release:

> The International Olympic Committee (IOC) wishes to reiterate its total commitment to the fight against doping, with the aim of protecting athletes' health and preserving fair play in sport. Any declarations which go against these principles are both wrong and misplaced.[4]

Although the IOC has long held these principles sacred, its influence over governing bodies was ineffective. The history of doping regulation in sport is littered with examples of governing bodies failing to draft their doping codes competently. Little thought was given to the compatibility of

---

4   Lausanne, 8 July 1999

doping rules between sports. Also, governing bodies seemed unaware of how previous doping rules of their own sport interacted with new provisions. As Michael Beloff QC, an arbitrator at the Court of Arbitration for Sport explained:

Beloff, M, 'Drugs, laws and versapaks'

... in my experience, rules of domestic or international federations tend to resemble the architecture of an ancient building: a wing added here; a loft there; a buttress elsewhere, without adequate consideration of whether the additional parts affect adversely the symmetry of the whole.[5]

As a result of this, sport has attempted to harmonise the doping regulations of the various national and international governing bodies. In the vanguard of this movement is the World Anti-Doping Agency (WADA). The rise of WADA can be seen as a response to the inadequacies of earlier regimes and a realisation that successful anti-doping policies come at a price.

Houlihan, B, 'The World Anti-Doping Agency: prospects for success'

The watershed in policy development that occurred in the late 1980s was due in part to the recognition by governments and sports organisations that doping was a much more intractable and complex problem than they had at first thought and in part to the increasing pressure of expectations that governments were placing on sports organisations. The regularity of scandal was important in keeping the issue in the public eye and reminding policy actors of the scale of the task that faced them and their own inadequacy. Thus at the same time that governments and sports bodies were acknowledging the greater prominence of doping on their respective agendas they were also increasingly aware that a number of factors were combining to move an effective policy response beyond their individual capacity. The first was the realisation of the likely cost of implementing a sustained anti-doping policy. Second, the reluctant acceptance that in-competition testing was pointless when steroids were being used primarily as training drugs and therefore were highly unlikely to be present in the athlete's urine at the time of competition. Anti-doping authorities, who were comfortable with in-competition testing which was relatively low cost and easily organised, were now faced with the prospect of having to manage a regime of out-of-competition testing with its attendant extra cost and complexity. The third factor was a consequence of the second and concerned the problems of undertaking testing among an elite group of athletes who were increasingly mobile and who were likely to be in their native country, and therefore accessible by their national doping control officers, for only part of each year. Indeed there was a growing number of athletes who spent most of their elite career outside their home country. For example, world class Australian road cyclists spent most, if not all, of their time in Europe where the major events and teams were located. Much the same could be said for the increasing number of South American and African track and field athletes who followed the American and European calendar of competitions. Such a high level of athlete mobility required a set of anti-doping regulations that would prevent athletes exploiting the loopholes and inconsistencies found in the anti-doping regulations of various countries and domestic affiliates of international federations. The final factor concerned the increasing willingness of athletes to challenge the sanctions imposed by anti-doping authorities. Legal challenges were often based on faults in the administration of urine collection or testing rather than the positive test result. A series of high profile court cases involving such athletes as the American, Harry Reynolds, the German Katrin Krabbe and the Australian Martin Vinnicombe emphasised the need for closer co-operation between anti-doping authorities. A successful legal challenge could not only call into question the reliability of the testing procedure and encourage other athletes to initiate court action, but could also prove disastrously expensive for the domestic federation.[6]

---

5   Beloff, M, 'Drugs, laws and versapaks', in O'Leary, J (ed), *Drugs and Doping in Sport* (2000), London: Cavendish, 40.
6   Houlihan, B, 'The World Anti-Doping Agency: prospects for success', in O'Leary, J (ed), *Drugs and Doping in Sport* (2000), London: Cavendish Publishing, 128

In order that doping and other sport-related disputes, as they arise, can be contained within the sporting world, the Court of Arbitration for Sport was conceived in 1981. A full analysis of the CAS and its jurisprudence can be found in Chapter 6. It is interesting to note at this point, however, that doping cases make up a significant proportion of the CAS caseload and much of the *lex sportiva* produced by the CAS is based on decision in doping cases. It is anticipated that doping cases will continue to provide the CAS with an important element of its workload.

THE WORLD ANTI-DOPING CODE

The development of harmonised, universally accepted anti-doping regulations reached a pinnacle in March 2003 when WADA revealed its anti-doping code in Copenhagen and the Copenhagen Declaration which followed suggested that governments, at least in theory, supported WADA's efforts. The Code, rather than being seen as a model set of regulations, should be viewed as a number of basic requirements with additional recommendations.

World Anti-Doping Code: Introduction

The *Code* is the fundamental and universal document upon which the World Anti-Doping Program in sport is based. The purpose of the *Code* is to advance the anti-doping effort through universal harmonization of core anti-doping elements. It is intended to be specific enough to achieve complete harmonization on issues where uniformity is required, yet general enough in other areas to permit flexibility on how agreed upon anti-doping principles are implemented.

As many of the provisions are general, governing bodies may wish to go beyond the provisions in the code. WADA will assist them in this endeavour with advisory models which can be implemented at the discretion of the governing body. The fundamental rational of the Code is:

World Anti-Doping Code: Introduction

. . . to preserve what is intrinsically valuable about sport. This intrinsic value is often referred to as 'the spirit of sport'; it is the essence of Olympism; it is how we play true. The spirit of sport is the celebration of the human spirit, body and mind, and is characterized by the following values:

- Ethics, fair play and honesty
- Health
- Excellence in performance
- Character and education
- Fun and joy
- Teamwork
- Dedication and commitment
- Respect for rules and laws
- Respect for self and other participants
- Courage
- Community and solidarity

Doping is fundamentally contrary to the spirit of sport.

By the Athens Olympics of 2004, most sports had adopted the WADA Code. The main exception to this blanket coverage is likely to be major US sports such as baseball, basketball and football which, it would appear, intend to remain independent not least because contracts between players and their employers are negotiated collectively under US anti-trust laws. It is understood that negotiations between WADA and these governing bodies are ongoing.

One of the major obstacles for anybody intent on implementing a rule for the whole world is that it must encompass a diverse range of religious, legal and social perspectives: the imposition at a global level of blood testing for EPO, for example, would cause enormous problems for Muslim nations. This next quote provided a warning for the IOC and applies equally now to WADA.

Boyes, S, 'The International Olympic Committee, transnational doping policy and globalisation'

In effect, what the IOC seeks is the 'globalisation' of its anti-doping policies and strategies, to penetrate and pervade both a broad spectrum of different sports and the different jurisdictions within which sporting activity takes place, to harmonise and homogenise the regulation of doping in sport on a global plane. However, the IOC has failed to recognise the process of globalisation as being 'two-way'. Though there has been a little acknowledgement of the mutual inter-penetration between the local and the global by the IOC, for the most part it has sought and continues to seek to impose its particular (localised) views at the global level. The resultant exclusions of and intrusions upon individual cultures and societies must be regarded as unsatisfactory for an organisation that would purport to support access to sport for everyone as being a basic human right. This clearly undermines the principle of protection of sports ethics as a basis upon which to regulate doping practices, when the ethics being protected are those of a small localised group and not inclusive of global society as a whole.

This ideological failure is compounded by the impracticality of the imposition of such a scheme. Where resistance to the global regime has arisen at a local level, whether as a result of cultural, social or legal disparities, this has had the effect of creating a situation of imbalance, where athletes are either subject to much stricter controls or effectively allowed to act irrespective of the rules 'imposed' by the global regulator. This is clearly debilitating to a policy of anti-doping so reliant on the principle of the 'level playing field' as an underlying rationale and is also damaging to any attempt at justification on the grounds of the protection of health.

Combined with the divergence of economic and social backgrounds and even physiological attributes that can facilitate 'unfair advantage', the solution becomes clear.

The IOC must abolish attempts to enforce its anti-doping policy on a world-wide scale. The rationales underpinning the operation of such a policy do not stand up to scrutiny when the global context of sporting competition is considered. The IOC has failed to take so many other differentiating factors into account in other areas, that to take supposedly global action in this small niche smacks of inconsistency and tokenism.[7]

The Definition of Doping

A workable definition of doping is fundamental to an effective system of doping control. Articles 1 and 2 of the World Anti-Doping Code define doping offence *inter alia* as the presence of a prohibited substance or its metabolites or markers in an athlete's body specimen. Article 2.1.1. makes it clear that it is the athlete's responsibility to ensure that no prohibited substances enter his or her body and that intent and fault are irrelevant.

---

7   Boyes, S, 'The International Olympic Committee, transnational doping policy and globalisation', in *op cit*, fn 5, O'Leary (2000), p 178.

In the past there have been two very different definitions of doping offences, the first of which is illustrated by the WADA World Anti-Doping Code; the second (included here largely for an historical perspective) is taken from the International Shooting Union (UIT) rules criticised by the Court of Arbitration for Sport in 1995:[8]

WADA Article 2: Anti-Doping Rule Violations

The following constitute anti-doping rule violations:

2.1 The presence of a *Prohibited Substance* or its *Metabolites* or *Markers* in an *Athlete's* bodily *Specimen*.

2.1.1 It is each *Athlete's* personal duty to ensure that no *Prohibited Substance* enters his or her body. *Athletes* are responsible for any *Prohibited Substance* or its *Metabolites* or *Markers* found to be present in their bodily *Specimens*. Accordingly, it is not necessary that intent, fault, negligence or knowing *Use* on the *Athlete's* part be demonstrated in order to establish an anti-doping violation under Article 2.1.

ART2 UIT Anti-Doping Regulations

Doping means the use of one or more substances mentioned in the official UIT anti-doping list with the aim of attaining an increase in performance by injection, oral or other means, and whether the drug is administered by the competitor himself or the substance is transmitted to the competitor's body by another person . . .

The distinction between the two lies in the fact that a competitor has committed a breach of the WADA Code if he or she tests positive. Under Art 2 of the UIT regulations a positive test is insufficient on its own. In addition, the governing body would have to show that the competitor or another person transmitted into the competitor's body a banned substance with the *aim* of achieving an increase in performance. It is not necessary under Art 2 of the UIT regulations that the substance did actually increase performance – merely that this was the competitor's objective by transmitting or allowing the substance to be transmitted into his body.

Clearly, the WADA Code provides an easier means of establishing a doping offence than the old UIT regulations. The WADA Code operates a system of strict liability. In the case of Dougie Walker, one of a number of high profile nandrolone cases that have also involved famous international athletes such as Linford Christie, Dieter Baumann, and Merlene Ottey, Walker escaped a ban from UK athletics. David Moorcroft, Chief Executive, confirmed that Walker was cleared because he made no knowing attempt to enhance his performance. This conclusion is rather confusing given the strict liability nature of the then IAAF regulations.

The concept of *mens rea* or 'guilty mind' is well known to criminal lawyers. Although there is a considerable difference between doping proceedings and criminal trials, some lawyers have suggested that the strict liability provisions of many sports governing bodies are fundamentally unjust. Strict liability in doping regulations allows a governing body to ban an athlete without showing that the athlete intended to take the substance – a positive test is sufficient. Despite the obvious concerns over a rule of this nature, both the CAS and the English High Court have held that a strict liability rule is lawful, bearing in mind that it may be the only way to effectively police the doping problem. It may therefore seem a little odd that Walker should be cleared and understandable why the IAAF would be perplexed at the decision. The IAAF certainly thought so and Walker was subsequently banned.

A rule that a positive test leads to an automatic ban is attractive in its clarity and simplicity but denies what many of us would view as the fundamental right of an opportunity to show a lack of

---

8 Arbitration CAS 94/129, *USA Shooting & Q International Shooting Union (UIT)*, award of 23 May 1995.

fault, knowledge or intent. In practice this means that even if an athlete could prove that the consumption of the drug was accidental or a result of malice on the part of another, he would still be found guilty.

Strict liability may appear to be a draconian provision. The reason for it is a fear that rules requiring proof of intent would be impossible to implement: it is feared that athletes would find little difficulty in producing someone prepared to take responsibility and vouch for the athlete's innocence.

Quigley v UIT CAS 94/129

It is true that a strict liability test is likely in some sense to be unfair in an individual case, such as that of Q, where the Athlete may have taken medication as the result of mislabeling or faulty advice for which he or she is not responsible – particularly in the circumstances of sudden illness in a foreign country. But it is also in some sense 'unfair' for an Athlete to get food poisoning on the eve of an important competition. Yet in neither case will the rules of the competition be altered to undo the unfairness. Just as the competition will not be postponed to await the Athlete's recovery, so the prohibition of banned substances will not be lifted in recognition of its accidental absorption. The vicissitudes of competition, like those of life generally, may create many types of unfairness, whether by accident or the negligence of unaccountable Persons, which the law cannot repair.

Furthermore, it appears to be a laudable policy objective not to repair an accidental unfairness to an individual by creating an intentional unfairness to the whole body of other competitors. This is what would happen if banned performance-enhancing substances were tolerated when absorbed inadvertently. Moreover, it is likely that even intentional abuse would in many cases escape sanction for lack of proof of guilty intent. And it is certain that a requirement of intent would invite costly litigation that may well cripple federations – particularly those run on modest budgets – in their fight against doping.

Gasser v Stinson and Another Lexisnexis 15 June 1988

Scott J: Mr Blackburne submitted with great force that a rule which did not permit an athlete even to try to establish his or her innocence, either in resisting conviction or in mitigation of sentence was unreasonable and unjustifiable. But the consequences if the absolute nature of the offence was removed or if the length of the sentence became discretionary and not mandatory must be considered.

Suppose an athlete gives evidence that he or she did not take the drug knowingly and that it must therefore be inferred that the drug was digested unknowingly. How is the IAAF to deal with such an explanation? How can credibility be tested? Suppose a third party, perhaps a member of the athlete's team of coaches, perhaps a medical adviser, perhaps a malicious prankster, gives evidence that he or she administered the drug to the athlete and that the athlete had no knowledge that this was being done. How is the credibility of the third party's evidence to be tested? The pressure for success in international athletics, as well as domestic athletics and the national pride and prestige which has become part of international athletics has to be borne in mind. Will the credibility of the athlete or the third party vary depending on the nation to which he or she belongs? If a competitor or third party from nation A is believed, what will be the position when similar evidence is given by a competitor or third party from nation B? The lengths to which some people will go in order to achieve the appearance of success for their nation's athletes in athletics competitions is in point. The long jump in last year's World Championship illustrates the point. Cynicism, sadly, abounds. Mr Holt in his evidence, said that in his view, if a defence of moral innocence were open, the floodgates would be opened and the IAAF's attempts to prevent drug-taking by athletes would be rendered futile. He had, in my opinion, reason for that fear.

Mr Blackburne submits that it is not justifiable that the morally innocent may have to suffer in order to ensure that the guilty do not escape. But that is not a submission that is invariably acceptable. The criminal law in this country (and in, I would think, all others) has various absolute offences and various mandatory sentences.

For my part I am not persuaded that the IAAF's absolute offence and mandatory sentence applicable to an athlete who is found to have dope in his or her urine is unreasonable.[9]

Scott J is correct when he states that there are a number of examples of English criminal sanctions that are strict in their liability.[10] The Misuse of Drugs Act 1971, however, the criminal provision that most closely parallels the WADA Code, does not impose strict liability:

Misuse of Drugs Act 1971, s 28

(2) Subject to subsection (3) below, in any proceedings for an offence to which this section applies it shall be a defence for the accused to prove that he neither knew of nor suspected nor had reason to suspect the existence of some fact alleged by the prosecution which it is necessary for the prosecution to prove if he is to be convicted of the offence charged.

(3) Where in any proceedings for an offence to which this section applies it is necessary, if the accused is to be committed of the offence charged, for the prosecution to prove that some substance or product involved in the alleged offence was the controlled drug which the prosecution alleges it to have been and it is proved that the substance or product in question was that controlled drug, the accused:

(a) shall not be acquitted of the offence charged by reason only of proving that he neither knew or suspected nor had any reason to suspect that the substance or product in question was the particular controlled drug alleged; but

(b) shall be acquitted thereof:

(i) if he proves that he neither believed nor suspected nor had reason to suspect that the substance or product in question was a controlled drug; or

(ii) if he proves that he believed the substance or product in question to be a controlled drug or a controlled drug of a description, such that, if it had in fact been that controlled drug or a controlled drug of that description, he would not at the material time have been committing any offence to which this section applies.

In addition to Art 2.1 of the code which deals with a positive test, there are a number of other situations where a doping offence may occur:

Article 2: Anti-Doping Rule Violations

2.2.1 The success or failure of the *Use* of a *Prohibited Substance* or *Prohibited Method* is not material. It is sufficient that the *Prohibited Substance* or *Prohibited Method* was *Used* or *Attempted* to be *Used* for an anti-doping rule violation to be committed.

2.3 Refusing, or failing without compelling justification, to submit to *Sample* collection after notification as authorized in applicable anti-doping rules or otherwise evading *Sample* collection.

2.4 Violation of applicable requirements regarding *Athlete* availability for *Out-of-Competition Testing* including failure to provide required whereabouts information and missed tests which are declared based on reasonable rules.

2.5 *Tampering*, or *Attempting* to tamper, with any part of *Doping Control*.

2.6 *Possession* of *Prohibited Substances* and *Methods*:

2.6.1 *Possession* by an *Athlete* at any time or place of a substance that is prohibited in *Out-of-Competition Testing* or a *Prohibited Method* unless the *Athlete* establishes that the *Possession* is pursuant to a therapeutic use exemption granted in accordance with Article 4.4 (Therapeutic Use) or other acceptable justification.

9   Lexisnexis, 15 June 1988

10   Such an example is s 58(2) of the Medicines Act 1968 which provides that no person shall sell by retail specified medicinal products except in accordance with a prescription given by a medical practitioner.

2.7 *Trafficking* in any *Prohibited Substance* or *Prohibited Method*.

2.8 Administration or *Attempted* administration of a *Prohibited Substance* or *Prohibited Method* to any *Athlete*, or assisting, encouraging, aiding, abetting, covering up or any other type of complicity involving an anti-doping rule violation or any *Attempted* violation.

If it is accepted that elite sporting competition is predicated on natural inequality then the distinction between fair and unfair competition is further confused by provisions within doping regulations that allow for exceptional use of substances, which would otherwise give rise to a doping offence, on medical grounds. An obvious example of this is the use of inhalers to assist asthma sufferers.

Article 4.4: Therapeutic Use

WADA shall adopt an *International Standard* for the process of granting therapeutic use exemptions.

Each International Federation shall ensure, for *International-Level Athletes* or any other *Athlete* who is entered in an *International Event*, that a process is in place whereby *Athletes* with documented medical conditions requiring the *Use* of a *Prohibited Substance* or a *Prohibited Method* may request a therapeutic use exemption. Each *National Anti-Doping Organization* shall ensure, for all *Athletes* within its jurisdiction that are not *International-Level Athletes*, that a process is in place whereby *Athletes* with documented medical conditions requiring the *Use* of a *Prohibited Substance* or a *Prohibited Method* may request a therapeutic use exemption. Such requests shall be evaluated in accordance with the *International Standard* on therapeutic use. International Federations and *National Anti-Doping Organizations* shall promptly report to *WADA* the granting of therapeutic use exemptions to any *International-Level Athlete* or national-level *Athlete* that is included in his or her *National Anti-Doping Organization's Registered Testing Pool*.

WADA, on its own initiative, may review the granting of a therapeutic use exemption to any *International-Level Athlete* or national-level *Athlete* that is included in his or her *National Anti-Doping Organization's Registered Testing Pool*. Further, upon the request of any such *Athlete* that has been denied a therapeutic use exemption, *WADA* may review such denial. If *WADA* determines that such granting or denial of a therapeutic use exemption did not comply with the *International Standard* for therapeutic use exemptions, *WADA* may reverse the decision.[11]

Proof of Doping

The standards of proof in establishing a doping infraction are prescribed in Article 3 of the WADA Code.

Article 3.3.1: Burdens of Proof

The *Anti-Doping Organization* shall have the burden of establishing that an anti-doping rule violation has occurred. The standard of proof shall be whether the *Anti-Doping Organization* has established an anti-doping rule violation to the comfortable satisfaction of the hearing body bearing in mind the seriousness of the allegation which is made. This standard of proof in all cases is greater than a mere balance of probability but less than proof beyond a reasonable doubt. Where the *Code* places the burden of proof upon the *Athlete* or other *Person* alleged to have committed an anti-doping rule violation to rebut a presumption or establish specified facts or circumstances, the standard of proof shall be by a balance of probability.

This Article needs to be read in conjunction with Art 3.2.1, which establishes a rebuttable presumption that the accredited laboratory conducted the analysis correctly. The effect is that once a positive finding had been made by the laboratory, the athlete faces an uphill task to disprove the

---

11   See Hamilton, B, 'Inhaled beta agonists: ergogenic, dangerous and against the spirit of sport: fact or fallacy?' (2004) 12 (2) Sport and the Law Journal 4.

allegations. The idea that the standard of proof is pitched somewhere between balance of probability and reasonable doubt might seem like a reasonable position in that the standard on governing bodies is higher than that required in a civil case but lower than the criminal standard of proof. In practice, however, this definition may prove difficult to apply: does the balance lie exactly in the middle of the two standards? How, in practical terms, is this concept to be elucidated?

Testing

The governing body or its agent[12] is under considerable pressure to ensure that the WADA Code or the governing body's own enhanced version of the Code is implemented scrupulously. Although a minor error in sampling or transportation may not prove fatal, an accumulation of a number of seemingly insignificant oversights may result in the overturning of a ban inasmuch as they cast doubt on the overall findings.

5.1 Test Distribution Planning

Anti-Doping Organizations conducting *Testing* shall in coordination with other *Anti-Doping Organizations* conducting *Testing* on the same *Athlete* pool:

5.1.1 Plan and implement an effective number of *In-Competition* and *Out-of-Competition* tests. Each International Federation shall establish a *Registered Testing Pool* for *International-Level Athletes* in its sport, and each *National Anti-Doping Organization* shall establish a national *Registered Testing Pool* for *Athletes* in its country. The national-level pool shall include *International-Level Athletes* from that country as well as other national-level *Athletes*. Each International Federation and *National Anti-Doping Organization* shall plan and conduct *In-Competition* and *Out-of-Competition Testing* on its *Registered Testing Pool*.

5.1.2 Make *No Advance Notice Testing* a priority.

5.1.3 Conduct *Target Testing*.

. . .

6.1 Use of Approved Laboratories

Doping Control Samples shall be analyzed only in *WADA*-accredited laboratories or as otherwise approved by *WADA*. The choice of the *WADA*-accredited laboratory (or other method approved by *WADA*) used for the *Sample* analysis shall be determined exclusively by the *Anti-Doping Organization* responsible for results management.

The effectiveness of doping procedures was successfully challenged by the lawyers representing Butch Reynolds before the USA Track and Fields Doping Control Review Board. The Board concluded that as the doping control room was not secured and guarded, the doping control officer had left the control station (even though by then the sample had been safely processed) and there was doubt as to whether unauthorised persons had been allowed into the station, the validity of the procedures had been undermined.

In a similar vein, lawyers for Katrin Krabbe argued unsuccessfully that a sample collected from the athlete in South Africa which was transported to Cologne and which had been left at Cologne airport for two days before collection was proof that the chain of custody had been breached making the results unreliable.[13]

---

12 In the UK, the Drug-Free Sport Directorate operates under the auspices of UK Sport. It co-ordinates drug testing on behalf of sports governing bodies in the UK administering both in and out of competition testing – www.uksport.gov.uk.

13 Gay, M, The Sports Council Doping Control Unit Seminars on Doping Control, 1994 and 1996.

The 'A' test of Diane Modahl showed significant levels of testosterone in her body. Testosterone makes an athlete stronger and more aggressive. It does little to aid endurance: one of the key characteristics of a successful middle distance runner. Modahl emphatically denied taking any drug. An alternative explanation, that she was producing the testosterone herself because of a medical condition, was eliminated.

Even before the 'B' test began there were grounds for questioning the validity of the 'A' test. First, the chain of custody documents were missing. These are the documents that not only map the movements and storage of the samples[14] but also identify the person responsible for their security at any time. Secondly, when the seal of the 'B' sample was broken a strong smell of ammonia was present. In many laboratories the test would not be undertaken with a sample so corrupted. The 'B' sample showed a pH reading of nine. As a normal sample should have a pH of five, the sample had obviously undergone enormous change. However, the Portuguese laboratory insisted on going ahead with the test on the basis that the pH reading would not have a bearing on a test for testosterone. The result of the 'B' test confirmed the result of the 'A' test.

Ultimately it may prove impossible to produce just but effective procedures. The WADA Code wrestles with two irreconcilable requirements: a rigorous testing system, and the rights of competitors to lead as normal a life as possible.

Verroken, M, 'A time for re-evaluation: the challenge to an athlete's reputation'

If we were serious about eradicating drugs from sport, there are more drastic actions that could be considered. These actions would protect our athletes and their reputations, but is the sporting world really ready to use them? For example,

- Storing urine and blood samples and await the technology being available to show that an athlete has competed drug free.

- Athletes could be housed in a sterile environment for six months before a major event and nutrition and training controlled.

- Athletes could submit their samples daily, these samples would be stored and a random selection be tested and validated by DNA analysis. If a drug is detected the preceding samples could be submitted to determine how long the substance had been present.

- Athletes who had been denied a medal or a place in a competition because of another athlete using drugs could be legally aided to challenge that athlete and claim loss of earnings, reputation and opportunity – provided they also would produce the evidence that they competed drug free.

- Lottery funding should be refused to athletes who have been found to have committed a doping offence

- Every event in the UK be open to independent testing

Ultimately there are measures that will resolve the problems of doping in sport. However there is a balance to be achieved; one that satisfies the various parties and their range of interests.[15]

---

14   For an analysis of the evidential validity of the chains of custody documentation see Grayson, E, 'Drugs in sport: chains of custody' (1995) New Law Journal, 20 January.

15   Verroken, M, 'A time for re-evaluation: the challenge to an athlete's reputation', in *op cit*, fn 5, O'Leary (2000), p 37.

Disciplinary Procedures

Most governing bodies operate a system of suspensions following a positive test but prior to the hearing.

Article 7.5: Principles Applicable to Provisional Suspensions

A *Signatory* may adopt rules, applicable to any *Event* for which the *Signatory* is the ruling body or for any team selection process for which the *Signatory* is responsible, permitting *Provisional Suspensions* to be imposed after the review and notification described in Articles 7.1 and 7.2 but prior to a final hearing as described in Article 8 (Right to a Fair Hearing). Provided, however, that a *Provisional Suspension* may not be imposed unless the *Athlete* is given either: (a) an opportunity for a *Provisional Hearing* either before imposition of the *Provisional Suspension* or on a timely basis after imposition of the *Provisional Suspension*; or (b) an opportunity for an expedited hearing in accordance with Article 8 (Right to a Fair Hearing) on a timely basis after imposition of a *Provisional Suspension*.

In the USA the national governing body has felt obliged to allow athletes to compete pending a hearing because of potential conflict with national law. Sandra Farmer-Patrick was allowed to compete in the 400 metre hurdles in the Atlanta Olympics although she had recently failed a doping test. The IAAF, however, insists that the regulations are followed strictly in some other countries where there is no incompatibility with national laws.

Athletes' procedural safeguards are based on Art 8 of the WADA Anti-Doping code, which deals specifically with the right to a fair hearing.

Article 8: Right to a Fair Hearing

Each *Anti-Doping Organization* with responsibility for results management shall provide a hearing process for any *Person* who is asserted to have committed an anti-doping rule violation. Such hearing process shall address whether an anti-doping violation was committed and, if so, the appropriate *Consequences*. The hearing process shall respect the following principles:

- a timely hearing;
- fair and impartial hearing body;
- the right to be represented by counsel at the *Person*'s own expense;
- the right to be fairly and timely informed of the asserted anti-doping rule violation;
- the right to respond to the asserted anti-doping rule violation and resulting *Consequences*;
- the right of each party to present evidence, including the right to call and question witnesses (subject to the hearing body's discretion to accept testimony by telephone or written submission);
- the *Person*'s right to an interpreter at the hearing, with the hearing body to determine the identity, and responsibility for the cost, of the interpreter; and
- a timely, written, reasoned decision . . .

Diane Modahl's hearing into the test results was heard before a panel under the auspices of the British Athletic Federation. Rather than adopting an inquisitorial style which may appear the most appropriate for such a tribunal hearing, the style was adversarial, with the BAF both judge and prosecutor. Modahl's defence attempted to establish reasonable doubt as to the credibility of the test procedure and result. By this time it had been established that the test had lain unrefrigerated for two days in the Lisbon heat. This would have accounted for the changes in pH. It was also argued that taking testosterone would have produced a reaction in the liver causing the production of metabolites. No metabolites were discovered in the sample. To explain the high testosterone level, the defence called an expert medical witness who explored the theoretical possibility that bacteria could have caused the corrupted sample to produce testosterone. The panel took two hours to reach a unanimous verdict that a doping offence had been committed. The panel was unconvinced that the theoretical arguments altered the balance of probability. A four year ban was imposed.

Diane Modahl's appeal against her ban was heard by the Independent Appeal Panel. The same evidence was put forward. By this time, however, the defence could show that the bacterial transformation theory could be replicated under laboratory conditions. On this ground the panel held that the drug taking allegations could no longer be sustained on the balance of probabilities. The finding was overturned and the ban quashed. Modahl brought an action against the BAF claiming that the hearing panel of Sir Arthur Gold, Dr Lucking and Mr Guy were biased against her.

Modahl v British Athletics Federation Ltd 2001 WL 1135166

Lord Justice Latham:

55. The first question which has to be answered is whether or not those proceedings have to be looked at overall, or whether there was a separate obligation to deal with the proceedings before the Disciplinary Committee fairly, even if no criticism can be made of the Independent Appeal Panel. Second, if the obligation required fairness at the Disciplinary Committee stage and there was a breach, what consequences should follow? The appellant, in this context, challenges the conclusions of the judge that there was no bias on the part of Sir Arthur Gold either actual or apparent, or bias on the part of Dr Lucking or Mr Guy again either of actual or apparent, which could properly characterise the proceedings of the Disciplinary Committee as being in breach of the obligation of fairness.

56. In submitting that the respondent was under a discrete obligation of fairness in relation to the Disciplinary Committee, Mr Julius relies in part on a passage in an affidavit sworn by Professor Radford, the respondent's Executive Chairman, in the course of the proceedings. At paragraph 52 he said:

'BAF also agrees that it would be a term of any contract that those responsible for selecting the Disciplinary Committee and that those sitting on the Disciplinary Committee would act in a bona fide manner and would not be biased . . .'

57. He further relies on the fact that the adverse decision of the Disciplinary Committee resulted in his client being declared ineligible for the period between the Disciplinary Committee hearing and the hearing before the Independent Appeal Panel for which the rules themselves provide no remedy. He submits, accordingly, that unless there is a discrete obligation in relation to the Disciplinary Committee, any unfairness at that stage would leave her without any remedy for any loss which she may have sustained as a result of that unfairness between the hearings.

58. Mr Flint however submits that the structure put in place by the Rules is, in itself, a discharge of the obligation on the part of the respondent to act fairly. The appeal to the Independent Appeal Panel is the safeguard which both the respondent and the athlete have accepted as the means of dealing with any deficiencies at the Disciplinary Committee stage. Precisely because the Rules make no reference to any entitlement of the athlete to a remedy by way of costs or damages in the event of the Independent Appeal Panel reversing a decision of the Disciplinary Committee, it must have been the intention of the parties that this was the method by which any such deficiencies were to be resolved.

59. Both Mr Julius and Mr Flint rely on the opinion of the Privy Council in *Calvin v Carr & Others* [1979] 2 All ER 440. In that case the appellant was part owner of a racehorse which ran in a race in Australia. A steward's inquiry found that there had been a breach of the Rules of Racing; and the appellant was disqualified for a year and his membership of the Australian Jockey Club forfeited. He appealed to the Committee of the Club but his appeal was dismissed. He then brought an action seeking a declaration that his disqualification was void on the basis that the stewards had failed to observe the rules of natural justice and that there was accordingly no jurisdiction in the Appeal Committee to hear his appeal. The opinion of the Privy Council, given by Lord Wilberforce, was that there was no absolute rule that defects in natural justice at an original hearing could or could not be cured by appeal proceedings, and that where a person had joined an organisation or body and was deemed on the rules of that organisation in the context in which he joined to have agreed to accept what in the end was a fair decision notwithstanding some initial defect, the task of the courts was to decide whether in the end there had been a fair result reached by fair methods.

60. The problem for the court was set out in the following terms by Lord Wilberforce at page 448:

> First there are cases where the rules provide for a rehearing by the original body, or some fuller or enlarged form of it. This situation may be found in relation to social clubs. It is not difficult in such cases to reach the conclusion that the first hearing is superseded by the second, or, putting it in contractual terms, the parties are taken to have agreed to accept the decision of the hearing body, whether original or adjourned ...

At the other extreme are cases, where, after examination of the whole hearing structure, in the context of the particular activity to which it relates (trade union membership, planning, employment etc) the conclusion is reached that a complainant has the right to nothing less than a fair hearing both at the original and at the appeal stage. This is the result reached by Megarry J in *Leary v National Union of Vehicle Builders.* In his judgment in that case the judge seems to have elevated the conclusion thought proper in that case to rule a general application. In an eloquent passage he said:

> 'If the rules and the law combined to give the member the right to a fair trial and the right of appeal, why should he be told that he ought to be satisfied with an unjust trial and a fair appeal? ... As a general rule ... I hold that a failure of natural justice in the trial body cannot be cured by a sufficiency of natural justice in an appellate body.'

In their Lordships' opinion this is too broadly stated. It affirms a principle which may be found correct in a category of cases; these may very well include trade union cases, where movement solidarity and dislike of the rebel, or renegade, may make it difficult for appeals to be conducted in an atmosphere of detached impartiality and so make a fair trial at the first (probably branch) level an essential condition of justice. But to seek to apply it generally overlooks, in their Lordships' respectful opinion, both the existence of the first category, and the possibility that, intermediately, the conclusion to be reached on the rules and on the contractual context, is that those who have joined in an organisation, or contract, should be taken to have agreed to accept what in the end is a fair decision, notwithstanding some initial defect.

In their Lordships' judgment such intermediate cases exist. In them it is for the court, in the light of the agreements made, and in addition having regard to the course of proceedings, to decide whether, at the end of the day, there has been a fair result, reached by fair methods, such as the parties should fairly be taken to have accepted when they joined the association. Naturally there may be instances when the defect is so flagrant, the consequences so severe, that the most perfect of appeals or rehearings will not be sufficient to produce a just result. Many rules (including those now in question) anticipate that such a situation may arise by giving power to remit for a new hearing. There may also be cases when the appeal process is itself less than perfect; it may be vitiated by the same defect as the original proceedings, or short of that there may be doubts whether the appeal body embarked on its task without predisposition or whether it had the means to make a fair and full enquiry, for example where it has no material but a transcript of what was before the original body. In such cases it would no doubt be right to quash the original decision. These are all matters (and no doubt there are others) which the court must consider. Whether these intermediate cases are to be regarded as exceptions from a general rule, as stated by Megarry J, or as a parallel category covered by a rule of equal status, is not in their Lordships' judgment necessary to state, or indeed a matter of great importance. What is important is recognition that such cases exist, and that it is undesirable in many cases of domestic disputes, particularly in which an inquiry and appeal process has been established, to introduce too great a measure of formal judicialisation. While flagrant cases of injustice, including corruption or bias, must always be firmly dealt with by the courts, the tendency in their Lordships' opinion in matters of domestic disputes should be to leave these to be settled by the agreed methods without requiring the formalities of judicial processes to be introduced.

61. It seems to me that in cases such as this, where an apparently sensible appeal structure has been put in place, the court is entitled to approach the matter on the basis that the parties should have agreed to accept what in the end is a fair decision. As Lord Wilberforce said, this does not mean that the fact that there has been an appeal will necessarily have produced a just result. The test which is appropriate, is to ask whether, having regard to the course of the proceedings, there has been a fair result. As Lord Wilberforce indicated, there may be circumstances in which by reason of corruption or bias or such other deficiency, the end result cannot be described as fair. The question in every case is the extent to which the deficiency alleged has produced overall unfairness.

62. The case for the appellant depends upon her being able to establish bias sufficient to produce such unfairness. As I have said, she challenges the findings of Douglas Brown J which exonerated Dr Lucking, Mr Guy and Sir Arthur Gold of both bias and apparent bias. I cannot see any justification for concluding that the judge was wrong to acquit Mr Guy and Sir Arthur Gold of both actual and apparent bias. There was wholly insufficient evidence to justify those allegations. Nor do I consider that the appellant can challenge the conclusion of the judge that Dr Lucking was not in fact biased. There was ample material from the witnesses who were members of the Disciplinary Committee to justify that conclusion. Equally, there was nothing about the decision itself which could in any way suggest it was infected by bias. The judge rightly concluded, in my view, that there was no real prospect of any different decision being reached on the material before the Disciplinary Committee, by any other Committee, however constituted.

63. The appellant is, however, on stronger ground in arguing that the judge was wrong to hold that Dr Lucking was not infected by apparent bias. This concept has to be approached with some caution in a contractual context. It is essentially a precautionary concept intended to exclude the risk of bias, hence the definition in domestic law enunciated by Lord Goff in *R v Gough* [1993] AC 646E. At page 668C, he expressed the test in the following well known words:

> In my opinion, if, in the circumstances of the case (as ascertained by the court), it appears that there was a real likelihood, in the sense of a real possibility, of bias on the part of a justice or other member of an inferior tribunal, justice requires that the decision should not be allowed to stand.

64. It is clear that Lord Goff envisaged that the court should examine all the facts whether they be known or unknown to anyone considering the matter at the time of the original hearing. As Sir Thomas Bingham MR (as he then was) said in *R v Inner West London Coroner ex parte Dallaglio* [1994] 4 All ER 139 at page 162g:

> 'the famous aphorism of Lord Hewitt CJ in *R v Sussex Justices ex parte McCarthy* [1924] 1 KB 256 at 259 ... "justice ... should manifestly and undoubtedly be seen to be done" it is no longer, it seems, good law, save of course in the case where the appearance of bias is such as to show a real danger of bias.'

65. This approach has been modified, it seems to me, in relation to decisions of public bodies by the effect of the Human Rights Act 1998, as explained in the judgment of the Master of the Rolls in Director General of Fair Trading the Proprietary Association of Great Britain and the Proprietary Articles Trade Association given on the 21st December 2000. The court there concluded that the provisions of Article 6 entitling a person to a fair public hearing by an independent and impartial tribunal in the determination of his civil rights and obligations required a modest adjustment to the test in *Gough*. In paragraph 86 of the judgment the Master of the Rolls said:

> 'When the Strasbourg jurisprudence is taken into account, we believe that a modest adjustment of the test in *Gough* is called for, which makes it plain that it is, in effect, no different from the test applied to most of the Commonwealth and in Scotland. The court must first ascertain all the circumstances which have a bearing on the suggestion that the judge was biased. It must then ask whether those circumstances would lead a fair minded and informed observer to conclude that there was a real possibility, or a danger, the two being the same, that the tribunal was biased.'

66. It is clear that this test, whichever way it is formulated, is intended to obviate both the appearance of unfairness, and the risk of unfairness. As far as the appearance of fairness is concerned, that is an essential ingredient of public justice in order to ensure a respect for the administration of justice, and is clearly an appropriate concept also for the supervision of public bodies. It may also be an appropriate tool in certain circumstances for the supervision of domestic bodies. For example a court may well consider it appropriate to interfere by way of injunction to prevent a particular person or persons from hearing disciplinary proceedings where a real danger of bias could be established on the basis that it might produce a real risk of unfairness.

67. But it does not seem to me to be appropriate to apply this test after the event to the determination of the question of whether or not there has been a breach of contract giving rise to a claim for damages. One returns at that stage to ask the question posed in *Calvin v Carr* (supra). The court's task is to determine whether or not, on the evidence, there has been a fair result. In a case such as the present, where the danger of bias can be evaluated and excluded, I consider that taken together with a wholly untainted appellate process, a fair result has been achieved. Any apparent bias on the part of Dr Lucking did not amount to a breach of the obligation on the disciplining body to provide a fair hearing overall.

68. If I am wrong in approaching the matter on this basis, I am prepared to accept that Dr Lucking was tainted by apparent bias. An informed person, that is a person knowing, as the judge found, that Dr Lucking had in 1991, albeit in the heat of the moment, asserted that athletes were guilty unless they were able to prove that they were innocent of doping, would consider that there was a risk that he might, albeit unconsciously, be affected by that attitude. His comments after the decision by the Independent Appeal Panel could not have allayed any such concern, so that, in my view, it would be likely that such a person would conclude that there had been a real risk of bias absent any further inquiry into the way the hearing was in fact conducted. If, contrary to my preferred view, this, of itself, produced unfairness amounting to a breach of contract, the judge's findings of fact however conclusively establish that that breach caused no loss. Whatever Dr Lucking's state of mind, the evidence of the other three members of the Committee who gave evidence satisfied the judge that they were not in any way infected by Dr Lucking, and came to a wholly independent judgment on the evidence which was fully justified by the material before them. The judge was correct, as I have already indicated, in concluding that the only basis for the decision of the Independent Appeal Panel in the appellant's favour was the new material giving support for what had previously merely been assertion as to the possibility that bacterial contamination could affect the testosterone reading.

69. But for the reasons I have already given, I consider that the appeal should be dismissed.

It is interesting to note that the approach of the Court of Appeal is similar to that taken by the Court of Arbitration for Sport which relies on the notion that 'all's well that ends well'. What should be considered is the impact of the hearing, the time between the hearing and appeal, and the impact on the athlete's career.

In many instances the Code does attempt to provide the athlete with rights akin to those one might expect in a national court of law. However, this cannot be guaranteed, as:

> The athlete facing doping charges is in many cases unable to invoke the rules of procedural fairness, unlike his fellow citizens in proceedings before governmental bodies, if the regulations of the IF in force in his particular branch of sport do not provide these.[16]

Banned Substances

In order for a governing body to regulate doping in sport it is necessary that it is able to identify accurately those substances which are not permitted. The WADA banned list is exhaustive; giving not

---

16   Soek, J, 'The fundamental rights of athletes in doping trials', in *op cit*, fn 5, O'Leary (2000), p 73.

only a list of substances outlawed but also their metabolites (further substances present as a result of the body converting banned substances) and other 'related' substances. In most cases this prevents the athlete's representatives from distinguishing the substances discovered from those specified in the schedules.

Many drugs which feature on the WADA banned list also appear in Schedule 2 of the Misuse of Drugs Act 1971. The MDA 1971 is the principal legislation criminalising the consumption of drugs in Britain and contains a list of various prohibited drugs. There are substances banned under the Code however, the consumption of which does not amount to a criminal offence.[17] The list of banned substances and techniques goes far beyond the scope of national criminal provisions.

For the first time in sport the WADA Anti-Doping Code attempts to give logical criteria for a substance's inclusion on the list. Although some may favour an attempt to justify logically why certain substances are on the list, others will see Art 4 as an attempt to justify the unjustifiable. After all, the preferred response to finding yourself in a hole is to stop digging. Inclusion on the banned list is dependent on satisfying two of the three categories for inclusion and we shall see whether the caveat in Art 4.3.3 is sufficient to deter those who test positive from challenging the logic of Art 4 in the courts.

Article 4.3.3: Criteria for Including Substances and Methods on the Prohibited List

WADA shall consider the following criteria in deciding whether to include a substance or method on the Prohibited List.

4.3.1 A substance or method shall be considered for inclusion on the Prohibited List if WADA determines that the substance or method meets any two of the following three criteria:

4.3.1.1 Medical or other scientific evidence, pharmacological effect or experience that the substance or method has the potential to enhance or enhances sport performance;

4.3.1.2 Medical or other scientific evidence, pharmacological effect, or experience that the Use of the substance or method represents an actual or potential health risk to the Athlete;

4.3.1.3 WADA's determination that the Use of the substance or method violates the spirit of sport described in the Introduction to the Code.

. . .

4.3.3 WADA's determination of the Prohibited Substances and Prohibited Methods that will be included on the Prohibited List shall be final and shall not be subject to challenge by an Athlete or other Person based on an argument that the substance or method was not a masking agent or did not have the potential to enhance performance, represent a health risk, or violate the spirit of sport.

It is very difficult to define the 'spirit of sport'. Some cynics may conclude its violation encompasses any unacceptable conduct not caught by the other two categories. On the basis of Article 4.3.3, it is unlikely that the CAS will be of assistance in it clarifying its boundaries. Such nebulous phrases do little to enhance the credibility of the code. On the other hand, the concepts of unfair advantage and risk to health are well rehearsed.

Enhancing Sport Performance

On a philosophical level it is argued that taking drugs will give the taker an advantage over a competitor who has not taken drugs and therefore constitutes cheating.[18] Therefore, there are two

---

17 Steroids, for example.
18 Simon, RL, *Fair Play: Sports, Values and Society* (1991), Boulder: Westview Press, Chapter 4.

grounds on which the prohibition of performance enhancing drugs may be justified. First, they give some athletes an unfair advantage over other athletes.[19] Secondly, they give the athlete an unfair advantage over the sport. Governing bodies run the risk that the image and validity of their sport would be undermined by a belief that their sport was conducted on an uneven playing field; this knowledge would lead to a damaging loss in popularity.

Following the drugs revelations surrounding Ben Johnson, the Canadian sprinter, a governmental inquiry chaired by Mr Justice Charles Dubin concluded:

de Pencier, J, 'Law and athlete drug testing in Canada'

The use of banned performance enhancing drugs is cheating, which is the antithesis of sport. The widespread use of such drugs has threatened the essential integrity of sport and is destructive of its very objectives. It also erodes the ethical and moral values of athletes who use them, endangering their mental and physical welfare while demoralising the entire sport community.[20]

Whilst we may concur with these sentiments, eradicating all the unfair advantages that one participant may have over another may not only be impossible but also undesirable. Competitive sport is all about one athlete being better than another and therefore it is beneficial to have physiological and psychological differences between the participants.

There are many advantages inherent in, for example, the nationality of an athlete. The skier raised in Austria or Switzerland has an advantage over one raised in Belgium; the runner living at altitude over the runner at sea level; the height advantage of the average American basketball player over the average oriental player; or the technological, training and dietary advantages of the rich nation over the impoverished third world county. All of these factors are advantages and may be considered unfair in terms of sporting equality. The argument that the above examples are natural advantages compared to the artificial advantage of drug taking is countered in the following extract:

Gardner, R, 'On performance enhancing substances and the unfair advantage argument'

In the first case we do not object to differences in the endurance capabilities of athletes resulting from increased haemoglobin count, provided that increase is the result of high-altitude training. In the second case, we do not object to discrepancies in the size of skeletal muscles, providing that size results from genetic endowment or training (eg weight lifting). In each case, we are not objecting to the advantage but to the way in which the advantage is gained. So what is it about blood doping or human growth hormone that somehow distinguishes these methods of securing an advantage and seems to render their effects unacceptable? The obvious difference is the advantages gained by blood boosting and HGH are achieved through the use of a (supplemented) substance. However if the basis of our objection is to be that using a substance is an unacceptable means to gaining an advantage, then the inconsistencies are more than apparent.

There are many legal substances used by athletes in their attempt to gain an advantage over competitors for example, amino acids, protein powders, vitamin and mineral supplements (sometimes injected), caffeine (legally limited to 12 micrograms per millilitre of urine, about seven cups of coffee), glucose polymer drinks and injections of ATP (a naturally produced chemical involved in muscle contraction). The list could go on and on. Clearly we do not object to gaining an advantage through the use of a substance; it is only particular substances to which we are opposed. This being the case, it seems that

---

19 Gardner, R, 'On performance enhancing substances and the unfair advantage argument (1989) XVI Journal of the Philosophy of Sport 59; Brown, WM, 'Drugs, ethics and sport' (1980) VII Journal of the Philosophy of Sport 15; Brown, WM, 'Fraleigh performance enhancing drugs in sport' (1985) XI Journal of the Philosophy of Sport 23; Brown, WM, 'Comments on Simon and Fraleigh' (1984) XI Journal of the Philosophy of Sport, 14.

20 de Pencier, J, 'Law and athlete drug testing in Canada' (1992) 4(2) Marquette Sports Law Journal 259.

some form of definitive criteria would have to be established in order to differentiate between permissible and prohibited substances. Yet, such criteria do not seem to exist.[21]

An alternative argument is that, rather than cheating fellow competitors, the drug taker is cheating 'the sport' itself. Clearly the essence of a sport would be compromised by certain breaches of the rules. It would be totally unacceptable for Linford Christie to be beaten in an Olympic 100 metres final by a competitor riding a horse or for Tiger Woods to lose the Masters to a player with a radio controlled golf ball. As Gardner has questioned, 'would allowing unrestricted use of steroids in the 100 metres be somewhat like providing the participants with motorcycles?'[22]

There are two problems with an affirmative answer. First, not all tactical or technical deviations from the norm are prohibited. Carbon fibre racquets have dramatically altered the game of tennis and it is unlikely that Cathy Freeman would have worn her one-piece running suit in the final of the women's 400 metres at the Sydney Olympics if it did not enhance her performance, yet these developments were accepted by the respective sports. Secondly, the question presumes that performance enhancing drugs are an extrinsic aid unrelated to the skills and physical condition of the athlete. However, as their name would suggest, these drugs enhance performance, that is, they allow the athlete to reach their full potential; and so parallels with motorcyclists are difficult to sustain.

Can a competitor truly claim victory if it is achieved with the assistance of drugs? Victory is inextricably linked to rules. It is questionable whether the drug taking athlete has competed in the first place. Successful athletes are afforded a unique place in society. Sporting heroes are society's heroes. By heralding the success of a drugs assisted athlete we are in danger of undermining society itself.[23]

Perhaps the most acceptable reason for prohibiting performance enhancing drugs is that otherwise sporting competition fails to be a test of persons:

Simon, R, 'Good competition and drug enhanced performance'

Where athletic competition is concerned, if all we are interested in is better and better performance, we could design robots to run the 100 yards in three seconds or hit a golf ball 500 yards when necessary. But it isn't just enhanced performance that we are after. In addition, we want athletic performance to be a test of persons. It is not only raw ability we are testing for; it is what people do with their ability that counts at least as much. In competition itself, each competitor is reacting to the choices, strategies and valued abilities of the other, which in turn are affected by past decisions and commitments. Arguably, athletic competition is a paradigm example of an area in which each individual competitor respects the other competitors as persons. That is, each reacts to the intelligent choices and valued characteristics of the other. These characteristics include motivation, courage, intelligence and what might be called the metachoice of which talents and capacities are to assume priority over others for a given stage of the individual's life.

However if outcomes are significantly affected not by such features but instead by the capacity of the body to benefit physiologically from drugs, athletes are no longer reacting to each other as persons but rather become more like competing bodies. It becomes more and more appropriate to see the opposition as things to be overcome – as mere means to be overcome in the name of victory – rather than persons posing valuable challenges. So, insofar as the requirement that we respect each other as persons is ethically fundamental, the prevailing paradigm does enjoy a privileged perspective from the moral point of view.[24]

---

21 *Op cit*, fn 18, Gardner (1989), p 59.
22 *Ibid*.
23 *Ibid*, p 68.
24 Simon, RL, 'Good competition and drug enhanced performance' (1994) XI Journal of the Philosophy of Sport, p 13.

Health Risk to the Athlete

There is no doubt that doping can damage your health[25]. To some sporting participants the side effects of these drugs outweigh the advantages of taking them. At the highest level, however, the competitive instincts of many participants may blind them to the dangers.

Goldman, B and Klatz, R, *Death in the Locker Room*

The desire to win is so great that people sometimes lose the concept of right and wrong due to being single-minded driven individuals. Sometimes it is very difficult to view life as a whole, as sports goals for the obsessed individual are the only true tangible goal. It can totally dominate your life and effectively shut out any vision of the world beyond. Mental perceptions of right and wrong may become misty and clouded and your attempts at experiencing the ethics and fun of sport are so nebulous, that it is hardly worth mentioning, let alone planning for in your mind. In some athletes' minds, the present is a set of stair steps of relatively minor competitions leading up to the moment when they have the opportunity to be the best in their designated sport.

There is great uncertainty in their minds about life-beyond-victory and that is one of your toughest challenges as an athlete. To be a good sports champion and leader you must not only compete successfully but also have an overview of your true life goals.

An example of this mindset was the results of a poll performed by Gabe Mirkin MD, author of *The Sports Medicine Book*. He is a devoted runner and in the early 1980s polled more than a hundred top runners and asked them this question, 'If I could give you a pill that would make you an Olympic champion and also kill you in a year would you take it?' Mirkin reported that more than half the athletes he asked responded that yes, they would take the pill. I was stunned by Mirkin's survey and wondered whether this indicated the willingness to die was universal among athletes; perhaps it was idiosyncratic to runners.

I performed a series of polls on athletes in the mid and late 1980s, those in combative and power sports such as weightlifting, track and field competitors, discus throwers, shot putters, jumpers, football players, etc. I found these competitors were just as crazy as runners.

I asked 198 top world class athletes a question similar to Mirkin's, 'If I had a magic drug that was so fantastic that if you took it once you would win every competition you would enter, from the Olympic decathlon to the Mr Universe, for the next five years but it had one minor drawback, it would kill you five years after you took it, would you still take the drug?' Of those asked, 103 (52%) said yes, that winning was so attractive, they would not only be prepared to achieve it by taking a pill (in other words through an outlawed, unfair method that is, in effect, cheating) but they would give their lives to do it.[26]

So how justified are governing bodies in taking a paternalist approach to protect the welfare of sporting participants?[27] Traditional paternalist jurisprudence would argue that such approach is only valid if the effect of the prohibition is to protect those unable to make an informed and rational judgment for themselves or to prevent harm to others. An obvious example of the former would be a ban on the taking of performance enhancing drugs by children and junior athletes, yet the extension of the ban beyond this point is more difficult to justify. If the governing bodies genuinely wished to protect the health of sportsmen and women would they not introduce a provision which forbade a

---

25 Although what is debatable is the quantities needed to do so.

26 Goldman, B and Klatz, R, *Death in the Locker Room 2* (1992), Chicago: Elite Sports Medicine Publications Inc, p 23.

27 Simon, RL, 'Good competition and drug-enhanced performance' (1984) XI Journal of the Philosophy of Sport 6; Brown, WM, 'Paternalism, drugs and the nature of sports' (1984) XI Journal of the Philosophy of Sport 14; Lavin, M, 'Sports and drugs: are the current bans justified?' (1987) XIV Journal of the Philosophy of Sport 34; and Fairchild, D, 'Sport abjection: steroids and the uglification of the athlete' (1987) XIV Journal of the Philosophy of Sport 74.

competitor competing whilst injured? Women's gymnastics would also need to be reviewed bearing in mind the incidence of arthritis and other diseases of the joints suffered by competitors in later life. There are also a number of contact sports which, by the nature of the activity, are likely to cause injury. No doubt the governing bodies of sport would argue that the risks of injury in certain sports are well known and that competitors are in some way consenting to the possibility of harm. The difficulty with this argument is that it could apply equally to doping.

Mill, JS, *On Liberty*

The object of this essay is to assert one very simple principle, as entitled to govern absolutely the dealings of society with the individual in the way of compulsion and control, whether the means used be physical force in the form of legal penalties or the moral coercion of public opinion. That principle is, that the sole end for which mankind are warranted, individually or collectively, in interfering in the liberty of action of any of their number, is self protection. That the only purpose for which power can be rightfully exercised over any member of a civilised community, against his will, is to prevent harm to others. His own good, either physical or moral, is not a sufficient warrant. He cannot rightfully be compelled to do or forbear because it will be better for him to do so, because it will make him happier, because, in the opinions of others, to do so would be wise or even right. These are good reasons for remonstrating with him or reasoning with him or persuading him or entreating him but not for compelling him or visiting him with any evil in case he do otherwise. To justify that, the conduct from which it is desired to deter him must be calculated to produce evil to someone else. The only part of the conduct of any one, for which he is amenable to society, is that which concerns others. In the part which merely concerns himself, his independence is, of right, absolute. Over himself, over his own body and mind, the individual is sovereign.[28]

It can be argued that drugs are not taken freely. Athletes are coerced into taking them by a belief that without them they would have little chance of sporting success.[29] However, there are many training regimes which athletes can and do reject on the basis that they may cause long term physiological damage: if injury is the mischief it is difficult to understand why drug taking should be treated differently.

On what basis then can society be justified in favouring the prohibition of performance enhancing drugs when as Mill argued, intervention in an athlete's life can amount to a greater wrong than the risk of illness voluntarily accepted?

Brown, WM, 'Paternalism, drugs and the nature of sport'

Often, too, we stress human factors such as determination, fortitude and co-operativeness over risk taking and technology. But in other cases skiing, mountain climbing, hang gliding risk and technology dominate. We believe in the capacity of sports to promote health and fitness but many originate in the practice of war and routinely involve stress and injury, sometimes death. We fashion rules and continually modify them to reduce hazards and minimise serious injury but few would seek to do so entirely. Perhaps we are tempted to require in athletes only what is natural. But our sports have evolved with our technology and our best athletes are often unnaturally, statistically, endowed with abilities and other characteristics far beyond the norm. It seems artificial indeed to draw the line at drugs when so much of today's training techniques, equipment, food, medical care, even the origin of the sport themselves, are the product of our technological culture.

---

28   Mill, JS, *On Liberty* (1962), London: Fontana. See also Dworkin, G, 'Paternalism' (1972) in The Monist, 56, 64–84; Dworkin, G, *Paternalism: Some Second Thoughts* (1983); Satorius, R (ed), *Paternalism*, Minneapolis: University of Minnesota Press; and Feinberg, J (1971) Legal Paternalism Canadian Journal of Philosophy 106–24

29   Thomas, CE, *Sport in a Philosophic Context* (1983), Philidelphia: Lea & Febiger; Wertheimer, A, *Coercion* (1989), Princeton: Princeton UP.

Nevertheless, something more may be said for the claim that sports reflect a broader set of values. In discussing the justification of paternalism in coaching the young, I have stressed the formation of the values of honesty, fairness and autonomy, values central to my conception of personhood. But they are not the only ones that might be stressed. Obedience, regimentation, service to others or sacrifice might have been proposed. These, too, in the proper context, might also be developed together with the skills of athletics. The values, perhaps even a conception of what is good for human life, are associated with sports, not because of their nature but due to the way we choose to play them. We can indeed forbid the use of drugs in athletics in general, just as we do in the case of children. But ironically, in adopting such a paternalistic stance of insisting that we know better than the athletes themselves how to achieve some more general good which they myopically ignore, we must deny them the very attributes we claim to value: self-reliance, personal achievement and autonomy.[30]

If it is difficult to sustain an argument for the prohibition of performance enhancing drugs taken by adults, perhaps a stronger argument is to ban them on the basis that they undermine the sporting ethic by giving some participants an unfair advantage over others or over the sport itself.

No matter how comprehensive the list of banned substances, however, there is always the danger that the 'dirty chemist' will be one step ahead, altering the chemical structure of compounds so as to distinguish the drug from those encompassed by the regulations. An alternative to the ever-increasing list system would be to look generally for abnormalities in samples. This was proposed by administrators in the sport of swimming. It has been suggested that the world governing body assemble a panel of medical and legal experts who would examine samples for irregularities, decide whether they are 'anti-doping substances', irrespective of whether they appear on lists of banned substances and sanction the competitors accordingly.

This proposition, although clearly attractive in many ways, is fundamentally flawed. An athlete could argue that it becomes impossible to act within the rules of the governing body if it is unclear exactly what those rules are until they are broken. Whilst it is accepted that the introduction of such a system would enable WADA to ensnare the 'cheats', it may be at the expense of many innocent athletes.

The reported decrease in positive tests at the Sydney Olympics could be accounted for by a strategic move by some competitors away from detectable drugs to undetectable ones such as human growth hormone. At the World Swimming Championships in Australia in January 1998, events were overshadowed by the alleged discovery of synthetic human growth hormone in the luggage of Chinese breast-stroke swimmer Yuan Yuan. Yuan and her coach received 15 year bans for trafficking in performance-enhancing drugs. Human growth hormone is favoured by drug-taking athletes over anabolic steroids because it produces greater improvements in performance and is also difficult to detect. However, human growth hormone is significantly more expensive than other drugs on the banned lists of sports governing bodies. Steroids are becoming the poor man's alternative. If this theory is correct, we would expect to see a decrease in positive tests among first world countries but a maintained level of positive tests among poorer athletes from poorer nations. As Andrew Jennings predicted before the 1996 Atlanta Games:

Jennings, A, *The New Lords of the Rings*

Two classes of dopers can be expected in Atlanta. Rich athletes can afford the drugs that don't show up in tests: human growth hormone, erythroproetin – which increases the number of red blood cells and so provides more oxygen in competition – and other hormonal drugs taken in dosages so low that they

---

30 Brown, WM, 'Paternalism, drugs and the nature of sport' (1994) XI Journal of the Philosophy of Sport 22.

clear the body in hours. They'll stay ahead of the testers with new versions of steroids coming out of commercial and illicit labs. Poor athletes who rely on steroids that show up in tests and who don't come off them well before competition are the most likely to be caught.[31]

Equally, the list contains some substances that would appear to have nothing but a negative effect on sporting performance – the so-called 'recreational drugs' being good examples.

Welch, R, 'A snort and a puff: recreational drugs and discipline in professional sport'

A clear line of demarcation should be drawn between drugs which are considered performance enhancing and those which should be more properly be considered as recreational. Whilst there are clearly problems both practical and philosophical in banning sports participants for taking the former, it is contended that consumption of the latter should cease to be the concern of regulatory bodies. Such bodies did not come into existence to act as moral watchdogs, and it is clearly debatable whether, today, such bodies are in touch with public opinion and thus the opinion of many of those who pay money to view particular sports. For example, with respect to the Dallagio affair there was discussion whether, even had the allegations be proven to be true, Dallagio's career should have been jeopardised for simply doing what many other individuals do, or have done at some time in their lives.[32] And this was with respect to rugby where arguably the followers of the game are more conservative in their moral outlook than is the case with football fans where the links with other forms of popular culture are much more overt. Take, for example, the number of musicians and actors who appear as guests on Sky's 'Soccer AM' programme on a Saturday. It is also the case that regulatory bodies, along it seems with politicians, ignore the increasingly widespread view, particularly amongst those who reached adulthood in the 1960s or during the decades since, that some or all drugs should be legalised or at least their possession decriminalised.[33]

Sanctions

The regulations covering sanctions represent the most complex part of the WADA Code as they attempt to deal with a number of variables distinguishing between teams and individuals, and different types of doping infractions.

For individuals, Art 10.1 invalidates any result achieved by the athlete where the positive result was obtained during a competition. The sanctions applied will depend on the doping infraction committed.

Article 10.2: Imposition of Ineligibility for Prohibited Substances and Prohibited Methods

Except for the specified substances identified in Article 10.3, the period of Ineligibility imposed for a violation of Articles 2.1 (presence of Prohibited Substance or its Metabolites or Markers), 2.2 (Use or Attempted Use of Prohibited Substance or Prohibited Method) and 2.6 (Possession of Prohibited Substances and Methods) shall be:

First violation: Two (2) years' Ineligibility.
Second violation: Lifetime Ineligibility.

However, the Athlete or other Person shall have the opportunity in each case, before a period of Ineligibility is imposed, to establish the basis for eliminating or reducing this sanction as provided in Article 10.5.

---

31 Jennings, A, *The New Lords of the Rings* (1986), London: Simon & Schuster.
32 See Freedland, J, 'Across that white line' *The Guardian*, 26 May 1999; Reeves, R, 'Free the cocaine two' *The Observer Review*, 27 August 1999.
33 Welch, R, 'A snort and a puff: recreational drugs and discipline in professional sport', in *op cit*, fn 5, O'Leary (2000), p 88.

Article 10.3: Specified Substances

The Prohibited List may identify specified substances which are particularly susceptible to unintentional anti-doping rules violations because of their general availability in medicinal products or which are less likely to be successfully abused as doping agents. Where an Athlete can establish that the Use of such a specified substance was not intended to enhance sport performance, the period of Ineligibility found in Article 10.2 shall be replaced with the following:

First violation: At a minimum, a warning and reprimand and no period of Ineligibility from future Events, and at a maximum, one (1) year's Ineligibility.

Second violation: Two (2) years' Ineligibility.

Third violation: Lifetime Ineligibility.

However, the Athlete or other Person shall have the opportunity in each case, before a period of Ineligibility is imposed, to establish the basis for eliminating or reducing (in the case of a second or third violation) this sanction as provided in Article 10.5.

Article 10.4: Ineligibility for Other Anti-Doping Rule Violations

The period of Ineligibility for other anti-doping rule violations shall be:

10.4.1 For violations of Article 2.3 (refusing or failing to submit to Sample collection) or Article 2.5 (Tampering with Doping Control), the Ineligibility periods set forth in Article 10.2 shall apply.

10.4.2 For violations of Articles 2.7 (Trafficking) or 2.8 (administration of Prohibited Substance or Prohibited Method), the period of Ineligibility imposed shall be a minimum of four (4) years up to lifetime Ineligibility. An anti-doping rule violation involving a Minor shall be considered a particularly serious violation, and, if committed by Athlete Support Personnel for violations other than specified substances referenced in Article 10.3, shall result in lifetime Ineligibility for such Athlete Support Personnel. In addition, violations of such Articles which also violate non-sporting laws and regulations, may be reported to the competent administrative, professional or judicial authorities.

10.4.3 For violations of Article 2.4 (whereabouts violation or missed test), the period of Ineligibility shall be at a minimum 3 months and at a maximum 2 years in accordance with the rules established by the Anti-Doping Organization whose test was missed or whereabouts requirement was violated. The period of Ineligibility for subsequent violations of Article 2.4 shall be as established in the rules of the Anti-Doping Organization whose test was missed or whereabouts requirement was violated.

The bans described above have been drafted with the intention of ensuring a consistency of duration. They are not however, drafted to provide a consistency of sanction. A two year ban for athletes in some sports where the sporting career is short, gymnastics for example, is akin to a life ban. In other sports noted for the longevity of a competitor's career, equestrianism for example, the sanction merely interrupts a career. This is particularly so in individual competition where there is nothing to prevent the competitor from practising and refining their skills during their interregnum. The logic for equality of sanction length is proffered by notes accompanying the WADA Code:

A primary argument in favor of harmonization is that it is simply not right that two Athletes from the same country who test positive for the same Prohibited Substance under similar circumstances should receive different sanctions only because they participate in different sports. In addition, flexibility in sanctioning has often been viewed as an unacceptable opportunity for some sporting bodies to be more lenient with dopers. The lack of harmonization of sanctions has also frequently been the source of jurisdictional conflicts between International Federations and National Anti-Doping Organizations.[34]

---

34 Notes accompanying Art 10.

This may be true enough, but could still, nevertheless, be a reflection of the underlying prioritisation of anti-doping over justice to participants.

Bans do not only prevent participation in events.

Article 10.9: Status During Ineligibility

No Person who has been declared Ineligible may, during the period of Ineligibility, participate in any capacity in a Competition or activity (other than authorized anti-doping education or rehabilitation programs) authorized or organized by any Signatory or Signatory's member organization. In addition, for any anti-doping rule violation not involving specified substances described in Article 10.3, some or all sport-related financial support or other sport-related benefits received by such Person will be withheld by Signatories, Signatories' member organizations and governments. A Person subject to a period of Ineligibility longer than four years may, after completing four years of the period of Ineligibility, participate in local sport events in a sport other than the sport in which the Person committed the anti-doping rule violation, but only so long as the local sport event is not at a level that could otherwise qualify such Person directly or indirectly to compete in (or accumulate points toward) a national championship or International Event.

The word 'activity' makes it clear that, as well as being banned for competing in competitions in that particular sport, the ban extends to other involvement such as coaching, and to other sports.[35] Article 11 deals with team sanctions.

Article 11: Consequences to Teams

Where more than one team member in a *Team Sport* has been notified of a possible anti-doping rule violation under Article 7 in connection with an *Event*, the Team shall be subject to *Target Testing* for the *Event*. If more than one team member in a *Team Sport* is found to have committed an anti-doping rule violation during the *Event*, the team may be subject to *Disqualification* or other disciplinary action. In sports which are not *Team Sports* but where awards are given to teams, *Disqualification* or other disciplinary action against the team when one or more team members have committed an anti-doping rule violation shall be as provided in the applicable rules of the International Federation.

The WADA Code does provide for a power to reinstate athletes in exceptional cases. The degree of reduction in the period of ineligibility is dependent on the degree of culpability. The circumstances in which a competitor may successfully invoke these 'exceptional circumstance' are seen to be restrictive once the Code is interpreted in the light of the accompanying notes.

Article 10.5: Elimination or Reduction of Period of Ineligibility Based on Exceptional Circumstances

24.3.1 No Fault or Negligence

If the Athlete establishes in an individual case involving an anti-doping rule violation under Article 2.1 (presence of Prohibited Substance or its Metabolites or Markers) or Use of a Prohibited Substance or Prohibited Method under Article 2.2 that he or she bears No Fault or Negligence for the violation, the otherwise applicable period of Ineligibility shall be eliminated. When a Prohibited Substance or its Markers or Metabolites is detected in an Athlete's Specimen in violation of Article 2.1 (presence of Prohibited Substance), the Athlete must also establish how the Prohibited Substance entered his or her system in order to have the period of Ineligibility eliminated. In the event this Article is applied and the period of Ineligibility otherwise applicable is eliminated, the anti-doping rule violation shall not be considered a violation for the limited purpose of determining the period of Ineligibility for multiple violations under Articles 10.2, 10.3 and 10.6.

---

35   As long as that other sport is a signatory to the Code.

24.3.1 No Significant Fault or Negligence

This Article 10.5.2 applies only to anti-doping rule violations involving Article 2.1 (presence of Prohibited Substance or its Metabolites or Markers), Use of a Prohibited Substance or Prohibited Method under Article 2.2, failing to submit to Sample collection under Article 2.3, or administration of a Prohibited Substance or Prohibited Method under Article 2.8. If an Athlete establishes in an individual case involving such violations that he or she bears No Significant Fault or Negligence, then the period of Ineligibility may be reduced, but the reduced period of Ineligibility may not be less than one-half of the minimum period of Ineligibility otherwise applicable. If the otherwise applicable period of Ineligibility is a lifetime, the reduced period under this section may be no less than 8 years. When a Prohibited Substance or its Markers or Metabolites is detected in an Athlete's Specimen in violation of Article 2.1 (presence of Prohibited Substance), the Athlete must also establish how the Prohibited Substance entered his or her system in order to have the period of Ineligibility reduced.

Article 10.5 is meant to have an impact only in cases where the circumstances are truly exceptional and not in the vast majority of cases.

To illustrate the operation of Article 10.5, an example where No Fault or Negligence would result in the total elimination of a sanction is where an Athlete could prove that, despite all due care, he or she was sabotaged by a competitor. Conversely, a sanction could not be completely eliminated on the basis of No Fault or Negligence in the following circumstances: (a) a positive test resulting from a mislabeled or contaminated vitamin or nutritional supplement (Athletes are responsible for what they ingest (Article 2.1.1) and have been warned against the possibility of supplement contamination); (b) the administration of a prohibited substance by the Athlete's personal physician or trainer without disclosure to the Athlete (Athletes are responsible for their choice of medical personnel and for advising medical personnel that they cannot be given any prohibited substance); and (c) sabotage of the Athlete's food or drink by a spouse, coach or other person within the Athlete's circle of associates (Athletes are responsible for what they ingest and for the conduct of those persons to whom they entrust access to their food and drink). However, depending on the unique facts of a particular case, any of the referenced illustrations could result in a reduced sanction based on No Significant Fault or Negligence. (For example, reduction may well be appropriate in illustration (a) if the Athlete clearly establishes that the cause of the positive test was contamination in a common multiple vitamin purchased from a source with no connection to Prohibited Substances and the Athlete exercised care in not taking other nutritional supplements.)

The most likely person to administer a substance to the athlete against their wishes will be one of the competitor's entourage (not a competitor). The accompanying notes explain that it will not be adequate for a total remission of sanction to blame such a person. This caveat severely restricts the possibility of a successful appeal under Art 10.

More fundamentally, even a successful claim by the athlete, that they were sabotaged and no fault can be ascribed to them, will result in an elimination of the sanction only – the infraction still stands. The code claims that Article 10.5 is consistent with principles of natural justice but it is arguable that such justice could only be achieved if no fault meant no infraction. Such a result may appease some athletes but many would be aggrieved that the 'doper' label remained.

Prior to the introduction of the WADA Code, a combination of strict liability doping definitions allied to fixed sanctions resulted in an inflexible system where the inevitable subtleties and grey areas were lost. However, the Court of Arbitration for Sport had shown itself adept at mitigating the severity of sanctions. For example, in a case where the swimmer's coach admitted giving the swimmer a headache remedy which, unbeknown to them, contained a substance on the banned list, the coach's two year ban was commuted to seven months on the grounds that the mistake was an innocent one and the swimmer had gained no unfair advantage.[36] Further, a swimmer's and a water

---

36 Arbitration CAS 95/150, V/*Federation Internationale de Natation Amateur (FINA)*, award of 28 June 1996.

polo player's bans were quashed after it was established that the breaches were for lack of notification of the use of asthma remedies and therefore, were breaches of a technical nature only.[37] The WADA Code now covers these eventualities so, to a certain degree, the CAS may now become less important as a mitigating body. It will be interesting to see whether the CAS will be active in future in ameliorating other aspects of the WADA Code.

THE ATHLETES' PERSPECTIVE

Ironically, one perspective that is often overlooked in the doping hiatus is the view of the athletes themselves. The mere allegation of a doping misdemeanour may be enough to cloud a sporting career. A positive test, as Diane Modahl discovered, can be fatal. Athletes both welcome and fear drug tests. They are welcomed inasmuch as they do not allow cheating athletes to prosper. They are feared because once a positive result is established the chances of them being able to explain away those test results are remote.[38]

Curtis, A, 'Running scared: an athlete lawyer's view of the doping regime'

I fear failing a drugs test for several reasons, and this fear has been heightened by the recent questionable nandrolone cases. The first is the shame that it would bring upon me and anybody associated with my performances, a stigma which seems to attach regardless of an end finding of guilt or innocence. Secondly, it would prevent me from taking part in the sport that I love. This would be especially difficult for a disabled person to accept as there are limited where a disabled person is allowed to compete on a level playing field and feel good about oneself and one's contribution to society generally. Thirdly, it would mean the loss of my income, which would affect my wife and children. Fourthly, it may affect my ability to secure employment as it would be seen as a black mark against my name, a drug offence being a serious matter in whatever walk of life.[39]

This fear has heightened following the Diane Modahl case which appears to have instilled feelings of insecurity amongst athletes. McArdle's survey of the views and opinions of elite level fencers revealed a scepticism about the doping regime.

McArdle, D, 'Say it ain't so, Mo. International performers' perceptions of drug use and the Diane Modahl affair'

One can argue that the views of these athletes are evidence of an unnecessary cynicism and stem from a fundamental lack of knowledge that can be rectified by the more effective use of educational programmes. That may well be the case, especially if one agrees that it is ultimately the athlete's responsibility to find out which substances are proscribed and to know what side effects, if any, those substances may have. But this survey indicated far more than a mere lack of awareness of banned substances. The fencers' scepticism about the science of drug testing, their perception of hypocrisy and incompetence among the governing bodies and their cynicism about the way in which testing programmes are couched in terms of 'cheating' rather than addressing legitimate health concerns are unlikely to be eased by more drug-awareness campaigns.

The effect of the Diane Modahl case on these athletes cannot be overstated. For some it had heralded a fundamental shift in perceptions, while for others it merely reinforced a pre-existing lack of faith in the

---

37 Arbitration CAS 95/141, C/*Federation Internationale de Natation Amateur (FINA)*, award of 22 April 1996 and Arbitration CAS 96/149, C/*Federation Internationale de Natation Amateur (FINA)*, award of 13 March 1997.

38 See, for example, the case of contaminated pork offal: Arbitration CAS 2000/A/270 *Meca-Medina & Majcen v FINA*.

39 Curtis, A, 'Running scared: an athlete lawyer's view of the doping regime', in *op cit*, fn 5, O'Leary (2000), p 117.

whole testing procedure. Not one of those interviewed expressed much faith in the testing regime. Until the athletes' fears of double standards, dodgy science and flawed reasoning are adequately addressed, questions such as how many athletes are actually using drugs, whether sports should test for recreational drugs and what penalties should be imposed on users are rendered irrelevant. The fencers thought the governing bodies and the testing authorities needed to provide definitive scientific evidence as to the efficacy of their procedures to the athletes' satisfaction (as opposed to the satisfaction of the media and other moral agents) if drug testing was to regain any vestige of credibility.

If exhortations of fair play mean little to elite-level performers, it would be pointless to use such arguments to justify banning the possession and supply of anabolic steroids under the Misuse of Drugs Act, 1971. So far as the fencers were concerned, the only possible justifications for bans would be on health protection grounds. Banning substances because their use was 'unfair' seemed indefensible. Banning them if they were shown to be harmful had more merit, but this had to be backed up by more effective education and health awareness programmes that have moved away from reliance on the 'cheating' argument. So far as this sport was concerned, those at the sharp end – the individuals who compete internationally and who are likely to be tested – lacked confidence in the procedure and science of drugs testing and in the organisations who carried it out.

Many of the fencers' comments might be wrong or ill-conceived, but if their perceptions are replicated in other sports, rebuilding British athletes' trust and confidence in the wake of the Diane Modahl affair is likely to be a very long process indeed. [40]

On the basis that prevention is better than cure (the curative provisions consume most of the WADA Code), Art 18 introduces matters of athlete education.

Article 18: Education

18.1 Basic Principle and Primary Goal

The basic principle for information and education programs shall be to preserve the spirit of sport as described in the Introduction to the Code, from being undermined by doping. The primary goal shall be to dissuade Athletes from using Prohibited Substances and Prohibited Methods.

18.2 Program and Activities

Each Anti-Doping Organization should plan, implement and monitor information and education programs. The programs should provide Participants with updated and accurate information on at least the following issues:

- Substances and methods on the Prohibited List

- Health consequences of doping

- Doping control procedures

- Athletes' rights and responsibilities

The programs should promote the spirit of sport in order to establish an anti-doping environment which influences behavior among Participants.

Athlete Support Personnel should educate and counsel Athletes regarding anti-doping policies and rules adopted pursuant to the Code.

---

40   McArdle, D, 'Say it ain't so, Mo. International performers' perceptions of drug use and the Diane Modahl affair', in *op cit*, fn 5, O'Leary (2000), p 108.

It is a pity that Art 18 is not couched in the same terms as many of the Articles preceding it. Article 18 appears to impose little in the way of compunction on a governing body to provide education. This is rather startling bearing in mind that health is one of the three reasons cited for a substance's qualification for the banned list. If doping in sport is such an axiomatically terrible thing, then a good programme of education should significantly reduce the number of offenders (and thereby protect their health). Article 19 looks at research and *inter alia* lists education as a suitable subject for research funding. We wait with interest to see how much of WADA's nearly $4 m research budget this year will be allocated to preventative research and how much to curative.[41]

CONCLUSION

The above analysis of the Code illustrates clearly that the rights of athletes to compete freely and the rights of sport to regulate competition are irreconcilable. As sport strengthens its anti-doping regulatory framework so, inevitably, the rights of competitors diminish. As the rights of competitors diminish, so the duty on sport to regulate fairly increases.

Antonio Rigozzi, A, Kaufmann-Kohler, G, Malinverni, G, 'Doping and fundamental rights of athletes: comments in the wake of the adoption of the World Anti-Doping Code'

WADA's effort might be seen by some as the latest attempt of the sports world to immunise sports from state control. The situation is more complex, however. The adoption of a Code, which complies with the fundamental rights of athletes, was only made possible thanks to a broad consultation of all stakeholders. Indeed, as a result of such consultation, the concerns about fundamental rights were duly taken into account in the course of the drafting process. This represents a major step forward as opposed to an approach that ignores fundamental rights requirements and, thus, leaves the enforcement of such rights to the courts. In that situation, the only rights protected are those of the individual athlete who has access to a court willing to interfere in sports matters and who can afford legal proceedings. By contrast, all the athletes will benefit from the fundamental rights protection incorporated into the Code.[42]

It is difficult to understand why it appears that only 'fundamental rights' are at issue. Why shouldn't a broader raft of rights, such as the right to be treated reasonably, fairly and equitably, be considered? The above authors claim that the code is not designed to immunise against the intervention of law but then justify the Code only in terms of identifiable legal rights. Certainly, in its preamble WADA does not attempt to promote the Code as a document protecting athletes' rights. Indeed, the only 'fundamental right' that the Code acknowledges athletes deserve is to 'participate in doping-free sport and thus promote health, fairness and equality for 'Athletes worldwide'.

There is a danger that WADA's utilitarian approach to athletes' rights, exemplified by the Code, and justified by that most nebulous of concepts, 'the spirit of sport', has resulted in an imbalance between sport and the rights of its most precious commodity.

---

41 On privacy issues and drug testing, see Malloy, D and Zakus, D, 'Ethics in drug testing in sport: an invasion of privacy justified?' (2002) 17 (2) Sport, Education & Society 203; Donnellan, L, 'The right to privacy and drug testing (2002) 10 (5) Sports Law Administration & Practice 11.

42 ISLR 2003, 3(AUG), 39–67.

KEY SOURCES

Houlihan, B, *Dying to Win; Doping in sport and the development of anti-doping policy* (1999) Strasbourg, Council of Europe Publishing

Mottram, DR, *Drugs in Sport* (2003), London: Routledge.

O'Leary, J, (ed), *Drugs and Doping in Sport* (2000), London: Cavendish.

Reeb, M, *Digests of CAS Awards 1986–1998*, Berne, Staempfli Editions SA, 1998–2000, New York: Aspen Publishers; 2001–2003, New York: Aspen Publishers

Waddington, I, *Sport, Health and Drugs* (2000), London: Spon.

THE COMMERCIAL REGULATION OF SPORT

CHAPTER 8

SPORT AND MONEY: ACCOUNTABILITY AND REGULATION

INTRODUCTION

This chapter will explore some of the concerns that have developed regarding the relationship between sport and money. This relationship has been examined at some length concerning the particular characteristics of 'sports business' earlier in the book. The financial dynamics in sport are often idiosyncratic. [1]

The first section will consider the 'growing pains' when there is a transformation from an amateur to a professionalised sport, which invariably involves fragmentation, leading to litigation and many legally related problems. The changes in the late 1970s with cricket and the mid-1990s in rugby will be explored.

The second section will examine the darker side of the relationship between sport and money. In recent years financial scandals have arisen in a number of sports on the national and international stage. As with other forms of business, there is a need for financial probity. The corruption scandals in English football will be discussed, together with the attempts to eradicate it. Additionally, the recent match fixing allegations in world cricket and in English football will be examined. The financial scandals of the International Olympic Committee will be briefly discussed.

The third section will focus on the relationship between sport and gambling. The relationship is almost a marriage in heaven. A major characteristic of sport is its unpredictability. It provides the ideal scenario for betting on the outcome. Gambling has a long related history with sports such as horse and greyhound racing. A modern development has been the increasing betting on a whole range of other immeasurable factors, for example, runs scored by a particular batsman in cricket or the winning margin in a basketball match. The development of methods such as spread betting and new mediums such as via the internet has changed the dynamics of gambling.

PROFESSIONALISATION AND THE END OF AMATEURISM

Will Carling's famous view of the Rugby Union Football Committee as '57 old farts' crystallises the legacy of the past in sports administration and governance. However, rugby union has gone through a dramatic change over the last few years – it has *really* entered the professional world – but not without a struggle:

'Shamateurism's end: taking the money and running'

The timing could not have been more ironic: on the very weekend rugby league was celebrating its centenary, rugby union announced it too was now a professional game. Rugby league was launched 100 years ago tomorrow by 21 union clubs, which wanted to pay their players for taking time off from work to play, but failed to persuade other union clubs to go along. It led to the two separate rugby codes – one openly professional and the other where payments were not supposed to be made. Slowly but inexorably, union's amateur status has become a sham. First came expenses, then came lucrative PR jobs

---

1   See earlier, pp 50–53.

with big companies, and then full blown product endorsement (so long as there was no direct mention of the individual player's links with rugby). Other countries went much further than the home nations. France began paying some of its top players in the thirties. But it was television – and the large audiences generated by the 1987 and 1991 World Cups – that tolled the final amateur bell. Rugby has become a multi-million pound business. Just before the start of this year's world cup, Murdoch's News Corporation struck a £360 million deal with the rugby unions of Australia, New Zealand and South Africa.

It was the fear of Murdoch – or his rival Kerry Packer – grabbing control of the sport that finally forced the International Rugby Union Board to move this weekend. Some rugby union officials were expressing regret yesterday. They should not have been. The new system will end the hypocrisy of the old. It will allow a few – and it will only be a few – top players to a share in the game's growing riches. They deserve that. The main core of the sport – just as in tennis, golf, even soccer – will remain amateur. Remember, even within rugby league, the vast majority of players have another job as well as playing rugby. Our own sports reporters put the number of union players who are likely to receive direct payments at between 60 and 100. Even within this group, few are likely to be full-time rugby players. The risks are too great – both from injury and loss of form. Big policemen and massive army officers are still likely to be found in the pack. Although payments can be made at any level, few clubs are likely to be in a position to offer them. Even the most successful club, Bath, holds fewer than 10,000. Compare that to United's 40,000 plus.[2]

This change in the status of the game[3] has brought obvious changes: sports agents,[4] professional players' union,[5] television revenues. However there have been those who lament the end of the amateur ethos.[6]

Similar changes have occurred in athletics:

Downes, S and Mackay, D, *Running Scared: How Athletics Lost Its Innocence*

Athens was also the venue in 1982 for the greatest revolution in a century of modem athletics. There were no races run, no jumps leaped nor implements thrown: the revolution took place in a conference hall, where the IAAF took the first tentative steps towards allowing athletics to go professional.

The process had begun at the IAAF's conference in Moscow prior to the 1980 Olympics. There, the Federation established a nine man working group on 'eligibility' – in other words, to examine the amateur status of athletes.

During the 1960s and 1970s amateurism, although increasingly regarded as an anachronism in the modern sporting world – cricket had abandoned its 'Gentlemen and Players' distinction, and the Wimbledon tennis championships had gone open – had still been strictly applied by the International Olympic Committee, first under the autocratic leadership of the American, Avery Brundage, and then under the Irish peer, Lord Killanin. The Games were still the most important event in any amateur sportsman's career, so no athlete could risk being banned for receiving money. But with Michael Killanin set to retire as IOC president in July 1980, the ground was laid for a moderniser to succeed him. The Spaniard Juan Antonio Samaranch duly became the IOC's first full-time president. Fittingly, he was to preside over a period which made it increasingly possible for Olympic competitors to become full-time, professional athletes.

---

2   'Shamateurism's end: taking the money and running' *The Guardian*, 28 August 1995.
3   'Small change for most Rugby Union players' *The Guardian*, 28 August 1995, p 3; 'The Rugby revolution: amateurism'.
4   'The future starts here: Rugby sports agents' *The Observer*, 31 December 1995, p 26.
5   'Moon is the man as sun sets on amateurism' *The Guardian*, 20 December 1995, p 21.
6   'Rugby Union: top club official quits over "ethos" ' *The Guardian*, 1 September 1995, p 23.

The mood at the IAAF's congress in Moscow had reflected this turning point in world sport. When the IAAF working party on eligibility delivered its report to the governing council when it met in Cairo the following March, its findings were hardly a surprise. The tone of the report was categorical: the very future of the IAAF was in the balance. The shamateur game was up, according to the working party. 'The year 1980 has brought to a head the fact that the future of the IAAF and its members is at stake,' the report began. 'It is felt that at international level, athletics is a semi-professional (in the widest sense) sport already, with many leading athletes in top countries training for at least 30 hours per week. The Group aims, however, to make a clear distinction between a professional sport and athletics, which, by its very nature, can never become this. It is recognised that there is dissatisfaction among the elite athletes and meeting organisers with the present rules on eligibility, and in different countries, violations of the rules occur, which causes accusations of hypocrisy to be levelled against the whole sport of athletics.'

Conscious of the need to prevent an amateur-professional schism in the sport, but also subjected to political pressures from the eastern bloc nations – who wanted the status quo maintained, so that their State-funded athletes would maintain their apparent advantage over part-time western athletes the working party proposed a set of rule changes which would openly allow payments to athletes, through a system of prize-money and trust funds. The recommendations, though, were only a majority view of the working party.

The proposed new eligibility rules were debated heatedly when put before the IAAF Conference held just before the European Championships in Athens in September 1982. The reactionaries on the working party, who wanted to avoid change, seemed to have swung opinion among the IAAF Congress – the sport's 'parliamentary' body, made up of representatives of every national member federation, with the authority to make or change the sport's rules.

Compromise was offered. Although the working party had favoured prize-money over appearance fees ('an athlete receiving money merely because he is a champion is felt to be an unfair and unworthy system for the sport. Appearance money inevitably takes the stimulus away from competition, just as it may be argued that prize money gives added stimulus'), it was the latter, appearance money scheme which had attracted more support. Yet even moves towards this new system of appearance payments seemed to have stalled until a rousing address by a member of the British delegation. The man who turned the day in favour of appearance fees was Andy Norman.

Before breakfast, sensing that the mood of the Congress might reject all proposals for athletes' payments at that afternoon's debate, Norman had banged on the door of the hotel bedroom of The Guardian reporter, John Rodda. After a typically journalistic late night, Rodda was feeling a little fragile when he was awoken by the knock on the door from the policeman, but he was persuaded nonetheless to help Norman by writing what Rodda later described as 'a blatantly provocative speech' in favour of change.

Standing in front of all the IAAF's power brokers at the Athens conference, and with Rodda's speech to guide him, Norman warned that if the national governing bodies continued to pretend that under-the-counter payments were not happening, then what they all feared most – a breakaway, professional circuit – might happen. Norman 'knew what the athletes wanted', Rodda recalled, 'and how it was obtainable'.

'Rule 17 – Athlete's Funds', the new payment rule, went through by 367 votes to 16 . . . the tide had turned professionalism's way.[7]

Although the enormous amount of amateur sporting activity, often in the form of recreational activity, must never be forgotten in these discussions, virtually all of elite modern sport is clearly professional.[8] The general commercialisation and commodification of sport has been shown to be

---

7   Downes, S and Mackay, D, *Running Scared: How Athletics Lost Its Innocence* (1996), Edinburgh: Mainstream, pp 100–02.

8   See Strenk, A, 'Amateurism: the myth and the reality', in Segrave, JP and Chu, D, *The Olympic Games in Transition* (1988), Champaign, Illinois: Human Kenetics, pp 307–21; Holt, R, 'Amateurism and its interpretation: the social origins of British sport' (1992) 5(4) Innovation 19.

influential in this process.[9] The law is never far behind in these circumstances, and the commercial origins of much legal intervention in sport are clear to see.

A good deal of elite sport is played on the world stage. The quadrennial Olympic Games and football World Cup are clear examples. The two processes of globalisation, where social activities and processes are increasingly ceasing to be explained purely in national terms, and professionalisation of sport, can be seen as advancing hand in hand. Changes in cricket at the end of the 1970s and in both codes of rugby will be discussed to illustrate these developments.

CRICKET WARS: THE PACKER LEGACY

The development of World Series Cricket sponsored by Kerry Packer as a challenge to established Test Cricket in Australia had major implications and consequences for world cricket. The mid-1970s cricket world was ideally placed for commercial exploitation. Although there was a semi-professional game in Australia and professional game in England, wages were very low compared with other similar sports and the television rights were cheap. In Australia the top players who played Test cricket were continually in dispute over pay. Kerry Packer, who owned a series of commercial TV stations in Australia, was under pressure to increase audiences and televised sport was seen as a cheap way to achieve this. He had successfully obtained exclusive rights to golf; he saw cricket as even more appropriate in terms of the ability to fit in commercial breaks.

Television rights had been presented to the non-commercial channel Australian Broadcasting Corporation (ABC) since the 1950s ritually on a non-exclusive basis with local commercial TV bids then being made. This process had kept down the price paid for rights. Packer wanted to buy exclusive rights to Test cricket. Even though in 1976 he was prepared to pay over six times the price that ABC had agreed with the Australian Cricket Board, he failed in his bid. Effectively closed out of established cricket, he decided to develop a rival international cricket competition and began to sign up established Australian test cricketers such as Ian Chappell and to approach established international starts from England, the West Indies, Pakistan, India and talented South African players excluded from international cricket because of sporting bans induced by apartheid. Instrumental in the recruitment of a number of these players was Tony Greig, then the England Test captain. One legal issue that needed to be reconciled was first what name could be used: the term 'Supertest' was viewed as sufficiently distinct. Also:

Haigh, G, *Cricket War: The Inside Story of Packer's World Series Cricket*

Benaud worried, though, that the Laws of Cricket themselves might have a legal character. The MCC did hold their copyright. It would be important to play a form of stand alone rules 'based on' the Laws to avoid further legal troubles.[10]

The vast majority of the world's best players were signed up and the 'Packers Circus', as the press described it, was launched in May 1977. The plan met a lot of resistance from the cricket establishment and although there were attempts at a compromise between the Packer organisation and International Cricket Conference (now Council) (ICC), the international governing body, the

---

9   See Chapter 2, p 40–55.
10   Haigh, G, *Cricket War: the Inside Story of Packer's World Series Cricket* (1993), Melbourne: Text Publishing Company, p 82.

issue of exclusive rights to Tests in Australia proved insurmountable. This led over two months later to:

> Reports ... of an International Cricket Conference ultimatum issued the previous evening at Lord's: WSC players should be barred from all first class and Test Cricket if they did not shred their contracts before 1 October 1977. Though the Test and County Cricket Board's Doug Insole and Donald Carr had received Queen's Counsel advice that enforcement would be legally difficult, the counties were passionate. Glamorgan's Ossie Wheatley went into the TCCB minute book expressing the view: 'Our duty is to drive this wedge of uncertainty into the player's mind.' Insole echoed: 'War situation. We must make sure this thing does not get off the ground.'[11]

The World Series Cricket (WSC) matches that were to be played during the winter of 1977–78 in Australia were then scheduled to be played at the same time as the test series between Australia and the West Indies. The contracted players would not be available for test selection whatever the moves of the ICC. The view was that:

> The ICC's self-appointing as cricket's sole promoter could not go unchallenged and barring signatories from first class cricket appeared an unenforceable restraint of trade ... CPH (Packer's Consolidated Press Holdings), it was decided, would back Greig, Snow and Proctor in a High Court challenge to the ICC.[12]

The High Court in London became the focus of attention that October:

> WSC, Greig, Proctor and Snow were litigants; the defendants were the Test and County Cricket Board and chairman Doug Insole – the ICC had no legal personality. A barrage of lawyers and twenty one star witnesses were gathered to impress Justice Sir Christopher Slade.

> The sole absentee was Sir Donald Bradman. Ray Steele arrived in his stead. 'He was such a shrewd little bugger of course,' Steele chuckles. Nobody relished the fiery court wicket with hostile Queen's Counsels from both ends: WSC's Robert Alexander downwind, the ICC's Michael Kempster coming uphill but making Greig flinch as testimony began. Ross Edwards was struck at how detested Greig had become. 'Jeez, he was like Lord Haw-Haw,' says Edwards. 'He was very bad meat.'

> 'For some reason, I felt like a criminal,' Greig recalled. 'Especially when I was first attacked by the opposition counsel. My initial impulse was to tell all our opposition to go jump in the lake ... It became like a battle, with the opposition trying to pull me apart and Alexander protecting me.'[13]

The decision was in favour of the players. The ICC's only gratification came in Justice Slade's observations that cricket administrators were a thoroughly decent breed who, 'believed that they acted in the best interests of cricket'. The judge could also understand the sense of betrayal at Greig's recruiting role, but retaliation had 'strained the bounds of loyalty'. In fact, they should have foreseen events:

> The very size of profits made from cricket matches involving star players must for some years have carried the risk that a private promoter would appear on the scene and seek to make money by promoting cricket matches involving world class cricketers.[14]

Greig v Insole [1978] 1 WLR 302

The question for decision has been whether the particular steps which the ICC and TCCB took to combat what they regarded as the threat from world series cricket were legally justified. The long investigation

---

11   *Ibid*, p 114.
12   *Ibid*, p 85.
13   *Ibid*, p 101.
14   *Ibid*, p 120.

has satisfied me that the positive demonstrable benefits that might be achieved by introducing the ICC and TCCB bans and applying them to players who had already committed themselves to contracts with world series of contracts were at best somewhat speculative. On the other hand there were, as has been mentioned, a number of demonstrable disadvantages if the bans were to be applied in this way. They would preclude the players concerned from entry into the important fields of professional livelihood. This would subject them to the hardships and injustice of essentially retrospective legislation. They would deprive the public of any opportunity of seeing the players concerned playing in conventional cricket, either at test or at English county level, for at least a number of years. By so depriving the public, they would carry with them an appreciable risk of diminishing both public enthusiasm for conventional cricket and the receipts to be derived from it. Furthermore the defendants by imposing the bans, in the form which they took and with the intentions which prompted them, acted without adequate regard to the fact that world series cricket had contractual rights with the players concerned, which were entitled to the protection of the law. The defendants acted in good faith and in what they considered to be the best interests of cricket. That, however, is not enough to justify in law the course which they have taken. In the result, I find for the plaintiffs in both actions.[15]

The legal costs of the ICC amounted to nearly £200,000. World Series Cricket was played over a period of about 18 months mainly in Australia but also in the West Indies. A mixture of 'Supertests' and one-day internationals led to many innovations such as improved televising and day-night games that have become a norm of the modern game. Detractors point to the increased gamesmanship in the form of 'sledging' and intimidatory fast bowling stimulated by WSC. What is not in doubt is that this period of history led to the financial contours of the game changing at the elite levels of cricket. It is an example of how development in one country triggered change in that sport on the world stage: the globalisation of sport.[16]

RUGBY WARS

Rugby perhaps more than any other world game has gone through enormous change since the early months of 1995. This has happened in both the codes of the game – union and league. Rugby, whose exact historical origins are open to some contention,[17] developed in the first half of the 1800s when one game of football divided into two, rugby and association, primarily due to the emergence of carrying of the ball as a legitimate practice. Rugby has continued to be identified primarily with the higher strata of the social hierarchy, although there was a split at the end of the 19th century between rugby union as the mainly middle class and amateur game in the South of England and rugby league as the working class and professional game in the North. An exception to this is in South Wales where the working class was absorbed into rugby union, largely as Hargreaves suggests, due 'to the game's representation and articulation of Welshness against the English outweighing any class antagonism'.[18]

The two games are international ones with union's main powerhouses in Australasia, South Africa, Britain and France. League has its presence similarly in Australia and England. However, in England, compared to union, it has the vast majority of its presence in the northern counties of Yorkshire and

---

15 *Greig v Insole* [1978] 1 WLR 302, *per* Slade LJ, pp 364–65.
16 Also see McFarline, P, *A Game Divided* (1977), Richmond: Marlin Books.
17 See Holt, R, *Sport and the British* (1989), Oxford: Clarendon; Farrell, R, 'The beginning (and the end?) of the bifurcation of Rugby' (1995) 3(2) Sport and the Law Journal 8.
18 Hargreaves, J, *Sport, Power and Culture* (1984), London: Polity.

Lancashire. After over 100 years of bifurcation between the two rugby codes, there is a view that the two codes might well be united in the not too distant future. How has this come about?

The Birth of 'Super League'

The catalyst for this change was the battle between the media tycoons Rupert Murdoch and Kerry Packer. Interestingly, Packer was on the side of the establishment resisting changes to the status quo. The story starts in March 1995 when it was announced by News Limited (the Australian division of Murdoch owned News Corporation International) that a new rugby league competition was to be launched in competition to that operated under the auspices of the Australian Rugby League (ARL), by signing up clubs and players that were contractually bound to the ARL. Contracts were being offered that were three to four times the value of those that were in existence. As Peter Fitzsimons in his book, *The Rugby War*, states:

> 'Super League' – a naked attempt by the corporate forces of Rupert Murdoch to take over Australian domestic rugby league competition – had been launched.[19]

In similar circumstances to the Packer affair, the catalyst of this move was the battle emerging in 1995 between rival pay television consortiums, Opus Vision aligned with Packer, and Foxtel aligned with Murdoch. The two were due to go on air at the end of 1995 and were looking for material to sell subscriptions. As with BSkyB television in Britain, sport was seen as a very attractive product. Rugby league was seen as a prime target. The problem for Murdoch and Foxtel was that Packer held both free-to-air and pay television rights to broadcast the ARL's competition right up until the start of the next millennium. Murdoch's response was to start his own competition and in essence try to buy up the game of rugby league. News Limited started litigation challenging the ARL's right to restrict competitors' entry into the game in Australia. Court proceedings were initiated by News Corporation, which claimed that loyalty agreements signed between the ARL and the New South Wales Rugby League and its 20 clubs in November 1994 and February 1995 were invalid.[20]

The ARL counter-sued, giving 29 reasons why Super League should not start a rival competition before 31 December 1999 – when Packer's TV rights were due to end. After a 51 day hearing, Justice James Burchett in Sydney found in favour of the ARL on all major points of contention and ordered the eight breakaway Super League clubs to return to the ARL.[21] It seemed impossible that its competition in Australia for 10 clubs would not start as planned. This led to mixed views. Mark O'Brien, lawyer for the ARL, said: 'There is no way Super League will get under way. Murdoch has tried to hijack the game and failed'. But Maurice Lindsay, the English game's chief executive, insisted: 'The judgment will not affect the European Super League. Our contract with BSkyB is also unaffected.'

Lindsay said he had been assured by Ken Cowley, chairman and chief executive of News Corporation, that its commitment to the rest of the world was 'unshakeable'. With considerable understatement, Cowley admitted that the judge's ruling was 'a setback', but he said News Corporation's 'commitment to our players, clubs and followers is unchanged'.[22] The case was appealed

---

19   Fitzsimons, P, *The Rugby War* (1996), Sydney: HarperSports.
20   See Garnsey, D, 'A league of their own' (1995) 5(2) Anzsla Newsletter.
21   See Doyle, B, 'News from Down Under Super League case' (1996) 4(1) Sport and the Law Journal 17.
22   See 'Court casts doubt on Super League' *The Guardian*, 24 February 1996.

to the Full Federal Court:

'Anzsla News Ltd's Super League appeal success'

On 15 November 1996, the High Court of Australia refused the application of the Australian Rugby League (ARL) for special leave to appeal from the decision of the Full Federal Court given on 4 October 1996 in the 'Super League' case. Thus ended the most significant and publicised case involving sports interests in Australia's history, a case which plunged the sport of rugby league into chaos and a very uncertain future. In a dramatic reversal, the Full Federal Court had unanimously overturned the judgment of his Honour Mr Justice Burchett and consequently freed News Limited and its associated companies to organise and participate in the Super League rugby league competition in opposition to the competition conducted by the ARL. The three members of the Full Court drew many different conclusions from the primary facts and deemed unnecessary for their consideration the issue which dominated Burchett J's analysis of the case, namely the definition of the market within which to view the alleged anti-competitive behaviour of News Limited. Perhaps the most significant finding of Lockhart, Von Doussa and Sackville JJ was their decision that the so-called Commitment Agreements and Loyalty Agreements contained 'exclusionary provisions' as defined in the Trade Practices Act 1974 (Cth), and were therefore void. According to the Full Court, the agreements contained exclusionary provisions because:

- the ARL clubs were in competition with each other for the services of News Limited as a rival competition organised when the agreements were entered into;
- the clubs and the ARL had entered into a 'contract, arrangement or understanding' within the meaning of the Act;
- a substantial purpose for them entering into the Commitment and Loyalty Agreements was to restrict the supply of rugby league teams and players available to the rival competition, this being a prohibited purpose under the Act.

They said 'It is plain that the League and ARL brought the clubs together, in circumstances that were redolent of great urgency, for the purpose of arresting the nascence of News as a real competition organiser'.

Also contrary to Burchett J, the Full Court held that the relationship between the ARL and the 20 clubs admitted to the national competition in 1995 was not such as to create reciprocal fiduciary obligations among those parties. In particular, on their reading of the evidence, the members of the Full Court did not believe that there was the degree of 'mutual trust and confidence' that is to be found among partners in a commercial venture. They found that the ARL and each of the clubs had conflicting commercial interests in relation to sponsorship and marketing opportunities and that the ARL exercised considerable control over the clubs, notably through the annual admission process (no club was entitled to enter as of right and any club could be excluded). Finally, a club's right of withdrawal was inconsistent with the existence of fiduciary duties, as that right left a club free to act in its own interests. The Full Court also disagreed with Burchett J's analysis concerning the alleged breaches of contract by News Limited. According to the Full Court, the only breaches by the so-called 'rebel' clubs were of the term implied in the 1995 competition contract requiring the clubs to do everything reasonably necessary to enable the 1995 competition to be carried on in a manner which allowed the ARL to receive the benefit of that competition. The Full Court found breaches of that term by the rebel clubs in:

- making public their proposed alignment with Super League;
- participating in the promotion of Super League;
- encouraging players to sign secretly with Super League.

The Full Court upheld the trial Judge's findings that News Limited and the Super League companies had induced the rebel clubs to breach the implied term; however the remedies available to the ARL were to be confined to an award of damages, as the ARL had the benefit of an injunction for the 1996 season.

The Full Court also considered the following matters:

In making orders directly affecting the rights and obligations of Super League players and coaches when those players and coaches were not parties to the litigation, there had been a breach of the principle that persons should be joined as parties if orders are to be made which affect them. Those orders were consequently set aside.

Burchett J erred in as much as he indicated that he would have refused relief on discretionary grounds, even if News Limited had established contravention of the Trade Practices Act, because he had found News Limited had induced breaches of contract and procured the 'corruption of fiduciaries'. A breach of the Trade Practices Act makes an agreement void and the Full Court stressed that was not an area for the exercise of discretion . . .

. . . In short, leaving aside the differences of opinion relating to the trade practices matters, the Full Federal Court strongly disagreed with Burchett J's conception of the co-operative nature of ARL style rugby league, which gave rise to fiduciary duties and constructive trusts, and his view that the alleged impropriety of News Limited's corporate tactics made it undeserving of a remedy from the Court. However it is probably also fair to say that the Full Court's judgment is not particularly remarkable in terms of the legal principles to be found in it . . . [23]

One of the consequences of the Full Federal Court's decision was the creation of two separate national rugby league competitions in Australia in 1997. The conflict that followed between the ARL and News Ltd over control of the game brought rugby league to its knees in Australia. Spectator bitterness and disinterest saw match attendances and sponsorships drop precipitously, with the Australian Football League Sydney Swans enjoying a significant increase in popularity in Sydney at the league's expense. By 1998 it was clear to both parties that if league was to survive, or perhaps if the ARL was to survive, the two competitions had to be merged.

The Merger Agreement that eventuated in December 1997, and was formalised in February 1998, between the ARL and News Ltd saw the establishment of the National Rugby League, owned equally between the ARL and News Ltd. The NRL was to establish a new reduced (from 20 teams) 14 team competition to be known as the National Rugby League competition by the year 2000. This was considered to be the optimal size for the new competition by the NRL.

In order to arrive at a 14-team competition, the NRL adopted a formula that took into account a number of factors including:

1 basic criteria to be applied to all clubs including detailed business plans setting out sponsorship details and other sources of finance related to solvency and playing facilities;

2 qualifying criteria which only applied to Brisbane, Newcastle and Auckland; and

3 selection criteria including mergers, crowd numbers (home games), crowd numbers (away games), competition points, gate receipts (home games), sponsorship and other income and profitability.

On the basis of this information, the NRL determined which clubs could participate in the 2000 competition. Four of the clubs that were admitted were clubs in which News Ltd had a stake:

1 Melbourne Storm, which it provided A$3 million in 2000, without which they would not have survived;

---

23 1997 (7 (1) Anzsla Newsletter; also see Leeming, M, 'The Super League Case', Parliamentary Paper 23, www.aph.gov.au/library/pubs/rp/1995–96/96rp23.htm#MAJOR.

2 North Queensland Cowboys; it took over the club in July 2001 after they recorded a loss of A$4.5 million;

3 Canberra, who are struggling for sponsorship support because they have the rugby union Super 12 champions, ACT Brumbies to contend with; and

4 Brisbane Broncos, who were one of the only clubs to report a profit in 2000.

The remaining 10 clubs, of which six are precariously placed financially, are:

1 New Zealand Auckland Warriors, who lost A$2.8 million before being wound up last year and are now under a new owner;

2 Northern Eagles, the result of a merger between Norths and Manly, who are to be wound up at the end of the 2001 season as they are not financially viable;

3 St George Illawarra, the result of a merger between St George and Illawarra which lost A$800,000 in 2000;

4 Wests Tigers, the result of a merger between Wests and Balmain which lost $2.4 million in 2000 after receiving a A$3 million leagues club grant;

5 Newcastle, who lost A$1.7 million in 2000, largely as a result of a failed leagues club (gambling) venture;

6 Sharks, who lost A$1.1 million after a A$1.7 million grant in 2000;

7 of the rest one club that is close to self sufficiency (Parramatta) and three clubs that are financially sound (Penrith; Bulldogs; and Sydney Roosters).

South Sydney was excluded. While they had met the NRL basic criteria, it was argued that they had failed to meet the selection criteria. As a result of their exclusion South Sydney challenged the decision of the NRL and took News Ltd to the Federal Court, losing at first instance but winning on appeal in the Full Federal Court, successfully arguing that there had been a breach of s 45 of the Trade Practices Act 1974 (Cth).[24] On appeal to the Australian High Court, News Ltd won and South Sydney's exclusion was confirmed:

News Limited v South Sydney District Rugby League Football Club Limited [2003] HCA 45

There is nothing novel in the wish, for not only commercial reasons, but also to achieve better and excellent standards of sporting achievement, that organizers of sporting contests might, as here, by reference to objective criteria, the seasons, and the capacity of operators to accommodate a certain number of contestants only, decree that a certain number of teams only may compete.[25]

The Super League has therefore been able to move ahead in Australia. In the European league there have been attempts to broaden out the scope of rugby league from its traditional roots in a relatively small area in the north of England, in Yorkshire and Lancashire. An additional London club, the London Broncos participates and from 2006 the French club, Perpignan, will join the competition.[26] Although the move to Super League has been free from any major legal resistance, there were plans mooted to merge long standing teams, which were met by vociferous opposition. Murdoch and BSkyB have been able to literally buy the game and significantly change its form. Some may see this

---

24 *South Sydney District Rugby League Football Club Ltd v News Limited* [2001] FCA 862.
25 13 August 2003, *per* Callinan J at para 210.
26 The French club 2006 Paris St Germain and Gateshead in the north-east of England competed in Super League in the 1990s.

as an example of 'sports hijacking'. Whether it will be in the long term interests of rugby league is open to speculation.

The Professionalisation of Rugby Union

At the same time as the birth of Super League, the world of rugby union was about to enter a period of monumental change. Packer, with the threat of the ARL losing all of its best players to Murdoch and left with a very second class competition, was persuaded:

> ... to switch their attention to rugby union. Maybe it was a time to set the genuinely worldwide up on a truly professional basis and then return to choke the living daylights out of Murdoch's rugby league, which, by comparison, was quite simply a piss-ant parish pump game.[27]

This led to a small band of executives, a business advisor, a consultant accountant and a lawyer acting on behalf of Packer trying to interest potential backers in the sports and television world to the potential of this plan. This plan would become the embryonic World Rugby Corporation. In competition, a rival vision was beginning to take shape originating in the fear of the southern hemisphere rugby unions that Super League was going to rob them of all their best players. Rugby union had to be able to meet the financial rewards that Super League could offer. They saw Murdoch as possibly being interested in a complementary rugby union world competition. Clearly the spirit of amateurism was in its death throes:

Fitzsimons, P, *The Rugby War*

> Since rugby league's very beginnings it had fought a long-running guerilla war against the amateurs of rugby union. For the last century or so, the monied war lords of league had made an art form out of periodically tearing down from the hill tops on hit and run raids, where they lured away whichever union player took their fancy with promises of enormous amounts of moolah.

> For just as long, the war had been more or less manageable, with rugby union able to hold most of its favoured players with the persuasive argument that rugby was the truly international game which offered the best benefits overall. If it was money you were after, no other game anywhere offered even half the contacts with the rugby-mad business community, and let us not forget the honour and glory, the glory and honour, the honour and glory.

> This Super League thing, Richie Guy concluded, was something else again. Even run of the mill rugby league players were being offered up to four times more than they had been earning previously, and it simply did not bear thinking about what some of his star All Black players might now be offered to defect.

> They were already getting paid to a certain extent. The best of the All Blacks that year could expect around NZ$130,000 through endorsements and promotions – raised largely through the marketing of the All Black name – but that was clearly not going to be enough any more. 'I think we realised immediately', Guy says, 'that we had to give the All Blacks vastly larger incomes. The first provisional figure we talked about was another five million dollars to protect the All Blacks and obviously the protection needed to be much wider than just the national team, so we started thinking we would need to initially target 150 players, to have them getting a good income too. The question I was thinking a lot about then was where would we get the money from?'[28]

> All of the broadsheets and tabloids alike were still chock-a-block with the enormous brouhaha that had been created by a comment the English rugby captain Will Carling had made on a British television

---

27 *Op cit*, fn 19, Fitzsimons (1996), p 4.
28 *Ibid*, pp 9–10.

program the week before. 'What gets me and a lot of players now is the hypocrisy of the situation', Carling had said as the cameras rolled. 'Why are we not just honest and say there is a lot of money in the game? If the game is run properly, as a professional game, you do not need 57 old farts running rugby.'

Well they never! Carling was immediately dropped from the captaincy for his troubles, causing the controversy to enormously escalate. But other of Carling's comments, and the response to them, also give a feel for the temper of the times: 'There seems to be an awful lot of things the Union now does to make money out of the sport', Carling said, 'but there is still this feeling that the players should not make any money out of it. Everyone seems to do very well out of rugby union except the players. It has become more than a fun game. You do not have a World Cup for fun and recreation'.

The English Rugby Football Union Secretary Dudley Wood had said in reply: 'We believe we are running a sport as a recreation for players to play in their spare time. I think money is a corrosive influence.'

This enormous gap between the attitudes of the players and those of the officials, Turnbull says, was absolutely typical of what he discovered around the world. 'It was just extraordinary', he says now, 'how everybody I talked to agreed that the players really disliked the officials, and that the officials simply did not understand what the players were on about'.[29]

So the lines were drawn:

... the fights between the World Rugby Corporation and the national rugby unions was a clash of generations, of footballing ideologies, of one set of business interests against another. Most of all it was about a violent difference of opinion between revolutionaries, as to what form the revolution should take.[30]

As with Packer's World Series Cricket, WRC began, in clandestine fashion, to sign up the top rugby union talent.[31] That this should largely take place during the 1995 Rugby Union World Cup added to the drama.[32] However, the rival group representing the power base of the world national rugby unions was in no mood to capitulate. Different national unions brought pressure upon their players to give up their WRC contracts.[33] In South Africa this led to a court case where the WRC claimed the South African Rugby Football Union induced South African players to break their contracts with them. Clearly the Unions were determined to fight back on a global scale and in addition to this specific legal defeat:

... the Australians were wavering, England still had only 10 players of their World Cup Squad signed, legal advice had been received that indicated that the Federation Française de Rugby had the overwhelming weight of French law on its side – in that any such 'rebel' organisation as WRC was outright illegal in that country ... all up, it was plainly not going to be possible to do this thing without there being an enormous split in the ranks of world rugby.[34]

Every sport has its own culture and, of course, the two – sport and culture – feed off the other. While the World Rugby Corporation to this point had been amazingly successful in getting the top players around the world to sign contracts – the culture as a whole simply refused to be so lassoed. And it was not just that the rugby union public remained clearly against it ...

---

29   *Ibid*, pp 43–44.

30   *Ibid*, p 53.

31   'Rugby union: rebels weigh up options' *The Guardian*, 18 July 1995, p 18.

32   'Rugby union: World Cup players warn that Packer is serious' *The Guardian*, 20 July 1995, p 20.

33   'Rugby union: home unions hit back at Packer' *The Guardian*, 25 July 1995, p 22; and 'Rugby union: Packer seeks to strike deal with the unions' *The Guardian*, 28 July 1995, p 19.

34   *Op cit*, fn 19, Fitzsimons (1996), pp 293–94.

From the beginning, Levy and Turnbull's plan required the Rugby Union administrators around the world to see sweet reason – to see either that the WRC scheme was truly visionary and should be embraced or alternatively to see that they were so heavily outgunned in terms of player manpower that they simply must wave the white flag so as to salvage what they could.

This did not transpire. Why? In part, because the WRC were uniformly dealing with rugby men, and it is a point of honour among rugby men, never to give in to intimidation. The ethos runs strongly through rugby veins that you should never back down and at the very least it is taken as given that if you cannot actually beat an intimidatory opponent you must at least try and take a piece of him home with you.

Thus with the possible exception of some slight wavering among individuals in New Zealand, at no point in any of the WRC manoeuvres did it ever seem even remotely possible that the national unions around the world would give in to them.[35]

No world rugby union competition transpired. However, the move to professional status in Britain has not occurred without a good deal of bloodshed and a six year turf war between different factions of the English Rugby Football Union (RFU), the representative body of the professional clubs (who have mutated through at least four representative bodies during this period) and the players associations, as to the right to govern the sport.[36] Peace broke out in early summer 2001 with the RFU, faced with considerable player discontent, having at last climbed down and ceded more power to the clubs:

> ... club rugby was on the verge of disintegrating because owners had reached the point when they were prepared to walk out unless they were able to run their clubs on proper business lines.[37]

The last few years has witnessed significant movement of players between the two codes. The situation has moved on since the mid-1990s when the Sports (Discrimination) Bill was presented as a Private Members' Bill by the Wakefield MP David Hinchliffe, aiming to end the power of the Rugby Football Union to ban for life any player who defected to play rugby league.[38] In the spring of 1995 the National Heritage Parliamentary Select Committee, chaired by the Labour MP Gerald Kaufman, looked at relations between rugby union and rugby league, particularly the issue of amateurism and distinctions in the way players from each sport are treated.[39]

The media determined wars in both rugby codes have brought about change that was probably only a question of time. This story raises a number of questions. Should media and TV companies be able to essentially buy complete sports in this way? Should there be more effective protection for established leagues to resist the setting up of 'rival or breakaway leagues'? In terms of rugby, is it inevitable that the two codes will at some point merge?

The Impact of Television

Media companies and their ever developing new technologies are very much the 'driving force' in changes in the contemporary sports world.[40] Perhaps the best example is the change that BSkyB television has had in the UK. The business model it employed to grow its business was based

---

35   *Ibid*, p 298.
36   See 'World becomes weary of English civil war' *The Guardian*, 5 April 2001.
37   'How union men gave peace a chance' *The Guardian*, 28 July 2001.
38   'Rugby Union: Union cuts life ban on league players' *The Guardian*, 15 March 1995, p 21.
39   'Amateur status "not accurate"' *The Guardian*, 17 March 1995, p 21 and 'Commentary: time to tackle the thorny question of "shamateurs"' *The Guardian*, 17 March 1995, p 24.
40   Whannel, G, *Fields in Vision: Television Sport and Cultural Transformation* (1992), London: Routledge, pp 1–2.

primarily on availability of first-run movies and live premiership football. It brought enormous amounts of 'new money' into the game. Companies such as BSkyB have small shareholdings in a number of Premier League Teams. In 1998 a £623 m takeover bid by BSkyB for Manchester United was turned down by Secretary of State for Trade and Industry, Stephen Byers, on the recommendation of the Monopolies and Mergers (MMC). The MMC was asked by the Office of Fair Trading to investigate the merger. Their report was unequivocal in its opposition to the merger. There were five main areas of concern:

- first, that the merger would be anti-competitive in the pay TV market because it would give BSkyB an unfair advantage in the negotiation of Premier League and other TV rights;

- second, the already dominant position of BSkyB and the market power of Manchester United would exacerbate such an advantage;

- third, any advantage that BSkyB might gain could not be overcome by the imposition of 'Chinese walls' (barriers to the flow of information such as between subsidiary and parent boards), non-exclusive deals or even exclusion from the rights negotiations;

- fourth, the merger would also damage the quality of British football by increasing the 'wealth gap' between richer and poorer clubs through a greater retention of TV revenue by the most popular clubs;

- and fifth that the merger would give BSkyB additional influence over Premier League decisions which would be against the long-term interests of the game.[41]

Not only was there considerable political and media condemnation of the possible takeover,[42] Manchester United fan groups were vociferous in their opposition. Manchester United obviously still remains a prize asset, however. In 2005, US billionaire and owner of 2003 Super Bowl winners Tampa Bay Buccaneers, Michael Glazier, now controls the club after a hostile takeover.

SPORT BABYLON: FRAUD AND CORRUPTION

What seems certain is that the increased money in sport leads to more opportunities for fraudulent and corrupt activities. This section will examine the variety of ways in which this can happen. A recurring issue is how best these nefarious activities can be challenged and attempts made to eradicate their occurrence and alter the behaviour of participants in both the playing and administration of sport. Governance is once again the crucial issue. How can the values and characteristics discussed in Chapter 4 be developed to help ensure financial probity within sport?

IOC and Ethics

The International Olympic Committee is clearly the most powerful international sports organisation. It has immense power and influence. Some of its activities have fallen under the spotlight in recent years.[43]

---

41 British Sky Broadcasting Group Plc and Manchester United Plc: A report on the proposed merger CM 3045 9 April 1999, available at www.competition-commission.org.uk

42 Brown, A and Walsh, A, *Not For Sale: Manchester United, Murdoch and the Defeat of BskyB* (1999), Edinburgh: Mainstream.

43 See Jennings, A, *The Great Olympic Scandal: When the World Wanted Its Games Back* (2000), London: Simon & Schuster; Bose, M, *Sports Babylon* (1999), London: Carlton.

Boyes, S, 'International Olympic Committee corruption and bribery scandal'

The International Olympic Committee has been embarrassed by a swathe of allegations of corruption and bribery amongst its ranks, stemming from the selection of Salt Lake City as the venue for the 2002 Winter Olympic Games. The accusations have led to the discovery by an IOC ad hoc inquiry of inducements totalling over US$500,000, presented to a significant number of IOC members by Salt Lake City during the bidding process. IOC rules state that members may not accept gifts above the value of $150 from cities bidding to host the Games. The inducements took the form of all expenses paid holidays for members and their families, support for the accommodation, employment and education of relatives of IOC members as well as other lavish gifts. The findings of the ad hoc inquiry implicated twenty-two IOC members, six of whom have been expelled: Lamine Keita (Mali); Agustin Arroyo (Ecuador); Jean-Claude Ganga (Congo); Zein El Abdin Abdel Gadir (Sudan); Sergio Santander (Chile); and Seiuli Paul Wallwork (Samoa). Four others resigned over the affair prior to the meeting: Pirjo Haggman (Finland); Bashir Mohamed Attarabulsi (Libya); David Sibandze (Swaziland); and Charles Mukora (Kenya). Nine IOC members were warned and three exonerated. The decisions were taken at an extraordinary meeting of the IOC on the 17 and 18 March 1999.

It is becoming increasingly apparent that the Salt Lake City affair is not an isolated incident. The Japanese Olympic Committee has revealed that IOC members broke the rules of the bidding process in the run up to the selection of Nagano for the 1998 Winter Games. Sydney, the venue for the 2000 Summer Games, has also found itself embroiled in the controversy. The Australian Olympic Committee revealed that it had offered funding for training and other sports related purposes to eleven African nations, dependent upon Sydney securing the 2000 Games. The Australian Olympic Comittee have denied that these offers were intended as bribes, highlighting the distinction between inducements paid to individuals and funding aimed at supporting sport in developing countries. The Australian Olympic Committee voluntarily proffered the information in order to distance itself from the scandal, but it now seems significant that Sydney won the right to stage the 2000 Games by only two votes. It has also been reported that Sydney frequently breached IOC guidelines in their treatment of visiting IOC members, presenting them with gifts and hospitality. However, this is not thought to be similar in scale or seriousness to the bribery and corruption in the Salt Lake City affair. However, a report into Sydney highlighted that, in any case, the guidelines governing the activities of cities bidding for the Games were vague and ambiguous, and that the IOC had demonstrated little interest in policing them.

The row has brought to a head increasing concerns over the capacity of the IOC President, Juan Antonio Samaranch, to meet the demands of the position. There have been widespread calls for Samaranch's resignation. Despite this Samaranch received an almost unanimous vote of confidence from the IOC at the extraordinary meeting in March. It was suggested Samaranch was facing more internal opposition in his attempts to reform the process by which Olympic venues are selected. Host cities are currently selected by a full vote of the IOC's members. The change involves a 'filter' process whereby bids are screened by a committee which reduces the field to two competing cities. The full membership of the IOC will then decide which of the two should be successful. The filter committee consists of sixteen representatives of the IOC membership, athletes, the International Winter Sports Federation, the Association of National Olympic Committees, the IOC President and the Chairman of the Evaluation Committee. It appears that, despite the can of worms opened by the Salt Lake City affair, many of the IOC's members are reluctant to give up their voting rights. However the IOC membership did vote unanimously for a proposal to ban members from visiting cities in the 2006 bidding process.

The affair has brought into question wider concerns relating to the transparency and accountability of what is perhaps the world's most influential and important sporting organization, with widespread calls for the IOC to take the appropriate steps to restore its blemished credibility. The IOC has also come under pressure from its corporate sponsors to restore its image. To this end the IOC Executive Committee has proposed the establishment of an 'Ethics Commission', consisting of both IOC and non-IOC representatives. This Commission would have the role of ensuring the integrity of the IOC and maintaining the basic principles of 'fair play'. It would also have the role of establishing a code of ethics, enforcing that code and considering and proposing further reforms within the IOC. The IOC has also recently published its financial accounts for the first time in many years in an attempt to demonstrate greater transparency.[44]

The Ethics Commission produced a wide ranging Code in 1999.

IOC, Code of Ethics

I Dignity

1 Safeguarding the dignity of the individual is a fundamental requirement of Olympism.

2 There shall be no discrimination between participants on the basis of race, sex, ethnic origin, religion, philosophical or political opinion, marital status or other grounds.

3 No practice constituting any form of physical or mental injury to the participants will be tolerated. All doping practices at all levels are strictly prohibited. The provisions against doping in the Olympic Movement Anti-Doping Code shall be scrupulously observed.

4 All forms of harassment against participants, be it physical, mental, professional or sexual, are prohibited.

5 The Olympic parties shall guarantee the athletes conditions of safety; well being and medical care favourable to their physical and mental equilibrium.

II Integrity

1 The Olympic parties or their representatives shall not, directly or indirectly, solicit, accept or offer any concealed remuneration, commission, benefit or service of any nature connected with the organization of the Olympic Games.

2 Only gifts of nominal value, in accordance with prevailing local customs, may be given or accepted by the Olympic parties, as a mark of respect or friendship. Any other gift must be passed on to the organization of which the beneficiary is a member.

3 The hospitality shown to the members and staff of the Olympic parties, and the persons accompanying them, shall not exceed the standards prevailing in the host country.

4 The Olympic parties shall avoid any conflict of interest between the organization to which they belong and any other organization within the Olympic Movement. If a conflict of interest arises, or if there is a danger of this happening, the parties concerned must inform the IOC Executive Board, which will take appropriate measures.

5 The Olympic parties shall use due care and diligence in fulfilling their mission. They must not act in a manner likely to tarnish the reputation of the Olympic Movement.

6 The Olympic parties must not be involved with firms or persons whose activity is inconsistent with the principles set out in the Olympic Charter and the present Code.

7 The Olympic parties shall neither give nor accept instructions to vote or intervene in a given manner within the organs of the IOC.

III Resources

1 The resources of the Olympic parties may be used only for Olympic purposes.

2 The income and expenditure of the Olympic parties shall be recorded in their accounts, which must be maintained in accordance with generally accepted accounting principles. These accounts will be

---

44 Boyes, S, 'International Olympic Committee corruption and bribery scandal' (1999) 2(2) Sports Law Bulletin 14.

checked by an independent auditor. They may be subjected to auditing by an expert designated by the IOC Executive Board.

3   The Olympic parties recognize the significant contribution that broadcasters, sponsors, partners and other supporters of sports events make to the development and prestige of the Olympic Games throughout the world. However, such support must be in a form consistent with the rules of sport and the principles defined in the Olympic Charter and the present Code. They must not interfere in the running of sports institutions. The organization and staging of sports competitions is the exclusive responsibility of the independent sports organizations recognized by the IOC.

IV Candidatures

The Olympic parties shall in all points respect the IOC Manual for cities bidding to host the Olympic Games. Candidate cities shall, *inter alia*, refrain from approaching another party, or a third authority, with a view to obtaining any financial or political support inconsistent with the provisions of such Manual.

V Relation with States

1   The Olympic parties shall work to maintain harmonious relations with state authorities, in accordance with the principle of universality and of political neutrality of the Olympic Games. However, the spirit of humanism, fraternity and respect for individuals which inspires the Olympic ideal requires the governments of countries that are to host the Olympic Games to undertake that their countries will scrupulously respect the fundamental principles of the Olympic Charter and the present Code.

2   The Olympic parties are free to play a role in the public life of the states to which they belong. They may not, however, engage in any activity or follow any ideology inconsistent with the principles and rules defined in the Olympic Charter or set out in the present Code.

3   The Olympic parties shall endeavour to protect the environment on the occasion of any events they organize. In the context of the Olympic Games, they undertake to uphold generally accepted standards for environmental protection.

VI Confidentiality

The Olympic parties shall not disclose information entrusted to them in confidence. Disclosure of information must not be for personal gain or benefit, nor be undertaken maliciously to damage the reputation of any person or organization.

VII Implementation

1   The Olympic parties shall see to it that the principles and rules of the Olympic Charter and the present Code are applied.

2   The Olympic parties shall notify the Ethics Commission of any breach of the present Code.

3   Each year, the Ethics Commission will submit to the IOC President and Executive Board a report on the application of the present Code, noting any breaches of its rules. The Commission will propose to the IOC Executive Board sanctions, which might be taken against those responsible.

4   The Ethics Commission may set out the provisions for the implementation of the present Code in a set of byelaws.[45]

---

45   See www.olympic.org/ioc/e/org/ethics.

Do such Codes have a meaningful impact upon the dominant cultures in organisations such as the IOC? Are there effective mechanisms in place to make sports bodies such as the IOC properly accountable for their actions?[46] How about international sports federations?

Football: Bungs and Brown Paper Bags

The 'bung' became part of public parlance in the 1990s. These payments, not declared for tax purposes and made to facilitate or sweeten particular transactions, have been common in sport.[47] They have been very much the tradition of 'doing business' in sport. It is football, the most commercialised of British sports that has the most infamous history as far as questionable financial payments are concerned.[48] There are historical examples that date back to the early days of the professional game. Call them what you will, bungs, sweeteners or plainly illegal payments, they have been made to ensure deals are concluded. The illegality derives from the fact that they are secretive and not disclosed for tax purposes. A major question is whether they are illegal just as far as the internal rules of football or whether they are also illegal as far as the law.

The development of the professional game was in fact first initiated by 'illegal payments' to players by Preston North End in 1884. The payments were contrary to the rules of the Football Association at the time, but as the scale of payments by other clubs in the north of England increased, this led to the professional football primarily developing in the north of England. In 1919, Leeds City was expelled from Division Two for illegal payments to players. Leeds United was formed to replace them. Until the 1960s and the introduction of a minimum wage for professional footballers, largely achieved by the campaign of Jimmy Hill of the Professional Footballers Association, the wages were reasonable in terms of average wages, but in no way comparable with wages of footballers today. In the context of the insecurity, risk of injury and short term nature of the job, the scope for additional backhand payments was obvious.

There are more recent examples of tax-free (*ex-gratia*) payments, often involving collusion between clubs. In the early 1990s, the Swindon Town chairman was given a prison sentence after he was found guilty of conspiracy to defraud the Inland Revenue. It arose that a number of other clubs had colluded with Swindon concerning transfers between the clubs. The other clubs agreed that as part of the transfer Swindon would pay thousands of pounds direct to the player. To disguise the payment, the selling club agreed to act as a conduit for the money by describing it as a signing-off fee, which they were paying their player. This payment would be disguised as a lump sum payment terminating the services of the player. To facilitate this, the funds (from Swindon) would be routed through the club that was selling the player.

The position of taxation in sport has always been problematic. There are many opportunities for tax evasion. In addition there have been continued claims that sport should not be subject to the formal application of taxation, especially VAT, in the same way as other businesses.[49] There has been a concerted campaign for non-profit making suppliers of sports services to be zero rated for VAT.[50]

---

46 See 'Buying the Games', Panorama, BBC TV, 4 August 2004; see transcript at http://news.bbc.co.uk/nol/shared/spl/hi/programmes/panorama/transcripts/buyingthegames.txt.

47 *Op cit*, fn 7, Downes and Mackay (1996), pp 16–17.

48 See Burrell, I and Palmer, R, 'Taxman blows whistle on football's fiddles' *The Sunday Times*, 6 June 1993, p 7.

49 See Grayson, E, *Sport and the Law* (1999), 4th edn, London: Butterworths.

50 Connor, G, 'A review of recent UK developments in taxation relating to sport' (2001) 4(1) Sports Law Bulletin 11.

As Baldwin argues:

Despite expressing vigorous support for sport and exhorting us all to participate in what is good for us, successive governments for the last 25 years have done little to alleviate the significant tax burden that the tax regime places on sport. The Sports Council estimates that for every £1 contributed by Central Government to sport, it returns £5 in tax to the Exchequer – not a bad return![51]

The bigger clubs use more sophisticated methods to avoid paying tax such as offshore tax havens. Agents invariably play a significant part in any transaction. The one modern incident that has led to financial dealings coming under the gaze of the law is that involving Tottenham Hotspur.

Williams, R, *Football Babylon*

June 1992 saw a routine check of Tottenham Hotspur's PAYE files by the Inland Revenue which revealed serious financial irregularities – a can of worms had been opened. As the taxmen probed deeper into the club's affairs, more and more irregularities were uncovered and a full scale Inland Revenue investigation began. Spurs commissioned city accountants Touche Ross to do a thorough review of the club's affairs. The irregularities under Irving Scholar's regime were numerous and scandalous. Amongst the revelations uncovered were *ex-gratia* payments to players that would result in considerable back tax liabilities for Spurs. Belgian Nico Claesen had been given a secret payment of £42,000 when he joined Spurs in 1986 which had not included the statutory PAYE deductions. Icelandic international Gudni Bergsson also benefited from a payment which was, like Claesen's, made via his former club. Irving Scholar authorised both payments.

Paul Gascoigne's and Chris Waddle's pension papers were backdated by two years and loans to both players used to buy houses around London were illegal. Scholar also gave a secret undertaking to both players, guaranteeing them *ex-gratia* payments of up to £120,000 after they had left Spurs. A letter from Scholar to Gascoigne's agent Mel Stein promised to pay the player '£70,000 net of all UK taxes, up to a maximum of £120,000 gross'. The implications of such payments were, in the words of Touche Ross, 'like having a gun held to the club's head'. The special inquiry at Tottenham began on 17 July 1992. A few months later, in November, the Inland Revenue demanded a payment of £500,000, with the promise of more to come.

The transfers of Chris Waddle to Marseille and Paul Gascoigne to Lazio both involved payments to the football agent Dennis Roach who, as The Sunday People reported, was being paid by both sides in the deals which was in total breach of FIFA, UEFA and FA regulations. Scholar brought Roach into the equation and, even after Italian fixer Gino Santin was detailed to finalise Gascoigne's Lazio transfer, he received a pay-off payment of £27,500. However this was not the end of the line for Roach who continued to receive money. A Spurs document stated: 'It would appear that Mr Roach has been on the payroll of the club, unknown to Mr Solomon and Mr Berry, having been paid £64,400 in the year ending 31 May 1991. It would also appear that Lazio may also be paying Mr Roach in connection with the Gascoigne sale. This is forbidden both under Football League and FIFA regulations.'

Most damaging of all were the irregular payments made over three transfers: the £250,000 transfer of Mitchell Thomas from Luton to Spurs in 1986; the £425,000 signing of Paul Allen from West Ham in 1985 and the £387,500 transfer of Chris Fairclough from Nottingham Forest in 1987. Thomas had been given a £25,000 loan when he joined Spurs but papers forwarded to the Football League Tribunal at the time of transfer omitted to mention it. Thomas also received a letter stating that, in effect, the money was never going to have to be repaid. The loan was made three weeks before he actually became a Spurs player. Allen and Fairclough also received loans before joining Spurs – £55,000 and £25,000 respectively – and neither payment was disclosed to the Transfer Tribunal.

---

51   Baldwin, R, 'Taxation of sport' (1996) 4(3) Sport and the Law Journal 95.

When Irving Scholar left Spurs the club was in big trouble. Terry Venables desperately searched for a business partner to save the club from financial ruin and certain closure. His knight in shining armour (or so he thought) was Amstrad boss Alan Sugar, a man with a bruising business reputation. It was not long before Sugar became concerned about the goings on at Spurs, the result of a combination of rumours and Inland Revenue facts. The relationship between Venables and Sugar became increasingly uneasy. Venables was dismissed by Sugar in a blaze of publicity and in 1993 the two men slugged it out in the High Court as Venables took legal action against his former partner. The legal proceedings were the usual claim and counterclaim, including evidence suggesting that some managers accept cash bungs as part and parcel of transfer deals. Alan Sugar knew that Tottenham's troubles with the Inland Revenue were to be laid directly at Scholar's door, yet Venables felt that Sugar consistently tried to portray him as the bad guy. As manager of the team under Scholar, Venables was employed by Tottenham Hotspurs FC, a subsidiary of Tottenham Hotspurs PLC and each organisation had its own independent board of directors. The FA examined the evidence and cleared Venables of any wrong doing. They must have been satisfied because, two years later, they appointed him England coach.[52]

An FA Commission of Inquiry ruled Tottenham Hotspur were guilty of 'avoidance and evasion of fees' concerning transfers. They were fined £600,000, had 12 points deducted from the next season's FA Carling Premiership total and were barred from the 1994–95 FA Cup. The subsequent three-man FA Appeals Board cut the 12 point deduction to six. The ban on the club's participation in the 1994–95 FA Cup remained and the fine was increased from £600,000 to £1.5 million.[53] Tottenham then considered taking the FA to the High Court but agreed to go to arbitration in keeping with the guidelines of FIFA, the sport's world governing body. The independent arbiters made a confidential decision but decreed that the FA acted outside its jurisdiction.[54] Subsequently the FA ruled that Tottenham still had to pay the £1.5 million fine imposed for financial irregularities but it was confirmed that the FA Cup ban and six point deduction from their FA Carling Premiership total had been annulled.[55] It was the end of that particular saga.

The 'Bungs' Inquiry

Certainly 'the bung' has become part of football parlance. Allegations were made in the High Court in a case between Terry Venables and Alan Sugar surrounding the transfer of Teddy Sheringham from Nottingham Forest to Tottenham Hotspur, concerning allegations of illegal payments made to Venables and the Nottingham Forest manager, Brian Clough. This court action was the culmination of a drawn out feud between Venables and Sugar and ongoing allegations as to the fitness of Venables' acting in financial dealings.[56] Some bemoaned this as another example of the malaise of football and sport in general. Questions were raised in parliament, primarily by the Labour MP Kate Hoey.[57] Many people in football said that this was all part of the culture and tradition. In another court case involving Terry Venables, the former Scottish international Frank McLintock, whose First Wave Agency acted in the Sheringham transfer, was paid £50,000 in cash on an invoice that did not mention

52   Williams, R, *Football Babylon* (1996), London: Virgin, p 139.
53   'Tottenham save six points but pay £1.5 m' *The Times*, 7 July 1994, p 44.
54   'Arbiters give Tottenham new hope of cup reprieve' *The Times*, 26 November 1994, p 48.
55   'FA upholds Spurs' £1.5 m fine' *The Times*, 14 December 1994, p 42.
56   See Harris, H and Curry, S, *Venables: The Inside Story* (1994), London: Headline, for further details; and *Panorama*, BBC TV, 16 September 1993.
57   'Why I'm so angry: bungs are tainting the game I love' *The Observer*, 5 November 1995, p 10.

his help in transfers. Justifying the payment, he said at the trial that:

> This is used by a number of clubs to get out of what they consider to be the antiquated laws of the Football Association. Some agents call it merchandising and have done no work of that kind whatsoever, but we have at least done some genuine work, which we can prove.[58]

The bung allegations led to an FA investigation carried out by an inquiry team consisting of the Premier League chief executive Rick Parry, Robert Reid QC and ex-player, Steve Coppell. After more than three and a half years of investigation, the Report was published in September 1997.[59] The main 'prosecution' made under FA rules was against the then Arsenal manager, George Graham. The investigation of Graham followed disclosures made in *The Mail on Sunday* and an investigation by the Inland Revenue was convened to look into the whereabouts of £50,000, which had allegedly gone missing from the £2.1 million transfer of Teddy Sheringham from Clough's Nottingham Forest to Tottenham in 1992. But here the inquiry immediately met the problem that would plague it again and again: an allegation followed by a denial – and few powers to get to the truth. Over the following months, more and more allegations were referred to the Inquiry. Three years, 60 witnesses, tens of thousands of pages of evidence and over £1 million later, few individuals were the subject of any FA proceedings. As far as the alleged £50,000 bung in the Sheringham transfer, the Report concluded, 'We are satisfied that cash payments were made from the £50,000 to members of staff at (Nottingham) Forest'.[60] A cash culture was exposed as existing at Forest, with members of the management and coaching team regularly receiving money-filled brown envelopes after transfers.

Graham received a national and international ban lasting for one year.[61] The police and the Serious Fraud Office (SFO) continued to be interested in some of the events investigated but no further action arose. The Premier League acted in a multi-agency approach with the police, the SFO, the Inland Revenue and overseas fraud police.[62] Graham quickly returned to the world of football at the end of his ban.[63] Ronnie Fenton, the assistant manager at Nottingham Forest at the time of the allegations and chief scout, Steve Burtenshaw, were charged with misconduct. Due to his ill health, no further action was taken against Brian Clough.

So was the Inquiry, as some would suggest, merely a cosmetic exercise? The Report is over 1,000 pages in length. It certainly exposed the lack of financial probity within English football. What seems to be clear is that many of the dealings investigated cannot really be characterised as any form of villainy. It does seem to be a part of football culture, albeit a part that needs to be challenged and exposed.

The Report also looked at the transfers of all foreigners to England between 1992 and 1994, around 35 cases and the increasing influence that agents were having on financial transactions.

---

58 'Soccer: clubs often dodge FA rules – McLintock' *The Guardian* 13 December 1995, p 22.

59 The Bungs Report, *The FA Premier League Inquiry into Transfers* (1997), London: FA Premier League.

60 See 'Bung-busters prepare to act on "cult of dishonesty" ' *The Daily Telegraph*, 20 September, p 28.

61 'FA hands Graham one-year ban' *The Times*, 14 July 1995, p 40; 'Ban Graham for life, says UEFA Chief' *The Guardian*, 4 March 1995.

62 See 'Sourness in new "bung" inquiry' *The Guardian*, 6 March 1995.

63 'The resurrection of brother George' *The Observer*, 7 April 1996 and 'Soccer: Leeds forget past and pin faith on Graham' *The Guardian*, 11 September 1996, p 20.

REGULATION OF SPORTS AGENTS

The bung saga has been influential in calls for a greater regulatory framework for football agents. FIFA first introduced regulations in 1994. They have evolved to the current form where a potential agent has to compete an examination. FIFA's agent regulations give it the power to punish clubs with a ban on all national and or international footballing activity.[64] That would mean clubs being suspended from the Premier League and banned from Europe.

Players' agents have been active in sport for a significant period of time. They are the 'fixers' for their clients and are invariably the contact for anyone wanting to do business with their client. For the client they are there to provide advice on and negotiate contracts and commercial endorsements, etc. There are a number of large agencies such as the SFX group with Jon Holmes prominent in the UK and the International Management Group established by the late Mark McCormack. There are a number of lawyers who act as agents: one of the most high profile is Mel Stein who acts for Paul Gascoigne.[65] There are issues of conflict of interest that can arise, but lawyers have the professional code of ethics as guidance. Players' associations as forms of trade unions increasingly have an active role in representing players as their agents. The Professional Footballers Association, formed at the end of the 19th century, represents the vast majority of professional footballers in England. Newer bodies have recently been formed in boxing, rugby and athletics. A greater form of collective representation of professional sportsmen and women, often representing the interests on an individual as well as collective level, is developing, perhaps in response to the greater commercialisation of modern sport.

In comparison with the United States, sport agency is not highly regulated in Europe. It is an example of an unregulated area of private entrepreneurial activity. It has attracted a variety of individuals into the industry, some whose business practices and ethical stances are questionable. A developing issue has been what regulatory framework is appropriate: for example, if there should be increased licensing, registration or certification.

Agents act in many sports – but it is in those that are most professionalised and commercialised that agents have most impact. Since the professionalisation of rugby union in the mid-1990s, agents have become more common. But transfers in rugby, a major source of business, are rare. In cricket, the England and Wales Cricket Board have indicated that they want individuals acting as agents to register with then and agree to abide by its regulations. Concern has grown over some agents who know little about professional cricket and come primarily from a football background. This form of registration can have a clear conflict of interest.

FIFA Regulations

Football is the most regulated sport in terms of agents in Britain. The current regulatory framework has replaced the requirement of the depositing of a CHF200,000 bank guarantee. Since *Bosman*, it's been far easier for dubious practice. Players know that they can start speaking legally to other clubs six months before the contract expires. The player is often persuaded by their agent not to re-sign with his existing club in his final year because he can earn huge sums of money by way of sign-on fee if he leaves to go as a free agent to a new club when his contract expires.

---

64   See Miller, F, 'Not every agent is a bad guy' (1996) 4 Sport and the Law Journal 36, for details of old regulations and how they have been incorporated within English national footballing regulations.

65   'Stein convicted' *The Daily Telegraph*, 15 July 1997.

There is clearly a problem with unlicensed agents. There are more than 500 FIFA agents in the world, but there are many more that work without licenses. In addition, the many unregistered agents who operate in the business are only after the highest possible commissions.

Bower, T, *Broken Dreams: Vanity, Greed and the Souring of British Football*

Lured by easy money, the number of football agents in England had proliferated. In 1995, agents had been legalized but were required to be registered by FIFA ... by 2002 there were 179 licensed agents in England, compared to 92 in Germany, 88 in France and 54 in Italy. Hundreds of others fluttered around as unofficial agents. Sharp dealers, operating from mobile telephones, encouraged players to initiate a transfer by feigning unhappiness of illness, with the assurance that the agent's fees would usually be paid by the clubs, not the players.[66]

Whether the business dynamics of football or more generally sports agents amount to any legal wrongdoing is questionable but certainly there are highly unethical practices.[67] In addition, there have been increasing concerns about the links that exist between clubs and certain agents and agency firms leading to potential conflicts of interest.[68] Some of the main provisions of the FIFA regulations are:

FIFA Player Agent Regulations

- Players and clubs are forbidden from using the services of a non-licensed players' agent. The ban does not apply if the agent acting on behalf of a player is a parent, a sibling or the spouse of the player in question or if the agent acting on behalf of the player or club is legally authorised to practise as a lawyer in compliance with the rules in force in his country of domicile.

- The applicant must have an impeccable reputation otherwise his application will be disregarded.

- The national associations shall set written examinations twice a year which the applicant must pass.

- Every candidate who has passed the examination is required to sign a Code of Professional Conduct.

- A licensed players' agent is required:
  - to adhere, without fail, to the statutes and regulations of the national associations, confederations and FIFA;
  - to ensure that every transaction concluded as a result of his involvement complies with the provisions of the aforementioned statutes and regulations;
  - never to approach a player who is under contract with a club with the aim of persuading him to terminate his contract prematurely or to flout the rights and duties stipulated in the contract;
  - to represent only one party when negotiating a transfer.[69]

In America many States have regulatory legislation concerning sports agents:

Gray, J, 'Agent regulation in the United States'

With the advent of multi-million dollar American professional athlete salaries, problems have occurred regarding the handling and investment of these significant sums of money. Some athletes have encountered financial problems because their agents were dishonest or unscrupulous. Others have experienced problems because they do not possess the requisite business or negotiations skills necessary

---

66 Bower, T, *Broken Dreams: Vanity, Greed and the Souring of British Football* (2003), London: Pocket Books, p 252.

67 'FIFA to probe Kewell deal', 15 July 2003, www.bbc.co.uk/sport.

68 See for example 'United cut Ferguson agency link', 25 May 2004, www.bbc.co.uk/news and *Fergie and Son*, BBC 3, 27 May 2004; after the airing of the programme concerning transfer dealings between Manchester United and Elite Sports agency run by manager Sir Alex Ferguson's son Jason, Alex Ferguson has vowed never to give interviews to BBC reporters.

69 See www.fifa.com/en/regulations for full regulations.

to protect their personal and business financial interests from their advisors and other business partners. Over the last twenty years, American athletes have lost their sports-related fortunes while investing in highly speculative business ventures such as gas, oil, music groups and restaurants. In an attempt to protect professional athletes from financial ruin and from unscrupulous agents and advisors, a number of regulatory schemes in the United States have been developed and implemented.

State Athlete Agent Registration Laws

Over the last ten years, American states that have big-time college football and men's basketball passed athlete agent registration laws. The states which passed athlete agent registration laws include: Alabama, Arkansas, California, Florida, Georgia, Indiana, Iowa, Kentucky, Louisiana, Maryland, Michigan, Minnesota, Mississippi, Nevada, North Carolina, Ohio, Oklahoma, Pennsylvania, Tennessee, and Texas. The authority of states to enact athlete agent registration laws exists through the states' 'police power'. In the past, the states have used this police power to regulate the professional conduct of lawyers and doctors. Typically, these laws require a player agent to complete a state athlete agent registration application, pay a registration fee, file a surety bond, obtain state approval of agent/athlete contract forms, establish a maximum agent fee, and prohibit inducing college athletes with prospective professional careers which result in making these athletes ineligible for National Collegiate Athletic Association competition.

Athlete Labor Union Regulation of Agents

Likewise, professional athletes who are represented by a union have established an agent certification and regulation program. The player union's authority to regulate agents is found in the National Labor Relations Act ('NLRA'). The NLRA provides the player unions with the authority to ensure that they certify every agent before the agent can negotiate an employment contract with any unionized team. Under the NLRA, the player unions have the power to be the exclusive representative for all employees in such unit. (See 29 USC §159(a)–(e) (1982).) As the exclusive representative of players, the union can then delegate individual contract negotiations to certified player agents.

The exclusive use of union certified player agents is addressed in the league's collective bargaining agreements. For example, the NFL collective bargaining agreement under Article VI states that both the owners and players recognize that the union regulates the conduct of all agents who negotiate contracts for players with NFL teams. Under no circumstances can a non-certified agent negotiate an employment player contract with a team. If this rule is violated, the NFL shall impose a $10,000 fine on a club who negotiates a player contract with a non-certified agent.

In general, the requirement for union certification of player agents includes the completion of an application which requests information regarding an agent's education, professional and employment background. In order to maintain certification, the payment of an annual union fee is required along with annual attendance at a union-sponsored continuing education seminar addressing player contract negotiations and collective bargaining interpretations made by leagues, unions, and arbitrators.

Prohibited agent activities include: the offering of money in order to induce an athlete to become a client of an agent, providing false information on the union's agent certification form, and charging in excess of the union's established contract negotiation fees. All disputes between athletes and agents are required to be settled by the arbitration system, as established by the unions.

National Collegiate Athletic Association Regulation of Agents

The rules governing athletic eligibility for most college and university athletes in the United States are implemented and enforced by the National Collegiate Athletic Association ('NCAA'). Further, the NCAA has the responsibility to maintain the ideals of amateurism as well as uphold the integrity of intercollegiate sports. On the other hand, most agents recruit athletes who participate in NCAA sponsored sports. As a result, a tension and uneasiness occurs between the NCAA, the college athlete and an agent during the transition of the athlete from an amateur to a professional career.

In order for a college athlete to retain his eligibility, he must remain an amateur athlete as defined by the NCAA. If an active athlete is found to be represented by an agent or an athlete has received any financial compensation from a prospective agent, the NCAA will declare that athlete ineligible from any future competition. Eligibility is important for prospective professional athletes because college competition prepares them for a potential professional sports career. Once an athlete loses NCAA eligibility, the prospects for a professional career are dim. Further, the NCAA can impose significant economic sanctions against their member schools when an ineligible athlete competes during a game.

While NCAA has the power to impose penalties over its member schools and their individual athletes, the NCAA does not possess any mechanism to control the recruiting actions of agents. As a result, agents can act with impunity relative to NCAA rules so long as agent NCAA rule violations are not codified and enforced in the state athlete agent registration laws or the player union agent certification program.

Conclusion

There is an old adage that 'Money is the root of all evil'. Truer words were never spoken in the context of large sums of money, unscrupulous player agents and unsophisticated professional athletes. The three agent regulation schemes currently used have met with mixed results. For example, paltry government enforcement and investigatory budgets limit the effectiveness of state athlete agent registration laws. This problem is worsened by the public perception that professional athletes are viewed as pampered, spoiled and immature and that limited public resources should be expended on crime prevention, adequate housing and job creation instead.

In comparison, player union agent certification programs can directly punish a player agent for misconduct by limiting his ability to negotiate player employment contract within unionized American sports leagues. However, those athletes without the benefit of a unionized league, such as golfers, tennis players and figure skaters, are left to their own resources in dealing with player agents.[70]

Should the UK introduce regulatory legislation such as that in the United States? Where is the balance to be struck in allowing a highly entrepreneurial activity to flourish, but protecting the vulnerable from exploitation?

MATCH FIXING IN SPORT – IT'S JUST NOT CRICKET

There have been incidents of match fixing in sport over many years. One of the most notorious was the fixing of the 1919 baseball World Series. In English football, although certainly not the first, the scandal involving Peter Swan, David Layne and Tony Kay in 1964 led to prison sentences.[71] The most recent corruption scandal in football concerned the allegations of match fixing against Bruce Grobbelaar, Hans Segers and John Fashanu.[72] At their first trial, the prosecution allegations were that Grobbelaar whilst playing for Liverpool FC, and Segers for Wimbledon FC, let in goals to try to achieve certain results and thereby fix matches in Premier League games during the 1993–94 season.

70 Gray, J, 'Agent regulation in the United States' (2000) 3(6) Sports Law Bulletin 9; also see Focus, special section on 'Sports agents and agency' 16(2) Journal of Sport and Social Issues, especially Roberts, G, 'Agents and agency: a sport's lawyer's view'; Cohen, G, 'Ethics and representation of professional athletes' (1993) 4(1) Marquette Sports Law Journal; Arkell, T, 'Agent interference with college athletics: what agents can and cannot do and what Institutions should do in response', and Shulman, J, 'The NHL joins in: an update on sports agents regulation in professional team sports' (1997) 4(1) The Sports Lawyers' Journal; Champion, Jr, W, 'Attorneys qua sports agents: an ethical conundrum', and Stiglitz, J, 'A modest proposal: agent deregulation', both in (1997) 7(2) Marquette Sports Law Journal. Also note film, *Jerry Maguire*, starring Tom Cruise, about the US sports agent of same name.
71 See Tongue, S, 'Bribery and corruption: English football's biggest ever match fixing scandal' *Total Sport*, March 1997, p 52.
72 Also note conviction of the former president of Olympic de Marseille, Bernard Tapie for match fixing, 'Tapie just a scapegoat for Paris' *The Guardian*, 16 May 1995, p 22.

In addition it was alleged that there was a conspiracy involving Fashanu acting as a middle-man in the payment of sums to the two goalkeepers for a Malaysian businessman, Heng Suam Lim. At their first trial, lasting 34 days, the jury could not reach a verdict.[73] At their second trial, with the prosecution only relying on the conspiracy to defraud charges, the four were acquitted. It has been estimated that the two trials cost more than £10 million.[74]

Football is not the only game to have allegations raised as far as match fixing is concerned. Horse and greyhound racing periodically are subject to such scandals.[75] There have been allegations in sports as diverse as boxing[76] and snooker.[77] The common theme is sports where gambling and betting are common. Cricket has also come under the spotlight of allegations concerning match fixing. Cricket and horse racing will be the focus of this section.

There have been many concerns over a number of years that match fixing is prevalent in professional cricket. Cricket is an ideal vehicle for all types of betting. You don't have to persuade all eleven players to throw a match to make illicit money from cricket. The rise of spread betting makes it much easier for corrupt players, gamblers or bookmakers to 'make a killing' on a match. In 'traditional' fixed odds betting, a punter can usually put money only on which team will win the game, or who will be top batsman. But spread betting allows you to bet on much smaller events, such as how many runs an individual player will score, how many wickets a bowler will take or how many wides there might be in an innings. The admissions in 2000 by the ex-South African Captain, Hansie Cronjé, of his involvement in match forecasting and the charges of his involvement in match fixing have validated those concerns.

During the 1980s and 1990s there have been sporadic rumours concerning irregularities in international matches, usually focused on one-day internationals. These matches have dramatically grown in frequency over the last 20 years. Many of these allegations, although not all, surround games involving Pakistan and India. Allegations often involve payment of sums of money to players to provide information or to perform badly and impact upon the result. One day matches provide many betting opportunities. In recent years they are all televised and shown around the world on subscription channels. Tournaments in places such as Singapore and Sharjah have become regular events. Gambling is almost universally prohibited, as is detailed above, in countries such as Malaysia, India, Pakistan and Sri Lanka. There is however huge underground betting activity and cricket has become a very attractive product. It is estimated that up to many millions of pounds can be bet on just a single one-day international.[78]

---

73   See Gardiner *et al*, *Sports Law*, 2nd ed (2001), pp 359–362, for further analysis.

74   See *Grobbelaar v News Group Newspapers Ltd* [2002] 4 All ER 732 – in November 1994 *The Sun* newspaper published a series of very prominent articles charging Grobbelaar with corruption. He promptly issued writs claiming damages for libel. After some delay caused by the intervening criminal prosecution of the appellant and others, these libel proceedings came before Gray J and a jury. The jury found in favour of the appellant and awarded him compensatory damages of £85,000. On the newspaper's appeal against this decision the Court of Appeal (Simon Brown, Thorpe and Jonathan Parker LJJ) set it aside as perverse in November 1994. The House of Lords allowed an appeal against the Court of Appeal but awarded Grobbelaar nominal damages of only £1.

75   See 'Racing' and 'New arrests In Hong Kong race fixing scandal' (1998) 1(6) Sports Law Bulletin; 'Sports corruption: floodlight failures and betting scandal' (1999) 3(1) Sports Law Bulletin 3.

76   See 'ABA concerned about referee cash allegation' *The Daily Telegraph*, 3 December 1996.

77   See 'Scan: bunged out' *The Guardian*, 28 April 1995, p 4, concerning a match between Jimmy White and Peter Francisco, prompted by what were officiously described as 'irregular betting patterns'.

78   Anti-Corruption Unit, *Report on Corruption in International Cricket* (2001), London: ACU – a figure of US$150 million has been estimated but in games between certain teams, eg India and Pakistan, it is likely to be many times more.

In domestic English cricket allegations have also been made. Don Topley, the ex-Essex player, claimed that there had been collusion between Essex and Lancashire in two matches in 1991. In the Sunday League match a win for Lancashire helped their aspirations to win the League that year. A day later in a County Championship match, Lancashire made a generous declaration that led to an Essex victory, which greatly assisted towards winning the County Championship that season by 13 points. Topley claimed that there had been collusion in advance to fix these results. The allegations were investigated, but no further action was taken.[79]

The English cricket team has also been involved in suspect matches. In 2000, the Fifth Test of the South African tour was affected by rain for the first four days. An agreement was made between the captains to forfeit each team's first innings at the start of the final day's play. England won the match by two wickets in a dramatic finale. This was the first time in 122 years of Test cricket that each side had forfeited its first innings. Subsequently it has arisen that the South African Captain, Hansie Cronjé, was approached by a bookmaker with the suggestion of achieving a result in this way. In August 1999, the ex-England all-rounder Chris Lewis was allegedly approached by an Indian sports promoter to influence a number of team mates to perform poorly in the rest of the Test series in return for £300,000. Lewis has also made allegations that three well known England international cricketers had been involved in match fixing. Again a subsequent investigation failed to provide any evidence to support further action.[80]

The Story Unfolds

There is a complex chronology of how the match fixing revelations have unfolded.[81] The following are the main events. From the mid-1990s onwards investigations had taken place in Pakistan, India and Australia concerning allegations of match fixing. A number of international players have reported being approached by bookmakers seeking information on issues such as pitch conditions, team selection and current form of players. During the Singer World Series of one day internationals in Sri Lanka in September 1994, it subsequently has transpired that Australian players Mark Waugh and Shane Warne accepted money from an Indian bookmaker, known to them as 'John'. Information was provided on a match between Pakistan and Australia in Colombo. In the subsequent Test series in Pakistan in October 1994, Warne and Tim May subsequently claimed that the Pakistani Captain, Salim Malik, approached them offering money if they bowled badly. A subsequent inquiry reported that a Lahore bookmaker had paid a total of US $100,000 to Malik and leg spinner Mushtaq Ahmed to ensure that Australia won a further one day international later in October 1994. In the match, the Pakistanis, batting second, collapsed dramatically when victory seemed to be easily in their grasp.

Warne, Waugh and May waited a number of months before they reported what had happened in Sri Lanka and Pakistan. In February 1995, after an internal report by the Australian Cricket Board (ACB),[82] Waugh was fined a sum of Aus$10,000 and Warne, Aus$8,000, concerning their involvement. The International Cricket Council (ICC) agreed at the time to the ACB's request to keep the details of the players' actions and penalties confidential.

---

79   *Ibid.*
80   *Ibid.*
81   See www.cricket.org/link_to_database/ARCHIVE/CRICKET_NEWS/FEATURES/MATCH-FIXING_APR2000 for a comprehensive chronology of suspected matches and links to published reports; also see *Not Cricket!* Panorama BBC TV, 20 May 2001: http://news.bbc.co.uk/1/hi/programmes/panorama/1328802.stm.
82   ACB Executive Report (February 1995).

In March 1995, Malik was sacked as Pakistani captain and although initially suspended from all first class cricket, was reinstated pending a Pakistani Cricket Board (PCB) investigation. The inquiry headed by Justice Fakhruddin Ebrahim concluded, in October 1995, that Malik had no case to answer and stated that the allegations made by Waugh, Warne and May were concocted. In April 1997, the Pakistani international Amil Sohail was banned from international cricket by a PCB disciplinary committee for allegations he had made against fellow team mates concerning match fixing. It seems that in the world of cricket, whistle blowing has not been encouraged.

In recognition of the mounting allegations surrounding betting and match fixing, in July 1995 the ICC added a clause to its Code of Conduct that specifically outlaws players and administrators' direct or indirect involvement in betting, gambling or any form of unofficial speculation on the outcome of any cricket match.

In June 1997, the Indian magazine *Outlook* published revelations made by former Indian international Manoj Prabhakar concerning match fixing and Indian players. The Board of Control for Cricket in India (BCCI) asked the former Chief Justice of India, Mr YV Chandrachud, to conduct a wide ranging inquiry. In November 1997, he concluded his investigation, and although his views were not publicly released for a further two and a half years, he stated that although there is a great deal of cricket-related betting occurring in India, he failed to find that any Indian player or official has been involved in betting activities.[83]

In August 1998, a further PCB appointed panel headed by Justice Ijaz Yousuf investigated match fixing and concluded that the conduct of Malik, Wasim Akram and Ijaz Ahmed has been suspicious. It recommended a further detailed investigation take place. A new government initiated Commission of Inquiry headed by Lahore High Court Judge, Malik Mohammad Qayyum was instituted and started its investigation. In October 1998, Mark Taylor, the Australian captain and Mark Waugh gave evidence to the Inquiry.

In December 1998, the ACB admitted it secretly fined Waugh and Warne in 1995. It stated that both players agreed that they 'were stupid and naïve' but denied they gave information concerning team line-ups or tactics. The ACB convened an independent inquiry into any other possible involvement of players headed by former Chairman of the Queensland Criminal Justice Commission, Rob O'Regan. In February 1999, the O'Regan Inquiry pronounced no evidence of Australian players' involvement in the practice of match fixing and reported that players had always played to their optimum potential. The Report was critical of the ACB's handling of the Waugh/Warne affair. In October 1999, the Qayyum Inquiry was concluded and the findings handed to the Pakistani Government.

The Hansie Cronjé Affair

In April 2000, the lid was blown off the whole issue of cricket match fixing. On 7 April, the Indian police claimed they had evidence that four South African cricket players, including the then captain Hansie Cronjé, had taken money for match fixing during their series against India in March 2000. In the course of a separate investigation, they had intercepted mobile phone calls between Cronjé and an Indian bookmaker, Sanjay Chalwa. Criminal charges were laid down against Cronjé, Herschelle Gibbs, Pieter Strydom and Nicky Boje. Cronjé initially denied the allegations. However, on 11 April he admitted that he had not been 'entirely honest' in his earlier denials he had taken nearly US$15,000 from bookmakers for 'providing information and forecasting'. The United Cricket Board of South

---

83 See Magazine, P, *Not Quite Cricket* (2000), London: Penguin.

Africa (UCBSA) together with the South African Government set up the King Commission to carry out an investigation.

The ICC in its Lords' May 2000 meeting announced the initiation of new regulations and potential bans concerning players found guilty of being involved in match fixing. The sentences include:

- Five year ban or an unlimited fine for a bet on any match or event in which such player, umpire, referee, team official or administrator took part or in which the member country of any such individual was represented.

- Five year ban and unlimited fine for inducing and encouraging any person to bet on any match or series of matches or to offer the facility for bets to be placed. That ban will only apply if the investigation is satisfied the bet was placed for the benefit of the individual against whom the charge was found, otherwise they will face a two year ban. An unlimited fine may also be imposed.

- Five year ban and unlimited fine for gambling or entering into any other form of financial speculation on any match or event.

- Life ban for any person who was a party to contriving or attempting to contrive the result of any match.

- Life ban for any person who failed to perform to his merits in any match owing to an arrangement relating to betting on the outcome of any match.

- Five year ban for receiving money, benefit or other reward (whether financial or otherwise) for the provision of any information concerning the weather, the teams, the state of the ground, the status of, or outcome of the match unless such information has been provided to a newspaper or other form of media and disclosed in advance to the cricket authority of the relevant member country. That ban will only apply if the investigation is satisfied the bet was placed for the individual against whom the charge was found, otherwise they will face a two year ban and/or an unlimited fine.

- Life ban and/or unlimited fine for receiving any money, benefit or other reward (financial or otherwise), which could bring the game into disrepute.

- Life ban and/or unlimited fine for providing any money, benefit or other reward (financial or otherwise), which could bring the person or the game into disrepute.[84]

In late May 2000 the Qayyum Report was finally published.[85] Judge Qayyum conducted the inquiry from September 1998 to October 1999 and about 70 players, officials and alleged bookies testified. The commission's finding was that there was no planned betting and match fixing as a whole by the players of the Pakistan cricket team. However, doubts of varying intensity were cast on the integrity of some members of the team in their individual capacity. Judge Qayyum said the censured players should be kept under observation. Its main recommendations were a life ban on former captain Salim Malik and a fine of US$6,000 for former captain Wasim Akram. Akram was given the benefit of the doubt. The Report states, 'He cannot be said to be above suspicion. It is, therefore, recommended that

---

84   See Gardiner, S, 'Measures to fight match fixing in cricket' (2000) 3(3) Sports Law Bulletin 1.
85   The report can be found at www.ricket.org/link_to_database/NATIONAL/PAK.

he be censured and be kept under strict vigilance'. On Malik, Judge Qayyum said:

> In the light of evidence to support allegations made by Shane Warne and Mark Waugh, the commission recommends that a life ban be imposed on Salim Malik and he be not allowed to play cricket at any level ... He should not be allowed to even associate himself with any cricketing affairs as he may be able to influence the new generation.

In addition to the ICC Code of Conduct Commission, in late June 2000, former Commissioner of the Metropolitan Police, Sir Paul Condon (now Lord Condon), became the head of the International Cricket Council's new anti-corruption unit, with a brief to investigate match fixing allegations worldwide. It published an Interim Report in May 2001.[86]

The King Commission

In the wake of the allegations against the South African players and Cronjé's admissions, the King Commission of inquiry into match fixing and related matters completed its first session of hearings in Cape Town on 26 June 2000. An interim report was submitted in August 2000 to the South African Sports Minister Ngconde Balfour and South African President Thabo Mbeki. In December 2000 a second interim report was submitted and a final report in July 2001.

The first three weeks of the hearings were notable for Cronjé's admissions that he had been talking to bookmakers or people involved in match fixing since 1995. Cronjé said that he had repeatedly lied to cover his tracks, and then went on to detail a five year flirtation with bookmakers that yielded tens of thousands of dollars. He admitted to inducing Herschelle Gibbs and Henry Williams to help him throw a match and to approaching several other players. He denied, however, that he had ever thrown a match. Cronjé said in his testimony that he had decided to sever all his ties with the game, pre-empting what is also certain to be a life ban imposed on him by the authorities. The cases of Gibbs and Williams are more problematic, as both claimed in mitigation that they failed to follow through with their arrangements with Cronjé.

Another important witness was the UCBSA managing director Ali Bacher who implicated Pakistan, Bangladesh and India in World Cup matches that were fixed in 1999 and who also accused Pakistan umpire Javed Akhtar of being on the payroll of a bookmaker. How much the UCB knew of match fixing prior to April remains a moot point, with particular reference to the 1996 team meeting in Bombay at which an offer to throw a game was debated in some detail. Although Bacher admitted that Cronjé briefly referred to the offer, he denied having believed it to be serious and also denied reading a newspaper report about the offer in 1998.

Disciplinary hearings were held for all four players. Cronjé received a life ban for all playing and related activities in September 2000. He failed in his challenge of the life ban in the South African High Court.

Le Roux, R, 'The Cronjé Affair'

> His legal team argued that his life ban was unconstitutional since he was not given an opportunity to state his case and that the ban constituted an unreasonable restraint of trade. They argued that the constitutional right to fair administrative action also applied to private bodies ... [[At] the time of the UCBSA's imposing of the life ban, its contract with Cronjé had already been terminated. The court did not accept that the ban was in effect disciplinary and punitive, but held that the UCBSA was merely relying upon its constitutional rights of non-association. The court also held that banning Cronjé from

---

86 See below, p 322.

activities of the UCSBA was not an unreasonable restraint of trade. He may, for instance coach, sponsor or promoter cricket in schools not affiliated to the UCBSA. Prior to the decision it was generally expected that the court would extend the constitutional right to fair administrative action (such as the right to be heard), applicable to public bodies, to private bodies such as the UCBSA. The court unequivocally stated that the UCBSA is a private body and in the absence of a binding contractual term, it was under no legal obligation to give Cronjé an opportunity to be heard before the resolution to ban him for life was passed. The public and private law divide therefore continues to exist in respect of South African sports bodies.[87]

Gibbs, Williams and Strydom all received a six month ban from international cricket.[88] After the failure of his legal action, Cronjé indicated he would disclose 'the truth' in a future book. He was initially granted immunity from criminal prosecution in South Africa on condition he told the whole truth about his involvement in the affair. In June 2001 that was withdrawn.[89] Cronjé died in a plane crash in June 2002.[90] Conspiracy theories were rife that his death was linked to the match fixing scandal. In a report by South Africa's Civil Aviation Authority, it was subsequently held that human error and bad weather were the cause of the crash.[91]

The Indian CBI Report

In July 2000, in the wake of the Indian police investigation, a series of nationwide tax raids on the homes and offices of top Indian cricketers, officials and bookmakers uncovered alleged direct evidence of match fixing. In November 2000, the Indian Central Bureau of Investigation presented a report concerning match fixing allegations in Indian cricket.[92] It named a number of Indian cricketers, most notably Mohammad Azharuddin, and also a number of former international team captains including Alec Stewart, Brian Lara and Martin Crowe. This was based on allegations made by another Indian bookmaker, Mukesh Kumar Gupta. There have been attempts to get him to repeat the allegations under oath, but he refused to do this by a given deadline. Azharuddin was given a life ban by the BCCI in December 2001.

A number of investigations have taken place in Test playing countries in the light of these allegations:

Australia: the CBI Report named Mark Waugh and Dean Jones. The Australian Cricket Board appointed Greg Melick, a Barrister to investigate. Melick submitted an interim report to the Australian Cricket Board in early August 2001. Melick said that, based on his findings, Waugh had 'no case to answer' in relation to the allegations.[93]

---

87 Le Roux, R, 'The Cronjé Affair' (2002) 2 The International Sports Law Journal 11.

88 Gibbs refused to tour Indai with the South African team in 2004 as the Indian police authorities indicated they would want to carry on investigations to match fixing allegations if he was in the country; see 'Gibbs set to skip India long-term', 22 November 2004, www.bbc.co.uk/sport.

89 'Cronjé immunity deal off', www.bbc.co.uk/sport, 21 June 2001; also see Gouws, D, ' . . . And Nothing But the Truth?' (2000), Cape Town: Zebra.

90 'Thousands mourn Cronjé', 5 June 2002, www.bbc.co.uk/news.

91 For further discussion of the Cronjé affair, see Alfred, L, Lifting the Covers: the Inside Story of South African Cricket (2001), Claremont: Sperahead; Oosthuizen, A and Tinkler, G, The Banjo Players: Cricket's Match Fixing Scandal (2001), Hout Bay: Riverside.

92 The report can be found at www.cricket.org/link_to_database/NATIONAL/IND/NEWS/CBI-REPORT.html.

93 The report can be found at www.cricket.org/link_to_database/NATIONAL/AUS.

England: the ECB asked the ACU to investigate the allegations relating to Alec Stewart. An interview took place in June 2001 and he was cleared in an announcement by Gerard Elias QC, the chairman of the ECB's Discipline Standing Committee.

New Zealand: the New Zealand Cricket Board appointed a Commission of Inquiry headed by Sir Ian Barker, a former High Court judge, to examine allegations against Martin Crowe. Crowe was exonerated of charges in late July 2001.[94]

Sri Lanka: the Board of Control for Cricket in Sri Lanka appointed Desmond Fernando, Presidents Counsel, as their Special Investigator. Ranatunga and De Silva who were named in the CBI Report were cleared of involvement in mid-July 2001.

Pakistan: the Pakistan Cricket Board had already taken robust action against a number of players, as a result of the Commission of Inquiry by Mr Justice Qayyum and felt that no residual action arose from the CBI Report for them. Salim Malik was given a life ban.

The West Indies: Brian Lara was implicated in the CBI Report and Elliott Mottley QC was appointed by the West Indian Cricket Board to investigate the allegations. He was cleared of allegations in November 2002.[95]

United Arab Emirates: the other country to have been heavily implicated in the CBI Report, relating to matches in Sharjah. The UAE Cricket Board commissioned an inquiry headed by George Staple QC from England, assisted by Clive Lloyd, the former Captain of the West Indies and Brigadier Mohammed K Al Mualla from Sharjah.

CRICKET MATCH FIXING: THE ANTI-CORRUPTION REPORT

In April 2001 the ACU produced its Report on Corruption in International Cricket. The Report is far ranging and represents a consolidation of the other world wide investigations. The Report's author Lord Condon stated:

Anti-Corruption Unit, *Report on Corruption in International Cricket*

4 This report will make disturbing reading for all those who love and follow the game of cricket. It describes at least twenty years of corruption linked to betting on international cricket matches. Corrupt practices and deliberate under-performance have permeated all aspects of the game.

5 I am confident that recent measures, including the creation and work of the ACU, have stopped much of this corrupt activity. I also believe, however, that corruption continues to happen and the potential for a resurgence of corruption in cricket remains a real threat.

6 International cricket is at a critical point of development. If the ICC continues as a loose and fragile alliance it is unlikely to succeed as a governing body. It must become a modern, regulatory body with the power to lead and direct international cricket. All the constituent cricket boards, in the member countries, must show equal determination to deal with the ongoing challenge of corruption.[96]

Section 1 concerns the role and work of the Anti-Corruption Unit. It details the relationship between cricket match fixing and organised crime.

---

94   A summary of the report can be found at www.nzcricket.co.nz.

95   'West Indies Board clears Lara of match-fixing charge', 12 November 2002, www.thatscricket.com/news/2002/11/12/lara_matchfixing.html.

96   *Op cit*, fn 78, Anti-Corruption Unit (2001), paras 4–6.

11 Within days of taking up this new appointment, it became clear to me that many people within cricket had significant information about corruption within the game. However, the prevailing culture was not helpful. As a result of the interviews carried out by my unit I realised the allegations in the public domain were only the tip of the iceberg. Many people had not reported attempts to corrupt them or suspicions about other people they believed to be corrupt.

15 The most disturbing aspect of the tolerance of corruption is the fear that some people have expressed to me about their own personal safety or the safety of their families. I have spoken to people who have been threatened and others who have alleged a murder and a kidnapping linked to cricket corruption. In order to respond to these anxieties I have interviewed some people away from their normal lifestyles.[97]

It reported on the findings from the self-declaration forms sent to international players (including former players still playing first class cricket), team officials, umpires, referees, curators (groundsmen) and certain senior employees and administrators of national boards. This policy had been initiated at the ICC meeting in May 2000.

ICC, 'Players' Declaration Form'

This is a copy of the Players' Declaration form issued to all international cricketers by the ICC. Similar forms have been issued to all cricket administrators, team officials, coaching staff and groundsmen/curators. Completed Declarations are lodged with the ICC Anti-Corruption Unit for recording and analysis.

CONFIDENTIAL – PLAYERS TO BE WRITTEN ON THE HEADED NOTEPAPER OF THE BOARD OF EACH MEMBER COUNTRY

Form of Declaration

This form applies to every international player, to whom the ICC Code of Conduct applies, involved in the playing of the game of cricket and is to be treated as a supplement to any contract with your Board.

This form requires you to declare in the interest of protecting the good name of cricket, whether you have been approached to be involved in cricket corruption in any form.

1 Have you taken part in, or been approached to take part in, any arrangement with any other person involved in the playing or administration of the game of cricket which might involve corruption in any form? YES/NO

2 Have you for personal reward or for some other person's benefit agreed, or been approached, in advance of or during a match to act in deliberate breach of the Laws of Cricket, the ICC Standard Playing Conditions, the ICC Code of Conduct or contrary to the spirit of the game of cricket? YES/NO

3 Have you for personal reward or for some other person's benefit agreed, or been approached, to give information concerning the weather, the ground, team selection, the toss or the outcome of any match or any event in the course of a match other than to a newspaper or broadcaster and disclosed in advance to your Board? YES/NO

4 Have you ever for personal reward or for some other person's benefit, deliberately played, or agreed to play or been approached to play, below your normal standard, or encouraged any other person to play below his normal standard, in order to contrive an event during the course of a match? YES/NO

5 Have you for personal reward or for some other person's benefit been involved, or approached, in any attempt to pervert the normal outcome of a match? YES/NO

Where an answer of yes is given full details should be provided to Head of the Anti-Corruption Unit of ICC.

---

97 *Ibid*, paras 11 and 15.

I hereby declare that I will not be involved in the future in any of the conduct described above and I will immediately inform the Chief Executive of my Board either directly or though the Team Manager and/or the Head of the Anti-Corruption Unit of ICC if I receive any approach to be involved in any such conduct.

NOTE – IF YOU KNOWINGLY ANSWER ANY OF THESE QUESTIONS INCORRECTLY OR IF YOU FAIL TO TELL THE HEAD OF THE ANTI-CORRUPTION UNIT OF ICC OF ANY CHANGE TO YOUR ANSWERS, YOU WILL BE LIABLE TO BE DISCIPLINED BY YOUR BOARD AND HEAVY PENALTIES MAY APPLY. I HEREBY DECLARE THAT THE ANSWERS I HAVE GIVEN TO THE ABOVE QUESTIONS ARE TRUE AND NOT MISLEADING ...

The ACU Report presented the following data from the forms:

55 Some 911 completed declarations have been received by the Anti Corruption Unit and of these 21 indicated a yes or positive answer about involvement or knowledge of corruption. The unit as a result of previous contact, reports and investigations, already knew 10 of these positive responses. The remaining 11 positive responses were scrutinized and 6 do not require follow up action. The remaining 5 positive responses are being investigated.[98]

However the ACU have argued that this approach was methodologically flawed. There were concerns voiced by players over confidentiality of the forms after they had been completed. In addition, this approach of self-incrimination is likely to have low levels of success in identifying perpetrators. What is the advantage of admitting wrong doing, especially in the context of the bans being implemented? The ACU advised that this approach should not be repeated.

Section 2 of the ACU Report concerns the 'analysis of corruption in cricket'.

The Seeds of Corruption

64 It has been suggested to me that the seeds of corruption in cricket were sown in the 1970s when county and club games in domestic tournaments, in England and other countries were allegedly fixed by teams to secure points and league positions. Players were not bribed with money but relied on mutual interest. If a match was of vital importance to one team and not to the other then an accommodation would be reached between the teams as to who would win. Similar arrangements would be made to secure bowling and batting points, if applicable. The movement of players around the world gave players from a number of countries experience of these 'friendly' fixed matches. As a result, in a number of matches the ethic of winning or losing on merit was replaced by a pragmatic arrangement to divide the points and/or agree in advance who would win.

. . .

74 My unit has received allegations from a number of different sources of the following being pre arranged or fixed in order to allow a betting coup to take place.

- The outcome of the toss at the beginning of a match.

- The end from which the fielding captain will elect to bowl.

- A set number of wides, or no balls occurring in a designated over.

- Players being placed in unfamiliar fielding positions.

- Individual batsmen scoring fewer runs than their opposite numbers who batted first.

- Batsmen being out at a specific point in their innings.

- The total runs at which a batting captain will declare.

---

98   *Ibid*, para 55.

- The timing of a declaration.
- The total runs scored in a particular innings and particularly the total in the first innings of a One Day International.

Why Has Corruption Developed in Cricket?

79 I have taken every opportunity to allow people involved in cricket to explain to me why they think corruption established such a strong foothold. Whilst the explanations and excuses have varied in emphasis they embrace some or all of the following:

- International cricketers are paid less than top soccer players, golfers, tennis players or formula one drivers and are therefore more vulnerable to corrupt approaches.
- During the last World Cup and other major events the cricketers received a low single figure percentage of the proceeds from the event and resent the distribution of profits elsewhere.
- Cricketers have little say or stake in the running of the sport and limited recognition of their representative bodies, where they exist.
- Cricketers have relatively short and uncertain playing careers, often without contracts and some seek to supplement their official earnings with money from corrupt practices.
- Some administrators either turn a blind eye or are themselves involved in malpractice.
- Cricketers play a high number of One Day Internationals and nothing is really at stake in terms of national pride or selection in some of these matches.
- Cricketers can take money from potential corruptors in return for innocuous information and yet refuse to fix matches.
- Whistle blowing and informing on malpractice was ignored or penalised rather than encouraged.
- There was no structure in place to receive allegations about corruption.
- Cricketers were coerced into malpractice because of threats to them and their families.
- It was just too easy.

. . .

90 The spectre of a more sinister regime of fear and coercion has been raised to explain some aspects of cricket corruption. The Central Bureau of Investigation (CBI) in India, has an investigation underway into the links between organised crime and cricket. My unit has met people who have made allegations about threats to their life as a result of exposing cricket corruption and I have met a number of people who were, in my opinion, genuinely frightened of the consequences if it became known they were cooperating with the Anti Corruption Unit.

. . .

98 I believe the blatant cases and excesses of cricket corruption have been stopped. I know from the work of the ACU that most of the preliminary approaches to players, umpires, groundsmen and others, to sound out their willingness to be drawn into corruption, have stopped. What is left is a small core of players and others who continue to manipulate the results of matches or occurrences within matches for betting purposes. They may be doing so out of greed, arrogance or because they are not being allowed to cease. Some may fear their previous corruption will be exposed if they try to stop and some may fear threats of violence if they stop. It will take some time before those who have developed a corrupt lifestyle within cricket have sufficient fear of exposure and punishment to stop.[99]

---

99   *Ibid*, paras 64, 74, 79, 90 and 98.

The final s 3 of the ACU Report is comprised of 'Recommendations to the ICC'. There is an emphasis on the education of players. A number of practical steps are suggested such as controlling the use of mobile phones by players during matches and limiting access to players. A clear indication in the Report concerns the need for significantly improved governance. The ICC must be more open, transparent and accountable:

> ... the ICC has tried to address 'conflict of interest' issues for those who serve on the Executive Board of the ICC. The matter has not been resolved satisfactorily and needs to be revisited.[100]

There has been controversy over the role that the ex-Chief Executive, Jagmohan Dalmiya has had in the award of TV rights. This is another clear example of the conflict that sports governing bodies have in governance over commercial issues and sporting rules.[101] The former needs to clearly comply with external regulatory norms. The latter need to be competently regulated by the ICC. The Report suggests that players and ex-players should have a 'more productive relationship with the ICC'.[102] The ICC Code of Conduct Commission has responded to the ACU Report.

ICC Code of Conduct Commission, 'Report of Official Inquiry'

A panel of the Code of Conduct Commission of the International Cricket Council (ICC) has been invited by the President of ICC to review the report of the Anti-Corruption Unit (ACU) of the ICC presented by Sir Paul Condon QPM, Director of the ACU, and report thereon to the Executive Board of ICC.

The Panel members are Lord Griffiths, Chairman, Mr Richie Benaud, Sir Oliver Popplewell, Chief Justice Nasim Shah and Sir Denys Williams.

Before meeting to discuss the report we had each read the report. We met for a full day to discuss the report on Tuesday 15th May and continued our discussions on Wednesday 16th May. During the first day we met with Sir Paul Condon and had the opportunity to question him on various aspects of the report and on the investigations of the ACU both past and ongoing. We are very grateful to Sir Paul for the assistance we received from him. Obviously we can not reveal in this report all the information he gave us as much of it was of a confidential nature which if revealed would prejudice ongoing investigations by the ACU and by the other National Boards that have instituted enquiries into alleged corruption or are about to institute such enquiries.

This is an excellent but most disturbing report. It traces the insidious growth of the corruption of international cricketers by the illegal betting industry in the 1980s and 1990s after televised cricket had stimulated an enormous increase in illegal gambling on cricket matches. At first the authorities took little action and when it came to the attention of ICC they mistakenly decided it better to hush the matter up rather than bring it into the public domain; at that time they thought they were dealing with isolated incidents rather than a growing cancer. But now the public realises the grave extent of the problem and the damage that has been done to the game. Vigorous action has been taken by some of the National Boards to bring retribution to those who have been guilty of corrupt practices in the past. The Pakistan Cricket Board has banned Salim Malik and Ata-ur-Rehman for life, stripped Wasim Akram of the captaincy and also imposed fines on other players. The Board of Control for Cricket in India has banned the Indian cricket captain Mohammed Azharuddin and Ajay Sharma for life and has imposed 5 year bans on Manoj Prabhakar, Ajay Jadeja and on the team physiotherapist Dr Ali Irani. The United Cricket Board of South Africa has imposed a life ban on Hansie Cronjé and six months bans and fines on Gibbs and Williams.

Inquiries are proceeding by the National Boards in Sri Lanka, Australia, New Zealand and the West Indies and we understand a further inquiry will also be undertaken by Pakistan. These may result in the

---

100 *Ibid*, para 135.
101 See earlier, pp 163–70.
102 *Op cit*, fn 78, Anti-Corruption Unit Report (2001), para 120.

exposure and punishment of other players, umpires or administrators for past corrupt behaviour. But it can at least be said that three of the principal villains have been removed from the game.

However, what we find particularly worrying is, that despite the public disgrace of the banned players, Sir Paul believes that certain persons are still continuing this corrupt association with illegal gambling in cricket. When these persons read Sir Paul's report and realise the effort and resources that are now being devoted to exposing them and others tempted to follow their example and the retribution that will follow exposure, we hope they will think hard before continuing their corrupt activities; particularly now that so much money is coming into international cricket from television that it should be possible for international cricketers to be much more highly rewarded.

The report convinces us that however much we may regret the past and in some cases the difficulties of proving past corruptions, it is upon the present and the future we must concentrate and that every practical measure must be taken to break the links between cricketers and unlawful gambling and return to a game where every player gives of his best.

The report contains 24 recommendations. We recommend that ICC should adopt them all, although we realise that some may be easier to implement than others. We will comment briefly on some of the recommendations.

Education and Awareness

There are 5 recommendations under this head and we endorse them all.

Recommendation 4 refers to encouraging the reporting of improper approaches. Nobody likes the idea of having to tell tales about his colleagues but stern measures are necessary to stamp out corruption and we repeat the advice we have already given in an earlier report that there should be an obligation on a player to report any corrupt approach to another player of which he becomes aware. We cannot find any such obligation in November 2000 Code of Conduct. If it is meant to be achieved by incorporating Appendix A of the ICC Code of Conduct Commission Terms of Reference into paragraph C of the Code of Conduct paragraphs 9 and 10 we doubt if this achieved the object and it is in any event a very clumsy way to set out an important if unpalatable obligation. We suggest a redraft of the Code of Conduct without resorting to the Terms of Reference of the Code of Conduct Commission.

In addition to this recommendation we suggest that match referees should be instructed to report to ICC any suspicious or unusual characteristics in the conduct of the game as for example very slow batting when a run race was obviously required to win the match, reckless batting when wickets were at a premium, bowling excessive numbers of wides and no balls, or a very large number of lbw decisions against one side; this is not an exhaustive list but illustrative of matters that may give rise to suspicion.

Security and Control

There are 4 recommendations under this head. These recommendations are aimed at preventing contact between players and bookmakers or gamblers. They are of the utmost importance in breaking the links between cricketers and unlawful gamblers.

For the future, an essential ingredient of the ICC's structure should be that the Security Unit be provided with funds, offices and whatever else might be necessary to prevent and detect corruption.

The ICC must accept that a proper percentage of the money, which they have, coming in from television rights and all other sources, has to be put into the prevention of corruption and match fixing.

Every national authority should take immediate steps to ensure the security of their players' dressing rooms at home or on tour. It is difficult to envisage hotel security ever being totally adequate and, in any case, players need space for relaxation and quiet. Draconian measures such as totally banning mobile phones may be difficult to enforce. However, there should be written into the players' contracts in every country, that players will be prepared to make available to the ICC's Security Unit, printouts of any mobile phones of which they have use.

These security measures will require the players to surrender some degree of privacy and freedom of action, and in our view they must be looked at together with recommendation number 10. The security measures require the full co-operation of the players themselves and we emphatically support recommendation number 10 which urges ICC to bring the players themselves through their representative body into greater involvement in the administration of the game so that they can share the responsibility for the health of the game and take a real part in the solution of its problems.

Prevention and Investigation of Corruption

For the immediately foreseeable future the ACU in its present form must continue to operate as envisaged in recommendations 16 and 17. Once security managers have been appointed by ICC and the National Boards, further thought will have to be given to the structure of the ACU and the scope of its operations as foreshadowed in recommendation 19.

The Future of ICC

It has become apparent that the present structure of ICC is inadequate to run international cricket and to manage the vast sums of money it now receives from television rights and other sources. It is essential that the ICC, within the next 12 months, be geared to provide the best possible infrastructure for control, finance and, in the case of matches under its control, corruption. There is no point in lamenting that this has not been the case in past years; it is a matter of getting it right now and for the future. To this end the recommendations in this report for the future of ICC must be tackled as a matter of urgency.

It is time for all countries, which after all make up the ICC, to ensure that cricket as a game again becomes paramount, and that in the fight against corruption and match fixing, national pride and embarrassment come a poor second.[103]

What are the Legal Implications?

Bans that the ICC have put into place are likely to be enforceable. All professional players' contracts will usually include an express term that a player should play to the best of his ability and not bring the game into disrepute. If not, a court will readily imply such a term.[104] An employer can also sue a player for any damages that might flow from any such breach. However, the length of ban may be able to be challenged. There are restraint of trade issues. Playing bans as a consequence of positive drugs tests have been successfully challenged in some national courts. Consequently in 1997, the IAAF reduced mandatory bans from four years to two. A second positive doping offence is however met with a life ban. Is there a distinction between the enforceability of bans between those who are found guilty of doping on the one hand and match fixing on the other? Should a ban cover all activities in cricket or just playing?

There are some privacy issues for players. Do the suggestions in the ACU Report concerning restriction of movement and the use of mobile phones infringe privacy rights? In the second King Commission Interim Report published in December 2000, wider powers were suggested including random lie detector tests for players, room and luggage searches and the right of the UCBSA to monitor all players' phone calls and email messages. Additionally it was proposed that only mobile phones issued to players by the UCBSA should be allowed and possession of an unauthorised mobile

---

103 ICC Code of Conduct Commission, 'Report of Official Inquiry', see www.cricket.org/link_to_database/ NATIONAL/ICC/MEDIA_RELEASES/2001/CONDON_REPORT/CODE_OF_CONDUCT_REPORT_20010523. html.

104 See later, Chapter 12.

telephone should be a punishable offence.[105] Are such powers for an employer and/or governing body legitimate?

In addition to any civil law measures, a player could be subject to criminal liability. Cronjé was charged in India with criminal conspiracy, fraud and cheating. Proof can however be a problem. The prosecutions of Grobbelaar and Segers failed where expert evidence from top past-goalkeepers such as World Cup 1966 England keeper, Gordon Banks, supported the view that there was no evidence that the goalkeepers threw the game. In addition, there will always be problems over admissibility of evidence; for example bookmaker Gupta's allegations, which have been the basis of the CBI Report claims, have not been repeated on oath and therefore could not be used in a court of law.

There may be arguments for imposing formal liability on governing bodies. It is not only the ICC that needs to take much more responsibility. The national cricket boards around the world need to review their procedures and be more responsible for the actions of players within their supervision. The move to all Test playing countries centrally contracting with their players seems a positive move to develop an appropriate relationship of accountability on the players' part and responsibility on the part of the governing body.

The ACU and IIC have put into place an extensive regulatory framework and continue to be vigilant. At the time of the 2003 World Cup in South Africa, Lord Condon indicated he believed that match fixing had been eradicated. But it is clear that match fixing has been a part of international cricket in its recent past. The question is whether it has been eradicated or not. Spasmodic allegations by players continue to be made not so much on fixing of matches but players facilitating events in matches that have significant amounts of money laid on them, for example the score after 15 overs of an innings. In summer 2004, the Ebrahim Report was published, which recommends a five year ban for former Kenyan captain Maurice Odumbe after a hearing on charges that he had received money, benefits or other rewards that could bring him or the game of cricket into disrepute.[106]

HORSE RACING – THE SPORT OF KINGS

Horse racing has never been a stranger to allegations of financial corruption. The growth of racing in numerous countries is inextricably linked to the regulatory regimes of gambling which has allowed on- and off-course gambling. This has been shown to be a worldwide phenomenon with periodic reports and investigations concerning allegations of corruption.

Such a scandal has enveloped racing n the UK over the last few years. In November 2002, the former national hunt jockey, Graham Bradley was banned for eight years (reduced on appeal to five years) for corruption offences, following quickly on the heels of the screening in October 2002 of a *Panorama* programme on horse racing, which claimed that the sport was 'institutionally corrupt'.[107] Allegations were made that links existed between criminal gangs and leading jockeys and trainers and that betting was used as a way of laundering drug-related money.

The programme revolved round Roger Buffham, the Jockey Club's former head of security who acting as a 'whistle-blower' made allegations against various individuals; jockeys, trainers and

---

105 King Commission. See www.cricket.org/link_to_database/ARCHIVE/CRICKET_NEWS/FEATURES/MATCH-FIXING_APR2000.

106 See report at www.icc-cricket.com/corruption/.

107 See 'The Corruption of Racing', *Panorama*, BBC TV, 6 October 2002, http://news.bbc.co.uk/1/hi/programmes/panorama/default.stm.

outside criminals. He also alleged a lack of action on the part of the Jockey Club to address the issues he had raised. The Jockey Club is the guardian of racing's rules formed by a band of enthusiasts in the Star and Garter pub in Pall Mall in 1751. Initially its 'Rules of Racing' applied only to Newmarket but they soon gained wide acceptance. Within a few years it was the sole authority in British racing, and retained its regulatory powers after the formation of the British Horseracing Board in June 1993.

Before the *Panorama* programme aired, the Jockey Club had sought an injunction in the High Court to ban Buffham from providing the BBC with what was alleged as 'confidential incriminating information'.[108] Refusing to award the injunction, Mr Justice Gray ruled that it was in the public interest for this information to be disclosed even though Buffham had signed a confidentiality agreement, on leaving his employment, and been given a 'golden handshake' of £50,000. The Judge held that the 'public interest' in disclosing this information outweighed the Jockey Club's right of privacy because it revealed '... the existence, or apparent existence, of wide scale corruption in racing.' And this was of 'legitimate concern to a large section of the public who either participate in racing or follow it, or who bet on the results of races.' The view of the court was that the right to privacy protected by Art 8 of the European Convention on Human Rights is not an absolute one. It is subject to the needs of a democratic society to know certain things in the interests of, amongst others, morals, the prevention of crime and the protection of the rights and freedoms of others.[109]

The Jockey Club itself is no stranger to controversy or the courts. It has long been active in defending its right to regulate the affairs of the racing world without any outside interference. This is also of course true of many other sports governing bodies that jealously guard their right to self-regulation.

In July 2003, a Security Review Group, jointly carried out with the British Horseracing Board, focused on the identification of the nature of the threats to the integrity of horse racing in Great Britain, assessing the breadth and depth of such threats and considering how best the Security Department of the Jockey Club should be structured and organised to deal with the threats to racing's integrity. A number of recommendations ensued.[110]

In addition to a major overhaul of its security operation, one proposal that was seen as controversial by jockeys was a ban on the use of mobile phones on a racecourse during racing from about half an hour before the first race. A number of jockeys raised the argument that such a move could be a denial of rights of privacy and a possible restriction of trade.[111]

In addition, trainers will not be able to bet on any horse on betting exchanges. The club will also assume responsibility for weighing-room security, and install an improved closed-circuit TV system in the stables at Britain's 59 racecourses.

Bradley appealed to the High Court in 2004 against the disqualification from racing. He challenged the imposition of the penalty, contending that it was disproportionate and unlawful. It was further argued that a proportionate penalty would have been measured in weeks or months rather than years. In reviewing the role of the Appeals Board decision in reducing the initial eight year disqualification to one of five years, there were no findings either that Bradley did not receive a fair hearing, suffered procedural unfairness or that the decision was perverse. The main contention that the penalty imposed was disproportionate.

---

108 *The Jockey Club v Buffham & BBC* [2002] EWHC 1866.
109 For more on the case, see earlier Chapter 5, p 221.
110 See 'Joint BHB/Jockey Club Security Review Group Report', 3 July 2003, www.thejockeyclub.co.uk/news.
111 'Phone row could end in court', 14 September 2003, www.bbc.co.uk/sport.

Bradley v The Jockey Club (2004) EWHC 2164

Per Richards J: In my judgment the Board was fully entitled to conclude, as the final result of its balancing exercise, that a period of five years' disqualification was a proportionate penalty. Such a conclusion was within the limits of the discretionary area of judgment open to the Board in the application of the test of proportionality; it was within the range of reasonable responses to the question of where a fair balance lies between the conflicting interests. In my judgment there is no basis for the court, in the exercise of its supervisory jurisdiction, to hold that the Board acted unlawfully in imposing that penalty.[112]

This decision provides the Jockey Club with significant means to penalise those found to have been involved in corrupt practices. However, again it will depend on how effectively the problem is policed and investigated in the first place.[113] Police investigations continue into the extent of involvement of jockeys, trainers and others connected to the racing industry. In autumn 2004, the champion jockey Kieren Fallon was arrested during ongoing police inquiries.[114]

Gambling has been identified as being at the root of match fixing. The ethics of sports athletes gambling on games and events they participate in have also been increasingly addressed. The days when international cricketers could openly bet against their team winning as Dennis Lillee and Rod Marsh did in the famous 1981 Headingley Test Match between England and Australia (at massive odds of 500 to 1) are long gone. Sports governing bodies are required to have specific rules prohibiting players betting on matches to protect the integrity of the game, providing effective investigation and policing of such actions.

The regulatory approach to gambling in the UK is now considered.

GAMBLING AND SPORT

Gambling and sport have almost been inseparable and gambling has been subject to considerable regulation by the State. Gambling has close links with the general commercialisation of sport and with corrupt practices in sport. An extended extract on gambling follows, again looking at its historical context, with an aim to understanding its vast significance within modern sport:

Mason, T, *Sport in Britain*

Gambling has always been a part of the modern sporting world, although the public response to it has varied from one period to another. Gambling was endemic in 18th century Britain, but before 1850 a puritanical reaction had begun, aimed particularly at working class betting. The greatest achievement of

---

112 See SLJR (2004) 12(2) Sport and the Law Journal 105. This case seems to clarify the ambiguity of decision in *Colgan v Kennel Club* (2001, unreported) in indicating that the court is not entitled to put itself in the position of the tribunal in sentencing. A decision on length, for example, of sentence may be wrong, but the court may only interfere with the decision when the tribunal stepped outside its discretionary area of judgment; also see Stoner, C, 'A question of proportionality: the determination of fines and sanctions in disciplinary matters' (2003) 10(4) Sports Law Administration and Practice 1.

113 On wider issues of governance in racing see Chapter 9, p 377 and OFT investigation into hosre racing and the role of the British Horseracing Board and The Jockey Club; also see 'OFT reaches provisional agreement with BHB over reform of British horseracing', press release 94/04, 10 June 2004, www.oft.gov.uk/News/Press+releases/2004/94-04.htm; 'BHB and OFT Reach Agreement on How Racing Should be Modernised', June 2004, www.britishhorseracing.com/inside_horseracing/about/press/view.asp?item=001818; and Vamplew, W, 'Reduced Horse Power: The Jockey Club and the Regulation of British Horseracing' (2003) 2(3) Entertainment Law 94.

114 'Fallon slams fixing claims', 3 September 2004, www.bbc.co.uk/news.

the anti-gambling lobby was probably the Street Betting Act 1906, but it remained a powerful and influential opponent certainly up until the second Royal Commission on the subject in 1949. Since then gambling on sport has been increasingly raided by governments to provide income for the State and has also played a crucial role in the financing of the major sports of football and horse racing.

Betting had always been a part of rural sports, both those involving animals, such as cock fighting and bear baiting, and those involving contests between men. Pedestrianism, for example, probably began in the 17th and 18th centuries, when aristocrats and gentry promoted races between their footmen. These men had been used as message carriers between town house and country residence, although this function lapsed as roads improved and coaches became speedier and more reliable. Their masters often gambled heavily on the results of such races. Sometimes the young master ran himself. Pedestrianism, like prize-fighting, seems to have enjoyed a fashionable period from about 1790–1810. It could almost be characterised as the jogging of the early 19th century. Its most famous gentlemanly practitioner was Captain Barclay, a Scottish landowner whose real name was Robert Barclay Allardice. He was prepared to bet 1,000 guineas in 1801 that he would walk 90 miles in 21 and a half hours. He failed twice and lost his money each time. But on 10 November 1801 he did it, for a stake of 5,000 guineas.

Betting on horses was also commonplace, often taking the form of individual challenges between members of the landed classes. In the 18th century it was the usual practice to ride your own horse, but the employment of a professional jockey became increasingly common. Betting added another dimension of excitement to the uncertainty of sport itself and it was excitement, which the leisured rural classes were especially seeking, particularly in a countryside whose range of more conventional pursuits soon began to pall in the eyes of the young, married, leisured, pleasure seeking males.

Cricket was another rural pastime that the landed bucks found attractive. By the beginning of the 18th century newspaper advertisements told of forthcoming matches 'between 11 gentlemen of a west part of the county of Kent, against as many of Chatham, for 11 guineas a man'. With money at stake it was important to reduce the chances of disagreement by drawing up a body of rules and regulations by which both sides would abide. In this way gambling made its contribution to the development of the laws of cricket. In fact, in the code of 1774 it was specifically mentioned:

> If the Notches of one player are laid against another, the Bet depends on both Innings, unless otherwise specified. If one Party beats the other in one Innings, the Notches in the first Innings shall determine the Bet. But if the other Party goes in a Second Time then the Bet must be determined by the numbers on the score.

Football was, of course a very attractive proposition both to bookmakers and punters. Before 1900 some newspapers had offered prizes for forecasting the correct scores as well as the results of a small number of matches and early in the 20th century a system of betting on football coupons at fixed odds had developed in the north of England. It has been suggested that the early pools might have been partly emulating the pigeon pools by which a prize fund was collected for a particular pigeon race, with each competitor subscribing. The owner of the winning bird collected.

Newspapers began publishing their own pools coupons (until the Courts declared the practice illegal in 1928) and individual bookmakers offered a variety of betting opportunities. By the end of the 1920s, the football pools, and particularly Littlewoods, under the entrepreneurial guidance of the Moores brothers, had begun to thrive. The pool for one week in 1929–30 reached £19,000. By the mid-1930s the firm was sponsoring programmes on Radio Luxembourg which broadcast the results of matches on Saturdays and Sundays. The football coupon asked backers to forecast the results of a given number of matches from a long list or a selected short list. The latter was given attractive names like 'family four' and 'easy six', 'three draws' or 'four aways'. In January 1935 the penny points was introduced and soon became the favourite pool with the largest dividends, consisting of fourteen matches chosen for their special degree of difficulty. The eight draw treble chance replaced it as the most popular pool after 1945. By 1935 estimates put the number of punters at between five and seven million and it was 10 million by the time war broke out. In 1934 those companies founding the Pools Promoters' Association had a turnover of about £8 million which had increased by 1938 to £22 million of which the promoters retained a little over 20%. This is not the place to animadvert on the place of the pools in British society.

By the mid-19th century, therefore, betting and sport were firmly established as the closest of associates. But the middle class evangelicalism of the new urban industrial Britain was already beginning to take steps against what was increasingly characterised as a social evil. Gambling was typical of a corrupt aristocracy and it served them right if it led to the sale of their estates and the impoverishment of ancient families. But when the poor were led to emulate those who should have set a better example then something had to be done. By 1850 the State was being pressurised into doing it. The arguments used by the opponents of working class betting remained more or less unchanged for the next 100 years. Betting by the poor led to debt, which led to crime. Even where crime was avoided, deterioration of character was not, especially among the young and women. Spending sums on betting which could not be afforded weakened the material basis of family life thereby making a major contribution to poverty. Finally gambling undermined proper attitudes to work. As *The Times* so succinctly put it in the 1890s, it 'eats the heart out of honest labour. It produces an impression that life is governed by chance and not by laws'. These arguments carried most days until the Royal Commission of 1949–51.

The anti-gamblers' first legislative success was an Act of 1853 to suppress betting houses and betting shops, which had been springing up in many places, very often inside public houses. In future, bookmakers operating from such places, exhibiting lists or in any way informing the public that they were prepared to take bets were liable to a fine of £100 and a six month prison sentence. The Bill went through both Houses without a debate. Betting shops may have found difficulty in surviving: betting itself moved outside to the streets and places of employment. The expansion of horse racing in particular, with after 1870, the electric telegraph and a cheap press providing tips and results, provoked the opposition to organise itself, which eventually resulted in the formation of the National Anti-Gambling League. It was in its heyday in the two decades or so before 1914. Sociologists such as BS Rowntree, the economist JA Hobson and radical politicians like J Ramsay MacDonald contributed to its publications. They saw the working class gambler exploited by the bookmaker and those upper class sportsmen who supported him. After failing with the law the League turned to Parliament with the clear aim of eradicating street betting. It was this off-course variety which was responsible for the bulk of working class gambling. A House of Lords Select Committee first examined the matter in 1901–02. In 1906 came the legislation.

The Street Betting Act of 1906 has gained some notoriety as an example of class biased legislation. It was not aimed at all off-course betting. A person who could afford an account with a bookmaker who knew his financial circumstances well enough to allow him to bet on credit did not have a problem. This ruled out many working men and women. It was ready money betting of the sort they went in for that was to be prosecuted. In future it was to be an offence for any person to frequent or loiter in a street or public place on behalf of himself or any other person for the purpose of bookmaking or betting or wagering or agreeing to bet or wager or paying or receiving or settling bets.

It is unlikely that the Act did much to diminish the amount of betting. It did of course enhance the excitement of it all, especially at those times and in those places where local magistrates decided that the full rigour of the law must be enforced. Moreover it placed the police in an increasingly difficult position trying to enforce a law for which there was little popular support. Allegations that they frequently looked the other way or had an agreement with local bookmakers to prosecute a runner from each of them in turn were commonplace. By 1929 the police were very critical of both the law and their role in enforcing it and said so before the Royal Commission which was examining the police service in that year. It took the liberalising impact of the Second World War and the relatively buoyant economic circumstances which eventually succeeded it to bring about a more relaxed attitude to gambling. This was also facilitated by the Royal Commission of 1949–51 having relatively sophisticated economic and statistical apparatus which enabled it to show that personal expenditure on gambling was only about 1% of total personal expenditure, that gambling was then absorbing only about 0.5% of the total resources of the country and that it was by then rare for it to be a cause of poverty in individual households. They still regarded gambling as a fairly low level activity and were not impressed by the amount of intellectual effort some enthusiasts brought to it. But they were in favour of the provision of legal facilities for betting off the course and the licensed betting shop reappeared in 1960, 107 years after it had first been made illegal. Six years later the government's betting duty reappeared too.

Gambling's relationship with sport has been significant in two other respects: as a motive for malpractice and corruption and as a source of finance for sporting activities. The latter is closely connected to the growth of football pools of which more in a moment. Not all sports lend themselves to result fixing with equal facility. The team games should, in theory, prove the most difficult, because there are so many more players who would have to be 'squared' if an agreed result was to be secured. In the early 19th century the relatively small number of professionals could exert a disproportionate influence on some cricket matches and they were occasionally bribed or removed from the game by false reports of sickness in the family. One professional was banned from Lord's in 1817 for allegedly 'selling' the match between England and Nottingham. The gradual assumption of authority by the MCC and the county clubs, the improvement in the material rewards of the average professional cricketer and the increasing opportunities to bet on other sports – notably horse racing and, after 1926, greyhound racing – probably killed off gambling on cricket by cricketers. Today the Test and County Cricket Board (TCCB) has a regulation forbidding players to gamble on matches in which they take part. It was thought to be overly cynical even by late 20th century standards when Dennis Lillee and Rodney Marsh won £5,000 and £2,500 respectively by betting against their own team, Australia, in the Leeds Test of 1981. By then, of course, betting by spectators could be encouraged because it brought in revenue. Ladbrokes had been allowed to pitch their tent at Lord's since 1973.

Football has occasionally been shaken by allegations that matches have been thrown, usually in the context of championship, promotion or relegation struggles. Attempts to fix the results of matches in order to bring off betting coups appear to have been very rare but in 1964, 10 players received prison sentences for their part in a so-called betting ring. Three of the players were prominent English internationals and they were banned from football playing and management for life. Two, Peter Swan and David Layne, were later re-instated on appeal but by then were too old to take up where they had left off. Certainly the FA and the Football League were anxious to keep betting and football apart. When coupon betting first appeared in the North of England, before 1914, the FA Council threatened to suspend permanently any player or official who could be proved to have taken part in it. In 1913 they failed, but in 1920 succeeded in getting Parliament to push through a Bill forbidding ready money betting on football matches.

Football itself had not profited from the growth of pools. But it seems clear that early in 1935 discussions were taking place between the League's Management Committee and representatives of the Pools Promoters' Association about the possibility of the pools making a payment to the League for the use of their fixtures. But the public attitude of many of the leaders of League football was that the pools constituted a menace to the game and should be suppressed either by the action of the football authorities or by State intervention via an Act of Parliament. The negotiations broke down, perhaps because the pools promoters did not wish to pay what was being asked so long as there was some doubt about whether the fixtures were copyright. All out war was declared and an attempt made to damage the pools by secretly changing the fixtures on two consecutive Saturdays at the end of February and the beginning of March 1936. Unfortunately for the Football League, dissention in the ranks led to the plans being leaked and the scheme sank. They had no better luck with a Private Members' Bill to abolish the pools, which was easily defeated in the Commons in the same year. Moreover, the League felt it did not need tainted money from the pools, whose promoters therefore kept their hands in their pockets. They did not take them out again until 1959 (although they offered to, briefly, at the end of the war).

It is hard to escape the feeling that not only football but sport in Britain missed a real financial opportunity, although it is clear that it would have required government help to have realised it. In the 1930s the private firms running British football pools set up offices and agencies in several European countries. In Sweden, for example, where betting on pools was illegal, around 200,000 people were completing coupons every week, the stake money swelling the profits of Littlewoods and Vernons among others. The Swedish government acted to stop it in 1934 by establishing the Swedish Betting Corporation to run a State owned pool. Switzerland and Finland soon followed and by 1950 similar State run pools had begun in Norway, Spain, Italy, West Germany, Denmark and Austria. Later Poland, Czechoslovakia, Belgium and Holland adopted similar schemes. After administration and prize money had been found, much of what remained was channelled into the support not merely of football but of sport and physical recreation in general. For example £8 million had been so raised by the Swedish government over a three year period at the end of the 1930s. There were three moments when a similar scheme might have been set up in this country.

The first was early in the Second World War when it was clear that some rationalisation of existing commercial institutions in a range of fields would have to take place. The Secretary of the Football Association, Stanley Rous, together with Sir Arthur Elvin, who ran Wembley Stadium, proposed the creation of an independent pools company, half of whose profits would go to football. Nothing came of it. Instead the government agreed to an amalgamation of the existing companies for the duration. It was known as Unity Pools.

Rous returned to the problem with even more radical proposals in 1943. Reconstruction was in the air and he had been finding out about Sweden in particular. Rous proposed that appropriate government departments should be approached with the suggestion that part of the proceeds from the pools should go into a centrally administered fund, out of which would come money for sports grounds, gymnasia, recreation rooms and sports centres. Again nothing came of it.

The subject was raised for a third time during the sitting of the Royal Commission on Betting Lotteries and Gaming 1949–51. The English, Scottish and Welsh Football Associations all supported the idea of a non-profit-making football pool under government control. But the Commission disagreed, partly because they felt a considerable body of public opinion would not like it, partly because of practical difficulties and partly because of the loss of revenue to the government. If there had been a moment for such radical change, it must have been during those reforming years of the third Labour government. By 1951, its legs were very shaky indeed. Moreover it had been the Labour government that had instituted a 10% tax on the pools in 1947 and increased it to 30% in 1949. Football, of course, could always do its own deal with the pools and in the summer of 1959 it did. In the previous October the Football League had issued a writ against Littlewoods claiming that the League fixtures for the following season were its copyright. In May 1959 a judge agreed. By July an agreement had been signed, to last for 10 years, by which the Pools Promoters' Association was to pay the Football League and the Scottish League a royalty of 0.5% on total stake money, which would not be less than £245,000 a year. There have been several subsequent agreements, the latest a 12 year one signed in December 1984 which ensures the Football League £5 million per year. This, though, is but a small proportion of the income of the pools companies, three of whom – Littlewoods, Vernons and Zetters – paid the government £220 million in tax in 1984–95 but still made a profit of £17 million.

The treatment of football was different to that of horse racing. The government did not introduce a tax on gambling on horse racing until 1966. In 1985 it was still being levied at only 8%. As we saw above, the tax on pools betting came much earlier and was much higher: 42% in 1985. When betting shops were legalised the government established a Horserace Betting Levy Board, allegedly to compensate racecourses for the fall in attendance that would ensue. Its role was to assess and collect a levy from bookmakers and the tote and use the money for the benefit of racing. According to the leading authority on the subject, the Levy Board saved racing in this country. Perhaps there should be a Football Betting Levy Board. It is not clear why there has not been. British sport has had to get on terms with gambling in the 20th century; it seems that the terms could have been better.[115]

---

115 Mason, T, *Sport in Britain* (1988), London: Faber & Faber, pp 59–68.

Betting on sport is growing in popularity, with many new forms such as spread betting.[116] Specialist companies now operate to give advice and odds.[117] The current law on betting is to be found in the Betting, Gaming and Lotteries Act 1963, which, despite its title, no longer deals with gaming and lotteries. Betting is not defined by statute, but is generally regarded as entering into a contract by which each party undertakes to forfeit to the other, money or money's worth if an issue, in doubt at the time of the contract, is determined in accordance with that other party's forecast. Unlike a lottery, a bet may involve skill or judgment. No person may act as a bookmaker without the authority of a permit issued by the licensing justices. The essential test applied by the licensing justices in considering an application is whether or not the applicant is a fit and proper person. A bookmaker operating from a betting office requires a licence for the premises issued by the licensing justices. From 1 September 1997 the duration of betting permits and licences has been extended from one to three years. A licence may be refused on the grounds that there are already sufficient licensed betting offices in the locality to meet the demand for betting. No person under 18 years may be admitted to a betting office.

The regulatory framework of the British betting industry has been liberalised during the first half of the 1990s. The advertising of individual betting offices and their facilities was originally prohibited under the 1963 Act but from 1997 the ban has been relaxed to allow advertisements in material form, for example, in newspapers, journals and posters. The ban remains on broadcast advertising of betting offices.

The Principles of Gambling Legislation in the UK

The government set up a Gambling Review Body in 1999 under the chairmanship of Sir Alan Budd.[118] A wide ranging review of the legislation on gambling in Britain, it submitted its report in June 2001. New legislation was introduced in autumn 2004 to liberalise the regulatory framework in the UK. It has three main objectives:

- gambling remains crime-free;

- players know what to expect and are not exploited; and

- there is protection for children and vulnerable people

A continued worry in horse racing has been the relationship between gambling and organised crime:

The Jockey Club, 'Submission to the Gambling Review Body'

The Jockey Club is concerned about the vulnerability of horseracing to criminal behaviour and other undesirable activity as a consequence of betting, and the submission to the Gambling Review Body makes the case for greater regulation of betting and changes to the criminal law so as to maintain the public's confidence in the integrity of the sport. Principal concerns stem from the fact that, by comparison with other forms of gaming and gambling, the business of bookmaking (including spread betting) is under-regulated and lacks the necessary measures to deter corruption and thus renders racing vulnerable to malpractice.

---

116 'Bookies bet on a football bonanza' *The Observer*, 7 January 1996, p 6.

117 See Hunter, W, *Football Fortunes: Results, Forecasting, Gambling and Computing* (1996), Harpenden: Oldcastle; 'A good bet', *Fair Game*, Channel 4, 22 May 1995.

118 *Gambling Review Report* (2001), London: The Stationery Office; it can be found at www.culture.gov.uk/gambling_and_racing.

There is evidence that betting and racing are being used for money laundering purposes. The Police have indicated that there is some corruption within racing by criminals and that illegal betting, to the detriment of both government and racing revenues, is being carried out on a large scale.[119]

Sports related gambling has exploited new technologies with internet betting exchanges having proliferated together with the opportunities provided by interactive services via digital television. A number of betting exchanges have signed contractual agreements with specific sports bodies designed to provide more effective monitoring of betting irregularities and transfer of information.

Gardiner, S and Gray, J, 'Can sport control its betting habit?'

Since the dawn of sport, gambling has been its constant companion. Ancient drawings on primitive cave walls find that gambling has existed for thousands of years. During modern times, sports betting is the most popular form of gambling worldwide, with Internet-related gambling generating over $3 billion in annual revenues in 2002.

Gambling and sports creates an 'unholy alliance.' Gambling has enhanced sport's popularity, particularly on television whereby bettors are more interested in the point spread, not the outcome of a contest. While sports leagues welcome the popularity that gambling provides, they must guard against match fixing, point shaving, and bribery of athletes and referees because the public appeal of sport also rests on the integrity of the contest.

Computers, technologies, and the Internet have facilitated a sophisticated and popular way to gamble on sports events known as 'betting exchanges.' In essence, betting exchanges allows people to swap bets. For instance, one can serve as a 'bookmaker,' offering odds to other Internet users concerning a sports competition or event. Betting exchanges have created a fundamental change in gambling because now anyone with a credit card can make money from either a horse, a player, or a team by offering odds on the web site and then keeping the stakes when people fail to beat the odds. However, there is a realistic fear that people who have privileged or 'insider' information – knowing for certain that a horse, a player, or a team is going to lose – are offering odds on betting exchanges and then maximising their revenues on unsuspecting gambling customers.

In the United Kingdom, the market leader is Betfair.com. This web site claims to be 'the world's largest online betting company' with an estimated turnover of £50 million per week. Betfair simply serves as a broker, matching people who want to bet with people prepared to offer odds and bringing them together on its website. Betfair makes its money by charging a commission to those who win their bets.

Horseracing is a major attraction for Internet betting exchange gambling. Recently in the United Kingdom, as a result of horseracing betting exchange abuses, there has been a succession of inquiries by the Jockey Club into suspicious betting practices around horse races. Similarly, it has been reported that the Association of Tennis Professionals ('ATP') has discovered that bets of up to £80,000 were being placed on individual matches and that there had been irregular betting patterns around matches involving players not ranked in the top 100. It is alleged that tennis players have been able to profit from insider information concerning their matches.

Betfair has responded to these concerns by signing a 'Memorandum of Understanding' with several sport governing bodies. This has included the Jockey Club and ATP, whose security departments will have access to individual identities and betting records of Betfair gamblers when a race or match produces unusual betting patterns or competition results.

Betfair points out that by developing internal policing relationships with relevant sport governing bodies, sports corruption will be deterred because electronic transactional records will help investigators

---

119 Find the submission at www.thejockeyclub.co.uk/jockeyclub/html/racing/gambling.htm.

catch any wrongdoers, and, therefore create 'safe' Internet gambling sites. The downside is that if an exclusive commission is paid to sport governing bodies when they recommend that gamblers deal with 'official' or 'approved' betting exchanges a conflict of interest is created where a sports contest integrity is sacrificed in order to maximise sports related gambling revenues.

As with the regulation of gambling generally, there are a number of differing regulatory regimes ranging from prohibition, on the one hand, through to very liberal licensing. Since 2001, for example, in the United Kingdom, an extensive consultation process has taken place that generally supports a more liberal regime. Further, in April 2003, the Department for Culture, Media and Sport produced a position paper, 'The Future Regulation of Remote Gambling' (see www.dcms.gov.uk). The stated objective is to have 'effective regulation [that will] see Britain become a world leader in the field of on-line gambling.'

In contrast, the United States has passed federal anti-gambling legislation. This includes the Professional and Amateur Sports Protection Act of 1992 (28 USC §3702) that prohibits the expansion of state-sanctioned, authorized, or licensed gambling on amateur and professional sporting events in the United States. Similarly, the Comprehensive Internet Gambling Prohibition Act of 2002 (s 3006) was proposed to prohibit all Internet gambling.

Striking a balance between sports competition and Internet gambling is a tricky proposition. The early indication is that Internet betting exchanges are creating opportunities for lucrative 'remote gambling' while resulting in gambling anonymity that may ultimately endanger the integrity of sports competition.[120]

The match fixing scandal in cricket shows that there is a need for an effective regulatory framework concerning gambling and sport. In some countries around the world, gambling is essentially prohibited. It of course flourishes as an 'illegal undergound activity'. It is prohibited in some areas and regulated in others through strong and enforceable government legislation. In the United States, there are many instances of specific sports gambling legislation to govern the behaviour of people within and outside sports. In a third grouping of countries a liberal regulatory framework exists. In Britain, over the last few years an increasingly liberal approach has been adopted.

At a time when the administration of sport has become more complex than ever before, and vast amounts of new money are flowing into sport, it is essential that more effective regulatory frameworks are developed in the sporting world to counter the impact of gambling on particular sports and players. It is also vital that there is effective policing of these new regulatory frameworks.

CONCLUSION

What this chapter has shown is that elite sport is subject to immense commercial and financial pressures. The spirit of sport as an activity in its own terms, and not merely as a form of entertainment, is in some danger in the face of these pressures. The law's involvement in regulating sports commercial structure is seen by some as adding to those pressures, and by others as necessary and as a mechanism to bring order. There are clearly some important governance issues in sport that need to be addressed to improve its financial probity.

---

120 Gardiner, S and Gray, J, 'Can sport control its betting habit?' (2004) 89 Sport Business International 55.

KEY SOURCES

Fitzsimons, P, *The Rugby War* (1996), Sydney: HarperSports.

Gambling Review Report (2001), London: The Stationery Office – www.culture.gov.uk/ gambling_and_racing.

'The Corruption of Racing', *Panorama*, BBC TV, 6 October 2002, http://news.bbc.co.uk/ 1/hi/programmes/panorama/2290356.stm.

Jennings, A, *The Great Olympic Scandal: When the World Wanted its Games Back* (2000), London: Simon & Schuster.

For full details and access to cricket match fixing Reports, see www.cricket.org/link_to_database/ ARCHIVE/CRICKET_NEWS/FEATURES/MATCH-FIXING_APR2000.

CHAPTER 9

SPORT AND COMPETITION POLICY

INTRODUCTION

The focus of this chapter is on European competition law and policy. This is deliberate because it is European law that has had the most profound effect and will continue to have such an effect on the development of modern sports governance within the UK. There will however be an analysis of the interventions that the UK Competition Commission has made into sport in recent years.

What seems to be clear on both the UK and European levels is that competition law and policy will only involve itself in those areas of sport which has a commercial aspect and not those aspects of sports governance which seeks to regulate sport:

Schaub, A, 'Sports and competition: broadcasting rights of sports events'

The Commission is not, in general, concerned with genuine 'sport rules'. Rules, without which a sport could not exist – that is, rules that are necessary for the organization of a sport or its competitions – should not, in principle, be subject to the application of EC competition rules. Sport rules applied in an objective, transparent and non-discriminatory manner do not constitute restrictions of competition.[1]

Similarly, Ungerer argues, 'there must be a clear separation between sports regulation and the commercialisation of sport.'[2] Just like the issues surrounding the effect of the *Bosman* case on the transfer rules in football dominated debate on the role of competition policy in sport in the recent past, and the Fédération International de l'Automobile (FIA) governance issues, detailed below, so the issue of broadcasting rights has come to dominate the discussion of the role of competition policy today.

These instances will not be isolated. The more popular sport becomes globally, the more significant the European competition rules become. It will be noted from these comments that European competition policy has an impact beyond the jurisdictional limits of the European Union. Therefore an understanding of European competition policy provides an essential foundation for understanding the inter-relationship between sport's economic aspects and anti-trust in any legal system. In the EU the additional dimension of the cultural aspects of sport is also part of the consideration when applying anti-trust doctrine to sport.

This chapter is divided into two essential parts – that are inter-related. The first part deals with the application of the competition rules to sport generally while the second deals with its application to broadcasting.

The application of European competition policy to the commercial aspects of sport is now a well-established phenomenon. Essentially competition regimes exist to regulate economic activity within countries and are usually predicated on the notions of 'fair play'. Most competition regimes aim to avoid anti-competitive behaviour of cartels and prevent firms from abusing their dominance in any particular market.

In the case of cartels, competition law outlaws price fixing and collusion in business activities which might distort competition in any particular market thereby preventing new competitors from entering a market or competing fairly in a market which includes output restrictions and market

---

1   Schaub, A, 'Sports and competition: broadcasting rights of sports events', Madrid, 26 February 2002.
2   Ungerer, H, 'Commercialising sport: understanding the TV rights debate', Barcelona, 2 October 2003.

partitioning. The rules regulate abusive behaviour of monopolies or firms that have a strong position in a particular market from imposing unfair prices, discrimination and unfair foreclosure of competitors or even potential competitors in the market. The irony of the free market is that rules are required to keep markets open as far as possible – or to use a sporting metaphor – to create a 'level playing field'.

Finally, competition policy also regulates mergers between firms as these may affect a broad range of socio-economic issues such as employment and may have the effect of reducing choice to consumers and thereby lessening or eliminating competition. The rationale for regulating the market through *inter alias* competition policy is to improve efficiency and competitiveness in any particular economy. The benefits are to be seen in economic growth and lower prices and more choice – all of which are to the benefit of consumers.

Competition policy may also have other objectives depending on the contExt of the economy of each country. It may have several other objectives as well. In the past, for example, much of European competition policy was motivated by realising the objective of the single market within the European Union. Competition policy has now shifted to reflect consumer interest such as access to products, the prevention of agreements the effect of which is to limit output, and promoting price competition: '. . . consumer interest (is) the central goal of competition policy . . . Consumer interest has a bearing in priority setting. Cases that directly affect consumer interests have been given preference'.[3] Competition policy should not be seen in isolation but within the contExt of the liberalisation of markets which appears to have gathered pace since the demise of communism – or more accurately – since the Berlin wall 'came down' in 1989.

Competition law may still be seen as a hostile factor affecting some of the traditional monopolistic commercial transactions in sport. The structure of sports governance in Europe and elsewhere has attracted the attention of various competition authorities. Most sports are governed by a single authority. While these authorities, such as FIFA in football for example, regulate the rules of the game and questions of discipline, their entry into the economic sphere has grown considerably. This situation was accepted unquestioningly in the past; it now finds less acceptance within sport and very limited approval within competition authorities. Evidence of the latter is especially noticeable in football in the field of broadcasting rights where the Commission is playing a leading role in regulating and shaping agreements between sports bodies and broadcasters. The emphasis falls on increasing output of games and increasing the number of actors in product delivery, especially providing for the 'new media' such as mobile telephones and internet access. The reason for challenging the role of sports authorities lies precisely in the fact that these authorities exercise a monopolistic hold over the lives and fortunes of sportspersons and those entities that want to enter the fast growing sports market. The latter is particularly visible in the field of sports broadcasting, whereas the former can be seen in the challenge to the transfer system and access to participation in sport. Broadcasting provides a fast growing source of revenue for some sports, especially football. Since football is a truly global sport, it provides the most vivid examples of the development of competition policy in sport. A recent report on the English Premiership Football Clubs shows that the proportion of revenue from broadcasting grew from 12% in the 1995/96 season to 31% in the 1999/2000 season. By comparison the revenue from match day takings during the same period fell from 47% to 34% and income from commercial activities such as merchandising fell from 41% to 35% in the same period. This pattern is probably also true for other premier leagues in Europe. Thus in the 1995/96 season the Premiership clubs in England earned 53% of their income from commercial

---

3   Monti, M, 'A reformed competition policy: achievements and challenges for the future', Center for European Reform, Brussels, 28 October 2004.

activities and broadcasting; by the 1999/2000 season this had grown to 66%. The actual revenue coming into the English Premiership clubs has almost doubled during the same period.[4]

The growth of revenue in football and in sport generally has attracted the attention of the EU Competition Directorate. In a 1999 speech, Jean-François Pons explained that there had been a growth of cases before the Commission connected to sport. He advanced two reasons for this:

- the growth of broadcasting of sports events; and
- the consequences of the *Bosman* ruling[5] which liberalised the transfer rules of football and, more importantly, confirmed to all interested parties that sport was subject to Community law (including competition law) in so far as it constitutes an economic activity.[6]

The commercial significance of broadcasting sport has grown for both sports authorities and broadcasters as noted by the Commission recently:

Schaub, A, 'Sports and competition: broadcasting rights of sports events'

... the value of TV rights of the Olympic Games jumped from 308 million Euro for the Los Angeles games in 1984 to 1.4 billion Euro for the Sydney Games in 2000. In 1992, broadcasters paid 434 million Euro for the TV rights of the English Premier League for five seasons. In 2000 they paid 2.6 billion Euro for three seasons.[7]

Ungerer, H, 'Commercialising sport: understanding the TV rights debate'

Football is significant for broadcasters. It represents 30–65% of their total rights expenditure. It is indispensable for high ratings. Football accounts for nearly 80% of all sports programming and, most important, in nearly all Member States, is a key driver for TV development. In the UK, 65% of subscribers have indicated that sports are a major reason for subscribing to pay-TV; in Spain this figure is even 85%.
... TV is of high significance for football clubs. 30–70% of football clubs' revenue come from TV, and this explains why sometimes our efforts (*the Commission*) to bring joint selling into line with Competition law requirements meet a certain anxiety – even bitterness – on the side of some leagues, and are initially misunderstood.'[8]

Pons' analysis and exposition of competition policy involvement in sport is now of historic interest, and is still true today, although the emphasis has fallen on broadcasting.

Pons, JF, *Sport and European competition policy*

Reasons for the increasing intervention of European Policy in the Sports Sector

(1) The strong growth in economic activities connected with sport

Those with an interest in this sector will be well aware of the most striking examples of such growth: the increase in salaries and transfer fees of professional sportsmen, the rise in the value of broadcasting rights as well as an increase in the sponsorship and advertising costs. This growth results principally from television's technological revolution, with the development of cable television, subscription channels and, more recently, of 'package' subscriptions and pay-per-view. That technological revolution has, of course, been accelerated with the advent of digital technology. The growth in the number of

---

4   See Deloitte & Touche, *England's Premier Clubs* (2001), 12; www.footballfinance.co.uk/publications.

5   The judgment is dealt with in detail elsewhere in this book.

6   Pons, JF, *Sport and European Competition Policy*, Fordham Corporate Law Institute, 26th Annual Conference on International Antitrust Law and Policy, New York, 14–15 October 1999; see www.europa/comp/dgiv.

7   *Op cit*, fn 1, Schaub (2002).

8   *Op cit*, fn 2, Ungerer (2002).

subscription channels and package subscriptions, the increased competition within television as well as the significant investment which must be recouped, and the pressures from advertising and sponsorship have all resulted in a search for more attractive programmes, notably for live broadcasts of high profile sports events (Olympic Games, important football matches and Formula One motor racing, in particular). For example, the value of television rights for the Olympic games jumped from 287 million dollars for Los Angeles (1984) to 907 million for Atlanta (1996) and is estimated at around 1,350 million dollars for the forthcoming games in Sydney (2000). A similar explosion of television rights for the Italian League has jumped from 29 billion liras for the period 1984–87, to 571 billion for the 1993–96, and to 1,278 billion for 1996/99.

According to the most recent global economic date (1997), sport's estimated world-wide turnover was in the region of 100 billion Euros, of which 44 billion resulted from ticket-sales, 37 billion from the award of television rights and 13 billion from the award of sponsorship rights. European sport represented some 36% of those receipts against 42% for the United States.

The strong growth in sports-related economic activities in Europe has been accompanied by a transformation in the structure and behaviour of large professional clubs and their federations, which are now managed as large industrial organisations or services. For example, 18 football clubs in Britain are now quoted on the Stock Exchange, with a total capital value on 30 June 1999 or around 1 billion Pounds (1.6 billion Euros). In Europe, sport is organised on the basis of a single federation by discipline and by country; together these national federations form a European federation.

Since 1974 (the *Walrave* judgment), the European Court of Justice has made clear on several occasions that 'the practice of sport is subject to Community law insofar as it constitutes an economic activity'.

The increasing application of competition rules of the Treaty of the European Union to sporting activities and undertakings results therefore from the development of sports-related economic activities, a number of which I have already mentioned.

However, Community competition rules do not apply to the more traditional aspects of sport, in relation to which the economic impact is limited, including mass participation in sporting activities (involving one European in three) and the vast majority of the 545,000 sports clubs in the European Union. But it is necessary to underline that high level professional sport has links with amateur sport and a clear impact on it; notably a part of the resources supporting the development of amateur sport come from professional one.

(2) The Bosman judgment

The judgment in 1995 of the European Court of Justice in the *Bosman* case, which concerned transfer rules of footballers, has had important repercussions on that sport in Europe. More significantly, it marked, in the eyes of the sporting and political world as well as in those of the general public, the intrusion of Community rules into sport.[9]

EU Competition Commission's Policy to Sport

The Commission has made it clear since the *Bosman* judgment that it recognises the special nature of sport. The special nature of sport is confirmed by almost every inter-governmental conference of the EU. Perhaps the Helsinki Declaration has been the most significant. Although there is no Treaty provision dealing with sport at present, the Draft Constitutional Treaty makes an express reference to sport. If this aspect of the draft Treaty emerges unscathed, sport will have a legal basis within the

---

9   *Op cit*, fn 6, Pons (1999) pp 3–4.

enlarged European Union.[10] Up till now the Commission has tied in sport with culture and education. The Commission, through the Education and Culture Directorate General and that of the Competition Directorate General, has been anxious to strike a balance between preserving the essential structures of sport and at the same time to bring the governance of sport in line with the Treaty provisions. In this regard sports authorities have been urged to reform their regulatory frameworks to bring these more in line with the norms espoused in the EC Treaty.

Jean-François Pons provided the guideline that the Commission has thus far followed.

Pons, JF, 'Sport and European competition policy'

(1) When dealing with competition cases in the sports sector the Commission must take into account the special character of sport in at least three respects:

- The rules for the organisation of sporting competitions are very different from those for competition between industrial firms. For instance, it is essential that no clubs participating in an annual championship should drop out prematurely as this would distort the final results. Rules are then necessary to ensure a minimum level of solidarity and equality between the strongest and the weakest teams in a championship and to guarantee the uncertainty of the results.

- Sport is not only an economic activity, it is also a social activity practised by millions of amateurs and one which plays a positive role in society ... A part of these social aspects of sport is financed by resources coming from economic activities: resources from the strongest clubs, television rights and sponsoring. Thus some form of distribution of resources from top to the bottom of the sporting pyramid is to be welcomed.

- Sport organisations (federations) have a role of regulation as well as being involved in economic activities (selling of television rights, of tickets, licensing of their logos, etc).

(2) In applying the competition rules to sport, the Commission is seeking to distinguish as clearly as possible between compliance with the principle of competition and the requirements of sports policy ...

The Commission will try to put a stop to the restrictive practices of sport organisations, which have significant economic impact and which are unjustified in the light of the goal of improving the production and distribution of sport events or with regard to the specific objectives of a sport. The Commission will, however, accept those practices of sport organisations which do not give rise to problems in the light of the competition rules of the Treaty either because they are inherent in the sport or necessary for its organisation or because they are justified in terms of the positive objectives referred to above.

It is not always easy to identify the intrinsic sporting nature of certain rules, either because they have significant economic consequences or because the rule, originally established for purely sporting reasons, has taken on more of an economic character as a result of the development of the economic activities associated with the sport. It may also be difficult to establish whether a rule is necessary to the organisation of sport or to the organisation of competitions. For these reasons it is only gradually on a case-by-case basis that the Commission and/or the Court of Justice on a basis of preliminary questions presented by national courts will be able to clarify what must be regarded as a rule inherent in sport or a rule necessary for the organisation of sport or sporting competitions. I would not be surprised if, in their future application of competition rules to sport, these institutions reached the conclusion that the following practices would fall outside the scope of Article 81(1) of the Treaty:

- The 'rules of the game'.
- Nationality clauses in competitions between teams representing countries (national teams).

---

10 Parrish, R, 'The EU's draft constitutional treaty and the future of EU sports policy' (2003) (3) The International Sports Law Journal 2.

- National quotas governing the number of teams or individuals per country participating in European and international competition.
- Rules for selection of individuals on the basis of objective and non-discriminatory criteria.
- Rules setting fixed transfer periods for the transfer of players, provided that they ensure some balance in the general structure of the relevant sports.
- Rules needed to ensure uncertainty as results, where less restrictive methods are not available.[11]

A recent example of the Commission's concern with preserving the distinctiveness of sport can be seen in the approval of the Union des Associations Européennes de Football's (UEFA) broadcasting regulations, which were amended by UEFA in July 2000. The rules allow national football associations to block the broadcasting on television of football during two and a half hours either on Saturday or Sunday to protect stadium attendance and amateur participation in the sport. The question of joint selling of broadcasting rights is still being investigated. The present Commissioner Monti noted that:

> The present decision reflects the Commission's respect of the specific characteristics of sport and of its cultural and social function in Europe in trying to play the role of an impartial referee between the different interests of broadcasters and football clubs.[12]

In this decision the Commission clearly stated that the UEFA broadcasting regulations did not fall within Art 81(1) as it was a matter dealing mostly with protecting the game of football and the restrictions pursued – to protect attendance at games – was 'justifiable and acceptable'.

The Commission has pursued the approach outlined by Pons above consistently. In March 2001 agreement was reached about the transfer rules (discussed below) and there is a Commission decision regarding the FIA. The nature of the agreement shows that the Commission and FIA have managed to negotiate a settlement that satisfies both. FIA has notified the agreement in terms of Art 19(3) of Regulation 17/1968 (now replaced by Regulation 1/2003). Essentially a division is created between the rules necessary to regulate motor racing which FIA retain and the commercial aspects of the sport which have been hived off to a commercial organisation for exploitation.

The current Commissioner for Competition has certainly pursued the policy outlines above and this can be seen in the new transfer deal in football and the new arrangements regarding FIA. It should be noted that the Commission recently expressed its satisfaction with the Formula One/FIA arrangements and has terminated its monitoring of the 2001 settlement.[13]

Scope of Involvement

The scope for the involvement of competition law in the economic areas of sport was clearly identified by Pons and has been subsequently repeated. These are:

- Distribution of sporting goods: exclusive distribution cannot be used to prevent parallel imports.

- Sponsoring must be organised in an objective, open and transparent manner otherwise competition law will apply.

---

11   *Op cit*, fn 6, Pons (1999).
12   *Op cit*, fn 3, Monti (2004).
13   IP/03/1491 of 31 October 2003.

- Sports equipment: standards for such equipment which are set to meet objective criteria to improve spectator appeal, or promote fairness of competition amongst participants for reasons of safety will not attract competition law intervention. But where the standards imposed are arbitrary, discriminatory or otherwise abusive on the part of governing bodies the competition rules will apply.

- Issues linked to the organisation of sport such as:

  (a) ticketing arrangements;

  (b) transfer rules.

The approach of the Commission and the European Court of Justice to the issues identified will be considered below in greater detail.

THE EUROPEAN COMPETITION RULES

The competition rules of the EC Treaty are set out in Arts 81 and 82 (formerly Arts 85 and 86, respectively).

The Regulation of Cartels

EC Treaty, Art 81

(1) The following shall be prohibited as incompatible with the common market: all agreements between undertakings, decisions by associations of undertakings and concerted practices which may affect trade between Member States and which have as their object of effect the prevention, restriction or distortion of competition within the common market, and in particular those which:

  (a) directly or indirectly fix purchase or selling prices or any other trading conditions;

  (b) limit or control production, markets, technical development, or investment;

  (c) share markets or sources of supply;

  (d) apply dissimilar conditions to equivalent transactions with other trading parties, thereby placing them at a competitive disadvantage;

  (e) make the conclusion of contracts subject to acceptance by the other parties of supplementary obligations, which, by their nature or according to commercial usage, have no connection with the subject of such contracts.

(2) Any agreements or decisions prohibited to this Article shall be automatically void.

(3) The provisions of paragraph 1 may, however, be declared inapplicable in the cases of:

  – Any agreement or category of agreements between undertakings;

  – Any decision or category of decisions by associations of undertakings;

  – Any concerted practice or category of concerted practices.

Which contributes to improving the production or distribution of goods or to promoting technical or economic progress, while allowing consumers a fair share of the resulting benefit, and which does not:

  (a) impose on the undertakings concerned restrictions which are not indispensable to the attainment of these objectives;

(b) afford such undertakings the possibility of eliminating competition in respect of a substantial parts of the products in question.

Article 81 deals with cartels – that is, where there is an agreement or arrangement tacit or otherwise between two or more undertakings which affects trade between Member States or is likely to do so by distorting competition in a number of ways. These are listed in Art 81(1). The rule is 'effects based' in that the effects of behaviour are paramount rather than the form of agreement. Thus formal contracts are not required. A pattern of behaviour may be sufficient to attract condemnation. The various ways in which anti-competitive conduct is manifested are listed in Art 81(1)(a) to (e). These are broadly worded to cover most anti-competitive conduct by cartels; but should not be seen as exhaustive, but merely indicative.

There must be an appreciable effect on trade between Member States, in that, 'in order to come within the prohibition imposed by Art 81(1), the agreement must affect trade between Member States to an appreciable extent'.[14]

The European Court of Justice (ECJ) explained that:

... the prohibition in Article 81(1) is applicable only if the agreement in question has as its object or effect the prevention restriction or distortion of competition within the common market. Consequently an agreement falls outside the prohibition in Article 81 when it has only an insignificant effect on the markets, taking into account the weak position which the persons concerned have on the market of the product in question. Thus an exclusive dealing agreement, even with absolute territorial protection, may, having regard to the weak position of the persons concerned on the market in the products in question in the area covered by the absolute protection, escape prohibition laid down in Article 81(1).[15]

The word 'undertakings' is deliberately used and has a broad application. A single person may constitute an undertaking. It is clear that sports bodies fall within the ambit of undertaking where they are engaged in economic activity. In the *Italia* case the Commission considered that the various bodies concerned with ticketing arrangements were undertakings under Art 81(1). FIFA as well as the Italian Football Association were considered as undertakings by virtue of the economic activity they were engaged in:

Italia Case OJ L 326/31 (1992), [1994] 5 CMLR 253

47. FIFA is a federation of sports associations and accordingly carries out sports activities. However, FIFA also carried out activities of an economic nature, notably as regards:

– the conclusion of advertising contracts,

– the commercial exploitation of the World Cup emblems, and

– the conclusion of contracts relating to television broadcasting rights.

. . .

49. It must therefore be concluded that FIFA is an entity carrying on activities of an economic nature and constitutes an undertaking within the meaning of Article [81 EC].

50. The Federazione Italiana Gioco Calcio (FIGC) is the national Italian football association, appointed by FIFA to organise the 1990 World Cup.

51. The FIGC was accordingly responsible for the entire organisation of the event in accordance with the provisions of the 1990 World Cup regulations and had in particular the task of ensuring that grounds were in order, press facilities provided, parking spaces laid out, etc.

---

14   Case 5/69 *Volk v Vervaecke* [1969] ECR 295; [1969] CMLR 273.
15   *Ibid*, pp 302 and 282 respectively.

52. For the purpose of financing such expenditure, the FIGC had a share in the net profits of the competition and was able to exploit commercially in Italy the 1990 World Cup emblem, which it had itself created.

53. The FIGC thus also carries on activities of an economic nature and is consequently an undertaking within the meaning of Article [81 EC].[16]

The other area of considerable dispute in competition cases both under Arts 81(1) and 82 is what constitutes the relevant market, or – to put it differently – what is the product market in which the anti-competitive behaviour has taken place. The definition of the relevant or product market will often determine whether or not there has been an infraction of the rules. On the whole, the Commission and the ECJ have drawn or defined the markets narrowly and this has allowed them to set standards of acceptable behaviour. The issue of relevant market will be mentioned again below.

Article 81(2) renders all agreements offending Art 81(1) null and void and therefore, unenforceable in any court within the European Union's Member States.

Article 81(3) allows the Commission to exempt certain agreements that offend Art 81(1) provided certain requirements are met. For example, some agreements may appear anti-competitive at first sight, but if allowed to continue may in the long run actually promote competition. When BSkyB television started out in the early 1990s satellite technology was new and BSkyB was taking a risk. BSkyB, in partnership with the BBC, concluded restrictive and exclusive agreements with the English Premiership for televising live football matches for a period of five years. Other broadcasters were excluded. The agreement was approved because BSkyB's risk was appreciated by the Commission and it was clear that it would not have been prepared to make the investment unless it could get some return on its investment. Since that initial agreement broadcasting technology has undergone a revolution and with the advent of digital technology there are many more broadcasters in the market. Notably the Commission has not been prepared to countenance BSkyB's continued monopoly and has insisted that the agreement between itself and the English Premiership League for televising live matches be considerably restructured allowing for diverse 'packages' of broadcasting rights, increased output of televised matches and access for other media.[17]

Thus Art 81(3) is a tool which has been used by the Commission to develop competition policy in the EU. However, an exemption will only be granted if the Commission feels that consumers will derive a fair share of the benefit and that there will be economic development and/or technological development. Finally, even if such an exemption should be given the agreement should not be more restrictive than is necessary for the achievement of the aim of the agreement, and it should not have the effect of eliminating competition. In this regard it is notable that the Commission recently granted such an exemption to UEFA's Champions League.[18]

Monopolies and Abuse of Dominance in the Market

European Treaty, Art 82

Any abuse by one or more undertakings of a dominant position within the common market or in a substantial part of it shall be prohibited as incompatible with the common market in so far as it may

---

16 Distribution of Package Tours During the 1990 World Cup OJ L 326/31 (1992), [1994] 5 CMLR 253.

17 This is discussed in greater detail below, but see Whittaker, J McDonnell, P and Singh, T, 'United we stand: collective media rights sales under challenge in England' (2003) (3) ISLJ 11; also see Notification 2004/C 115/02 which deals with the Commission's objections and the revisions made by the FA Premier League; and Harbord, D and Szymanski, S, 'Football trials' (2004) European Competition Law Review.

18 This is discussed below, p 364.

affect trade between Member States. Such abuse may, in particular, consist in:

(a) directly or indirectly imposing unfair purchase or selling prices or unfair trading conditions;

(b) limiting production, markets or technical development to the prejudice of consumers;

(c) applying dissimilar conditions to equivalent transactions with other trading parties, thereby placing them at a competitive disadvantage;

(d) making the conclusion of contracts subject to acceptance by other parties of supplementary obligations, which, by their nature or according to commercial usage, have no connection with the subject of such contracts.

The issue of dominance was considered in:

Case 85/76 *Hoffman-La Roche & Co AG v Commission* [1979] ECR 461

38 The dominant position thus referred to relates to a position of economic strength enjoyed by an undertaking which enables it to prevent effective competition being maintained on the relevant market by affording it the power to behave in an appreciable Extent independently of its competitors, its customers and ultimately of its consumers.

39 Such a position does not preclude some competition, which it does where there is a monopoly or quasi-monopoly, but enables the undertaking which profits by it, if not to determine, at least to have an appreciable influence on the conditions under which that competition will develop, and in any case to act largely in disregard of it so long as such conduct does not operate to its detriment.[19]

In the same case the question of abuse is explained:

91 The concept of abuse is an objective concept relating to the behaviour of an undertaking in a dominant position which is such as to influence the structure of the market where, as a result of the very presence of the undertaking in question, the degree of competition is weakened and which through recourse to methods different from those which condition normal competition in products or services on the basis of the transactions of commercial operators, has the effect of hindering the maintenance of the degree of competition still existing in the market or the growth of that competition.

A good illustration of abuse of dominance can be seen in the France 1998 World Cup case.

Case IV/36.888 1998 *Football World Cup*

The Decision concerns arrangements relating to the sale to the general public in 1996 and 1997 of entry tickets for the 1998 Football World Cup finals tournament by the officially appointed local organising committee.

The Comite Français d'Organisation de la Coupe du Monde de Football 1998 (CFO) was established as a non-profit-making organisation on 10 November 1992 by the Fédération Française de Football (FFF) with the agreement of the Fédération Internationale de Football Association (FIFA), specifically for the purpose of carrying on all activities relating to the technical and logistical organisation of the 1998 World Cup finals tournament in France, in compliance with various operational constraints laid down by FIFA.

As holder of all rights relating to World Cup tournaments, FIFA establishes regulations outlining the general organisational framework of both preliminary and final competitions. In relation to organisational arrangements relating to the 1998 Football World Cup finals tournament, FIFA established

---

19   Case 85/76 *Hoffman-La Roche & Co AG v Commission* [1979] ECR 461; [1979] 3 CMLR 211.

regulations providing that the CFO, subject to approval of the overall arrangements by FIFA, was responsible for all matters relating to the price, distribution, and sale of entry tickets for final matches.

In total, some 2,666,500 entry tickets were made available by the CFO for subsequent distribution either directly or through officially appointed sales channels.

LEGAL ASSESSMENT

Pursuant to Article 82 of the EC Treaty and Article 54 of the EEA Agreement, any abuse by an undertaking of a dominant position within the common market or in a substantial part of it shall be prohibited as incompatible with the common market in so far as it may affect trade between Member States. Such abuse may, *inter alia*, consist of direct or indirect imposing of unfair trading conditions or limiting markets to the prejudice of consumers.

Dominant position

The CFO represented the sole outlet for blind sales to the general public in 1996 and 1997 of Pass France 98 and individual entry tickets. As such, and in view of its ability to act independently and, therefore, free from competitive restraint, the CFO held a dominant position on the relevant markets.

Taking particular account of the significant difference between the demand for and supply of Pass France 98 and individual tickets sold by the CFO to the general public in 1996 and 1997, the CFO was, as a *de facto* monopolist, under a prima facie obligation to ensure that entry tickets sold in 1996 and 1997 for finals matches were made available to the general public under non-discriminatory arrangements throughout the EEA.

Abuse

In view of (a) the conditions of sale which applied in relation to CFO sales of blind tickets in 1996 and 1997, (b) the sales information made available by the CFO on its official World Cup website and on which the general public outside France could have reasonably been expected to rely, and (c) the restrictive means made available to the general public outside France for reserving entry tickets, the CFO abused its dominant position on the relevant markets because its behaviour had the effect of imposing unfair trading conditions on residents outside France which resulted in a limitation of the market to the prejudice of those consumers.

The general public outside France was free to purchase entry tickets direct from the CFO on condition that they provided a postal address in France to which the tickets could be delivered.

At the time of CFO sales of Pass France 98 and individual tickets, the general public resident in France had little difficulty in providing an address to which tickets could be delivered. However, only by entering into wholly arbitrary, impractical and exceptional arrangements could most of the general public resident outside France have obtained tickets direct from the CFO in 1996 and 1997. While it is questionable whether the general public outside France had ever been adequately informed that tickets could be purchased direct from the CFO, the effect of the requirement to provide a postal address in France was to discriminate specifically against the general public resident outside France, given that those resident in France were significantly better placed to meet that requirement.

This discrimination amounted in practice to an imposition by the CFO of unfair trading conditions on residents outside France and resulted in a limitation of the market to the detriment of those consumers in relation to CFO sales of 393,200 tickets through Pass France 98 and 181,000 tickets relating to the opening match, quarter and semi-finals, third and fourth-place play-off and the final, contrary to Article 82 of the EC Treaty and Article 54 of the EEA Agreement.

Effect on trade between Member States

In relation to ticket sales on the relevant product markets, the CFO imposed conditions of sale on the general public, which had the effect of denying the overwhelming majority of residents outside France access to those markets. Thus, such a procedure appreciably affected trade between Member States.

THE DECISION OF THE COMMISSION

The Comité Français d'Organisation de la Coupe du Monde de Football 1998 (CFO) has infringed Article 82 of the EC Treaty and Article 54 of the EEA Agreement by applying discriminatory arrangements in 1996 and 1997 relating to the sale to the general public of entry tickets for World Cup finals matches. Those arrangements involved the imposition of unfair trading conditions on consumers outside France which resulted in a limitation of the market to the prejudice of those consumers in relation to the sale of 393,200 tickets through Pass France 98 and 181,000 tickets relating to the opening match, quarter and semi-finals, third and fourth-place play-off and the final.[20]

There has been considerable concern amongst sports organisations that the competition rules are inappropriately applied to sport. The Commission has gone to a lot of trouble to explain its policy towards sport and set down guidelines for sports bodies to follow. It is necessary to consider these guidelines and comment on the tExts emanating from the Commission.

But first, how are the competition rules implemented? The emphasis in current competition law is to encourage compliance or at least to negotiate compliance in the case of Art 81(1) infractions. In the case of Art 82 infractions the Commission is often more severe and may impose substantial fines. It has the power to impose a fine of up to 10% of the offending undertaking's turnover. In the sports cases mentioned the fines have been more symbolic in nature since the Commission appreciates the fact that the sporting world needs time to come to terms with the impact of the competition rules. This was certainly the case with the World Cup cases in Italy and France.

Enforcement and Exemptions

The purpose of this section is not to offer an exhaustive account of enforcement procedures, but rather show how compliance is achieved. Regulation 17/1968 provided for the enforcement of the competition rules of the EU. This regulation has now been repealed and replaced by reg 1/2003 which came into effect as of May 2004.[21] In the past, agreements likely to offend Art 81(1) were notified to the Commission. This was usually done on the A/B form. The notification was then published in the Official Journal and interested parties were invited to comment or object. The Commission considered these comments and objections and might have had objections of its own. If the Commission objected to the agreement then those objections were similarly published in the Official Journal. The undertakings involved then had to alter their agreements in order to meet the objections raised. In many cases this long process could be avoided by undertakings sending their lawyers to the Commission in Brussels where the details and problems of an agreement were thrashed out to ensure compliance with the competition laws.

Notification was a formal process. There were several responses to notification as already indicated. The Commission might issue a 'comfort letter' or say nothing at all. A comfort letter indicated that the Commission was not going to take matters further. The same applied to the opposition procedure. If nothing was heard from the Commission six months after notification then

---

20   Council Directive (00/12/EC): Commission Decision of 20 July 1999 relating to a proceeding under Art 82 of the EC Treaty and Art 54 of the EEA Agreement (Case IV/36.888 – *1998 Football World Cup*) OJ L 5, 8 January 2000, pp 55–74.

21   The essence of this regulation will be dealt with at the end of the chapter; more particularly its possible effect on competition policy in sport. See Gauer, C *et al*, 'Regulation 1/2003 and the Modernisation Package fully applicable since 1 May 2004', (2004) 2, Competition Policy Newsletter.

it could be assumed that the Commission had no objection. Notification had a temporary and limited benefit of immunity from fines.[22]

Where the Commission has given attention to the agreement and stated its objections then the undertaking is entitled to a hearing, which means an oral hearing where it can put its case.

Abusive conduct under Art 82 is prohibited and where there has been a complaint or the Commission has acted on its own, it is obliged to indicate to the offending party the nature of the abuse and afford it a hearing before imposing either periodical fines when abusive behaviour continues, or imposing a single fine.

UEFA's notification of its agreements regarding broadcasting is a good example of how the notification procedure worked. The example below is a notification by UEFA of an application for negative clearance in terms of the now repealed Art 2 of reg 17/1968. Negative clearance constitutes a formal decision by the Commission by which it certifies that on the basis of the facts provided there are no grounds to proceed either under Art 81 or 82 for action on its part. The notification below was given in 1999. However, it is significant that UEFA chose to notify the Commission of its agreement since many undertakings prefer not to do so and pursue illegal agreements – until caught out.

Case 37.632 *UEFA Rule on 'Integrity of the UEFA Club Competitions: Independence of Clubs'*

The Union des Associations Européennes de Football (UEFA) applied for negative clearance or, failing this, for exemption pursuant to Article 81(3) of the EC Treaty in respect of the rule named 'Integrity of the UEFA club competitions: independence of the clubs'.

According to UEFA it is of fundamental importance that the sporting integrity of UEFA club competitions be protected. To achieve this aim, UEFA reserves the right to intervene and take appropriate action in any situation in which it transpires that the same individual or legal entity is in a position to influence the management, administration and/or sporting performance of more than one team participating in the same UEFA club competition.

The notified UEFA rule establishes that: 1 no club should have a financial or management interest in another club which participates in the same UEFA competition, 2 no person should be involved in the management of more than one club participating in the same UEFA competition, and 3 no person or company may control more than one club participating in the same UEFA competition.

The UEFA arguments for negative clearance

According to UEFA the rule: 1 is designed to preserve the integrity of competition and the uncertainty of outcome in the international club competitions it organises, 2. seeks to achieve this objective by avoiding the 'conflict of interests' which would result if an individual or a company was able to influence the sporting performance of two (or more) teams participating in the same competition and which might lead to the manipulation of results, 3 is not concerned with economic or commercial activities but is concerned with football as a sport, 4 the rule falls outside the scope of the competition provisions of the EC Treaty because it pursues a sporting objective; the rule does not restrict competition but even if it was held to restrict competition on the market for ownership interests in football clubs capable of taking part in UEFA competitions, the rule would not still violate Article 81 of the EC Treaty as it is needed for the proper functioning of sporting competition.

Contrary to other types of business, in the sports business consumer welfare requires that numerous clubs remain on the market and achieve the highest possible economic and sporting balance between them.

---

22   Council Regulation 17/68, Art 15(5), now repealed and replaced by Council Regulation 1/2003.

Furthermore, UEFA refers to Paragraph 107 of the Opinion of Advocate-General Alber in Case C-176/96, *Lehtonen* (delivered on 22 June 1999). Here Mr Alber points out, on the basis of the case law of the Court of Justice, that EC competition rules shall not be assessed in the abstract and that they always depend on economic conditions in the relevant markets. Rules restricting freedom of action which, by their effect, are necessary to the creation of competition on the relevant market can therefore be compatible with Articles 81 and 82 of the EC Treaty, so long as they are necessary and appropriate to attain this objective.

In the submission of UEFA, the rule is a balanced and proportionate measure to ensure that competition is genuine and is seen to be genuine because it does not prevent investment in clubs (from other than clubs participating in UEFA competitions or owners of such clubs), but simply prohibits clubs under common control from playing in the same UEFA competition.

Taking into account what the Court of Justice has recognised in the *Bosman* Case as legitimate objectives in view of the considerable social importance of football in the Community, the Commission considers that the restrictions imposed by the rule may not be subject to the prohibition laid down in Article 81(1) of the Treaty. In order to establish whether this preliminary conclusion can be upheld or not, the Commission has to know if such restrictions are limited to what is necessary to preserve the integrity of the UEFA club competitions and to ensure the uncertainty as to results. In other words, the Commission must confirm whether or not there are less restrictive means to achieve the same objective.

With this in view, the Commission invites third parties to send their observations.[23]

Below is a notification by the Commission that it objects to the UEFA arrangements regarding the televising of games. It has also issued a memorandum.

European Commission, 'Commission opens proceedings against UEFA's selling of TV rights to UEFA Champions League'

The European Commission has sent a statement of objections to European football organisation UEFA challenging UEFA's current arrangements for the selling of the rights to televise the UEFA Champions League. The Commission is concerned that UEFA's commercial policy of selling all the free and pay-TV rights on an exclusive basis to a single broadcaster per territory for a period lasting several years may be incompatible with EC competition law and should be improved to ensure that European sports fans can benefit from a wider coverage of top European football events.

UEFA (Union des Associations Européennes de Football) notified its Regulations concerning the joint selling of the commercial rights to the UEFA Champions League to the European Commission in 1999 requesting clearance under European Union competition rules. This statement of objections relates only to the UEFA Champions League TV rights.

Joint selling on an exclusive basis has a number of effects that threaten affordable access to football on TV unless certain safeguards are taken. UEFA sells all the TV rights to the final stages of the UEFA Champions League on behalf of the clubs participating in the league. One effect of this is that only bigger media groups will be able to afford the acquisition of and exploitation of the bundle of rights. In turn, this leads to unsatisfied demand from those broadcasters who are unable to obtain TV rights to football. This lack of competition may also slow down the use of new technologies, because of a reluctance of the parties to embrace new ways of presenting sound and images of football.

The Commission fully endorses the specificity of sport as expressed in the declaration of the European Council in Nice in December 2000, where the Council encourages a redistribution of part of the revenue from the sales of TV rights at the appropriate levels, as beneficial to the principle of solidarity between all

---

23   Communication made pursuant to Art 19(3) of Council Regulation 17/68 concerning request for negative clearance or for exemption pursuant to Art 81(3) of the EC Treaty (Case 37.632 *UEFA Rule on 'Integrity of the UEFA Club Competitions: Independence of Clubs'*) OJ C 363, 17 December 1999, pp 2–4.

levels and areas of sport. However, the Commission considers that the current form of joint selling of the TV rights by UEFA has a highly anti-competitive effect by foreclosing TV markets and ultimately limiting TV coverage of those events for consumers. The Commission considers that joint selling of the TV rights as practised by UEFA is not indispensable for guaranteeing solidarity among clubs participating in a football tournament. It should be possible to achieve solidarity without incurring anti-competitive effects.

The Commission will examine carefully any constructive proposals to render the current arrangement compatible with EC competition law and to guarantee open access to TV coverage of football.

The sending of a Statement of Objections does not prejudge the final outcome of the investigation and respects the rights of the notifying party and other interested parties to be heard.

UEFA has a total of three months to reply to the Commission's objections and can also request the organisation of a hearing at which it would be able to submit its arguments directly to the representatives of the national competition authorities.[24]

It should be noted that the Commission granted UEFA an exemption in respect of the television rights of the Champions league. The essence of the exemption is discussed below.

APPLICATION OF THE COMPETITION RULES TO SPORT

The Approach to Exemptions

The Commission has indicated on several occasions that when applying the competition rules to sport it will take into account the special nature of sport. Most recently Mario Monti, the Commissioner for Competition remarked that the Commission was aware of the different natures of sport and economic competition and that in the case of the former weaker competitors are preserved:

> A contest is required between a number of teams and participants. The interdependence between competing adversaries and the need to maintain a balance between them are features specific to sport.[25]

This view is premised on the belief that in sport, 'uncertainty of results' must be preserved together with a degree of equality in sporting competitions. The Commission was not concerned with 'genuine sporting rules' – those rules inherently necessary for the sport and its organisation – and in principle were therefore not subject to the competition rules:

> Sporting rules applied in an objective, transparent and non-discriminatory manner do not constitute restrictions of competition.[26]

In this regard the *Deliège* case[27] provides an excellent example of how the rules of the game are distinguished from the economic aspects of sport in EU law. Similarly rules to preserve the essential

---

24 IP/01/1043, Brussels, 20 July 2001, 'Commission opens proceedings against UEFA's selling of TV rights to UEFA Champions League' (note: TV broadcasting rights (radio broadcasting rights as well as stadium tickets are sold by the individual home clubs), sponsorship, suppliership, licensing and IPR).

25 Monti, M, 'Competition and sport: the rules of the game' (2001); see www.governance-in-sport.com.

26 *Ibid.*

27 Cases C–51/96 and 191/97 *Deliège v Liège Ligue Francophone de Judo and Others*. This case is discussed elsewhere in this book. In that case the court confirmed that the selection rules applied by the federation for participation of professionals and semi-professionals in the relevant sport would inevitably limit the number of competitors who could participate in an event. These limitations do not in themselves restrict the freedom to provide services. The rules derive from an inherent need for organising the sport and participation in events.

social and cultural benefits of sport are not likely to be affected by Art 81. Where rules are made to promote solidarity in a sport – in the case of football, this may mean rewarding smaller clubs for their investment in training – these rules may either fall outside the scope of Art 81(1) or be exempted under Art 81(3). However, these rules are only likely to be exempted if the sporting body imposing them can justify them. It must be shown that the rules are necessary for achieving the said objectives. In short, the rules (if they tend to be restrictive in nature) need to be proportionate to the objectives pursued.

In summary therefore the Commission has clearly indicated the following:

• The Commission is not interested in the rules of the game – rules which are essential for the organisation of the sport and which define issues such as discipline and playing rules and competition selection rules. In the case of the latter the rules need to be clear and be applied in an objective manner. By applying the selection rules, certain athletes may be disadvantaged economically – but this does not mean that there is any infringement of the Treaty.

• Where rules of a sporting organisation have an economic impact or effect prohibited by Art 81(1) then it will either not be affected by the said Article or it will be given exemption in terms of Art 81(3). This will only happen when it can be shown by the sporting organisation that the rule is necessary to achieve specific sporting objectives, which will benefit the sport, and those who participate in it. Usually the public also needs to derive some benefit from agreements or rules of a restrictive nature. The implication is that if the rules go too far in trying to achieve the justifiable objectives of the sport, then they will offend Art 81(1) and will not be given exemption under Art 81(3). In short the rules must be proportionate to the objectives stated and go no further than is necessary.

• There now appears be a clear indication by the Commission that where a sport is governed by a single federation which is responsible for both organisation and regulation of the sport it should seek to avoid commercial conflicts of interest.

The approach indicated above may appear relatively simple, but it may well be impossible for any sporting organisation to know whether the Competition Commission will share its interpretation of its rules and objectives. This matter will have to be considered on a case by case basis.

The approach of the Commission can be illustrated with the following examples. First, FIA and the Commission have recently reached an agreement in terms of which FIA's commercial interests are disposed of for 100 years allowing FIA to concentrate on regulating the sport and organising events.[28] As indicated above, the Commission is satisfied that there is compliance with this arrangements and therefore it no longer monitors the arrangement.

Second, UEFA and the notified rules (see above) forbidding clubs with one owner from competing in the same competition. The rule is intended to preserve the integrity of UEFA competitions by maintaining some independence between clubs. The Commission has taken a preliminary view (in July 2001) that these rules are not likely to cause it competition problems.[29]

Third, the Commission has announced new transfer rules in football. This happened after a protracted debate with FIFA and UEFA (but without agreement of Fédération International des Footballeurs Professionels (FIFPro), which represents the players). The new transfer rules tend to be

---

28 See later, p 372.
29 As indicated above, the Commission then awaits possible objections by third parties.

restrictive, but this is justified through the solidarity arguments. The issue of transfers will be considered below.[30]

Exclusivity

Other cases that the Commission has to deal with involve 'exclusivity'. Commercial transactions in sport do not make much sense unless there is some exclusivity. Generally speaking, the less exclusive the rights given, the less commercial value, and therefore the less the club gets in terms of money. The Commission recognises the commercial need for exclusivity. The Commission is more concerned that the exclusive rights are given on the basis of objective selection criteria and for a fixed period of time. Depending on the nature of the exclusivity the contract should not be for too long, for example in the case of broadcasting not for more than three years, and there should be no clause in the agreement allowing automatic renewal. It seems that the problem of exclusivity is largely a question of transparent and objective processes and a contract that is not excessive in length. In recent cases the Commission has also been concerned with agreements restricting output and establishing different packages of rights in the case of broadcasting. This approach, in the view of the Commission, allows for maximum participation in broadcasting especially in the case of the 'new media' that is internet and mobile telephony. The Commission has concentrated also on allowing consumers an increased benefit from exclusive agreements.

In a case involving sponsorship, the Danish Tennis Federation agreed to launch a transparent non-discriminatory call for tenders every two years in order to select a sponsor.[31] In the distribution of sporting goods the Commission took two decisions relating to the distribution of tennis balls. The Commission held that a system of exclusive distributions could not be used to prevent parallel imports. If this were allowed to happen it would affect competition between manufacturers and would limit consumer choice.[32]

One of the early cases involving exclusivity was the Football *Italia* case where package tours were arranged on an exclusive basis.

Italia Case OJ L 326/31 (1992), [1994] 5 CMLR 253

On 28 November 1989, the Commission received a complaint from the travel agency Pauwels Travel BVBA ('Pauwels Travel') against:

- FIFA Local Organising Committee Italia '90,
- '90 Tour Italia SpA,
- NV CIT Belgique.

The complaint, based on the provisions of Article 3 of Regulation No 17 (now repealed), related to the ticket distribution system applied during the FIFA World Cup held in Italy in 1990.

Pauwels Travel wanted to put together and sell in Belgium World Cup package tours comprising transport, accommodation and entrance tickets to the stadia in which the various matches were to be played. However, it found that the ticket distribution system that had been decided on did not allow travel agencies to acquire stadium entrance tickets for the purpose of putting together package tours.

---

30 See later, p 371.
31 Press release of 15 April 1998, IP/98/355. Also see *op cit*, fn 6, Pons (1999).
32 See Commission Decision of 18 March 1992, OJ L 364, 12 December 1992, p 58 (Dunlop Slazenger); Commission Decision of 21 April 1994, OJ L 378, 31 December 1994, p 45 (Tretorn).

The attempts made by Pauwels Travel to sell such package tours by procuring entrance tickets through parallel channels resulted in an action to cease and desist being brought before the Belgian national Courts by the travel agency authorised by the World Cup organisers to sell package tours in Belgium.

This Decision does not relate to the whole of the ticket distribution system, but only to the contracts through which the World Cup organisers conferred on the company '90 Tour Italia world exclusive rights for the supply of stadium entrance tickets for the purpose of putting together package tours.

The market on which the effects of the contracts must be assessed is thus that for the sale of package tours to the World Cup held in Italy.

THE DECISION OF THE COMMISSION

FIFA, the FIGC, the local organising committee Italia '90, CIT SpA, Italia Tour SpA and 90 Tour Italia SpA have infringed Article 85 (1) (81(1)) of the EEC Treaty as regards the provisions of the contracts of 26 June 1987 and 11 February 1988 concluded between the local organising committee Italia '90 and CIT SpA and Italia Tour SpA, on the one hand, and '90 Tour Italia SpA, on the other, which provided for the exclusive supply at world level to '90 Tour Italia SpA of ground entrance tickets for the purpose of putting together package tours to the 1990 World Cup. Such tickets formed part of a general system for the distribution of ground entrance tickets developed and implemented by the local organising committee Italia '90 in accordance with the instructions of the FIGC and FIFA, after approval by FIFA, a system which prohibited the sale of tickets for the putting together of such package tours, thus making it impossible for other tour operators and travel agencies to find sources of supply other than '90 Tour Italia SpA.[33]

In the *Italia* case other tour operators were effectively excluded from the business of arranging package tours for the Football Italia event. Clearly, in order to offer a package tour the tour operator would have had to be able to offer tickets to football games offered at the several Italian venues. They were thus precluded from doing so since the contracting parties had determined that such tickets would only be made available to '90 Tour Italia SpA. The exclusivity precluded competition in the market of package tours to the Football Italia events. The market being narrowly defined as package tours to Football Italia, which included tickets to the matches.

Exclusivity is recognised as a commercial necessity for promoting sport, yet it is clear that the parameters of exclusivity have to be carefully delineated:

- The length of the exclusive contract must not be too long.

- The range of rights granted (especially in broadcasting) must not be too wide.

- There must be no foreclosure of competition in the relevant market.

- Longer periods of exclusivity may be allowed if justified by entry into a new market or developing new technology.

Transfer Rules

The transfer rules in football have been the subject for considerable debate. Although the ECJ's Bosman ruling was based on the free movement of persons, the court ignored the competition aspects. The transfer rules have been settled by agreement between FIFA and the Commission. What follows is of historic interest.

In professional football, as well as a few other sports, players are tied to a club by a contract of employment. When a player wants to leave one club for another club, either at the end or during his

---

33 92/521/EEC: Commission Decision of 27 October 1992 relating to a proceeding under Art 85 (now 81) of the EEC Treaty (Cases IV/33.384 and IV/33.378 *Distribution of Package Tours during the 1990 World Cup*) OJ L 326, 12 November 1992, p 31–42.

contract, the home club has to agree that the player can move to the new club. The player's registration is then transferred from the old to the new club on payment of a transfer fee. The *Bosman* ruling[34] specified that when a player came to the end of his contract no transfer fee was payable where that player moved from a club in one country to a club in another country in the EU. This ruling effectively brought transfer fees to an end in EU countries when players had completed their contracts. The result of the *Bosman* ruling appears to have encouraged players to move clubs during their contracts – thus in effect avoiding the implications of the *Bosman* judgment. The principle of that judgment *inter alia* is that the transfer fee imposed at the end of the contract affected free movement of persons under the Treaty and was therefore unlawful. The *Bosman* ruling has caused transfer prices to rise dramatically and has brought about some instability in top European football clubs. It seems that there is no respect for contracts and the registration system does not offer much protection. Clubs have virtually been forced to let players go in return for a substantial transfer fee.

Football contracts are currently governed by the labour law of each Member State. This leads to inconsistency of treatment of such contracts. In continental Europe, for example in the Netherlands, a contract of employment must be formally dissolved where the club is unwilling to lose its player. In England, on the other hand, the practicalities virtually allow a player to walk out on his contract without the club effectively being able to stop it. In fact players in England now threaten to see out their contract allowing them to move freely to another club without their old club receiving a transfer fee. The anomalies of the transfer fee have been dealt with elsewhere.

Advocate-General Lenz canvassed the competition issues that arose. His analysis is worthy of consideration in view of the agreement reached between FIFA/UEFA and the Commission on the new transfer rules.

Bosman – Opinion of Advocate-General Lenz

(d) *Restriction of competition*

262 In my opinion, it is also perfectly clear that the effect of the rules at issue in this case is a restriction of competition within the meaning of Article 81(1). The rules on foreign players restrict the possibilities for the individual clubs to compete with each other by engaging players. That is a restriction on competition between those clubs. The Commission has rightly observed that those rules 'share ... sources of supply' within the meaning of Article 81(1)(c). Analogous considerations apply to the rules on transfers. As the Commission has stated, those rules replace the normal system of supply and demand by a uniform machinery which leads to the existing competition situation being preserved and the clubs being deprived of the possibility of making use of the chances, with respect to engagement of players, which would be available to them under normal competitive conditions. If the obligation not to pay transfer fees did not exist, a player could transfer freely after the expiry of his contract and choose the club that offered him the best terms. Under those circumstances a transfer fee could be demanded only if the player and his club had contractually agreed that in advance. The current transfer system, on the other hand, means that even after the contract has expired the player remains assigned to his former club for the time being. Since a transfer takes place only if a transfer fee is paid, the tendency to maintain the existing competition situation is inherent in the system. The obligation to pay transfer fees therefore by no means plays that '*rôle neutre*' with respect to competition that UEFA ascribes to it. The rules on transfers thus also restrict competition.

The factual elements of Article 81(1) are fulfilled if the restriction of competition represents the purpose or the effect of the corresponding agreement. In the present case it is quite obvious that the restriction of competition is not only the effect of the rules in question, but was also intended by the clubs and associations.

...

---

34   Case C-415/93 *Union Royale Belge des Societes de Football Association ASBL* v *Jean-Marc Bosman* [1996] 1 CMLR 645.

268 ... The Court of Justice does not ... regard clauses which are objectively required for the performance of a specific contract which is not itself objectionable as restrictions of competition ... Moreover the Court also regards restrictions of competition as compatible with Article 81(1) if, taking all the circumstances of the particular case into account, it is apparent that without those restrictions the competition to be protected would not be possible at all.

269 ... Only restrictions of competition which are indispensable for attaining the legitimate objectives pursued by them do not fall within Article 81(1).

270 ... the field of professional football is substantially different from other markets in that the clubs are mutually dependent on each other. In view of those special features, the possibility cannot therefore be dismissed that certain restrictions may be necessary to ensure the proper functioning of the sector. However, it has not been shown in the present proceedings that precisely the rules on foreign players and rules on transfers ... are necessary and indispensable for that purpose. The possible beneficial effects of those provisions can therefore be examined only in the context of Article 81(3).

As regards the transfer rules, I have already explained in the contExt of the examination under Article 39 why they are not indispensable for attaining the objectives they pursue – in so far as those objectives are legitimate. There exist alternatives, such as redistribution of a proportion of income, for instance, which permit those objectives to be realised at least as well.

271 ... In UEFA's opinion the present case is a 'concealed wage dispute'. UEFA argues that the relationship between employer and employee is not, however, subject to the provisions of competition law, and also refers on this point to the example of American law.

272 The transfer rules do indeed relate directly to the relationship between the player and his (previous or future) employer. If then the sphere of employment law were not subject to competition law, it could be argued that that must also apply to the rules on transfers.

273 There is in my opinion no rule to the effect that agreements, which concern employment relationships, are in general and completely outside the scope of the provisions on competition in the EC Treaty. Nor is there any such rule, moreover, in the law of the United States, which UEFA relies on. From the judgments of the American Courts, which UEFA itself has produced to the Court, it can be seen that that exception applies to collective agreements between employers' associations and trade unions and the necessary prior agreements on the part of those involved. The statutory exemption of baseball from antitrust law is obviously a special case which is of no relevance for the present proceedings, if only because Community law does not have any corresponding provision for football (or any other sport).

...

275 ... As the Commission rightly stated at the hearing, this case does not concern *collective agreements* but simple *horizontal agreements* between clubs. For that reason alone UEFA's submission must fail: no reason can be seen why such agreements or decisions should not fall within the scope of Article 81.

(e) Article 81(3)

278 ... if such an application were made (for exemption from Article 81(1)), it would admittedly appear theoretically conceivable that the Commission might grant those rules, which are in breach of Article 39, an exemption from the prohibition in Article 81(1). Since such an exemption would, however, make no difference to the breach of Article 39, it would make sense for the Commission to take that factor into account in the exemption procedure. A uniform result ought to be aimed at in any case. That would mean that an exemption under Article 81(3) would also have to be ruled out.[35]

The comments made by Advocate-General Lenz in para 278 are of particular significance. The question arises whether the Commission could exempt football from a restrictive practice under Art 81(1), which would also mean breaching one of the foundations of the Treaty – the free movement of

---

35   *Ibid* Bosman [1996] opinion of Advocate-General Lenz.

persons. Lenz appears to think that this is not possible. If this is in fact so then the current agreement on transfer fees and contracts of football players needs to be considered in a new light.

The New Transfer Arrangements

In March 2001 the Commission, FIFA and UEFA agreed the new regime governing football contracts and transfers. These arrangements excluded the agreement of FIFPro – the federation representing professional football players. The new arrangement was seen as a triumph for the Education and Culture commissioner Viviane Reding. The football authorities did a deal with the Commission. On 1 September 2001 the new transfer rules came into effect.[36] Branco Martins has provided an analysis of the essence of the new transfer rules:

Martins, RB, *European Sport's First Collective Labour Agreement*

- Protection of minors: introduction of a code of conduct on international transfers of players under the age of 18. Sports training and schooling will have to meet certain criteria. Transfers are not forbidden. The circular noting the clubs' code of conduct on transferring players under the age of 18 has been added as an annex;
- Educational compensation for players up to the age of 23: clubs will receive compensation for training and education of players under the age of 23. Details of this compensation will be found in the annex;
- There will be two fixed transfer periods in each season;
- Duration of contracts: the minimum term for a contract will be 1 year, the maximum will be 5 years, in accordance with national law. Players younger than 28 must complete at least three years of their contract; older players must complete at least 2 years – the so-called stability period. In the event that clubs, players and /or acting managers do not abide by these terms, sanctions will be imposed. Unilateral breach of contract is only possible at the end of the season;
- A transfer will only be possible once a year, at the end of the season. Under certain conditions it will be possible to carry out a transfer during a brief period in the middle of the season. A player may only change clubs once a year;
- A player may terminate his contract unilaterally if his club uses him in less than 10% of the official matches in a season. This is the *'sporting just cause'* stipulation;
- Sports sanctions for breach of contract: suspension for four months and a transfer prohibition for 12 months for a club that urges a player to cancel his contract. The agent involved can also count on sanctions;
- When a club approaches another club about a player's transfer, the player must be informed immediately in writing. Failure to do so incurs a penalty of 50,000 Swiss francs (34,500 Euros);
- Claims about conflicts may not only be brought before national courts but also to the FIFA Disputes Committee . . . set up for this purpose. The Committee will render a decision within 60–90 days. Each decision of the Disputes Committee can be appealed to the Arbitration Tribunal for Football;
- An Arbitration Tribunal will be set up with an independent chairman and a rotating complement of representatives from clubs and players. There is also the possibility of bringing the claim before the national court;
- Also new are the solidarity funds: when an international transfer takes place during the contract's term, a solidarity contribution of 5% of each redemption fee will be paid to clubs where the player has played between the ages of 12 and 23;

---

36 See Martins, RB, *European Sport's First Collective Labour Agreement* (2002), TMC Asser Institute: The Hague, Netherlands, at 33.

- During the third season following implementation of this regulation, an evaluation will take place among groups from the football community, on the viability of the rules during the previous seasons;
- Contracts dates before September 1 fall under the old regime. However disputes fall under the current provisions.[37]

The Status of the New Transfer Arrangements

The question that arises is whether these rules go far enough not to offend the competition rules, in particular Art 81(1). It seems that these rules have the blessing of the Competition Commissioner and that the Commission will not act against FIFA of its own accord. However, the nature of the agreement reached is informal and the Commission has not issued a formal decision. The Commission has only given an undertaking. This may be sufficient for practical purposes. The Commission is not empowered to grant exemptions to agreements of an anti-competitive nature if such agreements violate the very foundations of which the EU is founded, for example, the free movement of persons.

It could be argued that on investigation of the new arrangements the Commission found on the basis of the 'rule of reason' and the specificity of sport that these new transfer rules fall outside the purview of Art 81(1). In view of the fact that FIFPro did not agree to these rules it may decide to challenge the legality of the arrangements either with the Commission, but more likely via national courts and the Court of Justice.

It remains to be seen whether the new arrangements will work and whether amicable resolutions of contracts will be the order of the day. The new rules do not provide for transfer fees but for compensation based on objective criteria. Since transfer fees bear no resemblance to the new compensation scheme, it may just happen that amicable determinations of contract will become common, with a large sum of money changing hands in order to achieve such amicability. It is too early to assess the impact of the new rules save to say that it appears that transfer fees are still increasing, thus resembling 'business as usual' in practice.

It is quite likely that the role of competition law in this saga of sport is still to show itself.

The FIA Compromise

During March 2001 FIA and the Commission reached an agreement about several of FIA's contractual arrangements with regard to regulating and controlling the commercial aspects of Formula One motor racing. These arrangements met with opposition from the Commission and after considerable negotiation FIA's Max Mosely and the Competition Commissioner Mario Monti reached an acceptable compromise. FIA substantially amended its agreements making FIA a less dominant force in these arrangements. These modifications to the three agreements detailed below were notified in June 2001 and the Commission indicated that its initial objections have been met by FIA and that it would consider the new agreements favourably. The Notice invites interested parties to comment on the agreements before approval by the Commission.

---

37   *Ibid*, 33–34.

Notice published pursuant to Article 19(3) of Council Regulation No 17 concerning Case COMP/35.163

2. THE PARTIES

FIA was founded in France as a non-profit-making association. It has at present more than 162 members (29 from EU countries). These are national automobile clubs, associations, and national motor sport federations (ASN's). The FIA members organise and regulate motor sport in their respective territories.

ISC is a company founded by Mr Bernie Ecclestone. Its principal activity was the marketing of television rights to FIA international series other than F1. In spring 2000, Mr Ecclestone sold the company to David Richards and the ISC is now charged with the promotion of the FIA World Rally Championship and the FIA Regional Rally Championships.

FOA/FOM, companies controlled by Mr Ecclestone, are engaged in the promotion of the FIA Formula One Championship. The term FOA/FOM, . . . includes FIA Formula 3000 International Championship Ltd, an Ecclestone family trust interest, which is engaged in the promotion of the FIA F3000 Championship. The 1998 Concorde Agreement provides that the FOA is the Commercial Rights Holder to the FIA Formula One Championship; FOA is thus responsible for televising and generally commercialising the Championship. On 28 May 1999, FOA changed its name to Formula One Management Limited (FOM) which manages the rights. The commercial rights themselves were taken over by an associated company, now named FOA.

3. PRODUCTS/SERVICES

These cases concern the following services and products: (a) the organisation of cross-border motor sport series; (b) the promotion of such series; (c) the certification/licensing of motor car sport events' organisers and participants; (d) the broadcasting rights of the FIA Formula One Championships.

4. THE NOTIFIED ARRANGEMENTS

(A summary of these arrangements:

4.1 The FIA rules which comprises its statutes; the International Sporting Code; General Prescriptions applicable to all FIA championships, challenges, trophies and cups; The Regulations of the FIA International Championships; Information contained in the FIA Yearbook and FIA Bulletin.

4.2 The notified agreements:

The Concorde Agreement; the Formula One Agreement; the Grand Prix contracts between FOA and local promoters; Broadcasting Agreements; the FIA/ISC Agreement.

These agreements were of a restrictive and anti-competitive nature as indicated below and were appropriately modified taking the Commission's objections into account:). . .

5. MODIFICATION AND UNDERTAKINGS BY THE PARTIES

The Commission's Statement of Objections issued in June 2000 made the preliminary assessment that FIA had a 'conflict of interest' in that it was using its regulatory powers to block the organisation of races which competed with events promoted or organised by FIA (ie those events from which FIA derived a commercial benefit). Moreover for a certain period of time, FIA may have been abusing a dominant position under Article 82 of the EC Treaty by claiming the TV rights to motor sport series it authorised. Analogous situation was created in formula one by the imposition of certain clauses in the Concorde Agreement. Finally certain notified contracts appeared to contravene Article 81 and/or Article 82 of the EC Treaty in that they raised further the barriers to entry for a potential entrant: the promoter's contracts prevented circuits used for formula one from being used for races which could compete with formula one for a period of 10 years; the Concorde Agreement prevented the teams from racing in any other series comparable to formula one; the agreements with broadcasters placed a financial penalty on them if they showed motor sports that competed with the F1 series. Certain agreements between the FOA and broadcaster appeared to restrict competition within the meaning of Article 81 of the EC Treaty by granting the latter exclusivity in their territories for excessive periods of time.

Although the parties do not agree with the Commission's Objections, they have nevertheless agreed to modify significantly certain of their agreements.

The modifications have the following objectives:

- to establish a complete separation of the commercial and regulatory functions in relation to the FIA Formula One World Championship and the FIA World Rally Championship where new agreements are proposed which place the commercial exploitation of these championships at arm's length,

- to improve transparency of decision-making and appeals procedures, and to create greater accountability,

- to guarantee access to motor sport to any person meeting the relevant safety and fairness criteria,

- to guarantee access to the international sporting calendar and ensure that no restriction is placed on access to External independent appeals,

- to modify the duration of free-to-air broadcasting contracts in relation to the FIA Formula One World Championship.

In order to achieve a more complete separation between sporting and commercial matters and in order to increase transparency, FIA proposes that Mr Ecclestone relinquish his seat on the FIA Senate and his role as FIA Vice-President for Promotional Affairs. FIA proposes to make Mr Ecclestone an honorary Vice-President of FIA. FIA is also prepared to stipulate that the representative of the formula one commission should not participate in any decision in the FIA World Motor Sport Council regarding the authorisation of any series, which is a potential rival.

Moreover, FIA will be prepared in principle to participate in the sporting management and attach the FIA's name to a series where the series' organiser wishes to form a partnership with FIA, where an organiser promotes the definitive competition in a particular discipline, where that organiser demonstrably properly manages that competition and where the discipline itself is sufficiently popular and developed.[38]

What follows are two examples of the proposed modifications, which FIA undertook to make. These serve as examples of the principles of transparency and access to competition that the Commission is keen to stress. Also observe that FIA had to avoid giving itself a privileged position vis-à-vis the contracts.

FIA/FOA Agreement dated 19 December 1995

The main proposed amendments to the FIA/FOA Agreement (is) to delete any reference to FIA favouring the FIA Formula One Championship or to FIA endorsing the Grand Prix (over other events) and guaranteeing that no provision in the agreement would prevent FIA from performing its regulatory functions.

Upon expiry of the above-mentioned agreement with FOA, FIA proposes to enter into a 100-year agreement with a commercial rights holder for the marketing of the FIA rights in relation to the formula one championship. All rights to organise and receive revenues from the championship will be transferred to this company for a fixed fee. FOA will not be automatically named as successor to the existing agreement. The draft agreement provides for the separation of commercial and regulatory functions in relation to formula one, allows FIA to use its logos etc for regulatory purposes, acknowledges FIA as the sole regulator of the championship over others.

---

38 COMP/35.163 – Notification of the FIA Regulations, COMP/36.638 – Notification by FIA/FOA of agreements relating to the FIA Formula One World Championship, COMP/36.776 – GTR/FIA and others, OJ C169/03, 13 June 2001. The underlined words (contd) indicate that each sport's special features are taken into account when deciding what is an acceptable practice. It can also be observed that exclusivity *per se* is not objectionable, but only the manner in which it is exercised.

FIA proposes to adopt a similar approach to the FIA World Rally Championship (FIA/ISC Agreement) and to any other commercially viable FIA series. FIA will enter into arms'-length commercial agreements which will provide for fixed payments to be made to FIA removing thus any incentive for FIA to discriminate in favour of any series for commercial purposes.

FOA broadcasting contracts

FOA has removed from its standard for TV contract the provision whereby broadcasters were afforded a discount of the rights fee payable if they did not broadcast any other form of open wheeler racing by letters dated 14 August 2000 to the two broadcasters in the European Union whose contracts contained such a clause FOA unilaterally waived its rights in relation to it. Where exclusive rights have been granted in relation to terrestrial television, FOA is now limiting the duration of these contracts to a maximum of five years in the case of host broadcasters; and to a maximum of three years in all other cases.

FOA undertakes to notify comparable rival broadcasters when exclusive free to air broadcasting arrangements for a given territory expires and to invite them to apply. FOA has agreed to consider applications for broadcast rights on a non-discriminatory basis.

6. ASSESSMENT

The proposed changes to the regulatory framework and to the commercial arrangements appear to the Commission to introduce sufficient structural remedies minimising the risk of possible future abuse and to set the basis for a healthy competitive environment in economic activities related to motor sport. The Commission considers that, *inter alia*, the following elements are of particular relevance to this assessment.

The new rules introduce a separation of commercial and regulatory activities in motor sport, which FIA intends to make effective, inter alia, through the appointment as from 2010 to a 'commercial rights holder' for 100 years, for each of the FIA Formula One and FIA World Rally Championships, in exchange of one-off fixed fee, payable at the outset. . . .

The modified rules provide that and the Commission has been assured that the FIA rules will never be enforced so as to prevent or impede a competition or the participation of a competitor, save for reasons inherently linked to FIA's regulatory role of maintaining safety standards . . . The reformed rules appear to provide satisfactory guarantees for a new regulatory environment where the FIA's licensing powers and the code's sporting and technical rules will be applied in an objective, non-discriminatory and transparent manner. The FIA will not object to the establishment of new events and the participation of circuits, teams and drivers in them, provided that the essential provisions contained in the code have been complied with. The FIA has in this respect confirmed that all those complying with the rules of the code will have their events listed on the international calendar as a matter of right. . . .

The new regulatory environment removes the previously identified obstacles to intra-brand and inter-brand competition. Competing events and series within the formula one discipline (and with other sport disciplines) will be possible. The reforms also create the possibility of increased inter-brand competition. New disciplines can be created, and events and series in potentially competing disciplines can be approved. FIA will have neither the commercial incentive not the regulatory power to limit the type and number of events it authorises, other than on the basis of objective criteria.

The notified agreements as amended will remove those barriers, which had prevented in the past the use of FIA licensed products and circuits or the participation of FIA licensees in different disciplines or in competing events in the same discipline. The proposed changes to the notified agreements will, for example, result in the availability of racetracks in Europe for rival series to use, even if these circuits already host FIA Formula One championship events.

The modified Concorde Agreement establishes the organisational structure of the FIA Formula One Championship and provides for the commercial arrangements aiming at marketing the series. As motor sport and especially formula one is a particularly complex technical activity requiring important investments in technological research and development, it is indispensable for all participants to agree on the way the series are organised. In this sport, for instance, all teams participate in all events at the same time. However, it is impossible to market in individual rights of each team participating in the race. As FIA, FOA, the teams, the drivers, the manufacturers and the local organiser or promoter may all have rights in the event, some arrangement between all of them for the sale or rights, especially the broadcasting rights, appears to be indispensable. The Concorde Agreement provides for FOA to be the commercial rights holder for the FIA Formula One World Championship and to negotiate on behalf of the teams and FIA the organisation of the races with the local promoters and the sale of broadcasting rights with broadcasters. These arrangements do not appear to affect prices or output in the market to any significant degree. Individual formula one events do not compete with each other as they are not broadcasting at the same time. Moreover all formula one events are available for broadcasting. . . .

All provisions in the notified agreements whereby FIA compelled licence holders to surrender to FIA their broadcasting rights have been removed. The agreements no longer contain any rule or mechanism, which would allow FIA to appropriate all media rights to a given championship.

The broadcasting arrangements for formula one, as amended, will bring periods of exclusivity granted to individual broadcasters to a length that does not exceed what seems reasonable in view of the nature of the rights and the obligations and investments undertaken by broadcasters, given the specific features of the sport. The pricing policy applied to contracts no longer penalises broadcasters who choose to broadcast open wheeler racing events other than Formula One.[39]

The modifications and undertakings of the parties described above substantially alter the legal and economic contExt as compared to that described by the Commission in its Statement of Objections. The Commission now intends to take a favourable view of the notified agreements.

While this notification invites comments from interested parties it clearly indicates that the Commission has heeded the specificity of sport. In the case of FIA one may even argue that it has taken the unique issues of motor racing into account and has sought to advance the growth of the sport. It has caused FIA to re-regulate itself so that it will avoid conflict of interests and will seek only to administer for the good of the sport. It will no longer use its regulatory role to impose abusive and anti-competitive contracts.

Where there is exclusivity at stake the exclusivity is usually commercially necessary – but the means by which it is granted must be based on objective criteria that are transparent. It must give all parties capable of tendering a chance to do so. Also, the exclusivity must not be excessive in length. The exclusivity preserves the commercial value of the service provided and provides adequate returns where there has been investment in technology and the like. It was pointed out above that the Commission is content with the compliance of the arrangement reached between FIA, the Commission and the other parties.[40]

UK COMPETITION ENVIRONMENT

The UK Competition Act of 1998 came into force in 2000. It replaced the Restrictive Trade Practices Act 1976. Under the new act the Competition Commission has replaced the Monopolies and Mergers Commission, with a similar primary role of monitoring mergers and takeovers.[41]

The Office of Fair Trading which has been in place for many years continues to be the investigative body concerning all forms of anti-competitive behaviour, including cartels and the

---

39 *Ibid.*

40 Commission ends monitoring of the FIA/Formula One compliance with 2001 settlement, IP/03/1491, 31 October 2003.

41 See earlier discussion on proposed takeover of Manchester United by BSkyB, Chapter 8, p 313.

abuse of market power under the Competition Act. When an infringement is found, the OFT has the power to apply appropriate penalties in accordance with our published guidance and in the light of developments in UK and EC case law. The OFT will refer to the Competition Commission (CC) mergers believed to result in a substantial lessening of competition in a UK market.

The Competition Enforcement (CE) Division of the OFT plays a key role:

- enforcing EC and United Kingdom competition laws including Articles 81 and 82 of the EC Treaty and the Competition Act 1998;

- stopping cartels and other damaging anti-competitive agreements;

- stopping any abuse of a dominant market position;

- promoting a strong competitive culture across a wide range of markets;

- informing business, through a widespread education programme, about changes in legislation; and

- working with the European Commission and national competition authorities of other EU Member States on Art 81 and Art 82 cases.

Since the enactment of the Competition Act, two major issues have fallen under the investigative gaze of the OFT. The first has involved the suspicion of a cartel between football replica shirt manufacturers, sports apparel retailers and a number of clubs. The OFT commenced informal investigation of the sector in the late 1990s. In 2002 they announced that they were instituting an investigation of a number of companies including Umbro, JJB Shirts and Manchester United who they alleged had 'entered into a number of agreements to fix the price of football kits manufactured and supplied by Umbro, infringing Chapter I of the Competition Act 1998'.[42] The investigation established price fixing and refusal to supply shorts to retailer who wanted to sell at a discount.

In August 2003, the OFT after concluding its investigation levied fines agaist a number of businesses including JJB Sports (£8.373 m), Umbro (£6.641 m), Manchester United (£1.652 m) and the FA (£198,000). The OFT may impose a penalty of up to 10% of UK turnover for a maximum of three years for infringement of the Competition Act 1998. In autumn 2004, the Competition Appeal Tribunal (CAT) dismissed the appeals brought by Allsports Ltd and JJB Sports plc.[43]

Horse Racing

The second major investigation by the OFT concerned the governance of horse racing in the UK. In 2001, a competition inquiry into the British Horseracing Board's supply of pre-race data to internet betting sites was launched. This followed a complaint from William Hill that BHB was abusing a dominant position as the sole provider of race and runner data on UK horse racing. The bookmaker alleged that this enabled BHB to set excessive and discriminatory pricing and restrictive licensing terms.[44] In April 2003, the OFT reported on this and wider issues of governance.[45]

---

42 'Football kit "price fixing" inquiry', 16 May 2002, www.bbc.co.uk/news.
43 Judgment at www.catribunal.org.uk/documents/Jdg1021Umbro011004.pdf.
44 Also see Chapter 10, p 429.
45 'The British Horseracing Board and The Jockey Club: a Summary of the OFT's case' April 2003 OFT 654–www.oft.gov.uk/nr/rdonlyres/aec00594-01eb-44b8-aa54-11b3f8f4e273/0/oft654.pdf.

Gardiner, S, 'The competition of horse racing'

The Office of Fair Trading (OFT) has told the bodies that run British horse racing that it believes some of their rules infringe competition regulations. The OFT has made its preliminary view that certain Orders and racing rules are anti-competitive because they:

- limit the freedom of racecourses to organise their racing, in particular by fixing how often and at what times they stage races and the type of racing they stage;

- fix the amounts that racecourses must offer owners to enter their horses in a race; [and]

- monopolise the supply of race and runners data to bookmakers by foreclosing competition from alternative suppliers.

The OFT is requiring the British Horseracing Board (BHB) and the Jockey Club to end these apparent infringements of the ACT and to increase the freedom of race courses operating under this regulatory regime to compete and open up the market for potential competition in the supply of race and runners data.

The OFT has recognised that there are non-commercial sporting rules, such as specifying the earliest age at which horses can run and how jockeys are allowed to use their whips that are unlikely to affect competition and are outside of its ambit. These are essentially sporting rules. This reflects the approach adopted by the European Commission in cases such as *Deliège* and the agreement reached with the FIA and Formula One Racing in 2001.

However the rules identified are considered by the OFT to have 'significant economic and commercial consequences' and are not compatible with Chapter I prohibition, which under the Competition Act 1998 provides indications of what are uncompetitive practices which prevent, restrict or distort competition. The OFT may exempt an agreement from the Chapter 1 prohibition if it is seen as contributing to the improvement of production or distribution or promotes technical or economic progress while allowing consumers a fair share of the resulting benefit. These two provisions assume that the agreement does not firstly contain any restrictions that are not indispensable to the attainment of those objectives or secondly allow the undertakings concerned substantially to eliminate competition.

The OFT state that consumers want 'orderly and trustworthy racing'. The Orders and Rules are viewed by the OFT as 'going beyond what is indispensable to ensure a viable, orderly and trusted British racing industry.'

Not surprisingly the response to this report from the racing authorities has been defensive. In an initial response, BHB chief executive Greg Nichols said the OFT had 'fundamentally misunderstood how and why British racing operates as it does [there would be] a comprehensive and robust response'.[46]

The OFT investigation focused on a number of agreements, including the Orders and Rules of Racing. These competition concerns arose from the high level of central control exerted by the BHB over how and when racecourses could offer horse racing and over the way BHB could exploit horse racing commercially through its control over racing data. The OFT was concerned that these agreements had the overall effect of restricting competition between racecourses, by preventing them from altering their racing in response to consumer demand, and prevented the emergence of alternative providers of racing data. After a period of consideration, the BHB responded with its view of future governance of racing.[47]

---

46   Gardiner, S, 'The competition of horse racing' (2003) 6(2) Sports Law Bulletin 1.

47   See BHB, 'The modernisation of British racing', June 2004 – www.britishhorseracing.com/images/inside_horseracing/media/The_Modernisation_of_British%20Racing.pdf.

BHB, 'The modernisation of British racing'

The Report recommends seven key changes to the structure of the sport:

  (i) the separation of the governance and commercial functions of the British Horseracing Board (BHB);

 (ii) the restructuring of the BHB Board;

(iii) changes to the management of racing's commercial interests;

 (iv) changes to the method of allocation and distribution of data income;

  (v) the establishment of a prize money agreement between racecourses and the recipients of prize money (owners, trainers, jockeys and stable staff);

 (vi) the introduction of greater competition between racecourses for fixtures;

(vii) the modernisation of the Orders & Rules of Racing.[48]

This plan was provisionally accepted by the OFT in June 2004. It reflects the developing criteria and framework for appropriate sports governance with a clear position on the desirability of the separation between the governance of the 'rules of the game' and the exploitation of the commercial interests in a given sport.

COMPETITION AND BROADCASTING

There are a few competition issues relevant in broadcasting of sporting events.[49] In order to create a product it must be decided what is to be sold and bought. Traditionally it has been the view of buyers and sellers of broadcasting rights that in order for the product to have value it can only be sold once to a principal buyer who may then decide to license certain rights in respect of the 'property' bought. In order to maximise value several products may be created from a specific event. If one considers football as an example one observes that usually the product being sold is the championship league – say the premier league matches. This is in any event true in the case of Germany, the UK, the Netherlands, while in Italy the clubs may sell individually as well as jointly. In Germany the view is that the product, that is, 'broadcasting rights', is owned by both the clubs and the league. This is also the case in the Netherlands, except in the latter case the primary right resides with the organiser and risk-taker of the event, whereas the Dutch Football Union has an equity interest in those rights.

In Germany, for example, a special provision was inserted into the German Competition Act permitting joint selling of federal league competition games by the German Football Union.

Anti-Cartel Act, s 31:

Section 1 shall not apply to the centralised marketing of rights to TV broadcasting of sports contests performed in accordance with the articles of association by sports associations which 'as a way of discharging the socio-political responsibility help promote amateur sports and are rewarded for this by an appropriate participation in the revenues resulting from the centralised marketing of those TV rights.'

The implication is that such rights – that is, selling broadcasting rights – can only be exercised in unison – jointly by the league association. This also means that the agreement precedent between the

---

48 *Ibid*, 4.
49 This section will not cover intellectual property rights as this is dealt with in Chapter 10.

league and the club, according to German law, does not restrict competition.[50] Dutch law holds a contrary view.[51] English law agreed with German law on this point.[52]

Several different products can be created out of the Premiership competition:

- live broadcasts in the UK. The contract usually specifies how many matches may be broadcast. The broadcaster may be able to license another European or international broadcaster to show a selection of matches live abroad;

- delayed broadcasts of matches – of less commercial value than live broadcasts;

- match highlights;

- per view on cable and satellite;

- the new media which includes mobile phones and the internet.

Technology has made the greatest contribution to the many different product markets that we now experience. Consider for example the importance of the internet, which allows viewers from all over the world to view a particular event. The advent of digital TV available on a number of delivery 'platforms' has further extended the options viewers have of watching sport. Sport has made a major contribution to the growth of satellite and digital technology. The advantage to sport is that there are many different products that are now susceptible to broadcasting.

The trick, from a competition point of view, is how to achieve an adequate balance between revenue and seeing to it that the output of sports events is not unduly restricted by collective agreements to sell broadcasting rights, and also how to give each medium adequate and fair access to broadcast sporting events, especially in football – the global sport – where these issues arise most readily.

The greatest source of revenue for sport comes from broadcasting. Some sports attract much larger audiences than other sports. Football, golf, tennis, rugby and motor racing are very popular viewing sports. Commercialisation is instrumental in expanding the appeal of sport and the growth of certain sports such as rugby football. In the US baseball, gridiron football and basketball have become regular viewing events amongst Americans.

In the EU there is recognition of sport's cultural aspect and there has been concern that commercialisation may preclude public access. The Commission has adopted the 'Television without Frontiers Directive' in terms of which each Member State may select the sporting events that are culturally significant to the people of that Member State. Wachmeister explained the justification for this Directive thus:

Wachmeister, AM, 'Competition newsletter'

I Priority for free-access television for the coverage of major sports events

1 There are advantages for viewers if important sports rights are broadcast by free-access television, so that consumers are not obliged to make additional payments for decoders, receiving equipment or cable

---

50 Schimke, M, 'Legal principles applicable to the centralised marketing of TV broadcasting rights in Germany' 2003 (3) ISLJ 15.

51 Olfers, M, 'Team sport and collective selling of TV rights: The Netherlands and European law aspects' [2004] 1 & 2 ISLJ 63.

52 *Op cit*, fn 17, Whittaker *et al* (2003) 11. Also see: Ferrari, L, 'Legal aspects of media rights on football events under Italian law: ownership, exploitation and competition issues' (2003) 3 ISLJ 4.

subscription to view such events, in particular, those in which their compatriot sports men and women take part in international events.

2 More generally, concern has arisen, with the growth and development of pay-TV, that viewers are being denied free-access to important national events because large subscription broadcasters have been buying up those rights to develop their own services. It is said that some sporting events are of such national or heritage importance, that they reflect common identity and value, so that broad free access should be given to them. The complaints are from 'public interest' or 'national heritage' concern, rather than on competition grounds, and a regulatory approach would be necessary to achieve the desired result.

3 Competition law is not the right instrument for achieving cultural or regulatory aims. As confirmed by the Eurovision judgment, competition rules are neutral with respect to different types of broadcasting and in principle, do not provide a legal base for favouring one category of broadcaster over others.

4 Further to an amendment by the European Parliament, the directive modifying directive 89/552/EEC ('television without frontiers') includes a new Article 3A. The purpose of this Article is explained in recital 18, which reads as follows:

> Whereas it is essential that Member States should be able to take measures to protect the right to information and to ensure wide access by the public to television coverage of national or non-national events of major importance for society, such as the Olympic Games, the football World Cup and the European football Championship; whereas to this end Member States retain the right to take measures compatible with Community law aimed at regulating the exercise by broadcasters under their jurisdiction of exclusive broadcasting rights to such events.

5 Article 3A paragraph 3 stipulates, moreover, that Member States shall ensure that broadcasters under their jurisdiction do not exercise the exclusive rights purchased by those broadcasters in such a way that a substantial proportion of the public in another Member State is deprived of the possibility of following events, which are designated by that other Member State, on free television. According to information supplied to the Commission by national delegations to the Contact Committee set up by the Directive, a large majority of Member States intend to notify their measures taken under Article 3A paragraph 1 in the course of 1998. All Member States have indicated timetables for transposition of Article 3A paragraph 3 by the deadline required by the Directive, ie 30 December 1998.

6 The procedure laid down in Article 3A paragraph 2 requires the Member States to notify their measures and the Commission to verify their compatibility with Community law within a period of three months. The Commission must seek the opinion of the Committee established by the Directive. Measures taken by Member States in order to guarantee the availability of coverage of certain events must be in accordance inter alia with Article 90 of the Treaty.[53]

In the UK, the Independent Television Commission (ITC) is the body that ensures that the listed events procedure works. Existing listed events rules, which were updated by the Broadcasting Act 1998, require that sport's 'crown jewels' must be shown either fully live on free to air, terrestrial television channels which at least 95% of viewers can receive (the BBC, ITV or C4) or in highlights form by one of those broadcasters.

The Category A list of events which must be screened live by one of those three broadcasters includes: the Olympic Games; the FIFA World Cup Finals Tournament; the FA Cup Final; the Scottish FA Cup Final (in Scotland); the Grand National; the Derby; the Wimbledon Tennis Finals; the European Football Championship Finals Tournament; the Rugby League Challenge Cup Final; and the Rugby World Cup Final.

---

53 Wachtmeister, AM, 'Competition newsletter', June 1998. Full version available at http://europa.eu.int/comm/competition/speeches/text/sp1998_037_en.html.

The Category B list of events that those broadcasters must be allowed to show highlights of includes: Test cricket matches played in England; non-finals play in the Wimbledon Tournament; all other matches in the Rugby World Cup finals tournament; Six Nations Rugby Tournament matches involving home countries; the Commonwealth Games; the World Athletics Championship; the Cricket World Cup – the final, semi-finals, and matches involving home nations' teams; the Ryder Cup; and the Open Golf Championship.

In July 2001, the House of Lords delivered a ruling in *R v Independent Television Commission ex p TVDanmark 1 Ltd*[54] concerning the sale of sports TV rights. The case arose out of a dispute between the ITC and TVDanmark 1. This Danish satellite cable service, based in London, broadcast Denmark's five away World Cup qualifying games even though they are listed events in Denmark. The ITC challenged this arrangement.

The Court of Appeal had earlier held that although 'the object of Art 3(a) is maximum coverage, it is not an object to be achieved at any cost'. Other factors have to be borne in mind, 'such as the need to sustain competition, and to prevent public service broadcasters becoming over dominant as well as the need to have regard to ordinary commercial realities'. Therefore, the Court of Appeal held that TVDanmark's holding the rights rather than the free to air broadcaster was lawful.

Overruling this decision, the House of Lords held that the Art 3(a) protection for certain designated events 'was not qualified by considerations of competition, [or] market economics'. The right of the public to have access to listed events is paramount.[55]

Where the major sports events such as the Olympic Games and World Cup are at stake Europeans have been guaranteed free to air coverage. The European Broadcasting Union has provided a service in co-ordinating broadcasts of significance to the citizens of the EU. However, for the first time the rights to the World Cup Finals in South Korea and Japan in 2002 were purchased by a private company, the German Kirsch Group. The latter has since gone into liquidation. They attempted to auction the rights to the highest bidder and realised less income than was anticipated.

Collective Marketing/Selling of Broadcasting Rights

Some of these issues – such as joint marketing and sales – have already been briefly considered. In 1998 the EU Competition Commission's Wachmeister detailed the issues that arise when competition rules apply to sports broadcasting.[56]

The most important competition issues relevant to sport's broadcasting include:

- assessing the relevant market;

- collective marketing/selling of broadcasting rights;

- the nature of the exclusivity granted – this includes issues such as sublicences.

There are several problems connected to collective marketing/selling of broadcasting rights. One issue, which has caused considerable problems, is who owns the rights to the events and therefore the proceeds of the event. The Treaty provides that each Member State shall apply its own definition of property ownership and what constitutes it. Therefore, the question of who owns the property rights in the sporting event is defined according to the property laws of each Member State. Usually

54   [2000] 1 WLR 1604.
55   See 'Listed sports events are protected against the TV rights market' (2001) 4(4) Sports Law Bulletin 1.
56   *Op cit*, fn 53, Wachmeister (1998). Parts of the text have been amended to take current developments into account.

ownership cannot subsist in a live event in itself. It must be recorded for copyright to subsist. However, the question of who controls access and right of access is usually capable of constituting legal rights.

In the case of sports the conundrum surrounding rights to broadcasting is solved through contractual means. Usually the sports association or federation gives itself the power to market and sell the broadcasting rights to the games or events of the competition. Such a stipulation is usually a condition precedent for participation in any of the association and/or federation's competitions and championships. It is this condition precedent to participation that has most often been challenged as being anti-competitive and/or an abuse of the dominant position of the association and/or relevant sports federation.

The argument is that the product being sold is the particular competition and not individual games. In competition terms the argument runs that all the clubs or associations form part of one entity and therefore there can be no question of restrictive agreements between members of the entity and therefore competition law does not apply. The rights belong to whoever is organising the competition or championship. This argument has been forcefully proffered by Gary Roberts.

Roberts, GR, 'The single entity status of sports leagues under section 1 of the Sherman Act: an alternative view'

It is important to understand that the product of a sports league is not merely a series of isolated, unrelated athletic contests. Rather, it is a season of totally interrelated games, all played within the structure and under the trademark of the league, none of which could be produced by any less than the entire league acting as a totally integrated whole. The NFL, for example, produces an annual series of interrelated football games involving all of its 28 member clubs, annual division championship races, a nine-game post-season playoff tournament, and ultimately a Super Bowl game and league champion. Only in this wholly integrated structure can the league product be produced and be a distinct and far more attractive product than any team or two teams could make acting alone.[57]

According single entity status to a sports league suggests only that because of its inherent co-productive nature and the need for total integration of its members' joint activity, a league should be treated as a single firm, incapable of conspiring with itself. For example, although the Buick, Chevrolet, Pontiac, Cadillac, and Oldsmobile divisions of General Motors may have their every business decision co-ordinated and controlled by the General Motors board of directors, if the board so chooses, this does not violate section 1 because General Motors is a single firm whose business decisions do not involve a plurality of actors.[58]

More neutrally stated, the single entity issue asks whether inherently co-producing sub-units of a sports league, none of which is capable of generating revenue or producing anything by itself, should be considered to be acting as a single firm or as independent conspirators when they as a league collectively determine where they will jointly produce their league product.[59]

However this approach has found no favour in the EU. Advocate-General Lenz commented in the *Bosman* case that anti-trust exemptions only applied in baseball because of a collective employment agreement between the players' unions and the team owners' union.[60] He expressed the view that

---

57 Roberts, GR, 'The single entity status of sports leagues under s 1 of the Sherman Act: an alternative view' (1986) 60 Tulane Law Review 562, p 569.

58 *Ibid*, p 577.

59 *Ibid*, pp 578–79.

60 Case C-415/93 *Union Royle Belge des Societes de Football Association ASBC v Jean-Marc Bosman*, 15 December 1995; see the extract of Advocate-General Lenz's opinion above, pp 404–06.

this approach did not apply in the EU, as no such collective employment agreements exist in sport. He also expressed the view that the EC Treaty made no provision for employment law to be exempt from the competition rules.

Roberts' argument has been used in recent cases. It was submitted in the *Bosman* case and more recently by the KNVB (the Dutch Football Association). In the case of the latter the Dutch club Feyenoord argued that it had the right to sell broadcasting rights for games at its home ground and had the right to retain the income raised. The Dutch competition authorities and subsequently the Dutch Court agreed with Feyenoord's contention arguing that the club took the risks attached to the home game and were therefore entitled to keep the proceeds of the game.

KNVB v Feyenoord (2000) International Sports Law Journal

In July 1998 an agreement was signed between the KNVB and the Dutch Premier League (Eredivisie NV). This agreement regulated inter alia media rights and other rights. The KNVB petitioned for a declaratory order to the effect that renditions of radio and TV recordings containing both summaries and matches organised by the KNVB jointly belong to all the clubs and KNVB. The KNVB also applied for an injunction against the unilateral and individual exploitation of those recordings. Alternatively, an injunction against individual exploitation by Feyenoord of TV rights to home games.

The Court said that the club derives income from its ticket sales for home matches. The match is a tangible event, which can only take place if a location is provided; the party providing the location is entitled to exploit the event.

Given the fact that the KVNB must be considered to be an 'entrepreneurial association' and in complete control of the market – causing the provisions concerned (its rules) concerned to limit competition in the Dutch market and enable them to adversely affect economic movement between EU countries. The agreement is void since it had not received any approval of the Dutch competition authorities.[61]

In the UK a different conclusion was reached under the (now repealed) Restrictive Trade Practices Act 1976 (RTPA) when applied by the Restrictive Trade Practices Court (RTCP).[62] This judgment rewards careful reading as it is a most detailed description of football and broadcasting. The Director General of Fair Trading objected to the restrictive nature of the Premier League (PL) and the BSkyB agreement. The PL granted BSkyB the exclusive rights to broadcast only 60 live matches of the league. The court found the agreement to be restrictive of competition but to be generally in the public interest.

Green, N, 'Collective selling of sports television rights'

The Judgment

Collectivity:

The Court was convinced by the point that the 'product' sold by the PL was the league championship as a whole and not just individual games; 'if a club were to withdraw from the PL for whatever reason it could not produce the derived product it helped produce as a member of the PL cartel'. The Court thus accepted the argument that each of the clubs in a league contributes to the creation of a single product – the championship – being a product that no one club could individually produce.

Collective Selling and Individual Selling of Television Rights:

A central tenet of the argument of the DGFT was that whilst collective selling is per se unobjectionable, clubs should be able to sell the unallocated rights themselves individually. The Court described this

---

61 (2000) International Sports Law Journal 9, 9 September 1999 (District Court of Rotterdam).
62 *Re FA Premier League Ltd.* Agreement Relating to the Supply of Services Facilitating the Broadcast of Premier League Football Matches (Restrictive Practices Court, 28 July 1999).

argument as 'fundamentally flawed' and 'facile'. As the Court concluded, it would be intolerable to find that both the PL and an individual club were attempting to sell the same television rights. No broadcaster would be willing to deal with either of them or, if he was willing, would pay one vendor a different price for the rights that might be sold by the other vendor to a different purchaser.

The Court also expressed the view that the right of the home club to veto who entered its ground to make a broadcast was not an answer to the question: who owned the right to sell the match, whether it was the home team, the visiting team or both. The court considered that a concurrence of two teams was required.

Competition Between Broadcasters: Exclusivity

The Court heard a great deal of technical, commercial and economic evidence about the broadcasting market. It concluded that competition was largely determined by the need to differentiate programming and that the ability to differentiate programmes was a key driver for Pay-TV subscriptions and hence a key means by which Pay-TV operators entered the broadcasting market and expanded, once in.

Exclusivity was a critical device to facilitate differentiation. Other facts in broadcasting competition included: terms of the agreements conferring exclusivity; the popularity of the sports competition; the timing of the programme and whether it is a repeat event week in week out, or an irregular event; quality of coverage; and the existence of a single seller.

The Court concluded that the fact that BSkyB had entered the market, and had done exceptionally well in the market had had the effect of 'sharpening' competition not dimming it.

Legal Conclusions:

The Court concluded that the restrictions . . . benefits outweigh the disadvantages.[63]

The UK Competition Act of 1998 came into force in 2000. The RTPA was a complicated piece of legislation. Although the court found the broadcasting agreement restrictive the agreement nevertheless passed through one of the 'gateways' that would make it permissible. The Act was rather formalistic; now the Competition Act is in line with the EC competition rules, this case may no longer constitute reliable law.[64] What is interesting, however, is that the RTPC applied the rule of reason, in essence, and approved of collective selling and a rather broad based notion of exclusivity. In this regard it is at odds with the German and Dutch courts.

There are two German cases that have been reported that have made the questions of collective selling problematic. The first decision is of the German Federal Supreme Court (Deutches Bundesgerichthof) of 11 December 1997.

Lentze, G, 'Collective marketing of football television rights'

On 2 September 1994, the German Federal Antitrust Authority [Bundeskartellamt] issued a prohibition order against the German Soccer Federation (DFB) prohibiting the collective sale of television rights to the home matches of German clubs participating in European competitions. The prohibition did not have any legal impact on the collective sale of television rights to matches of the German Bundesliga. The decision of the Kartellamt was affirmed by a Berlin Court on 8 November 1995. The Bundesgerichthof also ruled in favour of the Kartellamt in its decision of the 11 December 1997, also finding the collective marketing practice of the DFB a violation of German competition law.

---

63 Green, N in (2000) International Sports Law Journal 4–6. For a full discussion of the issues raised in the *BSkyB/PL* case see Spink, P and Morris, P, 'The battle for TV rights in professional football', in Caiger, A and Gardiner, S (eds) *Professional Sport in the EU: Regulation and Re-regulation* (2000), The Hague: Asser Press; Caiger, A, 'BSkyB/BBC TV deal upheld' (1999) 2(5) Sports Law Bulletin 4.

64 Also note that the attempted merger between BSkyB and Manchester United was decided before the Competition Act 1998; see Toms, N, 'Ownership and control of sports clubs; the Manchester United Football Club Buy-Out', in Greenfield, S and Osborn, G (eds), *Law and Sport in Contemporary Society* (2000), London: Frank Cass; Brown, A and Walsh, A, *Not for Sale: Manchester United, Murdoch and the Defeat of BSkyB* (1999), Edinburgh: Mainstream.

Facts

Until the end of the 1988–89 season, television rights to home games of the German clubs participating in the European competitions were marketed by the clubs individually. Since the beginning of the 1989/90 season, however, the DFB has marketed these rights centrally. During the two subsequent seasons, the DFB granted rights either for individual games or in blocks for multiple games to different TV stations. For the seasons 1992/93 till the 1997/98, the DFB granted exclusive world-wide (except Italy and Monaco) TV broadcasting transmission rights for the European games (except the Champions League and the final of the Cup Winners Cup) in a package to two sports rights agencies which sell the rights yearly. UFA, which belongs to the Bertelsmann Group and ISPR, which is equally owned by the Kirch Group and the Axel Springer Company, bought the rights for a total of DM360 million (an annual charge of DM60 million per season). There is a complex mechanism for distributing the income so derived among the clubs.

The Bundesgerichthof held that the collective sale of the television rights to the home games of the European competitions is likely to affect the conditions of the German market for television rights of sporting events and thus violates the prohibition on cartels imposed by §1 of the German Act Against Restraints of Competition. The Court reasoned that competition among the clubs as right owners for the marketing of the independent single games are restrained through the DFB regulations without reasonable justification.

Original ownership of the TV rights

Under German law, television broadcasting transmission rights for an event are generally owned by an event organiser. The crucial question for the Federal Supreme Court, therefore was to decide whether the DFB not being the organiser of an individual match, should be denied ownership of the TV broadcasting rights. The court reasoned that the main economic achievements for the individual games are created by the hosting clubs ... The court took these economic achievements and the general organisational and financial responsibility of the hosting clubs into account, finding them to be the natural participant in the market and, thus, the organiser of the football match. In Germany, competition law considerations are adjudicated upon original ownership.

Finally the Federal Supreme Court rejected the plaintiff's argument that the TV rights are originally owned by a non-trading partnership whose members include both the DFB and the participating clubs.

The match as an independent event

Central marketing of TV broadcasting rights to football matches is not justified by the 'joint venture idea' of German competition law.

The fact that a match is played within the framework of a competition and derives its economic value from the whole competition does not necessarily require that the rights to a single game be sold collectively in a package. Every game does have an independent economic value and, therefore, can still be the subject matter of individual marketing. Therefore, a distinction has to be made between the organisation of the whole competition and the marketing of an individual game. Until 1989 German clubs had marketed their rights individually, as is the case in other European states such as Italy and Sweden.

Maintaining a competitive balance

The DFB and the majority of clubs argued that central marketing and its 'watering can principle' by which all clubs financially participate in the profits from the sale is essential to maintain a competitive balance within the league and to preserve the existence of the smaller clubs. Although the Federal Supreme Court affirmed the necessity to maintain competitive balance within a professional sports league, it came to the conclusion that it merely is an indirect political aim that may not justify a restraint on competition ... The court determined that central licensing of the TV broadcasting rights to the

European games is not necessary to maintain the competitive balance among the Bundesliga clubs and to preserve the existence of smaller clubs.

Conclusion

The German Federal Supreme Court ruled that the collective marketing of the television rights for the home matches of the German clubs participating in the European competitions constitutes a cartel and thus violates German competition law. It concluded that competition among the clubs as original rights owners and actual, economic competitors for the marketing of the independent, single games is restrained without reasonable justification. In general, the Federal Supreme Court refused to apply economic law differently to sports enterprises.[65]

It has already been mentioned that the German Anti-Cartel law made a special exception for TV broadcasting of sport. This occurred subsequent to the aforementioned case. But in view of the attitude and application of EU law, the said exception is open to doubt as EU law takes precedence over domestic law where the latter clashes with EU law. Therefore, it is possible that even where collective selling of broadcasting TV rights does not offend the German competition rules, it may well fall fall of the EU provisions, that is, Art 81(1) and an exemption may be required in terms of Art 81(3) or an accommodation arrived at with the Commission as happened recently (see below).

Both the German and the Dutch courts appear to adopt a very orthodox approach in the application of competition law to sports broadcasting. In both cases the competition authorities argued Roberts' single entity theory outlined above. In both instances there was a resistance to accepting that theory. In retrospect it now appears short-sighted for that approach to be advocated by Roberts.[66] The problem attached to all these broadcasting agreements is the fact that governing sports associations and federations have used their regulatory powers in compelling overly restrictive and anachronistic agreements – in short, they have abused their dominant position as governing bodies and have sought to control and regulate all economic aspects connected to their particular sports. This can be observed in several instances such as the case of FIA detailed above. Caution must be exercised with regard to the BSkyB/Premier League case, since the decision was based on a (now) repealed statute.

However, it can be said with a degree of certainty that the Roberts approach of the single entity theory is now largely academic since the Commission has refused to endorse it. Collective sales of broadcasting rights are *prima facie* anti-competitive in EU law. These agreements must be restructured to meet Commission approval and in some cases must be granted an exemption.

One should guard, however, against using the specificity of sport as a carte blanche for restrictive practices. The Commission has clearly showed in its analysis of the FIA and other agreements that each case must be decided on its own merits. Whereas the Commission was happy to accept central marketing of broadcasting rights for FIA it indicated that this was the only practicable way of dealing with the issue for Formula 1 motor racing. It would, therefore, be wrong to conclude that the same arguments might hold for football, rugby, golf or tennis. In all these assessments into restrictive agreements with regard to broadcasting, the basic questions at the bottom of all competition cases is whether these restrictions are justified, has the process of conferring exclusivity been objective and

---

65   Lentze, G, 'Collective marketing of football television rights' (1998) 5(1) Sport Law Administration and Practice 9.

66   It should be pointed out that amongst some sports lawyers and academics the 'single entity' approach enjoys a lot of support. See *op cit*, fn 51, Olfers (2004).

transparent and what are the implications for competition – is there foreclosure of the market or not? In this regard the time frame of the agreements will be relevant. Whether the agreement is for a fairly lengthy period such as five years will depend on various factors that may be unique to a particular sport and the current state of broadcasting technology.

In 1998, the German Regional Court of Frankfurt pronounced on the collective selling of broadcasting rights with regard to the European Truck Racing Cup, which had been arranged by FIA. The result was different from the football case and deserves closer considerations.

Lentze, G, 'Governing bodies and the ownership of television rights'

The FIA case

In its decision of 18 March 1998, the Regional Court Frankfurt am Main found in favour of FIA concluding that the collective sale by FIA was not anti-competitive. The court decided that FIA might sell the rights collectively because of its position as 'co-owner' of the television rights.

Background

AE TV, a German television production and marketing company televised races of the European Truck Racing Cup and sold rights to various TV stations. Contracting with the organisers of each individual event of the series. AE TV was given the right to broadcast an event in consideration for disposal of a free copy of the broadcast to the event organisers.

In 1995 and 96 FIA amended Article 26 of its International Sporting Code (note that the Commission objected to aspects of FIA's International Sporting Code and required amendment of the same. It does not appear as if Article 26 has been altered, but in view of the fact that FIA is shortly no longer going to be involved in commercial aspects of its sport – it may well be that Article 26 will be administered by the FOA). Under the amended code, television rights to all international motor racing series, including the European Truck Racing Cup, were to be owned by FIA from the beginning of January 1997 and it was made a condition of holding such series that the television rights would be marketed centrally by FIA.

Subsequently FIA entered into an exclusive marketing contract for all its motor racing series with International Sportsworld Communications Ltd (ISC) (This company is within the control of Mr Ecclestone, who before his recent resignation, was a vice-president of FIA. The Commission objected to various aspects of FIA's commercial agreements – one of which was that the exclusivity was not sufficiently transparent. See the FIA notification above). As a consequence of these developments, AE TV lost its right for television coverage of truck racing events.

Injunction

AE TV issued proceedings in Germany on 4 June 1997, the Regional Court Frankfurt a M granted AE TV an interim injunction, based on a violation of Article 81 EC preventing FIA from marketing centrally the television rights to the European Truck Racing Cup.

On the return day the Court found for FIA.

Event organiser

The Court held that the local organisers of each individual event in the international motor racing series were event organisers and thus, original owners of the television rights to their events. The court stated that the finding of ownership on the part of local organisers does not give the final response as to ownership in television rights and that it was necessary to consider the concept of 'co-ownership' when deciding organisation of events and therefore ownership of television rights.

Joint venture

The court concluded that the television rights to the European Truck Racing Cup are owned both by FIA as the governing federation and the individual race organisers. The decision to entrust FIA with the marketing of the joint television rights fell within the affairs of the joint venture and was a mere internal allocation of tasks.

Conclusion

The central issue of the majority of cases that deal with the collective sale of television sports rights is whether the inherently anti-competitive collective sale is justified by an underlying public interest in the collective sale.

In this case however, neither public interest nor the impact of collective sale to the market was considered. The court held that the collective sale of television rights is not anti-competitive due to the co-ownership of FIA.[67]

Subsequent to this case the German government exempted the collective sale of television rights from competition law (see above).

This exemption is significant but it is not unconditional. It is clear that in order for the exemption to apply positive proof must be shown that there is a reasonable proportion of revenue 'trickling down' to the clubs. It is submitted that if insufficient proof of the solidarity elements is not shown, collective sales will not be exempt from the competition laws.

In the last case it was observed that the AE TV sued in a German court for contravention of Art 81 (EC). Article 81 of the Treaty is directly applicable and can be raised in all the courts of the Member States (see below). Most Member States now have competition regimes that are in line with the EU rules. It should also be observed that decisions of the Commission or the ECJ take precedence over those of courts in Member States in accordance with the principle of supremacy. This is an important point to remember since similar authorities and courts in Member States should follow EU competition policy.

From the cases dealt with it can be seen that collective sales are subject to the competition rules and policy. This is to be observed in various pronouncements emanating from the Commission.

The arguments raised above with regard to German football, have also been applied to radio broadcasts. This is a notification of a restrictive agreement involving collective selling of broadcasting rights.

Case IV/37.214 DFB, Central Marketing of TV and Radio Broadcasting Rights for Certain Football Competitions in Germany

Notification from the Deutsche Fussballbund (DFB) for a negative clearance or an exemption of the collective selling (or central marketing) of the television and radio broadcasting rights for the 'Bundesspiele' with participation of 'Lizensligamannschaften'.

The term 'Bundesspiele' refers mainly to the matches of the first national football league ('Bundesliga'), the second national league ('2 Bundesliga') and of the national cup competition ('DFB-Vereinspokal').

'Lizensligamannschaften' are professional football teams that participate in the Bundesliga or the 2 Bundesliga.

The DFB is the German national football association and a member of UEFA.

According to DFB statutes, it is the DFB, which has the right to conclude contracts about the broadcasting on TV and radio the matches in question. The DFB receives the revenues generated by these contracts and distributes them among the Lizensligamannschaften in a certain proportion (Bundesliga: 2 Bundesliga).

---

67 Lentze, G, 'Governing bodies and the ownership of television rights' (1998) 5(4) Sport Law Administration and Practice 9.

The three most important contracts that the DFB has concluded concern (1) the broadcasting rights for the matches of the Bundesliga and 2 Bundesliga on free TV in Germany and abroad; (2) the pay-TV rights for Germany of a limited number of matches per round in the Bundesliga and 2 Bundesliga for live broadcasting and (3) the rights for the matches of the cup competitions.

Arguments put forward by the DFB in favour of the central marketing system.

The DFB claims to be at least co-owner of the broadcasting rights with the clubs because it founded the competitions and delivers a wide range of organisational services. It argues that the collective selling system does not fall within the scope of Article 85(1) (now 81(1)) of the Treaty. The DFB contends that central marketing rationalises distribution of the broadcasting rights; it serves solidarity between financially stronger and weaker clubs by distributing the revenues equally. This is in the interest of preserving competitive professional football in Germany as well as supporting amateur and youth football. In the DFB's opinion collective selling is indispensable. Moreover, the DFB objects to the proposal of a solidarity fund because of the conflict of interests between the different clubs and also because of tax reasons.

The DFB disputes the existence of any effect on trade between Member States caused by its collective selling system because it is the sports rights agencies, which acquire the rights from DFB and later sell them to broadcasters in Germany and abroad.

In the view of the DFB, the consumers, ie primarily the broadcasters but also the viewers, are interested in the protection of a functioning championship competition and are allowed a fare share of the benefit resulting from the collective selling. Furthermore, collective selling does not eliminate competition.[68]

Previously it was noted that the Commission has objected to the arrangements made by UEFA to market the Champions League. Below is the unusual background note to explain their position. In view of this memorandum, has the DFB in the notification above provided sufficient justification for an exemption – or is the agreement objectionable? Below this outline of objections is the arrangement which was finally reached in 2003.

Australian Comparison

The single entity theory has also not found much favour in a recent Australian case.

In *News Limited v Australian Rugby League Limited*[69] (the *Super League* case), a full bench of the Federal Court of Australia overturned a lower court's ruling that there was a joint venture between clubs in the league and the league. The case arose out of an attempt of News Ltd to establish a new rugby league competition known as the Super League to rival the established national rugby competition held under the auspices of the New South Wales Rugby League Ltd or the Australian Rugby Football League Ltd (the ARL).[70]

During 1995 News Ltd entered into contracts with over 300 players and coaches to participate in the league competition. The signing took place after the ARL had concluded commitment and loyalty agreements with over 20 clubs. These agreements precluded these clubs from participating in any other competition not approved by the ARL for the next five years until the end of the 1999 season.

---

68   OJ C 6, 9 January 1999, pp 10–11.
69   (1996) ATPR 41–466.
70   See earlier, pp 311–13.

News Ltd attacked these agreements and argued *inter alia* that the exclusionary aspects of the agreement had the effect of lessening competition in various markets thus resulting in a breach of the Trade Practices Act 1974. News Ltd also claimed that the ARL had abused its significant market power by preventing the entry of the proposed Super League.

The ARL argued that News Ltd had *inter alia* induced players and coaches to breach their contracts and that rebel clubs breached their fiduciary duties arising from the 'joint venture' between the clubs and the leagues.

The trial judge found for the ARL and found that there was a 'joint venture' between the clubs and the ARL and that News Ltd had not proved the markets it pleaded existed. In his view the relevant market included other sports as well. Even if News Ltd could prove that there had been a breach of the Act, he would have to deny a remedy on discretionary grounds since News Ltd had induced breaches of contract. The matter went on appeal to a full bench of the Federal Court of Australia. The Full Court found that there was no joint venture between the clubs and the ARL and that some clubs were in competition with each other to retain their position in the national competition.

The commitment and loyal agreements the clubs had entered into with the ARL constituted arrangements or understandings between the parties – there had been concerted action to enforce the provisions of the ARL agreements. The purpose and the length of the ARL agreements (five years) had the result of preventing competition and were therefore contrary to the Act.[71]

Although this case does not expressly deal with issues of collective selling of broadcasting rights, it was News Ltd's intention to broadcast the new competition. The most important aspect of this case is that it appears that the 'single entity' theory has also not found much favour in Australia.

Recent Views on Collective Selling of Broadcasting Rights

Below is one of the most recent communications from the Competition Commission; another setting forth their objections to the manner in which UEFA intends to market television broadcasting for the Champions League. The memorandum also clearly shows the Commission's attitude to the manner in which UEFA is conducting the matter.

European Commission, 'The UEFA Champions League background note'

The Champions League is a tournament organised every year by Geneva-based UEFA between the top European football clubs – 72 clubs participate from both European Union and non-EU countries.

The Champions League is one of the most important sports events in Europe. It is also one of the most watched events on television, generating over 800 million Swiss francs in TV rights, approximately 80 percent of the Champions League's total revenues.

How does UEFA sell the television rights to the Champions League?

UEFA sells the TV rights to a single broadcaster per Member State on an exclusive basis for periods of three to four years (see table in annex). The rights are split into primary and secondary rights.

UEFA imposes minimum broadcasting obligations on the TV companies that win the rights. Champions League matches are currently played on Tuesdays and Wednesdays. In big football nations the broadcaster must televise a Tuesday match live on either free TV or pay-TV and a Wednesday match live on free TV.

---

71   See *Competition Issues Related to Sports*, OCDE/GD128, No 11, Competition Policy Roundtables, www.oecd.org.

The contract broadcaster must broadcast highlights on free TV both nights. In the smaller member associations the contract broadcaster must televise a Tuesday match live match on free TV on Tuesday if a club from that country is playing, and on Wednesday. Once the contract broadcaster has complied with its minimum broadcast obligations, it can exploit any additional rights by free TV or pay-TV.

Why is it the Commission's business how UEFA markets the TV rights to the Champions League?

The Commission initiated its investigation into the joint selling by UEFA of the TV rights because UEFA notified the arrangement to the Commission on 1 February 1999 seeking a legal guarantee that the agreement did not fall in the category of agreements that are prohibited by Article 81(1) of the EU treaty, or an exemption from EU competition rules.

Why is the Commission concerned about the current selling system?

Joint selling of free-TV and pay-TV rights combined with exclusivity has an important effect on the structure of the TV broadcasting markets since football is in most countries the driving force not only for the development of pay-TV services but it is also an essential programme item for free TV broadcasters. UEFA sells all the TV rights to the whole tournament in one exclusive package to one broadcaster per Member State. Because the winner gets it all, there is a fierce competition for the TV rights whose increasing value can only be afforded by large broadcasters. This may increase media concentration and hamper competition between broadcasters. If one broadcaster holds all relevant football TV rights in a Member State, it will become extremely difficult for competing broadcasters to establish themselves in that market. If different packages of rights were sold, several broadcasters would be able to compete for the rights, including smaller, regional or thematic channels.

Isn't this remedied by UEFA's sub-licensing policy?

No, UEFA's sub-licensing policy is rather exclusive and allows only one other broadcaster to show the UEFA Champions League matches that the main broadcaster itself is not showing. Thus a maximum of two broadcasters per Member State can televise the UEFA Champions League to the exclusion of all other broadcasters in that Member State, who cannot even show highlights of the matches.

Does this mean that the Commission wants to ban collective selling of football rights?

No, while joint selling arrangements clearly fall within the scope of Article 81(1), the Commission considers that in certain circumstances, joint selling may be an efficient way to organise the selling of TV rights for international sports events. However, the manner in which the TV rights are sold may not be so restrictive as to outweigh the benefits provided.

Have you received complaints from TV companies, individual clubs, sports fans or others on the current system? And if so what are their arguments?

The Commission has not received any formal complaints. However, it has received observations from a total of 65 national authorities, associations, football clubs, broadcasters and sport rights agencies in reply to a summary of the case published in the EU's Official Journal on 10 April 1999. Critical voices against central marketing are mainly to be found among broadcasters, sport right agencies and the national competition authorities. They contest that joint selling is necessary for the protection of the UEFA Champions League brand or for ensuring broadcasting on free TV. It is argued that central marketing leads to higher prices for consumers, less football on TV and that UEFA's solidarity measures are inefficient, insufficient and are conducted in a non-transparent way.

How are the champions league TV rights currently re-distributed between qualifying clubs?

Out of a total revenue of 800 million CHF, 75 per cent goes to the clubs and 25 percent remains with UEFA to cover organisational and administrative costs as well as for solidarity payments. This leaves approximately CHF 122 million for solidarity payments, CHF 105 million for operational costs and CHF 47.2 million for UEFA.

Is the Commission against a solidarity redistribution of funds among football clubs?

The Commission fully endorses the specificity of sport as expressed in the declaration of the European Council in Nice in December 2000, where the Council encourages a redistribution of part of the revenue from the sales of TV rights at the appropriate levels, as beneficial to the principle of solidarity between all levels and areas of sport. The statement of objections sent by the Commission does not put this principle into question.

Does the Commission believe that the current system leads to less football on TV and higher pay-TV subscription fees?

The Commission is convinced that furthering competition in the broadcasting market will lead to better quality TV coverage and lower subscription fees.

Could you explain how the current system slows down the use of new technologies (as mentioned in press release)?

In joint selling arrangements there is a reluctance to give licenses to apply new technologies such as the Internet and UMTS, because broadcasters fear that it will decrease the value of their TV rights.

What happens now that the Statement of Objections has been sent?

UEFA has 3 months to reply to the statement of objections and has the right to have an oral hearing to defend their case. If UEFA is to propose new ways of selling the TV rights, the Commission will naturally examine the proposals and discuss them with UEFA.[72]

The Commission has now approved the UEFA broadcasting arrangements and have granted it an exemption in terms of Art 81(3).[73] The Commission announced its clearance of the UEFA arrangements in a press release.[74] The essence of the arrangements is quoted here from the press release:

Commission clears UEFA's new policy regarding the sale of media rights to the Champions League IP/03/1105.

Uefa's new joint selling arrangement

As a result of the Commission's objections, UEFA proposed a new joint selling arrangement, which solves the Commission's concerns, and which is operational starting with the 2003/2004 football season. According to the new system:

- UEFA will continue to market centrally the rights to the live TV transmission of the Tuesday and Wednesday night matches. The main rights will be split into two separate rights packages (the gold and silver packages) giving the winning broadcasters the right to pick the two best matches.

- UEFA will initially have the exclusive right to sell the remaining live rights to the Champions League. However, if it does not manage to sell this so-called Bronze package within a certain cut-off date, the individual clubs will be able to market the matches themselves.

- The new joint selling system also affords opportunities to new media operators as both UEFA and the football clubs will be able to offer Champions League content to Internet and operators seeking to launch or boost the new generation of mobile phone services using the UMTS technology.

---

72 MEMO/01/271, Bruxelles, 20 July 2001.
73 Commission Decision of 23 July 2003, COMP/C2-37.398, OJ 8 November 2003, L291/25. This exemption deals with the subject in detail and may be found on the Web under the Competition Commission, Antitrust, Legislation.
74 Commission clears UEFA's new policy regarding the sale of media rights to the Champions League, IP/03/1105 of 24 July 2003.

- Individual football clubs will also, for the first time, have the right to exploit TV rights on a deferred basis and to use archive content, eg for the production of videos, therefore provide their fans with a better and more varied offer.
- UEFA will not sell the rights for a period longer than three years and will do so through a public tender procedure allowing all broadcasters to put in bids.

UEFA's new joint selling system represents an improvement on the preliminary compromise reached with the Commission. It particularly agreed that football clubs would not be prevented from selling live rights to free TV broadcasters where there is no reasonable offer from any pay-TV broadcaster.

There has been a particular problem with the FA Premier League and BSkyB to which the Commission objected. Although the TV broadcasting rights were subject to tender and were presented in 'packages' BSkyB won the major tenders. The cosy arrangements between the FAPL and BSkyB tends to create a restrictive environment for competition. In December 2002 the Commission issued a statement of objections saying that the arrangements amounted to price-fixing. These FAPL/BSkyB selling arrangements meant that less than 30% of Premier League matches were made available for live broadcast, and when this is coupled with exclusivity means that only big media groups can afford a bundle of rights. Harbord and Szymanski note that in the current UK climate there are simply too few buyers and that if these rights are sold to multiple buyers the FAPL will have to settle for a reduced income. They are critical of some of the reasoning of the commission, that is, splitting up exclusive rights into packages. Their argument is that the Commission is tackling the wrong kind of exclusivity:

Harbord, D and Szymanski, S, 'Football trials'

The problem is that the Commission is tackling the wrong exclusivity. In order to improve matters significantly, not only must the rights not be sold exclusively to a single broadcaster, but the same rights must be licensed non-exclusively to multiple broadcasters (eg to each pay-TV or platform). Abset this remedy, consumers are unlikely to benefit greatly from a reformed Premier league selling procedure.[75]

The Commission had the following objections to the FAPL/BSkyB arrangements and these are outlined briefly:

- Clubs are excluded from taking independent commercial actions with regard to the exploitation of rights since it is the FAPL who does all the negotiating concerning contracts pertaining to the exploitation of media rights.

- The arrangements restrict competition in the upstream markets for the acquisition of media rights of football. These markets are closely linked with downstream markets who ultimately provide the services to consumers – and this affects downstream markets, for example, those TV companies who do not have access to sports broadcasting are affected commercially by reduced advertising.

- The sale of large packages of media rights by the FAPL created barriers of entry to smaller competitors, restricted output, limited the development of products and markets which led to foreclosure in the downstream markets. The restrictions led to further media concentration and hampered competition between media operators.

The FAPL presented an outline of a new commercial policy, including rights segmentation for the exploitation of all media rights of the FAPL, including radio, television, internet and UMTS and physical media rights such as DVD, VHS, CD-ROM etc.

---

75 *Op cit*, fn 17, Harbord and Szymanski (2004).

Tender were invited for the 2003 to 2007 season for a number of media rights. At the end of the process BSkyB won all the rights, most notably four packages of live TV rights.

Once again the Commission expressed certain concerns, so the FAPL presented a revised rights proposal. The essence of this revised proposal is:

- The award of TV rights for the FAPL matches will be subject to a public bid by broadcasters. Contracts will not exceed three years.

- Some football matches will still be played on Saturday afternoon and will not be for broadcasting to retain the traditional character of the competition.

- The FAPL will present TV broadcasting in several packages; the number and rights in each package may vary over time. Near live packages of rights for those matches not broadcast live will be made available. There will be some free-to air available to terrestrial broadcasters.

- Near live matches include midnight Sunday for Saturday matches, and midnight the same day for all other matches. Both the FAPL and clubs can exploit deferred matches, but in the case of clubs the exploitation shall be 'club branded', and clubs can band together to share costs of production or distribution. Club rights can only be exercised on dedicated club channels.

- Clubs deciding not to exploit their rights via club channel can sell their home games to a broadcaster from midnight on the day after the match and these may be broadcast before the next FAPL feature. It is not the intention that the clubs should undermine the benefits of central selling: 'therefore, no more than two clubs may sell to the same broadcaster its home match out of any full fixture programme of 10 PL matches'.

- The FAPL will require separate bids for each package to be broadcast to the UK and Ireland.

The revised proposal means that more live rights under new contracts have been made available from the 2004 to the 2007 season: 138 matches will be broadcast live (previously 106). The near live TV rights were sold in one package of 242 matches. From 2007 onwards no single broadcaster will be able to buy all the rights of the centrally marketed live rights packages. Both the FAPL (in respect of all matches) and the clubs (in respect of the matches in which they participated) will have a right to provide video content on the internet as of midnight on the night of the match. Clubs will be able to provide mobile content as of midnight of the day following the match. The FAPL has increased radio broadcasting rights and has allowed two matches to be broadcast live nationally on Saturday afternoons.

The Commission has indicated that it awaits comments and is likely to take a decision now that reg No 1/2003 is in operation. It seems that no decision has yet been taken.[76]

In the case of the new marketing system for Bundesliga broadcasting rights in Germany, a settlement with the Commission has been proposed.

The draft settlement in a nutshell

- The DFL or an independent selling body will off packages in a transparent and non-discriminatory procedure. Applicants may resolve disputes through arbitration. No contract may cover more than three seasons.

- Two television packages contain live broadcasting rights. They can be acquired by both free TV and PPV providers. One package contains Saturday's first division matches and Sunday's first division games (the main match day package). The second package contains Sunday's first division games

---

76 Notice 2004/C115/02 OJ 30 April 2004. See IP/03/1748 Commission reaches provisional agreement with FA Premier League and BSkyB over football rights.

and Friday's second division matches (the secondary match package). Both packages will also contain other rights, including conference-call coverage of the other match day.

- The third package consists of free TV rights for the first highlights programme and the right to broadcast at least two Bundesliga first division games per season. The fourth package entitles the provider to broadcast second division matches live on free TV. Other packages cover secondary and tertiary exploitation rights for free TV. These packages may be shared out among free TV broadcasters.

- Centrally marketed Internet and mobile phone packages: various packages offering live and deferred broadcasting.

- Clubs' television rights: every club can sell its home games 24 hours after the match on free TV once.

- Clubs' mobile phone, Internet and audio rights: every club can may offer the latest clips through mobile phones and put extensive match highlights on its website. Furthermore, every club can market live excerpts of its matches on the radio and mobile phones and offer live audiostreaming on the Internet.

- Rights that the League is unable to market may be offered at the same time by the home club.

- Further league packages and club rights round off the draft settlement.[77]

The Commission still needs to take a decision on these proposals but it would seem that the Commission would be favourably disposed towards this draft settlement. It appears to allow much more competition than the FAPL proposals.

CONCLUSION

One of the major events on the Competition Commission's calendar is the modernisation of the implementation of competition policy in the EC with the entering into force of reg 1/2003 on the 1 May 2004. This regulation has already been mentioned and replaces reg 17/62. The new Regulation makes Art 81(3) directly applicable in Member States, which means that exemptions can now be enforced in Member States. Domestic competition authorities have also acquired powers through the network of competition authorities.[78] The advent of the new Regulation brings about shared competencies between competition authorities in Member States and the Commission. Since Art 81(3) is now directly applicable the Commission has set out detailed guidelines for the courts and competition authorities as to how Art 81(3) ought to be applied. This is necessary since there is a real danger that divergent competition policy will be followed in several Member States. The notification procedure has been abandoned leaving more time for the Commission to deal with key areas of anti-trust policy.[79] It is still too early to say what impact the Regulation will have on competition policy in the EC or on sports law. An assessment will be made in the nExt edition of this book.

The application of Competition policy to sport is today happening far more frequently than has been the case in the past. The *Bosman* ruling, while not pronouncing on the application of the

---

77   This extract is taken directly from the press release: New marketing system for the Bundesliga broadcasting rights IP/03/1106 dated 24 July 2003.
78   OJ L101 of 27 April 2004, pp 43–53.
79   Gauer *et al*, supra, provide a useful analysis of the new regulation.

competition rules to sport, nevertheless served as a catalyst for the application of EC competition policy to the area of sport. Such application has been criticised on the basis that it is inappropriate. Yet the competition rules provide for the recognition of the special features of sport. This happens either by applying the rule of reason to the application of Art 81(1) or in considering the purpose of the restrictive agreements in terms of Art 81(3). The Commission's activity has been particularly pronounced in the area of the marketing of broadcasting rights where it has played a much more active and activist role. Its concerns have been primarily to increase output of broadcasts, provide access to new competitors and potentially new competitors as well as the new media. In the case of the latter the Commission has tried to create a space for these competitors to enter. Most of the Commission's activism was motivated at cutting down exclusivity, or considerably modifying the nature of the exclusivity. Whether the activity of the Commission will seriously affect the revenues flowing from broadcasting rights is not yet certain. The argument has been made that in the UK there are just too few competitors to enter the big competition of transmitting live football games. An assessment of the success or otherwise of the Commission's activities will have to wait. Consumers ought to be happy at increased output. It does seem that the concept of exclusivity in broadcasting rights will continue, but considerably mediated by the Commission.

However, in the case of all restrictions the Commission requires a sense of proportionality from sports organisations – that is, that the restrictions must be justified and must go no further than is actually required. One may almost argue that the Commission requires a sense of reasonableness on the part of sports organisations. The competition rules require that sports bodies have transparent processes in their decision making in so far as their decisions may have an economic dimension. They are also expected, now, to account for their conduct, that is, they must justify restrictive agreements and it has become increasingly difficult to do so.

It should be apparent from what has been said above that each case involving the competition authorities will be considered on its own merits. In some cases collective selling/marketing may be essential to the sport – such as the case of FIA detailed above – in others collective selling may be problematic. The Commission has indicated that it is not against exclusivity or collective selling *per se*, but rather against some of the restrictive arrangements that are made.

Finally, it is fair to say that the demarcation between aspects of governance, that is, rules required for the discipline of the sport and those having commercial impact, have become a lot clearer in the minds of both sporting organisations and the Commission. There is less criticism of the Commission for not understanding the special nature of sport. The Commission has shown an insight and sensitivity with regard to the latter. This is progress indeed.

EC competition policy is likely to have a profound effect on the governance of sports with a global appeal. The principles of competition policy that have been outlined above and have considerable influence on sport which is at present is less of a global phenomenon. Competition policy may be seen as bringing the norms of the sports world in line with those in the rest of the commercial world.

KEY SOURCES

Caiger, A and Gardiner, S (eds), *Professional Sport in the EU: Regulation and Re-regulation* (2000), The Hague: Asser.

Eklund, E, 'Following the rules of the game? A competition law study of the collective sale of sports broadcasting rights', *EUI Working Papers*, Law No 99/1, European University Institute (1999).

For access to speeches and paper on EU competition policy see http://europa.eu.int/comm/sport/index.html and www.governance-in-sport.com.

Halgreen, L, *European Sports Law: a Comparative Analysis of the European and American Models of Sport* (2004), Gadjura: Thomson.

Furse, M, *Competition Law of the UK & EC* (2004), Oxford: OUP.

CHAPTER 10

INTELLECTUAL PROPERTY RIGHTS AND SPORT

INTRODUCTION

This chapter is intended to provide the reader with a general introduction to the legal nature of intellectual property rights, and their commercial application and use in the promotion and marketing of sports events (increasingly more international in nature), sportspersons and teams, as well as the ways in which they can be legally created, protected and exploited. Where appropriate, a practical and comparative approach is taken on this subject.

Sport as a Global 'Industry'

Sport is now a global industry accounting for more than 3% of world trade and around 2% of the GNP of the 25 Member States of the European Union (EU).[1] In the EU, the sports industry has created – directly and indirectly – more than two million jobs. In the UK, sport provides employment for some 420,000 people, and is worth £12 billion a year in consumer spending. With the advent of the internet and the mega sums being paid for broadcasting rights of prestigious sports events – for example, in the summer of 2000, the English Premier League sold its broadcasting rights for the next three seasons for a staggering sum of £1.3 billion – the sports industry has continued to grow despite the downturn in the world economy following the atrocities of 9/11 in New York and Washington.

Not only are broadcasters scrambling for sports rights, but so also are sponsors, who are prepared to pay in the region of US$50 million for an exclusive worldwide association with the Olympic Games, to promote their products and services. In 2003, the worldwide market for sponsorship, of which sports sponsorship forms a significant and increasing proportion, grew by some 7.5% over 2002 to reach an all time high of around $26 billion, whilst the Europe sponsorship market increased to around US$8.3 billion.[2] A three-year exclusive sponsorship of the English Premier League now costs £48 million. According to some commentators, the worldwide market for sponsorship is expected to show similar rates of growth during the next few years! With such huge sums to play for, it is crucial not only to understand sports sponsorship from a commercial and financial point of view, but also important to appreciate its legal niceties.[3]

Likewise, licensing and merchandising rights in relation to sports events are also 'hot properties', commanding high returns for the rights owners ('licensors') and concessionaires ('licensees') alike.[4] Sport is not only a business; it is also a product and a very valuable marketing, communications, public relations and corporate hospitality tool.

---

1   On 1 May, 2004, 10 new Member States joined the EU to enlarge it to 25 Member States with a combined population of some 450 million.
2   Sports Marketing Industry figures; and see Kolah, A, 'Maximising the value of sponsorship', SportBusiness Report, August 2003.
3   *Ibid.*
4   See Blackshaw, I, 'Sports licensing and merchandising – the legal and practical aspects' (2002) 2 The International Sports Law Journal, 22–25.

What is Intellectual Property?

Bill Cornish has defined intellectual property (IP) as 'the application of ideas and information that are of commercial value'.[5] IP is a product of the mind – the intellect – and has economic value in that, like any other kind of property, it may be bought, sold, licensed, assigned or otherwise exploited. The body of law that recognises and protects this species of property is known as IP law and the rights that IP gives rise to are known as IP rights (IPRs).

IPRs essentially comprise trade mark rights, copyright, patent rights and design rights. In the sports context, perhaps the most important IPRs are trade marks and copyright, although the other IPRs enjoy some significance too.

In What Ways can IP be Legally Protected?

IP can be legally protected by the general law, that is, in England, the system of the 'Common Law' (eg the law of 'passing off'), and by special laws or 'statutes' (eg the UK Trade Marks Act of 1994). At the EU level, the exploitation of IPRs are also subject to the EU rules on fair competition enshrined in Arts 81 and 82 of the Treaty of Rome.

IPRs and Sport

IPRs are important in business generally and in the sports business in particular. They have a value and importance in their own right and also as a marketing tool. The branding of sport, sports events, sports clubs and teams, through the application and commercialisation of distinctive marks and logos, is a marketing phenomenon which, in the last 20 years or so, has led to a new lucrative global business of 'sports marketing'.

For example, Manchester United Football Club and Team have been developed and marketed as a brand around the world. This brand is worth millions of dollars and a significant contributor to the value of the Club, in terms of earnings, shareholder dividends and capital appreciation. Manchester United is also a publicly quoted company on the London Stock Exchange becoming the first football club in the world to achieve a market capitalisation in 2000 of £1 billion.[6] As such it is a 'hot property'. Likewise, the value of the 'Olympic Rings' as a sports event mark is incalculable.

Before looking at the importance of branding in sport and sports events, let us address the issue of whether there are any IPRs inherent in sports events. Under English law, there are no legally recognised 'property' rights in a sports event, according to Latham CJ in the case of *Victoria Park Racing and Recreation Grounds Co Ltd v Taylor and Others*:

> **Victoria Park Racing and Recreation Grounds Co Ltd v Taylor and Others [1937] 58 CLR 479**
>
> **Latham CJ:** It has been argued that by the expenditure of money the plaintiff has created a spectacle and that it therefore has what is described as a quasi-property in the spectacle which the law will protect. What it really means is that there is some principle (apart from contract or confidential relationship)

---

5   Cornish, WR, *Intellectual Property: Patents, Copyrights, Trademarks and Allied Rights* (2003), 4th edn, London: Sweet & Maxwell.
6   See Blackshaw, I, 'BSkyB and sport on the net' *The Times*, 25 April 2000.

which prevents people in some circumstances from opening their eyes and seeing something and describing what they see. The court has not been referred to any authority in English law which supports the general contention that if a person chooses to reorganise an entertainment or to do anything else which other persons are able to see he has a right to obtain from a court an order that they shall not describe to anybody what they see ... the mere fact that damage results to a plaintiff from such a description cannot be relied upon as a cause of action ... I find difficulty in attaching any precise meaning to the phrase 'property in a spectacle' ... A 'spectacle' cannot be 'owned' in any ordinary sense of that word.[7]

The position in the States is different as Judge Schoonmaker pointed out in the same year:

Pittsburgh Athletic Co et al v KQV Broadcasting Co (1937) 24 FSupp 490

The defendant operates a Pittsburgh radio broadcasting station known as KQV, from which it has in the past broadcast by radio play-by-play descriptions of the games played by the 'Pirates' at Pittsburgh, and asserts its intention to continue in so doing. The defendant secures information on which it broadcasts from its own paid observers whom it stations at vantage points outside Forbes Field on premises leased by the defendant ... This, in our judgement, amounts to unfair competition, and is a violation of the property rights of the plaintiffs ... For it is our opinion that the Pittsburgh Athletic Company, by reasons of its creation of the game, its control of the park, and its restriction of the dissemination of news therefrom, has a property right in such news, and the right to control the use therefrom, has a property right in such news, and the right to control the use thereof for a reasonable time following the games.[8]

In line with the English law approach, on 19 June 2000 the BBC lost its case against Talksport, who were broadcasting 'live' commentary of an 'Euro 2000' Football Championship on their radio station using the 'live' pictures from BBC television to enable them to do so. Such 'off tube' radio broadcasts do not infringe any property rights in the live television broadcast; the court refused to grant the BBC an injunction to stop such broadcasts by Talksport.

British Broadcasting Corporation v Talksport Limited [2000] TLR

Blackburne J: I have little doubt that in the minds of ordinary radio listeners, in which I would include myself, a live commentary of the sporting event means one by a person present at the event he is describing and able with his own eyes to see what he is commenting upon.[9]

He added (in the following paragraph):

Equally, I have little doubt, having listened to excerpts from a recording of Talksport's coverage last Monday evening's England v Portugal match, and to an uninterrupted recording of the first 12 or so minutes of that broadcast, that the average listener would think that he was listening to a live broadcast ie 'live' in the sense that I have described.[10]

It should be added that, even in the States, there is no unlawful misappropriation of an event organiser's property rights by transmitting 'real-time' game scores and statistics taken from television and radio broadcasts of games in progress, where some intellectual effort and skill have been expended in the compilation and dissemination of such sports statistics and information.[11]

---

7   [1937] 58 CLR 479.
8   [1937] 24 FSupp 490.
9   *British Broadcasting Corporation v Talksport Limited*, Official transcript no HC 00002692; [2000] TLR.
10 *Ibid.*
11 *The National Basketball Association and NBA Properties, Inc v Motorola, Inc and STATS Inc* [1997] 105 F3d 841.

The Importance of Branding

Peter York has likened the importance of branding in our consumer society to a new religion:

York, P, 'Branded'

> [T]he fastest-growing, most profitable, cleverest global corporations are organised around a new philosophy, a new religion and a new way of working. For these companies their brand is their central asset – physical products are secondary – and most of their quality time is spent making and reworking the brand – its meaning, attitude and social role, its values – because it's the brand that people buy, not the products. Products, so the thinking goes, are generic, copyable, discountable, vulnerable, but brands are unique magic.[12]

This philosophy has been successfully transferred and applied by clever marketers to sport and sports events as products competing for consumer attention and spending. Again, according to York:

> Nike isn't a maker of high-priced trainers but a world voice for sport as an agency of personal growth and achievement ... The Nike swoosh logo means precisely what the crucifix meant to an earlier generation in ghettos – it promises redemption, vindication and a way out.[13]

In a nutshell, a 'brand' is a badge of identification and, as such, a powerful and valuable marketing tool. A brand is also a valuable asset and as has been remarked, businesses are no longer being valued on their manufacturing ability but on the new and frequently used basis of 'intellectual capital'.

TRADE MARKS

A trade mark is defined as:

UK Trade Marks Act 1994 (TMA), s 1(1):

> ... any sign capable of being represented graphically which is capable of distinguishing goods or services of one undertaking from those of other undertakings. A trade mark may, in particular, consist of words (including personal names), designs, letters, numerals or the shape of goods or their packaging.

This definition is not exhaustive and so trade marks may also be granted in respect of distinctive colours and/or colour combinations, sounds and smells. For example, the Australian Football League has registered the sound of a football siren for football and associated services.[14] As regards the shape of goods, included in the above definition, it is reported that the Sports Café, based in Canada, has registered a door-handle shaped like a baseball bat as a trade mark for restaurant services.[15]

Registered and Unregistered Marks

Trade marks satisfying the requirements for registration (see below) may be registered in a public registry and, as such, gain full legal protection against similar or competing marks. Even if marks do not qualify for registration – often referred to as *'common law'* marks – if consistently and regularly used over a period of time to identify the goods and services of a particular individual or company

---

12 'Branded' *The Times*, 10 February 2001.
13 *Ibid.*
14 See 'Trademark protection issues – why register?' (1999) (1) Sports and Character Licensing 26.
15 *Ibid.*

will enjoy some legal protection under general principles of 'unfair competition' ('passing off' under English law).

After a certain period of time and commercial use, these unregistered marks may also acquire what is known as a 'secondary meaning' and qualify for registration and full protection. Where the mark is registered, it is advisable to follow the mark with the abbreviation 'R' in a circle, and/or use the legend: ' "X" is a registered trade mark of the ABC Company Limited' to give notice of your trade mark rights and discourage infringers. Likewise, where the mark is not registered, it is advisable to follow the mark with the abbreviation 'TM' to show that the mark is being used as a trade mark – to identify the source/origin of the goods and services concerned.

Even though the mark may be distinctive, it may be refused registration at the Trade Marks Registry on a number of grounds. For example, if the mark is:

- misleading (s 3(3)(b));

- descriptive (s 3(1)(c));

- geographical (s 3(1)(c));

- immoral (s 3(3)(a));

- against 'public policy' (s 3(3)(a)); and

- is a specially protected emblem (eg royal insignia) (s 3(5)&(4)).

Also, a mark may be prohibited under a specific UK or EU Law (s 3(4)) or if applied for in 'bad faith' (eg to block the application of another) (s 3(6)).

The registration procedure is laid down in ss 37–39 of the TMA. Once registered, the mark enjoys legal protection and the registration is renewable *ad infinitum* on paying the registration fee each time the period for renewal comes up. In the UK, the original registration and renewal periods are 10 years. If, however, the mark is not used, its registration can be challenged by someone else who wishes to use that mark or a similar one. Again, if infringers of the mark are not legally challenged, the mark may become '*generic*' (ie lose its distinctiveness as a badge of origin) and so be usable by anyone. This happened with 'hoover' and 'aspirin', which became general names for vacuum cleaners and analgesics. Likewise, the 'cola' part of the trade mark 'Coca-Cola' denotes a general kind of carbonated beverage. The mark may also be lost if the trade mark owner fails to exercise quality control over its representation and use on goods, packaging and advertising materials.

Territoriality

Trade marks, in general, are territorial in nature in the sense that they are granted for a specific geographical territory, for example, for the UK. If not registered outside that territory, generally speaking, they cannot be legally protected from infringers in that other territory. Also, trade marks are registered in respect of designated goods and services. Thus, generally speaking, if a mark is registered for shoes only, it cannot be legally protected on leather goods. In both cases, there are special rules for so-called 'famous marks', but these are beyond the scope of this section. Suffice to say that, under s 10(3) of the TMA, a person infringes a registered trade mark if

... he uses in the course of trade a sign which –

- is identical with or similar to the trade mark, and

- is used in relation to goods or services which are not similar to those for which the trade mark is registered,

- where the trade mark has a registration in the United Kingdom and the use of the sign, being without due cause, takes unfair advantage of, or is detrimental to, the distinctive character or the *repute* of the mark [emphasis added].

For example, the well-known trade mark 'Coca-Cola' benefits from and is protected under these provisions. The doctrine of 'famous marks' applies in many other countries too.[16]

There are 42 classes in which it is possible to register a trade mark – 34 for goods and 8 for services.[17] So, for example, if you wish to register the mark for sports clothing and shoes, the class concerned is Class 25, which covers:

Articles of sports clothing; foot wear; leisure wear; underwear for men, women and children; slippers; socks; ties, headgear; gloves; scarves; sweatshirts; T-shirts; sweaters; articles of clothing for babies; bibs; dungarees; pyjamas; tracksuits.

Likewise, if you wish to register the mark for corporate hospitality services at a sports event, the class concerned is Class 42, which covers:

Providing of food and drink; temporary accommodation; services that cannot be placed in other classes.

As will be seen, Class 42 is also the class for so-called *'miscellaneous services'* that do not fall within any of the other classes – a 'catch all' category.

International and Regional Marks

It is possible to register an international trade mark, which will have validity and, therefore, protection in several countries. This is done under the auspices of the World Intellectual Property Organisation (WIPO) in Geneva under the Protocol to the Madrid Agreement of 28 June 1989.[18] The procedure, which is beyond the scope of this book, seems to be efficient, but it does take some time for the international mark to be granted. Registration depends upon having a valid registration in one of the countries that has ratified the International Trade Mark Convention.[19]

It is also possible to register trade marks which have legal force in regions, such as the Benelux (Belgium, the Netherlands and Luxembourg) under the Uniform Benelux Law on Marks of 1971 and the EU (which on 1 May 2004 was enlarged from 15 to 25 Member States) under the Community Trade Mark Act of 1993.[20]

Registration of the mark in one of the Benelux countries gives protection in the others as well, without the need to register in those other countries. Registration is relatively quick – the procedure usually takes less than six months – and favourable tax treatment under the Netherlands 'participation exemption' leads many foreign companies to hold their worldwide trade marks through a Dutch-based 'holding company'. The same principle of multiple protection applies in the

---

16 See Art 6b of the Paris Convention for the Protection of Industrial Property, 20 March 1883, as amended. See also *Adidas-Salomon AG v Fitnessworld Training Ltd* (C408/01) *The Times*, 31 October 2003 (ECJ (6th Chamber)).
17 Nice Classification of Goods and Services, 1962.
18 WIPO Publication No 204 (E).
19 For further information, see Davidson, S, 'International trademark protection programmes – strategies and pitfalls' (1999/2000) 2 Sports and Character Licensing 30–32.
20 Council Regulation (EC) No 40/94, 20 December 1993.

case of the so-called 'Community Trade Mark'. The EU Trade Mark Office is based in Alicante, Spain ('OHIM'). The procedure to obtain an EU Trade Mark is bureaucratic, slow and not inexpensive.

To effect a comprehensive trade mark programme of registration and protection can be quite costly and time consuming, although individual applications, unless there is opposition from the Trade Mark Office, where there is prior examination, or third parties, are not in themselves expensive. The costs do mount up according to the number of countries and the number of classes in which the mark is registered and maintained. Renewal fees are also payable.

Sporting Trade Marks

Sporting Slogans and Mottoes

Provided the basic requirement of distinctiveness is satisfied, it is possible, in principle, to register sporting slogans and mottoes as trade marks. For example, Eric Cantona, the footballer, successfully registered the slogan 'Ooh aah Cantona' as a trade mark. According to the circumstances, it may be necessary to use a distinctive script in which to express the slogans and mottoes and also combine them with a distinctive logo to ensure registrability.

Event Names and Logos

Again, depending upon establishing distinctiveness, it is possible to register the names and associated logos of sports events as trade marks. However, the name 'Euro 2000' failed the requirement of distinctiveness, but, *prima facie*, would be registrable as a trade mark if made part of a distinctive logo.[21] Likewise, an attempt in 1998 to register the name 'World Cup' as a trade mark also failed through lack of distinctiveness.[22] Even so, unregistered marks do acquire value and some legal protection (eg under 'passing off' and other forms of 'unfair competition') through consistent use over a period of time. As far as a team name or logo, it is easier to obtain registration where the team name and logo are combined in the same mark. The 'mascot' of a sports club or a sports event would qualify, in principle, for registration as a trade mark. Again, distinctiveness is the basic requirement.

Sports Personality Names and 'Nicknames'

In principle, it is possible to register a 'personal name' as a trade mark. For example, Eric Cantona has registered the name 'Cantona 7' (the 'seven' referring to his playing position). It seems to be easier, however, to register a 'nickname' as a trade mark. Thus, Paul Gascoigne has registered 'Gazza'; David Seaman has registered 'Safe Hands'; and Australian Olympic swimmer, Ian Thorpe, has won the right, after a four-year battle against the Australian company, Torpedoes Sportswear, to register his 'nickname' 'Thorpedo' as a trade mark.[23] Similarly, Damon Hill, the ex-Formula One driver, has registered the image of his eyes looking out from the visor of his racing helmet as a trade mark. Also, a famous name is less likely to be registrable in respect of souvenirs and memorabilia because such goods will be 'about' rather than 'from' the personality concerned. In other words, the name will not be considered as an indicator of 'trade origin'. Essentially, a trade mark is a badge of origin.

---

21   On registration generally, see 'Trademark protection issues – why register?' (1999) 1 Sports and Character Licensing 26.

22   *Ibid.*

23   See *Torpedoes Sportswear Pty Ltd v Thorpedo Enterprises Pty Ltd* [2003] FCA 901 (Australia) (27 August 2003).

Generally speaking, it is advisable to apply for trade mark registration early on in the career of a sports personality and also to put in place official merchandising programmes before unauthorised traders capitalise on that personality's celebrity status.

Sports Personality Autographs

In principle, it should be possible to register the distinctive autograph of a famous sportsperson as a trade mark. This can be used on, for example, golf clubs, as an endorsement of them (eg clubs bearing the signature of Nick Faldo). Such signatures would also qualify for copyright protection as 'artistic works' (see below).[24]

Sporting 'Techniques'

The England rugby football team fly half, Jonny Wilkinson, who scored the winning drop kick goal in the 2003 Rugby World Cup Final in Australia, has reportedly registered as a trade mark his distinctive so-called 'cradle' action when kicking for goal. This is very much in line with the wide statutory definition of a trade mark mentioned at the beginning of this section.

Sports Club Names

Tottenham Hotspur Football Club applied to the UK Trade Marks Office to register the name 'Tottenham' as a trade mark for merchandising purposes. This application was opposed by a couple of match day traders, who sell football memorabilia outside Premier League grounds in London. Since 1969, they have sold merchandise branded 'Tottenham' on stalls near the Club's ground. Their objections were dismissed. Although Tottenham was a geographical area, the name Tottenham had, over the years, come to mean the Football Club rather than the location.[25] This decision could lead to other clubs successfully registering their geographical names as trade marks contrary to s 3(1)(c) of the TMA (see above), which disallows geographical names generally.

In the US case of *Pro-Football, Inc v Harjo*,[26] a group of Native Americans sought to cancel trade mark registrations owned by the Washington Redskins football team, claiming that the Redskins' trade marks disparaged their people or brought them into contempt or disrepute contrary to s 2(a) of the Lanham Act. The court rejected these claims and added that the Redskins had made substantial financial investment in their marks over 25 years.[27]

The Olympic Rings

The five interconnected rings in blue, yellow, black, green and red symbolising the Olympic Movement enjoy special trade mark protection at the international and national levels in many countries around the world. At the international level, the Olympic Rings are protected by the

---

24 See later p 410.
25 See Trade Mark Opposition Decision by Tottenham Hotspur to register 'Tottenham' 0/150/02 on Application 2130740.
26 2003 US Dist Lexis 17180 (2003).
27 Also see litigation on use of WWF 'brand' between *World Wide Fund for Nature (formerly World Wildlife Fund) v World Wrestling Federation* (2002) on use of WWF 'brand'.

Nairobi Agreement.[28] At the national level in the UK, they are protected by the Olympic Symbol (Protection) Act 1995. Under this Act, they can only be used with the prior consent of the British Olympic Association (BOA). Otherwise, infringers will face civil and criminal consequences. The BOA is also custodian of the Olympic Motto (*'Citius Altius Fortius'* – 'Faster Higher Stronger') and certain other words and expressions, such as *'Olympic(s)'*, *'Olympiad(s)'* and *'Olympian'*.

Olympic Symbol etc (Protection) Act 1995

Section 2

(1) The Olympics association right shall confer exclusive rights in relation to the use of the Olympic symbol, the Olympic motto and the protected words.

(2) Subject to ss 4 and 5 below, the rights conferred by subsection (1) above shall be infringed by any act done in the United Kingdom which:

   (a) constitutes infringement under section 3 below; and

   (b) is done without the consent of the person for the time being appointed under s 1(2) above (in this Act referred to as 'the proprietor').

(3) The proprietor may exploit the rights conferred by subsection (1) above for gain, but may not make any disposition of or of any interest in or over them.

(4) This section shall not have effect to permit the doing of anything which would otherwise be liable to be prevented by virtue of a right:

   (a) subsisting immediately before the day on which this Act comes into force;

   (b) created by:

      (i) the registration of a design under the Registered Designs Act 1949 on or after the day on which this Act comes into force; or

      (ii) the registration of a trade mark under the Trade Marks Act 1994 on or after that day.

(5) Consent given for purposes of subsection (2)(b) above by a person appointed under section 1(2) above shall, subject to its terms, be binding on any person subsequently appointed under that provision: and references in this Act to doing anything with or without the consent of the proprietor shall be construed accordingly.

Section 3

(1) A person infringes the Olympic association right if in the course of trade he uses:

   (a) a representation of the Olympic symbol, the Olympic motto or a protected word; or

   (b) a representation of something so similar to the Olympic symbol or the Olympic motto as to be likely to create in the public mind an association with it (in this Act referred to as 'a controlled representation').

(2) For the purposes of this section, a person uses a controlled representation if, in particular, he:

   (a) affixes it to goods or the packaging thereof;

   (b) incorporates it in a flag or banner;

   (c) offers or exposes for sale, puts on the market or stocks for those purposes goods which bear it or whose packaging bears it;

   (d) imports or exports goods which bear it or whose packaging bears it;

   (e) offers or supplies services under a sign which consists of or contains it; or

   (f) uses it on business papers or in advertising.

It is a precondition for hosting the Olympic Games for there to be special legislation protecting the Olympic Rings, the Motto and other Olympic Marks in the host country.

---

28   Agreement on the Protection of the Olympic Symbol, 1981.

Other Trade Mark Issues

Comparative Advertising

'Comparative advertising' or 'knocking copy', as it is known in the advertising industry, is permitted by s 10(6) of the TMA where there is a reference to a registered trade mark, provided that it is in accordance with honest practices in the trade or industry concerned and does not take unfair advantage of or cause damage to the distinctive character or reputation of the mark.

Apart from trade mark infringement, 'comparative advertising' may give rise, according to the facts and circumstances of the case, to actions for passing off, copyright infringement or complaints to the UK Advertising Standards Authority for breach of the British Code of Advertising and Sales Promotion.

Assignment and Licences

Any assignment, that is transfer, of the trade mark must be made in writing and signed by or on behalf of the assignor.[29] The assignment must be noted on the Trade Marks Register, otherwise it will not be binding upon a third party who is not aware of the assignment. Likewise any entire or partial licence to use the trade mark granted to another party must be made in writing and signed by or on behalf of the party granting the licence.[30] Again, the licence must be noted on the Trade Marks Register, failure to do so producing the same effects as noted in the previous section.

Furthermore in the UK and certain other 'Common Law' jurisdictions, it is necessary, when licensing another party to use a registered trade mark, to enter into a separate 'Registered User Agreement' and register this at the Trade Marks Office. Failure to do so could result in the trade mark being challenged and cancelled on the grounds of failure to use by the trade mark owner.

Remedies for Infringement

A registered trade mark owner enjoys the same legal remedies for the infringement of any other property right, namely:

- damages;
- injunctions;
- accounts.[31]

Special remedies include:

- an order for erasure of the mark or destruction of the infringing goods, materials or articles[32] or
- an order for the delivery up of infringing goods, materials or articles, subject to a six year limitation period.[33]

---

29   TMA 1994, s 24(3).
30   *Ibid*, s 24(2).
31   Ibid, s 14.
32   *Ibid*, s 15(1).
33   *Ibid*, s 16(1).

It should be noted that the granting of injunctions and the ordering of accounts are, under English law, *'equitable'* remedies and, as such, are always granted at the discretion of the court in accordance with the individual circumstances and merits of each particular case. It should also be noted that, a trade mark owner, or his representative, who makes unjustified threats of infringement, may be subject to the following legal actions:

- a declaration that the threats are unjustifiable;

- injunctive relief; and/or

- a claim for damages.[34]

These statutory remedies may be supplemented by the common law remedy of 'passing off' (see below).

COPYRIGHT

Copyright means literally the right to copy something, in which 'copyright' exists. According to s 1(1) of the UK Copyright Designs and Patents Act 1988 (CDPA), copyright subsists in:

(a) original literary, dramatic, musical or artistic works;

AList2:(c) the typographical arrangement of published editions.

Unlike trade marks, there is no registration requirement for copyright to subsist in a work. In the US, however, it is necessary to register copyright at the Library of Congress in order to secure full legal protection. Ownership of copyright is distinct from ownership of the material in which it subsists.

Originality

For copyright to subsist in literary, dramatic, musical and artistic works, they must be 'original'. In *Ladbroke (Football) Ltd v William Hill (Football) Ltd*,[35] the court held that the word 'original' requires only that 'the work should not be copied but should originate from the author'.

In other words, to claim copyright protection, an author needs to show that he has used his own skill and judgment to produce the work).[36] So, an author may use the same source of information as someone else to create his own work, but must not copy someone else's work. He must act and be able to demonstrate that he acted independently to avoid a copyright infringement claim being successful. In practice, however, the courts are less likely to accept a defence of independent creation the more complex the copyright work and the greater the similarity between that work and the alleged infringing work. There is no copyright in an idea, but only in the particular expression of that idea.

Protected Works

Section 3(1) of the CDPA defines 'literary work' as any work, other than a dramatic or musical work, which is written, spoken or sung, and includes a table or compilation and a computer program.

---

34   *Ibid*, s 21.
35   [1964] 1 WLR 273.
36   *Interlego AG v Tyco Industries Inc* [1988] RPC 343.

A literary work need not have any particular literary merit. Thus, case law has established that other forms of information, such as football pools coupons, football fixture lists and television programme listings, can be the subject of copyright protection. However, sports results that are in the public domain are not subject to copyright protection. But in *Walter v Steinkopff*,[37] a news service that copied *verbatim* the material from another news service infringed that other's copyright. Where the same information is used, but not the wording, there is no infringement of copyright.

The names of sports events will not usually qualify for protection as literary works. If combined with a distinctive logo, they may qualify as 'artistic works'.[38] Section 3(1) of the CPDA defines a 'dramatic work' as including a work of dance or mime. Thus, it may be possible to claim copyright protection in a choreographed sequence in a sport such as dance gymnastics and ice dancing. However, despite the amount of work coaches and players put into set piece moves in sport, however 'dramatic' the effect may be, the lack of any certainty in the outcome of that move may preclude any copyright protection. Also, sports performances by sportspersons on the field of play – however elegant or dramatic – do not qualify for protection as 'performers' rights' under s 194 of the CDPA. Such rights are restricted to performances of a theatrical character, such as dance, mime, musical and recitals of a literary work.[39]

Again, s 3(1) of the CPDA defines a 'musical work' as a work consisting of music, exclusive of any words or action intended to be sung, spoken or performed with the music. In other words, copyright in musical works is in the composition itself. Thus musical copyright can subsist in the music of the Olympic Anthem and literary copyright in its lyrics. The score for this Anthem, which was approved by the IOC at its 55th Session in 1958 in Tokyo, has been deposited at the headquarters of the IOC in Lausanne, Switzerland. By way of further example, the music that introduces televised transmissions of the 'UEFA Champions League' also benefits from copyright protection as a musical work. 'Artistic work' is defined as:

CDPA 1988, s 4(1)

(a) a graphic work, photograph, sculpture, collage, irrespective of artistic quality;

(b) a work of architecture, being a building or a model for a building; or

(c) a work of artistic craftsmanship.

Thus, works of architecture, such as sports stadia, enjoy copyright protection and may not be copied without authorisation. Likewise photographs of sportspersons and sports events benefit from copyright protection as artistic works. Although photographs may not be copied, the scenes they represent may be independently photographed. The owner of the photograph, not the person photographed, is the owner of the copyright, unless there has been an assignment of the copyright in the photograph to the person photographed. Also, a specially designed logo or graphical symbol, intended to represent a sportsperson, may also attract copyright protection as an artistic work. For example, as part of his new endorsement deal with Adidas, signed in 2004, David Beckham now has his own logo – a stylised representation of him taking a free kick. This logo will attract copyright protection.

---

37   [1892] 2 Ch 489.

38   See later, p 445.

39   CDPA 1988, s 180(2).

39   *Ibid*, s 7.

Sound Recordings, Films, Broadcasts and Cable Programmes

A sound recording is defined as:

CDPA 1988, s 5(1)

(a) a recording of sounds, from which the sounds may be reproduced; or
(b) a recording of the whole or of any part of a literary, dramatic or musical work, from which sounds reproducing the work or part may be produced.

A film is defined as:

CDPA 1988, s 5B(1)

a recording on any medium from which a moving image may by any means be produced.

This covers videos, CD-ROM, interactive media and the visual aspects of computer games, which in the sporting context have become very popular.

A broadcast is defined as:

CDPA 1988, s 6(1)

. . . a transmission by wireless telegraphy of visual images, sounds or other information which:

(a) is capable of being lawfully received by members of the public; or
(b) is transmitted for presentation to members of the public.

So-called 'broadcast rights' do not arise until the broadcast of a live event is made. The CDPA defines a cable programme as any item included in a cable programme service, which is defined as a service consisting wholly or mainly in sending visual images, sounds or other information by means of a telecommunications system, that is, by electronic means.[40] Clearly these definitions are crucial when arranging the broadcasting of sports events and compiling sports programming and content to be transmitted electronically, especially through the new media, such as the internet.

Copyright also exists in 'archive material', which is a very valuable 'asset' of many international sports bodies, such as the IOC, and needs to be reserved and protected as such. Copyright also exists in 'compilations'.

Duration of Copyright

In literary, dramatic and musical works copyright lasts for 70 years from the end of the year in which the author dies. As for sound recordings, copyright lasts for 50 years from the end of the year in which the recording was made or, if not released immediately, from the end of the year in which it was released. In films, the copyright lasts for 70 years from the death of the last survivor of the principal director; the author of the screenplay; the author of the film dialogue; and the composer of the film music. As far as broadcasts and cable programmes are concerned, copyright lasts for 50 years from the end of the year in which the broadcast was made or the programme included in a cable programme service.

---

40   CDPA 1988, s 7.

Defences

'Fair Dealing'

One of the defences to a claim of copyright infringement – unauthorised copying of the protected material – is 'fair dealing'. What amounts to fair dealing is problematical in practice and depends on the circumstances of each case. The famous English Judge of the last century, Lord Denning, has described fair dealing as 'a matter of impression'. Fair dealing is not a *carte blanche* to reproduce copyright works. The CDPA allows 'fair dealing':

- with a literary, dramatic, musical and artistic work for research and private study;[41]

- with a work for criticism and review. In such cases, an acknowledgment must be given;[42]

- with a work (other than a photograph) for news reporting does not infringe the copyright in that work. No acknowledgment is required where such reporting occurs in a sound recording, film, broadcast or cable programme. However, in practice, an acknowledgment ('on screen') is usually given (eg 'pictures from Sky Sport').[43]

For example, in *BBC v British Satellite Broadcasting Ltd*,[44] BSB used excerpts from the BBC's World Cup football coverage in their news broadcasts. They gave an acknowledgment to the BBC. The court held that, although they were mainly of the goals, the excerpts amounted to 'fair dealing'. This case led to the issue of the 'Sports News Access Code of Practice',[45] which governs the use of excerpts by the major broadcasters from sports broadcasts.

Incidental Use

Another statutory defence is that the use of the copyright material was incidental: 'Copyright in a work is not infringed by its incidental inclusion in an artistic work, sound-recording, film, broadcast, or cable programme.'[46] The word 'incidental' is not statutorily defined, but has been judicially defined in *FA Premier League & Ors v Panini UK Ltd*.[47] Panini distributed an unofficial football sticker album and sticker collection including Premier League players bearing the logo of their clubs and that of the Premier League. Panini was sued for copyright infringement as it was not licensed to use these logos and claimed that this use was 'incidental'. In other words, they were entitled to include incidentally one copyright work in another one. The Court of Appeal disagreed, holding that the use in this particular case was not 'incidental' as, in order to produce a collectable sticker, it was necessary for the players to appear in them in authentic club strip. In other words, the use was substantial and fundamental and, therefore, not 'incidental' within the meaning of the statutory exception.

---

41 CDPA 1988, s 29.
42 *Ibid*, s 30(1).
43 *Ibid*, s 30(2).
44 [1991] 3 WLR, 174.
45 Formulated in 1992.
46 CDPA 1988, s 90(3).
47 [2003] 4 All ER 1290; see also Blackshaw, I, 'Sports merchandising and copyright infringement', www.sportbusiness.com; and Shrivastar, R, 'Case comment on the FA Premier League and Panini case' [2003] R6(4) IPD 26022 (Ch D), Intellectual Property Quarterly, 2003, 3, 355–359.

Public Interest

Another defence to a copyright infringement claim is that of 'public interest'. This is not a statutory defence, but one developed by the courts in decided cases. The basis of the defence is that the disclosure of the information is necessary. The courts have drawn a distinction between what is interesting to the public, which does not come within the defence, and what is in the public interest, which does come within this exception.[48]

Assignments and Licences

The owner of copyright, like the owner of any other species of property, can transfer it to another party. To be fully effective legally, any assignment of copyright must be in writing.[49] In the sports context, for example, if an event organiser commissions a graphic artist to design an event logo, the artist owns the copyright in this work. So, as part of the commission, there is an agreement that the artist will assign his copyright in the logo to the event organiser.

An owner of copyright in a particular work may license another party to commercially exploit the copyright in that work.[50] In this case, the licence is merely a permission or authorisation to use the copyright, rather than to transfer its ownership. Without such authorisation, the use would constitute an infringement of the copyright concerned. The licence may be exclusive or non-exclusive and must be in writing to be legally valid.[51] Thus, in the above example, once the event organiser has obtained copyright in the event logo, he may license others to use it commercially, for example, as part of a sponsorship or merchandising programme.

Other Copyright Issues

Moral Rights

The Copyright Designs and Patents Act 1988 introduced into English law the concept of 'moral rights', which have long been recognised on the Continent and elsewhere. The basic 'moral right' is for the author to assert his authorship of the copyright work concerned – in other words to be credited with being the author.[52] The author of a work is the first owner of any copyright in it.[53] Another important 'moral right' protects the integrity of the copyright work. In other words, the work may not be altered without the author's consent. This is particularly important in the case of sculptures.

---

48   See *Lion Laboratories Ltd v Evans* [1984] 2 All ER 417.

49   CDPA 1988, s 90(3).

50   On the subject of control over copyright generally by a copyright owner, see Aitman, D and Jones, A, 'Competition law and copyright: has the copyright owner lost the ability to control his copyright?' (2004) 26(3) European Intellectual Property Review 137.

51   CDPA 1988, s 90(1).

52   *Ibid*, s 77.

53   *Ibid*, s 11.

Copyright Conventions

There are a number of international conventions on copyright. They lay down minimum standards for the protection of copyright owners in the countries that have ratified them. Under the Universal Copyright Convention (UCC), the copyright work must include the copyright symbol – © – together with the name of the copyright owner and the year of first publication. In addition, it is advisable to add the words 'all rights reserved' to ensure legal protection in those countries that have not ratified the UCC. Also, in the European Union, proposals are well advanced for the harmonisation of copyright law.[54]

Remedies for Copyright Infringements

Breach of copyright can give rise to civil and criminal consequences for the infringer.

Civil remedies include:

- damages;
- an account of profits;
- injunctions; and
- delivery up and destruction of the infringing copyright materials.

Certain criminal remedies are contained in s 107 of the CDPA. These include search warrants and delivery up. Offences under the Trade Descriptions Act of 1968 may also be committed. This Act makes it a criminal offence to apply a false trade description to goods or offer to supply such goods. There are also elaborate procedures and remedies in relation to the importation and sale of counterfeit goods.[55] In the sporting context, these measures need to be invoked, from time to time, in relation to cheap imitation sports clothes and shoes, usually emanating from the Far East, bearing imitation and unauthorised well-known designer names and labels.

PATENTS

A patent is regarded as the strongest form of intellectual property. As with trade marks, its legal force derives from registration in a Public Registry – the Patent Office. Like a registered trade mark, it is a statutory monopoly right for the period of its legal duration. In the UK, patents are governed by the Patents Act of 1977 (PA), which deals with, *inter alia*, what may be patented and what constitutes an infringement of a registered patent.

Section 1 of the PA lays down the requirements of patentability. In order to qualify for the grant of a patent, an invention must be:

- new;
- involve an inventive step;

---

54 Part of the Single Market Harmonisation Programme leading eventually to the introduction of a Community-wide Copyright Protection (see EU Directive 93/98/EEC, 29 October 1993, on Copyright Term of Protection). As part of this EU harmonisation process, attention is also being paid to copyright protection in the EU on the internet – so-called 'electronic copyright' (see proposal for a Directive on Copyright and Related Rights in the Information Society (COM 997) 628)).

55 See CPDA 1988, ss 107-110 and 198 as well as ss 107A and 198A, introduced by the Criminal Justice and Public Order Act 1994.

- capable of industrial application; and

- not of a nature whereby a patent grant is excluded.

On the last point, schemes, rules or methods for playing games would not qualify for the grant of a patent. Patents may be granted for a new product – a 'product patent' – or for a new way of making an old or a new kind of article – a 'process patent'.

Registration

In order for a patent to be granted, an application to register it must be filed at the Patent Office. The application must be followed by a statement of 'claims', which must be filed within 12 months of the patent application. The 'claims' set out the technical information and details on which the application for patentability of the product or process is based. The detailed procedure for patent applications is beyond the scope of this book, suffice to say that these applications are very technical, long and arduous. Also, professional assistance from qualified patent agents is needed.

Like trade marks, patents are territorial in nature. They are granted by national authorities and apply within national boundaries. However, for many years now, it has been possible to apply for a European patent, with wider geographical scope and application, to the European Patent Office in Munich, pursuant to the provisions of the European Patent Treaty. Patents are generally granted for a defined period, namely 20 years. In the case of pharmaceutical patents, this period is 25 years. At the end of these statutory periods, the patent is available for anyone to work without charge.

Patents and Sport

Unlike trade marks and copyright, patents, generally speaking, are of limited application and importance in the sports arena. However, there are instances where patent applications are relevant and worth obtaining. Depending on the facts and provided the legal requirements for patentability are satisfied, it may be possible to obtain a patent for certain items of sports equipment. For example, a new design of a golf club, a new way of manufacturing golf balls and a new design of a football boot could qualify for patent protection.

It may be possible to obtain patents in connection with the building and operations of new sports installations and facilities; for example, a retracting roof of a stadium or some other piece of machinery or mechanism or engineering feature. Patent lawyers, like sports lawyers, need to be inventive and creative, always looking for ways and means of legally protecting their clients and 'stealing a march' on their competitors!

The last point is certainly apposite in relation to moves in the United States to extend patent protection to so-called sports 'movements' or 'moves'. These are the distinguishable ways in which athletes go about their business. For example, golfer Bernard Langer's 'inverted putting grip'; rugby player Johnny Wilkon's 'cradle kick'; Australian cricketer Shane Warne's 'flipper'; high jumper Dick Fosbury's 'Fosbury flop'; and former basketball player Kareem Abdul Jabbar's 'sky hook' scoring shot.

Patentability of these sports 'movements' in the States could also apply elsewhere, although, according to some commentators, it is not thought likely that the UK Patent Office would play ball and allow the registration of sports 'movements'.[56] Nonetheless, an interesting idea!

---

56   See Ford, A, 'Whose move is this' *The Times*, 30 July 1996.

Remedies for Infringements

A product patent is infringed if anyone, without the patent owner's consent, makes, disposes of, offers to dispose of, uses or imports the product or keeps it whether for disposal or otherwise.[57]

Private and non-commercial acts and those carried out for experimental purposes do not constitute patent infringements. An infringer is liable for damages and, in appropriate cases an injunction may be obtained to stop the infringement. Of course, an alleged infringer may 'deny the validity' of the patent, arguing that it should not have been granted in the first place. It should be noted, however, that a patent owner could be liable for damages to the alleged infringer if he makes groundless threats of infringement proceedings!

In order to avoid a claim by the infringer that he did not know and had no reason to believe that the patent existed, the owner of the patent must not only mark the article or articles concerned with the word 'patented' but must include the number of the patent as well.[58]

DESIGNS

For the sake of completeness, a brief mention should be made about rights in designs. This is also a complex area of law. Registered designs protect decorative articles or the decorative component of them, whereas a design right protects functional articles and the functional component of them.

Design right is a creature of the CDPA of 1988. Section 213(2) defines 'the design' as meaning the design of any aspect of the shape or configuration of the whole or part of an article. Thus, the overall functional appearance or form is protected rather than, in the case of a registered design, particular features having eye appeal of the article concerned. However, it should be noted that those features can have a functional use as well as their aesthetic appeal. Thus, the bumps and recesses, which lock together the toy 'LEGO' bricks, serve a dual purpose – a functional and aesthetic one – and, therefore, qualify the bricks for registered design protection.[59] A design right lasts for 15 years following the end of the calendar year in which the design was first placed in tangible form. A registered design lasts for five years following registration and can be renewed for up to a total period of 25 years.

A claim for infringement of a registered design can be met by the defence that the alleged infringer did not know and had no reason to believe that the design was actually registered. To overcome this defence, the proprietor of the registered design must not only mark the article or articles concerned with the word 'registered' but must also include the number of the registered design (s 9 of Sched 4 of the CPDA).

In the sporting context, these design rights are not likely to be of much relevance or significance, except in those cases where a patent right might be possible and useful; for example, in manufacturing and engineering businesses that have an impact on sport. They may also have some application to sports 'strips' and 'mascots' and also sports equipment.

---

57 PA, s 60(1)(a).
58 Ibid, s 62(1).
59 *Interlego AG v Tyco Industries Inc* [1989] AC 217.

CONFIDENTIAL INFORMATION

Although *in strictu senso* confidential information is not an IPR, a word or two needs to be written about it in the context of the granting of sports rights and their legal protection and enforcement. As will be seen, confidential provisions figure quite importantly in sports marketing and sports rights agreements, not least because the international sports bodies like to keep their contents, especially the financial provisions, confidential.[60] They even like to keep the fact that they have entered into or, indeed, are negotiating to conclude such agreements strictly confidential too.

Thus, in proposals and tenders for sports rights, options, rights of first refusal and preliminary agreements, obligations of secrecy are generally imposed on the parties. These can be quite complex and extensive, particularly where negotiating exclusivity applies for a defined period of time. Under English law, confidentiality is not so very well developed as a general concept and most secrecy obligations arise under contracts and, as such, are enforced as contractual rights and obligations. Accordingly, the terms and extent of the confidentiality need to be well defined. In general, a claim for breach of confidence can only legally arise in the following circumstances:

- the information disclosed must be of a confidential nature;

- the claimant must own the confidential information;

- that information must have been received by the other party in such circumstances give rise to an obligation of secrecy; and

- there has been, to the detriment of the claimant, an unauthorised use or disclosure of that information by the recipient or someone else who has received it from the recipient.[61]

Limitations on the protection of confidential information also need to be well understood by the parties to sports agreements. For example, there is no obligation to maintain secrecy once the confidential information has passed into the 'public domain' (ie has become general knowledge) through no fault of the party bound by the obligation of secrecy or someone acting on his behalf. Likewise, there are other circumstances where the law actually requires disclosure – for example, in connection with court proceedings. Again, a party bound by a secrecy provision must be permitted to disclose the confidential information to his legal adviser, especially where advice is sought on the legal interpretation and enforceability of a contract or one of its particular terms.

Express provisions are usually included in the confidentiality clause to cover these contingencies and also – equally importantly – about the holding of 'press conferences' and disclosures generally to the media. The law of confidentiality is better defined and more developed on the European Continent under civil law doctrines and provisions, and, in some countries, for example, Switzerland, breaches of confidentiality obligations not only give rise to civil consequences, but also to criminal penalties.

SPORTS PERSONALITY RIGHTS

Sport is not only a global business; it is also a significant part of the global entertainment industry. Sports personalities enjoy incomes and celebrity status on a par with Hollywood film stars. We are

---

60   See later pp 438–39.
61   *Fraser v Thames Television Ltd* [1984] QB 44.

now witnessing footballers, like David Beckham formerly of Manchester United fame but currently of Real Madrid, earning mega sums, not only from playing football, but also by exploiting their popularity and notoriety through lucrative product endorsement and other promotional deals. However, sportspersons taking part in sporting events are not 'performers' or taking part in a 'dramatic performance' for UK copyright law purposes.[62]

In the UK – much less so on the Continent and elsewhere, including the United States, where personality rights are more generally legally recognised and better protected – sports stars, like the Beckhams of this world, are seeking ways and means of protecting their celebrity status and image rights from unauthorised commercial exploitation by others.[63]

Protectability

In the UK, there is no specific law protecting personality rights as such. A personality can only take legal action 'if the reproduction or use of [his/her] likeness results in the infringement of some recognised legal right which he/she does own.'[64] Famous persons, therefore, have to rely on a 'rag bag' of laws, such as trade mark and copyright law and the common law doctrine of 'passing off'.[65]

As previously mentioned, a number of sports personalities have registered their names and likenesses as trade marks under the Trade Marks Act 1994 and taken other measures to protect their personalities. For example, the British athlete, David Bedford, a former 10,000 metres world record holder, won a ruling against a phone directory company, 'The Number', over its advertising of its service ('118–118') featuring two runners in 1970s running kit. The UK communications regulator 'OfCom' held that The Number had caricatured Bedford's image – drooping moustache, shoulder length hair and running kit – without his consent contrary to r 6.5 of the UK Advertising Standards Code.[66] The decision is a significant one for sports personalities seeking to protect their image rights. The Number had argued that the characters featured in the advert were generic 1970s runners as opposed to being caricatures of Mr Bedford. But OfCom rejected this argument in the following uncompromising terms:

Appeal by The Number regarding Complaint by David Bedford

[W]e readily concluded that although the advertisements do not portray David Bedford or refer to him, they do indeed include a caricature of him, and not merely a generic representation of runners from the 1970s. It is our view that each of the twin Runners is a comically exaggerated representation of David Bedford looking like he did in the 1970s, sporting a hairstyle and facial hair like his at the time, and wearing running kit almost identical to the running kit that was distinctively worn by him at the time.[67]

In France and Germany, for example, it is much easier to protect sports personalities from unauthorised commercial exploitation of their names, images and likenesses.[68] For example,

---

62   CDPA 1988, s 180(2) (see earlier).

63   See Blackshaw, I (ed), *Sports Image Rights in Europe* (2005), The Hague: TMC Asser Press.

64   *Per* Laddie J in *Elvis Presley Trade Marks* [1997] RPC 543, 548.

65   See later, p 420–23.

66   *Appeal by The Number regarding Complaint by David Bedford*, 27 January 2004, see decision at www.ofcom.org.uk/bulletins/adv_comp/content_board/?a = 87101.

67   27 January 2004; see decision at www.ofcom.org.uk/bulletins/adv_comp/content_board/?a = 87101.

68   On the European Continent generally, image rights are protected by special provisions in the constitutions of the countries concerned – see Blackshaw, I, 'Protecting the images of sporting celebrities' (2004) The European Lawyer 12 March.

Eric Cantona was awarded damages by a French court for the unauthorised use of his image on the cover of a video.[69] And, in Germany, a court ruled that the use of the names and images of well-known footballers in a stickers album infringed their rights of privacy.[70] The claim that this use was for educational and informative purposes failed – the images were clearly used to sell stickers to children.

In many of the States in the US, especially California, the law on personality rights is also well developed and enforced. The rationale for the recognition and legal protection of these rights is as follows: first, the right to publicity recognises the economic value of an individual's identity; second, the publicity right is an incentive for creativity, encouraging the production of entertaining and intellectual works; and finally, the right prevents unjust enrichment of those who usurp the identity of another. Thus, for example, a number of ex-baseball stars filed a 'class action' to stop the use of their names in fantasy league games and video games. However, there are some limits on these so-called 'rights of publicity'.[71]

However, since the coming into force in the UK on 2 October 2000 of the Human Rights Act of 1998, which incorporates directly into English law the provisions of the European Convention on Human Rights, sports stars, in future, will be better able to protect themselves legally against unauthorised commercial exploitation of their celebrity status.[72] A body of legal decisions concerning public figures and celebrities including sportsmen and women is developing in remedy of breach of confidentiality that can be seen as a move along towards a right of privacy.[73]

Under the European Convention on Human Rights, sports personalities in the UK are now able to invoke directly before the courts the provisions on privacy (Art 8) and the right to personal property (Protocol 1, s 1) in order to protect the unauthorised exploitation of their names, images and likenesses.[74]

Celebrity Endorsements and Advertising Codes

In the UK, the advertising industry is self-regulating. Advertisers are subject to a number of Codes of Practice. The basic requirement is that all forms of advertising must be 'legal, decent and honest'. Under the British Code of Advertising and Sales Promotion, advertisers are required to obtain prior written permission if they wish to use a personality in an advertisement. Persons with a high profile must not be portrayed in 'an offensive or adverse way', and advertisements must 'not imply an endorsement where none exists'.[75]

---

69 See Harrington, D, 'Unauthorised commercial use of a sports star's image in the UK and internationally – a level playing field?' 1999/2000 1 & 2 Sports and Character Licensing.

70 *Ibid.*

71 See, for example, the case of *ETW Corporation v Jireh Publishing, Inc.* (2003 US App LEXIS 12488, 20 June 2003); see 'SportBusiness International'(August 2003), 54, in which a painting entitled 'The Masters of Augusta' commemorating Tiger Woods' 1997 victory, produced and sold by Jireh without Woods' consent, was held by the court not to infringe his 'right of publicity'.

72 See Blackshaw, I, 'Privacy for the famous', *The Times*, 23 May 2000.

73 See *Campbell v MGN Ltd* [2004] 2 WLR 1232; *A v B* [2003] QB 195; *Theakston v MGN Ltd* [2002] EMLR 22; *Ashworth Hospital Authority v MGN Ltd* [2002] 1 WLR 2033; *Venables v News Group Newspapers Ltd* [2001] 2 WLR 1038; *Douglas v Hello ltd* [2001] QB 967.

74 See Blackshaw, I and Boyes, S, 'Levelling the playing field – sport and human rights' *The Times*, 12 September 2000.

75 British Code of Advertising and Sales Promotion, r 13.

It may also be possible for a sports personality to sue for defamation where he or she is depicted in an advertisement in a derogatory way. In the classic English case of *Tolley v Fry*,[76] Mr Tolley, an amateur golfer, was depicted in an advertisement for Fry's chocolate with a bar of chocolate sticking out of his pocket. This advertisement implied that he had endorsed this product and had compromised his status as an amateur sportsman. Although this kind of case is not likely to be repeated in the present climate of widespread professionalism in sport, the principle, nevertheless, is well made and still valid. However, this principle was applied 60 years later in the case of an Australian footballer, who successfully argued that publishing, without his consent, a photo of him naked in the shower implied that he was the kind of person who would consent to having his photo taken in such circumstances and also to the photo being published in a magazine and that ordinary members of the public would think less of him if they thought that he was that kind of person.[77]

It may be added that, when dealing with endorsements of products and services by sports personalities, it is advisable to check that the personality has no objection to the product or service – in one case a personality, who was a teetotaller, endorsed an alcoholic drink! It is also prudent to include a clause in the endorsement agreement giving the right to terminate in the event of the sports personality acting illegally or immorally; for example, testing positive for banned performance enhancing drugs.[78]

UNFAIR COMPETITION

In the UK, unlike Continental Europe (for example, in France, Germany, Spain and Switzerland), there is no specific law on unfair competition, which will protect sports personalities from unfair marketing and other unjust practices. In the UK, apart from trade mark and copyright protection, sports personalities have to rely on the common law doctrine of 'passing off', which does not always provide them with the required relief. It is of limited protection and value in most cases.

'Passing Off'

The tort of 'passing off' consists essentially of one trader 'passing off' his goods or services as those of the claimant. The tort is designed to protect the 'goodwill', defined in the case of *IRC v Muller & Co's Margarine Ltd* as 'the attractive force that brings in custom',[79] that the claimant has built up in his field of business, and the resulting reputation that he enjoys in the market place. Goodwill is an intangible property right, whose legal nature has been described as:

Bulmer Ltd v Bollinger SA [1978] RPC 79

Buckley LJ:

A man who engages in commercial activities may acquire a valuable reputation in respect of the goods in which he deals, or the services which he performs, or of his business as an entity. The law regards such a reputation as an incorporeal piece of property, the integrity of which the owner is entitled to protect.[80]

---

76   [1931] AC 333.
77   See *Ettingshausen v Australian Consolidated Press* [1991] 23 NSWLR 443.
78   See Blackshaw, I, 'Damage limitation?' (2003) SportBusiness International, December/January 2004, 54.
79   [1901] AC 217.
80   [1978] RPC 79.

The claimant must show that there has been misrepresentation and the public has been deceived into believing that the goods or services of the trader are those of the claimant. Damage as a result of the 'passing off' must also be established; see the judgment of Lord Oliver in the case of *Reckitt & Colman Products Ltd v Borden Inc.*[81] These three elements required to constitute 'passing off', namely, (1) reputation or goodwill acquired by the plaintiff in his goods, name, mark, (2) misrepresentation by the defendant leading to confusion (or deception), causing (3) damage to the plaintiff have been described as 'the classical trinity' by Nourse LJ in the *Parma Ham* case.[82] It should be noted, however, that there is no legal requirement for the misrepresentation to be intentional or deliberate. In other words, innocence is no defence to a claim in 'passing off'.[83]

As will be seen, this is a limited right of protection – not a general one – and will depend on the individual facts and circumstances of each particular case.[84] For example, a children's radio personality, 'Uncle Mac', was unable to stop a cereal manufacturer from using his name on their product, because there was no 'common field of activity' between the claimant and the manufacturer. 'Uncle Mac' was not in the business of manufacturing and selling cereals; he was purely a radio presenter. So, there was no risk of confusion to consumers.[85] The former 'Spice Girl', Geri Halliwell, suffered the same fate when she tried to sue in 'passing off' the manufacturer of stickers bearing her name and likeness. She was an entertainer and not in the business of manufacturing, selling or endorsing stickers. Again there was no 'common field of activity'. And so consumers would not be misled.[86]

Likewise, the High Court held that potential purchasers of merchandise bearing the words 'Arsenal' and 'Gunners', as well as the distinctive Arsenal badge and cannon logos, all of which Arsenal had registered as trade marks, sold by Matthew Reed, an Arsenal fan, would not be misled into thinking that the merchandise originated from Arsenal or was, in some way, sanctioned or licensed by Arsenal. This was particularly as Reed's stall displayed a prominent disclaimer to the effect that his merchandise was not endorsed by Arsenal. Neither was there any representation that the merchandise was 'official'.[87] This is an interesting case on 'passing off' and also raises a novel point on trade mark law as the following summary of the case shows:

Arsenal Football Club Plc v Matthew Reed (2001) All ER (D) 67

The claimant brought actions in passing off and registered trademark infringement under s 10(1) and s 10(2)(b) Trade Marks Act 1994 against the defendant who, for 31 years, had been selling football souvenirs both inside and outside the claimant's ground. The claimant was also known by its nickname, 'the Gunners'. It had for a long time been associated with two graphics or logos; the first consisted of a shield and was referred to as the 'Crest Device', the other, referred to as the 'Cannon Device' depicted an artillery piece ('the Arsenal signs').

The claimant derived considerable income from the sale of souvenirs, which it sought to control by licensing. Its licensees were required to describe the claimant's products as 'official' and to mark them in

---

81   [1990] RPC 341, 406.
82   [1991] RPC 351, 368.
83   *Parker-Knoll v Knoll International Ltd* [1962] RPC 265.
84   The courts have moved away from the more lenient approach taken in the 'Ninja Turtles' case – *Mirage Studios v Counter-Feat Clothing* [1991] FSR 145. See also the 'Elvis' case – 'In re Elvis Presley' *The Times,* 22 March 1999.
85   *McCullogh v May* [1946] 65 RPC 58.
86   *Halliwell & Ors v Pannini & Ors,* 6 June 1997 (unreported).
87   *Arsenal Football Club PLC v Matthew Reed* [2001] All ER (D) 67.

a way that complied with the claimant's current labelling requirements. The claimant had registered the words 'ARSENAL' and 'GUNNERS' and the Arsenal signs as trademarks. The court had to decide:

... whether sales by the defendant of certain unlicensed souvenirs or memorabilia would mislead the public into the belief that those goods were the products of the claimant or were goods associated or connected with or licensed by the claimant because they bore one or more of the Arsenal signs;

whether an employee of the defendant had attempted to deceive customers by falsely representing that unlicensed products were 'official' products, made by or with the licence of the claimant;

whether, from the average customer's perspective, the defendant's words and devices were used as trademarks and whether, on a proper construction of s 10 of the Act, the defendant's sign must be used as a trademark for the relevant goods; and

whether the claimant's trademarks were all invalid and should be revoked under s 46 of the Act because they had not been used within a relevant five-year period or revoked under s 47 of the Act because they were incapable of distinguishing the claimant's goods in a trademark sense and therefore offended s 1(1) and s 3(1)(a) of the Act. HELD: (1) Passing off was designed to prevent damage being caused by deception to the goodwill of the claimant and the business, which benefited from that goodwill. *Warnink BV v J Townend & Sons* [1980] RPC 31 followed. The claimant had failed to produce evidence to support its case of likelihood of confusion. It was difficult to believe that any significant number of customers wanting to purchase licensed goods could reasonably think that the defendant was selling them, except when they were expressly marked. In the absence of relevant confusion, the claimant had also failed to show that it had suffered relevant damage as a result of the defendant's activities.

(2) There was no evidence to support the claimant's case in passing off.

(3) The Arsenal signs on the defendant's products would be perceived as a badge of support, loyalty or affiliation to those to whom they were directed. They would not be perceived as indicating trade origin. To succeed on trademark infringement, the claimant had to rely on the non-trademark use of those signs, a wide construction of s 10 of the Act. Use of a sign in a non-trademark sense could infringe a registration. *Phillips Electronics Ltd v Remington Consumer Products* [1998] RPC 283 followed. The law on this point however was not settled and needed to be resolved by the European Court of Justice.

(4) If the claimant had only used the signs in the way that they had been used on the defendant's products, there would have been no relevant trademark use. The claimant's use of the signs was not, however, so limited and they had been used on swing tickets, packaging and neck labels in just the way that one would expect a trademark to be used. The argument of non-use failed.

(5) There was no reason why the use of the Arsenal signs in a trademark sense, for example, on swing tickets and neck labels, was not capable of being distinctive. The fact that the signs could be used in other non-trademark ways did not automatically render them non-distinctive.[88]

This case went to the European Court of Justice for a preliminary ruling on the trade mark issue: whether the use by Reed was a trade mark use as a badge of origin, or were the marks being used merely as a badge of allegiance and support for Arsenal fans? Eventually, when the case came back to the British courts, the Court of Appeal decided,[89] following guidance from the European Court of Justice,[90] that – irrespective of whether or not a mark was being used as a badge of allegiance – *prima facie* it would infringe an identical registered trade mark if it was liable to jeopardise the guarantee of

---

88 Also reported in *The Times*, 26 April 2001; also see Blackshaw, I (2001) 4(3) Sports Law Bulletin 7.
89 *Arsenal Football Club Plc v Reed* [2003] 3 All ER 865.
90 ECJ judgment of 12 November 2002, Case C-206/01.

origin that the registered mark provided.[91] In other words, the use by the defendant of the plaintiff's marks on the defendant's goods – legally speaking – constituted a trade mark use, and, not having been authorised, amounted to a trade mark infringement.

To succeed in a 'passing off' action, sports personalities need to show that they actively exploit their reputation by licensing their name and likeness in relation to a range of goods and services, to the extent that the other party's activity would lead to consumers associating the sports personality with the business of the other party; in other words, into thinking that the sports personality had authorised the use of his name and likeness for the kind of product concerned.

However, this rather strict approach has – to some extent – been relaxed in the subsequent High Court decision in the case of *Irvine v Talksport Limited*.[92] In that case, the court unequivocally recognised – for the first time – that a well-known sportsperson can prevent third parties from exploiting their name or image in circumstances where members of the public will be confused into thinking that the sportsperson concerned has endorsed or in some way authorised/licensed such use by that party, which was not, in fact, the case. The court also held that the proper measure of damages would be the equivalent of the reasonable licence fee that the claimant could have demanded had a licence been granted in respect of the unauthorised activity. The High Court awarded damages of £2,000; whereas, on appeal, the damages were increased to £25,000 by the Court of Appeal.[93]

In Commonwealth jurisdictions, such as Australia, the courts are more relaxed in making the connection between the personality and the unauthorised products. Thus, in the case of *Hogan v Pacific Dunlop*,[94] the actor, Paul Hogan, who played 'Crocodile Dundee', successfully sued the defendants in passing off for using the 'knife scene' from the film *Crocodile Dundee* to advertise their shoes. The court held that there was a misrepresentation because the 'Dundee' character was seen to be sponsoring the shoes, even though no authorisation to do so had, in fact, been given by him.

Ambush Marketing

Another form of unfair marketing practice that has arisen in connection with sports events is so-called 'ambush marketing'- also known as 'parasite marketing'. This occurs when a party claims an association with a sports event, which it does not have and, perhaps more importantly, for which it has not paid a penny. This kind of marketing occurs at all the major sports events, not least the Olympics, and involves major corporations. The IOC has adopted a 'naming and shaming' approach to expose 'ambush marketers' to the world's media. In appropriate cases, the IOC will apply to the courts for relief. This it did at the Albertville Winter Games in 1992 to stop an unfair comparative advertising campaign by American Express, which was not a sponsor, against Visa, which was the official sponsor of the Games in the credit card category.

In the 2000 Sydney Summer Games, the IOC mounted a comprehensive brand protection programme to combat 'ambush marketers', which proved to be quite successful. At the Salt Lake City

---

91 Aldous LJ, with whose judgment Clarke and Jonathan Parker LLJ agreed, said of Laddie J's first instance judgment: 'I accept the judge's finding that the trade marks upon the goods are considered to be badges of allegiance, but all the evidence suggests that the trade marks do also designate origin of the goods to a substantial number of consumers.' So, the correct question to be asked was whether a mark operates as a guarantee of origin.

92 [2002] 1 WLR 2355.

93 See Scanlan, G (2003) 25(12) European Intellectual Property Review 563.

94 [1989] 21 IPR 225.

Winter Games in 2002 and the Athens summer Games in 2004, the Organising Committees established and operated a similar programme.[95]

New Media and Sports Rights

The development of new media, especially the internet, has had – and will continue to have – a significant impact on sport and, in particular, the delivery of sports programming and content. The subject is of such importance that the IOC convened a special World Conference on 'Sport and the New Media' in late 2000. The Conference was chaired by Dick Pound, at that time Vice President of the IOC but now the Chairman of WADA, who said:

> It is more than 10 years since the IOC last organised a conference on this scale and then the subject was television. That we have chosen to take this route reflects the importance we attach to new media issues in sport . . . New media has the potential to fundamentally alter the way the world relates to and consumes sports as entertainment.[96]

He described the relationship between sport and the internet as 'critical'.

INTERNET

The internet is very difficult to regulate and has been generally described as 'the new wild west' and also 'the world's photocopying machine'. As a source of information it is a particularly valuable communications and marketing tool for sport, not least sports, clubs and sports personalities. As with all leading sports clubs, Manchester United has its own website, ManUtd.com and is reputed to receive some 8 million 'hits' a month from a worldwide fan base of some 25 million! The famous Mr Beckham also has his own web site, which he uses for promotional and marketing purposes. In doing so, he is increasing the value of his own 'brand' for commercial exploitation in licensing, merchandising and other promotional deals. The internet has also developed into an important vehicle for the sale and purchase of a wide variety of goods and services – 'e-commerce' – including sporting ones. As such, it has been described as a 'sophisticated sales and marketing tool'.[97]

'Domain names', of which there are now many millions around the world and which identify and allow access to websites, can be protected by registration at a special registry established for this specific purpose. They can also be registered as trade marks, provided they are distinctive and not descriptive. For example, the domain name www.football.com is a unique name, but is not likely to be registrable as a trade mark, because it is descriptive of the services it offers.

From time to time, disputes arise concerning the ownership and use of domain names. Such disputes can be resolved in a number of ways. Legal action can be taken, where appropriate, for trade mark infringement, passing off and false and misleading advertising. It can also be taken under specific internet legislation, such as the US Anti-Cybersquatting Consumer Protection Act of 1999. 'Cybersquatting' occurs where a party registers a domain name comprising the name and/or trade

---

95 As to the different forms of and the ways and means of fighting 'ambush marketing' see Chapter 11, pp 459–73.

96 Foreword to Conference Report, published by the IOC in association with SportBusiness Group. For copies of the presentations made at this Conference, see www.iocnewmedia.com.

97 See Laura, E and McArdle, D, 'Selling your sole: e-Europe, EU law and sports' in Caiger, A and Gardiner, S, (eds) *Professional Sport in the EU: Regulation and Re-regulation* (2000) The Hague: TMC Asser Press; also see Smith, T, 'Sports internet – distribution and control of sports content' (2001) 14 Sports and Character Licensing.

mark of a third party, with a view to extracting a substantial sale price for the transfer of the name to that other party. Complaints by that party to the domain name registry concerned will result in the first registration being cancelled and a new registration being granted to the 'rightful' owner. The Olympic Movement has taken action in the States, under the above Act, against thousands of unauthorised websites using the names 'Olympic' and 'Olympiad' which, according to Dick Pound of the IOC, belong to the Games and the Olympic Athletes. These sites are claiming an association with the Olympics that they do not have, and, as such, this is another example of 'ambush marketing'.

Other disputes can be quickly resolved by the domain name registry through a kind of mediation process administered by the Arbitration & Mediation Center the World Intellectual Property Organization, based in Geneva, Switzerland.[98] Here are some recent examples.

'Soccer Players and Wembley Stadium Win Internet Domain Disputes'

The Internet Age has created new concepts of intellectual property, the most conspicuous being domain names. The right to use a particular domain name (the Internet address) has resulted in considerable legal wrangling, so much so that a new system of resolving disputes was created under international agreement in 1999 – an independent arbitration procedure created under the World Intellectual Property Organization (WIPO). This policy, called the Uniform Dispute Resolution Policy (UDRP) has resulted in a quick and relatively inexpensive adjudication.

Two Dutch soccer players and the operators of Wembley Stadium were the beneficiaries of that system when they won the the right to use their names as Internet addresses in November 2000. The UDRP panel ruled in favor of Jaap Stam and Pierre van Hooijdonk as well as the famed London stadium. Stam, who plays for Manchester United, won the rights to www.jaapstam.com. Losing control of the site is Oliver Cohen of Pittsburgh (*Jaap Stam v Oliver Cohen* Case No D2000–1061). Van Hooijdonk, who plays for Portugal's Benfica, won the rights to www.pierrevanhooijdonk.com from Sam Tait of Airdrie, Scotland (*Pierre van Hooijdonk v SUB Tait* Case No D2000–1068). The two players were among seven Dutch stars who took their cases to the World Intellectual Property Organization (WIPO). The other cases were terminated, which usually means the parties reached an agreement.

According to the Associated Press, Stam and van Hooijdonk told WIPO they had registered their names as trademarks in the registry that covers the Netherlands and their names were widely recognized. Cohen told WIPO that Stam could not claim his name was well-known worldwide. In the United States, he said, the name was familiar only to 'a minuscule number of esoteric people'. He said he had never offered to sell the address and had turned down a request to buy it.

Arbitrator James Bridgeman said he was satisfied that the people who registered the domain names would have been aware of the Dutch players. WIPO also ordered the transfer of www.wembleystadium.net to the company that owns and operates the stadium, which is about to be demolished and rebuilt.

The problem which resulted from the easy registration of domain names was a practice called 'cybersquatting' where anyone could pick a name out of a hat, even one that is trademarked or one that parrots the name of an actual person. In the United States, there is a law against cybersquatters who use those registered names as selling bait. But that law often involves costly litigation. The UDRP system, faster and cheaper, has been used in over 1,000 disputes and has a 60-day turnaround time between filing and resolution.[99]

---

98 See Blackshaw, I, 'Crushing sports cybersquatters', (2004) SportBusiness International, November, 23; Blackshaw, I, 'Settling sports disputes in cyberspace' (2004) 1/2 The International Sports Law Journal 20.

99 'Soccer players and Wembley Stadium win internet domain disputes' (2001) 4(3) Sports Law Bulletin 19; also see Harrington, D, 'Resolution of sports domian name disputes' (2003) 10 (5) Sports Law Administration and Practice 8.

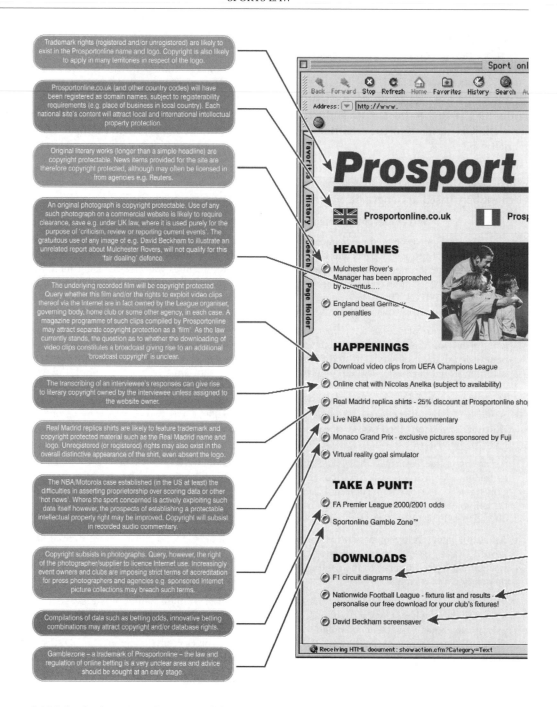

Trademark rights (registered and/or unregistered) are likely to exist in the Prosportonline name and logo. Copyright is also likely to apply in many territories in respect of the logo.

Prosportonline.co.uk (and other country codes) will have been registered as domain names, subject to registerability requirements (e.g. place of business in local country). Each national site's content will attract local and international intellectual property protection.

Original literary works (longer than a simple headline) are copyright protectable. News items provided for the site are therefore copyright protected, although may often be licensed in from agencies e.g. Reuters.

An original photograph is copyright protectable. Use of any such photograph on a commercial website is likely to require clearance, save e.g. under UK law, where it is used purely for the purpose of 'criticism, review or reporting current events'. The gratuitous use of any image of e.g. David Beckham to illustrate an unrelated report about Mulchester Rovers, will not qualify for this 'fair dealing' defence.

The underlying recorded film will be copyright protected. Query whether this film and/or the rights to exploit video clips thereof via the Internet are in fact owned by the League organiser, governing body, home club or some other agency, in each case. A magazine programme of such clips compiled by Prosportonline may attract separate copyright protection as a 'film'. As the law currently stands, the question as to whether the downloading of video clips constitutes a broadcast giving rise to an additional 'broadcast copyright' is unclear.

The transcribing of an interviewee's responses can give rise to literary copyright owned by the interviewee unless assigned to the website owner.

Real Madrid replica shirts are likely to feature trademark and copyright protected material such as the Real Madrid name and logo. Unregistered (or registered) rights may also exist in the overall distinctive appearance of the shirt, even absent the logo.

The NBA/Motorola case established (in the US at least) the difficulties in asserting proprietorship over scoring data or other 'hot news'. Where the sport concerned is actively exploiting such data itself however, the prospects of establishing a protectable intellectual property right may be improved. Copyright will subsist in recorded audio commentary.

Copyright subsists in photographs. Query, however, the right of the photographer/supplier to licence Internet use. Increasingly event owners and clubs are imposing strict terms of accreditation for press photographers and agencies e.g. sponsored Internet picture collections may breach such terms.

Compilations of data such as betting odds, innovative betting combinations may attract copyright and/or database rights.

Gamblezone – a trademark of Prosportonline – the law and regulation of online betting is a very unclear area and advice should be sought at an early stage.

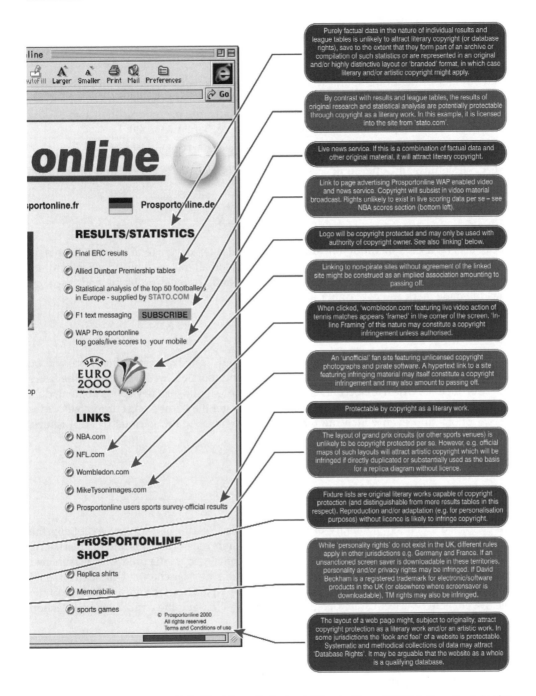

Sports and Character Licensing, published by Informa Professional, Gilmoora House, 57/61 Mortimer Street, London W1N 8JX, Tel +44 (0) 207 453 2154, Fax +44 (0) 207 631 3214, www.informalaw.com

Sports Website Issues

Website Content

The design, layout and content of a sports website raise a number of intellectual property issues, including trade mark and copyright protection, 'passing off' and database rights[100] (as to which, see later). Many sports bodies have their own websites, especially for promoting their events and competitions, many of which are controlled in-house, for example, 'UEFA.com'.[101]

The issues are well illustrated in the following 'IP rights in website content' feature.[102]

As will be seen, designing and operating a successful sports website is a legal and operational minefield!

Web-casts

The internet can also be used a medium for downloading 'real time' coverage of sporting events. In 1999, BSkyB showed the first live web-cast of an international football match (England v Scotland) on the internet.[103] Such 'web-casts' can give rise to their own kinds of legal problems and disputes. These may include trade mark and copyright issues.

Wap Phones

As the technology develops and becomes more and more sophisticated, access to the 'web' will be less by personal computers and more by other means, including mobile phones, especially the faster internet access '3G' models, which are becoming more common. These will carry sports content, data and eventually programming. For example, one will be able to get the latest cricket or football scores on one's mobile phone and even watch the matches themselves! Again, various IP legal issues, especially copyright ones, are raised by these developments.[104]

Sport and other 'New Technologies'

'Interactive TV'

Media convergence – defined as 'the ability of different network platforms to carry essentially the same kind of information' – is fundamentally influencing the kinds of sports rights and the marketing strategies of their holders and exploiters. For example, a new converged media product was launched on 22 August 1999, when Sky Digital subscribers tuning into the Manchester United v Arsenal Premiership match were treated to a new interactive experience. Apart from the normal footage of the match, viewers were able to select camera angles, read players' biographies, run their own 'action replays' and view news and results from other sports events.

---

100 See p 429.
101 See Fourtoy, A, and Britcher, C, 'UEFA controls and shoots for EURO 2004 SportBusiness International', 18 March 2004; Burton, S, 'Sports portals' (2001) 14 Sports and Character Licensing.
102 Couchman, N, 'IP rights in website content' (2000) 7 Sports and Character Licensing 16-17.
103 See feature on 'Sports internet' (2001) Sports and Character Licensing, Issue No 14, March 2001.
104 See de la Fuente, JP, 'Download now' (2003) Football Business International August 19; see also 'Mobile technologies: the opportunities for sport', a SportBusiness Report, 2004 – www.sportbusiness.com.

Likewise, subscribers to Bernie Ecclestone's 'F1 Super Signal' are able to choose the camera angles and follow the drivers they select. BBC television viewers during the 2001 Wimbledon Championships have been able to choose which of five matches taking place simultaneously they wish to watch. This is the first time that armchair spectators have had an interactive service on terrestrial television. These developments have been likened to the introduction of colour television in the late 1960s. Peter Salmon, the BBC director of sport has commented, 'This is a fundamental development and might in time change sport broadcasting'. Such developments open up unlimited opportunities for creative sports marketers and, again, as with any new technology or product, legal issues also arise, not least IP ones.[105]

Computer Games

Computer games would seem to be 'tame' in comparison with the above new media products. But computer sports games continue to be popular and more sophisticated in terms of visual excitement and otherwise. From a legal point of view, it is something of a nightmare to cover the rights to the various elements that go into the average sports computer game, including the obtaining of any and all relevant 'releases' from the various rights owners.

Again, a knowledge and appreciation of IP rights is essential to produce a product that does not infringe other party's legal rights, not least those of sports personalities involved. In Germany for example, Arts 1 and 2 of the Constitution protect image rights. In 2003, Oliver Khan, the German national team goalkeeper, successfully sued Electronic Arts (EA), the electronic games manufacturer, for using his image and name in an official FIFA computer football game. EA claimed that collective consent had been obtained from the national (VdV) and international (FIFPro) football players' unions; but not, in fact, from individual players, including Khan himself. This, the Hamburg District Court ruled, was not enough.[106] Further legal complications, especially copyright issues, also arise as many of these games are sponsored/endorsed by sports personalities and also contain advertising materials.

Database Rights

Database rights may be a powerful new intellectual property right, which sports governing bodies could exploit commercially. The case of *BHB and Others v William Hill Organisation Limited*[107] had held, at first instance, that the database information of BHB, comprising lists of runners, names of jockeys, jockeys' colours, the racing calendar and details of every horse licensed to race in the UK, which William Hill was posting on its internet site for online betting purposes, infringed BHB's rights. However, as a result of a subsequent ruling by the European Court of Justice in response to some detailed questions referred to it by the UK Court of Appeal, to whom William Hill had appealed, it is now doubtful that William Hill's particular activities in the BHB case will be held to infringe their database rights.[108] The Court of Appeal, in the light of the European Court of Justice ruling found in favour of William Hill.[109]

---

105 See 'Interactive TV: the opportunities for sport' SportBusiness Report 2004 – www.sportbusiness.com.

106 *Kahn v Electronic Arts GmbH,* unreported, 25 April 2003 (Germany).

107 [2001] RPC 612.

108 See Case C-203/02, 9 November 2004, The Grand Chamber of the European Court of Justice.

109 See *British Horseracing Board Ltd v William Hill Organisation Ltd* (CA (Civ Div)) [2005] RPC 35.

Database rights legally protect any data or information derived from a database and also raw data even when taken out of its database context. And these rights derive from the Copyrights in Database Regulations of 1997, which, in turn, implement EC Directive 96/9. Under the Regulations, a database will only be protected as a 'copyright work',[110] where there is intellectual creation in the selection or arrangement of the data in the database. However, the contents of a database will also be protected by database rights, where there is substantial investment in obtaining, verifying or presenting the data in the database. Under the Regulations, database rights enjoy protection for a term of 15 years. Where a further substantial investment in obtaining, verifying or presenting data has made, a new term of protection comes into effect.

The protection and exploitation of sports databases has also been the subject of a leading case in the US involving the online publication of 'real-time' golf scores. In a dispute between a communications company and the PGA,[111] the company wanted to exploit commercially golf scoring information that the PGA had spent money in gathering, but had not fully enjoyed the benefits of this investment. The US court held that the PGA had a property right in its real-time scoring system and that this information was not yet in the public domain for free exploitation, because the PGA had not yet reaped its reward, nor foregone that possibility. Thus, the PGA enjoyed a legal interest in these scores and could stop others from exploiting them commercially without their consent. In other words, this legal interest could be invoked by the PGA to stop would-be free riders unfairly capitalising on its product.

Of course, the manner in which sports governing bodies regulate the release and use of their database rights, especially as regards the terms and conditions of the licences they grant, may give rise to competition law/anti-trust challenges, especially from third parties who may not be able to obtain the particular data from other sources.

CONCLUSION

Sport is not only big business, but is also a product that is being commercialised in a variety of creative ways. This phenomenon has led to what some commentators have called the 'commodification' of sport, which also extends to sports persons themselves, who have also become 'hot properties' for sale, purchase and hire in their own right. The advent of the Internet Age and the appearance of new forms of media marketing platforms, including 'wap' phones, have also led to the creation and exploitation of new sports related rights and, in turn, added further appreciable value to sports business.

So, the role played by intellectual property law in the modern sporting arena is a very significant and valuable one, providing protection not only for the mega sums being invested in sport, but also the considerable financial returns on those investments. It is a dynamic and evolving branch of the law presenting a challenge not only to sports lawyers and legislators, but also to sports administrators, broadcasters and many others involved in the organisation and promotion of and participation in sport and sports events around the world.

---

110 For a shorter period (see earlier, p 409).
111 *Morris Communications Corporation v PGA Tour, Inc* [2002] 235 FSupp 2d 1269 (MD Fla).

KEY SOURCES

Armstrong, Marc, 'The 3 Lions, a case study in character/mascot licensing' (2001) 15 Sports and Character Licensing.

Blackshaw, Ian, (ed), *Sports Image Rights in Europe* (2004), The Hague: TMC Asser Press.

Griffith-Jones, D, *Law and the Business of Sport* (1997), London: Butterworths.

Hennigan, J, 'Altered image rights' (2003) Entertainment Law Review 14(7) 161–163.

Verow, R, Lawrence, C and McCormick, P, *Sport, Business and the Law* (2005), 2nd edn, Bristol: Jordan Publishing Limited.

CHAPTER 11

SPORTS MARKETING, SPONSORSHIP AND AMBUSH MARKETING

INTRODUCTION

Sport is now a product and successfully marketed and packaged as such in a variety of creative and lucrative ways around the world. This has developed over the last 25 years or so and led to the establishment of a discrete sports marketing industry. Much of the pioneering work was done by Horst Dassler of the sports goods manufacturer, ADIDAS, through ISL, standing for 'The International Sport Leisure and Culture' Company, which he founded.[1] He revolutionised the marketing of the Olympic Games, introducing a unified and global approach, and other major sporting events, including basketball, football and track and field, through the development of sponsorship, merchandising and other commercial and promotional techniques.

In this chapter the main forms of sports marketing – sponsorship, merchandising, endorsements of products and services and corporate hospitality – will be examined. The phenomenon of 'conflict marketing' or 'ambush marketing' – a form of unfair marketing practice, which is a by-product of the successful marketing of major sports events on a global basis, such as the Summer and Winter Olympic Games – will also be covered.

ENDORSEMENT AGREEMENTS

Under these agreements, companies use well-known sports persons to endorse and promote their products and services, which usually – but not necessarily – have a sporting connection. For example, a famous golfer, such as Nick Faldo, to promote golf clubs, or a sports personality, such as the Manchester United footballer, David Beckham, to promote the sale of sunglasses under the brand name 'POLICE'.

The commercial rationale for this kind of business arrangement is that potential purchasers of the products and prospective users of the services will be attracted by the endorsement of them by the sports personality concerned. Because 'Becks' wears these sunglasses they must be good, and his fans will want to emulate him and buy them too! In other words, the name and reputation of the person endorsing the product or service concerned is used to lure potential customers into purchasing that particular product or service. It is a kind of image transfer.

As part of the endorsement agreement, the company may use the sports celebrity's name, likeness and autograph in connection with the promotion and sale of the product(s) and services(s) concerned. As such, the agreement may involve the licensing of trade marks and the commercial exploitation of other intellectual property rights, such as copyright, belonging to the sports personality concerned.

As with all agreements that involve the commercial exploitation of intellectual property rights, the rights granted need to be carefully defined in the 'grant of rights' clause. To supplement such rights, endorsement agreements often require the sports personality to grant certain advertising and

---

1   In the summer of 2001, ISL were declared bankrupt by a Swiss Court with debts reputedly of £350 million. The insolvency was largely due to ever increasing financial guarantees given in connection with the marketing of international sports events, which it could not fulfil.

promotional rights as well, including personal appearances at stores and events to promote the sale of the products and services concerned.

The value of the endorsement and, therefore, the agreement depends not only on the continued success of the sports personality in his/her particular sporting discipline, but also on his/her general behaviour on and off the 'field of play'; for example, Mike Tyson biting off part of Evander Holyfield's ear during a fight in September 1997; and Eric Cantona's 'infamous' assault on a spectator at Selhurst Park on 25 January 1994 following a 'sending off'. Bad behaviour by the sports personality can have a negative effect on the association between that personality and the company seeking his/her endorsement of its products and/or services. Thus, it is essential to include so called 'morality provisions' in endorsement agreements.[2]

Under such provisions, which need to be precisely defined to avoid them being held to be legally unenforceable on the grounds of vagueness and uncertainty, if the sports personality behaves in an anti-social, dishonest or illegal manner, for example, tests positive for performance enhancing drugs and is suspended from competition or, indeed, uses illegal recreational drugs, if either of these particular contingencies are expressly covered in the agreement. Such conduct can – and, indeed, should – be expressly made a ground for termination of the endorsement agreement.[3]

To introduce precision in the clause, yet at the same time make it comprehensive and flexible, wording along the following lines could be used:

Model morality clause

The Sports Personality shall, at all times, during the period of this Agreement act and conduct himself/herself in accordance with the highest standards of disciplined and professional sporting and personal behaviour and shall not do or say anything or authorise there to be done or said anything which, in the reasonable opinion of the Company is or could be detrimental, whether directly or by association, to the reputation, image or goodwill of the Company or any of its associated companies. The Sports Personality shall not, during the term of this Agreement, act or conduct himself/herself in a manner that, in the reasonable opinion of the Company, offends against decency, morality or professionalism or causes the Company, or any of its associated companies, to be held in public ridicule, disrepute or contempt, nor shall the Player be involved in any public scandal.

The term 'associated companies' will need to be defined. The advantage of such a clause is that it lays down objective standards/norms of good behaviour whilst, at the same time, giving the sponsor the freedom to decide whether or not those standards/norms have been breached.

To ensure compliance with a 'morality clause', either a 'stick' or 'carrot' approach can be taken by the sponsor. Under the former, a financial penalty will be exacted for any breach. This raises the 'hoary chestnut' of whether the amount involved is an unenforceable contractual 'penalty' or an enforceable 'liquidated damages' provision. Apart from this, such a provision may be difficult in practical terms to enforce as an 'after the fact' type of sanction. On the other hand, it may be better to use the latter approach and award a 'bonus' payment for 'good behaviour'. This should act as an incentive and encourage compliance with the terms of the 'morality clause'. Put the other way round, an attractive 'bonus' payment should act as a disincentive to bad behaviour.

It is useful and advisable to supplement a 'morality clause' with a contractual provision requiring that, in the event of any breach, the offending party shall hand over to the company the management

---

2   See Korman, A, 'Sponsorship – moral dilemmas' (2000) 11 Sports and Character Licensing 20–21; see also Blackshaw, I, 'Damage limitation' (2003) 4 SportBusiness International Magazine, December/January 54; and Mitan, D, 'Contract killers' (2004) 1/2 SportBusiness International April 34.

3   See Blackshaw, I, 'It's just not cricket!' (2003) – www.sportbusiness.com.

and control of a public relations damage limitation exercise, to enable the company, as far as and to the extent possible, to mitigate any loss of goodwill or reputation as a result of the breach. Such a campaign will also include a press charm offensive!

Of course, the ultimate sanction for any breach of a 'morality/good behaviour' clause is termination of the endorsement agreement, and this right should be expressly reserved in all cases. Remember that this is a right – and not an obligation – and so the company is free to decide, according to the circumstances of each particular case, whether or not to exercise it. One important factor is the effect the breach of the 'morality/good behaviour' clause may have on an ongoing marketing, promotional and advertising programme in which the particular endorsement is a key component. It is also usual to require in endorsement agreements 'exclusivity' from the sports personality, in the sense that he/she will not enter into similar contracts with competitors during the term of the agreement, and also to define the geographical territory in which the endorsement rights may be exercised.

Criticism of the endorsed products by the sports personality may also need to be expressly covered in the agreement. Such criticism may be express or, perhaps more commonly, implied. For example, a sports personality seen in public consuming a competitor's products. In either case, this kind of behaviour undermines the exclusivity value of the endorsement. This kind of provision may need to be extended beyond the term of the agreement. But *cave*, post-termination restrictions often raise competition law issues.

Other important clauses are the financial and payment terms and conditions, and, as previously mentioned, the termination provisions, including the legal and practical effects of termination, especially in relation to the post-termination sale of existing stocks of 'endorsed' products. Finally, it should be made expressly clear that the endorsement agreement does not constitute an employment, partnership or joint venture relationship, with the corresponding legal, financial and practical consequences, but is merely an agreement to provide personal services on the part of the sports personality, who is acting as an 'independent contractor'. As such, the agreement will automatically terminate on the death or other physical or mental incapacity of the sports personality to perform the agreed services.

The need to negotiate clear terms and conditions and incorporate them into a well drafted agreement cannot be overemphasised. Agreements involving the contracting of personal services are notoriously difficult to draw up and enforce in practice. Before drafting the agreement, it is good practice to draw up a 'checklist' of the various legal, financial, commercial and practical matters to be included on both sides.

A sample of such a 'checklist' follows:

- Parties and their capacities to contract.
- Preliminary approvals and preconditions.
- Warranties and conditions.
- Rights and product/service category exclusivity.
- Registration and use of intellectual property rights.
- Territory/ies.
- Duration.
- Payment terms and conditions.
- Tax issues including Vat sales and withholding taxes.
- Personality's obligations.

- Company's obligations.
- Termination.
- Proper law and dispute resolution.
- Post-termination obligations.
- 'Belt and Braces' clauses.
- Appendices.

CORPORATE HOSPITALITY AGREEMENTS

Corporate hospitality has developed into a multi-billion dollar industry around the world. The UK corporate hospitality market is the most developed and worth around £750 m a year – and it is growing. Globally, the market is worth between $6.6 and $13.5 billion a year, with 75% of this expenditure attributable to North America, Europe and Australia.

Companies wishing to entertain their clients and customers and also to reward employees, especially sales and marketing executives for reaching their financial targets, have seen the advantage of capitalising on the popularity and power of sport and have developed sophisticated hospitality packages in relation to prestigious sporting events, such as Wimbledon and Henley at the national level, and the FIFA World Cup and the Olympic Games at the international level.[4]

As there is a considerable amount of corporate pride – if not 'oneupmanship' – riding on such forms of hospitality, and a considerable amount of goodwill resting on the success of the sporting events concerned, it is very important for the organisers and users of the hospitality to get things right – not only from an operational and commercial point of view, but also from a legal point of view. A well negotiated and drafted hospitality agreement is, therefore, a *sine qua non*. Essentially, corporate hospitality agreements are exclusive distribution contracts and, as such, may be subject to the EU Rules on Fair Competition.

As with all sports marketing agreements, one of the most important clauses is the 'grant of rights' clause. This defines the extent of the rights granted by the event organiser to the provider of the hospitality and any restrictions on the exercise of those rights. For example, there will be a requirement that the party providing the hospitality must use event sponsors' products, such as drinks and snacks, and not those of competitors. Thus, if Coca-Cola is the title sponsor of the event, the hospitality provider will not be allowed to serve Pepsi. Again, there need to be restrictions on 'give-aways' ('premiums') so that there is no conflict between these items and those of the event sponsors.

To secure the financial performance of the corporate hospitality provider's obligations, bank guarantees and bonds may be required. Indeed, it has been proposed, following some spectacular bankruptcies, that corporate hospitality companies should be part of a bonding scheme, rather like the ABTA scheme covering travel agents who organise and sell package holidays. Also, it could be advisable for the event organiser and the corporate hospitality provider to enter into a joint venture company to deliver the corporate hospitality. Such an arrangement would give both parties better legal control over infringers of their respective rights.

The corporate hospitality agreement will also need to contain appropriate 'warranties'; for example, from the event organiser that it owns the rights being granted and that the event will be

---

4 On the commercial advantages generally of organising and implementing corporate hospitality programmes relating to sporting events, see Kolah, A, 'Maximising the value of hospitality' (2004 SportBusiness Report).

held by the corporate hospitality provider, as well as quality control provisions regarding the use of the 'event marks' and 'official designations'. The agreement will also need to contain appropriate *'force majeure'* provisions to cover the legal, financial and practical consequences of the hospitality not being provided, as a result of the sporting event having to be cancelled or postponed for some unforeseen cause or other. In this connection, claims from suppliers for cancelled contracts and claims for 'disappointment' from invited guests need to be considered and factored into the agreement. Suitable insurance arrangements also need to be put in place to cover such contingencies and appropriate endorsements of interests on the policy concerned need to be expressly made. Again, the agreement will need to contain express provisions as to the applicable law and the settlement of disputes, especially where foreign elements are involved. In this connection, the use of alternative forms of dispute resolution should be considered.

From a practical point of view, to ensure the success of any hospitality programme, the event organiser needs to have legal and actual control over the venue, especially in the areas where the hospitality will be provided, in order to prevent and/or deal particularly with conflict and ambush marketing situations. One final point: in certain jurisdictions the provision of corporate hospitality – particularly on a lavish scale with expensive corporate mementoes/souvenirs – may be regarded as a bribe and, therefore, constitute a criminal offence.

INTERNATIONAL SPORTS LOGO LICENSING AGREEMENTS

Licensing logos of prestigious international sports events, such as the FIFA World Cup and the Olympic Games, on a wide range of merchandise, can be money spinners, not only for the event organisers, who grant the licences, the licensors, but also for the firms who take them, the licensees.[5] Sports licensing is reputed to be worth more than $125 billion in global sales.[6] And the US, Far East and Western Europe represent 85% of the global licensing market.[7] As Nic Couchman states:

> Capturing the intangible value associated with sport ... and successfully converting it into sales of consumer products is now an extremely diverse and highly creative process.[8]

The success of sports logo licensing not only depends on negotiating the best possible commercial and financial arrangements, but also on drafting the corresponding licence agreements.[9] Badly drafted agreements lead to uncertainties and misunderstandings, which, in turn, lead to disputes, which can – and often do – prove costly, in terms of time and money, not least for the licensees.

In this section, we will take a look at some of the contractual provisions in sports logo licence agreements that require special consideration and can cause problems in practice. Before doing so, however, what do we mean by sports logos and what legal status do they enjoy?

Sports Logos

Essentially, sports logos are designs used for identifying and promoting the sports event concerned. They often incorporate the name of the particular sports event in distinctive lettering as part of the

---

5   See Finlay, A, 'Sydney strikes gold' (2000) 8 Sports and Character Licensing 14–18.
6   Sports marketing industry figures.
7   *Ibid.*
8   Couchman, N, 'Introduction' (1999) 1 Sports and Character Licensing 3.
9   See Blackshaw, I, 'Licence to thrill' (2000) 5 Sports and Character Licensing 6–8.

design. In so far as they are distinctive, they are registrable as 'device marks' under trade mark law. A licensee will need to check, therefore, whether the logo has been registered as a trade mark, or, if not, whether an application for registration has been filed, or, again, if no application is pending, whether the logo is legally registrable at all.

In addition or as an alternative to registration as a trade mark, logos can also be legally protected by copyright law as an 'artistic work'. Again, the legal status needs to be checked, because, if the logo does not enjoy trade mark and/or copyright protection, anybody can use it and the licence is worth less. If the logo is registered as a trade mark, the licensee will need to check in which countries trade mark protection has been obtained – trade mark rights are territorial in nature – and also for which classes of goods they have been registered. For example, if the licence is to cover clothing, the logo will need to be registered in Class 25 of the Nice Classification, which covers 'clothing, footwear and headgear'. As a further example, if the logo is to be used on sports bags, it will need to be registered in Class 18.

Assuming the logo is properly registered as a trade mark, in certain jurisdictions, including the UK, a separate registered user agreement will have to be entered into and filed at the Trade Marks Registry. This will ensure that the licensee's use of the mark will count as legal user by the trade mark owner, to avoid the mark being vulnerable to cancellation through non-use.

Sports Logo Licence Agreements

Some of the main contractual provisions in sports logo licence agreements will now be considered.[10] Perhaps the most important provision in any licence agreement, and not least in one dealing with sports logos, is the so-called 'grant of rights' clause. This clause defines the nature and the scope of the rights granted by the licensor to the licensee in respect of the logo relating to the particular sports event. In particular, the clause will specify whether the licence granted is an exclusive or a non-exclusive one. It will also define the goods ('the licensed product(s)') to be included in the licence, as well as the distribution channels (for example, retail, mail order) through which they may be sold – this is essentially a matter of 'positioning' (to use a marketing term) of the licensed products and can affect materially their selling prices. The clause will also specify the geographical territory or territories in which the products can be sold, and also the duration (term) during which the licence will operate. The clause often includes other restrictions on the use of the licensed products, for example, as 'premiums', 'give-aways', or other items for sales promotional purposes. As the logo that is being licensed relates to a particular event, there will also be a specific prohibition against using or permitting the logos from being used in any manner contrary to public morals, or which compromises or reflects unfavourably on the good name, goodwill, reputation, standing and image of the sports body, its event and the sport itself. Likewise, the grant of rights will be made subject to the rules of the sports body concerned; for example, in the case of an Olympics merchandising programme, the Olympic Charter.

If the licence agreement is an exclusive one – in other words, only the licensee (not even the licensor) may exploit the licensed products in a particular territory during the term of the agreement – it is usual and most prudent to impose a minimum annual sales performance on the licensee, in order to maximise the financial returns from the licence. If the sales of the licensed products do not reach this minimum, the licensor, at his option, may terminate the licence agreement. Combined with such a performance clause is an express undertaking by the licensee to 'actively

---

10   See Blackshaw, I, 'Sports licensing and merchandising' (2001) 4/5 The International Sports Law Journal 41–44.

stimulate the demand for and promote the sale of the licensed products within the territory during the term'.

In settling the precise terms of the performance requirement, the licensor and licensee should agree on realistic and reasonably achievable targets, and objective criteria for determining whether the minimum sales have been achieved, according to all the circumstances of the particular case. Often a performance clause is accompanied by an obligation on the part of the licensee to supply certain quantities of the licensed products to the licensor in connection with the organisation and promotion of the sports event concerned. From both parties' points of view, the limits of this obligation need to be clearly laid down, especially, as is often the case, if the supply of products is to be *gratis* or at 'cost price'. Incidentally, a performance clause also has trade mark protection implications, in that, under trade mark law in the UK and elsewhere, the validity of a registered trade mark depends upon its being commercially exploited.

An equally important provision in any licence agreement is the 'consideration' clause. The financial *quid pro quo* for the licence can either be a lump sum (licence fee) and/or periodic payments (royalties). In the latter case, the basis on which the royalties are to be calculated needs to be precisely defined. If, as is usual, they are to be charged on the 'net invoice price' of the licensed products, this needs to be carefully defined. For example, what about trade discounts; what about sales to 'associated companies' (which also need to be defined) of the licensee; what about defective and returned goods; and so on?

Likewise, there need to be provisions on sales accounting, delivery of royalty statements and the right of the licensor (or its agent) to inspect the licensee's accounting records. There also need to be provisions defining when the royalty is earned (accrues) and when and where (specified bank account) the royalty is to be paid (settlement). In the case of international licence agreements, it will also be necessary to specify the currency of obligation and the currency of payment of the licence fee and/or the royalties, as well as the corresponding exchange rate for converting from one currency to the other. Royalties may accrue and be calculated in one currency but paid in another. Furthermore, provision will also need to be made for exchange control implications for payments from those countries that limit the transfer of funds abroad, especially hard currency such as the US dollar, and require governmental approvals of licence agreements (for example, Turkey). A supplementary provision will need to be included to cover the case of failures to obtain exchange control approvals and their practical consequences (for example, termination of the licence agreement). The question whether payments are to be made free or subject to any required withholding of tax also needs to be addressed and provided for in the agreement. Finally, the question of the right of set-off between the licensor and the licensee and the right to claim interest, and at what rate, on late payments of licence fees and/or royalties will also need to be expressly provided for in the agreement.

Another important clause in a sports logo licence agreement is the 'quality control' one. For trade mark and other commercial reasons, the licensor will need to exercise control over the quality of the licensed products and also, of equal importance, over the advertising and promotional material for them. Samples of the products need to be approved by the licensor before being put on the market by the licensee and appropriate requirements spelled out in the licence agreement. In this connection, the licence agreement should also include a provision requiring the licensee to mark the licensed products, and also their packaging, with trade mark and copyright legends, the wording of which also needs to be previously approved by the licensor. As regards advertising and sales promotion materials for the products, again, the licensor's requirements need to be specified in the agreement. In practice, to avoid bureaucratic delays in obtaining the necessary approvals, which should always be required in writing, provision is often made in the licence agreement for approval to be 'deemed' where, after a certain period of time (eg five working days) there has been no express disapproval, merely silence. Provision should also be made for approval in one format to be 'deemed' to cover approval in a similar format, provided the context remains essentially the same. Without such quality control approvals, the value of the logo may suffer and also its marketability.

Related to quality control is product liability, which, in view of the strict (that is, no fault) liability which applies within the European Union, needs to be addressed in the licence agreement. For the purposes of the European law, there is a wide definition of the term 'manufacturer', which includes those who affix or allow to be affixed their name or mark to products manufactured by someone else under their authority. In other words, licensors can also be held legally liable for defective products produced by their licensees, which cause harm to consumers. This could be a particular problem where, for example, toys and novelty items for children are licensed. It is usual to include indemnity provisions in favour of the licensor in the licence agreement and back them up with product liability insurance requirements on the part of the licensee.

Like other licence agreements, sports logo licence agreements are entered into on a personal basis, in the sense of the personal characteristics, for example, technical competence and financial standing, of the licensee. Accordingly, the licence agreement should be expressly stated to be a contract *intuitu personae* that can be terminated in the event that such personal characteristics cease to exist. For example, this can occur on a change of ownership or control of the licensee, rendering the new owner of the licensee unsuitable for some commercial or financial reason. As a further protection, it is also usual not to allow any assignment or sub-licence of the licence outside the licensee's corporate group, which needs to be defined, without prior written approval. In such cases, licensees will often require the inclusion of wording, where not legally implied, to the effect that such consent is not to be unreasonably withheld or delayed.

The consequences of termination or expiration of the licence agreement are particularly important in the case of a licence of a sports event logo. Due to the cyclical nature of sports events, for example, the FIFA World Cup takes place every four years, the circulation of out of date merchandise can cause confusion and thus commercial and marketing problems. It is usual, therefore, to include a provision in the licence agreement requiring the licensee to clear the market of licensed products within, say, six months of termination or expiration, after which any remaining products/stocks should be destroyed.

As with any other kind of product licensing agreement, for a sports logo licensing programme to be successful, it is necessary to include appropriate provisions in the licence agreement for protecting and defending the intellectual property rights concerned against infringements by third parties. Counterfeiting is particularly rife as far as consumer goods bearing prestigious sports event logos are concerned. As usual with counterfeiting, the Far East is often the source of these illicit products, but counterfeiting also occurs nearer home in Europe. In the European Union alone, it has been estimated that the loss to its economy from counterfeiting and piracy is in the order of £250 billion a year![11] It is necessary, therefore, to include clear provisions in the licence agreement for reporting and dealing with such infringements. To be successful, these provisions will call for a close liaison and collaboration between the licensor and the licensee, particularly as to who is responsible for taking what kind of action, including legal proceedings, and within what time scale. There will also need to be appropriate indemnities as to legal costs and other expenses where action is required by the licensee on behalf of the licensor. There are a number of legal measures, including invoking the

---

11   Sports marketing industry figures.

assistance of Trading Standards Officers and HM Customs & Excise, that can be taken in the UK against counterfeiting and counterfeiters.[12]

Another particularly important and sensitive problem area is confidentiality. Sports bodies like to control the dissemination of confidential information relating to their business activities. Thus, the licence agreement will include appropriate provisions on keeping the terms of the agreement strictly confidential, especially the financial details, and the handling of press inquiries and the making and contents of press releases relating to the licensing programme. Confidentiality is also an important matter for the licensee.

In licence agreements, which cover countries within the EU, particular attention needs to be paid to exclusive and territorial arrangements, which may fall foul of the EU competition rules,[13] which especially prohibit attempts to divide up the single market through restrictive agreements based on nationally granted intellectual property rights. For example, anti-competitive trade mark licensing agreements have received a great deal of attention from the EU competition authorities over the years. Where agreements are found to infringe the competition rules, substantial fines, up to 10% of the worldwide group turnover of the offender, can be imposed, even where the breach is committed by a small EU subsidiary. In certain circumstances, it is possible to get an individual or a so-called 'block' exemption from the competition rules under Art 81(3).

In international sports logo licensing agreements, another important clause to include is one on 'force majeure'. This can be especially relevant where the licence covers developing countries. The clause will be a full blown one in US and UK agreements, where everything, including as they say the 'kitchen sink', needs to be covered, to short form clauses, in the case of licences for civil law countries, under whose civil or commercial codes' full blown *force majeure* provisions are implied.

Likewise, where the sports logo licensing arrangements transcend national boundaries, it is also necessary to include 'proper law' and 'dispute resolution' clauses in the licence agreement. Rather than leave the matter to chance under the rules of private international law, it is advisable for the parties to expressly agree in advance in the licence agreement on the law, which will apply in the event of a dispute. English and Swiss law are popular choices in international sports logo licence agreements. Likewise, the parties need to include an express provision in the licence agreement on the manner in which any disputes will be settled, choosing between the courts, arbitration and other forms of dispute resolution, including mediation.[14]

Conclusions

Although it has not been possible to go into very much detail, the EU competition aspects alone merit an entire book to themselves, it is clear that sports logo licence agreements have certain peculiarities and characteristics, which need to be taken into account when negotiating and drafting them, especially international ones.

Whilst such licensing programmes can and do deliver financial benefits to licensors and licensees alike, there are many traps for the unwary. The need for specialist legal advice, therefore, cannot be overstated or underestimated. This is an area where the old adage 'prevention is better than cure' is particularly apposite.

---

12   These measures are summarised in Everitt, C, 'Fighting the fakes' (2000) 8 Sports and Character Licensing 22–25.

13   Now enshrined in EC Treaty, Arts 81 and 82.

14   See earlier, Chapter 6.

MAXIMISING THE FINANCIAL RETURNS FROM INTERNATIONAL SPORTS LICENSING

One area of sports business that is growing significantly, year on year, is commercial licensing related to major international sports events, such as the Olympic Games and the FIFA World Cup.[15] The right to brand merchandise with well-known and prestigious sports event logos, symbols, emblems and a mark, such as the five interlinked Olympic rings, is a much sought after and very valuable one.

This is particularly and increasingly so in our electronic and internet age, which has spawned sports computer games. These have grown into a multi-billion-dollar worldwide industry. In several sports, licensed games are now generating more revenues than traditional forms of sponsorship and are catching up with the mega sums being paid for sports broadcasting rights.[16]

Not only is a well negotiated licensing deal crucial to maximising returns, but so also is a well drafted licensing agreement. This is a specialised field containing traps for the unwary and inexperienced. So, in this section, the ways and means, contractually speaking, of maximising the financial returns from sports licensing agreements will be discussed. But first of all, a word or two about getting the basic deal right, from a business and financial point of view.

Getting the Deal Right

The most important point to be clear about is the nature and scope of the rights being granted, especially the products and territories that can be commercially exploited, and whether they are exclusive or not. A badly constructed deal, lacking clarity and precision on these matters – and, indeed, on other matters too – will inevitably produce a badly drafted legal agreement. This will lead to uncertainties and misunderstandings, and, in turn, to disputes, which could well turn out to be lengthy and costly to resolve. If the deal does not make commercial sense it often does not make legal sense either. In other words, it is difficult – if not impossible – to draft a meaningful and legally enforceable agreement.

Due Diligence

Allied to being clear about the rights to be granted is the need to do some basic 'due diligence'. In particular, the prospective licensee needs to check on the legal ownership of the rights being licensed. This can be difficult in some sports (for example, deducing title to 'Formula 1' or the 'World Cup'). And also the extent needs to be checked to which these rights can be legally protected, by intellectual property law (eg as trade marks or as copyright material) and/or otherwise (here the law on unfair competition and 'passing off' may well be relevant), against any claims or unauthorised actions by third parties.

The legal nature of the rights to be granted and their legal strength or vulnerability are subjects in their own right and would need a chapter to themselves to do justice to them. Suffice to say that the outcome of these investigations will affect the value of the rights to be granted and the amount to be paid for them. In some cases, they may even make the licensing deal unattractive financially to a prospective licensee and too risky to pursue. At the end of the day, it is a risk assessment and management exercise.

---

15 See McAuliffe, S, 'Non-football sports licensing: the hardest game in the world' (2000) 9 Sports and Character Licensing 22.

16 See Couchman, N, Chue, J and Dorrett, S, 'Computer games licensing' (2000) 2 Sports and Character Licensing 12.

Timing

From the point of view of the licensor, in an international sports licensing programme, careful consideration should be given to the timing of the release of the various rights in the various territories and the granting of various rights, especially so-called 'electronic rights' (internet and other new media), to suitable prospective licensees, on a 'horses for courses' basis, in order to maximise the financial returns. Furthermore, sponsorship and celebrity endorsement of computer games can add further significant value to the licences granted by sports bodies and other rights holders for sports related computer games. Advertising can also add value to the licensed products.

Tax Structuring

Another important financial consideration for optimising the financial returns on international licensing transactions is the 'domicile' of the Licence Agreement for tax purposes. If possible, the licensor should take advantage of any no or low taxation jurisdiction. For example, it may be worth tax sheltering the royalties through a 'Holding Company' in The Netherlands, taking advantage of their favourable tax treatment of such corporate entities and also their extensive network of double taxation agreements around the world.

The structuring of the licensing deal, from a tax mitigation point of view, is not only legal (tax evasion only is illegal – in fact, it is a criminal offence), but also prudent. However, as legal and administrative costs are involved in any tax avoidance scheme, especially where it is necessary to form intermediary companies, a cost–benefit analysis should be made to ensure that, in the final analysis, there are real financial savings to be made.

Getting the Agreement Right

There are a number of provisions that can – and, indeed, should – be included in sports licence agreements that will help to protect the financial side and maximise the returns to the licensor from the deal. A brief look at them follows.

Consideration and Payment

One of the most important clauses in any commercial agreement is the 'consideration' clause. And this is also true in the case of sports licence agreements, especially international ones – that is, those whose rights and obligations transcend national boundaries. Sport and sports events tend now to be global in nature and scope.

The 'consideration' clause defines the *quid pro quo* in return for which the licence is granted. The consideration is usually a financial one, rather than a mere exchange of mutual promises, which, in English contract law, is a sufficient basis on which to make the agreement legally binding. In other words, the consideration clause defines the 'price' of the licence and the payment terms. In a licence agreement, the payment for the rights granted is usually in the form of periodic payments ('royalties'), but can be a lump sum ('licence fee'), or, on occasions, a combination of both.

In the former case, the basis, on which the royalties are to be calculated, needs to be precisely defined. If, as is usual, they are to be charged on the 'net invoice price' of the 'licensed products' (as defined in the licence agreement), the former term also needs to be carefully defined. For example, what about 'trade discounts'; what about sales to 'associated companies' (which also need to be defined) of the licensee; what about defective and returned goods; and so on? In practice, it may aid clarity to set out any royalty formula, particularly a sliding scale one, in mathematical terms in an Appendix to the licence agreement.

There should also be provisions defining when the royalty is earned ('accrues') and when (the 'periodic payment dates') and where ('named bank account') the royalties are to be paid ('settlement'). In the case of transfer of funds internationally, the form (eg electronic transfer) and who bears the corresponding costs (normally the licensee) are also matters to be specified in the Licence Agreement.

Accounting and Audits

Likewise, there need to be provisions on sales accounting, delivery of royalty statements and the right of the licensor (or its agent) to inspect and audit the licensee's accounting records. Incorrect accounting can be the result of human error, misinterpretation of the relevant contractual provisions, or intentional and fraudulent under accounting on the part of the licensee. In practice, it is normally either of the first two causes rather than the third one.

As the majority of under-accountings are not obvious from the royalty statements issued by the licensee, the auditing provision is thus an important one, in practice, for safeguarding the financial interests of the licensor. As Mike Skeet, a partner in the Royalty Compliance Organisation, has pointed out:

> Undertaking an audit does not have to be confrontational; it is merely good business practice, which ... can be beneficial to all parties involved.[17]

Currency

In the case of international licence agreements, it may also be necessary to specify the 'currency of obligation' (that is, the currency in which the right to payment accrues) and the 'currency of payment' (that is, the currency in which the payment must be made) of the licence fee and/or the royalties when the two are different.

For example, where the licensed goods are sold in CFAs (Central African francs) and the royalties calculated on this basis, but the payment of them is to be made in US dollars. In such cases, the exchange rate to be used, or the method of calculating it, for making the conversion from the one currency to the other also needs to be specified in the licence agreement. The African Continent is becoming increasingly important as a venue for the holding of major sports events and licensing deals there are likewise growing in popularity. If FIFA decide to 'rotate' the venues for the World Cup, the African Continent is tipped to be the first to benefit from such a scheme.

Exchange Control

Furthermore, provision will also need to be made for exchange control implications for payments from those countries that limit the transfer of funds abroad, especially 'hard currency' (in international licensing agreements usually US dollars), and require governmental approvals of licence agreements. A supplementary provision will need to be included to cover the case of failures

---

17   Skeet, M, 'Royalty accounting – fact or fiction' (2000) 5 Sports and Character Licensing 10.

to obtain exchange control approvals within a specified period of time (say 90 days) and their consequences; for example, the right to terminate the licence agreement and the corresponding legal and practical effects.

Force Majeure

Payments abroad may also become impossible for reasons other than exchange control – for example, strikes, civil commotion, and even war. In such cases, a *'force majeure'* clause covering what happens in such situations will need to be included in the licence agreement.

In England and other countries following the common law tradition (for example, the US), all the possible contingencies and their legal and practical effects will need to be spelled out in this clause. Whereas in civil law countries, reference to the provisions in the corresponding civil or commercial code dealing with cases of *'force majeure'* only needs to be made in the licence agreement, as these provisions will be incorporated by reference and apply automatically.

Withholding Tax

Another important financial issue that needs to be taken care of in the licence agreement is whether payments are to be made free or subject to the deduction of any required withholding tax (often 10% in the case of royalties). To make such a clause effective, in practice, requires a number of formalities and procedures to be expressly laid down in the agreement and strictly followed by the licensee.

As a practical point, it may be useful to set out these and other procedures (for example, payment instructions), particularly as these may change during the term of the licence agreement, in a separate document to the licence agreement. This could be dealt with by the following suggested clause:

> From time to time, Licensor shall issue to Licensee separate written instructions of a procedural or administrative nature, in order to give practical effective to the concepts and principles laid down in this Agreement and Licensee hereby agrees to conform to and comply with any and all such instructions, which shall be deemed to form an integral part of this Agreement.

Set-Off and Interest

Also, the question of the 'right of set-off' – a highly controversial and technical matter in several jurisdictions not least in the UK – between the licensor and the licensee needs to be considered and specifically provided for in the licence agreement. In the experience of the writer, it is generally advisable to expressly exclude any such right in sports cases to avoid accounting problems and disputes.

The right to claim interest on late payments of licence fees and/or royalties will also need to be considered. In the opinion of the writer, this is generally advisable. Therefore, the right will need to be reserved and the rate specified in the licence agreement. But *cave*, in certain jurisdictions, high rates of interest may be legally unenforceable as 'penalties' (for example, in England) or as 'usury' (for example, in Arab countries applying 'Shariah' law).

Sporting Integrity

One final point. To preserve the integrity of the particular sport and/or sports event and its governing body, and, at the same time, to safeguard the intrinsic value of the Sports Licence

Agreement itself, it is usual to include a general provision requiring the licensee, in exercising its rights under the licence agreement, not to do or fail to do anything that might bring the sport, the sports event or the sports governing body into disrepute or contempt.

This clause covers a multitude of possible sins, including producing 'licensed products' of an inferior quality or doubtful taste. However, being of a subjective and broad nature, to aid its legal enforceability – vague terms may be held to be void for uncertainty – it would be advisable to spell things out and preface the clause with some qualifying words such as:

> In the absolute and uncontrolled discretion and opinion of Licensor, whose decision shall, in all cases, be final and binding, Licensee shall not ...

Allied to this need to protect the value and image of the 'licensed products' is the need to control the 'distribution channels' through which they are sold (eg luxury retail outlets rather than mail order catalogues, or even supermarkets, the legal issue in the pending *Tesco Stores/Levi Strauss Jeans* case). In January 2000, Warnaco, the manufacturer and seller of Calvin Klein branded jeans, reached an out of court settlement with Calvin Klein himself over cut-price jeans sold through discount shopping malls in the States.[18]

Conclusions

As will be seen from the above, there are a number of financial, fiscal and accounting matters that need to be addressed and taken into account when negotiating and drafting international sports licensing agreements. Getting these matters right from the outset is vital for maximising the financial returns from such a licensing venture. To ignore or be unaware of them is sheer commercial and financial folly. It is very much a case, therefore, of taking the time and the trouble of paying particular attention to them and being precise. It is a question of being wise before rather than after the event, when, sadly, it may well be too late.

SPORTS SPONSORSHIP AGREEMENTS

Sponsorship is perceived, in many business quarters, as a more attractive alternative to other forms of traditional advertising and promotion, particularly in terms of cost effectiveness, which is always high on the corporate agenda. This is particularly true in the field of sports sponsorship, in which an ever-increasing range of prestigious national and international sports events are on offer for commercial exploitation. What is sponsorship in general and sports sponsorship in particular?

Sponsorship is a commercial arrangement whereby a sponsor pays a certain sum of money (the sponsorship fee) and/or provides certain products, services or other facilities (value in kind) to the sponsored party, in return for which the sponsor is granted certain rights of association with the sponsored party, through which the sponsor can promote the image of the sponsor and sale of the sponsor's products and/or services.

In the sporting context, the sponsor's association is generally with the sponsored party's sports event and usually with the emblems, logos and mascot (the event marks), which identify and distinguish the particular sport's body and its event. For example, in the case of the Olympic Games,

---

18 See 'Speedo maker seeks debt shelter' *The Guardian*, 12 June 2001.

the Olympic Rings of the International Olympic Committee and the particular distinctive emblems, incorporating the Rings, of the Organising Committee of the Host Nation and the National Olympic Committees participating in the Olympic Games. Combined with the sponsorship rights are usually 'designations' – the right of the sponsor to describe itself as 'Official Sponsor of the XYZ Event' in all advertising and promotional literature and also on all product packaging, labelling and merchandising materials.

Commercial Opportunities

Sports sponsorship offers a wide range of commercial rights and opportunities, including:

- Title sponsorship.
- Event sponsorship.
- Broadcast sponsorship of the event.
- Team and individual sponsorship (including corporate logos on team and individual athletes' clothing).
- Official designations (such as official airline and official credit card to the event).
- Official supplierships (such as sports goods and equipment for the event).
- Franchise (such as the exclusive sale of the sponsor's soft drinks at the event) and display rights (the right to mount displays of the sponsor's goods at the event).
- Official programme sponsorship.
- Product and character merchandising (such as official event and team mascots).
- Commemorative items (such as official stamps, pins, coins, stickers).
- Premiums and other promotional items (such as key rings bearing the event marks).
- Corporate hospitality.
- Tickets and access to VIP areas (such as 'The Paddock Club' in Formula 1).

The list is almost limitless depending on the marketing and promotional creativity and ingenuity of the event organisers, sponsors and their advertising agencies and public relations consultants. With the advent of sponsorship of television and radio programmes on 1 January 1991 under the UK Broadcasting Act, there is a possibility of confusion arising in the mind of the general public between an event sponsor and the event broadcast sponsor. This happened in the case of the 1991 World Rugby Football Cup, where Sony was perceived to be the sponsor of the event, whereas, in fact, Sony was the sponsor of the television coverage of the event, much to the discomfiture of Heinz, the sponsor of the event, who had paid a substantially larger sum for the privilege! Rival companies have deliberately used such confusion on subsequent occasions in relation to other sporting events as a form of 'ambush marketing'.[19]

Likewise, title sponsorship of an event adds a further complicating dimension, which needs careful handling, both commercially and legally, to avoid 'conflict marketing' and thereby diluting the value of the sponsorship rights granted. In view of the wide range of sports events, as well as the variety of the 'rights packages' on offer, a sponsor needs to match very carefully the event, the kind of

---

19   See below, p 457 *et seq.*

association and the type of rights acquired with the image of the sponsor company and that of its products/services.

For example, a particular brand of cigarettes may be successfully 'teamed' with an international global sailing event, whereas a particular brand of popular car may 'sit' more comfortably with a football competition. Incidentally, tobacco sponsorship of sporting events in Europe became illegal at the end of 2004 under specific EU legislation.[20] Positioning in marketing, in general, is very important and this is equally true of sponsorship, in particular. Sports sponsorship is, to use a sporting metaphor, is, therefore, very much a matter of 'horses for courses'.

Legal Issues

Apart from the marketing aspects, attention also needs to be paid to the legal aspects of sports sponsorship, especially the contents and the drafting of the corresponding contracts. The sponsorship agreement will need to cover, amongst other things, the following matters:

- The rights being granted.
- Product and/or service category (where there are multiple concurrent sponsorships).
- Territorial issues.
- Warranties (especially by the event organiser regarding broadcast coverage of the event).
- Duration options and renewals of the sponsorship rights.
- Financial terms and conditions.
- Obligations of the event organiser.
- Obligations of the sponsor.
- Public and product liability.
- Insurance.
- Indemnities.
- Access to the venue and accreditations.
- Event cancellation and 'force majeure'.
- Termination.
- Post-termination arrangements and restrictions.
- Options to renew.
- Applicable law and dispute resolution.

Perhaps the most important of the above legal matters is the definition of the rights to be granted to the sponsor and the obligations to be undertaken by the sponsored party (the event organiser). These obligations will include, for example, ensuring 'clean' stadia for the exercise of franchise and advertising rights and 'clean' broadcast signals for the television coverage of the event. Otherwise, the sponsor may find that exclusivity is compromised through a competitor also being associated with the event in some other way, for example, one soft drinks company sponsoring the event, whilst a rival soft drinks company is the title sponsor of the event.

---

20 See below, p 451.

Potential conflicts between other classes of sponsor, within a particular sponsorship hierarchy, also need to be anticipated and suitable provisions included in the corresponding contracts. Thus, the rights and obligations of the parties need to be spelled out in the sponsorship agreement and nothing left to chance or to the parties' goodwill. In particular, the product or service category granted to the sponsor needs to be carefully defined. For example, does the 'soft drinks category' include sports and isotonic drinks and what about mineral waters? If these rights are to be granted to some other sponsor, they need to be expressly excluded from the grant of rights clause in the contract.

Likewise, the sponsor needs to be satisfied that the sponsored party can show a good title to the rights being granted, especially intellectual property rights, such as trade marks and copyright, and also that any rights being retained or reserved by the sponsored party, for any reason or purpose whatsoever, are precisely defined in the contract. Proving title to commercial rights in a sporting event may be easier in theory than in practice. Take the FIFA World Cup, for example; the sponsor of the broadcast coverage of the event will be faced with the following bald statement:

FIFA Statutes, Art 48.1

FIFA, its member associations, confederations and clubs own the exclusive rights to broadcasts and transmissions of events coming under their respective jurisdiction via any audiovisual and sound broadcasting media whatsoever – whether live, deferred or as excerpts.

Inquiries beyond this statement will produce a blank. However, at the very least, the sponsorship agreement should contain a 'warranty' by the sponsored party to the effect that it is free and able to grant the particular sponsorship rights, and this 'warranty' should be supplemented by a corresponding indemnity covering the sponsor against the legal and financial consequences of any breach of it.

As the value of any sports sponsorship will largely depend upon the extent of the broadcast coverage of the event concerned, it is also advisable to include suitable 'warranties' by the sponsored party on the minimum television coverage of the event and also, where appropriate, an obligation on that party to procure that any broadcaster of the event refers to the event using the name of the title sponsor (for example, the 'Coca-Cola such and such sporting event'). Failure to reach the minimum television coverage will be a ground for termination by the sponsor of the sponsorship agreement.

Likewise, the sponsored party should also 'warrant' that the event will be held at the agreed venue and on the agreed date(s). In the event of cancellation and 'force majeure', the circumstances constituting which in an English agreement should be spelled out (in civil law countries this is not necessary as the conditions are implied under the relevant code), appropriate provisions should be included in the contract for a corresponding suspension and/or reduction of the sponsorship fee, if not termination of the contract, depending upon the seriousness and length of time the particular contingency lasts.

As mentioned earlier, in lieu of or in addition to a sponsorship fee, a sponsor may provide the sponsored party with a non-monetary benefit, but nevertheless having value. This is called 'value in kind' (VIK) and needs to be defined for contractual purposes and valued for tax purposes (as to which, see later). In particular, the extent of the sponsor's obligations to provide the value in kind concerned need to be spelled out in the sponsorship agreement. For example, in an 'official office equipment' sponsorship category, the number and type of computers, photocopiers and other specified items of office equipment to be supplied to the event organisers and their officials and the terms of their maintenance, if appropriate, need to be stated.

Often sponsors require an option to renew or extend the sponsorship agreement on its expiration or a right of first refusal. Such clauses need to be carefully drafted too. In the first case, care must be taken not to use loose wording that, in effect, grants an option to renew or extend in perpetuity. For example, to avoid this result, the following wording should be used:

Model extension clause

The Sponsor shall have the right to extend this Agreement for a further period of ... [state the length of time in words and figures] on the same terms and conditions of this Agreement *with the exception of this present clause* ... [emphasis added].

Without the qualifying words, the agreement may be extendable for one year periods for ever. As to rights of first refusal, these are usually accompanied by a 'matching option', which also needs to be carefully worded. Also, depending on the particular circumstances, such a 'matching option', also known as the 'English clause' may raise competition law issues, if the effect is to exclude competitors of the sponsor being able to bid for the sponsorship.

In view of the international nature of sports sponsorship, particular attention also needs to be paid to the legal system which will govern the relationship between the parties, as well as the method and place for resolving any disputes. Alternative forms of dispute resolution, such as mediation by the UK Sports Disputes Resolution Panel or the IOC Court of Arbitration for Sport, rather than traditional ones through the courts or arbitration tribunals, are proving popular and cost effective in practice.

The EU Dimension

The sponsorship of international sports events in Europe also raises the spectre of EU law, especially the Fair Competition Rules.[21] EU competition law needs to be taken seriously, as breaches can lead to fines being imposed by the Commission and the European Court of Justice of up to 10% of the group worldwide turnover of an offending party. Since the decision of the European Court in 1974 in the case of *Walrave & Koch v Association Union Cycliste Internationale*,[22] where the Court held that 'the practice of sport is subject to Community Law in so far as it constitutes an economic activity', sports marketing arrangements generally need to take the EU dimension seriously and fully into account.

In particular, this also applies to sports sponsorship agreements. For example, in 1992, Dunlop Slazenger International were fined 5 million ECUs for applying a general ban on exports of certain squash and tennis balls.[23] And in the *Danish Tennis Federation (DTF)* case,[24] the DTF authorised three manufacturers to label their balls as 'official' and only such balls could be used in DTF tournaments. To qualify for 'official' status did not require any particular technical criteria to be satisfied: the arrangement was purely a revenue-raising exercise. The Commission found the practice as being anti-competitive and ordered the DTF to allow other manufacturers to participate in the scheme.

Exclusivity, territorial and other potentially competitive restrictions in sports sponsorship agreements need, therefore, to be carefully considered and drafted to ensure that they pass muster under the EU competition rules. Apart from fines, breaches of these rules render the agreements concerned void and unenforceable. Using a special procedure, however, agreements that may be problematical from an EU competition law point of view can be 'notified' to the Commission for examination and, even if found to be anti-competitive, fines will be avoided because of such 'notification'. As the 1995 European Court decision in *Bosman* and its aftermath shows, the evolving policy of the European Union in the sports field needs to be taken seriously by all parties involved in

---

21 Now enshrined in EC Treaty, Arts 81 and 82.
22 Case 36/74 [1974] ECR 1405.
23 Case T-43/92 *Dunlop Slazenger v EC Commission* [1994] ECR II-441.
24 OJ C 138/7, 1996.

the practice and commercialisation of sport.[25] In the UK, the Competition Act of 1998 contains similar provisions to the EU competition rules on restrictive agreements and abuse of dominant positions contained in Arts 81 and 82 respectively of the EC Treaty. The 'public interest' aspect is now of very limited application and can be invoked only in exceptional circumstances.

One further matter should be mentioned, namely the vexed question of sponsorship by tobacco companies of sporting events in the EU. This is a complex subject with a long history. The present state of affairs may be summarised as follows. Following the annulment by a ruling of the European Court of Justice on 5 October 2000[26] of the old EU Directive on advertising and sponsorship of tobacco products of 1998,[27] the EU Commission introduced a new proposal on 31 May 2001 to ban tobacco advertising and sponsorship by tobacco companies. This new ban was in force by the end of 2004. Tobacco advertising was already banned in Belgium, Finland, France, Italy, Portugal and Sweden.

Tax Aspects

In view of the mega sums involved in sports sponsorship – a global sponsor of the Olympics is now paying around US$50 million for exclusivity in its particular product or service category – the impact of tax – especially VAT – on both the sponsored party and the sponsor is also of increasing importance. Attention should, therefore, be paid to structuring sponsorship deals in the most tax efficient manner possible.

Fees payable by the sponsor to the sponsored party under international sports sponsorship agreements – that is, those that transcend national boundaries – may be subject to withholding taxes. These vary from country to country and in some countries are not levied at all – for example in The Netherlands. Basically, withholding tax is a payment on account of the tax, which might ultimately be levied. These taxes may be reduced under the provisions of double taxation agreements between the country of the payer of the sponsorship fee and the country of the recipient.

However, double taxation agreements do not apply to VAT which is payable on sponsorship fees and VIK. For this reason, a value needs to be placed on VIK and this value expressed in the sponsorship agreement. Of course, the tax authorities can check this value and, if necessary, put a higher value on VIK to reflect its actual and realistic value. The issue here is whether the cost price or the normal retail price of the VIK is the proper basis for tax assessment purposes. The treatment can vary from country to country.

Taxation is a complex subject and beyond the scope of this section. It is suffice to say that those involved in sports sponsorship agreements – especially international ones – need to take specialist advice to mitigate the effects of tax on their arrangements. From the sponsored party's point of view, a clause can be included in the sponsorship agreement along the following lines:

Model tax free clause

All payments under this Agreement shall be made free of all taxes, levies and imposts of any kind whatsoever, including, but not limited to, withholding, corporation, capital gains and valued added taxes.

---

25 For a comparative examination of issues surrounding sports sponsorship agreements, see Vieweg, K, 'Sponsorship, international sports associations, and litigation – from the perspective of German law' (1998) Nottingham Law Journal 53-60.

26 Case C-376/98; for further information see Pearl, I, 'Kicking the habit' (2001) 4(1) Sports Law Bulletin 15.

27 Council Directive (98/43/EC).

As far as the sponsor is concerned, at the very least, the sponsor should ensure that all payments under the sponsorship agreement qualify as tax deductible expenses for corporation tax purposes and that any other legitimate measures to reduce the tax burden are taken by structuring the sponsorship arrangements accordingly and taking advantage of any applicable Double Taxation Agreements, as well as any low tax jurisdictions.[28]

CORPORATE NAMING RIGHTS

Originating in the States, sports sponsorship has spread across the world and grown into a multi-billion dollar business, as companies and firms have come to realise the value of associating themselves and their products and services with prestigious sports events. As one leading International Sports Marketing Agency has observed:

> ... sports sponsorship has evolved to form an integral part of brand marketing, mature enough for even the most conservative companies to recognise it as a natural, indispensable ingredient in their marketing mix.[29]

In fact, sports sponsorship is now widely perceived as a more attractive alternative to other forms of traditional advertising and promotion, particularly in terms of cost effectiveness, which in these highly competitive times is a crucial consideration. Similar to sports sponsorship, another kind of marketing phenomenon, delivering equally attractive benefits at considerably less cost than traditional advertising, has grown up in the States. This is corporate naming of sports stadiums and arenas. It has been described by one of its users as, 'the new wave in sponsorship ... [which] benefits everybody'.[30]

In this section, the reasons for the rise in popularity of attaching corporate names to stadiums and arenas will be examined, and also at some of the contractual legal issues that the granting and exploitation of the corresponding corporate naming rights can give rise to in practice.

Corporate Naming of Stadiums and Arenas

The modern practice of unconnected corporations buying naming rights of stadiums and arenas seems to have originated in the purchase by the Great Western Bank of the naming rights to the Los Angeles Forum in 1987. Previously, a number of stadiums had been named after their corporate founders, for example, the 'Busch Stadium' in St Louis. The practice of naming stadiums and arenas after corporations has grown over the years, not only in the United States, but also in Canada, and not only in relation to new stadiums and arenas, but also to refurbished ones.[31]

The practice not only provides income to the stadiums and arenas concerned, but also provides the corporations, who hold the naming rights, with very valuable advertising, promotional and public relations benefits. Indeed, without the revenues from the sale of corporate naming rights, many stadiums and arenas, without any financial support from the public sector, would never be

---

28 See website for specimen form of Event Sponsorship Agreement, which will provide the reader with a useful precedent and checklist for negotiating and drafting a sports sponsorship agreement.
29 ISL Corporate Brochure.
30 See Blackshaw, I, 'Corporate naming rights – a new phenomenon in sports marketing' (2002) 1 The International Sports Law Journal April 18-21.
31 See Greenberg, M and Gray J, *The Stadium Game* (1996), Milwaukee: National Sports Law Institute.

built and local communities would suffer by being deprived of modern sports facilities. The sale of corporate naming rights also benefits publicly owned sports facilities by providing additional income that can be used for enhancing them. So, what are the benefits to corporations in holding naming rights of sports facilities?

Corporations benefit from naming rights in a number of ways. The use of a corporate name on a sports stadium or an arena receives exposures and impressions, which are difficult, if not impossible, to quantify in financial terms. Television, radio and the print media all refer to the corporation's name when reporting on events held at that facility. The name of the stadium also appears on tickets, programmes and other consumer items. Also, people can see the name on the external signage when attending, walking, driving, or even flying past the facility.

All of this adds up to a cost effective form of advertising for corporations and their products and services. For example, in 1991, America West Airlines purchased the naming rights to a new arena being built for the 'Phoenix Suns' at a cost of US$550,000 for the first year, with an annual uplift of 3%. During the 1993 NBA Finals, when the 'Suns' hosted the 'Chicago Bulls', a single 30 second commercial spot on NBC cost US$300,000. America West's name and logo were seen countless times at a cost of US$583,495, less than the cost of a one minute television commercial, namely US$600,000.[32]

Corporate naming rights also confer a unique and exclusive kind of benefit on those who hold them, in that they are attached to a relatively limited number of major sports facilities. They enjoy, therefore, a certain enviable *cachet*. They also create goodwill for corporations by allowing them to project a positive image in the community in which the sports stadiums and arenas are located. In other words, they confer certain public relations benefits.

Naming rights can also be the vehicle for raising public awareness of corporations and their products and services in regions where they are starting up or expanding their business operations. Naming rights also allow for cross-promotion through 'product tie-ins' at the sports facilities. For example, in the case of a bank owning the naming rights, they will have the right to have ATMs placed in the stadium or arena. Naming rights often bring with them the right for the corporation to receive, or purchase, a so called 'sky box' or a suite at the stadium or arena for corporate hospitality purposes. Finally, and perhaps most important of all, the costs of purchasing the naming rights can be used by the corporation as tax deductible advertising expenses, under the relevant provisions of the US Internal Revenue Code. These costs are tax deductible in many other countries too, including the UK if reasonably and necessarily incurred.

In order to enjoy the benefits of corporate naming arrangements, the rights themselves need to be well defined and incorporated in, as far as legally possible, water tight agreements. We will now take a look at some of the contractual legal issues that need to be addressed in order to achieve these results and gain the full benefits of the naming rights concerned.

Contractual Legal Issues

As with any kind of rights agreement, perhaps the most important provision of all is the 'grant of rights' clause. This defines the nature and scope of the rights granted, and needs to be drafted very carefully and precisely, to avoid any ambiguities and uncertainties, which can lead to

---

32 See Greenberg, M and Gray, J, *Sports Law Practice* (1998), New York: LEXIS, Chapter 8, s 8.09 (Corporate Naming Rights).

misunderstandings and differences, which, in turn, can lead to disputes, which can be time consuming and costly. For example, are the rights exclusive or non-exclusive? And what is included in the rights package? And equally important, what is excluded?

As part of a growing trend, in addition to the naming rights granted, other commercial opportunities are included as part of a marketing package. These additional rights could include rights to 'sky boxes' or suites for corporate entertaining, franchise rights, including so-called 'pouring rights', particularly important in the case where a soft drinks company is concerned, team sponsorship rights, and even facility financing rights, where a bank or other financial institution is involved. Such 'tying' arrangements may, however, give rise to anti-trust problems in certain circumstances.

For example, in 1995, 'Pepsi' acquired quite a comprehensive package of marketing and promotional rights, as part of its naming deal in relation to a new sports facility for the 'Denver Nuggets' and the 'Rocky Mountain Extreme'.[33] For an undisclosed sum, believed to be between US$35 and 68 million, 'Pepsi' acquired the exclusive naming and distribution rights for the facility, plus sponsorship rights for the 'Nuggets' and the 'Extreme', joint marketing opportunities on television and radio, as well as exclusive marketing rights at other tourist attractions within the entertainment complex surrounding the arena. Quite a stitch up!

Allied to the 'grant of rights' clause is the 'duration' clause, which is equally important. Naming rights can be granted for any length of time ('term'). The longer the term, the greater the value and, of course, the greater the price. In general, however, the rights tend to be granted on an annual renewable basis. If they are granted for a fixed term, an option to renew is often included in the naming rights agreement (see later). Rights granted in perpetuity can cause legal problems – interminable agreements are generally frowned on by the courts and also anti-trust/competition authorities.

Naming rights packages need to be accompanied by certain 'warranties' by the owner of the stadium or arena, to ensure that they are worth the vast sums paid for them. For example, these rights are not worth very much if the stadium or arena does not stage many events in the course of a year. The presence of a professional or collegiate team playing its home games at the facility is normally a contractual requirement in naming rights deals, because it guarantees a minimum number of dates that a facility is in operation. This is covered by warranties on the part of the owner of the facility, who warrants its active use during the term of the naming rights agreement. Of course, in the case of multi-use facilities, that is, those that stage sports and other events, such as concerts, the need for such warranties is not so important. The legal effects and practical consequences of any breaches of such warranties need to be spelled out in the naming rights agreement.

Another important clause in any commercial agreement is the 'consideration' clause. This defines the *'quid pro quo'* for the rights granted. This need not always be money, but can in sponsorship type deals, such as naming rights arrangements, be in non-monetary form, that is, value in kind. This could, for example, in the case of a soft drinks company, be the supply of free product to a sponsored team. In any case, the amount of the monetary consideration and the value of the benefit in kind need, in each case, to be clearly defined. So also do the payment arrangements – when and where they are to be made. Often, in naming rights deals, instead of a lump sum fee, an annual rights fee is payable, subject to a yearly uplift to cover inflation. This also needs to be spelled out in the naming rights agreement, especially if the uplift is linked to some 'cost of living index'. The payment of

---

33   *Ibid.*

interest for late payments, the rate of interest and when it accrues also need to be covered in the agreement.

The 'termination' clause is also an important contractual provision. The grounds for termination, who may terminate and the effects of termination need to be precisely stated in the agreement. A provision is often included whereby non-material breaches can be remedied by the party in default within a specified period of time, say, 15 days, failing which the other party may terminate the agreement. What is material and what is not material needs to be defined and also whether 'days' are natural days or working days.

On expiration of the naming rights agreement, the naming rights automatically come to an end by 'effluxion of time'. So, what happens then? In theory, the owner of the stadium or arena can grant the rights to someone else. But this may prove costly to the owner, who would have to incur the expense of repainting or replacing signs, reprinting tickets, producing new seat tags and other items, such as plastic cups and paper napkins, and so on, depending on the extent of the 'branding'. It is more likely that the owner will seek to do a new deal with the former holder of the naming rights.

From the point of view of the rights holder, it is prudent and advisable to include in the naming rights agreement an option to renew the agreement, or, at the very least, a right of first refusal to be granted the naming rights. Any such pre-emptive right should be accompanied by a 'matching option' in favour of the former holder of the naming rights. In other words, if the conditions for granting the rights for a new term are refused by the former holder of them, because they are financially unacceptable, then the rights owner cannot offer a third party better terms than those he refused from the former holder of the rights, without first offering the same deal to the latter. It will be appreciated that options to renew, rights of first refusal and matching options need to be very carefully drafted. In particular, the periods of time and the manner in which they are to be exercised need to be precisely defined – for example, notices to be given. Options and pre-emptive rights can also raise anti-trust/competition law issues.

Another important contractual provision to include in a naming rights agreement is a 'confidentiality' clause. For business reasons, the parties to the agreement will wish to keep the terms confidential, especially the financial ones. They will also wish to control releases of information to the media, as well as the holding and conduct of any press conferences. Any secrecy obligations will be subject to any requirements by law to disclose any confidential material to third parties, for example, in court proceedings. Furthermore, any information of a confidential character that is already in or subsequently enters the public domain, through no fault of the parties to the agreement, is not subject to the secrecy obligations undertaken by them.

Lastly in the naming rights agreement, the parties can – and should – include a provision stating the form of dispute resolution that is to apply in the event of a dispute. This provision should also include other practical details, such as, in the case of mediation, the body that will organise the mediation and appoint the mediator and where the mediation will take place and other practical arrangements.[34] The dispute resolution clause may include a number of alternative forms of dispute resolution, specifying the circumstances in which they will apply. For example, the clause may provide for expert determination for settling technical matters, such as intellectual property and

---

34 See earlier, Chapter 6 for further information. Mediation could be carried out by, for example, the IOC Court of Arbitration for Sport, based in Lausanne, Switzerland, and also by the London-based UK Sports Dispute Resolution Panel.

financial disputes, and mediation in all other cases. In any case, the parties can always agree on an ad hoc basis, but perhaps the most important point here is 'agree'. It is often better to agree in advance when the situation is less emotive.

The European Scene

As with many things, sports ideas and developments in the United States have a habit, in time, of spreading to the rest of the world – and not least to Europe. New sports stadiums and arenas, similar to the sports and entertainment complexes that are growing up in the States, are beginning to be developed in Europe; for example, the 'Hartwall Arena' in Helsinki, Finland. This seats up to 14,000 people and features 78 suites. It is a multi-purpose facility, and has established itself as the country's top location for sport, music and corporate events. It incorporates many media facilities, including state of the art broadcast production and editing suites. In the UK, Bolton Wanderers play at the 'Reebok' Stadium and Stoke City at the 'Britannia' Stadium.

The Oval cricket ground in London has been re-named 'The AMP Oval' after the Australian Financial Services Company 'AMP', which has paid £2 million for a five year exclusive naming rights deal.[35] Incidentally, it should be noted that the use of such naming rights has an impact on the traditional sports marketing model of a 'clean stadium' from a branding and promotional point of view.

Generally speaking, Europe tends to be soccer mad and tends to build only soccer stadiums rather than multidisciplinary and all purpose ones. However, the promoters of new soccer stadiums being planned and built, like the new Wembley Stadium in London, are beginning to realise that to rely only on gate receipts is not enough. These stadiums need to generate revenues from other activities. One solution to this financial problem is to incorporate arenas into them to attract other sports, such as track and field, and other events, such as pop concerts. The actual format/composition of the new Wembley Stadium continues to be a source of controversy.

As part of the funding process, additional revenues can also be generated from various kinds of sponsorship, including the sale of corporate naming rights. Arsenal have concluded a 15 year deal worth over £100 m with Emirates airlines for naming rights for its new 60,000-seater ground at Ashburton Grove, to be known as the Emirates Stadium.[36] As is increasingly happening in the States, naming rights are being combined with other marketing and promotional packages. However, packages, like the Pepsi one previously mentioned, may encounter anti-trust/competition law problems. In any case, we Europeans can, no doubt, learn from our American cousins how to deal with and overcome any legal threats of this or, indeed, any other kind. In many respects, that is exactly how the European Competition Rules have developed, based on the experience of the Anti-Trust Authorities in the States and adapted to the European situation.

Likewise, Europe can also learn from the practice in the States of granting naming rights to lending institutions that finance private sports facilities. In these cases, the bank or finance house arranging the finance acquires the naming rights to the new facility and uses the naming rights fees to reduce the debt repayments on the loan. It also acquires valuable promotional and marketing rights as part of the rights package as well. Furthermore new and existing stadiums and arenas in Europe will also need to learn from the States who are wiring up their facilities to allow spectators to take full

---

35 See (2001) 20(7) Sponsorship News, July.
36 'Arsenal name new ground', http://news.bbc.co.uk/sport1/hi/football/teams/a/arsenal/3715678.stm, 5 October 2004.

advantage of the digital and interactive age directly from their seats, allowing them, *inter alia*, to receive and send emails.[37] Such developments also offer further marketing opportunities for creative sports marketers.

Conclusions

Corporate naming rights, a new kind of sports sponsorship, are a growing marketing phenomenon in the States and are beginning to spread elsewhere, including Europe. They offer a wide range of benefits to stadium and arena owners and corporations wanting to associate themselves and their products and services with major sports and sports events.

As further investment in new sports facilities in Europe grows, to meet the increasing demands of event organisers, sports players and spectators alike, corporate naming rights packages are likely to increase in Europe, as they are continuing to do in the States, particularly those linked to financings of new stadiums and arenas. The new National Stadium, whether it is built at Wembley or elsewhere, could benefit financially from a corporate naming rights arrangement. Like other kinds of commercial arrangements, they need to be well defined and incorporated in well drafted agreements. And, where disputes do arise, these need to be settled by the most appropriate and effective means available, not forgetting the new forms of alternative dispute resolution especially mediation.

SPORTS SPONSORSHIP AND AMBUSH MARKETING

Although the marketing of sports events in the States is long and well established, a new sports marketing industry in Europe is fast developing. This is the result of a growing appreciation and recognition amongst marketing executives of European companies and firms of the value of associating themselves and their products and services with sport and sports events, as part of an integrated corporate marketing communications programme. Perhaps the most important part of the sports marketing mix is sponsorship, which has become a multi-billion dollar industry.[38]

An ever-increasing range of prestigious national and international sports events are on offer for commercial exploitation. Sports licensing is also growing in popularity as a corporate marketing tool. Whereas sponsorship involves the placing of a corporate trade mark on a sports product, licensing involves the placing of a sports trade mark on a corporate product. This section will examine what sports sponsorship is; what value it offers; why 'ambush marketing' has become a problem for sponsors and the organisers of sports events; and what can be done – legally or otherwise – about it.

What is Sports Sponsorship?

Sponsorship is a commercial arrangement, whereby a sponsor pays a certain sum of money (the sponsorship fee) or provides certain products, services or other facilities (value in kind or in sports

---

37   See 'Stadia take technological leap' (2000) 44 SportBusiness 44–45.
38   ISL Corporate Brochure.

marketing jargon 'vik') to the sponsored party, in return for which the sponsor is granted certain rights of association (official designation) with the sponsored party, through which the sponsor can promote its own image as well as the sale of its products and/or services.

In the sports context, the sponsor's association is with the sponsored party's sports event and also with the emblems, logos and mascots (the event marks) that identify and distinguish the particular sports body and its event, for example, the Olympic Rings of the IOC and the particular distinctive emblems (incorporating the Rings) of the Organising Committee of the Host Nation and the National Olympic Committees participating in the Olympic Games. Sports sponsorship results in a transfer of the essential values and properties of the sponsored party and its events to the sponsor's business organisation and, ultimately, to its products and/or services, thereby raising the sponsor's profile and standing in the community (offering public relations opportunities and advantages) and amongst its existing and potential customers.

In addition, sponsorship of sports events brings with it the right for the sponsors to be present and entertain employees, customers and others at the events. The ability to offer corporate hospitality at a prestigious sports event, such as the Olympic Games, is a very valuable commercial right and marketing tool.

What is the Value of Sports Sponsorship?

Sports sponsorship offers a wide range of commercial opportunities to sponsors.

Amongst other things:

- they can sponsor the event;
- they can have title sponsorship;
- they can sponsor the broadcast coverage of the event;
- they can sponsor the official programme;
- they can sponsor the official film;
- they can sponsor the official video;
- they can sponsor teams participating in the event; and
- they can sponsor the official commemorative book.

Its value also lies in the fact that the sponsor is given exclusivity in the particular product or service category in respect of which the sponsorship rights are granted by the owner of the rights. In view of the wide range of sports events, as well as the variety of rights packages, on offer, the best value to be gained from sports sponsorship depends on the sponsor matching the event, the kind of association and the rights acquired, with the image of the sponsor company or firm and that of its products and/or services it wishes to project to the world and the consumers it wishes to reach. For example, a particular brand of cigarettes or beer may be successfully 'teamed' with an international global sailing event, whereas a particular brand of popular car or a credit card may 'sit' more comfortably with a football competition. Matching, or convergence between the brand and the sports event, is crucial for sponsorship to deliver substantial commercial benefits to the sponsor.

Defining Ambush Marketing

The increasing popularity and value of sponsorship of high profile and media attractive international sports events, such as the Olympic Games, and the increasing sums being paid by sponsors for the privilege of being associated with them,[39] has spawned its own particular brand of unfair competition, called 'ambush marketing'.

Ambush marketing occurs when a company or firm claims an association with a sports event, which it does not have and, perhaps more importantly, for which it has not paid a penny. In such a case, sponsors do not get value for the considerable sums they have expended on the particular sponsorship. In fact, they get very angry with the event organisers when it occurs and look to them to stop it.

Mandel, N, 'Ambush marketing'

What impacts on sponsorship is when you don't get value. That happens when ambush marketing is allowed to occur. Let's get this straight. Ambush marketing is not clever marketing. It is stealing, it is thievery. Michael Payne [Marketing Director] of the IOC got it right when he called it 'parasite marketing'. You know what parasite means. It is when one organism lives off another with no benefit to the host.[40]

Ambush marketing not only adversely affects sponsors; it also prejudices sports events organisers. Mandel believes that this kind of unfair marketing practice dilutes events and causes confusion in the minds of consumers. Ambush marketing may take many forms. It may arise, for example, where one company is the event sponsor and another is event broadcast sponsor. This happened in the 1991 World Rugby Football Cup, where Sony was perceived to be the sponsor of the event, whereas Sony, in fact, was the sponsor of the television coverage of the event and Heinz was one of the major sponsors of the event, having paid a substantially larger sum for the privilege!

It may also occur as a result of a comparative advertising programme, as happened in the case of American Express in relation to the exclusive sponsorship by Visa (in the official credit card category) of the 1992 Albertville Olympic Games. In this case, an injunction was granted by the Paris High Court to stop American Express from continuing with its unlawful advertising campaign, to the effect that you can leave your Visa cards at home because American Express cards can take you to Albertville.

Ambush marketers also try to muscle in on prestigious sporting events by buying 'commercial air time' around the screening of the events, for sums considerably less than the costs of sponsorship packages, with a view to causing confusion in the minds of unsuspecting viewers and gaining an unfair marketing advantage over their competitors.

Verow, R, Lawrence, C and McCormick, P, *Sport, Business and the Law*

Examples Of Ambush Marketing

(a) Unauthorised use of intellectual property rights

This may involve the manufacture and sale of merchandise products bearing the name and logo of the event or of some or all of the participants in the event. Typically, an event organiser and some of its participants will appoint an official kit supplier who will be authorised to use identified intellectual property rights (typically registered or unregistered trade mark). The unauthorised supplier will effectively infringe these rights by illegally selling their own infringing merchandise. The remedies for

---

39   An exclusive global sponsorship package of the Olympics costs around US$50 million and the sponsor will have to spend four times that amount to make it work.

40   Remarks made by Norman Mandel, Business Affairs Counsel, the Coca-Cola Company, one of the world's leading marketing companies and biggest sponsors of international sports events, at the Global Sports Law Conference, Cardiff, November 1999.

such action tend to be an application for an injunction in the civil courts or else search and seizure using the various criminal remedies contained in trade mark and copyright legislation in the UK and abroad.

(b) Advertising

Advertising is a useful medium in which to 'ambush' an event. The bulk purchase of advertising in selected media in and around an event by an `unofficial' supplier seeking to take advantage of the name and reputation of the event is relatively straightforward. Indeed, such advertising need not even make specific reference to the event, but just to the sport or activity involved. Such reference is unlikely to infringe any intellectual property right but, if well managed by the ambusher, can result in a high identification on the part of the public with that advertiser and the sport or event in question.

Many important events will attempt to tie up advertising at a stadium, advertising on the route to and in the vicinity of the stadium as well as, to the extent permissible and possible, broadcast advertising. It is broadcast advertising which, if bought up by an unofficial supplier can saturate the official sponsor's exposure. In such a situation, there is unlikely to be any legal remedy unless the advertiser oversteps the mark. The best action tends to be preventative. That is to say, appropriate contractual obligations should be obtained by the rights holders to limit the sale of advertising space to competitors in and around events and, wherever possible, to offer a first option to official partners to broadcast advertising. Although great care must be taken by all the parties involved to avoid any competition or problems intrinsic in such extensive and exclusive arrangements it should be possible and is certainly desirable to do so.

(c) Broadcast sponsorship

Although broadcast sponsorship is increasingly coming within the control of rights owners who tend to deal with such rights when negotiating broadcast contracts, it remains a very effective way of ambushing the event without actually being an official partner of the event itself. Broadcast sponsorship can diminish and in the right circumstances even negate the value of event sponsorship. The most obvious solution to avoid this is to ensure that all the rights in broadcast events are dealt with together, at least giving an events sponsor the opportunity to cover the transmission and be its broadcast sponsor if it wants. If it chooses not to do that then a simple restriction ensuring that no competitor of the event sponsor can be the broadcast sponsor should provide the degree of comfort required.

(d) Joint promotions

Another more subtle form of ambush marketing can involve joint promotions between official sponsors and other businesses who have not paid to be a commercial partner. For example, the joint promotion between the official airline of an event and an insurance company of its choice could also give the impression that the insurer is an official supplier to the event. Joint promotions between official partners and any third parties are usually dealt with in the sponsorship agreement.

(e) Competitions and promotions

Although competitions and promotions between rights owners or official partners and other commercial partners are quite common, unauthorised competitions and prize promotions represent a useful and valuable method of exploiting the goodwill of an event or a sport. It is quite difficult to control many competitions and prize promotions as they may be little more than generic in their scope; ie, they are simply football competitions or rugby prize promotions and bear no relation to a particular event, except for the fact that they share a sport in common. Again, these situations are unlikely to give rise to an actionable legal wrong.

(f) Pourage agreement

The sale of products at events is a useful and high profile way for certain types of potential sponsors (usually soft drinks and fast food suppliers) to both raise their profile in association with a sport and also to sell products. A 'popular' form of ambush marketing (although it is perhaps not properly viewed as such) involves a commercial tie up between such a supplier and the owners of a venue. It is often the case that a rights owner will not own the venue where its competition takes place, so it must ensure that its agreement with the venue owner provides a 'clean' venue. The one category where this is likely to be very difficult to achieve is in the category of pourage agreement, where venues tend to conclude longer term agreements which provide certain commercial advantages to them. These are often in the nature of franchise or concession stands which are expensive to set up and maintain, and very often venue owners are not equipped or willing to manage such premises other than by such arrangement.

The important point for rights owners and their official partners is to ensure that the grant of such franchise or concessions does not go hand-in-hand with a grant of other commercial rights over the venue such as the right to re-name or the right to place a large number of advertising hoardings at the venue.

(g) Corporate hospitality and ticketing

A seemingly innocuous method of ambushing an event is to buy up tickets for the event and offer hospitality packages which are not being sanctioned or approved by the rights owners, who usually keep a tight control over such activities. The ability to control tickets and corporate hospitality is often an integral part of the attractiveness of an event to its official partners, who regard it as an important part of their package of rights and, effectively, an important competitive tool and method of 'oneupmanship' over their business rivals. Fortunately for rights owners and commercial partners, such unofficial activities do not tend to involve a significant misappropriation of the goodwill of an event.[41]

But whatever subterfuge and creativity 'ambush marketers' use to claim a false association with a major sports event with the intention of attracting some of its goodwill to themselves and their products and/or services, as Pound has remarked:

An increased vigilance is required to prevent such 'parasite' marketers from poisoning the well and firm action is necessary to expose instances of such activities to the public.

As major sports events proliferate and the costs of sponsorship packages soar through the roof, ambush marketing is not likely to go away. So, what can be done about it?

Combating Ambush Marketing

As happened in the *American Express/Visa* case, legal action can be taken to stop ambush marketing. In the United Kingdom, for example, the law of trespass may be invoked to stop ambush marketing activities near to or within the venue where the sports event is taking place. This would certainly be possible where the 'air space' at a venue is 'invaded' by advertising balloons or light aircraft pulling advertising streamers continually flying over a sports stadium during the staging of a sports event.

Depending on the facts and circumstances of the case, ambush marketing may possibly be prevented by actions for trade mark infringement (where event marks are misused) or 'passing off', the rather rigid principles of which the courts may be prepared to bend and extend to new forms of unfair competition in blatant and appropriate cases. But legal action may not be appropriate where immediate results are required to stop the ambush marketing.

---

41 Verow, R, Lawrence, C and McCormick, P, *Sports Business: Law Practice and Precedents* (1999), Bristol: Jordans, pp 279–80.

Mandel, N, 'Combating ambush marketing'

The legal option is not always the right one. It is not the desired response. Instead there has to be a story told to the general public which makes them care about a particular event. If the money from sponsorship is seen as only going to the players, who are already seen as wealthy, then there is no story. In many sports we do not pay enough attention to what happens to those sponsorship dollars. But the money may, for example, fund youth involvement in sport. If the parasites impact on that then they are stealing from our children and rights holders can issue press releases to tell the world.[42]

This approach of calling a press conference and 'naming and shaming' the ambush marketers has been used by the IOC in combating this form of unfair competition with some success. The power of the world's media can be an effective deterrent or remedy. As Mandel rightly points out, 'the fact is combating parasite marketing is doable. It just takes courage'.

However, it should be borne in mind that 'naming and shaming' may, according to the facts and circumstances of the particular case, fall foul of laws relating to trade libel, injurious falsehood and interference with contractual relations, when citing individual cases to the media or, indeed, to any third party, such as contractors who supply or distribute 'ambush' products. So an event organiser needs to be very sure of its facts and the legal position, before naming and shaming anybody, in order to avoid incurring any such adverse legal consequences and financial liabilities.

In any case, prevention, wherever possible, is better than cure. Anticipating problems and providing for them in advance is the name of the game. Thus, advanced planning helped to thwart 'ambushes' at Euro 2000 (UEFA European Football Championship held between 10 June and 2 July 2000 in Belgium and The Netherlands).[43] And for the Sydney Olympics, held in September 2000, the organisers established a comprehensive Olympic 'Brand Protection Programme' with government backing and the force of law.[44] This programme covered both ambush marketing and the sale of counterfeit merchandise, another kind of unfair marketing practice increasingly facing sporting events organisers.

In particular, the Australian Government passed special legislation to deal with these unfair practices. The Sydney 2000 Games (Indicia and Images) Act 1996 outlawed any unauthorised visual or aural representation suggesting a connection with the Games. The Act also provided protection against the wrongful use of words and images associated with the Games, including 'Olympic', 'Sydney 2000' and 'Summer Games'. The test being whether the use of those words implied that the user was a sponsor or provider of other support to the Games (eg official supplier of goods and services). Also, co-operation between the organisers of the Games and the Australian Customs Authorities also prevented counterfeit 'Olympic' merchandise entering the country. It would seem that these measures were reasonably successful in deterring would be and dealing with actual ambush marketers and counterfeiters taking unfair advantages at the Sydney Olympics, which were officially declared by the President of the International Olympic Committee 'the best Games ever'.

---

42 *Op cit*, fn 40, Global Sports Law Conference (1999).
43 See MacLaverty, O, 'How Euro 2000 organisers tackled ambush marketing' (2000) 8 Sports and Character Licensing 6–9.
44 See 'The fight for Olympic glory' *The Times*, 18 July 2000.

The following extract concerning the Salt Lake City Winter Games in February 2002 details the extensive 'Brand Protection Programme' that was in operation:

Naidoo, U, 'Salt Lake City Brand Protection Programme – ambush marketing and its repercussions'

The Salt Lake Organizing Committee for the Olympic Winter Games of 2002 (SLOC) has a contractual responsibility to protect the Olympic Brand and to provide value to legitimate rights holders. In order to fulfil these duties the organization has a dedicated Brand Protection Team. Besides ambush prevention for the Games the team also has the following objectives and functions:

- Ensure compliance with the Clean Venue Guidelines in the Olympic Charter.

- Protect Olympic Torch Relay presenting sponsors, Coca-Cola and General Motors, against ambush marketing.

- Prevent illegal distribution and sale of counterfeit merchandise.

- Protect intellectual property assets against misuse and infringement (SLOC currently has rights to 55 marks and 145 designations including 'Salt Lake 2002').

- Manage the use and approval of SLOC marks and designations for non-commercial applications.

Our marketing partners, sponsors, suppliers and licensees, make it possible to stage the Games by providing financial resources, technical support and value in kind. As of June 2001 we have 49 domestic sponsors/suppliers and they provide more than $800 million in revenue. This is more than 75% of SLOC's total operating budget. This is separate from International Olympic Committee (IOC) marketing, which has lined up approximately $550 million from worldwide sponsors including Coca-Cola, McDonalds, Visa and Kodak. In return for this huge commitment their products and services are officially associated with the 2002 Olympic Winter Games. Global recognition of the Olympic brand means that such an association is a valuable marketing tool for domestic and worldwide promotions.

Unfortunately, companies that do not have an official association with the Olympic movement engage in aggressive marketing campaigns which deliberately and falsely associate their products and services with the Olympics. This type of activity, known as ambush marketing, wrongly suggests that a company supports or is otherwise affiliated with our event, thereby permitting that company to usurp the benefits of association without paying an appropriate fee. Sometimes ambush marketing takes the form of overt use of protected marks, for which there are clear legal remedies. As equally pernicious are those campaigns where protected marks are not used but the campaign leaves one to infer an association.

If left unchecked, these ambush activities could potentially deprive our marketing partners of their exclusive contractual right to advertise their association with and contributions to the Olympic movement. They also affect the future of the Olympic Movement, as marketing partners are less likely to continue to devote resources if others, through deceptive advertising, can capitalize on the goodwill and favourable publicity of an Olympic association without contributing.

Ambush marketing also misleads the public. It leads consumers into believing a company is associated with the Olympic or Paralympic movement and, based on this false assumption and desire to support the Winter Games, consumers may give their patronage to that company. Working in co-operation with the United States Olympic Committee (USOC) and IOC, SLOC Brand Protection endeavours to prevent business practices which suggest a false, misleading or unauthorized association with the Olympics and Paralympics.

Brand Protection And The Effort to Combat Ambush Marketing

Illegal ambush marketing activities deceive the public, jeopardize programs that support Olympic and Paralympic athletes and teams, endanger the future marketing support for the Games, and hinder the successful staging of the Olympic and Paralympic Winter Games of 2002. The following are specific examples of unlawful ambush marketing practices:

- Commercial use of rights, benefits and privileges without authorization.
- Clear attempt to associate with the Olympic Games or Paralympic Games and benefit from the goodwill of the Games without a license.
- Unauthorized commercial use of copyrighted photographs, illustrations, film or satellite feed.
- Use of words, symbols or pictorials confusingly similar to Olympic or Paralympic marks.
- Use of words, symbols or pictorials covered under the Ted Stevens Olympic and Amateur Sports Acti.
- The production of print publications or television features about the Olympics by non-rights holders for commercial gain, beyond that which is considered appropriate for news and editorial coverage.
- Producing, selling, and distributing counterfeit merchandise.
- Sampling or selling competitive products in Olympic and Paralympics venues owned or leased by SLOC.
- False, misleading or deceptive advertising practices.
- Unfair trade practices.
- Registering website domain names using famous marks in bad faith with intent to profit.
- Warehousing domain names with the intent to profit.
- Using protected marks in 'metatags'.
- Using protected marks in trade names.
- Downloading copyrighted satellite feed of the official Olympic broadcast and transmitting it via the Internet without proper authorization.
- Unauthorized use of athlete appearances, images or likeness for advertising purposes during the Olympic Games in conflict with athlete agreements and Rule 45 of the Olympic Charter.

In the case of such unlawful activity, the Brand Protection team takes action to protect our marketing partners and SLOC's rights. We negotiate contractual agreements that are designed to block competitive activity. We use legal intervention where necessary and appropriate to ensure compliance. We work closely with law enforcement to investigate and prosecute offenders.

There are also many aspects of advertising which are lawful but which we would consider to be ambush marketing. These include:

- Displaying banners and billboards outside the perimeter of Olympic venues.
- Displaying or selling products and services through vendors located nearby.
- Running adverts and promotions in which visuals are used that relate to Olympic sporting events, without making any direct reference.
- Featuring former Olympians in adverts.
- Sponsorship of athletes, teams, National Governing Bodies, Olympic training facilities and other subcategories.
- Third-party tie-ins and promotions.

- Advertising gifts and donations made to the Olympics and related subcategories.

- Engaging in promotions coinciding with the Winter Games, which incorporate the use of validly purchased licensed merchandise and travel awards, which can be legitimately described within the context of advertising and promotions.

- Purchasing uncommitted commercial time on NBC's Olympic broadcast.

- Referencing the location of the Winter Games in print and internet adverts without direct infringement.

- Incorporating news and political commentary into public relations campaigns and news releases.

- Describing factual information only in promotions.

- Running advertising comparative to Olympic marketing partners.

Brighton Ski Resort is a competitor to our Olympic ski venues. It originally ran a billboard advertising campaign which proclaimed 'Proud Host of Zero Olympic Events'. After lengthy negotiations with SLOC's legal department, they were persuaded to change their slogans. They currently read 'No wonder we can't afford to be sued – Ski Passes $35 at Brighton', 'No one can take offence at this – Ski passes $35 at Brighton' and 'Brighton up the Games'.

Similarly local brewery company Wasatch Beer named one of their beers 'Unofficial beer of the 2002 Winter Games'. This was a direct ambush against our official sponsor Budweiser. After SLOC threatened action their beer label now reads 'Unofficial 2002 Amber Ale'. They also published a very clever notice in the local press, which stated, 'as the unofficial beer of a certain event that will take place a year after 2001, we cannot offer international logos or trademarks. We can, however, proudly offer this locally brewed amber ale. It may be unofficial, but we think you'll agree it tastes like a gold medal winner'. Both cases attracted a considerable amount of local Salt Lake City publicity. We have no power to prevent activities that do not directly infringe on SLOC's protected marks, so instead we concentrate our efforts on preventing ambush marketing by inserting anti-ambush provisions in contracts with companies that provide goods, services and property to SLOC. We have also engaged in an education campaign and we try to develop alternate strategies to prevent the ambush having a negative impact on our marketing partners. When we succeed in our endeavours we try to obtain publicity in the hope that this will discourage other ambush marketers.

Educating The Public: The Anti-Ambush Campaign

Our Anti-Ambush Campaign aims to educate and inform the public about brand protection issues and to deter ambush marketing. Three groups are being targeted: law enforcement, key business segments, and consumers. The campaign uses several tactics to communicate our message.

I: Direct Response

Educating on a one-on-one basis. Information is circulated to National Olympic Committees, International Federations, sporting goods trade associations, manufacturers, advertising agencies, and key competitors of our marketing partners. SLOC also attempts to reach conventional retailers, e-commerce sites, embroiders, silk screeners, printers and other businesses within the distribution channel in order to protect official merchandise licensees. Additionally, communications are targeted toward government officials and law enforcement agencies.

II: Presentations

Presentations are made to businesses, community groups, government agencies, venue managers, sponsors, and licensees to familiarize them with SLOC marks usage policies, IOC clean venue guidelines, governing laws, and Brand Protection's surveillance and enforcement procedures. Various conferences, trade shows, seminars, and workshops have been targeted to reach selected business segments in an effort to deter unlawful business practices.

III: Public Relations

With the assistance of SLOC's Media Relations Department, we educate the public through media exposure. A full-page colour advertisement was published in several national magazines and newspapers and on billboards. This lists our principal sponsors and requests that the public supports them. A special educational video 'The Protection of the Olympic and Paralympic Marks' was produced and distributed specifically for this purpose.

IV: Internet

The Brand Protection section of SLOC's saltlake2002.com website (click on 'Operations', then 'Brand Protection') includes information on SLOC marks usage policies, approval process, a Marks Approval Form, governing laws, frequently asked questions, and an Incident Report Form for reporting alleged violations. Official sponsors, suppliers and licensees are also listed on SLOC's website. Individual website owners who have infringing marks among their active content, domain names or 'metatags' are being contacted when warranted. In addition, marks usage policies and guidelines are being distributed via email to owners and operators of e-commerce sites that carry licensed merchandise.

V: Retail Point-of-Sale

We educate retailers on how to avoid counterfeit Olympic merchandise. Focusing primarily on conventional retail stores, we encourage the use of hang tags, labels, stickers, point-of-purchase material, window displays, and concept store merchandising techniques to readily identify Official Licensed Merchandise bearing the Salt Lake 2002 brand.

Conclusion

During the Games, one of Brand Protection's responsibilities will be to patrol in and around the venues to investigate and combat ambush activity. Our event has 10 competition venues in 5 different counties. We also have non-competition venues and celebration sites which need to be monitored. If ambush activity is encountered we take appropriate action to resolve matters through voluntary compliance. If the activity is unlawful and a serious violation of our marketing partners' rights then enforcement and/or legal proceedings may be considered. We aim to contribute to the successful staging of the Olympic Winter Games by ensuring the protection of SLOC's intellectual property assets and the contractual rights of our marketing partners.[45]

Other popular sporting events are also subject to attacks of 'ambush marketing'. In fact, the more popular and successful the event, especially in terms of media exposure, the more vulnerable it becomes. This is certainly true of the very popular London Marathon, which attracts thousands of participants and even more spectators who line the course, in addition to those who watch the event on television. In general, it is more difficult to protect an event from 'ambushers' in a public rather than a private venue. Here are some ideas from the Chief Executive of the London Marathon which have proved effective in practice.

Bitel, N, 'Ambush marketing'

It may seem surprising but some of the most effective controls are in the hands of the event organisers but are not used. They have the ability to control and regulate their own event but do not use it. Just consider some examples:

The sky above the finish of this year's New York City Marathon featured an unofficial air display of planes writing the legend 'Greenwich Mercedes Benz'. It will come as no surprise that Toyota were the

---

45   Naidoo, U, 'Salt Lake City Brand Protection Programme – ambush marketing and its repercussions' (2001) 4(4) Sports Law Bulletin 13.

official sponsor. Indeed as if to illustrate a point I made earlier, Mercedes had been the official car in 1995 but got fed up with the antics of unofficial operators. The result was this spectacular stunt. But it could have been avoided. At the London Marathon we have an air exclusion zone over the course partly because of police and television helicopters and partly at our request. I suppose in truth it also helps that any unauthorised low flying aircraft over our finish area, including Buckingham Palace and Parliament, are more likely to be shot down than sued. I was reminded of some clients of mine for whom we won a case against Gulf Oil. They then hired a plane and towed a sign saying 'Gulf exposed in fundamental breach' over the hospitality tent at the Cheltenham Gold Cup where Gulf were entertaining their most important clients. Unfortunately Lord Justice Parker found this to be a conspiracy to injure and immediately injuncted the miscreants (*Gulf Oil (UK) Ltd v Page and Others* [1987] 3 All ER 14). Well if it could work for Gulf, who had broken their contract, why not the event. After all, Mercedes are doing just the same; they are conspiring to injure the event by pretending they are authorised. Of course it is far better to prevent the infraction by control of the skies.

I have mentioned Nike's billboard campaign – well how did we react? First we ensured that the host broadcaster shot their pictures from angles which did not show the offending posters wherever possible. In the one case where this could not be achieved we placed some large mobile advertising boards and lots of balloons in front of their poster. The result of this self help was that not one billboard was seen by the television viewers. Nike's efforts at ambushing the London Marathon cost about £450,000. In this case their ambushing actually cost them more than the official rights and because of our efforts they certainly did not get value for money.

(1) The problem of the athlete as an advertising site is probably the area where most can be done. The winner of last year's Mercedes Championship was Mark O'Meara who is sponsored by Toyota. Thus for four days the television coverage concentrated on O'Meara who wore a sun visor emblazoned with the name of Toyota. We do not see this sort of ambush on the European Tour because there are rules which prevent players from wearing clothing which endorses competing marks. If you can do it in Europe why not America. In theory a football team could have an official boot and make the player wear those. I remember the 1975 FA Cup Final when Fulham did just that and found themselves in conflict with their Captain Bobby Moore who had a contract with a competing manufacturer. There followed an unedifying farce with the mark of one manufacturer being painted on the boots of another. But this only arose because this was a one off deal by Fulham especially for the final. If this was a condition in Moore's contract from the start then there should have been no problems. Why not try it – because players now believe this to be their right? How far does it extend? Ravinelli's goal celebrations involve him putting his shirt over his head. Ever quick to spot an opportunity, Nike got him to wear an undershirt with a massive Nike logo when playing for Italy – far larger than would be allowed under FIFA rules. Yet he got away with it because of official inaction. It would be so simple to stop this and other ambushes like it. Just introduce a rule modification making it ungentlemanly conduct to have any sponsor's name or mark anywhere on a player except the Club's own kit. Enforce breaches by bookings and sendings off and the message would soon get home.

(2) At the London Marathon, we have to contend with the BAF and IAAF rules which we do not make and we cannot therefore control what the athlete wears in the race. But we can and do control all other appearances. In our contracts we insist that athletes either wear official branded clothing or clothing with no brands at all at press conferences, interviews and photo calls. Old cat eyes would not have appeared at our press conference with his contact lenses! The manufacturers still try to get around this, dressing their athletes in logo festooned hats, pins and even sunglasses as soon as their athlete is about to mount the podium or join the press conference. We have to be vigilant and check the athlete closely before each such appearance. It can be done and for the sake of official sponsors it should.

(3) When selling television rights, event owners can probably insist on the right to prevent ambushers sponsoring the coverage. If we do not take control of this sector we are in danger of alienating the sponsors on whom the events depend. Watching the American coverage of the 1996 New York City

Marathon I got a glimpse of what life could be like here if we are not careful. The broadcaster had sold sponsorship rights not only to the overall coverage but only separately to the Men's results, Women's results, the start lists and so on. Thus Toyota were faced not only by Mercedes in the sky but also Jeep on the screen. How can we expect them to renew if we offer no protection.

(4) Taking this protection of television even further, the Australian rugby league has signed a deal with Channel 9 giving their sponsor, Quantas, first option to all break advertising during games. I said that organisers can only probably protect themselves from television ambush because I recognise that if, say, Sky are paying £670 million for the rights to Premier League Football they are going to want to be able to recoup a lot of that from, say Ford, for the broadcast sponsorship rights and many sports are just grateful to have their sports shown on television without being able to insist on anything. But one word of warning, there is one other problem and that is UK and European competition legislation. I have to say that the Australian example I think could be challenged here. It is one thing to control the advertising during the programme but to deny rivals advertising slots in between programmes might well be said to be a restrictive trade practice or anti-competitive.

(5) One other simple measure that can be taken to prevent ambushing is in relation to granting of rights to official merchandisers. I have seen in America examples where, say, one soft drink company was offering as part of a promotion free official merchandise, key rings, base ball hats and the like, where they were not the official soft drink. They had not produced pirate merchandise but had merely acquired from the official merchandisers the products. Subject to the same caveat about anti-competitive and restrictive trade practices this sort of pirate operation could be avoided by ensuring that in the contract with the official merchandisers provides they cannot supply rivals to official sponsors and suppliers.

(6) We should remember that many sponsors are not buying awareness. McDonalds are now the world's most recognised brand. When they sponsor an event surely their central aim is to sell more products. Therefore one of the most effective things that event organisers can do is to build a package of rights to help the sponsor achieve its aim. Only 2.8% of people may recognise Beefeater as the sponsor of the Boat Race but they are happy. Their package of rights has allowed them to reach their most important customers – the trade – and sell more product. Access to good hospitality and personal appearances by the athletes can be more important than awareness in securing contracts. Coming back to the London Marathon, the reason why our official shoe and clothing company, Asics, are not that upset by Nike's efforts is that Asics make a substantial sum from the official clothing, shoes and merchandise which they sell. This type of direct benefit is difficult for the ambusher to acquire and is therefore exactly the type of benefit that the event organiser has to incorporate in the rights packages which they make available to sponsors.[46]

The following account describes some traditional forms and highlights some new forms of 'ambush marketing', especially the so-called 'new age ambushers', and what can be done about them.

Reid, F, 'Combating traditional and "New Age" ambush marketing'

The high cost of and demand for sports sponsorship has led to the phenomenon of ambush marketing, which may be defined as:

> Engaging in promotions or advertising that trade-off the event or the property, goodwill and reputation of the event and that seek to confuse the buying public as to which company really holds the official sponsorship rights.

There are several reasons why companies do not become sponsors. It may be because they have failed to outbid their competitor for the rights or because they could not afford to or simply prefer to advertise without having to pay the rights fee. While some commentators view this practice as parasitic marketing,

---

46   Bitel, N, 'Ambush marketing' (1997) 5(1) Sport and the Law Journal 2.

since the ambushers are effectively using the goodwill generated by the event to promote their own products, others say it is simply creative marketing and only to be expected in any competitive industry. And sport has developed into a highly lucrative industry and a very competitive one too. Not surprisingly, therefore, ambush marketing assumes many different forms, taking advantage of an increasing range of traditional and new marketing platforms.

Tackling Traditional Ambush Marketing

It is virtually impossible to eradicate ambush marketing within the existing legal framework and protections available. Its impact, however, may be restricted. Given that its effect is to diminish the value of sponsorship rights and, thus, adversely affect the profits generated from an event's marketing programme, event organisers have now developed sophisticated anti-ambush marketing programmes.

There is no set procedure for dealing with ambush marketing. It is a mixture of contractual measures backed by common law remedies, together with careful planning and preparation by the event organiser. The bigger the event, the larger the rights fee, the more sophisticated this will be.

The IOC, in conjunction with the Sydney Olympic Organising Committee, set up an anti-ambush marketing committee to deal full time with this practice. It even went as far as introducing new Statutes to prevent the unauthorised use of the names, logo and insignia connected with the Olympics (Sydney 2000 Games Act and the Olympic Symbols Act 1998). In the UK, the Olympic Symbols and Insignia Act 1995 has a similar effect. Given the investment made by an official sponsor, such lengths are seen as fundamental to safeguard the IOC's marketing programme. No other event has the benefit of specific statutory protection.

If the rights holder has developed a set of protectable and discernible property rights it will immediately have grounds to bring an action against any unauthorised use by a third party. When there is an unauthorised use of a registered trademark, the rights owner does not need to establish any goodwill or prove that he has suffered damages. Otherwise, he would have to prove all three elements, which illustrates what a potentially more effective remedy trademark registration provides in the event of infringement. Perhaps, unsurprisingly, on the World Wide Web infringements are commonplace and companies are now specifically hired to monitor and deal with any actual infringements.

Conflict marketing can be controlled primarily by contractual means. All participating teams, clubs and individuals in an event should be asked to sign participation agreements, which impose rules of entry for the competition. These include restrictions on the exposure of sponsors' logos on equipment and competitors' apparel both on and off the field and during official press conferences and interviews.

In relation to freebies and give-aways any spectator who enters a stadium will purchase a ticket which should contain terms and conditions of entry, in particular, restrictions on products or advertising material being brought into the stadium. Obviously, it is easier for an event organiser to control events held in a stadium compared to ones staged outside, such as the London Marathon. The event rights owner will look to ensure that both the stadium and the surrounding area are 'clean for the event' so that no companies can acquire any advertising hoardings or promotional opportunities that provide brand exposure in or around the event.

During the Sydney Olympics, for example, the organising committee acquired all the advertising space around the centre of Sydney some four years before the event. The IOC worked together with local government agencies to prevent unauthorised merchandise being sold and to prevent companies trying to ambush the event. Given the number of events that comprised the Games and the number of venues used, this was a huge undertaking.

Prudent sponsors negotiate contractual provisions that reduce the sponsorship fees payable in the event sponsorship rights are devalued. Contractual provisions are also important for providing sponsors with the first option to become sponsors of the broadcast coverage and on other media, such as the official website.

The grey area for tackling ambush marketing lies in the area of indirect association. This is where companies with no direct interest in the sponsored subject are intent upon cashing in on its profile and goodwill to enhance their own product by suggesting some indirect association. Such conduct can raise issues of unfair competition, breach of contract, tortious interference with contractual relations and tortious interference with prospective business advantage.

A good example of the difficulties involved is the 1999 Rugby World Cup held in the United Kingdom and France. A leading brewing company used the strap line, 'Good luck to England we're right behind them. Enjoy x, a rucking good beer!' in a poster campaign. This strap line implied that there was some connection between the brewer and the England rugby team and/or the Rugby World Cup. There was no direct statement that the brewer was an official sponsor of the event or of the England team. The advertisement did not contain any registered trademarks: it did not contain the name of the World Cup or the logo of the England team, which are registered as trademarks, therefore, no trademark infringement had occurred. In other words, as there was no infringement of any tangible assets, the event rights holder had to establish actionable grounds against the brewer based upon the damage to its intangible assets – namely its goodwill. For this, the common law remedy of 'passing off' is available.

In order to establish 'passing off', a rights holder must show that there has been a misrepresentation causing confusion to the public and resulting in a loss or damage to the goodwill of the event. This is extremely difficult to prove unless an association is clearly made. For trademark infringement the rights holder merely has to prove confusion or the likelihood of confusion.

The rights holder must provide evidence to show confusion in the eyes of the public – that is, anyone reading the advertisement would believe that the brewer was a sponsor of the event. In addition, evidence must be produced to show the damage caused to the goodwill of the event. In the case of the brewer's advertisement, the rights holder would find it extremely unlikely, if not impossible, to succeed in an action for 'passing off'. Even if there were a subliminal association (as in the case of the brewer), an action in 'passing off' would probably not succeed. Furthermore, given the time and expense involved in those actions and, indeed, the difficulty in establishing a misrepresentation, 'passing off' is a commercially unattractive remedy. The rights holder is, therefore, left with a combination of other measures to defeat – or more likely to minimise – the success of ambushes in this field.

Finally, a non-legal measure and, in certain cases, more effective, is staging a press conference and 'outing' an ambusher. Bad PR can be a useful tool and a deterrent against ambushing events.

Tackling 'New Age' Ambush Marketing

The rapid development of new media technology has provided rights owners with new platforms to generate new revenue streams. These include the internet and the provision of 'e-commerce' activities; the introduction of Wireless Application Protocol (WAP) technology and the provision of 'm-commerce' services, all of which are driven by content. To attract subscribers to a new media service or traffic to a website, sports content is seen as vital, and used with and without the authorisation of the rights owner. Unofficial event websites spring up seeking to benefit indirectly from the goodwill generated by an event. Companies or entrepreneurs register 'domain names' similar to, or, in some cases, the same as the name of an event or sponsored property. Given the number of sports websites and the opportunities available on the Internet to reproduce material and information, rights owners must be especially vigilant of these 'new age' ambushers.

Whilst the Internet provides opportunities for rights holders to exploit new revenue streams it also provides opportunities for ambushers. There are numerous types and principally they concern the registration of 'domain names' and the setting up of unofficial websites.

Event websites are an important additional revenue source for events rights holders. They provide information on fixtures, results and statistics, further opportunities for sponsorships and offer other e-commerce activities, such as ticketing, merchandising and prizes/promotions.

There is little that a rights holder can do against unofficial sites unless they contain registered marks belonging to the event or contain copyright material such as fixtures and sports data owned by the rights holder. If a site has the same design, look and feel of an official site then copyright protection may also be available.

A major problem for rights holders on the Internet has been a practice referred to as 'cyber squatting' in relation to domain name registration. The domain name system (DNS) serves the central function of facilitating users' ability to navigate the Internet. It does so with the aid of two components: the domain name and its corresponding Internet Protocol (IP) number.

A domain name is the human-friendly address of a computer, usually in a form easy to remember or identify, such as www.wimbledon.com. Domain names are, effectively, addresses used to call up a location, such as a web page, on the Internet. There is nothing in traditional trademark law to prevent a business from using the same mark as that belonging to someone else, but using it for dissimilar goods or services, as long as it is not likely to cause confusion. Given there can only be one worldcup.com this raises serious problems for the rights holder if he is not first to register the domain name.

If the rights holder wishes to challenge the registration of the domain name and have that name transferred, a dispute resolution procedure is available under the World Intellectual Property Organisation (WIPO). In order to succeed, the complaint must include, and seek to prove, all of the following information:

(i) the manner in which the domain name(s) is/are identical or confusingly similar to a trademark or service mark in which the complainant has rights; and

(ii) why the respondent (domain name holder) should be considered as having no rights or legitimate interests in respect of the domain name(s) that is/are the subject of the complaint; and

(iii) why the domain name(s) should be considered as having been registered and being used in bad faith.

By way of illustration, the domain names worldcup.org and worldcup-tv.com were registered by a company called Metplus Communicate. A complaint was initiated by The Fédération Internationale de Football Association (FIFA) and ISL World-wide (FIFA's agents) to obtain a transfer of the domain name back to FIFA, the rights owner. In accordance with the criteria required, it was successfully argued that:

(i) the subject domain name was almost identical (and, therefore, confusingly similar) to its registered service mark, 'worldcup' (the class of good and services for which this mark was registered did not matter);

(ii) the respondent did not have any rights or legitimate interests in the domain name. (There had been an earlier settlement between the parties, arising out of the Respondent's use of the domain name worldcup.fr as part of which the Respondent agreed that it did not have any rights in the phrase 'worldcup');

(iii) the Respondent registered and used the subject domain name in bad faith, because it knew at the time of registration that the Claimant owned the service mark 'worldcup'.

The domain names were subsequently transferred back to FIFA.

Sites are also appearing under the name [x]sucks.com and whilst the principal purpose of these sites is a protest vehicle, the effect is that traffic is attracted on the back of the official site as with 'typo squatting'. Complaints against these types of domain name registrations need to prove that the domain name is 'confusingly similar'. The difficulty lies in establishing 'bad faith'. For instance, had the registered owner of worldcup.org been using the site for a legitimate purpose, then it would have been extremely difficult for FIFA to establish bad faith.

Keyword systems are technological systems permitting terms (keywords) to be resolved to a Uniform Resource Locators (URL) or an e-mail address. They assist Internet users to carry out searches for a particular site or sites that contain the information they require. For instance, in order to benefit from the goodwill generated by the FIFA World Cup, some website owners may use the words 'football' and 'worldcup' as meta tags for attracting traffic to the site. Trademark infringement, if available, would be the appropriate remedy.

The principal lesson to be learned from these illustrations is that the Internet provides new opportunities for rights holders but provides endless opportunities for ambushers. The initiation of careful vigilance and policing methods are prerequisites and should be backed up by utilising the dispute resolution procedures available.

Conclusions

Given the growth of sports marketing and the value of rights now sold, practices such as ambush marketing are viewed very seriously by rights owners.

Ambush marketing – traditional and 'new age' – will never be eradicated and, in some respects, it is arguable that it should be permitted since sponsors would have unfair monopolistic rights over their competitors. A fair balance must be maintained, although the current remedies available in England and Wales do not provide rights owners with adequate protection. In the United States, such marketing practices can violate the Lanham Act (typically, Section 43(a)) if, for example, they convey the false message that a company is an official sponsor when, in fact, it is not.

If England and Wales want to tackle the practice of ambush marketing more successfully in the future, and attract leading international sporting events, the introduction of US style anti-ambushing measures would be welcome. For the present, event rights owners need to develop a series of protectable rights to provide a proper framework against infringements. As already indicated, new media provide new opportunities not only for rights holders but also ambushers. The Internet is the latest battleground and the war against ambush marketers is far from over!

Some Ambush Marketing Terms:

Conflict Marketing

For example, Adidas was one of the principal sponsors of the 1998 World Cup having invested millions of pounds for the sponsorship rights and yet Nike (who were not an official sponsor) received more brand exposure due to their sponsorship of certain competing teams and players (Nike sponsored the Brazil and Dutch national teams and individuals such as Ronaldo endorsed their products). There is, therefore, a conflict between the marketing/sponsorship arrangements of the event with the marketing/sponsorship arrangements of the participating teams and players that has the effect of diminishing the value of the event's official sponsorship rights.

Medium Conflict Sponsors

Where the sponsor of the broadcast is a competitor of one of the event sponsors, this can cause significant damage to the value of the official sponsor's rights. Another source for potential conflict is the sponsorship of the event's official website.

Freebies/Give-Aways

Company promotions providing free products to spectators or event competitors in and around stadia during events, whereby such 'freebies' display the company's brand, are a cheap way of advertising, particularly when worn or consumed during the event (for example, *The Sun* newspaper distributed free hats outside Wembley Stadium during the European Football Championships in 1996).

Direct Association

A statement or misrepresentation that a company is an official sponsor or the use of logos or names of the event in a company marketing or merchandising activity without the authorisation of the rights holder.

Indirect Association

Where a company without using any of the tangible assets of the rights holder indirectly associates itself with the event so that the public believes that the company is connected with the event or even an official sponsor (for example during the 1999 rugby world cup a brewer launched an advertising campaign in all the daily papers with the strap line 'support English rugby' the brewer had not pertained the particular rights to, world cup sponsor or a team sponsor since Guinness was the official world cup sponsor and Tetley the official England team sponsor).

New Media

Cyber squatting

A practice where the name of a company or individual is registered as a 'domain name' by a third party with the purpose of benefiting from the goodwill generated by that name. If, say, newevent.com is registered by a third party before the event rights owner, the rights owner will potentially suffer revenue losses because traffic will be diverted to another site, which, in most people's eyes, will be the official site.

Typo squatting

When a 'domain name' is registered which is similar to the name of the event with a slight misspelling. For example, Wimbledone.com. Again, the 'domain name' owner is looking to benefit from the goodwill generated by the existing 'domain name'.

Keywords

Attempts to use the names of events as keywords or as meta tags that belong to another site, in order to attract more traffic. Effectively, sites incorporating these tags or using these keywords are hoping to improve their 'hit rate' by 'piggy backing' on the goodwill attached to well known events.[47]

A tough regime was put in place by the South African Government to protect the Cricket World Cup, which South Africa hosted in 2003, against ambush marketing. The measures included the introduction of a new criminal offence of 'making, publishing or displaying false or misleading statements, communications or advertisements which suggest or imply a contractual or other connection with a sponsored event or the person sponsoring that event', attracting imprisonment of up to two years for a first offence and up to five years for a subsequent offence.[48]

Strict anti-ambush marketing measures were also in place for the 2004 Athens Summer Olympic Games, and the IOC and the Games organisers cracked down on all those who improperly claim an association with the Games and who try to hitch a free ride on the backs of the official sponsors. As for the Summer Games in Beijing in 2008, there will be no hiding place for would be ambush marketers, as the Beijing Municipality has already introduced a Decree No 85 on 11 October 2001 to protect Olympic-related intellectual property, with severe civil and criminal consequences and penalties for infringers.[49]

---

47 Reid, F, 'Combating traditional and "New Age" ambush marketing' (2001) 4(4) Sports Law Bulletin 10; also see White, N, Couchman, N and Harrington, D, 'Ambush Marketing: major sporting events and the limits of the law' (2004) 11 (3) Sports Law Administration and Practice 1.

48 See Cornelius, S, 'South African measures to combat ambush marketing in sport' (2003) 1 The International Sports Law Journal 38.

49 See Blackshaw, I, 'Beijing introduces "ambush marketing" law for 2008 Olympics' (2003) 1 The International Sports Law Journal 29. This article also contains an English translation of the provisions of this new law.

FINAL REMARKS

Ambush marketing, which, as we have seen, takes a variety of forms, according to the ingenuity and creativity of the 'ambushers', robs sponsors of the benefits of the sponsorship rights that they have paid considerable sums to acquire and commercially exploit. It also undermines and dilutes the sports events themselves. Legal action, unless it can be swift and effective, may prove to be a blunt weapon and, therefore, to be avoided. On the other hand, a public relations approach in the form of a naming and shaming exercise may prove to be more effective. If the law is to play a useful part in combating ambush marketing cases, apart from the Lanham Trademark Act in the US, which affords some protection in trade mark infringement cases in sport, there would seem to be a need for a broader and universal law on this subject.

In effect, event organisers need to exercise strict control over everything within, and, as far as legally and practicably possible, everything around and outside the venue. That is quite a legal and practical challenge! In any case, the sports bodies and event organisers not only need to take whatever immediate and decisive action they can in ambush marketing cases, but also need to be seen to be doing so; not only by their sponsors, but also by the members of the general public, who also have an interest in seeing fair play done in sport – both on and off the field.

The marketing and promotion of sports events has come a long way since the early pioneering days of Horst Dassler of Adidas and ISL fame. It has grown into a sophisticated and complex multi-billion dollar global 'industry'. The part played by the law to date in these developments has been significant, and will continue to be of crucial importance in the future.

With the advent of the internet and digital age, providing innovative marketing and commercial platforms for sport, sports marketing is set to grow even further and reach even more dizzy heights in the future, offering new challenges to the creativity and resilience of sports administrators and marketers and placing further demands on the skills and resourcefulness of their legal and other professional advisers.

KEY SOURCES

Blackshaw, I, 'Sports sponsorship and ambush marketing' (2001) 151 NLJ 1011–12.

Couchman, N, 'Image rights – the state of play' (2001) 15 Sports and Character Licensing 11–28.

Griffith-Jones, D, *Law and the Business of Sport* (1997), London: Butterworths.

Seres, M, 'Sports and entertainment licensing' (2000) 11 Sports and Character Licensing 15–16.

Verow, R, Lawrence, C and McCormick, P, *Sports Business: Law, Practice and Precedents* (2005), 2nd edn Bristol: Jordans.

REGULATION OF THE SPORTS WORKPLACE

CHAPTER 12

SPORT AND CONTRACTS OF EMPLOYMENT

INTRODUCTION

Participants in sport fall into three main categories: a) amateurs; b) self-employed professionals; c) employed professionals. It is this last category that this and the following two chapters concentrate on. Professional sportsmen and sportswomen and those who coach and manage them, who are regarded in law as employees, will find themselves subject to and protected by the ordinary law of employment in both its common law and statutory forms. The major source of statutory employment rights is the Employment Rights Act 1996 (ERA) (previously the Employment Protection (Consolidation) Act 1978). This chapter will examine the formation and performance of the contract of employment, and will analyse the interaction between the core legal principles and the relationship between clubs and their employees in the world of sport. Detailed attention will be paid to legal rules that connect with or generate the specific regulation of professional sport.

WHO IS AN EMPLOYEE?

In order to ascertain which sports participants are covered by the law of employment it is necessary to understand the legal tests for defining an employee. This question is essential in the contexts of: a) statutory employment protection rights; b) contractual rights and duties; c) health and safety; d) vicarious liability. Surprisingly perhaps there is no useful statutory definition of an employee; s 230 of the ERA 1996 merely defines an employee as a person who has entered into or works under a contract of employment. Thus it is case law arising out of disputes concerning these practical issues that provide us with the tests to help resolve specific problems.

The 'control test' was the traditional common law means for ascertaining whether a person engaged in work was an employee. A person was controlled by an employer if that person was told not only what to do but also how to do it. Arguments that skills possessed by individual sportsmen took them beyond the control of clubs who paid them were quickly discounted.

Walker v Crystal Palace Football Club [1910] 1 KB 87 CA

Cozens-Hardy MR: It has been argued before us . . . that there is a certain difference between an ordinary workman and a man who contracts to exhibit and employ his skill where the employer would have no right to dictate to him in the exercise of that skill; eg the club in this case would have no right to dictate to him how he should play football. I am unable to follow that. He is bound according to the express terms of his contract to obey all general directions of the club, and I think in any particular game in which he was engaged he would also be bound to obey the particular instructions of the captain or whoever it might be who was the delegate of the authority of the club for the purpose of giving those instructions. In my judgment it cannot be that a man is taken out of the operation of the Act simply because in doing a particular kind of work which he is employed to do, and in doing which he obeys general instructions, he also exercises his own judgment uncontrolled by anybody.[1]

---

1   At p 92.

It is interesting to note the emphasis given to the authority of the team captain as the 'delegate of the authority of the club'. Is the notion of captain as 'foreman' consistent with the status and attitudes of the modern professional footballer? On the other hand, there is no doubt that the footballer who exercises too much individual initiative, contrary to instructions during training, is likely to find himself dropped from the first team.

Similarly cricketers are to be considered employees. Clause 5(a) of the Contract For Professional Cricketers requires the cricketer to ' . . . obey all the lawful and reasonable directions of the captain or deputy captain . . . '.[2]

Any problems for modern professional sport which might have been posed by relying on decisions at the start of the century have been pre-empted, as the control test in itself has long been regarded as inadequate. The modern emphasis is much more on whether an individual who provides a service is or is not working on his or her own account. This is determined not by a single test but by taking into account and weighing up a number of different factors.[3] It is clear from the decision in *Walker* that whilst control may be a significant factor in a given situation, an individual will still not be an employee if she or he bears the risk of loss. Compare professional footballers or cricketers with sports participants who are not considered in law to be employees – such as professional boxers or snooker or tennis players. These individuals, albeit under the guidance or even control of an agent or manager and subject to the rules of the sport, negotiate their own entry into matches and the consequent payment they receive.[4]

The method by which tax is paid is a relevant but by no means decisive factor.[5] It is clear from case law that club managers will generally be considered employees even if they were to be treated as self-employed for tax purposes. On the other hand, the decision in *Massey* might be applied to those who occupy special positions such as Director of Football, as exemplified in recent years by Kenny Dalglish at Blackburn FC or Terry Venables at Portsmouth FC. Both of these clearly possessed the bargaining power to enter into 'genuine agreements' concerning their employment status and indeed what precisely their roles at the clubs involved. This was especially true with Terry Venables who did not regard himself as under contract to Portsmouth and went on to buy the club for £1 (although his ownership of the club was subsequently disputed when Venables and Portsmouth parted company in 1998).

An interesting development in the context of employee status and sport is provided by the case of *Singh*.[6] One of the issues dealt with by the employment tribunal in the case is whether referees can be considered employees of the Football League and/or the Football Association and are thus, for example, eligible to claim unfair dismissal. In line with the authorities, established above, the tribunal placed no emphasis on the fact that referees are normally taxed as self-employed (though S had completed his tax returns as an employee). Similarly, the tribunal emphasised that there is no single test for determining the issue. Rather, a tribunal must 'stand back and consider all aspects of the

---

2   This standard contract of employment for professional cricketers was originally negotiated between the Test and County Cricket Board (TCCB), acting on behalf of County Cricket Clubs, and the Cricketers' Association, acting on behalf of professional cricketers. See further below, at p 483.

3   This 'multiple' approach is exemplified by the judgment of Mackenna J in *Ready Mixed Concrete (South East) Ltd v Minister of Pensions and National Insurance* [1968] 2 QB 497 QBD.

4   However, this position might not be so clear cut if a more flexible approach is taken to determining who is an employee. By way of comparison see Engelbrecht, G and Schinke, M, 'The social status of the sporting profession' (1996) 4(2) Sport and the Law Journal 16–19. In particular, consider the argument that in German law a competition organiser or a sponsor could be considered an employer.

5   Cf *Massey v Crown Life Insurance Co* [1978] ICR 509 CA with *Young and Woods Ltd v West* [1980] IRLR 201 CA.

6   *Singh v The Football Association Ltd, The Football League Ltd & Others* (2001) ET Case Number 5203593/99.

relationship between the applicant and the particular respondent with no single factor being decisive or determinative but seeking to appropriate weight to all relevant factors.' Thus the tribunal placed little emphasis on facts such as the requirement on referees to wear particular dress or on a referee's lack of entitlement to sick pay or holidays.

Recent case law, approved by the House of Lords in *Carmichael v National Power* [1998] ICR 1167, has placed much emphasis on the need for mutuality of obligations as part of the irreducible minimum required for the presence of a contract of employment. Thus in *Carmichael* guides 'employed' by National Power were held by the HL not to be employees on the basis that there was no obligation to offer them work and nor was there any obligation on the part of guides to accept any work that was offered. Similarly, referees are able to refuse to officiate a match on grounds of personal inconvenience. The tribunal, however, found there to be mutuality of obligations on the basis that there was an expectation that referees on the list would be offered work and they in turn were subject to the League's disciplinary control.

Thus as matters stand, that is unless in a relevant future case the Employment Appeals Tribunal (EAT) or a higher court takes the contrary view, referees must now be perceived as employees of the Football League (and where appropriate presumably the Premier League), and therefore fully in possession of statutory employment protection rights. However, the case also established that referees are not employees of the Football Association as the FA is only intermittently concerned with decisions over the refereeing of games – namely the FA Cup and FA Trophy matches. The irregularity and casual nature of the relationship between the FA and referees thus 'strongly militates against the existence of a contract of employment'.

The above judicial tests are also illustrated by an EAT decision[7] that a bar manager whose contract described him as self-employed was nevertheless an employee as the terms of his contract revealed that he could not be considered 'his own boss'. This case also serves as a reminder that generally sports employers will employ 'ordinary' employees as well as sportsmen and women. It should also be noted that s 23 of the Employment Relations Act 1999 empowers the Secretary of State to extend the protection conferred by statutory rights to other groups of workers, such as casual and agency workers, who may not be regarded as employees. (To date these powers have not been exercised.) The Working Time Regulations 1998 and Part-time Workers Regulations 2000 provide examples of rights given to workers as well as to employees.[8]

AGENTS AND MANAGERS

Of major importance in today's world of sport is the role and position of agents/managers engaged by individual sportsmen and women. A professional boxer in formal terms employs a manager despite in general being the subordinate party. The manager will enter into a contract of agency which will normally permit him to enter into similar contracts of his choice, and in reality will control the boxers who employ him. The boxer is in an analogous contractual position to professional musicians who to secure fame are dependent on securing a recording contract, but technically are in the position of principal in the agency relationship. Such professionals are excluded from employment protection rights, but receive some protection from the common law doctrine of restraint of trade.[9]

---

7   *Withers v Flackwell Heath Football Supporters Club* [1981] IRLR 307.
8   SI 1998/1833 and SI 2000/1551.
9   See below, pp 494–95.

Similarly, the professional footballer who has an agent is the principal in that relationship. The essential difference between the boxer and footballer is that the latter is an employee of his club, and is more genuinely employing an agent's services to assist in negotiations with the employer. The boxer, on the other hand, like the aspiring rock band, is dependent on the 'agent' for work and thus remuneration. Compare the boxer with, as examples, professional golfers, tennis players and snooker players, who generally more clearly possess the economic independence to be regarded as self-employed professionals. In so far as they employ agents they may be genuinely regarded as principals in what are essentially commercial relationships.

Individual sports participants who employ agents are bound by any contract entered into by the agent deemed to be within the scope of the latter's express and usual authority. The concept of usual authority covers any contract which it is reasonable for the third party to assume the agent to possess the authority to make in light of the norms of the commercial situation and other relevant factors. Usual authority may thus be wider than express authority. Therefore, for example, could a boxer ever object to a contract made by his manager to fight a particular boxer or to fight at a particular venue?

The Football League Contract

Clause 14(b)

The Club and the Player shall arrange all contracts of service and transfers of registration to any other Football Club between themselves and shall make no payment to any other person or agent in this respect.

This contractual provision is in accordance with the rules of the FA and the Premier and Football Leagues. Given the role currently played by agents in professional football, it would appear that cl 14(b) is more honoured in its breach than observance.[10] However, the clause should act to restrict the scope of an agent's usual authority. If this were so then, for example, a transfer agreed to by an agent in a footballer's absence would not bind the player.

FORMATION AND TERMS OF A CONTRACT OF EMPLOYMENT

In accordance with common law principle a contract of employment may, but need not, be in writing. In practice contracts entered into by sportsmen and sportswomen, irrespective of their employment status, will be in writing. Therefore, it can be noted in passing that sports participants, in so far as they are considered employees, are entitled to specified information in writing – ss 1–3 of the ERA 1996. This includes all the major contractual terms, the identity of any relevant collective agreements and copies of disciplinary rules and procedures.[11]

The ordinary rules of offer and acceptance apply to contracts of employment in the same way that they do to any other type of contract. However, in practice it is not that uncommon for an employment contract to be entered into informally through oral agreement, and the full contract is only later put into written form. The following two cases illustrate the problems this process can cause.

---

10 Strictly speaking, agents are only permitted to offer professional advice to players that employ them. In all probability, football agents do negotiate on behalf of their clients. Nevertheless, the agent has no authority to enter into a contract on a player's behalf.

11 It is interesting to note that in *Singh, op cit*, fn 6, the tribunal did not accept that it was significant, in determining whether Singh was an employee, that referees were not provided with a written statement of their terms and conditions of employment. (Indeed it would be rather ironic if employers who fail to comply with a statutory duty owed to employees could use that failure to establish the lack of an employment relationship.)

In *Stransky v Bristol Rugby Ltd*[12] the club's Director of Rugby was authorised to approach Joel Stransky, a former international player, to discuss his possible employment as a backs coach. Following these negotiations Stransky met the club's chief executive in a restaurant in Bath in April. The terms of the contract were discussed and agreed to over the meal. Stransky returned to his home in Leicester and informed his wife that he had a new job and thus they would be looking for a new home in the Bath/Bristol area. In the months after this meal, to the knowledge of the chief executive, preliminary steps were taken to secure a work permit for Stransky and he was introduced to the players. The chief executive was also asked to draw up the written contract for Stransky and his response indicated that he was intending to do so. In June, Stransky discovered that the club had decided not to employ him. In court the chief executive stated that he did not recall meeting Stransky for a meal let alone offering him employment. On the basis of the evidence this statement was rejected and the court concluded that a contract had been entered into during the meal in April. Thus the club was in repudiatory breach in refusing to employ Stranski for the agreed period.

In *White v Bristol Rugby Club*[13] White, a professional rugby player, signed a three year contract to move from his previous club to Bristol. The contract expressly stipulated that it was subject to an 'entire agreement' clause, so that no oral representations made in the course of negotiations applied in respect of its express terms and conditions. W subsequently decided not to join B and asserted that he had been told during pre-contract negotiations that he could opt out of the contract on repayment of the advance. The High Court held that the 'entire agreement' clause prevented W from relying on an oral opt-out term.

Trainees and Apprentices

Minors do not normally possess contractual capacity. This is however not a problem in sport, as a contract of employment or analogous contract for services is deemed to be for the minor's benefit.[14] It matters not that the contract contains particular terms which the minor regards as detrimental, providing that the contract taken as a whole is to the minor's benefit.[15]

Contracts of apprenticeship are important in, for example, professional football. Apprentices are in a special position. The contract must be in writing, and the contract cannot be terminated during its currency other than by reason of grave misconduct on the part of the apprentice. Note the apprentice may accrue statutory employment rights including the right not to be unfairly dismissed. However, ironically but nevertheless the norm in employment law, a dismissal may be fair even though it constitutes a breach of contract.[16] On the other hand, contrary to the normal principles of contract law, apprentices dismissed in breach of contract can receive damages for loss of future prospects as well as immediate financial loss.[17] Thus clubs are ill-advised prematurely to terminate an apprentice's contract

---

12   11/12/2002 QBD (Eady J), unreported.

13   [2002] IRLR 204. For further comment on this case see Blackshaw (2002) 5(1) Sports Law Bulletin, p 3.

14   For example, *Roberts v Grey* [1913] 1 KB 520, in which damages were awarded against a minor who broke a contract to accompany a professional snooker player on a world tour in order to receive training and develop experience.

15   See *Doyle v White City Stadium Ltd* [1935] 1 KB 520, in which a minor boxer was bound by rules permitting suspension and a fine for hitting his opponent below the belt. Indeed the court held that the rules were just as much for his protection as for the protection of his opponents. cf *De Francesco v Barnum* [1890] 45 Ch 430, in which a minor was released from her contract as a professional dancer where she was contracted to work only for the defendant, whilst he was under no duty to find her engagements, and her remuneration was deemed inadequate.

16   See *Finch v Betabake (Anglia) Ltd* [1977] IRLR 470.

17   *Dunk v George Waller & Son Ltd* [1970] 2 All ER 630.

Unless the contract of apprenticeship expressly permits dismissal for reason of redundancy such a dismissal will be in breach of contract. This will not be so if an employer can establish a complete closure of the workplace or a fundamental change in the nature of the business.[18] Short of, for example a football club going into liquidation, it is hard to conceive how these exceptions could apply in sport. However, it is clear that on expiry of the contract the apprentice cannot argue that he has been made redundant.[19]

Youth trainees, engaged by a club under a statutory training scheme, will not have the status of either employees or apprentices, and are thus generally excluded from the protection conferred by statutory employment rights. However, they are covered by health and safety legislation and the Sex and Race Discrimination Acts.

The FA and the Premier and Football Leagues, in conjunction with the Professional Footballers Association, provide written guidance to trainee players with respect to their contractual rights and duties.

The Code of Practice and Notes on Contract for FA Premier League and Football League Contract Players and Trainees[20]

Trainees

When a boy leaves school he may be registered by the Club as a Trainee Player. Sixteen year old school leavers will be registered for 104 weeks, or up to their 18th birthday whichever is the longer: seventeen year old school leavers for 104 weeks, or up to their 19th birthday whichever is the longer and for players who sign for a Club after leaving school and taking up employment elsewhere the period of registration shall represent the balance of 104 weeks or up to their 19th birthday whichever is the longer.

The Player will participate in Youth Training. This aims to provide training and coaching in the skills and abilities necessary to follow a career in Professional Football and to provide opportunities for acquisition of skills and knowledge in other occupations.

The managing agent for Youth Training in The FA Premier League and The Football League is The Footballers' Further Education and Vocational Training Society.

The payment to Trainees is geared to the Training Allowance laid down. Subject to a Club meeting the YT criteria and being granted placements the Club will receive re-imbursement for all or part of the Trainees' allowance. Under certain conditions travelling and lodging expenses may also be re-claimed. Clubs which fill all the placements granted may sign additional players as Trainees and pay the wages themselves.

The Trainees will be expected to perform certain menial tasks, eg cleaning boots and equipment, sweeping dressing rooms, preparing strip, and general dressing room duties. These duties should not take up more than ten hours per week, and should not include general stadium maintenance, groundsmanship or other ground work with the exception of the 2 day work experience in these areas.

The Trainee may be signed as a full Contract Player at any time on or after his seventeenth birthday.

Not less than two months before the end of the Player's Traineeship the Club must inform him in writing by recorded delivery whether or not it wishes to offer him terms as a Contract Player specifying (where applicable) such terms. It is important to note that Players who are released on the expiry of their Traineeship are entitled to receive two months notice. The Player is under an obligation to let the Club know within 21 days of receiving the offer whether or not it is acceptable. If the player rejects the offer he

---

18 *Wallace v CA Roofing Services Ltd* [1996] IRLR 435.

19 *North East Coast Shiprepairers v Secretary of State for Employment* [1978] IRLR 149.

20 Hereafter referred to as FA Code of Practice and Notes on Footballers' Contracts. A copy of the Code must be given to all players and trainees at the time they sign for a club.

may sign for the Club of his choice after his Traineeship has finished, but such Club will be liable to pay a compensation fee to the Club with which he was registered as a Trainee. Either Club may appeal to The Football League Appeals Committee to determine the compensation fee.

A Club which grants a Trainee Player's request for the cancellation of his registration may also demand compensation from any other Club signing the player as a Trainee or under a written contract within a two year period.

Trainees are governed by the same disciplinary rules as Contract Players. The sections headed 'Inducements' and 'Grievance Procedure' also apply equally to Trainees.

Where appropriate these provisions will apply equally to young players who have been offered a contract of apprenticeship.

Collective Bargaining

Trade unions and the world of industrial relations are not immediately associated in people's minds with the world of sport. (At least, this is so in Britain. In the USA, by way of contrast, professional sport is a heavily unionised sector of the economy.) However, the Professional Footballers' Association (PFA) is affiliated to the British Trade Union Congress (the major national trade union confederation) and cricketers also have their own trade union, the Professional Cricketers' Association. The role of both of these organisations, as is the case with any trade union, is to represent the individual and collective interests of their members.

Trade unions are most significant in the workplace when they are recognised by employers for the purposes of collective bargaining. The objective of collective bargaining is for trade unions to reach collective agreements with employers. In Britain such agreements are *presumed*, both at common law and under statute law, not to be legally binding on the respective parties, and thus normally do not have the status of contracts.[21] However, part or all of the content of a collective agreement can be incorporated into the individual contracts of employment of the employees on whose behalf the union was negotiating. (Note that this will normally be all relevant employees, not just those who happen to belong to the union.) A collective agreement so incorporated is, of course, legally enforceable between the individual employee and the employer.

The standard contract for professional cricketers is a major example of this process. The contract is derived from a collective agreement which was originally negotiated between the Professional Cricketers' Association and the Test and County Cricket Board. This contract is not legally binding on either of the organisations which negotiated it, but it is binding as an individual contract on any club which adopts it with respect to its individual players. Note both collective agreements and individual contracts derived from them can survive even if one of the parties, in formal terms, ceases to exist. Thus cricketers' contracts are not substantially affected by the fact that the TCCB was replaced by the England and Wales Cricket Board in 1997.

Another major role of trade unions is to represent individual members who have a grievance with or are being disciplined by the employer. Both professional footballers and professional cricketers have the contractual right to union representation at individual hearings.[22] Footballers may also be represented by the PFA before a transfer tribunal.[23]

---

21 See *Ford v AUEW* [1969] 2 QB 303, and s 179 of the Trade Union and Labour Relations (Consolidation) Act 1992.
22 Sections 10–15 of the Employment Relations Act 1999 gives all workers the statutory right to be represented at formal disciplinary and grievance hearings. If the worker so chooses the representative may be a trade union officer.
23 See below, pp 495.

The PFA has a higher public profile than the Professional Cricketers' Association, and like many trade unions also engages in active campaigning on behalf of its members. One of its most important and relatively successful campaigns in recent years has been 'Let's Kick Racism Out of Football'.[24]

If collective bargaining is not associated with the world of sport then this is even more the case with strikes. In 1996, however, the PFA balloted its members employed by clubs in the Football League on strike action. This would have involved the collective withdrawal of labour with respect to games to be broadcast live on television. The cause of the dispute was the decision by the Football League to terminate a 30 year agreement under which the PFA receives 10% of the income from television. This money is used by the PFA for the welfare of its members – particularly those who are forced by injury prematurely to end their careers. Strike action was ultimately averted as the dispute was resolved by agreement between the League and the PFA. However, the dispute was not permanently resolved as the PFA conducted and won a second strike ballot on this issue in the winter of 2001. The following extract considers the issues involved.

Welch R, 'Greedy footballers, trade disputes and the right to strike'

The early months of 2002 have witnessed the return of media headlines concerned with a rise in industrial conflict as rail workers, postal workers and teachers vote to take industrial action. Running in parallel to these developments was Tony Blair's much publicised speech denouncing those who are 'wreckers' of the public services. Despite his protestations to the contrary, many public sector trade unionists and some trade union leaders took this to be a reference to themselves. It is perhaps ironic that this concern over a return to industrial militancy was prefaced not in traditional industrial sectors but in the world of professional football.

In the latter months of 2001 the front as well as the back pages of the press were generally highly critical of the decision by footballers to take strike action, from December 1, at any game where a TV camera was present. Moreover, the Premier and Football Leagues came very close to seeking an injunction to prevent the strike from taking place. Thus professional footballers found themselves in a position very familiar to more traditional trade unionists. Firstly, a ballot for industrial action held in accordance with statutory requirements produces a large majority for strike action (in this case the ballot produced an unprecedented 99% majority in favour). Secondly, an employer and media onslaught is launched on 'greedy trade unionists for holding the public to ransom'. Thirdly, employers issue a threat to resort to use of legal action to prevent the strike from taking place. The purposes of this article are twofold. Firstly, to explain why litigation by the Football Leagues may have succeeded. Secondly, to discuss whether the proposed footballers' strike illustrates, albeit in an untypical context, that the law prevents industrial action which can be considered, at least in moral terms, to be legitimate.

The cause of the dispute was the breakdown in negotiations over the distribution of money secured from television companies. Under a fifty-year-old arrangement, the Professional Footballers Association (PFA) has received a share of the money earned from the televising of matches in return for players giving up individual appearance fees. This money is used by the PFA to provide hardship funds for players who are in financial difficulties or need to retrain for a new career having retired from the game. Such funds are particularly important for players in the lower leagues who are on comparable salaries with other members of the labour force; especially for players who are forced out of the game through physical injuries with long-term debilitating consequences.

Therefore, whichever side you are on (and I am not attempting to hide my sympathies with the players) it is important to clarify that players in the Premier League and First Division were not contemplating strike action to secure more money or benefits for themselves. To put it in an admittedly subjective

---

24 See chapter on discrimination, p 556.

manner such players were motivated by concern for their less fortunate colleagues and were prepared to take strike action in solidarity with them. (The view of the employers, on the other hand, was that these players could demonstrate their concern by increasing their individual subscriptions to the PFA as a source of increased revenue for the hardship fund.) The dispute was resolved though a last minute compromise but it is useful to examine what the legal outcome may have been had litigation taken place.

Since the end of the last century a tort first developed in *Lumley v Gye* (1853) 2 E & B 216 has been applied to the organisation of industrial action. Thus any trade union or trade unionist who persuades or calls on employees to take strike or most other types of industrial action is committing the tort of directly inducing those employees to act in breach of their contracts of employment. To this day this remains the position at common law. Thus the organisation of virtually any form of industrial action is unlawful in the sense that it is tortious and can be restrained by a court injunction. There is not and never has been any right to strike in the UK. However, since the Trade Disputes Act 1906 there has been statutory immunity from the above mentioned tortious liability providing the industrial action is in 'contemplation or furtherance of a trade dispute'. (It should be noted that since 1984 industrial action must also be sanctioned by a valid secret ballot if it is to attract statutory immunity. However, this was not an issue in the proposed players' strike for the reasons identified above.)

Under the original Trade Disputes Act and its successor, the Trade Union & Labour Relations Act 1974, a dispute could be regarded as a trade dispute provided it was *connected* to terms and conditions of employment even though it had a wider dimension such as a trade union campaign. Moreover, a dispute could be between employees and any employer. Thus in a case, *NWL Ltd v Woods* [1979] ICR 867, which has direct relevance to this discussion, the Law Lords held that the boycotting of a ship flying a 'flag of convenience' could be regarded as action taken in furtherance of a trade dispute and was thus lawful. The workers who took this action were not employed by the shipowner and nor did they benefit directly from it. The action was taken in support of the (ongoing) campaign by the relevant union, the International Transport workers Federation (ITWF), to improve the pay and conditions of crews recruited from third world countries.

However, in a case decided in 1982, *Universe Tankships Inc of Monrovia v ITWF* [1982] ICR 262, the Law Lords modified this conclusion where the taking of such action was resolved by the shipowner paying money into the Seafarers' International Welfare Fund. A majority of the Law Lords held that the payment of this money was not connected to the employment conditions of the crew or anyone at all. Rather the payment should be viewed as analogous to a political party or a revolutionary 'guerrilla group'. Having identified the absence of a trade dispute, the Law Lords were then able to apply the contractual doctrine of duress to grant restitution to the shipowner of the money paid into the welfare fund. Essentially the Law Lords concluded that money secured through industrial action which, was not in furtherance of a trade dispute, was money secured by duress. The decision also raises the possibility that such action could constitute the tort of duress. This development in tortious liability has yet to occur but it should be noted that statutory immunity for such liability does not and never has existed.

The parallels between *Universe Tankships* and the proposed PFA strike are obvious. Moreover, the definition of a trade dispute today is different to the 1974 definition that was the subject of the Law Lords' decision. As a result of amendments introduced by the Employment Act 1982 a dispute must be wholly or mainly related to terms and conditions of employment as against merely connected to such issues and must be between employees and their own employer. The House of Lords' decision in the subsequent case of *Dimskal Shipping v ITWF* [1992] IRLR 78 vividly illustrated that these amendments render action of the sort organised by the ITWF unlawful. In this case the industrial action was taken in a Swedish port and was lawful under Swedish law. However, the agreement to pay money into the welfare fund was governed by the English law of contract. Under the post-1982 definition of a trade dispute it was clear that statutory immunity was not available as the dispute was seen as a dispute between the union and the shipping company rather than between the latter and its employees. Thus, as in *Universe Tankships*, the remedy of restitution was granted to the shipowner.

In the context of the PFA dispute, on the basis of the balance of convenience test contained in *American Cyanamid v Ethicon* [1975] AC 396 . . . there would have been a strong chance that any club seeking an interlocutory injunction would have been successful. With respect to the future it should also be commented that, in the absence of a lawful trade dispute, a TV company could also seek an injunction. This is because such strikes constitute tortious interference with the commercial contract between the clubs and TV companies through the unlawful means of inducing the players to act in breach of their employment contracts.

It must be emphasised that it remains uncertain that the proposed strike was unlawful as the PFA may have succeeded in arguing that the distribution of TV money was wholly or mainly related to the terms and conditions of the employment contracts between players and their own clubs. However, I suspect this argument would have failed and, in my view, the whole incident illustrates why the current legal regulation of industrial action is unduly restrictive. For me, the likes of a very rich man such as David Beckham taking strike action on behalf of players for clubs such as Hartlepool and Macclesfield is worthy of praise not castigation. Equally, in the wider trade union world the taking of solidarity or as it is now known secondary action is a manifestation of the noblest form of trade unionism. It is also arguably the case that the taking of such action is a right protected by international law. Have our professional footballers provided the world of employee relations with a very good example of why, as is the case elsewhere in Western Europe, workers in the UK should be granted positive rights to strike?[25]

In line with the legal positions in and industrial relations systems of most Member States, the EU attaches rather more significance on consultation and negotiation with trade unions as social partners than has been the norm in Britain over the past few decades. Indeed the EC Treaty provides for the making of EU social law through agreement between European employers' associations and the ETUC. In this context it should be noted that FIFPro, with the support of the European Commission and the ETUC, is engaged in the social dialogue procedures contained in the EC Treaty with the ultimate objective of securing a European Collective Agreement for professional football.[26]

PERFORMANCE OF THE CONTRACT

Express Terms

The interplay between the standard terms in a sports professional's contract and general employment law is of central importance. This is particularly the case with the rights and duties of the contracting parties. As is generally the case with written employment contracts, many of the respective rights and duties of the parties derive from express contractual terms. For example, on the club's part there are normally express obligations to provide medical treatment and to continue to pay a player's basic wages during periods that he is injured or otherwise incapacitated. (Note for employees in general such rights may not be in their contracts, and there are no equivalent statutory duties imposed on employers.) Contracts could also contain provisions regulating marketing and sponsorship deals. Clearly, the personal terms agreed to by a player when he signs for a club will constitute part of the express terms of the contract.

On the player's part there are duties to behave in a professional manner and to abide by the rules of the game. Consider the practical implications and consequences of the following.

---

25 Welch R, 'Greedy footballers, trade disputes and the right to strike' (2002) 5(2) Sports Law Bulletin 14 – 15. Also see *The Guardian*, 15 October 1996 for a report on the possible legal implications of the original proposed strike.

26 FIFPro Press Releases of April 4 and November 19 2003, see www.fifpronet.com. Also see Branco-Martins, R, 'European sport's first collective labour agreement EFFC', Asser Instituut, 2003.

The Football League Contract

Clause 2 The Player agrees to play to the best of his ability in all football matches in which he is selected to play for the Club and to attend at any reasonable place for the purpose of training . . .

Clause 5 The Player agrees to observe the Rules of the Club at all times. The Club and the Player shall observe and be subject to the Rules and Regulations of the Football Association and the Football League. In the case of conflict such Rules and Regulations shall take precedence over this Agreement and the Rules of the Club.

Clause 7 . . . The Player shall at all times have due regard for the necessity of his maintaining a high standard of physical fitness and agrees not to indulge in any sport, activity or practice that might endanger such fitness . . .

Clause 13 . . . The Player may, save as otherwise mutually agreed and subject to the overriding obligation not to bring the game of Association Football into disrepute, contribute to the public media in a responsible manner. The Player, whenever circumstances permit, give to the Club reasonable notice of his intention to make such contributions to the public media in order to allow representations to be made to him on behalf of the Club if it so desires.

Clause 14(a) The Player shall not induce or attempt to induce any other player employed or registered by the Club, or by any other Football League Club, to leave that employment to cease to be so registered for any reason whatsoever.

Similar provisions to the above can be found in the standard Contract For Professional Cricketers and in the England and Wales Cricket Board's (formerly the TCCB) Rules and Regulations. Of particular interest, in both football and cricket, is the catch-all offence of 'bringing the sport into disrepute.'

Relate the above terms to the following much publicised incidents that have occurred over the past 20 years. The ban on Ian Botham after being convicted for the possession of cannabis; the alcoholism of Tony Adams and Paul Merson and the latter's addiction to cocaine and gambling; the short ban imposed on Chris Armstrong for smoking cannabis; the dismissal of Craig Whittington for the same offence; the dismissal of Roger Stanislaus for using cocaine; the termination of the cricketer Ed Giddins' contract for the same offence; the decisions by Chelsea FC and Manchester United FC not to impose club penalties on Dennis Wise and Eric Cantona after their respective convictions for assault; the fine imposed by the TCCB (and its subsequent lifting) on Ray Illingworth for publicising his version of the dispute with Devon Malcolm, after the latter was dropped from the England test team during the 1995 tour of South Africa.[27]

More recently, the convictions of Jonathan Woodgate and Lee Bower for acts of violence outside a Leeds night-club have not resulted in negative consequences for either player's career (including, in

---

27   The ongoing ramifications of the latter were evidenced by the criticisms of staff and students at Leeds Metropolitan University of the decision to award an honorary degree to Ray Illingworth. See *The Guardian*, 13 May 1997 and the *Higher Education Guardian*, 27 May 1997. With respect to dismissals for the use of drugs see next chapter, pp 521–22, and *The Guardian Sport 96*, 1 November 1996; *The Express*, 27 November 1996. In an article entitled 'Cocaine, the lurking danger' *The Guardian*, 26 November 1994, Christopher Elliott analyses the relationship between drug taking and the demands imposed on and lifestyles expected of the modern professional footballer. Also see *The Guardian*, 31 January 1996 ('Positive drug tests up by 15 per cent') for an analysis of the extent of drug taking in sport. Adrian Muto is the latest professional footballer to hit the headlines for proving positive in a drug test – for cocaine – see *The Guardian*, 19 October 2004. However, his consequent dismissal by Chelsea, after being suspended for seven months by the FA, has not had long-term repercussions for his career, as he subsequently signed a five year contract with Juventus – see *The Guardian*, 13 January 2005. This saga provides yet another example of different attitudes by different clubs to what arguably should not be seen as an issue for regulatory bodies such as the FA, though inevitably it is always likely to be an issue between an employer, including professional clubs, and its employees.

the case of Woodgate, selection for the national team). Similarly, allegations of sexual misconduct against a number of players during the 2003–04 season has not resulted in any disciplinary action at club level (though it must be emphasised that none of the allegations were proven). Many people have some sympathy with Rio Ferdinand, in light of his suspension for forgetting to attend a drug test, but again it is clear that this will not interfere with his career at club or international levels once the period of suspension has been served.

Clubs appear to have extremely wide discretion in these matters either towards lenience or towards harshness. This can be related to the range of reasonable responses test in unfair dismissal law.[28] Providing a player is not cheating, should not his private behaviour be his own affair? With respect to 'whistle-blowing' are we as the paying public (not to mention loyal and often long-suffering supporters) not entitled to be told what is happening behind the scenes? Although recently there appears to be a shift in football culture, there certainly seems to have been a different attitude taken towards drugs as against alcohol. The former may involve commission of a criminal offence, but is it as damaging, let alone more damaging, to a player's fitness than the 'refuelling' for which some professional footballers have been renowned. Drug-taking would also appear to be viewed more seriously than acts of violence on or off the field of play.[29]

With respect to cl 14(a) in the Football League Contract, it is a tort for any individual to induce another to act in breach of contract (as explained above, see p 485). A cynic might observe that in football the major culprits are the clubs themselves with respect both to players and managers. This is however a context where commodification plays a rather more important role in practice than juridification, given that private out of court settlements are the norm.[30]

JUDICIALLY IMPLIED TERMS

Judges are more prepared to imply terms in contracts of employment than is the case with contracts in general. The orthodox 'business efficacy' and 'officious bystander' tests are not without relevance,

---

28 See next chapter, pp 535–40.

29 The Football Association is even considering the introduction of a web-based tracking system so that footballers can be subject to random testing away from the workplace for traces of recreational drugs. See Chaudhary V, 'FA will deny drug users a place to hide' *The Guardian*, 26 May 2004.

30 See the following chapter for further discussion of this tort. One of the most controversial examples of alleged 'poaching' was when Mike Walker left Norwich to become the manager at Everton. For further controversy surrounding Mike Walker (after his return to Norwich), and an analysis of the legal issues concerning 'poaching', players' contracts and the transfer system, see Nash, M, 'The legality of poaching: footballers' contracts revisited' (1997) 5(1) Sport and the Law Journal 49–52. Also see Nash, M, 'Playing offside: footballers' contracts (1992) New Law Journal 1 July and 'Players and their promises: footballers' contracts (1993) Solicitors Gazette 15 October. Also see: *The Times*, 6 November 1993 for a report of threatened legal action by West Bromwich Albion after the club's manager, Ossie Ardiles, was appointed by Tottenham Hotspurs to replace Terry Venables; and *The Guardian*, 4 July 1995 for an article by Lawrence Donegan, 'New kicks on the block', on the poaching of young players and a dispute between Arsenal and Manchester United over an England schoolboy international, Matthew Wicks. For an analysis of the availability of equitable relief to prevent a player from acting in breach of contract through moving to another club, and a comparison with North American law, see McCutcheon, P, 'Negative enforcement of employment contracts in the sports industries' (1997) 17(1) Legal Studies 65–100.

The most recent instance of litigation around these issues was the long-running dispute between Middlesbrough FC and Liverpool FC over the transfer of Christian Ziege to Liverpool in the summer of 2000. A confidential out of court settlement has now resolved this matter – see *The Guardian*, 13 March 2004. Some of the legal issues underlying this dispute will be discussed in the following chapter.

but judges recognise that certain rights and duties arise naturally from the relationship between employers and their employees, and will identify and imply contractual terms accordingly.

Judicially Implied Duties of the Employer

The duty to provide work

Traditionally this duty applied only to those who were paid on a commission or piecework basis, or an exceptional category of employee who needed to work in order to establish and enhance a professional reputation, for example, an actor or a singer. For other employees, irrespective of their status, the following *dictum* applied:

> It is true that the contract of employment does not necessarily, or perhaps normally, oblige the master to provide the servant with work. Provided I pay my cook her wages regularly, she cannot complain if I choose to take any or all of my meals out.[31]

An alternative view was put forward by Lord Denning.[32]

> In these days an employer, when employing a skilled man, is bound to provide him with work. By which I mean that the man should be given the opportunity of doing his work when it is available and he is ready and willing to do it. A skilled man takes a pride in his work. He does not do it merely to earn money. He does it so as to make his contribution to the well-being of all. He does it so as to keep himself busy, and not idle. To use his skill, and to improve it.

Could (should) sports professionals be included in the traditional exceptional category of employees who need to work in order to develop a reputation? Lord Denning's reasoning may be of limited value as it was used to grant an injunction restraining a dismissal in the politically controversial context of the closed shop. Nevertheless, it seems more compatible with modern perspectives on the employment relationship than in the days where all employees were considered servants.[33] (Note the 'servant' Collier was employed as a sub-editor of a newspaper) If Lord Denning's view is to be followed it must surely cover professional footballers and the like. If this is the case to what extent is there a right to be selected for a competitive game, if only for a reserve team? Or will a club be fulfilling its duty in requiring a player to attend training sessions?

The most important recent developments with respect to a duty to provide work have come about through cases concerning the imposition of 'garden leave' by employers. Essentially, this is where employees are required to work out long notice periods before they are able to resign, but are instructed not to come to work. Typically this will be to prevent employees from continuing to access confidential information and/or have dealings with the organisation's customers. It has been held that in the absence of an express term permitting 'garden leave' the imposition of it constitutes a breach of the duty to provide work.[34] Such express terms will not be enforceable if they are deemed to be in restraint of trade. However, they will be enforced providing the employer has legitimate

---

31 *Per* Asquith J in *Collier v Sunday Referee Publishing Co Ltd* [1940] 2 KB 647, 650.

32 *Langston v AUEW* [1974] ICR 180, 190.

33 Lord Denning's view has received subsequent approval by way of *obiter dicta* in subsequent cases. See: *Breach v Epsylon Industries Ltd* [1976] IRLR 180 EAT.

34 *Provident Financial Group plc v Hayward* [1989] ICR 160 CA.

interests to protect and the clause is otherwise reasonable; for example, its duration is not longer than necessary to protect the employer's interests.[35]

The case of *Crystal Palace FC Ltd v Bruce*[36] has revealed that 'garden leave' clauses may be found in the employment contracts of some football managers. At the time of the case Steve Bruce was the manager of Crystal Palace. Bruce wished to leave the club to become the manager of Birmingham FC. Crystal Palace sought an injunction to enforce a 'garden leave' clause to prevent him from doing this. Burton J decided that Crystal Palace might well have legitimate interests to protect as it and Birmingham were both in the First Division and indeed were both rivals for a play-off position at the end of the 2001/02 season. Steve Bruce's departure to manage Birmingham would thus have been duly detrimental to Palace's prospects for the rest of the season. Moreover, the departure of a manager to another club not infrequently results in other members of the coaching and playing staff joining him shortly thereafter. The court granted an interlocutory injunction for a short period (around two months) to restrain Bruce from leaving Crystal Palace in breach of contract.

The duty to take reasonable care with respect to the health, safety and welfare of the employee

All employers are subject to this common law duty as well as various statutory duties imposed by legislation and the requirements of EC law. Such duties will normally be more than met by professional clubs, given that their employees will be perceived as valuable investments. (There is nothing more infuriating to the club – and the supporters – than learning that a valued player has received a serious injury during training). Contrary to the norm in employment law, it is the player's corresponding duty to the employer that is potentially of more practical significance.

The duty to maintain mutual trust and confidence

This duty is an example of the dynamism of judicial creativity in implying new terms into employment contracts. The duty was identified during the 1970s – particularly in order to expand the circumstances where a resignation by an employee could be construed as a dismissal.

The classic statement of the duty is provided by Browne-Wilkinson J.

Woods v W/M Car Services [1981] ICR 666 EAT

... it is clearly established that there is implied in a contract of employment a term that the employers will not, without reasonable and proper cause, conduct themselves in a manner calculated or likely to destroy or seriously damage the relationship of confidence and trust between employer and employee ... To constitute a breach of this implied term it is not necessary to show the employer intended any repudiation of the contract: the tribunal's function is to look at the employer's conduct as a whole and determine whether it is such that its effect, judged reasonably and sensibly, is such that the employee cannot be expected to put up with it ...[37]

---

35 For the leading case law on garden-leave and restraint of trade see *Credit Suisse & Asset Management Ltd v Armstrong* [1996] IRLR 450 & *FSS Travel & Leisure Systems v Johnson* [1998] IRLR 382. For further discussion on the doctrine of restraint of trade, see below pp 494–95

36 (2002) QBD (unreported). For further comment on this case and the granting of interlocutory injunctions see Welch R, (2002) 5(2) Sports Law Bulletin, pp 3–4. It is not known whether 'garden leave' clauses are typically to be found in managers' contracts but it has been reported that Barnet intended to enforce garden leave against Martin Allen when he walked out of the club to manage Brentford. However, the dispute was settled by an out of court settlement between the two clubs. See *The Independent*, 30 March 2004.

37 At pp 670–71.

Many of the decided cases in which employers have been found to be in breach of this duty have revolved around the issues of verbal and physical abuse and harassment. Given the oft-quoted statement (tautology) that professional football is a man's game, to what extent can the individual player be expected to tolerate swearing, barracking, public criticism (humiliation) and practical jokes from manager, team captain and team-mates? Generally, this could be considered part of the necessary 'locker room' culture to build and maintain team solidarity and spirit. However, in law, established workplace culture can still be found unlawful – particularly in the context of behaviour that constitutes racial or sexual harassment.[38] In football being required to accept a verbal 'bashing' may be one thing. It would be altogether different if, for example, a public dressing-down was tainted with racist language or innuendo.

Could a refusal to select a player for the first team ever constitute a breach of this duty? This could assume importance where a player is not being picked in order to punish that player, for example, for expressing a legitimate disagreement with a manager rather than for sporting or disciplinary reasons. In the context of a player seeking a transfer it could be counter-productive to leave a player to 'rot in the reserves' if this is adopted as a tactic to pressurise a player into staying with a club. If such a practice constitutes destruction of mutual trust and confidence on the club's part it would enable a player to claim he had been constructively dismissed and thus was now free to negotiate a new contract with any club of his choosing.[39]

As confirmed by the House of Lords in *Malik v BCCI*[40] this overriding duty can take a variety of forms from failing to treat employees with respect to adversely affecting an employee's reputation through operating a business in a dishonest and corrupt manner. Breach of this duty can give rise to an action for damages as well as enabling an employee to claim wrongful and unfair dismissal.[41]

Judicially Implied Duties of the Employee

The duty of obedience

An employee must obey all lawful and reasonable instructions of the employer. An instruction is reasonable if it is compatible with the job the employee is employed to do and is not excessive in terms of the demands imposed on the individual. It is clear that the duty can extend to personal factors such as appearance and dress, and to behaviour in the employee's own time.

In light of the clauses in the Football League Contract quoted above, consider what types of instructions can be issued to professional footballers beyond attending training sessions and reporting on match days; for example with respect to diet, family life and standards of personal behaviour. Cricketers owe an express duty not to 'engage in any activity or pursuit which is or may be prejudicial to the Club . . . ' – cl 6(e).

---

38   See chapter on discrimination pp 566–71.

39   Under the new transfer regulations adopted by FIFA, see below pp 512–19, players are permitted to terminate their contracts if they have 'sporting just cause'. A wilful refusal to select a player for first team matches is very likely to fall into this category even if it does not amount to a repudiatory breach of contract on the part of the employing club.

40   [1997] IRLR 462.

41   The fact that breach of this term can result in the awarding of a large sum of damages is illustrated by *Horkulak v Cantor Fitzgerald International* [2003] EWHC 1918 where an employee, who had been the victim of bullying, was awarded just under £1,000,000 in damages. The employee was employed as broker and thus, like many professional sports participants, was employed in a world where very high salaries are enjoyed.

The duty to take reasonable care

Given the financial consequences to a club if a player injures himself, a team-mate or in certain circumstances an opponent, and the high salaries that some sports professionals may command, it is at least conceivable that a club (or its insurance company) could require a player to indemnify it for such loss where it is the consequence of reckless conduct or negligence on the player's part. This might be especially so if the player concerned is no longer with the club, and therefore the effect on the player's morale would not be an issue for the plaintiff.

The employer's right to an indemnity was upheld by the House of Lords in *Lister v Romford Ice and Cold Storage Co Ltd*.[42] The decision has attracted much criticism because of the implications for good employee relations, and has been subjected to some judicial restriction.[43] However, in a 'non-industrial' context such as sport, contemporary judges might feel more inclined to apply the reasoning in *Lister* that an employee who breaks a contractual obligation of care, and thereby causes damage to the employer, is accordingly liable to compensate the employer, or perhaps more likely the club's insurance company.[44] The potential importance of *Lister* is now particularly significant in the light of high profile cases of litigation arising from fouls committed on the field of play.[45]

The duty of fidelity – exclusivity

Employees are under an obligation not to use or disclose confidential information obtained in the course of employment without the employer's consent. In other circumstances, however, there is no general obligation not to engage in 'moonlighting'. Employers who wish to secure the exclusive services of their employees will need to incorporate appropriate clauses into contracts of employment.

Clause 7 of the Football League Contract (above) prevents players from participating in their sport, or any other form of sporting activity, without the club's previous consent. Professional cricketers are subject to a wider restriction.

The Contract for Professional Cricketers

Clause 5(c)

... The Cricketer will ... Not without the prior consent in writing of the Club accept other employment or on his own account carry on any business calling or profession. Such consent will not be withheld where in the reasonable opinion of the Club the proper performance by the Cricketer of his obligations under this Agreement is not affected and where the interests of the club are not harmed.[46]

---

42 [1957] ALL ER 125.

43 See, for example, the Court of Appeal's decision in *Morris v Ford Motor Co* [1973] QB 792 which restricts the possibility of subrogation, ie, an insurance company substituting itself as the plaintiff to recover the money that it has paid to the insured.

44 Note that in *Morris* the majority of the Court of Appeal refused to accept Lord Denning's argument that an insurer should never be able to benefit from subrogation in an employment context.

45 See further, Chapters 15 and 16 on sportsfield violence.

46 On the other hand, cricketers had the contractual right to play international cricket if selected – cl 5(d). Indeed, today, as a result of the central contracts system, a player under contract to play for the England Test team may only play for his club with the permission of the ECB. Cf the position of footballers where a club may decide not to release a player whom the England manager has indicated he would like to select.

The duty of fidelity – maintaining confidentiality

Duties relating to confidential information are important in the context of 'whistle-blowing.' The scope of the implied duty of fidelity can be amplified by express terms in the contract, as in cl 13 of the Football League Contract (above). The concept of public interest may be invoked to justify a disclosure which would be otherwise a breach of contract.

Initial Services Ltd v Putterill **[1968] 1 QB 396 CA**

Lord Denning . . . disclosure must, I should think, be to one who has a proper interest to receive the information. Thus it would be proper to disclose a crime to the police; or a breach of the Restrictive Trade Practices Act to the Registrar. There may be cases where the misdeed is of such a character that the public interest may demand, or at least excuse, publication on a broader field, even to the press . . . [47]

The Public Disclosure Act 1998 also protects employees from dismissal or being subjected to any other detriment if they disclose information relating to, for example, criminal behaviour on the part of an employer. The statutory provisions override any contractual terms requiring employees to maintain confidentiality.

However, employers are still able to use employment contracts to a significant extent to conceal information which it can be argued the public have a legitimate interest in receiving. For example, the Act would make no difference to keeping confidential the details of the much publicised row between Devon Malcom and Ray Illingworth, even though the disclosure of such information could be seen as a matter of public interest. There is nothing in law that requires the public to be told why a player has been selected or dropped from a national team. Moreover, even where disclosure is permitted it will generally only be protected if it is made to the proper authorities rather than the media. For example, if a player or an agent or a manager discovered financial irregularities within a club, publication should be limited to bodies such as the Football Association/Football League or the England and Wales Cricket Board, and therefore might not necessarily enter the public domain.[48]

The Premier League Rules require players and agents to maintain confidentiality with respect to the personal terms in the player's employment contract. It was breach of this rule that led to the litigation between Middlesbrough FC and Liverpool FC over Christian Ziege.[49]

Confidentiality (Section K)

24. A contract between a Club and a Player shall be treated as being private and confidential and its contents shall not be disclosed or divulged either directly or indirectly to any Person whatsoever by either party thereto except:

    24.1 with the prior written agreement of both parties; or

    24.2 as may be required by any statutory, regulatory, governmental or quasi-governmental authorities or (where appropriate) any recognised stock exchange or as otherwise required by law or pursuant to these Rules, or

---

47 At pp 406.

48 However, rights to disclose information to the media may well have been extended as a result of the Human Rights Act 1998 and the incorporation of Art 10 of the European Convention on Human Rights into UK law. The actual legal position remains to be clarified through case law.

49 See above, fn 29.

24.3 in the case of the Player, to his duly appointed Agent and professional advisers including the Professional Footballers' Association; or

24.4 in the case of the Club, to its duly appointed Agent and its professional advisers or to such of its Officials or Auditors to whom such disclosure is strictly necessary for the purpose of their duties and then only to the extent so necessary.

RESTRAINT OF TRADE

The duty of fidelity applies whilst the contract subsists but ceases to apply on its termination except to information which comes within the category of a trade secret. Nevertheless, contract law permits express terms which affect an individual's freedom to work for whom he pleases once an employment contract has come to an end. Such clauses are *prima facie* in restraint of trade and thus void. However, a restraint is permitted if an employer has a legitimate interest to protect and the clause is reasonable in that it is no wider than necessary so as to protect the employer.

Sports professionals often begin their careers whilst young. They are thus in a similar position to entertainers such as pop/rock musicians in that in order to get a foot on the rung of the ladder of success they may sign a contract without fully understanding the practical implications of what they are agreeing to. Indeed, even if they do fully understand what the contract provides they may feel they have no option but to sign if their careers are to progress.[50]

The doctrine of restraint of trade is of particular significance in professional football in light of the transfer rules laid down by the Premier and Football Leagues. These rules used to apply to all professional players whose contracts with their clubs had come to an end. The position under the English law of contract was (is) that these rules are valid and thus enforceable.

Eastham v Newcastle United FC [1963] 3 All ER 139 Ch D

The transfer and retain system as it operated at the time was challenged by the footballer George Eastham as constituting an unlawful restraint of trade. Under the system on termination of a contract a club could decide to put a player on the retain list. As a consequence the player so retained could not play for any club in any country which was a member of FIFA. If the club refused to place him on the transfer list he had no choice but to accept the offer of a new contract from the club if he wished to work as a professional footballer. These regulations were declared in restraint of trade. However, the rules enabling a club to require a transfer fee were upheld.

Wilberforce J: The transfer system has been stigmatised by the plaintiff's counsel as a relic from the Middle Ages, involving the buying and selling of human beings as chattels; and, indeed, to anyone not hardened to acceptance of the practice it would seem incongruous to the spirit of a national sport. One must not forget that the consent of a player to the transfer is necessary, but, on the other hand, the player has little security since he cannot get a long term contract and, while he is on the transfer list awaiting an offer, his feelings and anxieties as to who his next employer is to be may not be very pleasant.[51]

---

50 For an analysis of the operation of the implications of the doctrine of restraint of trade for boxers' contracts, see Greenfield, S and Osborn, G, 'A gauntlet for the glove: the challenge to English boxing contracts' (1995) 6(1) Marquette Sports Law Journal 153–171. Of particular concern is the situation where a young boxer signs a contract under which the same person is 'employed' by the boxer to manage him and promote his fights.

51 [1963] 3 All ER 139, 145. Although it was decided that it was unlawful for clubs to retain players who were out of contract, it was this landmark case that decided that the transfer system, on its own, did not constitute a restraint of trade and was thus legal.

Despite this, Wilberforce J was prepared to uphold the transfer system taken alone as, although there was an element of restraint, a player could apply to have a transfer fee reduced or eliminated and could play professional football for a non-League club. The transfer system was protecting a legitimate interest as:

> ... within the League it provides a means by which the poorer clubs can, on occasions, obtain money, enabling them to stay in existence and improve their facilities; and, rather more generally, ... it provides a means by which clubs can part with a good player in a manner which will enable them to secure a replacement. One player cannot easily be exchanged for another; the transferee club may not – indeed by the nature of things probably will not – have a player to offer in exchange: by giving cash, the transferor club is able to look all around the League for a replacement. Given the need to circulate players, money is necessarily a more efficient medium of exchange than barter, and the system helps both money and players to circulate. Looked at in this way the system might be said to be in the interests of players themselves.[52]

There has been no indication on the part of the English courts in the years since *Eastham* that there has been any rethinking of the reasoning of Wilberforce J. However, as a result of changes that were introduced, in the wake of the *Bosman* ruling, at the start of the 1998/99 season, players who are aged 24 or over and who are out of contract are completely free to negotiate a new contract with any club.

For players who are under 24 and out of contract the position remains as follows. When a player's contract comes to an end he is not unconditionally free to negotiate a contract with a different club unless (and this is relatively unlikely with younger players who have successfully embarked on a professional career) he is given a free transfer. In this case he is literally a free agent who can move to a new club on whatever terms he (or his agent) can negotiate. Alternatively, and the more likely position in practice, the club can retain him as a registered player by offering a new contract on terms no less advantageous than the expired contract. The player is 'free' to negotiate a move to another club but this is subject to the clubs agreeing a transfer fee. If a fee cannot be agreed between the two clubs the issue may be referred to the Football League Appeals Committee whose decision on the value of the transfer fee is final. In practice, a player's desire to move may be frustrated if other clubs are not prepared to pay the required or prescribed transfer fee. Moreover, a player may submit to pressure to sign a new contract with a club to regain some security of employment.

FA Code of Practice and Notes on Contract

Retain and Transfer Rules

The Player's contract will run for a stated period. During that time the Club and Player have binding obligations to each other. These can be ended by agreement, so it is possible for the Club to suggest to the Player that he might like to consider joining another Club, and the Player can indicate to the Club that he would like to leave. Agreement of both sides is essential. No one is entitled in law to induce either a Club or Player to break a contract; such action is tortuous and could lead to an action for damages.

The aim of the current rules is to enable a Player to leave a Club freely at the end of his contract, but to recognise that the Club is entitled to compensation from the Club he joins, provided that this does not seriously hamper the Player's moving. It is implicit in the rules that the happy Club and Player should be able to continue their relationship smoothly. Contracts of any length are possible and a contract can be re-negotiated so that it runs for a further or a longer period.

---

52 [1963] 3 All ER 139, 149.

If, however, Player and Club decide to part at the end of a contract then the Player is free to look for another Club. He may do this even though his Club has made him a fresh offer. In three instances there will be no compensation payable:

(a) the Club has announced that he is free to move without fee,

(b) the Club has made no offer to him,

(c) the Club's offer is less favourable than his previous terms.

To calculate the position under (c) it is necessary to look at the most favourable year of the contract that has expired and to calculate the financial value and the bonus structure (the actual amount of bonus paid will of course depend upon appearances and results and is variable). If the previous contract contains a signing-on fee, paid in annual parts, the last part will be added unless the contract made clear that it was paid on a 'once only' basis. Players wishing to claim a Free Transfer on the basis that their offer of re-engagement is less favourable must make written application to The FA Premier League or The Football League (dependent on which League the Club is in membership) with a copy to their Club, by 30th June otherwise the Club's compensation rights will be retained. If there is a dispute over whether or not the terms are as favourable, the matter will be determined by the Board of the appropriate League and, on appeal, by The Football League Appeals Committee. A Player granted a Free Transfer is entitled to receive from his Club as severance payment his basic wage for a period of one month from the expiry date of his contract or until he signs for another Club, whichever period is the shorter, provided that where a Player signs for a Club within the month at a reduced basic wage then his old Club shall make up the shortfall in basic wage for the remainder of the month.

There is a time table for the various stages that must be followed:

(i) Third Saturday in May

This will usually be immediately after the end of the season. The Club must have made its offer by that date. Practice varies but it should be noted that some Clubs make a 'starting offer' at the old rates and negotiate, others decide what they regard as the contract they wish to make at the outset. It is important that during the period set aside for negotiation the Club officials (usually manager and secretary but often a director) and the Player are available. In special cases, eg where Clubs have outstanding fixtures affecting promotion or relegation, the notification may be delayed until no later than four days after the Club's last such fixture.

(ii) Period for consideration

The Player has at least a month (the offer may be sent early) to decide whether to accept the contract, to discuss it with the Club and to let the Club know his decision. Rules and Regulations provide that the Player must at the end of the period give the Club his decision. A list of these Players refusing offers (or free to move without compensation) will be circulated by the League concerned. It is in the interests of a Player who receives an offer of re-engagement with which he is dissatisfied to inform the Club in writing and in person in order to give the Club the opportunity to make a revised offer

(iii) Offer refused

If the Player turns down the offer he can approach other Clubs and they can talk to him. His Club too can ask other Clubs if they are interested in signing the Player.

As a matter of courtesy, Clubs intending to negotiate with Players who have not accepted offers of re-engagement, should give notice of approach to the Player's existing Club. It is essential that both Club and Player keep each other informed where serious enquiries are made or interest shown. It is not only courteous, it is essential for the proper working of the scheme. Copies of all firm offers made for a Player should be notified to The FA Premier League and/or The Football League as appropriate. A Player who has refused his Club's offer of re-engagement may notify The FA Premier League or The Football League and The Professional Footballers' Association of his refusal and his name will be circulated to all Clubs.

The Club may leave its offer open so that the Player may, after talking to other Clubs, decide to stay. On the other hand it is entitled to withdraw that offer (without losing the right to compensation) if it feels it must do so to finalise its squad of Players for the new season.

A Player is free to train with another Club during this period, even though his transfer has not been fully agreed or the compensation fee settled and paid.

(iv) Compensation Fee

The compensation fee is a matter between the Clubs and only affects the Player if it makes his transfer difficult or unlikely. The Clubs themselves will discuss and settle the fee. If no fee has been settled, then after 30th June the Clubs, or the Player to whom terms have been conditionally offered may appeal to The Football League Appeals Committee to determine the fee. The Player must have either signed for his new Club, or agreed terms subject to the fee being satisfactory.

(v) 30th June

All contracts apart from Monthly Contracts are dated to run out on this date. If the Player has not been transferred by this date the Club holding his registration may propose various action (*Sic*):

(a) the Club may enter into a 'conditional' contract with the Player. A 'conditional' contract allows a Player to continue playing for a Club until such time as another Club wishes to sign him in which case he must be released even if the two Clubs cannot agree on a compensation fee. A conditional contract should take the form of a normal contract with the Player's remuneration and incentives being subject to mutual agreement. The following clause should also be included to safeguard the Player's rights, "This agreement is signed with the proviso that, should another Club wish to acquire the Player's registration, the registration will be transferred for a fee determined in accordance with the provisions of The FA Premier League Rules and The Football League Regulations";

(b) the Club may continue to pay the Player the basic wage payable under the contract which shall have expired in which case the Player is not eligible to play for the Club nor is he subject to the regulations or discipline of the Club. A Club taking up this option is, by continuing to pay the Player, retaining its rights to a compensation fee. This need not go on indefinitely and on or after the first day of the season, the Club may apply to The Football League Appeals Committee to cease paying the basic wage, at the same time retaining its right to a compensation fee if it feels that circumstances warrant such action, for example, if the Player has, without good reason, refused offers of employment with another Club;

(c) where a Club is desirous of playing a Player who is 'in dispute' yet does not wish to enter into a conditional contract, it may agree in writing with the Player that he should continue to play for the Club on a week to week basis under the financial terms of his last contract until such time as either the weekly agreement is terminated by either party or another Club is prepared to sign the Player Copies of all weekly agreements must be forwarded to the League in which the Club is a Member and The Football Association and it is recommended that they take the following form: 'The Player agrees to continue playing for the Club on a week to week basis under the financial terms of his last contract unless the Club incentive schedule paid in accordance with that contract has been changed in which case the Player will receive the revised incentives, and to be subject to Club Regulations and discipline and to the Rules and Regulations of The Football Association and The FA Premier League/The Football League. The Player agrees to give the Club at least seven days' notice of his intention to terminate this agreement. It is understood that the notice need not apply where a Player chooses to join another Club in which case the agreement will terminate forthwith'. It would seem to be in the interests of all parties for the Player to continue playing for a Club as it gives other Clubs who may be interested in signing him a chance to assess him in a match situation;

(d) the Club may cease paying the Player in which case he becomes a free agent.

A Player who is paid under either option (b) or option (c) is entitled to fourteen days notice of the cancellation of his registration.

So that the Player is able to understand the options open to him he is advised, if in any difficulty, to contact his PFA representative or The PFA Office.

It should be noted that equivalent rules and procedures are contained in Section M of the Premier League Rules. However, the position in the Premiership is further complicated by the new transfer window restrictions on when transfers to Premier League clubs may take place.

Section M
Transfers of Players' Registrations

Transfer Windows

1 **'Transfer Windows'** means the 2 periods in a year during which, subject to Rule M 5, a Club may apply for the New Registration of a player or to have the registration of a player transferred to it.

2 The first Transfer Window in any year shall commence at midnight on the last day of the Season and shall end at 5.00 pm on 31st August next.

3 The second Transfer Window in any year shall commence at midnight on 31st December and shall end at 5.00 pm on 31st January next.

4 A Club making an application during the second Transfer Window must satisfy the Board that it is made for strictly sport related reasons or in exceptional circumstances.

5 Outside a Transfer Window the Board in its absolute discretion may:

5.1 refuse an application; or

5.2 grant an application and, if thought fit, impose conditions by which the Club making the application and the player shall be bound.

6 Except in the case of a Temporary Transfer, the transfer of a player's registration shall not be permitted more than once in the same Season.

It can be commented that the introduction of transfer windows, whilst in accordance with the new FIFA rules for international transfers, remains controversial and is certainly not universally liked either by clubs or their supporters.[53]

As stated above the 'older' professional, who is out of contract, is able to enter into negotiations with any clubs which express interest in signing him. This includes, of course, negotiations with his current club, and a player who is still wanted by his club is in a strong bargaining position to re-negotiate personal terms including a salary increase and loyalty bonuses. It should be noted that under the new rules players are free to commence negotiations with new clubs during the final six months of their contracts. Clubs also have a financial incentive to allow a player to move prior to the expiry of his contract in order still to be able to secure a transfer fee.

The way that even older players were able to play the old transfer system to their advantage is set out below in the extract from Gary Nelson's autobiography. Arguably, the downside from a player's perspective to the new freedom of contract is that, if a club is unable to reach a transfer agreement for

---

53 See 'Window gets the thumbs down from the pros' *The Guardian*, 1 February 2003. This certainly was the experience of Portsmouth FC in its first season in the Premiership (2003–04) where the manager, Harry Redknapp, frequently claimed that the club's fortunes on the field of play were unduly hampered by injuries in circumstances where new players could not be brought in.

that player with another club, and that player's contract has now expired, his position is now the same as any other type of employee employed under a fixed term contract that has expired. In short, the immediate future might be unemployment, as the player may be free to move but without a club to move to. As a lesser evil, the player may find employment with a new club, but on inferior personal terms to those that he previously enjoyed. There is, however, the possibility, if a fixed term contract is not renewed, of being able to claim unfair dismissal or a statutory redundancy payment.[54] With respect to the latter, the player's contract may contain provision for a rather more generous severance payment in the event of the contract not being renewed.[55]

As explained in the final part of this chapter, under pressure from the European Commission, FIFA agreed to a major overhaul of the international transfer sytem with effect from the start of the 2001/02 season. Although initially the new system only applies to international transfers, it is anticipated that sooner rather than later national football associations will adopt rules based on the new FIFA regulations. Failure to do so, at least by football and indeed other sports authorities within the EU, may well result in a legal challenge of the sort threatened by Nicolas Anelka.[56]

Nelson, G, *Left Foot Forward*

Transfer tribunals were the logical and inevitable consequence of the PFA gaining 'freedom of contract' rights for players. Their coming into being arose from the need for an independent body to reconcile the 'legal rights' of the parties – existing employer club, employee player, would be employer club – involved in negotiations/dispute as an existing contract comes to its end. A player's current club have two options. They can dispense with a player – ie give him a 'free' – or retain him. Crucially, to retain him they must offer him a new contract that is at least as favourable as the one just ending. This does create problems for Boards. With players who are doing the business well enough to justify the original outlay on them and justify their first team selection, the club will not want the contract to expire. Every attempt will usually be made to offer a new one that is sufficiently attractive for the player to want to sign. But he (and certainly, where applicable, his agent!) will appreciate that he is negotiating from a position of strength. What he now considers 'attractive' may be a considerable escalation on his previous terms.

But the player may not be such an obvious asset. He may be getting long in the tooth, no longer performing at his former level. This may not weaken his bargaining position as much as might appear at first glance. Initially, he may have been signed for a large transfer fee plus a huge signing-on fee and very substantial wages. The common sense move now may be to sell him. But in order to be able to command a transfer fee (as opposed to giving him the free and writing off all their past investment), the club must have him on their books. That's to say, they must renew his contract on at least the same terms. Knowing a good thing when he sees it, the player is almost certain to re-sign at once. The club are now paying the same high level of monies as before to a player they don't really want but whom, if they want to balance their books at all, they need to sell at the same top end of the market they bought him in.

'Freedom of contract' has made it possible for players to let their contracts expire and yet put themselves in an enhanced bargaining position. Consistently good form should clearly earn appropriate reward – no problem, you would think. But in many cases clubs offer even on-song players the legal limit they are obliged to – the same terms the players are already on. The Board's hope in such instances is that, not attracting any interest from other clubs, the player will be forced to re-sign on the old terms. But if there is outside interest and the player has more than one option, the club's gamble is more than likely to misfire. The player has leverage. He can wait to see what is the best offer on the table; even play both ends against the middle.

---

54 See next chapter, pp 551–53.
55 Pages 7–10 of the Notes provide guidance to footballers on the operation of the transfer system.
56 See below, pp 511–12.

If, finally, a player refuses to re-sign with his existing club and signs for another, a transfer fee still has to be agreed between the two clubs. If they don't agree – and usually they don't – by now there's likely to be a lot of acrimony flying about and the transfer tribunal enters the equation. It will arbitrate and decide the fee.[57]

The major impetus for the reform to the English transfer system in 1998 and the FIFA system in 2001 was the preliminary ruling given by the European Court of Justice (ECJ) in *Bosman*.

THE *BOSMAN* CASE

The European Court's ruling in this case is based on its interpretation of Art 39[58] of the Treaty of Rome which provides for the right of EC nationals to work and reside in any Member State on equal terms with the nationals of that State. This Article is directly applicable and thus enforceable by national courts and tribunals. The Article takes precedence over any conflicting national laws. Under Art 234 of the Treaty of Rome, at the request of either party, or at its own discretion, a national court may decide to request a preliminary ruling from the European Court of Justice on the meaning of Art 39 (or any other EC law). The European Court is not deciding the case on appeal but is answering the questions put to it by the national court. This court will then decide the case by applying the interpretation of the Article contained in the European Court's ruling, and any relevant national law which does not conflict with it, to the facts of the case. The opinion of an Advocate General to the European Court is highly influential, but not binding, on any ruling (or decision) that the Court gives.

This case came about because Bosman, a Belgium national, was placed on the transfer list by his club, RC Liege, once he refused to accept a new contract at a lower wage. Bosman wished to move to a French club, US Dunkerque, but RC Liege ultimately refused to process the transfer as it doubted US Dunkerque's ability to pay the agreed fee. Subsequently, the Belgian Football Association and UEFA became parties to the case as both bodies argued that their respective rules requiring transfer fees were lawful. The Cour d'Appel, Liege requested a preliminary ruling from the European Court. One question put to the European Court was whether Art 39 is to be interpreted as:

> . . . prohibiting a football club from requiring and receiving payment of a sum of money upon the engagement of one of its players who has come to the end of his contract by a new employing club.

The Opinion of Advocate General Lenz was in the affirmative on the basis that:

> . . . the transfer rules directly restrict access to the employment market in other Member States . . . under the applicable rules a player can transfer abroad only if the new club (or the player himself) is in a position to pay the transfer fee demanded. If that is not the case, the player *cannot* move abroad. That is a *direct* restriction on access to the employment market.[59]

---

57 This extract, from Nelson, G, *Left Foot Forward* (1995), London: Headline: London, pp 261–63, provides a useful insight into the view the professional footballer takes of the transfer system.

58 The Treaty of Amsterdam has renumbered the articles of the EC Treaty. At the time of the ruling what is now Art 39 was Art 48. Similarly, Art 81 was Art 85. My commentary will use the contemporary references to Treaty Articles.

59 Paragraph 210 of the Opinion of Advocate General Lenz. This reasoning was adopted by the European Court in its preliminary ruling. The Advocate General also argued that the transfer system was contrary to Art 81, which prohibits anti-competitive practices within the EC. However, this position did not form part of the European Court's ruling. For an analysis of this dimension of Bosman, and further discussion of restraint of trade, see Morris, PE, Morrow, S and Spink, PM, 'EC law and professional football: Bosman and its implications' (1996) 59 Modern Law Review 893–902; Caiger, A and O'Leary, J, 'The end of the affair: the '*Anelka Doctrine*' – the problem of contract stability in English professional football', pp 197–216, in Caiger, A and Gardiner, S (eds), *Professional Sport in the EU: Regulation and Re-regulation* (2000) The Hague: Asser Press.

In reaching his conclusion the Advocate General considered and rejected, *inter alia*, the need to protect smaller clubs and providing compensation to clubs for training players as constituting grounds for justifying the retention of the transfer system. In so far as these objectives were legitimate they did not meet the requirement of proportionality as they could be achieved through a redistribution of income from larger to smaller clubs. In short, any legitimate interests could be achieved by means other than a transfer system impeding rights of freedom of movement.

ASBL Union Royale Belge des Societes de Football Association & others v Jean-Marc Bosman [1996] 1 CMLR 645 (Case C-415/93)

A number of points have been put forward as justification of the transfer rules. The most significant of them is in my opinion the assertion that the rules on transfers are necessary in order to preserve a certain financial and sporting balance between clubs. It is argued that the purpose of those rules is to ensure the survival of smaller clubs. At the hearing before the Court of Justice URBSFA expressly submitted in this connection that the transfer fees paid guaranteed the survival of the amateur clubs.

That argument amounts to an assertion that the system of transfer rules is necessary to ensure the organization of football as such. If no transfer fees were payable when players moved, the wealthy clubs would easily secure themselves the best players, while the smaller clubs and amateur clubs would get into financial difficulties and possibly even have to cease their activities. There would thus be a danger of the rich clubs always becoming even richer and the less well-off even poorer.

If that assertion was correct, then in my opinion it could indeed be assumed that the transfer rules were compatible with Article 48. Football is of great importance in the Community, both from an economic and from a sentimental point of view. As I have already mentioned, many people in the Community are interested in football; the number of spectators in stadiums and in front of television screens emphatically confirms that. In some towns the local football team is one of the big attractions which contribute decisively to the fame of the place. Thus in Germany there are probably only a few interested contemporaries who do not associate the town of Mönchengladbach with football. The big clubs have in addition long since become an important economic factor. It would thus be possible, in my opinion, to regard even the maintenance of a viable professional league as a reason in the general interest which might justify restrictions on freedom of movement. In this connection it should be observed that I share the opinion – as moreover do the other parties to the proceedings – that a professional league can flourish only if there is no too glaring imbalance between the clubs taking part. If the League is clearly dominated by one team the necessary tension is absent and the interest of the spectators will thus probably lapse within a foreseeable period.

Even more important is the field of amateur sport. There are currently a great many amateur clubs in which young people and adults are given an opportunity for sporting activity. The importance for society as such of the availability of a sensible leisure occupation needs no further explanation. If the transfer rules were necessary to guarantee the survival of those amateur clubs, that would without doubt be an imperative reason in the general interest, relevant in the context of Article 48.

It must therefore be examined whether the rules on transfers in fact have the significance attributed to them by URBSFA, UEFA and others. A distinction must be drawn between the effects on amateur clubs on the one hand and professional clubs on the other hand.

As regards the amateur clubs, no specific arguments, let alone figures, have been submitted to support the assertion that the abolition of the transfer rules would have life-threatening consequences for those clubs or at least for some of them. But the question need not be considered further in any case. The corresponding question submitted by the Liege Cour d'Appel for a preliminary ruling relates to the situation under the transfer rules of a player whose contract expires. What is concerned is thus the transfer of a professional player to another club. As I have stated above, there is thus no need to clarify in the present proceedings whether it is compatible with Community law that a transfer fee is payable on the transfer of an amateur player to a professional club. The present question is thus confined to professional football. It cannot be seen what effect the answer to the question of the lawfulness of the rules on transfers in that field could have on amateur clubs.

As regards the professional clubs too the interested associations have produced little convincing, specific material to support their argument. In my estimation the report on English football by Touche Ross, submitted by UEFA and already mentioned above, has the greatest significance for the examination required here. In England there is of course a four-level professional league divided up into – from top to bottom – the Premier League and the First, Second and Third Divisions. From the figures given in that report it can be seen that in the period used as a basis the clubs in the Premier League spent a total of about £18.5 million net (that is, after deducting income from transfer fees received by them) on new players. After deducting that sum from total receipts, the clubs were still left with a total profit of £11.5 million. The clubs in the First Division, by contrast, made a surplus on transfer deals of a good £9.3 million, those in the Second Division a surplus of just £2.4 million and those in the Third Division a surplus of around £1.6 million. It is noteworthy in addition that for the latter three divisions there was in each case a loss on ordinary trading which was more than covered by the income from transfers.

Those figures are an impressive demonstration of what an important role the lower divisions play as a reservoir of talent for the top division. They also show that income from transfers represents an important item in the balance sheets of the lower division clubs. If the transfer rules were to be regarded as unlawful and those payments thus ceased, one would expect those clubs to encounter serious difficulties.

I thus entirely agree with the view, once more put forward clearly by URBSFA and UEFA at the hearing before the Court, that it is of fundamental importance to share income out between the clubs in a reasonable manner. However, I am nevertheless of the opinion that the transfer rules in their current form cannot be justified by that consideration. It is doubtful even whether the transfer rules are capable of fulfilling the objective stated by the associations. In any event, however, there are other means of attaining that objective which have less effect, or even no effect at all, on freedom of movement.

With reference to the question of the suitability of those rules for achieving the desired objective, it must first be observed that the rules currently in force probably very often force the smaller professional clubs to sell players in order to ensure their survival by means of the transfer income thereby obtained. Since the players transferred to the bigger clubs are as a rule the best players of the smaller professional clubs, those clubs are thereby weakened from a sporting point of view. It is admittedly true that as a result of the income from transfers those clubs are placed in a position themselves to engage new players, in so far as their general financial situation permits. As has been seen, however, the transfer fees are generally calculated on the basis of the players' earnings. Since the bigger clubs usually pay higher wages, the smaller clubs will probably hardly ever be in a position themselves to acquire good players from those clubs. In that respect the rules on transfers thus strengthen even further the imbalance which exists in any class between wealthy and less wealthy clubs. The Commission and Mr Bosman correctly drew attention to that consequence.

Mr Bosman has also submitted with some justification that the rules on transfers do not prevent the rich clubs from engaging the best players, so that they are only suitable to a limited extent for preserving the sporting equilibrium. The obligation to expend a sometimes substantial sum of money for a new player is indeed no great obstacle for a wealthy club or a club with a wealthy patron. That is emphatically shown by the examples of AC Milan and Blackburn Rovers.

The financial balance between the clubs is moreover also not necessarily strengthened by the rules on transfers. If a club engages players from clubs in other Member States or non-member countries, the funds required for the purchases flow abroad without the other clubs in the same league as the club in question benefiting therefrom.

Above all, however, it is plain that there are alternatives to the transfer rules with which the objectives pursued by those rules can be attained. Basically there are two different possibilities, both of which have also been mentioned by Mr Bosman. Firstly, it would be possible to determine by a collective wage agreement specified limits for the salaries to be paid to the players by the clubs. That possibility was described in more detail by Mr Bosman in his observations. He observed, however, that that possibility is not as effective as the alternative, which I am about to discuss. In view of what I am about to say, it is thus not necessary for me to say any more on this possibility. Secondly, it would be conceivable to distribute the clubs' receipts among the clubs. Specifically, that means that part of the income obtained by a club from the sale of tickets for its home matches is distributed to the other clubs. Similarly, the income received for awarding the rights to transmit matches on television, for instance, could be divided up between all the clubs.

. . . It can scarcely be doubted that such a redistribution of income appears sensible and legitimate from an economic point of view. UEFA itself has rightly observed that football is characterized by the mutual economic dependence of the clubs. Football is played by two teams meeting each other and testing their strength against each other. Each club thus needs the other one in order to be successful. For that reason each club has an interest in the health of the other clubs. The clubs in a professional league thus do not have the aim of excluding their competitors from the market. Therein lies – as both UEFA and Mr Bosman have rightly stated – a significant difference from the competitive relationship between undertakings in other markets. It is likewise correct that the economic success of a league depends not least on the existence of a certain balance between its clubs. If the league is dominated by one overmighty club, experience shows that lack of interest will spread.

If every club had to rely on financing its playing operations exclusively by the income it received from the sale of tickets, radio and television contracts and other sources (such as advertising, members' subscriptions or donations from private sponsors), the balance between the clubs would very soon be endangered. Big clubs like FC Bayern Munchen or FC Barcelona have a particular power of attraction which finds expression in high attendance figures. Those clubs thereby also become of great interest for television broadcasters and the advertising sector. The large income resulting from that permits those clubs to engage the best players and thereby reinforce their (sporting and economic) success even more. For the smaller clubs precisely the converse would happen. The lack of attractiveness of a team leads to correspondingly lower income, which in turn reduces the possibilities of strengthening the team.

Mr Bosman has admittedly pointed out that there are those who consider that the necessary balance results as it were automatically, since by reason of the facts described above no club can be interested in achieving an overwhelming superiority in its league. Experience shows, however, that club managements do not always calculate in that way, but may at times allow themselves to be led by considerations other than purely sporting or economic ones. It therefore is indeed necessary, in my opinion, to ensure by means of specific measures that a certain balance is preserved between the clubs. One possibility is the system of transfer payments currently in force. Another possibility is the redistribution of a proportion of income.

Mr Bosman submitted a number of economic studies which show that distribution of income represents a suitable means of promoting the desired balance. The concrete form given to such a system will of course depend on the circumstances of the league in question and on other considerations. In particular it is surely clear that such a redistribution can be sensible and appropriate only if it is restricted to a fairly small part of income: if half the receipts, for instance, or even more was distributed to other clubs, the incentive for the clubs in question to perform well would probably be reduced too much.

Neither URBSFA nor UEFA disputed that that solution is a realistic possibility which makes it possible to promote a sporting and financial balance between clubs. If I am not very much mistaken, they did not even attempt to rebut the arguments put forward by Mr Bosman in this connection.

It seems to me that that is not a matter of chance. The associations too can scarcely dispute that that possibility is an appropriate and reasonable alternative. The best evidence for that is the circumstance that corresponding models are already in use in professional football today. In the German cup competition, for example, the two clubs involved each to my knowledge receive half of the receipts remaining after deduction of the share due to the DFB. The income from awarding the rights of television and radio broadcasts of matches is distributed by the DFB among the clubs according to a specified formula. The position is presumably much the same in the associations of the other Member States.

A redistribution of income also takes place at UEFA level. Under Article 18 of the UEFA statutes (1990 edition), UEFA is entitled to a share of the receipts from the competitions it organizes and from certain international matches. A good example is the UEFA Cup rules for the 1992/93 season, which have been produced to the Court by URBSFA. Under those rules UEFA receives for each match a share of 4% of gross receipts from the sale of tickets and 10% of receipts from the sale of the radio and television rights. For the two legs of the final UEFA's share is increased to as much as 10% and 25% respectively.

While that system serves to cover the expenditure of UEFA and thus only indirectly – by means of corresponding grants by UEFA to certain associations or clubs leads to a redistribution of income, the case is different with the 'UEFA Champions League'. That competition, which took the place of the earlier European Champions' Cup, was introduced by UEFA in 1992. A UEFA document produced to the Court by Mr Bosman provides information on the purpose and organization of that competition. The objective is stated to be the promotion of the interests of football. It is specifically noted that the profit is not only to be for the benefit of the clubs taking part, but all the associations are to receive a share of it.

A balance of the 1992/93 season makes that clear. According to that, the eight clubs which took part in the competition each kept the receipts from the sale of tickets for their home matches. In addition to that, the competition produced an income of 70 million Swiss francs from the marketing of television and advertising rights. That amount was divided up as follows. The participating clubs received SFR 38 million (54%). A further SFR 12 million (18%) was distributed to all the clubs which had been eliminated in the first two rounds of the three UEFA competitions for club teams. SFR 5.8 million (8%) was distributed between the 42 member associations of UEFA. The remaining SFR 14 million (20%) went to UEFA, to be invested for the benefit of football, in particular for the promotion of youth and women's football.

The example of the Champions League in particular clearly demonstrates, in my opinion, that the clubs and associations concerned have acknowledged and accepted in principle the possibility of promoting their own interests and those of football in general by redistributing a proportion of income. I therefore see no unsurmountable obstacles to prevent that method also being introduced at national level or at the level of the relevant association. By designing the system in an appropriate way it would be possible to avoid the incentive to perform well being reduced excessively and the smaller clubs becoming the rich clubs' boarders. I cannot see any negative effects on the individual clubs' self-esteem. Even if there were such effects, they would be purely of a psychological nature and thus not such as to justify a continued restriction on freedom of movement resulting from the transfer system.

Finally, it must be observed that a redistribution of a part of income appears substantially more suitable for attaining the desired purpose than the current system of transfer fees. It permits the clubs concerned to budget on a considerably more reliable basis. If a club can reckon with a certain basic amount which it will receive in any case, then solidarity between clubs is better served than by the possibility of receiving a large sum of money for one of the club's own players. As Mr Bosman has rightly submitted, the discovery of a gifted player who can be transferred to a big club for good money is very often largely a matter of chance. Yet the prosperity of football depends not only on the welfare of such a club, but also on all the other small clubs being able to survive. That, however, is not guaranteed by the present rules on transfers.

In so far as the rules on transfers pursue the objective of ensuring the economic and sporting equilibrium of the clubs, there is thus at least one alternative by means of which that objective can be pursued just as well and which does not adversely affect players' freedom of movement. The transfer rules are thus not indispensable for attaining that objective, and thus do not comply with the principle of proportionality.

The second important argument on which the associations concerned base their opinion that the transfer system is lawful consists in the assertion that the transfer fees are merely compensation for the costs incurred in the training and development of a player. The Italian and French Governments have also adopted that argument. It is of course closely connected with the first argument, which I have just discussed.

However often that view has been repeated in the course of these proceedings, it still remains unconvincing.

The transfer fees cannot be regarded as compensation for possible costs of training, if only for the simple reason that their amount is linked not to those costs but to the player's earnings. Nor can it seriously be argued that a player, for example, who is transferred for a fee of one million ECU caused his previous club to incur training costs amounting to that vast sum. A good demonstration that the argument put forward by the associations is untenable can be found in the DFB transfer rule, described above, for the transfer of an amateur player to a professional club. As we have seen, under that rule a first division club had to pay a transfer fee of DM 100 000, whereas a second division club had to pay only DM 45 000 for the same player. That shows that the amount of the transfer fee quite evidently is not orientated to the costs of training.

A second argument against regarding transfer fees as a reimbursement of the training costs which have been incurred is the fact that such fees – and in many cases extraordinarily large sums – are demanded even when experienced professional players change clubs. Here there can no longer be any question of 'training' and reimbursement of the expense of such training. Nor does it make any difference that in such cases it is often 'compensation for development' (not compensation for training) which is spoken of. Any reasonable club will certainly provide its players with all the development necessary. But that is expenditure which is in the club's own interest and which the player recompenses with his performance. It is not evident why such a club should be entitled to claim a transfer fee on that basis. The regulations of the French and Spanish associations have, quite rightly in my opinion, drawn the conclusion that – at least after a specified moment in time – no transfer fees can be demanded any more.

Finally, it is self-evident that the training of any player involves expense. Reimbursement of that expenditure would thus depend on whether or not that player was transferred to another club. That too shows that the reasoning advanced by the interested parties does not hang together.

That does not mean, however, that a demand for a transfer fee for a player would, following the view I have put forward, have to be regarded as unlawful in every case. The argument that a club should be compensated for the training work it has done, and that the big, rich clubs should not be enabled to enjoy the fruits of that work without making any contribution of their own, does indeed in my opinion have some weight. For that reason it might be considered whether appropriate transfer rules for professional footballers might not be acceptable. Mr Bosman himself concedes that such transfer rules might be reasonable as regards transfers of amateur players to professional clubs. That question need not be discussed further in the present proceedings, which concern only changes of clubs by professional players. The Commission, however, suggested quite generally that a reasonable transfer fee may be justified.

Such rules would in my opinion have to comply with two requirements. First, the transfer fee would actually have to be limited to the amount expended by the previous club (or previous clubs) for the player's training. Second, a transfer fee would come into question only in the case of a first change of clubs where the previous club had trained the player. Analogous to the transfer rules in force in France, that transfer fee would in addition have to be reduced proportionately for every year the player had spent with that club after being trained, since during that period the training club will have had an opportunity to benefit from its investment in the player.[60]

---

60 The new FIFA rules concerning the calculation of compensation for the training of younger players would appear to conform to these principles; see below, pp 517–19.

The transfer rules at issue in the present case do not meet those requirements, or at best meet them in part. Moreover, it is not certain that even such a system of transfer rules could not also be countered by Mr Bosman's argument that the objectives pursued by it could also be attained by a system of redistribution of a proportion of income, without the players' right to freedom of movement having to be restricted for that purpose. The associations have not submitted anything which refute that objection. It should be noted, moreover, that the above-mentioned DFB rules on the transfer of amateur players to professional clubs, for instance, appear to follow basically similar considerations with their differing standard amounts.

In addition to the above arguments a number of other considerations have also been put forward as justification for the rules on transfers; they must now be considered.

UEFA has submitted that the payment of transfer fees enables and even encourages the clubs to search for talented players, an activity which is vital for football. Even if that is the case, I do not see why it should be necessary for that purpose to make the transfer of players depend on the payment of a transfer fee. The possibility already referred to several times, of redistributing a share of income would also give clubs the financial means for the discovery and training of talented young players. Such a system of redistribution can also very well be designed in such a way as to allow incentives to be maintained for seeking out talent and providing a good training.

The argument, also advanced by UEFA, that transfer fees make it possible for the clubs to take on staff – which probably did not only mean players – I do not find convincing. As I have already shown, there are other possible methods of financing open to the clubs which do not affect the freedom of movement of players.

The argument that the payment of transfer fees must be permitted in order to compensate clubs for the amounts they themselves have had to spend on transfer fees when engaging players requires no further discussion: that argument contains a *petitio principii*. So does the argument that the purpose of the transfer fee is to compensate the loss which the club incurs because of the player's departure: that presupposes precisely that a player can be regarded as a sort of merchandise for the replacement of which a price is to be paid. Such an attitude may correspond to today's reality, as characterized by the transfer rules, in which the 'buying' and 'selling' of players is indeed spoken of. That reality must not blind us to the fact that that is an attitude which has no legal basis and is not compatible with the right to freedom of movement.

Mr Bosman has expressed the supposition that the transfer rules are intended to serve the purpose of reserving the sums in question for the clubs: according to the view he has put forward, the abolition of the transfer rules would lead to a general increase in players' wages. There is something to be said for that view. If the transfer rules really were – inter alia – based on that (economic) purpose, it would in any event not be such as to justify the consequent restriction on freedom of movement, since no interest of the clubs deserving of legal protection can be discerned in their paying lower salaries than would be payable in normal circumstances in the absence of the transfer rules and thereby benefiting at the expense of the players.

URBSFA has submitted that the present rules on transfers pursue the aim of guaranteeing the quality of football and promoting sporting activity and the sporting ethos. That argument appears to me to be directed essentially to the amateur sphere, which – to repeat it once again – is not concerned by the present proceedings. Moreover, it is not evident in any case how the transfer rules are supposed to help attain those very generally stated objectives. I also have considerable doubts as to whether a system which ultimately amounts to treating players as merchandise is liable to promote the sporting ethos.

A more important objection is that the continued existence of those rules is necessary to guarantee the maintenance of the worldwide organization of football. The question of the compatibility of those rules with Community law is of significance for world football only in so far as the associations in the Community are affected. It is thus clear that the decision in the present case will apply to those associations only. If the Court follows the opinion I am advancing, it will no longer be possible within the Community to make the transfer of a professional footballer whose contract has expired and who is a national of a Member State to a club in another Member State depend on the payment of a transfer fee. It will, on the other hand, be open to associations in non-member countries to maintain those rules. That would have the result that a club in the Community wishing to engage a player who previously played for a club in a non-member country would still have to pay a transfer fee – even if that player was a national of one of the Member States of the Community. That could well create difficulties.

Those difficulties must not be exaggerated, however. The example of France (and to a certain degree Spain) shows that even now the system of transfer fees can be largely dispensed with within a Member State while continuing to be applicable to relations with other countries. There is thus nothing to prevent the Community being treated as a unit within which transfer fees are to be dispensed with, while being maintained for transfers to or from non-member countries. Moreover, that altogether corresponds in my opinion to the logic of the internal market.

Finally, I must mention the fear that the abolition of the existing rules on transfers would lead to dramatic changes in football or even to an expropriation. The view I have put forward would certainly mean that considerable changes would have to be made to the organization of professional football in the Community. In the medium and long term, however, no insuperable difficulties should arise. As the introduction by UEFA of the Champions League shows, for instance, the associations are perfectly capable of taking the measures necessary for the good of football. In the short term the abolition of transfer fees will certainly entail some hardships, especially for those clubs which have only recently invested money in such transfer fees. There can be no question of an expropriation, however. If someone regards players as merchandise with a monetary value, whose value may in some cases even be included in the balance sheet, he does so at his own risk. Moreover, it must be observed that the abolition of transfer fees will at the same time bring a club benefits, by giving it the possibility of taking on new players without having to pay a transfer fee. As to the clubs which have only just 'bought' new players, it must be noted that the contracts concluded with the players run for a specified term, during which those players can leave the club only with the club's agreement. The ending of transfer fees will thus become noticeable for those clubs only when that period has expired.[61]

It is interesting to reflect with the benefit of hindsight on the fact that many of the initial responses to the *Bosman* ruling concentrated on the extent to which it would still be 'business as usual'. There was a strong argument that the ruling would not affect the transfer system then operating within the Premier, Football and Scottish Leagues. It was assumed by almost everyone (including this writer) that *Bosman* had no implications for players who wished to secure transfers whilst still under contract.[62] On the other hand, whilst the actual legal position has not been and in practice never may be clarified, there were arguments that *Bosman* did impact on transfers within Member States and thus the changes voluntarily introduced in Britain were necessary to avoid the threat of legal challenge.

---

61 The ECJ's ruling was delivered on 15 December 1995. For an immediate reaction to the ruling see press reports of 16 and 17 December 1995. On the personal fate of Jean-Marc Bosman and a survey of a responses across the EC to the ruling, see *The Independent On Sunday* 18 February 1996. For the definitive academic analysis of *Bosman*, see Blanpain, R and Inston, R, *The Bosman Case The End of the Transfer System?* (1996), London: Sweet & Maxwell, Leuven: Peeters.

62 See, for example, the contribution by Robert Reid to the 'FA Premier League Seminar' on the *Bosman* case, 8 January 1996, organised in conjunction with the British Association for Sport and Law. Indeed, the overall view of the speakers at the seminar was that the *Bosman* case could not have arisen in Britain as it would not have been permissible to retain a player on a lower wage. Moreover, the ruling did not explicitly cover the situation where a player wishes to move to another club within the same country. Thus, it was argued, the Premier and Football Leagues should not be panicked into making changes to the current transfer fee system.

Gardiner, S and Welch, R, 'The winds of change in professional football: the impact of the *Bosman* ruling'

It must be emphasised that in adopting the reasoning of Advocate General Lenz the European Court did not rule that a transfer system operating within the territory of a single Member State violates Article 48. Indeed, The European Court stated:

> '... the provisions of the Treaty concerning the free movement of workers, and particularly Article 48, cannot be applied to situations which are wholly internal to a Member State, in other words where there is no factor connecting them to any of the situations envisaged by Community law.'[63]

The ruling only expressly covers transfer systems that require a transfer fee to be paid before an out of contract player is able to move to a club in a different Member State. Nevertheless, as will be detailed below, voluntary reform to the UK transfer system has recently occurred in the wake of the *Bosman* ruling. However, it has been argued that the ruling had no direct impact on this transfer system as it stood where an out of contract player was seeking to move to another club within the UK. It is useful to identify arguments which, if correct, would contradict this perspective.

One possibility is provided by human rights law. This equates freedom of movement with freedom of choice as it requires states to permit nationals to move freely within their own country as well as recognising their rights to leave and return to it.[64] Arguably, this freedom is effectively being denied to an out of contract player if he is forced to move abroad if this is the only way in which he can evade the transfer system. On this point it is interesting that various rulings by the European Court interpreting Article 85 have made it clear that anti-competitive practices within a Member State can adversely affect trade in other Member States. If Article 85 can apply to a course of conduct in one Member State why should this also not be the case with Article 48? In short, it could be argued that a transfer system operating within a Member State is not 'wholly internal' to that state if it restricts the operation of Article 48 as far as that Member State's own nationals are concerned.[65]

Another argument supporting the proposition that the UK transfer system was in violation of Article 48 is derived from the concept of indirect discrimination. In the context of employment Article 48 prohibits discrimination against nationals of Member States on grounds of their nationality. Whilst this would normally be understood as protecting individuals who are nationals of other Member States from discrimination, arguably, there is no logical reason why this should not also protect nationals of the Member State concerned. Under *Bosman* it is clear that an English club could not prevent an English player (just like any other player possessing EU nationality), on the termination of his contract, from moving to another club within the EU. However, it is likely that many English players would prefer to move to another club within the UK rather than one in another Member State.

EC law prohibiting sex discrimination in employment[66] stipulates that an employer who imposes a requirement that adversely affects a greater number of employees of one sex as against the other has committed an act of indirect sex discrimination. This discrimination is unlawful unless it can be justified by reference to objective business or organisational interests and these are not outweighed by the impact of the discrimination.[67]

---

63 Paragraph 89 of the European Court's Ruling.

64 These rights were first proclaimed by Art 13 of the United Nations Universal Declaration of Human Rights in 1948 and are enshrined in Art 12 of the International Covenant on Civil and Political Rights 1966. The rights were incorporated into the European Convention on Human Rights by Arts 2 & 3 of the Fourth Protocol which was adopted by the signatory governments in 1963.

65 Cases illustrating how practices by undertakings within a single Member State can adversely affect interstate trade contrary to Art 81 include *Re German Ceramic Tiles Discount Agreement* [1971] CMLR D6 and *Brasserie de Haecht v Wilkin and Wilkin* [1968] CMLR 26.

66 The Equal Treatment Directive (76/207/EC) and Art 141 (formerly Art 119) of the EC Treaty which prohibits sex discrimination in the context of pay.

67 These principles were laid down by the European Court in *Bilka-Kaufhaus GmbH v Weber von Hartz* [1987] ICR 110.

Applying this approach to the above situation it could be argued that it is indirect discrimination, contrary to Article 48, for a club effectively to require an out of contract player to move to a club in another Member State if he is seeking to exercise the right to freedom of movement conferred by Article 48. The reason being that this might have a deterrent effect on British players, as against players of other nationalities, who for family and/or other reasons might regard it as detrimental to work outside of the UK and thus feel they have no practical option other than to accept that any transfer will be subject to a transfer fee being agreed. If the requirement that a transfer fee be paid before an out of contract British player could move to another UK club was found to constitute indirect discrimination then this would be unlawful unless it could be justified objectively.

It is however possible that the transfer system in the UK met the criteria for justifying indirect discrimination as the specifics of this transfer system were different to the Belgian system challenged by *Bosman*. Firstly, a British club lost the right to retain the registration of an out of contract player unless it offered him the same or a higher salary to that he was receiving under his former contract. Secondly (as referred to above), if the player was offered a contract by another club, but the amount of the transfer fee could not be agreed by the two clubs concerned, the player was entitled to have the amount of the fee determined by an independent transfer tribunal. Bosman had no recourse to such a tribunal, and, in any case, if UK rules had applied RC Liege would have lost the right to retain him as the immediate cause of Bosman's dispute with the club was the imposition of a wage cut as part of the new contractual terms offered to him.

Indeed, for these reasons it has been argued that had a similar case to *Bosman* arisen in this country it would have been found that the principle of proportionality required by Article 48 would have been satisfied, and the UK system would not have been found to have been in violation of EC law.[68] If this is correct then logically, even it was possible to argue that the transfer system indirectly discriminated against British players, the same reasoning could have been used to justify such discrimination.[69]

The *Bosman* ruling did and does not directly apply to players recruited from outside of the EU and EEA. Players from, as examples, European States outside of the EU,[70] the Americas, most African countries, Asia and Australia are not protected by Art 39. As a matter of historical record it should be noted that FIFA decided with effect from 1 April 1997 to change its rules to permit any player to move to other clubs within the EU on free transfers once their contracts expire.[71] Thus a British club still had to pay a transfer fee to import a player from, for example, a Brazilian club. However, if it retained that player until his contract expired a transfer fee could not be claimed unless that player negotiated a move to a club outside of the EU.

The significance of the 1997 FIFA decision has been dwarfed by the overhaul of the international transfer system agreed by the Executive Committee of FIFA on 5 July 2001. Before examining the new system it is valuable to consider the other main contention that has emerged in the wake of *Bosman* (and again a contention that has not been resolved by judicial decision); that is, the view that EU law requires a club to release a player's registration where a player breaks his existing contract of employment in order to sign a new contract with a new club.

---

68   See Sir John Wood's contribution to the FA Premier League Seminar on the *Bosman* Case.

69   (1998) 3(4) Contemporary Issues in Law 289–312.

70   It should be noted that the enlargement of the EU, which took place on 1 May 2004, has not automatically resulted in freedom of movement throughout the EU for nationals of the new Member States, other than those of Cyprus and Malta. Member States have until 2009 (or in special circumstances 2011) to lift work permit restrictions. Moreover, contrary to some expectations the ECJ has given no indication that it believes nationals of third countries, which have associate status, are protected by Art 39. These issues will be considered further in Chapter 14.

71   See *The Guardian*, 27 March 1997.

If it is correct to restrict *Bosman* to players who are out of contract[72] then, whilst the transfer rules as they currently operate in Britain continue to apply, it is possible for clubs to introduce new contractual devices to maximise the possibility of securing a transfer fee for a player who wants to leave the club, or is no longer wanted by it. One possibility is to use 'long' fixed term contracts. Another is to introduce lengthy notice periods with 'garden leave' provisions. However, the latter may offend the duty to provide work. Both devices are subject to the doctrine of restraint of trade.[73] This is particularly the case for the younger player, although arguably not where the contract is negotiated by an agent who genuinely has his client's best interests at heart.

It is interesting to compare the promising young footballer with, for example, the young musician or even an established rock band. In *Schroeder Music Publishing Co Ltd v Macaulay*[74] an unknown musician was released from a contract which was perceived as tying the individual to the company for five years, with an option for the company to extend this to ten years, whilst the company was required to give very little in return.

Schroeder Music publishing Co Ltd v Macaulay [1974] 3 ALL ER 616

Lord Diplock: . . . salutary to acknowledge that in refusing to enforce provisions of a contract whereby one party agrees for the benefit of the other party to exploit or to refrain from exploiting his own earning-power, the public policy which the court is implementing is not some 19th century economic theory about the benefit to the general public of freedom of trade, but the protection of those whose bargaining power is weak against being forced by those whose bargaining power is stronger to enter into bargains that are unconscionable . . .

So I would hold that the question to be answered as respects a contract in restraint of trade . . . is: was the bargain fair? The test of fairness is, no doubt, whether the restrictions are both reasonably necessary for the protection of the legitimate interests of the promisee and commensurate with the benefits secured to the promisor under the contract. For the purpose of this test all the provisions of the contract must be taken into consideration.

In *Clifford Davis Management v WEA Records and CBS Records Ltd*[75] the band Fleetwood Mac was able to invoke this reasoning to secure release from a recording contract which tied the band to the appellant recording company for a five year period and which again contained a provision for the company to extend this by another five years. Interestingly, although at the time of the decision Fleetwood Mac had not attained the mega star status they were to go on to attract they were already an established band with significant chart success and some knowledge of the workings of the music industry. However, the court placed emphasis on the fact that they had not received independent advice prior to signing the contract with Clifford Davis.

Clearly, the approach taken in these cases has some potential repercussions for professional football or indeed other sports where 'long' contracts are used to tie players to clubs. This must particularly be the case with a trainee signing his first professional contract or indeed any young player who is eager to maintain a professional career. Arguably, given the experience of Fleetwood Mac, the doctrine of restraint of trade could even operate to protect the more experienced player who is still in his early twenties.

---

72 Paragraph 246 of the Opinion of Advocate General Lenz, see above pp 506–07, does seem quite explicit on this point.
73 See *op cit*, p 506, Gardiner and Welch (1998), pp 297–302.
74 [1974] 3 All ER 616.
75 [1975] 1 All ER 237.

A decisive factor in the Fleetwood Mac case was that the members of the band lacked any business experience. Clubs intending to tie young players to them are perhaps thus well advised to ensure that the individual player is properly advised by an agent and/or the PFA before deciding to sign. In this respect it is important to reiterate the advantages 'long' contracts can have for players given Lord Diplock's emphasis on the need to take all the provisions of a contract into account. It is rare for a player to find that his contract is being terminated as a result of serious injury, at least providing there are reasonable prospects that he will play again. Certainly, there are some players who benefit from the fact that their contracts continue and their salaries continue to be paid even though they are unlikely to be picked for first team football. In other sectors of employment employees who have become surplus to requirements are more likely to incur the risk of dismissal.

Overall the major problem with the doctrine of restraint of trade is that it is hard to identify principles of general application from decided case law. As illustrated by the difficulties George Michael faced when he tried to have his contract with Sony declared invalid, these types of claims tend to be decided on a case by case basis.[76] However, these arguments become academic if players are entitled to break their contracts providing compensation is paid to the employing club. If both the transfer rules and contract law are overridden by EU law, ie Articles 39 and/or 81 of the EC Treaty, then national associations will have no option other than to adopt the new transfer rules agreed to by FIFA. This is particularly so given that the European Commission has, at least informally, approved these rules as being compatible with EU law.[77]

The initial background to introduction of the new FIFA rules was the announcement by Nicolas Anelka in the summer of 1999 that he no longer wanted to honour his contract to play for Arsenal FC. Anelka wished to leave the UK and play for the Italian club, Lazio. At the time of this announcement Anelka had another four years of his contract to run. The problem for Anelka was that Arsenal was not prepared to release him from his contractual obligations, and Lazio was not prepared to pay the sizeable transfer fee that Arsenal required.

This situation generated legal debate (initiated by Jean-Louis Dupont, the Belgian lawyer who advised Bosman) that to prevent a player from terminating his employment contract, as the transfer system does, is as much a restraint on a player's freedom of movement as where a player is prevented from moving to another club on the expiry of his contract. The argument on behalf of Anelka was that he should have the right to break his contract providing he was prepared to pay compensation to Arsenal by reference to the normal contractual principles for calculating damages.

Interestingly, estimations of the actual amount of compensation to which Arsenal would have been entitled varied from around £5 m to a figure nearer the £22 m transfer fee that Arsenal required. The position with respect to Anelka was ultimately resolved when Arsenal accepted a transfer bid submitted by Real Madrid. However, the incident cast doubt on the original assumption, in the aftermath of *Bosman*, that Art 39 only applied to out of contract players.

---

76 For further discussion of restraint of trade see *op cit* fn 59, Morris *et al* (1996). With respect to the music industry specifically, see Greenfield, S and Osborn, G, 'Sympathy for the Devil? Contractual Constraint and Artistic Autonomy in the Entertainment Industry' (1994) 15(1) Journal of Media Law and Practice 117–27.

77 See Commission press release of 5 March 2001 on the outcome of discussions between the Commission and FIFA/UEFA on FIFA Regulations on international football transfers. Also see the statement by Mario Monti, the Competition Commissioner, of 11 June 2003 stating that the Commission had closed its investigation into the validity of the new rules. FIFPro, on the other hand, has stated that in its view there may still be issues to resolve – see press release of 13 June 2003 – www.fifpro.org. See the following chapter, pp 525–26, for discussion of the impact of these new regulations where players unilaterally terminate their current contracts. Revised rules were adopted by FIFA in October 2003 and came into force on 1st July 2005. However, the salient features of the rules remain the same.

The legal situation was further complicated by a complaint to the Commission by the Italian club Perugia. The basis of the club's complaint was that it wished to recruit an Italian player, Massimo Lombardo, from the Swiss club, Zurich Grasshoppers. Although Lombardo was at the end of his contract with Grasshoppers, *Bosman* did not directly apply to his situation, as Switzerland is not covered by EC law. In December 1998 the Commission ruled that the transfer system in its entirety, not just on expiry of a player's contract, violated EC competition law. This resulted in FIFA coming under considerable pressure to formulate proposals for reform, although the Commission had also emphasised it was not seeking the complete abolition of the transfer system as it recognises the 'specificity of sport'.[78]

It is not absolutely clear that the new rules conform with EC law, as the ECJ has yet to rule on the issue, and litigation challenging the rules could still occur in the future. For example, Andrew Caiger and John O'Leary have provided a particularly intriguing argument supporting the contention that *Bosman* applies to players denied a mid-contract transfer.[79] They argue that any player who unilaterally breaks his contract should be considered to be out of contract. Thus, in line with *Bosman*, the employing club has no option other than to release his registration. The club's only remedy is to seek damages for breach of contract. Caiger and O'Leary also stress that to permit professional footballers to act in this way is simply to allow them to act as any other employee under any other contract of employment is able to do.

These arguments are certainly cogent. However, as will be examined in the next chapter, there are mechanisms that can be used by an employer to restrain an employee from acting in breach of contract, or from working for a competitor on termination of an existing contract. Thus it is not always the case that an employee is always free to walk away from a job by unilaterally breaking the contract of employment. It is also debatable whether a player who terminates a contract through committing a unilateral breach can be regarded as being 'out of contract' in the sense that that concept was used in *Bosman*. The general tenor of the ruling was that an 'out of contract' player is a player whose contract has run its course and thus expired.

It remains to be seen whether the correct legal position will ever be clarified by a ruling from the ECJ. For the time being, the position is at least now clear for players who enter into new contracts after the new FIFA rules came into force, on 1 September 2001, and who then wish to terminate their contracts to move to a club in a different country.[80]

---

78 For a general discussion of the issues see Caiger, A and O'Leary, J (1999) 2(5) Sports Law Bulletin 2; Tsatsas, N, 'Anelka's costly walk-out case has a hole in it' *The Guardian*, 23 July 1999. On applicability of Art. 39, see *The Helsinki Report on Sport*, European Commission (COM(1999)644 – C5-0088/2000) and the Opinion to the European Parliament of the Committee on Legal Affairs and the Internal Market (A5-0208/2000). For an account of the 'Lombardo case' see 'Sports focus: the end of transfer fees' *The Observer*, 3 September 2000. For reference to the Commission's views on the compatibility of the transfer system with EC law see the speech of Commission Member Viviane Reding to the European Parliament on 7 September 2000 (Speech/00/290).

79 *Op cit*, fn 59, Caiger and O'Leary (2000).

80 For discussion of the background to the introduction of the new rules see Mcauley, D, 'They think it's all over . . . It might just be now: unravelling the ramifications for the European football transfer system post-*Bosman*' (2002) 23(7) European Competition Law Review 331–340. For an interdisciplinary analysis see Morris, P and Spink, P, 'The new transfer fee system in professional soccer: an interdisciplinary study' (2000/21) 5(4) Contemporary Issues in Law 253–281. Also see MacDonald, M, 'Transfers, contracts and personhood – an anthropological perspective' (2003) International Sports Law Review, 3–10 for an analysis on the relationship between transfer markets and the legal status of players as employees.

Principles for the amendment of FIFA rules regarding international transfers

Preamble

All players who have reached the end of their contracts are free to move internationally throughout the world subject to the provisions of paragraph 2 below concerning training compensation.

1 Protection of minors

In order to provide a stable environment for the training and education of players, international transfers or first registration of players under the age of 18 shall be permitted subject to the following conditions:

(a) the family of the player moves for reasons not related to football into the country of the new training club, or

(b) within the territory of the EU/EEA and in the case of players between the minimum working age in the country of the new training club and 18 suitable arrangements are guaranteed for their sporting training and academic education by the new training club. For this purpose a code of conduct will be established and enforced by the football authorities.

2 Training compensation for young players

In order to promote player talent and stimulate competition in football it is recognised that clubs should have the necessary financial and sporting incentives to invest in training and educating young players. It is further recognised that all clubs which are involved in the training and education process should be rewarded for their contribution according to the following principles:

2.1 The training and education of a player takes place between the ages of 12 and 23. Training compensation shall be payable as a general rule up to the age of 23 for training incurred up to the age of 21, unless it is evident that a player has already terminated his training period before the age of 23.

2.2 When a player signs his first contract as a professional a sum of compensation shall be paid to the club(s) involved in the training and education of the player.

2.2 Compensation shall be paid on each occasion the player changes club up to the time his training and education is complete, which as a general rule occurs when the player is 23 years of age.

2.4 The amount of compensation to be paid for training and education shall be calculated in accordance with the parameters set out in Annex I.

2.5 When a player signs his first contract as a professional, or when a player moves as a professional at the end of his contract but before reaching the age of 23, the amount of compensation shall be limited to compensation for training and education, calculated in accordance with the parameters set out in Annex I.

2.6 If a player moves during the course of a contract but before reaching the age of 23, compensation for training and education shall be paid and shall be calculated in accordance with the parameters set out in Annex I. However, in the case of unilateral breach of contract, this provision is without prejudice to the application of paragraph 3.2 below.

2.7 If a link between the player and his former club cannot be established, or if the training club does not make itself known within two years of the player signing his first professional contract, training compensation is paid to the national football association of the country where the player was trained. This compensation shall be earmarked for youth-football development programmes in the country in question.

3 Maintenance of Contractual Stability in Football

Contracts shall have a minimum and maximum duration of respectively one and five years, subject to national law.

It is recognised that contractual stability is of paramount importance in football, from the perspective of clubs, players, and the public. Contractual relations between players and clubs must be governed by a regulatory system which responds to the specific needs of football and which strikes the right balance between the respective interests of players and clubs and preserves the regularity and proper functioning of sporting competition.

3.1 Respect for contracts

   a In the case of all contracts signed up to the 28th birthday of the player: if there is unilateral breach without just cause or sporting just cause during the first 3 years, sports sanctions will be applied and compensation shall be payable.

      In the case of contracts signed after the 28th birthday, the same principles shall apply but only during the first 2 years.

      With regard to contracts as defined in the preceding two paragraphs, unilateral breach without just cause or sporting just cause is prohibited during the season.

   b Unilateral breach without just cause or sporting just cause after the first 3 years or 2 years will not result in the application of sanctions, with the exception of possible sports sanctions against a club and/or a players' agent inducing a breach of contract. Compensation shall be payable.

      A breach of contract as defined in the preceding paragraph is prohibited during the season.

      Disciplinary measures may be applied if appropriate notice is not given.

3.2 Compensation

   Unless provided for in the contract, and without prejudice to paragraph 6, compensation for breach of contract (whether by the player or the club) shall be calculated with due respect to applicable national law, the specificity of sport, and all objective criteria which may be relevant to the case, such as:

   (1) Remuneration and other benefits under the existing contract and/or the new contract,
   (2) Length of time remaining on the existing contract (up to a maximum of 5 years),
   (3) Amount of any fee or expense paid by or incurred by the old club, amortised over the length of the contract.
   (4) Whether the breach occurs during the 'protected period', as defined in 3.1a, or in the period described in 3.1b.

3.3 Sports sanctions

Other than in exceptional circumstances (such as recurring breach by a club or a player), sports sanctions for unilateral breach of contract without just cause or sporting just cause shall:

In the case of the player:

- If the breach occurs at the end of the first or the second year of contract:

Be a restriction on his eligibility to participate in any official football matches, except for the club to which he was contracted, for an effective period of 4 (four) months as from the beginning of the national championship of the new club.

There will be no sanction for unilateral breach at the end of the third year of contract, except if no notice is given in due time after the last match of the season. In such a case the sanction must be proportionate.

In the case of aggravating circumstances, such as failure to give notice or recurrent breach, sports sanctions may go up to, but not exceed, an effective period of 6 months.

- In the case of the club breaching a contract or inducing such breach:

Be a prohibition on registering any new player, either domestically or internationally, until the expiry of the second transfer window following the date on which the breach became effective. In all cases no restriction for unilateral breach of contract shall exceed a period of 12 months following the breach or inducement of the breach.

A club seeking to register a player who has unilaterally breached a contract during the 'protected period' as defined in 3.1a will be presumed to have induced a breach of contract.

Without prejudice to the foregoing general rules, other sanctions of a sporting nature may be imposed on clubs where appropriate and may include, but shall not be limited to, the following:

- fines,
- deduction of points,
- exclusion from competition.

In the case of a players' agent involved in such breach

Sanctions can also be imposed on players' agents being involved in a breach of contract in accordance with FIFA' s players' agents regulations.

Sports sanctions shall be imposed by FIFA's Player Status Committee, with a right of appeal to the Football Arbitration Tribunal, referred to under section 6 hereunder.

3.4 Sporting just cause

In addition to termination for just cause, it will also be possible for a player to terminate his contract for a valid sporting reason ('sporting just cause').

Sporting just cause will be established on a case by case basis. Each case will be evaluated on its individual merits taking account of all relevant circumstances (injury, suspension, field position of player, age of player, etc). Furthermore, it is understood that the existence of sporting just cause shall be examined at the end of the football season and before the expiry of the relevant transfer window.

The arbitration system shall determine whether compensation is payable and the amount of any such compensation when a contract is terminated for sporting just cause.

3.5 Amicable resolution

Any amicable resolution of a contract shall be notified to the national association responsible for the issuance of the international transfer certificate.

4 Solidarity Mechanism

If a player moves during the course of a contract, after reaching the age of 23 or after his second transfer (whichever comes first), a proportion (5%) of any compensation paid to the previous club will be distributed to the club(s) involved in the training and education of the player. This distribution will be made in proportion to the number of years the player has been registered with the relevant clubs between the age of 12 and 23.

5 Transfer Windows

In order to protect the regularity and proper functioning of sporting competition two unified transfer windows per season will apply, with a limit of one transfer per player per season. The mid season transfer window shall be limited to transfers for strictly sport related reasons, such as technical adjustments of teams or replacement of injured players, or exceptional circumstances.

6 Dispute Resolution, Disciplinary and Arbitration System

Without prejudice to the right of any player or club to seek redress before a civil court, a dispute resolution and arbitration system shall be established, which shall consist of the following elements:

- Conciliation facilities offered by FIFA, through which a low cost, speedy, confidential and informal resolution of any dispute will be explored with the parties by an independent mediator. If no such solution is found within one month, either party can bring the case before FIFA's Dispute Resolution Chamber.
- Dispute Resolution Chamber, with members chosen in equal numbers by players and clubs and with an independent chairman, instituted within FIFA's Player Status Committee, establishing breach of contract, applying sport sanctions and disciplinary measures as a deterrent to unethical behaviour

(eg to sanction a club which has procured a breach of contract), determining financial compensation, etc. In addition, the Dispute Resolution Chamber can review disputes concerning training compensation fees and shall have discretion to adjust the training fee if it is clearly disproportionate in the individual circumstances. Rulings of the Chamber can be appealed by either party to the Football Arbitration Tribunal.

- Football Arbitration Tribunal, with members chosen in equal numbers by players and clubs and with an independent chairman, according to the principles of the New York Convention of 1958.

For the avoidance of doubt, the Dispute Resolution and Arbitration System will take account of all relevant arrangements, laws and/or collective bargaining agreements, which exist at national level, as well as the specificity of sport as recognized recently, for instance, in the relevant Declaration appended to Presidency conclusions of the European Council at Nice in December 2000.

7 Entry into Force

The principles set out above shall enter into full force and effect only for contracts concluded after the date of formal adoption of these principles by the appropriate authority.

8 Review

In the third season following the adoption of these principles FIFA will, as part of a more general review of these principles, analyse in particular the application of training compensation during the first two seasons, and review its findings with the various members of the football family.

Thus the salient features of the new system are as follows.

- The rules only apply to international transfers and do not affect contracts currently in force.

- International transfers of players under the age of 18 are restricted to protect the families and the education of the player concerned.

- Clubs will be able to receive compensation for players under the age of 23 who move during the currency or at the end of their contracts.

- This compensation will no longer be in the form of a negotiated transfer fee but calculated according to agreed criteria set out in an annex to the new rules (see below). These criteria generally reflect the principles set out by Advocate General Lenz in *Bosman* for compensating clubs for training players.[81]

- Contracts should be for a minimum of one year and a maximum of five years.

- There will be one transfer period per season, and a further limited mid-season window, with a limit of one transfer per player per season.

- In the case of a contract signed up to the 28th birthday of a player, a unilateral breach in the first three years will give rise to rights to compensation and the application of sports sanctions restricting a player's ability to play immediately for his new club.

- In the case of a contract signed after a player's 28th birthday, the above will apply but only during the first two years of the contract.

- Players may be prevented for playing for another club for up to one year if that club, or others such as the player's agent, has induced the player to act in breach of his contract.

---

81   See para 239, above pp 503.

- Players will be permitted to terminate contracts if they have due or a 'sporting just' cause.

- A new arbitration system will be established to provide an effective and quick alternative to civil litigation. This will not prevent players or clubs from pursuing a legal action in a national court.

The consequences of these rules for players who unilaterally break their contracts or who are induced to do so by an agent or another club will be examined in the next chapter.

ANNEX I to Principles for the amendment of FIFA rules regarding international transfers

Training compensation for young players

A Principles

1   The training period of a player for which the new club has to pay compensation should start at the age of 12 and end when the player reaches the age of 23 (in order to ensure uniform treatment, for the purposes of calculating compensation, the training period starts at the beginning of the season of his 12th birthday or the later age as the case may be and finishes at the end of the season of his 23rd birthday).

2   Compensation for training is due:

2.1 For the transfer of players (up to the age of 23) who are not under contract or who are at the end of their (training or professional) contract (in the case of the transfer of players (up to the age of 23) who are still under contract, in addition to the compensation for training, the rules regulating contractual stability shall also apply).

2.2 For the first time, when the player acquires non-amateur status (FIFA Regulations), ie when he signs his first (professional or training) contract.

2.3 Afterwards, for every transfer up to the age of 23, however according to the status of the player, ie:

- from amateur to professional (non-amateur) status

- from professional (non-amateur) status to professional (non-amateur) status.

3   Compensation for training is not due:

3.1 For transfers from amateur status to amateur status.

3.2 For transfers from professional status to amateur status (reacquisition of amateur status).

3.3 If a club unilaterally terminates a player's contract without just cause.

4   Payment of the compensation for training:

As a general rule, the amount to be paid shall reflect the costs which were necessary to train the player and should be paid for the benefit of all clubs which have contributed to the training of the player in question, starting from the age of 12.

4.1 First payment (as mentioned in 2.2): The amount to be paid is for the benefit of all clubs which have contributed to the training of the player in question, starting from the age of 12. The money would be distributed on a pro rata basis according to full years of proper and proven training.

4.2 In cases of subsequent transfers (as mentioned in 2.3) from clubs belonging to the third or fourth categories (as defined hereinafter in paragraph B 1 c and d) the new club has to pay and/or reimburse to the old club the 'training costs' incurred or paid by the old club.

In the case of a player moving from a club belonging to the third or fourth categories to a club in a higher category, a cascade principle will apply as defined in paragraph 6 below.

For the avoidance of doubt, in the case of a player moving from a club in category first or second, the amount of training compensation payable shall be the training cost of the previous club.

B Calculation

Since it is impossible to calculate the effective training costs for every single player, flat training rates should be set and the clubs should be categorised in accordance with their financial investments in the training of players.

Establishment of 4 categories:

a) Category 1 (top level, eg high quality training centre):
   - all clubs of first division of National Associations investing as an average a similar amount in the training of players. These National Associations will be defined based on effective training costs and this categorisation can be revised on a yearly basis.

b) Category 2 (still professional, but on a lower level):
   - all clubs of second division of the National Associations of category 1
   - all clubs of first division of all other countries having professional football

c) Category 3:
   - all clubs of third division of the National Associations of category 1
   - all clubs of second division of all other countries having professional football

d) Category 4:
   - all clubs of fourth and lower divisions of the National Associations of category 1
   - all clubs of third and lower divisions of all other countries having professional football
   - all clubs of countries having only amateur football

2　Establishment of the amount which is necessary to 'train' one player in each of these categories for one year (ie costs for the training of one player multiplied by an average 'player factor')
   a) Category 1: [to be defined]
   b) Category 2: [to be defined]
   c) Category 3: [to be defined]
   d) Category 4: [to be defined]

The 'player factor' is the ratio between the number of trainees and the number of professional players. FIFA/UEFA will establish and quantify the factors such as categorisation and the player factor, taking into account relevant data and expertise.

For the avoidance of doubt, the salaries paid to any player (no matter what his age is) who has ever played in the first team may not be included for the purposes of calculating training costs.

3　The calculation in case of first contract and/or transfers of young players would be:

The amount fixed under point 2 corresponding to the category of the training club for which the player was registered multiplied by the number of years of training from 12 to 21. For the avoidance of doubt, this amount shall be paid until the season during which the player becomes 23.

In order to ensure that training compensation for very young players is not set at unreasonably high level, this compensation will always be category 4 for the 12 to 15 years old.

4　General principle: compensation for training is based on the costs of the category of the new club.

However, within the EU/EEA area: compensation for training is based on the costs of the training club. The following rules apply:
   a) player is transferred from a lower to a higher category: calculation is the average of the training costs for the two categories
   b) player is transferred from a higher to a lower category: calculation based on training costs of lower category club
   c) player is transferred from a club in category 1,2 or 3 to a club in category 4: no compensation for training is payable

5   Ceiling: There shall be a ceiling to be defined objectively to ensure that training compensation fees levied by the training clubs are not disproportionate. FIFA in consultation with UEFA will regularly establish and quantify the ceiling for the EU/EEA area.

6   Cascade

    a) In any transfer of a player from a club in the third or fourth categories to a club in a higher category, 75% of the amount exceeding the costs of the category of the 'old' club, shall be redistributed on a pro-rata basis to all the clubs having trained the player from the age of 12 onwards.

    b) In any transfer between two clubs of the same category, 10% of the amount calculated as described under point 3 shall be redistributed on a pro-rata basis to all the clubs having trained the player from the age of 12 onwards.

7   Further, in the EU/EEA, if the training club does not offer the player a contract this should be taken into account in determining the training fee payable by the new club.

Finally, as exemplified by the introduction of the above new rules, although the *Bosman* ruling has had particular significance for professional football, it must be remembered that *Bosman* applies to any professional sport played within the EC where a transfer system operates. Indeed, as shown by the *Malaja* and *Kolpak* cases,[82] *Bosman* has already impacted on the worlds of professional basketball and handball.

KEY SOURCES

Opinion of Advocate-General Lenz in *ASBL Union Royale Belge des Societes de Football Association & others v Jean-Marc Bosman* [1996] 1 CMLR 645 (Case C-415/93).

Blanpain, R and Inston, R, *The Bosman Case: The End of the Transfer System?* (1996), London: Sweet & Maxwell; Leuven: Peeters.

Gardiner, S and Welch, R, 'The winds of change in professional football: the impact of the *Bosman* ruling' (1998) 3(4) Contemporary Issues in Law 289–312.

Morris, P and Spink, P, 'The new transfer fee system in professional soccer: an interdisciplinary study' (2000/21) 5(4) Contemporary Issues in Law 253–81.

MacDonald, M, 'Transfers, contracts and personhood – an anthropological perspective' (2003) International Sports Law Review 3–10.

---

82   See Chapter 14, pp 582–88.

CHAPTER 13

TERMINATION OF CONTRACTS OF EMPLOYMENT IN SPORT

INTRODUCTION

Sporting contracts can be lawfully terminated in exactly the same way as any other type of contract, that is by mutual agreement, performance or expiry. However, there are special rules, primarily as a result of statutory rights of unfair dismissal, that apply to all contracts of employment including those entered into by professional sports participants. This chapter will explain the relevant common law and statutory rules and discuss their applicability to professional sport. Particular attention will be paid to cases involving sport in which these rules have applied as well as issues of particular importance to the world of sport such as contract-jumping, poaching players and the possible legal consequences of footballers unilaterally terminating their contracts in accordance with the new FIFA transfer rules.

COMMON LAW

Any employment contract can be terminated without cause if due notice is given. This can be the case with fixed-term contracts although the normal expectation is that such contracts will end on the date of their expiry. Non-renewal would not constitute a dismissal.

A summary dismissal, where no notice or inadequate notice is given or a fixed-term contract is terminated prior to its date of expiry, is *prima facie* a breach of contract and thus a wrongful dismissal by the employer unless the employee is guilty of gross misconduct. For this to be the case the employee must be in breach of a term – express or implied – which is at the root of the contract (or have repudiated the contract in its entirety). From a contractual perspective the dismissal is simply the employer communicating to the employee that the latter's breach has discharged the employer from his obligations under the contract, and the employer has consequently elected to regard the contract as terminated.

Disobedience of a lawful and reasonable instruction by the employer *may* constitute gross misconduct. On the other hand, it may be that an employee's disobedience, though misconduct, is not sufficiently serious to constitute a repudiatory breach. It is clear that there is no standard test for ascertaining whether misconduct is gross. The circumstances of the case must be taken into account in determining whether or not the employee has committed a repudiatory breach of contract. Only if this is the case is the employer justified in treating the contract as at an end.[1]

Examine the clauses in footballers' and cricketers' contracts.[2] In what circumstances could sports professionals be regarded as repudiating their employment contracts? Roger Stanislaus and Adrian Mutu were clearly regarded by Leyton Orient and Chelsea respectively as being guilty of gross misconduct once they had been found guilty by the FA of having tested positive for cocaine. A similar view was taken by Sussex County Cricket Club with respect to Ed Giddins. However, Sussex claimed

---

1   For contrasting cases on gross misconduct, see *Laws v London Chronicle Ltd* [1959] 2 All ER 285 CA; *Wilson v Racher* [1974] IRLR 114 CA; *Pepper v Webb* [1969] 2 All ER 216. Taken together these cases demonstrate just how difficult it is to predict in advance whether employee misconduct will constitute gross misconduct.

2   See previous chapter, pp 487–88.

that it had not dismissed Giddins. His contract was deemed to have terminated automatically as a result of the cancellation of his registration by the Test and County Cricket Board (TCCB). Does this frustrate the contract? If so, how? A term of imprisonment can frustrate a contract of employment. Should a ban for a lengthy period be considered analogous on the basis that it is qualitatively different to a ban for several matches? A short ban would be considered a normal occupational hazard.

For the manager of a professional football club instant dismissal is certainly par for the course. It is rarely based on allegations of gross misconduct. Indeed it is often the result of pressure from fans, who sometimes rightly and no doubt sometimes wrongly, hold the manager to blame if their team's performances are below expectations. The function of contract law here is essentially to provide a legal framework within which an out of court settlement can be negotiated; an action for wrongful dismissal is thereby precluded.[3]

However, the following case both shows how the concept of wrongful dismissal can relate to football managers and discusses the interplay between contractual duties imposed on both employers and employees through the judicially implied terms discussed in the previous chapter.

Macari v Celtic Football and Athletic Co Ltd Court of Session, Case 0/309/6/98

Luigi (aka Lou) Macari was appointed manager of Celtic in October 1993. In March 1994 the club was taken over by a consortium headed by Fergus McCann. The latter made it clear from the outset that he did not want Macari as manager and excluded him from meetings of the Board (which, under the previous regime, Macari had attended). In June 1994 Macari was summarily dismissed for wilful acts of disobedience. In particular, a failure to comply with a residence requirement to live in or near to Glasgow (Macari had previously been the manager of Stoke FC and his family home remained in Stoke), and his consequent frequent absences from Celtic Park. The Court of Session accepted that the club's treatment of Macari amounted to destruction of mutual trust and confidence. However, the Court rejected his claim for wrongful dismissal as it did not accept that the club's breach of contract justified Macari's wilful failure to obey the reasonable instructions of his employer.

Lord President: . . . The defenders' breach of the trust and confidence term was a material breach of contract on their part which the pursuer would have been entitled to accept by leaving his employment and suing them for damages. In fact he did not do so: he remained and drew his salary under his contract but failed to comply with the instructions given to him by the managing director. Of course, as the defenders pointed out, the pursuer did not refuse to obey these instructions because he had lost trust or confidence in the defenders. Rather, he deliberately chose not to comply with them, believing that he knew best what was involved in managing a football club and being determined to do it in his own way. In itself that point would not assist the defenders: whatever his reasons, the pursuer would not have been in breach of contract if any breach of the implied term by the defenders meant that they were not entitled to insist on him complying with their instructions.

As his counsel acknowledged, if sound, the argument for the pursuer would have potentially far-reaching consequences. If it were the case that a breach of the implied term of trust and confidence meant that an employee was entitled to ignore his employer's instructions, then it would mean, for instance, that he could continue working and draw his salary but refuse to obey instructions relating to matters of health and safety. The true position seems to me to be that, if an employee is faced with a breach of the trust and confidence term by his employer but chooses to continue to work and draw his salary, he must do the work in accordance with the terms of his contract. That in turn means that, as regards his work, he must obey any lawful and legitimate instructions which his employer gives him. It is in return for such work in

---

3   See *The Guardian*, 12 November 1994 for an article by David Lacey on the rash of dismissals of managers – as highlighted by the dismissal of Mike Walker by Everton a mere ten months after he had left Norwich to join the club. Over the course of the subsequent ten years speculation as to which manager is next due for the 'sack' (or indeed first to lose his job in the early weeks of a season) has become part of the staple diet of football punditry both in newspapers and on television.

conformity with the contract that the employer is obliged to pay the employee his salary under the contract. On the other hand, in no relevant sense can it be said that an employee's obligation to do his work in accordance with the lawful and legitimate instructions of his employer is, in the words of Lord Jauncey, 'the counterpart of' his employer's obligation under the implied term. I note en passant that similarly, on the approach of Lord Maclaren in Sivright, the employee's right is not 'conditional with respect to' that obligation of his employer. Nor does the employee undertake to work in accordance with his employer's instructions 'in exchange for' his employer's performance of his obligation under the implied term (to apply the test in 'ESE Financial Services'). So, where the employee chooses to continue to work under the contract, his employer's breach of the implied term does not entitle the employee to disregard the employer's lawful and legitimate instructions as to his work. In the present case the pursuer continued to work as manager of the club and to draw the salary for that work. The defenders' managing director gave him instructions about residence, attendance and reporting, all of which were lawful and legitimate and related to his work under the contract. For the reasons which I have given, the pursuer was obliged to comply with those instructions and his persistent failures to do so were not only breaches but material breaches of his contract with the defenders.

In any event, the pursuer had an obligation under a specific term of his contract, rather than by virtue of any instruction, to reside within 45 miles of George Square. When asked what obligation the defenders had breached which was the counter part of this obligation, counsel for the pursuer could refer only to the general implied obligation of trust and confidence. But there is nothing in the residence obligation which relates to that implied obligation, or makes it the counter part of that obligation. Therefore any breach of the implied term would not disable the defenders from insisting that the pursuer should comply with the residence clause.

For all these reasons in June 1994 the pursuer was in material breach of contract by reason of his failure to comply with the residence clause, by reason of his failure to comply with the instruction to attend more regularly at Celtic Park and by reason of his failure to comply with his undertaking to report to Mr McCann on a weekly basis. Referring to the undated fax sent in reply to Mr McCann's letter of 10 June, the Lord Ordinary describes the situation in the strongest possible terms: 'it seems to me that by the defiant, contumacious terms of that letter and of his subsequent telephone conversation, the pursuer was indicating that he was not intending to be bound by the directions of his employer and was opposing his lawful authority. I consider that the circumstances were then such, having regard also to his flouting of specific directions in particular in respect of residence, attendance at Celtic Park and the provision of weekly reports, as to entitle the employer to consider his employee's conduct was indicative of an intention not to fulfil his obligations under the contract and as an intimation of a repudiation of it, justifying his dismissal.'

Not surprisingly, counsel for the pursuer accepted that, if the general law of contract applied, in that situation the defenders were entitled to dismiss the pursuer. Analysing the matter more formally, under the general law they would be entitled to accept the pursuer's material or repudiatory breach with the result that they would thereafter be released from their obligations to the pursuer under the agreement with him.

This decision clarifies that, despite the overriding nature of the duty on the employer to maintain mutual trust and confidence, if the employee affirms a breach of his employment contract by continuing to work under it then he must continue to obey any instructions given by the employer which are in themselves reasonable. The case also illustrates that, providing any contractual procedures are adhered to, the failure to follow normal disciplinary procedures[4] will not be decisive

---

4   For example, the disciplinary procedures as set out in the ACAS Code of Practice. However, from 1 October 2004, a failure to follow minimum statutory procedures will normally result in damages being increased by between 10 to 50% in the event of a successful wrongful dismissal claim before an employment tribunal (but not a court) – see below, pp 540–44.

in an action for wrongful dismissal. If, in court, the employer can establish that the employee did commit a repudiatory breach of contract then the dismissal cannot be wrongful as the employer was entitled to choose to treat the contract as at an end.

REMEDIES FOR WRONGFUL DISMISSAL

The normal remedy for a wrongful dismissal, that is, a dismissal in breach of contract, is damages for actual financial loss suffered. In the case of fixed term contracts, which are the norm in professional sport, this will, subject to the normal duty of mitigation, be loss of earnings for the period of time that the contract had left to run. Therefore, in professional sport there is an obvious potential for the awarding of high levels of damages. However, for the reasons given above, in the circumstances where actions for wrongful dismissal would be most likely to occur clubs typically seek to ensure the issue is dealt with by agreement.

Now that behaviour by professional sports participants – both on and off the field of play – has become an issue of national interest or concern it is perhaps only a matter of time before a player who has been dismissed summarily brings an action for wrongful dismissal. However, as was the case with Ed Giddins (who was signed to play for Warwickshire once he had served his ban), the issue might be effectively resolved by a rival club employing the player who has been dismissed. If nothing else this shows that clubs, who may regard themselves as occupying the moral high ground, are upholding their own standards rather than standards observed within the sport as a whole.[5]

Injunctions

It is a fundamental legal principle that courts will not compel performance of a contract of employment or any contract which involves the provision of personal services. Ever since the actress Bette Davis sought to break her contract with her film studio,[6] it has been clear that this principle applies to the entertainment industry. On the other hand, injunctions will not be granted where their effect is in practice to compel performance of a contract.[7] Thus it may be very difficult to secure injunctions in the context of sport[8] unless the sports participant is in a position to earn an equally remunerative living by other means, such as acting or television work, for the duration of his contract.

Recent case law suggests a very strong reluctance on the part of modern judges to follow the decision in *Warner Bros*. In *Warren v Mendy*[9] the Court of Appeal refused an injunction to restrain the defendant from inducing Nigel Benn to break his contract with his manager by participating in a match arranged by the defendant. The court held that it was unrealistic to conclude that a boxer could choose between his sport and alternative employment. This case was cited and followed by the High

---

5   See *The Guardian*, 1 November 1996 for a discussion of the Ed Giddins affair and the fact that, once Sussex terminated his contract, he was approached by 10 of the 17 other first class counties. The report also suggests that it was the general view of his fellow professionals that, in sporting terms, he had done nothing wrong.

6   *Warner Brothers Pictures Incorporated v Nelson* [1937] KB 209.

7   *Page One Records Ltd v Britton* [1968] 1 WLR 157.

8   [1989] ICR 525. Note US courts are much readier to prevent professional sports participants from 'jumping contracts'. See McCutcheon, P, 'Negative enforcement of employment contracts in the sports industries' (1997) 17 Legal Studies 65.

9   [1989] 1 WLR 853.

Court in *Subaru Tecnica International Inc v Burns & Others*.[10] The court refused an injunction which would have prevented Richard Burns, the 2001 World Rally Champion, from breaking his contract with Subaru by driving for Peugeot.

On the other hand, an injunction was granted for a short period to enforce garden leave provisions in Steve Bruce's contract with Crystal Palace.[11] This does suggest that there may be circumstances in which the courts will accept that sports employers have legitimate interests to protect, and that these interests can only be protected effectively by court injunctions.

It should be noted that in *Warren v Mendy* the injunction was sought not against Nigel Benn but against another promoter seeking to induce Benn to act in breach of contract. Thus the action was based on the tort of direct inducement to act in breach of contract as established in *Lumley v Gye*.[12] The elements of the tort require the claimant to establish the following conditions:

- that the defendant persuaded or procured or induced the breach of contract;

- that the defendant when so acting knew of the existence of that contract;

- that the defendant intended to persuade, procure or induce a breach of that contract;

- that the plaintiff had suffered more than nominal damage; and

- that the plaintiff could rebut any defence of justification put forward by the defendant.[13]

With respect to football, this tort is of potential significance where one club induces a player to break his contract with his current club. Even if it can be argued that Art 39 permits a player to jump contracts[14] it seems unlikely that, arguments over freedom of movement notwithstanding, a court would accept that EC law has overridden this long established tort.

The new FIFA transfer rules regulating international transfers are of significance in this regard. The rules provide for a voluntary system which does permit the imposition of sport's sanctions where a player seeks to move to another club in breach of contract or is induced by another to do so. Effectively, these rules protect the employing club for the remainder of any season currently under way and for some or all of the following season.[15]

As far as domestic transfers are concerned, it seems that British football clubs would be better protected by the FIFA rules than is the case under the law of contract, in circumstances where a player wished to jump contracts. However, in the here and now this point remains academic given that the current national rules prevent a club securing a player's registration whilst he is still under contract unless a transfer fee is agreed. In contrast with the FIFA rules, this applies irrespective of the length of the contract and the age of the player.

With respect to sport in general, it could be argued by way of analogy to the sanctions contained in the FIFA rules that a court should grant an injunction for a period in that sport, which would equate as a competitive period to a football season, on the basis that there are legitimate sporting

---

10 (2001) Ch D (unreported).

11 See previous chapter, pp 489–90.

12 (1853) 2 E&B 216.

13 These elements of the tort were most recently confirmed in *Timeplan Education Group Ltd v NUT* [1997] IRLR 457.

14 See Caiger, A and O'Leary, J, 'The end of the affair: the *"Anelka Doctrine"* – the problem of contract stability in English professional football', pp 197–216, in Caiger A and Gardiner, S (eds), *Professional Sport in the EU: Regulation and Re-regulation* (2000) The Hague: Asser Press.

15 The norm will be the first four months of the next season where a player chooses to break his contract, but up to 12 months where the player is induced to do so by the club that then signs him; see previous chapter, pp 514–15.

interests to protect. This is particularly the case where a sports participant has been induced to act in breach of contract as it can be argued that he (or she) is only being specifically restrained from working for the party who has committed the tort. The injunction would not in itself prevent the individual sportsman (or sportswoman) from still walking out and seeking employment elsewhere – particularly where the player has good reason to believe a number of clubs, promotors or sponsors are interested in his services if he becomes a free agent.[16]

In the context of international transfers, the FIFA rules permit players to terminate their contracts immediately where they have due cause or a 'sporting just cause'. Clearly, the former position is in accordance with English contract law if a club is in repudiatory breach and thus the player is able to establish constructive dismissal. However, there is no automatic correlation between the notion of a 'sporting just cause' and a club acting in breach of contract. Failure to secure selection for first team matches on a long term basis may constitute an example of 'sporting just cause'. It is however difficult to establish any breach of contract by a club in this respect providing selection decisions are in good faith. For example, the player's position is filled by another player genuinely perceived to be in better form and/or better suited to the tactics that the team coach has decided to deploy.

It remains to be seen whether clubs will be prepared to forego any contractual rights and remedies where a player, for sporting reasons, is deemed entitled to terminate his contract and have his registration transferred to a new club. It similarly remains to be seen whether clubs will refrain from litigation once a contract ceases to be protected after the third year of its duration (or after the second year in the case of a player who was aged 28 or over at the date the contract was entered into). In these circumstances the inclusion of negative restraint clauses and the arguments over whether injunctions can be secured to enforce them remain of practical importance in football, as well as in other professional sports.

It should be noted that it is also possible for employees to secure injunctions to prevent their employers from acting in breach of contract. This has been particularly the case where injunctions have also been sought to restrain dismissals in breach of disciplinary procedures contained in the employment contract. In *Dietman v Brent LBC* [17] the High Court confirmed that an injunction could be so granted if:

(i)   the plaintiff acts quickly as otherwise the employee will be deemed to have accepted the termination of the contract;

(ii) mutual trust and confidence have not been destroyed;

(iii) damages are inadequate. This might be the case if the dismissed employee could show that were he allowed to plead his case at a hearing the employer might decide against dismissal.

Both professional footballers and cricketers have contractual rights of appeal against dismissal to the appropriate authorities. A player could seek an injunction where these procedures are not followed, but it might be in sport that the necessary mutual trust and confidence will have been destroyed. If this were the case, an injunction would be refused.[18]

---

16 There does seem to be some discrepancy between the reluctance of the courts to hold entertainers to their contracts, as exemplified by *Warren v Mendy* despite the latter having committed a tort, and a greater readiness to enforce lengthy garden leave clauses or post-employment restraints to protect an employer's interests in protecting their trade secrets or clientele. Generally, such clauses will be upheld providing they are reasonable as to their duration and area of geographical and/or commercial application.

17 [1987] IRLR 259.

18 Furthermore, in *Boyo v Lambeth LBC* [1995] IRLR 50 the Court of Appeal indicated support for a more restrictive view that a dismissal, even in breach of contract-based procedures, automatically terminates the contract of

Damages

The calculation of the compensation to which a club should be entitled presents another difficulty in circumstances where a player acts or is induced to act in breach of contract. The underlying principle in contract law for calculating damages is that the claimant should be awarded a sum of money which would put him in the same financial position that he would have enjoyed had the contract been properly performed. In some circumstances, for example where a player jumps contracts, the amount of damages that may be awarded may be smaller than anticipated.[19] It is possible for a clause to be inserted into a player's contract that specifies the amount of compensation to be paid in the event of the player breaking that contract. However, if the stipulated sum is excessive a court will regard it as a penalty and the clause will be declared void. It will then be for the court by reference to normal principles to determine the amount of damages to be awarded.

Some indication as to how the courts may calculate damages is provided by the decision of the Court of Appeal in the action for breach of contract brought by Middlesbrough FC against Liverpool as a result of their signing of Christian Ziegle.[20] This case revolves around the legal principles upon which damages will be calculated for breach of the contract entered into between all football clubs in the Premiership whereby they agree to abide by the rules of the Football Association Premier League (FAPL). The relevant rules were at the time of the case contained in s J of the FAPL's Rules.

Rule J.1.2 prohibited a club from approaching a player under contract without the prior permission of his club. Rule J.5 prohibited a player under contract from approaching another club with a view to negotiating a contract without the prior consent of his club. Rule J.22 provided that a contract between a player and his club is confidential and thus disclosure of its contents to any other person is a breach of contract.

A Commission of Inquiry appointed by the FAPL found that both Liverpool FC and the player Christian Zeigle were in breach of these rules and thus Liverpool had acted in breach of contract. The specific cause of the complaint was that the personal terms between Middlesbrough FC and Ziegle contained a clause under which Middlesbrough agreed that if any other club offered at least £5.5 million for Ziegle Middlesbrough would permit him to discuss personal terms with that club and, if these were agreed, would permit him to transfer to that club. Through relying on this term in his contract Ziegle was able to secure his release from Middlesbrough whilst still under contract with the club and become a Liverpool player. The Court of Appeal agreed with the Commission of Inquiry that there must have been a breach of Ziegle's contractual duty not to disclose confidential terms of his employment contract with Middlesbrough. This was because in the normal way of things Liverpool's transfer bid would have been either below or above £5.5 million rather than the specific sum required to trigger the clause in Ziegle's contract under which Middlesbrough was bound to release him.

---

employment. Were this position to be endorsed by the House of Lords, then even as a theoretical possibility injunctions would cease to be available, and the only remedy would be damages for wrongful dismissal. However, in the case of cricketers' and footballers' contracts this might include the length of time the player would still have been employed if the dismissal had not occurred until after contractual procedures had been followed. In this case even if a player was guilty of gross misconduct he would be entitled to some compensation on the basis that his dismissal was procedurally wrongful.

19 See *op cit*, fn 14, Caiger and O' Leary (2000), pp 209–211. They argue that damages would include neither the loss of a transfer fee nor the cost of replacing a player.

20 *Middlesbrough Football & Athletic Co v Liverpool Football & Athletic Grounds plc* [2002] EWCA Civ 1929.

On the basis of this breach of contract, Middlesbrough argued it was entitled to be granted damages from Liverpool as a result of the financial loss suffered by it. This loss was either (a) the loss of a chance to sell Ziegle at a higher sum, or (b) the loss of a chance to have enjoyed a financially more successful season (2000/01) had Ziegle remained a Middlesbrough player. In the High Court, Astill J dismissed Middlesbrough's claim with respect to (a) as effectively Middlesbrough had given up any right to negotiate a transfer fee providing £5.5 million was offered. The judge dismissed Middlesbrough's claim with respect to (b) on the grounds that it 'was wholly speculative'.

The CA upheld Middlesbrough's appeal as whilst it could not be said that at full trial Middlesbrough would succeed in either of their claims for damages, neither could the claims be struck out because there was no real prospect of establishing any entitlement to damages. The CA's decision thus illustrates the old contractual rule that a court cannot refuse to award damages on the basis that quantification of loss is difficult to establish because loss is based on events that may or may not have occurred. In the view of the CA it was feasible that Liverpool may have offered more than £5.5 million if the club had not known about the confidential clause in Ziegle's contract. Similarly, Middlesbrough may have had a more successful season had there not been a 'business interruption' to his staying with the club.[21]

UNFAIR DISMISSAL

The right not to be unfairly dismissed is a statutory right which has been in existence since 1971. The right was contained in the Employment Protection (Consolidation) Act 1978 (EPCA). This has been replaced with the Employment Rights Act 1996 (ERA) which came into force in August 1996.[22] Employees' rights are based on statutory principles which operate independently and often in contradiction to the principles of contract law – although it is more than possible that a summary dismissal will be both wrongful and unfair. Claims for unfair dismissal must be presented to employment tribunals (formerly called industrial tribunals) no later than three months from the effective date of termination of the contract of employment – normally the date on which the dismissal took effect. This time limit is increased by a further three months where new statutory procedures concerning disciplinary and grievance issues apply (see below).

Employment tribunals have jurisdiction over a number of areas of employment law which are governed by statute law – particularly the rights contained in the ERA and in the area of discrimination law (see following chapter). Tribunals have a distinctive composition. The chair of the tribunal must be legally qualified and will often be a practising solicitor or barrister. The other two

---

21 Similarly, in *Stransky* (see previous chapter, p 481) the court rejected the argument that Stransky was entitled only to nominal damages as there was no guarantee that he would have secured a work permit and thus in a position to take up employment with the club. Consequently, Stransky was entitled to damages for loss of earnings for the period of the contract.

The case of *Murphy v Southend United Football Club* (1999, unreported) also provides a useful example of how damages may be calculated in a sporting context. Murphy, who was the manager of Southend United, left the club in breach of contract. He successfully sued for money that the club owed him as a result of the sale of Stan Collymore. However, in accordance with a term in his contract the equivalent of 6 months' salary was deducted from his damages to reflect the club's loss through Murphy's premature termination of his contract. For further discussion of this case see (1999) 2(3) Sports Law Bulletin 3.

22 Thus a number of important cases are based on provisions of the EPCA. However, as the ERA merely further consolidates the law, the cases remain authoritative interpretations of the statutory rights.

members will be selected from panels drawn up by employers' associations and employees' bodies – in particular the British Trades Union Congress (TUC). Any individual has the right of audience before an employment tribunal, and therefore employees are often represented by officials of trade unions or appropriate professional associations. Although costs can be awarded against the losing party it is normal for the parties to bear their own costs.[23] As is the case with most types of tribunals, legal aid is not available.

An appeal from a tribunal is permitted on points of law only. The appeal will be heard by the Employment Appeals Tribunal (EAT). The composition of the EAT is similar to that of an employment tribunal, although the Chair will be a High Court judge. Legal aid is available in proceedings before the EAT. Further appeals lie to the Court of Appeal and the House of Lords. Decisions of the EAT (and relevant decisions of the Court of Appeal and the House of Lords) are often reported in the specialist Industrial Cases Reports (ICR) and the Industrial Relations Law Reports (IRLR).

Continuity of Employment

Only employees with one year's continuous employment can claim unfair dismissal. Such continuity can be acquired by a series of fixed term contracts. Employers are no longer able to rely on waiver clauses, such as that (originally) contained in the Cricketer's Contract, whereby employees give up the right to claim unfair dismissal in the event of the contract not being renewed. Similarly, such clauses are no longer enforceable in so far as they relate to statutory redundancy payments. Employees must have two years' continuity of employment to be eligible for such payments.

A cricketer may be employed on season by season basis. Does such a break in employment break continuity so that a player is never able to secure statutory rights? Under s 212 of the ERA, weeks during which the employee has no contract of employment still count if the employee's absence from work is because of a 'temporary cessation of work'. Should the close season period be considered a 'temporary cessation' so that a cricketer employed on a seasonal basis can in the due course of time establish continuity through a succession of fixed term contracts?

Ford v Warwickshire CC [1983] ICR 273 HL

A part-time college lecturer was made redundant after ten years' employment. She was not employed during the summer period between academic years. The Law Lords held that this period constituted a temporary cessation and thus she secured statutory rights.

Lord Diplock: . . . the length of successive fixed term contracts on which part-time lecturers are employed and the intervals between them vary considerably with the particular course that the part-time lecturer is engaged to teach; so it by no means follows that a similar concession would be made or would be appropriate in each of their cases. It also follows from what I have said that successive periods of seasonal employment of other kinds under fixed term contracts, such as employment in agriculture

---

23 Rule 14 of the Employment Tribunals (Constitution and Rules of Procedure) Regulations 2001, SI 201/1170, permit costs to be awarded where the bringing of a claim or conduct of proceedings is deemed by a tribunal to be 'misconceived'. The definition of 'misconceived' includes 'having no reasonable prospects of success'. The maximum costs that can be awarded against either employee or employer has been increased from £500 to £10,000. Arguably, the sums of money involved will constitute less of a deterrent to those involved in the world of professional sport than is the case with employees in less remunerative occupations.

during harvest-time or in hotel work during the summer season, will only qualify as continuous employment if the length of the period between two successive seasonal contracts is so short in comparison with the length of the season during which the employee is employed as properly to be regarded by the industrial tribunal as no more than a temporary cessation of work in the sense that I have indicated.[24]

This 'mathematical' approach might operate against a cricketer given the length of the out of season period (generally mid-September to mid-March). However, the Law Lords have also espoused what has been described as the 'broad brush' approach where the whole history of the employment has to be taken into account.[25] Through applying the latter, it could be argued that a cricketer who has been with a county for a number of years has established continuity despite the lengthy breaks between seasons. Certainly, it would seem unjust if a player who had stayed loyal to a particular club was to discover that, in the event of dismissal during a season, and thus during the currency of his contract, he had no statutory rights through a lack of continuous employment.

This issue was considered in the case of *Singh* (2001).[26] One of Singh's claims against the Football League was that he was unfairly dismissed. A barrier to this claim succeeding could have been that he was not employed by the League outside of the football season (which runs from August to May). However, the tribunal found Singh did have the necessary continuity of employment. The tribunal decided that the close season period could be considered a 'temporary cessation' which under s 212(3) of the ERA did not constitute a break in continuity. This conclusion was reached on the basis of the fact that during the close season there was an ongoing relationship between the League and its listed referees.

It seems likely that there is similar continuity of employment between cricketers and their clubs, despite the longer close season period. The problem of continuity does not arise, of course, where (as is the norm for professional footballers) a cricketer is employed for a period of years. Here, the contract continues during the out of season period and thus there is no break in the continuity of employment.

It should be noted that the Fixed Term Employees (Prevention of Less Favourable Treatment) Regulations 2002, which were introduced to implement the EU's Directive on Fixed Term Work, apply to the use of fixed term contracts in sport.[27]. The purpose of the Directive is to prohibit the differential treatment of workers on fixed term contracts in comparison with employees on 'indefinite' contracts. In this context, the Regulations will not impact on players' contracts, as typically they are all 'fixed term employees'. However, the Regulations may also convert fixed term contracts into ordinary indefinite contracts (terminable by notice) once a contract or series of contracts has lasted four years. This will not apply if the employer can justify the continued use of fixed term contracts. It is presumed that, should this issue ever arise, such justification will be available to clubs for sporting and commercial reasons.

---

24 [1983] ICR 273 HL, 286.
25 *Fitzgerald v Hall, Russell & Co Ltd* [1970] AC 984.
26 See previous chapter, pp 478.
27 Council Directive 1999/70/EC.

Claiming Unfair Dismissal

Section 95(1) of the Employment Rights Act 1996

For the purposes of this Part an employee is dismissed by his employer if . . .

(a) the contract under which he is employed is terminated by the employer (whether with or without notice),

(b) he is employed under a contract for a fixed term and that term expires without being renewed under the same contract, or

(c) the employee terminates the contract under which he is employed (with or without notice) in circumstances in which he is entitled to terminate it without notice by reason of the employer's conduct.

A dismissal with notice, and thus in accordance with the contract, may still be unfair. Similarly non-renewal of a fixed-term contract, which is of no legal consequence at common law, may constitute an unfair dismissal. Resignation may constitute a constructive dismissal only where it is the employee's response to a repudiatory breach by the employer. Unreasonable conduct by the employer will not in itself convert a resignation into a constructive dismissal.[28]

Contracts of employment can be terminated by means other than dismissal (or resignation). For example, contracts may be terminated by mutual agreement or through frustration. Consider the position of Ed Giddins after he tested positive for cocaine, and the argument by Sussex CCC that the cancellation of his registration by the Test and County Cricket Board automatically terminated his contract. Case law has established that the courts will not permit a dismissal to be disguised as termination of the contract through mutual agreement.[29]

Clause 2(c) of the Cricketers' Contract states that ' . . . this Agreement will terminate immediately if the Board cancels or terminates the registration of the Cricketer by the Club'. Do these decisions render this clause unenforceable? If so, then surely Ed Giddins was dismissed by Sussex CCC as, in reality, the decision not to continue to employ him was taken unilaterally by the club and thus, in law, constituted a dismissal.

Although unreasonable behaviour by an employer cannot turn a resignation into a constructive dismissal, it must be remembered that a breach of the duty to maintain mutual trust and confidence will constitute the requisite repudiatory breach of contract. As discussed in the previous chapter,[30] this could include a refusal to select a player where this is motivated by reasons other than merit; for example to pressurise a player to agree to go on to or to leave the transfer list.

Destruction of mutual trust and confidence clearly includes any form of unlawful discrimination on grounds of race, sex, sexual orientation or religious belief.[31] This includes subjecting an employee to harassment or abuse. A particular problem for sport (and also for other occupations such as the police) is the tradition of 'locker-room' behaviour where players are subjected to levels of banter and practical jokes that would probably not be tolerated in more typical forms of employment. It is very likely that a club will be in breach of contract if such behaviour gets out of hand and the club does not

---

28 See Lord Denning's judgment in *Western Excavating Ltd v Sharp*[1978] ICR 221 CA, in which he clarified that the 'contract test' is the only test that can be used to determine whether a resignation by an employee can in law constitute a constructive dismissal.

29 See *Tracey v Zest Equipment Co* [1982] IRLR 268; and, in particular, the Court of Appeal decision in *Igbo v Johnson Matthey* [1986] IRLR 215.

30 See p 491.

31 See following chapter, pp 571–74.

discipline the culprits. Abuse of a player by a team captain, coach or manager constitutes a similar problem area. Certainly, there will be a breach of contract if 'banter' and the like crosses the line with bullying and the club fails to protect the player who is the victim in such circumstances.

Grievance Procedures and Constructive Dismissal

The new statutory procedures covering disciplinary and grievance issues are of relevance here. These procedures were introduced by the Employment Act 2002 and came into effect on 1 October 2004 under the Employment Act 2002 (Dispute Resolution) Regulations 2004.[32] The primary purpose of the Regulations is to encourage employers and employees to resolve problems internally rather than regarding tribunal claims as a first course of action. Thus in general terms employees who have a grievance should not resign in order to claim constructive dismissal until the employer has been given an opportunity to provide appropriate redress through internal procedures.

However, the statutory procedures do not apply to prevent tribunal applications in circumstances where the employee has been subject to harassment and has 'reasonable grounds to believe that following the procedure would result in further harassment'. Regulation 11(4) defines harassment as 'conduct which has the purpose or effect of (a) violating the person's dignity, or (b) creating an intimidating, hostile, degrading, humiliating or offensive environment for him.' This includes instances of racial and sexual harassment but is also clearly wide enough to include bullying or other humiliating treatment by employers or other employees.

The statutory procedures contain the minimum procedure employees and employers must follow. The modified procedure, set out below, applies where the employee has ceased to be employed, and both parties agree in writing to use the modified rather than the standard procedure. Section 32 of the Employment Act 2002 renders inadmissible a claim to a tribunal until the employee has complied with Step 1 and waited 28 days before applying to the tribunal. Where failure to complete a grievance procedure is wholly or mainly attributable to one of the parties this will result in any award granted by a tribunal being increased or reduced, as considered just and equitable by the tribunal, by between 10 to 50 per cent.[33] An outline of the new procedures is contained in the revised ACAS Code on Disciplinary Rules and Procedures.

ACAS Code Annex C

Standard statutory grievance procedure

(This is a summary of the statutory procedure which is set out in full in Schedule 2 to the Employment Act 2002)

Step 1

Statement of grievance

- The employee must set out the grievance in writing and send the statement or a copy of it to the employer.

---

32 SI 2004/752. For detailed guidance on the regulations see www.dti.gov.uk/resolvingdisputes.
33 Awards can also be increased in harassment cases where the employer can be regarded as responsible for the employee's decision not to invoke the statutory grievance procedure.

Step 2

Meeting

- The employer must invite the employee to attend a meeting to discuss the grievance.
- The meeting must not take place unless:
- the employee has informed the employer what the basis for the grievance was when they made the statement under Step 1; and
- the employer has had a reasonable opportunity to consider their response to that information.
- The employee must take all reasonable steps to attend the meeting.
- After the meeting, the employer must inform the employee of their decision as to their response to the grievance and notify them of the right of appeal against the decision if they are not satisfied with it.
- Employees have the right to be accompanied at the meeting . . .

Step 3

Appeal

- If the employee does wish to appeal, they must inform the employer.
- If the employee informs the employer of their wish to appeal, the employer must invite them to attend a further meeting.
- The employee must take all reasonable steps to attend the meeting.
- After the appeal meeting, the employer must inform the employee of their final decision.
- Where reasonably practicable, the appeal should be dealt with by a more senior manager than attended the first meeting (unless the most senior manager attended that meeting).
- Employees have the right to be accompanied at the appeal meeting . . .

ACAS Code Annex D

Modified statutory grievance procedure

(This is a summary of the statutory procedure which is set out in full in Schedule 2 to the Employment Act 2002)

Step 1

Statement of grievance

- The employee must set out in writing:
- the grievance; and
- the basis for it.
- The employee must send the statement or a copy of it to the employer.

Step 2

Response

- The employer must set out their response in writing and send the statement or a copy.

The above statutory procedures do not apply where an alternative procedure is contained in a collective agreement between two or more employers or an employers' association and an independent trade union. The grievance procedure contained in clause 19 of the standard Footballer's Contract would appear to meet these criteria. Therefore once a player has raised a grievance in writing with the Club

Secretary he is free to pursue a tribunal application after 28 days have elapsed. However, normally such an application will not be made until the appropriate League board has heard any appeal and any final appeal has been heard by the Football League Appeals Committee. As above, there is no statutory bar to a tribunal application where the procedure is not followed but the player can establish that he has reasonable grounds to fear ongoing harassment.

The Meaning of Unfair Dismissal

Section 98 of the Employment Rights Act 1996

(1) In determining for the purposes of this Part whether the dismissal of an employee is fair or unfair, it is for the employer to show –

    (a) the reason (or, if more than one, the principal reason) for the dismissal, and

    (b) that it is either a reason falling within subsection (2) or some other substantial reason of a kind such as to justify the dismissal of an employee holding the position which the employee held.

(2) A reason falls within this subsection if it –

    (a) relates to the capability or qualifications of the employee for performing work of the kind which he was employed by the employer to do,

    (b) relates to the conduct of the employee,

    (c) is that the employee was redundant, or

    (d) is that the employee could not continue to work in the position which he held without contravention (either on his part or on that of his employer) of a duty or restriction imposed by or under an enactment.

(3) In subsection (2)(a) –

    (a) 'capability', in relation to an employee, means his capability assessed by reference to skill, aptitude, health or any other physical or mental quality, and

    (b) 'qualifications', in relation to an employee, means any degree, diploma or other academic, technical or professional qualification relevant to the position which he held.

(4) Where the employer has fulfilled the requirements of subsection (1), the determination of the question whether the dismissal is fair or unfair (having regard to the reason shown by the employer) –

    (a) depends on whether in the circumstances (including the size and administrative resources of the employer's undertaking) the employer acted reasonably or unreasonably in treating it as a sufficient reason for dismissing the employee, and

    (b) shall be determined in accordance with equity and the substantial merits of the case.

Under s 98(1) the burden of proof is on the employer to show the reason (or the principal reason) for the dismissal. If the employer cannot satisfy the tribunal that the reason was one or more of the above then the dismissal must be unfair. The case of *Singh*[34] illustrates this, as the tribunal found that his dismissal was the product of unlawful race discrimination, and therefore the Football League was unable under s 98 of the ERA to prove the dismissal was for a potentially fair reason.

The only other possibility, in accordance with s 98(1)(b), is that the employee was dismissed for some other substantial reason of a kind such as to justify the dismissal of an employee holding the position which the employee held.' As explained in the previous chapter, footballers whose contracts expire after they have reached the age of 24 must be allowed to move to a new club if they so wish.

---

34 See previous chapter pp 478–79, and following chapter p 560.

Conversely, as the retain and transfer rules no longer apply, there is no mechanism to encourage a club to retain on its books a player it no longer wants. It remains to be seen whether an unfair dismissal claim will ever be brought by a player who does not want to be released by a club. Such a claim would certainly be possible in law. The club would then have to show that it was acting reasonably in reaching a decision that it no longer wanted a player's services and thus the dismissal was fair by reference to 'some other substantial reason'. This point of course applies to cricketers and any other type of sports participant now that that clauses can no longer be incorporated into fixed term contracts to prevent unfair dismissal claims from being presented.

Dismissal for 'some other substantial reason' is also of potential relevance to sport in the situation where behaviour by an employee, whilst not strictly misconduct, is disruptive to working relationships.[35] Given the homophobic culture apparently prevalent in sport, as evidenced by the reaction to Justin Fashanu when he 'came out', clubs might be tempted to dismiss a player on the basis of his (or her) sexual orientation. However, today, such a dismissal would certainly be unfair, as it would also offend Regulations, which came into force in December 2003, prohibiting discrimination on grounds of sexual orientation.[36]

In the main, it is the categories of incapability and misconduct which are clearly the most important in sport. Such dismissals will still be unfair if an employment tribunal does not consider that the employer acted reasonably in deciding to dismiss. The decision as to the fairness of the dismissal is for the tribunal to make. The burden of proof is neutral. However, as a point of law, it is of primary importance that a tribunal does not substitute its views for that of the reasonable employer. Employers may operate within a range of reasonable responses. Only if a dismissal is outside of this range will it be unfair.

British Leyland (UK) Ltd v Swift [1981] **IRLR 91 CA**

Lord Denning MR: The correct test is: was it reasonable for the employer to dismiss him? If no reasonable employer would have dismissed him, then the dismissal was unfair. But if a reasonable employer might reasonably have dismissed him, then the dismissal was fair. It must be remembered that in all these cases there is a band of reasonableness within which one employer might reasonably take one view; another quite reasonably take a different view ... if it was quite reasonable to dismiss him, then the dismissal must be upheld as fair: even though some other employers may not have dismissed him.[37]

Iceland Frozen Foods Ltd v Jones [1982] **IRLR 439 EAT**

Browne-Wilkinson P: . . . (1) the starting point must be the words [of the section] themselves; (2) in applying the section an Industrial Tribunal must consider the reasonableness of the employer's conduct, not simply whether they (the members of the Industrial Tribunal) consider the dismissal to be fair; (3) in judging the reasonableness of the employer's conduct an Industrial Tribunal must not substitute its decision as to what was the right course to adopt for that of the employer; (4) in many (though not all) cases there is a band of reasonable responses to the employee's conduct within which one employer might reasonably take one view another quite reasonably take another; (5) the function of the Industrial Tribunal, as an industrial jury, is to determine whether in the particular circumstances of each case the decision to dismiss the employee fell within the band of reasonable responses which a reasonable

---

35   For example, in *Treganowan v Knee* [1975] IRLR 247 a secretary upset other office staff by boasting about her sexual exploits. Her dismissal was accepted as being for 'some other substantial reason' and was considered by the tribunal to be fair.

36   See following chapter, p 573.

37   [1981] IRLR 91 CA, 93.

employer might have adopted. If the dismissal falls within the band the dismissal is fair, if the dismissal falls outside the band it is unfair.[38]

It is clear that a dismissal may be reasonable, even if a particular tribunal regards it as harsh, if it can be shown that other employers, particularly those in the same line of business, would regard dismissal as an appropriate penalty. This test has been subjected to recent judicial criticism by the EAT. However, it is clear from subsequent decisions by the Court of Appeal that the test is still the correct law.[39] Indeed, and unfortunately in the view of many employment lawyers including this author, it is clear that the test can now only be overruled by the Law Lords or through legislation. However, given that clubs like most employers vary in their responses to acts of misconduct by their employees, it is useful to take note of the reasons given by the EAT for the test to be disregarded.

Haddon v Van Den Burgh Foods [1999] ICR 1150 EAT

Morison J: . . . First the question for the tribunal is the reasonableness of the decision to dismiss in the circumstances of the particular case having regard to equity and the substantial merits. Because the tribunal are applying an objective test, that is, a test of reasonableness, it is not sufficient for them simply to say 'well, we would not have dismissed in those circumstances'. They must recognise that, however improbable, their own personal views may not accord with the reasonableness. Just asking 'what would I have done' is not enough. However, it is neither reasonable nor realistic to expect the objective question to be asked and answered without the members of the tribunal having first asked 'what would we have done'. And provided that they do not stop there, we see nothing wrong with that approach.

The mantra 'the tribunal must not substitute their own decision for that of the employer', is simply another way of saying that the tribunal must apply the reasonableness test by going somewhat further then simply asking what they themselves would have done. It is likely however that what the tribunal themselves would have done will often coincide with their judgment as to what a reasonable employer would have done. The tribunal is, after all, composed of people who are chosen to sit as an industrial jury applying their own good sense of judgment. The task of the tribunal is to pronounce judgment on the reasonableness of the employers' actions and whenever they uphold an employee's complaint they are in effect 'substituting their own judgment for that of the employer'. Providing they apply the test of reasonableness, it is their duty both to determine their own judgment and to substitute it where appropriate.

The second point simply recognises that there may be cases where a decision not to dismiss would be reasonable and a decision to dismiss would also be reasonable. This point is based upon logic. Because course A would have been reasonable, it does not follow that every other course is unreasonable. In other words, in some marginal cases, the tribunal might well consider that a dismissal by the particular employer was reasonable even though another reasonable employer might not have dismissed. The mantra 'the band or range of reasonable responses' is not helpful because it has led tribunals into applying what amounts to a perversity test, which, as is clear from *Iceland* itself, was not its purpose. The moment that one talks of a 'range' or 'band' of reasonable responses one is conjuring up the possibility of extreme views at either end of the band or range. In reality, it is most unlikely in an unfair dismissal case involving misconduct that the tribunal will need to concern itself with the question whether the deployment of each of the weapons in the employers' disciplinary armoury would have been reasonable. Dismissal is the ultimate sanction. There is, in reality, no range or band to be considered, only whether the employer acted reasonably in invoking that sanction. Further, the band has become a band or group of employers, with an extreme end. There is a danger of Tribunals testing the fairness of the dismissal by reference to the extreme.

---

38 [1982] IRLR 439 EAT, 442.

39 In *Post Office v Foley* and *HSBC Bank plc v Madden* [2000] IRLR 827 the Court of Appeal confirmed the range of reasonable responses test and ruled that it is binding on the EAT.

In our view the approach taken in *Gilham* is to be followed. The statute is clear and unambiguous. The two points referred to above are no more than obvious statements which flow from the natural and ordinary meaning of the words of the subsection. In other words, we respectfully suggest that tribunals now return to the task in hand which is to apply the section without embellishment, and without using mantras so favoured by the lawyers in this field.

Mr Freer suggested to us that the tribunals, and the courts in particular, had difficulty in coming to terms with this piece of social legislation which changed the balance of power between employer and employee [the master/servant relationship]. Employers are no longer free to dismiss with impunity those whom they judge to be worthy of dismissal. As Lord Justice Roskill observed, the right to dismiss is tempered by the right of the individual not to be unfairly dismissed and the balance between the two is to be struck by the industrial jury.

We believe this balance will be best achieved by the industrial jury, the Employment Tribunals, applying the statute as it stands, no more and no less.

There is some anecdotal evidence with which we were presented which suggests that 'conduct' is the most frequent reason in contested Employment Tribunals unfair dismissal cases and that employees lost more than 50% of them, but that where they did succeed it was almost always because of the procedure being found faulty. Mr Freer points out, we think with justification, that a combination of the judicial embellishments upon the statute has led tribunals to adopt a perversity test of reasonableness and to depress the chances of success for applicants.

An application of the range of reasonable responses test, in the wake of its reinstatement by the Court of Appeal, in a sports related situation is provided by the following case.

Post Office v Liddiard CA Tuckey LJ, Latham LJ, Arden LJ 7 June 2001

This was an appeal by the Post Office from the decision of the Employment Appeal Tribunal ('EAT') dated 16 June 2000, which summarily dismissed the Post Office's appeal from the Employment Tribunal's finding that it had unfairly dismissed the respondent. The respondent was employed as a coder in the Post Office and worked nights. He commenced his employment in 1986 and had a good record of employment. In 1998, following riots involving English football hooligans attending the World Cup, the respondent was arrested and convicted in France of offences amounting to football hooliganism. He was sentenced to 40 days' imprisonment. Following the violence in France, there was widespread condemnation by the Prime Minister and the press of those involved in the violence. The respondent was identified in a national newspaper as being a Post Office employee and being involved. The Post Office suspended the respondent pending disciplinary proceedings, alleging gross misconduct that brought the Post Office into disrepute.

The respondent was dismissed in January 1999 and issued proceedings claiming unfair dismissal. The Employment Tribunal took into account the fact that the respondent had had an excellent employment record, the incidence for which he had been convicted in France had no relation to his employment, and that he was employed within the Post Office and not in contact with the public. The Tribunal also took into account the fact that the proceedings in France had a number of anomalies, that the respondent's manager who had dismissed him had admitted that he had been influenced by the press involvement, that the respondent had no previous convictions, and, although convicted, had denied the offences. On those grounds, the Tribunal found that the respondent had been unfairly dismissed. An appeal before the EAT was summarily dismissed. This was the Post Office's appeal from that dismissal on the grounds that the Tribunal misdirected itself, or alternatively, reached a perverse decision.

HELD: (1) At the date of the hearing before the Tribunal, the law regarding unfair dismissal, in particular s 98(4) *Employment Relations Act 1996*, was uncertain. The approach to s 98(4) of the 1996 Act that was to be adopted was given guidance in *Iceland Frozen Foods v Jones* (1983) ICR 17 when the decision of Iceland Frozen Foods was preferred over the approach in *Van Den Bergh Foods v Haddon* (1999) ICR 1150.

(2) *Iceland Frozen Foods* stated, *inter alia*, that the Tribunal was to determine an employer's decision in each case to dismiss an employee in the band of reasonable responses. That approach was approved in *Post Office v Foley* (2000) ICR 1283.

(3) The decision of *Foley* was given after the dismissal of the Post Office's appeal by the EAT. The Tribunal in the instant case took the approach adopted in *Haddon*, and it was clear from the determination of the Tribunal that there was no reference to the band of reasonable response tests.

(4) The central issue that the Tribunal should have addressed was whether it was reasonable for the respondent to have been dismissed for reasons that amounted to gross misconduct which brought the Post Office into disrepute. That question was not addressed by the Tribunal which preferred to take the Haddon approach, an approach which was expressly criticised in *Foley*, and accordingly, the Tribunal's determination could not stand.

It is clear that Liddiard's claim would have stood a far better chance of being upheld if the EAT's reasoning in *Haddon* could have been applied. The case itself is, arguably, a good example as to how the range of reasonable responses test is loaded in favour of the employer. To succeed in claiming unfair dismissal it is clear the employee will still need to show that no reasonable employer could have reached a decision to dismiss. In cases such as *Liddiard*, it could be argued that an employee's conduct outside of an employment is only the concern of the employer where it impacts on the employer's commercial reputation and thus its business or trade. However, the case shows that tribunals will generally have to accept that it is within the range of reasonable responses to dismiss employees whose private conduct generates adverse publicity for the employer.

However, other factors do have to be taken into account. A reasonable employer will normally take into account an employee's length of employment and previous record. Consistency of treatment is also an important factor in determining whether an employer has acted within the range of reasonable responses. These issues were considered in cases, which were not dissimilar to that of *Liddiard*.

T Doherty v Consignia plc & M Doherty v Consignia plc[40]

These cases are discussed together though there were some factual differences and the cases were heard at different times by differently constituted tribunals. Thomas Doherty (TD) and Michael Doherty (MD) were both Arsenal fans. Both also worked as stewards for Flight Options, a travel company, assisting fans travelling to and from football matches in countries outside the UK. Neither brother had any record of football hooliganism and both were highly regarded by Flight Options. The cases arose out of violence that preceded the 2000 UEFA cup final between Arsenal and Galatasary played in Copenhagen. It was established at the time that it was the Galatasary fans who initiated the violence as they attacked a square set aside for use by Arsenal supporters. Subsequent video footage did show TD kicking a Turkish fan but the footage was less clear with respect to MD. The footage did not identify either of the brothers as Post Office employees. However, subsequent coverage in the tabloid press did and it was decided to initiate separate disciplinary proceedings against both of them.

In deciding to dismiss MD and TD the Post Office failed to consider the previous impeccable employment records of both of the brothers. (This was particularly the case with MD who had 13 years' exemplary service and had put himself at risk defending the Post Office against armed robbery.) Moreover, in the case of TD, the employer failed to take into account its treatment of other Post Office employees, accused of acts of hooliganism in Copenhagen. In one of these cases disciplinary action was dropped for want of evidence, even though the individual concerned was shown in the same newspaper article as that concerning TD to be throwing a bicycle. The employer also failed to take into account that

---

40   (2001) Case Number 2204805/00; (2001) Case Number 2205635/00.

it had earlier reinstated an employee who was a Millwall fan and had been sentenced to nine months' imprisonment for football hooliganism. Thus the dismissals of both Doherty brothers were deemed unfair in that no reasonable employer would have reached a decision to dismiss in the circumstances of either case.

The cases also establish that the best hope for employees claiming unfair dismissal for offences committed away from the workplace is where evidence supporting the decision to dismiss is primarily derived from newspaper stories. The managers conducting the investigations and hearings placed undue reliance on the media coverage and the testimony of anonymous witnesses and failed to give sufficient weight to the testimony of the Doherty brothers, their colleagues and Flight Options. It should also be noted that both brothers exercised their rights of internal appeal but the separate employment tribunals found that the appeal hearings did not rectify the procedural errors that occurred in the original proceedings.[41]

The case of *Beck v Lincoln City FC* [42] provides an example of a dismissal which would probably be regarded as fair even on the basis of the more flexible approach advocated in *Haddon*. The case echoes that of *Macari* (see above) in that Beck was dismissed for taking an unauthorised leave of absence to go on holiday. However, initially, Beck made misleading statements about the reasons for his absence, claiming first bereavement and then a breakdown in the relationship with his girlfriend. Beck had previously received two written warnings for other forms of misconduct. The tribunal decided that Beck's dismissal was reasonable and fair in light of his breach of contract, subsequent prevarications and misleading statements with respect to the reason for his absence and previous record.

The continuing fundamental importance of the range of reasonable responses test means that the essential questions remain a) who constitutes the reasonable employer, and b) what stance will this elusive person take in response to misconduct etc on the part of an employee? The answers are no clearer in sport than in any other field of employment. In recent times the quite different reactions of football clubs to the use of drugs by their players – particularly those deemed recreational in nature and consumed in a social not sporting context – is a good example of the problem.[43] An alternative basis (to misconduct) for dismissing a player who has become addicted to drugs, be they legal or illegal, is incapability. Of particular importance in this respect are clauses in players' contracts requiring them to maintain appropriate standards of fitness, form and health.

To date clubs have shown what could be viewed as remarkable tolerance of players convicted for violent offences on, off or adjacent to the field of play. Does this mean that the dismissal of a player in the future for such an offence should be regarded as beyond the range of reasonable responses and thus unfair? It is perhaps significant that all the names that immediately spring to mind are 'star'

---

41   The importance of this principle is explained below in considering the unfair dismissal claim brought by the footballer, Dennis Wise. See pp 544–45.

42   IT Case No 2600760/98 (unreported) – see (1998) 1(6) SLB, p 6 for further comment on this case.

43   See previous chapter, p 000. Contrast the dismissals of Craig Whittington (Huddersfield) and Roger Stanislaus (Leyton Orient) with the lenient decision by Barnsley FC to take no further action with respect to Dean Jones who was banned for three months by the FA for taking an amphetamine-based substance. Of particular interest, with respect to possible inconsistency of treatment, was the decision by Charlton Athletic FC to dismiss Jamie Stuart after he had tested positive for marijuana and cocaine. Previously, the club had retained the services of Chris Armstrong and Lee Bowyer when, whilst Charlton players, they had received short bans from the FA after testing positive for cannabis. See Welch, R, 'A snort and a puff: recreational drugs and discipline in professional sport', in O'Leary, J (ed), *Drugs and Doping in Sport* (2000), London: Cavendish, pp 75–90, for a discussion of these issues and the view that clubs should not dismiss players for taking recreational, as against performance enhancing, drugs unless such decisions are taken on fitness grounds. If the latter is the case then clubs should not differentiate between illegal drugs and legal intoxicants such as alcohol.

footballers from leading sides in the Premier League. Could a player employed by a Cambridge United or a Crewe Alexandra anticipate such a lenient response in similar circumstances – particularly if his absence through suspension and/or imprisonment had significant repercussions for the fortunes and/or finances of the club concerned? Would the reasonable club adopt a policy of the greater the 'star' the greater the latitude that will be given?[44] Is violent conduct by a player more or less acceptable in other professional sports such as rugby or cricket?

Professional sports participants are obviously particularly prone to absence through physical injury, which may be long term in nature. Again there are clauses in their contracts dealing with the rights of clubs and players respectively in this situation. The Cricketers' Contract expressly permits a club to dismiss a player who, having been injured in the previous season, is still unfit for play at the start of the new season – cl 8. Given the presence of such a contractual term it is likely, although by no means in all circumstances definite, that such a dismissal would be considered within the range of reasonable responses and thus fair.

A long term and certainly a permanent injury can terminate the contract through frustration in which case, as there is no dismissal, the player has no statutory rights which can be pursued. However, cl 10 of the Football League Contract gives the player contractual rights to termination through notice in the event of permanent injury.

PROCEDURAL FAIRNESS

A reasonable employer will develop and comply with proper disciplinary procedures. Model procedures are provided by the Advisory Conciliation and Arbitration Service (ACAS).[45] Whilst the detailed procedures in the Code can be regarded as being based on recognised good practice, the statutory procedures outlined below, which were contained in the Employment Act 2002 and implemented by the 2004 Regulations, constitute minimum standards with which employers must comply. Failure to do so will render any dismissal automatically unfair under s 98A(1) of the Employment Rights Act (inserted by s 34 of the Employment Act 2002). In such cases tribunals will normally grant a minimum basic award of 4 weeks' pay, and will increase any compensatory award by between 10 to 50 per cent.[46]

In limited cases where the employer is entitled summarily to dismiss the employee on grounds of gross misconduct the employer is only obliged to follow the modified procedure set out below. The modified procedure will only apply where it is 'reasonable in the circumstances for the employer to dismiss the employee before enquiring further into the circumstances in which the conduct took

---

44 Mark Bosnich provides an example of one 'star' footballer who did have his contract terminated in January 2003 by Chelsea FC, having tested positive for cocaine. However, Bosnich was not as this time the club's first choice goalkeeper, and there has been some speculation of continued Premiership interest in him, for example, on the part of Charlton FC – see *Sunday Mirror Sport*, 25 July 2004. Nevertheless, Chelsea's dismissal of Adrian Mutu does demonstrate evidence of consistency of treatment as far as that particular club is concerned, and this would enable tribunals to regard future dismissals by Chelsea for drug offences as being within the range of reasonable responses.

45 See ACAS Code of Practice 1: Disciplinary Practice and Procedures in Employment

46 See below, pp 551–53 for explanation of the basic and compensatory awards. It should be noted that the new rules also apply to claims for wrongful dismissal if such claims are presented to tribunals, and thus damages could be increased or reduced where statutory procedures are not followed. However, in sport the amount of damages being claimed will often necessitate an action for wrongful dismissal being heard by a court rather than being taken to a tribunal.

place.' However, under reg 3(2) the modified procedure does not have to be followed if the employee presents a claim for unfair dismissal before the employer has informed the employee in writing of the reason(s) for the dismissal.

ACAS Code Annex A

Standard statutory dismissal and disciplinary procedure

(This is a summary of the statutory procedure which is set out in full in Schedule 2 to the Employment Act 2002)

This procedure applies to disciplinary action short of dismissal (excluding oral and written warnings and suspension on full pay) based on either conduct or capability. It also applies to dismissals (except for constructive dismissals) including dismissals on the basis of conduct, capability, expiry of a fixed term contract, redundancy and retirement . . .

Step 1

Statement of grounds for action and invitation to meeting

- The employer must set out in writing the employee's alleged conduct or characteristics, or other circumstances, which lead them to contemplate dismissing or taking disciplinary action against the employee.
- The employer must send the statement or a copy of it to the employee and invite the employee to attend a meeting to discuss the matter.

Step 2

The meeting

- The meeting must take place before action is taken, except in the case where the disciplinary action consists of suspension.
- The meeting must not take place unless:
    i) the employer has informed the employee what the basis was for including in the statement under Step 1 the ground or grounds given in it; and
    ii) the employee has had a reasonable opportunity to consider their response to that information.
- The employee must take all reasonable steps to attend the meeting.
- After the meeting, the employer must inform the employee of their decision and notify them of the right to appeal against the decision if they are not satisfied with it.
- Employees have the right to be accompanied at the meeting . . .

Step 3

The appeal

- If the employee wishes to appeal, they must inform the employer.
- If the employee informs the employer of their wish to appeal, the employer must invite them to attend a further meeting.
- The employee must take all reasonable steps to attend the meeting.
- The appeal meeting need not take place before the dismissal or disciplinary action takes effect.
- Where reasonably practicable, the appeal should be dealt with by a more senior manager than attended the first meeting (unless the most senior manager attended that meeting).
- After the appeal meeting, the employer must inform the employee of their final decision.
- Employees have the right to be accompanied at the appeal meeting . . .

ACAS Code Annex B

Modified statutory dismissal and disciplinary procedure

(This is a summary of the statutory procedure which is set out in full in Schedule 2 to the Employment Act 2002)

Step 1

Statement of grounds for action

- The employer must set out in writing:

  i) the employee's alleged misconduct which has led to the dismissal;

  ii) the reasons for thinking at the time of the dismissal that the employee was guilty of the alleged misconduct; and

  iii) the employee's right of appeal against dismissal.

- The employer must send the statement or a copy of it to the employee.

Step 2

Appeal

- If the employee does wish to appeal, they must inform the employer.

- If the employee informs the employer of their wish to appeal, the employer must invite them to attend a meeting.

- The employee must take all reasonable steps to attend the meeting.

- After the appeal meeting, the employer must inform the employee of their final decision.

- Where reasonably practicable the appeal should be dealt with by a more senior manager not involved in the earlier decision to dismiss.

- Employees have the right to be accompanied at the appeal meeting . . .

Regulation 5(2) permits an alternative system of appeal where this is agreed between one or more employers or an employers' association and an independent trade union. The following appeal procedures contained in the standard Footballer's Contract would appear to meet these criteria. However, the right to a hearing conducted by the employer, prior to any appeal, as contained in the statutory procedures still apply. Therefore, it is important that clubs ensure that their internal procedures do comply with the statutory minimum if they are to avoid any dismissal of a player to be found to be automatically unfair.

FA Code of Practice and Notes on Footballers' Contracts

A Player is governed by four principal sets of rules, which will be found to overlap to a large extent – The Football Association and The FA Premier League Rules or The Football League Regulations, the Club rules and the provisions of the contract (Clause 5). Obviously whilst playing, a Player is subject to the Laws of the Game (Clause 4). The Club will provide the Player with an up-to-date copy of all the Rules and Regulations, the Club rules and the provisions of the contract (Clause 5). The Player must also be given a copy of any insurance policy conditions affecting him that he needs to be aware of.

These rules are underpinned by a system of discipline. Each Club may operate its own system, although The FA Premier League, The Football League and Professional Footballers' Association have drawn up a disciplinary schedule containing recommended guidelines for Clubs to follow. It is essential that the method adopted is both consistent and fair. If rules are laid down they must be followed. The Player must always be made clear as to what is being alleged and he must be given a proper opportunity to state his case. Some Clubs have found that discipline on minor matters can be enforced with the help of a Club Committee including Players and Officials. Representations on behalf of a Player by his PFA representative should always be considered. Rarely will manners need to go further than the dressing room level. It is important to keep records.

The contract, however, lays down a formal system of discipline and punishment, with a system of appeals. Offences are divided into two categories:

- Serious (Clause 16) or persistent misconduct: serious or persistent breach of the rules of the club or terms of the contract (which incorporates Football Association and FA Premier League Rules and the Football League Regulations). If the Player is found to be guilty then his contract may be terminated by 14 days' notice being given. The Club must set out its reasons in writing and notify the Player.

- Less Serious (Clause 18) misconduct: breach of training or disciplinary rules or lawful instructions, breach of the provisions of the contract (which incorporates Football Association and FA Premier League Rules and the Football League Regulations). The player may be suspended, with or without pay, for up to 14 days or fined up to 14 days' basic wages. The Club must set out its reasons in writing and notify the Player.

A Club may, if it so wishes, treat conduct that might be classed as serious under Clause 16 as a lesser transgression under Clause 18 so as to impose a lesser penalty. Each action by a Club under Clauses 16 and 18 carries with it the right of appeal and the penalties are suspended until the appeal procedure is exhausted. A fine may be paid directly by the Player or may be stopped from his wages. If this procedure is used then the sum deducted in any week should not be greater than half the Players' basic wage (Clause 18). Under this procedure, for example, a two week fine (the maximum) would be deducted over four weeks.

The appeals procedure has two stages once the matter progresses beyond the level of the Club (Clause 16):

- To The FA Premier League or The Football League Board.
- By either Club or Player, depending of course on the outcome of the first appeal, to The Football League Appeals Committee.

In each case the appeal must be lodged within seven days of the formal notification of the previous decision. The Football League Appeals Committee has to hear a case within 14 days of its receipt.

The Football League Appeals Committee consists of an independent chairman and one member nominated by each of The Professional Footballers' Association and the Institute of Football Management and Administration together with a Football League and/or a FA Premier League representative for cases involving their member Clubs. It meets usually in London and Manchester or elsewhere convenient to the Club and Player.

In all appeals the Player will be able to obtain advice and representation from the PFA (Clause 20) if he so desires. [47]

Previous editions of this text have emphasised the importance of the decision of the House of Lords in *Polkey v AE Dayton Services Ltd*[48] with respect to the legal status of the ACAS Code. The Law Lords held that a failure to follow the Code did not automatically render a dismissal unfair. However, such a dismissal would normally be procedurally unfair unless an employer could show that in the circumstances of the case adhering to the Code could be considered by the reasonable employer to be futile or useless. An employer was not able successfully to argue that had the procedure been

47   FA Notes on Contract, pp 4–5.
48   [1988] ICR 142.

followed a decision to dismiss would still have resulted. A similar position applied where employers failed to follow their own procedures – particularly, as is often the case in sport, where such procedures have contractual force.[49]

The new s 98A(2) in the ERA (inserted by s 34 of the Employment Act 2002) constitutes a statutory reversal of this aspect of *Polkey*. Thus the 'no difference' approach is now the correct law where an employer complies with the statutory minimum procedures, but does not comply with other procedures contained in the ACAS Code or the employer's own disciplinary policy. An employer will now be allowed to show that, on a balance of probabilities, had full procedures been followed the decision to dismiss would still have been reached. In such circumstances, tribunals should regard the procedural deficiencies involved as making no difference to the employer's decision to dismiss. For example, a dismissal may still be procedurally fair, even though it is based on facts not known to the employer at the date of dismissal, if facts subsequently come to light to show that the employee was guilty. Similarly, a dismissal may be fair even though the employee was denied rights to be accompanied by a trade union representative or a colleague, but the tribunal accepts this would not have affected the outcome.[50]

It should be clarified that for a tribunal to reach a finding of fair dismissal in such circumstances, it will still be necessary for the substantive decision to dismiss to be within the range of reasonable responses. It remains to be seen whether this change in the law will result in different decisions in cases in the future which are similar to the cases discussed in this chapter. It is also important to remember that where disciplinary procedures are incorporated into players' contracts a failure to observe them will constitute wrongful dismissal and may entitle the player to claim damages or even secure an injunction to restrain the dismissal.[51]

A claim for unfair dismissal, brought by the famous footballer Dennis Wise (and now player-manager of Millwall), illustrates the very important principle that even where rights of appeal are exercised a dismissal will still be unfair if the decision to dismiss is based on initial procedural irregularities. This case provides a good example of a dismissal which would probably still be found to be unfair today because of a failure to adhere to the ACAS Code, even if what now constitute the minimum statutory procedures were followed.

Wise v Filbert Realisations Respondent (Formerly Leicester City Football Club) (In Administration)[52]

In July 2002, during a pre-season training club tour of Finland Dennis Wise was involved in an incident with a team-mate, Callum Davidson. As a result of a blow or blows in the face administered by Wise, Davidson sustained a fractured cheekbone with bruising and swelling around the right eye. Initially, the club manager fined Wise two weeks' wages and sent him home. However, the club decided to take disciplinary proceedings. On 22 July Wise was suspended pending an investigation into allegations of serious misconduct. A disciplinary hearing took place before the club chairman, Mr George, on 26 July. That hearing was conducted in a way which the employment tribunal found to be procedurally unfair in a number of respects. The club decided to dismiss Wise with 14 days' notice on 1 August, as provided for in clause 16 of his contract of employment.

---

49   See *Stoker v Lancashire CC* [1992] IRLR 75.
50   This right is provided by s 10 of the Employment Relations Act 1999 and applies irrespective of whether an employer recognises an employee's union. Both professional cricketers and footballers are permitted union representation by established procedures regulating disciplinary and grievance hearings.
51   See above, pp 524–28.
52   EAT/0660/03 9 February 2004.

Wise's contract provided for a 2-stage appeal process detailed above. Wise exercised his right of appeal to the Football League Disciplinary Committee (FDC). The panel decided to conduct a full rehearing. Oral evidence was given by Wise, who pleaded self-defence and Davidson and Matt Elliott, the club captain, were also called. The panel preferred the evidence of Davidson and Elliott, rejecting the plea of self-defence advanced by Wise. They found as fact that Wise had gone into Davidson's room looking for trouble and had struck him twice, causing the injuries earlier mentioned. Even applying the criminal standard of proof, the panel was satisfied that Wise had committed an assault occasioning Actual Bodily Harm. On these findings, the panel found that Wise was guilty of serious misconduct under clause 16 of the contract. Having done so, the panel proceeded to find that the sanction of dismissal was disproportionate and substituted a penalty of two weeks' loss of gross wages.

The Club appealed to the Football League Appeals Committee (FLAC) against the FDC decision. The main point of appeal was that, having found serious misconduct, the FDC had no power to say that dismissal was disproportionate, and in any event, FDC was wrong because dismissal was the appropriate penalty. The appeal came before a FLAC panel on 18 September 2002. FLAC agreed with the Club that, having found serious misconduct, the FDC was clearly wrong to substitute a two-weeks' wages fine for dismissal. They took into account the various factual findings made by FDC as to the assault itself and upheld the original dismissal.

The EAT upheld the appeal by Wise by applying the principle that in order to cure initial procedural failings the appeal process must be by way of rehearing and not review of the initial decision.

Clark J: In the present case the first instance decision at Club level was procedurally flawed. The FDC appeal was by way of rehearing and was conducted fairly; it was capable of curing the earlier procedural deficiencies. However, and this in our view is the crux of the appeal, the FDC hearing did not result in a decision which upheld the original dismissal decision; had it done so, we are satisfied, the Tribunal's decision would be unimpeachable; that hearing resulted in the dismissal being overturned. It was the subsequent FLAC hearing, itself, we accept, taking the form of a review of the FDC decision and not a rehearing, which reinstated the original Club decision to dismiss.

. . . In these circumstances . . . the Respondent cannot rely, either on the FDC rehearing which imposed a sanction short of dismissal, nor the FLAC decision, which followed a review, to cure the procedural irregularities at the

initial hearing . . . fairness requires not only that the sanction falls within the range of reasonable responses, but also the procedure by which that sanction was reached. It is on this latter requirement that the Respondent falls down. The dismissal is unfair.

. . . It follows that the Tribunal fell into error in their approach . . . They were not entitled to amalgamate the two levels of appeal and take the final sanction of dismissal at the review stage (FLAG) where the panel rehearing the case (FDC), after hearing the witnesses, found not only that the Appellant was guilty of serious misconduct, but that such misconduct did not merit dismissal.

It is clear from the ACAS Code that in many circumstances penalties short of dismissal should be imposed in the event of first-time and/or offences short of gross misconduct. By virtue of contract law and s 13(1) ERA[53] an employee should not be suspended without pay and/or fined unless this is permitted by an express term in the contract of employment. Clause 18 of the Football League Contract and cl 13(a) of the Cricketers' Contract incorporate the necessary provisions. Indeed the use of such penalties is much more common in professional sport than in many other fields of employment. It should be noted that the statutory dismissal and disciplinary procedures also apply to clubs intending to impose these sorts of penalties rather than dismissal.

---

53   Formerly s 1(1) of the Wages Act 1986.

Strictly speaking neither the statutory procedures nor other procedures contained in, or based on, the ACAS Code need be followed where an employer decides on a penalty short of dismissal. However, a dismissal based on a series of offences by an employee will be unsafe if in the earlier stages proper procedures were not followed. Thus there should be an investigation and the holding of a formal hearing each and every time an employee is disciplined. Moreover, in the cases of cricket and football, players have contractual rights of appeal against the imposition of suspensions and fines. Note further that under the ACAS Code a disciplinary decision should not stay permanently on an employee's record. The norm is that it should be removed if the employee 'keeps a clean sheet' for one year.

Procedural Fairness and Disciplinary Investigations

One of the central aspects of the ACAS Code is that a reasonable employer will form an appropriate view of the facts before reaching a decision to dismiss. The conducting of a reasonable investigation by the employer should be, therefore, a prerequisite to both the convening of a formal hearing and the reaching of a decision by the employer. As a general rule, failure to conduct an investigation, or one that in the circumstances will be considered adequate by a reasonable employer, will render a dismissal unfair. The cases involving the Doherty Brothers are a good illustration of this.[54]

British Home Stores v Burchell [1980] ICR 303 EAT

Arnold J: First of all, there must be established by the employer the fact of that belief; that the employer did believe it. Secondly, that the employer had in his mind reasonable grounds upon which to sustain that belief. And thirdly, we think, that the employer, at the stage at which he formed that belief on those grounds, at any rate at the final stage at which he formed that belief on those grounds, had carried out as much investigation into the matter as was reasonable in all the circumstances of the case. It is the employer who manages to discharge the onus of demonstrating those three matters, we think, who must not be examined further. It is not relevant, as we think, that the tribunal would themselves have shared that view in those circumstances.[55]

It is clear from *Burchell*[56] that if an employer satisfies this three staged approach his view of the facts must be accepted by an employment tribunal. A tribunal cannot substitute its view of the facts for that of the reasonable employer. It does not follow, however, that an employer who fails to conduct an investigation must have acted unreasonably, and therefore that a dismissal, not preceded by an investigation, must be unfair. This is even more the case today, given that under the new s 98A(2) of the ERA an employer can show that had an investigation been held a decision to dismiss would still have been reached.

For example, an employee is caught removing the employer's property from the workplace and is dismissed summarily 'on the spot'. The failure to conduct a formal investigation will be of no legal significance if the employee is guilty, even though the employer has not sought to establish the facts. However, this is also the type of situation where an employer, having summarily dismissed the employee, will be required to follow the modified disciplinary procedure under which the employee has a right of appeal. Thus, prior to dismissal the employer would be well advised at least to check that permission had not be given by a superior for the employee to take home the property

---

54 See above, pp 538.
55 [1980] ICR 303 EAT, 304.
56 It should be noted that the Court of Appeal approved this approach in *Foley* and *Madden*, *op cit*, fn 39.

concerned. This is because the employer is only safe in using the modified procedure where it is reasonable to dismiss without making further inquiries. An inappropriate use of the modified procedure will result in the dismissal being automatically unfair.[57]

If an appropriate investigation does establish that it is reasonable to view an employee as guilty of misconduct a dismissal will stand as fair (providing relevant statutory procedures are followed) even if, by the time of the tribunal hearing, the employee's innocence has been established. For example, a drugs test proves positive. By the time of the tribunal hearing new medical evidence, not available to an employer at the time of dismissal, reveals that the test was in some way flawed.

In professional sport it will often be the sports regulatory bodies who carry out investigations and hold hearings prior to imposing a penalty on a participant. This is very much the case with respect to a positive drugs test, or to a player who has committed a serious offence on the field of play. These procedures are exemplified by the Discipline Committee Regulations as originally drawn up by the TCCB for cricket.

Discipline Committee Regulations

1 Jurisdiction

I.I The Discipline Committee (the 'Committee') shall have jurisdiction in disciplinary matters over:

1.1.1 all registered cricketers;

I.1.2 any other cricketers involved in any cricket match controlled by or conducted under the auspices of the Board (a 'Match') (other than cricketers involved in any cricket match as a member of an official touring team representing a member of the International Cricket Council) including but not limited to all matches in which one of the participants is a team (whether a First or Second XI or a representative team under a particular age or at any other level) representing England or one of the Members of the Board or Scotland or Ireland or Holland or Oxford or Cambridge or British Universities or any official touring team representing a member of the International Cricket Council or, in a first-class match, the MCC;

1.1.3 all Members of the Board who shall be responsible not only for their own decisions, acts or omissions and those of their governing bodies, but also for any decisions, acts or omissions of any committees or sub-committees, any member of their governing body or of any committees or subcommittees, any officers, employees or agents, and any other such person over whom a Member exercises control;

1.1.4 all persons who serve as members of the committees of the Board including selectors and observers;

1.1.5 all umpires contracted to the Board and any other umpire who officiates in a Match (an Umpire);

1.1.6 any other person who has agreed in writing to be bound by all or any of the Board's Rules, Regulations, Directives and Resolutions for the time being in force.

For the avoidance of doubt, such jurisdiction shall extend to any person who has ceased to be within any of the foregoing categories, but was subject to the jurisdiction at the time when the matter occurred in respect of which such jurisdiction is to be exercised.

---

57 However, the surviving part of the *Polkey* decision may still operate here to the employer's advantage. This permits tribunals to reduce compensation by up to 100% where this is just and equitable. This would be the likely position of a tribunal where by the time of the tribunal hearing it can be established that the dismissed employee was guilty of theft.

I.2 For the purposes of these Regulations the terms 'Cricketer' and 'Cricketers' shall mean a cricketer or cricketers falling within the ambit of Regulations 1.1.1 and I.1.2 hereof and, in the case of the Minor Counties Cricket Association, the term 'Member of the Board' shall be deemed to include each and every member of the Minor Counties Cricket Association.

2 Initial Procedure

2.1 Any disciplinary matter may be referred to the Committee by any member of the Committee or by the Chairman or Chief Executive of the Board either of his own volition or upon request of any member of the Board.

2.2 The Chairman or a Deputy Chairman of the Committee shall decide whether the matter shall be referred to:

2.2.1 a Summary Panel, in which case the procedure set out in Regulation 3 shall apply; or

2.2.2 the Committee, in which case the procedure set out in Regulation 4 shall apply.

2.3 The disciplinary matters which may be referred in accordance with the procedure set out in Regulations 2.1 and 2.2 above include:

2.3.1 matters the subject of the Board's Directive on Conduct (paragraph 2 of Appendix D) or the Board's Directive on public statements (paragraph 3 of Appendix D);

2.3.2 matters contained in a formal report to the Board pursuant to Law 42.13 in respect of a Cricketer's conduct in a Match;

2.3.3 a positive doping control test within Regulation 17 of the Anti-Doping Regulation (Appendix L); and

2.3.4 any other alleged breach of any of the Board's Rules, Regulations, Directives and Resolutions for the time being in force.

3 Summary Panel Procedure

3.1 If any disciplinary matter shall be referred to a Summary Panel pursuant to Regulation 2.2, the Chairman or a Deputy Chairman of the Committee shall appoint three persons (who, subject as mentioned below, shall be members of the Committee) to constitute the Summary Panel. If a Cricketer is involved and it is reasonably practicable in all the circumstances, a person whose name appears on the list furnished to the Board from time to time by the Cricketers' Association for this purpose shall be included as one of the three persons on the Summary Panel.

3.2 The Summary Panel shall take all necessary steps to investigate the matter as quickly as possible in all the circumstances. The Summary Panel shall determine its own procedure and may require any person subject to the jurisdiction of the Committee:

3.2.1 to attend upon it or any of its members;

3.2.2 to produce any books. letters, contracts, papers or other documents within his possession or power relating to the subject matter of the proceedings;

and any person so required shall take all necessary steps to secure such attendance and production.

A person required to attend before a Summary Panel to answer a disciplinary matter may request, either that he be allowed to be accompanied by a legal or other representative of his choice, or that the matter be referred immediately to the Committee without any hearing by the Summary Panel. Any such request must be made promptly to the Chief Executive of the Board and shall be referred to the chairman of the Summary Panel whose decision thereon shall be conclusive and final. No person required to attend before a Summary Panel shall be entitled to be accompanied by a legal or other representative unless the chairman of the Summary Panel in his sole and unfettered discretion allows. If any person against whom any proceedings are brought pursuant to these Regulations remains silent during any such proceedings or, without good reason, fails to amend before the Summary Panel or to produce documents within that person's possession or power, the Summary Panel may construe such silence and/or failure in such manner as it thinks fit.

3.3 After such investigation as the Summary Panel shall think necessary, the Summary Panel shall decide that either:

3.3.1 the matter does not require any further action; or

3.3.2 a disciplinary offence has been committed with which the Summary Panel will deal; or

3.3.3 disciplinary charges should be laid before the Committee.

3.4 Any decision of the Summary Panel will be by a majority of its members. The Summary Panel shall communicate forthwith to the Chief Executive of the Board the Committee and to all other persons concerted any decision taken pursuant to Regulation 3.3.

3.5 In the event that the Summary Panel determines that a disciplinary offence has been committed the Summary Panel shall determine and shall be entitled to impose upon the person or persons concerned such penalty or penalties by way of official reprimand caution, as to future conduct, fine, or suspension or any combination thereof as it thinks fit PROVIDED ALWAYS that no fine shall exceed £1,000 and in the case of a Cricketer or Umpire the period of suspension shall not exceed four playing days. Any fine imposed shall be paid by the person or persons concerned within 28 days of that person or persons being notified of the fine. The Summary Panel shall be entitled to suspend any penalty imposed pursuant to these Regulations for such period and upon and subject to such other terms and conditions as it shall think fit.

3.6 Any person upon whom any penalty has been imposed by the Summary Panel as aforesaid shall be entitled, by giving written notice to the Chief Executive of the Board within 14 days of being notified of the decision of the Summary Panel, to appeal to the Committee, in which case the matter shall be referred to and re-heard by the Committee in accordance with the procedure laid down in Regulation 1 and any penalty imposed shall be suspended pending the re-hearing of the matter or withdrawal or disposal of the appeal.

3.7 In the event of any such appeal or if the Summary Panel shall decide under Regulation 3.3.3 that disciplinary charges should be laid before the Committee, the Summary Panel shall make available to the Chief Executive of the Board its notes of the hearing and all other documents relevant to the manner and shall advise the Chief Executive as to the disciplinary charges which in its opinion should be laid before the Committee. The Chief Executive shall act as prosecutor and shall be responsible (with full power to delegate) for the formulation of the charges and the conduct of the proceedings before the Committee on behalf of the Board. Notwithstanding the provisions of Regulation 4.3 on any appeal to it from the Summary Panel the Committee shall not be entitled to impose any penalty or penalties in excess of the penalty or penalties which the Summary Panel is entitled to impose.

4 Committee Procedure

4.1 The Committee shall determine its own procedure for any hearing. Unless otherwise determined by the Board or by the Committee, the quorum for any hearing shall be five members of the Committee one of which shall be appointed Chairman PROVIDED ALWAYS that any person who shall have been a member of a Summary Panel which dealt with a particular disciplinary manner in respect of which a chance has been laid before the Committee shall not sit as a member of the Committee at any hearing at which that matter is considered. If a Cricketer is involved and it is reasonably practicable in all the circumstances, a person whose name appears on the list furnished to the Board from time to time by the Cricketers' Association for this purpose shall be appointed as one of the members of the Committee.

4.2 The Committee may, in connection with any disciplinary manner falling within its jurisdiction, require any person subject to the jurisdiction of the Committee:

4.2.1 to attend at a hearing or hearings of the Committee; and

4.2.2 to produce books, letters, contracts, papers or other documents within his possession or power relating to the subject manner of the proceedings;

and any person so required shall take all necessary steps to ensure such attendance and production.

Any party to the proceedings attending a hearing of the Committee may call witnesses and may be accompanied by a legal or other suitable representative of his choice. If any person against whom any proceedings are brought pursuant to these Regulations remains silent during any such proceedings or fails, without good reason, to attend before the Committee or to produce documents within that person's possession or power, the Committee may construe such silence and or failure in such manner as it thinks fit.

4.3 Any decision of the Committee will be by a majority of its members. In the event that the Committee is unable to reach a majority the Chairman shall have a second and casting vote. The Committee, at the conclusion of any hearing by it of any matter falling within its jurisdiction, may impose such penalty or penalties or any combination thereof as it thinks appropriate in the circumstances including:

4.3.1 in the case of a Cricketer, a reprimand suspension from playing in any Match or Matches, suspension or termination of registration, suspension of eligibility for selection for England or fine;

4.3.2 in the case of a Member of the Board, a fine, suspension of the Member from any competition for which the Board is responsible, or variation of results of the Member's matches in any such competition or of points awarded to the Member in relation to any such competition;

4.3.3 in the case of a person who serves as a member of a committee of the Board (including selectors), a reprimand, fine or suspension or removal from the committee on which he serves;

4.3.4 in the case of an Umpire, a reprimand, suspension, fine or dismissal by the Board;

4.3.5 in any case, an order that any party to any such hearing shall make such contribution as the Committee shall determine to each of the Board's or any other party's costs and expenses (including legal costs) of or in connection with the hearing.

Any fine, costs and expenses imposed shall be paid by the person or persons concerned within 28 days of that person being notified of the amounts thereof. In addition, the Committee shall be entitled to suspend any penalty imposed pursuant to these Regulations for such period and upon and subject to such other terms and conditions as it shall think fit.

It should be noted that a further right of appeal lies to an 'Appeals Sub-Committee'. Given the detailed nature of these procedures, it would seem that, for example, a finding of illegal drug use would be a context in which a club could dismiss without making further inquiries of its own. Compare this with the view taken by Sussex CCC that the finding of the TCCB that Ed Giddins had taken cocaine automatically terminated his contract of employment, and thus further procedures by the club were superfluous.[58]

Irrespective of whether a club could justify not conducting its own investigation, it would still need to permit a player to exercise a right of appeal in accordance with the modified statutory disciplinary procedure. It is also important to remember that any dismissal will only be fair if it is within the range of reasonable responses. It is only through a formal appeal that a player will have the opportunity to argue that factors such as past loyalty to the club or personal problems should be taken into account. Moreover, as explained above, consistency of treatment is another relevant factor to be considered within the context of the range of reasonable responses. Thus clubs which in the past have taken a lenient or liberal view of the use of drugs by their players (such as Arsenal in the case of recreational drugs) might find it harder to justify, as fair, decisions to dismiss other players – at least for first-time offences.

---

58 For further discussion of the Giddins affair and drug testing and appeal procedures, see O' Gorman, T, 'Ed Giddins vs TCCB' (1997) 5(1) Sport and the Law Journal 23–25. The holding of internal hearings are perhaps of particular importance with respect to positive drugs tests given the controversies surrounding their accuracy as far as performance enhancing substances are concerned. See various contributions in *op cit*, fn 43, O' Leary (2000).

REMEDIES FOR UNFAIR DISMISSAL

Reinstatement and Re-engagement

Sections 114 and 115 of the ERA provide for the tribunal orders of reinstatement and re-engagement. The difference between the two is that a reinstated employee returns to the job he or she was doing prior to dismissal, whereas re-engagement requires the complainant to be engaged in comparable employment. This could be with an associated employer. A reinstated employee must receive arrears of pay and the full restoration of rights, including seniority and pension rights. The tribunal sets out the terms on which an employee must be re-engaged. Where either of these orders is granted and a dismissal is automatically unfair because of an employer's failure to follow statutory disciplinary procedures then tribunals must normally award four weeks' pay (subject to the statutory maximum).[59]

In practice it is relatively rare for either remedy to be awarded. However, with respect to the Doherty brothers[60] both tribunals took the view that they should be reinstated as had the employer acted reasonably on the basis of the evidence available, and consistently with respect to how the brother's colleagues were treated, neither would have been dismissed. Moreover, the tribunals took into account that there was strong support for the reinstatement of both amongst the workforce, and the relevant managers had either changed or could be expected to respond professionally by accepting that the decisions to dismiss had been mistaken. Therefore, the issue of trust and confidence was not a barrier to the practicality of reinstatement.

Orders may be refused on the basis that it is not just and equitable to require an employer to take back an employee who has contributed to the dismissal through misconduct or incapability, or on the basis that it would not be reasonably practicable for the employer to comply. The latter ground might be less significant in professional sport than in other areas of employment given that the norm is for there to be a squad of players, and reinstatement would simply require a player to be returned to the squad. As always, he would have no 'right' to be selected for the first team (or possibly even the reserves).

However, employers are not obliged to comply with either of these orders. Failure to do so will entitle the employee to basic and compensatory awards plus an additional award of between 26 and 52 statutory weeks' pay. A tribunal order notwithstanding, in most cases a club would be able to afford to compensate a player that it did not wish to take back.

Basic Award

Under s 119 of the ERA this is calculated by reference to age, actual completed years of employment and a statutory week's pay. The latter reflects gross pay but is subject to a statutory maximum. In 2004 this was £270 – well below the actual weekly wage of many salary earners, let alone professional sportsmen. Only the last 20 years of employment can be credited, although such a length of employment will be uncommon in professional sport. Alan Knight, the Portsmouth goalkeeper (known as 'The Legend' to the Portsmouth 'faithful'), is one of the few players in recent times who has come anywhere near this period of service with a single club.

---

59   This is the result of s 34(3) of the Employment Act 2002 which inserts new subss (5) and (6) into s 112 of the ERA.
60   See above, pp 538–39.

Three scales apply: half a week's pay for every year completed aged under 22; one week's pay for every year completed aged 22 to 40; one and a half week's pay for every year completed aged 41 or more. With some obvious exceptions, such as Graham Gooch who was still playing for Essex CCC when he was in his early forties, the highest scale will be rarely of relevance in sport.[61] In cases of automatic unfair dismissal, through failure to follow statutory procedures, tribunals will normally grant a minimum basic award of four weeks' pay.[62]

A statutory redundancy payment is calculated in the same way as the basic award, although years worked under the age of 18 are not taken into account. Thus with the necessary two year period of continuous employment, an employee must be at least 20 to qualify for a statutory payment. Redundancy is not normally an issue in sport. However, in recent years a number of football clubs have come perilously close to insolvency. Were a club ever so to fold all its employees would be redundant. Their entitlements to payments would be calculated on the above basis. Players would also be redundant if a club reduced the number of players it employed, for example to reduce the wages bill, as against not renewing a player's contract because it wished to replace him with a different player.[63]

Compensatory Award

Section 123(1) of the ERA specifies: 'the amount of the compensatory award shall be such amount as the tribunal considers just and equitable in all the circumstances having regard to the loss sustained by the complainant in consequence of the dismissal in so far as that loss is attributable to action taken by the employer'.

Section 123(4) applies the common law rule of mitigation. The function of the compensatory award is thus to compensate the dismissed employee for the actual financial loss suffered, and has the equivalent purpose to damages for breach of contract. However, unlike damages, loss of future earnings and pension rights can be taken into account, that is, to cover the period after due notice or a fixed term contract has expired. There is a statutory ceiling, but this was increased significantly by the Employment Relations Act 1999 to £50,000. In 2004 the ceiling was £55,000. This upper limit is still far below the salary of many professional footballers. However, the new levels of compensation may make claiming unfair dismissal more of an attractive option to players in the lower divisions, or indeed to participants in less well paid sports such as cricket and rugby. If a player is dismissed with due notice, or is faced with the non-renewal of a fixed term contract then, of course, a claim for unfair dismissal is the only legal course of action open to him.

Both basic and compensatory awards can be reduced as the tribunal considers just and equitable by reference to the contributory conduct of the dismissed employee. Such a deduction from the compensatory award should be made from the actual loss the individual incurs. Only after such deduction should the reduction to the statutory maximum figure take place. Moreover, under s 123(1)

---

61 It should be noted that as part of its proposals to tackle age discrimination in employment the government may decide that all redundancy payments should be calculated on the basis of one week's pay, and thus these age bands will disappear.

62 Section 34(6) of the Employment Act 202 inserts new subss (1A) and (1B) into s 120 of the ERA.

63 It is likely that a number of out of contract players were so redundant at the end of the 2001/02 season when a significant reduction in television income and the collapse of ITV Digital created severe financial problems for a number of clubs – particularly in the lower leagues. The loss of income to the Nationwide League clubs was in the region of £178 million – see Lacey, D, 'January sales were more about beggars than choosers' *Guardian Sport*, 1 February 2003.

it is permissible to reduce the compensatory awards to nil where this can be considered by a tribunal to be just and equitable. A tribunal might decide to do this, in line with the decision in *Polkey*, where misconduct discovered after the dismissal retrospectively justifies it. Such a dismissal may be technically unfair but the employee may not receive any compensation whatsoever. In the Dennis Wise case[64] the EAT noted that such *Polkey* reductions might be appropriate, but it was remitted to the tribunal to decide, on the basis of the evidence before it, what the extent of any such deductions should be.[65]

KEY SOURCES

Macari v Celtic Football and Athletic Co. Ltd [1999] IRLR 787 Court of Session.

Middlesborough Football & Athletic Co v Liverpool Football & Athletic Grounds plc [2002] EWCA Civ 1929; [2002] WL 31523286.

Wise v Filbert Realisations Respondent (Formerly Leicester City Football Club) (In Administration) EAT 0660/03/RN; [2004] WL 343779.

McCutcheon, P, 'Negative enforcement of employment contracts in the sports industries' (1997) 17(1) *Legal Studies* 65–100.

DTI Guidance on the Employment Act 2002 (Dispute Resolution) Regulations 2004, www.dti.gov.uk/resolvingdisputes.

---

64 See above, pp 544–45.

65 As a result of the statutory reversal of *Polkey* by s 98A(2) of the ERA (see above, p 000) the maximum *Polkey* reduction after 1 October 2004 should be 50% where statutory procedures are followed but other provisions in the ACAS Code, or an employer's own procedures, are not adhered to. This is because if, on a balance of probabilities, failure to follow procedure makes no difference to the decision to dismiss, the dismissal should be considered fair. However, where a dismissal is automatically unfair under s 98A(1), reductions of 100% are still possible as s 98A(2) does not then apply.

CHAPTER 14

SPORTS PARTICIPANTS AND THE LAW OF DISCRIMINATION

INTRODUCTION

The world of sport remains a highly segregated one – particularly between men and women and the fully-abled and disabled. With respect to the latter, events such as the Paralympics and the London Marathon notwithstanding, professional sport is predominantly and inevitably restricted to the fully-abled – indeed generally to the super fit. Therefore the Disability Discrimination Act 1995 will not be discussed as part of this chapter, although its provisions do of course apply to those employed by clubs in a variety of positions not concerned with sports participation.[1]

Inroads have been made in the context of race as more and more professional sportsmen (but not women) come from the Afro-Caribbean and Asian communities. However, there is more than a nagging suspicion that racism remains a major problem for sport, albeit for different sports in different ways – the lack of professional footballers of Asian origin being a clear example.

Chaudhary, V, 'Asians can play football, too'

Why is there no Indian or Pakistani John Barnes playing the professional game? When the Premier League season kicks off on Saturday, there will not be a single professional footballer of Asian origin on the field around the country. While Afro-Caribbean players continue to make their mark in the highest echelons of the game, both at a domestic and international level, Asian players have remained largely invisible. Black players make up almost 20 per cent of the 2,000 professionals currently playing in the Premier and Football Leagues. But the prospect of an Asian John Barnes remains as distant as England winning the World Cup.

There are currently around 60 Asian footballers playing in semi-professional high-level amateur teams and six professional apprentices of Asian origin. But that's about it. Just why there is a dearth of Asian professionals is an enigma. If racism is endemic within football, why do black players do so well?

A project due to begin at the end of August will examine how and why Asians are being overlooked by the football industry. The project is backed by the Sports Council and the Commission for Racial Equality. Raj Patel, aged 35, and Jas Bains, aged 31, the project directors, were both keen amateur footballers in the Midlands and gained first-hand experience of how Asian footballers are marginalised. Bains says: 'Scouts never watch the Asian teams play, and Asian players are hardly ever asked for trials. When I was playing, old stereotypes like Asians aren't big enough and can't physically compete, were always mentioned. It's just nonsense.'

---

1   Note in general terms the Disability Discrimination Act operates on similar principles to the Sex Discrimination and Race Relations Acts. For possible potential implications of the Act for sports participants with specific disabilities, such as heart complaints or diabetes, see Bitel, N and Bloohn, J, 'Fair play for disabled people in sport' (1997) 5(1) Sport and the Law Journal 8–11. Currently, the Disabilities Discrimination Act does not cover persons with non-symptomatic HIV. Employers are therefore not acting unlawfully in refusing employment to a person who has been diagnosed as HIV positive. A sports club that refused to sign, or dismissed, a player who had been tested HIV positive would not be committing an unlawful act of discrimination. Moreover, a dismissal would be fair if the club was deemed to have acted within the range of reasonable responses; see previous chapter, pp 535–40. The government is proposing to make changes to the Act. These proposals include adding being diagnosed as HIV positive to the list of disabilities covered by the Act. In the USA, the Americans with Disabilities Act 1990 does protect athletes who are HIV positive. See, Wolohan, JT, 'An ethical and legal dilemma: participation in sport by HIV infected athletes' (1997) 7(2) Marquette Sports Law Journal 373–397.

... Both men believe it is not simply a matter of racism. The problem, they claim, lies between stereotyping of Asian players at all levels of the game and a reticence towards professional sport by older members of the Asian community. Unlike the black communities in Britain and America, sport has never been seen as a path to improving social status. Asian parents have, traditionally, coaxed their children towards commerce or professions like law or medicine.

... However, they maintain that the crux of the problem lies in the attitude of coaches, managers and scouts. One young Asian footballer, who had trials at Chelsea, says: 'From the moment I got on the pitch I didn't stand a chance. I got abused by other players and was played out of position by the coach. Maybe I didn't have the talent to make it, but how do I know when I was never given fair treatment?'

Sally Westwood, a senior lecturer at Leicester University and a member of the research advisory group for the project, spent several weeks studying a mixed Asian-Afro-Caribbean football team in 1991. She says: 'The stereotyping of Asian players is linked with the way South Asians are seen as culturally more different. White society sees them as "not like us", whereas Afro-Caribbeans are seen as conforming more to North European values.' She found that while some black players in the team were offered trials with Leicester City, Asian players of similar ability were overlooked.

Patel and Bains are confident that the football industry will eventually recognise the wealth of talent in the Asian community. After all, they maintain, it's less than 10 years since 12 English first division managers said – in an article by the Sunday Times's Rob Hughes – they would not sign a black player because, 'they lack bottle, are no good in the mud and have no stamina'. Back in 1975 not a single black player represented England at any level and there were fewer than 20 black professionals.

'We are not asking for special treatment, just a chance for our youngsters to be given a fair chance,' says Bains ... [2]

The problem of racism is of course partly, but only partly, derived from the attitudes of sections of the paying public. That issue is beyond the scope of this chapter.[3] The concern here is for the more covert forms of racism and other forms of discrimination that may exist at the level of the sports club as an employer. Moreover, the institutions and structures of sport are such that the law as it stands can play only a limited role in regulating and eroding discriminatory attitudes and practices. This section is thus as much about the limits of the law as the protection it provides. This is particularly the case with the huge gulf in status which exists between men and women participants in sports such as football, rugby, cricket and indeed, albeit to a lesser extent, in tennis and golf.

Williams, J, 'Support for all?'

According to FIFA, 20 million women play organised football worldwide. In Scandinavia, where views about women as athletes, and almost anything else, are at least post-Jurassic, football is the most popular sport for females. Most local clubs cater for both male and female teams and foreign stars such as the USA's Michelle Akers are brought over to join semi-professional ranks. No surprise, then, that Norway won the recent women's World Cup in Sweden and that they and Denmark are as tough as they come in international competition. England? Well, you reap what you sow; in Sweden we were simply outclassed by, no avoiding it now, the Germans.

... And what, generally of the women's game today? Well, things looked ready for major take off as far back as 1989. Then, Channel 4, looking for cheap and 'exotic' alternatives to mainstream sport, showed

---

2   Vivek Chaudhary, 'Asians can play football, too' *The Guardian*, 17 August 1994. It is a matter of concern that this piece is as pertinent today as when it was first written ten years ago.

3   The 'Kick it out (originally Let's Kick Racism Out of Football) Campaign', established by the Commission for Racial Equality in conjunction with the PFA, is primarily concerned with combating racism amongst football supporters. For an account of the Campaign, see 'Kicking racism out of football' (1995) 84(4) Labour Research. Also see pp 128–40.

the Women's FA Cup Final. This was pre-Sky, of course, and fans, 2.5 million of them, a record for sport on C4, gobbled it up . . .

Now? Well, serious TV coverage has pretty much disappeared. *Serie A* arrived on C4. The BBC, desperate for soccer action, disgracefully provided the barest highlights of the recent women's World Cup and always around midnight. On Sky you can watch N Ireland v Scotland schoolboys live to your heart's content, but no female coverage. Why is at least some female coverage not part of the new TV deal? . . . Without media coverage, serious sponsorship for the women's game is pretty much out of the question.

Whilst some clubs, like Southampton, have taken female teams on board, here again progress is slow and uneven. Only Arsenal offer female players a full time paid coach/manager and a real level of integration into the male club. Not surprisingly, the Arsenal women have produced recent successes, and media coverage, to match this commitment. A few others – Wimbledon, Millwall, Wolves – have shown a real interest in the women's game and cash and staff support to match . . .

But, at best, even large professional clubs still tend to offer a kit, use of some gym space and the occasional mention in the matchday magazine in the hope that some women will keep out of their hair and provide the club with some good PR. And, off the WFCs troop to the park or local leisure complex to perform in front of 60–100 diehard fans and family members who can manage to track down the kick-off time. The 'blue riband' Women's FA Cup Final still struggles for a prestige venue (recently, Crewe, Watford, Oxford, Tranmere, Millwall) while, recently, the German women's final took place immediately before the men's equivalent in the Olympic Stadium, Berlin. Ho hum.

This all provides for real equivocation about the development of the top level of the women's game here. Is the FA devoting enough resources to the women's game? Are we really improving and what, exactly, is the plan? . . .

. . . The PFA's Community programme has done some great work in promoting football for girls over the past few years and in starting up female teams in connection with professional clubs. We have female players who could inspire the next generation. Kerry Davies and Hope Powell of Croydon and their former team mates Brenda Sempare, Doncaster captain Gillian Coulthard, and the charismatic Marianne Spacey of Arsenal have all served the women's game here with verve and distinction. We need them, and others, *working* in English football as coaches. Is anybody listening? You do *want* to beat the Germans, don't you?[4]

THE SEX AND RACE DISCRIMINATION ACTS

The Sex Discrimination Act 1975 (SDA) prohibits discrimination on the basis of gender – s 1, and/or on the basis that a person is married – s 3. Discrimination against a married mother (or father) will contravene the latter section as married persons will find it considerably harder to meet a requirement to be childless.[5] There is nothing in the Act that expressly gives similar protection to single parents. However, refusing job opportunities to a mother on the basis that she is a lone parent probably constitutes indirect discrimination against women.[6] If this is so, an employer would then be obliged to treat single fathers in the same way as single mothers. It is important to emphasise that EU law also regulates sex discrimination.[7] Where possible the SDA must be interpreted to conform with The Equal Treatment Directive and appropriate rulings of the ECJ.

---

4   Williams, J, 'Support for all?' *When Saturday Comes*, March 1997, No 121, pp 32–33.
5   *Hurley v Mustoe* [1981] IRLR 208.
6   See below, pp 560–64.
7   For discussion of the impact of the Equal Treatment Directive and other relevant areas of EU law, see below, pp 571–76.

The Race Relations Act 1976 (RRA) prohibits discrimination on racial grounds or by virtue of a person's membership of a racial group. 'Racial' covers colour, race and nationality or ethnic or national origins – s 3(1).[8]

Mandla v Dowell Lee [1983] ICR 385 HL

Lord Fraser: . . . It is not suggested that Sikhs are a group defined by reference to colour, race, nationality or national origins. In none of these respects are they distinguishable from many other groups, especially those living, like most Sikhs, in the Punjab. The argument turns entirely upon whether they are a group defined by 'ethnic origins' . . .

For a group to constitute an ethnic group in the sense of the Act of 1976, it must, in my opinion, regard itself, and be regarded by others, as a distinct community by virtue of certain characteristics. Some of these characteristics are essential; others are not essential but one or more of them will commonly be found and will help to distinguish the group from the surrounding community. The conditions which appear to me to be essential are these: (1) a long shared history, of which the group is conscious as distinguishing it from other groups, and the memory of which it keeps alive; (2) a cultural tradition of its own, including family and social customs and manners, often but not necessarily associated with religious observance. In addition to those two essential characteristics the following characteristics are, in my opinion, relevant; (3) either a common geographical origin, or descent from a small number of common ancestors; (4) a common language, not necessarily peculiar to the group; (5) a common literature peculiar to the group; (6) a common religion different from that of neighbouring groups or from the general community surrounding it; (7) being a minority or being an oppressed or a dominant group within a larger community, for example a conquered people (say, the inhabitants of England shortly after the Norman conquest) and their conquerors might both be ethnic groups.[9]

The scope of unlawful discrimination in employment covers arrangements for recruiting employees; refusal of employment; the terms on which employment is offered; opportunities for promotion or training; access to benefits, facilities or services; dismissal; subjection to any detriment. Unlike the Employment Rights Act, protection is not restricted to 'employees' but covers employment under a contract 'personally to execute any work or labour' – s 82(1) of the SDA; s 78(1) of the RRA.[10] This extension of the meaning of 'employment' is of obvious importance in sport, as it covers any competition or sponsorship deal that involves a sportsman or sportswoman entering into a contract to perform – be it in a match or a marketing activity. The legislation also prohibits discrimination by qualifying bodies that can confer authorisation or qualification for engagement in a particular trade. This covers sporting authorities that are empowered to restrict participation in professional sport to those to whom a licence has been granted by the authority concerned. This is illustrated by the successful case brought by the boxer, Jane Couch (see below).

The Sex Discrimination Act 1975 and the Race Relations Act 1976 operate on similar principles with respect to defining direct and indirect discrimination.

---

8   It should be noted that the new definition of 'racial group' contained in s 1(1A), and which only applies to employees, excludes colour and nationality. It remains to be seen whether this will be of any practical importance.

9   At p 390. Applying the above test the Law Lords decided that Sikhs were an ethnic as against simply a religious group. Similarly: Jews (*Seide v Gillette Industries*[1980] IRLR 427); Gypsies (*CRE v Dutton* [1989] QB 783); and the Welsh (*Gwynedd CC v Jones* [1986] ICR 833) have been held to be ethnic groups. Conversely, Rastafarians have been held not to have an ethnic status different to that of the wider Afro-Caribbean community (*Dawkins v Department of the Environment* [1993] IRLR 284).

10 Employee status is of significance where employees wish to complain of unlawful discrimination on grounds of sex, race, disability, sexual orientation, religion or belief. This is because such claims are subject to the statutory grievance procedures explained in the previous chapter. Tribunal claims will not be admissible until the employee has provided the employer with a written statement of the complaint of discriminatory treatment and waited a further 28 days.

Direct Discrimination

Section 1 of the Sex Discrimination Act 1975

A person discriminates against a woman in any circumstances relevant for the purposes of any provision of this Act if:

on the ground of her sex he treats her less favourably than he treats or would treat a man . . .

Section 1 of the Race Relations Act 1976

A person discriminates against another in any circumstances relevant for the purposes of any provision of this Act if:

on racial grounds he treats that other less favourably than he treats or would treat other persons . . .

In *James v Eastleigh Borough Council*[11] the House of Lords decided that Mr James was directly discriminated against when he was charged a higher price than his wife for admission to a swimming pool. The sole reason for the differential treatment was that the concessionary cheaper price was for pensioners only. Although Mr and Mrs James were both aged 61 she was a pensioner and he was not. Clearly, there was no discriminatory intent and motive on the part of the Council. Nevertheless, but for the fact that Mr James was a man he would have been treated the same as his wife.

As a result of the 'but for' test direct discrimination is in theory easier to establish as it is not necessary to establish an intention to discriminate and direct discrimination cannot be justified. However, there is a very real practical difficulty with regard to proof. As a result of an EC Directive[12] the burden of proof formally shifts to the employer where the evidence enables the tribunal to draw inferences of discrimination. Where this is the case, the tribunal must find discrimination proven if the employer is not able to provide an adequate explanation of his decisions or actions by reference to non-discriminatory factors.

However, the employer might be able to show that the decision not to appoint the applicant was taken for grounds that are not discriminatory, such as the applicant's perceived personality. Indeed, it is the fact that subjective value-judgments are so inherently connected to employers' decisions over matters such as recruitment and promotion that makes a direct discrimination claim so hard to win. Even where there is evidence of discrimination, as a result of what the employer writes or says, a claim is not guaranteed of success.

In *Saunders v Richmond Borough Council*[13] the applicant, a former women's golf champion, was rejected for the post of professional golf coach. Despite questions such as: 'So you'd be blazing a trail, would you? Do you think men respond as well to a woman golf professional as to a man?; If all this is true, you are obviously a lady of great experience, but don't you think this type of job is rather unglamorous?', she was not able to prove sex discrimination. Possibly the tribunal was influenced by the fact that the interviewer was a woman. Nevertheless, the reasoning is that there are cases when it is appropriate or least permissible to inquire into whether a person's gender, or race/ethnic grouping, may affect their suitability for a particular job.

---

11 [1990] ICR 554.
12 To implement EC Directive 97/900 the Sex Discrimination (Indirect Discrimination and Burden of Proof) Regulations 2001 No 2660 inserted a new s 63A into the SDA. This formal shift in the burden of proof is of limited practical importance as pre-existing case law under the RRA and SDA already permitted tribunals to draw inferences of discrimination in appropriate circumstances.
13 [1977] IRLR 362.

The case of *Singh*[14] provides an example of how direct race discrimination may succeed as a result of a tribunal drawing inferences of discrimination. The basis of Mr Singh's complaint was that he was withdrawn from the Football League's 'National List' of referees at the end of the 1999/99 season and thus ceased to be eligible to referee professional football matches. At this time he was the only person of Asian ethnic origin on the List. The reason given for the decision not to re-appoint him was that there had been a marked deterioration in his position on the merit list over the previous three years. Singh denied that there had been any such deterioration in his performance and successfully claimed direct race discrimination under s 1 of the RRA against the Football League.

Part of Singh's argument was that there is a subculture in professional football that generates institutionalised (and often unconscious) racism. The tribunal decided that it was unable to take judicial notice of the submission that a racially biased and stereotyped perception of Asians existed in high circles in football. Nevertheless, it was able to accept that there was evidence that individual respondents in this particular case were influenced by a stereotypical assumption that the applicant could never be a top-performing referee by virtue of his ethnic origin. Relevant evidence here included a comment by one of the individual respondents, who was Secretary of the National Review Board'[15] established to ensure consistency of refereeing, that 'We don't want people like him [Mr Singh] in the PL [Premier League]'. This comment was viewed as a race-specific statement by the tribunal and, as such, formed part of the evidence that led to the tribunal deciding that there had been a sustained 'whispering campaign' against S from which the inference of racism could be drawn. Consequently, though S was unable to prove that his ethnic origin was the specific reason for his removal from the National List, the tribunal was able to accept his complaint of direct race discrimination on the basis that a hypothetical white referee, with the same performance record as S, would not have been so treated.

Indirect Discrimination

The statutory definitions of indirect discrimination are now dependent on whether the claimant is in law to be regarded as an employee. The following original definitions still apply to non-employees.

Section 1(1)(b) of the Sex Discrimination Act 1975

A person discriminates against a woman in any circumstances relevant for the purposes of any provision of this Act if :

... he applies to her a requirement or condition which he applies or would apply equally to a man but:

which is such that the proportion of women who can comply with it is considerably smaller than the proportion of men who can comply with it and

which he cannot show to be justifiable irrespective of the sex of the person to whom it is applied and

which is to her detriment because she cannot comply with it.

---

14 See Chapter 12 pp 478–79 and Chapter 13 p 530.
15 The National Review Board was also one of the respondents in the case as it is this body that decides which referees should be added or removed from the National List. It was thus liable under s 12 of the RRA. This section regulates bodies that can confer authorisation or qualification. It is interesting to note that another part of the evidence from which the tribunal inferred racism was that officials of the NRB denied there was any racism in football beyond racist abuse from the terraces. This was despite the fact that the FA's 'Kick It Out' campaign recognises the under-representation of certain ethnic groups in the game. Thus the tribunal refused to believe that individual respondents were 'colour blind' when it came to decisions concerning the refereeing of matches.

Section 1(1)(b) of the Race Relations Act 1976

A person discriminates against another in any circumstances relevant for the purposes of any provision of this Act if:

he applies to that other a requirement or condition which he applies or would apply equally to persons not of the same racial group as that other but :

which is such that the proportion of persons of the same racial group as that other who can comply with it is considerably smaller than the proportion of persons not of that racial group who can comply with it and

which he cannot show to be justifiable irrespective of the colour, race, nationality or ethnic or national origins of the person to whom it is applied and

which is to the detriment of that other because he cannot comply with it.

In the case of an employee indirect sex discrimination is now defined as set out below.

Section 1(2)(b) of the Sex Discrimination Act 1975 (as amended)

A person discriminates against a woman in any circumstances relevant for the purposes of any provision to which this subsection applies if:

he applies to her a provision, criterion or practice which he applies or would apply equally to a man, but –

... which is such that it would be to the detriment of a considerably larger proportion of women than of men, and

which he cannot show to be justifiable irrespective of the sex of the person to whom it is applied, and

which is eto her detriment.

Indirect race discrimination against employees is defined as follows.

Section 1(1A) of the Race Relations Act 1976 (as amended)

A person also discriminates against another if . . . he applies a provision, criterion or practice which he applies or would apply equally to persons not of the same race[16] or ethnic or national origins as that other, but:

... which puts or would put persons of the same race or ethnic or national origins as that other as a particular disadvantage when compared with other persons,

... which puts that other at that disadvanatage, and

... which he cannot show to be a proportionate means of achieving a legitimate aim.

The case of *Price v Civil Service Commission*[17] provides a good illustration of the concept of indirect discrimination. The Civil Service advertised a vacancy. Applications were restricted to persons with one A level aged 28 or less. The EAT accepted statistics which showed: 'the economic activity of

---

16 As commented above, see fn 8, the reference to colour is omitted from this definition of racial group. This could be a particular problem in professional sport where many players are of mixed race and racist comments are likely to be specifically aimed at their colour rather than their race or ethnic or national origins.

17 [1978] ICR 27.

women with at least one Advanced Level falls off markedly about the age of 23, reaching a bottom at about the age of 33, when it climbs gradually to a plateau at about 45.' The reason for this was: 'that a considerable number of women between the mid-twenties and the mid-thirties are engaged in bearing children and in minding children . . . '.[18]

Price was discriminated against not only by reference to her age but as a woman. The Civil Service was unable to justify the age requirement and Price won her claim of unlawful indirect sex discrimination.

One consequence of the new definition of indirect discrimination for employees is that it is clear that any policy or practice of an employer can form the basis of an indirect discrimination claim. Arguably restrictive interpretations of 'requirement or condition', which stated that failure to meet an employer's criteria must constitute an 'absolute bar' to appointment etc, will cease to be applicable to employees.[19]

Much difficulty has surrounded the 'pool of comparison' a tribunal should use in determining whether indirect discrimination has occurred. The approach to be followed (in sex discrimination cases) was set out by the Court of Appeal in *Jones v University of Manchester*.[20]

First, the relevant totals are all women (WT) and all men (MT) who would qualify were it not for the requirement or condition complained of. It is then necessary to calculate in percentage terms what proportion of women in their group (WY) do comply in comparison to the number of men in their group who do so (MY). This is achieved by dividing WT into WY and MT into MY and converting the figures into percentages.

For example:

$$WT = 50, WY = 25; MT = 50, MY = 45.$$

$$WY \text{ is } 50\% \text{ of } WT \text{ and } MY \text{ is } 90\% \text{ of } MT$$

This reveals that as a percentage the proportion of the former (WY) is considerably smaller then the proportion of the latter (MY). On this basis there is indirect discrimination. There is no doubt that a similar method is to be used in cases of alleged indirect race discrimination.

Whilst this approach conforms with the words of s 1(1)(b), it does permit the possibility of allowing requirements to be imposed which may have a discriminatory impact against women. For example, Jones argued that an age requirement discriminated against women, as women mature students tend to graduate at an older age than their male counterparts. The court took the view that the pool of comparison was all graduates with relevant experience. Mature students were merely a sub-group within this pool, not a pool of comparison in their own right.

It remains to be seen whether the new definitions of indirect sex and race discrimination for employees will require a more flexible and less restrictive approach to be taken.

Even where indirect discrimination is so established the employer may be able to justify it. The test for justification is today derived from EC law and is used in both sex and race discrimination cases.[21]

---

18 *Per* Phillips J at p 31.
19 See *Perera v Civil Service Commission*[1983] ICR 428. However, this approach was rejected by the EAT in *Falkirk Council v Whyte* [1997] IRLR 560. In the EAT's view if particular criteria were in practice 'decisive factors' in a selection process then they should be regarded as constituting a 'requirement or condition' within the meaning of s 1(1)(b). If this latter interpretation is correct than effectively the legal position is the same for all claimants under the SDA and the RRA even though the new definitions apply only to employees.
20 [1993] IRLR 218.
21 *Hampson v Department of Education and Science* [1989] ICR 179.

As propounded by the European Court of Justice in *Bilka-Kaufhaus Gmbh v Weber von Hartz*,[22] the employer must establish:

(a) that there is an objective economic or operational need for the discriminatory practice; and
(b) the discriminatory effects are no greater than necessary to secure the employer's objectives.

The requirement of proportionality means that even where an employer can establish genuine commercial objectives the discrimination will not be justified if it produces merely marginal advantages.

Indirect discrimination in employment occurs typically with respect to issues such as job-sharing, part time working[23] and forms of dress and appearance. These sorts of issues are not likely to occur in the context of sport – at least as far as participants are concerned. On the other hand, age restrictions, which will become unlawful in 2006, will almost certainly be justifiable given that most sports professionals retire in their late thirties. Moreover, clubs need to maintain a pool of younger players and trainees. Age, of course, is not a significant factor in being employed as a manager or coach. It remains to be seen whether match officials will be able to challenge compulsory retirement. For example, professional football referees must currently retire at the age of 48.

The potential problems in determining the presence of indirect discrimination can be illustrated by this hypothetical situation. A sports club decides that it would prefer to select its players from those born and/or who have lived in the locality for most of their lives. The club announces that 'outsiders', however, will be considered. X is a member of a particular ethnic group and has only lived in the locality for six months. Under the new definition of indirect discrimination for employees X should be able to establish that the issues of birth and residence constitute ' criterion' for selection, and therefore should succeed in establishing this element of indirect discrimination. (Even if X is not an employee, on the basis of the wider approach adopted in the *Falkirk Council* case, X may be able to show indirect discrimination.)

However, under the old or new definitions, X may still have a problem in identifying the correct pool of comparison. For example, different ethnic groupings, including his own, live in the area in similar numbers. Thus it would not be possible for X to show statistically that the residence requirement indirectly discriminated against the ethnic group to which he belonged. Nevertheless, the majority actually selected by the club come from one particular ethnic group. Members of the group to which X belongs are eligible for selection, but choose not to apply.

The hidden, even unconscious, reason, why X is not selected is his membership of a particular ethnic group, as there is a perception that members of that group are not interested in and/or lack ability or the perceived necessary temperament for that particular sport. In reality, X is being discriminated against as a result of belonging to that group whilst having a minority interest in the sport concerned. The over formalistic approach confirmed in *Jones* precludes this form of cultural racism from being exposed.[24]

---

22 [1987] ICR 110.
23 It should be noted that the EU Part-time Work Directive (97/81/EC) requires Member States to introduce legal rules prohibiting discrimination against part-time workers (not just employees). In the UK the Directive has been implemented by The Part-time Workers (Prevention of Less Favourable Treatment) Regulations SI 2000/1551. This enables part time workers to compare their terms and conditions of employment, including pay, with full-time colleagues, including those of the same sex. The Regulations do not, however, entitle full time workers to move to part time contracts or to job-share.
24 In *London Underground Ltd v Edwards* (No 2) [1998] IRLR 364 the Court of Appeal refused to apply a pool considered to be unrepresentative. Edwards was a single mother. She was one of a handful of women drivers on the London

footnote continued on next page

Even if X could establish indirect discrimination there would still be the possibility of justification. For example, what if the club says we are part of the local community and we want to contribute to tackling local unemployment; or it can show that local people are less likely to move and therefore will be potentially more loyal to the club?

Could not the above add up to a policy which in crude terms is actually saying members of this ethnic group need not apply? X could, of course, argue that he has been the victim of direct discrimination, but how can this be proved if he is no more but no less talented than those actually selected?

Even if X could establish direct discrimination there is a further statutory 'sting in the tail'.

Section 39 of the Race Relations Act 1976

Nothing in Parts II to IV shall render unlawful any act whereby a person discriminates against another on the basis of that other's nationality or place of birth or the length of time for which he has been resident in a particular area or place, if the act is done:

in selecting one or more persons to represent a country, place or area, or any related association, in any sport or game or

in pursuance of the rules of any competition so far as they relate to eligibility to compete in any sport or game.[25]

If X is a woman, it is necessary to consider the situation where a club might impose factors based on physical strength and stamina, rather than on, or in addition to, nationality or residence. Whilst it might be easier to establish indirect discrimination in this context, it could be predicted that justification would be similarly easier for clubs to plead, given the perceptions that still exist that most men are stronger than most women. Scope for re-evaluating these arguably bigoted perceptions are unlikely given the sports exemption contained in the SDA.

Section 44 of the Sex Discrimination Act 1975

Nothing in Parts II to IV shall, in relation to any sport, game or other activity of a competitive nature where the physical strength, stamina or physique of the average woman puts her at a disadvantage to the average man, render unlawful any act related to the participation of a person as a competitor in events involving that activity which are confined to competitors of one sex.

This overt manifestation of sexist prejudice, of course, ignores the fact that professional sports participants are by definition not average men and women. With specialist weight training and coaching, women in sport can match the strength and stamina with that of many, albeit not all, men. Moreover, all of us can think of, for example, top class professional footballers whose brilliant ball skills may not be matched with a 'Charles Atlas' (or even Vinnie Jones) physique. Should an Act

---

Underground. The Court decided that this meant that the normal pool in such circumstances, that is all drivers employed by London Underground, was unrepresentative and should not be used. The Court then held that as the majority of single parents are women a shift system that discriminated against single parents was unlawful sex discrimination against Edwards even though all the other drivers, the women as well as the men, were able to work the new hours. Arguably, EU law requires the flexibility exemplified by this decision. If this is so, then under the new definition of indirect discrimination for employees, X, in the scenario discussed in the text, should be able to establish indirect discrimination. The selection criteria would then only be lawful if the club could justify them.

25 This section has not generated any case law and its scope could be restricted by the interpretation of 'represent'. As noted by Osborn and Greenfield: 'Clubs and leagues do not represent as opposed to cover geographical areas.' They nevertheless conclude: 'Overall s 39 permits a very wide measure of discrimination that appears difficult to rationalise.' Osborn, G and Greenfield, S, 'Gentlemen, players and the 6' 9" West Indian fast bowler' 2(3) *Working Papers in Law and Popular Culture*, Manchester Metropolitan University, p 28.

intended to eliminate sex discrimination legitimise the sexist assumptions long ago questioned in popular culture by the likes of the film *Gregory Girl* and the British television series *The Manageress*?

For the time being, sport remains segregated on a gender basis – particularly where it is played as a professional game. Moreover, media interest and thus national/international prestige and the 'big' money remains focused on the game as played by men. Desegregation might not be appropriate in all sports, that is those where physical strength is at the core of the sport, but should not women at least be given the option to compete on equal terms where skill with hands and/or feet is the essence of the game concerned?

If traditional attitudes persist as far as players and thus managers are concerned, inroads have at least been made when it comes to referees and officials.

Petty v British Judo Association [1981] ICR 660 EAT

Petty argued unlawful discrimination when the British Judo Association refused to permit her to referee an All-England's men's contest. The association pleaded s 44 on the basis that a woman would not have the strength to separate two male combatants.

Browne-Wilkinson J stated:

> It is common ground that judo is a sport in which men and women ought not to compete one with the other. Section 44 saves from being unlawful 'any act related to the participation of a person as a competitor in that activity,' ie judo ... we cannot see how provisions as to referees relate to the 'participation' of the competitors in the contest ... We think the words should be given their obvious meaning and not extended so as to cover any discrimination other than provisions designed to regulate who is to take part in the contest as a competitor. Any other construction would lead to great uncertainty: for example, would the section be extended to discrimination against the lady in the box office at a football ground? .... [26]

Today, of course, in football the 'lady' may be found not only in the box office but on the pitch as a match official. We still await the day when the 'lady' will also be present as a member of a mixed-sex professional club side.

It has been clarified that s 44 cannot be invoked as a defence where the relevant sports participants are of the same gender. In *Couch v British Board of Boxing Control*[27] it was held that the decision of the Board to withold a licence to box professionally from Jane Couch, the women's world welterweight champion, constituted unlawful sex discrimination. The decision of the Board was criticised for being based on 'gender-based stereotypes and assumptions', and s 44 was of no assistance to the Board in circumstances in which Couch was seeking a licence to participate in professional boxing bouts with other women. The section only applies where women are seeking to compete with men.[28]

The other defence to direct discrimination in the Sex Discrimination Act relates to gender as 'a genuine occupational qualification.' Section 7 makes an exception 'where the job needs to be held by a man to preserve decency or privacy because .... the holder of the job is likely to do his work in circumstances where men might reasonably object to the presence of a woman because they are in a state of undress or are using sanitary facilities.' Without doubt, dressing room team talks and locker

---

26 At pp 665–666.
27 Unreported, Case No 2304231/97. For further discussion of this case see Felix, A, 'The "Fleetwood Assassin" strikes a blow for female boxing' (1998) 1(3) Sports Law Bulletin 1, 6 and the 'In my Opinion' Column by Ferris, E, Vice-President of The Olympians in the same edition of the Sports Law Bulletin 2.
28 See *Bennett v Football Association* (1978) unreported CA Transcript 591; also see discussion of case and s 44 of the SDA in McArdle, D, *From Boot Money to Bosman: Football, Society and the Law* (2000), London: Cavendish.

room culture are integral aspects of professional sport, but one hopes, indeed assumes, that if the barriers erected by s 44 are ever overcome, this provision will not be permitted to act as the final bastion of a male preserve. It should not be beyond the wit or resources of professional clubs to provide the separate facilities to be found in any municipal swimming pool, whilst allowing players of both genders to mix once appropriately enrobed in the team kit.

Both the SDA and RRA inherently prohibit positive discrimination. Therefore, it would be unlawful, for example, for a football club to recruit a player for the specific reason that he was a member of the Asian-British community. However, positive action is permitted by the legislation and is indeed increasingly encouraged by EU law.[29] Thus it would be permissible for a club deliberately to seek to increase the number of players it employs from ethnic groups under-represented in the sport or club concerned. This could be done by, as examples, targeting schools containing high numbers of members of the relevant ethnic groups, or advertising in languages spoken by and/or in media popular with members of under-represented groups. The club may emphasise that it welcomes applicants from the ethnic group(s) concerned. However, specific decisions to recruit one individual as against another must be made on objective criteria and not motivated by a desire to engage in positive discrimination.

The main remedies available under the Acts are declarations and compensation. The latter covers actual financial loss and is not subject to any statutory maximum figure.[30] Moreover, compensation can include an element of aggravated damages where injury to feelings is caused by a deliberate intention to discriminate.

RACIAL AND SEXUAL HARASSMENT

The gender segregated nature of professional sport means that the problem of racist rather than sexist behaviour is of greater significance. However, this may not always be the case, and harassment of women employees who are not sports participants also needs to be considered as a possibility. Moreover, cases decided under the RRA are strong persuasive precedents for cases brought under the SDA and vice-versa.

The display of racist attitudes by white players to black team-mates, at least in football, is thankfully becoming a thing of the past. Similarly, there has been in recent years a significant reduction in racist chanting at most football grounds, although individual racists still appear uninhibited in racially abusing individuals. The most likely context in professional sport in which black players will be subject to racist abuse is on the field of play by members of the opposing team. Moreover, it would be wrong to conclude that racism within all clubs in all sports has disappeared. Thus case law on the problem of racial and sexual harassment in employment is one which this chapter must include.[31]

---

29 In *Badeck v Hessischer Ministerprasident* [2000 IRLR 432 the ECJ ruled that positive action is not contrary to EU law unless it requires women to be afforded automatic and unconditional preference over men (or vice-versa). The new EU Directives on Discrimination, see below p 572, encourage Member States to take positive steps to compensate for disadvantages produced by past forms of discrimination.

30 Cf the ERA 1996 and remedies for unfair dismissal; see previous chapter, pp 551–53.

31 It should be remembered that employees wishing to pursue harassment claims before employment tribunals will not normally have to follow the statutory grievance procedure – see previous chapter, pp 532–33. However, where the inadequacy of grievance procedures in protecting employees from ongoing harassment can be attributed to the employer this will normally result in an increase of between 10 to 50% in any compensation that the tribunal awards.

Neither the Sex Discrimination Act nor Race Relations Act as originally enacted specifically defined sexual or racial harassment as unlawful discrimination. Therefore, it was through case law that acts of harassment were deemed to constitute a detriment on grounds of sex or race and thus unlawful direct discrimination. However, judicial perceptions of what types of comments or behaviour constitute harassment have a somewhat chequered history. For example, in the case of *De Souza*[32] it was held that a racist comment may be no more than an insult and this is not sufficient to constitute an act of harassment.

In contrast, cases decided under the SDA did suggest the above approach is wrong. Thus it has been held that a single act of sexual harassment can constitute a detriment;[33] and that the subjective perceptions of the employee should be taken into account.[34] The latter decision is however double-edged in that it permits a woman's style of dress and sexual attitudes to be examined as evidence as to whether or not in fact a detriment has been suffered. Nevertheless, these cases do suggest that a single act of sexist or racist abuse could now constitute a 'detriment' within the meaning of the RRA.

Ironically, in the context of sexual harassment only, a recent decision of the Law Lords[35] does suggest echoes of the reasoning in *De Souza*. Their Lordships stated that harassment is only unlawful sex discrimination where an employee is treated differently by reference to her or his sex, and the fact that harassment is gender-specific does not automatically establish this is the case. Therefore, if disparaging remarks concerning anatomy were made to both women and men it would seem this is no longer to be regarded as sex discrimination.

This view of the law could have had very serious consequences for how racist abuse in sport is perceived. Potentially it could have reinforced (not uncommon) arguments that insulting a player by referring to his skin colour is no more significant than referring to his size, weight or hair colour, particularly when such comments are made 'in jest' or in the heat of competition. It is contended that the realities of racism in Britain are such that it is qualitatively different to be called, for example, 'a black bastard' as against being called one from a region of the country such as Yorkshire or even a different country such as Denmark. In the latter context it is true that the player's different nationality is referred to, but Danes in Britain do not have the collective memory and ongoing legacy of centuries of oppression, rooted in the slave trade and the spread of Empire, that remains the experience of the Afro-Caribbean and Asian communities. Racism in sport is as much derived from this history as it is in any other area of society.[36]

The continuing problem of racism in football is illustrated by the Bobby Gould incident and a case concerning the player-manager, Kevin Ratcliffe. The former concerned the decision of Nathan Blake to refuse to play for Wales after the manager, Bobby Gould, had made racist statements about

---

32 *De Souza v Automobile Association* [1986] IRLR 103. In this case the claimant overheard a colleague refer to her as 'the wog' but the Court of Appeal regarded this insult rather than harassment.

33 *Bracebridge Engineering v Darby* [1990] IRLR 3.

34 *Wileman v Minilec Engineering* [1988] IRLR 144.

35 *Macdonald v AG for Scotland; Pearce v Mayfield School* [2004] 1 All ER 339.

36 For an analysis of racism in football see Greenfield, S and Osborn, G, 'When the whites go marching in? Racism and resistance in English football' (1996) 6(2) Marquette Sports Law Journal 315–335. For comparative analysis and an examination of the experiences of black athletes in the USA, see Williams, P, 'Performing in a racially hostile environment' (1996) 6(2) Marquette Sports Law Journal 287–314.

For a discussion of the role of racism in undermining the interest in cricket in the British Afro-Caribbean Community and the decline in the West Indian test team see Steen R, 'Calypso Collapso' *Observer Sport*, 25 July 2004. Of particular interest is the long shadow cast by the public criticism of Devon Malcolm by Ray Illingworth in 1995 – see Chapter 12 fn 27. It was also at the start of the 1995 season that Wisden Cricket Monthly published an attack on black cricketers by Robert Henderson for not being 'unequivocal Englishmen'.

opponents in the dressing room. This incident was particularly revealing as initially Gould was not even capable of understanding that he had voiced racist sentiments, or, at least, why this should upset one of his own players.[37]

Arguably, even more disturbing is the case of *Hussaney v Chester City FC and Kevin Ratcliffe*.[38] Hussaney was an apprentice at Chester and had played for the youth and reserves team. On one occasion, when he was due to play for the Chester City Reserves against Oldham Athletic Reserves, he was called a 'black cunt' by the first team manager, Kevin Ratcliffe, who was also due to play for the reserves. Hussaney had put the wrong sized studs into Ratcliffe's football boots. Hussaney made a formal complaint to the club. Shortly after this incident, Hussaney was informed he would not be offered a professional contract. The club agreed that Ratcliffe made the alleged racial abuse, but denied it amounted to racial discrimination. Ratcliffe made some attempts to provide an apology to Hussaney. The tribunal held that the abusive language amounted to discrimination by both Ratcliffe and the club on grounds of race and made a compensatory award of £2,500 for injury to feelings.

This case illustrates how, as is the case with any employer, a professional club will be directly liable for acts of racist abuse on the part of those in managerial positions. The case also highlights the difficulties of establishing whether decisions are racially motivated albeit unconsciously. Hussaney brought a second claim against Chester FC stating that he had been victimised contrary to the Act for bringing the claim against Ratcliffe. The victimisation consisted of the decision by the club not to offer him a professional contract. The tribunal rejected this claim as it found that the decision was made 'purely on footballing grounds'. In January 2001, the EAT upheld Hussaney's appeal on the basis that the tribunal had provided insufficient reasons as to why it had reached the conclusion that there was no unlawful unconscious motivation. The tribunal had over-relied on the club's view that Ratcliffe had simply relied on his experience as an assessor of footballing skill in recommending that Hussaney not be offered a contract.[39]

It can be anticipated that in the future it will be easier to establish that racist abuse constitutes unlawful discrimination. This is because, as a result of EC law, the Race Relations Act now includes a statutory definition of racial harassment.[40]

Section 3A Race Relations Act 1976

(1) A person subjects another to harassment in any circumstances . . . where, on grounds of race or ethnic or national origins, he engages in unwanted conduct which has the purpose or effect of:

    a) violating that other person's dignity, or

    b) creating an intimidating, hostile, degrading, humiliating or offensive environment for him.

(2) Conduct shall be regarded as having the effect specified in paragraph (a) or (b) of subsection (1) only if, having regard to all the circumstances, including in particular the perception of that other person, it should reasonably be considered as having that effect.

---

37 As reported in *The Guardian*, 2 April 1997; also see Mitchell, K, 'Gould has the gift of the gaffe' *The Observer*, 6 April 1997. The most recent example of how influential people in sport find it difficult to distinguish between racist language and racism is provided by the incident where Ron Atkinson, believing himself to be off-air, described the Chelsea defender, Marcel Desailly, as a 'fucking lazy, thick nigger'. See Edoba, M, editor of New Nation, *The Observer*, 25 April 2004 for a response to this by a leading member of the black community.

38 Unreported, IT Case No 2102426\97.

39 See (2001) 4(3) Sports Law Bulletin 5 for case note.

40 Directive 2000/43 implementing the principle of equal treatment between persons irrespective of racial or ethnic origin. Directive 2000/78 establishing a general framework for equal treatment in employment and occupation has resulted in similar definitions in the new Regulations prohibiting discrimination on grounds of sexual orientation and religious belief – see below, pp 572–73. The Sex Discrimination Act was amended by the Empolyment Equality (Sex Discrimination) Regulations 2005 to incorporate an equiviliant definition.

On the basis of the above definition it would seem to be the case that any racist abuse perceived by the victim to be 'degrading' or 'offensive' will constitute racial harassment, contrary to the RRA, even if this was not the actual purpose or intention of the perpetrator. However, (as noted above) there remains an element of doubt as to whether abuse which based exclusively on a person's colour, rather than race, can constitute unlawful discrimination.

It has long been clear that a sustained campaign of verbal and/or physical racist harassment designed to force a player to leave a club will constitute an unlawful detriment under the RRA. The above case notwithstanding, if such behaviour was to occur in a club it is more likely to come from team-mates than the club management. A club is potentially liable in such a situation by virtue of the imposition of statutory vicarious liability.

Section 32 of the Race Relations Act 1976

Anything done by a person in the course of his employment shall be treated for the purposes of this Act as done by his employer as well as by him, whether or not it was done with the employer's knowledge or approval . . .

. . . In proceedings brought under this Act against any person in respect of an act alleged to have been done by an employee of his it shall be a defence for that person to prove that he took such steps as were reasonably practicable to prevent the employee from doing that act, or from doing in the course of his employment acts of that description.[41]

An employer will avoid vicarious liability if disciplinary codes prohibit acts of racial and sexual harassment, the rules are properly communicated to employees and complaints of harassment are investigated and otherwise properly acted upon.[42] It is clear that clubs which recognise the importance of tackling racism, were it to occur within the club, and display a practical commitment to doing so are likely to receive the protection of ss 3.[43]

The effectiveness of these provisions was potentially and seriously undermined by the heavily criticised decision of the EAT in the case of *Jones v Tower Boot Co*. In this case the applicant was subjected, at the workplace, to a series of brutal acts. It was clear that the employees responsible were motivated by racism. It was decided that the company could not be vicariously liable on the basis that the employees could not be regarded as acting within the course of their employment.

This reasoning required the conclusion that the more extreme the acts of racism (or sexism), the easier it becomes for an employer who takes no action nevertheless to evade liability. These criticisms were taken on board by the Court of Appeal in reversing the EAT decision.[44] Waite LJ clarified it was wrong to apply the common law concept of vicarious liability to the Race Relations and Sex Discrimination Acts, as the purpose of the Acts is to make employers vicariously liable where in a work context they fail to protect employees from racist or sexist behaviour. It is now clear that only the pro-active employer who takes reasonable steps to stamp out racism and sexism will escape vicarious liability.

It has also been held that the scope of an employer's vicarious liability potentially includes behaviour when employees are 'socialising' with one another as part of workplace culture. This was

---

41   Section 41 of the SDA contains equivalent provisions.
42   *Balgobin v Tower Hamlets LBC* [1987] IRLR 401.
43   The FA Code of Practice and Notes on Contract specifies that racial harassment is a disciplinary offence. This is defined as including: 'physical abuse, offensive language or jokes, offensive graffiti or posters and enforced isolation on the grounds of an individual's colour, race, ethnic or national origin or nationality.' See p 12.
44   See [1997] IRLR 168. The EAT decision is reported in [1995] IRLR 529.

decided in a case[45] concerning a police party in a pub. This case has implications for professional clubs as sport, like the police force, is a form of employment, where club culture and team-bonding may require or at least put pressure on players to participate in post-training or post-match social activities.

In *Burton v De Vere Hotels Ltd*[46] it was held that an employer will be directly liable for the acts of *third parties*, if its degree of control over a situation is such that it can take steps to protect employees from third party racist abuse and fails to do so. (In this case the hotel management failed to protect black staff from racist 'jokes' by Bernard Manning by, for example, withdrawing them from the function during Manning's speech.) In *Macdonald*[47] this decision was disapproved by the Law Lords. The correct position is apparently that an employer can now only be liable for third party harassment where the failure to protect the employee is itself racially motivated. The factor of control is no longer in itself sufficient to establish employer liability.

In professional sport the issue of third party racist abuse is most likely to arise during a match. Such abuse will either come from spectators or members of the opposing team. Clubs, of course, have less control once their players are on the field of play. However, with respect to racist chanting or racist abuse of individual players by spectators it seems that, in the light of *Macdonald*, even if there is a failure to implement efficient stewarding operations to clamp down on such behaviour a club will not incur liability under the RRA.

With respect to racist abuse by opponents on the field of play, clubs cannot take any effective measures to prevent this, short of not fielding or substituting a player (which would be self-defeating from the perspectives of both player and club). The decision in *Macdonald* is of no consequence for this particular issue. Rather the problem demonstrates a major lacuna with respect to the Race Relations Act, as the Act does not require employers to take disciplinary action against employees who engage in racist behaviour towards individuals outside of the employing organisation. It is worth noting that were racial harassment ever to give rise to liability in tort, then the case law on vicarious liability might become of some relevance, as the opposing player's club could then be rendered legally responsible for any racist behaviour by that player during a match.

However, in the here and now the law is unable to provide a solution to an important problem. Incidents of such racist abuse will occur partly because a player, who as an individual is racist, will be less inhibited about expressing his racism to an opponent as against a team-mate. Moreover, such racism may be used as a cynical and calculated act of 'gamesmanship' to wind up an opposing player to put him off his game and/or provoke him into committing a foul or offence which results in the victim of racism rather than its perpetrator being sent off.

It is, of course, primarily the referee or umpire who is in control during the course of a match, and it should be the job of the match officials to deal with any racist conduct committed by players. In the context of football, measures proposed by the Football Task Force,[48] if implemented, to make racism a

---

45 *Chief Constable of the Lincolnshire Police v Stubbs & Others* [1999] ICR 547.
46 [1997] ICR 1. For further discussions of issues concerning harassment and third party liability see Sinclair, A and Kelly, J, 'Employer liability to an employee for third party encounters of an unpleasant kind' Employee Relations Review 99; and 'Sexual harassment of employees by customers and other third parties' 2000 31(3) Texas Tech Law Review 807–867.
47 See above, fn 35.
48 See Gardiner, S, 'In my Opinion' and Welch, R, 'Anti-racist clauses in footballers' contracts' (1998) 1 (4) Sports Law Bulletin p 2 and pp 8, 15 respectively for further discussion of the Football Task Force's Report.

red card offence and to incorporate anti-racist clauses into players' and managers' contracts would be of assistance in countering racism during a match.

These measures should operate in a two-pronged and mutually reinforcing manner. First, referees will be obliged to send off players who are guilty of racism during the course of a game. Secondly, clubs can regard such players as having acted in breach of their employment contracts and can take disciplinary action against them accordingly. The fact that the racist player has been sent off and consequently damaged his team's prospects of success will, hopefully, encourage his club to subject him to disciplinary proceedings. Similarly, clubs will begin to demand that referees are consistent in regarding racism as a red card offence. Anti-racist clauses in managers' contracts will also deter the more cynical manager (should he exist) from encouraging his players to engage in racist 'gamesmanship'. Clearly, such clauses are of importance in situations such as those discussed above involving Bobby Gould and Kevin Ratcliffe. It can be argued that such measures should be adopted not only in football but also in all professional sports.

Though changes to the law that strengthen the regulation of harassment are to be welcomed, it can be concluded overall that the law is not a completely effective instrument for protecting employees from racial (and indeed sexual) harassment. However to reiterate, overt racism *within* football clubs at least appears to be on the wane. The reasons for this are probably the emergence of black icons such as Ian Wright and Les Ferdinand (not to mention Thierry Henry) and the relative success of the 'Kick It Out' campaign. If there are problems within clubs in other professional sports then it is perhaps what has happened in football, rather than relying on the law, which shows the way forward.

Football itself still has a long way to go, of course, in completely eliminating racist behaviour by sections of 'fans' (currently a small minority) and by opponents on the field of play, and in eradicating the insidious attitudes on which more overt racism is actually based.[49]

DISCRIMINATION AND EUROPEAN LAW

Sexuality

Until December 2003, discrimination against gays and lesbians in sport was not directly prohibited. Indeed, until very recently, in appropriate circumstances it was even permitted. As established in *Saunders*[50] it may have been within the range of reasonable responses for clubs to dismiss gay players. A dismissal could have been regarded as reasonable and thus fair if the presence of an openly gay player was causing tensions within the team and/or hostility from the paying public. The latter point is of particular significance when it is remembered that in *Saunders* emphasis was placed on the attitudes of parents. By analogy, gay professional players coaching young children or simply existing as role models could be perceived by parents as a potential source of corruption. That this confusion between gay sexuality and paedophilia is based on a misconception, which can best be described as

---

49   For an analysis of racism in sport see Gardiner, S and Welch, R, 'Sport, racism and the limits of "colour blind" law', in Carrington, B and McDonald, I (eds), *'Race', Sport and British Society* (2001) London: Routledge. For evidence of the coninuing problem of racism in football see Chaudhary, V, 'Race bias still rife in football' *The Guardian*, 20 May 2004. This reports on a survey carried out by the Commission for Racial Equality which shows that 'football is predominantly a white men's (sic) game', and that this is particularly the case outside the Premiership and the first division.

50   *Saunders v Scottish National Camps Association* [1981] IRLR 174.

superstitious bigotry, was not for a tribunal to find once it was clear that the reasonable employing club may have acted to preserve its reputation and paying support.

By the same token, however, it is clear that dismissal of an employee on the grounds of that person's sexual orientation is contrary to Art 8 of the European Convention on Human Rights 1950. It is also potentially contrary to the Article for an employer to succumb to homophobia on the part of sections of its workforce (and presumably third parties such as its customers).

The trigger for an historic change in the law rendering discrimination on grounds of sexual orientation to be unlawful was the decision of the European Court of Human Rights in *Lustig-Prean and Beckett v the United Kingdom*.[51] In this case the ECHR ruled that it was contrary to Art 8 of the European Convention on Human Rights, which protects rights to a private life, to discharge individuals from the Royal Navy on the sole ground that hey were homosexuals. The wide-sweeping consequences of this decision were immediately clear as the European Court rejected arguments from the Ministry of Defence that the presence of homosexuals in the armed forces 'can cause offence, polarise relationships, induce ill-discipline and, as a consequence, damage morale and unit effectiveness', and therefore any discrimination could be justified by the interests of national security.

As a result of this decision it has become impossible for any clubs to argue that discrimination against a gay player is justified by reference to the reaction of his team-mates or the club's supporters. However, the impact of the decision in *Lustig-Prean* was significantly reduced by the fact that the Human Rights Act only permits rights guaranteed by the European Convention to be enforced directly against public bodies. Moreover, discrimination against an employee on the basis of his or her sexuality cannot be considered unlawful either under the Sex Discrimination Act[52] or under the Equal Treatment Directive.[53]

The original legal basis for the new law is contained in Art 13 of the Treaty of Amsterdam. This empowered the Council of Ministers by unanimous agreement to approve legislation drafted by the Commission to prohibit a variety of forms of discrimination. Such legislation has now been adopted. In the case of race discrimination the Directive[54] came into force in July 2003. The Framework Directive,[55] which prohibits discrimination on grounds of religion or belief, sexual orientation, disability and age, came into force in December 2003, although Member States will have until 2006 to introduce measures on age[56] and disability.

---

51 [1999] IRLR 734.

52 *Smith v Gardner Merchant Ltd* [1998] IRLR 510. In *Macdonald v Ministry of Defence; Pearce v Governing Body of Mayfield Secondary School* [2003] ICR 937 it was accepted, before the House of Lords, by the employees that, despite s 6 of the HRA, the SDA can still not be interpreted as covering sexuality as well as gender. The Law Lords held that there is no direct sex discrimination where employers treat male and female homosexual employees in the same way.

53 In *Grant v South-West Trains Ltd* [1998] ICR 449 it was ruled by the ECJ that EU law prohibiting sex discrimination did not cover discrimination by an employer on grounds of an employee's sexual orientation.

54 Council Directive 2000/43/EC.

55 Council Directive 2000/78/ EC of 27 November 2000 establishing a general framework for equal treatment in employment and occupation.

56 The nature of professional sport means that compulsory retirement is not the issue that it is in most sectors of employment. However, it was generally thought that Jeff Winter was not 'over the moon' at being forced to retire from professional football refereeing at 48. Similarly, there has been speculation that Pierlugi Collina, regarded by many as the best football referee in the world, might officiate in the Premiership as a result of being too old at the age of 45 to continue to referee international matches – see *The Daily Mail*, 29 January 2004.

With respect to sexual orientation and religious belief the provisions of the Directive are implemented by statutory instrument.[57] It seems unlikely, though not impossible, that the latter will be of much significance in the world of sport. The Sexual Orientation Regulations render it unlawful to discriminate directly and indirectly against, or harass, a person on grounds of sexual orientation.

The Employment Equality (Sexual Orientation) Regulations 2003

Interpretation

2 (1) In these Regulations, 'sexual orientation' means a sexual orientation towards –

   (a) persons of the same sex;

   (b) persons of the opposite sex; or

   (c) persons of the same sex and of the opposite sex.

Discrimination on grounds of sexual orientation

3 (1) For the purposes of these Regulations, a person ('A') discriminates against another person ('B') if –

   (a) on grounds of sexual orientation, A treats B less favourably than he treats or would treat other persons; or

   (b) A applies to B a provision, criterion or practice which he applies or would apply equally to persons not of the same sexual orientation as B, but –

      (i) which puts or would put persons of the same sexual orientation as B at a particular disadvantage when compared with other persons,

      (ii) which puts B at that disadvantage, and

      (iii) which A cannot show to be a proportionate means of achieving a legitimate aim.

   (2) A comparison of B's case with that of another person under paragraph (1) must be such that the relevant circumstances in the one case are the same, or not materially different, in the other.

Harassment on grounds of sexual orientation

5 (1) For the purposes of these Regulations, a person ('A') subjects another person ('B') to harassment where, on grounds of sexual orientation, A engages in unwanted conduct which has the purpose or effect of –

   (a) violating B's dignity; or

   (b) creating an intimidating, hostile, degrading, humiliating or offensive environment for B.

   (2) Conduct shall be regarded as having the effect specified in paragraph (1)(a) or (b) only if, having regard to all the circumstances, including in particular the perception of B, it should reasonably be considered as having that effect.

In addition to the rights and remedies provided by the Regulations, it should be noted that any dismissal on grounds of sexual orientation would be an unfair dismissal under the Employment Rights Act. A player who resigns in response to being subjected to homophobia at the workplace will succeed in a claim for constructive and wrongful and/or unfair dismissal. However, action taken against a player for sexual misconduct will not be covered by the Regulations and a dismissal on such grounds may well be considered within the range of reasonable responses and thus fair.[58]

---

57 The Employment Equality (Sexual Orientation) Regulations 2003, SI 2003/1661 and The Employment Equality (Religion or Belief) Regulations 2003, SI 2003/1600 came into force on 1 December and 2 December 2003 respectively.

58 See *X v Y* Court of Appeal [2004] EWCA Civ 662.

Transsexuals

That the stigma attached to homosexuality is also attached to transsexuality is shown by the problems encountered by the professional tennis player Dr Renee Richards who prior to a sex change operation had been Dr Richard Rasskind.[59] However, in *P v S and Cornwall County Council*[60] the ECJ ruled that dismissal of an employee was contrary to the Equal Treatment Directive where the reason for the dismissal was that the employee proposed to undergo gender-reassignment surgery. The EAT's view had been that such discrimination is not by reason of gender providing male and female transsexuals are treated in the same way. The ECJ's view was the sex discrimination arises from 'comparison with persons of the sex to which he or she was deemed to belong before undergoing gender reassignment.' Alternatively such discrimination constitutes: 'failure to respect the dignity and freedom to which he or she is entitled, and which the Court has a duty to safeguard.'

Assuming such discrimination cannot be justified in the context of professional sport, and the ultimate position taken with respect to Renee Richards would suggest there can be no such justification, this ruling is as important in sport as it is for employment law in general. It should be noted that the SDA had been amended by statutory instrument[61] so that the Act now expressly protects transsexuals. As is the case with gay and lesbian players, the most likely form of discrimination against transsexuals in sport is likely to be in the form of harassment. It was held in *Chessington World of Adventures v Reed*[62] that employers will incur direct or vicarious liability if they fail to protect transsexual employees from harassment by co-workers.

A specific problem could occur around the issue of changing rooms. As a result of a case decided by the Court of Appeal,[63] it appears that an employer will not be committing unlawful discrimination in providing for separate toilet facilities for pre-operative transsexuals. It would seem logical to apply this decision to changing rooms, shower facilities and the like. However, according to the European Court of Human Rights,[64] a post-operative transsexual is entitled to have his or her new sex fully recognised through a change in that person's birth certificate. Thus it would seem that should a sports professional change sex and continue to participate in the sport in his or her new gender, other participants of that sex would not be able to object to sharing changing rooms with that person on the grounds that he was once a man, or vice-versa.

PREGNANCY AND MATERNITY RIGHTS

Article 2 of the Equal Treatment Directive[65] provides: 'the principle of equal treatment shall mean that there shall be no discrimination whatsoever on grounds of sex either directly or indirectly by reference in particular to marital or family status.'

In accordance with the norms of EU law the Directive is only directly enforceable within the UK by state employees. Nevertheless, through the preliminary ruling process, the ECJ has delivered a

---

59 See Grayson, E, *Sport and the Law* (1994), London: Butterworths, pp 240–241.
60 [1996] ICR 795.
61 The Sex Discrimination (Gender Reassignment) Regulations 1999, SI 1999/1102.
62 [1998] ICR 97.
63 *Croft v Royal Mail Group Plc* (CA) [2003] IRLR 592.
64 *Goodwin v UK* [2002] IRLR 664.
65 Council Directive 76/207/EC.

number of significant rulings which have conferred protection on women employees which may not have been provided for by national legislation. In the UK this has been particularly significant in the context of maternity rights. These rights should be appreciated by professional clubs who employ women either as players or in a variety of managerial or administrative capacities. Such rights are also relevant to women employed as match officials.

In the landmark rulings of *Dekker v VJV Centrum* and *Hertz vAldi Marked*[66] the ECJ ruled that refusal of employment to or dismissal of women on grounds of pregnancy is contrary to the Directive. These rulings were subsequently accepted as appropriate interpretations of the SDA by the House of Lords in *Webb*.[67] However, at the time of this decision it remained unclear whether it was unlawful to refuse employment to a pregnant woman under a temporary contract where she would be unable to fulfil all or most of that contract. As referred to by Lord Keith in his judgment in *Webb*, this could be relevant in sport with respect to the Wimbledon fortnight or the Olympic Games. Similarly, it could be of relevance where a woman would not be available for selection by a club for the large part of a current season. That such arguments are not available to employers, clubs or sporting bodies is clarified by the ECJ ruling in *Brandt-Nielson*.[68] This ruling states that refusal of employment to a woman because she is pregnant will be unlawful in all circumstances, irrespective of the economic consequences for the employer.

As a result of s 99 of the Employment Rights Act, which implements the EC Pregnancy Directive,[69] dismissal of a woman is automatically unfair if it is by reason of her pregnancy. This protection lasts during pregnancy and during the period of maternity leave to which she is entitled. Under the Maternity and Parental Leave Regulations[70] all women are entitled to 26 weeks' maternity leave. For women with at least 26 weeks' continuous employment there is entitlement to an additional 26 weeks. It should also be noted that parents, that is fathers as well as mothers, with one year's service, are entitled to 13 weeks' unpaid leave to care for a child under the age of 5.[71]

The above provisions concerning dismissal during pregnancy and maternity leave protect all professional sportswomen who have entered into a contract of employment. Sportswomen who are not employees are still protected by the SDA and Equal Treatment Directive. Ironically perhaps, a woman who has rights under the ERA and the Regulations might prefer to bring a claim under the SDA. This is because compensation is not subject to any statutory maximum limit. For highly paid professionals, therefore, a claim under the SDA will incorporate compensation for loss of any career opportunities. In all likelihood this will be far greater than the basic and compensatory awards available under the ERA.[72]

Although there has not been a sports specific case in the English courts, it is clear that the law gives significant rights to professional sportswomen in the context of pregnancy and maternity. In

---

66   [1991] IRLR 27, 131.
67   *Webb v EMO Air Cargo (UK) Ltd* [1993] ICR 175 HL.
68   The *Tele Danmark (Brandt-Nielson)* Case [2001] IRLR 853.
69   Council Directive 92/85/EC.
70   SI No 3312/1999. The Regulations are designed to implement the Parental Leave Directive, Council Directive 96/34/EC.
71   The Paternity and Adoption Leave Regulations 2002, SI 2002/2788 also permit fathers, with 26 weeks' continuous employment, to take two weeks' paid paternity leave to care for a newborn child or support its mother.
72   See previous chapter, pp 551–53.

Australia, recent case law has suggested restricting participation of a pregnant player will be unlawful.[73]

Equal Pay

Article 141 of the EC Treaty, as amplified by the Equal Pay Directive,[74] provides for the right of equal pay for work of equal value. In the UK this right is implemented by the Equal Pay Act 1970. As is the case with the SDA (and RRA), an applicant need not be an employee, but may be any individual who has entered into contract to perform work. As a directly applicable treaty provision, Art 141 can be relied upon as the basis of a claim in an industrial tribunal. Claims can thus be brought under EC law, or the Equal Pay Act or both. In recent years, in particular, this area of law has been driven by rulings of the ECJ.

However, one of the problems with the law as a mechanism of achieving equal pay for women is that both Art 141 and the Equal Pay Act require the applicant to identify a male comparator. In the segregated context of professional sport with different competitions and different teams for men and women this is generally a non-starter. This has long been an issue in, for example, professional tennis, where women players generally earn less than their male counterparts.[75]

Moreover, performance related pay and salary structures determined by market forces are legitimate grounds for pay differentials, even where the equal pay laws are applicable. In sport, these factors often render pay differentials the norm between members of the same team. For example, the pay that an individual footballer earns will be very much linked to the transfer and/or signing-on fee that a club is prepared to pay to secure his services. This is similarly the case where a club wishes to persuade a player to re-sign for it on expiry of his contract. In the event of a mixed-sex team ever being fielded, these factors would make it extremely difficult for a female member of the team to compare successfully, in terms of a legal challenge, the pay she received with that of a male team-mate earning a higher salary.

The equal pay laws do, of course, protect women employed by clubs as administrators, public relations officers and the like. Moreover, they apply to paid match officials. However, for the sports participant, with whom this chapter is primarily concerned, equal pay law will generally remain of abstract relevance until and if mixed sport in terms of gender becomes a reality.

ARTICLE 39 OF THE EC TREATY

The main impact of EU law on professional sport has clearly been the ECJ's ruling in *Bosman*. One of Bosman's complaints was that UEFA's '3 + 2' rule violated Art 48. This rule restricted the number of foreign players whose names could be included on a team-sheet in a UEFA competition to three.

---

73 See *Gardner v National Netball League* [2001] FMCA 50 (18 July 2001) (www.austlii.edu.au/). Also see Taylor, S, 'In My Opinion – Netball Australia' (2001) 4(4) Sports Law Bulletin 2.

74 Council Directive 75/117/EC.

75 Equal prize money is awarded at the Australian and US Open Championships, but not at the French Open Championship or Wimbledon. For example in Wimbledon 2004 Roger Federer, the Men's Singles Champion, won £602,500 in contrast with Maria Sharapova's prize money of £560,000. For an interview with Billie Jean King on, *inter alia*, the issue of prize money, see *Observer Sport*, 6 July 2003. Also see 'Equal pay champion attacks "sexist" Wimbledon' *The Times*, 27 June 2002 for criticisms by several players and DTI Secretary and Minister for Women, Patricia Hewitt.

An additional two players could be included if they had played in a country for five years uninterruptedly, including three years in junior teams.

Bosman's argument was that this restricts the freedom of movement of players who are EC nationals as clubs with their 'full quota of foreign players' are likely to restrict new contracts to indigenous players. The ECJ agreed with the Opinion of Advocate General Lenz that this offends the rule that all EC nationals must be treated on an equal basis.

As seen above, EU law, in terms of general principle, permits discrimination to be justified. Arguments on this basis were considered and rejected by Advocate-General Lenz.

URBSFA v Jean-Marc Bosman [1996] 1 CMLR (Case C-415/93)

A number of further considerations have been advanced as justification for the rules on foreign players, and these must now be examined. Three groups of arguments can essentially be distinguished. First, it is emphasized that the national aspect plays an important part in football; the identification of the spectators with the various teams is guaranteed only if those teams consist, at least as regards a majority of the players, of nationals of the relevant Member State; moreover, the teams which are successful in the national leagues represent their country in international competitions. Second, it is argued that the rules are necessary to ensure that enough players are available for the relevant national team; without the rules on foreigners, the development of young players would be affected. Third and finally, it is asserted that the rules on foreigners serve the purpose of ensuring a certain balance between the clubs, since otherwise the big clubs would be able to attract the best players.

The arguments in the first group would appear to latch on to the Court's observation in Dona that matches from which foreign players can be excluded must have a special character and context. In this connection the representative ot the German Government spoke with particular emphasis at the hearing before the Court. He asserted that the 'national character of the performance' characterized first division professional football. A glance at the reality of football today shows that that does not correspond to the fact. The vast majority of clubs in the top divisions in the Member States play foreign players. In the German Bundesliga, for example, I am not aware of any club which does without foreign players altogether. If one considers the most successful European clubs of recent years, it becomes clear that nearly all of them have several foreign players in their ranks. In many cases it is precisely the foreign players who have characterized the team in question – one need only recall the AC Milan team in the early 1990s, whose pillars included the Dutch players Gullit, Rijkaard and Van Basten. There may indeed be certain differences from country to country with respect to the playing style or the mentality of players. That has, however, by no means prevented foreign players playing in the national leagues.

Even if the 'national aspect' had the significance which many people attribute to it, however, it could not justify the rules on foreign players. The right to freedom of movement and the prohibition of discrimination against nationals of other Member States are among the fundamental principles of the Community order. The rules on foreign players breach those principles in such a blatant and serious manner that any reference to national interests which cannot be based on Article 48(3) must be regarded as inadmissible as against those principles.

As to the identification of spectators with the teams, there is also no need for extensive discussion to show the weakness of that argument. As the Commission and Mr Bosman have rightly stated, the great majority of a club's supporters are much more interested in the success of their club than in the composition of the team. Nor does the participation of foreign players prevent a team's supporters from identifying with the team. Quite on the contrary, it is not uncommon for those players to attract the admiration and affection of football fans to a special degree. One of the most popular players ever to play for TSV 1860 Munchen was undoubtedly Petar Radenkovic from what was then Yugoslavia. The English international Kevin Keegan was for many years a favourite of the fans at Hamburger SV. The popularity of Eric Cantona at Manchester United and of Jurgen Klinsmann at his former club Tottenham Hotspur is well known.

The inconsistency of those who put forward that view is moreover apparent if one considers an argument advanced by URBSFA in this context. It is argued that since the clubs often bear the name of a town, the spectators should be able to see players of the same nationality in the team in question. However, if a club adopts a name which contains the name of a place, it could at most be expected or demanded that that club's players should come from the place in question. Yet it is a well-known fact that in the case of Bayern Munchen, for instance, only a few of the players come from Bavaria (let alone Munich). If nationals who come from other parts of the relevant State are accepted without question, one cannot see why that should not also be the case for nationals of other Member States.

Finally, it should be observed that the success and playing style of a team are largely determined by the manager. The Court has already held, however, that football trainers enjoy the right to freedom of movement under Article 48. It did not even consider that those persons might perhaps be subject to restrictions other than those expressly permitted by Article 48. In practice frequent use is in fact made of that right. The best-known example is probably FC Barcelona, which has had a Dutch manager for a long time. Hamburger SV achieved its greatest success with an Austrian manager, and Bayern Munchen has had a whole series of foreign managers in recent decades. A country's national team is not always managed by a national of that country either. Thus the manager of the Irish national team, for example, is an Englishman. That emphasizes that a 'national' characterization of football, in the sense that players and managers must be nationals of the country in which the club in question is based, hardly comes into question.

It is further argued that the clubs which are successful in the national leagues represent the Member State in question in the European competitions and must therefore consist of at least a majority of nationals of that State; and that the 'German champions', for example, can thus emerge only from a competition between club teams for which 'at least a minimum number of German players play'. That argument too fails to convince. Firstly, the proponents of that view are unable to explain why precisely the rules currently applied are necessary to ensure that. If what mattered was that a team should consist predominantly of nationals of the State concerned, with eleven players in a team it would suffice generally to allow up to five foreign players. And if only a 'minimum number' of players had to possess the nationality of the State concerned, even more foreign players would have to be allowed. Moreover, it should be observed that the concept of 'German champion' can be interpreted without difficulty in a different way from that sought by the proponents of that view. There is no reason why that term cannot be taken as designating the club which has finished in first place following the matches played in Germany.

The argument fails to convince, however, for another reason too. In Germany, for example, the rules on foreign players do not apply to amateur teams. Some of those teams take part in the cup competition organized by the DFB. It is thus theoretically possible for an amateur team consisting of 11 foreign players to win the DFB cup and thus qualify to enter the European Cup-Winners' Cup. That this is not a purely hypothetical case is shown by the example of the Hertha BSC Berlin amateurs who reached the German cup final in 1993. The weakness of the argument becomes even more apparent if one considers that an association such as Scotland has no rules on foreign players and the other British associations have special rules for their mutual relations. It can thus perfectly well happen that clubs from those associations use a large number of players from other Member States in the leagues and competitions organized by their associations, but are forced to limit the number of such players when they take part in UEFA competitions. I cannot see how in such a case the abovementioned argument could be used to justify professional footballers from the European Community being forbidden to take part in the European Cup competitions.

The arguments in the second group are not convincing either. Nothing has demonstrated that the development of young players in a Member State would be adversely affected if the rule on foreign players were dropped. Only a few top teams set store on promoting their own young players as, for instance, Ajax Amsterdam do. Most talented players, by contrast, make their way upwards via small clubs to which those rules do not apply. Moreover, there is much to support the opinion that the participation of top foreign players promotes the development of football. Early contact with foreign stars 'can only be of advantage to a young player'.

It is admittedly correct that the number of jobs available to native players decreases, the more foreign players are engaged by and play for the clubs. That is, however, a consequence which the right to freedom of movement necessarily entails. Moreover, there is little to suggest that abolition of the rules on foreign players might lead to players possessing the nationality of the relevant State becoming a small minority in a league. The removal of the rules on foreign players would not oblige clubs to engage (more) foreigners, but would give them the possibility of doing so if they thought that promised success.

The argument that the rules on foreign players are needed to ensure that enough players develop for the national team is also unconvincing. Even if that consideration were to be regarded as legitimate in the light of the Court's judgments in Walmve and Dona, it could not justify the rules on foreigners. As I have already mentioned, it is unlikely that the influx of foreign players would be so great that native players would no longer get a chance. It is also significant here that the success or failure of the national team also has an effect on the interest in the club matches of the country in question. Winning the World Cup, for instance, generally brings about increased interest of spectators in national league matches as well. It is therefore in a country's clubs' very own interests to contribute to the success of the national team by developing suitable players and making them available. The prestige which those players acquire in the national team also benefits the clubs as such. Moreover, the example of Scotland may be noted, where the lack of rules on foreign players has plainly not led to a shortage of players for the national team.

Moreover, the national teams of the Member States of the Community nowadays very often include players who carry on their profession abroad, without that causing particular disadvantages. It suffices that the players have to be released for the national team's matches, as is also provided for in the current rules of the associations. The best example is perhaps the Danish national team which won the European Championship in 1992. In the German national team which became world champions in 1990 there were several players who played in foreign leagues. It is therefore not evident that the rules on foreigners are necessary in order to ensure the strength of the national team.

Third and finally, it is argued that the rules on foreign players serve to preserve the balance between clubs. In the opinion of URBSFA, the big clubs would otherwise be able to secure the services of the best players from the entire Community and thereby increase further the economic and sporting distance between them and the other clubs. The interest thus given expression is – as I shall explain later – a legitimate one. Like Mr Bosman however, I am of the opinion that there are other means of attaining that objective without affecting the right of freedom of movement. Moreover, the rules are in any case only to a very limited extent appropriate to ensure a balance between the clubs. The richest clubs are still in a position to afford the best – and thus as a rule the most expensive – foreign stars. At the same time, such clubs have the opportunity to engage the best native players, without any comparable rule setting them limits.

This limb of *Bosman* has generated far-reaching effects in the years since the ruling was delivered. Clubs in European competitions now have a wide number of nationalities to select a team from. There is an obvious interface here with the ongoing relaxation of transfer rules as required first by the *Bosman* ruling and more recently by the European Commission. Indeed the only real restrictions will be derived from a Member State's immigration rules. For example, European footballers, who are not nationals of EU Member States, and players from outside of Europe are still required to be in possession of a work permit if they are to play for a club in the Premier and Football Leagues. Similarly, the regulations of national sporting associations may still impose quotas on the fielding of foreign players.

Welch, R, 'Swamping the British game?: Foreign footballers and the new work permit regulations'

Almost from the date the European Court of Justice gave its historic ruling in the *Bosman* case on 15 December 1995 there has been concern over the number of foreign players playing professional football in the football leagues in England and Scotland. The impact of *Bosman* on this situation is partly the result of the greater mobility that the ruling has given to footballers at the end of their employment contracts. However, it is the second limb of the ruling that has had rather more significance for the increased recruitment of non-British players by domestic clubs. This is because *Bosman* essentially permits clubs to field as many non-British players in any given team as they wish providing those players are nationals of other Member States of the EU and EEA (Liechtenstein, Iceland and Norway). Moreover, freedom of movement, as required by Article 39 of the EC Treaty (formerly Article 48), prohibits Member States from applying their normal immigration rules to players from these countries.

However, of course, EU law does not extend to players from the many high-ranking footballing countries around the globe, and, in the here and now at least, does not apply to European countries outside the EU/EEA. Thus players from these countries may only enter the UK to play for a British club if they have been granted a work permit. The rules concerning work permits were amended by the Government in July 1999 prior to the start of the current season. These changes were immediately criticised for constituting a tightening rather than relaxation of the rules. Thus Gordon Taylor, on behalf of the PFA, stated that the changes 'will open the way for cheap, foreign imports' and Frank Clark, on behalf of the League Managers' Association also expressed concern about 'the number of foreign players currently in the British game.' (See, The Guardian, Saturday July 3 1999) This article will outline the changes that have been made and seek to evaluate arguments for and against the work permit system.

Anyone seeking a work permit in the UK must meet criteria which are issued by the Department for Education and Employment. (The scheme is administered by the DEE's Overseas Labour Service under the Immigration Acts 1971, 1988.) Thus work permit rules apply to all areas of employment including professional sports. There are, for example, rules relating to cricket, ice hockey and rugby that are analogous to the rules governing football.

Prior to July 1999, a foreign footballer would not generally have been eligible for a work permit unless he was an international player who had played for his country's 'A' team for approximately 75% of competitive matches in the previous two seasons. He was also required to be one of the six highest earners for the British club concerned. The work permit only applied to a single season unless an extension was granted on the basis that the player had proven himself to be regular player for the club, and was thus making a significant contribution to the British game. Under the new regulations the wage requirement has gone and work permits apply to the whole of the player's contract. The requirement to be an international player is retained, and the FIFA ranking of the player's national side will now be taken into account. In *R v Secretary of State for Education and Employment ex parte Portsmouth Football Club* [1988] COD 142 it was held that the 75% test must not be applied too rigidly, as, for example, a player having missed international matches through injury should be taken into account. The new rules permit the requisite flexibility through provision of an appeals committee to consider an application where the player does not meet the criteria, but a club has provided evidence that he is of the highest calibre.

In announcing the changes (then) Minister of Sport, Tony Banks, stated: 'The criteria strike a sensible balance between allowing clubs to recruit the best available international talent and the need to provide opportunities for home grown young players.' The Employment and Equal Opportunities Minister, Margaret Hodge, described the new system as 'straightforward, open and transparent' which would 'ensure a faster and fairer application process.' (See DEE press release 307/99)

Since Bosman there has been a 1,800 per cent increase in foreign players in the Premiership. (See, The Guardian, 18 July 1999). As predicted by Gordon Taylor ('The World Cup, foreign players and work permits' 1998 5(4) Sports law Administration & Practice), the 1998 World cup finals has also contributed to this development. However, whether the new rules really represent a relaxation which will generate an even greater number of 'foreign imports' remains debatable. Certainly, the consequences of taking into account the FIFA ranking of a player's national side still need to be fully evaluated. The fact that a permit can now last for the period of a player's contract will make the prospect of playing in the UK more attractive to the overseas player, but then it seems fair and just that if a player is offered and accepts a contract his job security should not be jeopardised by the possibility that a work permit will not be renewed at the end of a given season.

It is contended that the problem with the debate over whether work permit rules should be tightened or relaxed, or as an alternative whether a system of quotas should be introduced, is that it obscures the question as to whether such systems are desirable in the first place. Much attention has been focused on whether the increase in foreigners in the Premiership is deleterious to the international prospects of the English team. The essence of the argument is that fewer Englishmen are able to play club football at the highest level and are forced to ply their trade in the lower divisions. Thus they do not develop the skills required at international level. However, casual observation appears to indicate that a significant number of foreign players currently in the Premiership, probably the majority, come from EU/EEA countries (not to mention other countries in the UK) and thus do not require work permits in the first place.

The increase in players not requiring work permits will be even more significant if the European Court ever rules that Article 39 applies to any country within EU trading areas, and to whose nationals the EU has agreed to extend equal employment rights once they gain employment in an EU member state. There are cases such as *Balog* and most recently *Malaja* (See, The Observer, 6 February 2000) which may well lead to the ECJ making such a ruling. This will extend the nationalities within the scope of Article 39 from 18 to around 40.

Moreover, there is an assumption that arguably the most important group in football, the paying public, collectively prioritise the success of the English team over the success of the club they support week in and week out, and pay good money to watch in all weathers. Speaking for myself, but believing myself to be a typical football fan, it is definitely a case of club over country. Equally, for many football fans (especially for those of us who support lower division clubs) it a pleasure to be able to watch the likes of Emmanuel Petit, David Ginola and Giafranco Zola on a regular basis rather than occasionally during international tournaments.

A political and philosophical objection to work permit rules and quota systems is that they are derived from immigration controls which it is contended – sporting issues aside – are objectively racist. This is so whether we are reflecting on the racist speeches of the likes of Enoch Powell, the infamous 'swamping' comments of Margaret Thatcher which contributed to her winning the 1979 general election or the current controversy over the numbers of asylum seekers 'flooding' into the UK. Moreover, the world of football is not yet totally free from the racism and xenophobic nationalism which has been associated with the game in recent decades. Irrespective of what is intended (and no-one can doubt the commitment of the PFA to combating racism in football) any statements which increase perceptions of foreigners as a problem tend to fan the flames of racism and, in turn, may give credibility to the English 'nationalist' posing as a genuine football fan.

Surely, one of the (few) beneficial consequences of globalisation should be, alongside the already free movement of capital, the free movement of labour throughout the globe. Would this present an insuperable problem for football and other professional sports? I think not. In any case, the best solution to reducing the number of foreigners that clubs are recruiting, as indeed Gordon Taylor has identified, is for clubs to redevelop their youth academies to develop cheap home grown and, indeed, local talent. Much as I love to watch him give me Pompey's own Stevie Claridge over Ginola any day![76]

In the immediate aftermath of *Bosman* the only clear conclusion that could be drawn was that a sports professional, who was an EU national and out of contract, had the right under Art 39 to move to another Member State to play for a new club. However, litigation brought by Balog, a Hungarian footballer, and Malaja, a Polish basketball player, generated speculation and discussion that rights to freedom of movement could be extended beyond EU nationals to nationals of any country with

---

76   Welch, R, 'Swamping the British game?: Foreign footballers and the new work permit regulations' (2000) 3(2) Sports Law Bulletin 6–7.

which the EU had entered into a trading agreement.[77] In fact, the *Balog* case was settled out of court and was thus never put to the ECJ (though the Opinion of Advocate General Stix-Hackle was in Balog's favour on the basis of EU competition law).[78]

The *Malaja* case was resolved by the French domestic courts but provided the basis for the subsequent ECJ ruling in *Kolpak*. This case has clarified that the actual legal position is rather less dramatic than initially anticipated. Essentially, nationals of a number of countries, which have entered into Association Agreements with the EU containing non-discrimination clauses ('Europe Agreements'), must be treated on an equal basis with nationals of the Member State in which they have secured employment. However, the ruling does not give such non-EU nationals the right to enter a Member State or to move from one Member State to another.

The facts of *Malaja* and *Kolpak* are fairly similar. Malaja was a Polish basketball player for the French club, *Racing Club de Strasbourg*, and Kolpak was a Slovakian goalkeeper for the German Handball club, *TSV Ostringen eV Handball*. Both Poland and Slovakia had entered into 'Europe Agreements'. According to the rules of the French Basketball Association, clubs were prevented from fielding more than 2 non-EU nationals. There was a similar rule imposed by the DHB, the German Handball Federation. The *Conseil d'Etat*, the highest administrative court in France, decided in Malaja's favour and thus a reference to the ECJ was not necessary.

The German court, on the other hand, decided to request a preliminary ruling before reaching a decision. The question put to the ECJ was whether, under Art 38 of the Europe Agreement between Slovakia and the EU, Slovakian workers were entitled to general equality of equal treatment with nationals of the relevant Member State. On 8 May 2003, the ECJ ruled in favour of Kolpak and thus, like Malaja, he was entitled to be treated as a national player for the purposes of the sport's rules. In short, he could not be considered ineligible for team selection because there were already two non-EU nationals selected for the game.

Case C-438/00 *Deutscher Handballbund eV v Maros Kolpak* [2003] ECR I-4135

The dispute in the main proceedings and the question submitted for preliminary ruling

Mr Kolpak, who is a Slovak national, entered in March 1997 into a fixed-term employment contract expiring on 30 June 2000 and subsequently, in February 2000, entered into a new fixed-term contract expiring on 30 June 2003 for the post of goalkeeper in the German handball team TSV Ostringen eV Handball, a club which plays in the German Second Division. Mr Kolpak receives a monthly salary. He is resident in Germany and holds a valid residence permit.

The DHB, which organises league and cup matches at federal level, issued to him, under Rule 15 of the SpO, a player's licence marked with the letter A on the ground of his Slovak nationality.

Mr Kolpak, who had requested that he be issued with a player's licence which did not feature the specific reference to nationals of non-member countries, brought an action before the Landgericht (Regional Court) Dortmund (Germany) challenging that decision of the DHB. He argued that the Slovak Republic is one of the non-member countries nationals of which are entitled to participate without restriction in competitions under the same conditions as German and Community players by reason of

---

77 For discussion of the issues surrounding *Balog* and *Malaja* and ongoing developments with respect to freedom of movement see Gardiner, S and Welch, R, 'Show me the money: regulation of the migration of professional sportsmen in post-*Bosman* Europe', pp 107–126, in Caiger, A and Gardiner, S (eds), *Professional Sport in the EU: Regulation and Re-regulation* (2000), The Hague: Asser Press. Also see Gardiner, S, 'Support for quotas in EU professional sport' (2000) 3(2) Sports Law Bulletin 1, 19.

78 See 'Balog: the new *Bosman* case' (2001) 4(3) Sports Law Bulletin 1.

the prohibition of discrimination resulting from the combined provisions of the EC Treaty and the Association Agreement with Slovakia.

The Landgericht ordered the DHB to issue Mr Kolpak with a player's licence not marked with an A on the ground that, under Rule 15 of the SpO, Mr Kolpak was not to be treated in the same way as a player who was a national of a non- member country. The DHB appealed against that decision to the Oberlandesgericht Hamm.

The Oberlandesgericht takes the view that the reference to Article 48 of the EC Treaty (now, after amendment, Article 39 EC) by Rule 15(1)(b) of the SpO must be construed as meaning that this latter provision covers only players who enjoy complete equality of treatment vis-à-vis Community nationals in respect of free movement of workers. According to this interpretation, Mr Kolpak is not entitled to be issued with a licence which does not contain the limitations resulting from the addition of the letter A, as such general equality of treatment does not feature in the association agreements concluded with the countries of Eastern Europe and the Mediterranean Basin, which include the Association Agreement with Slovakia.

... the Oberlandesgericht Hamm has decided to stay the proceedings and to refer the following question to the Court for a preliminary ruling:

> Is it contrary to Article 38(1) of the Europe Agreement establishing an association between the European Communities and their Member States, of the one part, and the Slovak Republic, of the other part – Final Act – if a sports federation applies to a professional sportsman of Slovak nationality a rule that it has adopted under which clubs may field in league and cup matches only a limited number of players who come from countries not belonging to the European Communities?

The question submitted for preliminary ruling

By its question the Oberlandesgericht Hamm is asking, essentially, whether the first indent of Article 38(1) of the Association Agreement with Slovakia is to be construed as precluding the application to a professional sportsman who is a Slovak national and is lawfully employed by a club established in a Member State of a rule drawn up by a sports federation in that State under which clubs are authorised, during league or cup matches, to field only a limited number of players from non-member countries that are not parties to the Agreement on the European Economic Area ('the EEA').

In order to reply to the question, as thus reformulated, it is necessary first of all to examine whether the first indent of Article 38(1) of the Association Agreement with Slovakia can be invoked by an individual before a national court and then, if the answer to that question is in the affirmative, whether that provision can be invoked in regard to a rule drawn up by a national sports federation such as the DHB. Finally, it will be necessary to establish the scope of the principle of non-discrimination which that provision lays down.

The direct effect of the first indent of Article 38(1) of the Association Agreement with Slovakia

It should be noted at the outset that, in paragraph 30 of its judgment in Case *C-162/00* Pokrzeptowicz-Meyer [2002] ECR I-1049, the Court has already recognised the first indent of Article 37(1) of the Europe Agreement establishing an association between the European Communities and their Member States, of the one part, and the Republic of Poland, of the other part, signed in Brussels on 16 December 1991 and approved on behalf of the Communities by Decision *93/743/Euratom*, ECSC, EC of the Council and the Commission of 13 December 1993 (OJ 1993 L 348, p 1) ('the Association Agreement with Poland'), as having direct effect.

It is to be observed, first, that the wording of the first indent of Article 38(1) of the Association Agreement with Slovakia and that of the first indent of Article 37(1) of the Association Agreement with Poland is identical.

Second, those two Association Agreements do not differ in regard to their objectives or the context in which they were adopted. Each has, according to the final recital in the preamble and Article 1(2), the aim, inter alia, of establishing an association to promote the expansion of trade and harmonious economic relations between the contracting parties so as to foster dynamic economic development and prosperity in the Slovak Republic and in the Republic of Poland respectively, in order to facilitate those countries' accession to the Communities.

That being so, just as Article 58(1) of the Association Agreement with Poland does not preclude the first indent of Article 37(1) of that Agreement from having direct effect (see Pokrzeptowicz-Meyer, cited above, paragraph 28), so Article 59(1) of the Association Agreement with Slovakia does not preclude the first indent of Article 38(1) of that Agreement from having direct effect, given the similarity of the provisions in question.

Furthermore, as with the first indent of Article 37(1) of the Association Agreement with Poland, implementation of the first indent of Article 38(1) of the Association Agreement with Slovakia is not subject to the adoption by the Association Council, set up by that Agreement, of additional measures to define the detailed rules governing its application (Pokrzeptowicz-Meyer, paragraph 29).

Finally, just as in the case of Article 37(1) of the Association Agreement with Poland, the words '[s]ubject to the conditions and modalities applicable in each Member State' in Article 38(1) of the Association Agreement with Slovakia cannot be interpreted in such a way as to allow Member States to make the application of the principle of non-discrimination set out in that provision subject to conditions or discretionary limitations inasmuch as such an interpretation would render that provision meaningless and deprive it of any practical effect (Pokrzeptowicz-Meyer, paragraphs 20 to 24).

In those circumstances, the first indent of Article 38(1) of the Association Agreement with Slovakia must be recognised as having direct effect, with the result that Slovak nationals who invoke it are entitled to rely on it before national courts of the host Member State.

The question whether the first indent of Article 38(1) of the Association Agreement with Slovakia applies to a rule laid down by a sports federation

As a preliminary point, it should be observed that, in regard to Article 48(2) of the Treaty, it follows from paragraph 87 of the Court's judgment in Case C-415/93 Bosman [1995] ECR I-4921 that the prohibition of discrimination laid down in that provision applies to rules laid down by sporting associations which determine the conditions under which professional sportsmen can engage in gainful employment.

In that connection, the Court pointed out, in paragraph 84 of Bosman, cited above, that working conditions in the different Member States are governed sometimes by provisions laid down by law or regulation and sometimes by agreements and other acts concluded or adopted by private persons, and that, if the scope of Article 48 of the Treaty were to be confined to acts of a public authority, there would therefore be a risk of creating inequality in its application.

With regard to the first indent of Article 38(1) of the Association Agreement with Slovakia, in order to determine whether that provision applies to a rule drawn up by a sports federation such as the DHB, it is necessary to examine whether the Court's interpretation of Article 48(2) of the Treaty may be transposed in this case to the above provision of the Association Agreement with Slovakia.

The Court has stated in this regard, in paragraphs 39 and 40 of Pokrzeptowicz-Meyer, that, although the first indent of Article 37(1) of the Association Agreement with Poland does not lay down a principle of free movement for Polish workers within the Community, whereas Article 48 of the Treaty establishes for the benefit of Member State nationals the principle of free movement for workers, it follows from a comparison of the aims and context of the Association Agreement with Poland, on the one hand, with those of the EC Treaty, on the other hand, that there is no ground for giving to the first indent of Article 37(1) of that Association Agreement a scope different from that which the Court has recognised Article 48(2) of the Treaty as having.

In that context, the Court stated in paragraph 41 of Pokrzeptowicz-Meyer that the first indent of Article 37(1) of the Association Agreement with Poland establishes, in favour of workers of Polish nationality, once they are lawfully employed within the territory of a Member State, a right to equal treatment as regards conditions of employment of the same extent as that conferred in similar terms by Article 48(2) of the Treaty on Member State nationals.

It follows from the foregoing and from the reasoning set out in paragraphs 25 to 30 of this judgment that the interpretation of Article 48(2) of the Treaty adopted by the Court in Bosman and referred to in paragraphs 31 and 32 of the present judgment may be transposed to the first indent of Article 38(1) of the Association Agreement with Slovakia. That being so, it must be concluded that the first indent of Article 38(1) of the Association Agreement with Slovakia applies to a rule drawn up by a sports federation such as the DHB which determines the conditions under which professional sportsmen engage in gainful employment.

The scope of the principle of non-discrimination set out in the first indent of Article 38(1) of the Association Agreement with Slovakia

According to the DHB and the Greek, Spanish and Italian Governments, the scope of the non-discrimination clause contained in Article 38 of the Association Agreement with Slovakia is not intended to place on an entirely equal footing workers who are nationals of the Slovak Republic and workers who are nationals of the Member States of the European Union. The free movement of workers provided for in Article 48 of the Treaty, as applied within the area of sport by the Bosman judgment, can, they argue, benefit only Community nationals or nationals of an EEA Member State.

Furthermore, all the parties which submitted observations to the Court agree that the prohibition of discrimination on grounds of nationality, set out in the first indent of Article 38(1) of the Association Agreement with Slovakia, applies only to workers of Slovak nationality who are already lawfully employed in the territory of a Member State and solely with regard to conditions of work, remuneration or dismissal.

On this point, the DHB and the Greek, Spanish and Italian Governments argue that the rule contained in Rule 15(1)(b) and 15(2) of the SpO relates to access of Slovak nationals to employment. Article 38(1) of the Association Agreement with Slovakia, they submit, cannot therefore preclude the application of such a rule.

Against this, Mr Kolpak, the German Government and the Commission submit that the facts in point in the main proceedings come within the first indent of Article 38(1) of the Association Agreement with Slovakia inasmuch as Mr Kolpak is not seeking access to the German labour market but is already lawfully working in Germany pursuant to domestic law and is suffering, in that connection, discrimination in working conditions by reason of the SpO.

In that regard, it must be observed, first, that, according to the wording of the first indent of Article 38(1) of the Association Agreement with Slovakia, the prohibition of discrimination on grounds of nationality laid down in that provision applies only to workers of Slovak nationality who are already lawfully employed in the territory of a Member State and solely with regard to conditions of work, remuneration or dismissal. In contrast to Article 48 of the Treaty, that provision does not therefore extend to national rules concerning access to the labour market.

According to the order for reference, Mr Kolpak is lawfully employed as a goalkeeper under a contract of employment signed with a second-division German club, has a valid residence permit and does not, under national law, require a work permit in order to exercise his profession. It thus appears that he has already had lawful access to the labour market in Germany.

In that context, with more particular regard to the question whether a rule such as that laid down in Rule 15(1)(b) and 15(2) of the SpO constitutes a working condition, it is necessary to point out that, in Bosman, the dispute in the main proceedings related to, inter alia, similar nationality rules or clauses drawn up by the Union of European Football Associations (UEFA).

It follows from paragraph 120 of the judgment in Bosman that clauses of that kind concern not the employment of professional players, on which there is no restriction, but the extent to which their clubs may field them in official matches, and that participation in such matches is the essential purpose of their activity.

It follows that a sports rule such as that in issue in the main proceedings relates to working conditions within the meaning of the first indent of Article 38(1) of the Association Agreement with Slovakia inasmuch as it directly affects participation in league and cup matches of a Slovak professional player who is already lawfully employed under the national provisions of the host Member State.

That being so, in order to establish whether the first indent of Article 38(1) of the Association Agreement with Slovakia precludes the application of a rule such as that laid down in Rule 15(1)(b) and 15(2) of the SpO, it remains to determine whether that rule involves discrimination prohibited by that provision of the Association Agreement.

In that regard, it must be observed, first, that, so far as Article 48(2) of the Treaty is concerned, it follows from paragraph 137 of Bosman that that provision precludes the application of rules laid down by sporting associations under which, in competition matches which they organise, football clubs may field only a limited number of professional players who are nationals of other Member States.

With regard to the interpretation of the first indent of Article 38(1) of the Association Agreement with Slovakia, it follows from paragraphs 25 to 30, 34, 35 and 44 of the present judgment that that provision introduces for the benefit of workers of Slovak nationality, on condition that they are lawfully employed in the territory of a Member State, a right to equal treatment as regards working conditions having the same scope as that which, in similar terms, nationals of the Member States are recognised as having by virtue of Article 48(2) of the Treaty, and that the rule in issue in the case in the main proceedings is similar to the nationality clauses in point in Bosman.

That being so, the interpretation of Article 48(2) of the Treaty applied by the Court in Bosman and set out in paragraph 48 of the present judgment can be transposed to the first indent of Article 38(1) of the Association Agreement with Slovakia.

Thus, the first indent of Article 38(1) of the Association Agreement with Slovakia precludes any application to Mr Kolpak of a rule such as that laid down in Rule 15(1)(b) and 15(2) of the SpO in so far as that rule gives rise to a situation in which Mr Kolpak, in his capacity as a Slovak national, although lawfully employed in a Member State, has, in principle, merely a limited opportunity, in comparison with players who are nationals of Member States or of EEA Member States, to participate in certain matches, that is to say, league and cup matches of the German federal or regional leagues, which constitute, moreover, the essential purpose of his activity as a professional player.

That interpretation cannot be called in question by the DHB's argument that the rule laid down in Rule 15(1)(b) and 15(2) of the SpO is justified on exclusively sporting grounds, as its purpose is to safeguard training organised for the benefit of young players of German nationality and to promote the German national team.

Admittedly, in paragraph 127 of Bosman, the Court pointed out that, in paragraphs 14 and 15 of its judgment in Case *13/76 Dona v Mantero* [1976] ECR 1333, it had recognised that the Treaty provisions on the free movement of persons do not preclude rules or practices excluding foreign players from certain matches for reasons which are not economic in nature, which relate to the particular nature and context of such matches and are thus of sporting interest only, such as matches between national teams from different countries.

In paragraph 128 of Bosman, however, the Court stated that nationality clauses do not concern specific matches between teams representing their countries but apply to all official matches between clubs and thus to the essence of the activity of professional players.

In that context, the Court pointed out that a football club's links with the Member State in which it is established cannot be regarded as any more inherent in its sporting activity than are its links with its locality, town or region. Even though national championships are played between clubs from different regions, towns or localities, there is no rule restricting the right of clubs to field players from other regions, towns or localities in such matches. Moreover, in international competitions participation is limited to clubs which have achieved certain sporting results in their respective countries, without any particular significance being attached to the nationalities of their players (Bosman, paragraphs 131 and 132).

Regard being had to that case-law, the discrimination arising in the present case from Rule 15(1)(b) and 15(2) of the SpO cannot be regarded as justified on exclusively sporting grounds inasmuch as it follows from those rules that, during matches organised by the DHB, clubs are free to field an unlimited number of nationals of EEA Member States.

Furthermore, no other argument capable of providing objective justification for the difference in treatment between, on the one hand, professional players who are nationals of a Member State or of an EEA Member State and, on the other, professional players who are Slovak nationals, resulting from Rule 15(1)(b) and 15(2) of the SpO and affecting the working conditions of the latter, has been put forward in the observations submitted to the Court . . .

Ruling

The first indent of Article 38(1) of the Europe Agreement establishing an association between the European Communities and their Member States, of the one part, and the Slovak Republic, of the other part . . . must be construed as precluding the application to a professional sportsman of Slovak nationality, who is lawfully employed by a club established in a Member State, of a rule drawn up by a sports federation in that State under which clubs are authorised to field, during league or cup matches, only a limited number of players from non-member countries that are not parties to the Agreement on the European Economic Area.

This ruling, explicitly based on the reasoning in *Bosman*, establishes that Articles in Europe Agreements, conferring individual rights, may take direct effect in the same way as Art 39 0f the EC Treaty. Therefore, once nationals of a relevant associate country[79] have secured work in a particular Member State they must be treated in the same way as nationals of that state. Thus quota restrictions on 'foreign players' will not apply to them as such restrictions constitute 'working conditions' for the purposes of non-discrimination clauses in relevant Europe agreements.

However, the ruling in *Kolpak* has not generated the more radical changes first anticipated when Tibor Balog initiated his legal action. In particular, Art 39 of the EC Treaty is inapplicable to the nationals of associate countries, and thus a transfer to a club in another Member State will still be subject to that State's immigration rules. Indeed, it remains to be seen whether national laws requiring work permits, on the expiry of a non-national's contract, still apply to nationals of countries with associate status. Presumably, this may well be the case given that full freedom of movement, and rights to remain in a Member State, are not guaranteed to the nationals of eight out of the ten new Member States until 2009.[80] Indeed, the significance of *Kolpak* is further limited by the enlargement of the EU, which took place on 1 May 2004, in that the number of relevant associate countries is reduced to seven.

---

79 In addition to the ten new Member States the *Kolpak* ruling applies to nationals from Algeria, Bulgaria, Croatia, Morocco, Romania, Tunisia and Turkey. *Kolpak* does not apply to other countries with some degree of associate status. Significantly, in the context of professional sport, these countries include Georgia, Russia and Ukraine.

80 Nationals of Cyprus and Malta have full freedom of movement. However, transitional arrangements restricting freedom of movement for nationals of the Czech Republic, Estonia, Latvia, Lithuania, Hungary, Poland, Slovenia and Slovakia can be applied as of right until 2006 and extended on notification to the European Commission for a further three years.

Arguably, it is disappointing that the ECJ has not in *Kolpak* delivered a ruling of the historic proportions of *Bosman*, but this was in hindsight unlikely given the negotiations on the enlargement of the EU and the consequent discretion given to Member States to restrict freedom of movement rights they grant to the new EU nationals. In what for the time being is thus a two-tier EU, it seems that for example nationals from non-EU States such as Croatia and Turkey will still be fully subject to national immigration controls and work permit rules. Nevertheless, despite enlargement, *Kolpak* is not without practical significance given that there is a strong correlation between Member States that have quotas on foreign players and Member States that have not as yet extended full rights under Art 39 to the new EU nationals.[81] It is unlikely in the short term that work permit rules for professional sports participants will be further relaxed, let alone abolished. Nevertheless, the ability of clubs, situated in the UK and other Member States, to recruit players from a variety of nationalities in the knowledge that a player has the right to be selected in the same way as an EU national, even if they do not have the same rights of entry to the country concerned, will further develop the fielding of multi-national teams that the *Bosman* ruling effectively initiated.

KEY SOURCES

Carrington, B and McDonald, I (eds), *'Race', Sport and British Society* (2001), London: Routledge.

McArdle, D, *From Boot Money to Bosman: Football, Society and the Law* (2000), London: Cavendish.

Opinion of Advocate General Lenz in *ASBL Union Royale Belge des Societes de Football Association & others v Jean-Marc Bosman* [1996] 1 CMLR 645 (Case C-415/93).

Hendrickx, F, 'The European non-EU Player and the *Kolpak* case' (2003/2) The International Sports Law Journal, 12–15.

IDS Handbooks on *Race and Religion Discrimination* and *Sexual Orientation Discrimination* (2004), London: Incomes Data Services Ltd.

---

81 At the time of writing only Britain and Ireland had announced that there would be no restrictions on freedom of movement (other than in relation to some social security benefits) accorded to new EU nationals. Sporting associations in these countries do not generally impose rules restricting the selection of non-EU nationals, though the Scottish FA only permits a club to have two non-EU players.

SAFETY IN SPORT: LEGAL ISSUES

CHAPTER 15

THE CRIMINAL LAW AND PARTICIPATOR VIOLENCE

INTRODUCTION

One of the more controversial examples of the juridification of sports has occurred in respect of the punishment of participator violence. Where once this was the domain of the governing body, its referees and disciplinary tribunal, the criminal law is now also being turned to by those who believe that a more stringent penalty should be imposed upon those who cause injury during the course of play. Sports participants are no longer prepared to accept that all of their injuries are necessarily an integral and inevitable part of the playing of sport. Where the perpetrator is at fault, they expect to see some form of punishment imposed by either the governing body or, with increasing regularity, the criminal law.

In this chapter, the criminalising of participator violence will be examined. The criminal process, offences committed, possible defences and the potential outcomes of the litigation will be explained to show how the criminal law operates in sports. However, the imposition of criminal liability on sports participants will also be questioned throughout to demonstrate the problems inherent in the use of the criminal law as a control mechanism for participator violence and how the law may evolve in the future.

CONTROLLING PARTICIPATOR VIOLENCE BY THE CRIMINAL LAW

It has been suggested that today's sports are more violent than those of the past and that for this reason there is a more urgent need for legal control than at any previous time.[1] Statistics show the increased number of appearances before disciplinary tribunals, the high incidence of career ending injuries or even the increase in litigation between sports participants. However, these statistics can also be used to show that the game is better regulated and safer to play than in the past. The increase in disciplinary tribunal activity can be ascribed to changes in the playing and safety rules of sports and stricter interpretations and applications of existing laws by referees and other officials, rather than a simple increase in foul play. Players are penalised more frequently for technical offences, whilst all forms of violence are punished more severely. For example in football, tackles from behind have been punished more seriously since the 1994 World Cup, as injury is more likely to occur from this kind of challenge. In rugby union the deliberate collapsing of scrums now results in an award of either a penalty or a penalty try.[2] The constant changing of the rules relating to bouncers and beamers has been a feature of the administration of cricket for the last 80 years. These rule changes and their stricter enforcement have made the games safer but have increased the likelihood of disciplinary action for players who transgress them.

The increase in the number of career ending injuries could also have a more innocent explanation. Modern players are bigger, faster, better trained and play more frequently than in the past. By the very nature of some contact sports, incidental injuries will be more serious than before. Although the

---

1   Grayson, E, *Sport and the Law* (1999), 3rd edn, London: Butterworths, Chapter 6 and Appendix 9.
2   Rule 26(3)(h).

statistics can lead to the inference that there is more foul play, it is possibly closer to the truth to say that dangerous play is being more harshly treated by referees and governing bodies, even if their motives are not always simply to protect those who play their sports.

The juridification of sport is occurring at a time when there is a greater knowledge and use of legal rights amongst the public in general.[3] However, where participator violence is concerned there is much debate over whether such legal regulation should be increased. On one side, the interventionists demand for the greater use of the criminal law to ensure that sport does not become even more violent and can instead be returned to being an activity of fair play and fun.[4] This argument culminates in the proposal of specific legislation, a Safety of Sports Persons Act, to outlaw all forms of violence in sports.[5]

The opposite argument prefers the ideal of self-regulation of a sport by its governing body. The disciplinary tribunal would be the sole arbiter of on-field misconduct, imposing fines and playing bans in lieu of criminal sanctions.[6] This allows the matter to be kept 'in-house' and is the preferred option of most players and governing bodies. A middle line can also be put forward, whereby greater self-regulation is encouraged alongside a more defined role for the criminal law. This would ensure that the majority of sports injuries were dealt with by the governing body but those that were truly criminal would be treated as such. Each of these views is valid and will be discussed further throughout the chapter.

Looking back to bygone eras or analysing injury statistics offers little practical assistance. Participator violence can only be put into perspective by looking at a particular sport in the context of contemporary society and deciding whether what occurs during a game is an acceptable way of playing it. If it is, from both a player's and society's point of view, then there is no problem. If either the participants or society believe that the level of violence in a sport is becoming unacceptable, then some form of regulation is necessary. The difficult task is to delineate the appropriate jurisdictions of sport and the law. What cannot be denied is that the criminal law is being used more frequently to punish participator violence than at any previous time.

What is Participator Violence?

Violence is a term that has a widely understood meaning that has little in common with the criminal law offences of assault. The difficulty here is in using a term that has a culturally accepted though ambiguous meaning on the one hand yet requires a specific definition in the criminal law. The term 'participator violence' has been chosen instead of the more generic concept of sports violence. This distinguishes between three very different types of violence associated with sport; participator violence, spectator violence and violence committed by participants that is not connected with the actual playing of the sport. This latter category would include incidents of domestic violence, sexual assault or any other assault not associated with the playing of the game. Spectator violence is a more

---

3   See earlier, p 84.

4   Grayson, E, 'On the field of play' [1971] NLJ 413 and, with Bond, C, 'Making foul play a crime' (1993) Solicitors Journal 693.

5   For a history of the development of this proposal and its full text, see *op cit*, fn 1, Grayson (1999), Appendix 6.

6   This viewpoint is typified by the following articles of Gardiner, S, 'Not playing the game: is it a crime?' (1993) Solicitors Journal 628; 'The law and the sports field' [1994] Crim LR 513; with Felix, A, '*Elliott v Saunders*: drama in court 14' (1994) 2(2) Sport and the Law Journal 1; 'Juridification of the football field: strategies for giving law the elbow' (1995) 5(2) Marquette Sports LJ 189; and with James, M, 'Touchlines and guidelines: the Lord Advocate's response to sports field violence' [1997] Crim LR 41.

culturally neutral description of what is more commonly referred to as hooliganism.[7] Participator violence extends only to injury-causing incidents that occur between co-participants during the course of the game.

When describing offences against the person, the criminal law does not explicitly recognise the concept of violence. Violent conduct is defined more specifically by making reference to unlawful touchings, or the threat thereof and the degree of bodily harm or injury that is inflicted on a victim.[8] 'Violence' as it is more widely understood can, therefore, encompass the assaults and batteries described by the existing criminal law and the more general academic and popular commentaries on the subject.

The common theme in discussions of violence is that there must be an assault of another person and an intention to cause that other injury. However, this is too narrow for a full discussion of this topic as it does not encompass the range of injury-causing conduct that can occur in contact sports, nor that which is recognised by the law. Participator violence must include, therefore, the intentional, reckless or negligent touching by one sports participant of another, which causes personal injury to that other and occurs during the course of participation in a sport.

This definition includes the three legally recognised categories of culpability; intention, recklessness and negligence. Although wide, and including both criminal and tortious harm, this definition allows for a full analysis of where the line between the criminal regulation and self-regulation of participator violence should be drawn and the extent to which players ought to be allowed to consent to injury.

The Relevance of the Rules of the Game

Obeying the rules is an integral part of playing any sport.[9] Once all participants agree to be bound by the constitutive rules of the game a contest can take place. In most cases, an accidental or unintentional rule violation will be punished adequately by the game's own disciplinary system to correct the lack of skill of the player. However, a player performing intentional rule violations cannot truly be said to be playing the game.

Simon, RL, *Fair Play*

As cheaters make moves not recognised by the constitutive rules of the sport, not only do they fail to prove themselves better players than their fellow competitors but they have not even succeeded in playing the game in the first place.[10]

To cheat is to cease to compete; it is not logically possible to compete within the rules of the game and to breach them intentionally and still be considered to be playing the sport.[11] It might be thought logical that if a participant is playing a sport within its rules, then they ought not to be guilty of an assault if they cause injury to another player. However, the rules of a game are not determinative of criminal liability by themselves. The legal standing of the informal rules of a game, its playing

---

7   See later, Chapter 17.
8   See later, p 598.
9   See further Morgan, W and Meier, K (eds), *Philosophic Inquiry in Sport*, 2nd edn (1995), Leeds: Human Kinetics, Chs 18–26 and Fraleigh, W, *Right Actions in Sport* (1984), Leeds: Human Kinetics, Ch 5.
10 *Fair Play: Sports Values and Society* (1991), Boulder, CO: Westview, p 15.
11 Delattre, E, 'Some reflections on success and failure in competitive athletics' (1975) 2 Journal of Philosophy of Sport 136.

culture, have not yet been fully explored.[12] However, playing by the rules is not proof of innocence, nor is committing a foul proof of guilt.

R v Bradshaw (1878) 14 Cox CC 83

During a football match, the defendant had charged the deceased after the ball had been played. The deceased died from the internal injuries caused from the defendant's knees catching him in the stomach and rupturing his intestines. The judge directed the jury that,

> The question for you to decide is whether the death of the deceased was caused by the unlawful act of the prisoner. There is no doubt that the prisoner's act caused the death and the question is whether the act was unlawful. *No rules or practice of any game whatever can make that lawful which is unlawful by the law of the land; and the law of the land says that you shall not do that which is likely to cause the death of another.* For instance, no persons can by agreement go out and fight with deadly weapons, doing by agreement what the law says shall not be done and thus shelter themselves from the consequences of their acts. Therefore in one way you need not concern yourselves with the rules of football. But on the other hand if a man is playing according to the rules and practice of the game and not going beyond it, it may be reasonable to infer that he is not actuated by any malicious motive or intention and that he is not acting in a manner which he knows will be likely to be productive of death or injury. But independent of the rules, if the prisoner intended to cause serious hurt to the deceased or if he knew that, in charging as he did, he might produce serious injury and was indifferent and reckless as to whether he would produce serious injury or not, then the act would be unlawful. In either case he would be guilty of a criminal act and you must find him guilty; if you are of the contrary opinion, you will acquit him.

The verdict was not guilty.[13]

Thus, the rules of a game are not conclusive when considering the legality of an act. They are instead an evidential tool to be used as a gauge for assessing the mental state, or *mens rea*, of a perpetrator of participator violence. A jury can infer more easily that a player who was playing within the rules and practices of a sport did not inflict criminal injuries on an opponent but was in fact trying to play the game by making or attempting a legitimate tackle. Alternatively, if an incident was clearly in breach of the rules of the game, then it is easier for the finder of fact to infer that there was some degree of culpability on the part of the perpetrator, for example, where a player is attacked off-the-ball. Where the injuries are inflicted with the requisite *mens rea*, an assault crime has been committed.

This case is the starting point for any discussion of the application of English criminal law to sport. It explains the legal relevance of playing by the rules and emphasises that unless consent can be pleaded successfully by a defendant he will be guilty of an assault. This approach is in sharp contrast to that of the United States of America, where the opposite conclusion was reached by the New York Court of Appeal.

People v Fitzsimmons (1895) 34 NYS 1102

The defendant killed his opponent by a punch thrown during a boxing exhibition match. In directing the jury on a charge of homicide, the judge stated that,

> If the rules of the game and the practices of the game are reasonable, are consented to by all engaged, are not likely to induce serious injury, or to end life, if then, as a result of the game, an accident happens, it is excusable homicide.

The punch was found to be within the rules of boxing and that those rules were reasonable and therefore lawful. The Defendant was found not guilty.

---

12 See later, p 606.
13 *Per* Bramwell LJ (emphasis added).

Although a similar outcome would be reached in most cases using either the American or the British formula, the emphasis of the law is very different. The American courts have concentrated on the reasonableness of the sport and whether the defendant was playing according to its rules and practices. Consent extends to any act that is within the rules and practices, or playing culture, of the sport in question provided that they are reasonable. The assumption is that injuries caused whilst playing sport are legal and that the only acts that are unreasonable are assaults which occur behind the play.[14] In English law, it is assumed that an injury-causing challenge will be criminal if the requisite *mens rea* is present. Although consent can operate to negate criminal liability in most cases where the rules are adhered to, this is not automatic, as it is in America.

Why Participator Violence Needs Controlling

It is an integral part of contact sports that participants will be exposed to a degree of interpersonal contact beyond that which occurs in most other activities in life. It is also widely appreciated by those who play sport that these inherent contacts may from time to time cause incidental injuries. These injuries are as much a part of sport as the challenges which cause them. However, the use of an unlimited degree of force and the deliberate infliction of injury is not permitted by either the law or the rules of most contact sports. The most compelling justification for controlling participator violence is that it is contrary to the rules of non-combat contact sports and therefore cheating. The law operates to protect those playing sport from prosecution because participation in sports is seen as being in the public interest for promoting health, discipline and competition.[15] Where play is outside of the rules, and therefore cheating, the sports exemption loses its basis. Where this type of play is not sufficiently controlled by the relevant sports body, the criminal law can be resorted to, ensuring a more stringent penalty is imposed. However, this is not the only reason for resorting to the criminal law.

Player Protection

The aim of the law of assaults is to protect people from being caused unnecessary harm and to deter others from causing criminal injury in the future.[16] The constitutive rules of most sports contain a variety of safety rules to ensure the players are not caused injury. When sports participants go beyond the accepted playing culture of a sport to cause injury to a co-participant, the criminal law operates as the ultimate sanction.[17] Sport should not be a licence to thuggery.[18] In these circumstances, the law has both an actual and a symbolic role to play; to punish those who cause injury and to be seen to be enforcing the aims of the criminal law.

Fair Play and Discipline

One of the most long standing and often quoted justifications for the continued special status of sport in society is that it instils in its participants a number of virtues which society holds to be important. Over 200 years ago, Sir Michael Foster explained that lawful sports should have a special legal status

---

14   Horrow, R, *Sports Violence* (1980), Arlington VA: Carrollton.
15   *Attorney-General's Reference (No 6 of 1980)* [1981] QB 715.
16   For further discussion, see Herring, J, *Criminal Law* (2004), Oxford: OUP, Ch 1.
17   *R v Billinghurst* [1978] Crim LR 553 and further, below.
18   *R v Lloyd* (1989) 11 Cr App R (S) 36.

in relation to the law of offences against the person because they were 'manly diversions' that were supposed to 'give strength, skill and activity and may fit people for defence, public as well as personal, in times of need'.[19] Additional virtues attributable to sports participation are fair play, better health and discipline. The improving of a person's discipline is often used to explain why participation in sport, and especially boxing, should be encouraged amongst young people. The training regime and ethos of sport encourage a healthy and disciplined approach to life as a whole, not just sport.[20] If participator violence is allowed to flourish then these basic ideals of sport are undermined and the public interest in protecting sports participants from the criminal law disappears. Violent conduct that goes beyond how the game should be played cannot be described as fair but is more closely associated with cheating and dishonesty. The criminal law can therefore be utilised to ensure that these justifications for sport's special status are preserved for the benefit of the participants.

Bringing the Game into Disrepute?

The symbiotic relationship between modern sport and commerce has led to many governing bodies promoting their sport as healthy pastimes. Their need is to avoid being perceived as violent for fear of losing future players and potential sponsors. The growth in the use of fair play charters or codes of conduct in recent years has seen many sports try to seize the initiative in the regulation of participator violence and during the game cheating.[21] Accompanying rule changes and awards for compliance have reinforced the need for participants, teams and their spectators to behave in a sporting way. These initiatives can help to demarcate more effectively the respective jurisdictions of the governing body and the State. If the players do not conform to the rules and codes of conduct of their sport, then this behaviour may be appropriate for criminal sanction. These codes are also used to control the 'win at all costs' mentality of some participants. By reinforcing the values of sport acknowledged by the law as being in the public interest, it again becomes easier to identify the behaviour suitable for criminal sanction. In sports where these regimens have not been implemented, or where the codes or charters contain only broad manifesto ideals and insufficient punishment to act as a deterrent,[22] then once again the criminal law can be used to restrain the behaviour in place of the governing body.

To ensure that sport continues to be played in a socially acceptable way, the players must ensure that the game is played in accordance with the values that make sports participation in the public interest. If these values are ignored, society will utilise its own regulatory mechanisms to ensure that the games are played in a socially acceptable way. The criminal law can be used to reinforce the inherent values of sports participation and promote these activities as being in the public interest.

Co-operation and Education

Finally, the threat of the use of the criminal law may force governing bodies and law enforcement agencies to work more closely together to control participator violence rather than be at odds with each other as is seemingly the case at present. This could prevent another *Bosman*-type[23] situation

---

19   *Crown Law* (1792), 3rd edn, p 260.

20   Gunn, M and Omerod, D, 'The legality of boxing' (1995) 15(2) Legal Studies 192 and below, p 620.

21   See, for example, the FIFA Fair Play Charter, www.fifa.com

22   James, M, 'Virtually foul or virtually fair? FIFA, fair play, fouling and football games', SLSA Conference Paper, Bristol 2001.

23   [1996] CMLR 645.

from occurring where the law was imposed on sport without proper consultation and discussion. If sport takes some action to obviate the need for recourse to the criminal law, participator violence could be controlled by self-regulation.

Alongside this, the law could be seen as having an educating effect on sports participants. The law would set the parameters within which a sport ought to be played. The governing bodies and participants themselves could then address the issues internally and eventually avoid the necessity of drawn out and damaging legal actions. The criminal law would be used initially as a control mechanism but in time would be reduced to having an educating influence on self-regulating sports.

Thus, participator violence in sport must be controlled for both sporting and legal reasons. On the one hand, it must be controlled to protect the integrity of sport itself and on the other it is in the public interest that it be controlled by the law to reduce the number and severity of the injuries caused. More effective self-regulation may eventually make recourse to the criminal law unnecessary; however, in the meantime it is a serious alternative control mechanism to sports rules and the governing bodies' disciplinary tribunals.

THE CRIMINAL LAW

When controlling acts of participator violence, the criminal law has the same aims as when it seeks to control all other forms of violence; to protect the individual from harm, to uphold the values of society and to punish offenders in a way which will deter them and others from following a similar course of conduct in the future.[24] Where participator violence is concerned, the potential for provoking crowd disturbance is also taken into consideration. Where this latter is a possibility, players can be bound over to keep the peace as a means of controlling their future behaviour. It is not just the effect on other participants that is taken into consideration, but the effect of the incident on society as a whole.

The criminal law also purportedly aims at producing a consistent approach to acts of violence in all walks of life. The criminal law is supposed to treat all assaults in the same manner, whether they are committed on the field of play or in the street. However, as will be seen, this aim is rarely fulfilled where participator violence is concerned.[25]

Breach of the Peace

A breach of the peace occurs where there is a threat to a person or his property.[26] The powers arise under s 115 of the Magistrates' Courts Act 1980 and the Justices of the Peace Act 1361. After hearing a complaint, the magistrates can bind over the defendant to keep the peace. A bind over is a promise of future good behaviour. A surety is paid into court either by the defendant, or on his behalf, where it is held for a specified period of time. If during that time the terms of the bind over are breached, either the surety is lost or the defendant can be sent to prison or both.

---

24 See further, Herring, J, *Criminal Law: Text & Materials* (2004), Oxford: OUP, Chapter 1.
25 For more detail on the law of assaults generally, see Herring, J, *ibid*, Chapter 9.
26 *R v Howell* (1982) 73 Cr App R 31. See also *R v Coney* (1882) 8 QBD 534, below p 621.

Butcher v Jessop 1989 SLT 593

Three professional footballers became involved in a goalmouth fight during Glasgow Rangers FC v Glasgow Celtic FC Scottish Premier Division match. Two were from the Rangers team, the other from Celtic. The fight took place in front of the end containing the Celtic supporters. No injuries were inflicted. Held, *inter alia;* that because of the history of sectarian violence between the rival fans (Rangers and Celtic are traditionally Glasgow's Protestant and Catholic teams respectively), the players' behaviour was likely to cause a serious breach of the peace in the form of crowd disturbance. One of the players was bound over.

Breach of the peace is very rarely used to control participator violence. It is unlikely to be used unless there are spectators present who are likely to react violently to the incident. Where they are not present the incident will usually be considered too trivial for legal intervention. Where injury is incurred, then one of the more serious aggravated assault offences is the more likely and appropriate charge.

Common Assault

Common assault is a common law offence which, according to s 39 of the Criminal Justice Act 1988, is a summary offence triable only in the Magistrates Courts. The offence has two forms; a technical assault and a battery. Assault is an act that causes the victim to apprehend the immediate infliction of unlawful personal force, that is, the threat of violence. Battery is the actual infliction of unlawful force to the body of another, that is, the use of violence.[27] Common assault is charged where little or no harm is caused to the victim. Thus, it is rarely used to control participator violence as such incidents will normally be controlled by the sport's playing or disciplinary rules and will have been consented to.

Despite its lack of use, it is important to understand the definition of common assault as it forms the basis for the aggravated assaults that are more usually charged. The *mens rea* for common assault is intention or recklessness as to the causing of the apprehension or the making of the contact.[28] Both of these states of mind have specific legal meanings. Intention is deliberately doing an act to bring about the consequences, here the apprehension or the contact. Without direct proof of the defendant's state of mind, for example from a confession, intention must be inferred from the evidence. After many confusing and contradictory statements, the House of Lords has now given further guidance on how intention can be proved.[29] First, intention should be given its normal meaning unless the defendant claims that he did not intend the criminal consequences of his act. Secondly, the jury must be satisfied that the criminal consequences, for example the contact, were a virtual certainty of the defendant's act, and that the defendant knew this. Finally, if the consequences are virtually certain, then the jury can find that the defendant did intend them when performing his act. Thus, the consequences are intended where they were deliberately brought about, or where the defendant foresaw their occurring as a virtual certainty.[30]

Recklessness is where the perpetrator of the act foresaw that there was a risk of causing the consequences associated with his act yet went on to take that risk.[31] For battery the risk to be taken is

---

27   *Fagan v MPC* [1969] 1 QB 539.
28   *Ibid.*
29   *R v Woollin* [1999] AC 82.
30   See further Criminal Justice Act 1967, s 8.
31   *R v Cunningham* [1957] 2 QB 396 and *R v Venna* [1976] QB 421.

the risk of touching the victim. Potentially, this could be a very problematical test to apply to sport. Every participant in a contact sport knows that there is a risk of making contact with an opponent almost every time that a challenge is made. Does this mean that an offence is committed in these circumstances? Usually, participants are not guilty of an assault every time that they make contact with an opponent because of the application of the rules on consent and because the contact was within the rules and/or playing culture of the sport. However, where a player intentionally or recklessly causes injury to an opponent, an aggravated assault will be the appropriate charge.

Offences Against the Person Act 1861, s 47

> Whosoever shall be convicted . . . of any assault occasioning actual bodily harm shall be liable . . . to be imprisoned.

The *mens rea* for s 47 is either an intention to make contact, or recklessness as to whether contact will be made with, the person of another.[32] There is no requirement that any degree of harm be intended or foreseen, only that contact be made.[33] The *actus reus* is that actual bodily harm be occasioned to the victim. ABH is any harm that interferes with the health or comfort of the victim.[34] This is a common charge for perpetrators of participator violence. It can cover a wide range of injuries from serious bruising to minor fractures and in addition the requirement that the harm be only occasioned and not intended or foreseen can make it relatively easy for a participant to commit this offence. Although the reported cases deal mainly with fights on the pitch, in a situation where consent did not apply, there is no reason why s 47 could not be charged for an on-the-ball challenge.[35]

R v Davies [1991] Crim LR 70

> Following a collision in a football match, the two players involved began to take up their positions for the resulting free kick. The defendant approached the other player and struck him in the face. Although the victim was able to play on for the remainder of the match, it was subsequently found that he had suffered a fractured cheekbone. Held, that it was an offence of the utmost seriousness if in the course of a game of football there should be an unprovoked and deliberate assault of this kind. As serious injury had resulted, a sentence of six months' imprisonment was justified.

Players are still reluctant to bring actions under this section because of the relatively minor nature of the injuries caused. They are often little more than players expect as an integral part of playing contact sports. There is little difficulty in applying the law to off-the-ball fights. The problem lies more with delineating reckless conduct that is a legitimate part of the game and that which is so reckless as to be nothing to do with sport. For example, in football, a sliding tackle that missed the ball and tripped the opponent up would be consented to as part of the game. However, a late knee high tackle with studs up would not. Without guidance from the higher courts, a strict interpretation of the law would mean that this latter challenge is criminal.

---

32 *Ibid, Venna.*
33 *R v Savage; R v Parmenter* [1992] 1 AC 699.
34 *R v Miller* [1954] 2 QB 282.
35 See also the cases on sentencing participator violence, below, p 617.

Offences Against the Person Act 1861, s 20

> Whosoever shall unlawfully and maliciously wound or inflict any grievous bodily harm upon any other person . . . shall be guilty of . . . an offence.

The *mens rea* of s 20 is also that there must be intention or recklessness as to whether contact is made with another person. In addition, at the time that the act is committed the defendant must foresee some injury as the result of his action. He need not foresee either a wound or grievous bodily harm, just some harm.[36] The resulting injury must be either a wound or GBH. A wound is when the continuity of the skin is broken.[37] GBH means really serious harm.[38] The degree of harm required for a s 20 charge is much more severe than for s 47.

R v Gingell [1980] Crim LR 553

Following an incident in a rugby union match, the defendant pleaded guilty to having repeatedly punched in the face an opponent who had been lying on the floor, fracturing his nose, cheekbone and jaw. Held, that even if the original blow was in some way provoked, there was no excuse for the following repeated blows. However, the original sentence of six months in custody was reduced to two months.

R v Moss [2000] 1 Cr App R(S) 64

The defendant and victim were both involved in a ruck in a game of rugby union. The ball was played and the other players moved away from where the ruck had been. The victim was the last man to gain his feet. As he did so, the defendant punched him in the face. The victim sustained a fractured right eye socket and required a titanium plate to be inserted to strengthen the bone and muscle. The defendant was sentenced to eight months in prison.

Again, the majority of charges under this section have resulted from fights or other off-the-ball incidents. However, once again the recklessness of a player's challenge may make it a criminal assault. For example, if a high tackle is performed in either code of rugby, it is beyond the rules of the game and will be penalised. It is also foreseeable that some degree of harm, from bruising to a facial fracture, could be inflicted on the victim. If consent is found not to apply to such a challenge, then once again, the assault is a criminal one.

Offences Against the Person Act 1861, s 18

> Whosoever shall unlawfully and maliciously by any means whatsoever wound or cause any grievous bodily harm to any person, with intent . . . to do some grievous bodily harm to any person . . . shall be guilty of an offence.

In contrast to the previous two offences, only intention can satisfy the *mens rea* requirements of s 18. First, it must be proved that the assault or battery was intended. Secondly, the resulting wound or GBH must also have been caused intentionally. The degree of harm caused is otherwise the same as for s 20. Cases involving s 18 will be unusual in sport. Even where the players intend to criminally assault each other, such as during a fight, it will be a rare case indeed where they also intend to cause each other the very high degree of injury necessary for this offence. It is even less likely that the

---

36 *R v Savage; R v Parmenter* [1992] 1 AC 699.
37 *Moriarty v Brooks* (1834) 6 C & P 684.
38 *DPP v Smith* [1961] AC 290.

requisite intent for s 18 would be present for an on-the-ball challenge and even where it is, the police will usually consider that a prosecution is not in the public interest.[39]

R v Johnson (1986) 8 Cr App R(S) 343

The defendant was legitimately tackled by the victim in a game of rugby union. As they grappled for the ball, the defendant bit the victim's ear lobe and tore it away. Held, that despite the heat of the moment and the defendant's previous good character, on-field violence needs discouraging as much as violence committed elsewhere. A sentence of six months in prison was imposed.

R v Calton [1999] 2 Cr App R(S) 64

During a rugby union match, a schoolboy kicked a prone opponent in the face with considerable force. The victim sustained a broken jaw. Held, that such a blow was clearly nothing to do with the playing of rugby union and was therefore a serious criminal assault. A sentence of 12 months' detention in a Youth Offenders Institution was reduced to three on appeal.

R v Blissett, The Independent, 4 December 1992

During a professional football match, the defendant and the victim both jumped to head the ball. In the course of the challenge, the victim sustained a fractured cheekbone and eye-socket, the result of which was that he was unable to play competitive football in the future. Although sent off for the challenge, the defendant was cleared of violent conduct by a Football Association inquiry and of a s 18 assault by the court. The court relied heavily on the evidence of Graham Kelly, the FA Chief Executive, who claimed that on average he would expect to see a challenge such as this some 50 times per match. The defendant was acquitted.

These examples highlight the conflict present in bringing cases of participator violence before the criminal courts. On the one hand, the courts are at pains to point out that participator violence is just as serious as the violence committed in any other walk of life and should be punished accordingly. However, evidence such as that put forward by Graham Kelly seems to suggest that if a certain type of act is committed regularly enough it will become legitimised and as such immune from both internal disciplinary and criminal sanctions. This conflict over what is an acceptable means of playing sport and when sport ends and crime begins has been the focus of much debate.[40] Without clarification of which acts a player can consent to, evidence such as that given above will continue to confuse the issues.

Homicide

Homicide is the unlawful killing of a living person under the Queen's peace. It can be subdivided into two separate offences of murder and manslaughter. The distinction between these two offences is in the *mens rea*. For murder, the *mens rea* is either the intention to kill or intention to cause GBH to a person who then dies.[41] To date, there have been no sports related cases that have resulted in a conviction for murder. In most sports, it would be very hard to prove murder except in the most extreme off-the-ball attacks.

There are two ways in which manslaughter can be committed.[42] Most applicable to sport is constructive or unlawful act manslaughter. This is defined as being an unlawful and dangerous act

---

39   See further, James, M, 'The trouble with Roy Keane' (2002) 1(3) Entertainment Law 72.
40   See pp 606–12.
41   *R v Maloney* [1985] AC 905.
42   *Op cit*, fn 24, Herring (2004), Chapter 5.

that causes the death of the victim. In sport, the unlawful act will usually be a battery. Dangerous means that the unlawful act is one that all sober and reasonable people would inevitably recognise must subject the other person to, at least, the risk of some harm resulting from it, but the harm foreseen need not be serious harm.[43] In most cases of assault there will be foresight of some non-serious harm occuring thus, where death occurs from participator violence, a manslaughter charge may lie.

R v Moore (1898) 14 TLR 229

The goalkeeper in a football match was in the process of clearing the ball when the defendant jumped, with his knees up against the back of the victim, which threw him violently forward against the knee of the goalkeeper. The victim died a few days later from his internal injuries. In summing up, the judge stated that the rules of the game were quite immaterial and it did not matter whether the defendant broke the rules of the game or not. Football was a lawful game but it was a rough one and persons who played it must be careful not to do bodily harm to any other person. No one had a right to use force which was likely to injure another and if he did use such force and death resulted the crime of manslaughter had been committed. A verdict of guilty was returned.

The severity of the injuries caused in this case is unlikely to be repeated except in the most extreme or unfortunate of cases. The same basic test was applied in *Moore* as had been formulated in *Bradshaw*.[44] These two cases demonstrate how difficult it is to predict the outcome of an action for participator violence. The former was convicted on the basis that his body charge was an unlawful assault beyond the scope of the game. The latter was acquitted for a similar move that was found not to be an assault but an inherent part of a physical game. These difficulties have not yet been settled. If any of the cases under ss 47 or 20 had ended in death, they too could have been convicted of manslaughter.

The alternative charge would be one of gross negligence manslaughter.[45] There are no cases where this type of manslaughter has been charged in connection with sport. Gross negligence requires that the defendant performed an otherwise lawful act so badly, with so little care for the safety of the injured party, that it goes beyond a matter of compensation and should be punished by the criminal law. The judging of the quality of a sports participant's play is generally a matter for the law of tort, discussed below. The criminal law is concerned with whether the defendant had the requisite *mens rea* and whether the act was one that could be consented to. In all likelihood, if a player had exhibited play of a grossly negligent quality, he would also be found to have acted recklessly, thus supplying the *mens rea* for constructive manslaughter. Gross negligence is unlikely to be considered an appropriate charge in the sports context because of the evidential difficulties that are likely to arise as compared to the more simple charge of constructive manslaughter.

DEFENCES

According to the provisions discussed above, every time that a sportsperson touches a co-participant, a battery is committed. With recklessness being an acceptable form of *mens rea* for batteries, every time that a player consciously runs the risk that an opponent may be touched during the game, an offence is committed. The offences become more serious depending upon the degree of injury inflicted. If this was the usual way that participator violence was dealt with by the courts, nobody would play contact sports as the risk of conviction would be too great. Sport would be unable to

---

43   *R v Church* [1966] 1 QB 59.
44   Above, p 594.
45   *R v Adomako* [1995] 1 AC 171.

continue in the forms that we presently know it and the sheer volume of cases before the courts could bring the criminal justice system to a halt. The one defence that prevents this from happening is consent. Others are appropriate in certain specific circumstances, such as self-defence, whilst the idea that some assaults are so ingrained in the training for certain sports that they are an involuntary reflex has been run in the USA.

Consent

Consent applies to most contacts that are an integral part of the playing of sport. Where injury is slight or expected, prosecutions do not occur. However, they are becoming more frequent where more serious injuries are inflicted despite the operation of the defence of consent. This can be explained partly by the fact that no higher court decision has accurately defined how consent should apply to sport. This aside, there are a number of judicial pronouncements from both sporting and non-sporting cases on this issue. Further, the Law Commission in its two reports on consent in the criminal law did pay particular attention to the problems associated with applying the law of offences against the person and consent to contact sports.[46]

The general rule is that nobody can consent to having actual bodily harm or greater inflicted on their person. Consent is only a defence to common assault, not to the aggravated assaults. However, the law is to be applied differently to certain activities where it is in the public interest to allow a greater degree of harm to be inflicted consensually. Boxing and contact sports are amongst these exempted activities.

R v Brown [1993] 2 WLR 556

Some sports, such as the various codes of football, have deliberate bodily contact as an essential element. They lie at a mid-point between fighting, where the participant knows that his opponent will try to harm him and the milder sports where there is at most an acknowledgment that someone may be accidentally hurt. In the contact sports each player knows and by taking part agrees that an opponent may from time to time inflict upon his body (for example by a rugby tackle) what would otherwise be a painful battery. By taking part he also assumes the risk that the deliberate contact may have unintended effects, conceivably of sufficient severity to amount to grievous bodily harm. But he does not agree that this more serious form of injury may be inflicted deliberately. This simple analysis contains a number of difficult problems, which are discussed in a series of Canadian decisions, culminating in *Cicarelli* on the subject of ice hockey, a sport in which the ethos of physical contact is deeply entrenched. The courts appear to have started with the proposition that some level of violence is lawful if the recipient agrees to it and have dealt with the question of excessive violence by enquiring whether the recipient could really have tacitly accepted a risk of violence at the level which actually occurred ... [In the present appeal] what we need to know is whether, notwithstanding the recipient's implied consent, there comes a point at which it becomes too severe for the law to tolerate. Whilst common sense suggests that this must be so and that the law will not license brutality in the name of sport, one of the very few reported indications of the point at which tolerable harm becomes intolerable violence is in the direction to the jury given by Bramwell LJ in *Bradshaw* that the act (in this case a charge at football) would be unlawful if intended to cause serious hurt.[47]

Although *Brown* is the leading case on consent in English law, it does not fully explain how or why contact sports are exempted from its operation. Reference is made to part of the judgment in

---

46   Law Commission Consultation Paper No 134, *Consent and Offences Against the Person* (1994), London: HMSO and Law Commission Consultation Paper No 139, *Consent in the Criminal Law* (1995), London: HMSO.

47   *Per* Lord Mustill, p 592.

Bradshaw,[48] that consent cannot extend to acts intended to cause serious harm. But that is only in respect of a limit needing to be imposed on the degree of injury to which a player can consent. There is no discussion of the kind of acts to which a sports participant can consent, no reference to the part of the judgment that discusses the role of the rules and practices, or playing culture, of a sport and no analysis of how those ideas have been developed by the persuasive authorities of the Canadian courts, discussed below. It also is at variance with comments in other cases.

Attorney General's Reference (No 6 of 1980) [1981] QB 715

It is not in the public interest that people should try to cause or should cause each other bodily harm for no good reason. Minor struggles are another matter. So, in our judgment, it is immaterial whether the act occurs in private or in public; it is an assault if actual bodily harm is intended and/or caused ... Nothing which we have said is intended to cast doubt on the accepted legality of properly conducted games and sports ... etc. These apparent exceptions can be justified as ... needed in the public interest.[49]

R v Billinghurst [1978] Crim LR 553

In an off-the-ball incident during a rugby union match, the defendant punched the victim, fracturing his jaw in two places. The only issue at trial was whether there was consent. Held, that players are deemed to consent only to force of a kind which could be reasonably expected to happen during a game. There is no unlimited licence to use force in the game. The jury may consider decisive whether the force used was in the course of play or outside the course of play but that this should not be the sole criterion upon which they base their decision. The defendant was convicted under s 20.

The former of these two decisions makes no mention of an upper limit of harm to which a sports participant can consent; nor does it mention the scope of the exemption, nor how to define the playing culture of sport. It would allow sport an exemption to the general rule so that consent would operate to cover the causing of ABH, whether intentionally or otherwise. The latter case mentions the reasonable expectations of the players, which would be an integral part of a definition of playing culture, but gives no indication of the basis on which the reasonableness or otherwise of an act is to be determined. Potentially, as was discussed in *Bradshaw*, any injury, apart from intentionally inflicted GBH, appears to be capable of being consented to provided the act is reasonable. The confusion has been added to by the Law Commission.

Law Commission Consultation Paper No 134

The role of consent in the case of sport is different from the role that it plays in, for instance, sadomasochistic encounters of the type that were in issue in *Brown*. In the latter case, the victim has consented to a specific course of conduct designed to produce physical contact or even injury and the primary question is simply whether his consent to that particular injury is a defence to a charge of inflicting that injury. In most sports and games, however, the most that the victim has consented to is the *risk* of incurring a particular type of injury in the course of the game.

The best that we can do, therefore, is to say that the present broad rules for sports and games appear to be: (i) the intentional infliction of injury enjoys no immunity; (ii) a decision as to whether the reckless infliction of injury is criminal is likely to be strongly influenced by whether the injury occurs during actual play or in a moment of temper or over-excitement when play has ceased or 'off the ball'; (iii) although there is little authority on the point, principle demands that even during play injury that results from risk-taking by a player that is unreasonable, in the light of the conduct necessary to play the game properly, should also be criminal.[50]

---

48   Above, p 654.
49   *Per* Lord Lane CJ, p 719.
50   *Op cit*, fn 46, Law Commission Consultation Paper No 134, paras 10, 17–18, emphasis added.

There are a number of problems with the Law Commission's discussion of consent. First, sports participants very much do consent to a specific course of conduct designed to produce physical contact. If they did not, then they would not be playing contact sports. Rugby and football players consent to be tackled, basketball players to be blocked and ice hockey players to be checked, even when the challenge in question is ultimately considered to be a foul. Secondly, it is jurisprudentially incorrect to talk of consenting to risks. Victims consent to specific acts or contacts being performed upon them. Further, the most that sports participants consent to is not the risk of incurring a particular type of injury in the course of the game. It is that a certain range of contacts specific to the sport that they are playing will be performed upon them. If those contacts cause injury, that too is 'consented to'. It is the contacts, not the associated risks that are the subject of the consent. Thirdly, the explanation of what is a reasonable risk to take in the name of sport is not described in any detail.

In their later Consultation Paper, the Law Commission would allow consent to injury caused within the rules of a game, to the infliction of serious injury where reasonable but not to the intentional infliction of serious disabling injury.[51] Although this avoids some of the problems raised above, little detailed guidance is given on what is reasonable conduct in sport nor to allowing participants to consent to contacts that are within the playing culture of their sport, not just the rules. The discussion also takes place in the context of the proposals made for a Draft Criminal Code, adding a further layer of confusion by using the Code's newly defined terms for assault and injury.

From the above cases, the law appears to be that a sports participant cannot consent to a s 18 assault being inflicted upon them but can consent to the infliction of assault under ss 47 and 20, provided that the injury is the result of an act that can be reasonably expected to occur in the game. From the Law Commission's discussions, consent will not extend to cover any deliberately inflicted injury.

Consent in sport is not expressly given. Participants do not state formally before taking part in a game that they accept that they may be injured as a result of playing. Consent is implied by a person's participation in sport. The closest legal analogy to this is the implied consent associated with everyday life. Contact with other people, such as bumping into someone on the street, is inevitable simply by the social nature of our existence. These contacts are not unlawful assaults; they are impliedly consented to.[52] In contact sports this would mean that challenges associated with the playing of the game would be legal because of the implied consent of the participants.

Players can therefore consent to some degree of contact in the name of sport but not to the deliberate infliction of actual bodily harm or greater. Only in combat sports can a participant consent to the deliberate infliction of an injury-causing battery.[53] Participants can even consent to deliberate contacts that produce serious injuries provided that the degree of harm was not intended and was reasonably expected as an inherent part of the playing of the game. Although the courts have held that sport does not have a licence for thuggery,[54] it is appreciated that some harm may occur in the normal course of playing sports. Conversely, off-the-ball violence is rarely, if ever, tolerated. Neither, on the face of it, is any deliberate violence.

Sport is treated differently from other activities because it is considered to be a socially acceptable activity and in the public interest, promoting physical fitness, team spirit and discipline. However, the law fails to address several important issues. What do sports participants believe that they consent

---

51   *Op cit*, fn 46, Law Commission Consultation Paper No 139, para 12.68.
52   *Collins v Willcock* [1984] 1 WLR 1172.
53   See further, p 620.
54   *R v Lloyd* [1989] Crim LR 513.

to? Is it the same as the law considers them to consent to? Should more attention be paid to the playing culture of a sport? Should the same rules apply in the same way to all sports?

In reality, serious injury is usually inflicted lawfully on the strength of a player's implied consent to an act that was an integral part of the playing of the game and carried only a risk of injury. Where an act carries so high a risk of injury that its taking is unreasonable, then consent is unlikely to cover the initial contact, rendering it an unlawful, reckless assault. The reasonableness of a risk that a player is allowed to run is decided by reference to the public interest by the House of Lords, who give guidelines on the behaviour that they feel is acceptable to society. The problem for sport is that to date, the House has not given a specific judgment on this issue. Although consent can operate to ensure immunity from prosecution, its boundaries are by no means settled. A degree of clarity would be introduced by the courts defining the scope of reasonable conduct in sport by reference to the concept of playing culture.

Playing Culture

The courts in England have not yet fully accepted the concept of the playing culture, instead of the rules, of a sport as being the basis of criminal liability. Although playing culture has been referred to obliquely on a number of occasions, the Law Commission's Consultation Papers still based its reasoning and proposals on play that was either within or outside of the rules. If playing culture was to be defined by the courts, it would help consent to be defined more precisely, would reflect more accurately the way that modern sport is played and could help reduce the number of criminal assaults by explaining more clearly the role of the law in this area.

What is Playing Culture?

The playing culture of a sport is the way that it is accepted as being and expected to be played by those who are intimately involved with the particular sport.[55] It enables players to consent to all contacts that are inherent in the playing of the game and run the consequential risks of being injured by them. It is not limited to the rules of the game but would include codes of conduct, tactics and commonly occurring incidents of foul play. This latter element is by far the most controversial. In effect it allows deliberate cheating to be included by the law as an acceptable means of playing sport. However, it can also be said to be a pragmatic response to the way that sport is now played. Although we may hope that sport is always played according to its rules and in a spirit of fair play, it is idealistic to believe that it is actually played that way and unrealistic to claim that the law is the most appropriate tool to achieve this sea change.

The concept of playing culture can also claim to have been at least notionally accepted by the courts for well over a century. In *Bradshaw*, Bramwell LJ told the jury that they should examine whether the defendant was playing within the 'rules and practices' of football in helping them to determine whether the defendant had the *mens rea* for manslaughter.[56] One hundred years later, the judge in *Billinghurst* directed the jury in terms of consent only extending to applications of force that 'were of a kind which could be reasonably expected to happen during a game'.[57] The only drawback

---

55   See later, p 637.
56   (1878) 14 Cox CC 83.
57   [1978] Crim LR 553.

for the development of the concept is that no court has taken the trouble to explain what is meant by the 'practices' of a sport nor what is to be 'reasonably expected' as part of the game.

Finally, there is a problem over who is to define the playing culture of a sport. Each of the groups associated with participator violence will have different ideas of whether or not a particular incident is an acceptable way of the playing of the game. The players, match officials, coaches, owners, governing bodies and sponsors will all have their own ideas of what is acceptable conduct. Each of these definitions is likely to differ from the standard of play expected by the law. The body that is best placed to oversee acceptable conduct in a sport is probably the governing body. However, where leadership in a sport is lacking in this area, the law should not hesitate to intervene and impose its own ideas of what is acceptable conduct in the name of sport.

Should Playing Culture be Incorporated into the Law?

There are two completely contrasting views as to whether the playing culture of a sport should be the basis on which sports participants' consent is defined, particularly if that extends to include some deliberate rule breaking. On the one hand, it is argued that only that which is within the rules of a sport is allowed and can be consented to. Anything beyond the rules is not playing the game and consent cannot extend to protect the perpetrator from the law. On the other, it is argued that some minor breaches of the rules, including both those that are intended and those that are not, are such an inherent part of the game that consent must encompass them. Only those incidents that are totally unconnected with the playing of the game or carry too great a risk of injury that their commission cannot be in the public interest should be criminal.

Edward Grayson has long been at the forefront of the argument that sport must be played in a Corinthian spirit of fair play.[58] He argues that all harm resulting from foul play is therefore criminal and cannot be consented to.

Grayson, E, 'Making foul play a crime'

If a person intentionally or recklessly causes harm to another in order to prevent them from reaching a ball or for reason of sheer thuggery, then these actions are in breach of the criminal law. Clearly, the administrators of sport have failed to control this evil within their own sports. The concept that sporting supervisory bodies should usurp the power of the courts and the system of British justice cannot be supported by any cogent argument. Why should offenders who commit a crime within their game not be punished for their villainy? The law of the land never stops at the touchline.[59]

Grayson even goes so far as to propose a specific Act of Parliament to cover sports assaults.[60] To some extent, this is backed up by the ideals of how sports governing bodies believe that their games *should* be played. Fair Play Charters, such as those published by FIFA, put an emphasis on playing fairly, respecting one's opponents and discouraging violence.[61] This is perhaps how we hope that sport should be played if at all possible. However, the opposite argument is equally well represented and is perhaps a more pragmatic response to the way that sport is in fact played.

---

58   *Op cit*, fn 1, Grayson (1999).
59   Grayson, E, 'Making foul play a crime' (1993) Solicitors Journal 693, with Catherine Bond.
60   *Op cit*, fn 1, Grayson (1999), appendix 6.
61   www.fifa.com/en/media/index/0,00,37246,00.html?articleid=37246.

Williams, G, 'Consent and public policy'

Games like football are not the same as fights or bouts, but they are similar in involving the use of force between players in accordance with the rules. In these games, the consent by the players to the use of moderate force is clearly valid, and the players are even deemed to consent to an application of force that is in breach of the rules of the game, if it is the sort of thing that may be expected to happen during the game. For this reason, the rules of the game are not admissible in evidence in favour of the prosecution on a charge arising out of the game. A player may, however, be convicted of battery or manslaughter if he does an act with intent to harm outside the bounds of the sport ... The rules of the game are admissible in evidence for the defence, to help to establish that the defendant's conduct was not reckless.[62]

R v Billinghurst [1978] Crim LR 553, commentary

The rules of the game provide some guide because the victim presumably consents to that degree of force which is necessarily involved in acts permitted by the rules – eg a rugby tackle or a shoulder charge in soccer. In *Bradshaw* the rules were held to be admissible in favour of the defence but in *Moore* the rules were held inadmissible in favour of the prosecution. Those who play games commonly agree that they consent to the infliction of some degree of force which is outside the rules because they know it is commonly practised ... It is unlikely that anyone consents to the deliberate infliction on himself of serious bodily harm ... Certainly a rugby player consents to take the risk of a slight degree of harm, but his consent is to the risk of that harm in the course of playing the game. In the present case, an off-the-ball incident, the harm was not caused in the course of playing the game. If, in a cricket match, a fast bowler bowls and hits his opponent on the head and causes serious bodily harm, it may well be held that the batsman validly consented to run the risk of that kind of harm; but the position is entirely different if, when the ball is 'dead', the bowler throws it at the batsman's head.

Gardiner, S, 'Not playing the game: is it a crime?'

Participants who cause actual bodily harm or worse to others within the reasonable application of the rules of the sport can rely on the victim's consent to potential harm within the rules. However many participants in sports will see physical contact and resulting harm as consensual which are within the normal course of events. So the commission of fouls in football due to illegal tackles and the consequential injury are likely to be seen as consensual. They have inevitability, and although they fall outside the legalistic interpretation of the rules, they come inside the working culture of the game.

The internal mechanisms of the game should operate where the force used by the offender is seen as being a part of the game ... that is within the rules and code of conduct. This would include in football on-the-ball incidents. Only where clear acts of force are used off-the-ball, often by way of retaliation, should the criminal law intervene if the internal measures are seen as ineffectual against persistent offenders.[63]

By analysing the playing culture of a sport, it is possible to determine how the sport is accepted and expected to be played. This will then reflect more precisely which contacts are consented to and which risks are run by its participants. If it is felt that a sport, or some aspect of it, is becoming too violent, then the courts could and should intervene. Where it is accepted as part of the game by those who play it, however, there seems little point in the law intervening as the participants themselves are unlikely to consider the criminal courts the appropriate forum for resolving such disputes. However, playing culture must not be used to make sport more violent. It should set the maximum limits of what is acceptable in the name of sport. It is also capable of being a fluid standard, which can change

---

62 Williams, G, 'Consent and public policy' [1962] Crim LR 74, p 80.
63 Gardiner, S, 'Not playing the game: is it a crime?' (1993) Solicitors Journal 628, p 629.

and develop over time to reflect the attitudes of those who play sport and the public interest as defined by parliament and the courts.

How Should Playing Culture be Defined?

In English law, there has been only passing reference made to ideas that could be developed into a legally enforceable concept of playing culture. However, in other common law jurisdictions, it has been accepted and defined much more explicitly. In Canada in particular, there is a long history of the criminal law being used to punish participator violence.[64] Playing culture has developed there as an integral part of consent. The same has occurred in Australia, but in the tort of trespass to the person, whilst in the USA, it has been incorporated into most States' tort legislation.[65]

The use of the criminal law to control participator violence in Canada has been particularly prevalent in ice hockey. This has occurred at all levels of the sport from the NHL downwards.[66] Participants are deemed to consent to conduct that is incidental to the sport, or inherent in and reasonably incidental to the normal playing of the game, or to conduct closely related to the play.[67] Participants are considered to foresee, expect and agree to the normal blows and collisions incidental to play but do not license the use of unlimited force against themselves. In 1989, two separate cases established a detailed set of criteria by which consent and acceptable conduct in ice hockey in particular and sport in general could be determined.

R v Cey (1989) 48 CCC (3d) 480

During a junior level ice hockey match, the victim was facing the boards around the edge of the ice attempting to retrieve the puck. The defendant skated towards him at speed and used his stick to push the victim's head and face into the boards. Contact with the victim's neck was held to be intentional. The victim suffered whiplash, concussion and injuries to his mouth and nose. The defendant was sin-binned for a five-minute penalty. At trial, the judge considered that this type of act was customary within the game and therefore should not be criminal.

On appeal by the Crown against the acquittal, it was held that consent could extend not only to contacts and resultant injuries that are permitted by the rules of the game but also to contacts and resultant injuries arising from breaches of the rules that fall within the accepted standards by which the game is played.[68] Further, it was held by the majority, that the consent of the victim should be implied and determined objectively. A retrial was ordered.

Ordinarily consent, being a state of mind, is a wholly subjective matter to be determined accordingly, but when it comes to implied consent in the context of team sports such as hockey, there cannot be as many different consents as there are players on the ice, and so the scope of the implied consent, having to be uniform, must be determined by reference to objective criteria. This is so with respect at least to those forms of conduct covered by the initial general consent.[69]

---

64 Barnes, J, *Sports and the Law in Canada* (1996), 3rd edn, Toronto: Butterworths.

65 See later, p 638

66 Two of the earliest decisions involved incidents at the same NHL match, *R v Maki* [1970] 14 DLR (3d) 164 and *R v Green* [1971] 16 DLR (3d) 137. For a review of the cases prior to 1989 see, White, D, 'Sports violence as criminal assault: development of the doctrine by Canadian Courts' [1986] Duke LJ 1030; and Barnes, J, *Sports and the Law in Canada* (1996), 3rd edn, Toronto: Butterworths, Chapter 10.

67 *Ibid*, White, p 1039.

68 *Per* Wakeling JA, p 483 and Gerwing JA, p 488.

69 *Ibid, per* Gerwing JA, p 490.

The conditions under which the game in question is played, the nature of the act which forms the subject-matter of the charge, the extent of the force employed, the degree of risk of injury, and the probabilities of serious harm are, of course, all matters of fact to be determined with reference to the whole of the circumstances. In large part, they form the ingredients which ought to be looked to in determining whether in all of the circumstances the ambit of the consent at issue in any given case was exceeded.[70]

R v Ciccarelli (1989) 54 CCC (3d) 121

During a National Hockey League match, the defendant was called offside immediately before the victim was about to body-check him into the surrounding boards. The victim was unable to stop himself from making contact with the defendant and charged him with force into the boards. The defendant turned on the victim and hit him on the head three times with his stick. The entire incident took less than four seconds and no injury was caused to either party. To define the scope of implied consent, the objective test from *Cey* was adopted and extended to include:

(a) the nature of the game played; whether amateur or professional league and so on;

(b) the nature of the particular act or acts and their surrounding circumstances;

(c) the degree of force employed;

(d) the degree of risk of injury; and

(e) the state of mind of the accused.[71]

[The trial judge] considered the nature of a NHL game as a fast, vigorous, competitive game involving much body contact. He had regard to the acts in question and their surrounding circumstances. He found that high-sticking was unusual. He concluded that striking the opponent's head with a hockey stick, whether blade or butt, was not a reasonable practice and fell outside of the ambit of the implied consent. He considered that the blows occurred after the whistle had halted the play according to the rules of the game. He considered the nature of the blows and that the blows had the capacity to injure, although no injury was caused. The trial judge considered the state of mind of the appellant. He found that Ciccarelli wanted to intimidate Richardson and was not trying to injure him. Ciccarelli was retaliating.[72]

Despite the lack of injury caused by the blows, hitting an opponent with a hockey stick was considered to be so potentially dangerous as to be outside of the normal playing and playing culture of professional ice hockey. Consent did not apply and the appeal against conviction and sentence, of one day and $1000, was dismissed.[73]

Consent cannot be determined unilaterally by each individual player. It is instead implied or deemed to exist to the same extent for each player by reason of their participation in the game and its extent is determined by reference to a series of objective criteria. The list of criteria to be used is not closed and can be added to as and when necessary. Others such as degree of skill or experience or age may be relevant on occasion. These can then be used by a court to establish whether the injury-causing act was an acceptable means of playing the sport. In other words, whether it was within its playing culture.

The courts also held that where there is too high a risk of injury, or where serious injury is deliberately inflicted, then the players cannot consent to the conduct.[74] Participants do not have a free

---

70   *Ibid*, p 491.
71   *Per* Corbett DCJ at p 126.
72   *Ibid*, p 127.
73   For a modern application of the law, see *R v McSorely* [2000] BCJ No 1994 and further, below.
74   *R v Ciccarelli* (1989) 54 CCC (3d) 121, p 490.

licence to commit assault in the name of sport, only to commit those acts that are within the rules or the objectively determined implied consent. By acknowledging this objective approach, the courts have been able to determine the playing culture of the same sport at very different levels; in *Cey*, the game was a local league match, whereas in *Ciccarelli*, the players were amongst the highest paid and best in the world.

In a recent English case, the Court of Appeal has begun to address some of these issues; however, the outcome of the case is not wholly satisfactory.

R v Barnes [2004] EWCA Crim 3246

The offence occurred during a local league football match. By the 70th minute, the appellant's team were losing 2–0. To waste time, the victim ran with the ball and shielded it from the appellant by the corner flag. The appellant fouled the victim and heated words were exchanged. The referee awarded a free kick to the victim and told the appellant to 'grow up'. About 10 minutes later, the victim collected the ball about 25 metres from goal. He ran forwards, shot left footed and scored from about 6 metres out. After the victim had kicked the ball, the appellant performed a sliding tackle on him from behind, making contact with his right ankle and breaking both the victim's right ankle and right fibula. As he got to his feet, the appellant said words to the victim to the effect of 'have that'. He was charged with assault under s 20 OAPA.

At trial, the prosecution described the tackle as a two-footed lunge from behind whilst the appellant maintained that the challenge was one that was hard but fair. The judge directed the jury that they must examine the quality of the appellant's tackle and that they should only find him guilty of assault if they found that the challenge was not done by way of 'legitimate sport'. In further explanation, the judge told the jury that they must decide whether the challenge was so reckless as to be above and over what is generally acceptable in a football game, or so reckless that it could not have been in legitimate sport and was therefore tantamount to an assault. The appellant was convicted and appealed.

In allowing the appeal, the Court of Appeal held that the judge should have given the jury further guidance on what he meant by 'legitimate sport'. This should have included examples of actions that could be regarded as 'legitimate sport' and those which were not. The judge should also have explained the importance of the distinction between the appellant going for the ball and his going deliberately for the man and that even when a player is sent off for a challenge, such behaviour can still be considered as acceptable conduct in that sport. For these reasons, the summing up was inadequate and the conviction unsafe.

This was an opportunity missed by the Court of Appeal to explain and develop the concept of playing culture in English criminal law. The court criticised the trial judge for failing to explain or to give examples of what is meant by legitimate sport and acceptable conduct in sport, yet failed to elaborate on these terms itself. Although passing reference is made to *R v Cey*, and in para 15 of the judgment a composite test is propounded that draws on *R v Ciccarelli* and discussions of playing culture in earlier editions of this book, it is then not applied to the instant case. Bearing in mind the positive light in which the court viewed the evidence of the match referee, it seems strange that if the court did take into account the 'type of sport, the level at which it is played, the nature of the act, the degree of force used, the extent of the risk of injury [and] the state of mind of the defendant' that Barnes could be acquitted.

The Court of Appeal's policy on sports cases is set out from as early as para 5 of the judgment. It considers that the first port of call for participator violence cases is a sport's own disciplinary tribunal, then the civil courts and only for the most serious cases should the criminal courts be resorted to. Its desire to ensure that the floodgates are not opened to such cases seems to have blurred its application of its own reasoning and prevented it from developing guidelines for future cases. Thus a significant grey area remains.

The current position can be summarised as follows:

i) All injuries inflicted by contacts unconnected with the playing of the game are criminal.

ii) All injuries caused by unreasonable contacts or contacts that carry an unreasonable degree of risk are criminal.

iii) All injuries caused by contacts that are part of the normal, reasonable playing of the game are not criminal.

In determining the reasonableness of the defendant's conduct, the court should take account of the sport being played, its rules and object, the level at which it is played, the nature of the act performed, the degree of force used, the extent of the risk of injury and the state of mind of the defendant. The court should also consider how connected with the game the challenge was and whether the defendant can be said to have been trying to play the ball or the opponent. This would then force the trial court to examine in detail the nature of the act in the context of the playing culture of the particular sport.

Other Defences

Few other defences are relevant to a charge of participator violence except in very specific circumstances. Self-defence can be relevant where players are protecting themselves from being attacked.[75] Involuntary reflex could be relevant where a player is claiming that he is so highly trained to react in a certain way that his actions were in effect unwilled and therefore lacking *mens rea*.

Self-defence

A person who honestly believes that they are being, or are about to be, attacked can use reasonable force to repel the attacker.[76] It can be relied upon by either the victim or somebody who is using force to protect the victim. The use of force must be necessary to prevent a sufficiently specific and imminent attack. The victim does not have to wait to be hit before defending himself and can act preemptively. The only limit on the force that can be used is that it must be reasonable in the circumstances. There is no requirement of proportionality in the response,[77] provided that the force used was only that which was instinctively believed to be necessary to avert the attack.[78] If the response was reasonable in the circumstances, as they were believed to be by the defendant, the defence will succeed. However, if the force used was excessive or unreasonable, the defence will fail.[79] If successful, self-defence is a complete defence resulting in an acquittal.

In sport, self-defence is only likely to be an issue in off-the-ball incidents. On-the-ball, for example a hand-off in rugby, the defence of consent will be more appropriate. The only problem that a defendant may face is that although self-defence is a defence to a criminal charge, it is not generally available before a governing body's disciplinary tribunal.

---

75 *Op cit*, fn 24, Herring (2004), pp 608–18.
76 *Beckford v R* [1988] AC 130.
77 *Palmer v R* [1971] AC 814.
78 *R v Whyte* [1987] 3 All ER 416.
79 *R v Williams* [1987] 3 All ER 411.

R v Hardy, The Guardian, 27 July 1994

Following a ruck in a rugby union match, there was a brawl between the players of both sides. During the course of this brawl, the defendant punched the deceased and knocked him out. The deceased fell and hit his head on the ground, which was still partially frozen following a recent frost. The deceased died two days later of a brain haemorrhage. The defendant was charged with manslaughter.

At trial, the prosecution alleged that the defendant had joined in a free-for-all, during which he had deliberately punched the deceased. The defendant claimed that after seeing team mates be hit and after receiving at least two blows to the back of his head he had struck out at his assailant in self-defence. He had lashed out at whoever was attacking him from behind but only for his own protection. The jury returned a verdict of not guilty.

Despite this verdict, Hardy was found guilty of violent conduct by the Rugby Football Union's disciplinary tribunal.[80] He was banned retrospectively to cover the period during which he had not played because of the impending trial. However, this could still be used as evidence of a violent disposition to increase the length of any future ban that is incurred.

A further difficulty is in trying to distinguish between genuine self-defence and retaliation. Retaliation would appear to be inconsistent with self-defence. The former is an intentional battery designed to cause hurt; the latter is a lawful act committed because of the apprehension of danger to oneself. In the heat of the moment it is hard enough for a referee to do this, let alone a jury many months after the incident has occurred. The argument then becomes whether the players are consenting to violent responses to violent play or acting in legitimate self-defence. The former is illegal,[81] the latter is not.

Involuntary reflex

The only reported use of involuntary reflex as a defence is in an American case. In some respects, it could be seen to be a sub-species of automatism; however, the degree of voluntary control still present in the action would see that particular defence fail as automatism requires a total destruction of voluntary control in the defendant. Impaired, reduced or partial control will defeat the claim.[82]

State v Forbes No 63280 (Minn Dist Ct, 12–9-75)

The defendant and victim were both professional ice hockey players in the NHL. The game had been played in a bad spirit and following an on-ice fight, both had been sin-binned for seven minutes. On returning to the ice at the completion of the penalties, angry words were exchanged. The defendant hit the victim in the face with the butt end of his stick. The stick caught the victim in the right eye and caused him to fall to the ice. The defendant then jumped on to the victim and continued to punch him and pummel his head on the ice until another player pulled them apart.

The victim suffered a fractured eye socket and required 25 stitches to close facial cuts. He later required further surgery to correct double vision. The defendant was charged with aggravated assault by use of a dangerous weapon.

At trial, the defendant raised the defence of involuntary reflex. The basis of this defence was that as ice hockey players are trained from a very early age to use violence as part of the game strategy, such

---

80   *The Daily Telegraph,* 19 September 1994.
81   See, eg, *R v Billinghurst* [1978] Crim LR 553.
82   *AG (No 2 of 1992)* [1994] QB 91.

violence when used is an instinctive reflex action lacking the necessary *mens rea* for a criminal assault. The jury was hung 9–3 in favour of prosecution and a mistrial was declared. The defendant was not retried.

In English law, involuntary actions, or automatism, must have been caused by some factor external to the defendant.[83] The external factor here could be the training received by the ice hockey player during his years of involvement in the sport, or the actions of the victim, and that this was simply the reaction expected of an elite level, highly trained participant to such a situation. Although the reaction has been learned, it has been learned to such a degree that the intent to or recklessness as to whether another would be assaulted are absent.

Such a defence is unlikely to be accepted by the courts in this country either because there is too high a degree of voluntary control of the act or because training to perform such actions gives rise to a reckless state of mind.[84] However, it could be developed to be an aspect of the playing culture of a sport. If it was reasonable to train a player to react in this way and the response was reasonable in the circumstances of the game, then consent instead may apply. The difficulty for the courts is that they would have to rule not only on the specific injury-causing incident but also the training methods, tactics and playing rules of the sport under consideration. To be able to undertake such an analysis effectively, a definition of playing culture would be required. Those responses that were within the playing culture would be lawful; those that were not would be criminal.

Conclusions

Despite the gravity of injury that can be inflicted from participator violence, comparatively few cases ever reach the courts. There are many possible reasons for this phenomenon. However, the simple lack of reported cases should not hide the fact that prosecutions are on the increase and that the criminalisation of in-game conduct is a growing threat.

Probably the most important filter on the number of prosecutions brought is the initial failure to report incidents by the victims to the police. In most cases, the minor nature of the injuries caused, that they are treated by the players as being an inherent part of the game and that players want to keep such matters 'in-house' prevents an explosion in prosecutions. Players believe that it is better to sort things out on the pitch, or let the referee or governing body deal with it, rather than report it to the police. Further, because of the continuing nature of many sports participants' relationships with their opponents, in that they will expect to play them over again, it is better not to be considered to be rocking the boat or complaining too loudly.

If a case is reported to the police, then there is no guarantee that it will end up being prosecuted. It is extremely difficult to prove the necessary *mens rea* for participator violence. This is partly because if the incident occurs during the course of play it is hard to prove that the defendant intended or recklessly committed an assault. Further, there is the problem of bias from the witnesses. In only a very few cases have players from the same team as the defendant been prepared to give evidence against their own side's player.

At big matches, the police are more concerned with crowd control than the activities of players. It is only where those activities are likely to have an impact on crowd control that the police are likely to

---

83   *Bratty v AG for Northern Ireland* [1963] AC 386.
84   *R v Bailey* [1983] 2 All ER 503.

become involved.[85] At the lower levels of sports participation, the police are either not present or are likely to consider that the matter would be better dealt with by the governing body. Participator violence, unlike spectator violence, is not considered to be 'real crime'.

If a case reaches the Crown Prosecution Service, it must pass a two stage test to determine whether or not a prosecution should follow. Although generally the second test, that the prosecution is in the public interest, is usually satisfied by acts of violence,[86] the first requires that there is 'enough evidence to provide a "realistic prospect of conviction" against each defendant on each charge'.[87] Again the difficulty will be in proving the *mens rea* of the offence. Without strong evidence that the challenge was outside of the playing culture of the game and therefore not consented to, any charge is likely to fail. If this test is passed, the next test can also prove to be a hurdle. Although violence in general is not in the public interest, when it occurs as part of lawful sport, it takes on a different aspect and appears to be at least tolerated rather than illegal. Where in-game punishments are considered to be sufficient, it seems that the CPS does not consider the cost of a prosecution to be in the public interest.

A potential solution could be to introduce a series of guidelines for the CPS.[88] These could describe the type of foul play that the law would want eliminated from sport. The gravity of the injury inflicted, the nature of available evidence, how to establish the playing culture of a sport and whether certain sports or certain fixtures should be targeted as potential sources of violence or breaches of the peace could all be addressed.

In Scotland this has been partly achieved by the Lord Advocate issuing instructions to the Scottish Chief Constables in 1996.[89] The Instructions begin by defining the usual roles of the police and governing bodies of sport. The former's first priority is crowd control, whilst the latter has initial control of player behaviour.[90] This latter is of particular importance to the extent that Procurators Fiscal should take into account any punishment imposed by the governing body when deciding to prosecute a player.[91]

The problems arise when the Instructions state that the police should only investigate an incident, which is 'well beyond' that which would be considered normal play in that sport.[92] This raises a number of problems relating to participator violence, not the least of which is the definition of what is normal play and what is well beyond it. It is also unclear who is to decide the meaning of these terms: the police, Procurator Fiscal, players, officials or governing bodies. Perhaps again a definition of playing culture might have helped to clarify the legal position of participator violence. Finally, if the Instructions are to provide guidance to the police, they are so broadly phrased that they merely remind the police to use the discretion already available to them in any situation. If they are to control violent play, the terms in which they do so are so vague that players will be left in the same position as they are currently, not knowing whether a particular incident will lead to prosecution. In general,

---

85 *Butcher v Jessop* 1989 SLT 593.

86 Code for Crown Prosecutors, paras 6.4–6.5.

87 *Ibid*, para 5.1.

88 See further James, M, 'The prosecutor's dilemma' (1995) 3(3) Sport and Law Journal 60.

89 See also Miller, S, 'Criminal law and sport in Scotland: the Lord Advocate's Instructions of 10 July 1996 to Chief Constables' (1996) 4(2) Sport and the Law Journal 40 and James, M and Gardiner, S, 'Touchlines and guidelines' [1997] Crim LR 38.

90 Instructions to the Scottish Chief Constables in 1996, paras 1 and 2.

91 *Ibid*, para 8.

92 *Ibid*, para 3.

these are common sense guidelines, which draw attention to off-the-ball incidents. They do not help where the incident was on-the-ball.

The use of the law is also undermined by the lack of a consistent approach to participator violence. On- and off-the-ball incidents are treated differently, with the former much less likely to result in prosecution. Further, similar incidents in different sports settings are treated differently by the law. If you punch an opponent in a rugby match, you can be sent to prison. If you do the same in ice hockey, you are unlikely to be more than sin-binned. Finally, there is inconsistency of treatment between participator violence and other types of violence. Even where a conviction results from an incident of participator violence, the outcome is likely to be a sentence of about one-third of that which could be expected in a non-sports setting.[93] Without a greater degree of consistency, players will continue to perceive that they have been unfairly treated when the criminal law intervenes in their case.

Ultimately, it must be asked whether the criminal law is an effective use of the State's resources when it is used to punish participator violence or whether instead it is fulfilling a symbolic function. If the sole aim of the criminal law is to control and punish participator violence then it is failing. Such incidents continue to occur regularly throughout the country. The criminal law is used too inconsistently to be of true value as a control mechanism. Thus, when a conviction is secured, many of those associated with the incident feel that the guilty player has been very harshly and unfairly treated.

For example, Duncan Ferguson had been imprisoned for three months for head butting John McStay in a Scottish Premier Division football match.[94] For his first match following his release from prison, Ferguson played for Everton FC's reserve team,[95] which would usually attract around 1,000 spectators. Ferguson's return was saluted by a Scottish pipe band and banners proclaiming his innocence in front of a crowd of 10,432. In a further example, the father of a schoolboy who had been convicted under s 18 of the Offences Against the Person Act 1861 for kicking a prone opponent in the jaw and smashing his face said that the sentence of imprisonment was unfair because his son was not a criminal.[96] For the law to command the respect necessary to control participator violence, its punishments must be taken seriously and be seen as just and fair.

Is the operation of the law having a symbolic effect on players? Again the answer in all probability is no. Participants believe themselves to be at little or no risk from prosecution. If they do not believe in the threat of criminal sanctions the law cannot affect their play. What participants are doing is reacting to a playing situation in the heat of the moment. Most players do not intend to injure their opponent but are intent on playing the game. Where the only truly considered consequence is the thought of making the challenge, securing the points or winning, the criminal law is rarely, if ever, going to be an effective deterrent unless it takes a more defined and pro-active role. Without that, it will continue to be seen as an ineffective knee jerk response to an incident.

However, the symbolism may instead attach to the law, not to sport. The use of the criminal law must take place on some level if the law is going to retain any semblance of authority over sport. Thus, although it may not act as a strong deterrent, it may in fact symbolise the potential power that the law can exert over sport. If the law is to play a more pro-active role in controlling participator

---

93 See later, p 617.
94 *Ferguson v Normand* [1995] SCCR 770.
95 See further *The Times*, 8 December 1995.
96 *R v Calton, Yorkshire Post*, 29 September 1998. See also earlier, p 610.

violence in the future, it can then point to a history of involvement in past incidents. It is this symbolic effectiveness that the governing bodies of sport should have a greater regard to as it is from here that the criminal law can build for itself an extended jurisdiction over contact sports.

The criminal law is often seen to be a cumbersome and inconsistent control mechanism for participator violence. It is not taken seriously, rightly or wrongly, by those involved in sport. When it does get involved it is considered to be arbitrary and unfair. However, with a little clarification and development of the law and the continued failure of governing bodies to take the potential role of the criminal law seriously, it could become a potent weapon in the control of violent play or violent sports.

CRIMINAL LAW PUNISHMENTS

Sentences

The sentences available to a court following a conviction for assault are supposed to be calculated following the same criteria, whether or not the assault was committed on the sports field. However, there is a great deal of inconsistency between how crimes of participator violence and 'real' crimes are treated. An offence committed on the sports field will be treated with a degree of leniency not otherwise shown to violent offenders. The fact that the offence committed was a sports assault is not formally acknowledged as a mitigating factor in sentencing. However, a sports field offender will receive a much lower sentence than that imposed on any other type of offender. Despite the gravity of the injuries often inflicted, an offence of participator violence will generally result in a sentence of around one third of that imposed on other offenders.[97] Sometimes, even this rule of thumb is ignored.

R v Brownbill, unreported, Preston Crown Court, 4 February 2004

The defendant had attacked an opponent whilst playing ice hockey in an English National U'19's League match. As his victim lay on the ice, the defendant hit him about the head and face causing him to lose two front teeth. He was charged under s 47 OAPA and it was alleged by the prosecution that he had used his stick to cause the injuries. In finding that he had not used his stick to inflict the injury, the defendant was acquitted of the s 47 offence and found guilty of common assault. He was fined £250 and ordered to pay £250 costs.[98]

For each of the three aggravated assaults, biting, kicking a person when they are on the ground and headbutting are all aggravating factors that will increase the length of the sentence imposed, as is the degree of injury caused.[99] Provocation and the use of a single blow can be considered to be a mitigating circumstance that can reduce the sentence. The sentences appropriate for each offence are governed by a series of guideline cases. For comparison purposes, one non-sports case for each offence will be highlighted. In *Marples*,[100] it was held that a four month sentence of imprisonment was appropriate for a s 47 assault that had broken the victim's nose. The Court of Appeal considered a sentence of two and a half years appropriate in *Jane*,[101] a s 20 case, where the defendant had kicked a prone victim in the head, leading to the loss of his left eye, whilst trying to escape from a shoplifting

---

97 See also the cases listed under the sections on assaults.
98 http://newswww.bbc.net.uk/1/hi/england/manchester/3463481.stm, accessed 5 July 2004.
99 For further detail see Murphy, P, *Blackstone's Criminal Practice* (2004), Oxford: OUP, B2.19 *et seq*.
100 [1998] 1 Cr App R (S) 335.
101 [1998] 2 Cr App R (S) 363.

incident. Finally, under s 18, it is recommended that a jail sentence of between three and eight years will always be appropriate.[102] In *Richards*,[103] where the defendant had kicked the victim in the face whilst he was lying on the ground and fractured his skull and left eye socket, the Court of Appeal recommended that a sentence of five years should be imposed if a plea of guilty was entered and one of seven years where the charge was contested. These guideline cases can be compared to the sentences imposed in the following sports related cases.

R v Lloyd (1989) 11 Cr App R(S) 36

The defendant kicked a prone player in the face during a rugby union match, causing a fractured cheekbone. Convicted of causing grievous bodily harm with intent (s 18). Sentence: 18 months' imprisonment.

Attorney General's Reference (No 27 of 1983) (1994) 15 Cr App R(S) 737

The defendant head butted an opponent in a football match, shattering his cheekbone and eye socket and causing a laceration to his face. Pleaded guilty to causing grievous bodily harm with intent (s 18). Sentence: six months' imprisonment.

R v Chapman (1989) 11 Cr App R(S) 93

The defendant kicked a prone player in a football match, causing swelling and a laceration. Pleaded guilty to unlawful wounding (s 20). Sentence: 12 months' imprisonment, with a further six suspended.

R v Shervill (1989) 11 Cr App R(S) 284

The defendant kicked a prone player in a football match, causing a wound that required stitching. Pleaded guilty to unlawful wounding (s 20). Sentence: two months' imprisonment.

These cases demonstrate that there is a considerable degree of inconsistency between how the courts treat cases of participator violence. The sentences imposed are not particularly lengthy, with 18 months being the longest term of imprisonment. The courts seem to believe that violence in sport should be regarded as criminal but not too criminal. These low sentences can be reduced further by arguing successfully what could be described as sports specific mitigation.

R v Birkin [1988] Crim LR 854

The appellant was playing football when an opponent made a late tackle on him. After the tackle, the appellant ran a few steps alongside the victim before striking him with a blow that broke his jaw in two places. The appellant pleaded guilty to assault occasioning actual bodily harm (s 47) and was sentenced to eight months' imprisonment.

On appeal, it was held that violence such as this, whether on or off the field of play, must result in an immediate custodial sentence. However as the incident had taken place *on the spur of the moment* and that *the seriousness of the injury was neither intended nor expected*, the sentence should be reduced to six months.[104]

R v Lincoln (1990) 12 Cr App R(S) 250

The appellant and victim were on opposing sides in a football match. As the appellant went to take a throw in, the victim took up a position directly in front of the appellant to restrict his ability to throw the ball as far. The appellant took the throw in and after running a few paces said to the victim, 'Nobody

---

102 *Attorney-General's Reference (No 33 of 1997)* [1998] 1 Cr App R (S) 352.

103 [1998] 1 Cr App R (S) 87.

104 Emphasis added.

does that to me', and punched the victim, breaking his jaw in two places. The appellant was found guilty of assault occasioning actual bodily harm (s 47) and sentenced to four months imprisonment.

On appeal, it was accepted by the court that there was only one blow and that was *struck on the spur of the moment and in the heat of the moment*. It was also accepted that the appellant had suffered a *momentary loss of* control in circumstances where he had considered that he had received a degree of provocation. As such, the court reduced the sentence to one of 28 days' imprisonment.[105]

R v Goodwin (1995) 16 Cr App R(S) 885

The incident took place during an amateur rugby league match. The victim was running towards the appellant with the ball. Just before reaching him, the victim chipped the ball over the appellant's head. The victim went to run past the appellant to retrieve the ball, however instead of tackling the victim, the appellant elbowed him in the face, causing him to suffer a fractured cheekbone, which extended to the jaw, a fractured palate and two fractured molars. The appellant was convicted of inflicting grievous bodily harm (s 20) and was sentenced to six months' imprisonment.

The court held that an important consideration is *whether the criminal violence occurred at or about the time that one or other of the parties was playing the ball*. Clearly, if the assault occurred then rather than when the ball was being played elsewhere on the field it may be possible to take a less serious view of the offence as in such circumstances, the claim that the seriousness was unintentional and unexpected may be made with more justification. Further, *as the appellant had been prohibited from playing rugby league for 14 months and had thereby lost an opportunity to play the game professionally*, the sentence was reduced to one of four months' imprisonment.[106]

In each of these three cases, the defendants had already low sentences reduced for little more than that these very serious injuries were inflicted in the course of playing sport. That the injuries were not expected or intended is already taken account of in the defendant's charge as an integral part of the *mens rea* of the offence. Provocation is not usually a mitigating circumstance where it is of such a trivial nature as making a tackle on an opposing player. Acting on the spur of the moment shows a lack of a pre-arranged plan to attack but does not mean that the *mens rea* of the offence is missing. The loss of the opportunity to earn a living is very much a part of criminally assaulting a person as going to prison. In each of these situations, the court is looking for a reason to justify a more lenient sentence than the degree of injury caused would otherwise suggest is appropriate. It would be better for all concerned if the courts were to say that they did not feel that participator violence is as serious as other forms of violence and sentence accordingly than to claim that it is just as serious and then allow spurious claims to reduce the sentence in mitigation. This simply adds to the confusion in an already unclear area.

In Canada, an interesting sports specific punishment has been utilised instead of sending the professional player-defendant to prison. The defendant hit an opponent on the head and was subsequently charged and convicted of assault with a weapon, his hockey stick. On conviction, the judge ordered that the defendant should not play in any future games against his victim. This is a particularly pertinent penalty as the two players involved were professionals, thereby imposing a considerable restraint on the defendant-player for the remainder of his professional career.[107]

---

105 Emphasis added.
106 Emphasis added.
107 *R v McSorely* [2000] BCJ No 1994.

COMBAT SPORTS

The legal status of combat sports is a difficult subject for both the law and legal theory. Why is fighting, which in any other context would be illegal, lawful and in the public interest when performed in the name of sport? Sports are supposed to be encouraged for all of the inherent and associated benefits that they bring to participants and spectators. Is fighting really a benefit to modern society? Can hitting another person with fists, feet or sticks even be considered to be sport? Sports such as boxing and wrestling and martial arts such as judo are accepted as being lawful activities. However, some sports, such as kick boxing and unlimited rules fighting (or Mixed Martial Arts), are of ambiguous status from the point of view of both sport and the law.

There has been much discussion on the status of such sports over the years, most of which can split into two diametrically opposed groups.[108] There are those who consider that everyone should be free to choose which sports they participate in and should also be able to consent to any degree of injury being inflicted upon them. The other side claims that such sports are barbaric and that people need to be protected from themselves and their rash choices. This group would see all such sports banned.

Mill, JS, *On Liberty*

The only purpose for which power can rightfully be exercised over any member of a civilised community against his will is to prevent harm to others ... His own good either physical or moral is not a sufficient warrant. He cannot rightfully be compelled to do or forebear because it will be better for him to do so, because it will make him happier, because in the opinions of others, to do so would be wise or even right.[109]

Thus, provided that full, freely given and informed consent is present, adults should be free to act as they wish provided that non-consensual harm is not caused to another. Accordingly, all combat sports that are voluntarily participated in should be lawful provided that the rules are adhered to, the relevant safety procedures are in place and the participants have given their full, free and informed consent.

Feinberg, J, *The Moral Limits of the Criminal Law Vol 1: Harm to Others*

Legal paternalism: It is always a good reason in support of a prohibition that it is probably necessary to prevent harm (physical, psychological, or economic) to the actor himself.

Strict legal moralism: It can be morally legitimate to prohibit conduct on the ground that it is inherently immoral, even though it causes neither harm nor offence to the actor or to others.[110]

According to both of these theories, regardless of the consent of the participants, combat sports should be banned. Paternalists advocate that it is not in a person's interest to have caused to themselves such a degree of harm and they must therefore be protected from themselves by an outright ban. This would accord with the British Medical Association's views that the seriousness of injuries caused in boxing bouts is so great that its legality can no longer be tolerated by society.[111] Alternatively, such sports are inherently immoral because they encourage the use of violence, which is criminal, and therefore should be banned.

---

108 See earlier, pp 108–19.
109 Mill, JS, *On Liberty, in Three Essays* (1975), London: OUP, Chapter 1.
110 Feinberg, J, *The Moral Limits of the Criminal Law Vol 1: Harm to Others* (1984), Oxford: OUP, pp 26–27.
111 *The Boxing Debate* (1993), London: BMA Professional Division Publications.

The law takes a somewhat ambiguous view of such sports, falling somewhere in the middle of the debate. This leads to boxing and some other combat sports being lawful, whilst others, such as kick boxing, are at best tolerated if not outright illegal.

The Legal Status of Boxing

Boxing occupies an anomalous position in English law. There is no doubt that boxing is lawful, provided that the participants perform within the rules of the game and that they are immune from both criminal and civil legal actions despite the potentially fatal injuries that can be inflicted. However, how boxing has acquired that immunity is more problematical. The result is that boxing is one of the few situations in which a person can consent to have more than actual bodily harm inflicted on themselves.

The basis for boxing's immunity from the law is thoroughly confused.[112] The courts spent much of their time trying to distinguish between sparring and prize fighting, rarely considering the degree of harm that fighters inflicted on each other but concentrating instead on the arena in which they fought. As Anderson has noted, '[The] illegality of prize fighting was based initially on the charges of unlawful assembly, riot and tumult and not on the question of physical risk' to the combatants.[113] This strange position clouds the issue of consent to injury in the course of boxing by focusing the discussion on the behaviour of the spectators instead of on the theoretical and policy reasons underpinning the arguments for and against the legality of fighting sports.

After several attempts to establish the legality of sparring and prize fighting,[114] the issue was returned to in the leading case, *R v Coney*.[115] This did not hold that boxing, or sparring as it was referred to, was lawful but that prize fighting was unlawful because of its tendency to cause a breach of the peace. Prize fights were contests where the protagonists fought, often bare-knuckle, for an unlimited period until one or other of them could no longer continue, usually for money. Sparring was considered to be a test of skill where gloves were normally used and where the object was to score more points from direct hits than your opponent, rather than simply beating him into submission.[116] The development of the Marquis of Queensbery's rules in 1865 saw sparring become the boxing that we see today. Only this form of fighting, where the object is to score more points than your opponent rather than render him physically incapable of continuing, appears to be subject to immunity from prosecution.

R v Coney (1882) 8 QBD 534

Cave J: [A] blow struck in anger or which is likely or intended to do corporal hurt, is an assault but that a blow struck in sport and not likely or intended to cause bodily harm, is not an assault and that, an assault being a breach of the peace and unlawful, the consent of the person struck is immaterial. If this view is correct a blow struck in a prize-fight is clearly an assault; but playing with single-sticks or wrestling do not involve an assault; nor does boxing with gloves in the ordinary way.[117]

---

112 Parpworth, N, 'Boxing and prizefighting: the indistinguishable distinguished?' (1994) 2(1) Sport and the Law Journal 5.

113 Anderson, J, 'Pugilistic prosecutions: prize fighting and the courts in nineteenth century Britain' http://www2.umist.ac.uk/sport/SPORTS%20HISTORY/BSSH/The%20Sports%20Historian/TSH%2021-2/Art3-Anderson.htm, accessed 5 July 2004.

114 In particular, *R v Young* (1866) 10 Cox CC 371 and *R v Orton* (1878) 14 Cox CC 226.

115 (1882) 8 QBD 534.

116 *Ibid, per* Hawkins J, p 554.

117 *Ibid*, p 539.

Matthew J: [No] consent can render that innocent which is in fact dangerous. This is as true of a prize-fight, as it is of a duel. The fists of a trained pugilist are dangerous weapons, which they are not at liberty to use against each other.[118]

Stephen J: [The] consent of the person who sustains the injury is no defence to the person who inflicts the injury, if the injury is of such a nature or is inflicted under such circumstances, that its infliction is injurious to the public as well as to the person injured. But, the injuries given and received in prize-fights are injurious to the public, both because it is against the public interest that the lives and the health of the combatants should be endangered by blows and because prize-fights are disorderly exhibitions, mischievous on many obvious grounds. Therefore the consent of the parties to the blows which they mutually receive does not prevent those blows from being assaults ... In cases where life and limb are exposed to no serious danger in the common course of things, I think that consent is a defence to a charge of assault, even where considerable force is used, as, for instance, in cases of wrestling, single-stick, sparring with gloves, football and the like.[119]

Hawkins J: [Every] fight in which the object and the intent of each of the combatants is to subdue the other by violent blows, is or has a direct tendency to, a breach of the peace and it matters not, in my opinion, whether such fight be a hostile fight begun and continued in anger or a prize-fight for money or other advantage. In each case the object is the same and in each case some amount of personal injury to one or both of the combatants is a probable consequence ... I have no doubt then, that every such fight is illegal ... The cases in which it has been held that persons may lawfully engage in friendly encounters not calculated to produce real injury to or to arouse angry passions in either are neither breaches of the peace nor are they calculated to be productive thereof.[120]

The aim of the House was to outlaw prize fights, though the reasons for doing so are not what might at first be expected. Only Matthew and Stephen JJ concentrate on the dangerous nature of prize fights and the degree of injury inflicted by the protagonists on each other. The remainder of the House was more concerned that prize fights encouraged disorderly groups of spectators to gamble and otherwise cause breaches of the peace and therefore should be banned on grounds of legal moralism. Thus, prize fighting was illegal because of the potential for crowd disorder. That the protagonists might cause each other serious injury, and should perhaps have been banned on paternalistic grounds, was only a subsidiary matter. Many of the judges drew an even simpler distinction between prize fighting and sparring; the former had the *mens rea* for assault, the latter did not as it was only a test of skill, lacking the intent to harm.

Whilst prize fighting was banned, sparring, wrestling and even fighting with single-sticks was lawful. But just how different is modern professional boxing from the prize fights of old? Money is paid to the fighters, who often knock each other out. Although the aim of boxing is to score more points than your opponent, through both attack and defence, the surest way to prevent your opponent from scoring further points is to knock him out.[121] There could be said to be an unnecessary premium on the knock-out punch at the expense of more skilful fighting. One of the reasons for the continuing legality of sparring was that intention to and likelihood of causing injury was missing. Modern professional boxing appears strikingly similar to the prize fights that the House was intent on banning.

Since *Coney*, prize fights have been considered to be contrary to the public interest and illegal, whilst boxing is a test of skill by implication considered to be legal. The line of cases from *R v*

---

118 *Ibid*, p 547.
119 *Ibid*, p 549.
120 *Ibid*, p 553.
121 LCCP 139, para 12.35.

Orton[122] to *R v Brown*[123] has not seriously disputed the legality of boxing. It is so firmly entrenched in our society that the only way its status can be changed is by parliament, a view firmly endorsed by the Law Commission.[124] The status of boxing has been discussed academically, though without any real intent to see it being banned. The discussions have either focused on the similarity of modern professional boxing to the long-banned prize fighting, or on the changes in attitudes towards violence leading to boxing being potentially no longer in the public interest.

Parpworth, N, 'Boxing and prize fighting: the indistinguishable distinguished?'

Thus, it does not seem possible to distinguish . . . between those fights which are assaults and thus deserving of the sanction of the criminal law and those which are not assaults on the basis of the intention of the parties, when in truth, both prize fighters and boxers seek the same end, 'to hurt the opponent more than he is hurt himself'.[125] McInerney J's efforts [in *Pallante v Stadiums Pty Ltd* [1976] VR 331] to formulate an intellectually satisfying explanation of the curious position of boxing *vis-à-vis* the criminal law have rightly been described as 'heroic', but the inevitable conclusion is that the apparent immunity of boxing from the sanction of the law defies rational logic. Boxers have been seriously injured in the course of fights and indeed some have died, but despite the innate brutality of the contest the law has not seen fit to intervene. Boxing remains outside the ordinary law of violence because society chooses to tolerate it,[126] but will such toleration persist in the future?[127]

Gunn, M and Ormerod, D, 'Despite the law: prize-fighting and professional boxing'

There is a strong argument that boxing is contrary to the public interest and therefore illegal since all fights involve the infliction or attempted infliction of actual bodily harm. But an argument that boxing is illegal is unlikely to get to court and would be unlikely to succeed in any event. There is a strong philosophical objection to banning boxing, and there is no apparent Parliamentary interest in doing so, as evidenced by the Health spokesman Tom Sackville, MP, when asked what proposals the government had to discourage people from engaging in the dangerous activity of boxing: 'None. Individuals should have the freedom to participate in the activities of their choice so long as they are within the law and are fully aware of the risks involved.'

Since a ban is unlikely, despite the weight of medical evidence, improvements in safety standards need to be introduced, even if these make dramatic changes to the current nature of the 'sport'.[128]

The only recent cases to have discussed boxing have not discussed the legality of the sport itself. *Watson v British Boxing Board of Control* discussed the role of the governing body in providing post-match medical assistance to injured boxers.[129] *Couch v BBBC* was questioning the legality of the ban on women boxers.[130] The most intriguing aspect of this case was the Board's manipulation of medical evidence to demonstrate how dangerous boxing was to women whilst remaining safe for men.

Boxing causes such problems for the law and for jurists because its object is to inflict force deliberately on one's opponent. Under normal circumstances, fighting is not considered to be in the

---

122 (1878) 39 LT 293.

123 [1993] 2 All ER 75.

124 *Op cit*, fn 46, Law Commission Consultation Paper No 139, para 12.38.

125 *R v Brown* [1993] 2 WLR 556, *per* Lord Mustill, p 592.

126 *Ibid.*

127 Parpworth, N, 'Boxing and prize fighting: the indistinguishable distinguished' (1994) 2(1) Sport and the Law Journal 5, p 8.

128 Gunn, M and Ormerod, D, 'Despite the law: prize-fighting and professional boxing', in Greenfield, S and Osborn, G, *Law and Sport in Contemporary Society* (2000), London: Frank Cass.

129 *Watson v British Boxing Board of Control and Others* [2001] International Sports Law Review 201 and later, p 650.

130 *Couch v British Boxing Board of Control Ltd* (1998) unreported and see earlier, p 575.

public interest.[131] Elsewhere in sport, the force applied is usually incidental to the object of the game rather than its main purpose. The difficulty for boxing in the future is to continue to convince policy makers and judges that this form of fighting should maintain its status as immune from the law on the grounds of public interest. Despite the repeated infliction of blows to which no other section of the community could legally consent and the potential for causing serious injuries, degenerative brain disorders and occasional fatalities, boxing will remain lawful for the foreseeable future.

Other Fighting Sports

The immunity granted to boxing is not automatically granted to other combat sports. Participants in popular sports as yet unrecognised by the four regional Sports Councils are still, theoretically at least, open to the possibility of prosecution arising from injuries caused in the course of a bout.[132]

Law Commission Consultation Paper No 134

It has been pointed out that some forms of martial arts recently introduced into this country, including Thai boxing, kick boxing and full contact karate, may be equally or more dangerous than (traditional) boxing. Under the present law and under proposals made later in this Paper, serious injuries deliberately inflicted during such contests would appear, in the absence of an express exemption such as that enjoyed by boxing, to be plainly criminal. The legal status of these sports is thus at present controversial and we would welcome further comment about these activities. At the moment we are minded to think that they, like boxing, should be the subject of special consideration by Parliament.[133]

At present there is no mechanism, legal or sporting, by which sports activities and their governing bodies can be judged to be lawful, except on a case by case basis before the courts. This can create much confusion over the legal status of an activity. Certain martial arts, such as Tae Kwon Do and Kendo, are recognised for funding and development purposes by the four Sports Councils but only boxing is formally immune from prosecution.[134] This leaves certain martial arts in the peculiar position of being actively encouraged by the State yet potentially open to condemnation by society for being too violent.

Law Commission Consultation Paper No 139

Our proposals in this Paper will provide no protection from the criminal law in relation to those who cause injuries to those who consent to injury or the risk of injury in the course of unrecognised activities of the type we have described, because they will not have the protection afforded to lawful sport. We see no reason why there should be any such protection under any new regime for the recognition of sports and martial arts unless those who are involved in the activity are willing to submit it to the discipline of a recognition procedure and to achieve the designation of a 'recognised sport'. From what we have described in this section, serious attention needs to be given to ensuring that the element of risk in some of these activities is both controllable and containable and until this is done those who cause injuries intentionally or recklessly while participating in them will and should have no defence if a criminal prosecution is brought against them because they are not participating in a 'recognised sport'.[135]

---

131 *AG's Reference (No 6 of 1980)* [1981] 2 All ER 1057.

132 Farrell, R, 'Martial arts and the criminal law' (1994) 2(2) Sport and the Law Journal 29 and 'Consent to violence in sport and the Law Commission – part two' (1996) 4(1) Sport and the Law Journal 5.

133 *Op cit*, fn 46, Law Commission Consultation Paper No 134, para 10.23.

134 See further, http://www.sportengland.org/recognition_of_activities#top.

135 *Op cit*, fn 46, Law Commission Consultation Paper No 139, para 12.50.

The Law Commission goes on to propose that a recognition system for lawful sports should be established. Where a sport is recognised as lawful, the boxing exemption will apply to it. Where it is not, then participation in it will be unlawful.

> It appears to us that if formal machinery were to be brought into existence to examine the rules and organisation of all those sports and martial arts activities in the course of which there is a risk of physical injury at the hands of another, this would go a long way towards resolving some of the difficulties that we identified in Part XII of this paper. It would also serve to meet the desirable policy aim that people ought to be free to participate in whatever sporting activities they choose, provided that the risks involved in those activities are properly controllable and containable. If the rules of a recognised lawful sport permit the intentional infliction of injury or even of serious injury, then the infliction of such injury should be sanctioned by the criminal law and it should be for the expert recognition body to ensure that such risks are appropriately controlled. Similarly, if a criminal court is faced with an allegation that serious disabling injury was caused by reckless conduct on a sports field, it will be very much easier for it to determine whether the risk of causing such injury was a reasonable one for the defendant to take if it has access to the rules of the sport which have been approved by the appropriate recognition body.

> [It] is our firm view, however, that if recognised sports are to enjoy the benefit of a partial exemption from the ordinary rules of the criminal law then the appropriate recognition machinery will have to be created to satisfy the courts and Parliament that the governing bodies of recognised lawful sports can be trusted to regulate their sports effectively.

> As to the martial arts activities that are not at present recognised by the Sports Council, the intentional infliction of injury in the course of such activities would be *prima facie* unlawful if our present proposals were implemented unless the activity and a recognisable governing body qualified for recognition. The Central Council for Physical Recreation told us that there was no reason why such activities should not qualify for recognition if those responsible for them made an effort to comply with such requirements as were laid down by the recognition body. It considered it would be wrong to set out a list of 'recognised' types of activity in a schedule to an Act of Parliament. The recognition body would be able to look at developing rules and practices and to recognise or, if necessary, de-recognise an activity depending on whether its rules and its performances measured up to its criteria for recognition. This is also the way we envisage that the recognition body will proceed.

> The effect of our provisional proposals would be . . . that if people wished to continue to organise and take part in sporting or martial arts activities to which the proposed recognition body is not willing to give the accolade of recognition, then the criminal law would not extend any exemption to those who inflicted injuries on others during the course of such activities and those who were responsible for organising them might be found guilty as accomplices in any offences that were committed. Even if it is now the case that such activities qualify as unlawful prize fights in themselves, the intentional or reckless infliction of injury in the course of them would constitute a criminal offence and the present obscurity and consequential unenforceability of the criminal law in this area would be removed.

> [We] therefore provisionally propose that in the context of our other proposals:

>> the expression 'recognised sport' should mean all such sports, martial arts activities and other activities of a recreational nature as may be set out from time to time in a list to be kept and published by the UK Sports Council (or other such body proposed by the responsible minister) in accordance with a scheme approved by the appropriate minister for the recognition of sports and the rules of a recognised sport should mean the rules of that sport as approved in accordance with the provisions of such a scheme.[136]

The system of recognition currently in place for granting funding to a sport includes many criteria that are not relevant for deciding whether a sport should be exempted from the operation of the

---

136 *Ibid*, paras 13.3–13.19.

criminal law. The Law Commission would wish to concentrate on issues of safety, the avoidance of risk and whether the procedures were in place to achieve these. The Law Commission concludes its discussion by identifying a potential recognition body, UK Sport that in conjunction with the appropriate Minister for Sports could develop a scheme that would determine whether a particular activity should be recognised as lawful. A court would then simply have to consult the register of recognised sports to determine the legality or otherwise of a defendant's acts. The acts would be criminal *per se* if the sport was not recognised despite the unlikelihood of the protagonists bringing actions against each other for injuries caused. These proposals have so far been completely ignored by the government. If implemented they would be a major clarification of the scope of the law in relation to sport.

Until this occurs, the biggest test for the criminal law is likely to come from one of the most unregulated of the modern combat sports. Mixed Martial Arts is a fast growing pay-per-view television sport that is trying to make inroads into the UK mainstream.[137] Rules are reduced to a minimum so that fighters from different disciplines can take part. The object of the bouts is to find the best fighter from across a range of disciplines. So, for example, a boxer could be pitted against a karate black belt. Generally, the rules usually ban specific moves, such as biting or eye-gouging or finger-breaking. Otherwise, unlimited attacking and defending moves are allowed.

There are various bodies that currently organise these competitions.[138] Serious injuries are not uncommon and some deaths have occurred, as they have in boxing. The justification of the sport is that it is at least as safe as boxing as there is not the premium associated with the knockout punch. Smaller, more skilful martial arts exponents usually win by inflicting soft tissue injuries on their opponents or by securing a submission. Pressure to joints rather than heavy blows to the head and torso are the most effective means of winning.

Is this any better or worse than boxing? Several such bouts have already occurred in this country. On the face of it, this sport is little more than a type of brawling that could never be seen as being in the public interest. However, if the arguments mentioned above are developed, then there is the basis for drawing a very strong analogy with boxing and thereby allowing MMA to claim the same immunity from the law. To date, there has been a number of these bouts in the UK and no resultant prosecutions. Whether MMA will ever reach the same degree of acceptance as boxing will be a real test of the public policy arguments for and against the continuance of combat sports in the UK.

CONCLUSION

Injuries will continue to be caused in the name of sport for as long as contact sports in all their forms are tolerated, accepted and encouraged by society. For many years they were considered to be an integral part of the game. If you didn't want to get hurt, you played something else. We are now entering a period where people are more aware of their legal rights and are less tolerant of those who cause injury to them. The use of the criminal law to control participator violence is growing, whilst at the same time not being considered to be a serious threat to the way that sport is played. If sport ignores this, the criminal law will continue to be used as a heavy-handed means of punishing those who are guilty of using violence in the name of sport. If, however, governing bodies were to take a more pro-active stance towards participator violence, they could not only prevent serious injuries

---

137 For further information on one such body, see http://cagewarriors.com/mmaguide.asp.
138 See Mitchell, K, 'Mortal combat' *Observer Sport Monthly*, April 2001.

being caused to those who play their sport but could remove the need for recourse to the criminal law in all but the most extreme cases. Until that occurs, we are likely to continue to see resort to the criminal law being turned to by the victims of participator violence.

KEY SOURCES

Anderson, J, 'Pugilistic prosecutions: prize fighting and the courts in nineteenth century Britain', http://www2.umist.ac.uk/sport/SPORTS%20HISTORY/BSSH/The%20Sports%20Historian/TSH%2021–2/Art3-Anderson.htm.

Barnes, J, *Sports and the Law in Canada* (1996), 3rd edn, Toronto: Butterworths, pp 251–68.

Gunn, M and Omerod, D, 'Despite the law: prize fighting and professional boxing', Chapter 3 in Greenfield, S and Osborn, G (eds), *Law and Sport in Contemporary Society* (2000), London: Frank Cass.

Gardiner, S, 'Tackling from behind: interventions on the playingfield', Chapter 6 in Greenfield, S and Osborn, G (eds), *Law and Sport in Contemporary Society* (2000), London: Frank Cass.

James, M, 'Sports Participation and the Criminal Law', in Lewis, A and Taylor, J, (eds), *Sport: Law and Practice* (2003), London: Butterworths, Ch.E6.

CHAPTER 16

TORT, COMPENSATION AND ALTERNATIVE DISPUTE RESOLUTION FOR PARTICIPATOR VIOLENCE

INTRODUCTION

The role of the law of tort is to compensate those who have suffered loss as a result of the fault of another.[1] Tort establishes who should be compensated, who should bear the loss and how much should be paid in damages. It compensates those who are caused damage, either physically or financially, by the actions of another person.

Where sport is concerned, tort can be used by an injured player to receive compensation for the injuries resulting from an act of participator violence. The damages awarded include amounts for pain and suffering and for lost income, whether from the playing of sport or from a non-sports related job. Although not usually a mechanism for punishing players who cause injury, the natural corollary of forcing a violent sports participant to pay compensation to their victim is that the former is also financially punished. Tort is a more effective means of securing compensation than the methods currently available in the criminal justice system.[2] Further, it is often resorted to by injured parties because of their lack of adequate insurance. Were this issue to be addressed by governing bodies, then the use of the law of tort could be made obsolete.

There are a number of potential causes of action that an injured sportsperson may wish to consider. The most obvious are actions in either trespass to the person or negligence against the opponent who caused the injury to them. Where professional sport is at issue, the opposing club side may be vicariously liable for the injuries caused by one of its employee-players or the training methods and tactics of its coach. However, there are other potential defendants and other causes of action. The match officials, occupier of the sports arena and governing body may also be liable for a player's injuries if they have not been acting in a reasonably safe manner in their respective organising and administrative roles. An action may also lie in unlawful interference with a player's contract of employment where it can no longer be fulfilled by a player who has been injured deliberately during the course of play.

Finally in this chapter, various methods of alternative dispute resolution are considered. In sport, a governing body's disciplinary tribunal must be examined. Outside of sport, the role of insurance and risk management must be explored to demonstrate how the impact of the law can be minimised in the future.

TORT

Trespass to the Person

Under English law every person's body is inviolate. Any touching of another person, however slight, can be a battery, though as in the criminal law allowance is made for the normal contacts inherent to everyday life.[3] However, unlike the criminal law, tort does not distinguish between different degrees

---

1   Lunney, M and Oliphant, K, *Tort Law: Text and Materials* (2003), 2nd edn, Oxford: OUP, p 18.
2   See further, https://www.cica.gov.uk.
3   *Collins v Willcock* [1984] 1 WLR 1172.

of injury. It completely prohibits the first and lowest degree of non-consensual touching. The effect is that everybody is protected against any form of non-consensual physical molestation.

In sport, the most appropriate form of trespass to the person is battery, which is defined in broadly the same terms as in the criminal law.[4] Following *Letang v Cooper*,[5] an action must be framed in either battery or negligence. There is no such thing as a negligent battery. Only a contact made intentionally is actionable as a tortious battery.[6] Once the force is applied, it is unclear whether the defendant is liable for all reasonably foreseeable injury,[7] or for all injuries that are the direct consequence of his actions.[8] In one of the few reported decisions on this issue, the claimant was pushed into a swimming pool and damaged his ankle.[9] The court held the defendant liable for all the injuries resulting from the battery, even though they were neither intended nor foreseen, that is, the directness test was used.

Only in very rare cases will battery be the chosen cause of action for a victim. In *Elliott v Saunders and Liverpool FC*,[10] this was explained as being because most insurance policies specifically exclude cover for deliberately inflicted injuries. Thus, if an action for battery is successful, the defendant will be personally liable and unable to rely on his, or his employer's, insurance. A claimant would not wish to restrict the pool of defendants in such a way. Thus, the trespass claim in *Elliott v Saunders* was dropped when it was realised that Liverpool FC's insurance would not pay out on a battery claim, leaving Elliott to concentrate on the claim in negligence. However, in Australia there have been a number of successful actions for battery.

McNamara v Duncan (1971) 26 ALR 584

The parties were on opposing teams in an Australian Rules Football match. Between two and three seconds after the claimant had kicked the ball, the defendant elbowed him in the side of the head, fracturing the claimant's skull.

It was held that consent extended to intentional acts performed within the rules and usages of the game but not to those done solely or principally with a view to causing sensible hurt not justified by those rules and usages. As this challenge was outside of the rules and usages of Australian Rules Football, consent did not apply and the trespass was established.[11]

The same problems arise here as do for criminal assaults.[12] The defendant will usually claim that his actions were part of the game and either unintentional, consented to or negligent. The difficulties in proving the mental element of trespass has ensured that negligence has established itself as the preferred cause of action for the recovery of damages for sports injuries.

Negligence

The basis of the tort of negligence is a claim that the defendant failed to observe the necessary standard of care owed to the claimant and that this negligent act caused the claimant's injuries.[13] The

---

4   See earlier, p 598.
5   [1965] 1 QB 232.
6   *Wilson v Pringle* [1987] QB 237 and *Fagan v MPC* [1969] 1 QB 439.
7   *The Wagon Mound (No 1)* [1961] AC 388.
8   *Re Polemis and Furness Withy & Co* [1921] 3 KB 560.
9   *Williams v Humphrey* (1975) *The Times*, 20 February.
10 (1994) unreported (HC). For further detail, see the *Sports Law* website.
11 See also *Rogers v Bugden and Canterbury-Bankstown* (1993) ATR 81–246, below, p 645.
12 See Chapter 15.
13 On negligence generally, see further, *op cit*, fn 1, Lunney and Oliphant (2003) Ch 3.

victim can claim for compensation for the injuries suffered and for any consequential financial loss, such as lost earnings and medical costs. The law of negligence has developed from the general 'neighbourhood principle' that was formulated in the 1930s through a number of sports specific cases to the test that is applicable today.[14] The injured claimant must first establish that the other players owed him a duty to take care not to injure him in the course of play. Secondly, it must be established that the defendant's play was of such a degree of negligence that the duty was breached and thirdly, that the claimant suffered reasonably foreseeable injury and loss as a result of that injury. Although this looks like a straightforward application of the law to acts of participator violence, there are several problems with the neighbourhood test as applied to sport, the cause of which was the dearth of sports specific case law.

The cases that have since been litigated have gone some way to clarifying the position; however, there are still a number of contentious issues surrounding claims involving participator violence. First, how badly must the game be played before a player's actions become negligent? Secondly, against whom is the standard of care owed by a player to be measured? Thirdly, what must be the state of mind of the player towards his victim-opponent? Finally, what role, if any, is played by the defences of consent and *volenti*?

Condon v Basi [1985] 1 WLR 866

It is said that there is no authority as to what is the standard of care which covers the conduct of players in competitive sports generally and, above all, in a competitive sport whose rules and general background contemplate that there will be physical contact between the players but that appears to be the position. This is somewhat surprising but appears to be correct. For my part, I would completely accept the decision of the High Court of Australia in *Rootes v Shelton* [1968] ALR 33. I think that it suffices, in order to see the law which has to be applied, to quote briefly from the judgment of Barwick CJ and from the judgment of Kitto J. Barwick CJ said at p 34:

> By engaging in a sport or pastime the participants may be held to have accepted risks which are inherent in that sport or pastime: the tribunal of fact can make its own assessment of what the accepted risks are: but this does not eliminate all duty of care of the one participant to the other. Whether or not such a duty arises and if it does, its extent, must necessarily depend in each case upon its own circumstances. In this connection, the rules of the sport or game may constitute one of those circumstances: but, in my opinion, they are neither definitive of the existence nor of the extent of the duty; nor does their breach or non-observance necessarily constitute a breach of any duty found to exist.

Kitto J [at p 37] added:

> [In] a case such as the present, it must always be a question of fact, what exoneration from a duty of care otherwise incumbent upon the defendant was implied by the act of the claimant joining in the activity . . . [The] conclusion to be reached must necessarily depend . . . upon the reasonableness, in relation to the special circumstances, of the conduct which caused the claimant's injury. That does not necessarily mean the compliance of that conduct with the rules, conventions or customs (if there are any) by which the correctness of the conduct for the purposes of the carrying on of the activity as an organised affair is judged; for the tribunal of fact may think that in the situation in which the claimant's injury was caused a participant may do what the defendant did and still not be acting unreasonably, even though he infringed the 'rules of the game'. Non-compliance with such rules, conventions or customs (where they exist) is necessarily one consideration to be attended to upon the question of reasonableness; but it is only one and it may be of much or little or even no weight in the circumstances.

---

14 *Donoghue v Stevenson* [1932] AC 562. For further detail, see the *Sports Law* website.

I have cited from those two judgments because they show two different approaches which, as I see it, produce exactly the same result. One is to take a more generalised duty of care and to modify it on the basis that the participants in the sport or pastime impliedly consent to taking risks which otherwise would be a breach of the duty of care. That seems to be the approach of Barwick CJ. The other is exemplified by the judgment of Kitto J, where he is saying, in effect, that here is a general standard of care, namely the Lord Atkin approach that you are under a duty to take all reasonable care taking account of the circumstances in which you are placed; which, in a game of football, are quite different from those which affect you when you are going for a walk in the countryside.

For my part I would prefer the approach of Kitto . . .

Having set out the test . . . I ought to turn briefly to the facts, adding before I do so that it was submitted by counsel on behalf of the defendant that the standard of care was subjective to the defendant and not objective and if he was a wholly incompetent football player, he could do things without risk of liability which a competent football player could not do. For my part, I reject that submission. The standard is objective but objective in a different set of circumstances. Thus there will of course be a higher degree of care required of a player in a First Division match than of a player in a local league football match.

It is not for me in this court to define exhaustively the duty of care between players in a soccer football game. Nor, in my judgment, is there any need because there was here such an obvious breach of the defendant's duty of care towards the claimant. He was clearly guilty, as I find the facts, of serious and dangerous foul play which showed a reckless disregard of the claimant's safety and which fell far below the standards which might reasonably be expected in anyone pursuing the game.

The appeal was dismissed and an award of £4,900 made to the claimant.

Although the Master of the Rolls thought that this was a simple application of the law of negligence to sport, his Lordship does little to clarify the legal position. In the final paragraph, his abdication of responsibility for legal development in this area is encapsulated by the claim that, 'It is not for me in this court to define exhaustively the duty of care between players in a soccer football game'. This would appear to be exactly the kind of situation where the court should have taken the opportunity to develop the law incrementally through its application to a novel situation. Instead, by leaving the test so ill-defined, it allowed much confusion to develop in the intervening years. His Lordship leaves open the possibility of two different means of establishing whether a duty arises between sports participants, dismisses the claim that its breach should be determined subjectively and leaves the serious problems of a variable standard and reckless disregard to be dealt with by later courts. Many of these issues were addressed in the following case which has come closest to defining the true scope of negligence in this area.

Caldwell v Maguire and Fitzgerald [2001] EWCA Civ 1054

The claimant and two defendants were professional jockeys riding in a novice hurdle race. A fourth party, Byrne, was riding the inside line closest to the rail. The two defendants began to overtake Byrne and pulled in front of him to take the inside, racing line. Both defendants pulled across in front of Byrne before they were fully clear of him causing his horse to veer suddenly away from the rails and unseat him. The claimant, who had been in fourth place, was unable to avoid the unseated rider and was also brought down sustaining very serious injuries that caused him to retire from being a jockey.

The Stewards of the Meeting found that the two defendants were guilty of careless riding, contrary to Rule 153(iii) of the Jockey Club Rules. Careless riding, the least serious of the offences of interference, is defined as failing to take reasonable steps to avoid interference or causes interference by misjudgement or inattention, and banned them both for three days. The claimant sued for the injuries and lost earnings caused by his fall.

At trial, the judge found five applicable propositions from earlier sports related cases:

1   Each contestant in a lawful sporting contest owes a duty of care to each and all other contestants.

2   That duty is to exercise in the course of the contest all care that is objectively reasonable in the prevailing circumstances for the avoidance of infliction of injury to such fellow contestants.

3   The prevailing circumstances are all such properly attendant upon the contest and include its object, the demands inevitably made upon its contestants, its inherent dangers, its rules, conventions and customs and the standards, skills and judgement reasonably expected of a contestant. In the particular case of a horse race, the prevailing circumstances will include the jockey's obligation to ride a horse over a given course competing with the remaining contestants for the best possible placing, the Rules of Racing, and the standards, skills and judgement of a professional jockey, as expected by co-contestants.

4   Given the nature of such prevailing circumstances, the threshold for liability is in practice inevitably high. Proof of a breach of duty will require more than proof of an error of judgement or momentary lapse of skill when subject to the stresses of the race. Such are no more than incidents inherent in the nature of the sport.

5   In practice, it will be difficult to prove a breach of duty without proof of conduct that in point of fact amounts to a reckless disregard for the other contestant's safety. However, it must be emphasised that there is a distinction between the expression of legal principle and the practicalities of the evidential burden.

The trial judge found that the two defendants were guilty of lapses of care or errors of judgement, but that these were only to be expected in the heat of a race where winning was still a prospect. Therefore, on the above test they were not guilty of negligence.

In dismissing the Claimant's appeal unanimously, the Court of Appeal upheld the reasoning of the trial judge that the test to be applied is negligence taking into account the prevailing circumstances.

The judge did not say that the claimant has to establish recklessness. That approach was specifically rejected by this court in *Smoldon*. As in *Smoldon*, there will be no liability for errors of judgement, oversights or lapses of which any participant might be guilty in the context of a fast-moving contest. Something more serious is required. I do not think that it is helpful to say any more than this in setting the standard of care to be expected in cases of this kind.[15]

In an action for damages by one participant in a sporting contest against another participant in the same game or event, the issue of negligence cannot be resolved in a vacuum. It is fact specific.

We are concerned here with a split-second, virtually instantaneous, decision made by professional sportsmen entrusted with powerful animals, paid and required by the rules of their sport to ride them at speed to victory, or failing victory the best possible placing: in other words to beat all the horses in the race, or endeavour to do so. The course has no lanes, nor is it straight. The horse has a will of its own. The demands on professional jockeys to ride at all are heavy. They require skill and physical and mental courage . . . they need determination, and concentration, the ability to rapidly assess and reassess the constantly changing racing conditions and to adjust their own riding and tactics accordingly – a quality that must depend in part on experience and in part on intuition or instinct.

Accidents and the risk of injury, sometimes catastrophic, both to horses and riders, are an inevitable concomitant of every horse race. All National Hunt jockeys know the risks. The Rules of Racing which bind them all and the jockeys' own responsibilities to each other during the race, properly fulfilled, are intended to reduce the inevitable risks. But they cannot extinguish them . . . Mistakes by riders and horses are inevitable

---

15   *Per* Tuckey LJ, para 23.

and fortune, good or bad, plays its part in each race, as it does in any other sporting event . . . Negligence is not established against the defendants.[16]

Although *Caldwell* addresses many of the issues raised by *Condon*, it is important to analyse how and why the application of the law of negligence to sport remains controversial. Below, the application of the duty of care to sport, whether the duty should be defined objectively or subjectively, whether a variable standard of care can be applied, the relevance of the playing culture of a sport and the concept of reckless disregard will all be examined.

The Application of the Duty of Care to Sport

By preferring the approach of Kitto J, the Courts of Appeal in *Condon* and *Caldwell* are simply applying the ordinary principles of negligence to sports participants. The generalised duty of care is the neighbour principle from *Donoghue v Stevenson*; a sports participant must take all objectively reasonable care to avoid causing foreseeable injury to the other players. The foreseeable victims are the co-participants. This is a normal application of the law of negligence. The same legal test, the second proposition from *Caldwell*, will apply regardless of whether the participants are playing tennis or ice hockey. It is only the circumstances in which the injury takes place, relevant for the determination of the breach of duty, that will vary. The circumstances would include, for example, the rules, playing culture, level of play, experience and age of the participants. The court will examine the expectations of the players and establish the kind of contacts and risks of injury that are accepted by them as an integral part of the playing of the particular sport. If injury was caused by a reasonable contact, then no liability will result as the duty will not have been breached. Thus, whereas a body check is an inevitable and lawful contact in ice hockey, it would be totally out of the ordinary and actionable in tennis.

This test is more appropriate than that set out by Barwick CJ. It is wrong to talk in terms of players consenting to risks. Sports participants consent to contacts that are an inherent part of playing the game and they run the risk that such contacts may cause injury. A contact that is not consented to is a battery. An unreasonably run risk is negligence. One cannot consent to the negligence of another. What *Caldwell* ensures is a clear incremental development of the law, based on actions that are negligent in all the circumstances, rather than a new cause of action for sports injuries.

Objective versus subjective standards of care

The courts in *Condon* and *Caldwell* held that the breach of the duty of care should be determined objectively. This is the only common sense position. All participants in a game must be deemed to consent to playing the same game according to the same standard of care. It is illogical that each participant should be able to determine which contacts are acceptable and which unlawful according to their own internally defined standards as that would completely change the nature of the sport being played. One can no more claim that a tackle is negligent because one prefers not to be tackled than one can claim that all tackles are lawful regardless of how well or poorly they are performed. An objectively determined standard allows all participants to play the game according to the same playing and legal rules based on the group's expectations of what is acceptable conduct in that sport.

---

16 *Per* Judge LJ, paras 30 *et seq.*

In respect of consent, where many of the same arguments are rehearsed, it has been argued that a subjective approach is more appropriate.[17] According to this argument, only players who consciously decide to act outside of the rules or playing culture of a sport should be liable. This argument would support the replacing of the negligence standard with reckless disregard. Even if this approach is followed, there must still be some overarching objective, externally defined set of criteria by which a participant's behaviour is judged. The rules are externally defined and playing culture must be objectively defined to avoid the possibility of each participant defining what is acceptable to themselves by purely self-referential standards. By defining the standard of care objectively, each player can be deemed to know and be expected to play to the same standard of care as each of the other participants in that sport or game. A failure to do so will be negligent.

The Variable Standard of Care – Different Standards for Different Leagues

One of the most serious areas of confusion that arose from the decision in *Condon* was that a higher degree of care was required of a player in a First Division, or national league, match than of a player in a local league football match.[18] This would introduce into the law a variable standard of care for an activity depending on the skill of the particular individuals involved in the incident. This would appear to be in direct conflict with the generally applicable test laid down in *Nettleship v Weston*,[19] where it was held that the driving of a learner driver is to be judged by the standard of the ordinary, reasonably competent (qualified) driver. However, it quickly became accepted that all participants ought to be judged by the same basic standard of the ordinary, reasonably competent participant in the particular activity.[20]

Although the existence of the variable standard was denied, allowance was made for different players at different levels within a sport having different skill levels and expectations of risk. The same standard of play is not expected of a local league player and a national league player; however, the same standard of care in the circumstances is expected. These two propositions appear to be irreconcilable, introducing a variable standard of care into the law in all but name.

The test applicable to sport requires a degree of consistency with that applied to other activities but also a degree of fluidity that can take into account the needs of different sports and the expectations of players of different skill levels. The basic test from *Nettleship v Weston* provides only the consistency with other activities. However, if applied uniformly throughout a sport it would either impose too strict a standard of care on players at the lower levels of a sport, or allow too great a degree of leniency to those at the higher levels of play. A justification can be provided for some degree of variance in the applicable test by the very nature of sports matches themselves if sport is contrasted with driving on the roads.

When driving on the roads, every driver owes every other driver the same duty of care, regardless of the individual skill of each particular motorist. Driving is a closed activity or occurs in a closed system. The same laws, rules and risks apply to every motorist regardless of their skill or experience. Therefore, a certain minimum level of skill is required of every driver. If that level is

---

17 Gardiner, S, 'Interventions on the playing field', in Greenfield, S and Osborn, G (eds), *Law and Sport in Contemporary Society* (2000), London: Frank Cass, pp 105 *et seq*. See further, below.
18 [1985] 1 WLR 866, p 868.
19 [1976] 2 QB 691.
20 *Elliott v Saunders and Liverpool FC*. For further detail, see the *Sports Law* website. See also Felix, A and Gardiner, S, '*Elliott v Saunders*: drama in court 14' (1994) 2(2) Sport and the Law Journal 1.

dropped below and causes injury, then liability will be imposed. In sport, the analogy only stretches as far as each individual game or at most each individual competition, not each entire sport. The pyramidal organisation of sport ensures that for the most part, players of similar skill levels play against each other. Thus, it is appropriate that those at the same level within the pyramid are expected to play to the same standard of skill and exercise the same standard of care.

However, that does not mean that those at the higher levels of play owe a higher duty of care. A higher degree of skill may be expected but so also would a higher degree of risk taking and the acceptance by all involved of those risks. The test remains the same; the standard of the reasonably competent player. But the circumstances in which a breach may occur change, the level of play being of particular relevance. This does not impose a higher degree of care on elite players but places a much greater degree of emphasis on the relevant circumstances when determining a possible breach of duty. The most appropriate means of measuring the changes in circumstances is by making reference to the playing culture of a sport.[21]

An alternative means of achieving a similar outcome would be to introduce a separate test for elite-level players based on their increased levels of performance by drawing an analogy with how the law has developed in cases of medical negligence. The vast majority of participants at the non-elite levels would all be judged by the same standard of the ordinary reasonably competent player. Any variation would be based on the playing culture of the sport where that could be said to be markedly different at different levels of the playing pyramid, for example in football and rugby where the numbers of participants are so large as to create many separate layers in the pyramid.

The difference at the elite level would be that the increased levels of skill and experience could be taken into account when trying to establish whether a breach of the duty had occurred. Provided that the defendant participant was playing the game in a manner that was acceptable to others of his profession, then liability would not be imposed. In the medical negligence cases, *Bolam* requires doctors to act according to a recognised body of medical opinion.[22] If they do act in that manner, there can be no liability unless to follow such a procedure is incapable of withstanding logical analysis.[23] If a similar test were developed in sport, then participants would not be liable for playing in a manner accepted and expected by other professionals. The reasonable body of 'sporting' opinion could be provided by players, coaches and/or governing bodies and liability would not attach to acts that were in accordance with this.

Such a test takes into account the apparent tensions between sport as it is played and the legal test for negligence. It makes reference to the way that professional sport is played, taking evidence from those who play and/or coach the game, and taking into account the potential misjudgments that elite level players can make in the heat of the moment. Provided the player was playing the sport in a manner that was acceptable to other players, then liability would not follow unless it was in the public interest for it to do so.

However, is this variable standard hypothesis really the negligence in all the circumstances and playing culture argument dressed up in different clothes? If all that is being taken into account is that elite level players are better trained, more skilful and have perhaps a greater desire to win, then these are merely circumstances to take into account when deciding whether the act was negligent enough to breach the duty of care imposed on all sports participants. A body of sporting opinion is simply the

---

21   See earlier, p 606.
22   *Bolam v Friern Hospital Management Committee* [1957] 1 WLR 582.
23   *Bolitho v City and Hackney Health Authority* [1998] AC 232.

expert evidence called to prove or disprove the breach of duty. In *Caldwell*, by partially defining the circumstances relevant to determining negligence liability and laying the foundations for examining the playing culture of a sport or game as one of those circumstances to be taken into account when deciding on the liability of a defendant participant, the law achieves the necessary consistency of approach and also the fluidity that sport requires at its different levels of participation.

The Playing Culture of Sport

Following *Caldwel*, the concept of the playing culture of sport is now similar in both the law of tort *and R v Barnes* and the criminal law.[24] Although many of the same considerations apply, when determining the breach of the duty of care owed by a sports participant, the playing culture of the sport is now possibly the most important circumstance to take into account. The playing culture of a sport is the way that it is accepted as being, and expected to be played, by those who are involved with the sport in question. It goes beyond the rules of the sport to include its aims, objectives, skills and tactics and includes some acts of foul play. It is the way that a sport is actually played rather than the way that it perhaps ought to be played on a strict interpretation of the rules.[25]

The third of the *Caldwell* propositions has developed playing culture into a concept capable of being applied at law. By generalising the circumstances identified as relevant in *Caldwell*, the following should be taken into account when analysing potential liability: the rules, conventions, customs and object of the game; the demands inevitably made upon contestants; the inherent dangers and the standards and skills reasonably expected of participants. This is not a closed list and other relevant circumstances could include: the age and experience of the participants; the degree of formality of the game and the level of the game within the sport's structure. Thus, a useful guide for determining acceptable conduct in sports is now in place.

In its most refined form, the playing culture of a sport can be formalised as a code of conduct that complements the rules of the game. This is particularly striking in skiing where the International Skiing Federation's (FIS's) '10 FIS Rules for Conduct' are considered to be determinative of civil and criminal liability.[26] A breach of these Rules is considered by the FIS to be so inherently dangerous that it should lead to liability being imposed. In particular, r 3 states that the skier in front, or downhill, has priority. The skier behind must give anyone in front sufficient room to carry out any manoeuvre. Under r 4, the skier behind is wholly responsible for completing the overtaking manoeuvre safely.

Lyon v Maidment [2002] EWHC 1227

The claimant and defendant were members of the same skiing party. A third member of the party headed off down the run first, attempting to go as fast as possible down the initial slope to gain sufficient momentum to ascend the upslope at the end of the run. The defendant was the second of the party to begin his descent and the claimant was the third. The claimant alleged that the defendant had cut across his path and skied over his skis causing him to fall and suffer serious injuries to his head and spine.

It was held that as a result of the claimant having suffered hypoxia as a result of the fall he had misremembered what had happened and had not established a breach of duty. The evidence given by the other witnesses implied that the claimant had lost his balance and fallen as a result of going too fast.

---

24 See also above p 611.

25 For further discussion of the position in Australia and the USA, see the *Sports Law* website.

26 http://www.fis-ski.com.rulesandpublications/10fisrulesforconduct.html.

Further, it was noted by the court that the Rules of Conduct of the FIS govern the conduct of skiers and that any injury-causing breach of those Rules would result in civil liability being established. According to the Rules, where one skier is following another down a slope, the burden is on the uphill skier to avoid the skier further down the slope. This ensures that if the downhill skier makes any sudden change of direction, for whatever reason, the uphill skier can take evasive action to avoid a collision. As the defendant was the downhill skier and had not breached the Rules, the action in negligence was not made out.

This concept has now been extended beyond formally organised sports and applied to informal play activities.[27] This is an important development as far as playing culture and informal sports and games are concerned. The court must look for negligence in all the circumstances. In particular it must examine any formal rules and conventions, and where those are lacking, it must examine the informal, ad hoc rules, tacit understandings and expectations of the players. Thus, playing culture applies not only to formally constituted sports, nor is it restricted to strictly defined codes of conduct. It can apply equally to informal games in the park, the street or on the beach.

Reckless Disregard and the Standard of Care

The most heated debates have occurred over the definition of the standard of care to be exhibited by a sports participant. The adversarial nature of the English civil justice system has led to two very distinct theories of liability emerging. On one side is the argument that sport should be treated no differently from any other activity and that the normal test of negligence in all the circumstances should be applied. The alternative is that simple negligence is too high a standard, too easily breached by sport participants who are playing fast-moving, physical games in the accepted way. Only those who drop a long way below that standard, by acting recklessly and dangerously towards a co-participant, or who show a reckless disregard for the health and safety of an opponent, not those who show mere negligence towards them, should be liable. This argument is used in particular by defendants who, naturally, will try to claim that their own standard of play should not be considered to be careless enough to have liability imposed upon them.

Felix, A, 'The standard of care in sport'

Ordinary negligence standards cannot be applicable to establishing the standard of care in the sporting context. The standard of care is determined by reference to the foreseeability of harm. In the context of sports and participants in sports, a greater degree of harm is foreseeable by reason of participation in the game. Therefore, the standard of care should be lower . . . This can be justified by reference to the fact that society as a whole regards participation in sport as a valid activity although risk can be foreseen. On this basis then, the lower reckless disregard standard set out in *Wooldridge v Sumner* must be regarded as the applicable law. Indeed with such a standard it would be extremely difficult for a defendant to raise the *volenti* defence since [the claimant] could not be regarded as assuming the risks beyond those which show a reckless disregard for his safety and thus once breach was established, liability would almost certainly follow.[28]

The reckless disregard theory is grounded in the judgment in *Wooldridge v Sumner*,[29] where a rider in an equestrian competition lost control of his horse and hit and injured a press photographer standing at the edge of the arena. It was claimed that the defendant had been negligent in riding as he had and

27 See *Blake v Galloway* [2004] EWCA Civ 814. For more detail, see the website.
28 Felix, A, 'The standard of care in sport' (1996) 4(1) Sport and the Law Journal 32, p 35.
29 [1963] 2 QB 43.

damages were claimed for the injuries caused. The court held that spectators accept the risk of a lapses of judgment or skill in competitors who are going all out to win but do not accept the risk of participants having a reckless disregard for their safety.

Further weight is claimed for this theory from cases involving participator violence rather than injuries caused to spectators. In *Condon v Basi*, the Court of Appeal held that the defendant had been guilty of dangerous foul play and having a reckless disregard for the claimant's safety.[30] In *Elliott v Saunders*, Drake J held that the ordinary negligence standard used in *Condon v Basi* was applicable but went on to find that the defendant was not guilty of dangerous and reckless play and was therefore not in breach of the duty of care owed. And in *Casson v MoD*, the injuries caused to a young army cadet were found to have been caused by an adult member of the opposing football team acting with gross negligence and recklessness.[31]

Whether a new standard of care can be read into these judgments is open to debate. The judges' statements are strictly *obiter dicta* as they were unnecessary for deciding the cases because the ordinary negligence standard was found to apply, and was applied, in each instance. However, whilst the judges professed to be using the ordinary standard of negligence, they appear to have given judgment in terms of the lower standard of reckless disregard or reckless and dangerous play. This could be for one of several reasons. The judges could be trying to introduce a new standard of care for sports participants, or they could be trying to ensure that their judgment is not overturned on appeal should a higher court decide that reckless disregard is the correct standard, or they could be using reckless disregard as a shorthand for negligence in all the circumstances.

The proponents of a new test argue that reckless disregard is a more appropriate standard by which to judge participator violence because it allows for a greater degree of careless conduct by the defendant before liability is imposed than does simple negligence. This would result in less pressure being put on participants to change their style of play simply because of the threat that a civil action might result from their on-field conduct. As players rarely intend to commit acts of violence and because most injuries occur through actions committed in the heat of the moment, with no thought of the outcome of the act apart from, for example, who is going to gain the advantage or win the game, they should have to adhere to a lower standard of care than people in other activities. Instead of having to fall below the standard of the ordinary reasonable sports participant, they must act with a reckless disregard for the safety of their co-participants to incur liability.

This argument concedes that players are often more concerned with playing the game than with the possibility of legal action. If they are playing to win, it is unlikely that they are fully considering the non-sporting consequences of their actions. Reckless disregard would allow greater leeway to players, punishing only a high degree of negligent and dangerous play as opposed to that which dropped below the standard of the ordinary player, a standard perhaps too easily satisfied in contact sports.[32]

The reckless disregard test also provides a more subjectivist approach to liability for participator violence. By requiring the defendant to act with a reckless disregard for an opponent, it is in effect requiring him to act consciously with respect to causing injury. To be liable, the defendant will have known of the risks of causing injury by his act, that the taking of such risks is unacceptable according

---

30 [1986] 1 WLR 866, p 868, and above.

31 *Bradford Telegraph & Argus*, 1 June 1999.

32 The majority of states in the USA where this has been litigated have chosen reckless disregard as the appropriate test. Only one, Wisconsin, has followed the negligence in all the circumstances test, *Lestina v West Bend Mutual Insurance Company* 501 NW 2d 28.

to the playing culture of that sport, he will have gone on to do the act in spite of this and will have caused injury by the act. The test attempts to reflect more pragmatically the actual state of the mind of the participant in judging whether liability should be imposed for the particular injury caused. However, despite the constant attempts of its proponents, reckless disregard has been rejected by the Court of Appeal in *Caldwell*.

Caldwell reinforces that the test to be used is negligence in all the circumstances. The fourth and fifth of the *Caldwell* propositions specifically reject reckless disregard as the appropriate legal standard of care in cases of sporting negligence. Reckless disregard is only a reflection of the amount of evidence potentially required to prove negligence in sport, not a new standard of care. In reality, there is little practical difference between reckless disregard and negligence in all the circumstances. If the latter is applied taking into account the playing culture, accepted styles of play, level of play and the heat of the moment as relevant circumstances, then sports participants would receive just as effective protection by using negligence in all the circumstances as the legal test as they would using the reckless disregard theory. This echoes the Australian position from a virtually identical case. The courts there have continued to express liability in terms of negligence and by defining the relevant circumstances ever more explicitly.

Frazer v Johnstone (1990) 21 NSWLR 89

Both parties were jockeys in a professional horse race. The defendant was on the outside overtaking two slower horses with about 400m to go. As he passed them, he crossed dangerously close in front of them causing them to severely compress the horses on the inside. As the horses compressed, the claimant ran out of room, clipped the horse in front and his mount fell, unseating him and causing him injury. The trial judge upheld the claim that the defendant had failed to take reasonable care for the safety of the claimant and that his actions constituted recklessness in that he had deliberately run an unjustifiable risk. The defendant appealed on the grounds that the applicable test was recklessness in the circumstances and that he had not been reckless, only negligent.

Held, following a review of the English and Australian decisions, the trial judge's formulation of the test was correct. The test is whether the defendant had ridden as a reasonable man riding as a licensed jockey in a horse race. The single standard of care remains but the response of the reasonable man is shaped by the particular situation in which the act takes place. Any formulation of the test which involves an ingredient of recklessness is inconsistent with trying to establish whether what the defendant did was reasonable. As the judge's findings of fact would not be interfered with and as he had found the defendant to be negligent, the appeal was dismissed.

Thus, the Australian courts came to the same decision as in *Caldwell* some eleven years earlier. The law is already used to applying the test of negligence to a wide range of activities, thus, it should be more than able to be applied to sport as long as the relevant circumstances are properly taken into account. The applicable standard is whether the defendant acted reasonably in all the relevant circumstances. Reckless disregard is a useful evidential tool for cases arising out of fast moving, high impact contact sports where errors, misjudgements and mistimed challenges are not just possible but likely consequences of playing the game but negligence in all the circumstances remains the applicable legal test.

The reckless disregard theory can be criticised further for blurring the distinction between liability in crime and tort. In general, crimes are defined subjectively and subjective recklessness is considered to be a state of mind of such culpability that it should be governed by the criminal law and punished accordingly. Negligence is a measure of when a person's conduct has failed to live up to that normally expected of someone in the defendant's position. The functions of crime and tort are different and the reckless disregard test unnecessarily blurs them, as it also blurs the distinction between negligence and trespass to the person. Further, by moving away from the more objective approach in negligence, there is a possibility that each participant in a sport would be able to define their own version of acceptable conduct. Each participant must play the same game to the same standard. Negligence is not self-referential but is objectively and externally defined and is applicable to all in the same way.

Defendants will now have to claim that their actions were a reasonably expected way of playing the game instead of arguing that they should be allowed to be more reckless just because they are playing sport. They can emphasise the need for a high degree of evidence before negligence is proved but cannot insist that liability can only be imposed on proof of their recklessness.

Further cases

It is not only in the more common contact sports, such as rugby and football, or the more dangerous activities like horse racing, where the law can become involved. Wherever a sportsperson is injured by the negligence of a co-participant, regardless of the sport being played or the formality of the game, then liability can follow.

Leatherland v Edwards (1999) unreported (HC)

The parties were on opposite sides playing a game of uni-hockey as part of a police officers' training course. The activity was supposed to be a fast, non-contact sport. It was against the rules for the sticks to be swung above waist height and the ball was not supposed to rise above pitch-level. The claimant was covering his goal when the defendant took a shot and followed through in such a way that he hit the claimant in the face. The claimant's eye imploded as a result of the impact.

Held, that the defendant had breached a safety rule of the game which was central to its spirit and purpose and in such circumstances was negligent and had caused foreseeable harm. The claimant was awarded £111,383 for pain, suffering and lost earnings.

Pearson v Lightning (1998) unreported (CA)

The claimant and defendant were playing golf on the same course on parallel holes that ran in the opposite direction to each other. The defendant was about to play a shot near some trees whilst the claimant was taking a shot from the rough. Both were aware of the other's presence. The defendant played his shot, hit a tree and his ball deflected into the eye of the claimant.

Held, given the difficulty of the shot and that it could have gone wrong, the likelihood of a deflection off the tree and the close presence of the claimant, the judge had been entitled to hold that there was a sufficient degree of foreseeability to find that a duty of care was owed and had been breached by the defendant.

Defences

There are two main defences tortious claims; consent and *volenti non fit injuria*. Both are complete defences and are based on the principle that if you want contacts made with you, or are prepared to run the risk that contacts might be made with you, you cannot seek compensation for any injuries caused by those acts. A defendant may also plead contributory negligence to a claim.[33] This entails arguing that the claimant was also negligent and that this at least partially caused their own injuries, for example, because they were not wearing the required protective clothing. If successful, the claim

---

33   Lunney and Oliphant (2003) pp 268–273.

will be reduced by a percentage equivalent to the amount that the claimant was considered to be at fault.

Consent

Consent is a defence to trespasses against the person. The act to which the claimant consents is one of a range of acts anticipated in advance of their occurrence. Thus, 'One who has invited or assented to an act being done towards him cannot, when he suffers from it, complain of it as a wrong'.[34] An effective consent is not an automatic bar to a claim in negligence. The contact itself can be consented to, such as a tackle in football, and a claim in trespass will be barred. However, if it is performed with such a degree of carelessness that it causes injury, then an action may lie in negligence because of the poor quality of the challenge.

The same basic rules of consent apply to tort as they do to the criminal law.[35] Consent is implied from a player's participation in a sport. At present, there is no direct authority on the degree of injury to which a participant can consent in tort. However, it is possible that a player may be able to consent to more injury being inflicted on him than under the criminal law. In *R v Coney*, Hawkins J held that, 'It may be that consent can in all cases be given so as to operate as a bar to a civil action; upon the ground that no man can claim damages for an act to which he himself was an assenting party'.[36] Thus, a participant could be prosecuted for an act that could not result in a civil action because of the victim's consent. Provided that the participant's consent was full, informed and freely given, it would appear that the victim will be unable to bring an action in trespass.

Players do not and cannot consent to force that goes beyond that which is normally expected, even if such conduct is a regular occurrence in that sport. Further, they do not consent to blows that are out of all proportion to the normal playing of the game, only to those which are a legitimate part of it or are part of its playing culture.[37] The problem for the law is where the line between playing the game and assaulting your opponent is to be drawn. Some, but not all, conduct beyond the rules of a game is lawful. The emergent guidelines from the criminal law cases would be applied by analogy to consent to tortious battery cases.

Volenti non fit injuria

Volenti non fit injuria means that no harm is done to one who has assumed the risk of injury.[38] It allows a person to assess the degree of risk involved with an activity and then to decide whether or not to participate. To raise this defence, a defendant must show that the claimant voluntarily assumed a risk that was known about in advance. This will usually be done by showing that the claimant had voluntarily participated in the sport in question. In *Rootes v Shelton*, the court held that *volenti* operated to exclude the duty of care from arising in the first place.[39] This cannot be the correct position. *Volenti* operates to exonerate a defendant from liability for what would otherwise be an

---

34   *Smith v Baker* [1891] AC 325, *per* Lord Herschell, p 360.
35   See earlier, p 603.
36   (1882) 8 QBD 534, p 553.
37   See earlier, p 606.
38   Lunney and Oliphant (2003) , pp 253–268.
39   [1968] ALR 33 and Cox, N, 'Civil liability for foul play in sport' (2003) 54(4) NILQ 351.

actionable breach of duty. The duty still arises and is imposed upon the defendant but it is not breached by performing an act that carries one of the inherent risks associated with participation.

Volenti operates as a defence to a claim of negligence only when a duty of care, its breach and consequent damage have all been established. As sports participants run the risk of, for example, being tackled in rugby or football games or charged in ice hockey, *volenti*, as the legal embodiment of risk taking, seems to be the appropriate defence. However, the majority of sports negligence cases turn on the issue of breach of duty rather than the need to establish a defence to a fully made out claim of negligence. Only if a claim of negligence is fully made out will the issue of *volenti* arise. If a sports participant is found not to have acted negligently, there is no issue of *volenti* because there is no breach of duty. Where a sports participant has been found to have acted negligently because their play was unreasonable and/or unexpected, again no issue of *volenti* arises because participants run the risk of injury only from such acts as can be reasonably expected from a player playing according to the reasonably accepted standard of play.

Post-*Caldwell*, *volenti* will almost always be consumed by the third of the Court of Appeal's propositions. If the act is part of the reasonable playing of the game, then there is no breach of duty; if there is no breach of duty, there is no need to raise *volenti*. If the injuries are caused by an act that is not one of the inherent risks of participation in the sport, *volenti* will not apply because the claimant will not have voluntarily run the risk of being injured by an act that goes beyond the scope of acceptable conduct in that sport.

EXTENDING TORTIOUS LIABILITY

In most situations where a participant is caused injury whilst playing sport, the cause of the harm and most obvious defendant will be the player who caused the injury. However, in certain circumstances, there may be other, more appropriate, defendants. An injured sports professional can join the defendant's employer to the claim on the basis of vicarious liability. Referees can be sued for failing to uphold the safety rules of a game, sports facility owners for inadequate playing surfaces or equipment,[40] governing bodies for failing to organize the sport safely and coaches for failing to train a player sufficiently. The claimant's employers can also sue the defendant's employers for unlawful interference with the contract of employment. In all but the last of these situations, the same basic rules of negligence apply and have been extended to encompass new classes of defendants. The impact of the few landmark cases that have developed this area of the law are of paramount importance to everyone who is connected with the playing, coaching, officiating and administrating of sport.

Vicarious Liability

The doctrine of vicarious liability provides that the employer of a defendant is liable for the defendant-employee's tortious actions if they were performed during the course of employment. A vicarious liability claim is, therefore, limited by the nature of its reliance on the contract of employment to those who are professional players employed by a club to play sport. An employer can be vicariously liable for the acts of an employee without any wrongdoing on the part of the employer. The justification for such liability is that as the employee is working for the benefit of the

---

40 See later, Chapter 17.

employer, the employer is responsible for any wrongdoing that occurs in the production of that benefit. From the claimant's perspective, it provides an additional defendant who is likely to be better able to pay any compensation either because the employer has more money or is better insured.

There are three stages to proving a vicarious liability claim. First, that the defendant-employee must have committed an actionable tort. Second, that the employee was employed by the employer and third, that the tort was committed during the course of the employee's employment. Where sports injuries are concerned, the first stage will be completed by the claimant proving that the defendant-player/employee caused the claimant's injuries negligently, in accordance with the principles discussed above.

For the second stage, an employee is one who provides his own work and skill in the performance of a service for remuneration and who agrees to be subject to the control of the employer.[41] A sportsperson who is paid to play for a club is an employee of that club, which is evidenced by the contract of employment between the player and the club.

Finally, it must be proved that the defendant-employee was acting in the course of his or her employment at the time that the tort was committed. Only if this final point can be proven will the employer be vicariously liable for the acts of the employee. An act is in the course of an employee's employment if it is within the scope of activities included in or incidental to the doing of the job.[42] The employer is also liable for injuries caused by authorised acts of an employee that are performed in an unauthorised manner. This would include injury-causing acts that are outside of the rules or playing culture of the game.[43] However, if the employee was acting for his own purposes by going on 'a frolic of his own',[44] as opposed to acting for the benefit of the employer, then the employer will not normally be liable. Thus, an employer is liable for injuries caused in the furtherance of the contract of employment, but not for the doing of an unauthorised act.[45]

In professional team sports, the employing club will generally be joined to an action following an injury-causing act of foul play, as foul play has formed the basis of the successful negligence actions in each of the reported cases.[46] Where professional players are concerned, the claim for vicarious liability is so uncontentious that it has not been fully debated in the sports context in the UK. In two recent cases, the employing club was the sole defendant to the action as it was considered to be a clear case of vicarious liability and therefore a single defendant was a way of keeping down the legal costs.[47] It would only be necessary to have separate representation if vicarious liability was at issue, for example, where the employing club was trying to distance itself from the acts of its employee because the player had attacked a match official.

In the USA and Australia, clubs have been found vicariously liable for acts of deliberate violent conduct where the employee-player was known to have a violent disposition or responded to the actions of the coach.

---

41 *Ready Mix Concrete (South East) Ltd v Minister for Pensions and National Insurance* [1968] 1 All ER 433.
42 *Ruddiman v Smith* (1889) 60 LT 708.
43 *McCord v Swansea City AFC Ltd, The Times*, 11 February 1997.
44 *Joel v Morrison* (1834) 6 CD 501, *per* Parke B, p 503.
45 *Poland v Parr and Sons* [1927] 1 KB 236.
46 For further detail, see below the discussions on *Rogers v Bugden and Canterbury-Bankstown* (1993) ATR 81–246 and *Watson and Bradford City FC v Gray and Huddersfield Town FC* (1998) unreported.
47 *Gaynor v Blackpool FC* [2002] CLY 3280 and *Pitcher v Huddersfield Town FC* [2001] WL 753397.

Tomjanovich v California Sports Inc [No H–78–243 (SD Tx 1979)]

During a National Basketball Association match, the claimant was punched in the face by an opponent, Kermit Washington, and caused serious injury. The claimant sued Washington and his employer, the Los Angeles Lakers, who were owned by the defendant company. The claimant succeeded in his claim that the club was vicariously liable for the injuries caused to him because it was aware of the violent disposition and playing style of Washington and had done nothing to discourage it and had continued to pick him despite it. The claimant was awarded $3.2 m damages.

Rogers v Bugden and Canterbury-Bankstown (1993) ATR 81–246

The claimant was a professional rugby league footballer with the Cronulla Sharks. The defendant Bugden was a professional rugby league player with Canterbury-Bankstown. Bugden broke the claimant's jaw with a high tackle during match between the two teams. The claimant underwent extensive dental work and the insertion of a plate was required. He experienced ongoing pain and distress, the inconvenience of an insensitive lower lip and chin, difficulty in opening his mouth wide and a 'clicking' when chewing. He also experienced feelings of anger and frustration about not being able to play rugby and about the manner in which he had been injured and publicly humiliated. The claimant sued Bugden and the club for damages in assault.

At trial, Bugden's claim that the injury occurred whilst he was executing a legitimate smother tackle was rejected. The judge found that Bugden aimed for the claimant's head, deliberately struck him with his outstretched forearm with the intention of hurting him and that this was contrary to the rules of the game and that the assault was proved. The claimant was awarded compensatory damages of A$68,154.60, which included general damages for pain, suffering and loss of amenities of A$25,000. Canterbury were held vicariously liable for the assault as Bugden's actions constituted a mode, albeit an improper one, of carrying out an authorised act that was within the scope of his employment; Bugden's job of professional rugby league player required him to use force to tackle opposing players. Canterbury's argument that it only authorised tackles made within the rules was insufficient to exclude its liability.

The claimant's alternative claim of vicarious liability, that the club had impliedly authorised the assault, was rejected. His argument that before the game, Bugden's coach had 'revved up' the players and told them to stop three specific players, one of whom was the claimant, was not proven on the facts.

Each of the three parties appealed against aspects of the decision. The liabilities of the defendants were upheld.

(1) The appeal against liability was dismissed. The trial judge's conclusion that the claimant's jaw was broken by a deliberate head-high tackle could not be disturbed. The finding was based not only upon videotape film and photographs but also upon the credibility of several witnesses. It was not established that the trial judge misused his advantage in seeing or hearing the witnesses or that his conclusions were at variance with objective facts reliably established thereby. On the contrary, the videotape evidence and the photographic evidence amply supported his Honour's conclusion.

(2) The finding that the club was vicariously liable was correct on the facts . . . There was no suggestion that Bugden acted from animosity towards the claimant or in furtherance of his own interests; he did what he did in the course of playing for the club and it could only be seen as intended to assist and in fact assisting, the club to defeat Cronulla and as doing so by achieving a result (stopping the claimant's progress) which could have been achieved by the proper mode of a legitimate tackle. Bugden had achieved it by the improper mode of a foul tackle. Although it was not established that the foul tackle had been authorised by the club, the risk that motivation would, in some, lead to the adoption of illegitimate means was plain. An employer which encouraged action close to the line would, in appropriate cases, have to bear the consequences of acts that were over the line.

It is uncertain whether similar actions would succeed under English law. Until recently, the law was clear that if a participant were to punch or attack an opponent in pursuance of a personal vendetta, then that would be acting outside of the scope of the employee's employment. The act is unauthorised and the employer is not responsible for it if, 'The act of assault by [the employee] was done by him in relation to a personal matter affecting his personal interests,' for example, a spontaneous act of retributive justice.[48] However, two recent non-sports cases have potentially changed this.[49] Where a defendant's propensity to violence is known to the employer, particularly where the employee is employed specifically because of that propensity, then the employer can be liable for any injuries caused by the defendant-employee. This is very similar reasoning to that put forward by the court in *Tomjanovich*. The employer is now under a duty to recruit, train, supervise and discipline the employee to ensure that they do not act in a violent manner, the latter two duties being extremely important where the employee is known to have violent tendencies. This raises many questions about tactics and styles of play in contact sports and calls into question the role of the traditional 'hard man' of a team and of intimidatory play. It is likely that sport would prefer to follow the earlier reasoning and claim that no vicarious liability arises; however, claimants backed by insurance firms may find the latter argument being advanced through them.[50]

The result of these cases is that a sports participant is authorised by his employing club to perform acts that are inherently connected with the playing of the game. This will include acts that are within the rules and playing culture of the sport and certain elements of foul play provided that they are committed in the furtherance of the employer's objectives, that is, to win the game. An employer can also be liable for an employee's acts despite having expressly forbidden their employees from acting in a certain manner.[51] For example, a rugby club would be vicariously liable for the high tackles of its players even if it had told the players that they were not to perform such tackles under any circumstances. The players are simply performing authorised acts, tackles, in an unauthorised way, above the shoulders. If the act is of a purely personal nature unconnected with the playing of the game, then the employer may not be liable. However, it is likely that if the employer knew about the employee's propensity to violence and had the opportunity to change this, then liability may be imposed. Although the doctrine of vicarious liability can enable an injured participant to sue the potentially richer employing club, or to claim on its insurance, it can only be applied where there is a relationship of employer and employee. For the vast majority of unpaid sports participants, this cause of action does not arise.

Liability of Match Officials

Whilst actions for co-participant liability were becoming more commonplace, it came as a surprise when, in 1996, the first case where a match official was sued for controlling a game incompetently succeeded. It was claimed in the media that this would signal the end of sport as we know it, that nobody would want to officiate because of the risk of litigation and that if people did not want to get hurt playing sport then they should not play it. In reality, although still a landmark decision, sport has not ended; officials still officiate and injured participants can pursue an additional avenue when seeking compensation where it is deserved.

---

48 *Warren v Henlys Ltd* [1948] 2 All ER 935, *per* Hilbery J.
49 *Lister v Hesley Hall Ltd* [2002] 1 AC 215 and *Mattis v Pollock* [2003] IRLR 603.
50 See further, James, M and McArdle, D, 'Player violence or violent players: vicarious liability for sports participants' (2004) E Priv LR, forthcoming.
51 *Rose v Plenty* [1976] 1 WLR 141.

Smoldon v Nolan and Whitworth [1997] ELR 249

The claimant was a flanker playing in an under-19s colts rugby union match. The game was a local derby and was described as being full of niggling challenges. One forward player on the opposition side had been sent off and, contrary to the rules in place for junior rugby, the referee had allowed uneven scrums to take place, with eight players on one side and seven on the other. Further, because of the regularity of scrums collapsing, the hooker on the claimant's team had swapped positions with the claimant because his neck was too sore to continue playing hooker.

An abnormally high number of scrums continued to collapse despite warnings from both coaches and touch judges. The referee failed throughout the match to implement the 'CTPE' procedure for the engagement of scrums, which requires the two packs to crouch, touch shoulders and pause before engaging the scrum. Shortly after half-time, the scrum collapsed yet again, breaking the claimant's neck and leaving him paralysed.

The court held that the law was as stated in *Condon v Basi* and *Elliott v Saunders*. Thus, it must be established whether a duty was owed by the referee to the players and whether he had breached that by being negligent in all the circumstances. It was held that a referee owes a duty to the players to exercise the degree of care for their safety that is appropriate in the circumstances and to act as would a reasonable and competent referee. Further, there are no public policy grounds that can operate to exclude the liability of sports officials.

To establish a breach of the duty owed by the referee, the court held that the threshold of liability is high and will not be easily crossed because of the inherently risky nature of contact sports such as rugby. However, by failing to operate the CTPE procedure, failing to ensure that there were equal numbers on both sides of the scrum, failing to take notice of the warnings of the coaches and the injury to the original hooker and failing to provide adequate instructions to the players to help them prevent collapsing the scrum, there was sufficient evidence that the referee was in breach of his duty. The rules of the game, particularly those relating to the engagement of scrums, were not definitive of liability but were part of the circumstances which must be taken into account when trying to establish a breach of duty. As a result, the defendant had failed to exercise reasonable care and skill in the performance of his duty and had therefore breached his duty by failing to act in the manner of a reasonable and competent referee.

Smoldon was awarded £1.8 million damages for his injuries but received only £1 million. The defendant was unable to meet the claim because his earnings were insufficient, as they would be for most sports defendants. The compensation received was the maximum available under the Rugby Football Union's insurance scheme which was in place to protect referees in such situations. If Smoldon had not been able to reach the RFU's policy, then his claim would have been a hollow victory. Since this case, the RFU have encouraged all clubs to have their own policies of insurance and have increased the maximum payout under its own policy to £5 million.[52]

This decision opened up a previously unexplored area of potential liability. The judge explained that his was a decision on the particular facts of the case and not of general applicability throughout sport. However, the case sets a precedent that where a referee negligently allows breaches of the safety rules of a sport, as opposed to the playing rules, then a player who is injured as a result of those breaches can bring an action in negligence against the referee. This principle has since been applied to adult rugby.

Vowles v Evans and The Welsh Rugby Union Limited [2003] EWCA Civ 318

The claimant was playing hooker for Llanharan RUFC. After 30 minutes of play, a Llanharan prop dislocated his shoulder and had to leave the field. The referee explained that if there was no specialist

---

52   See further http://www.rfu.com/pdfs/community/rfuclubscompulsoryinsurance.pdf.

front row replacement, he would order uncontested scrums, as per the rules, however, if this happened, no league points could be awarded to Llanharan if they won. A Llanharan flanker with some limited experience of propping offered to 'give it a go' as there was no recognised specialist replacement.

For the remainder of the game, most of the scrums collapsed or failed to engage correctly around 2 or 3 times each. Despite the inability of the replacement prop, the referee persisted with contested scrums. During injury time at the end of the second half, the scrum again failed to engage properly. The claimant sustained a dislocation of his neck causing permanent incomplete tetraplegia. The WRU admitted that if negligence was established against the referee, it would be vicariously liable. At trial, Morland J held that the referee owed the players a duty to take reasonable care of their safety and that the had breached that duty by failing to insist on either a properly trained front row substitute or by failing to award uncontested scrums. The defendants appealed.

The appeal was dismissed and the reasoning of the High Court was upheld. Firstly, no policy reasons can justify why rugby union referees should not have a duty of care imposed upon them. There is no evidence to suggest either that people will be discouraged from refereeing in the future or that the WRU should not acquire insurance for its referees. Secondly, it was acknowledged that although there is a degree of risk involved in playing rugby, particularly as a prop, a player does not accept that the referee should be absolved from liability for injuries caused by his own negligent failure to uphold and apply the safety rules of the sport. Thirdly, by allowing Llanharan to choose a replacement prop forward of inadequate experience instead of ordering uncontested scrums, the referee had breached his duty of care to the claimant. Fourthly, a clear link between the scrum collapses and misengagements and the inexperience of the replacement player established the necessary causal link between the breach of duty and the injuries caused. Appeal dismissed.

In upholding the liability of the defendants, the Court of Appeal was yet again not influenced by the baseless arguments that sport would be brought to an end by this decision. Instead, it ensures that the safety of the players and the upholding of the safety rules are given precedence over other considerations. The duty of care imposed on a referee is not an onerous one; it requires only that the referee run the game in the way that he has been trained to and to follow the safety rules and procedures as laid down by the governing body. The referee would have avoided liability by either ordering uncontested scrums on the basis that there was no suitable replacement, or having allowed the replacement a reasonable attempt to prove himself in the position, to have ordered uncontested scrums when it became clear that the replacement was not competent.

Although these precedents have not been used widely, they do ensure that where match officials cause injury to players by their negligent non-application of the safety rules of a sport, then they, and vicariously the appropriate governing body, will be liable for damages. Thus for example, where an official fails to control some dangerous aspect of a game, such as allowing too many late tackles in football or high sticking in hockey, and as a result of these breaches of the safety rules a player is injured, then the referee could be at least partly liable for the injuries caused. His liability may be shared with the player who directly caused the contact but the official could be at least partially liable nonetheless.

A further problem for officials could arise from the state of the playing surface. In most sports, the officials are responsible for checking the pitch to ensure that it is playable. If a pitch is too wet, too hard, too uneven, or has stones or glass on it and the game should not proceed, any player injured by the official's decision to allow the game to be played on an unplayable or otherwise unsafe surface could again find themselves liable in negligence for the resulting injuries.

The true scope of these decisions will only be established following further litigation. The potential liability of match officials could force the most changes on sport. The most immediate outcome of the decision is that all match officials, either individually or through a governing body scheme, should be covered by adequate insurance. The more pro-active governing bodies are already insisting on a greater degree of regulation and certification of their officials to ensure that they are of a higher overall quality and more aware of the relevant safety issues. This is the only real means by which sport's future appearances in court can be limited. Failing the implementation of such programmes, the law will continue to impose liability for injury-causing incompetence.

Liability of Coaches and Supervisors

Possibly the most unexplored area of sporting negligence is the potential liability of sports coaches. If a match official can be liable for the negligent application of the rules of a game, then by analogy, a coach could be liable for the negligent supervision of a player, failure to teach players the rules of the game or for inappropriate training methods or tactics. If a player is injured or causes injury because they have not been taught how to play the game correctly, then the coach would appear to be the most appropriate person to sue for the damage caused. The most analogous cases involve the liability of school sports instructors. For example, in *Gannon v Rotherham MBC*, a PE teacher was found to have failed to instruct a pupil how to perform a racing dive into the shallow end of a swimming pool. The local council were vicariously liable for the injuries caused to the child.[53] Similarly, in *Affutu-Nartoy v Clarke and the ILEA*,[54] the claimant, a 15 year old boy, brought a successful action against the defendant for injuries caused by a high tackle performed on him during a rugby union training match.

Without any clear authority on coaches' liability, only speculative conclusions can be drawn. It would seem that if a coach fails to teach a participant a relevant skill, or teaches a skill to be performed in an incorrect manner, then the coach will be liable for any injuries that result to the inappropriately trained participant. This could even be extended to cover situations where a participant injures an opponent because of an inadequate technique. In this case, the opponent could sue the coach for his negligent training of the participant. Where the coach was in a paid position, such as working for a club or governing body, then that club or governing body would be vicariously liable for the actions of the employee-coach.

This type of action could be extended to include situations where players are asked or even forced to play whilst recovering from injury. Any extension of the recovery period, or exacerbation of the injury, could be at least partly the fault of the coach, especially where the true nature of the injury is kept from the player to encourage him to play on. Liability could also be extended to cover medical practitioners who condone or assist the coach in coercing or encouraging a player to play through injury, or who give negligent advice to a player about his ability to restart training and playing. Although some of this may at first sight seem far-fetched, in an age where players are sometimes given painkillers as a matter of course, clubs will need to have more effective systems in place to ensure that players are told what they are taking, why they should take it and what the nature of their injury is.

Liability for Unsafe Playing Area

In certain circumstances it is possible for an injured sports participant to bring an action by using the specialised duty of care under the Occupiers' Liability Act 1957.[55] The occupier of a sports facility

---

53   (1991) unreported.
54   (1984) *The Times*, 9 February, QBD.
55   See Chapter 17 for a full discussion of this topic.

owes a duty to all users to ensure that it is safe to be used for the sports which are played there. This includes the playing surfaces and equipment necessary for each particular sport.

Cook v Doncaster BC (1993) unreported

The claimant was a professional jockey competing in a race at the Doncaster Race Course. The Course was owned and operated by the defendant. As the claimant's horse approached the finish line, it caught its front leg in a divot that had been made by a horse in a previous race. The horse stumbled, unseated the claimant and landed on top of him, fracturing his collarbone. The claimant was unable to race for the rest of the season and was also unable to perform a lucrative contract to race in Hong Kong. Held, that the Race Course was found to have been unsafe for the purposes of horse racing as the divots and hoofprints had not been removed from it.[56]

The claimant received almost £350,000 in damages for pain and suffering and lost earnings. This cause of action could be used in tandem with a claim against a referee who has failed to notice that the playing surface of the sports facility is unsuitable for a particular sport, again extending the number of potential defendants against whom a claimant can claim.

Liability of Governing Bodies

The ultimate responsibility for running a sport and ensuring that its rules and the participants are safe lies with the governing body. The law of negligence has developed incrementally to the point where a sports governing body has been successfully sued for failing to provide a reasonably adequate safety system to be used by organisers of specific sports fixtures. As with *Smoldon*, there is much scope for the principles espoused in this case to be developed further and used to ensure that a sports governing body takes full responsibility for all safety aspects of the sport over which it rules.

Watson v British Boxing Board of Control [2001] QB 1134

The claimant was a professional boxer fighting in a bout sanctioned by the defendant. The fight was stopped in the final round when the referee decided that the claimant could no longer defend himself. He returned to his corner and quickly became unconscious at 10.54 pm. At 11.01 pm, he was seen by the ringside doctor. He was received at the North Middlesex Hospital at 11.22 pm, where he was prepared for operation. He was finally transferred to St Bartholomew's where he was operated on at 12.30 am and a sub-dural haematoma removed. The claimant was paralysed on his left side and had further physical and mental disabilities. It was alleged that the defendant owed a duty of care to the claimant and had breached it by not providing adequate rules to boxing promoters on the correct medical provision to be present at each bout.

The Court held that the BBBC did not create the initial danger, from the punches, to the boxers. Further, only promoters who were licensed by the Board and who followed its safety rules and advice could hold a bout. As the BBBC is a body with specialised knowledge in matters of safety and this knowledge is relied on by those involved with the sport, including both boxers and promoters, it is therefore under a duty to ensure that its rules provide a safe system by which injuries incurred as a result of a fight can be properly treated. Further, as the safety advice is relied on by the boxers for their own safety, there is sufficient proximity between the Board and the boxers for a duty to arise in respect of the insufficiency of the guidelines regarding post-bout medical treatment.

The duty was breached by the Board failing to provide adequate guidelines on what medical personnel and equipment should be present at a bout. The guidelines that were available were not in accordance

---

56 *Cook v Doncaster* (1993) unreported, HC.

with current medical best practice. The most important time to begin treatment of a brain haemorrhage is in the minutes immediately following the initial injury. The longer the delay, the greater the likelihood that the injuries suffered would be exacerbated by the swelling damaging the brain. The ringside treatment should therefore be much quicker and should begin preparing the injured fighter for surgery. If it had been, then it is likely that the claimant's injuries would have been significantly reduced. As serious brain injury is a foreseeable though infrequent outcome of a boxing bout, there should be in place guidelines that reflect this risk and ensure that a boxer's health is protected as far as is possible.

By reason of its position as the governing body of the sport and that an important part of that role was to produce safety guidelines for bouts, the Board owed a duty of care to the claimant. That duty was breached by the inadequacy of the guidelines and this caused foreseeable harm by exacerbating a serious brain injury incurred during the course of the bout.

The BBBC was liable because it had ignored current medical practice, of which it was aware, and had not updated its guidelines to ensure that all boxing bouts complied with this as a minimum requirement. It had not acted as a reasonable and competent governing body by its failure to ensure that boxers fighting in bouts sanctioned by it were provided with the most up to date post-fight medical supervision. Thus, governing bodies have imposed upon them a duty of care to ensure that participants in their sport are not exposed to unnecessary risks to their health and safety. Surprisingly, this issue has resurfaced only once, in the context of motor sport.

Wattleworth v Goodwood Road Racing Company Ltd, Royal Automobile Club Motor Sports Association Ltd and Federation Internationale De L'Automobile [2004] EWHC 140

The claimant brought an action on behalf of herself and as administratrix of her husband's estate. She alleged that certain safety barriers in place at the Goodwood motoring racing circuit were not adequate, the result of which was that her husband was killed when he crashed into them. The actions were against the first defendant under the Occupier's Liability Act 1957 s 2, for breaching its duty to provide a safe place to race motor vehicles, and against the second and third defendants for their failure to carry out sufficient or adequate inspections of the Goodwood circuit, thereby breaching their duty of care towards users of the race track.

From around 1991, Goodwood Road Racing Company (GRRC) began to develop and renovate the Goodwood circuit to bring it up to the standards required to host International Racing Calendar vintage car races. At all times, they consulted with Royal Automobile Club Motor Sports Association (MSA) technical and safety managers and, when necessary, the Federation Internationale De L'Automobile's (FIA) Circuits and Safety Commissions. The MSA would eventually be required to licence the Goodwood track and the FIA specific interntaional events that GRRC was hoping to host. Between 1993 and September 1998, the MSA and the FIA conducted a number of inspections and submitted a series of technical reports to GRRC outlining the changes and developments that needed to be carried out to the Goodwood circuit to bring it up to FIA standard. On each occasion that a safety recommendation was made, these were implemented by GRRC. On 17 September 1998, the relevant licence was issued by the MSA as the GRRC had completed all safety works required of it by the MSA and the FIA. Following the first major international meeting at the circuit on 18–20 September, no further changes were required. It was considered that if the track met these international standards, it was more than adequately safe for lesser events, such as track days. On 5 November 1998, at a track day, the deceased crashed his car into the tyre and earth barrier on the Lavant bend of the circuit, suffering massive injuries from which he died.

The role of the MSA and FIA, for the purposes of this case, can be summarised as being to produce safety specifications for motor racing tracks, to inspect and make recommendations about safety issues and to issue licences to tracks that reach the appropriate level of safety for the relevant categories of race. The deceased was a motorsport enthusiast, who held a MSA Race National B Licence and who regularly took part in track days. On the day of the accident, the weather was fine and there were no other drivers obstructing the deceased. As he exited the first part of the Lavant bend, his wheels went over the grass verge, he lost control of the car and hit the tyre and earth bank on the opposite side of the track at between 60–70mph and was killed instantly.

Following the accident, the circuit was again inspected by the MSA and was again found to be acceptable and constructed in accordance with recognised custom and practice. On 8 December 1999 alterations to the safety wall at the Lavant bend were instituted by GRRC, not the licensing bodies, at the annual MSA inspection. These involved placing soft impact absorbing materials in front of the tyre and earth wall. These changes were made prior to the issue of the 2000 licence.

Liability of GRRC: it was accepted that a duty was owed under s 2 OLA 1957 to take such care as is reasonable in all the circumstances to ensure that visitors are reasonably safe for the purposes for which they are permitted to be on the premises. GRRC's claim that this duty was discharged because they treated safety as an issue of paramount importance, recognised their lack of expertise in this area and therefore relied reasonably on the expertise of the MSA and the FIA, was accepted by the court. The relevant bodies had been fully and properly instructed and their opinions reasonably relied on and acted on to ensure that the circuit was reasonably safe for the classes of events that it hosted.

Liability of the MSA: using a similar formulation to that used by the Court of Appeal in *Watson*, the court held that there was a sufficiently proximate relationship on which to base a duty of care. Thus, where A (MSA) advises B (GRRC) as to action to be taken which will directly and foreseeably affect the safety of C (the deceased), then a situation of sufficient proximity exists to found a duty of care on the part of A towards C. As the MSA's inspectors were aware that their advice would be used in respect of events licensed by the MSA and those that were not licensed, the imposition of a duty of care on the MSA was fair, just and reasonable in the circumstances. The crash site had been identified as a low risk site, which was backed up by the very few accidents that had occurred there, but the risk was still a foreseeable one. However, the recommendations on the choice of crash barrier made by the MSA inspectors were reasonably made after proper consideration. They were made for good cause and were ones that an inspector skilled in motor racing circuit safety matters would reasonably and properly make and approve. Therefore, the duty of care imposed on the MSA was not breached by the advice of its inspectors.

Liability of the FIA: the court held that at the time of the accident, Goodwood held only a MSA licence. Further, the FIA's structure ensured that the primary responsibility for safety and track licensing lay with the national body, the MSA, and that the FIA licensed only specific events. Thus, the relative lack of proximity between GRRC and the FIA ensured that no duty of care could be imposed upon the FIA.

For these reasons, all claims were dismissed by the court.

The form of the duty imposed on a governing body will vary dramatically from sport to sport. In *Watson*, the BBBC failed to provide the necessary post-match care, through guidelines to its promoters, to a boxer who had suffered a brain injury. This type of injury is a foreseeable result of boxing and it is further foreseeable that if it is not treated quickly the injuries will be exacerbated. In *Wattleworth*, the duty of the governing/licensing body, the MSA, was to ensure that motor racing tracks were reasonably safe for drivers and spectators. This duty was discharged by its inspectors having acted reasonably by carrying out the series of inspections. Although the reasoning for declining to impose a duty of care on the FIA is not convincing, if a duty had been imposed, it too would not have been breached in this case. The reasoning of the High Court of Australia in *Agar v Hyde*[57] was not followed in coming to this decision and should mean that the possibility of pursuing an international federation as opposed to a national governing body is still open under English law.

---

57   [2000] CLR 201.

How this rule applies to other sporting situations is open to question. Where governing bodies lay down strict safety rules and do not enforce them, or should lay down strict safety rules but do not, or do not update them, then liability will be imposed. Whether this should be extended to all sports where serious injuries are foreseeable is likely to be much more controversial. Is it reasonable to require all rugby games have doctors, stretchers and neck braces available in case of spinal injuries at collapsed scrums? Should hockey games have eye or dental treatment available in case a ball or stick causes facial injuries? What safety procedures should be in place at equestrian events?

These potential extensions refer only to the provision of medical treatment for relatively commonly occurring or foreseeable injuries. A governing body might avoid potential liability by the provision of adequate guidelines to leagues and clubs but only if these were enforced. It is one thing to give guidance, another to allow those supposedly guided to completely ignore the advice with impunity.

More dramatically for sport would be the possibility that liability could be imposed on a governing body for the inadequacy of its in-game safety rules. Where a specific injury, or injury from a specific act, is a common occurrence in a sport, it is possible that the governing body could be liable when those injuries are caused. The court in *Watson* held that one of the reasons why governing bodies exist is to provide guidance, conduct and disseminate research and educate all those involved in its sport about safety issues. For example, if it is known that bouncers in cricket are dangerous and can cause injury unless the rules are changed, an incremental development of the law from *Watson* could see cricket's governing bodies liable for their failure to ensure the safety of cricketers.

Unlawful Interference with Contract

Moving away from the law of negligence, the tort of unlawful interference with contract must be examined. This tort requires the defendant to interfere intentionally with an existing contract between the claimant and another by doing an unlawful act. There is much confusion over the precise definition of this tort as many of the cases are heard only at the interlocutory stage and are never fully argued at trial, though the main elements can be identified. The tort is only likely to be committed by and on professional sports participants.

A defendant must have knowledge of the existence of the contract. That knowledge can be imputed where the defendant is familiar with the particular industry in which the parties are employed. A professional footballer would be taken to know that other professional footballers would be employed on a broadly similar contract to his own. The contract must be breached by 'unlawful means'. 'Unlawful means' includes torts but there is no liability for negligently interfering with a contract.

The difficulty arises over the requirement that the defendant must have acted with an intent to bring about the breach. This has seen two different interpretations given to this element and as yet no appellate court has been asked to rule on it finally. In the more restrictive sense, the defendant must act with the specific intent to breach the contract; the unlawful act must be designed to bring about the breach. Alternatively, the defendant may be required only to foresee that a breach is an inevitable consequence of his intentional conduct; he does not intend the breach, just the act that will cause it.

In the one case in which this argument has been raised, the judge somewhat confusingly concentrated on a claim of whether recklessness was sufficient for the tort. It is not. Further, by his finding that the defendant-player had been only negligent in his challenge, the action should fail at that point without further discussion.

Watson and Bradford City FC v Gray and Huddersfield Town **FC (1998) unreported**

The first claimant and first defendant were both playing professional football in a competitive First Division match. The claimant had just passed the ball to a team-mate at which point the defendant attempted a sliding challenge on him. The challenge was poorly executed, coming in high and late on the claimant, seriously breaking his leg. Held, the defendant acted negligently in performing the challenge and the claimant received compensation for his injuries. The defendant's employer, Huddersfield Town FC, were vicariously liable for the damages.

It was further claimed by the second claimant that there had been an unlawful interference with their contract of employment with the first claimant. As the first claimant was injured for almost the entire duration of his playing contract, the second claimant claimed compensation for the cost of hiring a replacement and for the lost money spent on the transfer fee that brought him to the club. The judge dismissed the claim on the basis that no deliberate unlawful act within the definition of the tort had occurred.

Although negligence is not sufficient, if the injury is caused by a trespass, the claim could succeed. Professional players will know of the existence of contracts of employment between their opponents and their clubs. A trespass is an intentional tort and is a sufficiently unlawful act. The inability to perform the employment contract is inevitable if one player deliberately injures another to the extent that he cannot play for a period of time. Alternatively, if the trespass is proven, it could be argued more easily that where contact and injury were intended, so also would be the eventual inability of the injured party to fulfil their contract. It is entirely possible that such a claim may succeed in the future. This would enable a club whose player was injured to claim compensation and avoid suffering financial loss by shifting the burden of paying for a replacement player on to the shoulders of the defendant-player's employing club.

COMPENSATION IN TORT

The aim of tortious damages is to compensate the victim for losses that are incurred as a result of the tort by putting them in the position as though the tort had never happened.[58] A claim for damages can be a gamble for both parties to an action. Although the court can determine a claimant's pre-trial losses, future losses are much more a matter of speculation. If the claimant recovers more fully than expected, there is a risk of over-compensation. If the condition degenerates, there is a risk of under-compensation. This problem arises because the court will, in general, award the claimant a lump sum at the end of the trial to cover both pre-trial losses and the more speculative general damages. To combat these discrepancies, structured settlements are used where serious injuries have been incurred. Instead of paying a one-off lump sum to the claimant, a structured settlement makes a series of periodic payments, usually by way of a life assurance policy. However, they are usually only a viable alternative to traditional damages awards in instances of catastrophic injury or where a high level of damages are expected.[59]

Trespass to the person and negligence have one distinct difference between them when an action for damages is pursued. For actions in negligence, the claimant must prove that he has suffered

---

58   See further, *op cit*, fn 1, Lunney and Oliphant (2003), Ch 15.
59   See further, Goldrein and De Haas, 'Butterworths personal injury litigation sevice' (2004) London: Butterworths Para [1001] *et seq.*

physical and/or property damage.[60] Trespass is actionable *per se*, without proof of injury.[61] However, where injury is minor, only a small sum will be awarded to register the court's displeasure at the trespass.

Courts can award damages from three separate categories. The most common kind are compensatory damages. The other two categories, aggravated and exemplary damages, are rarely awarded by English courts and are not thought to be appropriate in cases of negligence. These heads of damage should be considered only following an actionable trespass to the person, specifically a battery, and must be specifically pleaded.

Compensatory Damages

The aim of compensatory damages is to compensate the claimant, as far as is financially possible, with an amount that will put him in the same position as he was before the tort occurred. An award of compensatory damages will usually be the claimant's largest and only claim from the defendant. The award is split into two further sub-categories of special and general damages. Special damages are losses that are precisely quantifiable pre-trial. They will include pre-trial loss of earnings, medical expenses and damage caused to any personal property, such as sports equipment, as a result of the tort.

General damages are more speculative in nature or incapable of exact calculation. The most common and usually the most important claims under this heading are first, compensation for the pain and suffering caused by the injury and for loss of amenity, or being unable to do things as a result of the injury that the victim could have previously done. The amount awarded is calculated by reference to a tariff-like system which gives a certain amount per injury depending on its severity and impact on the victim.[62] The second claim will be for loss of future earnings and any loss of future earnings capacity, such as not getting promoted or not being able to follow an equally remunerative employment as a result of the injury. Special and general damages make up the largest part of any claim for compensation.

Aggravated and Exemplary Damages

Aggravated damages are a sub-species of compensatory damages often confused with exemplary damages. Aggravated damages are not awarded to punish the defendant. They are awarded to reflect the greater degree of harm caused to the claimant by the circumstances in which the injury was inflicted. As Lord Hailsham has said:

> In awarding aggravated damages the natural indignation of the court at the injury on the [claimant] is a perfectly legitimate motive in making a generous rather than a more moderate award to provide an adequate solution. But that is because the injury to the [claimant] is actually greater and as the result of the conduct exciting the indignation demands a more generous solution.[63]

Aggravated damages can be awarded for the damage caused to one's pride or for the humiliation suffered during the commission of the tort. The circumstances in which the tort was committed could

---

60   *Donoghue v Stevenson* [1932] AC 562.
61   *Letang v Cooper* [1965] 1 QB 232.
62   *Kemp and Kemp Personal Injury Awards* (2004) (CD-ROM), London: Sweet & Maxwell.
63   *Cassell & Co Ltd v Broome* [1972] 1 All ER 801.

include that the tort was committed in public, in front of a large audience or whilst being broadcast on television. These factors could lead a court to consider that the damage suffered was more serious than the simple infliction of an injury.

Exemplary damages are purely punitive in nature. They are awarded only very rarely by English courts and are best described as a civil fine, payable to the claimant instead of the State. English courts prefer not to award exemplary damages as it is considered that they create a windfall that leads to the over-compensation of the claimant, by rewarding him for a loss that has not been suffered. Exemplary damages should only be awarded where the defendant has committed the tort in a manner that he knows will make him a profit in excess of the damages awarded to the claimant. Exemplary damages awards take the financial profit element from the defendant and award it to the claimant. However, they are not restricted to money-making and can be awarded to teach the defendant that breaking the law does not pay. Such damages are means tested and will be added on to the compensatory award only if the defendant can afford to pay them.[64]

The injury-causing situations associated with sport where aggravated and exemplary damages are appropriate are likely to be extremely limited. However, one case from Australia, where the courts undertake similar considerations to English courts, has considered awards under all three headings.

Rogers v Bugden and Canterbury-Bankstown (1993) ATR 81–246

[The facts of the case are detailed above, p 645.]

Rogers' claim for exemplary damages was rejected on the grounds that Bugden had been punished adequately by a 14-week suspension imposed on him by the Australian Rugby League for the tackle and that any award would necessarily be small having regard to Bugden's employment as a police constable and his limited capacity to pay. If not for these factors, the trial judge would have regarded this as an appropriate case for an award of exemplary damages. The claimant's claim for aggravated damages was overlooked by the trial judge as was the claim for exemplary damages against the club.

Each of the three parties appealed against aspects of the decision.

Held: the award of damages would be increased against both parties to include aggravated damages of A$8,000 . . . and the award was further increased against Bugden, but not against the club, to include exemplary damages of A$7,500 for the following reasons.

. . .

(5) The claimant was entitled to an additional award for aggravated damages for the injury to his feelings. The emotional impact of the claimant's realisation that he had been the public victim of a deliberate assault and its contribution to his frustration and anger was not reflected in the award of general damages.

(6) The trial judge erred in rejecting the claim for exemplary damages against Bugden. The matters which led the trial judge to refuse to award exemplary damages were relevant. However in referring to Bugden's earnings as a police constable the trial judge overlooked his earnings as a footballer. While his match payments ceased during his period of suspension, Bugden continued to receive his playing fees and remained in the game after he had taken the claimant out of the game. Notwithstanding the deterrent effect of the suspension, the tackle was deliberate, intended to hurt and unnecessary.

(7) No exemplary damages would be awarded against the club, although this was a borderline case. The evidence stopped short of establishing that the club had encouraged or incited Bugden to engage in unlawful conduct on the field. A club seeking to motivate its players and in particular to direct their efforts against particular opposing players ran the risk that it would be found to have

---

64   *Rookes v Barnard* [1964] 1 All ER 367.

authorised or induced illegitimate action, in which case an award of exemplary damages in the order of $150,000 may not have been inappropriate.

In the UK, claims for compensatory damages are the norm. A claim for exemplary damages is unlikely to succeed except in the most extreme cases of deliberate assault, with all of the associated evidential difficulties such a claim entails. In *Rogers*, where exemplary damages were used as an additional punishment against the defendant-player, and contemplated against the defendant-club, the amount of compensation could have been trebled, exactly the kind of windfall payment that English courts are reluctant to award.

Aggravated damages remain unexplored in the English cases. If the reasoning of the Australian court was followed, aggravated damages could be awarded where there is additional emotional hurt or humiliation caused by the infliction of the injuries. This is particularly relevant where the claimant is a professional sportsperson and the injury is either broadcast live on television, or numerous replays are shown of it, reinforcing the fact that injury has been caused. This controversial claim could see some compensation claims increased significantly.

Conclusions

Actions in negligence provide the best legal means of securing compensation for injuries caused when playing sport. The recent reforms to the civil justice system in England ensure that cases should now reach court more quickly and that the trial process itself is greatly simplified. Contingency fee arrangements have removed a degree of financial risk that was inherent in bringing a compensation claim. However, it is not ideal.

There remain great evidential difficulties in pursuing tortious claims. As with the criminal law, proving the intention to commit a trespass is problematic unless the incident takes place off-the-ball or is otherwise unconnected with the play. Injuries that occur from on-the-ball incidents are likely to continue to provoke diametrically opposed views on whether the challenge was negligent. Although the numbers of expert witnesses that can be called by each side has been significantly restricted under the Civil Procedure Rules, claimants will still need to call expert evidence on the poor quality of the tackle, future playing career prospects and potential earnings capacity. The defence will equally rely on expert evidence to rebut those claims. Members of the parties' respective teams giving eyewitness accounts are likely to continue to feel a degree of loyalty towards their team mate and be reluctant to give evidence against them.[65] Equally, expert and eyewitnesses are likely to continue to give wildly varying views on whether a particular challenge was the kind of tackle expected of a player at that level or the worst and most dangerous tackle ever seen.

Claimants will continue to be unlucky and unsuccessful in their actions. Paul Elliott was left with a £750,000 legal bill following his failed action against Dean Saunders. This sum is roughly equivalent to the amount that he received under his insurance policy, leaving him with nothing. Ben Smoldon and Richard Vowles received around half of the compensation they were awarded as only limited insurance policies were in place. The litigation surrounding Michael Watson's injuries has left the BBBC virtually bankrupt and unable to fully meet his claim. Perhaps a more effective system of compensation should be based on insurance for sports participants.

---

65   The high profile case of Vinnie Jones turning hostile witness in *Elliott v Saunders* is a notable exception.

ALTERNATIVE SYSTEMS OF CONTROL AND COMPENSATION

The legal regulation of participator violence is often a long, drawn-out and expensive process. Worse still, it lacks the general support of those for whose benefit it is supposed to operate; the players. Most sports have in place a system of dispute resolution based on their internal disciplinary procedures and tribunals. As their name suggests, however, these tribunals are for disciplinary purposes only and are not used as a means of determining liability to pay compensation. In this section, various possible alternative control mechanisms are examined.

Control by the Governing Body

The very nature of sport means that it requires a framework of rules within which to operate. Without the rules the game does not exist; they need to be enforced and infringements of them punished. This function is carried out by a combination of governing body appointed match officials and the governing body's disciplinary procedures.

During the Game – the Match Officials

Whilst play is in progress, the match officials are in charge of upholding the rules and punishing the transgressors. In-game penalties are not only there to ensure that the sport is played according to its rules and in the correct spirit but also to ensure that safety rules and procedures are observed. Match officials usually have a range of punishments at their disposal including for example, loss of possession, the deduction of points, a free shot at goal or point-scoring attempt, ejection for the whole or part of the remainder of the game and disqualification. These are the simplest and most immediate punishments for all forms of violent conduct. Where little or no injury is involved, they will usually be sufficient and no further sanction will be imposed.

Post-Game – the Disciplinary Tribunals

Most governing bodies run a quasi-judicial disciplinary process.[66] Players must submit to these procedures following more serious breaches of the rules when a more severe punishment is required. Players are notified that they must attend a hearing and of the charge against them. The hearing itself is run like a mini-court with evidence provided by both sides. Most governing bodies allow the player charge to be represented in some way, usually by a lawyer or union representative. If the charge is not proven, then the in-game punishment stands as the penalty. If found guilty, the player will usually be fined, suspended from playing, or a combination of the two. At the professional level, fines can often be far in excess of those that could be imposed by the criminal courts. However, it is suspension that is generally considered to be the more effective punishment. Amongst non-elite participants, sport is played for recreational purposes and the players do not want to be banned from their hobby. At the elite levels, bans can have a serious impact on a player's career and/or earnings.

Bans and fines are used by governing bodies to punish certain forms of conduct and to deter others from repeating it in the future. What they do not do is provide a mechanism for establishing liability in terms of awarding compensation to the injured party. The governing bodies of British sport

---

66 See further, Lewis and Taylor (2003), Ch A2.

have never considered that this potential usurpation of the traditional role of the courts falls within their own jurisdiction.

Effectiveness

The ideal of self-regulation and the threat of what can occur if it fails to live up to the standards required by the law have been succinctly expressed by Lord Denning.

Enderby Town FC v Football Association [1971] 1 Ch 591

Justice can often be done in [internal tribunals] better by a good layman than by a bad lawyer. This is especially so in activities like football and other sports where no points of law are likely to arise and it is all part of the proper regulation of the game. It is not at liberty to lay down absolute rules: 'We will never allow anyone to have a lawyer to appear for him' . . . The long and the short of it is that if a court sees that a . . . tribunal is proposing to proceed in a manner contrary to the rules of natural justice, it can intervene to stop it.[67]

Punishments imposed from a governing body are potentially the most effective method for controlling sports violence. It is the most immediate and direct form of punishment and contains the required effective symbolism. Players know that it will be imposed and to a greater or lesser extent it is imposed with a degree of consistency and certainty. Players play sports because they want to, whether for recreational or financial reasons. Bans not only restrict their opportunity to play but also remove their opportunity to repeat the offence for the period of the ban. The more often they are violent, the longer will be the ban until the stage is reached where the player is either deterred from acting violently or is banned for life. Internal sanctions are the clearest indication to law enforcement agencies that a governing body is in control of its sport and does not need legal intervention to deter participator violence.

Where a disciplinary tribunal is operated efficiently, delays between the act and the punishment can be kept to a minimum, maximising its symbolic impact, unlike the lengthy pre-trial wait should the law become involved. For example, the Rugby Football League holds all tribunals before the next round of matches are played, whilst the Football Association will generally hold its hearings within a month of the incident. Although a long delay can result in players attempting to manipulate the system and serve a ban when it is most convenient to themselves, the system is considered by those involved in sport to work well.

However, there are problems with these systems. First, until recently, many tribunals paid scant regard to the rules of natural justice. This is changing and will continue to do so in the light of the Human Rights Act 1998.[68] However, without any standard format for these procedures, further challenges are likely in the future. Secondly, an action for restraint of trade can be brought by a professional player if a ban is imposed for too long a period. The player may claim that it is unreasonably preventing him from earning his living from the sport.[69] Thus, the length of bans must be capable of being justified objectively. Thirdly, compared to criminal punishments, the judgments of a tribunal can seem somewhat trivial. If a governing body's punishment fails to reflect the seriousness of the player's act, then the criminal law will continue to have an impact on the whole of sport.

---

67   *Enderby Town FC v Football Association* [1971] 1 Ch 591, p 605.
68   See earlier, p 217 and in particular *Jones v Welsh rugby Union* (1998) *The Times*, 6th January.
69   See earlier, p 212 and in particular *Edwards v British Athletic Federation* [1998] 2 CMLR 363.

Finally, the inability of governing bodies to determine issues of compensation for injured players ensures that recourse to the civil law will continue for those injured whilst playing sport.

Legal Standing of Internal Sanctions

In English law, there is no formal relationship between criminal law punishments, tortious compensation and sport's internal disciplinary processes. This lack of coherence can cause serious problems for the perpetrator of participator violence. The player can be punished by the criminal law, the civil law, the match official, his club, the national team and the governing body. Even in Scotland, where there are guidelines for when the criminal law should be used, the only mention made of a governing body's tribunal's concurrent jurisdiction in the Lord Advocate's instructions states that the Procurator Fiscal should take into account any sports related punishment that the player has received when deciding whether to prosecute.[70]

This problem of potential double, or even multiple, jeopardy is great, but is one that is also present in other professions, such as the medical and legal professions, where both an internal tribunal and the courts can punish a wrongdoer. However, sports participants have been vociferous in their complaints at the unfairness of having to submit to multiple jurisdictions.

Before Duncan Ferguson's appeal to the Scottish Football Association (SFA) against his 12 match ban for head butting John McStay, his lawyer said that, 'Our case will be based upon the belief that Duncan has been punished once [by the criminal courts] already and that to impose a second form of punishment would be very unfair'.[71] After the appeal was dismissed, the then Everton FC chairman, Peter Johnson, summed up the feeling at the club by stating that, 'even muggers don't get punished twice'.[72] Although the ban was later overturned, it was not on the grounds of double jeopardy but because the SFA had not applied its own rules correctly when punishing Ferguson.[73] As far as the courts are concerned, the additional punishment is the one imposed by the governing body. Perhaps a more pressing problem for sports tribunals is the possibility that by judging a player before the courts have had the opportunity to do so, they are acting *sub judice*.

In general a governing body's decisions are not susceptible to judicial review.[74] The law treats the findings of internal tribunals as the activities of private bodies. Only the activities of public bodies are susceptible to judicial review. Once the governing body has ruled that a player should be fined or banned, the only route of appeal is through the sport's internal appeals structure.[75] The punishment mechanisms in place from within sport are potentially the most effective means of controlling participator violence. They are immediate, have a greater symbolic impact, remove the player from the context in which he has been acting violently and allow the governing body to determine the scope of the playing culture of their sport. However, the procedural aspects of these tribunals must continue to improve to insulate them from further legal challenges.

---

70 Lord Advocate's instructions, para 8.
71 *The Guardian*, 7 November 1995.
72 *The Guardian*, 9 November 1995.
73 See earlier, pp 212–21 for discussion on fairness of disciplinary procedures.
74 See further Chapter 5.
75 Contrast with the Scottish position in *Ferguson v SFA* (1996) unreported.

Insurance

The only widely available non-legal means of securing compensation for sports injuries is insurance. Insurance schemes could become the most effective means of compensating the victims of participator violence. However, at present, very few participants outside of the very highest levels of sport are covered by anything approaching adequate individual insurance cover.[76] The most important practical advantage of insurance cover is that it can guarantee some level of compensation without the need to go to court. However, it should not be seen as the answer to the faults of the civil justice system. There are a number of disadvantages to such schemes, particularly if implemented on a voluntary, as opposed to a compulsory, basis. It should also be remembered that the extent of the cover provided by any particular insurance scheme will depend partly on the terms of the policy purchased and partly on the sum paid by way of a premium. That said, some governing bodies, for example the Rugby Football Union and England Netball, have been extremely pro-active in developing and promoting insurance schemes available for the whole sport.[77] The sums paid in by the large number of clubs and organisations signed up to their policies has the benefit of providing one giant premium, enabling both bodies to purchase adequate cover for most matches organised under their auspices.

Personal Liability or Personal Accident Insurance

Personal liability insurance schemes cover the insured participant for injuries caused by him to his co-participants. Such schemes will cover all non-intentionally inflicted injuries. Injuries that have been intentionally inflicted are usually specifically excluded by the policy. Where such an injury is inflicted deliberately by the policy holder, the injured party will have to use the normal legal routes to recover compensation.

Personal Injury Insurance

Personal injury insurance schemes cover situations where the insured party has been injured whilst participating in sport. They can cover almost any kind of injury caused provided that the correct policy has been bought to cover the particular sport. Personal injury insurance can be wide enough to cover injuries received through participation in sport, training and travelling to and from a match or training session. This type of policy is the closest that an injured participant can get to a guarantee of a compensation.

Comprehensive and No Fault Insurance

Comprehensive insurance cover is, in effect, the combination of personal liability and personal injury insurance. A comprehensive scheme would ensure that a participant could recover compensation for injuries caused to himself and that he could pay compensation to those injured by him. Such schemes would again cover all injuries except those deliberately inflicted when a legal action would still usually be necessary.

---

76 James, M, 'No fault insurance: kill or cure for sport?' (1999) 2(1) Sports Law Bulletin 10.
77 See further, http://rfu.com/index.cfm/fuseaction/RFUHome.Community_Detail/StoryID/328 and http://www.england-netball.co.uk/dyncat.cfm?catid = 1104.

No fault insurance is a much-touted system of compensation for injuries suffered during sports participation. Its advantages are attractive and obvious. There would be a guaranteed payout to any participant for any injury regardless of its cause. Payouts could be made from a mass insurance policy or a central fund, which covered all participants, either in a given sport or perhaps even in all sports. If a workable administration system could be established, then no fault insurance could be the main compensation mechanism for sports injuries in the future. Its main disadvantage is establishing from where sufficient premiums will come.

Advantages and Disadvantages of Insurance Schemes

Despite their apparently attractive nature, the various insurance schemes are not without their own specific problems. If insurance is going to play a more important and effective role in this area, it must first address some fundamental issues. Although none of these mean that insurance should be discounted as a compensation mechanism, they do show that before its introduction on a wider scale, a fair and effective system must be devised. At the moment the main drawback is simply not having a policy in place at all. In one recent case, the defendant was not registered with a relevant club, leaving the claimant unable to claim against either team's insurance. Left only with the option of suing the defendant, his action was successful. He was awarded £20,000 compensation, an affordable sum to the defendant who had no individual insurance against which to claim.[78]

Insurance can only be an effective compensatory mechanism for sports injuries if one of the schemes discussed above is made compulsory. If it is not, then an injured participant will still run the risk that the person who caused the injuries was uninsured, leaving the victim with no option but to pursue a legal claim. Alternatively, without compulsory personal injury insurance, the victim will not even have his own policy to claim from. Compulsory insurance would appear to be essential, though even this has some specific drawbacks.

The foremost of these is that the burden of the additional expense of most insurance schemes will, in some way or another, fall on the participant. This will have the obvious effect of making some sports, particularly those where injuries are commonplace, much more expensive to play. For example, overall, footballers at all levels suffer the most injuries per season, whilst rugby union players suffer the most serious injuries.[79] Participants in these two sports could expect to have relatively high premiums. So also would those whose sport requires expensive equipment, such as cricket, or a relatively dangerous playing arena, such as ice-based sports. The value of premiums to be paid could have an impact both on overall participation in a sport and its demographic makeup. Compulsory insurance could produce a degree of financial elitism in participation in some sports. One proposed method of controlling spiralling premiums is for teams or national governing bodies to purchase block cover for an entire sport. If every participant contributed a fee, the individual's premium would be greatly decreased, whilst the overall premium would be greatly increased, thereby improving the degree of cover for the participants.

Another unwanted side-effect of compulsory insurance could be that it would actually lead to an increase in dangerous and violent play and more sports injuries. If players know any injury caused to a co-participant will be fully compensated by an insurance policy, part of the deterrent effect of a prospective legal action is removed. If compulsory insurance is to be introduced into sport, it should

78 *Cubbin v Minis* (2000) unreported. See Harvey, S, 'Amateur football and the law' (2001) 9(1) Sport and the Law Journal 103.
79 *The Daily Telegraph*, 12 April 1997.

really only be done so alongside a complete overhaul of the mechanisms by which participator violence is punished. The deterrent effect of the law must be replaced by one that comes from the governing bodies of sport to ensure that all injuries are both adequately compensated and adequately punished.

Finally, the introduction of compulsory insurance may not produce the desired restriction on litigation. Instead, it introduces an additional group of potential claimants and defendants; the insurers. Insurance companies may wish to challenge their need to make a payment on the grounds that, for example, the perpetrator intended to cause the injury, or that the injured party was at fault or contributed to the causing of his injuries. Insurers could sue each other through the participants or policyholders in order to claim indemnities off other insurance companies. Again, the law would be continuing to play a role that sport was trying to obviate.

Neither are no fault insurance schemes the panacea they are often claimed to be. For these schemes, the criticisms relate more to their administration as opposed to any fundamental objection to the scheme itself. The differing risks involved across sports suggests that each sport would require its own separate scheme. The source of funding the premiums must then be pinpointed. The premiums could come from players' subs or a levy on transfer fees or the sale of television rights. The problem with the latter two sources of funding is their variable nature; not all sports have a football-style transfer system and not all sports command large TV incomes.

It must also be established whether the scheme should apply to an entire sport or whether there should be different schemes in place for professional and amateur participants. A further distinction could be made between school sports and other participants and whether the former should be covered by such a general scheme or a more specific scheme for children. None of these problems are insurmountable; however, they are important issues that must be addressed fully before no fault insurance can be introduced effectively and efficiently.

Future Developments

The present systems of punishment and compensation for participator violence are ill-equipped to cope with the demands currently being put on them. A number of proposals have been put forward in recent years to cope with this growing problem. The following sections outline two procedures that appear to work well in other jurisdictions and, in the case of risk management, one that is likely to be developed further in the UK.

The Sporting Injuries Insurance Act 1978 of New South Wales, Australia

The introduction of the Sporting Injuries Insurance Act 1978 has guaranteed a level of compensation to all registered players of authorised sports throughout New South Wales.[80] The Act established a framework through which a payment fund is administered. Premiums are levied on organisations who wish to be registered and covered by the Act. The size of the premium for each organisation is determined by the number of participants in the sport and the degree of risk of injury involved with participation.

Players must be registered with the sports organisation, usually through their club, with the organisation being registered with the fund administrators. Any registered player who is injured in

---

80   http://www.workcover.nsw.gov.au/LawAndPolicy/Acts/sportinginjuries.htm.

the course of an event which has been sanctioned by the registered organisation can claim for compensation from the fund. Compensation can only be claimed for the injuries sustained during the sport and for any further losses relating to the playing of the sport. It does not cover lost earnings from non-sports related employment. This ensures that the fund can pay as much compensation for injuries to the maximum possible number of applicants. Any additional losses must be recovered either under the applicant's own insurance policy or by way of a civil action.

Waiver Clauses

In most of the States in the USA, waiver clauses are used by potential defendants to exclude or restrict their liability. A potential claimant must sign a release form that states that if he or she is negligently injured during the course of the activity, they will not sue the person at fault. Waiver clauses are contracts that realign the duties imposed on the parties. If a waiver clause is signed, the injured party does not have a tortious right of action against the perpetrator, so insurance cover is the norm.

The only limit on this type of clause is that it must not be contrary to public policy.[81] Where sports are concerned, such clauses will only be contrary to public policy where the waiver must be signed by the parent in respect of injuries that might be caused to a minor.[82] Thus, in most States of the USA, participants can waive their right to sue for injuries caused through participation in sport in advance.[83]

Such terms are unlawful in this country. No person can contract out of their rights to sue for personal injury caused by the negligence of another.

Unfair Contract Terms Act 1977

1 For the purposes of this Part of this Act, 'negligence' means the breach . . .

   (b) of any common law duty to take reasonable care or exercise reasonable skill (but not any stricter duty);

   . . .

2 A person cannot by reference to any contract term or to a notice given to persons generally or to particular persons exclude or restrict his liability for death or personal injury resulting from negligence.

Thus, nobody can waive their right to sue for negligently inflicted injuries under English law. Potential defendants can only escape liability is if they can raise *volenti* as a defence. If sports participants were allowed to contract out of their rights to sue, even to a limited degree, then again the emphasis would be placed firmly on the governing bodies to control participator violence, not the courts.

Risk Management Strategies

Risk management of participator violence is a largely unexplored preventative measure. It operates on the age-old theory that prevention is better than cure and is based largely on common sense. It is advice given to and methods used by those involved in a potentially dangerous situation, so that they can take action to ensure that the danger either does not arise or arises on a less frequent or less serious basis.[84] Risk management sets out to identify, evaluate and control the risks involved with

---

81 *Tunkl v Regents of the University of California* 20 Cal (2d) 92.
82 *Wagenblast v Odessa School District and Vuillet v Seattle School District* 119 Wash (2d) 845.
83 See further, Cotton, D, 'Analysis of sate laws governing the validity of sport-related exculpatory agreements' (1993) 3(2) JLAS 50, and 'Guidelines for writing or execution of exculpatory agreements' (1996) 6(2) JLAS 117.
84 Greenberg, M and Gray, J, 'Designing and implementing a sports based risk management programme' (1997) 5(2) Sport and the Law Journal 49.

sports participation. It is a more legally defensive way of organising sports that concentrates on participants' health and safety and the reduction of injury.

Risk is anything that adversely affects the health of a participant. Inherent risks are those that are an integral part of the game, are inevitable and acceptable, resulting only from the participant's decision to participate in sports; for example, falling awkwardly during a legitimate challenge and breaking one's arm. Unacceptable risks are those that go beyond the mere playing of the game; for example, being forced to play whilst injured or being provided with unsafe equipment.

Instead of relying on the reactive nature of legal actions and internal disciplinary tribunals, a more pro-active stance is taken. This could include the use of fair play charters and codes of conduct, the dissemination of information relating to commonly occurring sports injuries, the publication of internal disciplinary punishments in advance in a tariff form, compulsory insurance schemes or better coaching of physical contact techniques. The use of any of these risk management techniques could lead to a dramatic reduction in the incidence of sports injuries. If the number of injuries can be reduced, the need for legal intervention can also be reduced. Thus, the use of risk management techniques to control unnecessary sports injuries may slow down the advance of the law into the sports arena by making its use unnecessary.

Most risk management techniques are common sense provisions that require little or no explanation. Governing bodies or sports organisers should ensure that there are means of explaining the inherent risks involved in a sport to the participants so that they are aware of the dangers; inform the participants of their potential legal liability should they injure others; maintain a programme of certification, review and continuing education for all coaches and referees; outline medical procedures and rules to be utilised should an accident occur; develop and implement guidelines regarding the safe and proper conduct of participants and coaches. Owners of sports facilities should inspect the premises periodically and thoroughly to ensure that there are no potentially dangerous defects present; place warnings or protective devices at the site of any hazard and be sure that such warnings are understood by the participants; have qualified personnel on hand at events; inspect all equipment used on a regular basis and make sure that it complies with sport or industry standards; keep up to date with changes in the sport; obtain liability insurance; develop procedures to document and investigate injuries to participants and provide detailed medical emergency procedures. Coaches should never instruct a participant to commit an act which is outside the scope of rules and customs of the game; ensure that participants receive proper instructions regarding their sports and the equipment used in that sport and select competition and activities that are appropriate for your participants. If some of these points are taken on board by those most closely associated with sport, then injuries and litigation will be reduced and controlled.

CONCLUSION

At present most people who are injured during participation in sports receive little or no compensation. Generally, injuries are considered by most players to be part of the playing of the game and a risk worth taking. However, there is a growing trend amongst injured sports participants to turn to the law for assistance in recovering some compensation. Sports litigation has enabled the law to develop extremely rapidly. Tortious actions may lie against almost anyone associated with the playing, coaching and organising of sport and as the law becomes clearer actions will be brought more easily. Unless governing bodies and players' associations take a more pro-active stance towards sports injuries, litigation will continue apace. Insurance, risk management, certification and review procedures will all help to reduce the incidence of sports injuries. But, without a detailed and coherent approach to violent and injurious conduct, the law will remain the primary mechanism for dispute resolution and claims for compensation.

KEY SOURCES

Foster, K, 'How can sport be regulated?', Chapter 14, in Greenfield, S and Osborn, G (eds), *Law and Sport in Contemporary Society* (2000), London: Frank Cass.

Grayson, E, *Sport and the Law* (1999), 3rd edn, London: Butterworths, Chapter 6.

James, M and Deeley, F, 'Care on the court' (2001) 145(35) Solicitors Journal 864.

Kevan, T, 'Sports injury cases: footballers, referees and schools' (2001) 2 JPIL 138.

McCutcheon, JP, 'Sports discipline and the rule of law', Chapter 7, in Greenfield, S and Osborn, G (eds), *Law and Sport in Contemporary Society* (2000), London: Frank Cass.

CHAPTER 17

SPECTATORS, PARTICIPANTS AND STADIUMS

INTRODUCTION

For thousands of years people have gathered together to watch sporting events. The word 'stadium' derives from an ancient Greek measure of length, roughly the equivalent of a furlong which was used as the standard distance for foot-races. As buildings were erected from which to view the racing, they also became known as 'stadiums'. On the most simplistic level, such a gathering would have been in any place suitable for the event to be staged and formal, permanent arrangements would not have been considered. Even today, golf's Open Championship has no permanent home; it is shared amongst a number of links courses in England and Scotland with makeshift stands being constructed for the event. As society has developed, however, permanent structures have been developed from which to view and participate in organized and exploited sporting events.

Many stadiums and venues are now inextricably linked in the eyes of the public with a particular sport; The Currah and Aintree with horse racing, Crystal Palace and Gateshead with athletics, St Andrew's with golf and Lord's with cricket. On a national level our sporting teams have also become associated with particular venues such as The National Stadium Cardiff, Murrayfield, Wembley and Hampden Park. On a club level, Ibrox, Anfield and Old Trafford form part of the footballing folklore of Glasgow Rangers, Liverpool and Manchester United respectively. In effect the stadium has become synonymous with, and part of the sporting identity of, the club.[1] Many stadiums are situated in large cities so that they are accessible to spectators and are by their nature enclosed venues whereby the sporting event is divorced from its surroundings. This is necessary not only for the obvious reason that it allows for the efficient collection of revenue, but also because *inter alia* it allows for safety of spectators within a controllable environment.

Some sporting events such as the Round the World Yacht Race do not lend themselves to spectator participation and so perhaps have fallen outside what we now term stadium or arenas. However, it is vital that they should be included in any legal discussion, for tragedies that befall such sporting events are often as a result of factors comparable to those relevant in conventional stadium 'disasters'.

The importance of an appropriate venue for a sporting event cannot be underestimated. In professional football in England, a trend has developed in football for clubs to relocate to purpose-built stadiums outside of major conurbations. Stadiums such as the Stadium of Light and the Reebok Stadium are major investments by Sunderland FC and Bolton FC respectively. The ultimate aim of these developments is to maximise profit by increasing seating capacity and spectator comfort to levels unattainable at older, inner-city venues. The most recent example, Manchester City's move from Maine Road to the City of Manchester Stadium, is indicative of a trend towards US-style facility relocation. For most football clubs, a maximisation of facility revenue is a key factor in the maintenance of a financially successful club. From a legal perspective these venues must operate effectively and safely in order that potential revenue streams are not compromised.

This chapter focuses on stadium safety. Stadium safety is broader than spectator safety because while incidents concerning spectators are rightly an important element of any discussion of sporting venues and the law, they are but one consideration in a complex interaction involving owners,

---

1 See Bale, J, 'Playing at home: British football and a sense of place', in Williams, J and Wagg, S (eds), *British Football and Social Change: Getting into Europe* (1991), Leicester University Press.

players, spectators, police and local residents. As it will be seen, issues of law even extend to those spectators watching an event from the comfort of their own living rooms.[2]

In order to acquire an overview of the various legal considerations involved in facility management, reference should also be made to the relevant intellectual property issues raised elsewhere in this book.[3]

PARLIAMENT AND STADIUM SAFETY

Although on most occasions when the law becomes involved in sport the effects and implications are relatively minor, it is natural that much of the attention is drawn to major sporting disasters where there is injury and loss of life. These occurrences make up a fraction of the law's involvement in sport yet receive a high proportion of coverage. The latest in a long list of stadium disasters occurred at Hillsborough during an FA Cup semi-final between Liverpool and Nottingham Forest at Sheffield Wednesday's ground on 15 April 1989, as a result of which 96 lives were lost. The Hillsborough disaster is discussed in more detail later. It is pertinent at this stage to cite the words of Lord Justice Taylor whose opening words in his final report read:

> It is a depressing and chastening fact that mine is the ninth official report covering crowd safety at football grounds. After eight previous reports and three editions of the Green Guide, it seems astounding that 96 people could die from overcrowding before the very eyes of those controlling the event.[4]

This comment is one in a long line of indictments of our ability to ensure the safety of the public at sporting events. It is perhaps more chilling when considered alongside the comment of Mr Justice Popplewell, the author of the eighth report[5] in 1986 that 'almost all the matters into which I have been asked to inquire and almost all the solutions I have proposed have been previously considered in detail by many distinguished inquiries over a period of 60 years'.[6]

The first government report into ways of controlling and ensuring the safety of spectators, the Shortt Report,[7] was commissioned following concerns over crowd control highlighted by the massive overcrowding of Wembley Stadium for the 1923 FA Cup Final. It was the first time the stadium had hosted the final. However, it would be wrong to assume that this was the first occasion that safety at sports stadiums had been called into question. Indeed, there is considerable evidence of stadium inadequacies prior to 1923. Stands had collapsed causing injury at the Cheltenham National Hunt Festival in 1866,[8] Ewood Park in Blackburn in 1896[9] and at Ibrox in Glasgow in 1902 where 26 people were killed at a Scotland v England international.

The Shortt Report 1924 highlighted a lack of apportionment of responsibility between the police and the ground authority. It suggested that responsibility should lie in the hands of a single, competent officer. It also recommended the increased use of stewards. Issues such as police

---

2   *Alcock v Chief Constable of South Yorkshire* [1991] 4 All ER 907.
3   See Chapter 10.
4   The Hillsborough Stadium Disaster Final Report (Taylor Report) (1990) London: HMSO, Cm 962, p 4.
5   The Popplewell Final Report, Final report of the Committee of Inquiry into Crowd Safety and Control at Sports Grounds (1986) London: HMSO, Cm 9710.
6   *Ibid*, p 10.
7   *The Short Report, Report of the Departmental Committee on Crowds* (1924), London: HMSO, Cm 2088.
8   *Francis v Cockerell* [1870] 5 QB 501.
9   *Brown v Lewis* [1896] 12 TLR 455.

responsibilities and adequate stewarding would again come under the microscope following Hillsborough. The report also observed:

> We have been somewhat surprised to find that in many cases little or no precaution has been taken against the risk of fire in stands. We do not suppose that either the risk or the consequences of fire would be so serious in an open stand as in a closed building but we consider it most important that adequate arrangements should be made to deal with any outbreak which might occur.[10]

The tragic consequences of inadequate fire precaution became apparent following the Bradford City fire disaster in 1985, where the Main South Parade Stand was razed to the ground in nine minutes leaving 56 people dead.

If these issues could be identified in 1923 then why were adequate measures not taken in the intervening years to prevent the later disasters? One reason which is particularly pertinent to the Shortt Report is the unwillingness to view the events as a matter of governmental responsibility. The report concluded 'anaemically'[11] 'We are assured that these governing bodies are only too anxious to secure that their sport is carried on under conditions which will promote the public safety and we feel at this stage it is safe to leave the matter to them'.[12]

A good example of parliament's inability or disinclination to act was the response to the Moelwyn Hughes Report of 1946.[13] The report followed the disaster at Bolton Wanderers' ground in that year. Here a crowd of 85,000, far exceeding anything experienced or expected, had crammed into Burnden Park. Two barriers collapsed resulting in the death of 33 people. The Moelwyn Hughes Report recommended mechanical means of counting those entering the ground, scientific calculations of maximum attendances and inspections of enclosures. The report concluded:

> No ground of any considerable size should be opened to the public until it has been licensed by, I suggest as an appropriate licensing authority, the local authority. The issue of the licence would depend upon satisfying the authority as to the construction and equipment of the ground, its compliance with regulations and the proposed maximum figures of admission to the different parts.[14]

The issues raised by the Hughes Report in 1946 were finally addressed by the Safety of Sports Grounds Act 1975 following another disaster at Ibrox. The recommendations of the Moelwyn Hughes Report were not implemented. The reasons for this are unclear. Cost cannot be ignored as a factor. As the report concluded, 'Compliance with the recommendations of this report will cost money. They will involve grounds in a loss of gate money ... The insurance for greater safety for the public demands a premium'.[15]

Another important factor is the complexity of the issues involved. As the Lang Report 1969 commented, 'The working party was dealing with a subject which has been discussed almost *ad nauseam* during recent years. Not unexpectedly the working party has not found a single simple solution for a problem which is often due to a combination of factors'.[16] The Lang Report was commissioned to look into what was considered to be an increasing problem at football grounds: that

---

10   *Op cit*, fn 7, Cm 2088, para 40.
11   The description given by *The Moelwyn Hughes Report* (1946) London: HMSO, Cm 6846.
12   *Op cit*, fn 7, Cm 2088, para 47.
13   *Op cit*, fn 11, Cm 6846.
14   *Ibid*, p 11.
15   *Ibid*, p 12.
16   *The Lang Report, Crowd Behaviour at Football Matches: Report of the Working Party* (1969), London: HMSO, p 3.

of crowd behaviour. Subsequent major disasters such as Bradford and Hillsborough have highlighted that whilst hooliganism remains a worrying social condition it is in most instances a distinct problem from that of stadium safety.[17]

The Wheatley Report 1971 was commissioned following the disaster at Ibrox Park where inadequate stairways and handrails caused the death of 66 spectators.[18] The report is of great significance as it was the first of the reports to directly spawn an Act of Parliament, the Safety of Sports Grounds Act 1975. In his report Lord Wheatley was conscious of both the history of recommendations such as his and the economic arguments against imposing stringent safety conditions. He dismissed such misgivings emphatically:

The Wheatley Report

I recognise that a decision to introduce a licensing system for grounds along the lines I have recommended may cause anxiety to some football clubs and football administrators. As I see it, their misgivings are associated with a fear that such stringent conditions may be attached to the granting of a licence that many clubs may not be able to afford the cost and some may have to go out of business ... My answer to that is this. My task is to consider the problem of crowd safety at the grounds. Clubs which charge the public for admission have a duty to see that their grounds are reasonably safe for spectators. That is a primary consideration. It is accordingly necessary that some standards should be imposed and observed. This has been recognised by the football authorities themselves ... I have canvassed all the alternatives that have been proposed or which I personally thought were reasonable to consider and the one I decided was best to meet the situation in the interest of the public is a licensing system by a local authority. There is nothing new in this proposal. It has been mooted for almost 50 years. It can come as no surprise to the football world and in the light of happenings over the years the demand for an independent appraisal and determination of the safety of grounds becomes almost irresistible. I certainly cannot resist it.[19]

Other reports such as the Harrington Report,[20] The McElhone Report[21] which looked at *inter alia* the consumption of alcohol, and the Department of the Environment Working Group 1984 which was commissioned following violence by football supporters in Luxembourg in 1983 and France in 1984, all focused on what was perceived to be an increase in football crowd violence. None of these reports resulted directly in legislation. Popplewell J's Report published in the aftermath of the Bradford City fire disaster concluded:

The Popplewell Report

A study of all these reports (and there are numerous reports and discussion papers by other bodies) shows that the following are measures which have been frequently recommended: closed Circuit Television; membership cards; segregation; more seating at football grounds; encouragement of supporters' clubs; a ban on alcohol; involvement of the clubs with the community and heavier penalties. I too shall argue for these and related measures ... It is to be hoped they will be more vigorously pursued by the appropriate bodies than in the past.[22]

---

17 The Heysel Stadium disaster is an unusual example of where the issues of crowd management and crowd disturbances were both integral factors.

18 *The Wheatley Report* (1971) London: HMSO, Cm 4952.

19 *Ibid*, paras 66 and 67.

20 *The Harrinton Report, Soccer Hooliganism: A Preliminary Report* (1968), Bristol: John Wright and Sons Ltd.

21 *The McElhone Report, Report of the Working Group on Football Crowd Behaviour*, Scottish Education Department, HMSO 1977.

22 *Ibid*, Cm 9710, p 16.

Whilst the Popplewell Report is often perceived as being an inquiry into the Bradford Fire Disaster, its terms of reference were in fact wider. On the same day as the Bradford fire disaster, one supporter was killed and another 200 injured in violent clashes at Birmingham City's home ground, St Andrew's with rival supporters of Leeds United. During this period football violence was a high profile issue. Popplewell J was asked to inquire into both these events.

This tendency, to amalgamate issues of crowd management and crowd disturbances, sets a dangerous precedent. The incident at the Hysel Stadium, Brussels, before the 1985 European Cup Final between Liverpool and Juventus where 39 supporters were killed was also considered by Popplewell J. The incident represents a rare occurrence where fighting spectators (crowd disturbance) caused a concentration of people causing a wall to collapse (crowd management). Bradford and subsequently Hillsborough were disasters caused by an inability to house large numbers of people in safety and crowd disturbance played little if any part. One of the most significant developments following Hillsborough was the government's ill-fated attempt to introduce a membership system: a means of curbing crowd disturbances. Measures aimed at curbing crowd violence such as controlling the consumption of alcohol, increasing police powers of arrest and courts powers to punish, are very different from the measures needed to manage large numbers of spectators in an enclosed space. This calls for good stadium design, adequate safety margins and good stewardship.

In Britain the desire to address issues of safety in the light of the Popplewell and Taylor Reports is indicative of a more paternal approach towards spectator safety and, it has been suggested, British sporting grounds have never been as safe. The lasting impact of the Taylor report has been the introduction of all-seater stadiums. It is perhaps impossible to assess the safety implications of this proposal but there can be little doubt that all-seated stadiums have had a crucial impact on the character of football grounds. However, if Parliament continues to rely on the Green Guide – the advisory document detailing safety standards and specifications for sports grounds – rather than extending safety legislation, the safety of spectators remains in the hands of individual sports clubs and subject to their willingness to implement its provisions.[23]

STADIUMS AND NEIGHBOURS

Clearly legal issues relating to sporting venues are not contained within the stadium. One would need only to speak to residents living near to major sporting venues to appreciate that whilst the sporting action may be contained, legal issues, like spectators, tend to spill over and affect the surrounding environment. Legal protection for those outside the stadium is important for two reasons.

First, because in order to arrive at and depart from the stadium, spectators need to pass through residential areas. Large numbers of fans need to be managed in such a way as to avoid encroaching on the safety and peaceful enjoyment of the property of local residents.

Secondly, because what goes on inside the stadium directly impacts on those outside. Sir Garfield Sobers's six sixes in an over off Malcolm Nash at the St Helen's ground in Swansea is rightly recognised as a historic sporting moment, in no small measure because of the power and timing of some of Sobers' hits from long off to square leg, two of which cleared not only the boundary ropes

---

23 See Taylor, I, 'English football in the 1990s: taking Hillsborough seriously?' in Williams, J and Wagg, S (eds), *British Football and Social Change: Getting into Europe* (1991), Leicester: Leicester University Press.

but also the ground itself.[24] From a legal perspective such shots could have caused injury to property and persons and it is not beyond the realms of possibility that a passer by could have been killed. This problem is even more evident at the village green level where cricket grounds are often situated next to the highway or adjoining property where there is little or no protection.[25]

A less tangible concern but one which may impact on a greater number of local residents is the level of noise emanating from the stadium. This noise may be particularly acute if the stadium in question hosts motor or speedboat racing, for example, although these events tend to be held in less built up areas.

THE ARRIVAL AND DEPARTURE OF SPECTATORS

The problems of spectators as they arrive and leave sporting venues can be dealt with briefly. Any physical or property damage sustained by local residents will usually be dealt with by the criminal law or by claims in tort.

Sport-specific criminal provisions are discussed in more detail later. General criminal provisions aimed at crowd control are contained in the Public Order Act 1986 and the Criminal Justice and Public Order Act 1994, examples of which are given below.

Public Order Act 1986, s 4

(1) A person is guilty of an offence if he –

(a) uses towards another person threatening, abusive or insulting words or behaviour, or

(b) distributes or displays to another person any writing, sign or other visible representation which is threatening, abusive or insulting,

with intent to cause that person to believe that immediate unlawful violence will be used against him or another by any person or to provoke the immediate use of unlawful violence by that person or another or whereby that person is likely to believe that such violence will be used or it is likely that such violence will be provoked.

(3) A constable may arrest without warrant anyone he reasonably suspects is committing an offence under this section.

Public Order Act 1986, s 5

(1) A person is guilty of an offence if he –

(a) uses towards another person threatening, abusive or insulting words or behaviour or disorderly behaviour, or

(b) displays any writing, sign or other visible representation which is threatening, abusive or insulting, within the hearing or sight of a person likely to be caused harassment, alarm or distress thereby.

(4) A constable may arrest a person without warrant if –

(a) he engages in offensive conduct which the constable warns him to stop, and he engages in further offensive conduct immediately or shortly after the warning.

---

24 Although such feats of hitting are rare, Sobers' achievement was repeated by Ravi Shastri off the bowling of Tilak Raj in the 1984–85 Ranji Trophy and almost by Frank Hayes of Lancashire against Glamorgan in 1977 off the unfortunate Malcolm Nash (his second boundary was a four).

25 In a club game between Bath Cricket Association and Thornbury in 1902, Billy Hyman hit 359 runs in 100 minutes. Fortunately for local residents, even at club level, such Herculean feats are rare.

Criminal Justice and Public Order Act 1994, s 60

(1) Where a police officer of or above the rank of superintendent reasonably believes that -

    (a) incidents involving serious violence may take place in any locality in his area, and

    (b) it is expedient to do so to prevent their occurrence, he may give authorisation that the powers to stop and search persons and vehicles conferred by this section shall be exercisable at any place within that locality for a period not exceeding twenty four hours.

(4) This section confers on any constable in uniform power–

    (a) to stop any pedestrian and search him or anything carried by him for offensive weapons or dangerous instruments,

    (b) to stop any vehicle and search the vehicle, its driver and any passenger for offensive weapons or dangerous instruments.

(5) A constable may, in the exercise of those powers, stop any person or vehicle and make any search he thinks fit whether or not he has any grounds for suspecting that the person or vehicle is carrying weapons or articles of that kind.

In tort, claims against the stadium owners may prove problematic since, generally speaking, owners are not responsible for the actions of spectators outside the stadium. In *AG v Corke*[26] the defendant was held responsible under the principle in *Rylands v Fletcher*[27] for the nuisance created off his land by travellers staying on the land. The principle in *Rylands v Fletcher* is a variation on the tort of nuisance as it imposes strict liability for foreseeable damage caused by the escape from the defendant's land of things accumulated or brought there by the defendant which amounts to a non-natural use of the land.[28] Had this principle continued to be applied to human beings it may have proved to be a means by which local residents could have sought redress from stadium owners. Subsequent decisions suggest, however, that the rule is not applicable in these circumstances.[29]

NEIGHBOURS AND SPORTING EVENTS

The law relating to damage outside the stadium caused by the activities inside the stadium has resulted in many of the most famous sporting legal cases. It is a possibility in many sports that a ball may be hit out of the stadium: in football a defender's desperate clearance from an onrushing forward, in rugby a kick into touch to move play up-field. Incidents of these types of projectiles causing harm are rare. Much more likely, although not exclusively, is the potential damage from a golf ball[30] or a cricket ball.[31] Not only is a cricket ball hard but, by awarding six runs for a shot which clears the boundary, the game encourages big hits and potential danger. Any liability for such an occurrence is likely to be based on the torts of negligence and nuisance.

---

26   [1933] Ch 89.
27   [1886] LR 3 HL 330; [1861–73] All ER Rep 1.
28   *Cambridge Water v Eastern Counties Leather Plc* [1994] 1 All ER 53; *Read v J Lyons* [1947] AC 156.
29   *Smith v Scott* [1973] Ch 314; *Matheson v Northcote College Board of Governors* [1975] 2 NZLR 106.
30   In *Castle v St Augustines Links Ltd and Another* [1922] 38 TLR 615, a taxi driver was successful in an action for nuisance (although today would most probably be brought under the tort of negligence) against a golf club, when a golfer's wayward tee shot from the 13th tee smashed through the window of the plaintiff's taxi resulting in the loss of an eye. Williamson, DS, 'Some legal aspects of golf' (1995) 3(1) Sport and the Law Journal.
31   For example, see (1996) 39 *Legal Times* 24.

Negligence can be defined as the breach of a duty to take care, owed by the defendant, which causes harm to the claimant[32]. Private nuisance occurs where the use by the defendants of their land results in unreasonable interference with the claimant's enjoyment of their land. As nuisance requires the plaintiff to have an interest in land it follows that this tort can only be invoked by those with an interest in land in the vicinity of the stadium[33] whereas a claim in negligence can be made by property owners or unfortunate passers by.

In *Bolton v Stone and Others*[34] a visiting cricketer struck a six which had cleared the boundary, 75 feet from the wicket, a 17 foot fence and had travelled a further 100 yards before striking the plaintiff standing on the highway. The cricket ground had been used for 90 years and evidence from the last 30 revealed only six incidents of escaped balls with no damage having been caused by any. The House of Lords allowed the appeal on the basis that the likelihood of injury occurring was so slight that a reasonable man would be justified in ignoring it:

Bolton v Stone [1951] 1 All ER 1078

Lord Reid: This case, therefore, raises sharply the question what is the nature and extent of the duty of a person who promotes on his land operations which may cause damage to persons on an adjoining highway. Is it that he must not carry out or permit an operation which he knows or ought to know clearly can cause such damage, however improbable that result may be or is it that he is only bound to take into account the possibility of such damage if such damage is a likely or probable consequence of what he does or permits or if the risk of damage is such that a reasonable man, careful of the safety of his neighbour, would regard that risk as material? I do not know of any case where this question has had to be decided or even where it has been fully discussed. Of course there are many cases in which somewhat similar questions have arisen but, generally speaking, if injury to another person from the defendants' acts is reasonably foreseeable the chance that injury will result is substantial and it does not matter in which way the duty is stated. In such cases I do not think that much assistance is to be got from analysing the language which a judge has used. More assistance is to be got from cases where judges have clearly chosen their language with care in setting out a principle but even so, statements of the law must be read in light of the facts of the particular case. Nevertheless, making all allowances for this, I do find at least a tendency to base duty rather on the likelihood of damage to others than on its foreseeability alone . . .

. . . Counsel for the respondent in the present case had to put his case so high as to say that, at least as soon as one ball had been driven into the road in the ordinary course of a match, the appellants could and should have realised that that might happen again and that, if it did, someone might be injured and that that was enough to put on the appellants a duty to take steps to prevent such an occurrence. If the true test is foreseeability alone I think that must be so. Once a ball has been driven on to a road without there being anything extraordinary to account for the fact, there is clearly a risk that another will follow and if it does there is clearly a chance, small though it may be, that somebody may be injured. On the theory that it is foreseeability alone that matters it would be irrelevant to consider how often a ball might be expected to land in the road and it would not matter whether the road was the busiest street or the quietest country lane. The only difference between these cases is in the degree of risk. It would take a good deal to make me believe that the law has departed so far from the standards which guide ordinary careful people in ordinary life. In the crowded conditions of modern life even the most careful person cannot avoid creating some risks and accepting others. What a man must not do and what I think a careful man tries not to do, is to create a risk which is substantial. Of course, there are numerous cases

---

32 *Donoghue v Stevenson* [1932] AC 562; *Peabody Donation Fund v Parkinson* [1985] AC 210; *Smith v Littlewoods Organisation* [1987] AC 241; *Caparo Industries v Dickman* [1990] 1 All ER 568

33 *Hunter and Others v Canary Wharf Ltd; Hunter and Others v London Docklands Development Corporation* [1997] NLJ 634.

34 [1951] 1 All ER 1078.

where special circumstances require that a higher standard shall be observed and where that is recognised by the law but I do not think that this case comes within any such special category.

Lord Radcliffe: I can see nothing unfair in the appellants being required to compensate the respondent for the serious injury that she has received as a result of the sport that they have organised on their cricket ground at Cheetham Hill but the law of negligence is concerned less with what is fair than with what is culpable and I cannot persuade myself that the appellants have been guilty of any culpable act or omission in this case . . .

If the test whether there has been a breach of duty were to depend merely on the answer to the question whether this accident was a reasonably foreseeable risk, I think that there would have been a breach of duty, for that such an accident might take place some time or other might very reasonably have been present to the minds of the appellants. It was quite foreseeable and there would have been nothing unreasonable in allowing the imagination to dwell on the possibility of its occurring. There was, however, only a remote, perhaps I ought to say only a very remote, chance of the accident taking place at any particular time, for, if it was to happen, not only had a ball to carry the fence round the ground but it had also to coincide in its arrival with the presence of some person on what does not look like a crowded thoroughfare and actually to strike that person in some way that would cause sensible injury.

Those being the facts, a breach of duty has taken place if they show the appellants guilty of a failure to take reasonable care to prevent the accident. One may phrase it as 'reasonable care' or 'ordinary care' or 'proper care' – all these phrases are to be found in decisions of authority – but the fact remains that, unless there here has been something which a reasonable man would blame as falling beneath the standard of conduct that he would set for himself and require of his neighbour, there has been no breach of legal duty and here, I think, the respondent's case breaks down. It seems to me that a reasonable man, taking account of the chances against an accident happening, would not have felt himself called on either to abandon the use of the ground for cricket or to increase the height of his surrounding fences. He would have done what the appellants did. In other words, he would have done nothing. Whether, if the unlikely event of an accident did occur and his play turn to another's hurt, he would have thought it equally proper to offer no more consolation to his victim than the reflection that a social being is not immune from social risks, I do not say, for I do not think that that is a consideration which is relevant to legal liability.[35]

The fact that the ball had left the ground previously, and the chances of it doing so again had been guarded against to some extent by the fencing, shows that the decision was not based on foreseeability alone. The House of Lords was able to look at the history of cricket balls leaving the ground and concluded that there were some foreseeable risks that it was possible to ignore.

It is interesting to note that Mrs Stone's action was taken against those responsible for the ground and not the batsman. It will be no defence in this type of situation for those in control of the ground to shift responsibility on to the players. The onus remains with those who control the cricket ground or driving range to take action should the occurrence of balls leaving the ground reach an unacceptable level. The difficulty will be to set such a level.

The law is clear that the level of duty owed by sportsmen will be that of the reasonable sportsman with the level of skill and knowledge of the defendant. It is in this way that we can require a higher level of skill from doctors and other professionals[36]. Clearly then we cannot expect a child to have the knowledge and experience of a reasonable adult[37]. It is possible that a professional sportsman may be

---

35   *Ibid*, p 1084.

36   *Whitehouse v Jordan* [1981] 1 All ER 267 HL; *Phillips v Whiteley Ltd* [1938] 1 All ER 566; *Roe v Ministry of Health* [1954] 2 QB 661; *Nettleship v Weston* [1971] 3 All ER 581.

37   McHale v Watson [1966] 115 CLR 199.

liable in circumstances where a child who hits a ball from a playground cage may not. The potential liability of the owners of the stadium will depend on their assessment of the likelihood of risk taking into account the age and skill of the participants.

In *Hilder v Associated Portland Cement Manufacturers Ltd*[38] the defendant landowners allowed children to play on their land situated adjacent to a highway. During a game of football the ball was kicked over a small fence on to the highway. The husband of the plaintiff was killed as a result of avoiding the ball:

Hilder v Associated Portland Cement Manufacturers Ltd [1961] 1 WLR 1434

Ashworth J: In my judgment, a reasonable man would come to the conclusion that there was a risk of damage to persons using the road and that risk was not so small that he could safely disregard it. While it is true that a football itself is unlikely to damage a person or vehicle on the road in the way that might occur with a cricket ball or a golf ball, I think that the sudden appearance of a football in front of a cyclist or motor-cyclist is quite likely to cause him to fall or to swerve into the path of another vehicle and in either event sustain serious injury ... Accordingly, I find that the defendants failed to take reasonable care in all the circumstances and that this failure unhappily caused the death of the deceased. The claim in negligence therefore succeeds.[39]

It can be seen that it is often difficult to predict when liability will be imposed: *Bolton* and *Hilder* are difficult to distinguish. No reference is made in *Hilder* to the frequency with which the football left the field. It may well be that the reasonable man, with the knowledge that it is one of the objectives of the game of cricket to hit the ball off the playing field, may conclude that Bolton posed a greater risk than Hilder. The next extract is from *Overseas Tankship (UK) Ltd Miller SS Co Pty*,[40] commonly known as *The Wagon Mound (No 2)*. This is not a sport case but is the leading case in this area where Lord Reid made it clear that just because likelihood is remote does not mean that one has carte blanche to ignore it:

Overseas Tankship (UK) Ltd Miller SS Co Pty [1966] 2 All ER 709 Privy Council

Lord Reid: It does not follow that, no matter what the circumstances may be, it is justifiable to neglect a risk of such a small magnitude. A reasonable man would only neglect such a risk if he had some valid reason for doing so, eg that it would involve considerable expense to eliminate the risk. He would weigh the risk against the difficulty of eliminating it. If the activity which caused the injury to Miss Stone had been an unlawful activity there can be little doubt but that *Bolton v Stone* would have been decided differently. In their Lordships' judgment *Bolton v Stone* did not alter the general principle that a person must be regarded as negligent if he does not take steps to eliminate a risk which he knows or ought to know is a real risk and not a mere possibility which would never influence the mind of a reasonable man. What that decision did was to recognise and give effect to the qualification that it is justifiable not to take steps to eliminate a real risk if it is small and if the circumstances are such that a reasonable man, careful of the safety of his neighbour, would think it right to neglect it.[41]

It would seem that foreseeability and likelihood are part of a larger equation. Whereas the ground owner may be justified in ignoring a foreseeable risk of a rare occurrence if the outcome would cause limited damage, he may not be at liberty to ignore the same risk if the possible outcome is more serious. Does the law adequately protect the likes of Mrs Stone? It is important to note that, in *Bolton*,

---

38   [1961] 1 WLR 1434.
39   *Ibid*, p 1438.
40   Privy Council [1966] 2 All ER 709.
41   *Ibid*, p 718.

Lord Reid was of the opinion that the cost of remedial measures should not be taken into account when considering the standard of duty owed by the ground owners; however, in The Wagon Mound (No. 2) he appeared to conclude that the cost of prevention was a factor to be considered. It would be judicious for stadium owners to take all low cost safety precautions.

In the above cases liability centred on the tort of negligence; however, as the courts have stated, the likelihood of someone being injured is remote. Most wayward tee shots or six-hits will injure no one. However, for people dwelling beside stadiums and grounds the fear of damage to person and property can undermine the enjoyment of that property. In *Miller v Jackson*[42] the defendant cricket club had played cricket on a small ground for many years. A small housing estate was built on land abutting the cricket field so that, despite there being a boundary fence, some balls were bound to be hit into the houses or their gardens. The plaintiffs sued in nuisance and negligence in respect of cricket balls being hit into their garden:

Miller v Jackson [1977] 3 All ER 338 CA

Geoffrey Lane LJ: . . . have the plaintiffs established that the defendants are guilty of nuisance or negligence as alleged? The evidence . . . makes it clear that the risk of injury to property at least was both foreseeable and foreseen. It is obvious that such injury is going to take place so long as cricket is being played on this field . . . It is true that the risk must be balanced against the measures which are necessary to eliminate it and against what the defendants can do to prevent accidents from happening . . . In the present case, so far from being one incident of an unprecedented nature about which complaint is being made, this is a series of incidents or perhaps a continuing failure to prevent incidents from happening, coupled with the certainty that they are going to happen again. The risk of injury to person and property is so great that on each occasion when a ball comes over the fence and causes damage to the plaintiffs, the defendants are guilty of negligence.

In circumstances such as these it is very difficult and probably unnecessary, except as an interesting intellectual exercise, to define the frontiers between negligence and nuisance: see Lord Wilberforce in *Goldman v Hargrave*.

Was there here a use by the defendants of their land involving an unreasonable interference with the plaintiffs' enjoyment of their land? There is here in effect no dispute that there has been and is likely to be in the future an interference with the plaintiffs' enjoyment of No 20 Brackenridge. The only question is whether it is unreasonable. It is a truism to say that this is a matter of degree. What that means is this. A balance has to be maintained between on the one hand the rights of the individual to enjoy his house and garden without the threat of damage and on the other hand the rights of the public in general or a neighbour to engage in lawful pastimes. Difficult questions may sometimes arise when the defendants' activities are offensive to the senses, for example, by way of noise. Where, as here, the damage or potential damage is physical the answer is more simple. There is, subject to what appears hereafter, no excuse I can see which exonerates the defendants from liability in nuisance for what they have done or from what they threaten to do. It is true that no one has yet been physically injured. That is probably due to a great extent to the fact that the householders in Brackenridge desert their gardens while cricket is in progress. The danger of injury is obvious and is not slight enough to be disregarded. There is here a real risk of serious injury.

There is, however, one obviously strong point in the defendants' favour. They or their predecessors have been playing cricket on this ground (and no doubt hitting sixes out of it) for 70 years or so. Can someone, by building a house on the edge of the field in circumstances where it must have been obvious that balls might be hit over the fence, effectively stop cricket being played? Precedent apart, justice would seem to demand that the plaintiffs should be left to make the most of the site they have elected to occupy with all

---

42 [1977] 3 All ER 338 CA.

its obvious advantages and all its equally obvious disadvantages. It is pleasant to have an open space over which to look from your bedroom and sitting room windows, so far as it is possible to see over the concrete wall. Why should you complain of the obvious disadvantages which arise from the particular purpose to which the open space is being put? Put briefly, can the defendants take advantage of the fact that the plaintiffs have put themselves in such a position by coming to occupy a house on the edge of a small cricket field, with the result that what was not a nuisance in the past now becomes a nuisance? If the matter were res integra, I confess I should be inclined to find for the defendants. It does not seem just that a long established activity – in itself innocuous – should be brought to an end because someone chooses to build a house nearby and so turn an innocent pastime into an actionable nuisance. Unfortunately, however, the question is not open. In *Sturges v Bridgman* this very problem arose . . . That decision involved the assumption, which so far as one can discover has never been questioned, that it is no answer to a claim in nuisance for the defendant to show that the plaintiff brought the trouble on his own head by building or coming to live in a house so close to the defendant's premises that he would inevitably be affected by the defendant's activities, where no one had been affected previously: see also *Bliss v Hall*. It may be that this rule works injustice, it may be that one would decide the matter differently in the absence of authority. But we are bound by the decision in *Sturges v Bridgman*; it is not for this court as I see it to alter a rule which stood for so long.

Lord Denning MR (dissenting): In support of the case, the plaintiffs rely on the dictum of Lord Reid in *Bolton v Stone*: 'If cricket cannot be played on a ground without creating a substantial risk, then it should not be played there at all.' I would agree with that saying if the houses or road was there first and the cricket ground came there second. We would not allow the garden of Lincoln's Inn to be turned into a cricket ground. It would be too dangerous for windows and people. But I would not agree with Lord Reid's dictum when the cricket ground has been there for 70 years and the houses are newly built at the very edge of it. I recognise that the cricket club are under a duty to use all reasonable care consistent with the playing of the game of cricket but I do not think the cricket club can be expected to give up the game of cricket altogether. After all they have their rights in their cricket ground. They have spent money, labour and love in the making of it: and they have the right to play upon it as they have done for 70 years. Is this all to be rendered useless to them by the thoughtless and selfish act of an estate developer in building right up to the edge of it? Can the developer or a purchaser of the house say to the cricket club: 'Stop playing. Clear out.' I do not think so . . .

. . . I would, therefore, adopt this test. Is the use by the cricket club of this ground for playing cricket a reasonable use of it? To my mind it is a most reasonable use. Just consider the circumstances. For over 70 years the game of cricket has been played on this ground to the great benefit of the community as a whole and to the injury of none. No one could suggest that it was a nuisance to the neighbouring owners simply because an enthusiastic batsman occasionally hit a ball out of the ground for six to the approval of the admiring onlookers. Then I would ask: does it suddenly become a nuisance because one of the neighbours chooses to build a house on the very edge of the ground in such a position that it may well be struck by the ball on the rare occasion when there is a hit for six? To my mind the answer is plainly No. The building of the house does not convert the playing of cricket into a nuisance when it was not so before. If and in so far as any damage is caused to the house or anyone in it, it is because of the position in which it was built. Suppose that the house had not been built by a developer but by a private owner. He would be in much the same position as the farmer who previously put his cows in the field. He could not complain if a batsman hit a six out of the ground and by a million to one chance it struck a cow or even the farmer himself. He would be in no better position than a spectator at Lord's or the Oval or at a motor rally. At any rate, even if he could claim damages for the loss of the cow or the injury, he could not get an injunction to stop the cricket. If the private owner could not get an injunction, neither should a developer or a purchaser from him . . .

. . . In this case it is our task to balance the right of the cricket club to continue playing cricket on their cricket ground as against the right of the householder not to be interfered with. On taking the balance, I would give priority to the right of the cricket club to continue playing cricket on the ground, as they have done for the last 70 years. It takes precedence over the right of the newcomer to sit in his garden undisturbed. After all, he bought the house four years ago in mid-summer when the cricket season was at its height. He might have guessed that there was a risk that a hit for six might possibly land on his property. If he finds that he does not like it, he ought, when cricket is played, to sit on the other side of the house or in the front garden or go out: or take advantage of the offers the club have made to him of fitting unbreakable glass and so forth. Or if he does not like that, he ought to sell his house and move elsewhere. I expect there are many who would gladly buy it in order to be near the cricket field and open space. At any rate he ought not be allowed to stop cricket being played on this ground.

This case is new. It should be approached on principles applicable to modern conditions. There is a contest here between the interest of the public at large; and the interest of a private individual. The public interest lies in protecting the environment by preserving our playing fields in the face of mounting development and by enabling our youth to enjoy all the benefits of outdoor games, such as cricket and football. The private interest lies in securing the privacy of his home and garden without intrusion or interference by anyone. In deciding between these two conflicting interests, it must be remembered that it is not a question of damages. If by a million to one chance a cricket ball does go out of the ground and cause damage, the cricket club will pay. There is no difficulty on that score. No, it is a question of an injunction. And in our law you will find it repeatedly affirmed that an injunction is a discretionary remedy. In a new situation like this, we have to think afresh as to how discretion should be exercised. On the one hand, Mrs Miller is a very sensitive lady who has worked herself up into such a state that she exclaimed to the judge: 'I just want to be allowed to live in peace . . . have I got to wait until someone is killed before anything can be done?' If she feels like that about it, it is quite plain that, for peace in the future, one or other has to move. Either the cricket club has to move: but goodness knows where. I do not suppose for a moment there is any field in Lintz to which they could move. Or Mrs Miller must move elsewhere. As between their conflicting interests, I am of opinion that the public interest should prevail over the private interest. The cricket club should not be driven out. In my opinion the right exercise of discretion is to refuse an injunction; and, of course, to refuse damages in lieu of an injunction. Likewise as to the claim for past damages. The club were entitled to use this ground for cricket in the accustomed way. It was not a nuisance, nor was it negligent of them so to run it, nor was the batsman negligent when he hit the ball for six. All were doing simply what they were entitled to do. So if the club had put it to the test, I would have dismissed the claim for damages also. But as the club very fairly say that they are willing to pay for any damage, I am content that there should be an award of £400 to cover any past or future damage. I would allow the appeal, accordingly.[43]

The judgments given by the Court of Appeal have tended to muddy these waters rather than clear.[44] The two issues at stake were whether there was liability in negligence or nuisance by the cricket club in allowing balls to be struck regularly into neighbouring gardens and if there was liability, what would be an appropriate remedy? On the second issue the appellant sought an injunction: a discretionary remedy to prevent recurrence of the tortious act. They had been offered compensation by the club which was also prepared to undertake preventative measures such as the installation of safety glass. A fence had already been erected and expert advice had suggested weather conditions would make a higher fence unviable. However, damages would be unsatisfactory in these circumstances. What the appellant wanted was an end to the nuisance of cricket balls landing in her garden.

Geoffrey Lane and Cumming-Bruce LJJ thought that there was liability on the part of the cricket club; Lord Denning thought not. Geoffrey Lane LJ was prepared to grant an injunction – Lord Denning MR and Cumming-Bruce LJ were not. The public interest, thought Geoffrey Lane LJ, could

---

43 *Ibid*, p 342.
44 See Parpworth, N, *Lord Denning and the 'Other Cricket Ball Case'* (1994) 2(2) Sport and the Law Journal 4 and 'A further cricket ball case: Lacey v Parker and Bingle' (1994) 2(3) Sport and the Law Journal 9.

not be put before the rights of individuals to quiet enjoyment of their land. Lord Denning on the other hand thought that the public interest was such a vital consideration that it made the playing of cricket and the inevitable six hits into neighbouring gardens a reasonable activity that did not therefore attract liability in the first place. Cumming-Bruce LJ did not invoke the public interest to deny liability but considered it a factor in his refusal to grant an injunction. Geoffrey Lane LJ, whilst sympathetic toward the respondents' argument that the club had existed long before the housing estate was built, felt bound by precedent to disregard this consideration whereas the fact that the appellant had come to the nuisance appeared to be an important factor in Lord Denning MR's denial of liability. Cumming-Bruce LJ appearing to take a middle line felt that coming to the nuisance was an important factor in refusing the injunction.

Some of the issues that had concerned the Court of Appeal in *Miller* resurfaced in a different guise in *Kennaway v Thompson*.[45] Here the plaintiff lived in a house next to a lake on which there were water sports. The club had begun racing on the lake some 10 years before the plaintiff built and occupied her house adjoining the lake. She had always lived in the vicinity and had inherited the land from her father. Over the years immediately prior to and after this the use of the lake and the noise level increased considerably. In the Court of Appeal the defendants, a motor boat racing club, accepted that some of their activities caused a nuisance. The judge had awarded damages but refused an injunction. The Court of Appeal granted an injunction and applied the principle in *Shelfer v City of London Electric Lighting Co*:[46]

Kennaway v Thompson [1981] QB 88 CA

Lawton LJ: Our task has been to decide on a form of order which will protect the plaintiff from the noise which the judge found to be intolerable but which will not stop the club from organising activities about which she cannot reasonably complain.

When she decided to build a house alongside Mallam Water she knew that some motor boat racing and water skiing was done on the club's water and she thought that the noise which such activities created was tolerable. She cannot now complain about that kind of noise provided it does not increase in volume by reason of any increase in activities. The intolerable noise is mostly caused by the large boats; it is these which attract the public interest.

Now nearly all of us living in these islands have to put up with a certain amount of annoyance from our neighbours. Those living in towns may be irritated by their neighbours' noisy radios or incompetent playing of musical instruments; and they in turn may be inconvenienced by the noise caused by our guests slamming car doors and chattering after a late party. Even in the country the lowing of a sick cow or the early morning crowing of a farmyard cock may interfere with sleep and comfort. Intervention by injunction is only justified when the irritating noise causes inconvenience beyond what other occupiers in the neighbourhood can be expected to bear. The question is whether the neighbour is using his property reasonably, having regard to the fact that he has a neighbour. The neighbour who is complaining must remember, too, that the other man can use his property in a reasonable way and there must be a measure of 'give and take, live and let live'.

Understandably the plaintiff finds intolerable the kind of noise which she has had to suffer for such long periods in the past; but if she knew that she would only have to put up with such noise on a few occasions between the end of March and the beginning of November each year and she also knew when those occasions were likely to occur, she could make arrangements to be out of her house at the material times. We can see no reason, however, why she should have to absent herself from her house for many

45 [1981] QB 88 CA.
46 [1895] 1 Ch 287.

days so as to enable the club members and others to make noises which are a nuisance. We consider it probable that those who are interested in motor boat racing are attracted by the international and national events, which tend to have the larger and noisier boats. Justice will be done, we think, if the club is allowed to have, each racing season, one international event extending over three days, the first day being given over to practice and the second and third to racing. In addition there can be two national events, each of two days but separated from the international event and from each other by at least four weeks. Finally there can be three club events, each of one day, separated from the international and national events and each other by three weeks. Any international or national event not held can be replaced by a club event of one day. No boats creating a noise of more than 75 decibels are to be used on the club's water at any time other than when there are events as specified in this judgment. If events are held at weekends, as they probably will be, six weekends, covering a total of 10 days, will be available for motor boat racing on the club's water. Water skiing, if too many boats are used, can cause a nuisance by noise. The club is not to allow more than six motor boats to be used for water skiing at any one time. An injunction will be granted to restrain motor boat racing, water skiing and the use of boats creating a noise of more than 75 decibels on the club's water save to the extent and in the circumstances indicated.[47]

As Lawton LJ stated, actions of this kind depend to a degree on the reasonableness of the activities undertaken: it is a matter of give and take. The facts of *Kennaway* lend themselves more readily to a give and take solution than *Miller*. In *Kennaway* the club admitted that the extra activity of recent years amounted to a nuisance so liability was less of an issue than the appropriate remedy. The plaintiff had, in a sense, come to the nuisance for although she had lived in the area all her life, the land beside the lake on which she now lived had been inherited from her father approximately 10 years after the club had commenced activities on the lake. The court was able to reach a compromise solution therefore by granting the injunction to limit activities above and beyond that which the plaintiff was deemed to have accepted as normal when coming to the lake. This logic would not have been easy to apply in *Miller*. It would not have been possible to grant an injunction limiting the number of sixes every season. It could be argued that the courts have reached a level on consistency by granting an injunction only where the level of activity extends beyond what the claimant is deemed to have accepted in coming to the nuisance.

In *Tetley v Chitty*[48] the local authority had granted permission to a go-karting club to use land in a residential housing area. McNeill J held that the noise generated by go-karting activities was an ordinary and natural consequence of the operation of go-karts on the council's land. In the same way as it would be difficult to play cricket without hitting sixes it would be difficult to run a go-karting club without noise. The difference however would lie in the frequency of the nuisance. McNeill J granted an injunction against the local authority's allowing use of the land for the purpose which gave rise to a nuisance, effectively terminating the activity in that area.[49]

It is important to note that the local authority, as landlord, was liable for allowing the nuisance committed by its tenants. McNeill J cited the headnote from *White v Jameson*[50] which states 'Where the occupier of lands grants a licence to another to do certain acts on the land and the licensee in doing them commits a nuisance, the occupier may be made a defendant to the suit to restrain the nuisance'. The owners of sporting stadiums will not avoid liability merely because they are not legally the party controlling the sporting function.

---

47   *Ibid*, p 332.
48   [1986] 1 All ER 663.
49   Also note *Stretch v Romford FC* (1971) 115 Sol Jo 7461.
50   (1874) LR 18 Eq 303.

SPECTATOR SAFETY

Parliament's efforts to protect spectators at sporting events represent but a fraction of the law in this area. The issue of stadium disasters will be considered in more detail with an analysis of the issues raised by the Hillsborough disaster but legal issues can be spawned from less tragic circumstances. Incidents such as a collapsed seat, the spectator struck by the ball from a speculative and errant goal attempt or an altercation between rival supporters illustrate just as effectively the law's intervention in sport. Whilst most sports spectators return from their chosen event with no more injury than the pain of their team's demise, a minority will consider recourse to law. Their reason is likely to fall into one of three categories. The first but least frequent occurrence would be an injury caused by the overspill of occurrences taking place on the pitch. The second is injury caused by the stadium itself. This would cover both defective premises and faulty safety procedures. The third are those injuries inflicted by other spectators.

Overspill from the Area of Play

One only need consider the clamour for tickets at major sporting events to appreciate that two of the most important reasons for attending certain sporting functions are the intensity and importance of the competition. This is particularly so of top level professional sport where the participants are performing to the maximum of their endeavours. Such extremes of performance, if misjudged, can result in balls, pucks, cars and even the participants themselves coming into contact with spectators.

An early case that examined the issue of liability was *Hall v Brooklands Auto Racing Club*.[51] Brooklands owned a two mile oval racing track which held regular races. Spectators paid to gain access to the track and were provided with stands from which they could view. The race track itself was partitioned from the spectators by railings and spectators preferred to stand just outside the railings rather than sit in the stands. During one long distance race two of the competing cars touched causing one of them to be catapulted into the railings. Two spectators were killed and many others injured. The Court of Appeal allowed an appeal against the findings of a special jury at first instance that the club had failed to provide adequate safety facilities:

Hall v Brooklands Auto Racing Club [1933] 1 KB 205

Greer LJ: In my judgment both parties must have intended that the person paying for his licence to see a cricket match or a race, takes upon himself the risk of unlikely and improbable accidents, provided that there has not been on the part of the occupier a failure to take reasonable precautions. I do not think it can be said that the content of the contract made with every person who takes a ticket is different. I think it must be the same and it must be judged by what any reasonable member of the public must have intended should be the term of the contract. The person concerned is sometimes described as 'the man in the street' or 'the man in the Clapham omnibus' ... Such a man taking a ticket to see a cricket match at Lord's would know quite well that he was not going to be encased in a steel frame which would protect him from the one in a million chance of a cricket ball dropping on his head. In the same way, the same man taking a ticket to see the Derby would know quite well that there would be no provision to prevent a horse which got out of hand from getting amongst the spectators and would quite understand that he himself was bearing the risk of an such possible but improbable accident happening to himself. In my opinion, in the same way such a man taking a ticket to see motor races would know quite well that no

---

51 [1933] 1 KB 205.

barrier would be provided which would be sufficient to protect him in the possible but highly improbable event of a car charging the barrier and getting through to the spectators.[52]

It is interesting to note that the cause of action in this instance was breach of contract with the club in breach of an implied term to ensure that the spectators were safe. Greer LJ held that there was an implied term whereby the plaintiff agreed to take the risk of this kind of accident occurring.[53] Today such an action would be brought in negligence (an area of law that has developed considerably since 1933) or under the Occupiers' Liability Act 1957, rather than in contract. The Occupiers' Liability Act 1957 will be discussed in more detail later. It is appropriate where an action is commenced against the occupier rather than the participant. The Act provides that a common duty of care is owed 'to take such care as in all the circumstances is reasonable to see that the visitor will be reasonably safe in using the premises for the purpose for which he is invited or permitted by the occupier to be there'.[54] An action in negligence in those circumstances would also be appropriate. Negligence is wider in scope and is applicable should the action be maintained against the participant.

The principle enunciated in *Hall v Brooklands Auto Racing Club* was applied in *Murray and Another v Harringay Arena Ltd*.[55] There a six year old spectator was injured by a puck hit out of the playing area during an ice hockey match. The Court of Appeal held that the defendants, by installing nets at both ends of the rink only, had satisfied their duty in that the limited netting was in conformity with other ice hockey rinks. The child's injury, as a result of something incidental to the game, was held to be a risk the spectator accepted. Again this case was decided on contractual grounds with the two competing implied terms, first that it was implied into the contract that the occupier would take reasonable precautions to ensure safety and secondly that there was an implied term whereby the visitor would accept all risks beyond what was reasonable for the occupier to protect against. Singleton LJ commented 'It may strike one as a little hard that this should apply in the case of a six year old boy'[56] but considered it right that the implied term should be consistently applied. This works with contractual matters but gives rise to difficulties in negligence where the courts are more inclined to distribute fault by contributory negligence rather than to deny any recovery on the grounds that the plaintiff had accepted the risk. This is an important legal distinction. The concept of contributory negligence allows the court to find liability and apportion culpability. However, if the plaintiff has accepted the risk, the concept of *volenti non fit injuria*, then there is no liability and the defendant escapes entirely.

This issue was clarified in *Wooldridge v Sumner*[57] where the plaintiff, an official photographer, was injured at a horse show when a horse being galloped around the arena went out of control plunging through a bordered area and struck him. The facts differed materially from the above cases in two ways. First, the plaintiff was not a paying spectator, which meant that the issue could not be resolved in terms of implied contractual terms. Secondly, it was acknowledged that no fault could be attributed to the occupiers of the arena and so the action was brought against the owners of the horse through the negligence of their servant, the rider.

One of the issues raised by the defendants was *volenti*: that the plaintiff had volunteered to accept the inherent risk of injury. This would seem to be compatible with the earlier plaintiff's implied

---

52 *Ibid*, p 223.
53 *Ibid*, p 224.
54 Section 2(2).
55 [1951] 2 KB 529.
56 *Ibid*, p 536.
57 [1963] 2 QB 43.

contractual term to assume the risk. However *volenti* is a defence to negligence and implies that a *prima facie* case of negligence has been established. Under the old contractual actions, liability had always been denied on the basis that there had not been a breach of contract by the defendant in the first place. One of the problems facing the court was whether liability was to be denied on the basis that there was no *prima facie* negligence or whether there was *prima facie* negligence but with the successful defence of *volenti*. Sellers LJ considered the plaintiff's claim that the horse had been ridden too fast:

Wooldridge v Sumner [1963] 2 QB 43

Sellers LJ: In my opinion 'too fast' in these circumstances would only be an error of judgment of a highly competent rider all out to succeed. It is no doubt a misfortune for a skilled batsman to be bowled or caught in a supreme effort to hit a six. It is also a misfortune if, on the other hand, he succeeds in hitting a six and the ball hits someone over the boundary. The three-quarter who dives at speed over the line for a try at Twickenham or on occasions at Wembley or the opponent who dives into a tackle to prevent a try may and sometimes does roll over and come into heavy contact with the surrounding barrier sometimes to his own hurt and to the possible injury of an adjacent spectator. No court or jury would, I think, condemn such endeavour as negligent.[58]

On the issue of *volenti* he continued:

In my opinion a competitor or player cannot in the normal case at least of competition or game rely on the maxim *volenti non fit injuria* in answer to a spectator's claim, for there is no liability unless there is negligence and the spectator comes to witness skill and with the expectation that it will be exercised. But provided the competition or game is being performed within the rules and the requirement of the sport and by a person of adequate skill and competence the spectator does not expect his safety to be regarded by the participant.[59]

It would appear that *volenti* is unlikely ever to feature in sports spectator injury cases as legal issues would revolve around the establishment of negligence rather than defences to negligence. The spectator struck by a puck, ball or car, as long as it was done so as an accepted part of the game, is subject to a lower standard of duty owed by the plaintiff and will have impliedly accepted that lower standard.

At the other end of the spectrum, incidents where spectators are injured as a result of deliberate actions outside of the rules of the game will be subject to both the criminal and civil law. The infamous incident of Eric Cantona kicking a spectator, following his dismissal during Manchester United's FA Cup match against Crystal Palace FC at Selhurst Park in 1995, resulted in a criminal conviction for assault.[60]

It is in between these two extremes that the law is a little less clear. When will the actions of the participant fall below this lower standard of duty?

Wooldridge v Sumner [1963] 2 QB 43

Sellers LJ: If the conduct is deliberately intended to injure someone whose presence is known or is reckless and in disregard of all safety of others so that it is a departure from the standards which might reasonably be expected in anyone pursuing the competition or game, then the performer might well be held liable for any injury his act might cause. There would, I think, be a difference, for instance, in

---

58   *Ibid*, p 53.
59   Ibid, p 56.
60   See Chapter 3, p 131 and Gardiner, S, 'Ooh Ah Cantona: racism as hate speech' [1996] 23 CMJ 23. See also the Bosnich 'Nazi salute' incident, *The Times*, 16 November 1996.

assessing blame which is actionable between an injury caused by a tennis ball hit or a racket accidentally thrown in the course of play into the spectators at Wimbledon and a ball hit or a racket thrown into the stands in temper or annoyance when play was not in progress.[61]

Diplock LJ in Wooldridge was of the opinion that there would be no breach of duty 'unless the participant's conduct is such as to evince a reckless disregard of the spectators' safety'.[62] This test was also adopted by Lord Denning in *Wilks v Cheltenham Homeguard Motor Cycle and Light Car Club*.[63] R Phillimore and Edmund Davies LJJ in that case preferred 'reasonable care in all the circumstances'.[64]

It might appear that there would be no remedy even to a spectator who deliberately positions himself in such a place in a cricket ground that only a totally miss-hit six could cause him harm because as Diplock LJ stated in *Wooldridge* 'the duty which [the participant] owes is a duty of care, not a duty of skill'.[65] He continued, 'it may well be that a participant in a game or competition would be guilty of negligence to a spectator if he took part in it when he knew or ought to have known that his lack of skill was such that even if he exerted to the utmost he was likely to cause injury to a spectator watching him'. It would seem that the injudiciously located spectator struck by a miss-hit six from an England international would be unsuccessful in his action but the same spectator struck by a similarly miss-hit six from an incompetent cricketer, unable to do any better, may well be successful.

Sellers LJ's notion of actions within the rules of the game also causes problems. Singleton LJ in *Murray* spoke of the breach of ice hockey rules of a participant who deliberately hits the puck out of the rink when pressed and the two minute penalty it invoked but did not seem to consider it negligent. Yet in the criminal case of *R v Kirk*[66] a Scottish professional footballer was convicted of culpably and recklessly kicking a ball into a crowd of spectators injuring a young girl. There was no breach of football rules in such action but he was convicted because it was done out of anger, which the court found unacceptable, rather than in an effort to gain time.

It appears unsatisfactory that the law should allow a football to be kicked into the spectators (with resulting injuries) with impunity as long as it was done within a normal footballing context whilst the participant who kicks the ball out of frustration, with the same force and accuracy, should be held legally responsible for his actions. This is particularly so as it could well be argued that football spectators expect such behaviour. Utilising such considerations as the rules of the game or the mental state of the participant may satisfy a test of reckless disregard. Such a test does not take into account the subjective element of the lower standard of duty which may be expected of the participant and therefore, a test of 'reasonable care in all the circumstances' is to be preferred.

STADIUM SAFETY

The first recorded example of stadium occupiers being held liable for a defective stand was *Francis v Cockrell*[67] where part of a stand collapsed at the Cheltenham National Hunt Festival. The court upheld a claim for damages against the occupiers even though it was builders with whom the

---

61   *Wooldridge v Sumner* [1963] 2 QB 43, at 57.
62   *Ibid*, at p 68.
63   [1971] 1 WLR 668.
64   Note also *Caldwellv Maguire* (2001) All ER (D) 363 with disapproval of 'reckless disregard' test.
65   *Op cit*, fn 61, *Wooldridge*, 68.
66   Unreported, *Daily Telegraph*, 17 October 1995.
67   (1870) QBD 501.

occupiers had contracted to build the stand who were negligent. The courts held that a contract existed between the spectator and the occupier with an implied term ensuring a reasonable standard of safety. Today a cause of action would most likely lie in negligence, occupiers' liability or under one of the sports-specific Acts which have proliferated in recent years.

Occupiers of stadiums and sporting clubs quickly became aware of their potential liability for stadium defects. Football clubs and bodies which initially existed in legal form as unincorporated associations soon became incorporated as limited companies. In *Brown v Lewis*[68] the court held that members of the club committee were individually liable for £25 damages following the collapse of a stand at Blackburn Rovers Football Club. By this time the benefits of incorporation were widely known. Incorporation brings into being an entirely separate legal entity which means that liability in most cases will be limited to the club and its resources, the membership being protected by the 'veil of incorporation'.[69] It was not long before most sporting clubs took advantage of this. More recently, sporting clubs, like other commercial enterprises, have sought to exploit the benefits of limited liability by hiving off areas of business into separate subsidiary companies under the general umbrella of a holding or parent company. This has the effect of divorcing the liability of smaller economic units from the whole. The primary motive for this exercise is clearly not to avoid liability for injured spectators; however, it must form part of a greater design to ensure clubs' solvency. To this end sporting clubs may often not own their own ground. Although from a legal perspective the ground will be owned by a different person, that person will often be another company with some of the same directors and shareholders as the club itself. An attempt was made by Lord Denning[70] to start a trend of considering groups of companies as a whole but this movement has fallen from favour in recent years.[71] This does not mean that other companies in a group will not be liable, as the courts have construed the Occupiers' Liability Acts so that it is possible for there to be multiple occupancy of premises:[72]

Occupiers' Liability Act 1957, s 2

(1) An occupier of premises owes the same duty, the 'common duty of care', to all his visitors, except in so far as he is free and does extend, restrict, modify or exclude his duty to any visitor or visitors by agreement or otherwise.

(2) The common duty of care is a duty to take such care as in all the circumstances of the case is reasonable to see that the visitor will be reasonably safe in using the premises for the purposes for which he is invited or permitted by the occupier to be there.

(3) The circumstances relevant for the present purpose include the degree of care and of want of care, which would ordinarily be looked for in such a visitor, so that (for example) in proper cases–

(a) an occupier must be prepared for children to be less careful than adults; and

(b) an occupier must expect that a person, in the exercise of his calling, will appreciate and guard against any special risks ordinarily incident to it, so far as the occupier leaves him free to do so.

(4) In determining whether the occupier of the premises has discharged the common duty of care to a visitor, regard is to be had to all the circumstances, so that (for example)–

(a) where damage is caused to a visitor by a danger of which he had been warned by the occupier, the warning is not to be treated without more as absolving the occupier of liability, unless in all the circumstances it was enough to enable the visitor to be reasonably safe; and

---

68   [1896] 12 TLR 455.
69   *Salomon v Salomon & Co Ltd* [1897] AC 22 HL.
70   *DHN Food Distributors Ltd v Tower Hamlets LBC* [1976] 1 WLR 852.
71   *Woolfson v Strathclyde Regional Council* [1978] SLT 159; *Adams v Cape Industries Plc* [1990] 2 WLR 657.
72   *Wheat v Lacon* [1966] 1 All ER 582.

(b) where damage is caused to a visitor by a danger caused by the faulty execution of any work of construction, maintenance or repair by an independent contractor employed by the occupier, the occupier is not to be treated without more as answerable for the danger if in all the circumstances he had acted reasonably in entrusting the work to an independent contractor and had taken such steps (if any) as he reasonably ought in order to satisfy himself that the contractor was competent and that the work had been properly done.

(5) The common duty of care does not impose on an occupier any obligation to a visitor in respect of risks willingly accepted as his by the visitor (the question whether a risk was so accepted to be decided on the same principles as in other cases in which one person owes a duty of care to another).

The 1957 Act lays down in statutory form the standard of duty required of all sporting clubs inviting spectators on to their premises. The standard is similar to that for common law negligence. The occupier must also take into account that child supporters may be owed a higher duty than adults.

Following *White v Blackmore*[73] it appeared that s 2(1) allowed occupiers to avoid liability by warning notices. In that case the deceased was a competitor at a 'jalopy' meeting. Having competed in one race he watched another. In that race a car ran into a safety rope which, because it had been staked negligently, pulled at a rope segregating spectators, causing the deceased to be catapulted into the air sustaining injuries from which he died. The Court of Appeal held that warning notices placed at the entrance to the venue stating that the organisers would not be liable for accidents to spectators however caused had effectively excluded liability.

The Unfair Contract Terms Act 1977, which applies to business liability only, appears to have closed this loophole. Section 2(1) of the Act prevents the exclusion or restriction of liability by contractual term or notice for death or personal injury resulting from negligence. Section 2(2) extends this by stating that liability for other loss or damage caused by negligence can only be excluded or restricted where reasonable.

It is important to note that the duty is only owed to a visitor who is 'using the premises for the purposes for which he is invited or permitted to be there'.[74] Injury sustained through standing on a faulty seat which subsequently collapses or whilst running on the field of play to celebrate victory may transform the visitor into a trespasser for 'when you invite a person into your house to use the staircase, you do not invite him to slide down the banisters'.[75]

Trespassers such as these or spectators who have gained entry to a sporting event unlawfully are considered to be owed a lesser duty than lawful visitors. Until relatively recently[76] the law has had little truck with trespassers at all. Now they are governed by the Occupiers' Liability Act 1984. However, the 1984 Act is unlikely to have an important impact in the sporting context as s 3(a) states the duty is only owed where the occupier 'is aware of the danger or has reasonable grounds to believe it exists'. In the 1960s and 1970s one could have envisaged a scenario of supporters gaining access to derelict stands that littered our sports grounds and sustaining injury but with the general improvement in sporting facilities this now seems an unlikely occurrence.[77]

---

73   [1972] 2 QB 651.
74   Section 2(2).
75   *The Carlgarth* [1927] P 93, 110, *per* Scrutton LJ.
76   In 1972 the House of Lords in *British Railways Board v Herrington* [1972] AC 877 held that trespassers were owed a
       duty of 'common humanity'.
77   But note *Ratcliffe v McConnell* (1997) LTL 7/11/97 (unreported elsewhere)

In the area of stadium safety, prevention is clearly better than cure and in 1975, parliament enacted the Safety of Sports Grounds Act. The Act introduced a system of licensing of major sports grounds by local authorities. Section 1 of the Act as amended by s 19 of the Fire Safety and Safety of Places of Sports Act 1987 states 'The Secretary of State may by order designate as a sports ground requiring a certificate under this Act (in this Act referred to as a 'safety certificate') any sports ground which in his opinion has accommodation for more than 10,000 spectators'. The certificate is appropriate for a number of activities during an indefinite period or individual occasion.[78] Section 2 explains that 'a safety certificate shall contain such terms and conditions as the local authority consider necessary or expedient to secure reasonable safety at the sports ground when it is in use for a specified activity or activities and the terms and conditions may be such as to involve alterations or additions to the sports ground'. If the local authority believes that the ground or parts of the ground are a serious risk to spectator safety then they are empowered under s 10 to prohibit or restrict admission and direct the holder of the licence as to the steps that must be taken before the order will be lifted.

The local authority's licensing duties in relation to designated football matches are now overseen by the Football Licensing Authority. The duties and powers of this body are contained in the Football Spectators Act 1989. The Secretary of State's criteria for labelling designated football matches is unclear but will be no less stringent than under the provisions of the 1975 Act. The Football Licensing Authority has the power to grant licences[79] as well as 'keeping under review the discharge by local authorities of their function under the Safety of Sports Grounds Act 1975'.[80] This supervisory role was recommended by Lord Justice Taylor following his critical analysis of the local authority's performance of its functions under the 1975 Act.

A licensing system also operates for those sports grounds that are undesignated but provide covered accommodation in stands for 500 or more spectators. This system is provided for by the Fire Safety and Safety of Places of Sport Act 1987. Again the system is operated by the relevant local authority which has the power to issue a certificate for a regulated stand containing 'such terms and conditions as the local authority considers necessary'.[81]

Whilst the Acts put in place a structure for the certification of sports grounds they are couched in general terms and do not specify minimum safety measures. Reference therefore must be made to the Guide to Safety at Sports Grounds, known as the 'Green Guide'. The Green Guide is not a statutory provision but it forms the basis of local authority enforcement of a safety standard and could be adopted by the courts as the benchmark for safety standards. The Green Guide specifies such details as the capacity of stands, evacuation procedures and fire safety as well as general conditions and maintenance.

In its present form, the Green Guide is not without its critics. A joint executive of local authorities, the FA, the Football League and the Sports Council have criticised the latest Green Guide, revised following the Taylor Report. As well as questioning its ability to serve as both the minimum standard for existing stadiums and the blueprint for new ones, the Joint Executive reported:

Ground Safety and Public Order. **Report No 1 of the Joint Executive on Football Safety**

The Taylor Report recommended that although some aspects of the guide should become mandatory requirements in safety certificates, the guide should remain a non-mandatory set of guidelines. Lord

---

78 Section 1(3).
79 Section 10.
80 Section 13(1).
81 Section 27(1).

Justice Taylor felt that sports grounds varied greatly in their layout and fixtures and it should be open to local authorities to deviate in some respects at some grounds from the guide's recommendations. We recognise that in the assessment of new grounds, it might be necessary for interpretation to be used where the standards of the guide cannot feasibly be met in their entirety by a club. Nevertheless, we feel that minimum standards should be enforced but with clearly established procedures for standards to be 'waived' in special circumstances.[82]

CROWD DISTURBANCE, MANAGEMENT AND SPECTATOR SAFETY

The issues of crowd management and crowd disturbances have been responsible for more debate, media coverage, parliamentary time and official reports than any other stadium safety issue. Indeed, an analysis of official reports has shown a concerning trend to amalgamate these issues when, in fact, they are quite separate sporting problems. It is ironic that the introduction of all-seater stadiums, arguably the most important factor in reducing crowd disturbances in recent years, was recommended by the Taylor Report into the Hillsborough Disaster where hooliganism was not a major issue.

Although it has often been said that crowd control is the responsibility of the clubs and their stewards, it has equally been acknowledged that, in many instances, the police do assume *de facto* control as part of their policing duties. This debate as to the role of the police in crowd management formed an important part of the Taylor Report considered later. In *Harris v Sheffield United Football Club*[83] the club argued that by fulfilling their policing duties the police were doing no more than was required of them under their public duty and the club were not liable to pay for 'special police services' under s 15(1) of the Police Act 1964. In the High Court, Boreham J considered the extent of the police's duty:

Harris v Sheffield United Football Club (unreported) QBD 26 March 1986

Boreham J: . . . the police were not discharging their own duty to the public; they were in fact discharging the club's duties to the spectators whom the club invited to the ground. The club chose to invite large numbers to their private premises; it was the club's duty to provide for their safety, health and comfort. They could have employed a security firm as banks and others have to do to protect their interests; they chose to request the police to perform those duties knowing that the police expected payment . . . the police within the ground provided services which it was not within the scope of their public duty to perform. For instance, they assisted in crowd management and in the enforcement of such ground regulations as refused entry to those who tried to enter without paying or prohibited spectators encroaching on parts of the ground which their entry fee did not entitle them to enter. It may be . . . that the maintenance of law and order was the predominant aim but there were other services performed.[84]

The Court of Appeal did not examine this issue to the extent of Boreham J but in rejecting the club's arguments Neill LJ did say:

The club has responsibilities which are owed not only to its employees and the spectators who attend but also to the football authorities to take all reasonable steps to ensure that the game takes place in

---

82 Ground Safety and Public Order. Report No 1 of the Joint Executive on Football Safety 1991, London: ACC Publications.

83 [1987] 2 All ER 838.

84 QBD 26 March 1986.

conditions which do not occasion danger to any person or property. The attendance of the police is necessary to assist the club in the fulfilment of this duty.[85]

This seems to suggest that crowd management assistance from the police is something for which the club is paying although the legal division of responsibility between the police and the club for crowd management has yet to be satisfactorily defined. There may be circumstances where an injured spectator has recourse to the club, with the club having recourse subsequently to the police.[86]

Much of the recent sports related legislation has been aimed at dealing with the problems associated with football hooliganism. It has long been possible for convicted hooligans to have restrictions placed on their attendance at matches and football clubs are now taking a more active stance by banning convicted hooligans from their grounds.[87] The police have powers to arrest spectators for committing a wide range of criminal offences. The remainder of this exposition will concentrate on sports-specific law.

Parliament has adopted a dual approach to the problem of football hooliganism. The first approach is to increase the powers of the police and the courts to punish hooliganism. Principally, this has been achieved through the Football (Offences) Act 1991:[88]

Football (Offences) Act 1991

1 Designated football matches

(1) In this Act a 'designated football match' means an association football match designated or of a description designated, for the purposes of this Act by order of the Secretary of State.

(2) References in this Act to things done at a designated football match include anything done at the ground–

   (a) within the period beginning twenty four hours before the start of the match or (if earlier) two hours before the time at which it is advertised to start and ending one hour after the end of the match; or

   (b) where the match is advertised to start at a particular time on a particular day but does not take place on that day, within the period beginning two hours before and ending one hour after the advertised starting time.

2 Throwing of missiles

it is an offence for a person at a designated football match to throw anything at or towards–

   (a) the playing area or any area adjacent to the playing area to which spectators are not generally admitted; or

   (b) any area in which spectators or other persons are or may be present, without lawful authority or lawful excuse (which shall be for him to prove).

3 Indecent or racist chanting

(1) It is an offence to engage or take part in chanting of an indecent or racialist nature at a designated football match.

(2) For this purpose –

---

85 [1987] 2 All ER 838, 847.

86 The Hillsborough Disaster; see below, p 698.

87 *Bristol City v Milns* (1978) *Daily Telegraph*, 31 January and *R v Clark and Others* (1985) *Daily Telegraph*, 10 April.

88 For an analysis of arrests under the Act and in particular the effectiveness of s 3, see Greenfield, S and Osborn, G, 'When the whites go marching in? Racism and resistance in English football' (1996) 6 Marquette Sports Law Journal 315 and Gardiner, S, 'Ooh Ah Cantona: Racisim as hate speech' [1996] 23 CJM 23.

(a) 'chanting' means the repeated uttering of any words or sounds whether alone or in concert with one or more others; and

(b) 'of a racist nature' means consisting of or including matter which is threatening, abusive or insulting to a person by reason of his colour, race, nationality (including citizenship) or ethnic or national origins.

4 Going onto the playing area

It is an offence for a person at a designated football match to go onto the playing area or any area adjacent to the playing area to which spectators are not generally admitted, without lawful authority or lawful excuse (which shall be for him to prove).

Whilst s 1(2)(a) would appear to be of long enough duration to cover early arrivals and late leavers it is difficult to envisage when s 1(2)(b) would be invoked. If a match were not going to take place that day it is unlikely spectators would be admitted to the ground in the first place. Equally, whilst it is possible to envisage occasions on which spectators might spill over on to the playing area it is difficult to envisage a lawful excuse for the throwing of missiles.

Section 3(2)(a) as originally enacted made racist chanting an offence only if it were 'in concert with one or more others'. The first edition of this book commented, 'it is odd that the legislation should be limited to racist chanting rather than a wider definition including racist abuse from one spectator'. This fault has now been remedied with the substitution of the words 'whether alone or in concert with one or more others'.[89]

Section 4 makes it a specific offence to go on to the playing area. In the earlier case of *Cawley v Frost*[90] a spectator was charged with using threatening words and behaviour in a public place contrary to s 5 of the Public Order Act 1956 when supporters clashed on the speedway track between the stand and the pitch. The issue arose as to whether the speedway track was a public place. The Court of Appeal held that the stadium was a public place in its entirety allowing incidents that happen on the pitch to be subject to public order offences. Section 4 extends the law by disposing of any requirement for a further criminal act to take place on the pitch.

Other legislative provisions of recent years have been aimed at preventing disruption rather than dealing with its aftermath. The Public Order Act 1986, for the first time, provided courts with the power to make exclusion orders against convicted hooligans. These powers have now been superseded by Part 3 of the Football Spectators Act 1989 which allows courts to impose restriction orders preventing spectators convicted of relevant offences[91] from attending designated matches outside England and Wales. The 1989 Act has itself been amended significantly by The Football (Offences and Disorder) Act 1999 which introduced Domestic and International Football Banning Orders. This terminology was further amended by s 1 of The Football Disorder Act 2000 which has removed the distinction between domestic and international orders. Section 14E(3) of the 2000 Act imposes a requirement on the court to confiscate the passport of the person subject to the order, unless there are 'exceptional circumstances'. Banning Orders can be imposed for up to 10 years.[92]

---

89 Football (Offences and Disorder) Act 1999, s 9.

90 (1971) 64 CHR 20.

91 Those listed in Sched 1 of the Act, including offences under the Football Spectators Act 1989; the Sporting Events (Control of Alcohol) Act 1985; s 5 of the Public Order Act 1986; s 12 of the Licensing Act 1872; s 91(1) of the Criminal Justice Act 1967; and s 4 or s 5 of the Road Traffic Act 1988. Additionally under s 2 of The Football (Offences and Disorder) Act 1999, any offence under s 5 of the Public Order Act 1986 or any offence involving the use or threat of violence towards another person or property. Definitions of 'violence' and 'disorder' are given in s 14C of The Football Disorder Act 2000.

92 The Football (Offences and Disorder) Act 1999, s 4.

All of the above provisions relating to banning orders can only be imposed upon those found guilty of a football related offence. However, the 2000 Act goes further. Under s 14D, a banning order may be imposed by a magistrates' court following a complaint by the police. The court must be satisfied that the person in question has caused or contributed to violence or disorder in the United Kingdom or elsewhere and there are reasonable grounds for believing that a banning order would prevent violence or disorder at a regulated football match.

Additionally s 21A provides that if a police officer has reasonable grounds for suspecting that the person in question has caused or contributed to violence or disorder in the United Kingdom or elsewhere and there are reasonable grounds for believing that a banning order would prevent violence or disorder at a regulated football match, that person, on the authorisation of an inspector, may be issued with a notice requiring them to appear before a magistrates' court within 24 hours and in the meantime may not leave England and Wales. These powers apply only during a control period when international bans are activated.

Sections 14D and 21A of The Football (Disorder) Act 2000 represent a significant extension to the powers to ban travelling trouble makers and, in the light of the fact that they do not require a conviction to be imposed, challenge the degree of liberty and freedom that may be exercised by supporters.

Alcohol and Sports Disorder

Alcohol has long been identified by politicians as a major cause of football hooliganism. The main provisions are now contained in the Sporting Events (Control of Alcohol etc) Act 1985. The legislation also acknowledges that although alcohol consumed at matches could prove problematical, drunkenness before matches also needed to be addressed. As Lord Justice Taylor recognised, the match was only a part, albeit a central part, of a Saturday afternoon's recreation which, for many supporters, began with the consumption of alcohol in pubs close to the ground or on the journey to the ground. Therefore much of the drunkenness was a result of drinking prior to the match:

Sporting Events (Control of Alcohol etc) Act 1985

1 Offences in connection with alcohol on coaches and trains

(1) This section applies to a vehicle which–
    (a) is a public service vehicle or railway passenger vehicle; and
    (b) is being used for the principal purpose of carrying passengers for the whole or part of a journey to or from a designated sporting event.

(2) A person who knowingly knowingly causes or permits intoxicating liquor to be carried on a vehicle to which this section applies is guilty of an offence–
    (a) if the vehicle is a public service vehicle and he is the operator of the vehicle or the servant or agent of the operator; or
    (b) if the vehicle is a hired vehicle and he is the person to whom it is hired or the servant or agent of that person.

(3) A person who has intoxicating liquor in his possession while on a vehicle to which this section applies is guilty of an offence

(4) A person who is drunk on a vehicle to which this section applies is guilty of an offence.

2 Offences in connection with alcohol, containers, etc at sports grounds

(1) A person who has intoxicating liquor or an article to which this section applies in his possession –
    (a) at any time during the period of a designated sporting event when he is in any area of a designated sports ground from which the event may be directly viewed; or

(b) while entering or trying to enter a designated sports ground at any time during the period or a designated sporting event at that ground, is guilty of an offence.

(2) A person who is drunk in a designated sports ground at any time during the period of a designated sporting event at that ground or is drunk while entering or trying to enter such a ground at any time during the period of a designated sporting event at that ground is guilty of an offence.

(3) This section applies to any article capable of causing injury to a person struck by it, being–

(a) a bottle, can or other portable container (including such an article when crushed or broken) which–

(i) is for holding any drink; and

(ii) is of a kind which, when empty, is normally discarded or returned to or left to be recovered by, the supplier; or

(b) part of an article falling within paragraph (a) above.

Section 1 applies not only to the person in possession of the alcohol but also to the person who permits the alcohol to be carried on a public service vehicle. Section 1(2)(a) makes it clear that the offence will be committed by coach operators or the railway authorities and their staff. Although being drunk at the ground,[93] taking alcohol to the ground[94] and being in possession of alcohol whilst viewing the match, are all offences,[95] it is not an offence to drink alcohol before entering the ground nor to drink at the club's bars. It could be argued that the consumption of alcohol at a public house near the ground is a more effective measure of a person's intoxication than his mere possession of alcohol. Clearly the measures are aimed at preserving the individual right to moderate consumption of alcohol as well as protecting the business interests of public houses and restaurants but it is uncertain as to how effective the provisions can be. Effective enforcement of these measures at a Premier League football match where there may be in excess of 30,000 people is impossible. The Act makes no attempt to define 'drunk', unlike the road traffic provisions relating to drinking and driving, and so even extremely intoxicated but discreet supporters should evade detection. The only time that drunkenness is likely to be observed is if the spectator's behaviour is such as to draw the attention of the police. At this stage it is likely that other offences such as public order offences would have been committed thus negating the need for the Act. The main benefit of the Act may be to enable the police to filter out a small percentage of the most visibly or audibly drunk prior to admission.

Segregation of the rival spectators has been a principal means by which crowd disruption has been avoided. It was one of the most effective weapons in the armoury of the police in ensuring that football's Euro '96 was relatively trouble free within the confines of the stadiums. However, no matter how well seating allocation is handled by the clubs, their efforts could be undermined by ticket touts selling tickets indiscriminately to various parts of the ground. This problem is now dealt with by s 166 of the Criminal Justice and Public Order Act 1994.[96] The section makes it a criminal offence 'for an unauthorised person to sell or offer or expose for sale a ticket for a designated football match in any public place or place to which the public has access or, in the course of a trade or business, in any other place.[97] This section is augmented by s 10 of The Football (Offences and Disorder) Act 1999

---

93 Sporting Events (Control of Alcohol etc) s 2(2).

94 *Ibid*, s 2(1)(b).

95 *Ibid*, s 2(1)(a).

96 Bitel, N, 'Ticket rights' (1993) 1(1) Sport and the Law Journal; Bitel, N, 'Not quite the ticket' (1995) 3(1) Sport and the Law Journal; Greenfield, S and Osborn, G, 'Criminalising football supporters: tickets, touts and criminal justice and Public Order Act 1994' (1995) 3(3) Sport and the Law Journal; Farrell, R, 'Ticket rights – and wrongs' (1994) 2(1) Sport and the Law Journal.

97 Criminal Justice and Public Order Act 1994, s 166(1).

which makes it an offence to make unauthorised sales of tickets in England and Wales for designated matches played outside England and Wales.

Finally when considering preventative measures, it is necessary to consider the issue of identity cards. A national membership scheme, the brainchild of the Thatcher government, was enacted in the Football Spectators Act 1989[98] but no order was ever made to bring the relevant sections into force and the provisions have lain dormant on the statute books. In essence the intention of the scheme was to register football spectators and issue them with identity cards authorising the attendance at designated football matches. A conviction for a relevant offence would result in membership being withdrawn. The measures were roundly condemned by interested parties and following criticism by Lord Justice Taylor[99] the government reluctantly backed down. The main planks of criticism were that the scheme was logistically unworkable and that it was an affront to individual liberty. It is a pity however that a more formalised system for barring spectators following conviction could not have been salvaged from the wreckage.

PARTICIPANT SAFETY

In the clamour to consider public safety, the safety of the participant is often overlooked. Three facets of player safety are relevant here because they arise specifically as a result of activities within stadiums; injuries caused by spectators, injuries caused by the stadium itself, and medical treatment for injuries sustained.

Whilst intra-spectator violence has become a familiar if unacceptable sight at many large sporting occasions, spectator violence towards players is relatively rare. The Cantona incident and the stabbing of Monica Seles at a tennis tournament in Hamburg in April 1993 has served to heighten awareness of a further situation where the law, reluctantly, may become involved in sporting issues. The stabbing was particularly shocking because tennis is not a sport usually associated with violent spectators and subsequently many of the participants took the precaution of turning the chairs to face the spectators. This measure seems to have died out as the shock of the Seles incident recedes and today tennis players and spectators retain the same degree of proximity as always (albeit with heightened security).

Being within touching distance of sporting heroes remains an intimacy that many other nations have relinquished. It is precisely in order to protect this intimacy at sports events that laws have been introduced to outlaw racist chanting, the throwing of missiles, running on to the playing area and being drunk at certain sporting occasions. What is most likely to change the relationship between player and spectator would be successful legal action brought by players against the owners of sporting venues. The more frequent the attacks on players the more likely that courts will be prepared to conclude that stadium owners are negligent by ignoring a foreseeable risk to players' safety.

Player safety is recognised by the sports governing bodies as highly important and these sports have developed standard protective clothing and other safety measures to ensure that players remain safe. Injuries caused by deficiencies in the stadium or playing area, because they are much rarer, attract less attention. The lower parts of rugby posts are sometimes padded but often collisions with the stadium are considered to be a risk the players must accept. With top sportsmen's careers being increasingly well paid but brief, players may feel more inclined to pursue claims for injuries of this

---

98 Football Spectators Act 1989, part 1, ss 2–7.
99 *Op cit*, fn 4, Hillsborough Final Report, p 65.

nature more energetically. There is no legal reason why a player should not bring an action against the ground-owner, club or governing body for injuries sustained as a result of a frozen pitch or a slippery surface.

In an unreported case,[100] a long jumper was successful in an action for negligence against a local authority, the owners of an athletics stadium, for a knee injury sustained when jumping in a local competition. His claim that his leg was twisted as a result of jumping into wet sand was upheld in the county court. Cases such as this emphasise the importance of stadium owners fulfilling their duty to provide sporting surfaces that in all the circumstances afford athletes reasonable safety.

The Occupiers' Liability Act 1957 places such a duty on the occupiers of premises to all visitors. This would cover all participants irrespective of whether they were 'home' or 'away' players. The limitations of these provisions were exposed in *Sims v Leigh Rugby Club*.[101] The plaintiff was a winger for Oldham Football Club and was involved in an 'away' rugby league match against Leigh. In attempting to score a try, the plaintiff was bundled over the touch line which, he alleged, resulted in his colliding with a concrete wall more than seven feet from the touchline. The plaintiff sustained a broken leg and brought an action against the 'home' club for a breach of their duty under the Occupiers' Liability Act 1957. Wrangham J in the High Court rejected the plaintiff's claim because, on the balance of probabilities, the injuries were sustained as a result of the tackle rather that on the collision with the wall. Comments made *obiter* should be of great interest to all stadium occupiers and the standard of duty required of them under the Act:

Sims v Leigh Rugby Club [1969] 2 All ER 923

Wrangham J: Now what did the defendants actually do? The answer to that is, it provided a playing field which complied in all respects so far as the evidence goes with the requirements of the governing body of the game. The governing body of the game is the Rugby Football League and that league directs through a council which consists of representatives of each club. They have made (I do not know when) bylaws which govern the layout of the playing fields which clubs are to provide for the games they play. One of those rules is that there shall be a distance of not less than seven feet from the outside of the touch line to the ringside. This concrete post was seven feet three inches from the touch line. Therefore it complied with the bylaw of the governing body of the game. Nevertheless, it is said that the defendant which I suspect operates through a committee, ought to have been wiser than the governing body of this game and ought to have said to itself: 'although the governing body consider the barrier between the playing pitch and the spectator's area may be near the touch line as seven feet, we think it ought to be much further off and therefore we will set our barrier not at seven feet but much further away'. And it is said that the defendant ought to have assumed this greater wisdom although it had not got one jot or one tittle of evidence to support its opinion, because it is common ground that a serious accident arising from the too great proximity of the barrier to the touch line has not been known at all. No one has been able to assist me with evidence of a single case arising from a barrier being too close to the touch line. It is true that on quite a number of occasions players have stopped themselves at the barrier; they have run into the barrier in that sense and only just stopped themselves at it, perhaps even had to hurdle the barrier because they were running so fast that they could not stop themselves in time. But no one has suggested that, apart from this unfortunate accident, a single accident has been caused in this way. So that it amounts to this, that it is said that the defendant was unreasonable because it did not set up its opinion against that of the governing body of the sport, although such evidence as there was entirely supported the view of the governing body of the sport. I think that is wholly unreasonable criticism to make of the defendant.[102]

---

100 *The Times*, 10 July 1996.
101 [1969] 2 All ER 923.
102 *Sims v Leigh Rugby Club* [1969] 2 All ER 923, pp 926–27.

Even if his Lordship had been convinced of the breach of duty, the plaintiff would still have fallen at the final hurdle:

> The matter perhaps does not quite stop there, for by s 2(5) of the Occupiers' Liability Act 1957 it is provided that a duty of care does not impose on an occupier any obligation to a visitor in respect of risk willingly accepted by the visitor. Now, it is not in dispute, of course, that anyone accepts employment as a professional footballer by a club playing under the rules of the Rugby Football League willingly accepts the risk of playing football, risks which are by no means small because it is a game involving great physical effort by one side an the other. It seems to me that a footballer does not merely accept the risks imposed by contract with the players on the other side. He willingly accepts all the risks of playing a game on such a playing field as complies with the bylaws laid down by the governing body of the game. I am sure that footballers who go to the Leigh ground, go to that ground willingly accepting the risks that arise from playing the game under the rules of the league, on a ground approved by the league.[103]

Thus it would appear that liability revolves around compliance with the rules of the governing body of the sport. In the unlikely event that the court considers the standards of the governing body to be inadequate, the participant will still be held to have accepted the risks inherent in the stadium. The conclusion reached by the judge, that accidents involving collisions with partitions, walls or advertising hoardings are extremely rare, is nonsensical.[104] Keen observers of cricket, rugby union, rugby league, football, boxing or basketball will be all too familiar with the image of participants crashing into hoardings, etc after leaving the arena of play. It is suggested that Wrangham J's approach of considering injuries in rugby league is too narrow. Ayrton Senna's death when he crashed into a tyre wall at the 1994 San Marino Grand Prix at Immola serves to highlight the importance of boundary walls and fences and the danger to sportsmen should they prove inadequate. Although injuries of this kind may be rare, they are nevertheless frequent enough to put occupiers on notice that injuries are more that an unlikely eventuality.

The judgment assumes that standards set by governing bodies are adequate. In this instance, seven feet may well have been a reasonable distance but to assume as much is an abdication of the responsibilities of the court. Equally the judgment is of little use to the providers of recreational sporting facilities whose standards would not be governed by sporting bodies. In order for the law to be comprehensive, courts would need to start with the rebuttable presumption that, confronted with an injured participant, safety measures were inadequate.

Even if the plaintiff managed to overcome this hurdle he would still be faced with the view that, in continuing with his participation, he had accepted the risks of playing in an arena in conformity with the rules of the governing body. This is not broad enough to encompass the problems encountered by the recreational sportsman who is entitled to assume that adequate measures have been taken to assure his safety.

On a professional sporting level, the judgment fails to take into account the sportsman as employee. Faced with an ultimatum of play or dismissal many professional sportsmen, reluctantly, may decide to continue. The courts have often acknowledged this imbalance of power in the contacting relationship between employer and employee and, it is submitted, the judge was wrong in the circumstances to conclude that the plaintiff had 'willingly' accepted the risk.

---

103 *Ibid*, 927.
104 See the contradictory comments of Sellers LJ in *Wooldridge v Sumner* [1963] 2 QB 43, 53.

A potential source of liability in instances such as *Sims*, but which was not raised in that case, is the employer's statutory duty under the Health and Safety at Work Act 1974:

Health and Safety at Work Act 1974

2 General duties of employers to their employees

(1) It shall be the duty of every employer to ensure, so far as it is reasonably practicable, the health, safety and welfare at work of all his employees.

(2) Without prejudice to the generality of an employer's duty under the preceding subsection, the matters to which the duty extends include in particular –

   (a) the provision and maintenance of plant and systems of work that are, so far as is reasonably practicable, safe and without risks to health;

   (b) the provision and maintenance of a working environment for his employees that is, so far as is reasonably practicable, safe, without risks to health and adequate as regards facilities and arrangements for their welfare at work.

3 General duties of employers and self-employed to persons other than their employees

(1) It shall be the duty of every employer to conduct his undertaking in such a way as to ensure, so far as is reasonably practicable, that persons not in his employment who may be affected thereby are not thereby exposed to risks to their health and safety.

Section 2 covers 'home' players whilst s 3 covers visiting players. Section 2 would also cover home players in actions against their own employers for a failure to provide a safe system of work; although the stadium would not be under the control of the visiting employer, his duty towards his employees is non-delegable. While he may delegate the operation of the system of work he cannot avoid liability should that system prove inadequate.[105]

We are all familiar with the injured participant who is stretchered to the sidelines only to miraculously recover and return to the fray. Sometimes, however, participants are seriously injured and their wellbeing can depend in part on the skill and availability of medical treatment at the stadium. An injured participant who is poorly treated prior to removal to hospital may suffer prolonged rehabilitation, an end to their career, permanent disability or even death. The legal implications of these scenarios are critical. Outside of the sporting context, negligence claims against medical staff tend to hinge on the issue of causation rather than whether they owed a duty, that is, did the lack of emergency treatment or the poor quality of treatment cause the injuries sustained?

In *Hotson v East Berkshire AHA*,[106] Hotson, aged 13, fell from a tree and suffered an acute traumatic fracture of the left femoral epiphysis. He was not correctly treated for five days and suffered avascular necrosis, involving disability of the hip joint and the virtual certainty of osteoarthritis. The health authority admitted negligence. The trial judge assessed at 75 per cent the chance the avascular necrosis would have developed from the fall anyway, and awarded damages based on the loss of a 25 per cent chance of full recovery. The House of Lords allowed the Authority's appeal stating that, on the balance of probabilities, the treatment had not caused the disability. It is clear, therefore, that poor or non-existent medical treatment does not give rise to an action in itself. It is necessary to establish not only a causal link between the treatment or lack of it, and the resulting injury or disability, but that the treatment was a material contributory cause.

---

105 *McDermid v Nash Dredging Ltd* [1987] AC 906.
106 *Hotson v East Berkshire AHA* [1987] 3 WLR 232.

The issue of the medical provision provided at a facility to an injured participant arose in the case of *Watson v British Boxing Board of Control*.[107] Michael Watson, a professional boxer, sustained head injuries during a WBO world super-middleweight title fight against Chris Eubank. The fight was regulated by the British Boxing Board of Control (BBBC), the sole body controlling professional boxing in the United Kingdom. Watson received medical attention from doctors present at the fight as required by the board and was then taken to hospital where, some half an hour after the end of the fight, he was given resuscitation treatment. He was later transferred to a neurosurgical unit where he underwent surgery. By that time he had suffered permanent brain damage. Watson brought an action in negligence against the BBBC on the basis that the board had failed in its duty both to see that all reasonable steps were taken to ensure that he received immediate and effective medical treatment should he sustain injury in the fight, and by failing to require immediate resuscitation at the ringside which would have prevented him from sustaining permanent brain damage. Lord Phillips MR concluded that the standard of reasonable care required that there should be a resuscitation facility at the ringside, and in failing to require the provision of such a facility the board was in breach of its duty of care to the claimant. His Lordship further concluded that if ringside resuscitation had been available the outcome for the claimant would probably have been significantly better, which was sufficient to establish causation.

It should be noted that this is a decision based very much on its facts and should not be considered by other governing bodies as what his Lordship described as the 'thin end of the wedge'. Governing bodies, event organisers and facility managers need to assess their duties and responsibilities on an individual basis, adopting the criteria prescribed in the *Watson* case.[108]

THE HILLSBOROUGH DISASTER

The Football Association on 20 March 1989 had decided to hold that year's FA Cup semi-final between Nottingham Forest and Liverpool at the Hillsborough Stadium in Sheffield. The date for the match was fixed for 15 April. The match was to be policed by the South Yorkshire Constabulary. The police had agreed to perform this function on the condition that the ticket allocation was the same as in the corresponding semi-final between the two clubs seven years earlier. The Liverpool supporters were unhappy with this arrangement as they were allotted 24,256 places as against 29,800 for Nottingham Forest despite the latter's smaller average home attendance. To accommodate the Liverpool supporters at the larger end of the ground, argued the police, would involve rival supporters crossing paths and the consequent risk of crowd disturbance. Eventually Liverpool reluctantly agreed.

The stand allocated to Liverpool supporters is known as the West Stand or Leppings Lane end. It held 4,456 seated supporters behind terracing and the total capacity was stated as 10,100. It was fenced by eight foot high fences mounted on low walls. As well as having crush barriers running parallel with the goal line, the stand also had further barriers running at right angles. These were installed following the 1981 FA Cup semi-final between Tottenham Hotspurs and Wolverhampton Wanderers where crushing occurred and a disaster was prevented by hundreds of supporters climbing on to the pitch. At the time, the police had advised that the capacity in the Leppings Lane end was too high but, tragically, this warning was ignored.

---

107 *Watson v British Boxing Board of Control* [2001] QB 1134 CA – for fuller discussion, see Chapter 16 p 650.
108 But note *Wattleworth v Goodwood* [2004] EWHC 140, discussed in Chapter 16, p 651.

The effect of the crush barriers was to create seven pens. They had been constructed in stages in a piecemeal fashion. The south and east sides of the ground accommodating 29,800 were accessed through 60 turnstiles whilst the north and west sides with a capacity of 24,256 were accessed solely from the Leppings Lane end where there were only 23 turnstiles. Of those 23 turnstiles, seven (labelled A – G) provided access to the Leppings Lane terraces. Supporters gaining access through one of these turnstiles would find themselves on a walled concourse containing one exit gate, gate C. Supporters could then choose to access pens one and two or six and seven by walking around the outsides of the stand and gaining access from the sides. This would not have been obvious to the first-time visitor who would not have been helped by the poor signposting and lack of information on the tickets. A supporter unfamiliar with the ground would naturally have used the tunnel under the centre of the stand signposted 'standing'. This tunnel gave access to the two central pens, three and four.

The policing arrangements were under the supervision of Superintendent Duckenfield who had recently assumed this supervisory responsibility. He had 1,122 police officers at his disposal on that day: 38% of the total South Yorkshire force. The police were operating under their own 'Standing Instructions for the Policing of Football Grounds'. In addition Sheffield Wednesday FC provided 376 stewards and gate men.

A computerised turnstile system ensured that at any time an accurate count could be made of the number of supporters in any section of the ground and appropriate warnings given if a section neared capacity. In the west terracing this would mean a warning would be given when capacity reached 85% of the total 10,100. There were no means of monitoring the capacity of any individual pen. The crowd could be observed through five cameras with zoom facility which relayed pictures to the police control room. The cameras gave good views of the terracing and the turnstiles.

On the day of the match all the turnstiles were opened at midday. There was some debate amongst police officers whether the pens on the west terrace should be filled one by one but it was decided that the option should be left to supporters who would find their own level. At 2 pm it was observed that the Nottingham Forest end contained many more supporters than the Liverpool end where the central pens, three and four, were filling but pens one and two at one end and six and seven at the other were relatively empty. Although it was suggested that the Liverpool supporters had arrived in Sheffield in plenty of time but were reluctant to enter the ground, many did arrive late. There were roadworks on the M62; many coaches were pulled off the road and searched by police; and coaches were still queuing for the coach park half an hour before the kick off.

In the half hour preceding the three o'clock kick off, conditions worsened significantly. Pens three and four appeared full to the point that the numbers exceeded those recommended by the Green Guide although the pens at either end had spare capacity. The numbers of people attempting to gain access to the stand before kick off were concerning police officers on the ground. Pressure was building, both at the turnstiles, and, on the concourse as 5,000 supporters congregated.

With eight minutes to go before kick off and crowd congestion reaching a critical level permission was sought and obtained by officers on the ground to open exit gate C to relieve the pressure. Most of the supporters headed through the tunnel into the central pens. Although central control was unaware of it, there was evidence that some police officers had realised that the crush at the front of the pens was causing distress. Others however, unaware of what was happening, refused to allow worried fans to climb the front fence for fear of a pitch invasion. The pressure in pen three was now so great that two spans of crush barrier at the front gave way. This caused some supporters to fall and cause an increase in pressure on those at the front. Unlike normal football crowds the mass of supporters in the central pens could not step back after the initial surge. Lord Justice Taylor captured the horror of the moment when he wrote 'The pressure stayed and for those crushed breathless by it, standing or prone, life was ebbing away. If no relief came in four minutes there would be irreversible brain damage; if longer, death'.109

Still the danger of the moment went unrecognised. A senior police officer saw the crowding, but underestimated the gravity of the situation. When fans began to spill out of the pens, the immediate police reaction was to call up extra officers and dogs to prevent a pitch invasion. Their ignorance of the situation was shared by many of the supporters at the back of the terrace. Lord Justice Taylor commented 'Behind them, there were still many unaware of the crisis, watching the game. The football continued to joyous shouting and singing round the rest of the ground while those crushed and trapped slowly expired'.110 At five and a half minutes past three a senior police officer ran on to the pitch and instructed the referee to stop the match.

As attempts by police and supporters were made to rescue injured fans the enormity of what had happened became clear:

The Hillsborough Stadium Disaster (Interim Report)

It was truly gruesome. The victims were blue, cyanotic, incontinent; their mouths open, vomiting; their eyes staring. A pile of dead bodies lay and grew outside gate three. Extending further and further on to the pitch, the injured were laid down and attempts made to revive them. More and more walking survivors flooded out on to the pitch as the players left. The scene was emotive and chaotic as well as gruesome. As the enormity of the disaster was realised, many of the fans milling about were bitter and hostile to the police, blaming them for what had happened. Officers were confronted, abused, spat on and even assaulted. A small number of hysterical fans had to be subdued.111

Efforts were made by the fire brigade, the ambulance service, St John's ambulance brigade, medical staff in the ground and the supporters themselves to assist in the rescue operation. Senior FA officials went to the police control room for information and were told that exit gate C had been forced open by incoming supporters. Graham Kelly, Chief Executive of the FA, repeated this information on television a little later. Television cameras were at the ground to record the match for later broadcasting. BBC's Grandstand programme was interrupted to show pictures of the aftermath of the disaster, multiplying the impact of the tragedy. The code of ethics adopted by television authorities, which prevent the broadcasting of suffering by recognisable individuals prevented an even more painful scenario of friends and relatives viewing the suffering of those they knew.

The ground gymnasium was converted to a temporary mortuary and scenes of distress continued there with relatives attempting to revive deceased relatives and others desperately searching for missing friends and relatives:

The Hillsborough Stadium Disaster (Interim Report)

... [the pathologists] found that 88 of the victims were male and seven female. Thirty eight were under 20 years of age, 39 were between 20 and 29 years and only three were over 50. In virtually every case the cause of death was crush asphyxia due to compression of the chest wall against other bodies or fixed structures so as to prevent inhalation. In all but nine cases that was the sole cause. In one, pressure on the chest had been so great as to crush the aorta; in six cases there were also injuries to the head, neck or chest; in the remaining two cases, natural disease was a contributory factor. In 18 cases bones were fractured. Thirteen of those were rib fractures. However one was a fractured femur, one a fractured

109 *The Hillsborough Stadium Disaster 15 April 1989 (Interim Report)* Cm 765, London: HMS, para 77.
110 *Ibid*, para 79.
111 *Ibid*, para 83.

radius and the remaining three involved fractures of bones and cartilages round the voice box. These injuries suggest the victims may have been trodden while on the ground.[112]

This represented only the tip of the iceberg. As Coleman *et al* have stated in their report produced for Liverpool City Council, the grief and suffering extended far beyond the confines of the stadium:

Hillsborough and After: The Liverpool Experience

The officially-recorded statistics show that 95 people died, 400 received hospital treatment and 730 were injured. These statistics do not and cannot record the full extent of the disaster and its victims. It is clear from the experiences of many concerned with counselling survivors since the disaster that an inestimable number of people received actual physical injury but did not seek immediate medical help. Claims for compensation made to the Hillsborough Disaster Appeal Fund provide no more concrete or substantive indication of the numbers involved as a further inestimable number of people have declined to pursue claims for a range of reasons. In addition to the 'hidden figure' of physical injury is the massive number of people, many of whom were not at Hillsborough, who have suffered severe mental anguish and debilitating trauma. Again the evidence suggests that a substantial number have suffered alone and, typically, have refused to speak with anyone about their experiences. Others, however, cannot stop talking about their experiences as the disaster has come to dominate their lives. Recurrent nightmares and fundamental changes in behaviour are further, regular long-term effects endured by survivors, friends and relatives. Thus any attempt to establish the real 'extent' of the Hillsborough disaster is impossible if not futile. It remains apparent, however, that several thousand people have been deeply affected and it will be a long time before recoveries from physical and mental injuries will be made. For some, 'full recovery' will never be possible.[113]

THE INQUIRY

Two days after the disaster, Taylor LJ was appointed to conduct an inquiry into the incidents at Hillsborough. His terms of reference were 'To inquire into the events at Sheffield Wednesday football ground on 15 April 1989 and to make recommendations about the needs of crowd control and safety at sports events'.[114]

The Stadium

Taylor LJ was particularly critical of the layout and capacity of the Leppings Lane end. Following the crushing that occurred at the 1981 semi-final, additional fencing was erected which, in effect, segregated the terrace into three sections. Pens three and four formed the central section. Within the central section modifications were made to the layout with a number of barriers being removed. Although extensive modifications had been made, compensatory safety measures had not. Access to the central section could still be made through any of the turnstiles for that terrace. Therefore, although the turnstiles had been computerised, the system could give no information as to the number of supporters in any particular section.

---

112 *Ibid*, para 109.
113 *Hillsborough and After: The Liverpool Experience*, Report from the Centre for Studies in Crime and Social Justice, Edge Hill University College, prepared for Liverpool City Council, p 2. Also see Scraton, P, *Hillsborough: The Truth* (1999), Edinburgh: Mainstream Publishing.
114 *Ibid*, p 1.

Under s 1 of the Safety at Sports Grounds Act 1975 as amended by the Fire Safety and Safety of Places of Sport Act 1987, Hillsborough had been designated as a stadium requiring a safety certificate in 1979. Section 2(2)(a) of the 1975 Act as originally enacted[115] stated that the safety certificate 'shall specify the maximum number of spectators to be admitted to the stadium'. However, s 2(2)(b) stated merely that a safety certificate 'may specify the maximum number to be admitted to different parts of it'. The certificate for Hillsborough did not contain maximum numbers for the pens at the Leppings Lane end and although evidence showed that engineers were aware that the alterations to the terrace would impact on spectator numbers no alterations were made to the certificate.

Although s 2(2) had been repealed by s 19 of the Fire Safety and Safety of Places of Sports Act 1987, it was still effective because s 19 gave power to the Secretary of State to lay down terms and conditions for the granting of a certificate and, as no order had been made, the Home Office had recommended that certificates continued to be granted in accordance with the repealed section. According to s 2(2) of the 1975 Act, terms and conditions would include those relating to 'the number, strength and situation of any crush barriers'[116] and although it was not a mandatory requirement under the Act to specify capacity of the particular sections of the terrace there was a breach of the provisions in not amending the certificate to reflect the lowering of overall capacity.

Enforcing the Safety Provisions

Another weakness of the provisions became evident when the Inquiry considered how the local authority exercised their supervisory duties under the Act. The Officer Working Party, formed to comply with the regulations, was informal with no chair or record of decisions. The report commented that 'the attention given to this important licensing function was woefully inadequate'.[117] This illustrates the valuable point that the best intentions of parliament can be thwarted by inadequate application.

Crowd Control and the Role of the Police

On the issue of crowd control, Lord Justice Taylor concurred with Justice Popplewell's earlier report that 'it cannot be too strongly emphasised that it is upon the club or the occupier of the ground who is putting on the function, that the primary or continuing obligation rests'.[118] This causes certain problems. *Harris v Sheffield United Football Club* suggests that the money paid to police is for more than normal policing duties. On the assumption that both stewards and police will be present, how will their functions, in fact, be divided? Justice Popplewell acknowledged the reality of the police's *de facto* control but this does not resolve the problem of legal responsibility. In the interim report Lord Justice Taylor concluded:

The Hillsborough Stadium Disaster (Interim Report)

There remains, however, the question of whether there are some grounds or parts of grounds where the club may need to rely on the police (whom they pay to attend) to control the filling of pens and monitoring them for overcrowding. In other words, whilst the duty to in law to insure safety rests upon

---

115 Before it was amended by s 19 of the *Fire Safety and Safety of Places of Sport Act 1987*.
116 Safety at Sports Grounds Act 1975, s 2(2)(iii).
117 *Op cit*, fn 109, *Interim Report*, para 158.
118 *Ibid*, para 4.13.

the club, they may need and by arrangement be entitled, to employ the police as their agents in certain circumstances.[119]

It would appear that Lord Justice Taylor is concluded that clubs owe a non-delegable duty to spectators, the running of which may be delegated to the police. This would mean that an injured spectator's recourse in law would be with the club but would not resolve the legal position regarding the police's legal obligation to the club. Lord Justice Taylor's solution was a Written Statement of Intent:

The Hillsborough Stadium Disaster (Final Report)

I therefore repeat my recommendation that there should be a written document setting out the respective functions of club and police for crowd safety and control 'and in particular for the filling of each self-contained pen or other terraced area and the monitoring of spectators in each such pen or area to avoid overcrowding'. The aim should be for the club through its stewards to perform all those functions of controlling spectators of which they are capable having regard to the quality of the stewards, the layout of the ground and the nature of the match. Where they are not able to discharge any such function the police should perform it. As the proportion of seating at grounds increases, control by stewards should become the norm.

In making interim recommendation four,[120] I used the phrase 'written agreement'. This led to anxiety that what was required was a binding legal contract which would deprive the police of any flexibility in response to circumstances of the day. My intention was not to shackle either party by a binding contract; it was simply to have a document setting out how the functions were to be divided so that no misunderstanding would arise whereby one party thought that the other had undertaken some duty or vice versa. I am content that the document be referred to simply as a 'statement of intent', so it can be subject to alteration without breach of contract should circumstances so demand.[121]

However the agreement is titled or phrased, there may in fact be legal implications for such a document. There is clearly a contract between the club and the police and, according to *Harris*, this can be for the provision of a crowd control function. It is possible that a Statement of Intent could be used to evidence terms as to the extent of the police's contractual obligation.

THE LEGAL IMPLICATIONS

Civil Actions

Potential litigants could be divided into three categories: those physically injured in the crush at the Leppings Lane end; friends and family of the deceased now suffering psychiatric injury as a result; and police officers suffering from psychiatric illness witnessing the horrific scenes. The civil actions taken by victims against the police gave rise to important legal issues that have had repercussions extending far beyond the sporting context. It was one thing to establish that the police were negligent in their actions but entirely another to establish that they owed a duty to the 'indirect' victims, that is, those who did not suffer directly as a result of the alleged negligence.

There was little doubt that those who were injured would be able to claim. More contentiously, the South Yorkshire Police Force's insurers advised them to settle claims with police officers who had

---

119 *Ibid*, para 165.
120 *Ibid*, p 57.
121 *The Hillsborough Stadium Disaster (Final report)*, ('Taylor' Report) CM 962 (1990), paras 213 and 214.

suffered psychiatric illness. It was asserted on behalf of the officers that 'they accept the reasonable risks of their service but they should not be expected to deal with the appalling consequences of the negligent actions of others'.[122] In the light of earlier claims by relatives and friends the compensation awarded to police officers became a controversial issue.[123]

The fact that the police officers were successful in their claim reflects a gradual shift in attitude by the courts toward claims for psychiatric injury. Originally psychiatric injury could only be claimed successfully as an adjunct to physical injury.[124] There were two reasons for this. Firstly, there was the difficulty in substantiating a claim for psychiatric injury. The courts seemed concerned over the possibility of false claims. Secondly, there was the floodgates argument: the courts feared that anyone witnessing injury could potentially claim. The importance of this risk has been overemphasised. The courts have always found ways of limiting the scope of such claims with tests of foreseeability and proximity. Their caution is probably attributable to a fear of indeterminate liability, that is, where it is not known how many claimants may exist, rather than a fear of multitude of good claims.

The concessions made by the courts for secondary psychiatric illness have been most circumspect. Claims will be entertained only from applicants within a close familial proximity to the primary victims:[125] more distant relatives and friends are considered by the courts to have the 'reasonable phlegm'[126] to overcome such a vicissitude. It is a general principle of negligence that the injury must have been foreseeable by the defendant.[127] It has been successfully argued that although liability toward the primary victim has been established, liability cannot be extended to secondary victims because such an eventuality could not have been foreseen as a consequence of the tortfeasor's action.

Other ways of restricting claims have been to limit them to those who have personally witnessed the shocking scene rather than those told second hand.[128] The additional requirement that the secondary victim should suffer injury at approximately the same time as the injury to the primary victim have been relaxed following *McLoughlin v O'Brian*.[129] In that case, the plaintiff was informed of a road accident involving her husband and children approximately one hour after the incident. At the hospital, she was told that one child was dead and she saw the other injured members of her family. The House of Lords, relaxing the definition of proximity in time, gave judgment in favour of the plaintiff. Although she had not witnessed the accident, she had come to it in the immediate aftermath and this was sufficient to establish a claim.

Following the Hillsborough disaster, claims were brought by a number of plaintiffs. By the time the cases reached the House of Lords, that number had been reduced to ten. They represented a range

---

122 *The Guardian*, 4 June 1996.

123 *Ibid*. The Chairman of the Hillsborough Family Support Group commented, 'Obviously we accept that these police officers are human beings and they have human emotions the same as everyone else ... but these officers chose to be police officers. We did not choose to be victims'.

124 *Victorian Railways Commissioners v Coultas* [1888] 13 App Cas 222.

125 *Page v Smith* [1995] 1 WLR 644.

126 *Alcock v Chief Constable South Yorkshire* [1991] 4 All ER 907. Reported *sub nom Jones v Wright* [1991] 1 All ER 353 *per* Hidden J, 839c.

127 *The Wagon Mound (No 2)* [1967] 1 AC 617.

128 *Hambrook v Stokes Bros* [1925] 1 KB 141.

129 [1983] AC 410.

of familial relationships. Two were at the ground whilst others saw the horror unfold on television or listened to it on radio. All the appeals failed.

Alcock v Chief Constable of the South Yorkshire Police [1991] 1 WLR 814

Lord Keith: It was argued for the appellants in the present case that reasonable foreseeability of the risk of injury to them in the particular form of psychiatric illness was all that was required to bring home liability to the respondent. In the ordinary sense of direct physical injury suffered in an accident at work or elsewhere, reasonable foreseeability of the risk is indeed the only risk that need be applied to determine liability. But injury by psychiatric illness is more subtle . . . In the present type of case it is a secondary sort of injury brought about by the infliction of physical injury or the risk of physical injury, upon another person. That can affect those closely connected with that person in various ways. One way is by subjecting a close relative to the stress and strain of caring for the injured person over a prolonged period but psychiatric illness due to such stress and strain has not so far been treated as founding a claim in damages. So I am of the opinion that in addition to reasonable foreseeability liability for injury in the particular form of psychiatric illness must depend in addition upon a prerequisite relationship of proximity between the claimant and the party said to owe the duty.[130]

Their Lordships went on to explain that there were two elements to the concept of proximity: proximity of love and affection and then spatial proximity:

Lord Keith: As regards the class of persons to whom a duty may be owed to take reasonable care to avoid inflicting psychiatric illness through nervous shock sustained by reason of physical injury or peril to another, I think it sufficient that reasonable foreseeability should be the guide. I would not seek to limit the class be reference to particular relationships such as husband and wife or parent and child. The kinds of relationships which may involve close ties of love and affection are numerous and it is the existence of such ties which lead to mental disturbance when the loved one suffers a catastrophe. They may be present in family relationship or those of close friendship and may be stronger in the case of engaged couples than in that of persons who have been married to each other for many years. It is common knowledge that such ties exist and reasonably foreseeable that those bound by them may in certain circumstances be at real risk of psychiatric illness if the loved one is injured or put in peril. The closeness of the tie would, however, require to be proved by the plaintiff, though no doubt being capable of being presumed in appropriate cases.[131]

On the issue of spatial proximity, Lord Ackner explained:

Lord Ackner: It is accepted that the proximity to the accident must be close both in time and space. Direct and immediate sight or hearing of the accident is not required. It is reasonably foreseeable that injury by shock can be caused to the plaintiff, not only through the sight and hearing of the event but of its immediate aftermath. Only two of the plaintiffs before us were at the ground. However it is clear from McLoughlin's case that there may be liability where subsequent identification can be regarded as part of the 'immediate aftermath' of the accident. Mr Alcock identified his brother-in-law in a bad condition in the mortuary at about midnight, that is some eight hours after the accident. This was the earliest of the identification cases. Even if this identification could be described as part of the 'aftermath', it could not in my judgment be described as part of the immediate aftermath. McLoughlin's case was described by Lord Wilberforce as being upon the margin of what the process of logical progression of case to case would allow. Mrs McLoughlin had arrived at the hospital within an hour or so after the accident. Accordingly, in the post-accident identification cases before your Lordships there was not sufficient proximity in time and space to the accident.[132]

---

130 *Ibid*, 913.
131 *Ibid*, 914.
132 *Ibid*, 921.

Finally the court addressed the issue of those friends and relatives who witnessed the disaster on television. Lord Ackner was of the opinion that it was indeed possible to suffer psychiatric illness as a result of viewing pictures on the television and therefore there was a possibility of recovering damages for that shock. However, the Chief Constable would have been aware of the television restriction on showing pictures of individual suffering and 'although the television pictures certainly gave rise to feelings of the deepest anxiety and distress, in the circumstances of this case there were no such pictures'.[133]

Whilst many of the claimants[134] satisfied one of the elements of a successful claim none could satisfy them all. The case can be criticised for setting arbitrary and artificial limits on who can claim. However, the repercussions of extending the boundaries of liability are enormous and in an area such as nervous shock objective judgments will always have to be made to limit the claims.

THE LEGISLATION

Lord Justice Taylor's most important recommendation, that of all-seater football stadiums,[135] has ensured, arguably, not only a reduction in football hooliganism but, most importantly, there has been no repetition of the Hillsborough disaster. The effect of all-seater stadiums has also reduced the importance of ground capacity at football matches but other sporting grounds are not so well protected. The enactment of the Fire Safety and Safety of Places of Sport Act 1987 is to be applauded for its attempt to broaden the scope of the safety legislation to cover all sports grounds. However, as it has been seen, this was achieved at the expense of the original s 2 of the Safety of Sports Grounds Act 1975 which enshrined in statute the need for safety certificates to identify ground capacity and the option of stating stand or pen capacity. Section 27 of the Fire Safety and Safety of Places of Sport Act 1987 which deals with the contents of safety certificates for stands at undesignated matches states 'A safety certificate for a regulated stand shall contain such terms and conditions as the local authority consider necessary or expedient to secure reasonable safety'. The local authority can call upon the latest edition of the Green Guide but the Taylor Report advised against incorporating its provisions into statute. The Taylor Report highlighted the cursory adherence to the legislation by the local authority when that legislation merely gives a discretion rather than instruction. It is difficult to see, outside of football, any direct improvement in safety legislation.

The legislation spawned as a direct consequence of the Report was aimed not at the causes of the Hillsborough disaster but more at the problems of crowd disturbances. The restrictions on spectators travelling overseas under Part 3 of the Football Spectators Act 1989 and the provision contained within the Football (Offences) Act 1991 continued the trend of previous reports into stadium disasters of combining provisions relating to crowd management and crowd disturbance. Anyone with an understanding of the history of stadium disasters in Britain will appreciate the dangers of dealing with crowd disturbances to the detriment of crowd management.

---

133 *Ibid*, 921.
134 Including the rescuers; see *White and Others v Chief Constable of South Yorkshire Police & Others* [1999] 1 All ER 1
135 *The Hillsborough Stadium Disaster (Final Report)* Cm 962, p 12.

CONCLUSION

Much of this chapter is taken up by an examination of the liability of various parties following stadium-related incidents. For those unfortunate enough to get involved in such incidents, however, prevention is better than cure. Although it may pain lawyers that there would be a decrease in the amount of litigation relating to stadium injuries, in an ideal world, a chapter on stadium disasters in a book such as this would be superfluous. The hurt felt by families and communities caused by disasters such as Hillsborough does not diminish with time and cannot be underestimated.[136]

Over the years, parliament, through various reports, has considered the causes of death and serious injury at sports stadiums and latterly has responded to those reports with legislation. The reality, however, as Taylor LJ stated in his report, is that 'There is no panacea which will achieve total safety and cure all problems of behaviour and crowd control . . . '[137]

On 11 April 2001 at a football match between Kaizer Chiefs Football Club and Orlando Pirates Football Club at Ellis Park Stadium, Johannesburg, 43 people died and many more were injured in South Africa's worst football disaster. The Commission, chaired by Mr Justice Ngoepe heard that the deaths and injuries occurred as a result of crushing when too many spectators were crammed into the ground. The circumstances were frighteningly similar to those encountered at Hillsborough. The Commission recommended the adoption of legislation broadly similar to the English law.[138] Without suggesting that safety in the UK and South Africa was ignored prior to the respective disasters, it is unfortunate that it takes major losses of lives to galvanise authorities into taking appropriate measures. The similarities between the disasters suggest that legislation is necessary to ensure that the enthusiasm and excitement of sports spectators is channelled safely. This is easier said than done however and the problem with most legislative measures is that they impose a financial burden on clubs and stadium owners.

It may seem cynical to suggest that safety measures should be balanced against cost but it is a fact of life that the legal standard of reasonableness often involves such reasoning.[139] An examination of earlier UK Commission reports indicates that many of the issues and problems addressed in later reports were correctly identified at a much earlier time. They were not addressed in the form of legislation then because of a desire not to interfere in private business matters and a fear that the cost of such measures would force clubs out of business.

Cost is an important factor today: the Green Guide remains advisory, it is said, because of the disparate nature of our football grounds but this could also be in part due to the costs of enforcing safety specifications. The Sporting Events (Control of Alcohol) Act 1985 attempts to stop the consumption of alcohol on trains and buses going to the match and also prevents consumption whilst watching the match but allows consumption at pubs and bars in and around the ground. The only

---

136 See, for example www.contrast.org/hillsborough/home.shtm; also see O'Leary, J, 'Straw rules out new inquiry on Hillsborough' (1998) 1(1) Sports Law Bulletin, 1 (review of Lord Justice Stuart-Smith's 'Independent Scrutiny'); Scraton, P, 'Policing with contempt: the degrading of truth and denial of justice in the aftermath of the Hillsborough disaster,' (1999) 26(3) Journal of Law and Society 273–97.

137 *Op cit*, fn 135, Final report, para 61.

138 Commission of Inquiry into the Ellis Park Stadium Soccer Disaster 0f 11 April 2001, Report at www.polity.org.za/html/govdocs/commissions/2002/finalellispark.pdf.

139 *Op cit*, fn 34, *Bolton v Stone.*

logic for this is that the restrictions on the drinking habits of supporters are being balanced against the interests of local business. If the purpose of the legislation is to prevent drunkenness at football grounds it is indeed a sorry piece of work.

One example of an increase in costs was the introduction of all-seater stadiums. It has been argued that a move to all-seater stadiums has drastically reduced the likelihood of another Hillsborough type disaster. Certainly the government is convinced. In 2002 it reaffirmed its policy that all clubs in the Premiership and the Championship should provide seated accommodation only and grounds that have become all seated should remain so even if the club is subsequently relegated.[140] Of course, it is impossible to say whether the introduction of all-seater stadiums has done anything to reduce the incidence of stadium injury. However there is considerable logic in Taylor LJ's comments:

The Hillsborough Stadium Disaster (Final Report)

It is obvious that sitting for the duration of the match is more comfortable than standing. It is also safer. When a spectator is seated he has his own small piece of territory in which he can feel reasonably secure. He will not be in close physical contact with those around him. He will not be jostled or moved about by swaying or surging. Small, infirm or elderly men and women as well as young children are not buffeted, smothered or un-sighted by large and more robust people, as on the terraces. The seated spectator is not subject to pressure of numbers behind, nor around, him during the match. He will not be painfully bent double over a crush barrier. Those monitoring numbers will know exactly how many there are without having to count them in, or assess the density by, visual impression. There will still, of course, be scope for crowd pressure on standing whilst entering and, especially, when leaving but involuntary and uncontrolled crowd movements occasioned by incidents at the game are effectively eliminated.[141]

This has not prevented supporters calling for standing room to be restored at football grounds[142]. It is ironic that agencies established to prevent further stadium disasters should come under pressure to reverse safety measures by the very people that the measures are intended to protect. The Football Licensing Authority has examined the possibility of the introduction of KOMBI seating which can act as seats but also fold flat to provide a standing area. This system has been introduced at the Volksparkstadion in Hamburg. The FLA concluded:

The combination of 'Kombi' seats and removable barriers is an ingenious and well-engineered system that overcomes most of the disadvantages, in particular inadequate seats and restricted views while seated, of the standing/seating conversions installed at other German football grounds.[143]

Ultimately, as the report correctly identifies, a purchase and installation cost of £90 per KOMBI seat compared to £21 for a standard seat suggests this innovative idea will proceed no further. At the end of the day, even if legislation has no financial implications, laws are only as good as the ability and willingness of the actors involved to comply with them. What is the point of a stewarding system, for example, if stewards spend their time watching the match rather than the crowds? The adoption of a 'safety culture' cannot be brought about by the mere intervention of the law.

---

140 www.flaweb.org.uk/standing%20in%20seated%20areas.htm.
141 *Op cit*, fn 35, Final Report, para 62.
142 www.safestanding.com/safe/modules.php?op=modload&name=NS-SimPetition&file=petition&id=61.
143 www.flaweb.org.uk/Kombi%20Seating%20Report.htm.

KEY SOURCES

The Hillsborough Stadium Disaster (Final Report), Cm 962.

Alcock Chief Constable of South Yorkshire (1991) 4 All ER 907.

Scraton, P, *Hillsborough: The Truth* (1999), Edinburgh: Mainstream Publishing.

Home Office Guidance on Football-Related Legislation, HC 34/2000.

Hartley, H, *Disaster Law; A Socio-Legal Perspective* (2001) London: Cavendish Publishing.